Algorithm Design

A bestseller in its French edition, this book is original in its construction and its success in the French market demonstrates its appeal. It is based on three principles: (1) An organization of the chapters by families of algorithms: exhaustive search, divide and conquer, etc. On the contrary, there is no chapter devoted only to a systematic exposure of, say, algorithms on strings. Some of these will be found in different chapters. (2) For each family of algorithms, an introduction is given to the mathematical principles and the issues of a rigorous design, with one or two pedagogical examples. (3) For the most part, the book details 150 problems, spanning seven families of algorithms. For each problem, a precise and progressive statement is given. More importantly, a complete solution is detailed, with respect to the design principles that have been presented; often, some classical errors are pointed out. Roughly speaking, two-thirds of the book is devoted to the detailed rational construction of the solutions.

Algorithm Design

A Methodological Approach
150 Problems and Detailed Solutions

Patrick Bosc, Marc Guyomard and Laurent Miclet

CRC Press
Taylor & Francis Group
Boca Raton London New York

CRC Press is an imprint of the
Taylor & Francis Group, an **informa** business

A CHAPMAN & HALL BOOK

First edition published 2023
by CRC Press
6000 Broken Sound Parkway NW, Suite 300, Boca Raton, FL 33487-2742

and by CRC Press
4 Park Square, Milton Park, Abingdon, Oxon, OX14 4RN

ISBN: 978-1-032-36941-9 (hbk)
ISBN: 978-1-032-36939-6 (pbk)
ISBN: 978-1-003-33459-0 (ebk)

DOI: 10.1201/b23251

Typeset in URWPalladio font
by KnowledgeWorks Global Ltd.

Contents

Preface

What this book is

This is a book about algorithmics, and its goal is to teach this field and to help instructors to teach it. Algorithmics is, as generally admitted, "the science and art of designing algorithms to solve a given problem, preferably in minimal time". Consequently, this book aims at presenting efficient methods to design algorithms—mainly through examples.

It is structured according to two rules:

- Each chapter is devoted to a methodology of algorithm design, which can be applied to different data structures. For example, the chapter "Dynamic Programming" proposes problems on 2D arrays, on trees, on strings, as well as on graphs. As a matter of fact, some problems are proposed in two different chapters since they can be solved in different ways—which is particularly interesting to study. We have taken care for each problem to highlight different aspects of the methodologies: none of the 148 problems is just a rewriting of another one. The particular interest of each problem is shortly described at its beginning.

- Each chapter begins by an informal presentation on an example, then gives the technical bases of the methodology, and exposes a complete example. Then follows the main part, composed of detailed problems with their complete solution. Somewhat complex problems are tackled in a progressive manner in order to highlight the constructive process of the analysis leading to the solution. This solution is itself exhaustively detailed, concluding in programs written in pseudo-code. We do not give the coding in a specific programming language since the transcription from this pseudo-code into any usual one is generally straightforward. The correctness of all algorithms has been tested through code written by the authors.

What this book is not

This book is not a "data structures and algorithms" textbook. There are some necessary reminders about data structures in the first chapter, and they are intensively used in the book, but their actual implementation is not described. The reader is supposed to be aware of the good packages and classes she or he can use in her or his favorite programming language.

It is not a textbook on algorithms either, since it does not describe systematically how to solve a general problem, such as sorting or substring matching. It indeed exposes and solves a great variety of problems, but all the examples have been designed to help the reader to understand what is the efficient methodology that can be applied—not to give an exhaustive list.

Let us qualify it as "an example-based book on algorithm design methodologies".

What this book wishes to be

Algorithmics is, as we have said, "the science and art of designing algorithms". We wish the reader to reinforce these two skills. We would firstly like, when confronted with a new problem, the reader would have an "intuition" of the method to use, thanks to the numerous examples of the book. This would be the "art" or "craft" side of the matter. Secondly, we wish the reader to become able to prove the efficiency of the chosen method, as opposed to a naïve or more straightforward method. This would be the "science" side.

We have chosen to teach through examples, but it does not mean that we forsake rigour and mathematical proofs. Designing an algorithm is basically using methodically well-founded concepts, such as recurrence and computational complexity. There are generally lots of very nice problems in the middle and at the end of the chapters of the classical textbooks, but, too often, only those in the text itself are explicitly solved. Most of the time, the solution (if any) is given as a hint which is more a "haha" or a white rabbit out of a top-hat than an explanation. It baffles the reader and makes her or him feel that an algorithmic problem is just a brain-teaser. On the contrary, we believe that the rigorous and progressive construction of the solution will help the reader to master the designing process. Both deduction and induction are reasoning ways to be practiced in algorithmics as in many (if not all) fields.

We give a high value to the construction of the solutions: their total length is largely more than half of the book. Why is it so? One could argue, as we have read at the head of lecture notes on algorithms: "If you're a student, seeing the solution will rob you of the experience of solving the problem yourself, which is the only way to learn the material. If you're an instructor, you shouldn't assign problems that you can't solve yourself!" Well, this may be true for easy math exercises or puzzle quizzes, but we disagree with this opinion as far as algorithmics is concerned.

Murray Gell-Mann used to call the "Richard Feynman Problem-Solving Algorithm" the following sequence: (i) write down the problem; (ii) think very hard; (iii) write down the answer. Unfortunately, no student can use her or his fresh knowledge in such a way. Understanding an example during the course is different from reconstructing the process for solving a different problem. When the solution is explained, being not only a recurrence equation or a hint on the invariant, it is obviously fruitful for the student to follow its construction.

Lastly, let's take a comparison with the game of Sudoku: if you do not succeed in solving a certain puzzle, reading the solution grid doesn't bring anything in terms of learning. On the contrary, if the solution is commented (as it rarely happens) you may discover and memorize a new technique by the example. Concerning the instructors, a reference solution can also be very useful: the actual challenge is not "can you solve it yourself?", but rather "can you find a progressive and helping way to explain the solution?".

Who must read it ?

This is definitely not a book for beginners in computer science. Some knowledge of classical mathematics is required, as well as a solid initial formation in programming languages and data structures. It may be used by some classes of undergraduate students; however, it is obviously more suited for graduate studies, where it can be indicated as a textbook in algorithmics. It will also interest computer science professionals as a reference book.

The computer science instructors will find in this book a lot of useful material: the introduction of each chapter can be used as a reference for a lesson; the abundance of problems (along with their detailed solutions) will be an—almost—endless source for presenting to the students examples of methodical design. No problem is the exact rewriting of another one, and there is full freedom to transpose each of them in a different grounding.

Contents

As already pointed out, this book is organised to successively present the main methodologies of algorithm design. However, the first chapter "Mathematics and computer science: some useful notions" recalls mathematical bases, mostly proof principles, with an insistance on induction (recurrence) and combinatorial counting; it also gives a reminder in data structures (sets, bags, graphs, files, etc.) and provides 21 short problems and solutions. With the same goal, the chapter "Complexity of an algorithm" is a refresher on the basic ideas of the field and proposes seven problems, the last one being non-classical.

In the chapter "Specification, invariants, and iteration", we expose the principles of the rational design of a *while* loop and give 15 problems, some rather easy and others quite difficult. The (lengthy) solutions of the latter are examples of what we have previously called "practicing both deduction and induction". The following chapter, "Reduce and conquer, recursion", shows how to design recursive algorithms with the help of eight classical problems. We particularly insist on showing how the proof by induction theory can be applied to certify the exactness of a recursive procedure.

Chapter 5 describes the "Generate and test" methodology, also called "backtracking". We show how to obtain a recursive enumeration of the solutions to a combinatorial problem; we give the different patterns of a program according to its combinatorial nature. We give general principles to prune the tree of the solutions and illustrate them with 18 problems. The following chapter tackles the same kind of problems, but with the "Branch and bound" iterative technique. Here, four classical problems are given and resolved step by step.

Chapter 7 is devoted to "Greedy algorithms", suited to the same kind of combinatorial problems, but with no backtracking. The proof that they produce a good solution is obviously important to elaborate: we give the usual manners to check it, with 14 problems, some of which require an elaborate solution.

In Chapter 8, the fruitful "Divide and conquer" methodology is carefully analyzed and an original typology of the related algorithms is given. Their detailed construction is explained throughout 29 problems—some of them rather sophisticated.

Finally, Chapter 9 describes the "Dynamic programming" approach, often very efficient to elaborate an optimal (polynomial) solution to a combinatorial (exponential) problem. The richness and variety of its applications is displayed through 32 problems. Again here, some are classics and some are unexpected, some are easy and some are difficult.

To sum up, we describe seven methodologies of algorithm design, illustrated by 148 problems. Each problem is precisely described, often in a progressive organization, and the complete solution up to the pseudo-code is given in a methodical and rational manner.

Helping the reader

The section "Notations", on page 791 and following, describes the symbols we use in the mathematical formulas and in the algorithms. The reader is invited to refer to these pages every time she or he feels uneasy about the meaning of a symbol.

The problem and the solution are generally divided into several questions. A marginal note recalls the number of the problem and the number of the question in the problem. For example, this margin note would indicate the beginning of question 3 of problem 42. In the 42-Q3 solution, the answer to question 3 would be indicated in the same way with an A instead of a Q.

Every problem is given a double evaluation: one for its intrinsic interest, the other for its difficulty. There are four levels of increasing interest denoted by   ○ ○○ ○○ ○○○   and four levels of difficulty denoted by • •• •• ••• .

Attributing an intrinsic interest to a problem is a rather arbitrary task. We have used a mix of several criteria, the main being its pedagogical quality in illustrating the methodology of the chapter. The difficulty level takes into account the manner of describing the problem; an intrisically difficult problem can be gently proposed when its description is written as a gradual series of easier questions.

Sources and bibliography

The bibliography at the end of this book is deliberately composed of almost only textbooks. In other terms, we have not sought to quote the original articles where the presented algorithms have been published (if they have been). The reader interested in the personal history of such-and-such algorithm can consult the reference books by D. Knuth [22], G. Brassard and P. Bratley [8], T. Cormen *et al.* [9], E. Horowitz *et al.* [19], D. Stinson [33], S. Russell [31] and P. Norvig [31].

No algorithm in this book is completely original, but the problem formulation leading to the algorithm can be: sometimes it comes from the textbooks of the bibliography, it is a "folk" formulation, and sometimes it is our own. Every problem has nevertheless been rewritten and segmented in questions for pedagogical reasons. Many among them have indeed been "tested" on students by the authors and their colleagues at University of Rennes 1, France. Our originality does not lie in the material itself, but in formulating the problem and in carefully constructing its solution and at times in investigating the problem further than usual.

In his quite interesting book *Problem on Algorithms*, I. Parberry [28] gives a richly annotated bibliography on about 30 textbooks in the English language; the interested reader will take advantage of his advice. We are less aware of the English language literature on algorithms than of the French, so we apologize that this paragraph may be somewhat lacunar. We have the highest esteem for the books by T. Cormen *et al.* [9], J. Kleinberg and E. Tardos [21] and D. Knuth [22], the first two being suitable for beginners up to master's students, the latter exhausive and brillant but more difficult to read. The books by R. Johnsonbaugh and M. Shaeffer [20], E. Horowitz *et al.* [19], S. Baase and A. Van Gelder [3], R. Neapolitan and K. Naimipour [27], A. Levitin [24], S. Skenia [32] and T. Goodrich and R. Tamassia [13] are also general purpose texts of high interest. More recently, the four books by T. Roughgarden [30] have brought a nice contribution to the subject.

Coming to less comprehensive books, U. Manber [25], D. Gries [16], J. Edmonds [12] and J. Bentley [4, 5] have written quite interesting texts. The book by R. Graham, D. Knuth and O. Patashnik is a wonderful exposure to the so-called concrete mathematics and [23] gives a solid mathematical foundation to all domains of computer science. The books by G. Valiente [34] (trees and graphs) and M. Crochemore [10] (strings) are specialized on certain data structures. On the program construction itself, the book by P. Berlioux and P. Bizard [6] is a reference. If you can read French...and find them, the books by J. Arsac—for example [2]—have, up to our knowledge, no equivalent one in English.

1

Mathematics and computer science: some useful notions

Throughout this book, the framework considered is that of a *progressive* development of algorithms in which each step relies on a safe construction. In this perspective, a variety of tools are presented, intended for ensuring the validity of the constructions that are used. Moreover, during this development process, programs often call, on the one hand, on conditions expressed in the language of predicates, and on the other hand on data structures specified in the language of set theory. However, this approach is not sufficient to reach efficient solutions (especially from a temporal complexity viewpoint—see Chapter 2). Some refinement is then needed on the basis of tailor-made data structures. This is why this introduction is devoted to diverse mathematical tools and objects, as well as to the principal data structures used later on.

This chapter starts with notions related to reasonings frequently used in the remainder of the book: (i) propositional and predicate calculus, (ii) proof by contradiction and finally (iii) mathematical induction. Then, we raise the issue of recurrence relations (and the associated computations) which are a prominent part in Chapter 9. We take this opportunity to make explicit our acceptance of the terms recurrence, induction and recursion. The remainder of this chapter is organized mainly around the notion of set and we review the concepts of Cartesian product, multiset, relation, function as well as their principal related operators. We are interested in lists seen as an illustration of the notion of inductive structure derived from that of Cartesian product. We also focus on trees and graphs which originate numerous problems, before closing the chapter with the concept of priority queue whose interest will mainly appear in chapters 6 and 7, respectively dedicated to branch and bound technique and greedy algorithms.

For the interested reader, a thorough construction of classical logic and set theory can be found in [1]. As to formal refinement of data structures, [17, 7] can be profitably consulted.

1.1 Reasoning and proving

1.1.1 Propositional and predicate calculus

The predefined set $\mathbb{B}$ is defined as $\mathbb{B} \stackrel{\frown}{=} \{\textbf{true}, \textbf{false}\}$. These two values will sometimes be referred as T/F or t/f in arrays for space purposes. The "iff" expression stands for the

DOI: 10.1201/b23251-1

1

equivalence relation "if and only if" and can also be written "≡". If a and b are elements of $\mathbb{B}$, then:

- conjunction: "a **and** b" is **true** iff both a and b are **true**.

- disjunction: "a **or** b" is **false** iff both a and b are **false**.

- negation: "**not** a" is **true** iff a is **false**.

- logical implication: "a ⇒ b" is **false** iff both **not** a and b are **false**.

- logical equivalence: "a ⇔ b" is **true** iff a and b share the same value.

The existence of undefined expressions (for instance due to accessing a function out of its domain or dividing by 0) requires the use of "short-circuit" operators stopping the evaluation as soon as the result is known. The two short-circuit operators "**and then**" and "**or else**" are defined as follows:

- If a and b are defined:

  a **and then** b ⇔ a **and** b.

  a **or else** b ⇔ a **or** b.

- If a is defined whereas b is not:

  false and then b ⇔ **false**.

  true and then b is undefined

  false or else b is undefined.

  true or else b ⇔ **true**.

- If a is undefined, then whatever b:

  a **and then** b is undefined

  a **or else** b is undefined.

In the context of predicate calculus, quantifiers ∀ and ∃ are defined as follows:

- "∀x · (D ⇒ T(x))" is **true** iff, for any x in domain D then T(x) is **true**. Therefore, this formula is **true** if D is empty.

- "∃x · (D **and** T(x))" is **true** iff there is an x in domain D such that T(x) is **true**. Therefore, this formula is **false** if D is empty.

  The notation ∄ is a shorthand for **not** ∃.
  The double equivalence:

  $(a \Rightarrow b) \equiv (\textbf{not } a \textbf{ or } b) \equiv (\textbf{not } b \Rightarrow \textbf{not } a)$

is the foundation for reasoning by contraposition, where the validity of the implication **not** Q ⇒ **not** P is proven to show that P implies Q.

1.1.2 Proof by contradiction

The proof by contradiction relies on two principles of propositional logic:

- *excluded middle*, claiming that a property which is not false is necessarily true, then its conjunction with its negation is **false**,

- the definition of implication: $(P \Rightarrow Q) \cong (\textbf{not } P \textbf{ or } Q)$.

A consequence of these two properties is that $(\textbf{not } P \Rightarrow \textbf{false})$ is equivalent to P, which ensures the validity of the proof by contradiction. In effect:

$$(\textbf{not } P \Rightarrow \textbf{false})$$

$\Leftrightarrow$ definition of the implication

$$(\textbf{not}(\textbf{not } P) \textbf{ or false})$$

$\Leftrightarrow$ involutivity of the negation

$$(P \textbf{ or false})$$

$\Leftrightarrow$ property of the disjunction

$$P.$$

Proving a proposition P by contradiction encompasses two steps:

1. **not** P is assumed (i.e. the falsity of P),

2. a contradiction between this assumption and one of its entailments is pointed out.

It is important to note that when no contradiction can be exhibited, *nothing* can be concluded as to P (neither truth nor falsity).

First example

Let us consider the following proposition P: "there is no smallest rational number strictly greater than 0". In order to prove P by contradiction, the negation of P is assumed, namely: "there is a smallest rational number strictly positive r". From the negation of P, a contradiction is searched.

Let $s = r/2$. By construction, s is a rational number strictly greater than 0 and strictly smaller than r. This claim is in opposition to P, which states that r is the smallest rational number.

Thus, it can be concluded that proposition P is for sure true and that there is no smallest strictly positive rational number.

Second example

One would like to demonstrate that there is no rational number whose square is 2, in other words one wants to prove the following proposition P "the square root of 2 is an irrational number".

Proof. One first assume that there is an element $x = p/q$ of $\mathbb{Q}_+$ (the set of positive rational numbers) such that $x^2 = 2$, with p and q are relatively prime numbers (i.e. p/q is an irreducible fraction). One has:

$$\left(\frac{p}{q}\right)^2 = 2$$

$\Leftrightarrow$ arithmetics

$$p^2 = 2q^2$$

$\Leftrightarrow$ reformulation

2 divides p^2

$\Leftrightarrow$ any even square number is the square of an even number

2 divides p

$\Leftrightarrow$ $p = 2p'$

$\exists p' \cdot (p^2 = 4p'^2 = 2q^2)$

$\Leftrightarrow$ reformulation

2 is a divider of q^2

$\Leftrightarrow$ any even square number is the square of an even number

2 is a divider of q.

One can then deduce that 2 is a divider of both p and q, which entails that p and q are not relatively prime numbers which is in opposition to the fact p/q is an irreducible fraction.

In a similar way, it is possible to demonstrate that there is no negative rational number whose square is 2, otherwise its opposite would be a positive rational number whose square would be 2. As a consequence, the square root of 2 is an irrational number [1].

1.1.3   Proof by induction with one index

In this section, we deal with another type of demonstration, namely proof *by induction* with a single index. We successively review its most usual versions, in particular those used in chapters 4 and 8.

1.1.3.1   Proof by simple induction

This type of demonstration is also called proof by *weak* induction. Let us consider a property $P(n)$, depending on the positive integer $n \in \mathbb{N}$ to be proven.

If the following two properties can be demonstrated:

    Initialization $P(n_0)$ is true for a given $n_0 \in \mathbb{N}$

    Induction $\forall n \cdot ((n \geqslant n_0 \text{ and } P(n)) \Rightarrow P(n+1))$

then:

    Conclusion $\forall n \cdot (n \geqslant n_0 \Rightarrow P(n))$

The fact that $P(n)$ is assumed to be true constitutes the *induction hypothesis*, in order to (try to) prove $P(n+1)$. The initialization is also called the *base*.

Proof. The correction of the proof by induction can be made by reasoning by contradiction. Let $X = \{k \in \mathbb{N} \mid k \geqslant n_0 \text{ and } P(k) = \textbf{false}\}$, be the set of integers greater than k_0 such that property $P(k)$ is false. If X is non-empty, it encompasses a smallest element (since in any set of integers there is an element smaller than all the others), denoted as m. From the

---

[1]This proof was made by Euclide, about 250 B.C.

initialization, it is known that $m > n_0$. Therefore, $m - 1 \geqslant n_0$ and since m is the smallest element in X, $m - 1 \notin X$ **and** $P(m-1)$ is true. Using the induction step, it can be deduced that $P(m)$ is true, which contradicts $m \in X$. Consequently, X is empty.

Example

Let us prove by induction the formula:

$$\sum_{i=1}^{n} i = \frac{n(n+1)}{2}.$$

Initialization This formula is true for $n_0 = 1$, since we have:

$$\sum_{i=1}^{1} i = 1$$

and for $n_0 = 1$ the formula yields:

$$\frac{1(1+1)}{2} = 1$$

which is the same result.

Induction Let us assume that the formula is true for n, with $n \geqslant 1$, and let us try to prove that it is still true for $(n + 1)$. In other words, let us try to prove that the induction formula

$$\sum_{i=1}^{n} i = \frac{n(n+1)}{2}$$

entails

$$\sum_{i=1}^{n+1} i = \frac{(n+1)(n+2)}{2}.$$

Indeed, it is correct since:

$$\sum_{i=1}^{n+1} i$$

$$= \qquad\qquad\qquad\qquad\qquad\qquad\qquad \text{arithmetics } ((n+1) > 1)$$

$$\left(\sum_{i=1}^{n} i\right) + (n+1)$$

$$= \qquad\qquad\qquad\qquad\qquad\qquad\qquad \text{induction hypothesis}$$

$$\frac{n(n+1)}{2} + (n+1)$$

$$= \qquad\qquad\qquad\qquad\qquad\qquad\qquad \text{arithmetics}$$

$$\frac{(n+1)(n+2)}{2}.$$

Conclusion The formula is true for $n_0 = 1$. In addition, if it is true for n (where $n \geqslant 1$), then it is true for $(n + 1)$. Finally, this demonstration by induction has proven that the formula is true for any strictly positive integer.

Remark

This demonstration may also be used to prove a result concerning negative integers: if a formula is true for $n = 0$, and if the fact that it is true for $-n$, where $n \in \mathbb{N}$, entails that it is true for $(-n - 1)$, then it is true for any negative integer.

1.1.3.2 Proof by partial induction

$P(n)$ denotes a property depending on an integer $n \in \mathbb{N}$.

> If it is possible to demonstrate the two following properties:
>
> **Initialization** $P(1)$ is true
>
> **Induction** $\forall n \cdot ((k \in \mathbb{N} \text{ and } n = 2^k \text{ and } P(n)) \Rightarrow P(2n))$
>
> then:
>
> **Conclusion** $\forall n \cdot ((k \in \mathbb{N} \text{ and } n = 2^k) \Rightarrow P(2n))$

This variant concerns a proposition on integers that are powers of 2. It is also possible to prove a property on even numbers, or more generally on any infinite subset of $\mathbb{N}$ that may be built by induction (see section 1.3, page 15).

1.1.3.3 Proof by strong induction

The proof by *strong* (or *total* or *generalized*) induction seems to be more difficult to apply than the regular induction. However it is appropriate and rightly often used. Here again, one considers a property $P(n)$, depending on an integer $n \in \mathbb{N}$.

> If it is possible to prove the following property:
>
> **Induction** $\forall n \cdot ((n \geqslant n_0 \text{ and } \forall m \cdot (m \in n_0 \mathinner{..} n - 1 \Rightarrow P(m))) \Rightarrow P(n))$
>
> then:
>
> **Conclusion** $\forall n \cdot (n \geqslant n_0 \Rightarrow P(n))$

The correctness of this demonstration pattern directly stems from that of the regular (simple) induction.

Example

Let us prove the following property using strong induction:

Any integer strictly greater than 1 is the product of several prime numbers.

It is assumed that 1 (also called unity) is a prime number.

Induction Let us assume that any integer m less than n and greater than or equal to $n_0 = 2$ is the product of several prime numbers. For n, two exclusive cases are singled out:

- n is prime and then the product of unity and itself, therefore the product of two prime numbers.

- n has a divisor d, other than 1 and itself. According to the induction hypothesis, one has $n = d \cdot p$, where d and p are two integers less than or equal to n and strictly greater than 1. Each of them is the product of several prime numbers, and n is also the product of several prime numbers.

Conclusion Any integer strictly greater than 1 is the product of several prime numbers.

1.1.4 Partition induction

An important type of proof by induction is *partition induction* (also called DaC induction due to its role in the technique for designing algorithms called "Divide and conquer" which is the subject of Chapter 8).

One considers a predicate $P(i, s)$ depending on the two integers i and s such that $i \leqslant s$. The partition induction consists of proving that P holds over any interval $I = i .. s$: (i) by proving it for any element of I, and (ii) by proving that the correctness of P over each of the intervals $I_1 = i .. m$ and $I_2 = m + 1 .. s$ (partition of I) entails that of P over I.

If it is possible to prove the two following properties:

Initialization $\forall i \cdot (i \in \mathbb{N} \Rightarrow P(i, i))$

Induction $\forall (i, m, s) \cdot ((i \in \mathbb{N} \text{ and } s \in \mathbb{N} \text{ and } m \in \mathbb{N} \text{ and } m \in i .. s - 1 \text{ and } P(i, m) \text{ and } P(m + 1, s)) \Rightarrow P(i, s))$

then:

Conclusion $\forall (i, s) \cdot ((i \in \mathbb{N} \text{ and } s \in \mathbb{N} \text{ and } i \leqslant s) \Rightarrow P(i, s))$

The correctness of this demonstration procedure is now demonstrated.

Proof. We proceed by contradiction. Let F be the set of pairs for which P does not hold, i.e.:

$$F = \{(i, s) \mid (i, s) \in \mathbb{N} \times \mathbb{N} \text{ and } i \leqslant s \text{ and not } P(i, s)\}.$$

Assuming that $F \neq \varnothing$, let (j, k) be one of the pairs of F for which $l = (k - j + 1)$ is minimum. From the initialization, $l \neq 1$ and there is at least one value m such that $j \leqslant m < k$. The pairs (j, m) and $(m + 1, k)$ do not belong to F since $(m - j + 1) < l$ and $(k - (m + 1) + 1) < l)$. It comes that both predicates $P(j, m)$ and $P(m + 1, k)$ hold. From the induction, it can be deduced that $P(j, k)$ holds, which contradicts $(j, k) \in F$. Thus $F = \varnothing$ and $\forall (i, s) \cdot (i \in \mathbb{N} \text{ and } s \in \mathbb{N} \text{ and } i \leqslant s \Rightarrow P(i, s))$.

Remarks

1. Partition induction must be based on an initialization $P(i, s)$ for which $s - i + 1 = 1$. In particular, it cannot rely on an initialization where $s - i + 1 = 0$. As a matter of fact, in such a case there is no value for m such that $i \leqslant m < s$. Similarly, the induction cannot be based on an initialization $P(i, s)$ such that $s - i + 1 > 1$. Let us take the example of $P(i, i + 1)$ as the initialization and let us try to prove that $P(i, i + 2)$ holds. The only two possible values for m are $m = i$ and $m = i + 1$. If $m = i$, the first induction hypothesis is $P(i, i)$ and if $m = i + 1$, the second induction hypothesis is $P(i + 2, i + 2)$. None of these predicates is an instance of the initialization and then the related pattern is invalid.

2. The regular simple induction is a special case of partition induction obtained by taking $m = i$.

Example

One will once more demonstrate that:

$$\sum_{k=1}^{n} k = \frac{n \cdot (n+1)}{2}$$

but, this time, using the technique of partition induction. Let us denote $S(i,s) = \sum_{k=i}^{s} k$ and call $P(i,s)$ the predicate $S(i,s) = (s^2 - i^2 + s + i)/2$. If we succeed in proving that $P(i,s)$ holds, we will have more specifically $P(1,n)$ and it can be concluded that $S(1,n) = (n^2 + n)/2 = \sum_{k=1}^{n} k$.

Initialization For any i, one has: $S(i,i) = (i^2 - i^2 + i + i)/2 = i = \sum_{k=i}^{i} k$.

Induction hypothesis Let us choose $m = \lfloor (i+s)/2 \rfloor$. One has:

- $S(i,m) = \dfrac{m^2 - i^2 + m + i}{2}$,

- $S(m+1,s) = \dfrac{s^2 - (m+1)^2 + m + 1 + i}{2}$.

Induction itself Let us demonstrate that, on the basis of the two above hypotheses, $S(i,s) = (s^2 - i^2 + s + i)/2$ for $i < s$:

$$S(i,s)$$

$=$ definition

$$\sum_{k=i}^{s} k$$

$=$ arithmetics ($i < s$), with $m = \lfloor (i+s)/2 \rfloor$

$$\sum_{k=i}^{m} k + \sum_{k=m+1}^{s} k$$

$=$ definition

$$S(i,m) + S(m+1,s)$$

$=$ induction hypothesis

$$\frac{m^2 - i^2 + m + i}{2} + \frac{s^2 - (m+1)^2 + s + m + 1}{2}$$

$=$ arithmetics

$$\frac{s^2 - i^2 + s + i}{2}$$

Conclusion $\displaystyle\sum_{k=i}^{s} k = \frac{s^2 - i^2 + s + i}{2}.$

Remarks

1. One trick used in the example above consists in replacing a constant (1 as the lower bound of the quantification) by a variable (i). Such a technique will be encountered for the construction of iterations in the context of the "strengthening by introducing variables" (confer section 3.3.3, page 98) where *more than necessary* is proven in order to facilitate (in general) the demonstration.

2. When used for the design of algorithms called "Divide and conquer", the major difficulty with partition induction lies in the discovery of induction hypotheses and the way they may be combined to make the final solution, what will be called "gathering step".

1.1.5 Foundation of the proof by induction

In the preceding paragraphs, some proofs by induction have been exhibited, all of them relying on the natural order of integers. It is interesting and useful to extend this type of proof to properties no longer characterized by an integer but by an element in a totally ordered set.

The proof by induction comes from the following property.

Property 1:
Let E *be a totally ordered set by means of the relation* $\preceq$ *and* P *be a property depending on the element* x *of* E. *If the following property holds:*

$$\forall x \cdot (x \in E \text{ and } \forall y \cdot ((y \in E \text{ and } y \preceq x \text{ and } P(y)) \Rightarrow P(x))$$

then $\forall x \cdot (x \in E \Rightarrow P(x))$.

Proving this property is achieved as a simple transposition of that given in section 1.1.3 for simple induction.

1.1.6 Proof by induction with several indexes

Property 1 stated in the previous section allows (in particular) the justification of a proof by induction for properties depending on several integer indexes. In the case of two indexes, one considers a property (or formula) $P(m, n)$ depending on the two integers m and n, which is to be proven by induction. Several patterns can be used, among which:

If it is possible to prove the two following properties:

Initialization $\forall i \cdot (i \in \mathbb{N} \Rightarrow P(i, 0))$ and $\forall j \cdot (j \in \mathbb{N} \Rightarrow P(0, j))$

Induction $\forall (i, j) \cdot ((i \in \mathbb{N}_1 \text{ and } j \in \mathbb{N}_1 \text{ and } P(i-1, j) \text{ and } P(i, j-1)) \Rightarrow P(i, j)$

then:

Conclusion $\forall (m, n) \cdot ((m \in \mathbb{N} \text{ and } n \in \mathbb{N}) \Rightarrow P(m, n))$.

The correctness of this pattern stems from the fact the set $\mathbb{N}^2$ of pairs of integers is equipped with a total order (induced by the total order over $\mathbb{N}$), defined as follows:

$$(a, b) \preceq (c, d) \ \hat{=} \ a < c \text{ or } (a = c \text{ and } b \leqslant d).$$

Let us consider q the point whose coordinates are denoted by (i, j). The pattern proposed above aims at assessing that if P holds at any point: (i) of the rectangle $0..i-1, 0..j-1$ (the cases when $i = 0$ or $j = 0$ are covered by the initialization), (ii) from $(i, 0)$ to $(i, j-1)$ of row i and (iii) $(0, j)$ to $(i-1, j)$ of column j, then P holds at point (i, j) as well. In other words, if P holds at any point "lower" (according to $\preceq$) than point (i, j), $P(i, j)$ holds as well, which corresponds to the instance of property 1 for the pairs of $(\mathbb{N}^2, \preceq)$.

This demonstration pattern is used in problem 21, page 45. It may be transposed to $\mathbb{N}_1$ if needed with an initialization referring to $\mathbb{N}_1$ and the induction with $\mathbb{N}_1 - \{1\}$, the conclusion being:

$$\forall(m,n) \cdot ((m \in \mathbb{N}_1 \text{ and } n \in \mathbb{N}_1) \Rightarrow P(m,n)).$$

Others patterns are applicable to prove an induction with two (or more) indexes. Their correctness is ensured inasmuch as they comply with property 1 for a given order (see problem 8, page 37).

1.2   Recurrence relations

After introducing the concept of recurrence relation, several examples are provided and the topic of establishing a recurrence relation and its related algorithmic calculation is dealt with.

1.2.1   Generalities, examples and closed forms

By definition, a series (also called a sequence) $S(n)$, with $n \in \mathbb{N}$, is *defined by a recurrence relation* if, for n sufficiently large one has a relation of type: $S(n) = f(S(n-1), \ldots, S(n-p))$. Moreover, it is necessary to identify values allowing for initializing the calculation of S. Here only series valued as nonnegative integers are taken into account (especially because they are associated with complexity calculations).

In the recurrence relation defining Fibonacci numbers:

$$\begin{aligned} &\mathcal{F}(1) = 1 \\ &\mathcal{F}(2) = 1 \\ &\mathcal{F}(n) = \mathcal{F}(n-1) + \mathcal{F}(n-2) \end{aligned} \qquad\qquad n > 2$$

or in the one giving Padovan numbers:

$$\begin{aligned} &\mathcal{P}(1) = 1 \\ &\mathcal{P}(2) = 1 \\ &\mathcal{P}(3) = 1 \\ &\mathcal{P}(n) = \mathcal{P}(n-2) + \mathcal{P}(n-3) \end{aligned} \qquad\qquad n > 3$$

f is a linear function. On the other hand, the one appearing in the relation defining factorials (number of permutations in a set of n elements) is nonlinear:

$$\begin{aligned} &\text{Fact}(1) = 1 \\ &\text{Fact}(n) = n \cdot \text{Fact}(n-1) \end{aligned} \qquad\qquad n > 1.$$

Thanks to the theory of *generative functions* (see for example [14]), mathematics provide powerful tools to find *closed forms* (i.e. nonrecurrent) for some series defined by means of recurrence relations, especially when f is linear, but also in other cases. Thus, Fibonacci sequence is expressed under closed form as:

$$\mathcal{F}(n) = \frac{1}{\sqrt{5}} \left[\left(\frac{1+\sqrt{5}}{2} \right)^n - \left(\frac{1-\sqrt{5}}{2} \right)^n \right] \qquad n \geqslant 1.$$

Catalan numbers, which are the subject of problems 5, page 34, and 13, page 40, are defined by the recurrence relation:

$$\begin{vmatrix} Cat(1) = 1 \\ Cat(n) = \sum_{i=1}^{n-1} Cat(i) \cdot Cat(n-i) \end{vmatrix} \qquad n > 1$$

as well as by:

$$\begin{vmatrix} Cat(1) = 1 \\ Cat(n) = \dfrac{4n-6}{n} \cdot Cat(n-1) \end{vmatrix} \qquad n > 1.$$

It may also be expressed by the closed form [2]:

$$Cat(n) = \frac{(2n-2)!}{(n-1)! \cdot n!} = \frac{1}{n} \cdot C_{2n-2}^{n-1} \qquad n \geqslant 1.$$

From an algorithmic point of view, a closed form seems appealing since easy to compute. However, if this choice is reasonable for computing the nth Catalan number, it may be inappropriate as shown about Fibonacci numbers in problem 12, page 39.

A recurrence relation may serve as the definition of a series involving more than one index. For instance, Ackerman numbers are defined by means of the following two index nested recurrence:

$$\begin{vmatrix} A(0,n) = n+1 \\ A(m,0) = A(m-1,1) \\ A(m,n) = A(m-1, A(m,n-1)) \end{vmatrix} \qquad \begin{array}{r} n \geqslant 0 \\ m > 0 \\ m > 0 \text{ and } n > 0. \end{array}$$

Another example of two index recurrence is that of Stirling numbers, which correspond to the number of partitions with p blocks of a set of n elements. Here, the recurrence is much more simple than the previous one and Stirling numbers are studied in problem 16, page 41.

1.2.2 Establishing and computing a recurrence relation

1.2.2.1 Principles

We now deal with the establishment and the computation of series defined by recurrence relations. It turns out that numerous problems, for example related to enumeration, but also to the calculation of the optimal value of a function (see Chapter 9), can be solved in pointing out a recurrence allowing for computing the considered value. The recurrence must be complete, i.e. any situation likely to happen must be taken into account.

---

[2]It is assumed that closed forms may involve any type of quantifier, here the product underlying factorial calculation.

As closed forms are rarely known, the computational procedure aims at building an iterative program where a one (or more) dimensional array is used to store the successive values of the considered series. This approach is discussed and justified in chapter 4.

According to the principle adopted, the value of a cell is calculated from those already present in the array. Then the order for filling the array is of prime importance and the evolution of the calculation strongly depends on dependence relationships between elements. For one dimension recurrences, it is generally simple (increasing or decreasing index values), but multiple index recurrences require more attention. The examples given hereafter illustrate the proposed approach.

1.2.2.2 Some examples

Single index recurrence: binary trees with n nodes

The objective is to compute $nbBT(n)$ the number of binary trees (see section 1.6, page 27) that possess n nodes (including leaves). First, the recurrence defining this number is defined. It can be observed that there is only one tree without nodes: the empty tree. For establishing a recurrence for $nbBT(n)$, a binary tree with n nodes is decomposed into smaller trees. When n is positive, a tree with n nodes is made up of a root (one node), possibly a left subtree with i nodes and possibly a right subtree with $(n-i-1)$ nodes. Let us have a look at the possible ways to proceed to the decomposition:

- one can place no node in the left subtree (empty), which leads to $nbBT(0)(=1)$, and $(n-1)$ nodes in the right subtree (by definition) with $nbBT(n-1)$ possibilities , which makes finally $nbBT(0) \cdot nbBT(n-1)$ cases,

- one can place a single node in the left subtree and $(n-2)$ nodes in the right subtree, which leads to $nbBT(1) \cdot nbBT(n-2)$ cases,

- ...

More generally, one place i nodes in the left subtree, thus $nbBT(i)$ left subtrees, and $(n-i-1)$ nodes in the right subtree, thus $nbBT(n-i-1)$ right subtrees, which leads to $nbBT(i) \cdot nbBT(n-i-1)$ such trees. This works for all values of i from 0 to $(n-1)$. Finally, the number of trees with n nodes is:

$$
\begin{aligned}
nbBT(n) &= nbBT(0) \cdot nbBT(n-1) + nbBT(1) \cdot nbBT(n-2) + \cdots \\
&\quad \cdots + nbBT(i) \cdot nbBT(n-i-1) + \cdots \\
&\quad \cdots + nbBT(n-1) \cdot nbBT(0)
\end{aligned}
$$

from which comes:

$$
\left|
\begin{aligned}
&nbBT(0) = 1 \\
&nbBT(n) = \sum_{i=0}^{n-1} nbBT(i) \cdot nbBT(n-i-1) \qquad\qquad n \geqslant 1.
\end{aligned}
\right.
$$

After having checked (by enumeration) that $nbBT(1) = 1$ and $nbBT(2) = 2$, the next value is:

$$nbBT(3) = \sum_{i=0}^{2} nbBT(i) \cdot nbBT(n-i-1)$$
$$= nbBT(0) \cdot nbBT(2) + nbBT(1) \cdot nbBT(1) + nbBT(2) \cdot nbBT(0)$$
$$= 2+1+2 = 5.$$

Figure 1.1, page 13, shows all the binary trees for $n \in 0 .. 3$.

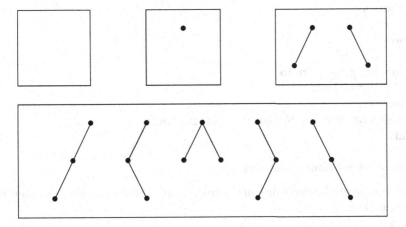

Fig. 1.1 – Vizualization of all binary trees of size 0, 1, 2 and 3, in respective numbers: 1, 1, 2 and 5.

In the absence of additional information, the computation of $nbBT(n)$ is achieved by filling the array NBBT$[0 .. n]$. Since the value of $nbBT(n)$ depends on lower index values, the calculation is evolving according to increasing index values once the cell NBBT$[0]$ is initialized (with 1). The resulting procedure is the following:

1. **constants**
2. $n \in \mathbb{N}_1$ **and** $n = \ldots$
3. **variables**
4. NBBT $\in 0 .. n \rightarrow \mathbb{N}_1$
5. **begin**
6. NBBT$[0] \leftarrow 1$;
7. **for** i **ranging** $1 .. n$ **do**
8. NBBT$[i] \leftarrow 0$;
9. **for** j **ranging** $0 .. i - 1$ **do**
10. NBBT$[i] \leftarrow$ NBBT$[i] +$ NBBT$[j] \cdot$ NBBT$[i - j - 1]$
11. **end for**
12. **end for**;
13. **write**(*the number of binary trees having* , n, *nodes is* , NBBT$[n]$)
14. **end**

An alternate solution for this calculation is presented in problem 13, page 40.

Single index recurrence: factorial

We now consider a situation where the (one dimensional) recurrence is given a priori. Here, one is interested in the computation of $n!$. It can be noticed that the only required value for the computation of $n!$ is $(n-1)!$. Moreover, it is unnecessary to store the successive values of factorial in an array, which simplifies the algorithm.

The following iterative procedure is devised without any storage of intermediate values:

1. **constants**
2. $n \in \mathbb{N}_1$ **and** $n = \ldots$
3. **variables**
4. $\mathsf{Facto} \in \mathbb{N}_1$
5. **begin**
6. $\mathsf{Facto} \leftarrow 1;$
7.   **for** i **ranging** $2 .. n$ **do**
8. $\mathsf{Facto} \leftarrow \mathsf{Facto} \cdot i$
9.   **end for;**
10.   **write(***for n =* , n, *the value of n! is* , Facto)
11. **end**

Two index recurrence: Delannoy numbers

We will emphasize on the evolution of the calculation of the two index recurrence defining Delannoy numbers:

$$
\begin{aligned}
nbDel(0,j) &= 1 && 0 \leqslant j \leqslant m \\
nbDel(i,0) &= 1 && 1 \leqslant i \leqslant n \\
nbDel(i,j) &= \begin{pmatrix} nbDel(i,j-1) + \\ nbDel(i-1,j) + \\ nbDel(i-1,j-1) \end{pmatrix} && \left\{ \begin{array}{c} 1 \leqslant i \leqslant n \\ \text{et} \\ 1 \leqslant j \leqslant m \end{array} \right. .
\end{aligned}
$$

In order to compute $nbDEL(n,m)$ where m and n are two integers, the array $NBD[0..n, 0..m]$ is associated with $nbDEL$. The computation of $NBD[i,j]$ (connected with $nbDEL(i,j)$, the general term of the recurrence), it is necessary to know: (i) the value of the cell with the same row index and the column index immediately lower, (ii) the value of the cell with the same column index and the row index immediately lower and (iii) the value of the cell with row and column immediately lower. One may then fill NBD according to rows (but columns or diagonals as well). After initializing row 0 with 1 (first term of the recurrence), rows are filled by increasing values of index i (until n is reached): cell $(i,0)$ is set to 1 (second term of the recurrence), then cells $(i,1)$ to (i,m) are filled using the last term of the recurrence.

1.2.2.3   Designing the algorithm associated with a recurrence

In general, given a (complete) recurrence formula for which no closed form is available, the computational procedure is built as follows:

1. Specification of the tabular structure (array) associated with the calculation (dimensions and size of each of them).

2. Determination of the dependence relationships that connect the left element and those present in the right part of the general term of the recurrence. An evolution of the calculation can then be deduced, which ensures that the computation of any element of the array calls only on previously computed elements (possibly using initialization terms of the recurrence).

3. Optionally, improvements of the computation, e.g. restriction of the calculation only to necessary elements.

4. Production of the code.

As it can be seen in the example of factorial (cf. also problem 12, page 39), the tabular structure may be replaced by a few appropriate scalar variables. Awareness is required about the representation of numbers, especially in the presence of a recurrence whose values grow very quickly. It is advisable to work with a floating point representation rather than with integers. For example, Ackerman numbers are such that $A(3, n) = 2^{n+3} - 3$ et $A(4, n) = 2^{2^{\cdot^{\cdot^{2}}}} - 3$ ($n + 3$ occurrences of 2), and this number becomes rapidly huge ($A(4, 2) = 2^{2^{2^{2}}} - 3 = 2^{16} - 3 = 2^{65536} - 3$). Last, the dependence relationship connecting left and right hand sides may be nontrivial. Here again, we refer to Ackerman numbers and the computation of $A(6, 1) = A(5, 65533)$.

1.3 Recurrence, induction, recursion, etc.

In the previous sections, proof by induction and recurrence have been dealt with and we now try to clarify a vocabulary often perceived as somewhat confusing.

Proof by induction

When algorithms based on this type of reasoning are built, we frequently use the generic term *inductive reasoning*, whose heart is *induction*. When reasoning on integers, it will be mentioned if it the underlying induction is a simple or a strong one. They constitute the two most often used variants in chapters 4 and 8.

Recursive program

An algorithm (as well as its coded form) is called recursive if it calls itself directly or by means of other algorithms. The function *Fact* in page 16 illustrates the notion of recursive algorithm, as well as numerous programs in chapters 4 and 8.

The "canonical" implementation of a recurrence is a recursive algorithm. However, it will be seen in Chapter 4 that, for efficiency purposes, an iterative version will be preferred where a tabular structure is filled (see preceding examples). This must not be confused with the fact that a recursive program can be transformed (automatically but with the explicit handling of a *stack*, see section 1.8) into an iterative one, which will have the same behavior (especially the same performances) as the initial recursive program.

Nonetheless, there is a type of recursive program that can interestingly be transformed into an iterative one: in the case of a *terminal* recursion. We will investigate this concept with functions, but this would apply to procedures as well. A function F is terminal recursive if it complies with the following pattern:

1. **function** $F(\ldots)$ **result** ... **pre**
2. ...

   3. **begin**
   4.   **if** C **then**
   5.   **result** V
   6.   **else**
   7.   **result** $F(\ldots)$
   8.   **end if**
   9. **end**

It is then possible to obtain an iterative program (whose execution is more efficient), which is achievable by an smart compiler.

Example

The function hereafter:

   1. **function** $Fact(p)$ **result** $\mathbb{N}_1$ **pre**
   2. $p \in \mathbb{N}_1$
   3. **begin**
   4.   **if** $p = 1$ **then**
   5.   **result** 1
   6.   **else**
   7.   **result** $p \cdot Fact(p-1)$
   8.   **end if**
   9. **end**

is not terminal recursive. It can be put into this form in the following way:

   1. **function** $Fact1(p)$ **result** $\mathbb{N}_1$ **pre**
   2. $p \in \mathbb{N}_1$
   3. **begin**
   4.   **result** $FactRecTerm(p, 1)$
   5. **end**
   6. **function** $FactRecTerm(p, q)$ **result** $\mathbb{N}_1$ **pre**
   7. $p \in \mathbb{N}_1$ **and** $q \in \mathbb{N}_1$
   8. **begin**
   9.   **if** $p = 1$ **then**
  10.   **result** q
  11.   **else**
  12.   **result** $FactRecTerm(p - 1, q \cdot p)$
  13.   **end if**
  14. **end**

Here, function $Fact1$ is nonrecursive and function $FactRecTerm$ is terminal recursive.

1.4   Sets

1.4.1   Basic notations

We begin with a particular formula called *pair* which will be frequently used in the following. A pair   is composed by two expressions separated by a comma or by the symbol $\mapsto$.

For example, the formula $x, y + 3$ is a pair. This pair may also be denoted by $x \mapsto y + 3$, or even $(x, y + 3)$. In this notation, the first element is called the *origin* and the second one is called the *end*.

$C \cong (x, y + 3)$ associates the name C to the object $(x, y + 3)$.

The relational operators $=$ and $\neq$, with their common meaning, are assumed available to compare two mathematical objects.

1.4.2   Definition of sets

Let E be a set, i.e. a collection of elements associated with the Boolean expression $x \in E$, which states that x is an element of set E. Its negation is denoted $\notin$. The set that contains no element (the empty set) is denoted by $\varnothing$. When E and F are two sets, the expression $E \times F$ denotes their Cartesian product which is defined by the equivalence $(a, b) \in E \times F \equiv (a \in E \text{ and } b \in F)$.

A set may be defined by the properties of its elements. This is the *intensional* definition. It is denoted by $\{x \mid x \in E \text{ and } P\}$, where E is a set and P a selection predicate. This defines the (sub)set of elements of E possessing the property P. Hence,

$$\{x \mid x \in \mathbb{N} \text{ and } \nexists \cdot (y \in \mathbb{N} \text{ and } x = 2 \cdot y)\}$$

defines the set of odd integers. The following property of the Cartesian product:

$$E \times F = \{(x, y) \mid x \in E \text{ and } y \in F\}$$

stems from the intensional definition of sets. The advantage of the second definition lies in the fact that it allows, *via* a *convention*, for easily pointing a particular element of a pair. As a matter of fact, let us consider the following definition of a point p in the Cartesian plane: $p \in \{(x, y) \mid x \in \mathbb{R} \text{ and } y \in \mathbb{R}\}$. It is then possible to use p.x (respectively p.y) for the abscissa (respectively ordinate) of p. This advantage is also exploited for inductive structures, in section 1.4.7, page 20, whereas the standard notation "$\times$" does not provide this facility.

A set may also be defined by means of the enumeration of its elements, which corresponds to the *extensional* definition. The associated notation is $\{1, 3, \textbf{true}, 1.4\}$. This latter set can also be written $\{1, \textbf{true}, 1.4, 3\}$ (the order of elements is irrelevant), or $\{1, 1, 3, \textbf{true}, 1.4, \textbf{true}, 3\}$ (an element is present or not, the number of occurrences does not matter inasmuch as the element is present). A set may also be defined in an inductive way. A set X defined inductively is a special case of a recursive set. The function serving for its definition has an inductive (or recurrent) nature, i.e.:

- some elements of X are explicitly given,

- the other elements are defined from elements already belonging to X.

For example, P the set of even numbers may be defined as *the smallest* subset of $\mathbb{N}$ complying with:

$$P = \{0\} \cup \{n \mid n \in \mathbb{N} \text{ and } ((n - 2 \in P) \Rightarrow n \in P)\}.$$

We will see later in this book several examples of sets defined inductively, especially trees. Often, properties of such sets are proven by an inductive reasoning.

$\mathbb{P}(E)$ stands for the powerset of set E and it is defined by

$$x \in \mathbb{P}(E) \Leftrightarrow \forall y \cdot (y \in x \Rightarrow y \in E).$$

Hence, if $E \cong \{1, 2, 3\}$, then $\mathbb{P}(E) = \{\varnothing, \{1\}, \{2\}, \{3\}, \{1, 2\}, \{1, 3\}, \{2, 3\}, \{1, 2, 3\}\}$.

1.4.3   Operations on sets

The reader is supposed aware of the definitions of the following set operations: $\cap$ (intersection), $\cup$ (union), $\subseteq$ (inclusion), $\subset$ (strict inclusion), $\not\subset$ (non inclusion), $\not\subseteq$ (non strict inclusion) ; the difference $a - b$ between two sets is defined as $\{x : x \in a \textbf{ and } x \notin b\}$.

For a finite set E, card(E) represents the *cardinality* (the number of elements) of E.

1.4.4   Special sets

Beyond $\mathbb{B}$, the set defined before for Booleans, the reader is assumed to be familiar with the following numeric sets: $\mathbb{N}$ (natural numbers), $\mathbb{Z}$ (integers), $\mathbb{R}$ (real numbers, i.e. "discrete reals" in computer representation), $\mathbb{C}$ (complex numbers).

Some subsets of the above sets have a specific notation. It is the case for $\mathbb{N}_1$ (which represents $\mathbb{N} - \{0\}$), $\mathbb{R}_+$ (which stands for the nonnegative elements of $\mathbb{R}$), $\mathbb{R}_+^*$ (representing the strictly positive elements of $\mathbb{R}$).

As to complex numbers, i is the constant such that $i^2 = -1$. The real componant of the complex number c writes re(c) and its imaginary part im(c). Hence, for $c \cong 1 - 2i$, $re(c) = 1$ et $im(c) = -2$.

If E is a totally ordered numeric set, the operator min(E) (respectively max(E)) represents the smallest (respectively largest) element of E. When E is empty, $min(E) = \infty$ and $max(E) = -\infty$.

We denote the intervals of $\mathbb{Z}$ by $exp_1 \mathrel{..} exp_2$. If $exp_2 < exp_1$ the interval corresponds to the empty set. Since $\mathbb{Z}$ is an ordered set, an interval may be seen as a list (cf. section 1.4.7, page 20). The same applies to the expression $exp_1 \mathrel{..} exp_2 - (F)$. This specificity is used in loops of type **for ... range** where, for instance, the range of the variable of the loop $1 \mathrel{..} 5 - \{3, 4\}$ corresponds to the set $\{1, 2, 5\}$, which is browsed in this order at runtime.

1.4.5   Relations, functions and arrays

1.4.5.1   Relations

Let E and F be two sets and $R \subseteq E \times F$. R is called a (binary) *relation* between the source E and the destination F. When $F = E$, the pair (E, R) is called *graph* (see section 1.5, page 22).

Functions are special binary relations and arrays are specific functions. It follows that notions defined for relations are valid for these latter two notions.

Let R be a binary relation between E and F. The inverse relation of R is denoted R^{-1} and it is defined as:

$$R^{-1} \cong \{(b, a) \mid (b, a) \in F \times E \textbf{ and } (a, b) \in R\}.$$

Let R be a relation between E and F. The domain of R is denoted by dom(R) and it is defined as the subset of E whose elements constitute the origin of at least one pair of R. More formally:

$$dom(R) \cong \{a \mid a \in E \textbf{ and } \exists b \cdot (b \in F \textbf{ and } (a, b) \in R)\}.$$

The co-domain of R is denoted by codom(R) and it is defined as the domain of R^{-1}. It is also the subset of F whose elements constitute the extremity of at least one pair of R.

Let E be a set, the identity relation over E is denoted id(E) and it is defined as follows:

$$id(E) \cong \{(a, b) \mid (a, b) \in E \times E \textbf{ and } a = b\}.$$

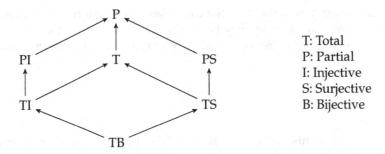

T: Total
P: Partial
I: Injective
S: Surjective
B: Bijective

Fig. 1.2 – Inclusion diagram of the various types of function. A → B means that type A functions are included in type B functions. From [1].

Let S be a relation between F and G, and R be a relation between E and F. The relation R ∘ S is called the composition of R and S. It is defined by:

$$R \circ S \cong \{(a,c) \mid (a,c) \in E \times G \text{ and } \exists b \cdot (b \in F \text{ and } (a,b) \in R \text{ and } (b,c) \in S)\}.$$

1.4.5.2 Functions

A *function* f from E to F is a relation where there is no pairs (a,b) and (a,c) such that $b \neq c$. One writes $f \in E \rightarrow F$. In the remainder, several types of functions will be singled out. Let $f \in E \rightarrow F$.

1. When f is a *partial* function, some elements of E may originate no pair of f.

2. When f is a *total* function, any element of E is the origin of one (and only one) pair of f.

3. When f is an *injective function* function, any element of F is the extremity of at most one pair of f.

4. When f is a *surjective* function, any element of F is the extremity of at least one pair of f.

5. When f is a *bijective function* function, f is both injective and surjective.

Let us notice that a total function is also a partial function. Figure 1.2, page 19, shows the inclusion relationships valid between the various types of function.

In the remainder, a predicate such as "$f \in E \rightarrow F$ and TI(f)" must be understood as "f is a total injective function from E to F".

1.4.5.3 Arrays

An *array* t is a total function from an interval $i .. s$ to a set F. One denotes $t \in i .. s \rightarrow F$. When i belongs to the definition domain of the array, $t[i]$ stands for the element having the index i of t. The set notation may be used, but when the context allows the determination of the bounds, the notation $[t_1, \ldots, t_n]$ may be used as a constant of type array. A *sub-array* (sometimes called *array slice*) defined on the domain $i..s$ is denoted by $t[i..s]$. Hence, if the interval $3 .. 5$ is included in the definition domain of t, $t[3 .. 5] \leftarrow [6, -1, 2]$ is a valid assignment. It is equivalent to $t[3 .. 5] \leftarrow \{3 \mapsto 6, 5 \mapsto 2, 4 \mapsto -1\}$. Besides, after the assignment, $\text{codom}(t[3 .. 5]) = \{-1, 2, 6\}$, whereas $\text{dom}(t[3 .. 5]) = \{3, 4, 5\}$.

A two-dimensional array is defined on the Cartesian product of two intervals. A constant value of a two-dimensional array may be represented as an array of array (for example $[[0, 1], [1, 1]]$), but the two-dimensional notation, easier to read, is more used (the same array: $\begin{bmatrix} 0 & 1 \\ 1 & 1 \end{bmatrix}$).

1.4.6 Bags

A bag (or multiset) of elements of the set E is a mathematical structure inside which the number of occurrences of a given element is meaningful. A bag S over E may be considered as a function s from E to $\mathbb{N}$, such that, for $v \in E$, $s(v)$ is the number of occurrences of v in S. In order to ease writing, we adopt an *ad hoc* notation instead of the set-oriented one. The notations used further and their set-oriented equivalent forms are listed hereafter.

Bags	Sets	Bags	Sets
$\Epsilon$	$\in$	$\not\sqsubset$	$\not\subset$
$\varnothing\!\!\!/$	$\varnothing$	$\sqsubseteq$	$\subseteq$
$\dot{-}$	$-$	$\not\sqsubseteq$	$\not\subseteq$
$\sqcap$	$\cap$	$|\dots|$	card
$\sqcup$	$\cup$	bmin	min
$\sqsubset$	$\subset$	bmax	max

bag(E) represents the set of finite bags of the finite set E and $[\![\dots]\!]$ is equivalent to the notation $\{\dots\}$ for sets defined in extension. Last, $\text{mult}(v, B)$ is the function returning the multiplicity (the number of occurrences) of v in the bag B.

1.4.7 Cartesian product and inductive structures

Inductive structures, i.e. structures defined by induction (see page 17), play an important role as data structures in this book. The two most typical cases are finite lists and finite trees. The latter are dealt with in section 1.6, page 27. Here, we restrict ourselves to the introduction of finite lists . What is the meaning of a formula such as:

$$\text{list} = \{/\} \cup \{(val, svt) \mid val \in \mathbb{N} \textbf{ and } svt \in \text{list}\}. \tag{1.1}$$

Informally, the set defined this way is the union between the empty list (denoted by /) and the set of pairs made of an integer and a list of integers. $(3, (1, (8, /)))$ is an example of such a list. In principle, such a linguistic structure – which is an *external representation* of lists – must not be confused with lists strictly speaking. In practice, this *external* notation will be authorized. It is necessary to add that we only deal with *finite* structures and that, in this context, a list is the *smallest* set obeying equation 1.1. Based on the use of the convention related to the dotted notation (see section 1.4.2, page 17), with the assignment $l \leftarrow (3, (1, (8, /)))$, one has $l.val = 3$ and $l.svt = (1, (8, /))$. Direct access to elements of lists is not permitted and it is always necessary to go through one of the fields (such as $l.svt.svt.val$ for instance).

In practice, the (more concise) notation $\langle \dots \rangle$ is used. Hence, $(3, (1, (8, /)))$ may also be noted $\langle 3, 1, 8 \rangle$. The concatenation of lists is denoted by $\cdot$.

1.4.8 Strings and sequences

Strings (or *sequences*, sometimes *words*) are (right-) flexible arrays whose left bound is implicitly 1. Their elements are usually called *letters* or *characters*. Thus, they are total functions for which set operators are available (dom, codom, etc.). The size (length) of the string c is denoted by |c|. The *concatenation* (denoted by ·) allows to extend a string by adding another string, as well as a character (which is converted into a string). If c = c[1]...c[n] denotes a string, $\bar{c}$ = c[n]...c[1] is the mirror of c. From an algorithmic point of view, a string c used as an input parameter implicitly conveys its definition domain (dom(c)). If c is a string defined over 1 .. n, the slice c[i .. s] is a string defined over 1 .. s − i + 1 provided that i .. s ⊆ 1 .. n. The *empty string* ε (neutral element for the concatenation) is defined over 1 .. 0. The declaration of a symbolic constant, a variable or a parameter c of type **string** is written c ∈ **string** with an implicitly vocabulary made up of letters, numbers and special symbols. Calling on a specific vocabulary Σ is achieved by c ∈ **string**(Σ). The following example illustrates the use of strings, especially constants not surrounded by quotation marks which require a special font.

```
1.  constants
2.     a = abcd /% symbolic constant of type string %/
3.  variables
4.     b ∈ string({a,b,c,d,1,2,3,4}) /% variable of type string over the vocabulary
       Σ = {a,b,c,d,1,2,3,4} %/
5.  begin
6.     write(Odd(a)) ; /% the function Odd(x) (see the code) delivers a string made
       of the elements of x having an odd index %/
7.     read(b) ; write(Odd(b)) ;
8.     b ← acbd · 1234 · a[3 .. 4] · a[1] ; /% example of a concatenation %/
9.     write(Odd(b))
10. end
```

```
1.  function Odd(x) result string pre
2.     x ∈ string and y ∈ string
3.  begin
4.     y ← ε ; /% y becomes an empty string %/
5.     for i ranging dom(x) do
6.        if 2 · ⌊i/2⌋ ≠ i then
7.           y ← y · x[i] /% extension of y by the next element of x having an odd
              index %/
8.        end if
9.     end for;
10.    result y
11. end
```

References to the notion of sequence

- The longest sub-sequence common to two sequences (page 635),

- Shuffling words (problem 21, page 45),

- The sluttering sub-sequence (problem 109, page 462),

- Distance or dissemblance between sequences (problem 107, page 452, problem 139, page 674 and problem 140, page 678),

- Shortest common super-sequence (problem 138, page 674).

1.5   Graphs

Intuitively, a *graph* is a set of points, some of them being pairwise connected. It is a fairly simple notion which allows for modeling numerous problems offering a great practical interest, such as the search of the best route to reach a vacation home with a GPS device.

Graph theory is also the source of many mathematical and/or computer science complex challenges such as the four color problem whose complete automated proof has been carried out by the proof assistant Coq.

More simply, for us, the notion of graph originates numerous interesting problems throughout this book.

Graph theory may be seen as an emanation of set theory (through the notion of binary relation). However, the two theories have developed separately, thus often use divergent vocabularies. In the following, directed graphs are first studied, then undirected ones. This overview ends with the case of weighted (valued) graphs. Only finite graphs are taken into consideration.

1.5.1   Directed graphs

A *directed graph* G is a pair (N, V), where N is a (finite) set and V a binary relation between N and N (V is therefore a finite subset of $N \times N$).

Elements of N are called *nodes* or *vertices*; those of V are called *arrows* or *directed edges*, or *(directed) arcs*. The cardinality of N is called the *order* of the graph.

Example

The pair G defined by:

$$G = \begin{pmatrix} \{a,b,c,d,e,f\}, \\ \{(a,b), (a,c), (a,f), (b,a), (b,c), (b,d), (c,e), (d,d), (d,f), (e,a), (e,f), (f,c)\} \end{pmatrix}$$

is a directed graph.

Figure 1.3 provides four possible representations for this graph. Schema (b), that has the form of a square matrix, is often used as a computer representation.

An arrow that connects a vertex s with itself is called a *loop over the vertex* s; it writes (s, s) with $s \in N$.

Let s be a vertex of a graph G. The *out-degree* (respectively *in-degree*) of s in G, denoted by $d_G^+(s)$ (respectively $d_G^-(s)$), is the number of arrows whose origin (respectively extremity) is the vertex s.

A directed graph $G' = (N', V')$ is a *subgraph* of the directed graph $G = (N, V)$ if $N' \subset N$ and $V' = \{(u, v) \in V \mid u \in N', v \in N'\}$. G' is also called the graph induced from G by the set of vertices N'.

In other words, a subgraph G' of a graph G is obtained by taking a strict subset N' of the set N of vertices of G, keeping only the arrows whose origin and extremity belong to N'.

Let $G = (N, V)$ be a directed graph and $s \in N$. The set of *successors* of s in G, denoted by $Succ_G(s)$ is the set of vertices reached from s through the relation V.

The set of *predecessors* of s in G, denoted by $Pred_G(s)$, is the set of vertices $Succ_{(N, V^{-1})}(s)$.

Example

In the example of graph G in figure 1.3, page 23, we have $d_G^+(d) = 2$, $d_G^-(d) = 2$, $Succ_G(a) = \{b, c, f\}$ and $Pred_G(c) = \{a, b, f\}$. It can be noticed that the arrow (d, d) is a loop (over d).

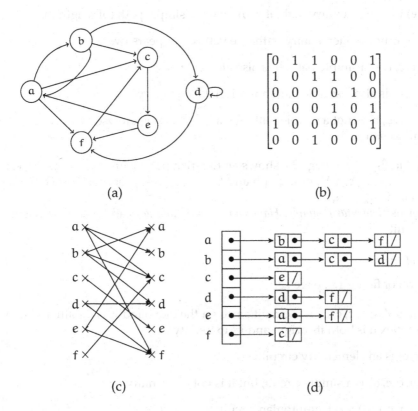

$$\begin{bmatrix} 0 & 1 & 1 & 0 & 0 & 1 \\ 1 & 0 & 1 & 1 & 0 & 0 \\ 0 & 0 & 0 & 0 & 1 & 0 \\ 0 & 0 & 0 & 1 & 0 & 1 \\ 1 & 0 & 0 & 0 & 0 & 1 \\ 0 & 0 & 1 & 0 & 0 & 0 \end{bmatrix}$$

(a)   (b)

(c)   (d)

Fig. 1.3 – Four representations of a directed graph. Schema (a) is the (usual) sagittal representation, (b) is the representation by an adjacency matrix, (c) is a bipartite representation and (d) is a representation by lists of successors.

The graph $G_1 = (\{a, b, d, f\}, \{(a, b), (b, a), (a, f), (b, d), (d, d), (d, f)\})$ is the graph induced from G by the set of vertices $\{a, b, d, f\}$.

If there is no ambiguity, the subscript G is omitted.

A *path* P in a graph $G = (\{s_1, \ldots, s_n\}, V)$ is a nonempty list of vertices $\langle s_{i_1}, \ldots, s_{i_q} \rangle$ such that any pair of adjacent vertices in P is an arrow of G $((s_{i_k}, s_{i_{k+1}}) \in V$ for $k \in 1 .. q - 1)$.

The *length* of the path $P = \langle s_{i_1}, \ldots, s_{i_q} \rangle$ is the number of arrows $(s_{i_k}, s_{i_{k+1}})$ which constitute it. It is denoted by $|P|$.

An *elementary path* is a path without any duplicate vertices.

A *simple path* is a path without arrows browsed more than once. Any elementary path is a simple one.

A *Hamiltonian path* is a path where every vertex (of the graph) is present once and only once. The list of vertices is a permutation of N.

An *Eulerian path* is a path which encompasses every arrow once and only once.

Examples of paths

In the graph of figure 1.3, page 23:

- $\langle a, b, a, c, e, a, b, d, d \rangle$ is a path. It is made up of the following list of arrows: $\langle (a, b), (b, a), (a, c), (c, e), (e, a), (a, b), (b, d), (d, d) \rangle$ and its length is 8. It is neither simple, nor elementary.

- $\langle b, c, e \rangle$ is an elementary path, it is therefore a simple path (of length 2).

- $\langle b, a, b \rangle$ is not an elementary path: the vertex b appears twice.

- $\langle a, b, c, e, f \rangle$ is a simple path. It is also elementary.

- $\langle a, b, a, c \rangle$ is also a simple path but it is not elementary.

- $\langle a, b, c, e, a, b \rangle$ is not a simple path: the arrow (a, b) is browsed twice. $\langle a, b, d, f, c, e \rangle$ is a Hamiltonian path.

Schema (a) in figure 1.4, page 24, shows an Eulerian path, namely $\langle d, b, c, a, b, e, d, c, e \rangle$.

Let $G = (\{s_1, \ldots, s_n\}, V)$ be a graph and $C = \langle s_{i_1}, \ldots, s_{i_q} \rangle$ be a path in G. C is a *circuit* in G if and only if $s_{i_q} = s_{i_1}$.

The terms *elementary, simple, Hamiltonian* and *Eulerian* can be easily transposed from path to circuit.

Examples of circuits

In the graph of figure 1.3, page 23:

- $\langle a, b, a, b, d, d, f, c, e, a \rangle$ is a circuit since on the one hand it is a path and on the other hand vertex a is both its origin and its extremity.

- $\langle c, e, f, c \rangle$ is an elementary circuit.

- $\langle a, b, a, c, e, a \rangle$ is a simple circuit, but it is not elementary.

- $\langle a, b, d, f, c, e, a \rangle$ is a Hamiltonian circuit.

In the graph (b) of figure 1.4, page 24, the path $\langle d, b, c, a, b, e, d, c, e, f, d \rangle$ is an Eulerian circuit.

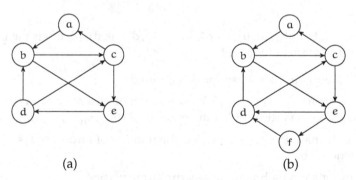

(a)   (b)

Fig. 1.4 – Two directed graphs. Graph (a) contains the Eulerian path $\langle d, b, c, a, b, e, d, c, e \rangle$, but no Eulerian circuit. Graph (b) contains at least one Eulerian circuit ($\langle d, b, c, a, b, e, d, c, e, f, d \rangle$).

$G^+ = (N, V^+)$ is the *transitive closure* of $G = (N, V)$ if and only if V^+ is the smallest transitive relation containing V.

In other words, G^+ is the transitive closure of G if, when there is a *path* between x and y in G, there is an *arrow* between x and y in G^+.

In the schema hereafter, graph (b) represents the transitive closure of graph (a). Dashed arrows are those stemming from the closure.

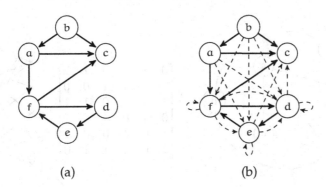

(a)   (b)

Let x be a vertex of a graph G. The vertex y is a *descendant* of x in G if there is an arrow (x, y) in G^+. The vertex x is then an *ascendant* of y.

Two directed graphs $G_1 = (N_1, V_1)$ and $G_2 = (N_2, V_2)$ are *isomorphic* if and only if there is a bijection f between N_1 and N_2 such that for any pair of vertices (i, j) of N_1:

$$(i, j) \in V_1 \Leftrightarrow (f(i), f(j)) \in V_2.$$

In the schema given hereafter, graph (a) is represented in the plan, whereas (b) (the grid "cylinder") proposes a three-dimensional representation. They are isomorphic graphs through the following bijection p:

$$p = \{(H, c), (G, b), (J, a), (I, d), (C, g), (D, f), (F, e), (A, h)\}.$$

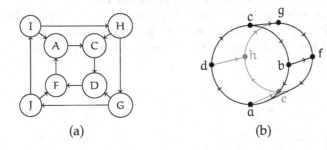

(a)   (b)

1.5.2   Undirected graphs

An *undirected graph* G is a pair (N, V), where N is a finite set and V a subset of the powerset of N with one or two elements.

As in directed graphs, the elements of N are called *vertices* or *nodes*. The elements of V are called *edges*, or *loops* if they involve a single vertex.

Example

The pair G defined by:

$$G = \begin{pmatrix} \{a,b,c,d,e,f\}, \\ \{\{a, b\}, \{a, e\}, \{a, f\}, \{b, c\}, \{b, d\}, \{d\}, \{c, e\}, \{a, f\}, \{e, f\}, \{d, f\}\} \end{pmatrix}$$

is an undirected graph. Figure 1.5 provides three possible representations for this graph.

The terms *string* and *cycle* for undirected graphs are the counterparts of those of path and circuit in directed graphs. The qualifiers *elementary*, *simple*, *Hamiltonian* and *Eulerian* apply to undirected graphs as well. The same applies to the definitions of a subgraph, a graph induced by a set of vertices and a transitive closure.

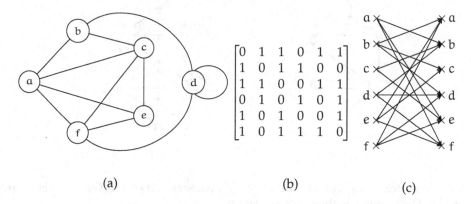

(a)   (b)   (c)

Fig. 1.5 – Three representations of an undirected graph. Schema (a) is the usual representation; (b) is the representation by an adjacency matrix (this matrix is always symmetric); (c) is a bipartite representation.

1.5.3   Weighted graphs

Intuitively, a *weighted* graph is a graph in which each arrow is provided with an attribute (most often an integer or a real number, but it may be any type of value). This attribute may stand for a distance, a duration, a cost, a potential, etc.

More formally, a *weighted directed graph* G is a triple (N, V, P), such that (N, V) is a directed graph and P is a total function from V to the set of values E.

Figure 1.6 considers the directed graph in figure 1.3, page 23, with arrows valued in $\mathbb{R}$ $(E = \mathbb{R})$.

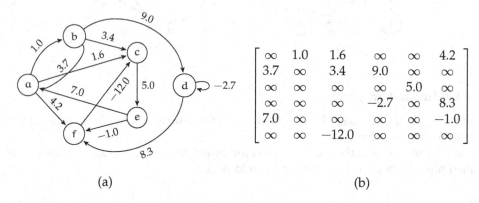

(a)   (b)

Fig. 1.6 – Two representations of a weighted directed graph. Schema (a) is the usual sagittal representation, (b) is the matrix representation where absent arrows are provided with a conventional symbol (here ∞).

An *undirected weighted graph* is a graph in which every edge is provided with an attribute.

More formally, *an undirected weighted graph* G is a triple (N, V, P) such that (N, V) is an undirected graph and P is total function from V to a set E of values.

In practice, the representation of a weighted graph may be restricted to that of N and P, as shown in schema (b) in figure 1.6.

References to the notion of graph

Among the countless problems related to graphs (search for shortest paths or strings between two vertices, or between a given vertex and all others, or between all pairs of vertices, the determination of the existence of an isomorphism between two graphs, coloring of a graph, etc.), some are tackled as problems in this book. Let us quote:

Nonweighted directed graphs:

- Moving a knight under constraints (problem 15, page 41).
- Exhaustive visit of a chessboard (problem 49, page 170).
- The knight's tour (problem 54, page 227).
- Eulerian circuits and paths (problem 55, page 230).
- Hamiltonian paths (problem 56, page 231).
- Graph isomorphism (problem 58, page 234).
- Graph coloring (problem 59, page 236).
- Tournaments and Hamiltonian paths (problem 85, page 370).

Weighted directed graphs:

- Optimal broadcast (problem 78, page 345).
- Best path in a conform graph (problem 131, page 660).
- Best paths from a source (problem 132, page 661).
- Best paths algebras (problem 133, page 664).
- Best path in an array (problem 134, page 667).
- Distance between sequences (problem 139, page 674).

Undirected weighted graphs:

- Optimal broadcast (problem 78, page 345).
- The traveling salesman (problem 57, page 233, and example page 314).

1.6 Trees

Beyond their intrinsic interest (compiling, automated proofs, natural language processing, etc.), trees are at the root of efficient representations for a wide range of data structures (sets, queues, priority queues, flexible arrays, etc. – see [22, 9]. Despite the use of numerous types of trees throughout this book (see for instance recursion trees, Chapter 5, page 197), here we restrict ourselves to binary and ternary trees. There are several ways to define this notion. Using graph theory is one of them. A binary or ternary tree is defined as a specific graph (an undirected connected loopless graph where a particular vertex – the root – is

dintinguished). However, our preference goes to an inductive definition more appropriate
for our use.

Figure 1.7, page 28, provides an example of both a binary and a ternary tree. They are *directed* graphs. On this issue, graph theory terminology and the one used here diverge since,
in graph theory, these structures would be called "arborescence". The term *path* is used according to its meaning in graph theory. We will use the term "path" for routes/itineraries
where the direction of arrows is not taken into account. As to the term *distance*, it is indifferently used for paths and "paths".

The example below shows how a *labeled* binary tree is defined in a recursive manner
(each node is associated with a value, a positive integer here)[3]:

1. **constants**
2. $ab = \{/\} \cup \{(l, n, r) \mid l \in ab \textbf{ and } n \in \mathbb{N} \textbf{ and } r \in ab\}$
3. **variables**
4. $t \in ab$
5. **begin**
6. $t \leftarrow /;$
7. $t \leftarrow (((/,0,/),1,/),3,(((/,4,/),5,(/,6,/)),7,(/,9,/)));$
8.   **write**(t.l)
9. **end**

ab is the set of all finite binary trees of integers. It is defined (line 2 in the code) as the union
of two sets: $\{/\}$ (the empty tree) and the set of triples (l, n, r), where l and r are binary trees
(respectively the left subtree and the right subtree) and n an integer. Line 4, t is a variable
defined as one of the elements the set ab. The instruction in line 6 assigns the empty tree
to t. That of next line assigns the tree of schema (a) in figure 1.7 to t. Line 8 displays (on a
regular terminal) the left subtree of t (denoted by t.l).

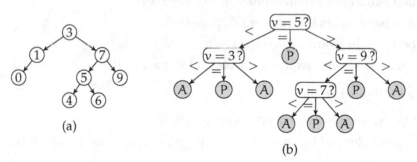

(a)

(b)

Fig. 1.7 – Schema (a): a binary tree and Schema (b) : a (decision) ternary tree (A: absent P: present).

In a binary tree, a *leaf* is a childless node (without any successor); a *simple point* is a
node with a single child. The *height* of a binary tree is the distance (i.e. the number of
edges) between the root and the furthest leaf. The *weight* of a binary tree is the number of
its nodes/vertices. Among all the possible simple "paths" in a nonempty binary tree, there
is (at least) one with maximum length. This length is called the *diameter*. A diameter does
not necessarily include the root (see problem 94, page 431).

---

[3]Even if, for convenience, they can be at the same place in the schemas, it is important to distinguish between
the *name* of a vertex or a node, which is an identifier, and the label, which is any type of value. The inductive
definition of trees allows for omitting the *name* of the node.

In the forthcoming schemas, "paths" connecting grey vertices are materialized by bold arrows. In schema (a) (respectively (b)), the considered "path" is made of 5 (respectively 7) arrows, so its length is 5 (respectively 7). The height of these two trees is 4, their diameter is 7. The bold "path" in schema (b) is a diameter.

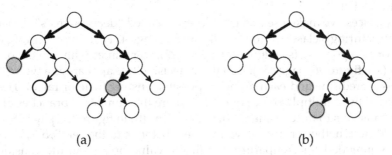

(a)   (b)

Most of the above definitions can easily be transposed to ternary trees. Among particular binary trees, let us cite *skinny* trees, *complete* trees, *full* trees and *perfect* trees. A skinny tree is a tree where no vertex has two children. A complete tree is a tree does not contain any simple point. Trees (a) and (b) in figure 1.8, page 29, are complete trees. This is not the case for the three others in this figure. A full tree is a tree where all leaves are located at the same height. It is the case for tree (b) in figure 1.8, page 29. It is the only tree of this type in this figure. A perfect tree is such that: (i) all leaves are located on the last two levels, i.e. the lowest levels, (ii) when the (perfect) tree is not a full one, i.e. when the leaves are spread over two levels, the leaves of the lowest level are left-gathered (iii) there is at most one simple point and it is located on the penultimate level. Schema (c) in figure 1.8 provides an example of a perfect tree. Tree (b) is also a specific perfect tree (because of the absence of a simple point). On the contrary, trees (d) and (e) in figure 1.8, page 29, are not perfect trees, the first one because it possesses two simple points, the second one because the leaves of the last level are left-gathered. Tree (a) is not a perfect tree. It is easy – and often useful – to give an inductive definition of the notions studied in this section (see problem 94, page 431). We draw the attention of the reader on the fact that definitions concerning trees are far from consensual.

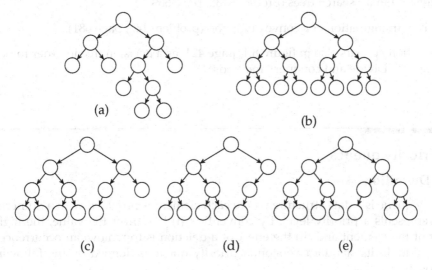

(a)   (b)

(c)   (d)   (e)

Fig. 1.8 – Complete, full and perfect trees—Examples and counter-examples.

A particular type of binary tree is worthy of a special attention, namely binary *search* trees (called bst for short). An bst is either an empty tree, or a binary tree whose nodes contain numeric values, and such that, if v is its root, its left (respectively right) subtree is a bst containing, if nonempty, values lower (respectively greater) than v. Tree (a) in figure 1.7, page 28, is a bst.

At many places, we make use of particular trees called "decision trees". A decision tree allows for structuring a classification (see figure 8.1, page 421), for representing the various executions of an algorithm (see figure 90, page 427), sometimes with aim of computing its complexity (see figure 96, page 433). Usually, a decision tree appears as a binary tree where each node is a predicate and each branch a possible answer (**true** or **false**). The predicate can be replaced by a multiple choice question where the number of branches of each node is that of the answers to the considered question. Tree (b) in figure 1.7, page 28, is a ternary tree for deciding whether or not a given value v belongs to the set $\{3, 5, 7, 9\}$. In this tree, each node is intended for comparing v with the value present in the considered node. Leaves answer the question associated with the decision tree (P: the numeric value present in the leaf belongs to $\{3, 5, 7, 9\}$, A : the numeric value present in the leaf does not appear in $\{3, 5, 7, 9\}$ – it is absent.)

References to the notion of tree

The notion of tree is the heart of several problems of this book. Let us quote the following titles (of problems):

- Binary, ternary and interpolation searches (problem 90, page 427).

- Local minimum in a binary tree (problem 93, page 431).

- Diameter of a binary tree (problem 94, page 431).

- Nuts and bolts (problem 96, page 433).

- The largest rectangle under a histogram (problem 116, page 480).

- The egg problem (2) (problem 130, page 657).

- Weighted binary search trees (problem 135, page 669).

- The best triangulation of a convex polygon (problem 142, page 681).

This notion appears also in figure 8.1, page 421, as a decision tree in order to point out a typology of "Divide and conquer" methods.

1.7   Priority queues

1.7.1   Definition

A priority queue is a data structure where each element is provided with a numeric value which represents a priority level. By convention (i) the lower the value, the higher the priority of the element and (ii) the effect of a deletion is to remove an occurrence of the lowest value. In its standard version, a priority queue is defined by the following five operations:

- *InitPQ*(q): procedure which empties the priority queue q.

- *HeadPQ*(q): function which delivers the priority element (the head) of the queue q. The precondition of this function is that the queue involves at least one element.

- *RemovePQ*(q): procedure that removes the priority element (the head of the queue) from the queue q. This procedure also has as a precondition that q contains at least one element.

- *AddPQ*(q, e): procedure which inserts the element e in the queue q (this element is assumed to convey its own priority).

- *IsEmptyPQ*(q): Boolean function which returns **true** if and only if the priority q is empty.

Sometimes, it is necessary to enrich this set of operations with additional ones, such as that consisting in modifying the priority of a given element of the queue (see for instance problem 78, page 345). The size of the queue q is denoted by $|q|$.

1.7.2 Implementations

Several more or less sophisticated implementations of priority queues are reported in the literature. Let us remind two of them for queues with n elements:

- Sorted lists for which the insertion operation is in $\mathcal{O}(n)$, the (re)initialization operation is in $\Theta(n)$ or $\Theta(1)$ depending on the fact that space is recovered or not. Other operations are in $\Theta(1)$. This type of solution is convenient only if n is small.

- Heaps. From a structural point of view, a heap is a perfect binary tree (leaves are located on – at most – two consecutive levels and those of the last level are left-gathered). As to the content, a heap is such that the value of any node is less than (or equal to) that of all its descendants.

An important characteristic is that a heap can beneficially be represented by an array T such that, for a given i, T[2i] and T[2i + 1], if they do exist, are the children of T[i].

The following schema (a) shows a heap defined on $\mathbb{R}_+$ according to its arborescent form. Schema (b) is the array representation of schema (a).

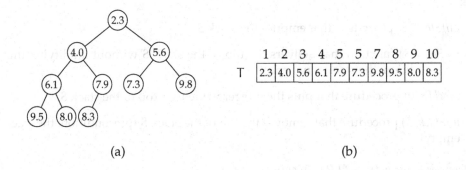

	1	2	3	4	5	5	7	8	9	10
T	2.3	4.0	5.6	6.1	7.9	7.3	9.8	9.5	8.0	8.3

(a)   (b)

In terms of visited vertices (or evaluated conditions), the cost of the operation *Delete* is in $\Theta(\log_2(n))$ and that of *Insert* is in $\mathcal{O}(\log_2(n))$. Other operations require a constant time.

References to the notion of priority queues

This notion is at the heart of two chapters of this book: Chapter 6 about the "Branch and Bound" technique and Chapter 7 devoted to greedy algorithms.

1.8   FIFO and LIFO queues

A FIFO (First In, First Out) queue may be considered as a particular priority queue whose elements do not bear any explicit priority. The handling of priority is performed in an implicit way, since an element is always inserted at the end of the queue and the head element (the oldest one entered in the queue) is removed for a deletion. FIFO(E) represents all the FIFO queues over elements belonging to E. Thus, if one writes $F \in$ FIFO($\mathbb{R}_+ \times \mathbb{R}_+$), it is a declaration of a FIFO queue F containing pairs of nonnegative real numbers. Operations used for dealing with FIFO queues are:

- *InitFifo*(F): procedure which empties the queue F.

- *HeadFifo*(F): if F is a FIFO queue of elements of type E, this function returns the head element without removing it from the FIFO queue. This function supposes (precondition) that F is not empty.

- *RemoveFifo*(F): this procedure removes the head element from the FIFO queue F. Here again, the precondition is that F is not empty.

- *AddFifo*(F, e): procedure which adds the element e at the end of the queue F.

- *IsEmptyFifo*(F): this function returns **true** if and only if the queue F is empty.

As for priority queues, it is sometimes useful to enrich this set of operations or to modify some of them.

A LIFO queue (hereafter called a *stack*) is a data structure designed to manage items according to the following strategy: the element to be removed is the last one that was introduced (hence the name LIFO: Last In First Out). Operations used to deal with stacks are:

- *initStack*(S) procedure that empties the stack S,

- *topStack*(S) function that delivers the top of the stack S without modifying this latter (precondition: the stack is not empty),

- *Stack*(S, v) procedure that puts the integer value v on top of the stack S,

- *unStack*(S) procedure that removes the top of the stack S (precondition: the stack is not empty),

References to the notion of FIFO queues

The notion of FIFO queue is used in Chapter 7 dedicated to greedy algorithms.

References to the notion of stack

The notion of stack is used in the problem 116, The largest rectangle under a histogram, page 480.

1.9   Problems

Problem 1.   Is a neutral element unique?   ○ •

This problem mainly aims at a thorough use of the proof by contradiction.

Let S be a set provided with an internal operator $\oplus$. Let $u \in S$ be a left neutral element for $\oplus$, i.e.:
$$\forall x \cdot (x \in S \Rightarrow u \oplus x = x).$$
Let v be a right neutral element for $\oplus$.

Question 1.   Prove in a direct way that if $\oplus$ is a commutative operator, one has $u = v$.   1 - Q 1

Question 2.   Prove this property by contradiction without calling on the commutativity   1 - Q 2
property of $\oplus$.

The solution is on page 46.

Problem 2.   Minimum element of a partially ordered set   ○ •

The interest of this problem is to demonstrate the same property by means of both a proof by contradiction and a proof by induction.

Let E be a finite set with a partial order relation denoted by $\preceq$ and F be a strict nonempty subset of E. A strict antecedent of x is an element y distinct from x such that $y \preceq x$. An element m of F is said to be *minimum* if m has no strict antecedent in F.

Question 1.   Prove by contradiction that F has at least one minimum element.   2 - Q 1

Question 2.   Demonstrate by induction that F has at least one minimum element.   2 - Q 2

Question 3.   One considers the set E made of pairs of integers and the partial order   2 - Q 3
relation $\preceq$ defined by:
$$(a, b) \preceq (c, d) \mathrel{\hat{=}} a \leqslant c \text{ and } b \leqslant d.$$
Let $F(\subset E) = \{(a, b) \mid a \in 1..3 \text{ and } b \in 1..2 \text{ and } a \neq b\}$. Enumerate the minimum elements of F.

The solution is on page 46.

Problem 3.   Factorial *vs* exponential   ○ •

In this problem, two results about the comparison of values of factorials and exponentials are established. The first one constitutes a result useful for the order of two related classes of complexity (see Chapter 2).

3 - Q 1   **Question** 1.   Prove by simple induction that:

$$\forall n \cdot (n \in \mathbb{N}_1 \Rightarrow n! \geqslant 2^{n-1}).$$

3 - Q 2   **Question** 2.   What is the minimum value n_0 such that:

$$\forall n \cdot ((n \in \mathbb{N}_1 \text{ and } n_0 \in \mathbb{N}_1 \text{ and } n \geqslant n_0) \Rightarrow n! > 2^{2n}) ?$$

The solution is on page 47.

Problem 4.   Currency change (1)   ○ ●

> *In this problem, we first validate a new schema for the proof by simple induction. Then, it is applied to a property about the construction of an amount of money. We also ask for making the demonstration with the proof by regular simple induction. It is the possible to decide whether one method is more "convenient" than the other one, noticing that the result holds for this problem only.*

4 - Q 1   **Question** 1.   Prove that the following alternate pattern for simple induction proof holds:

> If it is possible to demonstrate the two following properties:
>   **Initialization** $P(n_0)$ and $P(n_0 + 1)$ hold for a given $n_0 \in \mathbb{N}$
>   **Induction** $\forall n \cdot ((n \geqslant n_0 \text{ and } P(n)) \Rightarrow P(n + 2))$
> then:
>   **Conclusion** $\forall n \cdot (n \geqslant n_0 \Rightarrow P(n))$

4 - Q 2   **Question** 2.   Use this pattern to prove that any amount of money n over five cents can be obtained with two and seven cent coins.

4 - Q 3   **Question** 3.   Prove the same result by simple induction as given in section 1.1.3.1, page 4.

4 - Q 4   **Question** 4.   Which is the maximum number of seven cent coins used in each of these patterns?

4 - Q 5   **Question** 5.   In your opinion, which of these two proofs is easier to perform?

The solution is on page 47.

Problem 5.   Catalan numbers   ○ ●

> *In this problem, it is proven (by simple induction) that the closed form of the recurrence relation proposed for Catalan numbers is valid. An upper bound of the value of the nth Catalan number is also proposed.*

Catalan numbers have been previously addressed and defined by the following recurrence relation (see page 11):

$$\begin{vmatrix} Cat(1) = 1 \\ Cat(n) = \dfrac{4n-6}{n} \cdot Cat(n-1) \end{vmatrix} \qquad\qquad n > 1.$$

Question 1. Prove by simple induction that, for any positive integer n, the closed form of this recurrence relation is (see page 11):   5 - Q 1

$$Cat(n) = \frac{(2n-2)!}{(n-1)!\, n!}.$$

Question 2. Prove by simple induction that, for any positive integer n, one can write: 5 - Q 2

$$Cat(n) \leqslant \frac{4^{n-1}}{n}.$$

The solution is on page 48.

Problem 6. Erroneous proofs by simple induction   ○ •

> *This problem is intended for drawing the attention on the compliance with the hypotheses so as to perform a valid proof by induction. Two examples are successively proposed, where the proposition P to prove is obviously false. It is interesting to point out the fallacy in the reasoning suggested to make the proof.*

First case

We envisage to prove the following property P_1:

Any pair of integers is made of two identical integers.

The reasoning is performed on the maximum of the two numbers a and b, denoted by $\max(a, b)$.

Initialization If $\max(a, b) = 0$, then obviously $a = b = 0$.

Induction Suppose that property P_1 holds when the maximum of a and b is p. The induction hypothesis tells that:

if $\max(a, b) = p$ then $a = b = p$.

We have to demonstrate that P_1 holds when the maximum of a and b is $(p + 1)$. Let (a, b) be a pair of integers such that $\max(a, b) = p + 1$. The maximum of $(a - 1)$ and $(b - 1)$ is p. According to the induction hypothesis, one has: $a - 1 = b - 1 = p$, hence: $a - 1 + 1 = b - 1 + 1 = p + 1$, and finally $a = b = p + 1$.

Conclusion Property P_1 holds for any pair of integers.

Question 1. Where is the flaw?   6 - Q 1

Second case

We consider the following property P_2:

n arbitrary points of a plane are aligned.

The induction relates to the number of points n.

Initialization For $n = 2$, proposition P_2 holds, since two points are aligned.

Induction Suppose that property P_2 holds for p points (induction hypothesis). Let us prove that then the $(p + 1)$ points $A_1, A_2, A_3, \ldots, A_{p+1}$ are aligned. According to the induction hypothesis, the first p points $A_1, A_2, A_3, \ldots, A_p$ are aligned on a straight line (d_1) and the last p points $A_2, A_3, \ldots, A_{p+1}$ are aligned on a straight line (d_2). These two straight lines (d_1) et (d_2) have the points A_2 and A_3 in common and they are one and the same. One has $(d_1) = (d_2) = (A_2 A_3)$ and the points $A_1, A_2, A_3, \ldots,$ A_p, A_{p+1} are aligned.

Conclusion Proposition P_2 holds for any number of points strictly greater than 1.

6 - Q 2   **Question 2.**   Find the flaw.

The solution is on page 49.

Problem 7. Erroneous proof by strong induction   ○ **:**

> *Following the previous one, this problem aims at pointing out a flaw in a reasoning by induction. However, here, the formula to demonstrate is right and a direct appropriate proof is expected.*

It is proposed to demonstrate by simple induction that, for any strictly positive integer n, one has:

$$n = \sqrt{1 + (n - 1)\sqrt{1 + n\sqrt{1 + (n + 1)\sqrt{1 + (n + 2)\ldots}}}}$$

To start, it is assumed that the above expression makes sense, i.e. that it converges when n increases indefinitely (which is true, as we will see later).

The proof by strong induction is performed as follows:

Initialization For $n = 1$, the right part of the formula becomes:

$$\sqrt{1 + 0\sqrt{1 + 1(\ldots)}} = 1$$

and the equality holds.

Induction hypothesis For any $n > 1$:

$$(n - 1) = \sqrt{1 + (n - 2)\sqrt{1 + (n - 1)\sqrt{1 + n\sqrt{1 + (n + 1)\ldots}}}}.$$

Induction One has:

$$(n-1) = \sqrt{1 + (n-2)\sqrt{1 + (n-1)\sqrt{1 + n\sqrt{1 + (n+1)\ldots}}}}$$

$\Rightarrow$ squaring

$$(n-1)^2 = 1 + (n-2)\sqrt{1 + (n-1)\sqrt{1 + n\sqrt{1 + (n+1)\ldots}}}$$

$\Leftrightarrow$ remarkable identity

$$n^2 - 2n + 1 = 1 + (n-2)\sqrt{1 + (n-1)\sqrt{1 + n\sqrt{1 + (n+1)\ldots}}}$$

$\Leftrightarrow$ arithmetics

$$n(n-2) = (n-2)\sqrt{1 + (n-1)\sqrt{1 + n\sqrt{1 + (n+1)\ldots}}}$$

$\Leftrightarrow$ division by $n-2$ of the two members

$$\frac{n(n-2)}{n-2} = \sqrt{1 + (n-1)\sqrt{1 + n\sqrt{1 + (n+1)\ldots}}}$$

$\Leftrightarrow$ arithmetics

$$n = \sqrt{1 + (n-1)\sqrt{1 + n\sqrt{1 + (n+1)\ldots}}}.$$

We have demonstrated that the induction hypothesis entails the formula to be proven.

Question 1.   Where is the flaw in the above reasoning?   7 - Q 1

Question 2.   Yet, this formula is valid. Give a valid proof.   7 - Q 2

The solution is on page 50.

Problem 8. Alternate pattern for two indexes recurrence proof   ○ •

In section 1.1.6, page 9, a two indexes recurrence proof pattern was proposed. The objective of this problem is to validate another one.

Prove that the following pattern of proof is right:

If the following two properties can be proven:

Initialization $P(i, 1)$ holds for any $i \geqslant 1$ **and**
  $P(1, j)$ holds for any $j \geqslant 1$

Induction $\forall (i, j) \cdot \left(\left(\begin{array}{l} i \in \mathbb{N}_1 \text{ and} \\ j \in \mathbb{N}_1 \text{ and} \\ P(i, j) \end{array} \right) \Rightarrow \left(\begin{array}{l} P(i+1, j) \text{ and} \\ P(i, j+1) \text{ and} \\ P(i+1, j+1) \end{array} \right) \right)$

then:

Conclusion $P(m, n)$ holds for any pair of integers such that $m \geqslant 1$ and $n \geqslant 1$

The solution is on page 50.

Problem 9. Divisibility by 7   ○ •

> *This problem is devoted to the proof by induction of a property of the elements of a series of integers given under its closed form.*

Let $A(n,p)$ be the integer defined as:

$$A(n,p) = 3^{2n} - 2^{n-p} \qquad\qquad n \in \mathbb{N}_1 \text{ and } p \in \mathbb{N} \text{ and } n \geqslant p.$$

9 - Q 1   **Question 1.**   Prove by simple induction that whenever $A(n,p)$ is (respectively is not) a multiple of 7, $A(n+1,p)$ is (respectively is not) a multiple of 7.

9 - Q 2   **Question 2.**   What can be said about the divisibility (by 7) of the series of numbers $A(n,0)$, $A(n,1)$, $A(n,2)$ and $A(n,3)$?

The solution is on page 51.

Problem 10. Proof by induction *vs* direct proof   ○ •

> *Here, a series of numbers is under consideration. Two properties are proven, one by simple induction and the second one "directly". It turns out that the proof by induction does not appear to be the easiest one.*

We consider the following recurrence defining the series of numbers $A(n)$:

$$\left|\begin{array}{l} A(1) = 1 \\[2mm] A(n) = A(n-1) + \dfrac{n^2 - 3n + 1}{(n-1)^2 \cdot n^2} \end{array}\right. \qquad\qquad n \geqslant 2.$$

10 - Q 1   **Question 1.**   Prove by simple induction that the closed form of numbers $A(n)$ is $(n^2 - n + 1)/n^2$ for any integer $n \geqslant 1$. What can be deduced as to the nature of these numbers?

10 - Q 2   **Question 2.**   Prove that for any integer $n > 2$, $A(n)$ lies in the *open* interval $A(2) .. A(1)$.

The solution is on page 51.

Problem 11. The lizard sequence   ○ ⁝

> *In this problem, one tries to build an infinite sequence of binary numbers which equals that obtained by taking only one in three term, as well as that obtained by keeping the two in three remaining terms. Of course, the two trivial sequences made solely of 0's or 1's are discarded.*

Let $S = \langle s_1, s_2, \ldots, s_n, \ldots \rangle$ be the binary sequence other than the trivial one composed solely of 0's (respectively 1's). One denotes by $S/3$ the sequence built by taking one in three element of S as follows: $S/3 = \langle s_3, s_6, \ldots, s_{3n}, \ldots \rangle$. One denotes by $S - S/3$ the sequence remaining from S when S/3 is removed, which gives: $S - S/3 = \langle s_1, s_2, s_4, s_5, s_7, s_8, \ldots, s_{3n-2}, s_{3n-1}, s_{3n+1}, s_{3n+2}, \ldots \rangle$. For example, for $S = \langle 0, 0, 1, 1, 0, 0, 1, 1, 0, 0, 1, 1, \ldots \rangle$, one has:

$$S/3 = \langle 1, 0, 0, 1, \ldots \rangle \quad \text{and} \quad S - S/3 = \langle 0, 0, 1, 0, 1, 1, 0, 1, \ldots \rangle.$$

Question 1. Propose a reasoning by induction which allows the construction of the two sequence S_1 and S_2 (other than $\langle 0, 0, 0, \ldots \rangle$ and $\langle 1, 1, 1, \ldots \rangle$) such that $S = S/3 = S - S/3$. They are called the "lizard sequence" (see [11]).   11 - Q 1

Question 2. Give their first 20 elements.   11 - Q 2

The solution is on page 52.

Problem 12. Fibonacci sequence; about the closed form   8 •

> *This problem highlights the fact that even if a closed form of a recurrence formula is known, it can hardly be used in an algorithm.*

Let us remind that Fibonacci sequence of integer numbers is defined (see page 10) by the following recurrence:

$$\mathcal{F}(1) = 1$$
$$\mathcal{F}(2) = 1$$
$$\mathcal{F}(n) = \mathcal{F}(n-1) + \mathcal{F}(n-2) \qquad\qquad n > 2.$$

Its closed form is:

$$\mathcal{F}(n) = \frac{1}{\sqrt{5}} \left[\left(\frac{1 + \sqrt{5}}{2} \right)^n - \left(\frac{1 - \sqrt{5}}{2} \right)^n \right] \qquad n \geqslant 1.$$

Question 1. Explain why the above formula is not used to compute $\mathcal{F}(n)$ for a given n.   12 - Q 1

Question 2. Propose an iterative algorithm returning the nth Fibonacci number.   12 - Q 2

Remark

Several other ways for the computation of Fibonacci numbers are discussed in problem 89, page 425.

The solution is on page 53.

Problem 13. How many binary trees have n nodes?   ○ •

> *This problem is a complement to the example given page 12. Its objective is to design a variant of the algorithm computing the number of binary trees possessing n elements on the basis of a closed form, therefore expected to be more efficient.*

It has been established that the number of binary trees with n nodes is given by the following recurrence:

$$\left|\begin{array}{l} nbBT(0) = 1 \\ nbBT(n) = \displaystyle\sum_{i=0}^{n-1} nbBT(i) \cdot nbBT(n-i-1) \end{array}\right. \qquad n \geqslant 1.$$

13 - Q 1   **Question 1.**   Prove that this recurrence can also be written:

$$nbBT(n) = Cat(n+1) \qquad n \geqslant 0$$

where $Cat(n)$ is the nth Catalan number (see definition page 11).

13 - Q 2   **Question 2.**   Derive an iterative algorithm to compute $nbBT(n)$.

The solution is on page 53.

Problem 14. Identifying a closed form   ○ ⦂

> *This problem has a twofold interest. On the one hand, a practical way for the calculation of the elements of a two index recurrence is studied. On the other hand, a closed form is proposed and proven by means of a new pattern for two index proof by induction.*

The following two index recurrence is considered:

$$\left|\begin{array}{ll} a(0,j) = j+1 & j \geqslant 0 \\ a(i,0) = 2 \cdot a(i-1,0) + a(i-1,1) & i > 0 \\ a(i,j) = a(i-1,j-1) + 2 \cdot a(i-1,j) + a(i-1,j+1) & i > 0 \textbf{ and } j > 0. \end{array}\right.$$

14 - Q 1   **Question 1.**   Give the value $a(3,2)$. Propose a tabular structure and describe the evolution of the calculation of $a(i,j)$ $(i,j \geqslant 0)$.

14 - Q 2   **Question 2.**   Write an iterative program which computes the value $a(n,m)$ for a given pair (n,m).

14 - Q 3   **Question 3.**   Propose a closed form for $a(i,j)$ and prove its validity by induction. What is the interest of this expression from an algorithmic point of view?

The solution is on page 54.

Problem 15. Moving a knight under constraints   ◦ •

One considers possible moves of the knight (in the spirit of the chessgame) under constraint between the two extreme points of a board and their enumeration by means of a recurrence formula.

One is interested in the paths of the knight (according to chessgame) over a board with $n > 4$ rows and $m > 3$ columns. One wants to know the number of distinct ways to go from the square $(1, 1)$ (departure) to the square (n, m) (arrival). By convention, (i, j) stands for the square of the board located on row i and column j. In contrast to chessgame where the knight has eight possible moves (except if it would go outside the board), it is imposed that the knight moves only in order to increase the column index (the second one), as shown in figure 1.9.

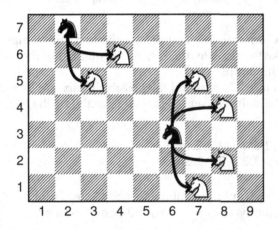

Fig. 1.9 – The knight located in $(7, 2)$ (respectively $(3, 6)$), plotted in black, can move to the two (respectively four) positions, plotted in white.

Question 1.   Let $\mathrm{nbRout}(i, j)$ be the count of distinct paths starting in $(1, 1)$ and ending   15 - Q 1
in (i, j). Give the complete recurrence for calculating $\mathrm{nbRout}(i, j)$.

Question 2.   Write the iterative algorithm derived from this formula for any given pair   15 - Q 2
of integers (n, m). Give the value of $\mathrm{nbRout}(5, 7)$.

The solution is on page 56.

Problem 16. How many partitions of n elements have p blocks?   ◦ •

The main goal of this problem is to establish the recurrence formula defining Stirling numbers.

We denote by $\mathcal{S}(p, n)$ the number of partitions with p blocks of a set having n elements. The values $\mathcal{S}(p, n)$ are called *Stirling numbers*. For example, $\{\{a, c\}, \{b, d\}\}$ and $\{\{b\}, \{a, c, d\}\}$ are two out of the seven partitions with two blocks of the four element set $\{a, b, c, d\}$.

16 - Q 1   **Question** 1.   Give all the partitions with one, two, three and four blocks of the latter four element set (a block cannot be empty).

16 - Q 2   **Question** 2.   What is the recurrence defining $S(p, n)$?

16 - Q 3   **Question** 3.   Propose a progression of the calculation of $S(p, n)$, then develop the corresponding iterative algorithm.

16 - Q 4   **Question** 4.   Give the values of $S(p, n)$ for $1 \leqslant p \leqslant 5$ and $1 \leqslant n \leqslant 7$.

The solution is on page 58.

Problem 17.   Climbing a staircase   ○ ●

> *The target of this problem is twofold: establishing a recurrence relation and optimizing its algorithmic computation by obviating some of the cells of the underlying array.*

One considers a m step staircase that can be climbed with jumps of a_1 or a_2 or ... or a_n steps. We would like to calculate $nbCL(s, m)$ the number of distinct ways for climbing *exactly* the m steps with s jumps.

For example, when $m = 12$ steps and the possible jumps are $a_1 = 2, a_2 = 3$ and $a_3 = 5$ steps, the 12 steps of the staircase can be climbed (exactly) by the following successions of jumps (among others):

$(2, 2, 2, 2, 2, 2), (2, 3, 2, 3, 2), (2, 2, 2, 3, 3),$
$(3, 3, 3, 3), (2, 2, 3, 5), (3, 2, 5, 2), (2, 2, 5, 3).$

17 - Q 1   **Question** 1.   Give two ways for climbing up the 12 steps (not more, not less) of a staircase using *exactly three* jumps of $a_1 = 2$ or $a_2 = 3$ or $a_3 = 5$ steps.

17 - Q 2   **Question** 2.   Give the recurrence relation for the calculation of $nbCL(s, m)$.

17 - Q 3   **Question** 3.   Propose a progression for this calculation, then the iterative associated program.

17 - Q 4   **Question** 4.   Give the values $nbCL(s, m)$ for $m \leqslant 12, s \leqslant 6, n = 2, a_1 = 2, a_2 = 5$.

17 - Q 5   **Question** 5.   In the previous example, it can be noticed that some portions of the array related to $nbCL$ are filled in with 0's. Explain why and suggest an improvement of the algorithm proposed in question 3.

The solution is on page 59.

Problem 18.   The Patagon game   ○ ⁝

> *This problem introduces the* Patagon game, *where a single player aims at accumulating the highest gain. One searches to count the "reasonable" ways of playing, which both comply with the rule of the game and are likely to lead to the maximum gain. problem 146, page 687 is devoted to the determination of a way of playing according to which the highest gain is reached.*

When playing the *Patagon game*, the player is in front of n objects, arranged in line. Each object possesses a given visible value. The player can take as many objects as he wants so as to accumulate a total value as large as possible. Obviously, there is a constraint (and only one): the player cannot take two of the objects of the initial configuration located side by side.

Question 1. What is the best choice with the following line of objects (where an object is represented by its value) ?   18 - Q 1

23	41	40	21	42	24

Question 2. The choice of the player is assumed to be represented by its n-sized characteristic vector (1 in position i if the ith object is taken, 0 otherwise). In the previous example, $[0, 1, 0, 1, 0, 1]$ represents a game yielding $0 + 41 + 0 + 21 + 0 + 24 = 86$ Patagon currency units. Prove that, for $n > 1$, there are strictly less than 2^n distinct ways of playing.   18 - Q 2

Question 3. Some ways of playing are, for sure, worse than others. For example, $[0, 1, 0, 1, 0, 0]$ (yielding 62) is worse than $[0, 1, 0, 1, 0, 1]$ (paying 86). A way of playing is said to be *reasonable*, if it does not leave objects that could have been taken (while obeying the rule of the game). Hence, playing $[0, 1, 0, 1, 0, 1]$ is reasonable, whereas playing $[0, 1, 0, 0, 0, 1]$ or $[0, 1, 0, 1, 0, 0]$ is not. How can the reasonable ways of playing be characterized?   18 - Q 3

Question 4. The objective of the remainder of the problem is to count the number of reasonable ways of playing, in other words, the number of n sized binary vectors related to all reasonable ways of playing. For a n sized game, $nbRWP_0(n)$ (respectively $nbRWP_1(n)$) denotes the number of reasonable ways of playing where the nth location of the vector is 0 (respectively 1). The total number of reasonable ways of playing, $nbRWP(n)$, is obviously the sum $nbRWP_0(n) + nbRWP_1(n)$.   18 - Q 4

Prove that:

$nbRWP_0(1) = 0,\ nbRWP_1(1) = nbRWP_0(2) = nbRWP_1(2) = nbRWP_0(3) = nbRWP_1(3) = 1$

and that for $n > 3$:

$nbRWP_0(n) = nbRWP_1(n-1)$
$nbRWP_1(n) = nbRWP_1(n-2) + nbRWP_1(n-3)$.

Question 5. Prove that: 18 - Q 5

$nbRWP(1) = 1,\ nbRWP(2) = 2,\ nbRWP(3) = 2$

and that for $n > 3$:

$nbRWP(n) = nbRWP(n-2) + nbRWP(n-3)$.

Question 6. Give the values of $nbRWP_0(n)$, $nbRWP_1(n)$ and $nbRWP(n)$ for n varying from 1 to 15. Independently of $nbRWP_0$, which relation ties $nbRWP$ and $nbRWP_1$? Would it have been possible to establish it before?   18 - Q 6

Question 7. Give the algorithm calculating $nbRWP(n)$ for a given value n.   18 - Q 7

The solution is on page 61.

Problem 19. The game of two stacks   ○ **⁝**

> In this problem, one is interested in the number nbWW of ways to win in a game where
> tokens located in two stacks are added or removed. A property of nbWW is pointed out and
> proven by induction.

Let us consider a game where two stacks P and Q containing respectively p and q tokens $(p, q > 1)$ are available. The goal is to reach one of the configurations $(p = 0, q = 1)$ or $(p = 1, q = 0)$, called *winning state* later. The evolution of the stacks obeys the following procedure: two tokens are removed from P (respectively Q), one is thrown away and the other is added to Q (respectively P).

Example. $(p = 4, q = 6) \longrightarrow (p = 2, q = 7)$ or $(p = 5, q = 4)$.

We want to know the number $nfg(p, q)$ of distinct ways allowing to reach one of the two winning states starting from a configuration where stack P contains p tokens and stack Q has q tokens.

19 - Q 1   **Question 1.**   Give the recurrence expression of $nbWW(p, q)$.

19 - Q 2   **Question 2.**   Propose a tabular structure associated with the calculation of $nbWWg$ as well as the progression of its filling.

19 - Q 3   **Question 3.**   Deduce an iterative algorithm for the computation of the number of distinct ways allowing to reach one of the two winning states of the game.

19 - Q 4   **Question 4.**   Use this algorithm to compute $nbWW(4, 2)$.

19 - Q 5   **Question 5.**   Prove that any element $nbWW(i, j)$, such that $|i - j|$ is a multiple of 3, is equal to 0 (excepted $nbWW(0, 0)$, which makes no sense).

The solution is on page 63.

Problem 20. The yellow coins   ○ **⁝**

> This problem raises the (apparently) simple problem of enumerating the distinct ways for
> forming one euro with yellow coins. It is shown that the intuitive approach based on a single
> index recurrence is not appropriate and that it is necessary to call on a double index one. The
> approach developed here has a follow up in problem 148, page 689.

One wants to know the number of distinct ways for forming the amount of one euro with yellow coins, in other words, using the six following coins of the European currency system: $1, 2, 5, 10, 20$ and 50 cents.

20 - Q 1   **Question 1.**   Let us first reason in order to form any amount ranging from one to nine cents. Obviously, there is a single solution to form the amount of one cent. For two cents, one can take a single coin (two cents), or a one cent coin and one cent remains to be formed. To form the amount s of three or four cents, one takes a one cent coin and the amount $(s-1)$ remains to be formed, or one takes a two cent coin and the amount $(s - 2)$ remains to be formed. To form five cents, one takes a single coin (five cents), or a one cent coin and the amount of four cents remains to be formed, or a two cent coin and the amount of three cents remains to be formed. Last, to form the amount s from six to nine cents, one takes a five cent coin and the amount $(s - 5)$ remains to be formed, or a one cent coin and the amount $(s - 1)$ remains to be formed, or a two cent coin and the amount $(s - 2)$ remains to be formed. One deduces the following recurrence defining nbWF1E(1), the number of ways for forming one euro:

$$
\begin{aligned}
&nbWF1E(1) = 1 \\
&nbWF1E(2) = 1 + nbWF1E(1) \\
&nbWF1E(i) = nbWF1E(i-1) + nbWF1E(i-2) && 3 \leqslant i \leqslant 4 \\
&nbWF1E(5) = 1 + nbWF1E(4) + nbWF1E(3) \\
&nbWF1E(i) = nbWF1E(i-5) + nbWF1E(i-2) + nbWF1E(i-1) && 6 \leqslant i \leqslant 9.
\end{aligned}
$$

Explain why this recurrence is not convenient.

Question 2. Propose a *double index* recurrence to calculate the number of ways for forming one euro with yellow coins.   20 - Q 2

Question 3. Check that there are two ways for forming three cents.   20 - Q 3

Question 4. Write the iterative program performing the computation of the number of ways for forming one euro with yellow coins.   20 - Q 4

Question 5. What is the number of ways for forming one euro with yellow coins?   20 - Q 5

Question 6. Prove that the number of ways for forming the amount m with *all yellow coins* grows with m.   20 - Q 6

The solution is on page 65.

Problem 21. Shuffling words   ◦ ⋮

> *We define the* shuffle *operation of two words and want to determine the number of possible shuffles of two given words. We also want to decide whether a word can be the result of the shuffle of two others.*

Let us take three words: u of length m, v of length n and w of length $(m+n)$. The word w is said to be a *shuffle* of the two words u and v if it obtained in shuffling the letters of u and v while preserving their order of the letters in u and v. For example, with u = *nose* and v = *lips*, the word w = *nolispse* is a shuffle of u and v, but not the word *nlsoipes*.

Question 1. Give a recurrence relation for the calculation of nbShuf(m, n) the number of distinct shuffles that can be obtained from u and v, or more generally from any pair of words of respective lengths m and n. What is the value of nbShuf(5, 4)?   21 - Q 1

Question 2. Prove by induction that $nbShuf(m,n) = (m+n)!/(m! \cdot n!)$. How could we have found this result directly?   21 - Q 2

Question 3. Write an algorithme which decides if a word w is a shuffle of the words u and v. Apply it to u = *abc*, v = *db* and w = *dabbc*.   21 - Q 3

The solution is on page 68.

1.10   Solutions

Answers to problem 1. Is a neutral element unique ? *The problem is on page 33.*

1 - A 1   **Answer 1.**   Since the operator $\oplus$ is commutative, one has:

$$\forall x \cdot (x \in S \Rightarrow u \oplus x = x \oplus u).$$

u is a left neutral element, then $u \oplus x = x$ and $x \oplus u = x$. It can be deduced that v is also the right neutral element.

1 - A 2   **Answer 2.**   Let us assume that the left neutral element u and the right neutral element v of $\oplus$ are distinct. Since u is a left neutral element, one has: $u \oplus v = v$. Similarly, since v is a right neutral element, one has: $u \oplus v = u$. Assuming that $u \neq v$ leads to say that operation $u \oplus v$ has two different results, which contradicts the definition of an internal operation. Consequently, since the assumption that u are v distinct leads to a contradiction, u and v are necessarily equal.

Answers to problem 2. Minimum element of a partially ordered set   *The problem is on page 33.*

2 - A 1   **Answer 1.**   Let us assume that any element x of F has at least one strict antecedent, i.e. for any $x \in$ F there is a element $a(x)$ such that $a(x) \neq x$ and $a(x) \preceq x$. In such a case, there is at least one element $a(a(x)) = a^2(x)$ and at least one element $a^n(x)$ for any integer $n \geqslant 1$. As soon as n exceeds the cardinality of F, in the series $a^n(x), \ldots, a(x)$ there is at least an element appearing twice (or more) [4]. Thus, one has a situation of the type $a_1 \preceq a_2 \preceq \ldots \preceq a_p \preceq a_1$, where all the elements $a_1, \ldots, a_p$ are distinct, which is impossible, since it contradicts the definition of a partial order relation whose antisymmetry property entails that $a \preceq b$ **and** $b \preceq a \Rightarrow a = b$.

The hypothesis according to which any element x of F has at least one strict antecedsent, is thus false. Consequently, F contains one element without any strict antecedent, i.e. a minimum element.

2 - A 2   **Answer 2.**   The demonstration is based on a proof by induction (simple recurrence) about the cardinality of F. $P(n)$ is the following property "any strict subset F of E whose size is n involves at least one minimum element".

Initialization   Any subset F of E whose cardinality is 1 involves one minimum element (the single element of F).

Induction   Let F be a strict subset of E with n elements that possesses a minimum element m (induction hypothesis). Let us now consider the set F with an additional element x (from E) that is not already in F. (x does exist since F is a strict subset of E). Three exclusive cases can be singled out:

- $x \preceq m$, and by transitivity (of the partial order relation $\preceq$), x is the minimum element of $F \cup \{x\}$,
- $m \preceq x$ and m becomes the minimum element of $F \cup \{x\}$,
- m and x are not tied via the order relation and m is the minimum element of $F \cup \{x\}$.

Conclusion $P(1)$ holds, and moreover $P(n) \Rightarrow P(n+1)$, so $P(n)$ holds for any integer n.

---

[4]This claim is a consequence of the "pigeonhole principle ", which states that when $(k + 1)$ objects (or more) are stored in k boxes, at least one box contains two (or more) objects.

Answer 3.   From the statement of the problem, one has: 2 - A 3

$$F = \{(1,2), (2,1), (3,1), (3,2)\}.$$

The element $(1,2)$ has no strict antecedent and is therefore a minimum of F. The same holds for $(2,1)$. F possesses two minimum elements.

Answers to problem 3. Factorial *vs* exponential   *The problem is on page 33.*

Answer 1.   We follow the steps of the simple induction reasoning.   3 - A 1

Initialization For $n = 1$, one has $1! = 1$ and $2^0 = 1$, the (non strict) inequality holds.

Induction Suppose that the inequality hols for $n \geqslant 1$ (induction hypothesis). For $(n + 1)$, one has:

$$(n+1)!$$
$$= \qquad \qquad \text{definition of the factorial}$$
$$(n+1) \cdot n!$$
$$\geqslant \qquad \qquad \text{induction hypothesis}$$
$$(n+1) \cdot 2^{n-1}$$
$$\geqslant \qquad \qquad n \in \mathbb{N}_1 \Rightarrow n \geqslant 1$$
$$2 \cdot 2^{n-1}$$
$$= \qquad \qquad \text{arithmetics}$$
$$2^n.$$

Conclusion The inequality holds for $n = 1$ as well as for $(n + 1)$ if it does for n. It can be deduced that $n! \geqslant 2^{n-1}$ for any strictly positive integer n.

Answer 2.   It is easy to observe that the inequality $n! \geqslant n^{2n}$ does not hold until $n = 8$ 3 - A 2 since $8! = 40320$ and $2^{16} = 65536$. On the contrary, it holds for $n = 9$ since $9! = 362880$ and $2^{18} = 262144$.
We now prove that for $n \geqslant 9$, if $n! > 2^{2n}$ then $(n + 1)! > 2^{2n+2}$. One has:

$$(n+1)!$$
$$= \qquad \qquad \text{definition of a factorial}$$
$$(n+1) \cdot n!$$
$$> \qquad \qquad \text{induction hypothesis}$$
$$(n+1) \cdot 2^{2n}$$
$$> \qquad \qquad n \geqslant 9$$
$$4 \cdot 2^{2n}$$
$$= \qquad \qquad \text{property of the exponential}$$
$$2^{2n+2}.$$

It can be deduced that the proposed property ($n! > 2^{2n}$) for any integer n strictly greater than 8.

Answers to problem 4. Currency change (1)   *The problem is on page 34.*

Answer 1.   The proof of validity of this pattern is made in a way similar to the one used   4 - A 1 in section 1.1.3.1, page 4.

4 - A 2   **Answer** 2.   First, this pattern is used to demonstrate the property claiming that any amount of money n (strictly) greater than five cents may be obtained with coins of two and seven cents.

Initialization We take $n_0 = 6$ since it is impossible to form the amount of five cents with the two considered coins. It is possible to obtain the amount of six (respectively seven) cents with three two cent coins (respectively one seven cent coin).

Induction Suppose that the property holds for any amount $n \geqslant 6$ (induction hypothesis). To form the amount $(n + 2)$, it is sufficient to add one two cent coin to the combination of coins serving for the amount n (which does exist according to the induction hypothesis).

Conclusion The property holds for any amount $n \geqslant 6$.

4 - A 3   **Answer** 3.   We now proceed to the demonstration using the "regular" proof by simple induction (see section 1.1.3.1, page 4).

Initialization The amount of six cents is obtained with three two cent coins.

Induction Assume that the property holds for a given value of n ($n \geqslant 6$). Two exclusive cases occur:

- The amount n has been obtained with at least one seven cent coin. This coin is discarded, four two cent coins are added and the amount $n + 1$ is thus formed.
- The amount n has been obtained only with two cent coins. Three of these coins are removed and one seven cent coin is added, which makes the amount $n + 1$.

Conclusion The amount of six cents can be formed with two cent coins and (no) seven cent coins and if it is possible to form the amount n, we know how to form the amount $(n + 1)$ with these coins. Hence, it is possible to form any amount strictly over five cents with two and seven cent coins.

4 - A 4   **Answer** 4.   According to the first pattern, only one seven cent coin can appear (precisely that used to form the amount of seven cents), since then only two cent coins are added. It is the same with the second pattern, since as soon as a seven cent coin appears, it is removed.

4 - A 5   **Answer** 5.   The first (respectively second) pattern requires to prove the validity of the property for n_0 and $n_0 + 1$ (respectively n_0). On the contrary, in this example, the proof of the induction step is shorter with the first schema where no distinction between situations has to be made.

Answers to problem 5. Catalan numbers *The problem is on page 34.*

5 - A 1   **Answer** 1.   We proceed using proof by simple induction.

Initialization For $n = 1$, the proposed closed form yields: $0!/(0! \cdot 1!) = 1$ (assuming that $0! = 1$).

Induction Assume that, for $n \geqslant 1$, the closed form is suitable (induction hypothesis). For $(n + 1)$, the general term of the recurrence relation yields:

$$Cat(n + 1)$$

$$= \qquad\qquad\qquad\qquad \text{general term of the recurrence relation}$$

$$\frac{4(n + 1) - 6}{n + 1} \cdot Cat(n)$$

$$= \qquad\qquad\qquad\qquad\qquad\qquad\qquad \text{induction hypothesis}$$

$$\frac{4n-2}{n+1} \cdot \frac{(2n-2)!}{(n-1)! \cdot n!}$$

$$= \qquad\qquad\qquad\qquad\qquad\qquad\text{arithmetics}$$

$$\frac{(4n-2) \cdot (2n-2)!}{(n-1)! \cdot (n+1)!}$$

$$= \qquad\qquad\text{numerator and denominator multiplied by } n$$

$$\frac{(4n^2-2n) \cdot (2n-2)!}{n! \cdot (n+1)!}$$

$$= \qquad\qquad\qquad\qquad\qquad\qquad\text{arithmetics}$$

$$\frac{(2n)!}{n! \cdot (n+1)!}$$

this latter expression being nothing but the closed form for $(n+1)$.

Conclusion The closed form holds for $n = 1$, and if it holds for $n \geqslant 1$, it does for $(n+1)$. It can be concluded that the closed form is suitable for any positive value n.

Answer 2. Here again, a proof by simple induction is performed. 5 - A 2

Initialization For $n = 1$, one has $Cat(1) = 1$ and $4^{n-1}/n = 1$; the property holds.

Induction Assume that, for $n \geqslant 1$, the property holds (induction hypothesis). For $n + 1$, one has:

$$Cat(n+1)$$

$$= \qquad\qquad\qquad\qquad\text{general term of the recurrence relation}$$

$$\frac{4(n+1)-6}{n+1} \cdot Cat(n)$$

$$\leqslant \qquad\qquad\qquad\qquad\qquad\qquad\text{induction hypothesis}$$

$$\frac{4(n+1)-6}{n+1} \cdot \frac{4^{n-1}}{n}$$

$$= \qquad\qquad\qquad\qquad\qquad\qquad\text{rewriting}$$

$$\frac{4n-2}{n} \cdot \frac{4^{n-1}}{n+1}$$

$$< \qquad\qquad\qquad\qquad\qquad (4n-2)/n < 4 \text{ for } n \geqslant 1$$

$$\frac{4^n}{n+1}$$

Conclusion The property holds for any integer n.

Remark

Equality occurs only for $n = 1$. Beyond, $4^{n-1}/n$ is a strict upper bound for $Cat(n)$. Hence, one has: $Cat(2) = 1 < 4^1/2 (= 2)$, $Cat(3) = 2 < 4^2/3 (\approx 5.33)$, $Cat(5) = 14 < 4^4/5 (= 51.2)$.

Answers to problem 6. Erroneous proofs by simple induction *The problem is on page 35.*

Answer 1. When we write: 6 - A 1

$$\text{If } \max(a,b) = 0, \text{ then } a = b = 0$$

we comply with the fact that the numbers under consideration are integers. The flaw is not there, but in the following line that does not comply with the induction hypothesis with $p \geqslant 0$:

$$\text{The maximum of } (a-1) \text{ and } (b-1) \text{ is then } p.$$

As a matter of fact, this line may produce negative numbers (when a or b equals 0): we are no longer in the scope of property P_1 applying to integers. Take the numbers $a = 0$ and $b = 1$. One has: $a - 1 = -1$ and $b - 1 = 0$. Their maximum is 0 whereas these two numbers are both equal to 0 (and therefore equal).

6 - A 2   **Answer** 2.   The fallacy lies in the following sentence:
    The two straight lines (d_1) and (d_2) have the two points A_2 and A_3 in common.
So that this claim is true, the number of points must be strictly over 2 ($p \geqslant 3$), in order to be able to use points A_2 and A_3. The induction hypothesis must start with $p > 2$. However, for $p = 2$, the straight line (d_1) is $(A_1 A_2)$ and the straight line (d_2) is $(A_2 A_3)$, and they have only one point (A_2) in common and generally they are not collinear.

Answers to problem 7. Erroneous proof by strong induction   *The problem is on page 36.*

7 - A 1   **Answer** 1.   The flaw appears when writing (implicitly for any $n \geqslant 2$):

$$((n-1)^2 - 1)/(n - 2) = n.$$

As a matter of fact, a division by $(n - 2)$ is performed, but this denominator is equal to 0 when $n = 2$, and the division is illegal.

7 - A 2   **Answer** 2.   For any $n \geqslant 1$, the following identity holds:

$$n = \sqrt{1 + (n-1)(n+1)}.$$

In the right member, let us replace $(n + 1)$ by $\sqrt{1 + n(n + 2)}$, it yields:

$$n = \sqrt{1 + (n-1)\sqrt{1 + n(n + 2)}}.$$

Now, let us replace $(n + 2)$ by $\sqrt{1 + (n + 1)(n + 3)}$, we get:

$$n = \sqrt{1 + (n-1)\sqrt{1 + n\sqrt{1 + (n+1)(n+3)}}}.$$

The substitution mechanism can be repeated for $(n + 3)$, then $(n + 4)$ and so on, and this results in the proposed formula, namely:

$$n = \sqrt{1 + (n-1)\sqrt{1 + n\sqrt{1 + (n+1)\sqrt{1 + (n+2)\ldots}}}}.$$

Answers to problem 8. Alternate pattern for two indexes recurrence proof   *The problem is on page 37.*

We use the total order relation over $\mathbb{N}_1{}^2$ given in section 1.1.6, page 9, namely:

$$(a, b) \preceq (c, d) \stackrel{\wedge}{=} a < c \text{ **or** } (a = c \text{ **and** } b \leqslant d).$$

The pattern suggested above aims at establishing that if P holds for any point of the rectangle $(1 \ldots m, 1 \ldots n)$ – $m = 1$ or $n = 1$ is accounted for in the initialization – then P holds also for any point $(m + 1, 1)$ to $(m + 1, n)$ and for any point $(1, n + 1)$ to $(m, n + 1)$; thus, P holds for all the points "lower" (in the sense of $\preceq$) than the point $(m + 1, n + 1)$. If, in addition, we prove that P holds in $(m + 1, n + 1)$, the newly proposed pattern of proof is an instance of property (1), page 9, for the pair $(\mathbb{N}_1{}^2, \preceq)$.

Answers to problem 9. Divisibility by 7   *The problem is on page 38.*

Answer 1. Let $A(n,p) = q$, where q is a nonnegative integer, then we have $3^{2n} = 2^{n-p} + q$. By definition: 9 - A 1

$$A(n+1,p) = 3^{2(n+1)} - 2^{(n+1)-p} = 9 \cdot 3^{2n} - 2 \cdot 2^{n-p}.$$

Replacing 3^{2n} by $(2^{n-p} + q)$ in the right part of the preceding expression, we get:

$$A(n+1,p) = 9 \cdot (2^{n-p} + q) - 2 \cdot 2^{n-p} = 7 \cdot 2^{n-p} + 9 \cdot q.$$

This latter expression is likely to produce a multiple of 7 only if q (indeed $A(n,p)$) is itself a multiple of 7. Thus, we have:

$$A(n,p) = q = 7k \quad \text{and} \quad A(n+1,p) = 7 \cdot (2^{n-p} + 9k).$$

Consequently, if $A(n,p)$ is a multiple of 7, $A(n+1,p)$ is also one and if $A(n,p)$ cannot be divided by 7, $A(n+1,p)$ cannot either.

Answer 2. From the previous answer, $A(n,p)$ is made of integers multiple of 7 if and   9 - A 2 only if the first term of the series $(A(n_0,p) = A(p,p))$ is a multiple of 7. The first term of each of the four proposed series is now considered:

- the first terms of the series $A(n,0)$ is $A(1,0) = 3^2 - 2^1 = 7$ and $A(2,0) = 77$ and the series is made of integers multiple of 7 for any positive integer n,
- the series $A(n,1)$ starts with $A(1,1) = 3^2 - 2^0 = 8$, and this series is not made of numbers multiple of 7 for any positive integer n,
- the first term of the series $A(n,2)$ is $A(2,2) = 3^4 - 2^0 = 80$, and this series is not made of multiples of 7 for any integer n strictly greater than 1,
- the series $A(n,3)$ starts with $A(3,3) = 3^6 - 2^0 = 728 = 7 \cdot 104$. It can be deduced that any element of the series $A(n,3)$ can be divided by 7 for any integer n strictly greater than 2.

Answers to problem 10. **Proof by induction *vs* direct proof** *The problem is on page 38.*

Answer 1. For $n = 1$, the suggested closed form yields $A(1) = 1$, which matches the   10 - A 1 value given by the recurrence formula. We will demonstrate that for any $n > 1$:

$$A(n+1) = \frac{(n+1)^2 - (n+1) + 1}{(n+1)^2} = \frac{n^2 + n + 1}{(n+1)^2}.$$

One has:

$$A(n+1) = A(n) + \frac{(n+1)^2 - 3(n+1) + 1}{n^2 \cdot (n+1)^2} = A(n) + \frac{n^2 - n - 1}{n^2 \cdot (n+1)^2}$$

and replacing $A(n)$ by its value given by the recurrence relation:

$$A(n+1) = \frac{n^2 - n + 1}{n^2} + \frac{n^2 - n - 1}{n^2 \cdot (n+1)^2} = \frac{n^4 + n^3 + n2}{n^2 \cdot (n+1)^2} = \frac{n^2 + n + 1}{(n+1)^2}$$

which is the expected expression.
The numerator and the denominator of the expression defining numbers $A(n)$ are integers, hence these numbers are rational ones.

On the other hand, they are positive since for any positive integer n:

$$A(n) = \frac{n^2 - n + 1}{n^2} > \left(\frac{n-1}{n}\right)^2 \geqslant 0.$$

10 - A 2   **Answer 2.**   The "direct" demonstration of the property:

$$\forall n \cdot ((n \in \mathbb{N}_1 \text{ and } n > 2) \Rightarrow (1 > A(n) > 3/4))$$

is easy and thus preferred to that by induction. First, let us work out $(A(n) - 3/4)$:

$$A(n) - \frac{3}{4} = \frac{n^2 - n + 1}{n^2} - \frac{3}{4} = \frac{n^2 - 4n + 4}{4n^2} = \left(\frac{n-2}{2n}\right)^2$$

expression whose value is strictly positive for $n > 2$. Let us now determine the sign of $(1 - A(n))$. One has:

$$1 - A(n) = 1 - \frac{n^2 - n + 1}{n^2} = \frac{n-1}{n^2}.$$

Yet, $((n-1)/n^2)$ has a strictly positive value for $n > 1$. One concludes that, for $n \geqslant 3$, $A(n)$ is strictly greater than $3/4$ ($A(2)$) and strictly less than 1 ($A(1)$).

Answers to problem 11. The lizard sequence   *The problem is on page 38.*

11 - A 1   **Answer 1.**   We denote by a and b the first two terms of a sequence S obeying the constraints of the statement. We will prove that, if we assume that the $(3k - 1)$ first terms of the sequence $S = \langle a, b, s_3, \ldots, s_{3k-1}, \ldots \rangle$ for $k \geqslant 1$ are known, the next three terms can be identified. Then, it will be possible to deduce that it is possible to build a lizard sequence S as long as desired. We use a proof by strong induction.

Induction For $k \geqslant 1$, the first $(3k - 1)$ terms of S are assumed to be known (induction hypothesis). Then:

$$S = \langle a, b, s_3, \ldots, s_{3k-1}, x, y, z, \ldots \rangle$$

and we want to determine the value of the terms x, y and z of respective rank $3k, 3k+1$ and $3k + 2$. More precisely, the three sequences are written:

$$S = \langle a, b, s_3, \ldots, s_k, \ldots, s_{2k+1}, s_{2k+2} \ldots, s_{3k-1}, x, y, z, \ldots \rangle$$
$$S/3 = \langle s_3, \ldots, x, \ldots \rangle$$
$$S - S/3 = \langle a, b, \ldots, y, z, \ldots \rangle.$$

It turns out that: (i) x is the kth term of $S/3$ and it should be equal to the kth term of S, so $x = s_k$ and s_k is known since $k \in 1..3k-1$, (ii) y is the $(2k+1)^{th}$ term of $S - S/3$ and it should be equal to the $(2k + 1)^{th}$ term of S, so $y = s_{2k+1}$. Now, $(2k + 1)$ is in the range $1 .. 3k - 1$ only if $k \geqslant 2$. However, for $k = 1$, the term s_{2k+1} is none other than x which we know from the above, (iii) z is the $(2k+2)^{th}$ term of $S - S/3$ and it should be equal to the $(2k+2)^{th}$ term of S, so $z = s_{2k+2}$. Now, $(2k + 2)$ is in the range $1..3k - 1$ only if $k \geqslant 3$. However, for $k = 1$, the term s_{2k+2} is none other than y which is known from the above, and if $k = 2$, the term s_{2k+2} is identified with x also known.

Conclusion It is possible to build a sequence S of any length given the first two terms a and b.

11 - A 2   **Answer 2.**   The first 20 elements of S are:

$$\langle a, b, a, a, a, b, a, b, a, a, b, a, a, a, a, b, a, b, a, a \rangle.$$

In addition to the two trivial sequence made solely of 0's or 1's, there are two lizard sequences, depending on the value (0 or 1) taken by a and b:

$$S_1 = \langle 0,1,0,0,0,1,0,1,0,0,1,0,0,0,0,1,0,1,0,0 \rangle$$
$$S_2 = \langle 1,0,1,1,1,0,1,0,1,1,0,1,1,1,1,0,1,0,1,1 \rangle$$

where S_2 (respectively S_1) is obtained from S_1 (respectively S_2) by the inversion of 0's and 1's.

Answers to problem 12. Fibonacci sequence; about the closed form *The problem is on page 39.*

Answer 1. Programming directly the proposed formula delivers a real number, not an integer value as expected. In the experiment that we have conducted with the language Ada provided by the Ideone platform, $\sqrt{5} = 2.236068$ and the simple precision number representation, a difference between the exact value and the integer part of the real result appears from $n = 68$.

12 - A 1

Answer 2. The computation of the nth Fibonacci number is performed in an iterative fashion based on the recurrence. It can be noticed that, as for the computation of a factorial, keeping values $\mathcal{F}(1)$ to $\mathcal{F}(n-1)$ is useless for the computation of $\mathcal{F}(n)$. Only three variables are necessary x, y and z, which play the role of $\mathcal{F}(n-2), \mathcal{F}(n-1)$ and $\mathcal{F}(n)$. The program is the following:

12 - A 2

```
1.  constants
2.     n ∈ ℕ₁ − {1,2} and n = ...
3.  variables
4.     x ∈ ℕ₁ and y ∈ ℕ₁ and z ∈ ℕ₁
5.  begin
6.     x ← 1; y ← 1;
7.     for i ranging 3 .. n do
8.        z ← x + y; x ← y; y ← z
9.     end for;
10.    write(𝓕𝑖𝑏𝑜𝑛𝑎𝑐𝑐𝑖 number of rank, n, is , z)
11. end
```

Answers to problem 13. How many binary trees have n nodes? *The problem is on page 40.*

Answer 1. Let $j = i + 1$, for $n \geqslant 1$, $\text{nbBT}(n)$ can be rewritten:

13 - A 1

$$\text{nbBT}(n) = \sum_{j=1}^{n} \text{nbBT}(j-1) \cdot \text{nbBT}(n-j).$$

Let $T(j) = \text{nbBT}(j-1)$, one has:

$$T(n+1) = \sum_{j=1}^{n} T(j) \cdot T(n-j+1).$$

Yet, the $(n+1)^{\text{th}}$ Catalan number is defined by:

$$\text{Cat}(n+1) = \sum_{i=1}^{n} \text{Cat}(i) \cdot \text{Cat}(n-i+1).$$

Since $nbBT(0) = Cat(1) = 1$, one has:

$$nbBT(n) = Cat(n+1) \qquad n \geqslant 0.$$

13 - A 2   **Answer 2.**   We have seen the closed form of Catalan numbers on page 11, namely:

$$Cat(n) = \frac{(2n-2)!}{(n-1)!\, n!} = \frac{1}{n} \cdot C_{2n-2}^{n-1} \qquad n \geqslant 1.$$

The value $nbBT(n)$ can be written thanks to the previous expression of the $(n+1)^{th}$ Catalan number:

$nbBT(0) = 1$
$nbBT(1) = 1$

$$nbBT(n) = Cat(n+1) = \frac{1}{n+1} \cdot C_{2n}^{n} = \frac{(n+2)\cdots 2n}{2\cdots n} \qquad n > 1.$$

The corresponding program is:

```
 1. constants
 2.   n ∈ N and n = ...
 3. variables
 4.   NBBT ∈ N₁ and Denom ∈ N₁
 5. begin
 6.   NBBT ← 1;
 7.   for i ranging n + 2 .. 2n do
 8.      NBBT ← NBBT · i
 9.   end for;
10.   Denom ← 1;
11.   for i ranging 2 .. n do
12.      denom ← Denom · i
13.   end for;
14.   NBBT ← NBBT/Denom;
15.   write(the number of binary trees having , n, nodes is , NBBT)
16. end
```

Answers to problem 14. Identifying a closed form   *The problem is on page 40.*

14 - A 1   **Answer 1.**   To compute $a(3,2)$, we need the values $a(2,1), a(2,2)$ and $a(2,3)$, which, in turn, require the knowledge of $a(1,0),\ldots,a(1,4)$. The calculation of these latter values is based on $a(0,0),\ldots,a(0,5)$, values obtained directly from the recurrence formula (first line).

The values are computed as follows: (i) elements whose first index is 0 and second index j ranges 0 .. 5, thanks to the first line of the recurrence formula, (ii) element $a(1,0)$ with the second line of the recurrence, and elements whose first index equals 1 and second index ranges 1 .. 4 using the third term of the recurrence, (iii) elements $a(2,1), a(2,2)$ and $a(2,3)$ with the third line, and last (iv) element $a(3,2)$ using once again the third line. From a concrete point of view, the computations will result in the (partial) filling of the array $A[0..i, 0..i+j]$ whose values are reported in figure 1.10, page 55.

The calculation of $a(i,j)$ corresponds to the filling of cell $A[i,j]$. We start with cells $A[0, \max(\{j-i, 0\})]$ to $A[0, j+i]$ (first line of the recurrence), then (when $i > 0$) cells $A[k, \max(\{j-i+k, 0\})]$ to $A[k, j+i-k]$ of any line whose index k is varying from 1

j	0	1	2	3	4	5
i = 0	1	2	3	4	5	6
1	4	8	12	16	20	
2		32	48	64		
3			192			

Fig. 1.10 – Array A associated with the calculation of $a(3,2)$.

to i, using the second (respectively third) line of the recurrence for the first cell when $\max(\{j - i + k, 0\}) = 0$ (respectively $\max(\{j - i + k, 0\}) > 0$) and the third line for all other cells.

Answer 2.   The following algorithm computes the value of cell $A[n, m]$ related to $a(n, m)$ according to the previously described progression.   14 - A 2

1. **constants**
2. $n \in \mathbb{N}$ and $n = \dots$ and $m \in \mathbb{N}$ and $m = \dots$
3. **variables**
4. $A \in 0..n \times 0..n + m \to \mathbb{N}_1$
5. **begin**
6.   **for** $j \in 0..m + n$ **do**
7. $A[0, j] \leftarrow j + 1$
8.   **end for;**
9.   **for** i **ranging** $1..n$ **do**
10.   **for** j **ranging** $\max(\{m - n + i, 0\})..n + m - i$ **do**
11.   **if** $j = 0$ **then**
12. $A[i, 0] \leftarrow 2 \cdot A[i - 1, 0] + A[i - 1, 1]$
13.   **else**
14. $A[i, j] \leftarrow A[i - 1, j - 1] + 2 \cdot A[i - 1, j] + A[i - 1, j + 1]$
15.   **end if**
16.   **end for**
17.   **end for;**
18.   **write(***the value of the sequence in* , $n, m,$ *is* , $A[n, m]$)
19. **end**

Remark

We invite the reader to design another version where a two row array A is used.

Answer 3.   It turns out that the formula $a(i, j) = (j + 1) \cdot 4^i$ for $i, j \geqslant 0$ holds over the   14 - A 3
whole array of figure 1.10, page 55.
So as to prove it by induction, it is necessary to use a valid proof pattern. A glance at the recurrence formula defining $a(i, j)$ leads to think that neither the pattern given in page 9, nor that proposed in problem 8 page 37 is suitable, since their initialization requires to demonstrate the validity of the formula for the first column of the tabular structure. From the partial order relation $\preceq$ over $\mathbb{N}^2$ defined in section 1.1.6, page 9:

$$(a, b) \preceq (c, d) \mathrel{\hat{=}} a < c \text{ or } (a = c \text{ and } b \leqslant d)$$

it is easy to show that the following pattern (of proof) is an instance of the property (1) page 9, for the pair $(\mathbb{N}^2, \preceq)$:

> If the two following properties can be proven:
>
> **Initialization** $P(0,j)$ holds for any $j \geqslant 0$
>
> **Induction** $\forall(i,j) \cdot \left(\left(\begin{array}{l} i \in \mathbb{N} \text{ and} \\ j \in \mathbb{N} \text{ and} \\ P(i,j) \end{array} \right) \Rightarrow \forall k \cdot \left(\begin{array}{l} k \in 0 .. j-1 \\ \Rightarrow P(i+1,k) \end{array} \right) \right)$
>
> then:
>
> **Conclusion** $P(n,m)$ holds for any pair of integers n, m such that $n \geqslant 0$ and $m \geqslant 0$.

It can be noticed that the proof to be done requires only an order over lines, but that the reference property (property 1), page 9) requires a total order. This pattern is now used to prove that

$$\forall(i,j) \cdot (i \in \mathbb{N} \text{ and } j \in \mathbb{N} \Rightarrow a(i,j) = (j+1) \cdot 4^i).$$

Initialization Let us consider the formula for the elements $a(0,j)$. By definition of the sequence, one has $a(0,j) = j+1$. Yet, $j+1 = (j+1) \cdot 4^0$ for any $j \geqslant 0$ and $a(0,j) = (j+1) \cdot 4^i$ holds for $i = 0$ and $j \geqslant 0$.

Induction Let us assume that the formula holds for any element whose first index is equal to n (induction hypothesis) and let us demonstrate that it does for element $a(n+1,j)$ (where j is an arbitrary nonnegative integer). Two cases can be singled out depending on the value of j:

- When $j = 0$, by definition $a(i,0) = 2 \cdot a(i-1,0) + a(i-1,1)$. From the induction hypothesis, one can write $a(i,0) = 2 \cdot (0+1) \cdot 4^{i-1} + (1+1) \cdot 4^{i-1} = 4 \cdot 4^{i-1} = (j+1) \cdot 4^i$.
- When $j > 0$, the last term of the recurrence states that $a(i,j) = a(i-1,j-1) + 2 \cdot a(i-1,j) + a(i-1,j+1)$. Using the induction hypothesis to rewrite each of the terms of the right hand side, we get:
$$a(i,j) = (j-1+1) \cdot 4^{i-1} + 2(j+1) \cdot 4^{i-1} + (j+1+1) \cdot 4^{i-1} = 4(j+1) \cdot 4^{i-1}$$
$$= (j+1) \cdot 4^i.$$

Conclusion Formula $a(i,j) = (j+1) \cdot 4^i$ holds for any nonnegative integers i and j.

The use of the closed form allows to build the following program computing $a(i,j)$:

1. **constants**
2. $n \in \mathbb{N}$ **and** $n = \ldots$ **and** $m \in \mathbb{N}$ **and** $m = \ldots$
3. **begin**
4.   **write**(*the value of the sequence in* , n, m, *is* , $(m+1) \cdot 4^n$)
5. **end**

both simpler and more efficient than the algorithm of the previous question.

Answers to problem 15. Moving a knight under constraints   *The problem is on page 41.*

15 - A 1   **Answer 1.** In general, there are four possibilities for reaching the square (i,j) in a single move: the knight was in $(i-2,j-1)$ or in $(i-1,j-2)$ or in $(i+1,j-2)$ or in $(i+2,j-1)$. It can be deduced that for $3 \leqslant i \leqslant n-2$ and $3 \leqslant j \leqslant m$:

$$nbRout(i,j) = nbRout(i-2,j-1) + nbRout(i-1,j-2) + nbRout(i+1,j-2) + nbRout(i+2,j-1).$$

This formula does not hold when i or j ar equal to 1 or 2 as well as when i is $(n-1)$ or n. This leads to the (complete) recurrence hereafter:

$$
\begin{array}{ll}
\text{nbRout}(1,1) = \text{nbRout}(3,2) = 1 & \\
\text{nbRout}(i,1) = 0 & 2 \leqslant i \leqslant n \\
\text{nbRout}(i,2) = 0 & 1 \leqslant i \leqslant n \text{ and } i \neq 3 \\
\text{nbRout}(1,j) = \text{nbRout}(3,j-1) + \text{nbRout}(2,j-2) & 3 \leqslant j \leqslant m \\
\text{nbRout}(2,j) = \text{nbRout}(3,j-2) + \text{nbRout}(1,j-2) + \text{nbRout}(4,j-1) & 3 \leqslant j \leqslant m \\
\text{nbRout}(n,j) = \text{nbRout}(n-2,j-1) + \text{nbRout}(n-1,j-2) & 3 \leqslant j \leqslant m \\
\text{nbRout}(n-1,j) = \begin{pmatrix} \text{nbRout}(n-3,j-1)+ \\ \text{nbRout}(n-2,j-2)+ \\ \text{nbRout}(n,j-2) \end{pmatrix} & 3 \leqslant j \leqslant m \\
\text{nparc}(i,j) = \begin{pmatrix} \text{nbRout}(i-2,j-1)+ \\ \text{nbRout}(i-1,j-2)+ \\ \text{nbRout}(i+1,j-2)+ \\ \text{nbRout}(i+2,j-1) \end{pmatrix} & \begin{cases} 3 \leqslant i \leqslant n-2 \\ \text{and} \\ 3 \leqslant j \leqslant m \end{cases}
\end{array}
$$

Answer 2.   The values of nbRout are stored in a n row, m column array, NR[1..n, 1..m]. Columns 1 and 2 are first initialized thanks to the first three terms of the recurrence. Due to the fact that the calculation of any other square call only on values located "on its left side", columns 3 to m are then dealt with: the four extreme elements (row index 1, 2, $(n-1)$ and n) are calculated by means of terms 3 to 6 of the recurrence, others using the last term of the recurrence (general case). This yields the following algorithm:

15 - A 2

1. **constants**
2. $n \in \mathbb{N}_1 - \{1..4\}$ **and** $n = \ldots$ **and** $m \in \mathbb{N}_1 - \{1..3\}$ **and** $m = \ldots$
3. **variables**
4. $NR \in 1..n \times 1..m \rightarrow \mathbb{N}_1$
5. **begin**
6. $NR[1,1] \leftarrow 1$;
7.   **for** i ranging 2 .. n **do**
8. $NR[i,1] \leftarrow 0$
9.   **end for**;
10.   **for** i ranging 1 .. n **do**
11. $NR[i,2] \leftarrow 0$
12.   **end for**;
13. $NR[3,2] \leftarrow 1$;
14.   **for** j ranging 3 .. m **do**
15. $NR[n,j] \leftarrow RP[n-1,j-2] + NR[n-2,j-1]$;
16. $NR[n-1,j] \leftarrow NR[n,j-2] + NR[n-2,j-2] + NR[n-3,j-1]$;
17. $NR[1,j] \leftarrow NR[2,j-2] + NR[3,j-1]$;
18. $NR[2,j] \leftarrow NR[1,j-2] + NR[3,j-2] + NR[4,j-1]$;
19.   **for** i ranging 3 .. n − 2 **do**
20. $NR[i,j] \leftarrow NR[i-2,j-1] + NR[i-1,j-2] + NR[i+1,j-2] + NR[i+2,j-1]$
21.   **end for**
22.   **end for**;
23.   **write**(*the number of ways for moving from* $(1,1)$ *to* $(, n, , , m,)$ *is* , $NR[n,m]$)
24. **end**

Running this algorithm for $n = 5$ and $m = 7$ leads to the following array:

	j	1	2	3	4	5	6	7
$i = 5$		0	0	1	0	2	3	10
4		0	0	0	2	2	5	7
3		0	1	0	2	1	8	10
2		0	0	1	1	3	4	9
1		1	0	1	0	3	2	11

Answers to problem 16. How many partitions of n elements have p blocks?

The problem is on page 41.

16 - A 1   **Answer 1.**   We have:

- one partition with one block: $\{\{a, b, c, d\}\}$,

- seven partitions with two blocks: $\{\{a, b\}, \{c, d\}\}$, $\{\{a, c\}, \{b, d\}\}$, $\{\{a, d\}, \{b, c\}\}$, $\{\{a\}, \{b, c, d\}\}$, $\{\{b\}, \{a, c, d\}\}$, $\{\{c\}, \{a, b, d\}\}$, $\{\{d\}, \{a, b, c\}\}$,

- six partitions with three blocks: $\{\{a\}, \{b\}, \{c, d\}\}$, $\{\{a, b\}, \{c\}, \{d\}\}$, $\{\{a, c\}, \{b\}, \{d\}\}$, $\{\{a\}, \{c\}, \{b, d\}\}$, $\{\{a, d\}, \{b\}, \{c\}\}$, $\{\{a\}, \{d\}, \{b, c\}\}$,

- one partition with four blocks: $\{\{a\}, \{b\}, \{c\}, \{d\}\}$.

16 - A 2   **Answer 2.**   The recurrence relation for $S(p, n)$ is defined as follows:

Special cases   For any n, there is a single partition with one block for a set having n elements, thus: $S(1, n) = 1$ for $n \geqslant 1$. Moreover, for any $p > 1$, when $n < p$, $S(p, n) = 0$, since the number of blocks cannot exceed that of the elements in the set (let us remind that no block can be empty). Last, for any $p > 1$, there is exactly one partition with p elements for a p element set, and $S(p, p) = 1$.

General case   When n increases by 1, the new element can constitute a new block (with this single element), and there are $S(p - 1, n)$ distinct possibilities, or added into one of the p preexisting blocks, and there are $p \cdot S(p, n)$ possibilities.

The following recurrence formula can be deduced:

$$\left|\begin{array}{ll} S(1, n) = 1 & n \geqslant 1 \\ S(p, p) = 1 & p > 1 \\ S(p, n) = 0 & p > n \\ S(p, n) = p \cdot S(p, n - 1) + S(p - 1, n - 1) & n \geqslant 1 \text{ and } p < n. \end{array}\right.$$

16 - A 3   **Answer 3.**   The array $S[1 .. p, 1 .. n]$ is used to compute the values associated with this recurrence. Observing the recurrence, we can notice that, in the general case (fourth term), the value of element $S[i, j]$ depends on those of the two elements located in the preceding column $(j - 1)$, which makes it possible to proceed by increasing values of the column index. Each column j is filled as follows: (i) cell $S[1, j]$ is initialized to 1 (first term of the recurrence), (ii) the general term is used for the calculation of any cell $S[i, j]$ where $i < j$ and $i \leqslant p$, (iii) when the cell $S[j, j]$ belongs to the array, it is set to 1, and finally (iv) any cell $S[i, j]$ where $i > j$ is set to 0.
The corresponding algorithm is:

1. **constants**
2. $n \in \mathbb{N}_1$ **and** $n = \ldots$ **and** $p \in \mathbb{N}_1$ **and** $p \leqslant n$ **and** $p = \ldots$

3. **variables**
4. $S \in 1..p \times 1..n \to \mathbb{N}$
5. **begin**
6. $S[1,1] \leftarrow 1;$
7.   **for** i **ranging** $2..p$ **do**
8. $S[i,1] \leftarrow 0$
9.   **end for;**
10.   **for** j **ranging** $2..n$ **do**
11. $S[1,j] \leftarrow 1;$
12.   **for** i **ranging** $2..p$ **do**
13.   **if** $i < j$ **then**
14. $S[i,j] \leftarrow i \cdot S[i,j-1] + S[i-1,j-1]$
15.   **elsif** $i = j$ **then**
16. $S[i,j] \leftarrow 1$
17.   **else**
18. $S[i,j] \leftarrow 0$
19.   **end if**
20.   **end for**
21.   **end for;**
22.   write(*the number of partitions with* , p, *blocks of a set having* , n,
       elements
23.   *is* , $S[p,n]$)
24. **end**

Answer 4.   For $p = 5$ and $n = 7$, the values obtained are reported in the array below: 16 - A 4

n	1	2	3	4	5	6	7
p = 1	1	1	1	1	1	1	1
2	0	1	3	7	15	31	63
3	0	0	1	6	25	90	301
4	0	0	0	1	10	65	350
5	0	0	0	0	1	15	140

Answers to problem 17. Climbing a staircase   *The problem is on page 42.*

Answer 1.   Two possible sequences of jumps are $\langle 5,2,5 \rangle$ and $\langle 2,5,5 \rangle$, which shows that   17 - A 1
the order of the jumps matters (when they are different).

Answer 2.   The recurrence relation is built according to the following observations: 17 - A 2

Special cases There is a single way to climb 0 steps with 0 jumps and therefore
    $nbCL(0,0) = 1$. Moreover, there is no way for jumping (at least one jump) without
    climbing (at least one step) and $nbCL(s,0) = 0$ for $s \geqslant 1$. Last, one has $nbCL(0,m) = 0$
    for $m > 0$, since it is impossible to climb at least one step without jumping.

General case Let us suppose that we are on step m of the staircase after s jumps, with s
    and m strictly positive. As $s > 0$, just before we made a jump (which led us to the step
    m) from one of the steps from which step m can be reached with a single jump. The
    count of ways to reach the step m with s jumps is thus equal to the sum of the ways
    we had to reach these steps.

We end up with the recurrence given below:

$$
\begin{vmatrix}
nbCL(0,0) = 1 \\
nbCL(0,m) = 0 & m > 0 \\
nbCL(s,0) = 0 & s > 0 \\
nbCL(s,m) = \displaystyle\sum_{\substack{i \in 1..n \text{ and} \\ (m-a_i) \geqslant 0}} nbCL(s-1, m-a_i) & s > 0 \text{ and } m > 0.
\end{vmatrix}
$$

17 - A 3   **Answer** 3.   To compute this recurrence, the array NBCL[0 .. s, 0 .. m] is used where the cell NBCL[i, j] is associated with the element $nbCL(i,j)$ of the recurrence. It can be observed that the calculation of the cell NBCL(s, m) calls only on values whose first index is immediately lower $(s-1)$. Hence, the calculation can progress by increasing values of row indexes inasmuch as the first row (index 0) is initialized, which is performed by means of the first two terms of the recurrence. Last, any row can be filled in from left to right after setting the first element to 0, according to the third term of the recurrence.

The n values of the possible jumps (a_i) are stored in the array A[1 .. n], in increasing order (without loss of generality). The corresponding algorithm is the following:

```
 1. constants
 2.    n ∈ ℕ₁ and n = ... and s ∈ ℕ₁ and s = ... and m ∈ ℕ₁ and m = ... and
 3.    A ∈ 1 .. n → ℕ₁ and A = [...]
 4. variables
 5.    NBCL ∈ 0 .. s × 0 .. m → ℕ
 6. begin
 7.    NBCL[0,0] ← 1;
 8.    for j ranging 1 .. m do
 9.       NBCL[0,j] ← 0
10.    end for;
11.    for i ranging 1 .. s do
12.       NBCL[i,0] ← 0;
13.       for j ranging 1 .. m do
14.          NBCL[i,j] ← 0;
15.          for k ranging 1 .. n do
16.             if j − A[k] ⩾ 0 then
17.                NBCL[i,j] ← NBCL[i,j] + NBCL[i−1, j−A[k]]
18.             end if
19.          end for
20.       end for
21.    end for;
22.    write(the number of ways for climbing , m, steps with , s, jumps
23.             is , NBCL[s,m])
24. end
```

A possible variant would consist in the suppression of lines 16 à 18 and the use of the array NF whose column indexes range from −A[n] to m, NBCL[0..s, −A[n]..−1] being initialized with 0's.

17 - A 4   **Answer** 4.   With the algorithm explicited above, for s = 6, m = 12, n = 2, $a_1 = 2$ and $a_2 = 5$, the following array NF is produced:

j	0	1	2	3	4	5	6	7	8	9	10	11	12
i = 0	1	0	0	0	0	0	0	0	0	0	0	0	0
1	0	0	1	0	0	1	0	0	0	0	0	0	0
2	0	0	0	0	1	0	0	2	0	0	1	0	0
3	0	0	0	0	0	0	1	0	0	3	0	0	3
4	0	0	0	0	0	0	0	0	1	0	0	4	0
5	0	0	0	0	0	0	0	0	0	0	1	0	0
6	0	0	0	0	0	0	0	0	0	0	0	0	1

Answer 5.   Using the array A whose values are increasing as previously stated, the 17 - A 5
number of steps reached with s jumps cannot be neither under $s \cdot A[1]$, nor above $s \cdot A[n]$,
which explains the 0's appearing in the cells connected with these cases (for example,
columns with index $j = 11$ and $j = 12$ for $i = 2$ and the last ten columns for $i = 5$).
Consequently, we can envisage a variant of the initial algorithm where, after the initialization of any row with 0's, the filling of row i is restricted to cells whose column index lies in
the interval $i \cdot A[1] .. \max(\{m, i \cdot A[n]\})$. Lines 11 to 21 of the previous algorithm are replaced
by:

```
1.  for i ranging 1 .. s do
2.     NBCL[i, 0] ← 0;
3.     for j ranging 1 .. m do
4.        NBCL[i, j] ← 0
5.     end for;
6.     for j ranging i · A[1] .. min({m, i · A[n]}) do
7.        for k ranging 1 .. n do
8.           if j − A[k] ⩾ 0 then
9.              NBCL[i, j] ← NBCL[i, j] + NBCL[i − 1, j − A[k]]
10.          end if
11.       end for
12.    end for
13. end for;
```

Answers to problem 18. The Patagon game *The problem is on page 42.*

The problem is on page 42.

Answer 1.   Of course, several choices are possible, but the one looking like the best one 18 - A 1
(intuitively for the moment or after the evaluation of all legal choices) is the sequence $\langle 23,$
$40, 42 \rangle$, yielding the total amount 105.

Answer 2. 2^n is the number of distinct subsets of a set having n elements, or the num- 18 - A 2
ber of distinct n sized binary vectors. This would be the number of unconstrained ways of
playing. But, for $n > 1$, there is at least one vector with two successive 1's; therefore the
legal ways of playing are strictly less than 2^n.

Answer 3.   Any binary vector cannot contain two successive 1's and a reasonable vec- 18 - A 3
tor cannot have three consecutive 0's either (in such a case, that of the middle could be
replaced by 1). In addition, it can neither start, nor end with 00.

Answer 4.   The first six expressions are established by enumeration. For a 1 sized 18 - A 4
game, the only reasonable possibility is to take its single object, and $nbRWP_0(1) = 0$
and $nbRWP_1(1) = 1$. For a 2 sized game, 01 and 10 only are reasonable choices, and
$nbRWP_0(2) = nbRWP_1(2) = 1$. Last, with a 3 sized game, the reasonable configurations

are: 010 et 101, therefore $nbRWP_0(3) = nbRWP_1(3) = 1$. The general term of the recurrence is developed in studying the four exclusive exhaustive cases of n-sized reasonable vectors with $n > 3$: $V_1 = [\dots, 0, 0, 1, 0]$, $V_2 = [\dots, 1, 0, 1, 0]$, $V_3 = [\dots, 1, 0, 0, 1]$, $V_4 = [\dots, 0, 1, 0, 1]$. It can be remarked that when removing the final 0 in V_1 and V_2, we obtain a reasonable vector with 1 in position $n - 1$, thus $nbRWP_0(n) = nbRWP_1(n - 1)$. It is not the case when removing the final 1 in vectors V_3 and V_4, since then, if $V_4' = [\dots, 0, 1, 0]$ is clearly a reasonable vector, $V_3' = [\dots, 1, 0, 0]$ is not. It is necessary to study carefully what happens when the last two elements of V_3 are suppressed. We then get $V_3'' = [\dots, 1, 0]$, which is a reasonable vector and it can be deduced that:

$$nbRWP_1(n) = nbRWP_0(n-1) + nbRWP_0(n-2) = nbRWP_1(n-2) + nbRWP_1(n-3)$$

using the definition of $nbRWP_0$ established before.

18 - A 5   **Answer 5.**   The values $nbRWP(1), nbRWP(2)$ and $nbRWP(3)$ are obtained by the corresponding values of $nbRWP_0$ and $nbRWP_1$, i.e.:

$$nbRWP(1) = nbRWP_0(1) + nbRWP_1(1) = 0 + 1 = 1,$$
$$nbRWP(2) = nbRWP_0(2) + nbRWP_1(2) = 1 + 1 = 2,$$
$$nbRWP(3) = nbRWP_0(3) + nbRWP_1(3) = 1 + 1 = 2.$$

For $n > 3$, using the definition one gets:

$$
\begin{aligned}
nbRWP(n) &= nbRWP_0(n) + nbRWP_1(n) \\
&= nbRWPr_1(n-3) + nbRWP_1(n-4) + nbRWP_1(n-2) + nbRWP_1(n-3) \\
&= nbRWP_0(n-2) + nbRWP_0(n-3) + nbRWP_1(n-2) + nbRWP_1(n-3) \\
&= nbRWP(n-2) + nbRWP(n-3).
\end{aligned}
$$

18 - A 6   **Answer 6.**   The values of $nbRWP_0(n), nbRWP_1(n)$ and $nbRWP(n)$ for n varying from 1 to 15 are gathered in the array below:

n	1	2	3	4	5	6	7	8	9	10	11	12	13	14	15
nfr$_0$	0	1	1	1	2	2	3	4	5	7	9	12	16	21	28
nfr$_1$	1	1	1	2	2	3	4	5	7	9	12	16	21	28	37
nfr	1	2	2	3	4	5	7	9	12	16	21	28	37	49	65

It can be observed that for $n > 2$: $nbRWP_1(n) = nbRWP(n - 2)$. This is not surprising since: (i) the form of their recurrence is the same, $nbRWP_1(3) = nbRWP(1) = 1$ and $nbRWP_1(4) = nbRWP(2) = 2$, (ii) in question 4:

$$nbRWP_1(n) = nbRWP_0(n - 1) + nbRWP_0(n - 2) = nbRWP_1(n - 2) + nbRWP_0(n - 2)$$
$$= nbRWP(n - 2).$$

Remark

As seen in page 10, the sequence whose general term is $\mathcal{P}(n) = \mathcal{P}(n - 2) + \mathcal{P}(n - 3)$ for any $n > 2$ where $\mathcal{P}(0) = \mathcal{P}(1) = \mathcal{P}(2) = 1$, defines the Padovan sequence. Its numbers are exponentially increasing in the order of $(1.324\cdots)^{n-1}$. More precisely, the nth number is the integer closest to $(1.324\cdots)^{n-1}/1.045\cdots$. For instance, $\mathcal{P}(20) = 200$.

The number $1.324\cdots$ is sometimes called *silver ratio*, by analogy with the *golden ratio* related to Fibonacci sequence.

18 - A 7   **Answer 7.**   The calculation of $nbRWP(i)$ requires only $nbRWP(i-2)$ and $nbRWP(i-3)$. To compute $nbRWP(n)$, the array $T[1 .. 4]$ is used to keep the last four values of $nbRWP$, thus the program:

1. **constants**
2. $n \in \mathbb{N}_1$ **and** $n = \ldots$
3. **variables**
4. $T \in 1 \ldots 4 \to \mathbb{N}_1$
5. **begin**
6. $T[1] \leftarrow 1; T[2] \leftarrow 2; T[3] \leftarrow 2;$
7.   **for** i **ranging** $4 \ldots n$ **do**
8. $T[4] \leftarrow T[1] + T[2];$
9.   **for** j **ranging** $1 \ldots 3$ **do**
10. $T[j] \leftarrow T[j+1]$
11.   **end for**
12.   **end for**;
13.   write(*the number of reasonable ways for playing with a game*
14.   *of size* , n, *is* , $T[4]$)
15. **end**

Answers to problem 19. The game of two stacks   *The problem is on page 44.*

Answer 1.   There is one and only one way to reach a winning state if one is already 19 - A 1
in this state: doing nothing. In the configuration $p = 1, q = 1$, it is no longer possible to
play, a winning state is unattainable and it is lost. When $p \geqslant 2$ and $q \geqslant 2$, two possible
ways of playing are open and the number of ways to reach a winning state is given by the
sum of the ways to win from the two configurations attained when playing ($p - 2, q + 1$ or
$p + 1, q - 2$). When p or q is less than 2, there is a single way of playing and the number of
ways to win from the configuration (p, q) equals that of the new configuration $(p - 2, q + 1$
when $q < 2$, $p + 1, q - 2$ when $p < 2$). The following recurrence can be derived, which
accounts for the symmetry of the problem:

$$
\begin{aligned}
&nbWW(0,1) = nfg(1,0) = 1 \\
&nbWW(1,1) = 0 \\
&nbWW(0,q) = nbWW(1, q - 2) && q > 1 \\
&nbWW(1,q) = nbWW(2, q - 2) && q > 1 \\
&nbWW(p,0) = nbWW(p - 2, 1) && p > 1 \\
&nbWW(p,1) = nbWW(p - 2, 2) && p > 1 \\
&nbWW(p,q) = nbWW(p - 2, q + 1) + nbWW(p + 1, q - 2) && p > 1 \text{ and } q > 1.
\end{aligned}
$$

Answer 2.   Due to the fact that the number p (respectively q) of tokens of stack P (re- 19 - A 2
spectively Q) may increase, the tabular structure cannot be reduced to an array with $(p+1)$
rows and $(q + 1)$ columns (or the reverse). Strictly speaking, an array with $(p + \lfloor q/2 \rfloor + 1)$
rows and $(q + \lfloor p/2 \rfloor + 1)$ columns would suffice, but for simplicity of the filling, a squared
tabular structure $T[0 \ldots p + q, 0 \ldots p + q]$ is used where $T[i, j]$ corresponds to $nfWW(i, j)$. As
to the general case, this array can be filled in by increasing diagonals of equation $(p + q)$,
since $nbWW(p, q)$ is located on the diagonal of equation $(p + q)$ and the two elements
required for its calculus are located on the diagonal of equation $(p + q - 1)$. Diagonals
of equation 1, 2 et 3 (0 is meaningless) are first initialized using the appropriate terms of
the recurrence. Then, elements of a diagonal are filled in thanks to the general term of the
recurrence, except the extreme four terms for which the terms associated with p or q less
than 2 are used.

Answer 3.   The algorithm below implements the above principles: 19 - A 3

```
1.  constants
2.      p ∈ ℕ₁ − {1} and p = ... and q ∈ ℕ₁ − {1} and q = ...
3.  variables
4.      T ∈ 0 .. p + q × 0 .. p + q → ℕ
5.  begin
6.      T[0, 1] ← 1; T[1, 0] ← 1;
7.      T[2, 0] ← 1; T[0, 2] ← 1; T[1, 1] ← 0;
8.      T[3, 0] ← 0; T[1, 2] ← 1; T[2, 1] ← 1; T[0, 3] ← 0;
9.      for k ranging 4 .. p + q do
10.         T[0, k] ← T[1, k − 2];
11.         T[1, k − 1] ← T[2, k − 3];
12.         T[k, 0] ← T[k − 2, 1];
13.         T[k − 1, 1] ← T[k − 3, 2];
14.         for j ranging 2 .. k − 2 do
15.             T[j, k − j] ← T[j − 2, k − j + 1] + T[j + 1, k − j − 2]
16.         end for
17.     end for;
18.     write(the number of ways for winning with two stacks having, p,
            and, q, tokens
19.             is, T[p, q])
20. end
```

19 - A 4   **Answer 4.**   The computation of $nbWW(4, 2)$ is performed in filling in the following array:

q	0	1	2	3	4	5	6
p = 0		1	1	0	1	1	0
1	1	0	1	1	0	2	
2	1	1	0	2	3		
3	0	1	2	0			
4	1	0	3				
5	1	2					
6	0						

and it can be seen that $nfWW(4, 2) = 3$.

19 - A 5   **Answer 5.**   The validity of the property mentioned in the statement can be observed in the array above (cells (i, j) located on a diagonal of equation $|i − j|$ multiple of 3 – $nbWW(0, 0)$ excepted – take a zero value). The proof is now performed by simple induction on n, the index of the diagonal of equation $(i + j = n)$. The induction hypothesis is: any element $nbWW(i, j)$ such that $|i − j|$ is a multiple of 3 and $(i + j = n)$ takes a zero value, cell $nbWW(0, 0)$ excepted.

Initialization For $n = 1$, $nbWW(0, 1)$ and $nbWW(1, 0)$ are the only elements such that $(i + j) = n$, but $|i − j| = 1$ is not multiple of 3. For $n = 2$, $nbWW(0, 2)$, $nbWW(2, 0)$ and $nbWW(1, 1)$ are such that $(i + j) = n$. The only element complying with $|i−j| = 3k$, is $nbWW(1, 1)$ whose value is 0 according to the second term of the recurrence. Thus, the property holds for $n = 1$ and $n = 2$.

Induction Let us assume that the property holds for $n \geqslant 2$, using the previously established recurrence, we will prove that any element $nbWW(i, j)$ such that $|i − j|$ is a multiple of 3 and $(i + j = n + 1)$ takes a zero value. We successively examine elements such that $(i + j = n + 1)$.

nbWW$(0, n+1)$ **and** nbWW$(n+1, 0)$ We have nfWW$(0, n+1) =$ nbWW$(1, n-1)$ (third term of the recurrence); the sum of the indexes of this latter element equals n and we can use the induction hypothesis. When $(|0 - (n+1)| = n+1)$ is a multiple of 3, $(|1 - (n-1)| = n-2)$ is also a multiple of 3 and nbWW$(0, n+1) =$ nbWW$(1, n-1) = 0$. The same reasoning applies to nbWW$(n+1, 0)$ due to the symmetry of the terms of the recurrence.

nbWW$(1, n)$ **and** nbWW$(n, 1)$ According to the fourth term of the recurrence, we have nbWW$(1, n) =$ nbWW$(2, n-2)$. The fact that the sum of the indexes of nbWW$(2, n-2)$ equals n allows to use the induction hypothesis. When $(|1-n| = n-1)$ is a multiple of 3, $(|2 - (n-2)| = |n-4|)$ is also a multiple of 3 and nbWW$(1, n) =$ nbWW$(2, n-2) = 0$. The same reasoning applies to nbWW$(n, 1)$ due to the symmetry of the terms of the recurrence.

General case for nbWW(i, j) **with** $i + j = n + 1, i > 1$ **and** $j > 1$ Such an element is the sum of nbWW$(i-2, j+1)$ and nbWW$(i+1, j-2)$, both such that the sum of their indexes is n; the induction hypothesis can be used. When $|i - j|$ is a multiple of 3, $(|i-2-(j+1)| = |i-j-3|)$ is also a multiple of 3, as well as $(|i+1-(j-2)| = |i-j+3|)$. It follows that nbWW$(i, j) =$ nbWW$(i-2, j+1) +$ nbWW$(i+1, j-2) = 0$.

Conclusion Any element nbWW(i, j) such that $|i - j|$ is a multiple of 3 takes a zero value – nbWW$(0, 0)$ excepted – for any pair (i, j) where $i \geqslant 0$ and $j \geqslant 0$.

Answers to problem 20. The yellow coins $\qquad$ *The problem is on page 44.*

Answer 1. We have nbWF1E$(1)(2) = 1 +$ nbWF1E$(1)(1) = 2$ and the suggested recurrence yields (i) nbWF1E$(3) =$ nbWF1E$(1) +$ nbWF1E$(2) = 3$ (whilst there are only two ways for forming three cents), (ii) nbWF1E$(4) =$ nbWF1E$(3) +$ nbWF1E$(2) = 5$ (whilst there are only three ways for forming four cents). Giving initial values for nbWF1E(1) to nbWF1E(4) $(1, 2, 2$ et $3)$ would not change the story since nbWF1E$(5) = 1 +$ nbWF1E$(4) +$ nbWF1E$(3) = 6$ would be false as there are only four distinct ways for forming five cents.

20 - A 1

The origin of the problem lies in the fact that some combinations of coins are counted more than once. Thus, when we convert "To form the amount s of three cents, one takes a one cent coin and the amount $(s-1)$ remains to be formed, or one takes a two cent coin and the amount $(s-2)$ remains to be formed", into nbWF1E$(3) =$ nbWF1E$(2) +$ nbWF1E(1), there is no guarantee that *distinct* ways are counted. In this example, the combination made of a one cent coin and a two cent coin is obtained (and counted) twice. In other words, the recurrence suggested does not take into account exclusive situations leading to distinct ways for forming the desired amount and in this respect this is not a valid recurrence.

Answer 2. Now, we envisage a double index recurrence and we denote by nbWF1E2(m, p) the number of distinct ways for forming the amount m with the coins numbered from p to 6. We proceed as follows. To form the amount m with coins numbered from p to 6 $(p < 6)$, we can: (i) take only coins ranked strictly over p (i.e. no coin of value value $v(p)$), or (ii) take a single coin of value $v(p)$ (if possible, i.e. if $m \geqslant v(p)$) and the amount $(m - v(p))$ remains to be formed with the coins whose rank ranges from $(p+1)$ to 6 according to the same mechanism, or (iii) if possible (i.e. if $m \geqslant 2 \cdot v(p)$) take two coins whose rank is p and the amount $(m - 2 \cdot v(p))$ remains to be formed with coins whose rank ranges from $(p+1)$ to 6 according to the same mechanism, (iv) and so on. In doing so, we are ensured that the ways for forming the amount m are different by construction since, in

20 - A 2

the first case the combination of coins involves no coin whose rank is p, in the second case a single such coin is inserted, in the third case two such coins appear, etc. Therefore, when $m \geqslant v(p)$, one can write:

$$nbWF1E2(m, p) = \sum_{i=0}^{\lfloor \frac{m}{v(p)} \rfloor} nbWF1E2(m - i \cdot v(p), p + 1)$$

or even:

$nbWF1E2(m, p)$

$=$ distinction of the first term

$$nbWF1E2(m, p + 1) + \sum_{i=1}^{\lfloor \frac{m}{v(p)} \rfloor} nbWF1E2(m - i \cdot v(p), p + 1)$$

$=$ variable change, $(i - 1)$ becomes j

$$nbWF1E2(m, p + 1) + \sum_{j=0}^{\lfloor \frac{m - v(p)}{v(p)} \rfloor} nbWF1E2(m - v(p) - j \cdot v(p), p + 1)$$

$=$ definition of $nbWF1E2$

$nbWF1E2(m, p + 1) + nbWF1E2(m - v(p), p)$.

When m is strictly less than $v(p)$, the only way for forming the amount m is to ignore coins of rank p and use those ranked from $(p + 1)$ to 6. So, we end up with the recurrence hereafter

$\left|\begin{array}{l}
nbWF1E2(0, p) = 1 \hfill 1 \leqslant p \leqslant 6 \\
nbWF1E2(m, 6) = 1 \hfill m \text{ is a multiple of } v(6) \text{ and } 1 \leqslant m \leqslant 100 \\
nbWF1E2(m, 6) = 0 \hfill m \text{ is not a multiple of } v(6) \text{ and } 1 \leqslant m \leqslant 100 \\
nbWF1E2(m, p) = nbWF1E2(m, p + 1) + nbWF1E2(m - v(p), p) \hfill m \geqslant \\
v(p) \text{ and } 1 \leqslant p < 6 \text{ and } 1 \leqslant m \leqslant 100 \; nbWF1E2(m, p) = nbWF1E2(m, p + 1) \\
m < v(p) \text{ and } 1 \leqslant p < 6 \text{ and } 1 \leqslant m \leqslant 100.
\end{array}\right.$

Remark 1

It is worth noticing that the order of the coins does not matter, the key point is to consider all of them and to calculate $nbWF1E2(100, 1)$. If it is assumed that the coins are ordered increasingly on their values, the last term of the recurrence can be replaced by $nbWF1E2(m, p) = 0$, since when m is less than $v(p)$, it is less than $v(p + 1)$ too.

Remark 2

One could consider $nbWF1E2(m, p)$ the number of ways for forming the amount m with coins 1 to p, in which case one would calculate $nbWF1E2(100, 6)$.

20 - A 3   **Answer** 3.   In the example aiming at forming three cents with yellow coins such that $v(1) = 20, v(2) = 5, v(3) = 10, v(4) = 1, v(5) = 50$ and $v(6) = 2$ (but any other ordering of the coins would be suitable as well), one has:

$nbWF1E2(3, 1) = nbWF1E2(3, 2); nbWF1E2(3, 2) = nbWF1E2(3, 3); nbWF1E2(3, 3) = nbWF1E2(3, 4);$

$nbWF1E2(3, 4) = nbWF1E2(3, 5) + nbWF1E2(2, 4)$.

Yet:

$$nbWF1E2(2,4) = nbWF1E2(2,5) + nbWF1E2(1,4) = nbWF1E2(2,6) + nbWF1E2(1,5) + nbWF1E2(0,4) = 1 + nbWF1E2(1,6) + 1 = 1 + 0 + 1 = 2;$$
$$nbWF1E2(3,5) = nbWF1E2(3,6) + nbWF1E2(1,5) = 0 + nbWF1E2(1,6) = 0 + 0 = 0.$$

Finally, $nbWF1E2(3,1)$ has the value 2, as expected.

Answer 4. The program performing the calculation uses the array $T[0..100, 1..6]$ asso- 20 - A 4
ciated with $nbWF1E2$, and the result is $T[100, 1]$. The value of the yellow coins are stored in
the array $V[1..6]$ in any order *a priori*. The recurrence defined before leads to a progression
according to decreasing value of the column index. We start with column 6 for which second
and third terms are used. Then, each column is filled in according to increasing values
of row index: the cell of index 0 thanks to the first term, next elements using fourth and
fifth terms. This results in the following program:

```
1.  constants
2.     V ∈ 1..6 → ℕ₁ and V = [1, 2, 5, 10, 20, 50]
3.  variables
4.     T ∈ 0..100 × 1..6 → ℕ
5.  begin
6.     for i ranging 0..100 do
7.        T[i, 6] ← 0
8.     end for;
9.     for i ranging 0.. ⌊100/V[6]⌋ do
10.       T[V[6] · i, 6] ← 1
11.    end for;
12.    for p ranging inverse 1..5 do
13.       T[0, p] ← 1;
14.       for m ranging 1..V[p] − 1 do
15.          T[m, p] ← T[m, p + 1]
16.       end for;
17.       for m ranging V[p]..100 do
18.          T[m, p] ← T[m, p + 1] + T[m − V[p], p]
19.       end for
20.    end for;
21.    write(the number of ways for forming one euro with yellow coins
          is, T[100, 1])
22. end
```

Answer 5. By running this program, it appears that there are 4562 distinct ways for 20 - A 5
forming one euro with yellow coins.

Answer 6. It has been seen that $nbWF1E2(m, 1)$ does not depend on the order accord- 20 - A 6
ing to which yellow coins are taken into account, therefore on the order of values in V.
Hence, it is possible to work with the vector $V = [1, 2, 5, 10, 20, 50]$. In this context, for
$m > 0$, $nbWF1E2(m, 1)$ is defined as the sum of $nbWF1E2(m, 2)$ and $nbWF1E2(m − 1, 1)$.
Since $nbWF1E2(m, 2) \geqslant 0$, one has:

$$nbWF1E2(m, 1) \geqslant nbWF1E2(m − 1, 1).$$

Another justification of this result can be found in realizing that the formation of the
amount m with the six yellow coins can begin with the formation of $(m − 1)$ followed
by the addition of a one cent coin to get m.

Remark

When all the values of T are displayed, it turns out that, as a matter of fact, $nbWF1E2(m, 1)$ grows with m, non strictly for the first four values and strictly after. However, it can be noted that, in general, $nbWF1E2(m, p)$ where $p \neq 1$ is not increasing.

Answers to problem 21. Shuffling words   *The problem is on page 45.*

21 - A 1   **Answer** 1.   Let us denote by $nbShuf(i, j)$ the number of distinct shuffles that can be built from the prefixes $u[1 .. i]$ and $v[1 .. j]$ of the words u and v. In the general case $w[i + j]$ can be either $u[i]$, or $v[j]$. In the first case, there are $nbShuf(i - 1, j)$ possible shuffles ending by $u[i]$, and in the second one there are $nbShuf(i, j - 1)$ possible shuffles ending with $v[j]$. When u (respectively v) is the empty word, there is a unique way for building the shuffle. Thus, the following recurrence is obtained:

$$
\begin{vmatrix}
nbShuf(i, 0) = 1 & 0 \leqslant i \leqslant m \\
nbShuf(0, j) = 1 & 0 \leqslant j \leqslant n \\
nbShuf(i, j) = nbShuf(i - 1, j) + nbShuf(i, j - 1) & 1 \leqslant i \leqslant m \text{ and } 1 \leqslant j \leqslant n.
\end{vmatrix}
$$

For example, for $m = 5$ and $n = 4$, $nbShuf(5, 4) = 126$ is calculated by means of the following procedure which fills in an array:

- initialization of the first row ($i = 0$) using the second term of the recurrence,

- filling of the other rows in increasing order of their indexes,

- in a row cells are filled in increasing order of the column index, the first one using the first term of the recurrence, the others with the third term.

The array below is then obtained:

j	0	1	2	3	4
i = 0	1	1	1	1	1
1	1	2	3	4	5
2	1	3	6	10	15
3	1	4	10	20	35
4	1	5	15	35	70
5	1	6	21	56	126

Remark

It can be observed that the array is symmetric with respect to the diagonal of equation $i - j = 0$, which is in coherence with the fact that the two indexes i and j play the same role in the recurrence.

21 - A 2   **Answer** 2.   For the proof by induction, the pattern given page 9 is used since it is well suited for this situation and we let $P(m, n) = (nbShuf(m, n) = (m + n)!/(m! \cdot n!))$.

Initialization For any integer i, one has:

$$
nbShuf(i, 0) = 1 = \frac{i!}{i! \cdot 0!}
$$

and for any integer j:

$$nbShuf(0, j) = 1 = \frac{j!}{j! \cdot 0!}.$$

Induction Let us assume (induction hypothesis) that for any pair (i, j) of positive integers:

$$nbShuf(i-1, j) = \frac{(i+j-1)!}{(i-1)! \cdot j!}, nbShuf(i, j-1) = \frac{(i+j-1)!}{i! \cdot (j-1)!}$$

it must be proven that:

$$nbShuf(i, j) = \frac{(i+j)!}{i! \cdot j!}$$

One has:

$$
\begin{aligned}
& nbShuf(i, j) \\
= & \qquad\qquad\qquad\qquad\qquad \text{general term of the recurrence} \\
& nbShuf(i-1, j) + nbShuf(i, j-1) \\
= & \qquad\qquad\qquad\qquad\qquad \text{induction hypothesis} \\
& \frac{(i+j-1)!}{(i-1)! \cdot j!} + \frac{(i+j-1)!}{i! \cdot (j-1)!} \\
= & \qquad\qquad\qquad\qquad\qquad \text{arithmetics} \\
& \frac{i \cdot (i+j-1)!}{i! \cdot j!} + \frac{j \cdot (i+j-1)!}{i! \cdot j!} \\
= & \qquad\qquad\qquad\qquad\qquad \text{arithmetics} \\
& \frac{(i+j) \cdot (i+j-1)!}{i! \cdot j!} \\
= & \qquad\qquad\qquad\qquad\qquad \text{definition of factorial} \\
& \frac{(i+j)!}{i! \cdot j!}.
\end{aligned}
$$

Conclusion $\forall(m, n) \cdot \left(m \in \mathbb{N} \text{ and } n \in \mathbb{N} \Rightarrow nbShuf(m, n) = \frac{(m+n)!}{m! \cdot n!} \right)$.

The preceding result is rewritten:

$$nbShuf(m, n) = \frac{(m+n)!}{m! \cdot n!} = C_{m+n}^m = C_{m+n}^n$$

in other words $nbShuf(m, n)$ is the number of combinations of n (or m) elements out of $(m+n)$ or even the number of ways to choose n (or m) distinct letters out of $(m+n)$. This result can be established directly as follows. Let ML be an array with $(m+n)$ cells. There are C_{m+n}^n ways for taking m cells of this array to assign the letters of u in increasing order of the index and in the order of the letters of u. For each way to place u, there is a single way for the placement of the letters of v inside ML and therefore the number of shuffles of u and v equals C_{m+n}^n.

Answer 3.   The requested decision algorithm is based on the recurrence isSHUF such   21 - A 3
that $isSHUF(i, j) = \textbf{true}$, if and only if $w[1 .. i+j]$ is a shuffle of $u[1 .. i]$ and $v[1 .. j]$. The reasoning for establishing this recurrence is similar to that of the first question (w is a shuffle of u and v only if its last letter is that of u or v). We get:

$$
\begin{array}{ll}
isSHUF(i, 0) = (w[1 .. i] = u[1 .. i]) & 0 \leqslant i \leqslant m \\
isSHUF(0, j) = (w[1 .. j] = v[1 .. j]) & 0 \leqslant j \leqslant n
\end{array}
$$

$$\text{isSHUF}(i,j) = \begin{pmatrix} (\text{isSHUF}(i-1,j) \textbf{ and } w[i+j]=u[i]) \\ \textbf{or} \\ (\text{isSHUF}(i,j-1) \textbf{ and } w[i+j]=v[j]) \end{pmatrix} \quad \begin{cases} 1 \leqslant i \leqslant m \\ \textbf{and} \\ 1 \leqslant j \leqslant n \end{cases}.$$

The related program uses the Boolean array $M[0..m, 0..n]$, filled as previously: increasingly in rows and, for a row, increasingly in columns, once row 0 is initialized. The expected result is found in cell $M[m,n]$. The code of the program is given hereafter:

```
1.  constants
2.     u ∈ string and u = ... and v ∈ string and v = ...
3.       and w ∈ string and w = ... and m = |u| and n = |v|
4.  variables
5.     M ∈ 0..m × 0..n → 𝔹
6.  begin
7.     M[0,0] ← true;
8.     for j ranging 1..n do
9.        M[0,j] ← M[0,j−1] and w[j] = v[j]
10.    end for;
11.    for i ranging 1..m do
12.       M[i,0] ← M[i−1,0] and w[i] = u[i];
13.       for j ranging 1..n do
14.          M[i,j] ← (M[i−1,j] and w[i+j] = u[i]) or (M[i,j−1] and w[i+j] =
              v[j])
15.       end for
16.    end for;
17.    write(it is , M[m,n], to say that , w, is a shuffle of , u, and , v)
18. end
```

The handling of the example where $u = abc$, $v = db$, $w = dabbc$, leads to the array below:

j		0	1	2
		ε	d	b
i = 0	ε	T	T	F
1	a	F	T	T
2	b	F	T	T
3	c	F	F	T

Since the cell $M[3,2]$ contains the value **true**, it can be concluded that $w = dabbc$ is a shuffle of $u = abc$ and $v = db$.

2

Complexity of an algorithm

> Fools ignore complexity. Pragmatists
> suffer it. Some can avoid it. Geniuses
> remove it.
>
> A. Perlis

2.1 Reminders

2.1.1 Algorithm

First, let us recall that an *algorithm* is defined as a set of rules intended for the resolution of a problem with input data. This set of rules defines exactly a sequence of operations which terminate in finite time.

For example, let us consider the multiplication of two positive integers written in base 10. We have learnt at school a certain algorithm to solve this problem, on the basis of a precise sequence of elementary operations, using multiplication of digits in base 10 and addition of numbers. We know that this algorithm allows to calculate the product of any pair of numbers in a finite time, depending on the length of the numbers. There exists other algorithms to solve this problem, sometimes founded on variations on the same principle (like the abacus technique), but also quite different, as is the so-called *Russian multiplication*[1] (see figure 2.1), which requires only multiplications and divisions by 2 (and additions).

These algorithms are simple enough to be learnt by most of people, and pretty efficient, in the sense that they deliver the expected result quickly and they require neither a large space, nor the writing of too numerous digits. At the contrary, observe the following naïve algorithm: to multiply n by m, write n lines each with m crosses, one below the other, then count the total number of crosses. This latter method requires only the ability to count, but it is much more costly in time and space.

2.1.2 Algorithmics, complexity of an algorithm

We just saw several methods (or algorithms) to perform the multiplication of two numbers. It is very often the case for numerous problems and it is useful to be able to compare the diverse algorithms which, equivalent from a functional point of view, can be very different in terms of performance. The main goal of *algorithmics*, the science for the design of algorithms, is to find an algorithm as efficient as possible for a given problem.

---

[1] Actually, it was already used in ancian Egypt.

DOI: 10.1201/b23251-2

```
              4 1                    4 1                3 3
          ×   3 3                    2 0                6 6
          -------                    1 0              1 3 2
            1 2 3                   5                   2 6 4
        +   1 2 3                   2                 5 2 8
          -------                   1           1   0 5 6
          1 3 5 3                              -----------
                                               1 3 5 3
```

Fig. 2.1 – Left: ordinary multiplication of 41 and 33. Right: Russian multiplication. On the left column, from top to bottom, one writes the finite sequence of the integer divisions of 41 by 2. On the right column, from top to bottom, one writes the sequence of the multiplications of 33 by 2. Line by line, the parity of the left number is checked. If it is even (marked in grey), the right number in the line is suppressed. Eventually, one adds all remaining numbers in the right column to obtain $41 \times 31 = 33 + 264 + 1056$.

Usually, the efficiency of an algorithm is measured as its *time* complexity (or *temporal*) and its *space* complexity (or *spatial*). However, since the size of computer memories has tremendously increased over the past years, space complexity is a less and less critical criterion. That is why, in the remainder of this book, time complexity prevails.

On the basis of this remark, the goal of algorithmics becomes essentially the search for an algorithm solving a given problem as quickly as possible. Hence, the key question raised is that of the *measurement* of this speed. Of course, it is highly desirable to measure the complexity of an algorithm independently of both the programming language used for implementation and the computer onto which it will be run. Thus, complexity is analyzed on the basis of one or several *elementary operation(s)*, which depend on the problem, but is (are) representative of what the considered algorithm does. In that respect, for an algorithm performing a search in an array, the elementary operation is the comparison, while for a sort algorithm two elementary operations come into play: comparison and exchange of data. Last, for the product of two matrices, the multiplication of (in general real) numbers constitutes the elementary operation.

A second important point is that complexity is expressed according to the *size of data* that are dealt with. This size is an integer characteristic of the problem. For an algorithm searching in an array or sorting an array, it is the number of elements (or size) of the array; for the product of two square matrices, it is the number of rows (or columns) of the matrices. It is often impossible to give the *exact* complexity of an algorithm in terms of a number of elementary operations depending on the size of the data. As a matter of fact, most of time complexity depends on data themselves. For example, some sort algorithms work very well when the array is already almost sorted and slowly if it is sorted backward. For this reason, exact complexity is not the target and the considered notions are those of *minimum* complexity (or *best case*) when data are supportive, and *maximum* complexity (or *worst case*). It is tempting to define an *average* complexity, but this is hardy feasible in general since statistical hypotheses about data distribution are required.

Another approach to time analysis is to use the notion of *order of growth*, which expresses the behavior of complexity when data size becomes "huge" (asymptotic complexity).

In the following two sections, we present the notions of minimum and maximum complexity, then complexity analysis by order of growth.

2.1.3 Minimum and maximum complexity of an algorithm

We present the concepts of *maximum* and *minimum complexity* through the example of the search in a dictionary. Let us suppose that we are looking for a word in a dictionary to get its definition if it is present, or to conclude that it is not in this dictionary. Let n be the size of data, i.e. the number of words in the dictionary. Here, the elementary operation is the comparison of two words[2] and the searched word is denoted by x.

A first algorithm consists in browsing the dictionary from beginning to end until completion which can take two forms: either the word is found and the number of comparisons is less than or equal to n, or it is absent and the entire dictionary has been read. A concrete technique for this latter case is the *sentinel trick*: the dictionary is extended with the searched word x. Hence, x is necessarily found in the dictionary and when it is at the $(n + 1)^{th}$ comparison we conclude that it is absent from the original dictionary. In the algorithm *RechDict1* below, the dictionary is the array $DIC[1..n]$ (at this time, no hypothesis is made about order over the words). When the word x is in DIC, the algorithm returns its position, otherwise the value $(n + 1)$.

1. **constants**
2. $n \in \mathbb{N}_1$ **and** $n = \ldots$ **and** $x \in$ **string and** $x = \ldots$
3. **variables**
4. $DIC \in 1..n + 1 \rightarrow$ **string and** $DIC = [\ldots]$
5. **begin**
6. $DIC[n + 1] \leftarrow x$; $i \leftarrow 1$;
7.   **while** $DIC[i] \neq x$ **do**
8. $i \leftarrow i + 1$
9.   **end while**;
10.   **if** $i < n + 1$ **then**
11.   **write**(*the word* , x, *is in position* , i, *in the dictionary*)
12.   **else**
13.   **write**(*the word* , x, *is not in the dictionary*)
14.   **end if**
15. **end**

What is the complexity of this algorithm? We already know that in the worst case (when x is not in the original dictionary), $(n + 1)$ comparisons are performed. In the best case, only one comparison is done, if luckily enough, x is the first word in the dictionary. The average complexity can be calculated under simple statistical hypotheses and it turns out that it is not $n/2$ (see problem 27, page 81).

If it is now assumed that the dictionary is sorted, obviously there is a quicker method for searching a word: binary search. There are many variants (see for example problem 90, page 427); we suggest the following iterative version. The word located "in the middle" of the dictionary is compared to x. If x is greater than (respectively lower than or equal to) the middle element according to the lexicographical order, the operation is repeated in the upper (respectively lower) half dictionary until a portion of dictionary containing a single word is reached. A positive decision is drawn if this word is the searched word x, otherwise x is not in the dictionary.

---

[2]Actually, a more elementary operation would be the comparison of letters, or even that of bits, but we keep with this one for obvious reasons.

The iterative program *RechDict2* hereafter implements what is previously described:

1. **constants**
2. $x \in$ **string and** $x = \ldots$ **and** $n \in \mathbb{N}_1$ **and** $n = \ldots$
3. **variables**
4. $beg \in \mathbb{N}_1$ **and** $end \in \mathbb{N}_1$ **and** $end \geqslant beg$ **and** $mid \in \mathbb{N}_1$ **and** $mid \geqslant beg$ **and**
5. $mid \leqslant end$ **and** $DIC \in 1 .. n \rightarrow$ **string and** $DIC = [\ldots]$
6. **begin**
7. $beg \leftarrow 1$; $end \leftarrow n$;
8.   **while** $beg \neq end$ **do**
9. $mid \leftarrow \left\lfloor \dfrac{beg + end}{2} \right\rfloor$;
10.   **if** $x > T[mid]$ **then**
11. $beg \leftarrow mid + 1$
12.   **else**
13. $end \leftarrow mid$
14.   **end if**
15.   **end while**;
16.   **if** $x = T[beg]$ **then**
17.   **write(***the word* , x, *is in position* , beg, *in the dictionary*)
18.   **else**
19.   **write(***the word* , x, *is not in the dictionary*)
20.   **end if**
21. **end**

In the case of this algorithm, there are neither best, nor worst situations. As a matter of fact, the number of comparisons (of words) depends only on the size n of the dictionary DIC, not on its contents. The size of search area is repeatedly divided by two and we will admit that the number of comparisons is in the order of $\lfloor \log_2(n) \rfloor$, the greatest integer less than or equal to $\log_2(n)$ (we come back on this statement later). If we admit that the average complexity of *RechDict1* is linear, *RechDict2* performing a logarithmic number of comparisons is better, as expected.

For a dictionary of English language, n is close to 200 000 and the number of comparisons of *RechDict2* ($\lfloor \log_2(n) \rfloor$) is 16.

Let us remark that the variant of *RechDict2* where the alternative distinguishes the equality of x and $T[mil]$ (and the program stops), may require a single comparison. However, it is convenient to notice that: (i) the favorable configuration differs from that for *RechDict1* and (ii) one more comparison is performed at each iteration step and in the worst case the number of comparisons becomes $2 \cdot \lfloor \log_2(n) \rfloor$.

2.1.4 Orders of growth

The most usual way to deal with time analysis is to use the notion of *order of growth* (also called *complexity class*). The function $f_A(n)$ expresses the maximum complexity of the algorithm A in terms of the size n of data that are considered. The idea is to inflate $f_A(n)$ by a function whose growth is (well) known. For this purpose, a certain number of functions serve as a reference:

- 1 (constant complexity),
- $\log_2(n)$ (logarithmic complexity),
- n (linear complexity),
- $n \cdot \log_2(n)$ (quasi linear complexity),
- n^2 (quadratic complexity),

- n^p ($p > 2$) (polynomial complexity),
- 2^n (exponential complexity),
- $n!$,
- n^n.

One could try to write formulas of type $f_A(n) \in \mathcal{O}(n^2)$ meaning (with some precautions that will be explicited) that $f_A(n)$ does not grow more rapidly than n^2 when n increases. However, this first attempt would be very restrictive since, for instance, $f_A(n) = n^2/2 + 3n/2 + 1$ or $f_A(n) = 2n^2 - 1$ would not comply with the definition. Hence, the meaning of $f_A(n) \in \mathcal{O}(n^2)$ is revised so that the two preceding examples become acceptable. For the first one, it will be said that $f_A(n)$ does not grow more quickly than the reference function (here n^2) when n increases, *from a given rank* n_0. Thus, it is possible to write $(n^2/2 + 3n/2 + 1) \in \mathcal{O}(n^2)$, since from $n_0 = 4$, it is true that $(n^2/2 + 3n/2 + 1) < n^2$. However, it is still illegal to write $(2n^2 - 1) \in \mathcal{O}(n^2)$ since for any $n > 1 : (2n^2 - 1) > n^2$. Yet, intuition tells that the order of growth is the same for both $(2n^2 - 1)$ and n^2, and it seems consistent to say $(2n^2 - 1)$ and n^2 grow the same way. Last, we say that $f_A(n) \in \mathcal{O}(n^2)$, if there is a constant C and an integer n_0 from which the inequality $f_A(n) \leqslant C \cdot n^2$ holds. Eventually, the following definition is adopted. Let g be a function: $\mathbb{N} \to \mathbb{R}_+$. We call *maximum order of growth* $\mathcal{O}$ of g the set:

$$\mathcal{O}(g) \stackrel{\wedge}{=} \{t : \mathbb{N} \to \mathbb{R}_+ \mid \exists(C, n_0) \cdot (C \in \mathbb{R}_+ \text{ and } n_0 \in \mathbb{N} \text{ and } \forall n \cdot \\ ((n \in \mathbb{N} \text{ and } n \geqslant n_0) \Rightarrow t(n) \leqslant C \cdot g(n)))\}.$$

According to this definition, $(n^2/2 + 3n/2 + 1) \in \mathcal{O}(n^2)$, as well as $(2n^2 - 1) \in \mathcal{O}(n^2)$ hold. Since $(2n^2 - 1) \in \mathcal{O}(n^2)$, $(2n^2 - 1) \in \mathcal{O}(n^3)$ also holds. In practice, we look for the *smallest* reference function rf such that $f_A(n) \in \mathcal{O}(rf(n))$. Once the set $\mathcal{O}(g)$ of the functions which grow at most as quickly as g (now with a precise meaning) has been defined, it is legitimate to define similarly the set $\Omega(g)$ of the functions which grow at least as quickly as g. The two notions $\mathcal{O}(g)$ and $\Omega(g)$ allow to provide upper and lower bounds for the behavior of an algorithm.

We call *minimum order of growth* of g the set:

$$\Omega(g) \stackrel{\wedge}{=} \{t : \mathbb{N} \to \mathbb{R}_+ \mid \exists(D, n_0) \cdot (D \in \mathbb{R}_+ \text{ and } n_0 \in \mathbb{N} \text{ and } \forall n \cdot \\ (n \geqslant n_0 \Rightarrow t(n) \geqslant D \cdot g(n)))\}.$$

Last, we call *exact order of growth* of g the set $\Theta(g)$ defined by the intersection of $\mathcal{O}(g)$ and $\Omega(g)$:

$$t \in \Theta(g) \stackrel{\wedge}{=} t \in \mathcal{O}(g) \text{ and } t \in \Omega(g)$$

or:

$$\Theta(g) \stackrel{\wedge}{=} \{t : \mathbb{N} \to \mathbb{R}_+ \mid \exists(C, D, n_0) \cdot (C \in \mathbb{R}_+ \text{ and } D \in \mathbb{R}_+ \text{ and } n_0 \in \mathbb{N} \text{ and } \forall n \cdot \\ (n \geqslant n_0 \Rightarrow D \cdot g(n) \leqslant t(n) \leqslant C \cdot g(n)))\}.$$

$f \in \mathcal{O}(g)$ (respectively $\Omega(g), \Theta(g)$) is often read "f is in big o of g" (respectively in Ω of g, in Θ of g).

Interesting result

Let $\mathcal{A}$ be an algorithm made of two consecutive parts $\mathcal{A}_1$ and $\mathcal{A}_2$, whose respective complexities are such that $f_{\mathcal{A}_1}(n) \in \mathcal{O}(f_1(n))$ and $f_{\mathcal{A}_2}(n) \in \mathcal{O}(f_2(n))$; then $f_{\mathcal{A}}(n) \in \max(\{\mathcal{O}(f_1(n), \mathcal{O}(f_2(n))\})$. In other words, the maximum order of growth of an algorithm is given by that of its part of highest maximum order of growth (see problem 23, page 79).

Remarks

1. $f \in \mathcal{O}(1)$ means that from a given rank n_0 there is a constant C such that $f(n) \leqslant C$.

2. The complexity function $f_A(n)$ of any algorithm $\mathcal{A}$ is such that $f_A(n) \in \Omega(1)$.

3. For any integer $a \geqslant 2$, one has: $\mathcal{O}(\log_a(n)) = \mathcal{O}(\log_2(n))$ and $\Theta(\log_a(n)) = \Theta(\log_2(n))$ since $\log_a(n) = \log_2(a) \cdot \log_2(n)$. In general, $\log_2(n)$ is taken as a reference function.

4. Stirling formula

$$n! \approx \sqrt{2\pi n} \cdot \left(\frac{n}{e}\right)^n$$

allows to write (by taking the logarithm of each member) that $\log_2(n!) \in \Theta(n \cdot \log_2(n))$.

5. An order of growth is not a limit. For instance, $f(n) = n^2 \cdot (2 + \sin^2(n)) \in \Theta(n^2)$ but it does not have a limit when n tends toward infinity. Moreover, functions concerned by orders of growth are not from $\mathbb{R}$ to $\mathbb{R}$, but from $\mathbb{N}$ to $\mathbb{R}_+$ since the size of data manipulated in a program is an integer and a complexity is positive by nature.

2.1.5 Some examples of complexity

In the forthcoming chapters, the complexity of the algorithms is studied systematically. Hence, here, we restrict ourselves to a few examples on the basis of some of the algorithms introduced so far. It is easy to deal with the following algorithms:

- factorial (see page 14) whose complexity in terms of multiplications is in $\Theta(n)$,

- the calculation of the number of binary trees having n nodes (see page 13) whose complexity in terms of multiplications is given by:

$$\sum_{i=1}^{n} \sum_{j=0}^{i-1} 1 = \frac{n \cdot (n+1)}{2}$$

thus in $\Theta(n^2)$,

- the calculation of a Delannoy number of order (m, n) given by the recurrence in page 14, whose complexity in terms of additions is expressed as:

$$\sum_{i=1}^{n} \sum_{j=1}^{m} 2 = 2 \cdot m \cdot n$$

thus in $\Theta(m \cdot n)$,

- the number of partitions with p blocks of a set having n elements (see problem 16, page 41) whose complexity in terms of additions (or multiplications) is given by:

$$\sum_{j=2}^{n} \sum_{i=2}^{j-1} 1 = \frac{(n-1)(n-2)}{2}$$

thus in $\Theta(n^2)$,

- algorithm *RechDict1* which is in $\mathcal{O}(n)$ comparisons,

- the naïve multiplication of two square matrices which is in $\Theta(n^3)$ multiplications of real numbers (more efficient algorithms exist).

For the variant of the algorithm *RechDict2*, we must compute $nbStepMax(n)$, the maximum number of steps in the loop. It is given by the recurrence:

$$
\begin{aligned}
&nbStepMax(1) = 1 \\
&nbStepMax(n) = 1 + nbStepMax\left(\left\lfloor\frac{n}{2}\right\rfloor\right) && n > 1
\end{aligned}
$$

whose solution is $nbStepMax(n) = \lfloor\log_2(n)\rfloor$. The maximum number of comparisons (of words) is thus $2 \cdot \lfloor\log_2(n)\rfloor + 1$; this algorithm is in $\mathcal{O}(\log_2(n))$.

This latter example highlights the central role (very often) of recurrence relations for the evaluation of complexity. They are used intensively, in particular for the complexity of recursive algorithms in chapters 4 and 8.

2.1.6 About elementary operations

In the remainder, notably in the problems, the focus is put on asymptotic time complexity of algorithms and sometimes on exact complexity. Frequently, the very nature of the algorithm leads to choose a unique elementary operation, but sometimes several elementary operations come into play. Two situations can occur:

- They are correlated and one of them is chosen; it is the case for the product of matrices where additions and multiplications are tied, but also for the computation of the sum of the elements of an array where the number of additions (the heart of the sum) and comparisons (related to the control of the loop) differ from only one unit,

- The operations are independent and, either they are counted separately or the one with the maximum number of occurrences is taken into account.

In the problems proposed and/or dealt with, elementary operation(s) are most of time made explicit in the statement. Sometimes, this aspect is willingly left in the dark and it must be appropriately detailed in the answer.

There are numerous sorting algorithms which, generally, call on two elementary operations: evaluation of condition and exchange (see for example problem 33 page 112). In some problems, sorting is an initial step and it will be assumed that one of the most efficient at worst is used, whose asymptotic time complexity is quasi linear ($n \cdot \log_2(n)$) in terms of comparisons and/or exchanges[3].

It may happen that we want to compare time complexity of several algorithms intended to solve a same problem. It is then important to choose one (or several) elementary operation(s) common to each of them so that the comparison makes sense.

The evaluation of conditions, simple (called comparisons) or complex, explicit (conditional statements or **while** loops) or implicit (**for** loops), play a prominent role in numerous algorithms. Henceforth, it can be rightly chosen as elementary operation, all the more as no other operation appears relevant for the considered algorithm.

2.1.7 Practical computing time

Each cell of the array below indicates the approximative size of data that can be dealt with by an algorithm whose exact complexity appears in the columns and run-time in rows, for

---

[3] see en.wikipedia.org/wiki/Sorting_algorithm

an instruction computer run-time of 1µs. For example, in an hour, the size of the problem that can be dealt with by an algorithm in n^3 is 1 500. An "astronomic" size is greater than the estimated number of atoms in the universe (10^{80}).

size	$\log_{10}(n)$	n	n^2	n^3	2^n	$n!$
duration = 1 s	astronomic: 10^{10^6}	10^6	10^3	10^2	19	10
1 mn	astronomic	6.10^7	8.10^3	4.10^2	25	11
1 h	astronomic	4.10^8	2.10^4	1 500	31	13
1 j	astronomic	9.10^{10}	10^5	4 400	36	16

For the same instruction run-time (1µs), the following array gives time necessary for an algorithm, whose exact complexity appears in columns, to with data whose size is indicated in rows. For example, a program in n^2 can deal with a problem of size 1 000 in one second. An "astronomic" time is greater than one trillion years.

complexity	$\log_2(n)$	n	$n\log n$	n^2	2^n
size = 10	3µs	10µs	30µs	100µs	1 000µs
100	7µs	100µs	700µs	1/100s	10^{14} centuries
1 000	10µs	1 000µs	1/100s	1s	astronomic
10 000	13µs	1/100s	1/7s	1,7mn	astronomic
100 000	17µs	1/10s	2s	2,8h	astronomic

2.1.8 Pseudo-polynomial problems

Let us remind that the order of growth is evaluated as a function of the size n of the problem, which is independent of the data manipulated by the algorithm. In that respect, the product of two matrices of real numbers ($n \times n$) can be computed by an algorithm in $\Theta(n^3)$ multiplications of real numbers, whatever the values of the matrices.

However, for some algorithms, complexity is evaluated considering data themselves. Without going into the details (what will be done in Chapter 9), the problem titled *currency change* (problem 148, page 689) aims at accumulate the amount N (cents) using a minimum number of coins in the context of the European currency system. For example, for N = 6, the best way is to take two coins: one cent and five cents, rather than – for example – three two cent coins. If we are provided with n distinct types of coins (unlimited in quantity), it turns out that no polynomial (in n) method is known which works for any currency system, but only an exponential one (thus in $O(2^n)$), called A_1.

In contrast, the algorithm (A_2) computes the expected optimal in $\Theta(N \cdot n)$. But beware, N is some data, not the size of the problem. Consequently, run-time depends on characteristics of each occurrence of the problem, which contradicts the principles and criteria of algorithm complexity evaluation.

One might think that the expression $\Theta(N \cdot n)$ shows that the problem is linear in n, thanks to algorithm A_2. But this is false, since N is not a constant and cannot be upper bounded *a priori* by a constant. For the amount $N = 2^{2^n}$ or $n!$, running A_2 would be less efficient than A_1 to produce the desired result. In contrast, when N is a reasonable (i.e. a rather small) amount (which is often the case in concrete applications), A_2 is better than A_1.

Algorithms like A_2, whose type of complexity is in $\Theta(N \cdot P(n))$, where $P(n)$ is a polynomial in n, and where N depends on the data, are said *pseudo-polynomial*. Of course, they can be studied and used, but we must keep in mind that their run-time depends directly and critically on the data of the considered problem.

Final remark

For some problems, data size can be evaluated as a function of several parameters, not a single one. For example, in chapter 9 we will see the "Choosing skis" problem, where each of the n skiers must receive the best pair of skis (among m). n and m are independent values, except the condition $m \geqslant n$. The order of growth of the best algorithm known for this problem is $\mathcal{O}(n \cdot m)$. Therefore, it is impossible to characterize its complexity on the basis of a single parameter: in such a case, the size of the problem is basically multi-dimensional and the order of growth is expressed as a multiple variable polynomial.

2.2 Problems

Problem 22. About some reference functions ⊗ •

This problem aims at deciding whether "close" reference functions characterize (or not) the same order of growth.

Let us consider the following claims (f is a function from $\mathbb{N}$ to $\mathbb{R}_+$):

1. $2^{n+1} \in \mathcal{O}(2^n)$
2. $(n+1)! \in \mathcal{O}(n!)$
3. $f(n) \in \mathcal{O}(n) \Rightarrow (f(n))^2 \in \mathcal{O}(n^2)$
4. $f(n) \in \mathcal{O}(n) \Rightarrow 2^{f(n)} \in \mathcal{O}(2^n)$
5. $n^n \in \mathcal{O}(2^n)$.

Are these propositions true or not?

The solution is on page 83.

Problem 23. About orders of growth ⊗ •

In this problem, an interesting property is established. It is related to the sum of two functions whose maximum or exact order of growth is known. This result is useful in practice to determine the maximum or exact order of growth of a program obtained by sequential composition of several components.

Let $f_1(n)$ and $f_2(n)$ be two functions from $\mathbb{N}$ to $\mathbb{R}_+$ such that:

$$\forall n \cdot (n \geqslant n_0 \Rightarrow f_1(n) \leqslant f_2(n)),$$

like $f_1(n) = \log_2(n)$ and $f_2(n) = n$, or $f_1(n) = n^2$ and $f_2(n) = 2^n$.

23 - Q 1   **Question 1.**   Demonstrate that if $g(n) \in \mathcal{O}(f_1(n))$ and $h(n) \in \mathcal{O}(f_2(n))$ then $g(n) + h(n) \in \mathcal{O}(f_2(n))$.

23 - Q 2   **Question 2.**   Prove that if $g(n) \in \Theta(f_1(n))$ and $h(n) \in \Theta(f_2(n))$ then $g(n) + h(n) \in \Theta(f_2(n))$.

The solution is on page 84.

Problem 24. Variations around the orders of growth   ○ ⦙

> *The main objective of this problem is to prevent from drawing hasty conclusions when dealing with orders of growth.*

Are the following two claims true:

    1. $f \in \Theta(s)$ **and** $g \in \Theta(s) \Rightarrow f - g \in \Theta(s)$
    2. $f \in \mathcal{O}(s)$ **and** $g \in \mathcal{O}(r) \Rightarrow f - g \in \mathcal{O}(s - r)$?

The solution is on page 84.

Problem 25. Order of growth: polynomials   ⦙ •

> *Very often, the order of growth of an algorithm is expressed as a polynomial. In this problem, it is shown that a simplified version is sufficient to express the order of growth.*

Let $\mathcal{A}$ be an algorithm whose complexity is expressed as a polynomial and we aim at finding out a "simplified" expression. First, two special cases are considered before moving to the general case.

25 - Q 1   **Question 1.**   Let us consider f from $\mathbb{N}_1$ to $\mathbb{R}_+$ and g from D to $\mathbb{R}_+$ (where $D = \mathbb{N} - 0..2$) the two following functions: a) $f(n) = n^3 + 3n^2 + 6n + 9$, b) $g(n) = n^3 - 3n^2 + 6n - 9$. Prove that both f and g belong to $\Theta(n^3)$.

25 - Q 2   **Question 2.**   Let $f(n) = a_p \cdot n^p + a_{p-1} \cdot n^{p-1} + \cdots + a_1 \cdot n + a_0$ be a function from D in $\mathbb{R}_+$, with $a_i \in \mathbb{N}$ and D the set $\mathbb{N}$ possibly deprived of its first elements for which f has a nonpositive value. Prove that for $a_p > 0, f(n) \in \Theta(n^p)$.

25 - Q 3   **Question 3.**   If a, b and k are integers, prove the inequality:

$$a^k + b^k \geqslant \left(\frac{a + b}{2} \right)^k . \tag{2.1}$$

Deduce that for $k \in \mathbb{N}$ **and** $n \in \mathbb{N}_1$, one has:

$$f(n, k) = 1^k + 2^k + \cdots + n^k \in \Theta(n^{k+1}).$$

The solution is on page 85.

Problem 26. Order of growth: paradox?

○ •

> *In problem 23, page 79, we have seen a property of the sum of two complexity functions. To extend it to a multiple sum seems legitimate, but beware of confusing the image of a function with the sum of functions.*

Question 1.   Prove that:

26 - Q 1

$$\sum_{i=1}^{n} i = (1 + 2 + \cdots + n) \in \mathcal{O}(n^2).$$

Question 2.   Let us consider the following reasoning. It is known that:

26 - Q 2

$$\sum_{i=1}^{n} i = \frac{n \cdot (n + 1)}{2}.$$

Yet:

$$\sum_{i=1}^{n} i \in \mathcal{O}(1 + 2 + \cdots + n)$$

and

$$\mathcal{O}(1 + 2 + \cdots + n) = \mathcal{O}(\max(\{1, 2, \ldots, n\})) = \mathcal{O}(n).$$

Hence:

$$\frac{n \cdot (n + 1)}{2} \in \mathcal{O}(n).$$

Where is the flaw?

The solution is on page 87.

Problem 27. Average complexity: an example

○○ ⋮

> *The objective of this problem is to proceed to an average complexity calculation. We highlight a result which, without being unexpected, is not definitely intuitive.*

The algorithm hereafter, close to that developed for the sequential search in a dictionary, looks for the value x in the array T of integers where the first n elements are distinct, the last one acting as a sentinel (its value is precisely x). The result returned is the rank of x when x is in $T[1 .. n]$, $(n + 1)$ otherwise.

1. **constants**
2. $x \in \mathbb{N}_1$ **and** $x = \ldots$ **and** $n \in \mathbb{N}_1$ **and** $n = \ldots$
3. **variables**
4. $T \in 1 .. n + 1 \rightarrow \mathbb{N}_1$ **and** $T = \ldots$ **and** $i \in \mathbb{N}_1$
5. **begin**
6. $i \leftarrow 1 \,; T[n + 1] \leftarrow x;$
7.   **while** $T[i] \neq x$ **do**
8. $i \leftarrow i + 1$
9.   **end while;**

10.   **write**(i)
11. **end**

27 - Q 1   **Question** 1.   Give the minimum and maximum complexity of this algorithm, in terms of comparisons.

27 - Q 2   **Question** 2.   The following probabilistic hypothesis is made: (i) the integer values in the array are drawn equi-probably between 1 and N, with $N \geqslant n$ and (ii) x is drawn equi-probably between 1 and N as well. What is the average complexity of the algorithm?

The solution is on page 87.

Problem 28.   The ford in the fog   8 ⁝

> *This problem shows how two strategies a priori analogous can produce algorithms of very different complexity. Ultimately, a solution with linear complexity is expected, but also an upper bound of the constant of proportionality, which is rather unusual.*

We are in front of a river with a dense fog. We know that there is a ford in the neighborhood, but we ignore if it is located on the left or on the right and at which distance (unbounded *a priori*). With this fog, the entrance of the ford can be seen only when we are just in front of it. How to proceed to cross the river?

We must successively explore left and right ways, while increasing the distance traveled at each direction change. Starting on the left or on the right does not matter, but both sides must be considered in a "balanced" fashion and the distance must be steadily increased so as to avoid to walk too far in the wrong way (where there is no ford).

A first method consists in walking one step on the right, coming back to the starting point, walking one step on the left, coming back to the starting point, walking two steps on the right, coming back to the starting point, walking two steps on the left, coming back to the starting point, walking three steps on the right, and so on until the ford is reached, according to the following schema:

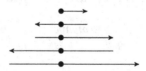

Let us suppose that the ford is situated 15 steps on the left. To reach it, the number of steps walked in total is 465, more than 30 times the 15 strictly necessary steps.

More generally, let us denote by n the distance (in steps) between the starting point and the ford, i.e. the minimum number of steps necessary to reach the ford.

28 - Q 1   **Question** 1.   Give the number of steps walked with the proposed method when the ford is located n steps on the left (respectively right) away from the starting point. What is the class of complexity of this method in terms of steps traveled? One would like to find a basically more efficient method (in the sense of class of complexity) ensuring that the ford is reached with less than 9n steps. The shortcoming of the previous method lies in a too "wise" increase in the number of steps. Adding a single step each time (arithmetic progression) is finally costly and one imagines to *double* the number of steps (geometric progression), which is reflected by the schema below:

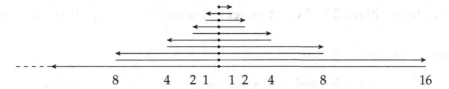

8   4   2 1   1 2   4   8   16

Question 2.   Give the number of steps walked depending on whether the ford is located 9 (respectively 15) steps away from the starting point on the left or on the right. Conclude.   28 - Q 2

Question 3.   Check that, with a progression according to the powers of 3 (instead of 2), the objective (in terms of steps walked) is not met.   28 - Q 3

Question 4.   Modify the method proposed in the second question, still progressing using the powers of 2, so that the constraint on the number of steps walked is met. It is asked to give the maximum number of steps walked as well as the minimum one, depending on n, the distance between the starting point and the ford.   28 - Q 4

The solution is on page 88.

2.3   Solutions

Answers to problem 22.   About some reference functions
The problem is on page 79.

The five claims are successively studied.

1. $2^{n+1} = 2 \cdot 2^n$, hence $2^{n+1} \in \mathcal{O}(2^n)$ (for $n_0 = 0$ and $C = 2$).

2. So that $(n+1) \in \mathcal{O}(n!)$, there must be a constant K such that, from a given rank n_0, one has $(n+1)! \leqslant K \cdot n!$. As $(n+1)! = (n+1) \cdot n!$, this would mean that, for any n greater than n_0, $n+1 \leqslant K$, which is impossible. We deduce that $(n+1)! \notin \mathcal{O}(n!)$.

3. If $f(n) \in \mathcal{O}(n)$, then $f(n) \leqslant C \cdot n$ from a given rank n_0 and $(f(n))^2 = C^2 \cdot n^2$, hence $(f(n))^2 \in \mathcal{O}(n^2)$ for $n_0' = n_0$ and $C' = C^2$.

4. We point out a counterexample to show the falsity of this proposition. Let us take $f(n) = 2n$. Then, we have $2^{f(n)} = 2^{2n}$, and it is sufficient to prove that there is no constant K such that for any n, $2^{2n} = K \cdot 2^n$. Yet, $2^{2n} = 2^{n+n} = 2^n \cdot 2^n = K \cdot 2^n$ if $2^n = K$, which is impossible whatever the value of K. Thus, the implication $f(n) \in \mathcal{O}(n) \Rightarrow 2^{f(n)} \in \mathcal{O}(2^n)$ is false.

5. So that $n^n \in \mathcal{O}(2^n)$, we should have $n^n \leqslant C \cdot 2^n$ for a constant C and n significantly large. Under these conditions, we should have $(n/2)^n \leqslant C$, which is impossible since the left member of this inequation increases with n. We conclude that $n^n \notin \mathcal{O}(2^n)$.

Answers to problem 23. About orders of growth *The problem is on page 79.*

23 - A 1   **Answer 1.**   As $g(n) \in \mathcal{O}(f_1(n))$:

$$\exists(C_1, n_1) \cdot (C_1 \in \mathbb{R}_+ \textbf{ and } n_1 \in \mathbb{N} \textbf{ and } \forall n \cdot (n \geqslant n_1 \Rightarrow g(n) \leqslant C_1 \cdot f_1(n))).$$

Similarly, as $h(n) \in \mathcal{O}(f_2(n))$:

$$\exists(C_2, n_2) \cdot (C_2 \in \mathbb{R}_+ \textbf{ and } n_2 \in \mathbb{N} \textbf{ and } \forall n \cdot (n \geqslant n_2 \Rightarrow h(n) \leqslant C_2 \cdot f_2(n))).$$

It can be deduced that:

$$\forall n \cdot (n \geqslant \max(\{n_1, n_2\}) \Rightarrow (g(n) + h(n)) \leqslant (C_1 \cdot f_1(n) + C_2 \cdot f_2(n)))$$

$$\forall n \cdot (n \geqslant \max(\{n_1, n_2\}) \Rightarrow (g(n) + h(n)) \leqslant 2 \cdot \max(\{C_1, C_2\}) \cdot f_2(n)))$$

which characterizes the fact that:

$$g(n) + h(n) \in \mathcal{O}(f_2(n)).$$

23 - A 2   **Answer 2.**   As $g(n) \in \Theta(f_1(n))$:

$$\exists(C_1, D_1, n_1) \cdot (C_1 \in \mathbb{R}_+ \textbf{ and } D_1 \in \mathbb{R}_+ \textbf{ and } n_1 \in \mathbb{N} \textbf{ and } \forall n \cdot$$
$$(n \geqslant n_1 \Rightarrow C_1 \cdot f_1(n) \leqslant g(n) \leqslant D_1 \cdot f_1(n))).$$

Similarly, since $h(n) \in \mathcal{O}(f_2(n))$:

$$\exists(C_2, D_2, n_2) \cdot (C_2 \in \mathbb{R}_+ \textbf{ and } D_2 \in \mathbb{R}_+ \textbf{ and } n_2 \in \mathbb{N} \textbf{ and } \forall n \cdot$$
$$(n \geqslant n_2 \Rightarrow C_2 \cdot f_2(n) \leqslant h(n) \leqslant D_2 \cdot f_2(n))).$$

We deduce that:

$$\forall n \cdot (n \geqslant \max(\{n_1, n_2\}) \Rightarrow$$
$$(C_1 \cdot f_1(n) + C_2 \cdot f_2(n)) \leqslant g(n) + h(n) \leqslant (D_1 \cdot f_1(n) + D_2 \cdot f_2(n)))$$

thus:

$$\forall n \cdot (n \geqslant \max(\{n_1, n_2\}) \Rightarrow$$
$$C_2 \cdot f_2(n) \leqslant g(n) + h(n) \leqslant \max(\{(D_1, D_2)\} \cdot (f_1(n) + f_2(n)))$$

and finally:

$$\forall n \cdot (n \geqslant \max(\{n_1, n_2\}) \Rightarrow$$
$$C_2 \cdot f_2(n) \leqslant g(n) + h(n) \leqslant 2 \cdot \max(\{D_1, D_2\}) \cdot f_2(n))$$

which characterizes the fact that:

$$g(n) + h(n) \in \Theta(f_2(n)).$$

Answers to problem 24. Variations around the orders of growth *The problem is on page 80.*

The two claims are successively studied.

1. Let $f(n) = n^3 + 2n^2$ and $g(n) = n^3 + n^2$. Then, $f(n) - g(n) = n^2 \in \Theta(n^2)$ and not $\Theta(n^3)$, which invalidates the first proposition.

2. Let $f(n) = 3n^3$, $s(n) = n^3 + 2n^2$, $g(n) = n^3$ and $r(n) = n^3 + n^2$. Obviously, $f(n) \in \mathcal{O}(s(n))$ and $g(n) \in \mathcal{O}(r(n))$. One has: $f(n) - g(n) = 2n^3$ and $s(n) - r(n) = n^2$ and thus $f(n) - g(n) \notin \Theta(s(n) - r(n))$, which contradicts the second claim.

These two claims are proven to be false.

Answers to problem 25. Order of growth: polynomials *The problem is on page 80.*

Answer 1. It must be proven that each of the functions f and g is upper and lower 25 - A 1 bounded by terms of the form $K \cdot n^3$. Let us first consider $f(n)$. One has:

$$\forall n \cdot (n \in \mathbb{N}_1 \Rightarrow (1 \cdot n^3 \leqslant f(n) \leqslant 18 \cdot n^3))$$

and thus $f(n) \in \Theta(n^3)$.

As to $g(n)$, $3n^2 - 6n + 9$ has a positive value for any $n \in D$ (and even for any $n \in \mathbb{N}$). Therefore, for $n \in D$, $g(n) \leqslant n^3$. Moreover:

$$g'(n) = g(n) - \frac{n^3}{3} = 2 \cdot \frac{n^3}{3} - 3n^2 + 6n - 9$$

is a function taking positive values (not necessarily integers) for any $n \in D$, hence $g(n) \geqslant n^3/3$. Eventually, we have established that for $n \geqslant 3$:

$$\frac{1}{3} \cdot n^3 \leqslant g(n) \leqslant 1 \cdot n^3$$

thereby $g(n) \in \Theta(n^3)$.

Answer 2. Here again, we will try to under and over estimate f by a polynomial. Let- 25 - A 2 ting $g(n) = a_p/2 \cdot n^p + a_{p-1} \cdot n^{p-1} + \cdots + a_1 \cdot n + a_0$, we can write:

$$f(n) = \frac{a_p}{2} \cdot n^p + g(n).$$

Let us examine $g(n)$. If c denotes the largest of the values $|a_i|$ for $i \in 0 .. p - 1$, one has:

$$
\begin{aligned}
&g(n) \\
={}& \\
&\frac{a_p}{2} \cdot n^p + a_{p-1} \cdot n^{p-1} + \cdots + a_1 \cdot n + a_0 \\
\geqslant{}& \\
&\frac{a_p}{2} \cdot n^p - c \cdot (n^{p-1} + \cdots + n + 1) \\
\geqslant{}& \\
&\frac{a_p}{2} \cdot n^p - \frac{c}{n-1} \cdot (n^p - 1) \\
>{}& \\
&\frac{a_p}{2} \cdot n^p - \frac{c}{n-1} \cdot n^p \\
={}& \\
&n^p \cdot \left(\frac{a_p}{2} - \frac{c}{n-1} \right).
\end{aligned}
$$

with right-column annotations: definition / arithmetics / value of the geometric series for $n \neq 1$ / arithmetics / arithmetics.

This latter expression is positive for $n \geqslant n_0 = 2 + (2c/a_p)$ and we can conclude that:

$$\forall n \cdot \left(n \in D \text{ and } n \geqslant n_0 \Rightarrow f(n) \geqslant \frac{a_p}{2} \cdot n^p \right).$$

Let us now try to find a polynomial overestimating f. Let b be the largest of the values $|a_i|$, for $i \in 0 \mathbin{..} p$. One has:

$$f(n) \leqslant b \cdot (n^p + n^{p-1} + \cdots + n^1 + 1) \leqslant b \cdot (p+1) \cdot n^p.$$

For $n \geqslant 2 + (2c/a_p)$, one has:

$$\frac{a_p}{2} \cdot n^p \leqslant f(n) \leqslant b \cdot (p+1) \cdot n^p$$

which proves that $f(n) \in \Theta(n^p)$.

25 - A 3 **Answer** 3.   As $(a + b) \leqslant 2 \cdot \max(\{a, b\})$, we can write:

$$(a + b)^k \leqslant (2 \cdot \max(\{a, b\}))^k.$$

Furthermore, one has:

$$(2 \cdot \max(\{a, b\}))^k = (\max(\{2a, 2b\}))^k \leqslant (2a)^k + (2b)^k$$

and by combination:

$$(a + b)^k \leqslant (2 \cdot \max(\{a, b\}))^k \leqslant (2a)^k + (2b)^k$$

which yields the expected inequality when replacing a (respectively b) by a/2 (respectively b/2).

Now, let us prove that $f(n, k) \in \Theta(n^{k+1})$. One has:

$$f(n, k) = 1^k + 2^k + \cdots + n^k \leqslant n \cdot n^k = n^{k+1}.$$

Furthermore:

$$
\begin{aligned}
f(n, k) &= 1^k + 2^k + \cdots + (n-1)^k + n^k \\
&= \frac{1^k}{2} + \frac{1^k}{2} + \frac{2^k}{2} + \frac{2^k}{2} + \cdots + \frac{(n-1)^k}{2} + \frac{(n-1)^k}{2} + \frac{n^k}{2} + \frac{n^k}{2} \\
&= \frac{1^k + 1^k + 2^k + 2^k + \cdots + (n-1)^k + (n-1)^k + n^k + n^k}{2} \\
&= \frac{1^k + n^k + 2^k + (n-1)^k + \cdots + (n-1)^k + 2^k + n^k + 1^k}{2}.
\end{aligned}
$$

Using formula 2.1, page 80, it comes:

$$
\begin{aligned}
f(n, k) &\geqslant \frac{1}{2}\left(\left(\frac{n+1}{2}\right)^k + \cdots + \left(\frac{n+1}{2}\right)^k \right) = \left(\frac{n}{2}\right)\left(\frac{n+1}{2}\right)^k \\
&\geqslant \frac{n^{k+1}}{2^{k+1}}.
\end{aligned}
$$

Finally:

$$\forall n \cdot \left(n \in \mathbb{N}_1 \Rightarrow \left(\frac{1}{2^{k+1}} \cdot n^{k+1} \leqslant f(n,k) \leqslant 1 \cdot n^{k+1} \right) \right)$$

which confirms that for $k \in \mathbb{N}$ **and** $n \in \mathbb{N}_1$, one has:

$$f(n,k) \in \Theta(n^{k+1}).$$

Answers to problem 26. Order of growth: paradox? *The problem is on page 81.*

Answer 1.   One has: 26 - A 1

$$\sum_{i=1}^{n} = 1 + 2 + \cdots + n = \frac{n(n+1)}{2} = \frac{n^2}{2} + \frac{n}{2}$$

therefore $\sum_{i=1}^{n} = 1 + 2 + \cdots + n \in \mathcal{O}(n^2)$.

Remark

We could have used the result established in the third question of the preceding problem by taking $k = 1$ for $f(n,k)$.

Answer 2.   The reasoning carried out operates on the image of the function and not   26 - A 2
on the function itself. As a matter of fact, the decomposition of the considered function in terms of a sum of functions yields:

$$f(n) = \sum_{i=1}^{n} i = \sum_{i=1}^{\infty} f_i(n)$$

where the function f_i is defined as $f_i(n) = i$ if $n \geqslant i$, 0 otherwise.
Indeed, here, we have an *infinite* sum, and the result established in problem 23, page 79, does not apply.

Answers to problem 27. Average complexity: an example   *The problem is on page 81.*

Answer 1.   The minimum complexity is 1, when $T[1] = x$. The maximum complexity is   27 - A 1
$(n + 1)$, when x does not appear in T.

Answer 2.   Now, we aim at establishing the average complexity of the search of x 27 - A 2
using the proposed algorithm. There are $N!/(N - n)!$ distinct arrays which are drawn equi-probably[4]. There are $(1/N) \cdot (N!/(N - n)!) = (N - 1)!/(N - n)!$ arrays where x is the head element. In such a case, a single comparison takes place. Thus, there are $N!/(N - n)! - (N - 1)!/(N - n)! = (N - 1)(N - 1)!/(N - n)!$ arrays which do not start with x. Among those, 1 out of $(N - 1)$ have x in second position, hence $(N - 1)!/(N - n)!$. In such a case, two comparisons are performed. It is easy to observe that there are always $(N - 1)!/(N - n)!$ arrays with x in position i, leading to i comparisons, for $i \in 1 .. n$.

---

[4]It is the number of *arrangements* of n objects out of N and not *combinations*, since the order according to which objects come matters. For example, there are 60 distinct arrays when $N = 5$ and $n = 3$.

$(N-n)(N-1)!/(N-n)!$ arrays remain where x cannot be found for which $(n+1)$ comparisons take place. Thus, the average number of comparisons is:

$$\frac{1}{\frac{N!}{(N-n)!}}\left(\left(\sum_{i=1}^{n}\frac{(N-1)!}{(N-n)!}i\right)+\frac{(N-n)(N-1)!}{(N-n)!}(n+1)\right)=(n+1)\left(1-\frac{n}{2N}\right).$$

In particular, for $N=n$, there are $((n+1)/2)$ comparisons in average. When N/n increases, the number of comparisons tends to $(n+1)$.

Answers to problem 28. The ford in the fog   *The problem is on page 82.*

28 - A 1   **Answer 1.**   Generally speaking, when the ford is located n steps on the left away from the starting point, the number of steps required by the suggested method is:

$$4\cdot\sum_{i=1}^{n-1}i+3n=4(n(n-1))/2+3n=2n^2+n.$$

If it is situated n n steps on the right, one must travel:

$$4\cdot\sum_{i=1}^{n-1}i+n=4(n(n-1))/2+n=2n^2-n$$

steps. In both cases, the number of steps is in $\Theta(n^2)$.

28 - A 2   **Answer 2.**   Using a geometric progression:
1. when the ford is 9 steps on the left away from the starting point, one does
$1+(1+1)+(1+2)+(2+2)+(2+4)+(4+4)+(4+8)+(8+8)+(8+16)+(16+9) = 101$
steps;
2. when the ford is 15 steps on the left away from the starting point, one does
$1+(1+1)+(1+2)+(2+2)+(2+4)+(4+4)+(4+8)+(8+8)+(8+16)+(16+15) =$
107 steps;
3. when the ford is 9 steps on the right away from the starting point, one does
$1+(1+1)+(1+2)+(2+2)+(2+4)+(4+4)+(4+8)+(8+8)+(8+9) = 69$
steps;
4. when the ford is 15 steps on the right away from the starting point, one does
$1+(1+1)+(1+2)+(2+2)+(2+4)+(4+4)+(4+8)+(8+8)+(8+15) = 75$
steps.

It can be observed that for the same distance, the ford is reached more quickly when it is on the right (unsurprisingly since we walk on the right first). Moreover, in the last three cases, the constraint bearing on the number of steps is met, since $107 < 9\cdot n$ ($9\cdot 15 = 135$), $69 < 9\cdot n$ ($9\cdot 9 = 81$), $75 < 9\cdot n$ ($9\cdot 15 = 135$), but not in the first case where $101 > 9\cdot n$ ($9\cdot 9 = 81$).

28 - A 3   **Answer 3.**   The proposed strategy consists in walking one step on the right, (if needed) coming back to the starting point and walking one step on the left, (if needed) coming back to the starting point and walking three steps on the right, (if needed) coming back to the starting point and walking three steps on the left, (if needed) coming back to the starting point and walking three steps on the right, (if needed) coming back to the starting point and walking three steps on the left, (if needed) coming back to the starting point and walking nine steps on the right, (if needed) coming back to the starting point and walking nine steps on the left, and so on. Thus, if the ford is located ten steps away from the starting point on the left, we walk $1+(1+1)+(1+3)+(3+3)+(3+9)+(9+9)+(9+27)+(27+10) = 116$ steps, therefore more then $9\cdot 10 = 90$. Consequently, this strategy is not appropriate with respect to the constraint imposed.

Answer 4.   The idea is to adopt the following schema, where the symmetry (left/right) is broken: 28 - A 4

In contrast to the previous two methods, the actual position of the ford on the left side is not a disadvantage. As a matter of fact, when the ford is 5 steps on the left, we have to walk $(1+1) + (2+2) + (4+4) + 5 = 19$ steps, whereas when it is 5 steps on the right $(1+1) + (2+2) + (4+4) + (8+8) + 5 = 35$ steps are necessary. In both cases, the number of steps is less than $10 \cdot 5 = 50$, which bodes well.

Let us evaluate the number N of steps to walk when the ford is located on the left of the starting point. When the ford is one (respectively two) steps on the left, it is reached with three (respectively four) steps and the constraint is met since $3 < 10 \cdot 1$ and $4 < 10 \cdot 1$. When it is located at a distance n greater than two steps, one has:

$$\exists p \cdot (p \in \mathbb{N}_1 \text{ and } 2^{2p-1} < n \leqslant 2^{2p+1})$$

yet:

$$\frac{2^{2p-1}}{n} < 1. \tag{2.2}$$

Relying on the schema describing the move strategy, the number of steps N is:

$$N = 2(2^0 + 2^1 + \cdots + 2^{2p}) + n. \tag{2.3}$$

In effect, we walk back and forth alternatively on the left and on the right until the ford is not reached. It comes:

$$
\begin{aligned}
&N \\
={}& && \text{formula 2.3} \\
&2(2^0 + 2^1 + \cdots + 2^{2p}) + n \\
={}& && \text{sum of a geometric series} \\
&2(2^{2p+1} - 1) + n \\
={}& && \text{arithmetics} \\
&8 \cdot 2^{2p-1} + n - 2 \\
={}& && \text{arithmetics with } n > 0 \\
&n \cdot (8 \cdot \frac{2^{2p-1}}{n} + 1) - 2 \\
<{}& && \text{formula 2.2} \\
&9n - 2.
\end{aligned}
$$

Let us study the values taken by N for $n \in 2^{2p-1} + 1 .. 2^{2p+1}$:
 - if $n = 2^{2p+1}$, $N = 3 \cdot 2^{2p+1} - 2 = 3 \cdot n - 2$,
 - if $n = 2^{2p+1} - 1$, $N = 3 \cdot 2^{2p+1} = 3 \cdot n$,
 - if $n = 2^{2p+1} - 2$, $N = 3 \cdot 2^{2p+1} + 2 = 3 \cdot n + 2$,
 - ...
 - if $n = 2^{2p-1} + 2$, $N = 8 \cdot 2^{2p-1} + 2^{2p-1} + 2 - 2 = 9 \cdot n - 18$
 - if $n = 2^{2p-1} + 1$, $N = 8 \cdot 2^{2p-1} + 2^{2p-1} + 1 - 2 = 9 \cdot n - 10$.

It can be seen that, in the interval $2^{2p-1} + 1 .. 2^{2p+1}$, we have: $3 \cdot n - 2 \leqslant N \leqslant 9 \cdot n - 10$. Since when the ford is only one step to the left, we have $N = 1 (= 9n - 6)$, it appears that: $\forall n \geqslant 1, 3n - 2 \leqslant N \leqslant 9n - 6$. This shows that, on the one hand, the number of steps walked is always less than $9n$ as requested, on the other hand, it varies in the proportion of 1 to 3.

The same result is obtained when the ford is located n steps to the right of the starting point (we study the values of n between two even powers of 2 after treating the case $n = 1$ separately, for which we have $N = 1$).

If we now consider the framework of a geometric progression of reason 3, a reasoning similar to the previous one shows that:

- when the ford is located one step to the left, $N = 3$,
- when the ford is located two steps to the left, $N = 4$,
- when the ford is located at a distance n, such that $3^{2p-1} \leqslant n \leqslant 3^{2p+1}$, with $p \geqslant 1, 2n - 1 \leqslant N \leqslant 10n - 10$.

It can be deduced that the objective assigned is not met since the number of steps walked can exceed $9n$, but that its lower bound is decreased compared to that obtained with a geometric progression of reason 2.

Complementary study

We will now show that, if we stick to geometric progressions, choosing the reason 2 is optimal. To this end, we choose a continuous rather than discrete frame and we evaluate distances, no longer in number of steps, but in divisible units, such as the meter. It is therefore considered that the ford is at a distance of n from the starting point, where n is this time a positive real number. If we explore on the side of the ford and turn back after having walked a length strictly less than n, the ford is by definition not yet reached.
Let us denote by E (real over 1.0) the reason for the geometric progression. So, the strategy consists in making 1.0 meter on the right, E meters on the left, E^2 meters on the right, etc. We will assume that the ford is on the right at a distance of 2.0 meters or more, but it does not matter as we have seen before. Let us look at the worst and the best cases, from the point of view of the N/n ratio, where N is the distance (this time in meters) walked before finding the ford.
For example, let $E = 3.0$ and $n = 9.01$. First we go one meter to the right, then we go back to the starting point (another meter), then we go to the left at the distance $E = 3.0$, we go back to the starting point (so far we have covered seven meters). We will now go nine meters to the right and just miss the ford by one centimeter. We turn back on the nine meters (provisional total: 25.0), we go back and forth to the left and we come back to the starting point for a total of $(25.0 + 2 \cdot 27.0) = 79.0$ meters. Only 9.01 meters to go and we will reach the ford. We then covered a total distance of $N = 88.01$ meters, with a ratio $N/n = 9.768 \cdots$. Now imagine that the ford was not at $n = 9.01$ meters, but at ten meters. We would have walked $N = 89.0$ meters, for a ratio N/n of 8.9, which would have been better than the previous one. The further the ford would have been to the right, at a distance less than or equal to 81.0 meters, the more this ratio would have decreased. The ford is here on the right, at a distance n such that $E^2 < n \leqslant E^4$. Generally speaking, if it is on the right, there is an integer p such that $E^{2p} < n \leqslant E^{2p+2}$ and the worst case (the one that maximizes the ratio N/n) is when $n = E^{2p} + \epsilon$ with ϵ as small as desired. The best case is when $n = E^{2p+2}$. The proof of validity of both statements is left to the reader.

In the worst case, the distance walked is:

$$N = 2(1 + E + E^2 + \cdots + E^{2p+1}) + E^{2p} + \epsilon = \frac{E^{2p}(2E^2 + E - 1) + E - 1}{E - 1} - \frac{2}{E - 1} + \epsilon.$$

N can be rewritten as:

$$N = \frac{2E^2 + E - 1}{E - 1}(E^{2p} + \epsilon) - 2\epsilon\frac{E^2 + 1}{E - 1} = \frac{2E^2 + E - 1}{E - 1}n - 2\epsilon\frac{E^2 + 1}{E - 1}.$$

So we can see that N is linearly related to n.

What is the best value of E to minimize this distance in the worst case? Deriving the term $(2E^2 + E - 1)/(E - 1)$, we see that it is minimum for $E = 2.0$ and in this case: $N = 9n - 10\epsilon$.

We assume that the ford is on the right at a distance $n \geqslant 2.0$. In the best case ($n = E^{2p}$), the number of steps is:

$$N = 2(1 + E + E^2 + \cdots + E^{2p-1}) + E^{2p} = \frac{E + 1}{E - 1}n - \frac{2}{E - 1}.$$

We can see that N is also in linear relation with n and for $E = 2$ we have: $N = 3n - 2$.

Note that replacing E by $E/(E-1)$ in the coefficient $(2E^2+E-1)/(E-1)$ leaves this coefficient unchanged. This results in identical limit values (L) of N/n, confirmed by the experiments carried out by the authors, an excerpt of which is given in the table below:

E	1.2	1.25	1.4	1.5	1.8	2	2.25	3	3.5	5	6
L	15.4	13.5	10.8	10	9.1	9	9.1	10	10.8	13.5	15.4

3

Specification, invariants, and iteration

> Le bonheur est désir de répétition
> (Happiness is a desire for repetition).
>
> M. Kundera

This chapter illustrates the principle of *reasoned* development of loops. It could seem at first sight that writing a loop is a straightforward task, but every programmer knows how tricky it can be. The *logical* approach that we propose here applies to a variety of problems and reveals the interest of its systematic and thorough nature. Several problems in Chapter 8 call also on loops and will supplement those proposed here. The main objective is to equip the reader with strong bases about the construction of loops by *invariant*, however without entering in too many sophisticated details.

3.1 Principle for the construction of loops by invariant

Generally speaking, the rational development of a program (algorithm) consists in considering it as a mechanism which transforms a "system" from an initial state called "precondition" to a final state named "postcondition" or "goal". This holds in particular for loops which constitute the particular class of programs handled in this chapter. The pair (precondition, postcondition) is called the *specification* of the program and we aim at the development of a program on the basis of its specification. The notation prec prog postc, used from now on, means that the program prog does come to an end and allows to go from the situation prec to the situation postc. In other words, prog being a program, prec and postc being predicates, prec prog postc means that if prog is run starting in a state complying with prec then it finishes and the state reached meets the predicate postc.

In order to ease the reasoning underlying the development of the program prog, its design is systematized by means of five components (in addition to precondition and postcondition):

1. **Invariant** It is a predicate standing for a characteristic property of the problem to be solved.

2. **Stopping condition** It is also a predicate.

3. **Progression** It is a piece of program/code.

4. **Initialization** It is a piece of program as well.

5. **Termination** This is an integer value expression[1].

---

[1]The terms "bound function" or "variant" are also used by some authors.

DOI: 10.1201/b23251-3

These components maintain the relationships described now.

1. First of all, the conjunction of the invariant and the stopping condition leads to the desired goal, which can be formalized by:

$$(\texttt{invariant } \textbf{and } \texttt{stopping condition}) \Rightarrow \texttt{postcondition}.$$

2. Moreover, the progression must:

    (a) *preserve* the invariant. More precisely, the progression is a fragment of program defined by the precondition "invariant **and not** stopping condition" and the postcondition "invariant". Here, the assertion is that the invariant holds before and after the progression is carried out. Of course, one must not conclude that the invariant holds during the whole execution of the progression.

    (b) *strictly* decrease the termination expression. More precisely, in looping situation (i.e. when the predicate "invariant **and not** stopping condition" holds), the (integer) value of the termination expression after one progression step is positive or zero and strictly less than its previous value. Thus, the stopping condition will be met after a finite period of time, which ensures that the program *finishes*.

3. The initialization must *establish* the invariant. It is a piece of program whose precondition is that of the problem to be solved and whose postcondition is the invariant.

It is worth noticing that the first two components (invariant and stopping condition) relate to *situations* while the next two (progression and initialization) are *actions*. Items 1, 2 and 3 clearly show that the *invariant* plays a central role since it appears in items 1, 2-a, 2-b and 3. It constitutes the cornerstone of the construction of loops, in other terms the glue which links the other components together. Hence, the development of a loop begins with the identification of the invariant.

Figure 3.1 summarizes the aspects discussed earlier.

The encoding of the corresponding generic loop is as follows:

1. initialization;
2. **while not** stopping condition **do**
3.   progression
4. **end while**

In this "minimal" notation, precondition, postcondition, invariant and termination expression do not appear. The last two elements are widely addressed in the design phase and, in general, only the fist two are featured in the code as comments (introduced by the keywords *PRE* and *POST*).

The complexity of a loop is expressed in terms of either conditions to be evaluated (for instance those related to its control), or sometimes an operation characteristic of the problem dealt with appearing in its body. Very often, loops have a linear complexity, but other situations (e.g. logarithmic or polynomial) can be encountered as well.

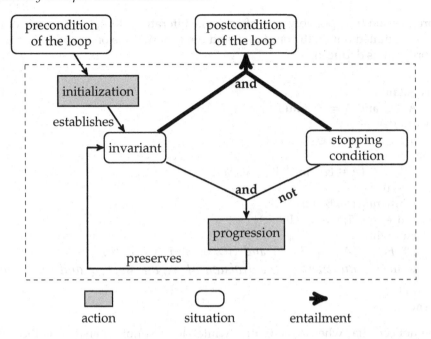

Fig. 3.1 – Articulation invariant/stopping condition/progression/initialization.

3.2 An introductory example: the Euclidian division

We consider the classical problem of the Euclidian division. We are interested in the calculation of the quotient of the "integer" division of A by B ($A \in \mathbb{N}, B \in \mathbb{N}_1$), knowing that we are not provided with a division operation. The specification of the program to design is given by the pair:

Precondition: $(A \in \mathbb{N})$ **and** $(B \in \mathbb{N}_1)$.

Postcondition: q is the quotient and r is the remainder of the division of A by B.

In order to make the postcondition "usable" (this point will be developed later), it is reformulated on the basis of the definition of the Euclidian division by:

$(A = B \cdot q + r)$ **and** $(0 \leqslant r < B)$.

From this expression, we take as invariant:

$(A = B \cdot q + r)$ **and** $(0 \leqslant r)$

and as stopping condition: $r < B$. The actions related to the progression and the initialization remain to be expressed, as well as the termination expression. As to the progression, it suffices to increment q of 1 and to decrement r of the value of B to restore the invariant (which is possible since the stopping condition is not met, hence $r \geqslant B$). The invariant is established from the precondition by the assignments: 0 to q and A to r. Concerning the termination expression, it can be observed that the expression $(A - q \cdot B)$ is equal to A after the initialization takes place and diminishes of B whilst being positive after each step of the progression (it is possibly zero after the last iteration step). On the basis of the five components pointed out on the one hand, and the generic code on the other hand, the following program is deduced:

1. **constants**
2. $A \in \mathbb{N}$ **and** $A = \ldots$ **and** $B \in \mathbb{N}_1$ **and** $B = \ldots$
3. **variables**
4. $q \in 0 .. A$ **and** $r \in 0 .. B - 1$
5. **begin**
6.   /% *PRE:* $(A \in \mathbb{N})$ **and** $(B \in \mathbb{N}_1)$ %/
7. $q \leftarrow 0; r \leftarrow A;$
8.   **while not**$(r < B)$ **do**
9. $q \leftarrow q + 1; r \leftarrow r - B$
10.   **end while;**
11.   /% *POST:* $(A = q \cdot B + r)$ **and** $(r \geqslant 0)$ **and** $(r < B)$ %/
12.   **write**(*the quotient of the division of* , A, *by* , B, *is* , q, *and the remainder is* , r)
13. **end**

It can be noticed that when $A = 0$, the "while" loop is not entered (it is the only case indeed). Moreover, when A is a multiple of B, the remainder r is 0.

3.3   Useful techniques

In the previous example, the problem was fairly simple thus easily handled, but it is not always so. Quite often, the precondition and/or the postcondition must be reformulated, and this must be done so that the correctness of the program developed *in fine* is ensured. We review some techniques allowing for *legal* transformations.

3.3.1   Sequential composition

We have seen that the construction of a program based on a loop is done in decomposing the problem into five sub-problems. There is another type of decomposition frequently used, namely that based on the sequentiality rule. It stipulates that if $\{P\}$ $prog_1$ $\{R\}$ and $\{R\}$ $prog_2$ $\{S\}$ then $\{P\}$ $prog_1; prog_2$ $\{S\}$. In this rule, the symbol ";" denotes the sequentiality operator; $\{R\}$ is called an intermediary situation. This rule can also apply to state that if we look for a program specified by the pair (P, S), it suffices to find out an intermediary situation R and two programs $prog_1$ and $prog_2$ such that: i) $\{P\}$ $prog_1$ $\{R\}$, and ii) $\{R\}$ $prog_2$ $\{S\}$. The sequential composition of $prog_1$ and $prog_2$ is an answer to the initial problem specified by (P, S).

Let us illustrate this process with the following example where we want to know if the element of index K in the array T is its unique minimum. We want to develop the program specified by:

Precondition: (T is a constant (non modifiable) array of N integers) **and** $(N \geqslant 1)$ **and** (K constant) **and** $(K \in 1 .. N)$.

Postcondition: $infk = $ (T[K] is strictly less than all other elements in T).

We want to elaborate a solution involving a single loop and where the array T is not necessarily entirely read. A brief analysis shows that two cases may occur:

- the array T involves a single copy of its minimum which turns out to be T[K], which requires the complete scan of T,

- T[K] is not the minimum value of T (a value strictly less than T[K] is encountered and the scan of T can stop), or T[K] is indeed the minimum of T and another value (T[i], i ≠ K) equal to T[K] is encountered, and once again the scan of T can stop).

In order to facilitate the design of a solution, in a first time, the variable infk is ignored and the following new postcondition is taken into consideration:

Postcondition: i is the lowest index of the interval 1 .. N different from K such that $T[i] \leqslant T[K]$ if it does exist, $(N + 1)$ otherwise

which stands for an intermediary situation (in the sense of sequential composition); the following approach is thus envisaged:

1. We construct the loop (LOOP) specified by:

   Precondition: (T is a constant array of N integers) **and** $(N \geqslant 1)$ **and** (K constant) **and** $(K \in 1 .. N)$

   Postcondition: i is the index of 1 .. N different from K such that $T[i] \leqslant T[K]$ (if such an i exists), $(N + 1)$ otherwise.

2. We build the complementary part (COMPPART) specified by:

   Precondition: i is the index of 1 .. N different from K such that $T[i] \leqslant T[K]$ (if such an i exists), $(N + 1)$ otherwise.

   Postcondition: infk = (T[K] is less than all other elements in T).

   The code related to COMPPART consists in assigning the value of the relational expression $(i = N + 1)$ to infk. As to that of LOOP, it relies on the following five components:

   1. Invariant $(i \in 1 .. N)$ **and** $(\forall j \cdot (j \in ((1 .. i - 1) - \{K\}) \Rightarrow T[j] > T[K]))$

   2. Stopping condition $(i = N + 1)$ **or else** $((i \neq K)$ **and** $(T[i] \leqslant T[K]))$

   3. Progression $i \leftarrow i + 1$

   4. Initialization $i \leftarrow 1$

   5. Termination $N + 1 - i$

It is easy to check that: (i) the conjunction of the invariant and the stopping condition entails the postcondition, (ii) the progression preserves the invariant, (iii) the termination expression decreases at each step whilst being nonnegative, and (iv) the initialization establishes the invariant, in other words that the relationships 1, 2-1, 2-2 and 3 are met. Eventually, the following program is built:

1. **constants**
2. $N \in \mathbb{N}_1$ and N = ... and $T \in 1 .. N \rightarrow \mathbb{N}$ and T = [...] and $K \in 1 .. N$ and K =
   . . .
3. **variables**

4. $i \in 1 .. N + 1$ **and** $\mathrm{infk} \in \mathbb{B}$
5.   **begin**
6.   /% *first part:* LOOP %/
7.   /% *PRE:* (T *is a constant array of* N *integers*) **and** (N $\geqslant$ 1) **and** (K
        constant) **and** (K $\in 1 .. N$) %/
8. $i \leftarrow 1$;
9.   **while not**$((i = N + 1)$ **or else** $((i \neq K)$ **and** $(T[i] \leqslant T[K])))$ **do**
10. $i \leftarrow i + 1$
11.   **end while**;
12.   /% *POST:* i *is the index of* 1 .. N *different from* K *such that* $T[i] \leqslant T[K]$ (*if such
        an* i *exists*), (N + 1) *otherwise* %/
13.   /% *second part:* COMPPART %/
14. $\mathrm{infk} \leftarrow (i = N + 1)$;
15.   **if** infk **then**
16.   write(*the element whose index is,* K, *in the array,* T, *is its unique
            minimum*)
17.   **else**
18.   write(*the element whose index is,* K, *in the array,* T, *is not its unique
19.   minimum*)
20.   **end if**
21. **end**

3.3.2   Predicate strengthening and weakening

The notion of strengthening of the predicate pred is often understood in a logical sense, i.e. we consider the predicate pred' (strengthening pred) since it complies with the property: pred' $\Rightarrow$ pred. This approach must reveal to be of particular interest when facing the specification (P, Q) it is easier to build the program prog' such that {P} prog' {Q'} where Q' $\Rightarrow$ Q (especially if Q' is defined by the addition of a conjunct to Q), than the program prog such that {P} prog {Q}. See for example the problem 42, page 122.

Conversely, we can talk about predicate weakening when considering a predicate pred'' (which weakens pred) meeting the property: pred $\Rightarrow$ pred''. This approach is of interest when in the presence of the specification (P, Q), it is easier to build the program prog'' such that {P''} prog'' {Q} where P $\Rightarrow$ P'' than the program prog such that {P} prog {Q}. It is notably the case if P'' if obtained by removing a conjunct from P.

3.3.3   Strengthening by the introduction of programming variables

Here, we consider a second type of predicate strengthening in which the state space of the problem (the set of its variables) is enriched with (at least) one variable. For example, let us consider the array T[1 .. N] (N $\geqslant$ 1) of positive integers and the predicate P $\stackrel{\frown}{=}$ "s stands for the sum of the elements of T". An equivalent formulation of P is P' $\stackrel{\frown}{=}$ "(s stands for the sum of the first i elements of T) **and** (i $\in 1 .. N$) **and** (i = N)". A new variable (i) is introduced and we have a strengthening of P, the initial predicate. The principal interest of this approach lies in the fact that at least one conjunction is part of the new predicate which will be exploited to find out an invariant for the considered problem. See for example problem 31, page 111.

3.4 Heuristics for the discovery of invariants

Programming is a goal-driven activity. The search for an invariant does not escape this rule, and the three heuristics proposed hereafter are founded on the relationship between the postcondition and the invariant. We successively review three concurrent basic techniques. The first one, the breakup of the postcondition, assumes that the postcondition has the form of a conjunction. As this case is seldom, it is frequently necessary to proceed to a prior strengthening of the postcondition so as to display several conjuncts. The second one, the hypothesis of the work carried out partly, leads (by its very nature) to an implicit strengthening of the postcondition with the introduction of variables. The last heuristics is the strengthening of the postcondition following that of the invariant.

3.4.1 Breakup of the postcondition

Due to the property associated with relationship A (see page 94), when the postcondition is expressed as a conjunction, it may be convenient to identify one of the conjuncts as the invariant and the other one to the stopping condition. The method applies as well when the postcondition involves *several* conjunctions. On the one hand, one (or several) conjunct(s) will form the invariant, on the other hand the stopping condition will be made with the remaining conjunct(s), which is formalized as follows:

Postcondition: B_1 and B_2 and ... and B_n
Stopping condition: B_i and ... and B_j
Invariant: B_1 and B_2 and ... and B_{i-1} and B_{j+1} and ... and B_n

There is no systematic way for breaking up the postcondition. However, the following suggestions can be useful:

- It is desirable that the stopping condition is syntactically expressed in a usual programming language, so that its negation plays the role of a loop condition. This excludes predicates with quantifiers such as $\forall j \cdot (j \in \cdots \Rightarrow \cdots)$.

- It is preferable that the invariant is easy to establish from the precondition. Hence, once the choice of the invariant made, the difficulty to establish it (the initialization phase) must be assessed.

- All the variables of the postcondition must appear in the invariant (in other words, the stopping condition must not contain "orphan" variables).

The approach is illustrated with the following example, where we look for the first zero in an array of numbers. We want to develop the program specified by:

Precondition: (T is a constant array of N integers) **and** (there is at least one zero in T).

Postcondition: The variable i indicates the zero of T whose index is the lowest (the "leftmost" zero).

Since there is at least one zero in T, it can be noted that $N \geqslant 1$. As this algorithm demands the total or partial scan of the array, we will build an iteration. Moreover, the postcondition is not under conjunctive form and it must be strengthened by replacing an *expression* exp (here N) by a *variable* v (here i) and adding the conjunct $(v = \exp)$. In the remainder, this type of transformation is called "transformation under constructive form". We reformulate the initial postcondition in:

Postcondition: $(i \in 1 .. N)$ **and** $(T[1 .. i - 1]$ contains no zero) **and** $(T[i] = 0)$.

It is then possible to breakup the postcondition and to apply the suggestions made above to divide it into two parts, the first one being the invariant and the second one the stopping condition:

1. Invariant The first two conjuncts are easy to establish and thus taken for the invariant:

$(i \in 1 .. N)$ **and** $(T[1 .. i - 1)$ contains no zero)

which can be graphically illustrated by:

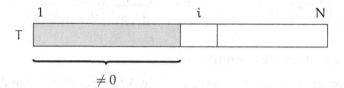

The conjunct $(T[i] = 0)$ has been discarded. It is indeed a predicate which is difficult to establish since it demands the localization of a zero!

2. Stopping condition The discarded conjunct is chosen, i.e. $T[i] = 0$. It can be noticed that this predicate involves no quantifier which makes it possible to integrate its negation into the loop condition.

3. Progression It is specified by:

Precondition: $(i \in 1..N)$ **and** $(T[1..i-1]$ contains no zero) **and not** $(T[i] = 0)$

PROGRESSION

Postcondition: $(i \in 1 .. N)$ **and** $(T[1 .. i - 1]$ contains no zero).

A possible idea for the progression is to move i one position to the right by the assignment: $i \leftarrow i + 1$. The invariant is fulfilled by the new situation since there is no zero in $T[1..i-1]$ and that there is necessarily one after $T[i-1]$ (according to the precondition) hence $i \leqslant N$ and $i \in 1 .. N$.

4. Initialization It is specified by:

Precondition: $(T$ is a constant array of N integers) **and** (there is at least one zero in the array T)

INITIALIZATION

Postcondition: $(i \in 1 .. N)$ **and** $(T[0 .. i - 1]$ contains no zero).

Moving from the precondition to the invariant, means that the following situation is reached:

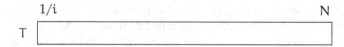

where the invariant is fulfilled since, when $i = 1$, it is instantiated as: $(1 \in 1 .. N)$ **and** $(T[1 .. 0]$ contains no zero). This can be obtained by the assignment: $i \leftarrow 1$.

5. Termination The expression $(N - i)$ is suitable, since it remains nonnegative and it diminishes at each step of the progression.

Eventually, we have built the following program:

1. **constants**
2. $N \in \mathbb{N}_1$ **and** $T \in 1 .. N \rightarrow \mathbb{N}$ **and** $T = [\ldots]$
3. **variables**
4. $i \in 1 .. N$
5. **begin**
6.   /% *PRE:* (T *is a constant array of* N *integers*) **and** (*there is at least one zero in the array* T) %/
7. $i \leftarrow 1;$
8.   **while not**$(T[i] = 0)$ **do**
9. $i \leftarrow i + 1$
10.   **end while;**
11.   /% *POST:* $(i \in 1 .. N)$ **and** $(T[1 .. i - 1]$ *contains no zero*) **and** $(T[i] = 0)$ %/
12.   **write**(*the index of the leftmost zero in* , T, *is* , i)
13. **end**

In the best case, this algorithm is in $\Theta(1)$ and at worst it is in $\Theta(N)$ in terms of comparisons.

In section 3.7, several problems are proposed in which the initial postcondition is not expressed in a conjunctive form. In such a situation that occurs very frequently in practice, the postcondition must first be turned into a "constructive" form, i.e. expressed as a conjunction which is to be broken up.

3.4.2   Hypothesis of the work carried out partly

One of the characteristics of the invariant is that it is a property which holds at each step of the loop. It is thus legitimate to exploit this specificity when looking for an invariant. Assuming that a part of the work is already done, the question of interest is:

"What situation are we in?"

whose answer is often the expected invariant.

This technique is illustrated by the "classical" simple example called "the Monaco flag", whose statement is the following. The initial situation is the array $T[1 .. N]$ $(N \geqslant 0)$ whose elements are either white or red and constitute the constant bag B. The final situation is the array forming the same bag B, inside which white (respectively red) elements are on the left (respectively right) hand side. It is imposed to go from the initial situation to the final one using a single loop, which scans the array from left to right. Changes in the array T are done only by exchanges between two elements of index i and j (*Exchange*(i, j)), which ensures the preservation of the initial values of the bag B.

We are searching for an invariant assuming that the work is carried out partly and that the configuration depicted in figure 3.2 is reached:

Formally, this configuration is defined by the formula:

$(\forall u \cdot (u \in 1 .. i - 1 \Rightarrow T[u] = \text{White}))$ **and** $(1 \leqslant i \leqslant k + 1 \leqslant N + 1)$ **and**
$(\forall u \cdot (u \in k + 1 .. N \Rightarrow T[u] = \text{Red}))$

This expression covers the following cases:

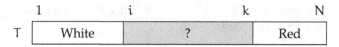

Fig. 3.2 – Situation in which the work is carried out partly.

- The initial situation where the content of T is unknown (neither white, nor red element localized), with $i = 1$ and $k = N$. As a matter of fact, the above formula which thus writes:

$$(\forall u \cdot (u \in 1 \mathinner{.\,.} 0 \Rightarrow T[u] = White)) \textbf{ and } (1 \leqslant 1 \leqslant N + 1 \leqslant N + 1) \textbf{ and }$$
$$(\forall u \cdot (u \in N + 1 \mathinner{.\,.} N \Rightarrow T[u] = Red))$$

  is evaluated to **true** and it expresses that nothing is known about each of the elements of T,

- The final situation where all elements are localized (white elements on the left, red ones on the right), with $k = i - 1$,

- A situation where there is at least one red element and no white one, with $i = 1$ and $0 \leqslant k < N$,

- A situation where there is at least one white element and no red one, with $1 < i \leqslant N+1$ and $k = N$,

- The case where T is empty ($N = 0$).

It reveals to be an invariant for the problem to solve.

From the starting situation (precondition) and the arrival situation (postcondition), we now define the five elements of the loop.

1. Invariant We take the expression associated with figure 3.2, namely:

$$(\forall u \cdot (u \in 1 \mathinner{.\,.} i - 1 \Rightarrow T[u] = White)) \textbf{ and } (1 \leqslant i \leqslant k + 1 \leqslant N + 1) \textbf{ and }$$
$$(\forall u \cdot (u \in k + 1 \mathinner{.\,.} N \Rightarrow T[u] = Red)).$$

2. Stopping condition The loop terminates when $k = i - 1$. It has been pointed out (see item 3.4.2) that then the conjunction of the invariant and the stopping condition entails the postcondition.

3. Progression The action to undertake in the progression depends on the color of $T[i]$. If $T[i]$ is white, i is incremented by 1 (which extends the zone containing white elements) and if $T[i]$ is red, it is exchanged with $T[k]$ and k is decremented by 1 (which enlarges the zone involving red elements).

4. Initialization Operations related to the initialization have been evoked in item 3.4.2, and they come down to two assignments: $i \leftarrow 1$ and $k \leftarrow N$.

5. Termination The expression $(k - i + 1)$ is suitable since it is equal to N after initialization, it decreases by 1 at each iteration step and its value is zero when the stopping condition is met.

Finally, we have the program hereafter:

1. **constants**
2. $N \in \mathbb{N}$ and $N = \ldots$ and $T \in 1 .. N \rightarrow \{White, Red\}$ and $T = [\ldots]$
3. **variables**
4. $i \in 1 .. N$ and $k \in 1 .. N$
5. **begin**
6.   /% *PRE:* $T[1 .. N]$ *is an array whose elements are either white, or red* %/
7. $i \leftarrow 1; k \leftarrow N$;
8.   **while** $k \neq i - 1$ **do**
9.   **if** $T[i] = White$ **then**
10. $i \leftarrow i + 1$
11.   **else**
12.   *Exchange*$(i, k); k \leftarrow k - 1$
13.   **end if**
14.   **end while**;
15.   /% *POST: white (respectively red) elements in* T *are in the left (respectively right) part of* T %/
16.   **write**(T)
17. **end**

This algorithm is in $\Theta(N)$ comparisons (N comparisons are about values of T and N for the control of the loop). It demands as many exchanges as there are red elements (whatever their initial position); hence, the algorithm is in $\mathcal{O}(N)$ exchanges.

As in most of problems, the invariant is not unique. The interested reader is invited to elaborate about the invariant which derives from the situation of the work carried out partly given in figure 3.3.

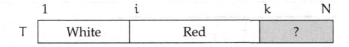

Fig. 3.3 – Another situation related to the hypothesis of the work carried out partly.

3.4.3 Strengthening the invariant

We have seen that the conjunction of the invariant P and the stopping condition B must entail the postcondition R:

$$(P \textbf{ and } B) \Rightarrow R.$$

It has been suggested to reformulate the postcondition by introducing one (or several) variable(s) in order to make a conjunction appear. In doing so, we have strengthened the initial postcondition by an auxiliary postcondition which *entails* it. However, it may happen that, for necessity reasons or by opportunity, the strengthening of the postcondition appears only during the development phase. In such cases, the strengthening of the postcondition is often expressed *indirectly* by the strengthening of the invariant. Thus, an additional conjunct P' is associated with the "natural" invariant so as to either ensure the progression, or express a stopping condition. More formally, we have:

$(P \textbf{ and } P' \textbf{ and } B) \Rightarrow (P \textbf{ and } B)$

$\Rightarrow$ one has either $(P \textbf{ and } B) = R$, or at worst $(P \textbf{ and } B) \Rightarrow R$

$(P \textbf{ and } P' \textbf{ and } B) \Rightarrow R.$

The approach adopted is made up of four parts:

1. The loop is first developed on the basis of the "natural" invariant.

2. It is observed that the value of an expression is missing to pursue the construction of the loop.

3. This value is assumed to be available (thanks to the introduction of a variable). This leads to add a new conjunct to the preexisting invariant.

4. The construction of the loop is resumed on the basis of the new invariant.

This approach is now illustrated to compute the sum of the elements located "on the left" of the maximum value (assumed to be unique) of an array. We want to build the program made up of a single loop and specified by:

Precondition: (T is a constant injective (all values in T are distinct) array of N integers) **and** ($N \geqslant 1$).

Postcondition: m is the position of the maximum in T and s is the sum of the elements $T[1 .. m-1]$.

The position of the maximum in $T[1 .. N]$ being m, the situation at the end of the program is expected to be the following:

$$T[m] = \max_{j \in 1..N} (T[j])$$

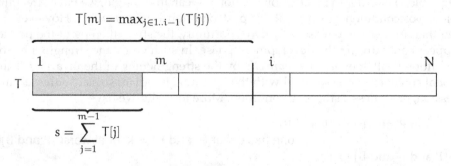

More formally, making the domain of the variables explicit, the postcondition is rewritten:

$$(m \in 1..N) \textbf{ and } (T[m] = \max_{j \in 1..N}(T[j])) \textbf{ and } (s \in \mathbb{Z}) \textbf{ and } \left(s = \sum_{j=1}^{m-1} T[j] \right).$$

First attempt

The postcondition is strengthened so as to obtain a conjunction on the basis of the following situation:

$$T[m] = \max_{j \in 1..i-1}(T[j])$$

First, let us examine the variation domain of variables i, m and s. So that m takes a value, the array $T[1..i-1]$ must be nonempty, which entails that i is not equal to 1. Hence, i is varying in the interval $2..N+1$, whereas $m \in 1..i-1$ and $s \in \mathbb{Z}$. Adding this information, we get:

Postcondition (version stemming from the strengthening of the previous postcondition):
$$(i \in 2..N+1) \textbf{ and } (m \in 1..i-1) \textbf{ and } (T[m] = \max_{j \in 1..i-1}(T[j])) \textbf{ and } (s \in \mathbb{Z}) \textbf{ and } (s = \sum_{j=1}^{m-1} T[j]) \textbf{ and } (i = N+1).$$

This postcondition opens to a first breakup attempt.

1. Invariant The first five conjuncts are easy to establish and they constitute the invariant:
$$(i \in 2..N+1) \textbf{ and } (m \in 1..i-1) \textbf{ and } (T[m] = \max_{j \in 1..i-1}(T[j])) \textbf{ and }$$
$$(s \in \mathbb{Z}) \textbf{ and } \left(s = \sum_{j=1}^{m-1} T[j] \right).$$

2. Stopping condition We keep the discarded conjunct: $i = N+1$.

3. Progression How to move from a situation where the invariant holds, as well as $\textbf{not}(i = N+1)$, to a situation where the invariant still holds, while advancing towards the postcondition of the statement? Let us have a look at $T[i]$. If i is not the position of the maximum of $T[1..i]$ there is nothing else to do but increment i (by 1). Otherwise, a solution is to compute (using a loop) and store (in s) the sum of the elements of $T[1..i-1]$. It is easy to guess that some of the sums will be calculated twice or more. the idea is to take advantage of the calculations already performed, and to this end, to consider that this sum is available in the variable v. Thus, the update of s demands no loop, s takes the value of v. Making this assumption is a strengthening of the invariant by the conjunct $v = \sum_{j=1}^{i-1} T[j]$. It is now necessary to rebuild the loop on the basis of the new invariant.

Second attempt

The invariant (and indirectly the postcondition) is strengthened by the addition of the conjunct $v = \sum_{j=1}^{i-1} T[j]$.

1. Invariant It becomes:
$$(i \in 2..N+1) \textbf{ and } (m \in 1..i-1) \textbf{ and } (T[m] = \max_{j \in 1..i-1}(T[j])) \textbf{ and }$$
$$(s \in \mathbb{Z}) \textbf{ and } \left(s = \sum_{j=1}^{m-1} T[j] \right) \textbf{ and } (v \in \mathbb{Z}) \textbf{ and } \left(v = \sum_{j=1}^{i-1} T[j] \right)$$

graphically:

$$(T[m] = \max_{j \in 1..i-1}(T[j])) \text{ and } \left(v = \sum_{j=1}^{i-1} T[j]\right)$$

$$s = \sum_{j=1}^{m-1} T[j]$$

2. Stopping condition We keep the same stopping condition: $i = N + 1$.

3. Progression The progression is specified by:

Precondition: $(i \in 2..N+1)$ **and** $(m \in 1..i-1)$ **and** $(T[m] = \max_{j \in 1..i-1}(T[j]))$ **and** $(s \in \mathbb{Z})$ **and** $(s = \sum_{j=1}^{m-1} T[j])$ **and** $(v \in \mathbb{Z})$ **and** $(v = \sum_{j=1}^{i-1} T[j])$ **and** **not**$(i = N+1)$

PROGRESSION

Postcondition: $(i \in 2..N+1)$ **and** $(m \in 1..i-1)$ **and** $(T[m] = \max_{j \in 1..i-1}(T[j]))$ **and** $(s \in \mathbb{Z})$ **and** $(s = \sum_{j=1}^{m-1} T[j])$ **and** $(v \in \mathbb{Z})$ **and** $(v = \sum_{j=1}^{i-1} T[j])$.

If i is the position of the new maximum in $T[1..i]$, s takes the value of v. The variables m and v are then updated, $T[i]$ is added to v and i is incremented by 1.

4. Initialization The initialization is specified by:

Precondition: $(T$ is a constant injective array of N integers$)$ **and** $(N \geqslant 1)$.

INITIALIZATION

Postcondition: $(i \in 2..N+1)$ **and** $(m \in 1..i-1)$ **and** $(T[m] = \max_{j \in 1..i-1}(T[j]))$ **and** $(s \in \mathbb{Z})$ **and** $(s = \sum_{j=1}^{m-1} T[j])$ **and** $(v \in \mathbb{Z})$ **and** $(v = \sum_{j=1}^{i-1} T[j])$.

The value 2 is assigned to i, which enforces other variables to comply with the following constraints:

$$(s = T[1]) \text{ and } (v = T[1]) \text{ and } (m = 1).$$

4. Termination The variable i is incremented at each step of the progression. The expression $(N + 1 - i)$ is suited to ensure the termination.

Eventually, the following program is built:

```
1. constants
2.    N ∈ ℕ₁ and N = ... and T ∈ 1..N → ℤ and T = [...]
3. variables
4.    i ∈ 1..N+1 and m ∈ 1..N and v ∈ ℤ and s ∈ ℤ
5. begin
6.    /% PRE: T is a constant injective array of N integers) and (N ⩾ 1)) %/
7.    i ← 2; s ← T[1]; v ← T[1]; m ← 1;
8.    while not(i = N+1) do
```

9.   if $T[i] > T[m]$ **then**

10. $s \leftarrow v; m \leftarrow i$

11.   **end if**;

12. $v \leftarrow v + T[i]; i \leftarrow i + 1$

13.   **end while**;

14.   /% POST: *m is the position of the maximum in* T *and s is the sum of the elements* $T[1 .. m-1]$ %/

15.   **write**(*the sum of the elements before that of index*, m, *is* , s)

16. **end**

This solution demands at worst and at best N iterations and $(2N + 1)$ comparisons.

3.5   About bounded linear search

Linear search is a class of algorithms looking for the smallest of the elements of a nonempty set fulfilling a predicate $P(i)$.

Bounded linear search is close to linear search, except that the set of solutions can be empty. Generally, the result returned in case of failure is either a conventional value outside the definition domain of P, or a Boolean.

3.5.1   An example

We want to know whether the sum of the elements of the constant array $T[1 .. N]$ is greater than a given value S, or not.

We want to build the program specified by:

Precondition: (T is an array of N natural numbers) **and** $(N \geqslant 0)$ **and** (S constant) **and** $(S \in \mathbb{N}_1)$.

Postcondition: $sgs = (\sum_{j=1}^{N} T[j] > S)$.

The postcondition is not in a constructive form, hence the expression $(N + 1)$ is replaced by the variable i and the postcondition becomes:

Postcondition: $(i \in 1 .. N + 1)$ **and** $(sgs = (\sum_{j=1}^{i-1} T[j] > S))$ **and** $(i = N + 1)$.

The presence of a quantification suggests that its evaluation as such will raise a difficulty and we proceed to a second strengthening with the introduction of the variable ps calculating the partial sum of the first $(i - 1)$ elements of T, hence:

Postcondition: $(i \in 1 .. N + 1)$ **and** $(ps = \sum_{j=1}^{i-1} T[j])$ **and** $(sgs = (ps > S))$ **and** $(i = N + 1)$.

Now, the development of the algorithm can begin.

1. Invariant The first three conjuncts are easy to establish and they serve for the invariant:

$$(i \in 1 .. N + 1) \text{ and } \left(ps = \sum_{j=1}^{i-1} T[j] \right) \text{ and } (sgs = (ps > S)).$$

2. Stopping condition We take the discarded conjunct: $(i = N + 1)$.

3. Progression The progression is specified by:

$(i \in 1 .. N + 1)$ **and** $(ps = \sum_{j=1}^{i-1} T[j])$ **and** $(sgs = (ps > S))$ **and** **not**$(i = N + 1)$

PROGRESSION

$(i \in 1 .. N + 1)$ **and** $(ps = \sum_{j=1}^{i-1} T[j])$ **and** $(sgs = (ps > S))$.

A solution to this specification is:

      1. $ps \leftarrow ps + T[i]$;
      2. $sgs \leftarrow sgs$ **or** $(ps > S)$;
      3. $i \leftarrow i + 1$

4. Initialization The initialization is specified by:

Precondition: (T is an array of N natural numbers) **and** $(N \geqslant 0)$ **and** (S constant) **and** $(S \in \mathbb{N}_1)$

INITIALIZATION

Postcondition: $(i \in 1 .. N + 1)$ **and** $(ps = \sum_{j=1}^{i-1} T[j])$ **and** $(sgs = (ps > S))$.

The three assignments 1 to i, 0 to ps and **false** to sgs answers this specification.

5. Termination $(N + 1 - i)$ is a suitable termination expression.

We can observe that the algorithm could stop as soon as sgs turns to **true**, which could diminish the number of iterations, thus complexity at worst. This remark leads to the modification of both the stopping condition and the progression in the preceding development. The stopping condition is modified accordingly and a new loop is built.

1. Invariant It remains unchanged.

2. Stopping condition We take: $(i = N + 1)$ **or** sgs.

3. Progression The second assignment of the progression is $(sgs$ **or** $(ps > S))$, whose evaluation is done in the context of the precondition of the progression (entailing that sgs is **false**), hence:

    sgs **or** $(ps > S)$

$\Leftrightarrow$ **not**(sgs) and propositional calculus

    $ps > S$

4. Initialization It remains unchanged.

5. Termination It is unchanged.

The following program is obtained:

    1. **constants**
    2. $N \in \mathbb{N}$ **and** $N = \ldots$ **and** $T \in 1 .. N \rightarrow \mathbb{N}$ **and** $T = [\ldots]$ **and** $S \in \mathbb{N}_1$ **and** $S = \ldots$
    3. **variables**
    4. $i \in 1 .. N + 1$ **and** $sgs \in \mathbb{B}$ **and** $ps \in \mathbb{N}$
    5. **begin**
    6.   /% PRE: (T is an array of N natural numbers) **and** $(N \geqslant 0)$ **and** (S constant) **and** $(S \in \mathbb{N}_1)$ %/
    7. $i \leftarrow 1$; $sgs \leftarrow$ **false**; $ps \leftarrow 0$;

8.   **while not**$((i = N + 1)$ **or** sgs$)$ **do**
9.   ps $\leftarrow$ ps $+ T[i]$; sgs $\leftarrow (ps > S)$; $i \leftarrow i + 1$
10.   **end while**;

11.   /% *POST*: sgs $= \left(\sum\limits_{j=1}^{N} T[j] > S \right)$ %/

12.   **write**(sgs)
13. **end**

The complexity of this algorithm is in $\mathcal{O}(N)$ comparisons.

3.5.2 Special case and related pattern

Problems resembling the previous one occur frequently and the identification of a programming pattern for bounded linear search is convenient. It provides the ability of instantiation rather than a development *ex nihilo*.

We consider the search for the first element (whatever the structure used, set, bag, array, etc.) among N for which a given property P is true; j contains the identity of this element or $(N+1)$ if it does not exist. In addition, we assume that property P, denoted LP(j), is "local" to element j, in the sense that its evaluation does not depend on the elements examined before it. Last, it may happen that, in contrast to the previous example, the property LP cannot be evaluated when $j = N + 1$. Consequently, the stopping condition uses a "short-circuiting" disjunction. The resulting pattern, used in problems 34, page 113, and 41, page 121, is the following:

1. **constants**
2. $N \in \mathbb{N}$ **and** $N = \ldots$
3. **variables**
4. $j \in 1 .. N + 1$ **and** $LP \in \mathbb{B}$ **and** $\ldots$
5. **begin**
6.   /% *PRE*: $\ldots$ %/
7. $j \leftarrow 1; \ldots$
8.   **invariant**
9. $\ldots$
10.   **termination**
11. $N + 1 - j$
12.   **while not**$((j = N + 1)$ **or else** LP$)$ **do**
13. $j \leftarrow j + 1$
14.   **end loop**;
15.   /% *POST*: $\ldots$ %/
16.   **if** $j = N + 1$ **then**
17.   **write**(*no element* $\ldots$)
18.   **else**
19.   **write**(*element*, j, $\ldots$)
20.   **end if**
21. **end**

3.6   Some key points to develop a loop

Building a loop starts with the search for an invariant which plays a central role for the design of the other components of the loop: initialization, stopping condition, progression and termination. The notion of invariant specifies the relationships between the variables of the loop. There is no recipe ensuring that an invariant will be found out, but we recommend to "derive" it from the postcondition of the program to build, which expresses the situation expected at the end of the execution of the loop. The conjunction of the invariant and the stopping condition *must* logically entail the postcondition. Therefore, a heuristics for the discovery of an invariant consists in splitting the postcondition so as to identify an invariant on the one hand and a stopping condition on the other hand. The postcondition may be strengthened by the introduction of new variables in order to facilitate such a breakup. Insofar as the invariant is a property which holds at each step of the loop, it can be discovered assuming that the work is carried out partly in formalizing the situation attained.

As to the precondition of the loop, it specifies the situation before the beginning of the loop. The role of the initialization is to establish the invariant, thus to move from precondition to invariant. The progression must preserve the invariant whilst making "progress" in the resolution of the problem. Last to ensure that the loop stops, a nonnegative integer expression is connected with the evolution of the loop, which must decrease at each step.

3.7   Problems

Problem 29.   White and red beans $\overset{\circ}{\circ}$ •

> *This famous problem by D. Gries [15] highlights the fact that it is possible to reason about a given algorithm (or program) by identifying its invariant.*

A can contains a number W of white beans and R of red beans ($W + R \geq 1$). We are provided with a reserve of red beans which suffices to perform the following operation while it is possible:

> Two beans are randomly taken from the can
> **if** they have the same color **then**
>   they are thrown away and one red bean is put back into the can
> **else**
>   the red bean is thrown away and the white bean is put back into the can
> **end if**

29 - Q 1   **Question 1.**   Why does this process stop?

29 - Q 2   **Question 2.**   What can be said about the color of the last bean remaining in the can?

The solution is on page 127.

Problem 30. From a coder's dustbin 8 •

> *This problem highlights the importance of a safe construction.*

We have found the following text in a dustbin of a computer science school:

Precondition: (T is a constant array of N natural numbers) **and** $(N \geqslant 1)$.

Postcondition: The variable sup contains the highest value in T.

1. Invariant: $(i \in 1 .. N)$ **and** $(\forall j \cdot (j \in 1 .. i - 1 \Rightarrow T[j] \leqslant sup))$.

2. Stopping condition: $(i = N)$.

3. Progression:
1. **if** $T[i] > sup$ **then**
2. $\quad sup \leftarrow T[i]$
3. **end if**;
4. $i \leftarrow i + 1$

4. Initialization: $i \leftarrow 2; sup \leftarrow T[1]$

5. Termination: $(N + 1 - i)$

Question 1. Which errors originate the rejection? 30 - Q 1

Question 2. Give a safe version. 30 - Q 2

The solution is on page 127.

Problem 31. Summing up the elements of an array ○ •

> *This problem is a simple application of the postcondition splitting principle in order to find out an invariant, once it is appropriately reformulated to be under constructive form.*

Question 1. Build the program specified by: 31 - Q 1
    Precondition: (T is a constant array of N natural numbers) **and** $(N \geqslant 0)$.
    Postcondition: s stands for the sum of the N elements of T.

Question 2. What is its time complexity in terms of additions? 31 - Q 2
The solution is on page 127.

Problem 32. Searching in a bidimensional array 8 •

> *This problem is dedicated to the "basic" problem of search of a value in a bidimensional array. A "natural" solution makes use of two loops, but it is shown that it is easy and elegant to proceed with a single one. The proposed approach can be easily extended to a higher number of dimensions. We will use the hypothesis of the work carried out partly.*

Let us consider the following specification:

Precondition: (T is a constant array of natural numbers with R rows and C columns) **and** (R > 0) **and** (C > 0) **and** (V is a natural number present in T).

Postcondition: (i, j) stands for an occurrence of V in T, i.e. T[i, j] = V.

32 - Q 1   **Question 1.**   Propose the elements of a single loop answering this specification, on the basis of the hypothesis of the work carried out partly.

32 - Q 2   **Question 2.**   Write the corresponding program and give its complexity in terms of comparisons.

Remark

We invite the reader to build the equivalent program made of two loops so as to compare it with the previous one, especially regarding the ease of design.
The solution is on page 129.

Problem 33.   Sorting by straight selection   ○ **:**

A sort program is now presented. Although it is not among "efficient" sorts, it is interesting from a pedagogic point of view. Moreover, in contrast to the previous problem, it relies on two nested loops according to an approach both simple and progressive.

We want to develop the program specified by:

Precondition: (T is an array of N natural numbers) **and** (S is the constant bag of the values in T) **and** (N ⩾ 1).

Postcondition: (T is sorted in ascending order) **and** (S is the bag of the values in T).

The second conjunct of the postcondition expresses that the content of T does not change but possibly the order of its elements. The exclusive use of the procedure *Exchange*(i, j) previously introduced (see section 3.4.2, page 101) guarantees the compliance with this property. In this way, this conjunct can be definitely dropped.
The postcondition is not under constructive form and it must be strengthened:

Postcondition: (i ∈ 1 .. N + 1) **and** (T[1 .. i − 1] is sorted) **and** (i = N + 1).

Assuming that the work is carried out partly, we are in the situation represented hereafter:

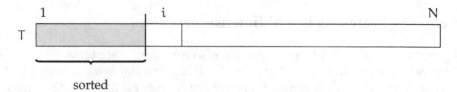

sorted

We can already glimpse that the progression will aim at doing so that $T[1 .. i]$ is sorted. We have two possible choices: i) to insert $T[i]$ in $T[1 .. i]$ at the right place, and ii) to keep $T[1 .. i-1]$ unchanged assuming that all the values in $T[i .. N]$ are greater than (or equal to) those of $T[1 .. i-1]$. The first option corresponds to the *sort by insertion* and we choose the second one, called *sort by selection*, because it requires to *select* the smallest value in $T[i .. N]$.

Question 1.   Give the postcondition associated with this option, then specify the components of the resulting loop, skipping the specification of the part related to the identification of the position m of the minimum in $T[i .. N]$.   33 - Q 1

Question 2.   We have now to handle the loop corresponding to the identification of the position m of the minimum in $T[i .. N]$. This fragment of program is specified by: 33 - Q 2

> **Precondition:** (i constant) **and** ($i \in 1 .. N$) **and** ($T[i .. N]$ is a nonempty array of natural numbers)
>
> IDENTIFICATION OF THE POSITION m OF THE MINIMUM IN $T[i .. N]$
>
> **Postcondition:** ($m \in i .. N$) **and** ($T[m] = \min_{j \in i..N}(T[j])$).

The array $T[i .. N]$ is nonempty since in the context of execution of this loop, we have: $i \in 1 .. N+1$ and $i \neq N+1$. So, we are sure to find a minimum value in $T[i .. N]$. The postcondition can be schematized by:

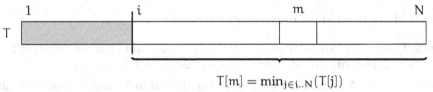

$$T[m] = \min_{j \in i..N}(T[j])$$

Propose a strengthening of this postcondition in order to put it under constructive form by the introduction of the variable k in the quantification of the minimum in connection with N.

Question 3.   Develop the corresponding loop.   33 - Q 3

Question 4.   Write the program achieving the sort by selection of the array $T[1 .. N]$.   33 - Q 4

Question 5.   What is its complexity in terms of number of exchanges?   33 - Q 5

The solution is on page 131.

Problem 34. Was it a car or a cat I saw   o •

> *The use of the pattern proposed for bounded linear search (see section 3.5, page 107) is illustrated through a simple example.*

Let $T[1 .. N]$ ($N \geqslant 0$) be a given character string (a word). T is a palindrome if the word (or sentence, spaces being ignored) it stands for, writes the same way from left to right and conversely. That is, T is the mirror string of itself.

34 - Q 1   **Question** 1.   Prove that, when T represents a palindrome, the following property holds:

$$\forall j \cdot ((1 \leqslant j \leqslant N) \Rightarrow (T[j] = T[N + 1 - j])).$$

34 - Q 2   **Question** 2.   Indicate why and how this problem can be solved with an adaption of the pattern featured in section 3.5.2, page 109.

34 - Q 3   **Question** 3.   Write the program which decides whether T stands or not for a palindrome.

34 - Q 4   **Question** 4.   Give its complexity in terms of evaluated conditions.

The solution is on page 133.

Problem 35. The Dutch national flag (variant)   8 :

> *This problem illustrates the use of the hypothesis of the work carried out partly. The Dutch flag is a classical problem, so named by its author, E.W. Dijkstra, because the original version is aimed at replenishing the colors of the flag of his country. The version dealt with here is slightly different since natural numbers are managed instead of colors. This algorithm is at the heart of quicksort which makes one of its major interests.*

We would like to build the program specified by:

Precondition: (T is an array of N natural numbers) **and** (S is the constant bag of the values contained in T) **and** (N $\geqslant$ 1) **and** (V = T[1]).

Postcondition: (S is the bag of the values contained in T) **and** (T is made of three parts, on the left values less than V, on the right values greater than V and in the middle all occurrences of V).

Roughly speaking, the postcondition appears as shown below (the middle zone is not empty since it contains at least one copy of V):

1		p	q	N	
< V		= V	> V		q > p

All the modifications of T will be done through exchanges (procedure *Exchange*(i, j) where i and j refer to indexes of elements of T). Therefore, as in problem 33 page 112, the first conjunct of the postcondition can be omitted from now on. The complexity of the solution(s) is evaluated in terms of calls to procedure *Exchange*. First, let us formalize the postcondition:

Postcondition (formalized version):
$\exists (p, q) \cdot ((p \in 1 .. N) \textbf{ and } (q \in p + 1 .. N + 1) \textbf{ and } (\forall j \cdot (j \in 1 .. p - 1 \Rightarrow T[j] < V)) \textbf{ and }$
$(\forall j \cdot (j \in p .. q - 1 \Rightarrow T[j] = V)) \textbf{ and } (\forall j \cdot (j \in q .. N \Rightarrow T[j] > V))$

This version of the postcondition cannot be used as such for a breakup. We will transform it (strengthen): we replace the variables of existential quantification p and q by the programming variables b and w (see section 3.3.3, page 98), hence:

Postcondition (second version):
$(b \in 1 .. N)$ **and** $(w \in b + 1 .. N + 1)$ **and** $(\forall j \cdot (j \in 1 .. b - 1 \Rightarrow T[j] < V))$ **and**
$(\forall j \cdot (j \in b .. w - 1 \Rightarrow T[j] = V))$ **and** $(\forall j \cdot (j \in w .. N \Rightarrow T[j] > V)).$

At this stage, there is no evidence for a breakup and we envisage the introduction of the variable r in association with one of the identifiers b, w and N do that a new conjunct appears.

Question 1. Give the expression of the postcondition resulting from the association of r with w, then the invariant for which a graphical representation is asked. 35 - Q 1

Question 2. Pursue the construction of the loop while identifying the cases where no exchange is needed and so that at most one exchange occurs for each step of the progression. 35 - Q 2

Question 3. Write the program stemming from this construction and specify its complexity in terms of exchanges. 35 - Q 3

The solution is on page 134.

Problem 36. 7s and 23s

> *This problem shows another example of use of the hypothesis of the work carried out partly. Here, the stopping condition is worthy of a special attention.*

Let $T[1 .. N]$ be an array of integers, with $N \geqslant 0$. We want to design a program performing a permutation of the values of T so that all 7s are located before the 23s. The final content of T must differ from the initial configuration only in the position of values 7 and 23. Like in the previous problem, the procedure $Exchange(i, j)$ is assumed to be available.

Question 1. Complement the schema hereafter in order to point out an invariant on the basis of the hypothesis of the work carried out partly. 36 - Q 1

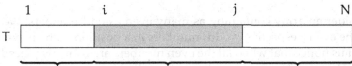

Question 2. What can be observed when $i = j$? Can we take this predicate as the stopping condition? 36 - Q 2

Question 3. Provide the three other components of the loop. 36 - Q 3

Question 4. Deduce the complexity of the associated program, in terms of both comparisons and exchanges. 36 - Q 4

The solution is on page 136.

Problem 37. The Mth zero ∘ :

> *In this problem, we illustrate a situation where a strengthening of the postcondition is made by the introduction of variables in the presence of a quantifier (count).*

We wish to build the program specified by:

Precondition: (M constant) **and** ($M \in \mathbb{N}_1$) **and** (T is a constant array of N integers) **and** (T contains at least M zeros).

Postcondition: i is the position of the Mth zero in T.

First of all, let us notice that the precondition entails that $N \geqslant M$. The quantifier # denotes the count quantifier. Hence:

$$\#j \cdot ((j \in 1 .. N) \text{ and } (T[j] = 0))$$

counts the number of zeros present in T. Then, the postcondition is formalized in this way:

Postcondition: $(i \in 1 .. N)$ **and** $(\#j \cdot ((j \in 1 .. i - 1) \text{ and } (T[j] = 0)) = M - 1)$ **and** $(T[i] = 0)$.

Although this postcondition is under a constructive form, we may think that the presence of a quantification will be embarrassing for the identification of an efficient invariant.

37 - Q 1   **Question 1.**   Propose a strengthened version of the postcondition in which the quantified expression calls on the variable p.

37 - Q 2   **Question 2.**   Build the loop on the basis of this new postcondition.

37 - Q 3   **Question 3.**   Deduce the program associated with the loop and give its complexity in terms of comparisons.

The solution is on page 137.

Problem 38. Alternating odd and even ∘ :

> *This problem illustrates the breakup of the postcondition after a sequence of strengthenings.*

Let us consider an array containing as many even as odd numbers. We would like to place each of the even (respectively odd) numbers in a position with an even (respectively odd) index. Let us notice that when all the even numbers are correctly placed, it is the same for the odd numbers (and conversely), hence the following specification:

Precondition: (T is an array of $2N$ natural numbers) **and** (S is the constant bag of values contained in T) **and** ($N \geqslant 0$) **and** (T contains N even natural numbers and N odd natural numbers).

Postcondition: (S is the bag of values contained in$T$) **and** [(positions with even indexes contain even values) **or** (positions with odd indexes contain odd values)].

As in the previous problem, evolutions of T are made via the procedure *Exchange*, which gets us free from the first conjunct of the postcondition. The postcondition is not in a conjunctive form, but it can be easily strengthened while preserving its symmetry:

Postcondition (second version which entails the first one): $((e \in 2 .. 2 \cdot N + 2)$ **and** $(e$ is even) **and** (positions with even indexes in the interval $2 .. e - 2$ contain even values) **and** $(e = 2 \cdot N + 2))$ **or** $((o \in 1 .. 2 \cdot N + 1)$ **and** $(o$ is odd) **and** (positions with odd indexes in the interval $1 .. o - 2$ contain odd values) **and** $(o = 2 \cdot N + 1))$.

However, it is not yet a conjunctive form and we must proceed to a strengthening of this version. To this aim, let:

$$P \cong \left(\begin{array}{l} (e \in 2 .. 2N + 2) \textbf{ and } (e \text{ is even}) \textbf{ and} \\ (\text{positions with even indexes of the interval } 2 .. e - 2 \\ \text{contain even values}) \end{array} \right)$$

$$Q \cong \left(\begin{array}{l} (o \in 1 .. 2N + 1) \textbf{ and } (o \text{ is odd}) \textbf{ and} \\ (\text{positions with odd indexes of the interval } 1 .. o - 2 \\ \text{contain odd values}) \end{array} \right)$$

which enables the rewriting of the postcondition hereafter:

Postcondition (rewritten second version): $(P$ **and** $(e = 2N))$ **or** $(Q$ **and** $(o = 2N + 1))$.

Question 1. Prove that:

$\qquad$ A **and** B **and** (C **or** D) $\Rightarrow$ (A **and** C) **or** (B **and** D).

38 - Q 1

Deduce a new version of the postcondition under constructive form entailing the second version.

Question 2. Give the elements of the loop built from this new postcondition. $\qquad$ 38 - Q 2

Question 3. Write the program solving the problem under consideration. $\qquad$ 38 - Q 3

Question 4. What is its complexity in terms of evaluated conditions and exchanges? $\qquad$ 38 - Q 4

Question 5. Justify the fact that it is also possible to build a loop from the following postcondition:

38 - Q 5

$\qquad$ $(e \in 2 .. 2N)$ **and** $(e$ is even) **and** (positions with even indexes of the interval $2 .. e - 2$ contain even values) **and** $(o \in 1 .. 2N + 1)$ **and** $(o$ is odd) **and** (positions with odd indexes of the interval $1 .. o - 2$ contain odd values) **and** $(e = 2N)$ **and** $(o = 2N + 1)$.

Question 6. Specify the resulting progression. $\qquad$ 38 - Q 6

The solution is on page 138.

Problem 39. The longest sequence of zeros $\qquad$ ○ **⋮**

> *This problem illustrates a case of a double strengthening, namely of the postcondition on the one hand (which is traditional), of the invariant (imposed by the progression) on the other hand. In addition, we highlight the fact that the approach proposed for the construction does not conflict with modifications aiming at the efficiency of the resulting program.*

We would like to build the program specified by:

Precondition: (T is a constant array of N integers) **and** $(N \geqslant 0)$.

Postcondition: lg is the length of the longest sequence of consecutive zeros in T.

The postcondition is not under conjunctive form; to achieve this, we introduce the variable i in the following way:

Postcondition (version stemming from the strengthening of the previous one): (lg is the length of the longest succession of zeros contained in the subarray $T[1 .. i-1]$) **and** ($i \in 1 .. N+1$) **and** ($i = N+1$).

First attempt

The preceding formulation suggests an invariant and a stopping condition:

1. Invariant The first two conjuncts are easy to establish and they are retained for the invariant:

> (lg is the length of the longest succession of zeros contained in the subarray $T[1 .. i-1]$) **and** ($i \in 1 .. N+1$).

In a graphical form, we get:

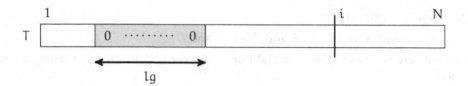

2. Stopping condition We take the discarded conjunct: ($i = N+1$).

3. Progression We must look for a fragment of program specified by:

Precondition: (lg is the length of the longest succession of zeros contained in the subarray $T[1 .. i-1]$) **and** ($i \in 1 .. N+1$) **and** **not**($i = N+1$)

PROGRESSION

Postcondition: (lg is the length of the longest succession of zeros contained in the subarray $T[1 .. i-1]$) **and** ($i \in 1 .. N+1$).

The value $T[i]$ exists since $i \neq N+1$. If $T[i] \neq 0$, i must be incremented. Otherwise ($T[i] = 0$), we have to express that $T[i]$ may be part of the longest string of zeros of the subarray $T[1 .. i]$ (before restoring the invariant), which can be achieved by the calculation (by means of a backward loop) of the length p of the longest string of consecutive zeros ending in i. However, we can remark that all elements of $T[1 .. i-1]$ have already been examined and that it would be damageable to scan them again (even partly). This length p will be assumed to be known, which leads to a new invariant, derived from the previous one by a strengthening which adds this hypothesis. The price to pay is the reconstruction of the loop on the basis of the new invariant.

Second attempt

We make the construction founded on the previous suggestion.

39 - Q 1   **Question 1.**   Specify the new invariant.

39 - Q 2   **Question 2.**   Taking ($i = N+1$) as the stopping condition, continue the construction of the loop (progression, initialization and termination expression).

Question 3.   Write the program. Give its complexity in terms of comparisons.   39 - Q 3

Question 4.   Propose and justify another stopping condition likely to improve the effi-   39 - Q 4
ciency of the loop.

The solution is on page 142.

Problem 40.   The majority element (iterative issue)

> *This problem about the search for a majority element in a bag is also addressed in chapter "Divide and conquer" (see problem 105, page 445). The solution developed here relies on an original technique. As a matter of fact, we often exploit the proven technique based on the strengthening of the postcondition for efficiency purposes. Here, in contrast, we will weaken the postcondition in order to get an algorithm which is simple but which provides only a possible solution requiring a "confirmation". The solution obtained is concise, efficient and elegant.*

If V is an array or a bag, the expression $\text{mult}(x, V)$ represents the multiplicity (i.e. the number of occurrences) of x in V. We consider the bag S of N ($N \geqslant 1$) strictly positive integers. S is called *majority* if there is an integer x such that:

$$\text{mult}(x, S) \geqslant \left\lfloor \frac{N}{2} \right\rfloor + 1;$$

x is called the *majority element* of S (it is unique). The problem posed is that of the search for the majority element in S. We would like to build a program whose specification is:

Precondition: (S is a bag of N values) **and** ($N \geqslant 1$).

Postcondition: x contains the value of the majority element of S if it exists, -1 otherwise.

The identification of a candidate who got the absolute majority in an election or the design of fault tolerant algorithms are possible applications of this problem.

A naïve algorithm

It is easy to specify a naïve algorithm, at best in $\Theta(N)$ and at worst in $\Theta(N^2)$ comparisons solving this problem (the comparison between two elements of S being the elementary operation). An element of S is arbitrarily selected and its number of occurrences in S is calculated. If it is not majority, another element of S is chosen, and so on until a majority element is found or half of the elements of S are treated without finding any.

A second approach

So as to enhance complexity at worst, we envisage a three step solution: first S is refined by the array T, then T is sorted, last a sequence of identical values of length greater than $\lfloor N/2 \rfloor$ is searched. The first step is in $\Theta(N)$, the second one in $O(N \cdot \log_2(N))$ and the last one is linear, hence a complexity at worst in $O(N \cdot \log_2(N))$.

An efficient iterative solution

The solution envisaged now is founded on an *abstract* data structure made of four bags. After a proposal for an invariant of the iteration, some of its properties are pointed out in order to build a "safe" program. Then, a refinement of the abstract data structure is undertaken by suppressing three out of the four initial bags and using only a constant array and scalar variables in the final algorithm.

Invariant

Let S be the bag of values for which a potential majority element is searched and its multi-set partition (according to the hypothesis of the work carried out partly) made of:

- R the bag of values "remaining to be treated",

- P a bag of pairs of values such that, the two values of any pair are different,

- C a bag called " bag of bachelors" where all elements have the same value.

Example

Let $S = [\![1,3,4,1,1,3,5,2,5,1]\!]$ and the possible configuration hereafter:

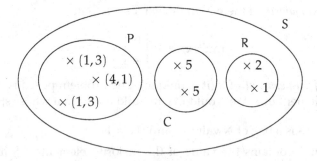

The partition of S (in particular in the above situation) complies with the following properties:

Property 2:
$|S| = 2 \cdot |P| + |C| + |R|$.

This property is trivial and we do not prove it.

Property 3:
If the bags R and C are empty, then S is not majority.

Property 4:
If the bag R is empty but C is not (let us call c the value present in C) then:

1. *if S has a majority element, it is c,*

2. *if S has no majority element, nothing can be said about c (not even that c is the element with the largest multiplicity in S).*

Question 1.   Prove properties 3 and 4.   40 - Q 1

Question 2.   We will build a loop whose invariant corresponds to a situation where S   40 - Q 2
is partitioned in P, C and R and in which the stopping condition occurs when R is empty.
Which conclusion can be then drawn?

Question 3.   Specify the precondition as well as the postcondition of the abstract loop   40 - Q 3
built upon the proposed invariant. How to answer the initial problem on the basis of this
loop?

Question 4.   Complete the construction of the abstract loop (progression, initialization,   40 - Q 4
termination).

Question 5.   How to refine the data structure using only scalar variables and one array?   40 - Q 5
Derive an iterative algorithm solving the problem of the search for a majority element of a
bag S. What is its complexity in terms of comparisons?

The solution is on page 144.

Problem 41. The celebrity problem   尚 **⠇**

> *In a way similar to the problem about the majority element (see problem 40, page 119), we*
> *envisage a solution where the postcondition is weakened. The solution partly calls on the*
> *bounded linear search (see section 3.5, page 107) and it turns out to be elegant and of linear*
> *complexity.*

In a group, a *star* is a person who is known by everyone and who knows nobody. We
consider a group of N (N ⩾ 1) people and we look for a star inside the group, if any.
By convention, a group made of a single person admits this person as a star. The only
authorized operation denoted by *Knows*(i, j) consists in choosing a person i who is asked
whether he/she knows the person j (i ≠ j) or not. The operation *Knows*(i, j) returns **true**
or **false** depending on the answer (mandatory and assumed to be truthful) of the person
who is questioned.

As there are $N(N-1)/2$ pairs of persons, the problem can be solved, for sure, by at
most $N(N-1)$ operations *Knows*. However, we are interested in a solution requiring less
operations, if possible a (small) multiple of N.

Question 1.   Prove that there is at most one star in any group.   41 - Q 1

Question 2.   Prove that, in the absence of any additional information, when the oper-   41 - Q 2
ation *Knows*(i, j) is performed:

- if the answer is **true**, then j can be the star, but i cannot,

- if the answer is **false**, then i can be the star, but j cannot.

Question 3.   Specify the precondition and the postcondition of the program solving the   41 - Q 3
problem posed.

Question 4.   Specify the constituents of a loop identifying a person likely to be the star   41 - Q 4
of a group, called "potential" star.

Question 5.   Specify the other components of the program determining the star of a   41 - Q 5
group or the fact that it involves no star. Write the program solving the initial problem.

41 - Q 6 **Question** 6.   What is its complexity when *Knows* (i, j) is taken as the elementary operation?

The solution is on page 145.

Problem 42. Weakening a precondition

> *In this problem, we are interested in weakening the precondition. This approach which is legitimate, consists in resolving a problem in reference to a more general one for which a solution is known. The weakening is made by the elimination of an hypothesis and we study the impact of this choice on the performances through two examples.*

We have seen in section 3.3.2 that it is legal that, trying to solve the problem specified by $\{P\}$ prog $\{Q\}$, we solve the problem specified by $\{P'\}$ prog$'$ $\{Q\}$ with $P \Rightarrow P'$. In other terms, the precondition is weakened and we can wonder about the impact of this approach on performances. Two examples are dealt with to shine a light on this matter.

Sorting increasingly an array ordered decreasingly

We want to build the program specified by:

> **Precondition:** (T is an array of N natural numbers) **and** (S is the constant bag of
>   values contained in T) **and** ($N \geqslant 1$) **and** (T is decreasingly ordered).

> **Postcondition:** (T is sorted increasingly) **and** (S is the bag of values contained in
>   T).

Two strategies can be envisaged: (i) to develop a specific algorithm accounting for the fact that T is decreasingly ordered or (ii) to *weaken the precondition* by suppressing the conjunct related to the fact that the array is already ordered.

42 - Q 1 **Question** 1.   Propose the principle of a solution of linear complexity in terms of exchanges in the context of the first option.

42 - Q 2 **Question** 2.   Which complexity is obtained with the algorithm proposed in problem 33, page 112? Can it be expected to do better with a "usual" sorting algorithm? Conclude.

Constrained variation array

We consider the program whose specification is:

> **Precondition:** (T is a constant array of N natural numbers) **and** (there is at least
>   one zero in T) **and** (the difference between two successive elements of T is
>   at most 1).

> **Postcondition:** The variable i identifies the zero of T with the lowest index.

This specification differs from that of the example dealt with in page 99, since here, we are provided with a property about the variation over the numbers contained in T. Once again, two strategies are feasible: specific program or use of the algorithm proposed in page 101. This second option corresponds to the weakening of the precondition of the problem where the third conjunct is ignored.

Question 3. Prove that when T is such that the difference between two consecutive 42 - Q 3 elements of T is at most 1, then:

$$(T[i] > 0) \Rightarrow \forall j \cdot (j \in i .. i + T[i] - 1 \Rightarrow T[j] > 0).$$

Question 4. Develop the specific solution based on a loop whose constituents will be 42 - Q 4 first explicited.

Question 5. What can be said about the impact of the choice in terms of complexity? 42 - Q 5

Question 6. We now consider the program specified by: 42 - Q 6

Precondition: (T is a constant array of N natural numbers) **and** (there is at least one zero in T) **and** (the difference between two successive elements of T is at least 1).

Postcondition: The variable i identifies the zero of T with the lowest index.

Elaborate on the following weakening of the initial precondition:

Precondition: (T is a constant array of N natural numbers) **and** (there is at least one zero in T).

Question 7. Compare the three previous weakening situations. 42 - Q 7

The solution is on page 148.

Problem 43. Halving a polygon ○ ⦂

> *The problem dealt with here is a somewhat sophisticated variant of the sequential search. Usually, in this kind of problem, using the technique called "stop as early as possible" does not impact asymptotic complexity. This is not what happens here, where this strategy is the backbone for the improvement of the efficiency obtained with respect to a naïve method. Moreover, this problem has a formulation in a two-dimensional space generally solved by two nested loops. Here, as in problem 32 page 111, the use of a single loop makes the design simpler.*

We consider an arbitrary polygon of finite order N (N > 2) whose vertices are labelled clockwise from 1 to N. We look for any arbitrary chord that separates (halves) the perimeter p of the polygon "as accurately as possible", i.e. such that the absolute value of the difference between the sum of the lengths of the sides bounded by the chord is minimum. Complexity is evaluated in terms of the number of visited vertices.

Definitions – Notations – Representation

Further, $|a|$ denotes the absolute value of a. The side which originates from vertex i is denoted by (i). The chord connecting vertices i and j is denoted by $\overline{(i,j)}$. The arc going from vertex i to vertex j is denoted by $\overset{\frown}{(i,j)}$. The length of the arc a is denoted by $\|a\|$.

A polygon of order N is represented by the array d (d $\in$ 1 .. N → $\mathbb{R}_+$) such that d[i] is the length of side (i). Figure 3.4 shows a polygon of order 9.

More formally, if the operator · denotes concatenation of adjacent arcs, a (nonempty) arc is inductively defined as a sequence of sides the following way.

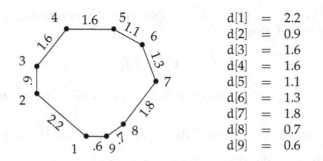

$$\begin{aligned}
d[1] &= 2.2 \\
d[2] &= 0.9 \\
d[3] &= 1.6 \\
d[4] &= 1.6 \\
d[5] &= 1.1 \\
d[6] &= 1.3 \\
d[7] &= 1.8 \\
d[8] &= 0.7 \\
d[9] &= 0.6
\end{aligned}$$

Fig. 3.4 – Example of a polygon of order 9 and its representation by the array d.

Definition 1 (Arc):

Base case :

$$\begin{cases} (i, \widehat{i+1}) = (i) & i \in 1..N-1 \\ (\widehat{N,1}) = (N). \end{cases}$$

Inductive case:

$$\begin{cases} (\widehat{i,j}) = (i, \widehat{i+1}) \cdot (\widehat{i+1,j}) & j \neq i+1 \text{ and } i \neq N \\ (\widehat{N,j}) = (\widehat{N,1}) \cdot (\widehat{1,j})) & j \neq 1. \end{cases}$$

Similarly, the length of an arc is defined as follows.

Definition 2 (Length of an arc):

Base case:

$$\begin{cases} \|(i, \widehat{i+1})\| = d[i] & i \in 1..N-1 \\ \|(\widehat{N,1})\| = d[N]. \end{cases}$$

Inductive case:

$$\begin{cases} \|(\widehat{i,j})\| = d[i] + \|(\widehat{i+1,j})\| & j \neq i+1 \text{ and } i \neq N \\ \|(\widehat{N,j})\| = d[N] + \|(\widehat{1,j}))\| & j \neq 1. \end{cases}$$

Definition 3 (Locally optimal chord):

The chord $\overline{(j,k)}$ *is locally optimal with respect to its origin* j *if:*

$$\left| \|(\widehat{j,k})\| - \|(\widehat{k,j})\| \right| = \min_{i \in 1..N-\{j\}} \left(\left| \|(\widehat{j,i})\| - \|(\widehat{i,j})\| \right| \right).$$

Definition 4 (Globally optimal chord):

The chord $\overline{(j,k)}$ *is globally optimal if:*

$$\left| \|(\widehat{j,k})\| - \|(\widehat{k,j})\| \right| = \min_{\substack{u \in 1..N \text{ and} \\ v \in 1..N \text{ and} \\ u \neq v}} \left(\left| \|(\widehat{u,v})\| - \|(\widehat{v,u})\| \right| \right). \tag{3.1}$$

The problem

The objective of the problem is to find out a globally optimal chord (the problem has at least one solution). A method consists in the evaluation of formula 3.1 and keeping one of the pairs of vertices which complies with it. The corresponding algorithm is in $\Theta(N^2)$. It is also possible to exploit the following identity so as to avoid useless calculations (p is the perimeter of the polygon):

$$\left| \|\widehat{(i,j)}\| - \|\widehat{(j,i)}\| \right| = 2 \cdot \left| \|\widehat{(i,j)}\| - \frac{p}{2.0} \right|. \tag{3.2}$$

The pairs of vertices (j,k) complying with formula 3.1 are also those which comply with:

$$\frac{\left| \|\widehat{(j,k)}\| - \|\widehat{(k,j)}\| \right|}{2.0} = \min_{\substack{u \in 1..N \text{ and} \\ v \in 1..N \text{ and} \\ u \neq v}} \left| \|\widehat{(u,v)}\| - \frac{p}{2.0} \right|.$$

But, since $|a - b| = |b - a|$, to visit all of the arcs, the variable v does not need to scan the whole set $1..N - \{u\}$. It is sufficient that it takes the values of the interval $u + 1..N \cup \{1\}$, hence:

$$\frac{\left| \|\widehat{(j,k)}\| - \|\widehat{(k,j)}\| \right|}{2.0} = \min_{\substack{u \in 1..N \text{ and} \\ v \in u+1..N \cup \{1\}}} \left| \|\widehat{(u,v)}\| - \frac{p}{2.0} \right|.$$

If $\overline{(j,k)}$ is a *locally* optimal chord issued from j, the value $\left(\left| \|\widehat{(j,k)}\| - p/2.0 \right| \right)$ is denoted δ_j. The lengths of the arcs intervening in the calculation can be gathered in the following triangular matrix (called triangle of lengths):

$$
\begin{array}{cccc}
\|\widehat{(1,2)}\| & \|\widehat{(1,3)}\| & \cdots\cdots\cdots & \|\widehat{(1,1)}\| \\
& \|\widehat{(2,3)}\| & \cdots\cdots\cdots & \|\widehat{(2,1)}\| \\
& & \vdots & \\
& \|\widehat{(i,i+1)}\| & \cdots\cdots & \|\widehat{(i,1)}\| \\
& & \ddots & \vdots \\
& & \ddots & \vdots \\
& & & \|\widehat{(N,1)}\|
\end{array}
$$

It can be noticed that the upper right corner of the triangle indicates the value of the perimeter $p = \|\widehat{(1,1)}\|$ of the polygon. In the case of the polygon of figure 3.4, page 124, $p = 11.8$, and this triangle is valued as follows:

	2	3	4	5	6	7	8	9	1
1	2.2	3.1	4.7	6.3	7.4	8.7	10.5	11.2	11.8
2		0.9	2.5	4.1	5.2	6.5	8.3	9.0	9.6
3			1.6	3.2	4.3	5.6	7.4	8.1	8.7
4				1.6	2.7	4.0	5.8	6.5	7.1
5					1.1	2.4	4.2	4.9	5.5
6						1.3	3.1	3.8	4.4
7							1.8	2.5	3.1
8								0.7	1.3
9									0.6

However, this type of triangle contains $(N(N+1))/2$ elements and their exhaustive evaluation leads once again to a solution in $\Theta(N^2)$. This result can be improved on the basis of the following four observations:

1. For a given vertex j, there is either one, or two locally optimal chords.

2. If the chord $\overline{(j,k)}$ is the first[2] locally optimal chord issued from j, then none of the chords $\overline{(j+1,j+2)}$, $\overline{(j+1,j+3)}$,...,$\overline{(j+1,k-1)}$ is globally as good as $\overline{(j,k)}$.

3. Let $\overline{(j,k)}$ be the first locally optimal chord issued from j. The chord $\overline{(j+1,k)}$, if it exists, may be better than $\overline{(j,k)}$.

4. When, for the vertex j, a locally optimal chord $\overline{(j,k)}$ is found out, it becomes useless to test the optimality of $\overline{(j,k+1)}$,..., $\overline{(j,N+1)}$ (according to the usual principle "stop as early as possible").

    As to observation 3, it is convenient to notice that other chords issued from the vertex $j+1$ can outperform the chord $\overline{(j+1,k)}$.

43 - Q 1   **Question 1.**   Demonstrate identity 3.2, page 125.

43 - Q 2   **Question 2.**   In which situation are there two locally optimal chords issued from the same vertex j ? Give an example.

43 - Q 3   **Question 3.**   Prove the proposition related to the third above observation.

43 - Q 4   **Question 4.**   In the example of figure 3.4, page 124, which are the arcs whose length intervenes in the calculation? Which globally optimal chord is found out?

43 - Q 5   **Question 5.**   Let us consider the following example:

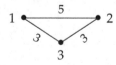

Specify (by means of a triangle of lengths) the arcs whose length intervenes in the calculation. What can be observed?

43 - Q 6   **Question 6.**   We decide to build an algorithmic solution on the basis of *a single loop*. Propose an invariant for this loop.

---

[2]The first one *encountered* according to a clockwise scan.

Question 7.   Complement the construction of the loop (stopping condition, progres-   43 - Q 7
sion, initialization, termination) and derive the code associated with this solution. What is
its complexity (in terms of visited vertices)?

The solution is on page 149.

3.8   Solutions

Answers to problem 29. White and red beans   *The problem is on page 110.*

Answer 1.   It is easy to see that, whatever the result of a draw, the number of beans in   29 - A 1
the box decreases by 1. After a while, the can contains a single bean and the process stops.

Answer 2.   Let us try to find an invariant in the procedure described in the statement of   29 - A 2
the problem. Let nbW (respectively nbR) be the number of white (respectively red) beans
present in the can before any draw. If two red beans are drawn, nbW does not change and
nbR diminishes by 1. If two white beans are drawn, nbW decreases by 2 and nbR increases
by 1. Last, if one white bean and one red bean are drawn, NBW remains unchanged and
nbR diminishes by 1. This shows a property of nbW about its parity which remains unchanged over time whatever the result of the successive draws. This is an invariant of the
mechanism described in the statement. It makes it possible to deduce that, if the initial
number of white beans is odd (respectively even), the last bean is white (respectively red).

Answers to problem 30. From a coder's dustbin   *The problem is on page 111.*

Answer 1.   A first mistake lies in the fact that the variable sup is used in the invariant   30 - A 1
without its prior definition. Another error impacts the stopping condition which prevents
the accounting for $T[N]$ in the search of the maximum.

Answer 2.   An acceptable version is based on the following invariant: 30 - A 2

$$(i \in 1 .. N+1) \textbf{ and } (sup \in \mathbb{N}) \textbf{ and } (\forall j \cdot (j \in 1 .. i-1 \Rightarrow T[j] \leqslant sup))$$

as well as on the stopping condition: $(i = N+1)$.

It can be noticed that the initialization establishes the invariant since it holds for $i = 2$ and
$sup = T[1]$ ($T[j] \leqslant sup$ is true for $j = 1$ – indeed, case of equality).

Answers to problem 31. Summing up the elements of an array *The problem is on page 111.*

Answer 1.   The initial expression of the postcondition is: $s = \sum_{j=1}^{N} T[j]$. It is not under   31 - A 1
conjunctive form and it will be strengthened by the replacement of $(N+1)$ by the *variable*
i, and the adjunction of the conjunct $(i = N+1)$. Thus, the postcondition becomes:

Postcondition : (s is the sum of the first $(i-1)$ elements of T) **and** $(i \in 1 .. N+1)$ **and** $(i = N+1)$.

The heuristics of the breakup leads to separate the postcondition and to suggest:

1. Invariant The first two conjuncts are easy to establish, so they are kept to form the invariant:

(s is the sum of the first $(i-1)$ elements of T) **and** $(i \in 1 .. N+1)$

graphically:

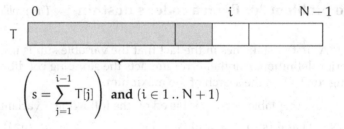

$$\left(s = \sum_{j=1}^{i-1} T[j]\right) \text{ and } (i \in 1 .. N+1)$$

2. Stopping condition The discarded conjunct is taken: $i = N+1$.

3. Progression It is specified by:

Precondition: $\left(s = \sum_{j=1}^{i-1} T[j]\right)$ **and** $(i \in 1 .. N+1)$ **and not** $(i = N+1)$

PROGRESSION

Postcondition: $\left(s = \sum_{j=1}^{i-1} T[j]\right)$ **and** $(i \in 1 .. N+1)$

In order to both "make the calculation progress" and restore the invariant, the progression chosen consists in the integration of $T[i]$ into the sum and the increment of i by 1. These two actions are possible since the formula $((i \in 1 .. N+1) \text{ and not}(i = N+1))$ ensures that both $T[i]$ exists and i can be increased. We are thus in the following situation:

$$\left(s = \sum_{j=1}^{i-1} T[j]\right) \text{ and } (i \in 1 .. N+1)$$

which is nothing but the invariant. So, we have built the progression: $s \leftarrow s + T[i]; i \leftarrow i+1$.

4. Initialization The initialization is specified by:

Precondition: (T is a constant array of N natural numbers) **and** $(N \geqslant 0)$

INITIALIZATION

Postcondition: $\left(s = \sum_{j=1}^{i-1} T[j]\right)$ **and** $(i \in 1 .. N+1)$.

As usual when the initialization is designed, the postcondition of the specification is the invariant of the loop under construction. Moving from the precondition to the invariant can be done in attaining the following situation where i is identified to 1:

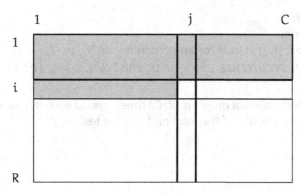

$$\left(s = \sum_{j=1}^{0} T[j] \right) \text{ and } (1 \in 1 .. N+1)$$

situation which can be established by the assignments 1 to i and 0 to s.

5. Termination The expression $(N + 1 - i)$ is appropriate: it remains nonnegative and decreases by 1 at each iteration step.

Finally, the following program is built:

```
1.  constants
2.     N ∈ ℕ₁ and N = ... and T ∈ 1 .. N → ℕ and T = [...]
3.  variables
4.     i ∈ 1 .. N + 1
5.  begin
6.     /% PRE: (T is a constant array of N natural numbers) and (N ⩾ 0) %/
7.     i ← 1; s ← 0;
8.     while not(i = N + 1) do
9.         s ← s + T[i]; i ← i + 1
10.    end while;
11.    /% POST: ( s = ∑ᴺⱼ₌₁ T[j] ) %/
12.    write(the sum of the elements of the array , T, is , s)
13. end
```

Answer 2. In terms of additions as well as comparisons related to the control of the loop, this algorithm is in $\Theta(N)$ in the best and in the worst case.   31 - A 2

Answers to problem 32. Searching in a bidimensional array   *The problem is on page 111.*

Answer 1. Let us assume that the work is carried out partly, which is schematized by: 32 - A 1

1. Invariant It matches the situation described above, namely:

$(i \in 1 .. R)$ **and** $(j \in 1 .. C)$ **and** (the value V is not in the rectangle $T[1 .. i - 1, 1 .. C]$) **and** (the value V is not in row $T[i, 1 .. j - 1]$).

2. Stopping condition The loop terminates as soon as $T[i, j] = V$.

3. Progression It is specified by:

Precondition: (the value V is not in the rectangle $T[1 .. i - 1, 1 .. C]$) **and** (the value V is not in the row $T[i, 1 .. j - 1]$) **and not**$(T[i, j] = V)$

PROGRESSION

Postcondition: (the value V is not in the rectangle $T[1 .. i - 1, 1 .. C]$) **and** (the value V is not in the row $T[i, 1 .. j - 1]$).

The progression of the indexes i and j is handled here in order to examine the next element (which exists according to the precondition and the fact that the stopping condition is not met): j is incremented by 1, and if it exceeds C, we move to the beginning of next line.

4. Initialization It allows to move from the precondition to the invariant, which is done in giving the value 1 to both variables i and j.

5. Termination We can take the area of the white zone of the schema as the termination expression since it decreases by 1 at each step of the loop: $(R - i) \cdot C + (C + 1 - j)$.

32 - A 2   **Answer** 2.   The corresponding program is:

```
1. constants
2.    R ∈ ℕ₁ and R = ... and C ∈ ℕ₁ and C = ... and V ∈ ℕ and V = ... and
3.    T ∈ 1 .. R × 1 .. C → ℕ and T = [...]
4. variables
5.    i ∈ 1 .. R and j ∈ 1 .. C + 1
6. begin
7.    /% PRE: (T is a constant array of natural numbers with R rows and C
         columns) and (R > 0) and (C > 0) and (V is a natural number present in
         T) %/
8.    i ← 1; j ← 1;
9.    while not(T[i, j] = V) do
10.       j ← j + 1;
11.       if j > C then
12.          i ← i + 1; j ← 1
13.       end if;
14.    end while;
15.    /% POST: (i, j) stands for an occurrence of, V, in, T, i.e. T[i, j] = V %/
16.    write(an occurrence of , V, is in the cell (, i, , , j, ) of T)
17. end
```

The loop is completed between one and $(R \cdot C)$ times, and at each iteration two comparisons take place (one for the control of the loop and one for testing j).

Answers to problem 33. Sorting by straight selection   *The problem is on* page 112.

Answer 1.   The postcondition stemming from the choice made is: 33 - A 1

Postcondition: $(i \in 1..N+1)$ **and** ($T[1..i-1]$ is sorted) **and** $(\forall j \cdot (j \in 1..i-1 \Rightarrow \forall k \cdot (k \in i..N \Rightarrow T[j] \leqslant T[k])))$ **and** $(i = N+1)$.

We now identify the five components of the loop to construct.

1. Invariant The first three conjuncts are easy to establish and they are retained for the invariant:

$(i \in 1..N+1)$ **and** ($T[1..i-1]$ is sorted) **and** $\forall j \cdot (j \in 1..i-1 \Rightarrow \forall k \cdot (k \in i..N \Rightarrow T[j] \leqslant T[k]))$

or graphically (omitting the variation domain of i):

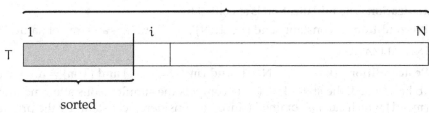

$$\forall j \cdot (j \in 1..i-1 \Rightarrow \forall k \cdot (k \in i..N \Rightarrow T[j] \leqslant T[k]))$$

2. Stopping condition We take the last conjunct: $(i = N+1)$.

3. Progression It is specified by:

Precondition: $(i \in 1..N+1)$ **and** ($T[1..i-1]$ is sorted) **and** $\forall j \cdot (j \in 1..i-1 \Rightarrow \forall k \cdot (k \in i..N \Rightarrow T[j] \leqslant T[k]))$ **and** **not**$(i = N+1)$

PROGRESSION

Postcondition: $(i \in 1..N+1)$ **and** ($T[1..i-1]$ is sorted) **and** $\forall j \cdot (j \in 1..i-1 \Rightarrow \forall k \cdot (k \in i..N \Rightarrow T[j] \leqslant T[k]))$.

A possible solution is to identify the position m of the minimum (one of the minima) in the subarray $T[i..N]$ before swapping elements in position i and m. The invariant is then restored by the incrementation of i.

4. Initialization The initialization is specified by:

Precondition: (T is an array of N natural numbers) **and** $(N \geqslant 1)$

INITIALIZATION

Postcondition: $(i \in 1..N+1)$ **and** ($T[1..i-1]$ is sorted) **and** $\forall j \cdot (j \in 1..i-1 \Rightarrow \forall k \cdot (k \in i..N \Rightarrow T[j] \leqslant T[k]))$.

Assigning 1 to i answers this specification: $T[1:0]$ is sorted; all the elements of this subarray are less than (or equal to) those of $T[1..N]$.

5. Termination If the search for the minimum in $T[i..N]$ comes to an end, it is the same for the loop under construction. $(N+1-i)$ is a suitable termination expression.

Answer 2.   The strengthening envisaged consists in replacing $(N+1)$ by k. Henceforth,   33 - A 2 $T[m] = \min_{j \in i..N}(T[j])$ becomes $T[m] = \min_{j \in i..k-1}(T[j])$ and it is necessary to specify the variation domain of k on the one hand and to carry forward the substitution in the term $m \in i..N$. We get:

Postcondition: $(k \in i+1..N+1)$ **and** $(m \in i..k-1)$ **and** ($T[m] = \min_{j \in i..k-1}(T[j])$) **and** $(k = N+1)$.

33 - A 3   **Answer** 3.   The components of the loop for the identification of a minimum in $T[i .. N]$ are now proposed.

1. Invariant The first three conjuncts are easy to establish and they constitute the invariant:

$$(k \in i + 1 .. N + 1) \textbf{ and } (m \in i .. k - 1) \textbf{ and } (T[m] = \min_{j \in i..k-1}(T[j])).$$

2. Stopping condition We take the remaining conjunct: $(k = N + 1)$.

3. Progression It is specified as follows:

Precondition: $(k \in i + 1 .. N + 1) \textbf{ and } (m \in i .. k - 1) \textbf{ and } (T[m] = \min_{j \in i..k-1}(T[j])) \textbf{ and } \textbf{not}(k = N + 1)$

PROGRESSION

Postcondition: $(k \in i+1 .. N+1) \textbf{ and } (m \in i .. k-1) \textbf{ and } (T[m] = \min_{j \in i..k-1}(T[j])).$

Progressing towards the postcondition is done via the update of m if $T[k]$ reveals to be the smallest element over $T[i .. k]$; the restoration of the invariant is achieved by incrementing k.

4. Initialization The initialization is specified by:

Precondition: $(i \text{ constant}) \textbf{ and } (i \in 1..N) \textbf{ and } (T[i..N] \text{ is an array of natural numbers})$

INITIALIZATION

Postcondition: $(k \in i+1 .. N+1) \textbf{ and } (m \in i .. k-1) \textbf{ and } (T[m] = \min_{j \in i..k-1}(T[j])).$

To be reached, the state $(k = i + 1)$ compels the simultaneous attainment of the state $(m = i)$ which can be obtained (since i is considered constant) by the program:

    1. $k \leftarrow i + 1 ; m \leftarrow i.$

5. Termination The variable k is incremented by 1 at each step of iteration. The expression $(N + 1 - k)$ is decreasing while being nonnegative, which ensures the termination.

33 - A 4   **Answer** 4.   Eventually, we obtain the following program:

```
 1. constants
 2.    N ∈ ℕ₁ and N = ...
 3. variables
 4.    T ∈ 1..N → ℕ and T = [...] and i ∈ 1..N+1 and k ∈ 2..N+1 and m ∈ 1..N
 5. begin
 6.    /% PRE: (T is an array of N natural numbers) and (N ⩾ 1) %/
 7.    i ← 1;
 8.    while not(i = N + 1) do
 9.       /% nested loop for the determination of m %/
10.       k ← i + 1; m ← i;
11.       while not(k = N + 1) do
12.          if T[k] < T[m] then
13.             m ← k
14.          end if;
15.          k ← k + 1
16.       end while;
17.       Exchange(i, m) ; i ← i + 1
18.    end while;
19.    /% POST: (T is increasingly sorted) %/
20.    write(T)
21. end
```

Answer 5.   The outer loop is achieved for i varying from 1 to N and the inner loop,   33 - A 5
which contains the exchange operation, for k varying from $(i + 1)$ to N. It can be deduced
that the number of exchanges is in $\Theta(N^2)$.

Answers to problem 34. Was it a car or a cat I saw   *The problem is on page 113.*

Answer 1.   Let us make a proof by contradiction. Let us consider the kth character of T   34 - A 1
starting from its beginning and its end, respectively $T[k]$ and $T[N - k + 1]$. Let us assume
that T is a palindrome and that these two elements are different, the word (or sentence,
spaces being ignored) represented by T does not read the same in both directions, hence
there is a contradiction.

Answer 2.   Let us remind that the pattern proposed in page 109 consists in deciding   34 - A 2
whether there is (or not) an element j in a structure of size N, that fulfills a given predicate
LP that does not depend on the elements preceding j. The result returned is either j itself,
or the conventional value $(N + 1)$ indicating that the structure has been exhausted without
finding an element for which property LP is met. For the problem of decision about a
(possible) palindrome, the approach can be used with:

$$LP(j) \mathrel{\hat=} (T[j] \neq T[N + 1 - j])$$

detecting a bad match leading to deciding that the string T is not a palindrome. However,
it should be noted that k never takes the value $N + 1$ since elements are pairwise examined.
Indeed, if T represents a palindrome, the algorithm comes to an end with a value of k equal
to (or exceeding by 1) that of $(N + 1 - k)$. For the same reason, the termination expression
must be adapted (see next question), although the generic expression suits well.

Answer 3.   Taking these adaptions into account, we get the program hereafter: 34 - A 3
```
 1. constants
 2.    T ∈ string and T = ... and N = |T|
 3. variables
 4.    j ∈ 1 .. N
 5. begin
 6.    /% PRE: (T is a constant string of N characters) and (N ⩾ 0) %/
 7.    j ← 1;
 8.    while not((j ⩾ N + 1 − j) or else (T[j] ≠ T[N + 1 − j))) do
 9.        j ← j + 1
10.    end while;
11.    /% POST: ((j ⩾ N + 1 − j) and (T represents a palindrome)) or ((j < N +
       1 − j) and (T does not stand for a palindrome)) %/
12.    if j ⩾ N + 1 − j then
13.        write(the string , T, represents a palindrome)
14.    else
15.        write(the string , T, does not represent a palindrome)
16.    end if
17. end
```

Remark

This solution allows for handling strings whatever the parity of their size (odd or even).

34 - A 4   **Answer 4.**   The number of conditions evaluated (for the control of the loop) is varying from 1 (immediate stop in case of bad match or N = 0) to $\lceil (N+1)/2 \rceil$ (T represents a palindrome). Thus, complexity is in $\mathcal{O}(N)$.

Answers to problem 35. The Dutch national flag (variant)   ☙ *The problem is on page 114.*

35 - A 1   **Answer 1.**   Replacing w by r in the second version of the postcondition, it yields:

Postcondition (new version):
$(b \in 1 .. N)$ **and** $(w \in b+1 .. N+1)$ **and** $(r \in w .. N+1)$ **and**
$(\forall j \cdot (j \in 1 .. b-1 \Rightarrow T[j] < V))$ **and** $(\forall j \cdot (j \in b .. w-1 \Rightarrow T[j] = V))$ **and**
$(\forall j \cdot (j \in r .. N \Rightarrow T[j] > V))$ **and** $(r = w)$.

The invariant can be made of the first six components (easy to establish):

1. Invariant $(b \in 1 .. N)$ **and** $(w \in b+1 .. N+1)$ **and** $(r \in w .. N+1)$ **and**
      $(\forall j \cdot (j \in 1 .. b-1 \Rightarrow T[j] < V))$ **and** $(\forall j \cdot (j \in b .. w-1 \Rightarrow T[j] = V))$ **and**
      $(\forall j \cdot (j \in r .. N \Rightarrow T[j] > V))$.

It can be schematized by:

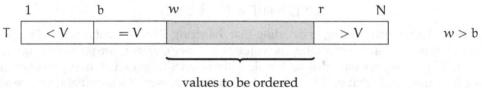

values to be ordered

35 - A 2   **Answer 2.**   We continue the construction of the loop with the four remaining elements.

2. Stopping condition The conjunct previously discarded is taken: $(r = w)$.

3. Progression It is specified by:
Precondition: $(b \in 1 .. N)$ **and** $(w \in b+1 .. N+1)$ **and** $(r \in w .. N+1)$ **and**
$(\forall j \cdot (j \in 1 .. b-1 \Rightarrow T[j] < V))$ **and** $(\forall j \cdot (j \in b .. w-1 \Rightarrow T[j] = V))$ **and**
$(\forall j \cdot (j \in r .. N \Rightarrow T[j] > V))$ **and** $\text{not}(r = w)$

PROGRESSION

Postcondition: $(b \in 1 .. N)$ **and** $(w \in b+1 .. N+1)$ **and** $(r \in w .. N+1)$ **and**
$(\forall j \cdot (j \in 1 .. b-1 \Rightarrow T[j] < V))$ **and** $(\forall j \cdot (j \in b .. w-1 \Rightarrow T[j] = V))$ **and**
$(\forall j \cdot (j \in r .. N \Rightarrow T[j] > V))$.

The area containing the values not yet sorted has two variable endpoints (w and $r-1$), which are exploited to fulfill the constraint of the statement related to exchanges. Let us review the various cases likely to happen:

  a) when $T[r-1] > V$, no exchange is needed and the invariant is restored by decrementing r by 1,

  b) when $T[w] = V$, here again, no exchange is required to restore the invariant, w is incremented by 1,

  c) when $T[w] < V$, $T[w]$ should be placed in the first area and the values at positions w and b are exchanged before the restoration of the invariant with the incrementation of these two variables by 1,

d) when $T[w] > V$, $T[w]$ should be placed in the right area and the values at positions w and $(r-1)$ are exchanged before the restoration of the invariant in decrementing r by 1.

Whatever the situation, it can be observed that at most one exchange takes place.

4. Initialization The initialization is specified by:

Precondition: (T is an array of N natural numbers) **and** $(N \geqslant 1)$ **and** $(V = T[1])$

INITIALIZATION

Postcondition: $(b \in 1 .. N)$ **and** $(w \in b+1 .. N+1)$ **and** $(r \in w .. N+1)$
$(\forall j \cdot (j \in 1 .. b-1 \Rightarrow T[j] < V))$ **and** $(\forall j \cdot (j \in b .. w-1 \Rightarrow T[j] = V))$ **and**
$(\forall j \cdot (j \in r .. N \Rightarrow T[j] > V))$.

The following situation must be reached:

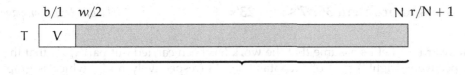

values to be ordered

which is done by the assignments:

$$b \leftarrow 1; w \leftarrow 2; r \leftarrow N+1$$

5. Termination The area of the values remaining to sort diminishes by 1 at each step of the loop. $(r - w)$ is thus a legal termination expression.

Answer 3.   Ultimately, the following program is built: 35 - A 3

```
1.  constants
2.      N ∈ ℕ₁ and N = ...
3.  variables
4.      T ∈ 1 .. N → ℕ and T = [...] and V ∈ ℕ and b ∈ 1 .. N and w ∈ 2 .. N +
        1 and r ∈ 2 .. N + 1
5.  begin
6.      /% PRE: (T is an array of N natural numbers) and (N ⩾ 1) %/
7.      V ← T[1]; b ← 1 ; w ← 2 ; r ← N + 1 ;
8.      while not(w = r) do
9.          if T[r − 1] > V then
10.             r ← r − 1
11.         else
12.             if T[w] = V then
13.                 w ← w + 1
14.             elsif T[w] < V then
15.                 Exchange(w, b) ; b ← b + 1 ; w ← w + 1
16.             else
17.                 Exchange(w, r − 1) ; r ← r − 1
18.             end if
19.         end if
20.     end while;
```

21. /% POST: (S is the bag of the values contained in T) **and** (T is made of three parts, on the left values less than V, on the right values greater than V and in the middle all occurrences of V) %/
22. **write**(*array,* T, *where the occurrences of the value,* V
23.   *are in the middle, those less than ,* V, *on the left*
24.   *and the others on the right*)
25. **end**

35 - A 4   **Answer** 4.   The length of the area containing the values remaining to sort diminishes by 1 at each step of the progression, while at the same time at most one exchange takes place. More precisely, the number of exchanges varies from 0 (if the array T contains a single value or if $\forall i \cdot (i \in 2 .. N \Rightarrow T[i] > T[1])$) to $(N-1)$ (if $\forall i \cdot (i \in 2 .. N \Rightarrow T[i] < T[1])$).

Answers to problem 36. 7's and 23's   *The problem is on page 115.*

36 - A 1   **Answer** 1.   Let us assume that the work has been carried out partly, i.e. that the "left" (respectively "right") part of T contains no 23 (respectively no 7), which is graphically represented below:

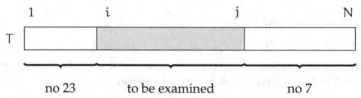

knowing that this array has been obtained by means of exchanges between pairs $(7, 23)$ or $(23, 7)$. Hence, the following invariant can be retained:

$(i \in 1 .. j+1)$ **and** $(j \in i-1 .. N)$ **and** $(T[1 .. i-1]$ contains no 23) **and** $(T[j+1 .. N]$ contains no 7).

36 - A 2   **Answer** 2.   When i and j are equal, the grey area contains a unique element which, whatever it is, is located at the right place (no exchange required). We could think of taking this predicate as the stopping condition, but if T is empty, we have $i = 1$ and $j = 0$ (according to the invariant) and the condition $(i = j)$ is not met. Therefore, we adopt the stopping condition $(i \geqslant j)$ which covers the case of a empty area either empty or containing a single element.

36 - A 3   **Answer** 3.   Now, we continue the design of the loop.

3. Progression   It is specified by:

Precondition: $(i \in 1 .. j+1)$ **and** $(j \in i-1 .. N)$ **and** $(T[1 .. i-1]$ does not contain any 23) **and** $(T[j+1 .. N]$ does not contain any 7) **and** **not**$(i \geqslant j)$

PROGRESSION

Postcondition: $(i \in 1 .. j+1)$ **and** $(j \in i-1 .. N)$ **and** $(T[1 .. i-1]$ does not contain any 23) **and** $(T[j+1 .. N]$ does not contain any 7)

The two indexes i and j will be managed simultaneously in the following synthesized way:

	$T[i] = 23$	$T[i] \neq 23$
$T[j] = 7$	*Exchange*(i,j); $i \leftarrow i+1$; $j \leftarrow j-1$	$i \leftarrow i+1$
$T[j] \neq 7$	$j \leftarrow j-1$	$j \leftarrow j-1$; $i \leftarrow i+1$

4. **Initialization** To reach the invariant from the precondition, it is sufficient to make the assignments: $i \leftarrow 1$ and $j \leftarrow N$.

5. **Termination** The expression $(j - i + 1)$ decreases by 1 or 2 at each step and it remains nonnegative.

Answer 4. The number of exchanges is at best zero (23's are all located after 7's) and at worst $\lfloor N/2 \rfloor$ (T contains a sequence of $\lfloor N/2 \rfloor$ (respectively $\lceil N/2 \rceil$) 23's followed by a sequence of $\lceil N/2 \rceil$ (respectively $\lfloor N/2 \rfloor$) 7's). Three comparisons are performed at each step of the loop (one for the control of the loop and two for the comparisons between $T[i]$ and $T[j]$). The number of steps is at best equal to $\lfloor N/2 \rfloor$ (when both indexes i and j evolve always together) and at worst $(N-1)$ (when only one of the two indexes i and j changes). Thus, complexity is in $\Theta(N)$ in terms of both comparisons and exchanges.

36 - A 4

Answers to problem 37. The Mth zero *The problem is on page 116.*

Answer 1. A new expression of the postcondition is:

37 - A 1

Postcondition: $(p \in 0 \,.\,.\, M-1)$ **and** $(i \in 1\,.\,.\,N)$ **and** $(p = (\#j \cdot ((j \in 1\,.\,.\,i-1)$ **and** $(T[j] = 0)))$ **and** $(p = M-1)$ **and** $(T[i] = 0)$.

Answer 2. We successively examine the five components of the loop.

37 - A 2

1. **Invariant** The invariant contains the first three conjuncts (including the quantified expression):

   $(p \in 0\,.\,.\,M-1)$ **and** $(i \in 1\,.\,.\,N)$ **and** $(p = (\#j \cdot ((j \in 1\,.\,.\,i-1)$ **and** $(T[j] = 0))))$.

2. **Stopping condition** It is made of the two discarded conjuncts:

   $(p = M-1)$ **and** $(T[i] = 0)$.

3. **Progression** It is specified by:

   Precondition: $(p \in 0\,.\,.\,M-1)$ **and** $(i \in 1\,.\,.\,N)$ **and** $(p = \#j \cdot (j \in 1\,.\,.\,i-1)$ **and** $(T[j] = 0))$ **and** **not**$((p = M-1)$ **and** $(T[i] = 0))$

   PROGRESSION

   Postcondition: $(p \in 0\,.\,.\,M-1)$ **and** $(i \in 1\,.\,.\,N)$ **and** $(p = \#j \cdot ((j \in 1\,.\,.\,i-1)$ **and** $(T[j] = 0))$.

   The following fragment of code answers this specification:

```
1. if T[i] = 0 then
2.     p ← p + 1
3. end if;
4. i ← i + 1
```

4. Initialization The initialization must comply with the following specification:

Precondition: (M constant) **and** (M $\in \mathbb{N}_1$) **and** (T is a constant array of N integers) **and** (T contains at least M zeros)

INITIALIZATION

Postcondition: $(p \in 0..M-1)$ **and** $(i \in 1..N)$ **and** $(p = \#j \cdot ((j \in 1..i-1)$ **and** $(T[j] = 0))$.

When i is equal to 1, p must take the value 0. This situation is attained from the precondition by the two assignments: $i \leftarrow 1$ and $p \leftarrow 0$.

5. Termination The expression $(N - i)$ diminishes by 1 at each step of the progression, while remaining nonnegative, which guarantees the termination.

37 - A 3   **Answer** 3.   The program associated with the loop is:

```
1. constants
2.    N ∈ ℕ₁ and N = ... and M ∈ 1..N and M = ... and T ∈ 1..
      N → ℕ and T = [...]
3. variables
4.    p ∈ 0..M − 1 and i ∈ 1..N
5. begin
6.    /% PRE: (M constant) and (M ∈ ℕ₁) and (T is a constant array of N
      integers) and (T contains at least M zeros) %/
7.    i ← 1 ; p ← 0 ;
8.    while not((p = M − 1) and (T[i] = 0)) do
9.       if T[i] = 0 then
10.          p ← p + 1
11.      end if;
12.      i ← i + 1
13.   end while;
14.   /% POST: i is the position of the Mᵗʰ zero in T %/
15.   write(the Mᵗʰ zero in , T, is located in position , i)
16. end
```

The loop is executed at most (respectively at least) N (respectively M) times. At each step, two comparisons are made, hence the complexity is in $\Omega(M)$ and $\mathcal{O}(N)$ comparisons.

Answers to problem 38. Alternating odd and even *The problem is on page 116.*

38 - A 1   **Answer** 1.   We have:

A **and** B **and** (C **or** D)
⇔   distributivity
(A **and** B **and** C) **or** (A **and** B **and** D)
⇒   (A **and** B) ⇒ A **and** (A **and** B) ⇒ B
(A **and** C) **or** (B **and** D).

Hence, we can deduce:

P **and** Q **and** $((e = 2N + 2)$ **or** $(o = 2N + 1))$
⇒
(P **and** $(e = 2N + 2)$) **or** (Q **and** $(o = 2N + 1)$).

Developing P and Q, the following postcondition is obtained:

Postcondition (third version entailing the second one): $(e \in 1 .. 2N + 2)$ **and** (e is even) **and** (positions with even indexes of the interval $1 .. e - 2$ contain even values) **and** $(o \in 1 .. 2N + 1)$ **and** (o is odd) **and** (positions with odd indexes of the interval $1 .. o - 2$ contain odd values) **and** $[(e = 2N + 2)$ **or** $(o = 2N + 1)]$.

Answer 2.   We successively review the five components of the loop.

38 - A 2

1. Invariant The first six conjuncts of the postcondition are easy to establish and they are retained for the invariant:

$(e \in 1 .. 2N + 2)$ **and** (e is even) **and** (positions with even indexes of the interval $2 .. e - 2$ contain even values) **and** $(o \in 1 .. 2N + 1)$ **and** (o is odd) **and** (positions with odd indexes of the interval $1 .. o - 2$ contain odd values).

2. Stopping condition We take the discarded conjunct:

$$((e = 2N + 2) \text{ or } (o = 2N + 1)).$$

3. Progression It is specified by:

Precondition: $(e \in 1..2N + 2)$ **and** (e is even) **and** (positions with even indexes of the interval $2..e - 2$ contain even values) **and** $(o \in 1..2N + 1)$ **and** (o is odd) **and** (positions with odd indexes of the interval $1 .. o - 2$ contain odd values) **and** **not**$[(e = 2N + 2)$ **or** $(o = 2N + 1)]$

PROGRESSION

Postcondition: $(e \in 2 .. 2N)$ **and** (e is even) **and** (positions with even indexes of the interval $2..e - 2$ contain even values) **and** $(o \in 1..2N + 1)$ **and** (o is odd) **and** (positions with odd indexes of the interval $1 .. o - 2$ contain odd values).

Before the progression, we are either in the following situation:

values with odd indexes are correctly placed

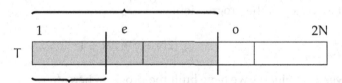

values with even indexes are correctly placed

or in this one:

values with even indexes are correctly placed

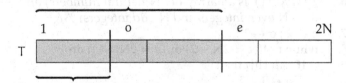

values with odd indexes are correctly placed

The relative positions of o and e do not play any role and we can indifferently take into consideration T[e] or T[o] (which, nevertheless, breaks the symmetry exploited until now) to propose the progression:

1. **if** *odd*(T[i]) **then**
2.   o ← o + 2
3. **else**
4.   *Exchange*(o, e) ; e ← e + 2
5. **end if**

assuming available the function *odd*(k) which returns **true** if k is odd, **false** otherwise. The preservation of the symmetry would require the review of the four possible cases (T[i] even and T[e] odd, T[o] odd and T[e] odd, etc.), which would lead to a somewhat unsightly progression.

4. Initialization It obeys the following specification:

Precondition: (T is an array of 2N natural numbers) **and** (S is the constant bag of values contained in T) **and** (N ⩾ 0) **and** (T contains N even integers and N odd integers)

INITIALIZATION

Postcondition: (e ∈ 2..2N) **and** (e is even) **and** (positions with even indexes of the interval 1..e − 2 contain even values) **and** (o ∈ 1..2N + 1) **and** (o is odd) **and** (positions with odd indexes of the interval 1 .. o − 2 contain odd values).

The following situation:

complies with the postcondition and the transition from the precondition is obtained with the assignments: o ← 1; e ← 2.

5. Termination One of the two variables o and e decreases by 2 at each step of the progression. In contrast, the following expression is nonnegative and it diminishes by 1 at each step of the progression:

$$(2N − e + 2N + 1 − o)/2.$$

38 - A 3   **Answer** 3.   Finally, we have built the program hereafter:

1. **constants**
2.   N ∈ ℕ and N = ...
3. **variables**
4.   T ∈ 1..2N → ℕ and T = [...] and e ∈ 2..2N + 2 and o ∈ 1..2N + 1
5. **begin**
6.   /% *PRE*: (T is an array of 2N natural numbers) **and** (N ⩾ 0) **and** (T contains N even integers and N odd integers) %/
7.   e ← 2 ; o ← 1 ;
8.   **while not**((e = 2N + 2) **or** (o = 2N + 1)) **do**
9.   **if** *odd*(T[i]) **then**
10.   o ← i + 2
11.   **else**
12.   *Exchange*(o, e) ; e ← e + 2
13.   **end if**
14.   **end while**;
15.   /% *POST*: (*positions with even indexes contain even values*) **or** (*positions with odd indexes contain odd values*) %/

16.   **write**(T)
17. **end**

Answer 4.   In terms of exchanges, this algorithm is in $\mathcal{O}(N)$. The number of evaluated   38 - A 4
conditions is in $\Theta(N)$ (one condition for the control of the loop and another one for testing
T[o] – odd or not).

Answer 5.   We have: 38 - A 5

$(e \in 2 .. 2N)$ **and** (e is even) **and**
(positions with even indexes of the interval $2 .. e - 2$
contain even values) **and** $(o \in 1 .. 2N + 1)$ **and** (o is odd) **and**
(positions with odd indexes of the interval $1 .. o - 2$
contain odd values) **and** $(e = 2N)$ **and** $(o = 2N + 1)$
$\Rightarrow$ **A and B** $\Rightarrow$ **A or B**
$(e \in 2 .. 2N)$ **and** (e is even) **and**
(positions with even indexes of the interval $2 .. e - 2$
contain even values) **and** $(o \in 1 .. 2N + 1)$ **and** (o is odd) **and**
(positions with odd indexes of the interval $1 .. o - 2$
contain odd values) **and** $((e = 2N)$ **or** $(o = 2N + 1))$,

this latter expression being nothing but the postcondition used before. The newly proposed
postcondition is thus a (logical) strengthening of the initial postcondition; hence, it can
serve as a basis for the construction of a loop appropriate to solve the problem.

Answer 6.   With this in mind, we can use the same invariant as before: 38 - A 6

$(e \in 1 .. 2N + 2)$ **and** (e is even) **and** (positions with even indexes of the interval
$2 .. e - 2$ contain even values) **and** $(o \in 1 .. 2N + 1)$ **and** (o is odd) **and** (positions
with odd indexes of the interval $1 .. o - 2$ contain odd values)

and take the discarded conjunct as stopping condition:

$((e = 2N + 2)$ **and** $(o = 2N + 1))$.

The progression is specified by:

Precondition: $(e \in 1 .. 2N + 2)$ **and** (e is even) **and** (positions with even indexes of the
interval $2 .. e - 2$ contain even values) **and** $(o \in 1 .. 2N + 1)$ **and** (o is odd) **and** (positions
with odd indexes of the interval $1 .. o - 2$ contain odd values) **and not**$((e = 2N + 2)$ **and** $(o =
2N + 1))$

PROGRESSION

Postcondition: $(e \in 2 .. 2N)$ **and** (e is even) **and** (positions with even indexes of the interval
$2 .. e - 2$ contain even values) **and** $(o \in 1 .. 2N + 1)$ **and** (o is odd) **and** (positions with odd
indexes of the interval $1 .. o - 2$ contain odd values).

Here again T[o] can be tested as to the fact that it is odd (or not), but since the stopping
condition is conjunctive, its negation is disjunctive. Therefore, we can be in the situation
where $o = 2N + 1$ (with $e \neq 2N + 2$) which means that odd values are all well placed.
The exchange must not be done ($2N + 1$ being an invalid index for T), but "force" the
variable p to its final value ($2N + 2$), since even values are necessarily well placed, hence
the progression:

1. **if** $o \neq 2N + 1$ **then**
2.   **if** *odd*(T[o]) **then**
3. $o \leftarrow i + 2$
4.   **else**

5.   *Exchange*(o, e) ; $e \leftarrow p + 2$
6.   **end if**
7. **else**
8. $e \leftarrow 2N + 2$
9. **end if**

It can be noticed that this progression is slightly more tricky to build than the previous one. Moreover, it is easy to see that the complexity of the program is the same in terms of exchanges, but that the number of evaluated conditions for each iteration is now 3 instead of 2 formerly.

Answers to problem 39. The longest sequence of zeros

The problem is on page 117.

39 - A 1   **Answer 1.**   The new invariant is:

(lg is the length of the longest succession of zeros contained in the subarray $T[1..i-1]$) **and** $(i \in 1..N+1)$ **and** $(p \in 1..i)$ **and** (p is the length of the longest succession of consecutive zeros finishing in $(i-1)$),

which can be schematized the following way:

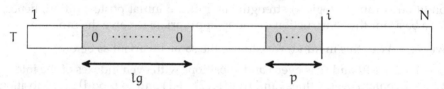

Despite appearances suggested by this schema, the subarrays associated with lg and p may effectively be confused.

39 - A 2   **Answer 2.**   The progression is specified by:

Precondition: (lg is the length of the longest sequence of zeros contained in the subarray $T[1..i-1]$) **and** $(i \in 1..N+1)$ **and** $(p \in 0..i-1)$ **and** (p is the length of the longest sequence of consecutive zeros finishing in $i-1$) **and not**$(i = N+1)$

PROGRESSION

Postcondition: (lg is the length of the longest succession of zeros contained in the subarray $T[1..i-1]$) **and** $(i \in 1..N+1)$ **and** $(p \in 0..i-1)$ **and** (p is the length of the longest sequence of consecutive zeros finishing in $i-1$).

It can be asserted that $T[i]$ exists and that the invariant holds. It follows that, if $T[i] = 0$ then p increases by 1, while lg becomes the greatest value between p and lg. Otherwise, lg remains unchanged whereas p is set to 0. Restoring the invariant is obtained by incrementing i by 1.

Hence, we have the following progression:

1. **if** $T[i] = 0$ **then**
2. $p \leftarrow p + 1$; $lg \leftarrow \max(\{lg, p\})$
3. **else**
4. $p \leftarrow 0$
5. **end if**;
6. $i \leftarrow i + 1$

The initialization is specified by:

> **Precondition:** (T is a constant array of N integers) **and** $(N \geqslant 0)$
>
> INITIALIZATION
>
> **Postcondition:** (lg is the length of the longest succession of zeros contained in the subarray $T[1 .. i - 1]$) **and** $(i \in 1 .. N + 1)$ **and** $(p \in 0 .. i - 1)$ **and** (p is the length of the longest succession of consecutive zeros finishing in $i - 1$).

Establishing the postcondition (the invariant of the loop) is achieved by the assignments: $i \leftarrow 1 ; lg \leftarrow 0 ; p \leftarrow 0.$

As to the termination, the expression $(N + 1 - i)$ is appropriate since it decreases by 1 at each step of the progression while remaining nonnegative.

Answer 3.   Eventually, we have built the following program: 39 - A 3

```
1.  constants
2.      N ∈ ℕ and N = ... and T ∈ 1 .. N → ℕ and T = [...]
3.  variables
4.      p ∈ 0 .. N and i ∈ 1 .. N + 1
5.  begin
6.      /% PRE: (T is a constant array of N integers) and  (N ⩾ 0) %/
7.      i ← 1 ; lg ← 0 ; p ← 0 ;
8.      while not(i = N + 1) do
9.          if T[i] = 0 then
10.             p ← p + 1 ; lg ← max({lg, p})
11.         else
12.             p ← 0
13.         end if;
14.         i ← i + 1
15.     end while;
16.     /% POST: (lg is the length of the longest succession of consecutive zeros
               contained in the array T) %/
17.     write(the length of the longest succession of zeros in , T, is , lg)
18. end
```

This solution demands N iterations since i is increased by 1 at each step of the progression. Thus, it is in $\Theta(N)$ comparisons (control of the loop and test of $T[i]$).

Answer 4.   The variable lg contains continuously (in the sense of the invariant) the   39 - A 4
length of the longest sequence of zeros. Carrying on the execution of the loop is meaningful only if the value of lg can evolve. However, the longest possible succession of zeros involving $T[i]$ is that which would encompass the p zeros situated before i and the (potential) $(N + 1 - i)$ zeros located between the positions i and N. When $(p + N + 1 - i)$ is less than (or equal to) lg, the value of lg will not change and thus the loop can stop. We can deduce that an alternative to the stopping condition $(i = N + 1)$ is $(p + N + 1 - i) \leqslant lg$. This latter enables an "early" termination, thus less iterations, hence a better efficiency. With this solution, the number of comparisons is in $O(N)$. It can be noticed that when the array T contains no zero, the two stopping conditions are equivalent and lead to browse the loop N times.

Answers to problem 40. The majority element (iterative issue) *The problem is on page 119.*

40 - A 1   **Answer 1.**   *Demonstration of property 3 page 120* The only possibility is that one element of P is majority. But, any element of P is present at most $|P|/2$ times (which, in this case, is equal to $|S|/2$ times) and thus S cannot be majority.

Demonstration of property 4 page 120, part 1 Letting $maj(S)$ be the predicate stating that S is majority and $maj(v, S)$ the predicate stating that v is a majority element in S, proposition 1 can be expressed a:

$$maj(S) \;\Rightarrow\; (c \in C \Rightarrow maj(c, S)),$$

proposition which will be proven by contradiction as follows:

$$\textbf{not}(c \in C \Rightarrow maj(c, S)) \;\Rightarrow\; \textbf{not } maj(S),$$

or (applying rules of the propositional calculus):

$$(c \in C \textbf{ and not } maj(c, S)) \;\Rightarrow\; \textbf{not } maj(S).$$

If c is not a majority element, is it possible that a random element x of P, different from c, is majority? The answer is negative since this element has a multiplicity at most equal to $|P|/2$, value which is less than $\lfloor |S|/2 \rfloor + 1$. Therefore, there is no majority element in S.

Demonstration of property 4 page 120, part 2 It is enough to consider the schema in which the bag R is empty: C contains the value 5, which is not a majority element, 1 is the value with the highest multiplicity in S but it is not a majority element.

40 - A 2   **Answer 2.**   When the loop stops, R is empty according to the stopping condition and:

- either C is also empty and according to property (3), page 120, it is known that S is not majority,
- or C is nonempty and according to property (4), page 120, the value c contained in C (in any number of occurrences) is the *majority candidate* of S, i.e. the only potential majority element for S, but nothing is sure.

40 - A 3   **Answer 3.**   The precondition and postcondition of the loop built with the proposed invariant are:

Precondition: (S is a bag of N values) **and** $(N \geqslant 1)$.

Postcondition: if C is nonempty, x contains the value of the majority candidate of S; if C is empty, S is not majority.

Therefore, this loop has a weakened postcondition with respect to that of the initial problem. In order to solve it, in the case where a possible majority candidate has been identified, it is necessary to check whether S is *actually* majority (or not).

40 - A 4   **Answer 4.**   We now give the progression, the initialization and the termination function.

Progression We choose an arbitrary element t of R which is withdrawn from R, and:

     (a) if C is empty, t is inserted in C,

     (b) if t is already in C, it is added to C,

     (c) if t is absent from C, t is paired with an arbitrary element of C (which is suppressed from C) and the couple is moved to the bag P.

Under the assumption of the negation of the stopping condition, this procedure is feasible and it maintains the invariant.

Initialization The bag S is copied into R. The two bags P and C are emptied, which establishes the invariant.

Termination The value of |R| decreases by 1 at each step of the progression, which guarantees that the loop finishes.

Answer 5. The bag C is refined by the pair (x, nbx), where x is the value present in C   40 - A 5
and nbx is its multiplicity. The bag R is refined by the pair (T, i), where T is an array of N elements and i is such that $i \in 1 .. N$. $T[i .. N]$ materializes the bag R. Last, the bag P disappears from the refinement since its components are never used. The following algorithm is deduced:

```
 1. constants
 2.    N ∈ ℕ₁ and N = ... and T ∈ 1 .. N → ℕ₁ and T = [...]
 3. variables
 4.    x ∈ ℕ₁ and nbx ∈ 0 .. N and i ∈ 1 .. N + 1
 5. begin
 6.    /% PRE: (S is a bag of N values represented by the array T[1..N]) and (N ⩾
        1) %/
 7.    nbx ← 0 ; i ← 1 ;
 8.    while i ≠ N + 1 do
 9.       if nbx = 0 then
10.          x ← T[i] ; nbx ← 1
11.       elsif T[i] = x then
12.          nbx ← nbx + 1
13.       else
14.          nbx ← nbx − 1
15.       end if;
16.       i ← i + 1
17.    end while;
18.    /% POST: if C is nonempty (nbx > 0), x contains the value of the majority
        candidate of S; if C is empty (nbx = 0), S is not majority %/
19.    if nbx = 0 or else mult(x, T) ⩽ ⌊N/2⌋ then
20.       x ← −1 ;
21.       write(No majority element in the array , T)
22.    else
23.       write(x, is the majority element of the array , T)
24.    end if
25. end
```

The expression $mult(x, T)$ requires a refinement using a loop over the array T, which is not made explicit here. This algorithm refined a second time evaluates $(N + 1)$ times the stopping condition of the first loop and at most $(N + 1)$ times that of the second loop; thus it is in $\Theta(N)$ in terms of comparisons.

Answers to problem 41. The celebrity problem   *The problem is on page 121.*

Answer 1. By convention, a group with a single person has a star, thus at most one   41 - A 1
star. The property is proven by contradiction for a group made of at least two people.

Let us assume that i_1 and i_2 are two stars of a group. Since a star is known by everyone, operations $Knows(i_1, i_2)$ and $Knows(i_2, i_1)$ both return **true**, which contradicts the fact that a star knows nobody in the group.

41 - A 2 **Answer** 2. Let us assume that the operation $Knows(i, j)$ is performed and that we are only provided with the answer to rule on the existence of a star. If the answer is positive, j can be the star of the group since he/she is known by i (who knows another member of the group and thus cannot be the star). If the answer is negative, j cannot be the star since he/she is not known by a member of the group, but i can be the star.

41 - A 3 **Answer** 3. The problem to solve is specified by:

Precondition: (We have group of N people) **and** $(N \geqslant 1)$

Postcondition: ((i is the star of the group) **and** $(i \in 1 .. N))$ **or** ((the group has no star) **and** $(i = N + 1))$.

41 - A 4 **Answer** 4. The program allowing for the identification of a "potential" star has a postcondition which is a weakened version of the initial problem, namely:

Postcondition: ((i is *perhaps* the star of the group) **and** $(i \in 1 .. N))$.

A "potential" star is identified by means of a loop whose specification is:

Precondition: (We have a group of N people) **and** $(N \geqslant 1)$.

Postcondition: ((i is *perhaps* the star of the group) **and** $(i \in 1 .. N))$.

The components of the loop are as follows:

1. Invariant The postcondition is strengthened in:

Postcondition: $(j \in 1 .. N + 1)$ **and** $(i \in 1 .. N + 1)$ **and** (i is *perhaps* the star of members $1 .. j - 1$ of the group) **and** $(j = N + 1)$.

The first three conjuncts are chosen for the invariant:

$(j \in 1 .. N+1)$ **and** $(i \in 1 .. N+1)$ **and** (i is *perhaps* the star of members $1 .. j - 1$ of the group).

2. Stopping condition The discarded conjunct is taken: $(j = N + 1)$.

3. Progression It is specified by:

Precondition: $(j \in 1 .. N + 1)$ **and** $(i \in 1 .. N + 1)$ **and** (i is *perhaps* the star of members $1 .. j - 1$ of the group) **and** $\textbf{not}(j = N + 1)$

PROGRESSION

Postcondition: $(j \in 1 .. N+1)$ **and** $(i \in 1 .. N+1)$ **and** (i is *perhaps* the star of members $1 .. j - 1$ of the group).

The progression must deal with member number j of the group. We will use the operation $Knows(j, i)$, i being the "potential" star. From question 2, if the answer is **true**, i keeps its status, otherwise it is replaced by j. Thus, we have the progression:

```
1. if not  Knows(j, i) then
2.     i ← j
3. end if;
4. j ← j + 1
```

4. Initialization In order to establish the invariant, it is sufficient to select person 1 as a possible star (and therefore to assign 2 to j), i.e. to make the assignments: $i \leftarrow 1$ and $j \leftarrow 2$.

5. Termination The expression $(N + 1 - j)$ is suitable since it decreases at each step of the loop while remaining nonnegative.

Answer 5.   At the end of the previous loop, i identifies a member of the group which   41 - A 5
may be the star. It remains to confirm that i is actually the star of the group, or that there is
no star inside it (thanks to the principle of sequential composition introduced page 96.
First of all, let us remark that we know that any member j, with j greater than i, knows the
"potential" star i. Member i is actually the star only if: i) any member j with j less than i is
such that $Knows(j, i)$ is **true**, and ii) any member j *other than* i is such that **not**$(Knows(i, j))$. It
is easy to observe that each situation corresponds to the special case described in section
3.5.2, page 109. Therefore, we will adapt the pattern given in page 109.
In the first loop, the generic property LP is identified to **not**$(Knows(j, i))$ and variable N to
$(i - 1)$. In the second one, LP is identified to $((j \neq i)$ **and** $Knows(i, j))$, hence the program:

```
 1.  constants
 2.     N ∈ ℕ₁ and N = ...
 3.  variables
 4.     i ∈ 1 .. N + 1 and j ∈ 1 .. N + 1
 5.  begin
 6.     /% first loop: identification of a "potential" star %/
 7.     /% PRE: (We have a group of N people) and (N ⩾ 1) %/
 8.     i ← 1 ; j ← 2 ;
 9.     while not(j = N + 1) do
10.         if not  Knows(j, i) then
11.             i ← j
12.         end if;
13.         j ← j + 1
14.     end while;
15.     /% POST: (j ∈ 1 .. N + 1) and (i ∈ 1 .. N) and (i is perhaps the star of
            members 1 .. j − 1 of the group) and (j = N + 1) %/
16.     /% second loop %/
17.     /% PRE: (i is perhaps the star of the group) %/
18.     j ← 1 ;
19.     while not((j = i) or else not Knows(j, i)) do
20.         j ← j + 1
21.     end while;
22.     /% POST: (i ∈ 1 .. N) and (j ∈ 1 .. i + 1) and ((j = i) and (i is perhaps the
            star of members 1 .. j − 1 of the group)) or ((j ≠ i) and the group has no
            star %/
23.     if j ≠ i then
24.         write(no star in the group)
25.     else
26.         /% third loop %/
27.         /% PRE: (i is perhaps the star of the group) %/
28.         j ← 1 ;
29.         while not((j = N + 1) or else ((j ≠ i) and (Knows(i, j)))) do
30.             j ← j + 1
31.         end while;
32.         /% POST: ((i is the star of the group) and (j = N + 1)) or ((the group
                has no star) and (j ∈ 1 .. N)) %/
33.         if j = N + 1 then
34.             write(i, is the star of the group)
```

35.   **else**
36.   **write**(*no star in the group*)
37.   **end if**
38.   **end if**
39. **end**

41 - A 6   **Answer** 6.   The first step (identification of a "potential" star) requires exactly $(N - 1)$ operations *Knows*. The second one requires between one (when member 1 does not know the "potential" star) and $(N - 1)$ (when $i = N$ and the first $(N - 1)$ members know the last one who is the "potential" star) operations *Knows*. The last step also needs between one (when membre i knows member 1) and $(N - 1)$ (when member i knows nobody in the group) operations *Knows*. Thus, the complexity is linear as expected.

Remark

The complete presentation of this problem as well as its background can be found in [25].

Answers to problem 42. Weakening a precondition *The problem is on page 122.*

Sorting increasingly an array ordered decreasingly

42 - A 1   **Answer** 1.   If the array T is ordered decreasingly, it can be transformed into an increasingly ordered array by means of a loop whose progression is inspired from that used in problem 34, page 113. Instead of testing the symmetry of the array, elements whose indexes j and $(N + 1 - j)$ are in "mirror" positions are exchanged. The stopping condition of the loop is $j \geqslant N + 1 - j$. The solution obtained requires $\lfloor N/2 \rfloor$ exchanges and it is in $\Theta(N)$.

42 - A 2   **Answer** 2.   The sort algorithm proposed in problem 33 page 112, is in $\Theta(N^2)$ exchanges. A lower asymptotic complexity $(\mathcal{O}(N \cdot \log_2(N)))$ can be reached with a more efficient sort algorithm such as "quicksort". However, whatever the choice of such an algorithm, if there is a gain in terms of design and construction of the program, there is a loss in terms of performances. It appears that weakening the precondition is not appropriate in this case.

Constrained variation array

42 - A 3   **Answer** 3.   Let $T[i] = k$ $(k > 0)$. Since the difference between two consecutive elements is at most 1, the most favorable case to find out a zero occurs with the program:

$$T[i] = k, T[i + 1] = k - 1, \ldots, T[i + k - 1] = 1, T[i + k] = 0.$$

It appears that all the elements of T with indexes i to $i + k - 1$ ($= i + T[i] - 1$) are strictly positive. When we have a longer sequence, to reach a zero the previous property over elements with indexes i to $(i + T[i] - 1)$ still holds. Formally, we have:

$$(T[i] > 0) \Rightarrow \forall j \cdot (j \in i .. i + T[i] - 1 \Rightarrow T[j] > 0).$$

42 - A 4   **Answer** 4.   We build the constituents of a loop in the spirit of those designed for the search of the first zero, taking advantage of the result established in the previous question.

1. Invariant   We take: $(i \in 1 .. N)$ **and** $(T[1 .. i - 1]$ contains no zero).

2. Stopping condition   It is $T[i] = 0$.

3. **Progression** From the property established previously, it is known that, since $T[i]$ is not equal to zero, it is possible to increment i by the value $T[i]$ with the guarantee that no zero is "missed" ($T[i + T[i]]$ may be equal to 0), hence the progression: $i \leftarrow i + T[i]$.

4. **Initialization** The initialization is restricted to the assignment $i \leftarrow 1$.

5. **Termination** The expression $(N - i)$ is appropriate.

Answer 5.   The specific algorithm which has been designed needs between one com-   42 - A 5
parison (if $T[1] = 0$) and N comparisons (if $T[1] = \ldots = T[N-1] = 1$ and $T[N] = 0$). It is the same for the algorithm given in page 101. The two solutions are situated in the same class of complexity $\mathcal{O}(N)$. However, in the specific algorithm the step of the loop is variable and it is always greater than or equal to 1. Thus, it is preferable to use it since it never does worse than the other one (even slightly better in general).

Answer 6.   The discarded conjunct (the difference between two consecutive elements   42 - A 6
of T is at least 1) expresses the fact that it cannot exist two consecutive elements of T with the same value, which does not help to resolve the problem of the search for the first zero. As a consequence, there is no (obvious) specific program in this case. It is thus recommended to use the program corresponding to the weakened precondition (see page 101), choice solving "at best" the problem in a performance perspective.

Answer 7.   The three examples treated previously show that weakening the precondi-   42 - A 7
tion can lead to:

- a solution whose class of complexity is worse than that of a specific solution,
- a solution of same class of complexity, but after all less efficient,
- a good solution if the discarded conjunct cannot be exploited for building a specific solution.

Answers to problem 43. Halving a polygon   *The problem is on page 123.*

Answer 1.   We have: 43 - A 1

$$\left| \|\widehat{(i,j)}\| - \|\widehat{(j,i)}\| \right|$$

$=$ arithmetics

$$\left| 2 \cdot \|\widehat{(i,j)}\| - (\|\widehat{(j,i)}\| + \|\widehat{(i,j)}\|) \right|$$

$=$ definition of p

$$\left| 2 \cdot \|\widehat{(i,j)}\| - p \right|$$

$=$ arithmetics

$$2 \cdot \left| \|\widehat{(i,j)}\| - \frac{p}{2} \right|.$$

Answer 2.   When the semi-perimeter having its origin in vertex j has exactly its end in   43 - A 2
the middle of a side, there are two optimal chords issued from vertex j. It is the case of the pentagon hereafter: there are two optimal chords issued from j: $\overline{(j, k)}$ and $\overline{(j, k+1)}$. The first one separates the pentagon into $\|\widehat{(j, k)}\| = 4$ units, and $\|\widehat{(k, j)}\| = 8$ units, the second one separates it into $\|\widehat{(j, k+1)}\| = 8$ units, and $\|\widehat{(k+1, j)}\| = 4$ units.

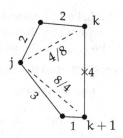

43 - A 3   **Answer** 3.   It is easy to prove that:

$$\forall l \cdot \left(l \in j+2 .. k-2 \Rightarrow \left| \|(j\overset{\frown}{+}1,l)\| - p/2.0 \right| > \left| \|(j,l\overset{\frown}{+}1)\| - p/2.0 \right| \right).$$

Consequently, it is sufficient to restrict the proof to the longest arc among the set of arcs $(j\overset{\frown}{+}1,j+2), (j\overset{\frown}{+}1,j+3),\ldots,(j\overset{\frown}{+}1,k-1)$, or $(j\overset{\frown}{+}1,k-1)$. Thus, we will demonstrate that $\left| \|(j\overset{\frown}{+}1,k-1)\| - p/2.0 \right| > \left| \|(j,\overset{\frown}{k})\| - p/2.0 \right| (= \delta_j).$

Denoting by q the extremity of the semi-perimeter issued from j, two situations must be singled out:

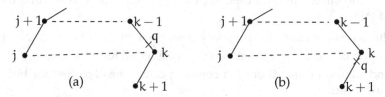

(a)   (b)

In both cases, we have:

$$\left| \|(j\overset{\frown}{+}1,k-1)\| - \frac{p}{2.0} \right|$$

$=$ $\qquad\qquad\qquad \frac{p}{2.0} > \|(j\overset{\frown}{+}1,k-1)\|$ and property of the absolute value

$$\frac{p}{2.0} - \|(j\overset{\frown}{+}1,k-1)\|$$

$=$ $\qquad\qquad\qquad\qquad\qquad\qquad\qquad\qquad\qquad$ development of $\frac{p}{2.0}$

$$\|(j,j\overset{\frown}{+}1)\| + \|(j\overset{\frown}{+}1,k-1)\| + \|(k\overset{\frown}{-}1,q)\| - \|(j\overset{\frown}{+}1,k-1)\|$$

$=$ $\qquad\qquad\qquad\qquad\qquad\qquad\qquad\qquad\qquad$ arithmetics

$$\|(j,j\overset{\frown}{+}1)\| + \|(k\overset{\frown}{-}1,q)\|.$$

In the first case (schema (a)), $\|(k\overset{\frown}{-}1,q)\| > \|(q,\overset{\frown}{k})\|$ since otherwise the chord $\overline{(j,k-1)}$ would be the *first* locally optimal chord for the vertex j. Therefore, it comes:

$$\|(j,j\overset{\frown}{+}1)\| + \|(k\overset{\frown}{-}1,q)\|$$

$>$ $\qquad\qquad\qquad\qquad\qquad\qquad\qquad\qquad\qquad$ arithmetics

$$\|(k\overset{\frown}{-}1,q)\|$$

$>$ $\qquad\qquad\qquad\qquad\qquad\qquad\qquad\qquad\qquad$ previous remark

$$\|(k,\overset{\frown}{q})\|$$

$=$ $\qquad\qquad\qquad\qquad\qquad\qquad\qquad\qquad\qquad$ definition of δ_j

$$\delta_j$$

and finally:

$$\left| \|(j+1,\overset{\frown}{k}-1)\| - \frac{p}{2.0} \right| > \delta_j.$$

In the second case (schema (b)), we have:

$$\|(j,\overset{\frown}{j}+1)\| + \|(k-\overset{\frown}{1},q)\|$$

$$=$$
    development of $\|(k-\overset{\frown}{1},q)\|$

$$\|(j,\overset{\frown}{j}+1)\| + \|(k-\overset{\frown}{1},k) + \|(k,\overset{\frown}{q})\|$$

$$>$$
    arithmetics

$$\|(k,\overset{\frown}{q})\|$$

$$=$$
    definition of δ_j

$$\delta_j$$

and we also have:

$$\left| \|(j+1,\overset{\frown}{k}-1)\| - \frac{p}{2.0} \right| > \delta_j.$$

Answer 4. First of all, let us notice that the chord $\overline{(j+1,k)}$ may not exist and we will come back to this point later (see question 5). To prove that the chord $\overline{(j+1,k)}$ may be better than $\overline{(j,k)}$ the first optimal chord issued from j, an example suffices. Let us consider the following pentagon:

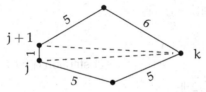

The chord $\overline{(j,k)}$ is locally optimal and it separates the perimeter into two parts of respective lengths 12.0 and 10.0. The chord $\overline{(j+1,k)}$ separates the perimeter into two equal parts of length 11.0. This division is optimal since the value of δ_{j+1} is 0.0 and it outperforms the previous one for which $\delta_j = 12.0 - 11.0 = 1.0$.

Answer 5. The value of the perimeter of the polygon is 11.8 and the value of its semi-perimeter is 5.9. The arcs whose length intervenes in the calculation are greyed-out as ■, as ▨ or as □ in figure 3.5.

We will go into the details of the calculations in order to highlight the properties and mechanisms used. In the case of the first line, the respective lengths of the arcs $(1,\overset{\frown}{2})$, $(1,\overset{\frown}{3})$, $(1,\overset{\frown}{4})$ and $(1,\overset{\frown}{5})$ are calculated. Their values are 2.2, 3.1, 4.7 and 6.3. The length of the arcs $(1,\overset{\frown}{6})$ to $(1,\overset{\frown}{1})$ is not calculated (according to the heuristics "stop as early as possible"), since the length of the arc $(1,\overset{\frown}{5})$ is greater than that of the semi-perimeter. The chord $\overline{(1,5)}$ associated with this arc (cell greyed-out as ■ in the schema) is retained as the (first) locally optimal chord from the vertex 1, since the comparison with the previous arc $(1,\overset{\frown}{4})$ is in favor of $(1,\overset{\frown}{5})$.

As for the arcs whose origin is vertex 2, it is useless calculating the length of the arcs $(2,\overset{\frown}{3})$ and $(2,\overset{\frown}{4})$ (see question 3). The evaluation begins with the arc $(2,\overset{\frown}{5})$ whose length is $\|(1,\overset{\frown}{5})\| - \|(1,\overset{\frown}{2})\|$ (or, 6.3 − 2.2 = 4.1). As a matter of fact, according to the definition of the length of an arc (definition 2 page 124, inductive case), if $j \neq i+1$ and $i \neq N$,

43 - A 4

43 - A 5

	2	3	4	5	6	7	8	9	1
1	2.2	3.1	4.7	6.3	7.4	8.7	10.5	11.2	11.8
2		0.9	2.5	4.1	5.2	6.5	8.3	9.0	9.6
3			1.6	3.2	4.3	5.6	7.4	8.1	8.7
4				1.6	2.7	4.0	5.8	6.5	7.1
5					1.1	2.4	4.2	4.9	5.5
6						1.3	3.1	3.8	4.4
7							1.8	2.5	3.1
8								0.7	1.3
9									0.6

Fig. 3.5 – Example corresponding to figure 3.4, page 124, showing the arcs whose length is actually calculated. The arcs greyed-out in ■ are those corresponding to locally optimal chords. The arcs ▨ correspond to those visited whose length is less than p/2.0. An arc $(\widehat{i,k})$ greyed-out as □ is, for a given origin i, the first arc whose length is greater than or equal to p/2.0, but which is not a locally optimal chord (whilst $\overline{(i, k-1)}$ is). The arcs on a white background (□) correspond to those not visited.

$$\|(\widehat{i,j})\| = d[i] + \|(\widehat{i+1,j})\|$$

$\Leftrightarrow$ first base case, definition 2, page 124

$$\|(\widehat{i,j})\| = \|(\widehat{i,i+1})\| + \|(\widehat{i+1,j})\|$$

$\Leftrightarrow$ arithmetics

$$\|(\widehat{i+1,j})\| = \|(\widehat{i,j})\| - \|(\widehat{i,i+1})\|$$

$\Rightarrow$ substitution (i by 1 and j by 5) and arithmetics

$$\|(\widehat{2,5})\| = \|(\widehat{1,5})\| - \|(\widehat{1,2})\|$$

$\Leftrightarrow$ numerical application

$$4.1 = 6.3 - 2.2.$$

We pursue with the arcs $(\widehat{2,6})$ of length 5.2 and $(\widehat{2,7})$ of length 6.5. This latter value is greater than the semi-perimeter, which leads to select $\overline{(2,7)}$ as the locally optimal chord issued from vertex 2 (the length of the following arcs – $(\widehat{2,8}), (\widehat{2,9}), (\widehat{2,1})$ – is not calculated applying the heuristics "stop as early as possible"). For the arcs starting at vertex 3, only length of the arcs $(\widehat{3,7})$ and $(\widehat{3,8})$ are calculated: $\left|\|(\widehat{3,7})\| - p/2.0\right| = 0.3$ and $\left|\|(\widehat{3,8})\| - p/2.0\right| = 1.5$. The comparison is in favor of $(\widehat{3,7})$; the chord $\overline{(3,7)}$ is thus declared to be locally optimal. The length of the arcs $(\widehat{3,9})$ and $(\widehat{3,1})$ is not calculated.

Vertex 7 is the starting point of the calculation related to arcs starting at vertex 4. We calculate the length of the chords $(\widehat{4,7}), (\widehat{4,8})$ and $(\widehat{4,9})$, whose respective values are 4.0, 5.8 and 6.5, which leads to take $\overline{(4,8)}$ as the locally optimal chord issued from vertex 4. The length of $(\widehat{4,1})$ is not calculated.

As for vertex 5, we calculate the length of the arcs $(\widehat{5,8}), (\widehat{5,9})$ and $(\widehat{5,1})$. Chord $\overline{(5,1)}$ of (maximum) value 5.5, is declared locally optimal.

From now on, in vertue of observation 3 in the statement of the problem, for each vertex i of the interval 6 .. 9, there is a single candidate arc $(\overset{\frown}{(6,1)}, \overset{\frown}{(7,1)}, \overset{\frown}{(8,1)}, \overset{\frown}{(9,1)})$; the related chord $(\overline{(6,1)}, \overline{(7,1)}, \overline{(8,1)}, \overline{(9,1)})$ is therefore locally optimal.

Eventually, the resulting global optimal chord is $\overline{(4,8)}$. Figure 3.5, page 152 confirms this result since, among all the values of the triangle of lengths, 5.8 is the one closest to 5.9, which is the length of the semi-perimeter.

Answer 6. The perimeter of this polygon is 11.0. Therefore, the value of its semi- 43 - A 6 perimeter is 5.5. For the arcs issued from the vertex 1, we have $\|\overset{\frown}{(1,2)}\| = 5.0$, value which does not allow for stopping the search for the locally optimal chord. On the contrary, the value $\|\overset{\frown}{(1,3)}\| = 8.0$ exceeds the semi-perimeter and we can stop the search for arcs whose origin is the vertex 1. Among these two values, $\|\overset{\frown}{(1,2)}\|$ is the best one and the chord $\overline{(1,2)}$ is the local optimum for vertex 1.

	2	3	1
1	5.0	8.0	11
2		3.0	6.0
3			3.0

However, to account for the arc whose origin is vertex 2, according to observation 3 of the statement, we should begin with the calculation of the arc $\|\overset{\frown}{(2,2)}\|$; yet, this one does not exist in the triangle of lengths. This special case shall be taken into consideration in the progression of the loop which will be built. It occurs when the row $(i+1)$ is dealt with and the locally optimal chord of line i is $\overline{(i,i+1)}$. So, this case is not specific to triangles, it is also the case of the quadrangle below for which the calculation for the arcs whose origin is the vertex 3 cannot be done from $\|\overset{\frown}{(2,3)}\|$ since the chord $\overline{(2,3)}$ is of type $\overline{(i,i+1)}$.

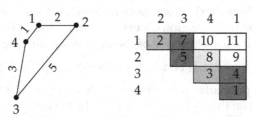

	2	3	4	1
1	2	7	10	11
2		5	8	9
3			3	4
4				1

Answer 7. Obviously, it is excluded to permanently dispose of the triangle of lengths 43 - A 7 and even to calculate the length of *all* its elements (otherwise, complexity would be in $\Theta(N^2)$). We will take advantage of observations 2, 3 and 4 of the statement (as it was done in the treatment of question 4, page 126) in order to avoid visiting some arcs in the course of iterations.

Figure 3.6, page 154, represents the situation reached in the context of the hypothesis of the work carried out partly with the graphic conventions of figure 3.5, page 152. Arcs hatched (▨) are those that remain to be treated.

The array D (respectively the scalar p) representing the length of the various sides (respectively the perimeter of the polygon) are constants. As such, they are not part of the invariant which is expressed as:

$i \in 1 .. N + 1$ **and** $j \in i + 1 .. N + 2$ **and**
the chord $\overline{(o,e)}$ is globally optimal over the portion of the triangle of lengths covering entirely rows 1 to $(i-1)$ and columns 1 to $(j-1)$ of line i **and**

the length of the related arc is $lgo = \|(\overset{\frown}{o,e})\|$ **and**

the length of the current chord is $lgc = \|(\overset{\frown}{i,j})\|$.

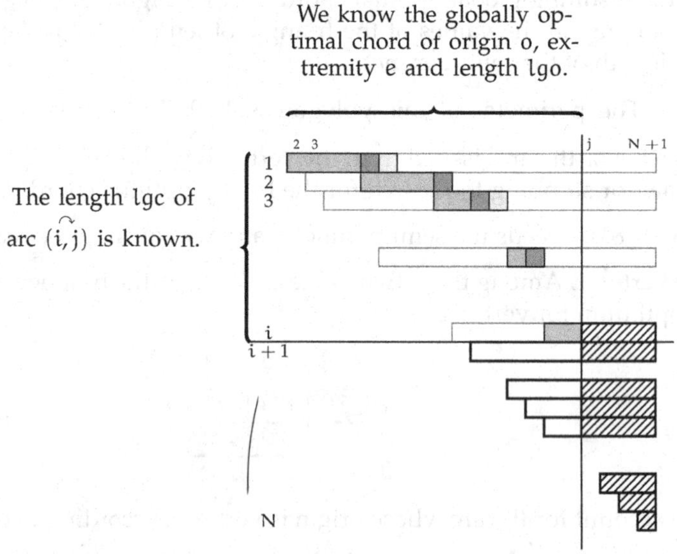

We know the globally optimal chord of origin o, extremity e and length lgo.

The length lgc of arc $(\overset{\frown}{i,j})$ is known.

Fig. 3.6 – An instance of the work carried out partly over the triangle of lengths.

43 - A 8   **Answer 8.**   Let us finish the construction of the loop.

Stopping condition According to figure 3.6, page 154, the loop ceases as soon as $i = N+1$.

Progression Two situations must be envisaged. Either we must consider a new row (see line 14 of the code hereafter), or we move forward on the same row (see line 31 of the code hereafter). The first situation occurs when the semi-perimeter is passed over (it is a first keypoint for the efficiency of the algorithm), or when $j = N + 1$. We must choose between the arcs $(\overset{\frown}{i,j})$ and $(i,\overset{\frown}{j-1})$ comparing $|lgc - p/2.0|$ and $|lgc - d[j - 1] - p/2.0|$. In the particular case where $i = N$ and $j = N + 1$, arc $(\overset{\frown}{N,N})$ does not exist. However, given that $lgc = d[N] = d[j - 1]$, the comparison works well since it leads to take $\overline{(N, N + 1)}$ as the locally optimal chord. Then, the best *globally* optimal chord is updated if necessary. Line 25 of the code allows for updating the value of lgc without recalculating it arc by arc. To do so, it is sufficient to subtract the value of $D[i]$ from the current value (it is the second keypoint concerning the efficiency of the algorithm). Line 27 of the code is the algorithmic expression of the point raised in question 5. Line 31 of the code deals with the case where we progress on the same row and it does not require specific explanations.

Initialization The invariant is established by the code lines 10 to 12 of the algorithm below, assigning the appropriate value to each of the variables o, e, i, j, lgc and lgo.

Termination In figure 3.6, the area of the surface occupied by zones bold outlined (□ ou ▨) diminishes at each step of the progression while remaining positive. This area is measured by

$$\frac{(N - i) \cdot (N - i + 1)}{2} + N + 2 - j,$$

which makes a suitable termination expression.

The code is as follows:

1. **constants**
2. $N \in \mathbb{N}_1$ and $N > 2$ and $N = \ldots$ and $D \in 1..N \rightarrow \mathbb{R}_+$ and $D = [\ldots]$ and
3. $\forall h \cdot \left(h \in 1..N \Rightarrow D[h] < \sum\limits_{k \in 1..N \text{ and } k \neq h} D[k] \right)$ and
4. $p \in \mathbb{R}_+$ and $p = \sum\limits_{k=1}^{N} D[k]$
5. **variables**
6. $lgo \in \mathbb{R}_+$ and $lgc \in \mathbb{R}_+$ and $o \in 1..N-1$ and $e \in o..N$ and
7. $i \in 1..N+1$ and $j \in i+1..N+2$
8. **begin**
9.   /% *PRE: we have a polygon with N sides (N > 2) of lengths* $D[1], \ldots, D[N]$ %/
10. $o \leftarrow 1 ; e \leftarrow 2$;
11. $i \leftarrow 1 ; j \leftarrow 2$;
12. $lgo \leftarrow D[1] ; lgc \leftarrow D[1]$;
13.   **while** $not(i = N+1)$ **do**
14.   **if** $lgc \geqslant \dfrac{p}{2.0}$ **or** $j = N+1$ **then**
15.   /% *The following condition compares the two arcs located on both sides of the semi-perimeter in order to choose the best one, including when* $i = N, j = N+1$ %/
16.   **if** $\left| lgc - \dfrac{p}{2.0} \right| > \left| lgc - D[j-1] - \dfrac{p}{2.0} \right|$ **then**
17. $lgc \leftarrow lgc - D[j-1]$;
18. $j \leftarrow j-1$
19.   **end if**;
20.   **if** $\left| lgc - \dfrac{p}{2.0} \right| < \left| lgo - \dfrac{p}{2.0} \right|$ **then**
21. $lgo \leftarrow lgc$;
22. $o \leftarrow i ; e \leftarrow j$
23.   **end if**;
24.   /% *The new value of* lgc *is obtained from the old one, not summing up the lengths of all its arcs* %/
25. $lgc \leftarrow lgc - D[i]$;
26.   /% *Treatment of the special case of question 5* %/
27. $j \leftarrow max(\{j, i+2\})$;
28.   /% *Following row/following vertex* %/
29. $i \leftarrow i+1$
30.   **else**
31. $lgc \leftarrow lgc + D[j] ; j \leftarrow j+1$
32.   **end if**
33.   **end while**;
34.   /% *POST: the chord* $\overline{(o, e)}$ *of length* lgo *separates the polygon at best* %/
35.   **write**(*the chord connecting vertices,* o, *and,* e, *of length,* lgo,
36.   *separates the polygon at best*)
37. **end**

The precondition (line 3) specifies the constraint that must be met by D so that it is the representation of a polygon (in fact, it is the extension to a polygon of the triangular inequality in the Euclidian metrics).

Complexity

The complexity, in terms of visited vertices, is in $\Theta(N)$. As a matter of fact, considering two consecutive rows i and $(i + 1)$ in the triangle of lengths (see for example, figure 3.5 page 152), visited vertices follow one another, with the possible exception of the overlapping of one or two vertices. Finally, N vertices are visited once and at most $(N - 2)$ are visited twice, hence at most $3(N - 4)$ visited vertices. The calculation of the perimeter p, present in the precondition, has no impact on the asymptotic complexity since it is performed in $\Theta(N)$.

Remark

It can be observed that triangles of lengths are a kind of triangular saddle (see problem 102, page 439): rows (respectively columns) are increasingly (respectively decreasingly) ordered. This property can be exploited to enhance the stopping condition of the loop and stop it when the locally optimal arc of origin i is $(\widehat{i, 1})$, that its length is less than or equal to the semi-perimeter and that it does not improve the globally optimal arc known so far. In the situation of figure 3.5, page 152, it is the case of $(\widehat{5, 1})$ which is such that $\|(\widehat{5, 1})\| = 5.5$.

Yet, 5.5 is worse than the length (5.8) of the best arc known $(\widehat{4, 8})$ and less than the semi-perimeter 5.9. It is useless evaluating all the arcs whose origin is a vertex greater than 5. The expression of the new stopping condition is left to the reader. It has no incidence on the asymptotic complexity since it is still necessary to reach the rightmost column of the triangle of lengths, thus to visit at least N vertices.

4

Reduce and conquer, recursion

Le caméléon n'a la couleur du
caméléon que lorsqu'il est posé sur un
autre caméléon (The chameleon has the
color of the chameleon only when
placed over another chameleon).

F. Cavanna

4.1 A few reminders about recursion

Numerous problems have a solution expressible easily and efficiently in a recursive way. It is important to make sure that the associated algorithms (programs) are correct and come to an end. In the simplest cases, similarly to a simple recurrence including a terminal case and a general term, a recursive procedure is written as a conditional statement with a stopping case on the one hand and a recursive call on the other hand. However, if this type of construction is desirable, it guarantees neither termination nor correctness of the procedure. Let us consider the following function:

```
1. function Calc(n) result ℤ pre
2.    n ∈ ℤ
3. begin
4.    if n > 100 then
5.       result n − 10
6.    else
7.       result Calc(Calc(n + 11))
8.    end if
9. end
```

When the parameter is strictly greater than 100, termination is obvious, but what happens otherwise? The reader can check in exercise 44, page 166, that, according to this hypothesis, this function always ends and that the returned result is the value 91.

We now give an example of a problem for which a recursive approach allows to design a simple elegant solution. Let us consider a series of positive integers terminated with a marker, either −1, or −2. If the marker is −1, the objective is to compute the sum of the preceding values, otherwise their product. The sequence of numbers must be read only once and it must not be explicitly stored (for instance in an array). Indeed, recursion will be used to collect each of the numbers read in the local variable nb. The appropriate operation (sum or product) associated with the marker (global variable $mark$) will be performed after the recursive call and, finally, the expected value (global variable res) is obtained by means of the following procedure:

1. **procedure** *SomProd* **pre**
2. $nb \in \mathbb{N}_1 \cup \{-1, -2\}$
3. **begin**
4.   **read**(nb);
5.   **if** $nb > 0$ **then**
6.   *SomProd*;
7.   **if** $mark = -1$ **then**
8. $res \leftarrow res + nb$
9.   **else**
10. $res \leftarrow res \cdot nb$
11.   **end if**
12.   **else**
13. $mark \leftarrow nb$;
14.   **if** $mark = -1$ **then**
15. $res \leftarrow 0$
16.   **else**
17. $res \leftarrow 1$
18.   **end if**
19.   **end if**
20. **end**

By doing so, no explicit storage is used for the numbers to be added or multiplied, those being stored in the execution stack related to the handling of recursion. Clearly, no space saving is achieved but this is not the objective in this case. It can be noticed that the procedure *SomProd* is not restricted to a conditional statement, although it involves one that singles out the terminal case and the recursive one.

4.2 Recurrence relation and recursion

In Chapter 1, we have seen that the solution of certain problems calls on a recurrence relation. The related implementation was expressed as an iterative procedure aiming at filling in a tabular structure. An alternative choice would be to write a recursive procedure. If such an approach is definitively legitimate, it is generally less efficient.

Let us take the example of the recurrence associated with the calculation of the number of binary trees having n nodes:

$$\left| \begin{array}{ll} nbBT(0) = 1 \\ nbBT(n) = \displaystyle\sum_{i=0}^{n-1} nbBT(i) \cdot nbBT(n-i-1) & n \geqslant 1. \end{array} \right.$$

The associated recursive procedure *nbBinTr*(n) is:

1. **function** *nbBinTr*(n) **result** $\mathbb{N}_1$ **pre**
2. $n \in \mathbb{N}_1$ **and** sum $\in \mathbb{N}$
3. **begin**
4.   **if** $n = 0$ **then**
5.   **result** 1
6.   **else**
7.   sum $\leftarrow 0$;
8.   **for** i **ranging** $0 .. n - 1$ **do**
9.   sum $\leftarrow$ sum $+$ *nbBinTr*(i) $\cdot$ *nbBinTr*(n − 1 − i)
10.   **end for**;
11.   **result** sum
12.   **end if**
13. **end**

and the computation of the number of binary trees with 15 nodes is made through:

1. **constants**
2. $n = 15$
3. **begin**
4.   **write(** *the number of binary trees having* , n, *nodes is* , *nbBinTr*(n)**)**
5. **end**

which delivers the same value as the one returned by the iterative program in page 13.

However, each number nbBT is computed several times. To realize this, it is sufficient to observe what happens for $n = 5$. The call *nbBinTr*(5) causes two calls to *nbBinTr*(0), *nbBinTr*(1), *nbBinTr*(2), *nbBinTr*(3) and *nbBinTr*(4). Except *nbBinTr*(0), these calls in turn cause pairs of new calls (for example *nbBinTr*(4) calls *nbBinTr*(0), *nbBinTr*(1), *nbBinTr*(2) and *nbBinTr*(3)), and so on. More precisely, nbMult(n) the number of multiplications required to calculate nbBT(n) is given by the recurrence:

$$nbMult(0) = 0$$
$$nbMult(n) = \sum_{i=0}^{n-1} (1 + nbMult(i) + nbMult(n - i - 1)) = 1 + 2 \cdot nbMult(n - 1) n \geqslant 1$$

whose solution is $nbMult(n) = (3^n - 1)/2$ for any $n \geqslant 1$ (this result can be proven by strong induction). The number of multiplications required by this algorithm is thus in $\Theta(3^n)$, whereas that in page 13 is in $\Theta(n^2)$.

Another illustration of the interest for an iterative implementation of the computation of a value defined by a recurrence relation is given in exercice 45, page 167.

4.3 "Reduce and conquer" and its complexity

In this section, the focus is put on a specific family of recursive procedures resolving a problem of size n, by calling on the resolution of identical problems of size $(n-1)$. Chapter 8 deals with the more general case where the (sub-)problems can have different sizes.

4.3.1   Presentation

We consider a one-dimensional problem of size n denoted by $Pb(n)$. To resolve it, we call on (i) a sub-problems of size $(n-1)$ (hence the term "reduce") of the same nature as the initial problem and (ii) the additional function f. This latter aims at the generation of the sub-problems on the one hand and at the "combination" of their results in order to obtain the final result on the other hand. There should be a size n_0 (most often $k = 0$, i.e. f is a function of constant complexity) for which the solution is known directly (the so-called elementary problem), i.e. without calling on sub-problems. So, we have the following generic reduction resolution pattern (also called reduction model):

$$Pb(0) \text{ or } Pb(1) \text{ elementary}$$
$$Pb(n) \to a \cdot Pb(n-1) + f(n) \qquad\qquad n > 0 \text{ or } n > 1.$$

When $a = 1$, we have a "classical" recursion which, most often, can be easily transformed into an iteration (see Chapter 1). In the general case, the structure of the program is:

```
1.  procedure ReduceAndConquer(n) pre
2.      n ∈ ℕ₁
3.  begin
4.      if n = ... then
5.          Resolve the elementary problem
6.      else
7.          ReduceAndConquer(n − 1);
8.              ...              /% a calling occurrences %/
9.          ReduceAndConquer(n − 1);
10.         Assemble
11.     end if
12. end
```

were the generic procedure *Assemble* composes the final result from the partial results returned by each of the invoked sub-problems. The initial call is made through the program:

```
1.  constants
2.      m ∈ ℕ₁ and m = ...
3.  begin
4.      ReduceAndConquer(m)
5.  end
```

The complexity of such a program is expressed in terms of an elementary operation representative of the considered problem. This operation is part of the general case of the reduction model (possibly inside function f) and/or in the elementary problem. Assuming that the complexity of f is in $\Theta(n^k)$ (most often $k = 0$, i.e. a function f of constant complexity), the complexity equation is written:

$$C(1) = d \quad (d \in \Theta(1))$$
$$C(n) = a \cdot C(n-1) + c \cdot n^k \qquad\qquad n > 1$$

whose general solution is $C(n) = a^{n-1} \cdot d + c \cdot \sum_{i=0}^{n-2} a^i \cdot (n-i)^k$; this solution can be obtained by the summing factor method. As a matter of fact, we have:

$$C(n) = a \cdot C(n-1) + c \cdot n^k$$
$$C(n-1) = a \cdot C(n-2) + c \cdot (n-1)^k$$
$$C(n-2) = a \cdot C(n-3) + c \cdot (n-2)^k$$
...
$$C(2) = a \cdot C(1) + c \cdot (2)^k$$
$$C(1) = d.$$

Multiplying the second line by a, the third one by $a^2, \ldots$, the penultimate one by a^{n-2}, the last one by a^{n-1} and summing up the left terms on the one hand and the right on the other hand, it yields:

$$C(n) + a \cdot C(n-1) + a^2 \cdot C(n-2) + \cdots + a^{n-2} \cdot C(2) + a^{n-1} \cdot C(1) =$$
$$a \cdot C(n-1) + c \cdot n^k + a^2 \cdot C(n-2) + a \cdot c \cdot (n-1)^k + a^3 \cdot C(n-3) + a^2 \cdot c \cdot (n-2)^k + \cdots + a^{n-1} \cdot C(1) + a^{n-2} \cdot c \cdot (2)^k + a^{n-1} \cdot d.$$

By simplifying, it comes:

$$C(n) = c \cdot n^k + a \cdot c \cdot (n-1)^k + \cdots + a^2 \cdot c \cdot (n-2)^k + \cdots + a^{n-2} \cdot c \cdot (2)^k + a^{n-1} \cdot d,$$

and finally:

$$C(n) = a^{n-1} \cdot d + c \cdot \sum_{i=0}^{n-2} a^i \cdot (n-i)^k.$$

Some particular solutions can be deduced:

$$k = 0 \text{ and } a = 1 \quad \longrightarrow \quad C(n) = d + c \cdot \sum_{i=0}^{n-2} 1, \text{ or } C(n) \in \Theta(n)$$

$$k = 0 \text{ and } a > 1 \quad \longrightarrow \quad C(n) = a^{n-1} \cdot d + c \cdot \sum_{i=0}^{n-2} a^i, \text{ or } C(n) \in \Theta(a^n)$$

$$k = 1 \text{ and } a = 1 \quad \longrightarrow \quad C(n) = d + c \cdot \sum_{i=0}^{n-2} (n-i), \text{ or } C(n) \in \Theta(n^2).$$

In order to ensure the correctness of the proposed solution, we will systematically rely on an inductive construction (most often a simple induction over $\mathbb{N}$ or $\mathbb{N}_1$) with three constituents: (i) the *base* where the elementary case is made explicit together with its related solution, (ii) the *induction hypothesis* where it is assumed that the problem of size $(n-1)$ can be resolved for $(n-1)$ greater than or equal to the value of the base, and (iii) the *induction* itself where it is demonstrated how to resolve the problem $Pb(n)$ of size n using the induction hypothesis. A fourth component of this type of proof will be omitted, the *termination*, which is guaranteed here inasmuch as the size of the problem is an integer at least equal to the value specified in the base (since starting with a positive integer greater than or equal to that of the base, the value of the base is obtained by constant subtractions of 1).

Through two examples, we now illustrate the cases $a = 1$ and $a = 2$ for $k = 0$.

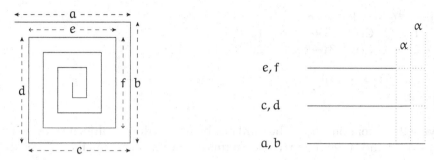

Fig. 4.1 – A spiral for $n = 4$.

4.3.2   Example 1: the spiral pattern

We want to make a "spiral" as illustrated in figure 4.1, using the approach "Reduce and conquer". Such a spiral is said to be of size n if the figure is composed of n nested "pseudo squares" ($n = 4$ in figure 4.1). We set $a = b, c = d = a - \alpha, e = a - 2\alpha$, with a given value of α. Moreover, the drawing is made from the outside to the inside; therefore, it starts by the upper horizontal segment of length a. Last, we have two primitives to make the drawing: *place*(x, y) which puts the pen down at the point of coordinates (x, y), and *draw*(x, y) which traces the segment from the current position of the pen to the point (x, y).

In order to continue the drawing, a first question is about the value of f (see figure 4.1). Since in the first step we have $a = b, c = d = a - \alpha$, so that the sub-problem being called upon is of the same nature than the initial problem, we must have $f = e = a - 2\alpha$.

Considering the nature of the drawing, n, a and α must meet a precondition so that the trace of the drawing of the spiral of size n can be executed. Indeed, the trace imposes that $(n - 1)$ times 2α can be subtracted from a; hence, we must have: $a > 2 \cdot \alpha \cdot (n - 1)$.

These preliminaries being laid out, we first specify the reduction model for this problem, then we propose a recursive procedure performing this drawing, called *SpiralDrawing*(n, x, y, a, α) where n is the number of "pseudo squares" to be drawn, x and y are the coordinates of the starting point of the drawing, a and α correspond to the symbols defined before. The construction of the drawing obeys the following inductive schema.

Base   We know how to make the spiral of size 0 which consists in doing nothing.

Induction hypothesis   We assume that, inasmuch as a is greater than $2 \cdot \alpha \cdot (n - 1)$, we know how to make the spiral of size $(n - 1)$ ($n - 1 \geqslant 0$) having an upper horizontal segment of length l equal to that of its right vertical segment and a lower horizontal segment and a left vertical segment of length $l - \alpha$.

Induction   We specify how to make the spiral of size n assuming that a is greater than $2 \cdot \alpha \cdot (n - 1)$. We begin with the trace of the upper horizontal segment of length a, then the right vertical segment of the same length. Then, we trace the lower horizontal segment of length $(a - \alpha)$, then the left vertical segment of the same length. Then, we trace the spiral of size $(n - 1)$ whose upper horizontal segment is of length $(a - 2\alpha)$, which is feasible from the induction hypothesis since:

$$a > 2 \cdot \alpha \cdot (n - 1) \quad \Rightarrow \quad a > 2 \cdot \alpha \cdot (n - 2),$$

and we have achieved our goal.

Consequently, the reduction model for this problem is:

SpiralDraw(0, a) elementary (nothing to do)

$$SpiralDraw(n, a) \rightarrow \begin{cases} SpiralDraw(n - 1, a - 2\alpha) \\ + \\ \text{tracing of the outer pseudo-square} \end{cases} \quad n > 0.$$

The drawing is performed by means of the procedure hereafter:

1. **procedure** *SpiraleDrawing*(n, x, y, a, α) **pre**
2. $n \in \mathbb{N}$ and $x \in \mathbb{R}_+^*$ and $y \in \mathbb{R}_+^*$ and $a \in \mathbb{R}$ and $\alpha \in \mathbb{R}_+^*$ and $a > 2 \cdot \alpha \cdot (n - 1)$
3. **begin**
4.   **if** $n > 0$ **then**
5. $draw(x + a, y)$;
6. $draw(x + a, y - a)$;
7. $draw(x + \alpha, y - a)$;
8. $draw(x + \alpha, y - \alpha)$;
9. $SpiralDrawing(n - 1, x + \alpha, y - \alpha, a - 2\alpha, \alpha)$
10.   **end if**
11. **end**

which is called by:

1. **constants**
2. $x_0 \in \mathbb{R}_+^*$ and $x_0 = \ldots$ and $y_0 \in \mathbb{R}_+^*$ and $y_0 = \ldots$
3. **begin**
4. $place(x_0, y_0)$;
5. $SpiralDrawing(7, x_0, y_0, 24.0, 1.5)$
6. **end**

and traces the spiral of size 7 whose initial upper side of length 24 cm starts at the point of coordinates (x_0, y_0). This call complies with the precondition evoked previously since $24 > 2 \cdot 1.5 \cdot 6 (= 18)$.

Remark

Here, we have a tail-recursive procedure and the actual implementation can be an iterative procedure rather than a recursive one (see Chapter 1).

Finally, we calculate the length of the trace depending on n, a and α assuming that the precondition $a > 2 \cdot \alpha \cdot (n-1)$ is met. The length of the trace is the solution of the recurrence:

$$\begin{aligned} LG(0, -, -) &= 0 \\ LG(n, a, \alpha) &= 2a + 2(a - \alpha) + LG(n - 1, a - 2\alpha, \alpha) \end{aligned} \quad n > 0$$

or, by summing up:

$$LG(n, a, \alpha) = \sum_{i=0}^{2n-1} 2(a - i\alpha) = \sum_{i=0}^{2n-1} 2a - 2\alpha \sum_{i=0}^{2n-1} i = 4an - 4\alpha n^2 + 2\alpha n.$$

For $n = 7$, we get $LG(7, a, \alpha) = 28a - 182\alpha$, i.e. 98 cm for $a = 10.0$ cm and $\alpha = 1.0$ cm.

4.3.3   Example 2: Hanoi towers

The Hanoi towers problem involves "reconstructing" a tower (also called a "pagoda") composed of a stack of n disks of bottom-up decreasing diameters. We have three pillars: (i) p_i where the initial tower is, (ii) p_f where the final tower shall be, and (iii) an auxiliary pillar p_a housing intermediate stacks of disks.

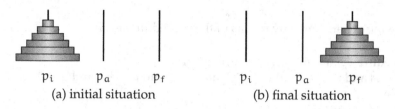

p_i p_a p_f p_i p_a p_f
  (a) initial situation   (b) final situation

Fig. 4.2 – Initial and final configurations for $n = 6$.

The following rules must be observed:

- we can move a single disk at a time thanks to the operation $move(p_1, p_2)$, where p_1 designates the pillar from which the upper disk is extracted and p_2 the pillar on top of which this disk is placed,

- a disk can be placed either on an empty pillar or over a larger disk.

An example of initial and final configurations is given in figure 4.2, for $n = 6$. We will build a solution to move any tower of n disks ($n \geqslant 1$) according to the inductive schema hereafter.

Base We know how to move a tower made of a single disk from a pillar to an empty one.

Induction hypothesis We assume that we know how to move a tower of $(n-1)$ $(n-1 \geqslant 1)$ disks of decreasing diameters from a pillar to either an empty one or to a pillar housing the largest disk using the auxiliary one which is initially empty.

Induction We show that we can move a tower made up of n disks of decreasing diameters from pillar p_i to pillar p_f (initially empty) using the auxiliary pillar p_a. To do this: (i) we move the tower made of the $(n-1)$ upper disks from p_i to p_a (see figure 4.3, page 164), which is feasible according to the induction hypothesis since the auxiliary pillar p_a is initially empty, (ii) then we move the last disk (the largest one) from p_i to p_f (see figure 4.4), which corresponds to an elementary move that can be made legally since the pillar p_f is empty, (iii) last we move the tower made of the $(n-1)$ disks on the pillar p_a to

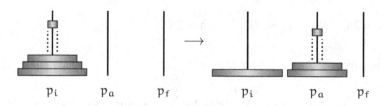

p_i p_a p_f p_i p_a p_f

Fig. 4.3 – The first step of the inductive process of move of a tower of Hanoi.

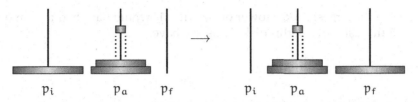

Fig. 4.4 – The second step of the inductive process of move of a tower of Hanoi.

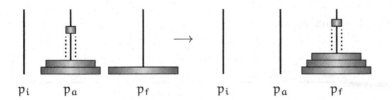

Fig. 4.5 – The last step of the inductive process of move of a tower of Hanoi.

the pillar p_f (see figure 4.5), which is feasible according to the induction hypothesis, noticing that, although nonempty, the arrival pillar p_f contains the largest disk at its base.

The following reduction model can be deduced:

$$
\begin{array}{l}
\text{hanoi}(1, p_i, p_f, p_a) \text{ elementary } (\text{move}(p_i, p_f)) \\[1ex]
\text{hanoi}(n, p_i, p_f, p_a) \rightarrow
\begin{cases}
\text{hanoi}(n-1, p_i, p_a, p_f) \\
+ \\
\text{move}(p_i, p_f) \\
+ \\
\text{hanoi}(n-1, p_a, p_f, p_i)
\end{cases}
\quad n > 1.
\end{array}
$$

Here, the generic function f consists in moving the largest disk from p_i to p_f. Choosing the move of a disk as the elementary operation, we calculate $\text{nbMV}(n)$, the number of moves of disks necessary to move a tower of n disks. The number $\text{nbMV}(n)$ is given by the recurrence:

$$
\begin{aligned}
\text{nbMV}(1) &= 1 \\
\text{nbMV}(n) &= 2 \cdot \text{nbMV}(n-1) + 1
\end{aligned}
\qquad n > 1
$$

whose solution is $\text{nbMV}(n) = 2^n - 1$; so, complexity is exponential.

We now show that this solution is optimal. Let $\text{minnbMV}(n)$ be the minimum number of disk moves required for a tower of n disks. The largest disk must be moved at least once. To be "legally" moved, this disk must be alone on its pillar and the destination pillar must be empty; all other disks must be placed, in right order, on the third pillar. Therefore, before the first move of the largest disk, a tower of size $(n-1)$ would have had to be moved. It is the same after the last move of this disk. Thus, we have:

$$minnbMV(n) \geqslant 2 \cdot minnbMV(n-1) + 1.$$

Since the algorithm designed before yields a number of moves which meets:

$$nbMV(n) = 2 \cdot nbMV(n-1) + 1,$$

this algorithm is optimal.

4.4   What should be reminded for "Reduce and conquer"

Resolving a problem of size n by the approach "Reduce and conquer" first requires to express it (in the general case) as the combination of several sub-problems of the same nature than the initial problem, of size $(n-1)$. For the size 0 or 1, the problem must have a direct solution, i.e. which does not call on sub-problems. In the pattern of resolution thus identified, an additional function appears whose goal is both to generate the sub-problems and to specify how the results of the sub-problems are combined to form that of the initial problem. The proof of correctness of the schema of resolution envisaged is made by induction. The base is the resolution of the case having a direct solution and the induction hypothesis assumes that it is known how to resolve the sub-problem of size $(n-1)$. Then, the temporal complexity of the associated algorithm can be established (it may be linear, polynomial or even exponential) and the algorithm can be written in the form of a recursive procedure modeled on the resolution pattern.

4.5   Problems

Problem 44.   A doubly recursive function   ○ ●

> *This problem focuses on recursion. Its interest lies in the way the termination of the considered recursive procedure is proven.*

We consider the function *Calc* whose code has been given at the beginning of this chapter. We will show that this function delivers the value 91 for any call parameter value strictly less than 102.

44 - Q 1   **Question 1.**   Establish that $Calc(100) = Calc(101) = 91$.

44 - Q 2   **Question 2.**   Prove by induction (simple induction over $k \in \mathbb{N}$) that, for any n in the interval $(90 - 11k) \mathinner{..} (100 - 11k)$, the call $Calc(n)$ returns the value 91.

44 - Q 3   **Question 3.**   What can be concluded about the termination of this function?

The solution is on page 174.

Problem 45. Fibonacci sequence; recursive computation ○ •

> *This problem aims mainly at the illustration of the soundness of a non-recursive implementation of a value defined by a recurrence relation.*

We denote by $\mathcal{F}(n)$ the current term of the Fibonacci series defined for n strictly positive. By definition:

$$\begin{vmatrix} \mathcal{F}(1) = 1 \\ \mathcal{F}(2) = 1 \\ \mathcal{F}(n) = \mathcal{F}(n-1) + \mathcal{F}(n-2) \qquad\qquad n \geqslant 2. \end{vmatrix}$$

Question 1. Write the recursive function $FiboR(n)$ modeled on this recursive definition to compute $\mathcal{F}(n)$.   45 - Q 1

Question 2. Give the total number of additions performed for $n = 6$.   45 - Q 2

Question 3. Calculate the number of additions generated by the call $FiboR(n)$.   45 - Q 3

The solution is on page 175.

Problem 46. Is this point inside the polygon? ○ •

> *This problem takes place in the framework of the Euclidian geometry. It presents no significant difficulties, except that the value associated with the base of the inductive reasoning used, is neither 0 nor 1, cases announced as "regular" in the presentation of this chapter.*

We want to determine whether or not a point is inside (broadly speaking) a convex n-sided polygon ($n \geqslant 3$). A Cartesian coordinate system xOy of the plane is considered.

Question 1. Given two points A and B of coordinates (x_A, y_A) and (x_B, y_B), give the principle of the Boolean function of header: 46 - Q 1

$SameSide(x_A, y_A, x_B, y_B, x_C, y_C, x_D, y_D)$ **result** $\mathbb{B}$

deciding whether or not points C and D of coordinates (x_C, y_C) and (x_D, y_D), are located on the same side of the line (AB). What is its complexity in terms of evaluated conditions?

Question 2. State an inclusion property of a point in an triangle and write the function: 46 - Q 2

$InTriangle(x_A, y_A, x_B, y_B, x_C, y_C, x_P, y_P)$ **result** $\mathbb{B}$

deciding whether or not the point P of coordinates (x_P, y_P) is inside (broadly speaking) the triangle (ABC). What is its complexity in terms of evaluated conditions?

Question 3. Derive a function of type "Reduce and conquer":   46 - Q 3

$InPolygon(n, x_P, y_P)$ **result** $\mathbb{B}$

deciding whether or not the point P is inside the convex polygon of n vertices of coordinates $(x_1, y_1), (x_2, y_2), \ldots, (x_n, y_n)$ with $n \geqslant 3$.

46 - Q 4   **Question 4.**   Give its temporal complexity at worst in terms of evaluated conditions.

46 - Q 5   **Question 5.**   Why does polygon convexity matter?

The solution is on page 176.

Problem 47.   Drawing nested double squares   ○ ⋮

> *The main interest of this problem lies in the design of the trace to be done, especially the identification of its starting point.*

We want to make the drawing presented in figure 4.6, inside which the base pattern is made of two nested squares. We are provided with the two usual primitives *place*(x, y) and *draw*(x, y) of example 4.3.2 page 162, and the drawing must be done under the following constraints:

- at the end of the drawing, the pen must be back to its starting position,

- the pen must not be raised during the drawing and no segment can be drawn more than once (neither idle time, nor useless work).

We want to make the drawing thanks to a procedure of type "Reduce and conquer" meeting these constraints. Here, the size n of the problem ($n \in \mathbb{N}$) corresponds to the number of double squares to be nested.

Fig. 4.6 – A drawing involving four nested double squares.

47 - Q 1   **Question 1.**   Identify the possible starting point(s) of the drawing.

47 - Q 2   **Question 2.**   Propose a strategy of type "Reduce and conquer" likely to make this drawing. Deduce the associated reduction model.

47 - Q 3   **Question 3.**   Write the procedure performing this drawing, invoked by the program:

    1. **constants**
    2. $m \in \mathbb{N}_1$ and $m = \ldots$ and $x_0 \in \mathbb{R}$ and $x_0 = \ldots$ and $y_0 \in \mathbb{R}$ and $y_0 = \ldots$ **and**
    3. $c_0 \in \mathbb{R}_+$ and $c_0 = \ldots$

4. **begin**
5. $place(x_0, y_0)$;
6. $NestDbSqDrawing(m, x_0, y_0, c_0)$
7. **end**

where x_0 and y_0 designate the coordinates of the starting point of the drawing, m is the actual number of double squares to be drawn and c_0 is the length of the side of the "outermost" square.

Question 4.   What is its complexity in terms of number of calls to the function *draw* and   47 - Q 4
how long is the trace?

The solution is on page 178.

Problem 48.   Drawing nested triangles   ○ ⦂

> *This problem is also a matter of drawing. It points out the construction of an optimal solution with a first approach which is not optimal. The final solution makes use of two procedures of type "Reduce and conquer".*

We would like to make the following drawing:

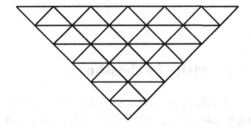

called "big inverted triangle". Each elementary triangle is a isosceles rectangle one (right-angled down), of height d issued from the right angle; the length of its horizontal base is thus $2d$. The above schema represents six "layers" of such triangles. The bottom layer involves a single triangle, that above two, and so on, up to six. As it can be seen, an assembly of n layers forms a big triangle similar to the elementary one, but whose sides are n times larger and such a figure is said of size n. In an elementary triangle, when the coordinates of the point associated with the right angle are (x, y), the coordinates of the other two vertices are $(x - d, y + d)$ and $(x + d, y + d)$. Here again, the two primitives $place(x, y)$ and $draw(x, y)$ defined in example 1 page 162 are supposed to be available. The drawing must start and finish at the point associated with the right angle whose assigned coordinates are (x_0, y_0).

Remark

The minimum number of elementary triangles to be drawn to get a triangle of size n is clearly $n(n + 1)/2$.

Question 1.   In a first step, suggest the principle of a solution of type "Reduce and conquer" where there is a single constraint: the pen must remain down during the whole tracing. Specify the reduction model that is used.

48 - Q 2   **Question** 2.   Write the code of the corresponding procedure which is invoked by the program:

> 1. **constants**
> 2. $m \in \mathbb{N}_1$ and $m = \ldots$ and $x_0 \in \mathbb{R}$ and $x_0 = \ldots$ and $y_0 \in \mathbb{R}$ and $y_0 = \ldots$ and
> 3. $d_0 \in \mathbb{R}_+$ and $d_0 = \ldots$
> 4. **begin**
> 5. $place(x_0, y_0)$;
> 6. $Triangle1(m, x_0, y_0, d_0)$
> 7. **end**

where m is the number of layers of triangles to be drawn, (x_0, y_0) represents the coordinates of the point associated with the right angle (bottom of the drawing) and d_0 is the height of the elementary triangle.

48 - Q 3   **Question** 3.   Which is the complexity of this procedure in terms of calls to the function *draw* and number of elementary triangles drawn?

48 - Q 4   **Question** 4.   So as to avoid useless tracing and to enhance efficiency, modify the previous strategy and propose the principle of a solution where: (i) the pen is never raised and (ii) no segment is drawn twice (or more).

48 - Q 5   **Question** 5.   Write the code of the new procedure $Triangle2(n, x, y, d)$ and prove its optimality.

The solution is on page 181.

Problem 49. Exhaustive visit of a chessboard   ○ ⁝

> *This problem highlights a family of chessboards which can be visited by the knight in an exhaustive simple way, each square being seen only once. It presents some features in common with problem 54 page 227, in Chapter 5.*

We consider a chessboard of side $s = 4m+1$ (with $m \geqslant 0$). We will show that the knight can visit it exhaustively while going through each square once and only once. Let us notice that this problem may have a solution for some other chessboards (of side different from $4m+1$), but this remains outside the scope of the problem. The knight obeys its usual move rules, i.e. when it is on the square (i, j), it may move to the following eight squares:

$$(i-2, j-1) \quad (i-2, j+1) \quad (i+2, j-1) \quad (i+2, j+1)$$
$$(i-1, j-2) \quad (i-1, j+2) \quad (i+1, j-2) \quad (i+1, j+2)$$

inasmuch as it does not move out of the chessboard. In this problem, i (respectively j) designates the row (respectively column) index.

49 - Q 1   **Question** 1.   Propose an exhaustive visit of a chessboard of side $s = 5$ ($m = 1$) starting from the square $(1, 1)$.

49 - Q 2   **Question** 2.   Generalize the visit to a chessboard of side $s = 4m+1$ ($m \geqslant 1$), still starting from the square $(1, 1)$.
Hint. Point out how to make the exhaustive visit of the outer crown of width 2 of the chessboard.

Question 3.   Specify the reduction model used.

49 - Q 3

The solution is on page 184.

Problem 50.   Drawing fractal curves   ○ ⦂

> *This problem highlights two problems of curve drawings where the construction of the solution goes beyond the strict framework of the "Reduce and conquer" method. Indeed, tracing these two families of curves is based on four procedures very similar in terms of structure, each of which of type "Reduce and conquer" with cross calls.*

Hilbert curves

We consider the curves of figure 4.7, where small circles appear on the starting points of the drawings. The function *draw* defined in example 1 page 162 is available.

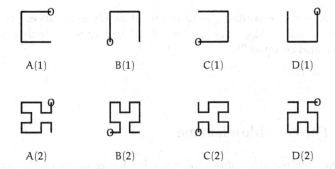

$$A(1) \qquad B(1) \qquad C(1) \qquad D(1)$$

$$A(2) \qquad B(2) \qquad C(2) \qquad D(2)$$

Fig. 4.7 – Curves $A(1)$ to $D(1)$ ($\alpha = 1$) and $A(2)$ to $D(2)$ ($\alpha = 1/3$).

Question 1.   On the basis of these curves, express $A(i+1)$, $B(i+1)$, $C(i+1)$ and $D(i+1)$ depending on $A(i)$, $B(i)$, $C(i)$, $D(i)$ and the four elementary segments "left stroke" (respectively "right stroke", "up stroke", " down stroke") denoted by l (respectively r, u, d) each of length α (given).

50 - Q 1

Question 2.   Draw the curve $A(3)$ called level-3 Hilbert curve.

50 - Q 2

Question 3.   Write the code of the procedure which draws any level-n Hilbert curve corresponding to $A(n)$.

50 - Q 3

Question 4.   Which is the complexity $C_A(n)$ for tracing $A(n)$ in terms of calls to the function *draw* ?

50 - Q 4

Question 5.   Determine the height and width of the drawing as a function of n and α.

50 - Q 5

W-curves

We now consider the curves defined as follows:

$$A(1) \;=\; r \quad B(1) \;=\; d \quad C(1) \;=\; l \quad D(1) \;=\; u$$

and for $i \geqslant 1$:

$$
\begin{array}{rclcccccccc}
A(i+1) & = & A(i) & d & r & B(i) & r & D(i) & r & u & A(i) \\
B(i+1) & = & B(i) & l & d & C(i) & d & A(i) & d & r & B(i) \\
C(i+1) & = & C(i) & u & l & D(i) & l & B(i) & l & d & C(i) \\
D(i+1) & = & D(i) & r & u & A(i) & u & C(i) & u & l & D(i) \\
W(i) & = & A(i) & d & r & B(i) & l & d & C(i) & u & l & D(i) & r & h
\end{array}
$$

where d, r, g, u represent the elementary strokes of length α previously introduced.

50 - Q 6 **Question 6.**   Draw the curves $W(1)$ and $W(2)$.

50 - Q 7 **Question 7.**   Establish the complexity for drawing the curve $W(n)$ $(n \geqslant 1)$ in terms of calls to *draw* as a function of n and α.

Remark

It can be proven that the curve $W(n)$ is bounded by a square of side $\alpha \cdot (2^{n+1} - 1)$.

Complement

The interested reader can examine the drawing of Sierpinski curves (see for example `https://en.wikipedia.org/wiki/Sierpiński_curve`), which also relies on the approach "Reduce and conquer").

The solution is on page 185.

Problem 51.   The countdown game

> *This problem presents the originality of a reduction model in which the number of sub-problems generated depends on the size of the decomposed problem. Unsurprisingly, the result has a complexity far beyond exponential.*

This problem is based on the TV game show *Countdown*. Thanks to usual arithmetic operations, one seeks to form a given number TG (natural) called *target*, from nbPl *plates* on each of which is a number (natural). These constitute a bag B of nbPl elements (in the TV game show nbPl $= 6$) whose values are taken (possibly with duplicates) from the set $\{1, 2, 3, 4, 5, 6, 7, 8, 9, 10, 25, 50, 75, 100\}$ and the number TG is taken in the range $101 .. 999$. It is imposed that any operation is carried out with positive integers and that division is only possible between numbers whose division is without remainder. Besides, it is not mandatory to use all numbers of B to form C.

51 - Q 1 **Question 1.**   First, we are considering a *simplified* version in which the only available operation is addition. Generally speaking, two numbers are replaced by their sum. Propose a set-oriented model of resolution based on the "Reduce and conquer" technique, showing a solution (if it exists).

51 - Q 2 **Question 2.**   We consider the following example: nbPl $= 4$, B $= [\![3, 10, 8, 3]\!]$, TG $= 18$. It is assumed that the first substitution leads to B' $= [\![13, 8, 3]\!]$, the next one to B'' $= [\![21, 3]\!]$, and so on. Give the call tree leading to the solution.

We now move on to the general case, i.e. addition, subtraction, multiplication and division can be used.

Question 3.   Specify the rules for replacing two numbers according to the arithmetic   51 - Q 3
operation under consideration.

Question 4.   Generalize the previously proposed reduction model.   51 - Q 4

Conceptually speaking, the answer expected from the game's contestants is an arithmetic
expression. So, for the plates $[\![3, 4, 8, 75, 10, 9]\!]$ and the target TG $= 756$, a possible result
would be:

$$(((3 + 4) + 8) - 9) + (75 \times 10).$$

This expression can be represented in at least two other ways. First, by a tree:

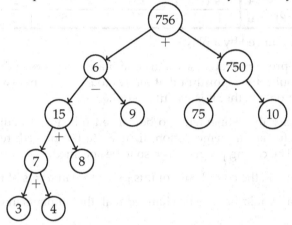

or by an array with $(nbPl - 1)$ rows and four columns in which are recorded the successive
choices of quadruples ⟨operator, operand-1, operand-2, result⟩ having led to the solution:

	operator	operand-1	operand-2	result
$(n =) 2$	1 (+)	6	750	756
3	2 (·)	75	10	750
4	3 (−)	15	9	6
5	1 (+)	7	8	15
$(nbPl =) 6$	1 (+)	3	4	7

It is in this second form (read from bottom to top) that a player announces his result. It
is also on this type of representation that we propose to work with[1]. The isomorphism
between the two representations then allows to take advantage of the vocabulary specific
to trees (notions of father, left or right son, descendant, etc.) to take into consideration the
rows of the array. We add to the table representation the following conventions: the root
of the tree is the first row (the top row) of the array and, if it exists, the father of a row is
located somewhere *above* that row. Furthermore, in order to take into account a problem
that may occur, we consider that the array may contain sterile rows, which therefore do
not contribute to the calculation of the result. Thus, for example, for the $[\![3, 75, 8, 10, 25, 10]\!]$
and the target TG $= 172$ we can obtain the following array:

---

[1]A solution based on the explicit construction and then the exploitation of the arithmetic expression tree is
also possible. We invite the reader to think about it.

	operator	operand-1	operand-2	result
(n =) 3	2 (−)	250	78	172
4	4 (·)	25	10	250
5	1 (+)	8	10	18
(nbPl =) 6	1 (+)	3	75	78

While row 5 is obviously sterile, only the "purged" array:

	operator	operand-1	operand-2	result
(n =) 3	2 (−)	250	78	172
4	4 (·)	25	10	250
(nbPl =) 6	1 (+)	3	75	78

would have to be announced by a player.

51 - Q 5   **Question 5.**   The problem that arises is the elimination of rows in the array that would prove to be sterile. Build the algorithm that allows to *qualify* or not (with a Boolean) any row of M depending on whether it is useful or sterile.

51 - Q 6   **Question 6.**   Specify the refinements to be carried out (in particular concerning set-oriented structures) for an implementation, then write the procedure *GoodCount* which solves the problem. The calling program is also to be specified.

51 - Q 7   **Question 7.**   Establish the complexity of this procedure in terms of recursive calls.

51 - Q 8   **Question 8.**   What would have to be changed if all the numbers in the bag B had to be used?

51 - Q 9   **Question 9.**   What would have to be changed to find all the ways to form the target TG from the bag B?

The solution is on page 189.

4.6   Solutions

Answers to problem 44. A doubly recursive function   *The problem is on page 166.*

44 - A 1   **Answer 1.**   The call *Calc*(101) leads to pass through the "then" branch of the conditional statement and it returns the value 91 (= 101 − 10). In contrast, the call *Calc*(100) passes through the "else" branch of the conditional statement and it generates the call *Calc*(*Calc*(111)). The call *Calc*(111) returns (111 − 10) = 101, then *Calc*(101) delivers the result 91. We do have *Calc*(100) = *Calc*(101) = 91.

44 - A 2   **Answer 2.**   As it is suggested in the statement of the problem, we proceed by induction over $k \in \mathbb{N}$ to examine any interval of the form $(90 - 11k) \, .. \, (100 - 11k)$ that is a basis for partitioning the whole interval $-\infty \, .. \, 100$.

Base For $k = 0$, we consider the interval $90 \, .. \, 100$ and the initial call *Calc*(n) for n inside this interval. The result is *Calc*(*Calc*(n + 11)). Since n + 11 > 100, *Calc*(n + 11) returns

$(n + 1)$. Indeed:

$Calc(90) = \ldots = Calc(100) = 91$ (from the previous question).

Induction hypothesis We assume that, for $k \geqslant 0$, we have:

$$n \in (90 - k) \ldots (100 - k) \Rightarrow Calc(n) = 91.$$

Induction We consider the call $Calc(n)$ where n belongs to the next interval, i.e. $(90 - 11(k+1)) \ldots (100 - 11(k+1))$. This call generates the call $Calc(Calc(n+11))$. As $(n+11)$ lies in the interval $(90 - k) \ldots (100 - k)$, $Calc(n + 11)$ returns 91. In turn, the call $Calc(91)$ delivers the same value 91.

So, for any value of n in the interval $-\infty \ldots 100$, the result of the call $Calc(n)$ is 91. In the previous question, we have proven that $Calc(101) = 91$, hence the result announced in the statement, namely that the function $Calc$ returns 91 for any call parameter strictly less than 102.

Answer 3. Since $Calc(n)$ returns 91 for $n < 102$ and $(n-10)$ for $n \geqslant 102$, we can deduce *a posteriori* that, whatever the actual parameter, any call terminates. 44 - A 3

Answers to problem 45. Fibonacci sequence; recursive computation *The problem is on page 167.*

Answer 1. The recursive function calculating the nth term of the Fibonacci series is given hereafter: 45 - A 1

```
1. function FiboR(n) result ℕ₁ pre
2.    n ∈ ℕ₁
3. begin
4.    if n = 1 or n = 2 then
5.        result 1
6.    else
7.        result (FiboR(n − 1) + FiboR(n − 2))
8.    end if
9. end
```

Answer 2. For $n = 6$, $FiboR(5)$ is called once, $FiboR(4)$ twice, $FiboR(3)$ three times, $FiboR(2)$ five times and $FiboR(1)$ three times, a total of 14 calls. Each of these calls, except those of the leaves, causes an addition, resulting in a number of additions equal to half of the previous one, i.e. 7. 45 - A 2

Answer 3. The number of additions generated by the call $FiboR(n)$, $nbAdd(n)$ is given by the recurrence: 45 - A 3

$$\begin{vmatrix} nbAdd(1) = 0 \\ nbAdd(2) = 0 \\ nbAdd(n) = 1 + nbAdd(n-1) + nbAdd(n-2) & n > 2. \end{vmatrix}$$

Adding 1 in the left and right hand sides, and letting $NB(n) = nbAdd(n) + 1$, this can be rewritten as:

$$\begin{vmatrix} NB(0) = 1 \\ NB(1) = 1 \\ NB(n) = NB(n-1) + NB(n-2) & n > 2. \end{vmatrix}$$

This brings us back to the Fibonacci series and:

$$NB(n) = \frac{1}{\sqrt{5}}\left(\left(\frac{1+\sqrt{5}}{2}\right)^n - \left(\frac{1-\sqrt{5}}{2}\right)^n\right)$$

hence:

$$nbAdd(n) = \frac{1}{\sqrt{5}}\left(\left(\frac{1+\sqrt{5}}{2}\right)^n - \left(\frac{1-\sqrt{5}}{2}\right)^n\right) - 1$$

i.e. the nth Fibonacci number diminished by 1. It can be checked that:

$$nbAdd(1) = nbAdd(2) = 0, nbAdd(3) = 1, nbAdd(4) = 2, nbAdd(5) = 4, nbAdd(6) = 7.$$

The absolute value of the term $(1 - \sqrt{5}/2)^n$ is less than 1 and its sign alternates depending on the parity of n. As a result, this term tends to 0 when n tends to infinity. So, it can be assumed that for n sufficiently large, the nth Fibonacci number is the integer closest to $(((1 + \sqrt{5})/2)^n)/\sqrt{5}$, i.e. $1.618^n/2.236$. It appears that the complexity of the recursive calculation is exponential in terms of additions. We will see in problem 89 page 425, that this result can be significantly improved.

Answers to problem 46. Is this point inside the polygon?   *The problem is on page 167.*

46 - A 1   **Answer 1.**   From the coordinates of the points A and B, we can determine the equation of the line (AB), namely:

$$y - a \cdot x - b = 0 \text{ where } a = (y_A - y_B)/(x_A - x_B) \text{ and } b = (x_A \cdot y_B - y_A \cdot x_B)/(x_A - x_B).$$

We then calculate $y_C - a \cdot x_C - b$ and $y_D - a \cdot x_D - b$. If one of these values is zero, the corresponding point belongs to the line (AB). If not, when these two values are of the same sign, C and D are on the same side of the line (AB), otherwise these points are located in each of the half-planes bounded by the line (AB). The function *SameSide* requires the evaluation of a single condition. Its complexity is therefore constant (in $\Theta(1)$).

46 - A 2   **Answer 2.**   The point P is inside the triangle (ABC) if: (i) A and P are on the same side of the line (BC), (ii) B and P are on the same side of the line (AC), and (iii) C and P are on the same side of the line (AB). This property can be observed on the figure hereafter and it can be easily proven by contradiction.

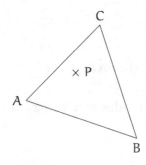

So, we can write the function deciding whether or not the point P is inside the triangle ABC:

1. **function** *InTriangle*$(x_A, y_A, x_B, y_B, x_C, y_C, x_P, y_P)$ **result** $\mathbb{B}$ **pre**
2. $\quad x_A \in \mathbb{R}$ **and** $y_A \in \mathbb{R}$ **and** $x_B \in \mathbb{R}$ **and** $y_B \in \mathbb{R}$ **and** $x_C \in \mathbb{R}$ **and**
3. $\quad y_C \in \mathbb{R}$ **and** $x_P \in \mathbb{R}$ **and** $y_P \in \mathbb{R}$
4. **begin**
5. $\quad$ **result** $\left(\begin{array}{l} SameSide(x_A, y_A, x_B, y_B, x_C, y_C, x_P, y_P) \text{ and then} \\ SameSide(x_A, y_A, x_C, y_C, x_B, y_B, x_P, y_P) \text{ and then} \\ SameSide(x_C, y_C, x_B, y_B, x_A, y_A, x_P, y_P) \end{array} \right)$
6. **end**

This function invokes *SameSide* at most three times and thus three conditions are evaluated and its complexity is constant (in $\Theta(1)$).

Answer 3. The function of type "Reduce and conquer" deciding whether or not the point P in inside any convex polygone of $n \geqslant 3$ sides, relies on the following inductive schema.

46 - A 3

Base When $n = 3$, the inclusion of P is decided thanks to the function *InTriangle*.

Induction hypothesis We assume that we know how to decide whether the point P is inside any convex polygon of $(n-1)$ sides $(n - 1 \geqslant 3)$.

Induction To decide about the inclusion of the point P in any convex polygon of n sides, we divide this polygon into a triangle and a convex polygon of $(n-1)$ sides. The inclusion of P in the triangle is first checked using the function *InTriangle*. If the answer is positive, we conclude that P is inside the polygon. If not, we check the inclusion of P in the convex polygone of $(n-1)$ sides, which can be done according to the induction hypothesis.

The corresponding reduction model is:

$InPolygon(3)$ elementary (function *InTriangle*)
$InPolygon(n) \rightarrow \begin{cases} \text{search in a triangle} \\ + \text{(possibly)} \\ InPolygon(n-1) \end{cases} \qquad n > 3.$

The vertices of the polygon are assumed to be numbered from 1 to n. We divide the polygon into the triangle of vertices 1, $(n-1)$ and n, and the polygon of $(n-1)$ vertices (numbered from 1 to $(n-1)$), according to figure 4.8, with an octagon where the successive chords used to form the triangles are called $c_1, \ldots, c_5$.

If the coordinates of the vertices of the polygon are stored in the arrays X (abscissas) and Y (ordinates), the following function decides whether or not the point P is inside the associated polygon:

1. **function** *InPolygon*(n, x_P, y_P) **result** $\mathbb{B}$ **pre**
2. $\quad n \in \mathbb{N}_1 - \{1, 2\}$ **and** $x_P \in \mathbb{R}$ **and** $y_P \in \mathbb{R}$
3. **begin**
4. $\quad$ **if** $n = 3$ **then**
5. $\quad\quad$ **result** *InTriangle*$(X[1], Y[1], X[2], Y[2], X[3], Y[3], x_P, y_P)$
6. $\quad$ **else**
7. $\quad\quad$ **result** *InTriangle*$(X[1], Y[1], X[n-1], Y[n-1], X[n], Y[n], x_P, y_P)$
8. $\quad\quad$ **or else** *InPolygon*$(n-1, x_P, y_P)$

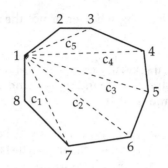

Fig. 4.8 – An example of division of an octagon into triangles.

9.   **end if**
10.   **end**

46 - A 4   **Answer** 4.   Knowing that the number of conditions evaluated in the function *InTriangle* is at most 3, the number of conditions evaluated at worst (i.e. when P is not inside the polygon), by the function *InPolygon* is given by the recurrence:

$$\begin{vmatrix} nbCond(3) = 1 + 3 = 4 \\ nbCond(n) = 1 + 3 + 1 + nbCond(n-1) = 5 + nbCond(n-1) \end{vmatrix} \qquad n > 3$$

therefore $nbCond(n) = 5(n-2) - 1$. In the best case (when P is inside the first triangle derived from the division of the polygon), five conditions are evaluated (two for *InPolygon* and three due to *InTriangle*). The function *InPolygon* has a linear complexity (in $\mathcal{O}(n)$).

46 - A 5   **Answer** 5.   The solution proposed concludes that P is inside the polygon if this point is inside one of the triangles obtained from two adjacent sides of the triangle and the associated chord. If the polygon is not convex, this principle does no longer hold since the triangle thus obtained can be outside the polygon, as illustrated hereafter:

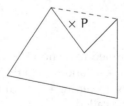

Answers to problem 47. Drawing nested double squares
The problem is on page 168.

47 - A 1   **Answer** 1.   It turns out that we must start the drawing of size n and that of size $(n-1)$ at points that are "analogous" from a geometric point of view. Therefore, it is necessary that, from the starting point of the drawing of size n, we can reach the "analogous" point of the drawing of size $(n-1)$. This requires that this latter is a "point of contact" between the drawings of sizes n and $(n-1)$, hence the four following possibilities: $A_1/A_2, B_1/B_2, C_1/C_2$ or D_1/D_2 (see figure 4.9).

47 - A 2   **Answer** 2.   If we start at point A_1 (B_1, C_1 or D_1), it is impossible to draw the "outer-most" double square "completely" before moving to the problem of size $(n-1)$ because

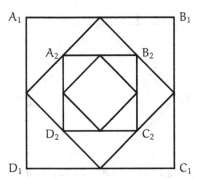

Fig. 4.9 – Correspondences between the four possible starting points of the drawing and their counterpart in the next double square.

of the two constraints imposed on the one hand and the answer to the previous question on the other hand. The drawing is made according to the following inductive schema.

Base We know how to make the nested double square drawing for $n = 0$ (there is nothing to do and the drawing constraints are obviously met).

Induction hypothesis We assume that we know how to make the nested double square drawing for $(n - 1)$ $(n - 1 \geqslant 0)$ pen down, without duplicating lines and the pen located at the same point at the beginning and at the end of the drawing.

Induction We describe how to make the drawing involving n nested double squares. We start at point A_1 (but everything that is to be said can be transposed to B_1, C_1 or D_1) and we want to reach point A_2. Obviously, we can proceed in several ways. We choose the shortest route, knowing that what is not done at this step should be on the way back. Once at point A_2, we know how to make the drawing of size $(n - 1)$, the pen coming back to A_2 (induction hypothesis). Then, we finish the "outermost" double square as shown in figure 4.10, and thus the pen is back to the starting point A_1. The two other constraints are fulfilled during the trace since the pen has never been raised and any segment is drawn only once for the whole drawing (the induction hypothesis ensures this for the "inner" part and figure 4.10 emphasizes it for the "outermost" double square).

Therefore, we have the following reduction model:

$\text{NestDbSqDr}(0)$ elementary (nothing to draw)
$\text{NestDbSqDr}(n) \rightarrow \begin{cases} \text{start the drawing of the "outermost" double square} \\ + \\ \text{NestDbSqDrb}(n-1) \\ + \\ \text{finish the drawing of the "outermost" double square} \end{cases} \quad n > 0.$

Here, the generic function f consists only of starting and finishing the the drawing of the "outermost" double square.

Answer 3. The following algorithm can be deduced: 47 - A 3

1. **procedure** *NestDbSqDrawing*(n, x, y, c) **pre**
2. $n \in \mathbb{N}$ and $x \in \mathbb{R}$ and $y \in \mathbb{R}$ and $c \in \mathbb{R}$

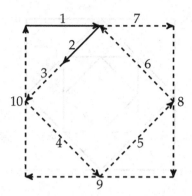

Fig. 4.10 – Example of a drawing strategy with numbers indicating the order according to which segments are drawn: solid line for the outward route, dashed line for the return route.

```
 3. begin
 4.    if n > 0 then
 5.       draw(x + c/2, y);
 6.       draw(x + c/4, y − c/4);
 7.       NestDbSqDrawing(n − 1, x + c/4, y − c/4, c/2);
 8.       draw(x, y − c/2);
 9.       draw(x + c/2, y − c);
10.       draw(x + c, y − c/2);
11.       draw(x + c/2, y);
12.       draw(x + c, y);
13.       draw(x + c, y − c);
14.       draw(x, y − c);
15.       draw(x, y)
16.    end if
17. end
```

47 - A 4 **Answer 4.** The complexity of this procedure in terms of calls to the function *draw* (nbDraw) is given by the recurrence:

$$\begin{vmatrix} nbDraw(0) = 0 \\ nbDraw(n) = nbDraw(n − 1) + 10 \end{vmatrix} \qquad n > 0$$

hence $nbDraw(n) = 10n$ and the proposed procedure has a linear complexity. As to the length of the trace as a function of n and c, it is expressed by the recurrence:

$$\begin{vmatrix} LGTR(0, −) = 0 \\ LGTR(n, c) = 4c + 2c\sqrt{2} + LGTR(n − 1, c/2) \end{vmatrix} \qquad n > 0$$

which yields $LGTR(n, c) = (4c + 2c\sqrt{2})(1 + 1/2 + 1/4 + \cdots + 1/2^{n-1}) = 2(4c + 2c\sqrt{2})(1 − 1/2^n)$. When n tends to infinity, $LGTR(n, c)$ tends to $4c(2 + \sqrt{2})$ and it is linear as a function of c.

Answers to problem 48. **Drawing nested triangles** *The problem is on page 169.*

The problem is on page 169.

Answer 1.   We rely on the following inductive schema to specify the drawing of any "big" inverted triangle of size n ($n \geqslant 0$).   48 - A 1

Base We know how to draw a "big" inverted triangle of size 0, which is indeed the empty one (nothing to do).

Induction hypothesis We assume that we know how to draw a "big" inverted triangle of size $(n-1)$ ($n - 1 \geqslant 0$), pen down and back to the starting point at the end of the drawing.

Induction We make the drawing of the "big" inverted triangle of size n as follows. We first draw the left side of the bottom triangle, then the "big" inverted triangle of size $(n-1)$ (which is feasible pen down and back to the starting point at the end of the drawing according to the induction hypothesis), then the horizontal side of the bottom triangle, then a second "big" inverted triangle of size $(n-1)$ (feasible for the reason explained before), last the right side of the bottom triangle, and the pen is back to its initial position (the point associated with the right angle of the bottom triangle).

This process is schematized hereafter:

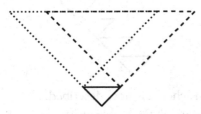

with the tracing of the lower triangle (respectively the first, second recursive call) as a solid (respectively dotted, dashed) line. This corresponds to the following reduction model:

$DrawTriang1(0, -, -, -)$ elementary (nothing to do)	
$DrawTriang1(n, x, y, d) \rightarrow$ $\begin{cases} \text{trace the left side of the lower triangle} \\ + \\ DrawTriang1(n-1, x-d, y+d, d) \\ + \\ \text{trace the base of the lower triangle} \\ + \\ DrawTriang1(n-1, x+d, y+d, d) \\ + \\ \text{trace the right side of the lower triangle} \end{cases}$ $n > 0.$	

where two similar (sub-)problems of size $(n-1)$ appear. The generic function f essentially comes down to draw the lower triangle.

Answer 2.   We deduce the following program: 48 - A 2

```
1. procedure Triangle1(n, x, y, d) pre
2.    n ∈ ℕ and x ∈ ℝ and y ∈ ℝ and d ∈ ℝ
3. begin
4.    if n ⩾ 1 then
5.       draw(x − d, y + d);
6.       Triangle1(n − 1, x − d, y + d, d);
```

7.   *draw*(x + d, y + d);
8.   *Triangle1*(n − 1, x + d, y + d, d);
9.   *draw*(x, y)
10.   **end if**
11.   **end**

Answer 3.   The number of calls to the function *draw* is given by the recurrence:

$$
\begin{aligned}
&\text{nbDraw}(0) = 0 \\
&\text{nbDraw}(n) = 2 \cdot \text{nbDraw}(n-1) + 3 \qquad\qquad\qquad\qquad n > 0
\end{aligned}
$$

hence $\text{nbDraw}(n) = 3(2^n - 1)$ and the number of elementary triangles actually drawn is $(2^n - 1)$. When $n = 5$, 31 elementary triangles are drawn instead of 15 strictly necessary.

Answer 4.   Avoiding the drawing of useless segments requires the replacement of the second "big" inverted triangle of size $(n-1)$ by a banner of size $(n-1)$ fitting exactly the necessary part of the drawing (see the example of the banner of size 4 below).

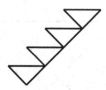

The new inductive resolution schema is now described.

Base We know how to draw the "big" inverted triangle as well as the banner of size 0, which are empty (nothing to do).

Induction hypothesis We assume that we know how to draw the "big" inverted triangle and the banner of size $(n-1)$ $(n-1 \geqslant 0)$, pen down without useless tracing, back to the starting point when the drawing is finished.

Induction We would like to draw the "big" inverted triangle and the banner of size n. The first one consists in tracing the left side of the bottom triangle, then the "big" inverted triangle of size $(n-1)$ (which is feasible according the induction hypothesis, without useless tracing, pen down, back to the starting point at the end of the drawing), then the horizontal side of the bottom triangle, then the banner of size $(n-1)$ (which is feasible according to the induction hypothesis, without useless tracing, pen down, back to the starting point at the end of the drawing), last the right side of the bottom triangle and so, we drew the "big" inverted triangle of size n under the imposed constraints. We can notice that the tracing of the left side of the lower elementary triangle, followed by the tracing of its horizontal side and that of the banner of size $(n-1)$, and last that of the right side of the lower elementary triangle make up a banner of size n, the pen being back to the starting point.

This process is illustrated by the schema hereafter:

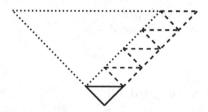

where the tracing associated with the lower triangle (respectively with the recursive call, with the call to *Banner*) is a solid (respectively dotted, dashed) line. The reduction model is:

$$
\begin{aligned}
&\text{DrawTriang2}(0,-,-,-) \text{ elementary (nothing to do)}\\[4pt]
&\text{DrawTriang2}(n,x,y,d) \rightarrow
\begin{cases}
\text{trace the left side of the lower triangle}\\
+\\
\text{DrawTriang2}(n-1,x-d,y+d,d)\\
+\\
\text{trace the base of the lower triangle}\\
+\\
\text{DrawBan}(n-1,x+d,y+d,d)\\
+\\
\text{trace the right side of the lower triangle}
\end{cases} \quad n>0\\[8pt]
&\text{DrawBan}(0,-,-,-) \text{ elementary (nothing to do)}\\[4pt]
&\text{DrawBan}(n,x,y,d) \rightarrow
\begin{cases}
\text{trace the left side of the lower triangle}\\
+\\
\text{trace the base of the lower triangle}\\
+\\
\text{DrawBan}(n-1,x+d,y+d,d)\\
+\\
\text{trace the right sidebof the lower triangle}
\end{cases} \quad n>0.
\end{aligned}
$$

In this resolution model, the drawing of a "big" inverted triangle references a single instance of the (sub-problem) of size $(n-1)$, and the role of the function f is the tracing of the elementary triangle and that of a banner of size $(n-1)$. For the banner, the function f comes down to the tracing of the elementary triangle.

Answer 5. The corresponding program is made up of two recursive procedures, *Triangle2* and *Banner* hereafter:

48 - A 5

1. **procedure** *Triangle2*(n, x, y, d) **pre**
2. $n \in \mathbb{N}$ and $x \in \mathbb{R}$ and $y \in \mathbb{R}$ and $d \in \mathbb{R}$
3. **begin**
4.   **if** $n \geqslant 1$ **then**
5. $draw(x - d, y + d)$;
6. $Triangle2(n - 1, x - d, y + d, d)$;
7. $draw(x + d, y + d)$;
8. $Banner(n - 1, x + d, y + d, d)$;
9. $draw(x, y)$
10.   **end if**
11. **end**

1. **procedure** *Banner*(n, x, y, d) **pre**
2. $n \in \mathbb{N}$ and $x \in \mathbb{R}$ and $y \in \mathbb{R}$ and $d \in \mathbb{R}$
3. **begin**
4.   **if** $n \geqslant 1$ **then**
5. $draw(x - d, y + d)$;
6. $draw(x + d, y + d)$;
7. $Banner(n - 1, x + d, y + d, d)$;
8. $draw(x, y)$
9.   **end if**
10. **end**

We now calculate the exact complexity of this solution in terms of calls to the function *draw*. The call *Banner*$(n - 1, x + d, y + d)$ generates exactly $3(n - 1)$ calls to *draw*. As to the number of calls associated with the call *Triangle2*$(n - 1, x - d, y + d, d)$, it is given by:

$$nbDraw(0) = 0$$
$$nbDraw(n) = nbDraw(n-1) + 3(n-1) + 3 \qquad\qquad n \geqslant 1$$

hence $nbDraw(n) = 3n(n+1)/2$, which corresponds to $n(n+1)/2$ triangles (minimum number) and proves that the proposed solution is optimal.

Answers to problem 49. Exhaustive visit of a chessboard *The problem is on page 170.*

49 - A 1   **Answer** 1.   We first study the case of a chessboard of side $s = 5$. We suppose that the visit starts at the square $(1,1)$, but it would be possible to choose another one. In the following figure, we show the first steps of the visit (the square $(1,1)$ is in the lower left corner):

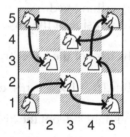

After seven moves, a first lap ends in the square $(3,2)$. The knight begins a new lap by a move to the square $(1,3)$ and it carries on as indicated hereafter:

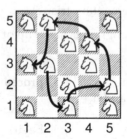

From the square $(3,1)$, the knight starts a third lap as follows:

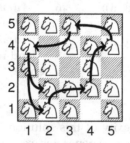

From the square $(2, 2)$, the last lap consists of the moves shown in the figure hereafter:

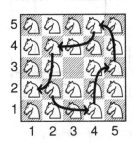

Thus, the knight has visited all the squares of the crown of side 5 and width 2. With a last move from $(2, 1)$ to $(3, 3)$, the knight will have covered the whole chessboard.

Answer 2. Dealing with the general case for $s \geqslant 1$ ($m \geqslant 0$) is fairly simple and it is based on the following inductive schema. **49 - A 2**

Base We know how to visit a chessboard of side $s = 1$ ($4m + 1$ with $m = 0$) exhaustively since it is sufficient to leave the knight on the single square of the chessboard.

Induction hypothesis We assume that we know how to visit a chessboard of side $s = 4(m - 1) + 1$ ($m - 1 \geqslant 0$) exhaustively, each square being seen only once.

Induction The exhaustive visit of a chessboard of side $s = 4m + 1$ is made by first visiting the crown of side $4m + 1$ and width 2 (see figure 4.11). The knight starts from the square $(1, 1)$ (lower left corner as before) and it makes the sequence of moves $(1, 1) \rightarrow (2, 3) \rightarrow (1, 5) \rightarrow \ldots \rightarrow (2, 4m - 12) \rightarrow (1, 4m + 1)$, then $(3, 4m) \rightarrow (5, 4m + 1) \rightarrow \ldots \rightarrow (4m - 1, 4m) \rightarrow (4m + 1, 4m + 1)$, then $(4m, 4m - 1) \rightarrow (4m + 1, 4m - 3) \rightarrow \ldots \rightarrow (4m, 3) \rightarrow (4m + 1, 1)$, then $(4m - 1, 2) \rightarrow (4m - 3, 1) \rightarrow \ldots \rightarrow (2, 4m - 1) \rightarrow (3, 2)$. Thus, the knight made its first lap. The rest of the moves obeys the principle described in the previous answer for $m = 1$, in particular the knight moves to the square $(3, 1)$ to start the second lap. At the end of the fourth lap, the knight is at the square $(2, 1)$. A last move leads it to the square $(3, 3)$ and here, we know how to visit the "remaining" chessboard of side $s = 4(m - 1) + 1 = 4m - 3$, exhaustively and without double visit according to the induction hypothesis. The objective assigned, the exhaustive visit of the initial chessboard of side $s = 4m + 1$, without visiting any square twice (or more), is reached.

Answer 3. Therefore, the resolution model is: **49 - A 3**

ExhVisitChess(0) elementary (nothing to do)
ExhVisitChess(m) $\rightarrow$ VisitCrown(m) + ExhVisitChess(m − 1) $\qquad\qquad$ m > 0

where VisitCrown(m) carries out the visit of the whole crown of side $(4m + 1)$ and width 2 (see figure 4.11).

Answers to problem 50. Drawing fractal curves $\qquad$ *The problem is on page 171.*

Answer 1. From these curves, it appears that: **50 - A 1**

$$
\begin{array}{llllllll}
A(2) & = & D(1) & l & A(1) & d & A(1) & r & B(1) \\
B(2) & = & C(1) & u & B(1) & r & B(1) & d & A(1) \\
C(2) & = & B(1) & r & C(1) & u & C(1) & l & D(1) \\
D(2) & = & A(1) & d & D(1) & l & D(1) & u & C(1).
\end{array}
$$

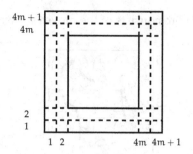

Fig. 4.11 – *A crown of side* $4m + 1$ *and width* 2.

Moreover, assuming that $A(0), B(0), C(0)$ and $D(0)$ are empty curves, we also have:

$$
\begin{array}{rcllllllll}
A(1) & = & D(0) & l & A(0) & d & A(0) & r & B(0) \\
B(1) & = & C(0) & u & B(0) & r & B(0) & d & A(0) \\
C(1) & = & B(0) & r & C(0) & u & C(0) & l & D(0) \\
D(1) & = & A(0) & d & D(0) & l & D(0) & u & C(0).
\end{array}
$$

The approach can be generalized by:

$$
\begin{array}{rcllllllll}
A(i+1) & = & D(i) & l & A(i) & d & A(i) & r & B(i) \\
B(i+1) & = & C(i) & u & B(i) & r & B(i) & d & A(i) \\
C(i+1) & = & B(i) & r & C(i) & u & C(i) & l & D(i) \\
D(i+1) & = & A(i) & d & D(i) & l & D(i) & u & C(i)
\end{array}
$$

for $i \geqslant 0$.

50 - A 2   **Answer** 2.   The level-3 Hilbert curve is shown in figure 4.12, on the basis that:

$$A(3) \;=\; D(2) \;\; l \;\; A(2) \;\; d \;\; A(2) \;\; r \;\; B(2),$$

and that the connecting elements l, d and r (of length α) appear as strokes.

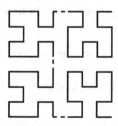

Fig. 4.12 – *The level-3 Hilbert curve.*

50 - A 3   **Answer** 3.   From the answer to the first question, we need four procedures to be called A, B, C and D, A corresponding to the Hilbert curve. We have:

1. **procedure** $A(n)$ **pre**
2. $n \in \mathbb{N}$
3. **begin**
4.   **if** $n > 0$ **then**
5. $D(n-1)\,;u \leftarrow u - \alpha\,;$
6. $draw(u,v);$
7. $A(n-1)\,;v \leftarrow v - \alpha\,;$
8. $draw(u,v);$
9. $A(n-1)\,;u \leftarrow u + \alpha\,;$
10. $draw(u,v);$
11. $B(n-1)$
12.   **end if**
13. **end**

1. **procedure** $B(n)$ **pre**
2. $n \in \mathbb{N}$
3. **begin**
4.   **if** $n > 0$ **then**
5. $C(n-1)\,;v \leftarrow v + \alpha\,;$
6. $draw(u,v);$
7. $B(n-1)\,;u \leftarrow u + \alpha\,;$
8. $draw(u,v);$
9. $B(n-1)\,;v \leftarrow v - \alpha\,;$
10. $draw(u,v);$
11. $A(n-1)$
12.   **end if**
13. **end**

1. **procedure** $C(n)$ **pre**
2. $n \in \mathbb{N}$
3. **begin**
4.   **if** $n > 0$ **then**
5. $B(n-1)\,;u \leftarrow u + \alpha\,;$
6. $draw(u,v);$
7. $C(n-1)\,;v \leftarrow v + \alpha\,;$
8. $draw(u,v);$
9. $C(n-1)\,;u \leftarrow u - \alpha\,;$
10. $draw(u,v);$
11. $D(n-1)$
12.   **end if**
13. **end**

1. **procedure** $D(n)$ **pre**
2. $n \in \mathbb{N}$
3. **begin**
4.   **if** $n > 0$ **then**
5. $A(n-1)\,;v \leftarrow v - \alpha\,;$
6. $draw(u,v);$
7. $D(n-1)\,;u \leftarrow u - \alpha\,;$
8. $draw(u,v);$
9. $D(n-1)\,;v \leftarrow v + \alpha\,;$
10. $draw(u,v);$
11. $C(n-1)$
12.   **end if**
13. **end**

The program:

1. **variables**
2. $u \in \mathbb{R}$ **and** $v \in \mathbb{R}$ **and** $\alpha \in \mathbb{R}_+^*$
3. **begin**
4. $u \leftarrow 15.0\,;v \leftarrow 20.0\,;\alpha \leftarrow 0.5\,;$
5. $place(u,v)\,;$
6. $A(5)$
7. **end**

invokes procedure A to draw the level-5 Hilbert curve at the starting point of coordinates $(15.0, 20.0)$, where the length of the elementary stroke (α) is half a centimeter.

Answer 4.   To calculate the complexity of the drawing of the level-n Hilbert curve, we first demonstrate – by induction – that the four procedures, A, B, C and D, have the same complexity for any level n ($n \geqslant 0$). We denote by C_A (respectively C_B, C_C, C_D) their respective complexity in terms of calls to *draw*.   50 - A 4

Base   We have $C_A(0) = C_B(0) = C_C(0) = C_D(0) = 0$.

Induction hypothesis   We assume that for $n-1$ ($n-1 \geqslant 1$), we have $C_A(n-1) = C_B(n-1) = C_C(n-1) = C_D(n-1)$.

Induction We have:

$$C_A(n) = C_D(n-1) + 2 \cdot C_A(n-1) + C_B(n-1) + 3 = 4 \cdot C_A(n-1) + 3$$
$$C_B(n) = C_C(n-1) + 2 \cdot C_B(n-1) + C_A(n-1) + 3 = 4 \cdot C_A(n-1) + 3$$
$$C_C(n) = C_B(n-1) + 2 \cdot C_C(n-1) + C_D(n-1) + 3 = 4 \cdot C_A(n-1) + 3$$
$$C_D(n) = C_A(n-1) + 2 \cdot C_D(n-1) + C_C(n-1) + 3 = 4 \cdot C_A(n-1) + 3$$

and using the induction hypothesis, we observe that $C_A(n) = C_B(n) = C_C(n) = C_D(n) = 4 \cdot C_A(n-1) + 3$.

We now establish the complexity of the drawing of the level-n Hilbert curve. From $C_A(0) = 0$ and $C_A(n) = 4 \cdot C_A(n-1) + 3$, we deduce that $C_A(n) = 4^n - 1$. The drawing of a Hilbert curve has an exponential complexity in terms of calls to *draw*.

50 - A 5   **Answer 5.**   For $n = 1$, the drawing requires a square of side α. For $n = 2$, the drawing needs a square of side 3α. More generally, since the level-n Hilbert curve is obtained as the horizontal and vertical juxtapositions – with a connecting element – of two Hilbert curves of level $(n-1)$, the drawing of the curve $A(n)$ has the same height and width, given by:

$$\begin{array}{l} \text{DrawHeight}(1, \alpha) = \alpha \\ \text{DrawHeight}(n, \alpha) = 2 \cdot \text{DrawHeight}(n-1, \alpha) + \alpha \hfill n > 1 \end{array}$$

hence $\text{DrawHeight}(n, \alpha) = \alpha \cdot (2^n - 1)$. The side of the square bounding the level-n Hilbert curve varies in an exponential way with n. It can be checked in figure 4.12, page 186, that the curve is bounded by a square of side 7α.

50 - A 6   **Answer 6.**   The drawing of the curves $W(1)$ and $W(2)$ is presented in figure 4.13, where the elementary connecting elements are strokes (of length α).

50 - A 7   **Answer 7.**   We first establish the complexity $C_A(n)$ (respectively $C_B(n), C_C(n), C_D(n)$) of the procedure drawing the curve A (respectively B, C, D) for $n \geqslant 1$. Looking at their code, we can reasonably think that the four procedures have the same complexity in terms of calls to *draw* or elementary strokes (d, r, l, u). Let us prove it by induction.

Base We have $C_A(1) = C_B(1) = C_C(1) = C_D(1) = 1$.

Induction hypothesis For $n - 1$ ($n - 1 \geqslant 1$), we assume that $C_A(n-1) = C_B(n-1) = C_C(n-1) = C_D(n-1)$.

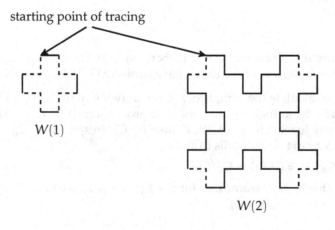

Fig. 4.13 – Level-1 and level-2 W-curves for the same value of α.

Induction We have:

$$C_A(n) = 2 \cdot C_A(n-1) + C_B(n-1) + C_D(n-1) + 5 = 4 \cdot C_A(n-1) + 5.$$

Similarly:

$$C_B(n) = 2 \cdot C_B(n-1) + C_C(n-1) + C_A(n-1) + 5 = 4 \cdot C_B(n-1) + 5 = 4 \cdot C_A(n-1) + 5.$$

The same type of calculation leads to conclude that $C_C(n) = C_D(n) = 4 \cdot C_A(n-1) + 5$, and then:

$$C_A(n) = C_B(n) = C_C(n) = C_D(n) = 4 \cdot C_A(n-1) + 5.$$

Let us calculate $C_A(n)$. We have:

$$C_A(n) = 4^{n-1} \cdot C_A(1) + 5 \cdot \sum_{i=0}^{n-2} 4^i = 4^{n-1} \cdot C_A(1) + 5 \cdot \frac{4^{n-1}-1}{3} = \frac{2}{3} \cdot 4^n - \frac{5}{3}.$$

Hence the complexity for drawing $W(n)$ is:

$$C_W(n) = 4 \cdot C_A(n) + 8 = \frac{2}{3} \cdot (4^{n+1} + 2).$$

It can be checked in figure 4.13, page 188, that $C_W(1) = 12$ et $C_W(2) = 44$. As for any Hilbert curve, drawing W-curve has an exponential complexity.

Answers to problem 51. The Countdown game   *The problem is on page 172.*

Answer 1. As suggested in the statement of the problem, two numbers are replaced by their sum for each pair of numbers present in S, resulting in a decrease in the number of numbers for subsequent combinations. We must therefore explore the C_n^2 pairs of type (a, b) that can be formed from the elements of S. The reduction model is therefore the following:

51 - A 1

LCEB1(S) (nothing to do)		$\|S\| = 1$
LCEB1(S) $\rightarrow$ $\begin{cases} \text{for each pair } (a, b) \text{ of } S, \text{ som} \leftarrow a+b \\ \text{if TG} = \text{som} \quad \text{we have a solution and the search is stopped} \\ \text{else } B' \leftarrow ((S \dot{-} [\![a, b]\!]) \sqcup [\![\text{som}]\!]); \text{LCEB1}(B') \end{cases}$		$\|S\| > 1.$

Answer 2. The call tree is given in figure 4.14, page 190.

51 - A 2

Remark

All leaves contain the value 24, sum of the elements of B.

Answer 3. We review the four operations that can be used with two of the positive integers a and b present in a bag:

51 - A 3

- the addition $(a + b)$ as the product $(a \cdot b)$ is achievable without proper constraints,
- regarding subtraction, it is important not to apply it in the presence of two equal numbers a and b, otherwise the condition applying to numbers present in a bag will not be met; we will make either $(a - b)$ if $a > b$, or $(b - a)$ if $b > a$,

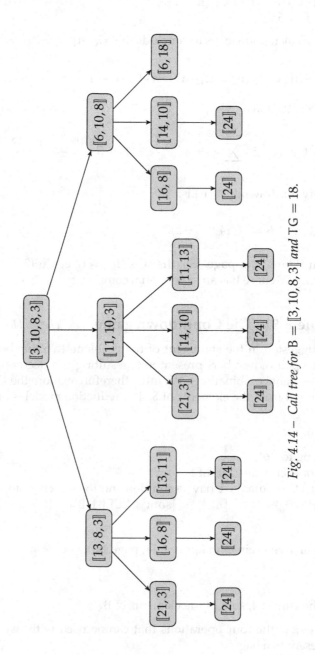

Fig. 4.14 – Call tree for B = [3, 10, 8, 3] *and* TG = 18.

• as mentioned, the division assumes that this operation only takes place in the presence of multiples, in which case (a/b) will be made if $a \geqslant b$ or (b/a) if $a < b$.

Note that, in general, it is useless to replace a pair (a, b) by a number c which is a or b. Indeed, in this case, the new generated bag will be included to the one it comes from and will only be able to produce substitutions that can be obtained from the latter. This happens for multiplication and division when a or b is equal to 1, but also for the difference when a (respectively b) is double b (respectively a) or for the division a/b when $a = b^2$. For example, with $B = [\![3, 9, 2, 10, 7]\!]$, dividing 9 by 3 leads to the new bag $B' = [\![3, 2, 10, 7]\!]$ and any operation on these four numbers can be performed from B as well.

In the same vein, it is clear that the presence of duplicate bags leads to the generation of identical bags by each of the substitution operations. So, the original bag $[\![3, 10, 8, 3]\!]$ actually gives rise to the two identical bags $[\![13, 8, 3]\!]$ and $[\![3, 13, 8]\!]$. However, avoiding the generation of identical configurations is not easy to implement and this point is left aside.

Answer 4. As before, the basic idea is, thanks to an arithmetic operation op, to replace two numbers a and b of B by another $r = op(a, b)$. From this perspective, it appears that the size of the problem is the number n of numbers to combine. On the one hand, we must explore the C_n^2 pairs of type (a, b) that can be formed from the elements of B, on the other hand we have to consider all *useful* operations between a and b (see above). The reduction model is therefore the following: **51 - A 4**

LCEB2(S) (nothing to do)	$\lvert S \rvert = 1$
LCEB2(S) $\rightarrow$ $\begin{cases} \text{for each pair } (a, b) \text{ of S and each useful operation op} \\ \text{if } TG = op(a, b) \text{ we have a solution and the search is stopped} \\ \text{else } B' \leftarrow ((S \doteq [\![a, b]\!]) \sqcup [\![op(a, b)]\!]); LCEB2(B') \end{cases}$	$\lvert S \rvert > 1.$

Answer 5. The principle of the algorithm to be constructed consists in marking all the lines of the table which enter in the construction of the solution (the so-called *qualified* rows). This is done by associating to the array M the joint array of Booleans Q which is such that Q[i] is **true** if and only if (for any i) the ith element of M is a "descendant" of the nth element (the "root"). More formally, this algorithm is specified as follows: **51 - A 5**

Precondition: $Q[n .. nbPl]$ is a variable array of Booleans. M is a constant array satisfying the conditions specified above.

Postcondition:

$$Q[n] \text{ and } \forall j \cdot \left(j \in n+1 .. nbPl \Rightarrow \left(Q[j] \Leftrightarrow \exists p \cdot \left(p \in n .. j-1 \text{ and } \left(\begin{array}{c} Q[p] \text{ and} \\ M[p, 4] = M[j, 2] \text{ ou} \\ M[p, 4] = M[j, 3] \end{array} \right) \right) \right) \right).$$

The processing to be carried out is based on a loop. We adopt the technique of the "work partly done" (rows of M located between n and $i - 1$ are processed) to build this loop.

Invariant Q[n] is **true** and all the rows of M between n and $i - 1$ are processed (they are qualified or not). In other words, Q[n] is **true** and, for any $j \in n + 1 .. i - 1, Q[j]$ is true iff row number j is a descendant of the node represented by row number n (the "root").

Stopping condition The processing is complete when $i = nbPl + 1$. The conjunction of the invariant and the stopping condition implies the postcondition.

Progression Row number i must be marked if and only if it is the son, left or right, of a row already marked (which is therefore located *above* in the array). The corresponding processing requires a second loop, nested with the first, at the end of which row number i is qualified or not (assignment of a Boolean value to Q[i]). Once again, we adopt the strategy of "the work partly done" to build this second loop.

> **Invariant** $j \in n .. i$ **and** row number i is not the "son" of any of the lines already qualified.

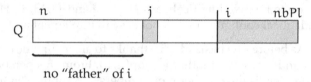

$$\text{no "father" of } i$$

Stopping condition There are two sub-cases to consider:

(a) Either $j = i$, which means that no qualified "father" has been found for row number i.

(b) Or row number j is the qualified "father" of row number i, which is characterized by:

$$Q[j] \text{ and } (M[i,4] = M[j,2] \text{ or } M[i,4] = M[j,3])$$

Note that a short-circuiting operator is required to constitute the stopping condition:

$$\left(\begin{array}{l} j = i \text{ or else} \\ \left(Q[j] \text{ and } \left(\begin{array}{l} M[i,4] = M[j,2] \text{ or} \\ M[i,4] = M[j,3] \end{array} \right) \right) \end{array} \right).$$

The conjunction of the invariant and the stopping condition implies the postcondition.

Progression It is restricted to $j \leftarrow j + 1$.

Initialization $j \leftarrow n$ establishes the invariant.

Termination The expression $(i - j)$ is suited to ensure termination.

At the end of this loop, Q[i] takes the value of the expression $j \neq i$ (Q[i] $\leftarrow j \neq i$).

Indeed, Q[i] takes the value **false** if and only if the row numbered i does not have a "father" or if its father is not qualified.

Let us now go back to the initialization of the main loop.

Initialization The invariant must be established. The following program is appropriate:

$i \leftarrow n + 1; Q[n] \leftarrow$ **true**.

Termination The expression $(nbPl - i + 1)$ is suited to ensure termination.

Note that it is possible to encode the outer loop with a *for* loop. This is the solution chosen below.

1. **procedure** *Qualification* **pre**
2. $j \in n .. nbPl$

3. **begin**
4.   /% *PRE:* Q[n .. nbPl] *is a variable array of Booleans* %/
5.   Q[n] ← **true**;
6.   **for** i ranging n + 1 .. nbPl **do**
7.   j ← n;
8.   **while not** $\left(\begin{array}{c} j = i \text{ \textbf{or else}} \\ \left(Q[j] \text{ \textbf{and}} \left(\begin{array}{c} M[i,4] = M[j,2] \text{ \textbf{or}} \\ M[i,4] = M[j,3] \end{array} \right) \right) \end{array} \right)$ **do**
9.   j ← j + 1
10.   **end while**;
11.   Q[i] ← j ≠ i
12.   **end for**
13.   /% *POST: row* i *is qualified if it is a descendant of row* n %/
14. **end**

Answer 6.   In order to implement the suggested model, several aspects need to be re-   51 - A 6
fined:

- the bag B (respectively B′) becomes the array T (respectively T′) of n elements,
- the enumeration of pairs of elements of B (now T) is done with two nested loops,
- operations are numbered: 1 for addition, 2 for $(a - b)$, 3 for $(b - a)$, 4 for multiplication, 5 for (a/b), 6 for (b/a),
- the construction of the bag B′ from B becomes the construction of the array T′ from (effective values) of array T thanks to a loop in which values are "padded" on the left, op(a, b) replacing a, b being suppressed.

The procedure *CountDown* resulting from these choices is as follows:

1. **procedure** *CountDown*(T, n) **pre**
2. $n \in \mathbb{N}_1$ **and** $a \in \mathbb{N}_1$ **and** $b \in \mathbb{N}_1$ **and** $T \in 1 .. n \to \mathbb{N}_1$ **and** $T' \in 1 .. n \to \mathbb{N}_1$ **and**
3. $Q \in 2 .. nbPl \to \mathbb{B}$ **and** op $\in 1 .. 6$ **and** res $\in \mathbb{N}_1$ **and** $p \in \mathbb{N}_1$ **and** $m \in \mathbb{N}_1$
4. **begin**
5.   **if** n > 1 **then**
6.   **for** i ranging 1 .. (n − 1) **do**
7.   **for** j ranging (i + 1) .. n **do**
8.   a ← T[i]; b ← T[j];
9.   **for** k ranging 1 .. 4 **do**
10.   **if not** stoploop **then**
11.   **if** k = 1 **then**
12.   res ← a + b; op ← 1
13.   **elsif** k = 2 **then**
14.   **if** a > b **then**
15.   res ← a − b; op ← 2
16.   **elsif** b > a **then**
17.   res ← b − a; op ← 3
18.   **else**
19.   /% *case* a = b *and operation* a − b *useless* %/
20.   res ← a
21.   **end if**
22.   **elsif** k = 3 **then**

```
23.                  res ← a · b; op ← 4
24.              else
25.                if Multiple(a, b) then
26.                    res ← a/b; op ← 5
27.                elsif Multiple(b, a) then
28.                    res ← b/a; op ← 6
29.                else
30.                    /% case a and b not multiples then division operation useless %/
31.                    res ← a
32.                end if
33.              end if;
34.              if res ≠ a and res ≠ b then
35.                  M[n, 1] ← op; M[n, 2] ← a; M[n, 3] ← b; M[n, 4] ← res;
36.                  if res = TG then
37.                      stoploop ← true;
38.                      /% qualification step of lines of M (see previous question) %/
39.                      /% before printing solution %/
40.                      Qualification;
41.                      PrintSol
42.                  else
43.                      p ← 1;
44.                      for m ranging 1 .. n do
45.                        if m = i then
46.                            T'[p] ← res; p ← p + 1
47.                        elsif m ≠ j then
48.                            T'[p] ← T[m]; p ← p + 1
49.                        end if
50.                      end for;
51.                      CountDown(T', n − 1)
52.                  end if
53.                end if
54.              end if
55.            end for
56.          end for
57.        end for
58.      end if
59.  end
```

The Boolean function *Multiple*(a, b) returns **true** if the division of a by b has no remainder, **false** otherwise. The procedure *PrintSol* prints the sequence of operations used to form TG, thanks to the array M which is explored from rows nbPl to n taking into account only *qualified* lines (i.e. whose associated value in Q is **true**). Since these two operations do not present any particular difficulty, they are not detailed. An example of call to this procedure is:

```
1. constants
2.     nbPl ∈ ℕ₁ and nbPl = ... TG ∈ 101 .. 999 and TG = ... and
3.     T ∈ 1 .. nbPl → {1, 2, 3, 4, 5, 6, 7, 8, 9, 10, 25, 50, 75} and T = ...
4. variables
5.     M ∈ 2 .. nbPl × 1 .. 4 → ℕ₁ and stoploop ∈ 𝔹
6. begin
7.     stoploop ← false;
```

8.   *CountDown*(T, nbPl);
9.   **if not** stoploop **then**
10.   write(*No solution for the proposed target value*)
11.   **end if**
12. **end**

Answer 7.   The number of recursive calls carried out in the body of the inner loop is between 1 (when $a = b = 1$ only addition is done) and 4 (numbers a and b are multiples, different and such that $a \neq 2b$ and $b \neq 2a$). Hereafter we calculate $nbRecCall(n)$ the *maximum* number of these calls: $\quad$ **51 - A 7**

$$nbRecCall(1) = 0$$
$$nbRecCall(n) = 2n(n-1)(nbRecCall(n-1)+1) \qquad n > 1.$$

Developing this recurrence, it comes:

$$
\begin{aligned}
nbRecCall(n) &= 2n(n-1) + 2n(n-1) \cdot nbRecCall(n-1) \\
&= 2n(n-1) + 2n(n-1) \cdot (2(n-1)(n-2) \cdot nbRecCall(n-2) + 1) \\
&= 2n(n-1) + 4n(n-1)(n-1)(n-2) + 4n(n-1)(n-1)(n-2) \cdot nbRecCall(n-2) \\
&= 2n(n-1) + 4n(n-1)(n-1)(n-2) + 4n(n-1)(n-1)(n-2) \cdot \\
&\qquad\qquad (2(n-2)(n-3) \cdot nbRecCall(n-3) + 1) \\
&= 2n(n-1) + 4n(n-1)(n-1)(n-2) + 8n(n-1)(n-1)(n-2)(n-2)(n-3) \\
&\quad + 8n(n-1)(n-1)(n-2)(n-2)(n-3) \cdot nbRecCall(n-3) \\
&= 2n(n-1) + 4n(n-1)(n-1)(n-2) + 8n(n-1)(n-1)(n-2)(n-2)(n-3) \\
&\quad + \cdots + 2^n n(n-1)^2 \cdots 3^2 \cdot 2^2 \cdot 1 \cdot (nbRecCall(0) + 1)
\end{aligned}
$$

hence in the end:

$$nbRecCall(n) = \sum_{i=1}^{n} 2^i \cdot \prod_{j=1}^{i} (n-j+1)(n-j) \qquad n \geqslant 1.$$

This is a class of complexity *far worse* than exponential, for which we have: $nbRecCall(1) = 0$, $nbRecCall(2) = 4$, $nbRecCall(3) = 60$, $nbRecCall(4) = 1464$, $nbRecCall(5) = 58600$, $nbRecCall(6) = 3516060$, which shows that this procedure is only practicable for very low values of n ($\ll 20$). Experiments conducted by the authors with $nbPl = 6$ show that the number of recursive calls varies from a few hundred to just over 650000, this latter value being reached in the absence of a solution.

Answer 8.   If all the numbers in B are to be used, the solution discovery in the elementary case must be *deported*; we have then to check that the (unique) number in T is TG. This leads to the following changes in the procedure *CountDown*: (i) remove lines 36 to 42 and line 53, and (ii) replace line 58 with "**elsif** T[1] = TG **then** (PrintSol) **endif**" (The qualification step of rows of M is unnecessary here since the $(nbPl-1)$ rows of M are to be printed. $\quad$ **51 - A 8**

Answer 9.   To get all the solutions, it is sufficient not to stop the loops, which leads to remove: (i) the declaration of the variable stoploop in line 5 of the calling program and its initialization in line 7, (ii) on the one hand the alternative formed by the pair of lines 10 and 54, on the other hand the assignment in line 37 in the procedure *CountDown*. $\quad$ **51 - A 9**

5

Generate and test

> Though patience be a tired mare, yet
> she will plod.
>
> William Shakespeare

The techniques applied in this chapter suppose a good understanding of the content of section 1.4.5.2, page 19 (Chapter 1 titled "Mathematics and computer science: some useful notions"). Most of the examples and problems proposed in this chapter belong to the class of NP-complete problems (see for example [9] for an introduction to complexity classes), which means that no polynomial algorithm is known to resolve them.

5.1 Fundamentals

5.1.1 Principle

Generate and test: a search problem

"Generate and test" programming technique (also called *backtracking*) is a method of search of solutions among a finite set of candidates. Similarly to the classical search paradigm (a typical example is the sequential search in a table), the principle of "Generate and test" consists of a *finite set of candidates* and a *selection predicate* which allows to decide whether or not a candidate is a solution to the considered problem. Then, we can determine the subset of candidates which are solutions (i.e. those candidates which comply with the selection predicate). In the framework of "Generate and test" as well in that of classical search, the basic algorithmic technique aims at successively examining all the candidates.

When the set of solutions is nonempty, a first variant is to search only *one arbitrary* solution to the problem, not all of them. A second variant is characterized by the search of the best solution (in a sense to be defined according to the problem).

The main characteristic of the "Generate and test" technique lies in the fact that, contrary to classical search, the set of candidates C is defined in comprehension (it is "built", "calculated", "generated" from its properties over the course of search). This set may be so large that the technique becomes impractical as such.

A first example

In this section, which is a kind of tutorial, a simple example is developed, which allows to discuss most of the aspects to be addressed later on, without going into the details. A methodological approach is outlined, then refined in the rest of this introduction to make it usable in the exercises of the chapter.

Given a set E of n ($n > 0$) elements of $\mathbb{Z}$, we search for all the subsets of E where the sum of the members is zero. The set C of candidates is $\mathbb{P}(E)$, the powerset of E and the selection predicate is "the sum of the elements of a candidate is zero". Therefore, we must examine once and only once (enumeration without duplicates) the 2^n subsets of E and, for each one, calculate the sum of its elements. We keep only the subsets of E which are a solution to the problem (here, there is at least one solution: the empty subset $\varnothing$, but this does not happen in general).

Concretely, the set E is represented by the array $T[1 .. n]$. For example, with $n = 6$ and $E = \{10, 0, -3, -7, 5, -5\}$, $T = [10, 0, -3, -7, 5, -5]$. Each candidate is implemented by its characteristic vector and here, the 2^6 vectors are $[0, 0, 0, 0, 0, 0]$ (for the empty set), $[1, 0, 0, 0, 0, 0]$ (for the set $\{10\}$), ..., $[1, 1, 1, 1, 1, 1]$ (for the whole set E). We can notice that each of these vectors is a function from the interval $1 .. 6$ to the interval $0 .. 1$. The expected solution is obtained through the calculation of the sum of the elements of T filtered by the characteristic vector in order to finally retain only the sub-arrays whose sum is zero.

Frame

When resolving this problem, the first difficulty is the successive production of all the candidates. One way to reach this goal is to make use of the tree (called *recursion tree*) whose leaves are the characteristic vectors. For $n = 3$, the recursion tree is that of figure 5.1.

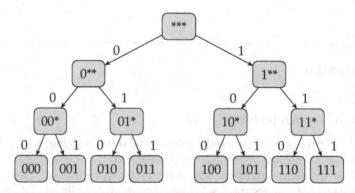

Fig. 5.1 – Recursion tree for the construction of all the total functions from the interval $1 .. 3$ to the interval $0 .. 1$. These functions cover the powerset of $\{1, 2, 3\}$.

The following algorithm meets our objective and it browses the recursion tree depth first,

```
 1. procedure GenSet1(i) pre
 2.    i ∈ 1 .. n
 3. begin
 4.    for j ranging 0 .. 1 do
 5.       X[i] ← j ;
 6.       if i = n then
 7.          write(X)
 8.       else
 9.          GenSet1(i + 1)
10.       end if
11.    end for
12. end
```

provided that it is invoked in the context:

1. **constants**
2. $n \in \mathbb{N}_1$ **and** $n = \dots$ **and** $T \in 1 \,..\, n \rightarrow \mathbb{Z}$ **and** $T = [\dots]$
3. **variables**
4. $X \in 1 \,..\, n \rightarrow 0 \,..\, 1$
5. **begin**
6.   *GenSet1*(1)
7. **end**

This algorithm constitutes the first step to the solution to our problem. It is the *frame* of the solution where X is the *enumeration vector*.

The formal proof of correction of this algorithm can be made using Hoare's axiomatics extended to recursive procedures [18]. It is founded on the following recursion invariant "$X[1 \,..\, i - 1]$ is constant, it is a total function from $1 \,..\, i - 1$ to $0 \,..\, 1$ and, if a node of the recursion tree meeting the condition $(i = n)$ is printed, then all the nodes fulfilling this condition have been printed". Thus, for example, if, in the schema of figure 5.1, we consider the subtree rooted in $X = [1,{}^*,{}^*]$ $(i = 2)$, we go in and out of the procedure with this value of X, and if a single leaf of this subtree has been printed, then the four leaves have been printed.

Selection

For now, we have only produced all the total functions from $1 \,..\, n$ to $0 \,..\, 1$. Our final objective is more ambitious since we want to identify the subsets for which the sum is zero. Therefore, we must select among the candidates. Let us assume that we have the Boolean function *ZeroSum* that checks whether the sum of the elements of T, filtered by X, is equal to zero. To get a solution to our problem, it is sufficient to complement the condition $(i = n)$ of the above invariant with the condition *ZeroSum*. We then obtain the following version *GenSet2*:

1. **procedure** *GenSet2*(i) **pre**
2. $i \in 1 \,..\, n$
3. **begin**
4.   **for** j **ranging** $0 \,..\, 1$ **do**
5. $X[i] \leftarrow j$;
6.   **if** $i = n$ $\boxed{\textbf{and } ZeroSum}$ **then**
7.   write(X)
8.   **elsif** $i \neq n$ **then**
9.   *GenSet2*(i + 1)
10.   **end if**
11.   **end for**
12. **end**

The recursive call must occur only when $i \neq n$. The condition in line 8 is clearly necessary. The newly inserted code is framed and this mechanism is systematically used later on in order to enhance readability.

Remark

Strictly speaking, the condition in line 6 could be restricted to the condition *ZeroSum*, as long as the vector X is padded with 0's. However, this approach is abandoned for didactic reasons.

Optimization

The procedure *GenSet2* is correct but not very efficient. As a matter of fact, it can be observed that invoking the function *ZeroSum* leads to redundant calculations. Avoiding them requires the strengthening of the invariant imposed by the introduction of the new variable CurrSum. The recursion invariant becomes: "$X[1 .. i - 1]$ is constant, it is a total function from $1 .. i - 1$ to $0 .. 1$, $CurrSum = \sum_{k=1}^{i-1} T[k]$ and if a node of the recursion tree meeting the condition $i = n$ has been printed, then all the nodes fulfilling this condition have been printed". In line 6 of the new procedure, the variable CurrSum must be updated and since this update is not automatically suppressed after the recursive call, we must also "undo" its effect by subtracting the value $j \cdot T[i]$ (added in line 5) from CurrSum. This yields the following version:

```
1.  procedure GenSet3(i) pre
2.    i ∈ 1 .. n
3.  begin
4.    for j ranging 0 .. 1 do
5.      X[i] ← j ; CurrSum ← CurrSum + j · T[i] ;
6.      if i = n and CurrSum = 0 then
7.        write(X)
8.      elsif i ≠ n then
9.        GenSet3(i + 1)
10.     end if;
11.     CurrSum ← CurrSum − j · T[i]
12.   end for
13. end
```

which is invoked in the context:

```
1.  constants
2.    n ∈ ℕ₁ and n = … and T ∈ 1 .. n → ℤ and T = […]
3.  variables
4.    X ∈ 1 .. n → 0 .. 1 and CurrSum ∈ ℤ
5.  begin
6.    CurrSum ← 0 ;
7.    GenSet3(1)
8.  end
```

Complexity and pruning

The number of total functions from $1 .. n$ to $0 .. 1$ is also the number of *leaves* of trees like the one in figure 5.1 page 198, i.e. 2^n. The number of calls to the function *GenSet* (whatever the version) corresponds to the number of *inner* nodes, i.e. $\sum_{i=0}^{n-1} 2^i = 2^n - 1$. This exponential complexity leads us to question the necessity of visiting all the leaves of the tree. One may think that the configuration of some nodes could avoid parsing exhaustively (also called "brute force" traversal) all the subtrees situated under these nodes. If this would be possible, the efficiency of the solution could be improved (nevertheless without being sure to reduce the order of complexity).

Generally, it is indeed not always necessary to examine all the possibilities of solutions: some can be removed before complete construction. That is the principle called *pruning* , which, when possible, by testing each partial candidate, avoids the development of candidates located beneath the current node, because it is certain that the partial candidate will never lead to a solution. When searching for an optimal solution, it is often possible to take advantage of the optimality criterion. As a matter of fact, when the function associated with it is increasing (respectively decreasing), we will try to underestimate (respectively overestimate) its final value so as to carry out pruning when it does not reach (respectively exceeds) the current optimal value.

For the problem under consideration, and for the version *GenSet3*, a possible pruning is founded on the following observation. At a certain point of the calculation, if the value of CurrSum is too high (positive) or too low (negative), i.e. it has no chance of becoming zero, the development of the current subtree is useless[1]. The following version implements such a pruning:

```
1. procedure GenSet4(i) pre
2.    i ∈ 1..n
3. begin
4.    for j ranging 0..1 do
5.       if |CurrSum| ⩽ (n − i + 1) · AbsExtT then
6.          X[i] ← j; CurrSum ← CurrSum + j · T[i];
7.          if i = n and CurrSum = 0 then
8.             write(X)
9.          elsif i ≠ n then
10.            GenSet4(i + 1)
11.         end if;
12.         CurrSum ← CurrSum − j · T[i]
13.      end if
14.   end for
15. end
```

provided that it is invoked in the following program (the constant AbsExtT is the absolute value of the extremum of T):

```
1. constants
2.    n ∈ ℕ₁ and n = ... and T ∈ 1..n → ℤ and T = [...]
3. variables
4.    X ∈ 1..n → 0..1 and CurrSum ∈ ℤ and
5.    AbsExtT ∈ ℕ and  AbsExtT = max ({max(codom(T)), |min(codom(T))|})
6. begin
7.    CurrSum ← 0;
8.    GenSet4(1)
9. end
```

Although, for some sizes of the problem, the effect of pruning is often impressive, experience shows that the gain obtained allows only to deal with problems whose sizes are slightly greater than the one originally envisaged. Exercise 53, page 225, constitutes an illustration among others.

Conclusion

In this section, we have outlined the approach we advocate to face a problem according to the method "Generate and test". The next two sections refine this approach to end up with a collection of "patterns" that can apply to a wide scope of situations.

---

[1]This remark is sufficient to carry out a *rough* pruning. It would be possible to refine it in diverse ways, for instance in taking into account the sign of CurrSum. In particular, the current development can be stopped when (CurrSum > 0 and (min(codom(T)) ⩾ 0 or else CurrSum > (n − i + 1).|(min(codom(T))|)).

5.1.2 Functions and related frames

In the previous section, we have filled up the frame of the algorithm able to enumerate all the total functions from the interval $1 .. n$ to $0 .. 1$, in order to resolve the problem of subsets whose sum is zero. In this section, we focus on this notion of frame, expanding the study to a wide range of functions such as total functions, surjective total functions, partial functions, injective partial functions, etc. in order to cover all the situations tackled in the problems of section 5.4 page 223. In the remainder of this section, we are looking for functions from $I = 1 .. n$ to $F = 1 .. m$.

5.1.2.1 Total functions

The general case: enumeration of total functions between two intervals I and F

This case generalizes the one studied in the example of section 5.1.1, page 197. We are looking for an algorithm able to produce all the total functions from $I = 1 .. n$ to $F = 1 .. m$. The frame:

1. **procedure** $T(i)$ **pre**
2. $i \in 1 .. n$
3. **begin**
4.   **for** j **ranging** $1 .. m$ **do**
5. $X[i] \leftarrow j$;
6.   **if** $i = n$ **then**
7.   **write**(X)
8.   **else**
9. $T(i+1)$
10.   **end if**
11.   **end for**
12. **end**

answers this objective provided that it is invoked in the program:

1. **constants**
2. $n \in \mathbb{N}$ **and** $n = \ldots$ **and** $m \in \mathbb{N}$ **and** $m = \ldots$
3. **variables**
4. $X \in 1 .. n \rightarrow 1 .. m$
5. **begin**
6. $T(1)$
7. **end**

The number of total functions from $1 .. n$ to $1 .. m$ is also the number of *leaves* of the recursion tree, i.e. m^n. The number of calls on the function T corresponds to the number of *inner* nodes, i.e. $\sum_{i=0}^{n-1} m^i = (m^n - 1)/(m - 1)$. The exponential nature of this function (in n) generally leads to algorithms whose temporal complexity restricts their practical interest. This is also true for the other frames studied in this section.

The example developed in section 5.2, page 215, concerns the case where I is a bag. The procedure T is well suited, however it produces all the sub-bags of I (generally with duplicates) in the form of a characteristic vector.

The case where the input set is a Cartesian product

How can we adapt the procedure T to the case where I is the Cartesian product of two intervals $1 .. n$ and $1 .. q$? The principle is simple: the enumeration *vector* X is transformed into an enumeration *matrix* and the procedure T is rewritten as follows (X is filled in top down from left to right):

```
1.  procedure T2D(l, c) pre
2.      l ∈ 1 .. n and c ∈ 1 .. q
3.  begin
4.      for j ranging 1 .. m do
5.          X[l, c] ← j ;
6.          if l = n and c = q then
7.              write(X)
8.          else
9.              if c = q then
10.                 T2D(l + 1, 1)
11.             else
12.                 T2D(l, c + 1)
13.             end if
14.         end if
15.     end for
16. end
```

The calling program becomes:

```
1.  constants
2.      n ∈ N and n = ... and q ∈ N and q = ... and m ∈ N and m = ...
3.  variables
4.      X ∈ 1 .. n × 1 .. q → 1 .. m
5.  begin
6.      T2D(1, 1)
7.  end
```

The transposition to functions other than total functions can be easily done.

Enumeration of surjective total functions

The recursion invariant is expressed:

"$X[1 .. i − 1]$ is constant. It is a total function from $1 .. i − 1$ to $1 .. m$ and, if a node of the recursion tree meeting the condition $(i = n)$ has been printed, then all the nodes complying with this condition have been printed".

It can be noticed that, in general, $X[1 .. i − 1]$ is not a surjective function. The production of all the surjectives functions is obtained by arranging the procedure T, with a technique similar to that used for optimizing the procedure *GenSet3*, page 200, the following way. Before a solution is written, it must be checked that it is actually a surjective one. To this aim, the global Boolean array B, containing the values of j stored in X, is updated. Checking surjectivity is specified by the universal quantification present in the condition of the conditional statement (line 7 of the frame TS). This part of the condition can be refined by means of a sequential search. Updating B, in line 6, must be "undone" when the treatment is finished, which is possible thanks to the use of the local variable Sav inside which the previous value is preserved.

```
1.  procedure TS(i) pre
2.      i ∈ 1 .. n and Sav ∈ B
3.  begin
```

4.   **for** j **ranging** $1 .. m$ **do**
5. $X[i] \leftarrow j$;
6. $Sav \leftarrow B[j]$; $B[j] \leftarrow$ **true** ;
7.   **if** $i = n$ **and then** $\forall k \cdot (k \in 1 .. m \Rightarrow B[k])$ **then**
8.   **write**(X)
9.   **elsif** $i \neq n$ **then**
10. $TS(i + 1)$
11.   **end if**;
12. $B[j] \leftarrow Sav$
13.   **end for**
14. **end**

The following program, which initializes the array B, enables to get the expected result:

1. **constants**
2. $n \in \mathbb{N}$ **and** $n = \ldots$ **and** $m \in \mathbb{N}$ **and** $m = \ldots$
3. **variables**
4. $X \in 1 .. n \rightarrow 1 .. m$ **and** $B \in 1 .. m \rightarrow \mathbb{B}$
5. **begin**
6. $B \leftarrow (1 .. m) \times \{\textbf{false}\}$;
7. $TS(1)$
8. **end**

For $n = 3$ and $m = 2$, the recursion tree is presented in figure 5.2, page 204.

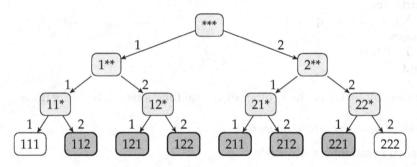

Fig. 5.2 – The recursion tree for the construction of all the surjective functions from $1 .. 3$ to $1 .. 2$. Leaves in white signal functions that are not surjective. Leaves in dark grey symbolize surjective functions.

In the frame TS, the enumeration of all the surjective total functions starts with the enumeration of all total functions. Consequently, the number of calls to function TS is still $((m^n - 1)/(m - 1))$.

In the forthcoming exercises, we will encounter situations where checking surjectivity is not mandatory, in other words, where the universal quantification in line 7 of TS can be omitted (see for example exercise 52, page 224). In such a case, the frame to be used is T.

Enumeration of injective and bijective total functions, production of permutations

An interesting extension of the procedure T consists in producing all the *injective* total functions from $I = 1 .. n$ to $F = 1 .. m$. The recursion invariant is "$X[1 .. i - 1]$ is constant, it is an *injective* total function from $1 .. i - 1$ to $1 .. m$ and, if a node of the recursion tree meeting the condition $(i = n)$ has been printed, then all the nodes fulfilling this condition have been printed". Injectivity is obtained by excluding the elements already present in

$X[1 .. i-1]$ from the interval $1 .. m$ onto which the loop takes its values. That is what is done by the frame *TI* hereafter:

```
1. procedure TI(i) pre
2.    i ∈ 1 .. n
3. begin
4.    for j ranging (1 .. m − codom(X[1 .. i − 1])) do
5.       X[i] ← j ;
6.       if i = n then
7.          write(X)
8.       else
9.          TI(i + 1)
10.      end if
11.   end for
12. end
```

This procedure is invoked in the context:

```
1. constants
2.    n ∈ ℕ and n = ... and m ∈ ℕ and m = ...
3. variables
4.    X ∈ 1 .. n → 1 .. m
5. begin
6.    TI(1)
7. end
```

Since the number of injections from a set of n elements to a set of k elements is equal to A_k^n (number of arrangements of k objects among n), the number of leaves visited by the algorithm is $A_m^n = m!/(m − n)!$, if $m \geqslant n$. As to the number of calls, (the proof is left to the reader), it is equal to:

$$\sum_{i=0}^{n-1} A_m^i \tag{5.1}$$

Figure 5.3, page 206 shows the recursion tree parsed by the procedure for $I = 1 .. 3$ and $F = 1 .. 4$. When $F = I$, this procedure results in the set of *bijections* from $I = 1 .. n$ to I and it allows to get the *permutations* of a set of values. Checking surjectivity is not necessary as a total injective function to itself is a bijection. Formula $\sum_{i=0}^{m-1} A_m^i$ gives the number of calls carried out.

In most programming languages, the loop above cannot be directly coded. So, how to refine this program? One solution (whose principle is similar to the solution applied to build the procedure *GenSet3*, page 200) consists in handling (in the form of an array for efficiency reasons) a function F (for "Free") defined on the interval $F = 1 .. m$ valued in $\mathbb{B}$ (or sometimes, for the sake of convenience, in the interval $0 .. 1$) such that $F[k]$ means that k is absent from $X[1 .. i − 1]$. The above schema is then refined in the following manner:

```
1. procedure TI2(i) pre
2.    i ∈ 1 .. n
3. begin
4.    for j ranging 1 .. m do
5.       if F[j] then
6.          X[i] ← j ; F[j] ← false ;
7.          if i = n then
```

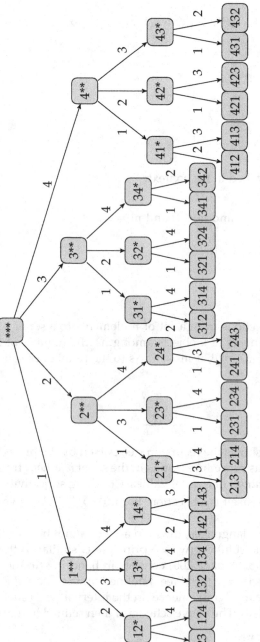

Fig. 5.3 – Recursion tree for the construction of all the total injections between the intervals 1 .. 3 and 1 .. 4.

```
8.              write(X)
9.          else
10.             TI2(i + 1)
11.         end if;
12.         F[j] ← true
13.      end if
14.   end for
15. end
```

This procedure can be called by the program:

```
1. constants
2.    n ∈ N and n = ... and m ∈ N and m = ...
3. variables
4.    X ∈ 1 .. n → 1 .. m and F ∈ 1 .. m → B
5. begin
6.    F ← (1 .. m) × {true} ;
7.    TI2(1)
8. end
```

Later this refinement is generally not made explicit.

5.1.2.2 The case of partial functions

The general case: enumeration of partial functions between two intervals I and F

We are looking for an algorithm able to produce all the partial functions from $I = 1 .. n$ to $F = 1 .. m$. From the pattern T, it is sufficient to add a shadow value to F (0 for example) such that any pair whose extremity is 0 is considered non-existent for the function (see figure 5.4).

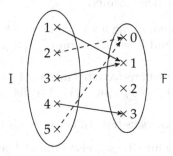

Fig. 5.4 – A partial function from $I = 1 .. 5$ to $F = 1 .. 3$. The partial feature of the function is obtained by creating a total function from I to the interval $0 .. 3$, then restricting the co-domain to the interval $1 .. 3$.

The frame:

```
1. procedure P(i) pre
2.    i ∈ 1 .. n
3. begin
4.    for j ranging {0} ∪ 1 .. m do
5.       X[i] ← j ;
6.       if i = n then
```

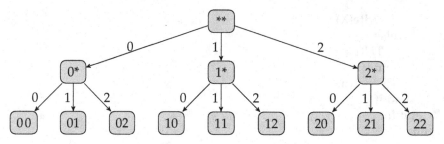

Fig. 5.5 – The recursion tree for the construction of all the partial functions from I = 1 .. 2 *to* F = 1 .. 2. *Any 0 in a node stands for the absence of a pair for the considered position.*

```
7.            write(X)
8.        else
9.            P(i + 1)
10.       end if
11.    end for
12. end
```

meets our objective. The invariant

X[1 .. i − 1] is constant. It is a total function from I = 1 .. i − 1 to F' = 0 .. m and, if a node of the recursion tree fulfilling the condition (i = n) has been printed, then all the nodes meeting this condition have been printed

is interpreted as

X[1 .. i − 1] is a partial function from the interval 1 .. i − 1 to F = 1 .. m and, if a node of the recursion tree fulfilling the condition (i = n) is printed, then all the nodes meeting this condition have been printed

provided that the entries of X containing 0's are ignored. The context of invocation is similar to that of T. For I = 1 .. 2 and F = 1 .. 2, figure 5.5 page 208 shows the recursion tree parsed by this pattern.

There are $(m+1)^n$ partial functions from the interval 1..n to 1..m, and the enumeration of all of them demands $((m+1)^n - 1)/((m+1) - 1)$ calls.

Enumeration of partial injective functions between two intervals I *and* F

Obtaining only partial injective functions is also achieved (as for simple partial functions) by the introduction of the shadow value 0. Because of its special status, this value must not be removed from the parsing interval of the loop, hence the following pattern:

```
1. procedure PI(i) pre
2.     i ∈ 1 .. n
3. begin
4.     for j ranging ((1 .. m) − (codom(X[1 .. i − 1]))) ∪ {0}) do
5.         X[i] ← j ;
6.         if i = n then
7.             write(X)
8.         else
9.             PI(i + 1)
10.        end if
```

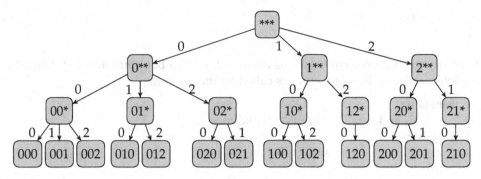

Fig. 5.6 – Recursion tree for the construction of the partial injective functions between the intervals $1 .. 3$ *and* $1 .. 2$.

11. **end for**
12. **end**

Figure 5.6 page 209 shows the recursion tree for $I = 1 .. 3$ and $F = 1 .. 2$. Any 0 stands for an absent pair. The number of partial injective functions between $1 .. n$ and $1 .. m$ is given by the following recurrence:

$$H(m, 0) = 1$$
$$H(1, n) = n + 1 \qquad\qquad\qquad n > 0$$
$$H(m, n) = H(m, n - 1) + m \cdot H(m - 1, n - 1) \qquad n > 0 \textbf{ and } m > 1.$$

We recognize the recurrence defining Stirling numbers of second type, i.e. the number of partitions of a set of m elements in n subsets (see also exercise 16, page 41). It is easy to prove by induction that $H(m, n) = m^n + P_{n-1}(m)$, where m is the unknown and $P_{n-1}(m)$ is a polynomial of degree less than or equal to $(n - 1)$. The number of calls to the frame *PI* is given by the expression (the proof is left to the reader):

$$\sum_{i=1}^{n-1} H(m, i).$$

The refinement of the loop in a conventional programming language is obtained as follows:

```
 1. procedure PI2(i) pre
 2.    i ∈ 1 .. n
 3. begin
 4.    for j ranging {0} ∪ (1 .. m) do
 5.       X[i] ← j ;
 6.       if j ≠ 0 then
 7.          F[j] ← false
 8.       end if;
 9.       if i = n then
10.          write(X)
11.       else
12.          PI2(i + 1)
13.       end if;
14.       F[j] ← true
```

15.   **end for**
16. **end**

Similarly to total injective functions (frame *TI2*), F is a Boolean array, but defined here on the interval $0 .. m$. This procedure is called by the program:

1. **constants**
2. $n \in \mathbb{N}_1$ **and** $n = \ldots$ **and** $m \in \mathbb{N}_1$ **and** $m = \ldots$
3. **variables**
4. $X \in 1 .. n \rightarrow 1 .. m$ **and** $F \in 0 .. m \rightarrow \mathbb{B}$
5. **begin**
6. $F \leftarrow (0 .. m) \times \{\mathbf{true}\};$
7. $PI2(1)$
8. **end**

It turns out that, whatever the frame retained, the number of candidates to be generated (and compared) is exponential. So is the complexity of the resulting algorithm, regardless of the elementary operation considered. Consequently, in the rest of this chapter, we do not dwell on complexity, except for pointing out some limitations (when simple and inexpensive from an algorithmic viewpoint) of the number of candidates generated.

5.1.3   Patterns for "Generate and test"

So far, we have been interested only in the search of *all* the solutions to a given problem. However, two variants are worthy of attention. The first one relates to a quality criterion of the solutions, so as to keep only the best one. For example, in section 5.1.1, page 197, the selection of the subsets of a set of integers E whose sum is zero, would become the search for the (one of the) solutions whose cardinality is the largest one. The second one consists of searching *a single* solution (of course, if there is at least one), for instance the one encountered first.

We will now combine the frames developed in section 5.1.2 with the three versions presented above (respectively called *AllSolutions*, *OptimalSolution* and *OneSolution*). This will lead us to envisage as many patterns as there are possible crossbreeds: *AllSolutions* and the frame *T* produce the pattern *AllT*, *AllSolutions* and the frame *TS* produce the pattern *AllTS*, etc. Nevertheless, all the crossbreeds are not developed hereafter: some are not used, while others are the subject of examples or exercises.

5.1.3.1   Patterns derived from "AllSolutions"

Three cases are now detailed: the crossbreed of "AllSolutions" and the frames *T*, *TS* and *TI*, which gives birth to the patterns *AllT*, *AllTS* and *AllTI* presented in figure 5.7, page 211.

In this figure, the procedures or functions *Satisf*, *Do*, *Undo* and *SolFound* are shared by the three patterns. As we saw in sections 5.1.1 page 197, and 5.1.2 page 202, the condition *Satisf* is used to introduce pruning, an optimization or a refinement. The procedures *Do* and *Undo* appear jointly. They are necessary for backtracking when global variables (other than the enumeration structure X) have been introduced, generally for pruning, or optimization, or refinement purposes. The condition *SolFound* (sometimes omitted) is added to the condition $(i = n)$ (which indicates that the enumeration structure is complete) in order to express that X meets the constraints proper to the problem. The condition $(i \neq n)$ is necessary only when the condition *SolFound* is present. It characterizes an incomplete enumeration structure. Then search for a solution must go on.

1. **procedure** *AllT*(i) **pre**
2. i ∈ 1..n
3. **begin**
4. **for** j **ranging** 1..m **do**
5. **if** *Satisf*(i,j) **then**
6. X[i] ← j ; *Do*(i,j) ;
7. **if** $\left(\begin{array}{l} i = n \text{ and then} \\ \left(SolFound(i,j)\right)\end{array}\right)$ **then**
8. **write**(X)
9. **elsif** i ≠ n **then**
10. *AllT*(i + 1)
11. **end if**;
12. *Undo*(i,j)
13. **end if**
14. **end for**
15. **end**

1. **procedure** *AllTS*(i) **pre**
2. i ∈ 1..n and Sav ∈ 𝔹
3. **begin**
4. **for** j **ranging** 1..m **do**
5. **if** *Satisf*(i,j) **then**
6. X[i] ← j ;
7. Sav ← B[j] ; B[j] ← **true** ;
8. *Do*(i,j) ;
9. **if** $\left(\begin{array}{l} i = n \text{ and then} \\ \left(\forall k \cdot (k \in 1..m \Rightarrow B[k])\right) \\ \text{and then } SolFound(i,j)\end{array}\right)$
   then
10. **write**(X)
11. **elsif** i ≠ n **then**
12. *AllTS*(i + 1)
13. **end if**;
14. B[j] ← Sav ; *Undo*(i,j)
15. **end if**
16. **end for**
17. **end**

1. **procedure** *AllTI*(i) **pre**
2. i ∈ 1..n
3. **begin**
4. **for** j **ranging** $\left(\text{codom}(X[1..i-1])\right)$ **do** (with $(1..m) -$)
5. **if** *Satisf*(i,j) **then**
6. X[i] ← j ;
7. *Do*(i,j) ;
8. **if** $\left(\begin{array}{l} i = n \text{ and then} \\ \left(SolFound(i,j)\right)\end{array}\right)$ **then**
9. **write**(X)
10. **elsif** i ≠ n **then**
11. *AllTI*(i + 1)
12. **end if**;
13. *Undo*(i,j)
14. **end if**
15. **end for**
16. **end**

Fig. 5.7 – Patterns of algorithms of type "Generate and test", for the search of all the solutions and when they are expressed as a total function from I = 1..n to F = 1..m. The pattern AllT (respectively AllTS, AllTI) deals with total (respectively total surjective, total injective) functions. The pattern AllTB (for bijections) is not developed since it corresponds to the pattern AllTI when F = I (i.e. when m = n). The case of the production of characteristic vectors of all the subsets of the interval 1..n can be obtained from the pattern AllT taking F = 0..1. For the three above patterns, the calling programs are similar to those given for the respective frames.

1. **procedure** *OptPI*(i) **pre**
2. $i \in 1 .. n$
3. **begin**
4.   **for** j **ranging** $((1 .. m) - \text{codom}(X[1 .. i - 1])) \cup \{0\}$ **do**
5.   **if** *Satisf*(i, j) **then**
6. $X[i] \leftarrow j$; *Do*(i, j) ;
7.   **if** $\begin{pmatrix} i = n \textbf{ and then} \\ SolFound(i, j) \end{pmatrix}$ **then**
8.   Found $\leftarrow$ **true** ;
9.   **if** *BetterSolution* **then**
10. $Y \leftarrow X$;
11.   *KeepCurrContext*
12.   **end if**
13.   **elsif** $i \neq n$ **then**
14.   *OptPI*(i + 1)
15.   **end if**;
16.   *Undo*(i, j)
17.   **end if**
18.   **end for**
19. **end**

1. **constants**
2. $n \in \mathbb{N}_1$ **and** $n = \dots$ **and**
3. $m \in \mathbb{N}_1$ **and** $m = \dots$
4. **variables**
5. $X \in 1 .. n \to 0 .. n$ **and**
6. $Y \in 1 .. n \to 0 .. n$ **and**
7.   Found $\in \mathbb{B}$
8. **begin**
9.   Found $\leftarrow$ **false** ;
10.   *OptPI*(1) ;
11.   **if** Found **then**
12.   **write**(Y)
13.   **end if**
14. **end**

Fig. 5.8 – Pattern and calling program of the algorithms of type "Generate and test", when searching for an "optimal" solution which is expressed as a partial injective *function from* $I = 1 .. n$ *to* $F = 1 .. m$. *When there is no solution, nothing is produced.*

The patterns *AllP* (respectively *AllPI*) corresponding to the crossbreeds of "AllSolutions" and the frame *P* for partial functions (respectively *PI* for partial injective functions) is not studied since useless later on.

5.1.3.2   Patterns derived from "OptimalSolution"

The version *OptimalSolution* assumes a total order relation over the candidates. Y is a global variable containing the current successive optimal solutions. The procedure *KeepCurrContext* uses global variables to save information useful for comparing solutions with each other. The pattern *OptPI* (optimal solution when the enumeration vector represents a partial injective function) is shown in figure 5.8, page 212. The pattern *OptT* (optimal solution when the enumeration vector represents a total function) is presented in the example of section 5.2, page 216.

A variant of the procedure *OptimalSolution* would consist in getting *all* the optimal solutions. The approach adopted to get all the solutions (see pattern *AllT*) cannot be transposed here since Y cannot be written all along the execution. It is necessary to wait for the end of the process to write the result, provided that all the optimal solutions are stored before in an *ad hoc* structure. This version is only mentioned, it is not used later.

5.1.3.3   Patterns derived from "OneSolution"

The last case, namely *OneSolution*, is coded with a **while** loop, that enables stopping as soon as the first solution is found out. We restrict ourselves to the two patterns *OneT* ("OneSolution" for *total* functions from $1 .. n$ to $1 .. m$) and *OneTI* ("OneSolution" for total

1. **procedure** *OneT*(i) **pre**
2.   i ∈ 1 .. n **and** j ∈ 1 .. m + 1
3. **begin**
4.   j ← 1 ;
5.   **while not**(j = m + 1 **or** Found) **do**
6.   **if** *Satisf*(i, j) **then**
7.   X[i] ← j ; *Do*(i, j) ;
8.   **if** $\left(\begin{array}{c} i = n \text{ and then} \\ SolFound(i,j) \end{array}\right)$ **then**
9.   Found ← **true** ;
10.   **write**(X)
11.   **elsif** i ≠ n **then**
12.   *OneT*(i + 1)
13.   **end if**;
14.   *Undo*(i, j)
15.   **end if**;
16.   j ← j + 1
17.   **end while**
18. **end**

1. **procedure** *OneTI*(i) **pre**
2.   i ∈ 1 .. n **and** d ∈ OrderedList(1 .. m)
3. **begin**
4.   d ← *DomVar*(1 .. m − codom(X[1 .. i − 1])) ;
5.   **while not**(d = ⟨ ⟩ **or** Found) **do**
6.   **if** *Satisf*(i, j) **then**
7.   X[i] ← d.val ; *Do*(i, j) ;
8.   **if** $\left(\begin{array}{c} i = n \text{ and then} \\ SolFound(i,j) \end{array}\right)$ **then**
9.   Found ← **true** ;
10.   **write**(X)
11.   **elsif** i ≠ n **then**
12.   *OneTI*(i + 1)
13.   **end if**;
14.   *Undo*(i, j)
15.   **end if**;
16.   d ← d.svt
17.   **end while**
18. **end**

Fig. 5.9 – Patterns of algorithms of type "Generate and test" when searching for the first solution which is expressed as a total function from I = 1 .. n *to* F = 1 .. m. *The pattern* OneT *(respectively* OneTI*) concerns total (respectively total injective) functions. In* OneTI, *the statement* d ∈ OrderedList(1 .. m) *defines* d *as an ordered list of values of the interval* 1 .. m *to be taken into account. The function* DomVar *invoked in line 4 builds the ordered list of the values involved in the set passed in parameter. By convention, the field* val *(see line 7) gives access to the head value of the list, while the field* svt *(see line 14) designates the rest of the list (see section 1.4.7, page 20). The pattern* OneTB *(case of bijections) is not developed, it corresponds to the pattern* OneTI *when* F = I *(i.e. when* m = n*).*

injective – and *bijective* when m = n – functions from 1 .. n to 1 .. m). These patterns are presented in figure 5.9, page 213. Calling an instance of these patterns must be preceded by the initialization of the Boolean variable Found with **false**.

The pattern *OneTI* raises a technical difficulty onto which we must focus. Whereas in the pattern *OneT*, the variable j ranges the beginning of (or the whole) interval 1 .. m, this is no longer true for the pattern *OneTI*, where this interval must be deprived of the values present in the slice X[1 .. i − 1]. The method used consists in building the ordered list of the possible values for i in the local variable d and to browse this list in the loop.

The pattern *OneTI* can be refined as shown in figure 5.10, replacing the list d by the Boolean array F, defined over the interval 1 .. m. The initialization of the loop must then calculate the value to be given to F (**true** if the position has to be accounted for, **false** otherwise).

5.1.3.4 Conclusion

In this section, we have shown how to deal with a problem according to the method "Generate and test". The approach advocated involves three steps:

```
1.  procedure OneTI2(i) pre
2.      i ∈ 1..n and j ∈ 1..m+1 and F ∈ 1..m → 𝔹
3.  begin
4.      F ← (1..m − codom(X[1..i−1]) × {true}) ∪ codom(X[1..i−1]) × {false} ;
5.      j ← 1 ;
6.      while not(j = m+1 or Found) do
7.          if L[j] and Satisf(i,j) then
8.              X[i] ← j ; Do(i,j) ;
9.              . . .
10.         end if;
11.         j ← j+1
12.     end while
13. end
```

Fig. 5.10 – Refinement of the pattern OneTI *obtained using a Boolean array. Line 9 is to be replaced by lines 8 to 14 of the pattern* OneTI.

1. Pattern Identify the type of pattern imposed by the problem. Let us recall that the choice of a pattern is based on the crossbreeding of a frame (i.e. a type of function) and the characteristics of the desired solutions (one, all or the best one).

2. Instantiation – pruning This pattern must be instantiated in order to meet the constraints proper to the problem. First of all, the predicate *SolFound* intended for the selection of the solutions among the candidates, must be specified. Then, cuts may be introduced by means of the predicate *Satisf*. This will avoid the development of some sterile branches. This pruning step can demand the strengthening of the recursion invariant, associed with the introduction of new variables. These latter are initialized before the first call, updated and restored in their initial state by the pair of procedures *Do* and *Undo*.

3. Optimization This step is optional. Generally, it is possible to improve the version obtained at point 2 by strengthening the recursion invariant as it was done in the introductory example. Most often, it becomes necessary to revise auxiliary procedures and functions *Satisf*, *Do*, etc.

Table 5.1 lists the possible patterns and, if appropriate, provides the page where the code appears.

	All solutions	Optimal solution	One solution
Total	*AT* (p. 211)	*OptT* (p. 216)	*OneT* (p. 213)
Total surjective	*ATS* (p. 211)	*OptTS*	*OneTS*
Total injective	*ATI* (p. 211)	*OptTI*	*OneTI* (p. 213)
Partial	*AP*	*OptP*	*OneP*
Partial surjective	*APS*	*OPS*	*UPS*
Partial injective	*TPI*	*OptPI* (p. 212)	*OnePI*

Tab. 5.1 – List of the 18 patterns for "Generate and test" along with the pages where the code appears. The case of bijective functions is obtained from those of injective functions.

The approach adopted throughout this chapter makes an intensive use of global variables, but it is not the only possible way of doing. Some solutions could more or less "move away" from the patterns presented in this section. However, as a principle, the solutions proposed for exercises in this chapter do not deviate from these algorithmic schemes.

In a different framework, a declarative paradigm such as *logic programming* would exempt from the use of global variables and especially from the explicit handling of backtracking (which is one of the basic features of such languages). In the context of constraint logic programming, modeling is done through relationships between the variables of the problem. These relationships are activated and propagated when resolving the problem. This programming paradigm applies particularly well to problems dealt with by the "Generate and test" approach. The reader is invited to use these various programming styles to the examples and exercises of this chapter.

5.2 An example: the optimal partition of an array

5.2.1 The basic problem

Let us take the search for an optimal solution as an illustration. We consider the array $T[1 .. n]$ $(n \geqslant 0)$ of natural numbers. We would like to get a partition of T into two bags B_1 and B_2 such that, denoting by $Sum1 = \sum_{i \in B_1} i$ and $Sum2 = \sum_{i \in B_2} i$, we have $Sum2 - Sum1 \geqslant 0$ and $(Sum2 - Sum1)$ minimum.

For example, for $n = 7$ and T defined as:

i	1	2	3	4	5	6	7
$T[i]$	6	8	2	7	9	4	1

one solution is to build the bag $B_1 = [\![8, 9, 1]\!]$, from $T[2]$, $T[5]$ and $T[7]$, with $Sum1 = 18$, and the bag $B_2 = [\![6, 2, 7, 4]\!]$ from $T[1]$, $T[3]$, $T[4]$ and $T[6]$, with $Sum2 = 19$. The bag B_1 (respectively B_2) can be represented by the characteristic vector $\overline{B_1} = [0, 1, 0, 0, 1, 0, 1]$ (respectively $\overline{B_2} = [1, 0, 1, 1, 0, 1, 0]$).

Letting $Sum = \sum_{i \in dom(T)} T[i]$:

$Sum2 - Sum1$

$=$ arithmetics

$Sum2 - Sum1 + Sum - Sum$

$=$ property of $Sum1$ and $Sum2$

$Sum2 - Sum1 + Sum - (Sum1 + Sum2)$

$=$ arithmetics

$Sum - 2 \cdot Sum1$.

So, the minimization of $(Sum2 - Sum1)$ comes down to that of $(Sum - 2 \cdot Sum1)$.

We are going to identify the set of sub-bags of the bag represented by T. It is sufficient to consider the interval $1 .. n$ and to take the powerset of $1 .. n$. The characteristic vectors obtained will indirectly give access to the expected result. Here, the convenient pattern is *OptT* (Optimal solution with the set of total functions). Let us take the opportunity of this exercise to introduce this pattern, in addition to those developed in section 5.1.3. Figure 5.11, page 216, is dedicated to this purpose. The existence of a solution is ensured and handling the Boolean Found, as in the pattern of figure 5.8, page 212, is useless.

```
1. procedure OptT(i) pre
2.    i ∈ 1 .. n
3. begin
4.    for j ranging 1 .. m do
5.       if Satisf(i, j) then
6.          X[i] ← j ; Do(i, j) ;
7.          if i = n and SolFound(i, j) then
8.             if BetterSolution then
9.                Y ← X ;
10.               KeepCurrContext
11.            end if
12.         elsif i ≠ n then
13.            OptT(i + 1)
14.         end if;
15.         Undo(i, j)
16.      end if
17.   end for
18. end
```

Fig. 5.11 – Pattern of algorithms of type "Generate and test" in the case where we search for an optimal solution expressed as a total function from $I = 1..n$ to $F = 1..m$. This version presupposes that there is at least one solution.

The pattern *OptT* is instantiated with $I = 1..n$ and $F = 0..1$ (so as to get all the characteristic vectors of all the subsets). Let *MinimalDif1* be this instance of *OptT*.

1. The first draft we develop is the following:

```
1. procedure MinimalDif1(i) pre
2.    i ∈ 1 .. n
3. begin
4.    for j ranging 0 .. 1 do
5.       ...
6.    end for
7. end
```

2. Let us move to the condition *Satisf* seen as a pruning condition. Can we stop exploring the tree before reaching a leaf, on the basis of the partial candidate under construction? The answer is positive. Let CurrSum1 and OptSum be respectively the current value of Sum1 and the current optimal value (both initialized to 0 before the initial call). When the value which will be added to CurrSum1 increases it beyond half of Sum (let us recall that T contains *positive* numbers), we can prune the subtrees at that point and explore another branch. The following second draft is obtained:

```
1. procedure MinimalDif1(i) pre
2.    i ∈ 1 .. n
3. begin
4.    for j ranging 0 .. 1 do
```

5. $\text{if} \left[\text{CurrSum1} + j \cdot T[i] \leqslant \left\lfloor \dfrac{\text{Sum}}{2} \right\rfloor \right] \text{then}$

6.   ...
7.   **end if**
8.   **end for**
9. **end**

3. Now, let us come to what corresponds to lines 6 and 12 of the pattern *OptT*. The instance of the generic procedure *Do* consists in updating the global variable CurrSum1 and that of the procedure *Undo* cancels what was done by *Do*:

1. **procedure** *MinimalDif1*(i) **pre**
2. $i \in 1..n$
3. **begin**
4.   **for** j **ranging** $0..1$ **do**
5.   **if** $CurrSum1 + j \cdot T[i] \leq \left\lfloor \dfrac{Sum}{2} \right\rfloor$ **then**
6. $X[i] \leftarrow j;$ $\boxed{CurrSum1 \leftarrow CurrSum1 + j \cdot T[i];}$
7.   ...
8. $\boxed{CurrSum1 \leftarrow CurrSum1 - j \cdot T[i]}$
9.   **end if**
10.   **end for**
11. **end**

4. *SolFound* is **true** when a leaf of the tree is reached, which is expressed by $i = n$, hence the following refinement:

1. **procedure** *MinimalDif1*(i) **pre**
2. $i \in 1..n$
3. **begin**
4.   **for** **ranging** $0..1$ **do**
5.   **if** $CurrSum1 + j \cdot T[i] \leq \left\lfloor \dfrac{Sum}{2} \right\rfloor$ **then**
6. $X[i] \leftarrow j; CurrSum1 \leftarrow CurrSum1 + j \cdot T[i];$
7.   **if** $\boxed{i = n}$ **then**
8.   ...
9.   **else**
10.   *MinimalDif1*$(i + 1)$
11.   **end if**;
12. $CurrSum1 \leftarrow CurrSum1 - j \cdot T[i]$
13.   **end if**
14.   **end for**
15. **end**

5. *BetterSolution* compares the current solution to the best one found so far. If it is better, this solution is preserved in the global variable Y, whilst the procedure *KeepCurrContext* updates the global variable OptSum.

1. **procedure** *MinimalDif1*(i) **pre**
2. $i \in 1..n$
3. **begin**
4.   **for** j **ranging** $0..1$ **do**
5.   **if** $CurrSum1 + j \cdot T[i] \leq \left\lfloor \dfrac{Sum}{2} \right\rfloor$ **then**

```
6.          X[i] ← j; CurrSum1 ← CurrSum1 + j · T[i];
7.          if i = n then
8.              if  CurrSum1 > OptSum  then
9.                  Y ← X ;  OptSum ← CurrSum1
10.             end if
11.         else
12.             MinimalDif1(i + 1)
13.         end if;
14.         CurrSum1 ← CurrSum1 − j · T[i]
15.     end if
16.   end for
17. end
```

The initial call of the procedure *MinimalDif1* is done in the following context:

1. **constants**
2. $n \in \mathbb{N}$ and $n = \dots$ and
3. $T \in 1 .. n \rightarrow \mathbb{N}$ and $T = [\dots]$ and
4. $\text{Sum} \in \mathbb{N}$ and $\text{Sum} = \sum_{i=1}^{n} T[i]$
5. **variables**
6. $X \in 1 .. n \rightarrow 0 .. 1$ and $Y \in 1 .. n \rightarrow 0 .. 1$ and
7. $\text{CurrSum1} \in \mathbb{N}$ and $\text{OptSum} \in \mathbb{N}$ and
8. $S_1 \in \mathbf{bag}(\mathbb{N})$ and $S_2 \in \mathbf{bag}(\mathbb{N})$
9. **begin**
10. $\text{OptSum} \leftarrow 0$; $\text{CurrSum1} \leftarrow 0$;
11.   *MinimalDif1*(1);
12.   **write**(Y)
13.   /% Construction of S_1 and S_2 %/
14. **end**

The actual construction of S_1 and S_2 from Y is easy to carry out. It is sufficient to distribute the values of T into S_1 or S_2 depending on the corresponding value in Y. This construction is not made explicit here.

Let us remark that, when there are several optimal solutions, this algorithm stores in Y, the first one according to the lexicographical enumeration. In the case of the example in page 215, the best solution found out is $Y = [0, 0, 1, 1, 1, 0, 0]$, not $Y = [0, 1, 0, 0, 1, 0, 1]$ (which corresponds to that proposed above).

5.2.2 The initial problem with a strengthened precondition and a strengthened postcondition

We now impose that n is even and that the two bags B_1 and B_2 are of the same size $n/2$. How can this constraint be introduced into the program without disrupting it?

A first solution consists in keeping the previous program and to generate the leaves of the tree in the same way, except those pruned by *Satisf*. The condition related to the equal size of B_1 and B_2 ($n/2$) is added to *SolFound*. To this aim, it is necessary to store the current size of B_1 by means of the global variable *Size1*. This variable will be incremented in *Do* and decremented in *Undo*.

1. **procedure** *MinimalDif2*(i) **pre**
2. $i \in 1 .. n$

3. **begin**
4.   **for** j ranging $0..1$ **do**
5.   **if** $\text{CurrSum1} + j \cdot T[i] \leqslant \left\lfloor \dfrac{\text{Sum}}{2} \right\rfloor$ **then**
6. $X[i] \leftarrow j; \text{CurrSum1} \leftarrow \text{CurrSum1} + j \cdot T[i]; \boxed{\text{Size1} \leftarrow \text{Size1} + j;}$
7.   **if** $i = n$ **and** $\text{Size1} = \dfrac{n}{2}$ **then**
8.   **if** $\text{CurrSum1} > \text{OptSum}$ **then**
9. $Y \leftarrow X; \text{OptSum} \leftarrow \text{CurrSum1}$
10.   **end if**
11.   **elsif** $i \neq n$ **then**
12.   *MinimalDif2*$(i + 1)$
13.   **end if**;
14. $\text{CurrSum1} \leftarrow \text{CurrSum1} - j \cdot T[i]; \boxed{\text{Size1} \leftarrow \text{Size1} - j}$
15.   **end if**
16.   **end for**
17. **end**

The initial call becomes:

1. **constants**
2. $N2 = \left\{ v \middle| v \in \mathbb{N} \text{ and } \left\lfloor \dfrac{v}{2} \right\rfloor \cdot 2 = v \right\}$ **and**
3. $n \in N2$ **and** $n = \ldots$ **and**
4. $T \in 1..n \rightarrow \mathbb{N}$ **and** $T = [\ldots]$ **and**
5. $\text{Sum} \in \mathbb{N}$ **and** $\text{Sum} = \displaystyle\sum_{i=1}^{n} T[i]$
6. **variables**
7. $X \in 1..n \rightarrow 0..1$ **and** $Y \in 1..n \rightarrow 0..1$ **and**
8. $\text{CurrSum1} \in \mathbb{N}$ **and** $\text{OptSum} \in \mathbb{N}$ **and** $\text{Size1} \in \mathbb{N}$ **and**
9. $S_1 \in \textbf{bag}(\mathbb{N})$ **and** $S_2 \in \textbf{bag}(\mathbb{N})$
10. **begin**
11. $\text{OptSum} \leftarrow 0; \text{CurrSum1} \leftarrow 0; \text{Size1} \leftarrow 0;$
12.   *MinimalDif2*(1);
13.   **write**(Y)
14.   /% *Construction of* S_1 *and* S_2 %/
15. **end**

This solution is correct, but it takes advantage of the new condition (related to the size of the bags B_1 and B_2) only when a candidate is completely built.

The key for an improvement lies in a new version of *SolFound*. It is actually possible not to wait the end of the construction of the vector X to check the equality of the sizes. As soon as one of the two bags reaches the size of $n/2$, we can just complete the vector X without finishing the exploration of the recursion tree. Let us respectively denote by Size1, Size2 and CurrSum2 the size of the bag S_1, the size of the bag S_2 and the partial sum of S_2.

1. The first draft of the procedure *MinimalDif3* does not change with respect to *MinimalDif1*:

1. **procedure** *MinimalDif3*(i) **pre**
2. $i \in 1..n$
3. **begin**
4.   **for** j ranging $0..1$ **do**
5.   **if** $\text{CurrSum1} + j \cdot T[i] \leqslant \left\lfloor \dfrac{\text{Sum}}{2} \right\rfloor$ **then**

6.   ...
7.   **end if**
8.   **end for**
9. **end**

2. Let us examine what corresponds to lines 6 and 15 of the pattern *OptT*. The instance of the generic procedure *Do* consists in updating the global variables CurrSum1, CurrSum2, Size1 and Size2 and the procedure *Undo* cancels what was done in *Do*:

1. **procedure** *MinimalDif3*(i) **pre**
2. $i \in 1 .. n$
3. **begin**
4.   **for** j **ranging** $0 .. 1$ **do**
5.   **if** $\text{CurrSum1} + j \cdot T[i] \leqslant \left\lfloor \dfrac{\text{Sum}}{2} \right\rfloor$ **then**
6. $X[i] \leftarrow j;$
7. $\text{CurrSum1} \leftarrow \text{CurrSum1} + j \cdot T[i];$
8. $\text{CurrSum2} \leftarrow \text{CurrSum2} + (1-j) \cdot T[i];$
9. $\text{Size1} \leftarrow \text{Size1} + j; \text{Size2} \leftarrow \text{Size2} + (1-j);$
10.   ...
11. $\text{CurrSum1} \leftarrow \text{CurrSum1} - j \cdot T[i];$
12. $\text{CurrSum2} \leftarrow \text{CurrSum2} - (1-j) \cdot T[i];$
13. $\text{Size1} \leftarrow \text{Size1} - j; \text{Size2} \leftarrow \text{Size2} - (1-j)$
14.   **end if**
15.   **end for**
16. **end**

3. *SolFound* means that a solution leading to a leaf can be directly built and that the corresponding vector is a solution (not necessarily optimal). There are two possibilities: either $\text{Size1} = n/2$ or $\text{Size2} = n/2$.

4. *BetterSolution* and *KeepCurrContext* consist in storing the solution vector just found out if it corresponds to a solution better than the current optimal value. It is also necessary to finish the construction of the partial solutions for which the size of one of the two arrays is less than $n/2$.

5. *SolStillPossible*, the predicate which allows to pursue the enumeration, boils down to $(i \neq n)$.

The final algorithm is:

1. **procedure** *MinimalDif3*(i) **pre**
2. $i \in 1 .. n$
3. **begin**
4.   **for** j **ranging** $0 .. 1$ **do**
5.   **if** $\text{CurrSum1} + j \cdot T[i] \leqslant \left\lfloor \dfrac{\text{Sum}}{2} \right\rfloor$ **then**
6. $X[i] \leftarrow j;$
7. $\text{CurrSum1} \leftarrow \text{CurrSum1} + j \cdot T[i];$
8. $\text{CurrSum2} \leftarrow \text{CurrSum2} + (1-j) \cdot T[i];$
9. $\text{Size1} \leftarrow \text{Size1} + j; \text{Size2} \leftarrow \text{Size2} + (1-j);$
10.   **if** $\text{Size1} = \dfrac{n}{2}$ **then**
11.   **if** $\text{CurrSum1} > \text{OptSum}$ **then**
12. $Y[1 .. i] \leftarrow X[1 .. i]; Y[i+1 .. n] \leftarrow (i+1 .. n) \times \{0\};$
13. $\text{OptSum} \leftarrow \text{CurrSum1}$
14.   **end if**

```
15.        elsif Size2 = n/2 then
16.            if CurrSum1 > OptSum then
17.                Y[1 .. i] ← X[1 .. i]; Y[i + 1 .. n] ← (i + 1 .. n) × {1};
18.                OptSum ← CurrSum1
19.            end if
20.        elsif i ≠ n then
21.            MinimalDif3(i + 1)
22.        end if;
23.        CurrSum1 ← CurrSum1 − j · T[i];
24.        CurrSum2 ← CurrSum2 − (1 − j) · T[i];
25.        Size1 ← Size1 − j; Size2 ← Size2 − (1 − j)
26.      end if
27.    end for
28. end
```

The calling program of the procedure *MinimalDif3* is carried out as follows:

```
1. variables
2.    /% cf. lines 2 to 6 of the calling program of MinimalDif1 %/
3.    OptSum ∈ ℕ and CurrSum1 ∈ ℕ and CurrSum2 ∈ ℕ and
4.    Size1 ∈ ℕ and Size2 ∈ ℕ and B₁ ∈ bag(ℕ) and B₂ ∈ bag(ℕ)
5. begin
6.    OptSum ← 0;
7.    CurrSum1 ← 0; Size1 ← 0; CurrSum2 ← 0; Size2 ← 0;
8.    MinimalDif3(1);
9.    write(Y)
10.   /% Construction of B₁ and B₂ %/
11. end
```

5.2.3 The initial problem with a strengthened precondition

We return to the previous problem with a precondition strengthened by the following proposition: the array T is increasingly ordered. Theory (see Chapter 3) tells us that, if we have a correct program for a given precondition R, then this same program is still correct for a stronger precondition P (i.e. when $P \Rightarrow R$). However, by not exploiting the new precondition, a more efficient version may be missed.

One could think that due to the order over the values of T, there is a linear or polynomial algorithm which resolves the problem. Indeed, algorithmicists believe that such an algorithm (which would probably be a *greedy* one, see Chapter 7) does not exist.

We therefore admit that, in order to get a version better than *MinimalDif3*, we must stay in the framework of "Generate and test". How does the fact that T is sorted allow new prunings?

We keep the global variables $Size1$, $CurrSum1$, $Size2$ and $CurrSum2$ of the previous version. When T is not sorted, the pruning condition is:

```
...
if CurrSum1 + j · T[i] ⩽ ⌊Sum/2⌋ then
    ...
end if
...
```

It just checks that the value $j \cdot T[i]$ added to $CurrSum1$ does not exceed $\lfloor Sum/2 \rfloor$. It can be refined in exploiting the fact that T is sorted. If, underestimating $Sum1$ by adding $j \cdot T[i]$ by anticipation, $\lfloor Sum/2 \rfloor$ is exceeded, or in a dual manner, if overestimating $Sum2$ in adding $(1-j) \cdot T[i]$ by anticipation, $\lfloor Sum/2 \rfloor$ is not reached, there is no hope for meeting the condition $Sum1 \leqslant Sum2$.

Indeed, at this stage:

- $(n/2 - Size1 - j)$ values remain to be stored into B_1 and $(n/2 - Size2 - (1-j))$ values to be placed into B_2,

- $((CurrSum1 + j \cdot T[i]) + (n/2 - Size1 - j) \cdot T[i+1])$ is a lower bound of $Sum1$, and $((CurrSum2 + (1-j) \cdot T[i]) + (n/2 - Size2 - (1-j))) \cdot T[n])$ overestimates $Sum2$.

Consequently, the pruning condition *Satisf* can be rewritten:

$$\cdots$$

$$\textbf{if } \left(\begin{array}{l} (CurrSum1 + j \cdot T[i]) + \left(\dfrac{n}{2} - Size1 - j\right) \cdot T[i+1] \leqslant \left\lfloor \dfrac{Sum}{2} \right\rfloor \textbf{ and} \\[2mm] (CurrSum2 + (1-j) \cdot T[i]) + \left(\dfrac{n}{2} - Size2 - (1-j)\right) \cdot T[n] \geqslant \left\lfloor \dfrac{Sum}{2} \right\rfloor \end{array} \right) \textbf{ then}$$

$$\cdots$$

end if

$$\cdots$$

The rest of the program remains unchanged. An additional pruning may take place: at each step, it can be checked that $OptSum$ can be still improved. Indeed, $(n/2 - Size1 - j)$ values can be still added to B_1 and to have the opportunity to make better than the current optimal value, it is necessary that, choosing $(n/2 - Size1 - j)$ times the largest value, $OptSum$ is strictly exceeded. Hence, *Satisf* can be completed as follows:

$$\cdots$$

$$\textbf{if } \left(\begin{array}{l} (CurrSum1 + j \cdot T[i]) + \left(\dfrac{n}{2} - Size1 - j\right) \cdot T[i+1] \leqslant \left\lfloor \dfrac{Sum}{2} \right\rfloor \textbf{ and} \\[2mm] (CurrSum2 + (1-j) \cdot T[i]) + \left(\dfrac{n}{2} - Size2 - (1-j)\right) \cdot T[n] \geqslant \left\lfloor \dfrac{Sum}{2} \right\rfloor \textbf{ and} \\[2mm] (CurrSum1 + j \cdot T[i]) + \left(\dfrac{n}{2} - Size1 - j\right) \cdot T[n] > OptSum \end{array} \right)$$

then

$$\cdots$$

end if

$$\cdots$$

We can further refine this algorithm noticing that, the proposed solution is based on the smallest ($T[i+1]$) or the largest ($T[n]$) among the remaining values. At the cost of a more expensive calculation, in the first condition, we could add $T[i+1] + \cdots + T[i + (n/2 - Size1 - j) - 1]$ (instead of $n/2 - Size1 - j) \cdot T[i+1]$) to $(CurrSum1 + j \cdot T[i])$. Likewise, in the second condition, we could add the sum $T[n/2 + Size2 - (1-j) + 1] + \cdots + T[n]$ to $(CurrSum2 + (1-j) \cdot T[i])$. Last, in the third condition, we could add the sum $T[n/2 + Size1 - j + 1] + \cdots + T[n]$ (instead of $(n/2 - Size1 - j) \cdot T[n]$) to $(CurrSum1 + j \cdot T[i])$.

Remark

In the absence of the assumption stating that T is sorted, we could, however, underestimate the future value of $Sum1$ as $CurrSum1 + j \cdot T[i] + (n/2 - Size1 - j) \cdot 1$. On the other hand, though, no overestimation of either Sum2, or OptSum would be possible without information concerning the elements of the slice $T[i + 1 .. n]$.

5.3 What should be remembered from "Generate and test"

The approach adopted in this chapter for "Generate and test" is original. As shown in the three-step development schema presented in section 5.1.3.4, page 213, it consists in establishing a clear boundary between the purely routine aspect of the development (the identification of a development pattern) and the creative aspect (the search for pruning and optimization techniques). This latter aspect often demands treasures of ingenuity to find out solutions more efficient than *brute force*. Generally, it is hard to measure the resulting gain in terms of performances.

The style of development advocated in this chapter is close to what is called "design pattern" in the area of software engineering, where the solution to a specific problem is instantiated from a proven generic framework. The major advantage of the approach resides in the fact that it is not necessary to build a solution *from scratch* for each new problem. On the other hand, by definition, it must be possible to reformulate the problem to make it compatible with the chosen "pattern".

5.4 Exercises
Problem 52. The n-queen problem ∘ ⦂

This exercise is a classic programming one, discussed here according to the "Generate and test" paradigm. The problem is to place n queens on a chessboard n × n, without any two of them being in capture. Two solutions are examined. In the first one, a square matrix is used as the enumeration structure and it represents all the total functions from the chessboard to Booleans. This solution is subject to some optimization. The second solution uses a vector (instead of a matrix) to represent all the bijections from the interval $1 .. n$ to itself.

Do you play chess? Do you know how to place eight queens on a chessboard so that they do not threaten each other? Let us recall that, in chess, a queen threatens any other piece located on the same rank, file or one of the two diagonals passing through its location (provided that it is not masked by an intermediary piece). This problem can be posed in a more general way: how to place n queens $(n \geqslant 4)^2$ on a chessboard of size $n \times n$ so that none is attacked by another one? For example, the following schema provides a solution for $n = 8$ (part (a)) and for $n = 4$ (part (b)):

---

[2]For $n = 1$, there is a single solution, for $n = 2$ and $n = 3$, there is no solution, and for $n \geqslant 4$ there are several solutions.

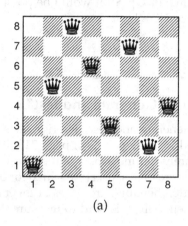

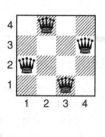

(a)   (b)

In the rest, we would like to get all the configurations of the chessboard answering the problem.

Question 1.   Let us take a chessboard $n \times n$ and two queens Q_1 and Q_2 located respectively on the squares (r_1, f_1) and (r_2, f_2). What is a necessary and sufficient condition characterizing the fact that they are on a same row, column or up (SW-NE) diagonal, or down (NW-SE) diagonal?

A first version

In this first version, the enumeration structure is chosen as the array X, defined over the Cartesian product $1 .. n \times 1 .. n$ valued in $\mathbb{B}$ (**false** (respectively **true**) meaning the absence (respectively the presence) of a queen in the considered position). If X is a solution, X is a total (each square of X originates a pair) surjective (n (respectively $n^2 - n$) pairs have **true** (respectively **false**) as their extremity) function. During its elaboration, the array X is a total *non surjective a priori* function since there may be no square valued as **false**. However, if X is a solution, it complies with the constraint proper to the problem stating that all the free squares of the chessboard are *in capture* by the n queens which are *not in capture* one another. This constraint entails the surjectivity of X, which has not to be checked (as it is done in the pattern *AllTS*, page 211). Therefore, the appropriate pattern is *AllT* (page 211), arranged from the frame *T2D* (page 203) so as to account for the bidimensional feature of the definition domain of the enumeration structure.

Question 2.   Identify the possible prunings and draw a significant portion of the recursion tree for $n = 4$.

Question 3.   For this version, we suppose that the four Boolean functions *FreeRank*(r, f), *FreeFile*(r, f), *FreeUpDiag*(r, f) and *FreeDownDiag*(r, f) are available (r and f represent respectively the rank number and the file number of the square where it is envisaged to place a queen), which return **true** iff the portion of rank, file or diagonal mentioned in the following schema contains no queens.

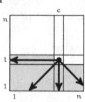

The procedure $NQueens1(r, f)$ attempts to place a queen in the square (r, f) knowing that the part of the chessboard delimited by the ranks from 1 to $r - 1$ constitutes a partial solution. Write this procedure specifying how each of the generic operations of the pattern *TT* are instantiated.

Question 4. The calls of the four Boolean functions mentioned above lead to redundant calculations. They can be avoided by their replacement by *arrays* of Booleans. Provide the procedure *NQueens2* which takes this remark into account.   52 - Q 4

A second version

We would like to improve the previous version by the refinement of the data structure in the following way. Considering the function X used above, it is clear that there is no loss of information if we keep only the pairs of the domain of X that are in relation with the value **true**. Since, if it exists, a solution must involve a single queen per rank, the relation X is a bijection of the interval $1 .. n$ to itself (or, if preferred, a permutation of the interval $1 .. n$). Therefore, the appropriate pattern is *TTI*, page 211, applied to the case where the domain and the co-domain of X is $1 .. n$. We must produce, not all the total functions as before, but only all the bijections from $1 .. n$ to $1 .. n$. By construction, in the context of the chessboard, these bijections represent a configuration involving one queen per rank and file. The filter related to diagonals remains to be carried out. To do so, we propose to use the technique of Boolean arrays (see question 4 above).

Question 5. Identify the possible prunings and draw a significant part of the recursion tree for $n = 4$.   52 - Q 5

Question 6. Implement this solution through the procedure $NQueens3(r)$ in which the parameter r is the index for the filling of the enumeration vector X.   52 - Q 6

Question 7. Compare the three solutions experimentally for some values of n.   52 - Q 7

The solution is on page 251.

Problem 53. The sentinels   ○ ⋮

> *Twin brother of the n-queen problem (see exercise 52), that is advisable to carry out beforehand, the present exercise differs from it on two points. On the one hand, this time, the enumeration vector does not represent a bijection, but a partial injection, and on the other hand an optimal solution is searched, not all of them.*
>
> *Two versions are studied. The first one is the direct transposition of the algorithms presented in the introduction of the chapter: the only data structure is the enumeration structure. In the second one, applying the strategy consisting in strengthening the recursion invariant, an ad hoc data structure aimed at improving the efficiency of the algorithm is added to the enumeration vector.*

We would like to place a *minimum* number of queens on a chessboard $n \times n$ so that:

- they are not in capture,
- all the squares of the chessboard are under their control.

Let us recall that a queen controls the squares of the rank and file on which it is standing, as well as the squares of the two diagonals passing through the square where it is located. Chessboard (a) in figure 5.12, page 226, illustrates a first configuration with six queens controlling all the squares of a chessboard 8×8 without any of them in capture. Chessboard (b) displays another configuration, this time with only five queens.

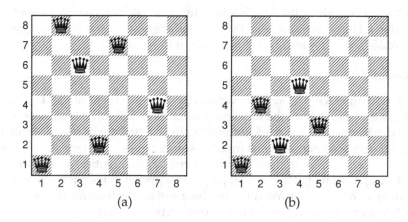

(a)   (b)

Fig. 5.12 – Two examples of chessboards with sentinels.

Configuration (b) is better than (a) from the point of view of the optimality criterion considered (the number of queens present on the chessboard), but we do not know if it is optimal. Actually, it is since there is no four-queen configuration allowing for the control of the whole chessboard. The reader will be able to check this assertion at the end of the exercise.

53 - Q 1 **Question 1.** For a chessboard $n \times n$, give a lower bound of the number of queens necessary to resolve the problem.

In the n-queen problem (see problem 52, page 223), two solutions were studied, the first one based on an enumeration matrix (see questions 2 and 3, page 224), whose efficiency can be improved, and the second one based on an enumeration vector representing a total injective function (see question 6, page 225), which significantly enhances the first solution, as shown by the results of question 7, page 256. Here, we discard the first solution to retain the counterpart of the second solution. However, given the nature of the problem and in addition to the fact that we are looking for an optimal solution, the pattern to instantiate is *OptPI* (see figure 5.8, page 212). Indeed, since there can be ranks without queens (see figure 5.12, page 226), some squares of the enumeration vector X may not represent a file. X therefore represents a partial function. It is injective since there cannot be more than one queen per file. Two variants are studied: the first one (*Sentinels1*) uses only the enumeration structure X and the optimal solution Y, in the second one (*Sentinels2*), some redundant structures are added to X, for efficiency purposes.

53 - Q 2 **Question 2.** Determine some possible prunings. For a chessboard 5×5, build a partial recursion tree including at least one pruning situation and one successful situation.

53 - Q 3 **Question 3.** As mentioned previously, the procedure *Sentinels1* is derived from the pattern *OptPI* (figure 5.8, page 212). Specify how the auxiliary operations of *OptPI* are instantiated. Write the code, as well as an example of call of the procedure *Sentinels1*. The consequence of the constraint imposed for this solution (exclusive use of X) is that the pair of operations *Do* and *Undo* is useless here.

Question 4.   The previous solution leads to repeat some calculations (such as the count   53 - Q 4
of free squares when a new queen appears). We want to refine this solution by the adjunction of the following elements:

- The array Capt, defined over $1 .. n \times 1 .. n$ valued in $0 .. n$, which, for a given
  configuration of X, counts, for each square of the chessboard, the number of
  times it is *in capture*. If position (r, f) is occupied (by a queen), $Capt[r, f] = 1$.
- The integer variable nbPlacedQueens which, for a given configuration of X,
  provides the number of queens on the chessboard.
- The integer variable nbFreeSquares which, for a given configuration of X,
  provides the number of squares that are not under the control of at least one
  queen.

Updated in an incremental manner, these structures avoid useless calculations.
List and specify the operations required to maintain the array Capt, then define the procedure *Sentinels2*, instance of the pattern *OptPI*. Write its code.

The solution is on page 256.

Problem 54. The knight's tour   ○ ⦂

> *One more problem about chessboards! This time, the result is not a specific configuration, but
> an order over knight moves. This exercise studies two variants of the exhaustive visit of all the
> squares of the chessboard by the knight before coming back to its starting point (see exercise
> 49, page 170). In the first part of the exercise, we are looking for all the solutions (routes) to
> go from square d (departure) to square a (arrival). A rough evaluation of the complexity is
> also required. The second part aims at determining an optimal solution.*

Determination of all the moves of the knight

We consider a chessboard $n \times n$ ($n \geqslant 1$, typically $n = 8$), one knight, d and a two distinct
squares of the chessboard. We are looking for all the elementary routes[3] that the knight
may ride from the starting square d to the arrival square a, respecting the rules of the
game of chess.

In the rest, we use indifferently the notation proper to chess (digit in ordinate, letters in abscissa, positions in the form letter/digit) or Cartesian to locate a square in the chessboard.

Reminder about chess rules for the knight: when the knight is in square (i, j), with one
move it can reach one of the eight squares hereafter:

$$(i-2, j-1) \quad (i-2, j+1) \quad (i-1, j-2) \quad (i-1, j+2)$$
$$(i+1, j-2) \quad (i+1, j+2) \quad (i+2, j-1) \quad (i+2, j+1), \tag{5.2}$$

provided it stays inside the chessboard. Schema (a) in figure 5.13 represents these possibles
moves for a knight initially located in position $(4, 4)$.

---

[3]I.e. courses without circuit (see Chapter 1 and exercise 55, page 230).

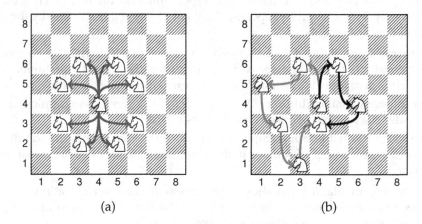

Fig. 5.13 – Possible moves of the knight in chess. (a): all the possibles moves of the knight. (b): two routes of the knight between positions $(4,4)$ *and* $(4,3)$.

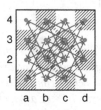

Fig. 5.14 – Graph of all moves of the knight on a chessboard 4×4.

Example

Schema (b) in figure 5.13 shows two routes to go from square $(4,4)$ to square $(4,3)$, one of length 5, the other one of length 3.

A first solution – that is not developed here – consists of a prior calculation of the graph of all possible moves, from any starting square of the chessboard. So, for $n = 4$, we would get the graph in figure 5.14.

The problem then becomes that of the search for all the elementary paths from a vertex to another one in a graph. The usual methods of search of all the elementary paths apply. However, the principle founding our solution is different, since in the framework of "Generate and test". It consists of the calculation of the squares within reach of the knight from its current position, on an as-needed basis. One possible specification of the problem is to consider that the knight's course is represented by an enumeration matrix X defined on the domain $1 .. n \times 1 .. n$ valued in $1 .. n \times 1 .. n$. The square $X[r, f]$ contains a pair which designates the square following the square (r, f) in the course. Such a matrix represents a *partial* function since all the squares are not necessarily attained. Moreover, it is *injective*, since an end square appears at most once. Two constraints must be mentioned: identity does not belong to the transitive closure (see definition 1.5.1, page 24) of X (so as to exclude circuits), but the pair (d, a) (departure and arrival squares) does. A possible refinement of this enumeration structure consists in placing on the chessboard the rank of the moves made by the knight during its course. For example, with a chessboard 4×4, to go from $a1$ to $b1$, one possibility would be to have the following route:

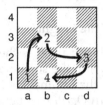

The enumeration structure still represents a partial function (since some squares do not appear in the route), injective (since a single square is associated with a given stage) from $1 .. n \times 1 .. n$ to $1 .. n^2$. It is an *a priori* possible candidate for the enumeration function we are looking for. However, our experience with this type of structure (see exercise 52, page 223), leads us to discard this solution. Due to the injective feature of this function, it is possible to take the inverse function, which is also injective, but this time, from $1 .. n^2$ to $1 .. n \times 1 .. n$. It is of importance to notice that an enumeration vector *under construction* represents a *total* function over the domain $1..i-1$, which allows to choose the pattern *AllTI* (see page 211) rather than *AllPI*. The above example is then in the form of an enumeration vector containing the chess coordinates of the squares that are reached:

1	2	3	4
$(a, 1)$	$(b, 3)$	$(d, 2)$	$(b, 1)$

In doing so, however, we have introduced an additional difficulty. It concerns the structure of the frames presented in section 5.1.2, page 202, in which the **for** loops ranges a *scalar* set whose values are stored in the enumeration structure. This is no longer the case here since the enumeration vector contains *pairs*. How to solve this problem? One solution would consist in using *two* loops to scan all the squares of the chessboard. However, there are better things to do as only (at most) eight locations are candidates to be the next stage of the course. At the cost of a slight twist of the pattern *AllTI*, it is sufficient to range the interval $1 .. 8$, to give an indirect access to candidate squares, which is obtained by means of the description 5.2, page 227.

Question 1. We consider a chessboard 4×4, with a knight located on the initial square $a1$ which tries to reach the final square $b1$. Continue the development of the leftmost branch of the recursion tree given below:

54 - Q 1

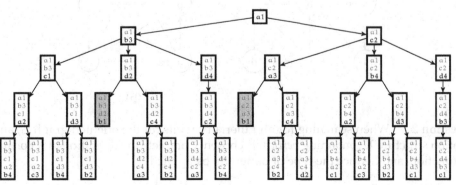

54 - Q 2 **Question 2.**   Proceed to the analysis of the problem and specify the components of the pattern *AllTI*. Provide the code of the procedure *Knight1*, instance of the pattern *AllTI* on the one hand, and a calling program on the other hand. Evaluate the complexity in the worst case in terms of number of nodes of the recursion tree.

Determination of an optimal tour of the knight

We now consider the following problem: what is the minimal number of moves for a knight to go from the square $d = (i, j)$ to the square $a = (k, l)$ (a and d being distinct)? To do this, we propose to search for the optimal course (or one of the optimal courses) of a knight by instantiating the pattern *OptPI* (see figure 5.8, page 212). The enumeration structure is assumed to be the same as previously.

54 - Q 3 **Question 3.**   Specify the diverse elements to be instantiated in the pattern *OptPI* in order to resolve this problem.

54 - Q 4 **Question 4.**   Give the algorithm *KnightOpt* calculating one of the optimal course of the knight.

The solution is on page 260.

Problem 55.   Eulerian circuits and paths   8 :

> *This exercise looks at Eulerian routes in a directed connected graph. Starting from the algorithm for searching for an Eulerian circuit in an directed graph obtained in the third question, we ask to transform it so as to search for an Eulerian path in an undirected graph. An application to one-line plots (i.e. plots for which the pen is not raised and the line is not crossed again) is being studied.*

We consider a directed graph $G = (N, V)$ where N is the set of vertices and V the set of arcs. Let $n = \mathrm{card}(V)$. First we study the problem of the Eulerian circuits, then the problem of the Eulerian paths (see definitions 1.5.1 and 1.5.1, page 24).

55 - Q 1 **Question 1.**   For each of the graphs hereafter, identify one of the Eulerian circuits, if any.

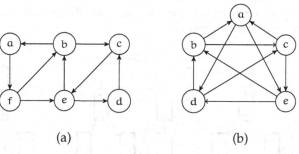

(a)   (b)

55 - Q 2 **Question 2.**   When searching for all Eulerian circuits for the oriented graph G, an enumeration structure X containing *vertices* is chosen. Complete the definition of X considered as a function, and deduce the type of pattern to be applied.

Question 3.   Instantiate the generic procedure *AllT*(i) (see figure 5.7, page 211), in order   **55 - Q 3**
to obtain an algorithm of type "Generate and test" displaying all the Eulerian circuits of a
directed connected graph.

Question 4.   The problem of tracing without raising the pen is posed differently from   **55 - Q 4**
the problem of finding a circuit in a directed graph. Indeed, a *undirected* connected graph
is provided and it is a matter of discovering an Eulerian *path* (i.e. a succession of vertices
which passes once and only once through each of the edges – either in one direction or in
another – without necessarily returning to the starting vertex. On the other hand, this path
can cross a vertex as many times as it is considered necessary).
Part (a) of the schema below represents the drawing that must be done without raising the
pen and without passing over the same line several times.

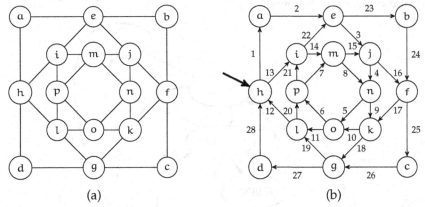

(a)   (b)

Part (b) shows a possible solution. It is an Eulerian path starting at the vertex h; this path
is a directed graph that is superimposed on the initial graph. Each arc is accompanied by
the sequence number of the path.

Explain the changes to be made to the algorithm of the third question in order to resolve
this variant of the initial problem.

The solution is on page 264.

Problem 56.   Hamiltonian paths   ○ ●

> *The interest of this exercise is to study an algorithm of type "Generate and test" for the classic*
> *problem of search for a Hamiltonian path in a graph.*

We consider the following game: a four-letter word (taken from a French lexicon) is
written on each of six dominoes. Two dominoes can be juxtaposed iff the last two letters
of the first one and the first two letters of the second one form a four-letter word of the
lexicon. The remainder is based on:

- the following lexicon, made of 13 words (proper nouns and conjugated verbs are ac-
cepted):

        TELE   TETE   MELE   MERE   CURE   CUBE   SEVE
        SETE   LESE   LEVE   MISE   MITE   MILE

- the following six dominoes, numbered from 1 to 6:

1	2	3	4	5	6
BETE	SEME	VECU	LESE	TELE	REMI

For example, the domino SEME can be put after the domino REMI, since MISE belongs to the lexicon. Such a game can be represented by a graph: the six dominoes correspond to the six nodes of the graph and an arc connects two nodes if it is possible to juxtapose the node origin and the node extremity.

Example

The graph of the game is as follows:

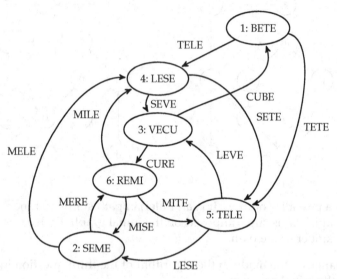

The label placed on each arc corresponds to the word of the lexicon obtained by concatenation of the words placed at the extremities of the arc, deprived of the first two characters of the first domino and the last two characters of the second domino. The goal of the game is to build a path using the six dominoes. One possible solution is:

BETE TELE VECU REMI SEME LESE.

Therefore, the five words resulting from this juxtaposition are:

TETE LEVE CURE MISE MELE.

More generally, the objective of this exercise is to instantiate one of the patterns of Table 5.1 page 214 in order to enumerate, in a given graph, all the paths that pass once and only once through each of the nodes of the given graph, i.e. all the *Hamiltonian* paths (see definition 1.5.1, page 23).

In the previous example, the words CUVE and MIRE would be ignored although they belong to the lexicon because they come from a loop on the words VECU and REMI. Indeed, loops are of no interest in the framework of Hamiltonian paths.

56 - Q 1   **Question 1.**   This question relates to a manual processing of the problem. To restrict the search space, it is imposed to start with domino number one (BETE), then take domino number five (TELE). Find all the solutions starting with these two dominoes. Is it possible to find other solutions, if not all of them, from those that have just been found?

In the following, it is assumed that the set M of the nodes of the graph (numbered from 1 to n) is available as well as the function $Succ(s)$ (see definition 1.5.1, page 22), such that $Succ \in 1..n \rightarrow \mathbb{P}(1..n)$ whose result is the set $Succ(s)$ of the successors of the node s (i.e. the set of words that can be juxtaposed to s). So, in the example of the statement of the problem, we have:

s	1	2	3	4	5	6
$Succ(s)$	{4,5}	{4,6}	{1,6}	{3,5}	{2,3}	{2,4,5}

Question 2. In the framework of the search for all the Hamiltonian paths, propose an enumeration structure X, provide its properties and choose the pattern to be instantiated.   56 - Q 2

Question 3. For the above example, provide the recursion tree obtained from node 1 (domino BETE) as the root.   56 - Q 3

Question 4. Provide an instance of the pattern *AllSolutions* that finds all the Hamiltonian paths in a n-node graph.   56 - Q 4

The solution is on page 267.

Problem 57. The traveling salesman

Classic example of the search for an optimal solution using "Generate and test", this exercise is easy to approach. Nevertheless, the existence of more efficient algorithms (such as the Held-Karp algorithm or the "Branch and bound" technique—see problem 71, page 322) limits its practical interest.

A traveling salesman must visit the n cities forming the vertices of an undirected connected graph whose edges are labeled by the distance of the two cities they join. The traveler departs from a certain city and should, if possible, return there after having visited all other cities once and only once. The question to be resolved by the program to be built is: what route must he take to make the shortest possible journey? Formally, starting from an undirected weighted graph G = (N, V, D), valued on $\mathbb{R}_+^*$ by the function D (distance), the objective is to find the shortest possible Hamiltonian cycle.

In the graph (a) in figure 5.15, the path $\langle 1, 2, 4, 3, 1 \rangle$ is the shortest, with a length of 11, while in the graph (b), 32 is the length of the best path, which is the value reached for the path $\langle 1, 2, 3, 4, 1 \rangle$. On the other hand, with the graph (c) (which does not have a Hamiltonian cycle), the problem posed has no solution.

Remark

With no loss of generality, any of the nodes of the graph can be choosen as the starting city.

Question 1. Assuming that the graph is complete (i.e. there is an edge between any pair of cities), how many Hamiltonian cycles exist from a given city?   57 - Q 1

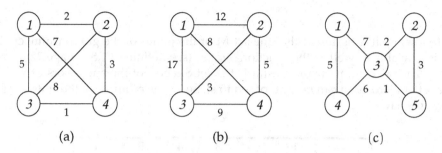

Fig. 5.15 – Examples of city networks.

57 - Q 2   **Question** 2.   In the graph (b) of figure 5.15, the path $\langle 1, 2, 3, 2, 4, 1 \rangle$ is a cycle, but it is not Hamiltonian (it goes twice through the vertex 2). Its length, 31, is less than the best Hamiltonian path found ($\langle 1, 2, 3, 4, 1 \rangle$). Show that if the triangular inequality does not hold in the graph, there may exist non-Hamiltonian cycles (i.e. passing more than once through a vertex) that are better than an optimal Hamiltonian cycle.

57 - Q 3   **Question** 3.   Propose an enumeration structure X to solve the considered problem and provide its properties. Deduce the appropriate algorithm pattern and provide its generic code if it is not one of those given in the introduction of this chapter.

57 - Q 4   **Question** 4.   Provide the recursion tree for the graph (a) in figure 5.15, page 234, starting at node 1. A pruning based on the length of the chains can easily be applied. Specify its operating mode and determine the expected effect on the recursion tree.

57 - Q 5   **Question** 5.   In this question, it is assumed that the array D of the graph edge lengths is available, as well as the function $Succ(s)$ which, for each node of the graph G, provides the set of successors of s. Instantiate the pattern provided in response to question 3 to produce an algorithm that determines the order in which the traveler must visit the cities so as to minimize the total length of the path traveled.

The solution is on page 269.

Problem 58. Graph isomorphism

> *This exercise concerns directed graphs. The algorithm considers two graphs for which an iso-morphism is searched. It works at two levels: it looks for a bijection over nodes (vertexes) which underlies a bijection over arcs. This characteristic originates a pruning which is gener-ally efficient.*

Let $G_1 = (N_1, V_1)$ and $G_2 = (N_2, V_2)$ be two directed graphs such that $\text{card}(N_1) = \text{card}(N_2)$ and $\text{card}(V_1) = \text{card}(V_2)$. Let B be a bijection between N_1 and N_2. G_1 and G_2 are *isomorphic* through B, if B induces a bijection between V_1 and V_2 (in other words if, applying the bijection, leads to rewriting G_1 using the vocabulary of G_2), more precisely if $B^{-1} \circ V_1 \circ B = V_2$ (or even if $V_1 \circ B = B \circ V_2$). For example, let us take $G = (N_G, V_G)$ and $H = (N_H, V_H)$, the two graphs in figure 5.16.

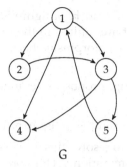 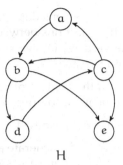

G   H

Fig. 5.16 – Two examples of graphs.

These two graphs are isomorphic through the following bijection between vertices:

$$B = \begin{array}{|c|c|c|c|c|} \hline 1 & 2 & 3 & 4 & 5 \\ \hline c & a & b & e & d \\ \hline \end{array}$$

Indeed, this relation actually induces a bijection over the arcs that can be represented by the table:

$(1,2)$	$(1,3)$	$(1,4)$	$(2,3)$	$(3,4)$	$(3,5)$	$(5,1)$
(c,a)	(c,b)	(c,e)	(a,b)	(b,e)	(b,d)	(d,c)

In the two schemas hereafter, a bipartite representation of relations is used. In the left hand-side schema ($V_G \circ B$), the arcs of V_G are in grey, relation B is dashed and the composition of the two relations is in black. The same conventions are used in the right handside schema ($B \circ V_H$).

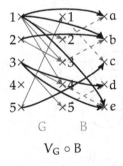 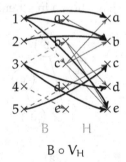

$V_G \circ B$ $B \circ V_H$

It can be observed that the two compositions of relations $V_G \circ B$ and $B \circ V_H$ are identical: the graphs G and H are isomorphic.

In the examples of figure 5.16, page 235, the out-degree (respectively in-degree) of node 1 of graph G is 3 (respectively 1). It is the same for the vertex c in graph H.

Question 1.   Give a table with the in-degrees and out-degrees of the vertexes of G and H of figure 5.16.   58 - Q 1

We would like to write an algorithm that takes as input a pair of graphs (G_1, G_2) with the same number n of vertices and the same number of arcs and delivers the number of possible isomorphisms between G_1 and G_2.

58 - Q 2   **Question 2.**   Let us consider again the two graphs G and H of figure 5.16, page 235. Enumerate all the bijections between N_G and N_H that are limited to the preservation of the arity of the vertices. Do we systematically obtain isomorphisms between G and H? Deduce a pruning strategy.

58 - Q 3   **Question 3.**   In the context of isomorphism counting, propose an enumeration structure X and provide its properties.

58 - Q 4   **Question 4.**   Give the pruned recursion tree for the example of figure 5.16, page 235.

58 - Q 5   **Question 5.**   Write a "Generate and test" algorithm to resolve this exercise. It is recommended to focus on the process ensuring that the enumeration vector corresponds to an isomorphism between G_1 and G_2. The function $d^+(s)$ (respectively $d^-(s)$) delivering the out-degree (respectively in-degree) of vertex s (see definition 1.5.1 page 22) is assumed to be available.

The solution is on page 272.

Problem 59. Graph coloring

> *This exercise deals with the problem of graph coloring. We limit ourselves to designing an algorithm that determines whether the graph can be colored with m colors.*

We consider an undirected connected graph $G = (N, V)$ where N is the set of vertices and V is the set of edges. Such a graph is said to be *painted* if a color is assigned to each vertex, i.e. if there is a total function X from the set of vertices N to a set C of m colors. A painted graph is said to be *colored* by X iff *none of the pairs* of vertices connected by an edge have the same color.

For example, the graph of schema (a) hereafter can be colored with the set of three "colors" $C = \{1, 2, 3\}$, as shown in schema (b):

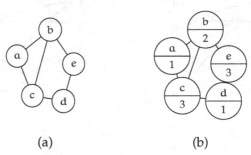

(a)   (b)

The coloring function can be represented by the enumeration vector $X[1 .. 5] = [1, 2, 3, 1, 3]$ whose first element is the color of the first node a, the second one, the color of the second node b, and so on for the five nodes.

59 - Q 1   **Question 1.**   For the graph (a) above, propose a coloring X' (distinct from X) obtained by a permutation P of the colors ($X' = P \circ X$). Propose a second coloring X'' that is not obtained by a permutation of the colors.

59 - Q 2   **Question 2.**   Let $G = (N, V)$ be a graph and Z a painting of G (i.e. a total function from N to a set of colors). Provide a set-oriented expression (on the basis of the relations Z and V) of the condition stating that Z is a *coloring* of G.

Question 3. Define the enumeration vector X and its properties for the search for a 59 - Q 3
coloring. Deduce the pattern that is applicable if it is decided to stop as soon as the first
coloring is encountered (see table 5.1, page 214).

Question 4. Provide the pruned recursion tree scanned for the first coloring of graph 59 - Q 4
(a) above.

Question 5. Given a graph G and a set C of m colors, no necessary and sufficient con- 59 - Q 5
dition is known as to the coloring of G by the m colors of C. Consequently, to determine
whether a given graph G can be colored with a set of m given colors, we must strengthen
the objective by *explicitly* looking for a coloring. Provide the code of the algorithm and
a calling program (the function $Succ(s)$ – see definition 1.5.1 page 22 –, that returns the
neighbors of the vertex s, is assumed to be available).

The solution is on page 274.

Problem 60. U.S. Presidential Elections ○ ⫶

> *In this exercise, we are interested in situations where the U.S. Presidential ballot does not
> allow for the election of a candidate due to a tie vote. The last questions relate to pruning
> made possible by the exploitation of symmetry.*

The American presidential elections are approximately as follows: in each of the 50
states, voters vote for one of two presidential candidates, Democrat or Republican. If the
Republican candidate outnumbers the other in votes in that state, the state will send to
Washington "delegates", all Republicans. If the Democrat candidate wins in this state, the
state will send to Washington the same number of delegates, all Democrats[4]. The number
of delegates depends on the population of the state. For the final stage of voting, the delegates gather in Washington and vote according to their political party. The president who
is elected is the one who gets the most votes from the delegates.

In the following, the states are coded on the interval $1 .. n$ ($n \geqslant 1$), SE is the table that
associates each state code with the number of electors assigned to that state and T is the
total number of delegates across the country.

The result of an election can be represented by a characteristic vector defined on the
interval $1 .. n$, valued in $0 .. 1$. The value 0 (respectively 1) means, by convention, that the
Democrats (respectively Republicans) are the winners in the respective state. The solution
to our problem is to review the power set of $1 .. n$ to determine if there is a tie.

Question 1. Define the enumeration vector X along with its properties. Deduce the 60 - Q 1
pattern to be applied (see table 5.1, page 214).

Question 2. Describe the components of the procedure *USElections* that enumerates all 60 - Q 2
configurations where both candidates have the same number of votes. What is the resulting
code? Provide an example of calling program.

Question 3. Prove that the number of such configurations is even. 60 - Q 3

Question 4. Propose a modification of the algorithm that produces only one of the two 60 - Q 4
matching configurations.

---

[4]We assume at this point that no tie occurs.

Question 5.   Propose a very simple modification of the U.S. constitution so that the election is always effective, that is to say that the two presidential candidates cannot have the same number of votes of delegates.

The solution is on page 276.

Problem 61. Crypto-arithmetics   ○ •

> *The major originality of this exercise lies in the fact that it is about producing* total injec-
> tions *between two sets. These injections constitute the potential solutions. One of the diffi-
> culties concerns complexity evaluation. Asymptotic complexity is not convenient here since
> the chosen parameter is varying in a finite interval. Nevertheless, calculations are proving
> quite difficult.*

Let Σ be the Latin alphabet of 26 letters: $\Sigma = \{\mathcal{A}, \mathcal{B}, \ldots, \mathcal{Z}\}$. Let $L \subset \Sigma$ be a subset of n letters ($n \leqslant 10$) and let $+$ be a formal addition, expressed with these letters, for example:

$$\mathcal{TWO} + \mathcal{TWO} + \mathcal{ONE} = \mathcal{FIVE}$$

that can be written:

$$
\begin{array}{r}
\mathcal{T}\ \mathcal{W}\ \mathcal{O} \\
+ \quad \mathcal{T}\ \mathcal{W}\ \mathcal{O} \\
+ \quad \mathcal{O}\ \mathcal{N}\ \mathcal{E} \\
\hline
\mathcal{F}\ \mathcal{I}\ \mathcal{V}\ \mathcal{E}
\end{array}
$$

The objective of the exercise is to find out all the total injections from L to the ten decimal digits, so that the substitution of each letter by its corresponding digit provides a correct arithmetic operation in base 10.

The above example has a solution that can be represented by the following partial bijection:

$$\{\mathcal{E} \mapsto 8, \mathcal{F} \mapsto 2, \mathcal{N} \mapsto 4, \mathcal{O} \mapsto 5, \mathcal{V} \mapsto 7, \mathcal{I} \mapsto 3, \mathcal{W} \mapsto 1, \mathcal{T} \mapsto 9\}$$

from $\{\mathcal{E}, \mathcal{F}, \mathcal{N}, \mathcal{O}, \mathcal{V}, \mathcal{I}, \mathcal{W}, \mathcal{T}\}$ to $\{8, 2, 4, 5, 7, 3, 1, 9\}$, since:

$$915 + 915 + 548 = 2\,378.$$

On the other hand, the solution corresponding to:

$$925 + 925 + 548 = 2\,398,$$

correct from the arithmetics perspective, is however not acceptable. Indeed, it comes from a function that is not injective, since the letters $\mathcal{W}$ and $\mathcal{F}$ are both in connection with 2 (the same applies to $\mathcal{T}$ and $\mathcal{V}$ that are both in connection with 9). As to the addition:

$$910 + 910 + 548,$$

it comes from a nonfunctional relation: $\{\ldots, O \mapsto 5, O \mapsto 0, \ldots\}$.

It will be assumed that there is a function *ExactCalc* that, starting from an injection from letters to digits, and a representation of the formal operation, returns **true** if, carried out through the injection, the operation is correct from an arithmetic point of view and **false** otherwise.

Question 1.   Give the principle of an algorithm allowing to find out all the solutions to any crypto-arithmetics problem. Which is the appropriate pattern (see table 5.1, page 214) assuming that, in a first step, no pruning is researched?   61 - Q 1

Question 2.   Define the instances of the different components of the pattern used (*Satisf, SolFound, Do* and *Undo*). Deduce the code of the procedure *CryptoArith*. Provide an example of calling program.   61 - Q 2

Question 3.   For a specific problem like that given above, how to improve the temporal complexity by introducing some prunings? Is it possible to discover general pruning conditions?   61 - Q 3

The solution is on page 278.

Problem 62.   Latin squares   ⁞

> *The originality of this exercise lies in the fact that, although the enumeration vector represents an injective function, restrictions of this function have a stronger property, that is worth being exploited.*

A *Latin square of order* n ($n \geqslant 1$) is a square table inside which squares contain the n elements of a set S, that are arranged in such a way that they appear once and only once in each row and in each column. Therefore, each of the rows and columns consists of a permutation of the n elements.

For example, with $n = 6$ and $S = \{1, 2, 3, 4, 5, 6\}$, we have (among $812\,851\,200$ solutions) the following three Latin squares:

$$
\begin{bmatrix}
1 & 2 & 3 & 4 & 6 & 5 \\
4 & 6 & 5 & 2 & 3 & 1 \\
3 & 4 & 6 & 1 & 5 & 2 \\
2 & 5 & 1 & 3 & 4 & 6 \\
5 & 3 & 2 & 6 & 1 & 4 \\
6 & 1 & 4 & 5 & 2 & 3
\end{bmatrix}
\quad
\begin{bmatrix}
3 & 6 & 2 & 1 & 4 & 5 \\
1 & 3 & 4 & 6 & 5 & 2 \\
6 & 4 & 3 & 5 & 2 & 1 \\
2 & 1 & 5 & 3 & 6 & 4 \\
4 & 5 & 1 & 2 & 3 & 6 \\
5 & 2 & 6 & 4 & 1 & 3
\end{bmatrix}
\quad
\begin{bmatrix}
1 & 2 & 5 & 3 & 6 & 4 \\
2 & 6 & 1 & 4 & 3 & 5 \\
5 & 4 & 3 & 2 & 1 & 6 \\
3 & 5 & 4 & 6 & 2 & 1 \\
6 & 1 & 2 & 5 & 4 & 3 \\
4 & 3 & 6 & 1 & 5 & 2
\end{bmatrix}
$$

The second square has a peculiarity: each of the two diagonals is entirely composed of identical elements. Such a Latin square is called *antidiagonal*. The third square has a different peculiarity: the elements of S appear in the same order on the first row and the first column. Such a Latin square is said to be *normalized*. There are 96 773 760 standard Latin squares and 76 640 antidiagonal Latin squares of order 6. Thereafter, the study is limited to the case where $S = 1 .. n$.

62 - Q 1   **Question 1.**   Knowing that we are looking for all Latin squares for a given n, define the enumeration structure X and provide its properties. Deduce the pattern that applies here. What can be concluded about the set that the variable j of the loop will go through?

62 - Q 2   **Question 2.**   Provide a portion of the recursion tree for a Latin square of order 3.

62 - Q 3   **Question 3.**   Provide the code of the procedure *LatinSquare*, as well as an example of calling program.

62 - Q 4   **Question 4.**   In the version of the previous question of the procedure *LatinSquare*, we exploit the fact that the variable j scans a "hole interval", i.e. a finite subset of $\mathbb{N}$ (and not a complete interval). This feature does not exist in most classical programming languages. In the procedure *MinimalDif3* of the introductory example (page 200), we saw how to get around this problem by strengthening the invariant with a data structure (CurrSum for the example in question) that is redundant with respect to X, the enumeration structure. On the basis of this example, modify the procedure *LatinSquare* to get an efficient version *LatinSquare2* (care should be taken to avoid sequential searches inside X).

62 - Q 5   **Question 5.**   Demonstrate that with the exception of the Latin square of order 1, there is no antidiagonal Latin square of odd order, then show how the procedure *LatinSquare* can be adapted to obtain the procedure *AntidiagonalLatinSquare*, the latter allowing to write all antidiagonal Latin squares of any order n.

62 - Q 6   **Question 6.**   Give the principle of a procedure to write all normalized Latin squares of a given order n.

The solution is on page 279.

Problem 63. The sudoku game

> *This exercise is about the sudoku game. In its final version (question 4), its originality comes from the fact that the enumeration structure is not empty at the start of the algorithm, since it must contain the numbers already placed on the grid.*

This game is an extension of the "Latin square" game. It is advisable to deal with the related exercise (see page 239) before tackling this one.

The purpose of the game is to fill with numbers a nine-sided square subdivided into as many identical three-sided squares, called *regions* so that each row, each column and each region contains once and only once the digits from 1 to 9. At the beginning of the game, some digits (called the *revealed squares*) are already in place.

In general, the starting grid represents a minimal sudoku[5].

Here is an example of a sudoku grid (the grid to complete on the left and its solution on the right):

---

[5]A grid with revealed squares is said to be minimal if, on the one hand, the solution exists and is unique, and on the other hand, the suppression of any revealed squares results in the loss of uniqueness.

	3			7				
6			1	9	5			
	9	8					6	
8				6				3
4			8		3			1
7				2				6
	6					2	8	
			4	1	9			5
				8			7	9

5	3	4	6	7	8	9	1	2
6	7	2	1	9	5	3	4	8
1	9	8	3	4	2	5	6	7
8	5	9	7	6	1	4	2	3
4	2	6	8	5	3	7	9	1
7	1	3	9	2	4	8	5	6
9	6	1	5	3	7	2	8	4
2	8	7	4	1	9	6	3	5
3	4	5	2	8	6	1	7	9

As a first step, we will consider grids *without* revealed squares. The objective is then to produce all possible sudoku grids.

Question 1.   Propose an enumeration structure X. Define its properties. What can we conclude about the set that the variable of the loop will go through? Among the patterns of the list in the table on page 214, which is the appropriate one for this case? 63 - Q 1

Question 2.   Write the code of the procedure *Sudoku1* (without revealed squares), as well as a calling program. There are about $7 \; 10^{21}$ solutions. Estimate the computing time of this program on a typical current processor. 63 - Q 2

Question 3.   In the previous version of the procedure *Sudoku1*, we exploit the fact that the programming language that is used allows to browse an incomplete interval (with "holes") which represents a finite subset of $\mathbb{N}$. Such a characteristic does not exist in most of languages used in practice. In the procedure *GenSet3* of the introductory example (page 200), we have seen how to obviate this problem by strengthening the invariant with a data structure redundant (CurrSum for the considered example) with the structure X. On the basis of this example, modify the procedure *Sudoku1* in order to be provided with an efficient version *Sudoku2* (it is recommended to avoid sequential searches inside X). 63 - Q 3

The grids considered now contain revealed squares. We are only interested in the variant of *Sudoku2* (in which an auxiliary data structure is used).

Question 4.   Modify the procedure *Sudoku2* (yielding *Sudoku3*) so as to deal with revealed squares. 63 - Q 4

Question 5.   How to adapt the result of the previous question so as to propose an operation checking that a grid is actually minimal. 63 - Q 5

Question 6.   In general, the grids displayed in magazines are evaluated according to their supposed level of difficulty, usually between *very easy* and *demonic*. However, the ranking on this scale depends on the strategy(ies) applied in the search for a solution. Thus, if we consider the average time to find the solution as the only difficulty criterion, the grid *Blond platinum* (cf. grid (a), figure 5.17) is often considered as one of the most difficult grids known to date, whereas a strategy using "Generate and test", such as the one implemented in the *Sudoku3* version, finds the solution in less than a second on a desktop computer. Conversely, for the grid (b) of the same figure, an algorithm of type "Generate and test" will struggle for about fifteen seconds before displaying the solution, whereas a specialist will classify this grid, at worst, in the category *difficult*. 63 - Q 6

In this question, it is asked to consider modifications to the solution of question 3 and to implement the new solution in order to calculate the number of recursive calls required

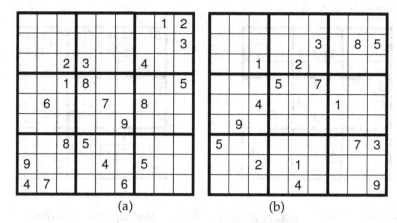

Fig. 5.17 – (a) The grid Blond platinum; *(b) A grid unfavorable for a "Generate and test" strategy.*

to find the solution. This value can be objectively considered as characterizing the level of difficulty in the context of resolution using "Generate and test". The algorithm thus modified will then be applied to the two grids in figure 5.17, for comparison purposes.

Calculating the level of difficulty of a grid based on a single run from the top left square may seem arbitrary. A more satisfactory solution is to start the search successively on the 81 squares of the grid and to calculate the average of the 81 values thus obtained.

63 - Q 7   **Question 7.**   Modify the procedure of the previous question to start the search on an arbitrarily chosen square.

63 - Q 8   **Question 8.**   Use the modification thus made to obtain a program that calculates the average number of recursive calls obtained by starting successively on the 81 squares of the grid. Apply the algorithm thus obtained to the two grids of figure 5.17, page 242.

63 - Q 9   **Question 9.**   Question 3 introduces a strengthening of the invariant (consisting of adding redundant data structures H, V, etc.). It is clear that this modification has no consequence on the asymptotic complexity of the solution, which is only due to recursive calls. However, the practical impact of this variant is questionable. Experimentally evaluate the gain (in terms of execution time) provided by the application of this strengthening by comparing the execution time of the versions *without* and *with* strengthening, over about twenty significant test sets. Conclusion?

The solution is on page 282.

Problem 64. Seven-Eleven

This exercise is a very interesting example whose naïve solution has a disastrous temporal complexity, while an ingenious transformation, based on a decomposition into prime factors, provides a solution whose efficiency is acceptable.

The neighborhood grocery store is open from 7 am to 11 pm, hence its name: the "7 - 11". We buy a set of four items $\{a_1, a_2, a_3, a_4\}$. At the cashier's desk, the bill amounts to 7.11$. A bill of 7.11$ at the grocery "7-11"! We mention the coincidence to the cashier and we ask him about the way he attained this amount: "Well, I simply multiplied the price of the four items". We calmly explain to him that he has to *add up* the price of the four items, not multiply them. He replies: "it does not matter, the bill would still be 7.11$". He is right. The objective is to determine the price of each item, knowing that the first solution encountered is convenient.

Question 1. Express in US cents, the sum (respectively the product) of the four prices.   64 - Q 1

Question 2. Assuming that any price is strictly over one cent and on the single basis of the properties of the addition, which is the interval of variation of the prices (in US cents again)?   64 - Q 2

Question 3. In order to design an algorithm solving this problem, propose an enumeration vector X and specify its properties. Which type of pattern is implied by this choice (see table 5.1, page 214) knowing that the first solution is searched?   64 - Q 3

Question 4. Write the procedure *SevenEleven1* that displays the first solution encountered. Improve the solution by strengthening the recursion invariant.   64 - Q 4

In order to improve the efficiency of an algorithm, the approach that consists in preprocessing the data often proves to be fruitful. While in the previous question all possible quadruples of prices were examined, we can decide to consider only quadruples whose product equals 711 000 000. To list such quadruples first of all requires the decomposition of 711 000 000 into a product of prime factors[6] (this constitutes the preprocessing here). It is easy to calculate that $711\,000\,000 = 2^6 \cdot 3^2 \cdot 5^6 \cdot 79$. Coding each of the items in the interval 1 .. 4, the problem comes down to finding a specific four-element partition of the bag $[2, 2, 2, 2, 2, 2, 3, 3, 5, 5, 5, 5, 5, 5, 79]$. So, for example, the partition $[[2, 2, 5, 5], [2, 2, 5, 5], [2, 3, 79], [2, 3, 5, 5]]$ corresponds to four items of respective prices 100, 100, 474 and 150. By construction, the produit of these four prices is 711 000 000, therefore, this verification becomes unnecessary. The remaining point is to find (one of) the partition(s) whose sum is 711.

Question 5. Use the preceding remark to define a new enumeration structure X and provide its properties. Deduce the pattern that applies (see table 5.1, page 214) and give its code if it does not appear in the introduction.   64 - Q 5

Question 6. Deduce the new version of the procedure *SevenEleven* that displays the first solution encountered. What can be said about the complexity of this solution?   64 - Q 6

The solution is on page 288.

Problem 65. Decomposition of an integer   ○ ⁞

> *Starting from a "brute force" solution, several optimizations and prunings are studied in this exercise. It is our major goal knowing that there are solutions much more efficient than those based on the "Generate and test" approach.*

Given an integer n (n ⩾ 1), the "decomposition" of n is the set of sets of positive natural numbers that sum up to n. For example, the decomposition of n = 6 is the set:

---

[6] As a bag, the decomposition is unique provided that 1 is excluded. That is the reason why prices are imposed to be at least two US cents.

$\{\{1,2,3\},\ \{1,5\},\ \{2,4\},\ \{6\}\}$ [7]. The objective of the exercise is to build diverse variants of the procedure that successively delivers all the elements of the decomposition of a given positive integer n.

65 - Q 1   **Question** 1.   Give the decomposition of $n = 10$.

65 - Q 2   **Question** 2.   In order to solve this problem in the "Generate and test" paradigm, define an enumeration structure X and provide its properties. Deduce its corresponding pattern.

65 - Q 3   **Question** 3.   In this question, we are interested in a "brute force" solution. Provide the procedure *DecompInteger1*, instance of the pattern chosen in the previous question, specifying how the function*SolFound* is instantiated.

65 - Q 4   **Question** 4.   A first pruning is possible when a branch has already exceeded the value n. What changes need to be made to the procedure *DecompInteger1* to implement this optimization?

65 - Q 5   **Question** 5.   For the moment, the calculation of the sum of the numbers represented in the vector X is systematically carried out during the evaluation of the condition corresponding to the generic function *SolFound*. It is clear that this leads to redoing the same calculations several times. The optimization considered here aims at the elimination of these redundant calculations. Make this improvement by adapting the technique of strengthening of the recursion invariant applied in the introductory example in this chapter (see page 197).

65 - Q 6   **Question** 6.   A last pruning is still possible. It is based on the fact that the search can be stopped as soon as the exact sum has been found for any number. How should the previous version be modified to get to this version?

The solution is on page 291.

Problem 66. Madame Dumas and the three Musketeers   ○ •

> *This exercise is a typical example of constrained production of permutations. Hereafter, if possible and for genericity purpose, we attempt to dissociate the aspect related to the production of permutations from that of accounting for constraints.*

Madame widow "Dumas Sr." is organizing a dinner in honor of d'Artagnan and the Three Musketeers. The five seats around the table are numbered from 1 to 5. Madame Dumas knows that:

1. Porthos prefers to be on seat number 1,

2. Athos prefers to be separated from d'Artagnan,

3. Aramis prefers to be separated from Athos,

4. Porthos prefers to be separated from Athos.

---

[7]There is the close notion of *partition* of an integer, where a set of *bags* is searched (an integer may appear several times in a sum). For example, the partition of 6 is: $\{[\![6]\!],\ [\![5,1]\!],\ [\![4,2]\!],\ [\![4,1,1]\!],\ [\![3,3]\!],\ [\![3,2,1]\!],\ [\![3,1,1,1]\!],\ [\![2,2,2]\!],\ [\![2,2,1,1]\!],\ [\![2,1,1,1,1]\!],\ [\![1,1,1,1,1,1]\!]\}$. Partition is more combinatorial than decomposition since any decomposition is a partition (but not every partition is a decomposition).

As for her, Madame Dumas prefers to be separated from d'Artagnan (preference number 5). How to help Madame Dumas establish her seating plan (i.e. answer the question "who is where?"), if possible respecting everyone's preferences? Hereafter, each participant is coded by a number of the interval $1..5$, according to alphabetical order (1: *Aramis*, 2: *Athos*, 3: *d'Artagnan*, 4: *Dumas*, 5: *Porthos*).

In the remainder, it is suggested to deal with preference 1 in an *ad hoc* way instead of the generic algorithm.

Question 1. Define the enumeration vector X and provide its properties. Among those proposed in table 5.1, page 214, which pattern applies here, knowing that we look for all possible solutions? 66 - Q 1

Question 2. Draw the recursion tree obtained when the root is *Porthos*. 66 - Q 2

Question 3. Propose a solution to handle the constraints of type "*Y* prefers to be separated from *Z*". 66 - Q 3

Question 4. Write the algorithm that displays all the seating plans compatible with the constraints. Give an example of calling program. 66 - Q 4

The solution is on page 293.

Problem 67. Mini Master Mind 8 :

> *Master Mind is a game that became famous in the 70's. Two players confront each other, one passive, the coder, proposes a code, which the second, the decoder, must discover. Inspired by this game, this exercise has a triple interest. First of all, in the first question, it leads to thinking about the properties of the proposals made by the decoder. A particularly efficient pruning is studied in a second step. Last, a third solution takes a totally different promising path.*

It is a two-player game, the *coder* and the *decoder*. The first one settles a permutation of n colors (here $n = 5$) black, navy blue, orange, red and violet, respectively coded B, N, O, R, V, that the second tries to discover.

To do this, the decoder proposes a list of five different colors and in response, the coder informs him of the number of correctly placed colors. If this is the case for all five colors, the game is over. Otherwise, the decoder makes another proposal which is rated in turn. The decoder must discover the code with as few proposals as possible. In doing so, he draws on information provided in response to his previous proposals. In this exercise, the program to be built plays the role of the decoder.

Figure 5.18 shows the history of a Mini Master Mind game with the code [V, R, N, O, B] where the game ends after seven propositions.

Question 1. Which necessary condition must a decoder proposal satisfy to be the permutation expected by the coder? Suggestion: consider the following question: "assuming that the proposal is the solution, how is it evaluated against the various history entries?" 67 - Q 1

In the following, the list of n colors to discover is represented by the table C, and the history H is in the form of a data structure (see figure 5.18 for an example) accessible through the following three operations:

N° Prop.	Propositions	Rating
1	[B,N,O,R,V]	0
2	[N,B,R,V,O̲]	1
3	[N,O,V,B̲,R]	1
4	[O,V,R,B̲,N]	1
5	[R,B,V,O,N]	0
6	[V̲,O,R,N,B]	1
7	[V̲,R̲,N̲,B̲,O̲]	5

Fig. 5.18 – History of the progress of a game for the initial coding [V, R, N, B, O]. Under-lined letters correspond to correctly placed colors. This information is not available to the decoder.

- **procedure** *InitHisto* that makes H empty,

- **procedure** *InsertHisto*(P, E) that inserts the permutation P evaluated to E into H,

- **function** *CompatHisto*(P) **result** 𝔹 that returns **true**, iff the permutation P complies with the necessary condition subject of the first question, **false** otherwise.

67 - Q 2 **Question** 2.   Define the enumeration vector X. Which of the patterns in table 5.1, page 214, applies? Deduce the procedure *PermutMasterMind1*(i) that builds (in the enumeration vector X) the next proposition of the decoder. Show how to use this procedure to play a game of Mini Master Mind (it is assumed that none of the players makes a mistake).

The procedure *PermutMasterMind1*(i) does not perform any pruning. However, it is possible to avoid constructing a complete occurrence of the vector X by noting that as soon as a permutation in progress, confronted with an entry in the history, produces a response (evaluation) superior to the responses (evaluations) present in the history, it is useless to continue the construction of X. This is the role assigned to the operation **function** *PossibleHisto*(c, k) **result** 𝔹, which verifies that the subvector X[1 .. k − 1] lengthened in k by the color c does not produce matches in excess of the answers recorded in the history. We propose to explore this strategy in the following two questions.

67 - Q 3 **Question** 3.   In this question, we assume that n = 4 and that the array of colors C is C = [B, O, R, V]. It is further assumed that:
- the permutation to be discovered is [R, O, V, B],
- at the moment of interest, the history is as follows:

N° Prop.	Prop.	Rating
1	[B, O, R, V]	1
2	[B, R, V, O]	1
3	[B, V, O, R]	0
4	[O, R, B, V]	0

- propositions produced by the decoder are made in lexicographical order and he stops his search as soon as a proposition is compatible with the history (as defined in question 1).

Give the pruned recursion tree that leads to the fifth proposition.

Question 4. Write the procedure *PermutMasterMind2* that implements this strategy. 67 - Q 4

Whether one uses *PermutMasterMind1* or *PermutMasterMind2*, these two procedures perform the search for the next proposition starting systematically from the same initial permutation. Obviously, this method leads to reconsidering permutations that have already failed. Thus, in the example of question 3, the two "Generate and test" procedures start the search with the code [B, O, R, V]. This one is discarded – along with all permutations already present in the history up to [O, R, W, G] – thanks to the condition *CompatHisto*. A better solution *a priori* would be to start from the permutation that follows (in lexicographical order) the last one that failed. For the example, we would start with the permutation after [O, R, B, V], which is [O, R, V, B].

In a first step, the objective is to construct an algorithm which, starting from a given permutation, produces the next one (always according to the lexicographical order), assuming (precondition) that it exists. For ease of reading, the explanations are provided with a nine-digit code from 1 to 9; the function $S(p)$ provides the permutation that follows p. $S([9,8,7,6,5,4,3,2,1])$ does not exist (the precondition is not satisfied). On the other hand, $S([1,2,3,4,5,6,7,8,9]) = [1,2,3,4,5,6,7,9,8]$. In effect, the number (without duplicate digits) following 123456789 is 123456798. Similarly, $S([5, 9, 8, 7, 6, 4, 3, 2, 1]) = [6, 1, 2, 3, 4, 5, 7, 8, 9]$, or $S([6, 1, 9, 8, 4, 7, 5, 3, 2]) = [6, 1, 9, 8, 5, 2, 3, 4, 7]$.

How can we achieve these results? Let us first observe that moving from a permutation to the next one can be done by exchanges only. The case $[5,9,8,7,6,4,3,1,2]$ is easy to handle: just exchange the digits 2 and 1. Consider the case $[5,9,8,7,6,4,3,2,1]$. Deprived of its first element (5), i.e. $[9,8,7,6,4,3,2,1]$, this code has no successor since the sequence of numbers is descending. $S([5,9,8,7,6,4,3,2,1])$ cannot begin with any of the digits $1,2,3$ or 4: the number would be less than the start code. Nor can it start with 5 since the digits that follow 5 are in descending order. It must begin with the digit in $[9,8,7,6,4,3,2,1]$ immediately greater than 5, i.e. 6. Let us swap 5 and 6. We get $[6,9, 8,7,5, 4,3,2,1]$. This is not the expected result because there are several codes that are interspersed between $[5,9,8, 7,6,4, 3,2,1]$ and $[6,9,8, 7,5,4, 3,2,1]$, such as $[6,9,8, 5,7,4, 3,2,1]$. The exchange alone is therefore not enough. What operation must be carried out following the exchange? Simply reverse the descending sub-array following the first digit. For the example, we get $[6,1,2, 3,4,5, 7,8,9]$, which is the expected result.

This approach applies to more complex cases such as $[6,1,9,8,4,7,5,3,2]$. Simply identify the longest descending code on the left ($[7,5,3,2]$) and, as above, look for the successor of $[4,7,5, 3,2]$. This one starts with 5. Let us exchange 4 and 5: $[5,7,4, 3,2]$. Let us reverse the last four digits: $[5,2,3, 4,7]$. The beginning of the code, $[6,1, 9,8]$, playing no role in the process, the result is $[6,1,9, 8,5,2, 3,4,7]$. Finally, it should be noted that this approach applies uniformly to all codes with a successor.

Question 5. Apply the above approach to get the code of the function $S(p)$ delivering the permutation that follows p in lexicographical order. The precondition for this function is that there is a permutation that follows. Evaluate its complexity. 67 - Q 5

Question 6. Show how to use this procedure to make a game of Mini Master Mind. 67 - Q 6

Question 7. What do you think is the most effective strategy? Support your answer with some experimental results on a 12-color Mini Master Mind. 67 - Q 7

The solution is on page 296.

Problem 68. Crossword puzzle

> *This exercise is based on a crossword puzzle. It is a typical example that highlights the gain afforded by an efficient pruning. The solution obtained with a sophisticated pruning brings a significant improvement with respect to that where a coarse pruning applies.*

"Crossword puzzle" is a game where the player is provided with both an empty grid and a bag of words to be placed on it. The objective of the player is to find a configuration where all the words are placed on the grid.

Example

Figure 5.19 gives an example where the empty grid accompanied with a lexicon of 24 words is on the left hand side and a possible completed configuration is on the right hand side. It should be noticed that *all* the words, including those with a single letter, are present in the lexicon.

D	BI	BEC
E	CA	DIS
E	ET	FER
E	IF	MIL
M	ME	EMUE
R	RU	IBIS
T	SI	LISIER
AI	AME	MARBRE

A statement (the empty grid and the lexicon)   A possible solution

Fig. 5.19 – Example of statement and solution for the "crossword puzzle" game.

The first approach that we investigate is limited to a coarse pruning. Its principle consists in filling in the grid horizontally taking into account at each step only words whose size equals that of the considered location (this constitutes the pruning used here). Then, once the grid is filled in, it is checked that the remaining words (not yet placed) are those appearing vertically on the grid. In the remainder, it is assumed that:

- the grid under consideration, Grid, has r rows and c columns,

- H is a constant which represents the number of horizontal locations, numbered from 1 to H (in the example of figure 5.19, H = 13),

- Dico is a constant array, defined on the interval 1 .. N, which represents the bag of the N words to be placed on the grid.

68 - Q 1   **Question 1.**   Which enumeration structure allows the implementation of this solution? What are its properties? Which of the patterns of table 5.1, page 214, is to be retained?

68 - Q 2   **Question 2.**   Give the recursion tree for the 3 × 3 problem of figure 5.20 (the search is stopped as soon as a solution is found.)

A	TA	TRI
I	TA	
AI	RIT	

Fig. 5.20 – Example of a 3 × 3 crossword puzzle.

In order to facilitate the processing, the following assumptions are made:

1. *HorLocLength*(i) is a function returning the length of the horizontal location i.

2. *VertWordsBag* is the function that, once the grid is complete, returns the bag of words placed vertically.

3. *Free* is the bag of words that are absent from the enumeration structure X. The multiset union of *Free* and the words present in X constitutes the set of words of Dico.

4. The function *BagConv* converts an array of words into a bag.

Question 3.   Write the procedure *CrosswordPuzzle1*(i) that looks for the first solution and writes it (the precondition of this procedure is that there is at least one solution). Give its complexity in the worst case (in terms of conditions evaluated).   68 - Q 3

This first solution is perfectible in terms of efficiency. We will now study and implement a pruning designed to bring an improvement in terms of temporal complexity. To do so, we propose not to wait until the end of the generation phase to perform a vertical verification. More specifically, as soon as a word is a candidate for horizontal placement, we check that it does not constitute an obstacle to the vertical placement of one of the words still available by making sure that each character of the candidate word is also a possible character for a vertical word.

Example

Let us consider the following configuration in which we are about to attempt to place the word **RUE** on the second-to-last horizontal location

while the bag of available words is [[**CRI, TALC, EU, OSE**]]. The placement of **RUE** is consistent with the vertical word **CRI**, the **R** being common. On the other hand, the **U** of **RUE** is incompatible with all free four-letter words since **TAU** is not the beginning of any free word of length 4. The placement of the word **RUE** is thus abandoned, which produces a pruning of the recursion tree.

Question 4.   For the example of figure 5.20, page 249, provide the recursion tree obtained by the pruning described above. Conclusion?   68 - Q 4

68 - Q 5 **Question 5.** The pruning presented above requires both horizontal and vertical access to the grid locations and words. For this reason, we decide to take the grid itself as an enumeration structure. Specify the operations necessary to implement the pruning, then provide the procedure *CrosswordPuzzle2* that implements that pruning.

The solution is on page 299.

Problem 69. Self-referent arrays

> *Self-reference (i.e. the property for an entity to refer to itself) is a notion that is encountered in many scientific domains such as linguistics, logics or mathematics. In the following exercise, the objective is to produce self-referent arrays. Two interesting prunings are applied.*

An array X of n (n > 0) elements, defined on the interval $0..n-1$ valued in the interval $0..n-1$, is said self-referent if, for any index i of the array, X[i] is the number of occurrences of the value i in the array. Formally:

$$\forall i \cdot (i \in 0..n-1 \Rightarrow X[i] = \#j \cdot (j \in 0..n-1 \text{ and then } X[j] = i)) \tag{5.3}$$

where # is the counting quantifier. For example, for n = 4, the array:

i	0	1	2	3
X[i]	1	2	1	0

is a self-referent array: 0 has one occurrence, 1 has two occurrences, and so on. For n < 7, it is easy to prove (by enumeration) that there is no solution for $n \in \{1, 2, 3, 6\}$, and that there is a single solution for n = 5.

69 - Q 1 **Question 1.** Give another self-referent array for n = 4.

69 - Q 2 **Question 2.** What can be said about the sum of the elements in a self-referent array? Justify your answer.

69 - Q 3 **Question 3.** For a given n, the objective is to produce all the self-referent arrays, using the "Generate and test" approach. What is the appropriate pattern from the list shown in figure 5.1, page 214? What pruning based on the result of question 2 can be applied to the instantiation of the generic function *Satisf*? How to represent the generic function *SolFound*? Deduce the procedure *AutoRefArr1* as well as a suitable calling context.

69 - Q 4 **Question 4.** A second pruning can take place. It is based on the fact that, if in the slice $X[0..i-1]$ the element j is already present X[j] times, it is useless to try to place j in location i. Thus, in the following example:

i	...	2	3	...	5	...	12	...	20	...	50
X[i]	...	5	5	...	3	...	5				

X[5] is equal to 3 and the value 5 is actually present 3 times in X[0..19]. It is therefore useless to try to place 5 in position 20, the attempt would be doomed to failure. Implement this pruning in the context of the procedure *AutoRefArr2*.

Question 5.   Prove that, for $n \geqslant 7$, self-referent arrays having the following structure: **69 - Q 5**

i	0	1	2	3	...	n − 5	n − 4	n − 3	n − 2	n − 1
X[i]	n − 4	2	1	0	...	0	1	0	0	0

$$\underbrace{}_{n - 7 \text{ times}}$$

are self-referent arrays.

Conjecture

The authors speculate that the sufficient condition which is the subject of question 5 is in fact a necessary and sufficient condition.

The solution is on page 303.

5.5   Solutions

Answers to problem 52. The n-queen problem *The problem is on page 223.*

Answer 1.   There are $(2n - 1)$ diagonals of each type. Queens $Q_1 = (r_1, f_1)$ and   **52 - A 1** $Q_2 = (r_2, f_2)$ are located on the same up (respectively down) diagonal iff $r_1 - f_1 = r_2 - f_2$ (respectively $r_1 + f_1 = r_2 + f_2$). Therefore, each of these diagonals can be identified by the value $r - f$ (respectively $r + f$). As it is illustrated in the schemas hereafter, these values are varying in the interval $1 - n .. n - 1$ for up diagonals and $2 .. 2n$ for down diagonals.

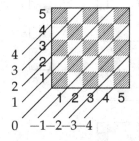
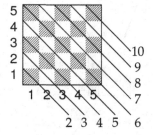

Answer 2.   Among the possible prunings, of course, there are those tied to the presence   **52 - A 2** of two queens on the same rank, file or diagonal. We must also think of the case where no queen is placed on a complete rank or file. The tree in figure 5.21, page 252, shows these various cases. Prunings due to queens *in capture* appear under the nodes with the symbol ✂; those due to the absence of queens on a rank are symbolized by ✖. The tree is incomplete and the subtrees still to be explored are dotted. For the clarity of the figure, white color is used to symbolize a free queen, while black is used when a queen is attacked by another one.

Answer 3.   The functions *FreeRank* and *FreeFile* can be easily built, while the functions   **52 - A 3** *FreeUpDiag* and *FreeDownDiag* can be implemented on the basis of the answer to question 1. The condition *Satisf* is true either when we are about to leave a rank or file with its last square unoccupied (it is the first term of the condition), or when a queen will be placed in

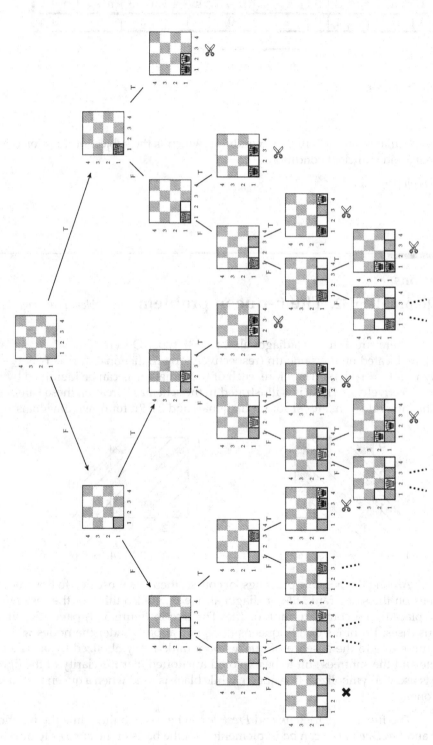

Fig. 5.21 – The four-queen problem, version "enumeration matrix" (incomplete tree). ✂: pruning due to a rank, file or diagonal conflict. ✗: pruning due to the absence of queen in a rank. On branches: T for **true** and F for **false**. The processed squares are framed. In this figure, no leaf solution is reached.

an unattacked position (it is the second term). This condition is sufficient to characterize a solution. The code is written:

```
1.  procedure NQueens1(r, f) pre
2.     r ∈ 1..n and f ∈ 1..n
3.  begin
4.     for j ranging B do
```

5.   **if** $\left(\begin{array}{l} \text{not } j \text{ and} \left(\begin{array}{l} (f = n \Rightarrow \textbf{not } FreeRank(r, f)) \textbf{ and} \\ (r = n \Rightarrow \textbf{not } FreeFile(r, f)) \end{array} \right) \\ \textbf{or} \\ j \textbf{ and} \left(\begin{array}{l} FreeUpDiag(r, f) \textbf{ and} \\ FreeDownDiag(r, f) \textbf{ and} \\ FreeRank(r, f) \textbf{ and} \\ FreeFile(r, f) \end{array} \right) \end{array} \right)$ **then**

```
6.       X[r, f] ← j;
7.       if r = n and f = n then
8.          write(X)
9.       else
10.         if f = n then
11.            NQueens1(r + 1, 1)
12.         else
13.            NQueens1(r, f + 1)
14.         end if
15.      end if
16.   end if
17.   end for
18. end
```

The associated calling program is:

```
1.  constants
2.     n ∈ N₁ and n = ...
3.  variables
4.     X ∈ 1..n × 1..n → B
5.  begin
6.     NQueens1(1, 1)
7.  end
```

Answer 4.   It is sufficient to take four global Boolean arrays FrR (for *free rank*), FrF (for *free file*), FrUD (for *free up diagonal*) and FrDD (for *free down diagonal*) initialized to **true** in the calling program, and to manage them as shown in both the schema of question 3, and the program below. Let us notice that the two procedures *Do* and *Undo* must be instantiated in this case.   52 - A 4

```
1.  procedure NQueens2(r, f) pre
2.     r ∈ 1..n and f ∈ 1..n
3.  begin
4.     for j ranging B do
```

5. if
$$
\left(
\begin{array}{l}
\text{not j and}
\left(
\begin{array}{l}
(f = n \Rightarrow \textbf{not } \text{FrR}[r]) \text{ and} \\
(r = n \Rightarrow \textbf{not } \text{FrF}[f])
\end{array}
\right) \\
\textbf{or} \\
\text{j and}
\left(
\begin{array}{l}
\text{FrUD}(r - f) \text{ and} \\
\text{FrDD}(r + f) \text{ and} \\
\text{FrR}(r) \text{ and} \\
\text{FrF}(f)
\end{array}
\right)
\end{array}
\right)
$$
then

6. $\boxed{X[r, f] \leftarrow j;}$

7. if j then

8. $\boxed{\text{FrR}[r] \leftarrow \textbf{false}; \text{FrF}[f] \leftarrow \textbf{false}; \text{FrUD}[r - f] \leftarrow \textbf{false}; \text{FrDD}[r + f] \leftarrow \textbf{false}}$

9. end if;

10. if $r = n$ and $f = n$ then

11. write(X)

12. else

13. if $f = n$ then

14. $NQueens2(r + 1, 1)$

15. else

16. $NQueens2(r, f + 1)$

17. end if

18. end if;

19. if j then

20. $\boxed{\text{FrR}[r] \leftarrow \textbf{true}; \text{FrF}[f] \leftarrow \textbf{true}; \text{FrUD}[r - f] \leftarrow \textbf{true}; \text{FrDD}[r + f] \leftarrow \textbf{true}}$

21. end if

22. end if

23. end for

24. end

The calling program is:

1. **constants**
2. $n \in \mathbb{N}_1$ and $n = \ldots$
3. **variables**
4. $X \in 1 .. n \times 1 .. n \rightarrow \mathbb{B}$ **and**
5. $\text{FrR} \in 1 .. n \rightarrow \mathbb{B}$ **and** $\text{FrF} \in 1 .. n \rightarrow \mathbb{B}$ **and**
6. $\text{FrUD} \in 1 - n .. n - 1 \rightarrow \mathbb{B}$ **and** $\text{FrDD} \in 2 .. 2n \rightarrow \mathbb{B}$
7. **begin**
8. $\text{FrR} \leftarrow (1 .. n) \times \{\textbf{true}\}; \text{FrF} \leftarrow (1 .. n) \times \{\textbf{true}\};$
9. $\text{FrUD} \leftarrow (1 - n .. n - 1) \times \{\textbf{true}\}; \text{FrDD} \leftarrow (2 .. 2n) \times \{\textbf{true}\};$
10. $NQueens2(1, 1)$
11. **end**
1

52 - A 5 **Answer 5.** The (incomplete) recursion tree is shown in figure 5.22. The only possible prunings concern the mutual capture of queens on diagonals. For the sake of clarity of the figure, the vector X is reinterpreted as a chessboard.

52 - A 6 **Answer 6.** The two arrays FrUD and FrDD are initialized to **true** meaning that the chessboard is empty.

1. **procedure** $NQueens3(r)$ **pre**
2. $r \in 1 .. n$

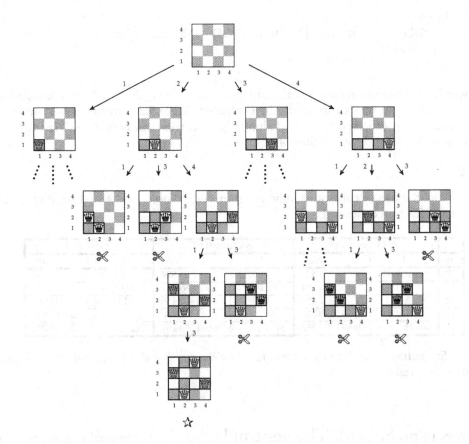

Fig. 5.22 – The four-queen problem, version "enumeration vector" (incomplete tree). ✂: pruning on a node due to a diagonal conflict. ☆: success. The squares processed are framed.

```
 3.  begin
 4.     for f ranging (1 .. n − codom(X[1 .. i − 1]) do
 5.        if  FrUD[r − f] and FrDD[r + f]  then
 6.           X[r] ← f;  FrUD[r − f] ← false; FrDD[r + f] ← false;
 7.           if  r = n  then
 8.              write(X)
 9.           else
10.              NQueens3(r + 1)
11.           end if;
12.           FrUD[r − f] ← true; FrDD[r + f] ← true
13.        end if
14.     end for
15.  end
```

The calling program is:

```
 1.  constants
 2.     n ∈ ℕ₁ and n = …
 3.  variables
 4.     X ∈ 1 .. n → 1 .. n and FrUD ∈ 1 − n .. n − 1 → 𝔹 and FrDD ∈ 2 .. 2n → 𝔹
```

```
5. begin
6.   FrUD ← (1 − n .. n − 1) × {true}; FrDD ← (2 .. 2n) × {true};
7.   NQueens3(1)
8. end
```

52 - A 7   **Answer 7.**   Theoretical complexities are those given in section 5.1.2, page 202 and the gain obtained by prunings can hardly be evaluated. Table 5.2 provides some numerical evaluations (unless otherwise stated, evaluations are carried out with a 2.8 GHz Intel Core i5 processor) for the three algorithms and for some values of n.

Remark

For $n = 256$, the use of constraint logic programming would find a first solution to this problem in a fraction of second ...

	NQueens1		NQueens2		NQueens3	
n	T	NbC	T	NbC	T	NbC
8	0.00934	21 824	0.00467	21 824	0.00182	1965
10	0.107	489 891	0.0445	489 891	0.00728	34 815
12	3.04	14 437 450	1.16	14 437 450	0.148	841 989
14	121.	543 118 736	43.	543 118 736	5.14	26 992 957
16	46608.	26 041 596 261	3438.	26 041 596 261	242.	1 126 417 791

Tab. 5.2 – Evaluation of the three algorithms. n: side of the chessboard, T: execution time in seconds, NbC: number of calls.

Answers to problem 53. **The sentinels**   *The problem is on page 225.*

53 - A 1   **Answer 1.**   In addition to the square where it is located, a queen controls $(n−1)$ squares in a rank, $(n−1)$ squares in a file and in the best case $(2 \cdot (n−1))$ squares in diagonal, in total at best $(4 \cdot (n−1)+1) = (4n−3)$ squares of the chessboard. To cover the $n \times n$ squares, at least x queens are necessary, x being the solution of the integer inequation $(x \cdot (4n−3)) \geqslant n^2$. So, it is necessary to have at least:

$$\left\lceil \frac{n^2}{4n − 3} \right\rceil$$

queens on the chessboard. This result is clearly too optimistic to be used for pruning: the number of branches suppressed on the basis of this criterion is too low to be of interest: one can think that the cost for evaluating the triggering condition of the pruning is likely to exceed the gain brought by the pruning.

53 - A 2   **Answer 2.**   A partial recursion tree is given in figure 5.23, page 257. Squares in black symbolize free squares (*not in capture*). For the clarity of the figure, white color is used to represent a "free" queen whereas black is used when a queen is attacked by another one (*in capture*). The queens are placed rank by rank (top down on the chessboard) and in a rank, file by file (from left to right). The rightmost leaf in the figure represents one of the solutions (with three queens). Since, by definition, the pattern *OptPI* does not place two queens in either a same rank, or a same file, the only envisageable pruning concerns the case where there is an attempt to place a queen on one of the diagonals passing through the square where a queen is already placed.

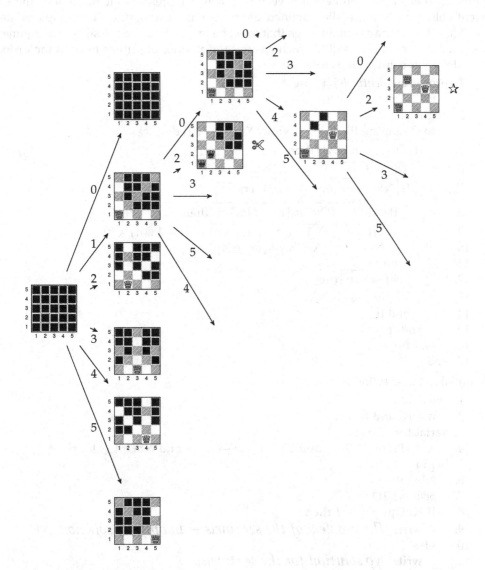

Fig. 5.23 – The sentinels. Recursion tree (incomplete) for a chessboard 5 × 5. Black squares correspond to unattacked free squares. ✂: pruning due to a conflict in a diagonal. ☆: success. The figure must be read top down from left to right. It can be noticed that, on a branch, a same number of file does not appear twice, except the "phantom" number 0 used to manage injectivity.

Answer 3. The function *Satisf* of the pattern *OptPI* becomes the function *FreeSquare*(r, f). This latter considers two situations: either f = 0, which means that no queen will be placed on rank r, either the square (r, f) is unoccupied and a queen can be put there. The condition *SolFound* is met when all the squares are either occupied by a queen, or under the control of at least one queen. This role is performed by the function *NbFreeSquares*(r). The condition *BetterSolution* means that the current solution

53 - A 3

is better (in terms of number of queens) than the best solution found out so far. This condition calls on the function *NbPlacedQueens*(r). The procedure *KeepCurrContext* consists in updating the variable NbOpt, which represents the best result achieved so far. It must be noticed that in the enumeration vector X, which represents (at this point) the best current solution, only the slice defined over 1 .. r is meaningful. The complementary slice (X[r + 1 .. n]) may contain slags that must be ignored, hence the second assignment, Y[r + 1 .. n] ← (r + 1 .. n) × {0}, which ensures the absence of queens beyond rank r in Y. The code of this solution is as follows:

```
 1. procedure Sentinels1(r) pre
 2.    r ∈ 1 .. n
 3. begin
 4.    for f ranging (0 .. n) − (codom(X[1 .. i − 1])) do
 5.       if  FreeSquare(r, f)  then
 6.          X[l] ← f;
 7.          if  NbFreeSquares(r) = 0  then
 8.             if  NbPlacedQueens(r) < NbOpt  then
 9.                Y[1 .. r] ← X[1 .. r] ; Y[r + 1 .. n] ← (r + 1 .. n) × {0};
10.                NbOpt ← NbPlacedQueens(r)
11.             end if
12.          elsif  r ≠ n  then
13.             Sentinels1(r + 1)
14.          end if
15.       end if
16.    end for
17. end
```

The initial call is as follows:

```
 1. constants
 2.    n ∈ ℕ₁ and n = ...
 3. variables
 4.    X ∈ 1 .. n → 0 .. n and Y ∈ 1 .. n → 0 .. n and NbOpt ∈ 1 .. n + 1
 5. begin
 6.    NbOpt ← n + 1 ;
 7.    Sentinels1(1) ;
 8.    if NbOpt ≠ n + 1 then
 9.       write(The problem of the sentinels − an optimal solution: ,Y)
10.    else
11.       write(No solution for the sentinels)
12.    end if
13. end
```

The development of the operations *FreeSquare*, *NbFreeSquares* and *NbPlacedQueens* is left to the reader.

53 - A 4   **Answer** 4.   By convention, if the position (r, f) is occupied by a queen, Capt[r, f] equals 1. This array is initialized to 0 before the main call, in order to account for the emptiness of the chessboard. Moreover, it is managed by two procedures:

- *Occupy*(r, f), whose precondition is the fact that position (r, f) is free (Capt[r, f] = 0). This procedure places a queen in position (r, f), updates the variable NbFreeSquares along with all the squares of Capt attacked by this queen.

- *Free*(r, f) is the dual procedure and it is used to *undo* what was done by the previous one. Its precondition is the fact that position (r, f) is occupied by a queen (Capt[r, f] = 1). This procedure removes this queen, updates the variable NbFreeSqares as well as all the squares of Capt which were attacked by this queen.

These two operations are easy to build and they are not detailed here. In addition to the fact that, with respect to the previous version, some operations become variables (NbPlacedQueens and NbFreeSquares), the two main changes concern the generic operations *Do* and *Undo*. *Do* must maintain the array Capt and the variable NbFreeSquares through the call to the procedure *Occupy*. *Do* must also directly update the variable NbPlacedQueens. The generic procedure *Undo* carries out the inverse task. It uses the operation *Free*. In the version below, the expression of the browsing domain of the **for** loop may be simplified using the whole interval 0 .. n since the predicate of the conditional statement that follows manages the restriction existing in the previous version.

```
1.  procedure Sentinels2(r) pre
2.     r ∈ 1 .. n
3.  begin
4.     for f ranging 0 .. n do
5.        if  f = 0 or else Capt[r, f] = 0  then
6.           X[r] ← f;
7.           if f ≠ 0 then
8.              Occupy(r, f); NbPlacedQueens ← NbPlacedQueens + 1 ;
9.           end if;
10.          if  NbFreeSquares = 0  then
11.             if  NbPlacedQueens < NbOpt  then
12.                Y[1 .. r] ← X[1 .. r]; Y[r + 1 .. n] ← (r + 1 .. n) × {0};
13.                NbOpt ← NbPlacedQueens
14.             end if
15.          elsif  r ≠ n  then
16.             Sentinels2(r + 1)
17.          end if;
18.          if f ≠ 0 then
19.             Free(r, f); NbPlacedQueens ← NbPlacedQueens − 1
20.          end if
21.       end if
22.    end for
23. end
```

The initial call is in the form:

```
1.  constants
2.     n ∈ ℕ₁ and n = …
3.  variables
4.     NbOpt ∈ 1 .. n + 1 and X ∈ 1 .. n → 0 .. n and Y ∈ 1 .. n → 0 .. n and
5.     Capt ∈ 1 .. n × 1 .. n → 1 .. n and
6.     NbPlacedQueens ∈ 0 .. n and NbFreeSquares ∈ 0 .. n²
7.  begin
8.     Capt ←  ⎡ 0  ⋯  0 ⎤
                ⎢ ⋮  ⋯  ⋮ ⎥  ;
                ⎣ 0  ⋯  0 ⎦
```

9.   NbOpt ← n + 1; NbPlacedQueens ← 0 ; NbFreeSquares ← n²;
10.   *Sentinels2*(1);
11.   **if** NbOpt ≠ n + 1 **then**
12.   **write**(*The problem of the sentinels − an optimal solution:* ,Y)
13.   **else**
14.   **write**(*No solution for the sentinels*)
15.   **end if**
16. **end**

Some experiments show that the gain between the first and the second solution is significant. So, for n = 10, the first solution returns a result in 143 s, whereas the second solution
reaches the same goal in 10 s. However, when n increases, the intrinsic complexity of the
approach makes the second version not more usable in practice than the first one.

Answers to problem 54. **The knight's tour**   *The problem is on page 227.*

54 - A 1   **Answer** 1.   The prefix $\begin{array}{c} a1 \\ b3 \\ c1 \\ a2 \end{array}$ is not included.

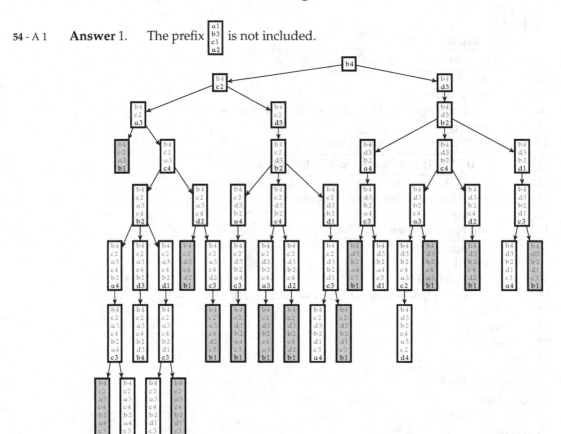

The leaves framed in a grey rectangle represent a success, while others materialize a dead
end. Indeed, the successors would introduce a circuit into the course.

54 - A 2   **Answer** 2.   The range of variation of j (the loop control variable) is the interval 1 .. 8,
of which we discard the elements that give access to a square already encountered. Two
constant joint arrays, A and B, defined on the interval 1 .. 8 specify the values that must be
added to the current coordinates of the knight in order to obtain the possible coordinates
after one move. The values taken by these two tables come from formula 5.2, page 227.

The condition *Satisf* of the generic procedure is instantiated as a Boolean expression which ensures that the new coordinates are located inside the chessboard. The condition *SolFound* checks that the position reached is the arrival square a.

The decision to store in the enumeration vector X the coordinates of the squares rather than the steps of the path complicates the expression on which k (the loop control variable) ranges. This makes it necessary to give some explanations about line 4 below. We must exclude from the interval $1..8$ all the values that represent squares belonging to the current path c and that are within knight reach of the extremity of c. The condition $X[l] = (X[l-1].abs + A[q], X[l-1].ord + B[q])$ means that $(X[l-1], X[l])$ is a step along the current course (and therefore that the square $X[l]$ is on the current course). The condition $X[l] = (X[i-1].abs + A[k], X[i-1].ord + B[k])$ specifies that from $X[l]$ the knight can reach one of the eight candidates for extending its course.

The following procedure *Knight1* can be deduced:

1. **procedure** *Knight1*(i) **pre**
2. $\quad i \in 1..n^2$
3. **begin**
4. $\quad$ **for** j ranging $1..8 - \left\{ k \,\middle|\, \exists l, q \cdot \begin{array}{l} k \in 1..8 \text{ and} \\ \left(\begin{array}{l} l \in 2..i-1 \text{ and } q \in 1..8 \text{ and} \\ X[l] = \begin{pmatrix} X[l-1].abs + A[q], \\ X[l-1].ord + B[q] \end{pmatrix} \text{ and} \\ X[l] = \begin{pmatrix} X[i-1].abs + A[k], \\ X[i-1].ord + B[k] \end{pmatrix} \text{ and} \end{array} \right) \end{array} \right\}$

$\quad$ **do**

5. $\quad\quad$ **if** $\left(\begin{array}{l} X[i-1].abs + A[j] \in 1..n \text{ and} \\ X[i-1].ord + B[j] \in 1..n \end{array} \right)$ **then**
6. $\quad\quad\quad X[i] \leftarrow (X[i-1].abs + A[j], X[i-1].ord + B[j])$;
7. $\quad\quad\quad$ **if** $\boxed{X[i] = a}$ **then**
8. $\quad\quad\quad\quad$ **write**$(X[1..i])$
9. $\quad\quad\quad$ **else**
10. $\quad\quad\quad\quad$ *Knight1*$(i+1)$
11. $\quad\quad\quad$ **end if**
12. $\quad\quad$ **end if**
13. $\quad$ **end for**
14. **end**

The calling program is in the form:

1. **constants**
2. $\quad$ Coord $= \{(abs, ord) \mid abs \in 1..n \text{ and } ord \in 1..n\}$ **and**
3. $\quad n \in \mathbb{N}_1$ **and** $n = \ldots$ **and**
4. $\quad A \in 1..8 \to -2..2$ **and** $A = [-2, -2, -1, -1, 1, 1, 2, 2]$ **and**
5. $\quad B \in 1..8 \to -2..2$ **and** $B = [-1, 1, -2, 2, -2, 2, -1, 1]$ **and**
6. $\quad d \in$ Coord **and** $d = \ldots$ **and** $a \in$ Coord **and** $a = \ldots$
7. **variables**
8. $\quad X \in 1..n^2 \to$ Coord
9. **begin**
10. $\quad X[1] \leftarrow d$;
11. $\quad$ *Knight1*(2)
12. **end**

A refinement of the procedure *Knight1* is needed so as to remove the set notation as well as the quantifier in line 4. One possibility is to update the global Boolean matrix L, defined on the domain $1..n \times 1..n$, that is such that $L[x, y]$ is **true** iff the square of coordinates (x, y) has not yet been visited (and therefore does not appear in $X[1 .. i - 1]$). The following version of the procedure and its calling program account for this remark. In this new version, the procedures *Do* and *Undo* must be instantiated. We also take this opportunity to factorize the calculations of the new position into the variables u and v.

```
 1. procedure Knight2(i) pre
 2.    i ∈ 1 .. n² and
 3.    u ∈ ℤ and v ∈ ℤ
 4. begin
 5.    for j ranging 1 .. 8 do
 6.       u ← X[i − 1].abs + A[j] ; v ← X[i − 1].ord + B[j] ;
 7.       if (u ∈ 1 .. n and v ∈ 1 .. n) and then L[u, v]  then
 8.          X[i] ← (u, v);  L[u, v] ← false;
 9.          if X[i] = a  then
10.             write(X[1 .. i])
11.          else
12.             Knight2(i + 1)
13.          end if;
14.          L[u, v] ← true
15.       end if
16.    end for
17. end
```

The short-circuiting operator in line 7 is mandatory. The procedure *Undo* must cancel the "occupation" of the square (u, v). The array L must be initialized to **true** before the initial call (see line 11 below):

```
 1. constants
 2.    Coord = {(abs, ord) | abs ∈ 1 .. n and ord ∈ 1 .. n} and
 3.    n ∈ ℕ₁ and n = ... and
 4.    A ∈ 1 .. 8 → −2 .. 2 and A = [−2, −2, −1, −1, 1, 1, 2, 2] and
 5.    B ∈ 1 .. 8 → −2 .. 2 and B = [−1, 1, −2, 2, −2, 2, −1, 1] and
 6.    X ∈ 1 .. n² → Coord and
 7.    d ∈ Coord and d = ... and a ∈ Coord and a = ...
 8. variables
 9.    L ∈ 1 .. n × 1 .. n → 𝔹
10. begin
                ⎡true  ⋯  true⎤
11.    L ←      ⎢  ⋮   ⋯    ⋮  ⎥ ;
                ⎣true  ⋯  true⎦
12.    X[1] ← d ;
13.    Knight2(2)
14. end
```

Complexity

The expression $\sum_{i=0}^{n-1} A_m^i$ (see formula 5.1, page 205) gives the number of calls demanded by the frame *TI* for the enumeration of all the total injective functions from $1 .. n$ to $1 .. m$. In the case of total injections from $(1 .. (n^2 - 1))$ to $(1 .. (n^2 - 1))$ (i.e. actually bijections), the formula is written: $\sum_{i=0}^{(n-1)^2-1} A_{(n-1)^2}^i$. However, as shown in the table below, for $d = (1, 1)$

and $a = (2,1)$, this result highly overestimates the actual number of calls to procedure *knight2*, since it does not take into account the specific constraints of the problem:

n	actual number of calls	$\displaystyle\sum_{i=0}^{(n-1)^2-1} A_{(n-1)^2}^i$
3	4	10
4	683	623 530
5	561 747	$3.59\ 10^{13}$
6	1 514 771 696 838	$2.66\ 10^{25}$

It can be observed that beyond $n = 5$ the algorithm cannot be used in practice.

Answer 3. This new procedure is largely inspired by *Knight1*, a designating the arrival square and *SolFound* testing if the square attained is a. *BetterSolution* and *KeepCurrContext* do not deserve any special comment.

We can wonder about the insertion of a pruning condition (for example, instead of the condition $i \neq n$ of the pattern *OptPI*). Since the knight moves no more than two squares in a given direction, the number of remaining moves is at least equal to half the distance in rank and file between the current square and the arrival square a. Hence, a pruning is possible when the condition

$$\left(i - 1 + \max\left(\left\lceil \left| \frac{X[i].abs - a.abs}{2} \right| \right\rceil, \left\lceil \left| \frac{X[i].ord - a.ord}{2} \right| \right\rceil \right) \right) \geqslant \text{CurrOptLg}.$$

is met, the global variable CurrOptLg representing the length of the current optimal route.

Answer 4. The code of the procedure *KnightOpt* is:

1. **procedure** *KnightOpt*(i) **pre**
2. $\quad i \in 1 .. n^2$ **and**
3. $\quad u \in -1 .. n + 2$ **and** $v \in -1 .. n + 2$
4. **begin**
5. $\quad$ **for** j ranging $1 .. 8 - \left\{ k \,\middle|\, \exists l, q \cdot \begin{array}{l} k \in 1 .. 8 \text{ and} \\ \left(\begin{array}{l} l \in 2 .. i - 1 \text{ and } q \in 1 .. 8 \text{ and} \\ X[l] = \begin{pmatrix} X[l-1].abs + A[q], \\ X[l-1].ord + B[q] \end{pmatrix} \text{ and} \\ X[l] = \begin{pmatrix} X[i-1].abs + A[k], \\ X[i-1].ord + B[k] \end{pmatrix} \text{ and} \end{array} \right) \end{array} \right\}$

   $\quad$ **do**
6. $\quad\quad u \leftarrow X[i-1].abs + A[j] \,; v \leftarrow X[i-1].ord + B[j] \,;$
7. $\quad\quad$ **if** $\boxed{u \in 1 .. n \text{ and } v \in 1 .. n}$ **then**
8. $\quad\quad\quad \boxed{X[i] \leftarrow (u, v) \,;}$
9. $\quad\quad\quad$ **if** $\boxed{X[i] = a}$ **then**
10. $\quad\quad\quad\quad$ **if** $\boxed{i - 1 < \text{CurrOptLg}}$ **then**
11. $\quad\quad\quad\quad\quad \boxed{Y \leftarrow X \,; \text{CurrOptLg} \leftarrow i - 1}$
12. $\quad\quad\quad$ **end if**

13.   **elsif** $\left(i - 1 + \max\left(\left\lceil \left| \dfrac{|X[i].abs - a.abs|}{2} \right| \right\rceil, \left\lceil \left| \dfrac{|X[i].ord - a.ord|}{2} \right| \right\rceil \right) \right) < \text{CurrOptLg}$ **then**

14.   *KnightOpt*$(i+1)$
15.   **end if**
16.   **end if**
17.   **end for**
18. **end**

The call is performed via the program:

1.   **constants**
2.   Coord $= \{(abs, ord) \mid abs \in 1..n$ **and** $ord \in 1..n\}$ **and**
3. $n \in \mathbb{N}_1$ **and** $n = \dots$ **and**
4. $A \in 1..8 \rightarrow -2..2$ **and** $A = [-2, -2, -1, -1, 1, 1, 2, 2]$ **and**
5. $B \in 1..8 \rightarrow -2..2$ **and** $B = [-1, 1, -2, 2, -2, 2, -1, 1]$ **and**
6. $d \in$ Coord **and** $d = \dots$ **and** $a \in$ Coord **and** $a = \dots$
7.   **variables**
8. $X \in 1..n^2 \rightarrow$ Coord **and** $Y \in 1..n^2 \rightarrow$ Coord **and** CurrOptLg $\in 1..n^2$
9.   **begin**
10. $X[1] \leftarrow d$;
11.   CurrOptLg $\leftarrow n^2$;
12.   *KnightOpt*(2) ;
13.   **if** CurrOptLg $\neq n^2$ **then**
14.   **write**(*An optimal course is* , Y[1 .. NbCpOpt])
15.   **else**
16.   **write**(*No solution for the knight course*)
17.   **end if**
18.   **end**

The refinement of this procedure is carried out in the same way as in the procedure *Knight1*.

Answers to problem 55. Eulerian circuits and paths   *The problem is on page 230.*

55 - A 1   **Answer 1.**   For the graph (a), there is no Eulerian circuit. On the other hand, there are Eulerian *paths*. One of them is represented by:

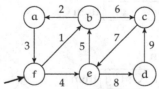

This path ensures that it is possible to draw the graph in a single stroke. However, the arrival point is different from the departure point. For the graph (b), there are Eulerian circuits, such as:

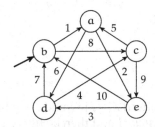

Answer 2.   The enumeration structure X is defined on the interval $1..(n+1)$ and valued   55 - A 2
in the set of nodes N. For a complete solution, the slice $X[1..n]$ is a total surjective function
from the interval $1..n$ to N, hence the choice *a priori* of the pattern *AllTS* (see figure 5.7,
page 211). When X is under development, $X[1..i-1]$ defines the graph $G' = (N', V')$
where $N' = \{X[1],\ldots,X[i-1]\}$ and $V' = \{(X[1],X[2]),(X[2],X[3]),\ldots,(X[i-2],X[i-1])\}$. G'
is a subgraph of G. The path $\langle X[1],\ldots,X[i-2],X[i-1]\rangle$ is an Eulerian one for the graph
G'. If on the one hand X is complete and on the other hand $X[1] = X[n+1]$, the path is an
Eulerian circuit. In such a situation, checking surjectivity is unnecessary. The pattern *AllT*
(simpler than *AllTS*) is sufficient.

Answer 3.   The set that the variable j runs through is the set of successors to $X[i-$ 55 - A 3
$1]$ in the graph G (line 4 of the procedure *EulerianCircuits1*). In line 5, $SetArcs(X[1..i-$
$1], G)$ represents the set of arcs of G stored in the slice $X[1..i-1]$. The instance of the
generic procedure*Satisf* (line 4 in the program below) consists in checking the arc under
consideration is not already used. In line 7, the condition $(i = n+1)$ verifies that there are
$(n+1)$ nodes in the Eulerian path of graph G. In the same line, the condition *SolFound* is
instantiated by the expression $X[1] = X[i]$ that checks that the last node of the path is the
same as the first one). This leads to the following program:

```
1.  procedure EulerianCircuits1(i) pre
2.      i ∈ 1..n+1
3.  begin
4.      for j ranging Succ_G(X[i−1]) do
5.          if (X[i−1],j) ∉ SetArcs(X[1..i−1],G) then
6.              X[i] ← j;
7.              if i = n+1 and X[1] = X[i] then
8.                  write(X)
9.              elsif i ≠ n+1 then
10.                 EulerianCircuits1(i+1)
11.             end if
12.         end if
13.     end for
14. end
```

The call is made through:

```
1.  constants
2.      m ∈ N and m = ... and
3.      N = 1..m and V ⊆ N × N and V = {...} and n = card(V) and
4.      G = (N,V)
5.  variables
6.      X ∈ 1..n+1 → N
7.  begin
8.      for s ∈ N do
9.          X[1] ← s;
```

```
    10.     EulerianCircuits1(2)
    11.   end for
    12. end
```

Remark

To be perfectly faithful to the pattern *AllT*, j would have had to pass through the interval
$1 .. n$ in the procedure *EulerianCircuit1* and then be filtered in the conditional statement to
take only values belonging to the set $Succ_G(X[i-1])$. The above solution is more efficient.

The search performed in the condition of line 5 of the procedure *EulerianCircuits1* can be
expensive. It is preferable to strengthen the recursion invariant of the procedure with the
following property: "L is a Boolean array defined on $1 .. m \times 1 .. m$ such that $L[x, y]$ is true
iff the arc (x, y) does not belong to G' (it does not appear in $X[1 .. i-1]$)". The following
solution is obtained:

```
    1. procedure EulerianCircuits2(i) pre
    2.    i ∈ 1 .. n + 1
    3. begin
    4.    for j ranging Succ_G(X[i − 1]) do
    5.       if  L[X[i − 1], j]  then
    6.          X[i] ← j ;  L[X[i − 1], j] ← false;
    7.          if i = n + 1 and  X[1] = X[i]  then
    8.             write(X)
    9.          elsif  i ≠ n + 1  then
    10.            EulerianCircuits2(i + 1)
    11.         end if;
    12.          L[X[i − 1], j] ← true
    13.      end if
    14.   end for
    15. end
```

This time, the two procedures *Do* (line 6) and *Undo* (line 12) are necessary. The calling
program becomes:

```
    1. constants
    2.    m ∈ ℕ and m = ... and
    3.    N = 1 .. m and V ⊆ N × N and V = {...} and n = card(V) and
    4.    G = (N, V)
    5. variables
    6.    X ∈ 1 .. n → N and
    7.    L ∈ 1 .. m × 1 .. m → 𝔹
    8. begin
```

$$
9. \quad L \leftarrow \begin{bmatrix} \text{true} & \cdots & \text{true} \\ \vdots & \cdots & \vdots \\ \text{true} & \cdots & \text{true} \end{bmatrix} ;
$$

```
    10.   for s ∈ N do
    11.      X[1] ← s;
    12.      EulerianCircuits2(2)
    13.   end for
    14. end
```

Remark

In graph theory, a theorem due to Euler provides a necessary and sufficient condition for the existence of (at least) one Eulerian circuit in a directed connected graph. This theorem asserts that an Eulerian circuit exists iff for each vertex s, there are as many arcs originated in s as there are arcs ending in s. This property – that is easy to check – is useful to avoid a costly search of Eulerian circuits where there are none.

Answer 4. Here, we are looking for an Eulerian *path* in an *undirected* graph. An edge is assumed to be represented by a pair of vertices. As to the aspect "string of edges" (see section 1.5.2, page 25), the change concerns line 7 of the procedure *EulerianCircuits2*, where it is no longer necessary to check that we go back to the starting point (vertex). To account for the fact that the graph is "undirected", it is sufficient to make sure that neither the arc $(X[i-1], j)$, nor the reverse arc $(j, X[i-1])$ belongs to the partial solution. The following code is associated with the procedure *EulerianPaths*:

55 - A 4

```
 1. procedure EulerianPaths(i) pre
 2.    i ∈ 1 .. n + 1
 3. begin
 4.    for j ranging Succ_G(X[i − 1]) do
 5.       if  L[X[i − 1], j] and L[j, X[i − 1]]  then
 6.          X[i] ← j;  L[X[i − 1], j] ← false; L[j, X[i − 1]] ← false;
 7.          if  i = n + 1  then
 8.             write(X)
 9.          else
10.             EulerianPaths(i + 1)
11.          end if;
12.           L[X[i − 1], j] ← true; L[j, X[i − 1]] ← true
13.       end if
14.    end for
15. end
```

Here, the array L plays a role similar to that it had in the procedure *EulerianCircuits2* and the calling program is similar to that of the procedure *EulerianCircuits2* (see page 266).

Remark

The search for Eulerian paths or circuits in a graph belongs to the class of polynomial problems. Therefore, algorithms more efficient than those presented in this exercise do exist. The reader is invited to build such algorithms.

Answers to problem 56. Hamiltonian paths *The problem is on page 231.*

Answer 1. There are three solutions starting with BETE, then TELE. Expressed with their numbers, these are $\langle 1, 5, 2, 4, 3, 6 \rangle$, $\langle 1, 5, 2, 6, 4, 3 \rangle$ and $\langle 1, 5, 3, 6, 2, 4 \rangle$.

56 - A 1

It can be noticed that the solution $\langle 1, 5, 2, 6, 4, 3 \rangle$ could be continued by the domino 1 and, by circular permutation, provide solutions starting with any node. However, some solutions do not start with node 1 and are not one of the circular permutations mentioned above, for instance $\langle 2, 6, 4, 5, 3, 1 \rangle$. Therefore, all the Hamiltonian paths *cannot* be deduced from those calculated with a given starting node.

56 - A 2   **Answer** 2.   The vector X[1 .. n] is a bijection from 1 .. n to 1 .. n (in other words a permutation of the interval 1 .. n) such that any pair (k, X[k]) is an arc of the graph. The slice X[1 .. i − 1] is a total bijective function from the interval 1 .. i − 1 to a subset of 1 .. n. Therefore, the appropriate pattern is *AllTI* (see figure 5.7, page 211) which goes through all the bijections if the domain and the codomain of X have the same cardinality.

56 - A 3   **Answer** 3.   The recursion tree appears in figure 5.24.

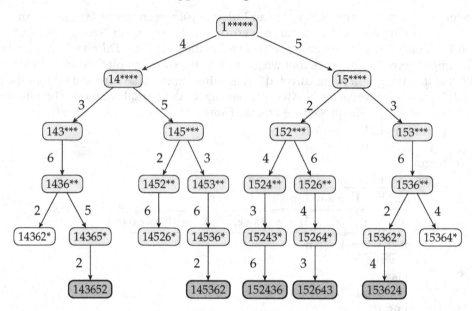

Fig. 5.24 – Hamiltonian path—The dominoes—Recursion tree. The white leaves represent dead ends. Other leaves are solutions.

56 - A 4   **Answer** 4.   The procedure to build, *Domino1*, is an instance of the procedure *AllTI* (All Total Injective functions, see figure 5.7, page 211), in which X is a function of the interval 1 .. n to itself (thus a bijection). The role of the condition *Satisf* is to check the specific property of the problem demanding that the current node j is actually a successor of the node X[i − 1]. We get:

```
 1. procedure Domino1(i) pre
 2.    i ∈ 1 .. n
 3. begin
 4.    for j ∈ (1 .. n − codom(X[1 .. i − 1])) do
 5.       if  j ∈ Succ(X([i − 1]))  then
 6.          X[i] ← j ;
 7.          if i = n then
 8.             write(X)
 9.          else
10.             Domino1(i + 1)
11.          end if
12.       end if
13.    end for
14. end
```

The following calling program provides all the solutions:

```
1.  constants
2.    n ∈ ℕ and n = ...
3.  variables
4.    X ∈ 1..n → 1..n
5.  begin
6.    for s ∈ 1..n do
7.      X[1] ← s ;
8.      Domino1(2)
9.    end for
10. end
```

A more efficient version of this procedure can be obtained by considering only possible successor nodes:

```
1.  procedure Domino2(i) pre
2.    i ∈ 1..n
3.  begin
4.    for j ∈ (Succ(X[i − 1] − codom(X[1..i − 1]))) do
5.      X[i] ← j ;
6.      if i = n then
7.        write(X)
8.      else
9.        Domino2(i + 1)
10.     end if
11.   end for
12. end
```

This version produces the tree of figure 5.24, page 268.

Remark

Although this problem seems close to that of the search for Eulerian paths or circuits, it belongs to the class of NP-complete problems. It is highly unlikely that a polynomial algorithm to solve it does exist.

Answers to problem 57. **The traveling salesman** *The problem is on* page 233.

Answer 1. There are $(n-1)!$ permutations of the n cities which start with a given city. 57 - A 1 Due to the fact that the graph is undirected, one might think of cutting the calculations in half (any path can be traveled one way or the other), but this remark cannot be exploited in the patterns dedicated to the search for an optimal solution.

Answer 2. Let us consider three cities x, y and z such that $D(x,z) > D(x,y) + D(y,z)$ 57 - A 2 and $\langle ..., y, ..., x, z, ... \rangle$ is an optimal Hamiltonian route. Obviously, replacing $\langle x, z \rangle$ by $\langle x, y, z \rangle$, a shorter journey is obtained.

Answer 3. We have to find a permutation of N that extends back to the starting node. 57 - A 3 X is thus a bijection of $1..n$ to $1..n$ (i.e. a permutation of the interval $1..n$), constrained by the fact that for any k, $(X[k − 1], X[k])$ is an edge of the graph. Therefore, the pattern to be instantiated is *OptTI*, applied to the bijective case (the domain and the codomain of X have the same cardinality). The code is obtained from that of *OptPI* (see figure 5.8, page 212) by replacing the set of the **for** loop in line 4 by:

$$(1 .. n) - \mathrm{codom}(X[1 .. i - 1]).$$

57 - A 4   **Answer 4.**   Each path is developed twice. The optimal overall path value is 11. We get the tree in figure 5.25, where: (i) the cost of each arc is mentioned on its right preceded by the sign $+$ and (ii) the cost of each path is affixed to the right of each node.

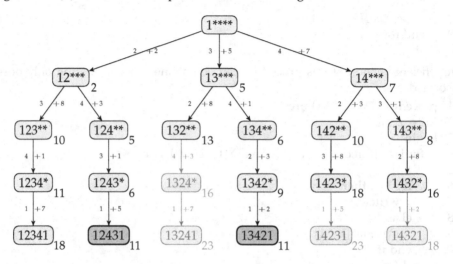

Fig. 5.25 – The recursion tree for graph (a) of figure 5.15, page 234.

A possible pruning consists in interrupting the course of a permutation if the provisional length exceeds the current minimum. On the tree in figure 5.25, the light grey portions correspond to parts of the tree that are undeveloped due to the triggering of the pruning condition.

Remark

Another pruning strategy can be added to the first one. It consists in using as a lower bound of the remaining length the number of elementary journeys to be made between two cities, multiplied by the smallest length between two cities that have not yet been visited. This heuristics is not implemented in the solution proposed hereafter.

57 - A 5   **Answer 5.**   We instantiate the pattern to list all the candidate cycles, that is, all the city permutations beginning with the starting city (without forgetting to add the return to the city of departure). Each permutation is associated with a length given by the sum of the lengths of the elementary paths composing it. The permutation that gives the shortest total path is retained.

The set traversed by j (the loop control variable) is the set of successors of node $X[i-1]$ minus the nodes already used. DepCity is the city of departure and Y is the optimal solution retained. The variable CurrLg contains the length of the path under construction, while the variable OptLg represents the length of the best Hamiltonian cycle already found.

The condition *Satisf* applies the first pruning mentioned before. The procedure *Do* computes the length of the path under construction. The condition $(i = n)$ means that all cities have been visited once and only once; returning to the departure city is taken into account by the condition *BetterSolution*. The condition *BetterSolution* is met if the length of the current path plus the distance necessary to come back to the departure city is shorter than the best solution already found. The procedure *Undo* is limited to subtract the previously added distance from CurrLg.

```
1.  procedure TravSalesman(i) pre
2.     i ∈ 1 .. n
3.  begin
4.     for j ranging Succ(X[i − 1]) − codom(X[1 .. i − 1]) do
5.        if  CurrLg + D(X[i − 1], j) < OptLg  then
6.           X[i] ← j ;  CurrLg ← CurrLg + D(X[i − 1], j);
7.           if i = n then
8.              if  CurrLgr + D(X[i], DepCity) < OptLg  then
9.                 Y[1 .. n] ← X ; Y[n + 1] ← DepCity ;
10.                OptLg ← CurrLg + D(X[i], DepCity)
11.             end if
12.          else
13.             TravSalesman(i + 1)
14.          end if;
15.           CurrLg ← CurrLg − D(X[i − 1], j)
16.       end if
17.    end for
18. end
```

The call of this procedure for the test set (a) in figure 5.15, page 234, is done as follows:

```
1.  constants
2.     N = {1, 2, 3, 4} and n = card(N) and
3.     DepCity = 1 and
```

$$
4. \quad D \in N \times N \to \mathbb{R}_+^* \text{ and } D = \begin{bmatrix} \infty & 2 & 5 & 7 \\ 2 & \infty & 8 & 3 \\ 5 & 8 & \infty & 1 \\ 7 & 3 & 1 & \infty \end{bmatrix}
$$

```
5.  variables
6.     X ∈ 1 .. n → 1 .. n and
7.     Y ∈ 1 .. n + 1 → 1 .. n and
8.     CurrLg ∈ N and OptLg ∈ N
9.  begin
10.    OptLg ← ∞ ; CurrLg ← 0 ;
11.    X[1] ← DepCity ;
12.    TravSalesman(2) ;
13.    if OptLg = ∞ then
14.       write(No solution for the traveling salesman)
15.    else
16.       write(Y)
17.    end if
18. end
```

The final value of the variable LgOpt is used to determine whether or not the problem has a solution.

Answers to problem 58. **Graph isomorphism**   *The problem is on page 234.*

58 - A 1   **Answer 1.**   The values of the in-degrees and out-degrees are given hereafter.

G :

	1	2	3	4	5
Out-degree	3	1	2	0	1
In-degree	1	1	2	2	1

H :

	a	b	c	d	e
Out-degree	1	2	3	1	0
In-degree	1	2	1	1	2

58 - A 2   **Answer 2.**   Given the constraints imposed by the question, nodes 1, 3 and 4 are compulsorily in correspondence with nodes c, b and e. On the other hand, node 2 (respectively 5) can be connected either with a, or with d. Consequently, the two following possibilities of correspondence are:

$$B = \begin{array}{|c|c|c|c|c|} \hline 1 & 2 & 3 & 4 & 5 \\ \hline c & a & b & e & d \\ \hline \end{array} \quad \text{and} \quad B' = \begin{array}{|c|c|c|c|c|} \hline 1 & 2 & 3 & 4 & 5 \\ \hline c & d & b & e & a \\ \hline \end{array}$$

As shown in the schemas below, the bijection B' is not an isomorphism (on the other hand, it is already known that B is actually an isomorphism between G and H).

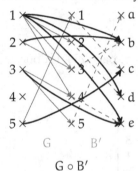

$G \circ B'$

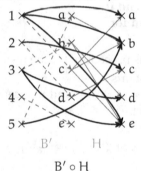

$B' \circ H$

It is clear that the mapping of vertices of the same degree is a condition necessary *but not sufficient* to guarantee that the relationship so defined establishes an isomorphism between the two graphs. However, this condition can serve as a pruning strategy.

58 - A 3   **Answer 3.**   The nature of the problem imposes an enumeration structure X that represents a total bijection (see paragraph titled "Enumeration of total injective and bijective functions, production of permutations", page 204). The convenient pattern is therefore *AllTI* (see figure 5.7, page 211). Vertexes of G_1 are numbered from 1 to n and we build the enumeration vector X of size n with the vertexes of G_2. Such a vector represents a bijection between the vertexes of N_1 and N_2; it corresponds to an isomorphism if $V_1 \circ X = X \circ V_2$. As it stands, this condition can be checked only after the vector X is complete. However, to avoid dead ends, the search space can be pruned by checking that in-degrees of the two vertexes in correspondence are the same as well as their out-degrees.

58 - A 4   **Answer 4.**   The recursion tree for the introductory example is presented in figure 5.26.

58 - A 5   **Answer 5.**   The patterns of figure 5.7, page 211, do not solve directly the problem posed since they enumerate the solutions, whereas a count is required here. We will instantiate the pattern *AllTI* (see figure 5.7, page 211) adapted so that the *number* of isomorphisms is displayed (not isomorphisms themselves). The condition *Satisf* verifies the equality of the in-degrees of the two vertexes in (possible) correspondence as well as their out-degrees. *SolFound* checks that once complete (containing n values), the vector X is actually an isomorphism between graphs G_1 and G_2.

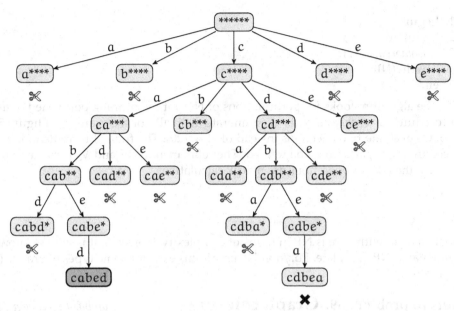

Fig. 5.26 – Graph isomorphism—Recursion tree for the case of figure 5.16, page 235. � *: pruning due to incompatible degrees.* ✖ *: leaf removed since not representing an isomorphism. The leaf in dark grey represents the unique solution.*

1. **procedure** *Isomorphism*(i) **pre**
2. $i \in 1..n$
3. **begin**
4.   **for** j **ranging** $N_2 - \text{codom}(X[1..i-1])$ **do**
5.   **if** $\boxed{d^+(i) = d^+(j) \quad \textbf{and} \quad d^-(i) = d^-(j)}$ **then**
6. $X[i] \leftarrow j;$
7.   **if** $i = n$ **and then** $\boxed{V_1 \circ X = Xb \circ V_2}$ **then**
8. $\text{NbIsum} \leftarrow \text{NbIsum} + 1$
9.   **elsif** $i \neq n$ **then**
10.   *Isomorphism*(i + 1)
11.   **end if**
12.   **end if**
13. **end for**
14. **end**

Above, the short-circuiting operator **and then** (line 7) is necessary for the correctness of the algorithm. The calling program is:

1. **constants**
2. $n \in \mathbb{N}_1$ **and** $n = \ldots$ **and**
3. $N_1 = 1..n$ **and** $N_2 = 1..n$ **and**
4. $V_1 \subseteq N_1 \times N_1$ **and** $V_1 = \{\ldots\}$ **and**
5. $V_2 \subseteq N_2 \times N_2$ **and** $V_2 = \{\ldots\}$ **and**
6. $\text{card}(V_1) = \text{card}(V_2)$ **and**
7. $G_1 = (N_1, V_1)$ **and** $G_2 = (N_2, V_2)$
8. **variables**
9. $X \in 1..n \rightarrow N_2$ **and**
10. $\text{NbIsum} \in \mathbb{N}$

11. **begin**
12. $NbIsum \leftarrow 0$;
13.   *Isomorphism*(1) ;
14.   **write**(NbIsum)
15. **end**

Basically, the algorithm looks for permutations of N_2, but the pruning performed in line 5 of the procedure *Isomorphism* avoids to enumerate them all (for the example of figure 5.16, page 235, we evaluate two bijections instead of $5! = 120$). The framed formula in line 7 of the procedure *Isomorphism* must be refined. The refinement of V_1 and V_2 is carried out by matrixes and the related operations are matrix calculations.

Remark

The problem dealt with here is NP in terms of complexity. However, it is not yet known if its polynomial or NP-complete. Polynomial algorithms exist for some types of graphs (e.g. planar graphs).

Answers to problem 59. Graph coloring   *The problem is on page 236.*

59 - A 1   **Answer 1.**   The graph $G_{X'}$ hereafter is obtained through the following permutation of colors: $\{2 \mapsto 1, 1 \mapsto 3, 3 \mapsto 2\}$. On the other hand, in the graph $G_{X''}$, the colors assigned to the vertices e and c are different; therefore, this coloring cannot correspond to a permutation of the colors initially chosen.

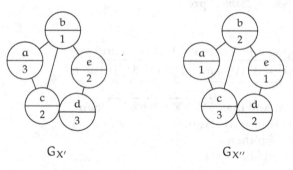

$G_{X'}$ $\qquad\qquad\qquad\qquad$ $G_{X''}$

59 - A 2   **Answer 2.**   If $(s, c) \in V \circ Z$, c is a forbidden color for the node s since it is assigned to one of its neighbors. Expressing that the colors of the nodes and their neighbors are different is formalized by the expression $Z \cap (V \circ Z) = \varnothing$. This can be observed on the schema hereafter applying to the graph $G_{X''}$.

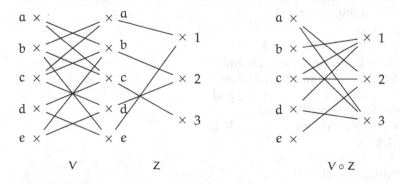

V $\qquad\qquad$ Z $\qquad\qquad\qquad\qquad$ V ∘ Z

Answer 3.   Nodes are assumed to be coded by the values of the interval $1 .. n$ and thus **59 - A 3**
the enumeration vector $X[1 .. n]$ represents a total function from the interval $1 .. n$ to $1 .. m$.
This function is neither surjective (a color may not be used), nor injective (several nodes
can be associated with the same color). To be a coloring, this vector must comply with the
property of the previous question. The partial vector $X[1 .. i-1]$ represents a coloring of
the graph restricted to the nodes labeled from 1 to $(i-1)$. The pattern that applies is *OneT*
(see figure 5.9, page 213).

Answer 4.   Limiting ourselves to applying brute force would be to verify in the generic **59 - A 4**
condition *SolFound* that the condition in question 2 is satisfied. A pruning is possible by
considering that, since $X[1 .. i-1]$ is a partial coloring, the treatment of the node i can be
limited to checking that none of its neighbors of number lower than i has the same color
as the one we are about to assign to i. The recursion tree applying this pruning is shown
in figure 5.27.

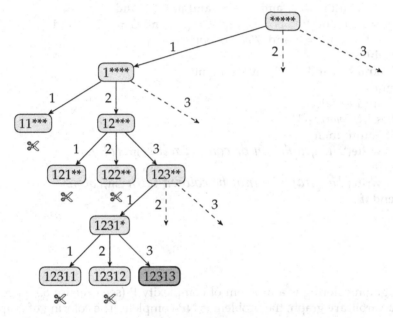

Fig. 5.27 – Graph coloring—Recursion tree. ✂: *pruning due to the impossibility to color the partial
graph. Dashed arcs represent unexplored branches. The leaf in dark grey represents the first solution
encountered through a left-right depth-first exploration of the tree.*

Answer 5.   We have to properly instantiate the pattern *OneT* (see figure 5.9, page 213) **59 - A 5**
since we are looking for a solution for a total function from the set of vertices to the set
of colors. The generic function *Satisf* in line 7 was commented in the previous question.
The refinement of the corresponding formula is left to the reader. There is no need for the
generic function *SolFound* (line 9) since, if $(i = n)$, all the vertices are colored. So we get the
following procedure:

1. **procedure** *PossibleColoring*(i) **pre**
2. $i \in 1 .. n$ **and**
3. $j \in 1 .. m+1$
4. **begin**
5. $j \leftarrow 1$;
6.   **while not**$(j = m+1$ **or** Found) **do**

```
7.      if  ∀k · (k ∈ Succ(i) and k < i  ⇒  j ≠ X[k])  then
8.          X[i] ← j ;
9.          if i = n then
10.             Found ← true
11.         else
12.             PossibleColoring(i + 1)
13.         end if
14.     end if;
15.     j ← j + 1
16.   end while
17. end
```

that is called by the program:

```
1. constants
2.    n ∈ ℕ₁ and n = ... and m ∈ ℕ₁ and m = ... and
3.    N = 1 .. n and V ⊆ N × N and V = {...} and G = (N, V) and
4.    V ∩ id(1 .. n) = ∅ and  /% No loop %/
5. variables
6.    Found ∈ 𝔹 and X ∈ 1 .. n → 1 .. m
7. begin
8.    Found ← false ;
9.    PossibleColoring(1) ;
10.   if Found then
11.      write(The graph can be colored with , m, colors)
12.   else
13.      write(The graph cannot be colored with , m, colors)
14.   end if
15. end
```

Remark

For $m = 2$, graph coloring is a problem of complexity P (see exercise 83, page 363). For $m > 2$ and an arbitrary graph, the problem is NP-complete. The coloring of graphs with a minimal number of colors has many applications, such as the allocation of frequencies in certain telecommunication networks or the resolution of sudoku grids. This latter problem is addressed through an ad hoc approach in exercise 63, page 240.

Answers to problem 60. U.S. Presidential Elections   *The problem is on page 237.*

60 - A 1   **Answer 1.**   The enumeration vector is nothing but that evoked in the statement of the problem. X is defined on the interval 1 .. n and valued on the interval 0 .. 1. No complementary property is required. Therefore, the convenient pattern is *AllT* (see figure 5.7, page 211).

60 - A 2   **Answer 2.**   The global variable NbRep represents the current number of Republican delegates (another correct solution is obtained by swapping the role of Republicans and Democrats). A desired configuration is such that this number is exactly equal to half of the total number T of electors and a leaf in the recursion tree has been reached. Pruning is carried out by watching in *Satisf* that the Republican party: (i) has not already a number

of delegates exceeding T/2 and (ii) can still reach a number of delegates at least equal to T/2. It is assumed that the expression T/2 is evaluated by providing the result as a *real* number (not the Euclidean quotient).

1. **procedure** *USElections*(i) **pre**
2. $i \in 1 .. n$
3. **begin**
4.   **for** j **ranging** $0 .. 1$ **do**
5.   **if** $\boxed{NbRep + j \cdot DEL[i] \leqslant \dfrac{T}{2} \text{ and } NbRep + j \cdot DEL[i] + \sum\limits_{j=i+1}^{n} DEL[j] \geqslant \dfrac{T}{2}}$

     then
6. $X[i] \leftarrow j \; ; \; \boxed{NbRep \leftarrow NbRep + j \cdot DEL[i]} \; ;$
7.   **if** $i = n$ **and** $\boxed{NbRep = \dfrac{T}{2}}$ **then**
8.   **write**(X)
9.   **elsif** $i \neq n$ **then**
10.   *USElections*$(i + 1)$
11.   **end if**;
12. $\boxed{NbDel \leftarrow NbRep - j \cdot DEL[i]}$
13.   **end if**
14.   **end for**
15. **end**

Calling the procedure *USElections* is done by the program:

1. **constants**
2. $n \in \mathbb{N}_1$ **and** $n = \ldots$ **and**
3. $DEL \in 1 .. n \rightarrow \mathbb{N}$ **and** $DEL = [\ldots]$ **and**
4. $T = \sum\limits_{k=1}^{n} DEL[k]$
5. **variables**
6. $X \in 1 .. n \rightarrow 0 .. 1$ **and** $NbDel \in 0 .. T$
7. **begin**
8. $NbDel \leftarrow 0 \; ;$
9.   *USElections*(1)
10. **end**

In the conditional statement of line 5, it is easy to avoid the systematic calculation of the sum: it is sufficient to refine it by an appropriate strengthening of the recursion invariant.

Answer 3.   The number of such configurations is even because every solution has a counterpart: the one where in each state the voters gave the majority to the other party.   60 - A 3

Answer 4.   It is sufficient to arbitrarily fix the choice of the first state, which leads to the calling program hereafter: 60 - A 4

1. **constants**
2. $n \in \mathbb{N}_1$ **and** $n = \ldots$ **and**
3. $DEL \in 1 .. n \rightarrow \mathbb{N}$ **and** $DEL = [\ldots]$ **and** $T = \sum\limits_{k=1}^{n} DEL[k]$
4. **variables**
5. $X \in 1 .. n \rightarrow 0 .. 1$ **and** $NbDel \in 0 .. T$
6. **begin**

7.   NbDel ← DEL[1] ;
8.   X[1] ← 1 ;
9.   *USElections*(2)
10. **end**

Answer 5.   It is enough to impose that the total number of delegates be odd.

Answers to problem 61. **Crypto-arithmetics**   *The problem is on page 238.*

Answer 1.   The algorithm is an instance of the pattern *AllTI* (see figure 5.7, page 211). The enumeration vector X is such that $X[1 .. i - 1]$ is an injection from the $(i - 1)$ first letters to $0 .. 9$. Since no pruning is envisaged, no other property of this injection has to be checked (before X be complete).

Answer 2.   Let us consider the pattern *AllTI*. The conditional statement associated with *Satisf* is useless (there is no pruning). The condition *SolFound* is limited to calling the function *ExactCalc*. The procedures *Do* and *Undo* do not apply. The corresponding procedure is:

```
1.  procedure CryptoArith(i) pre
2.     i ∈ 1 .. n
3.  begin
4.     for j ranging 0 .. 9 − (codom(X[1 .. i − 1])) do
5.        X[i] ← j;
6.        if i = n and then  ExactCalc  then
7.           write(X)
8.        elsif i ≠ n then
9.           CryptoArith(i + 1)
10.       end if
11.    end for
12. end
```

It is of importance to notice that the short-circuiting operator "**and then**" in line 6 cannot be replaced by a simple "**and**". Its presence is mandatory for the correctness of the algorithm. The following program allows to obtain all the solutions:

```
1.  constants
2.     L ⊂ Σ and L = {...} and n = card(L)
3.  variables
4.     X ∈ 1 .. n → 0 .. 9
5.  begin
6.     CryptoArith(1)
7.  end
```

Strings like $\mathcal{FIVE}$, $\mathcal{ONE}$, etc., formal arguments of the operation, do not appear in the code above; they are used and managed only by the procedure *ExactCalc*.

Answer 3.   We can look for constraints proper to the problem and use them for the design of pruning conditions. In the example of the statement, the constraints: (i) $(\mathcal{F} \leqslant 2)$, since $\mathcal{F}$ is the sum of three digits and (ii) $(O = 0 \text{ or } O = 5)$, since $O + O + \mathcal{E} = \mathcal{E}, ,$ are easy to point out. It is however difficult to imagine a systematic means for extracting this type of constraints, which rarely appear as independent equations.

Variant

The roles of letters and digits can be exchanged. The enumeration vector X is then a vector of *letters*, while E represents the set of ten digits. The principle consists in searching for a *partial* bijection between E and X: some digits have no image in the set of letters. Consequently, from an efficiency point of view, this variant is undoubtedly less interesting than the version developed above (see section 5.1.2.2, page 207, for counting partial injections).

Answers to problem 62. Latin squares

The problem is on page 239.

Answer 1. The enumeration vector represents a total function from the Cartesian product $(1 .. n \times 1 .. n)$ to $(1 .. n)$. However, on closer inspection, we can see that, restricted to a given row or column, the function is a *bijection*. Therefore, X is an array $n \times n$ valued in the interval $1 .. n$ such that any partial row (respectively column) $X[r, 1 .. c]$ (respectively $X[1 .. r, c]$) is an *injective* function into the interval $1 .. n$. So the pattern that applies here is *AllTI* (see figure 5.7, page 211) arranged in the manner of *T2D* (see page 203) to handle a two-dimensional definition domain.

62 - A 1

The set that j will go through is therefore the interval $1 .. n$, minus the values of X present before the considered element in the line on the one hand, and the values present above the considered element in the column on the other hand, i.e.

$$1 .. n - (\text{codom}(X[r, 1 .. c - 1]) \cup \text{codom}(X[1 .. r - 1, c])).$$

Answer 2. An incomplete example of recursion tree is proposed in figure 5.28, page 280. It illustrates the two possible cases: failure due to an empty search set and success.

62 - A 2

Answer 3. The code obtained by the instantiation of the pattern *AllTI* is the following:

62 - A 3

```
1.  procedure LatinSquare(r, c) pre
2.      r ∈ 1 .. n and c ∈ 1 .. n
3.  begin
4.      for j ranging 1 .. n − ( codom(X[r, 1 .. c − 1])
                                      ∪
                                 codom(X[1 .. r − 1, c]) ) do
5.          X[r, c] ← j ;
6.          if r = n and c = n then
7.              write(X)
8.          else
9.              if c = n then
10.                 LatinSquare(r + 1, 1)
11.             else
12.                 LatinSquare(r, c + 1)
13.             end if
14.         end if
15.     end for
16. end
```

The calling program is:

```
1.  constants
2.      n ∈ N₁ and n = ...
3.  variables
4.      X ∈ 1 .. n × 1 .. n → 1 .. n
```

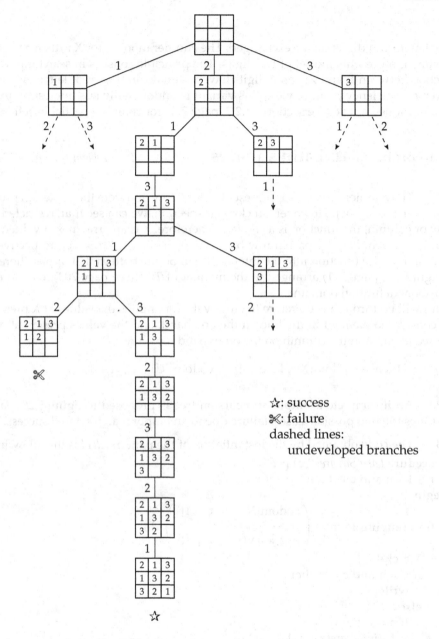

Fig. 5.28 – Recursion tree for a Latin square of order 3.

5. **begin**
6.   *LatinSquare*(1, 1)
7. **end**

62 - A 4   **Answer** 4.   It is of course possible to look to the left and above the position (r, c) to check that the element about to be placed there is not already present on the row portion or on the column portion. For efficiency reasons, it is preferable to strengthen the invariant by adding to X the Boolean arrays H and V defined on the Cartesian product $1..n \times 1..n$. H is such that $H[j, c]$ is **true** if and only if the value j is absent from the row portion $X[r, 1..c-1]$.

Similarly, V is such that $V[r, j]$ is **true** if and only if the value j is absent from the column portion $X[1 .. r - 1, c]$. The establishment and maintenance of these properties is done on the one hand in the call, and on the other hand in the procedures *Do* and *UnDo*. In the end, we get the following version:

```
 1. procedure LatinSquare2(l, c) pre
 2.    r ∈ 1 .. n and c ∈ 1 .. n
 3. begin
 4.    for j ranging 1 .. n do
 5.       if H[j, c] and V[r, j] then
 6.          X[r, c] ← j;  H[j, c] ← false; V[r, j] ← false;
 7.          if r = n and c = n then
 8.             write(X)
 9.          else
10.             if c = n then
11.                LatinSquare2(r + 1, 1)
12.             else
13.                LatinSquare2(r, c + 1)
14.             end if
15.          end if;
16.           H[j, c] ← true; V[r, j] ← true
17.       end if
18.    end for
19. end
```

and the calling program:

```
1. constants
2.    n ∈ ℕ₁ and n = ...
3. variables
4.    H ∈ 1 .. n × 1 .. n → 𝔹 and V ∈ 1 .. n × 1 .. n → 𝔹 and
5.    X ∈ 1 .. n × 1 .. n → 1 .. n
6. begin
```

$$
7. \quad H \leftarrow \begin{bmatrix} \text{true} & \cdots & \text{true} \\ \cdots & \cdots & \cdots \\ \cdots & \cdots & \cdots \\ \text{true} & \cdots & \text{true} \end{bmatrix} ; V \leftarrow \begin{bmatrix} \text{true} & \cdots & \text{true} \\ \cdots & \cdots & \cdots \\ \cdots & \cdots & \cdots \\ \text{true} & \cdots & \text{true} \end{bmatrix} ;
$$

```
8.    LatinSquare2(1, 1)
9. end
```

Answer 5.   Only the diagonals of the odd-order squares intersect in the central square. 62 - A 5
The four corners of the square should therefore be identical, which prohibits any other square than that of order 1 from being Latin, since the four corners are not confused but contain identical values.

To obtain only the antidiagonal Latin squares, a solution consists in arranging the procedure *LatinSquare* so as to introduce the conditional statement associated with the function *Satisf* after the beginning of the **for** loop. This is in the form:

$$CorrectNWSEDiag(r, c, j) \text{ and } CorrectSWNEDiag(r, c, j)$$

where these two new operations are specified as follows:

- *CorrectNWSEDiag*(r, c, v) is a Boolean function that returns **true** if the position (r, c) of the square X is not located on the diagonal running from the North-West corner to the SouthEast corner, or as the case may be, if the value v is identical to the value at the NorthWest corner of the square.
- *CorrectSWNEDiag*(r, c, v) is the counterpart of the previous function for the diagonal running from the SouthWest corner to the NorthEast corner.

The function *CorrectSWNEDiag* is as follows:

1. **function** *CorrectSWNEDiag*(r, c, v) **result** $\mathbb{B}$ **pre**
2. $r \in 1..n$ **and** $c \in 1..n$ **and** $v \in 1..n$
3. **begin**
4.   **result** $(r + c = n + 1$ **and** $r \neq 1) \Rightarrow (v = X[1, n])$
5. **end**

62 - A 6   **Answer 6.**   A possible solution is based on the same principle as the one applied in the previous question: when placing an element on the first column of the square (excluding the first row), we make sure that the value to be placed is the same as its symmetrical with respect to the NorthWest-SouthEast diagonal. The generic function *Satisf* is instantiated by the Boolean function *Column1EqualsLine1*(r, c, v) which delivers **true** if, when (r, c) designates a square of the first column (so we have $c = 1$), with the exception of the square $(1, 1)$, then v is equal to $X[1, r]$.

Answers to problem 63. **The sudoku game**.   *The problem is on page 240.*

63 - A 1   **Answer 1.**   It is a total function from the Cartesian product $1..9 \times 1..9$ to $1..9$. However, we can see that, restricted to a given row, column or region, the function is a *bijection*. Therefore, if (r, c) designates the square on which a value is about to be placed, X is a 9×9 array valued in the interval $1..9$ such that $X[l, 1..c-1], X[1..r-1, c]$ and the restriction to the region in which the position (r, c) is located are *injective* functions in the interval $1..9$. This is shown in the schema below for the square of coordinates (r, c).

c

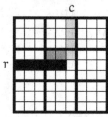

r

The part in ■ represents the portion of the row on the left of (r, c) whose values must be excluded from the interval $1..9$ for the loop; the part in ☐ represents the portion of the column above (r, c) whose values must be excluded from the set scanned by the loop $1..9$. Last, the part in ▨ represents the portion of the region involving (r, c) whose values must be excluded.

The set that j will go through is therefore the interval $1..9$ minus the values already produced on the considered row, column or region:

$$1..9 - \operatorname{codom} \left(\begin{array}{l} X[r, 1..c-1] \cup X[1..r-1, c] \cup \\ X\left[\left\lfloor \dfrac{r-1}{3} \right\rfloor \cdot 3 + 1..r-1, \left\lfloor \dfrac{c-1}{3} \right\rfloor \cdot 3 + 1..c-1 \right] \end{array} \right)$$

The pattern to be instantiated is therefore *AllTI*, laid out like *T2D* (see page 203), in order to account for the bidimensional nature of the definition domain of X.

Answer 2.   The procedure *Sudoku1* is presented hereafter. As said before, it is an instance of the pattern *AllTI* accounting for the fact that X is defined on a Cartesian product.   63 - A 2

1. **procedure** *Sudoku1*(r, c) **pre**
2. $r \in 1..9$ **and** $c \in 1..9$
3. **begin**
4.   **for** j **parcourant** $1..9 - \text{codom}\left(X\begin{bmatrix} X[r, 1..c-1] \cup X[1..r-1, c] \cup \\ \left[\left\lfloor \dfrac{r-1}{3} \right\rfloor \cdot 3 + 1 .. r - 1, \right. \\ \left. \left\lfloor \dfrac{c-1}{3} \right\rfloor \cdot 3 + 1 .. c - 1 \right] \end{bmatrix}\right)$ **do**
5. $X[r, c] \leftarrow j$;
6.   **if** $r = 9$ **and** $c = 9$ **then**
7.   **write**(X)
8.   **else**
9.   **if** $c = 9$ **then**
10.   *Sudoku1*(r + 1, 1)
11.   **else**
12.   *Sudoku1*(r, c + 1)
13.   **end if**
14.   **end if**
15.   **end for**
16. **end**

The calling program is as follows:

1. **variables**
2. $X \in 1..9 \times 1..9 \rightarrow 1..9$
3. **begin**
4.   *Sudoku1*(1, 1)
5. **end**

A rough experimental evaluation estimates the execution time of this program to be about 19 billion years, which is more than the age commonly attributed to the universe!

Answer 3.   For each possible value of j and for each square (r, c), it is necessary to know   63 - A 3
if j is likely to be placed there, taking into account the values already present in the row
r, in the column c and in the region where the square is located. For the sake of efficiency,
rather than performing a search, a data structure (whose properties strengthen the existing
invariant) is defined, consisting of three Boolean tables H, V and R, which, by *direct access*,
provide a quick answer. Specifically, H[r, j] (respectively V[j, c]) is **true** iff the value j is not
used in the row r (respectively in the column c). R[r, c, j] is **true** iff j is not used for the area
that houses the square (r, c). So, for example, for the configuration X below:

X:

5	3	4	6	7	8	9	1	2
6	7	2	1	9	5	3	4	8
1	9	8	3	4	2	5	6	7
8	5	9	7	6	1	4	2	3
4	2	6	8	5				

H:

f	f	f	f	f	f	f	f	f
f	f	f	f	f	f	f	f	f
f	f	f	f	f	f	f	f	f
f	f	f	f	f	f	f	f	f
t	f	t	f	f	f	t	f	v
t	t	t	t	t	t	t	t	t
t	t	t	t	t	t	t	t	t
t	t	t	v	v	v	t	t	t
t	t	t	t	t	t	t	t	t

V:

f	t	t	f	t	f	t	f	t
t	f	f	t	t	f	t	f	f
t	f	t	f	t	t	f	t	f
f	t	f	t	f	t	f	f	v
f	f	t	t	f	f	f	t	t
f	t	f	f	f	t	t	f	t
t	f	t	f	f	t	t	t	f
f	t	f	t	f	t	t	t	f
t	f	f	t	f	t	f	t	t

arrays H and V are given above. From the point of view of H, the value $j = 1$ can be placed in $X[5,6]$ since the value of the square $H[5,1]$ is **true** (is free). There is indeed (yet) no 1 on line 5. More generally, the contents of row 5 of H would allow one of the values 1,3,7 or 9 to be placed in $X[5,6]$ since these positions have the value **true** in line 5 of H. From the point of view of V, $V[1,6]$ is **false** (there is indeed already a 1 in column 6). More generally, the contents of column 6 of V authorizes the placement of any of the values 3,4,6,7 or 9 in $X[5,6]$ since these positions have the value **true** in column 6 of V. The array R is a three-dimensional array ($3 \times 3 \times 9$). The restriction to the first two dimensions applies to all nine regions, and for each of them, the third dimension refers to the availability of the value j. Also for the configuration X above, the region containing the square (5,6) (the middle region $R[2,2,.]$) looks like this: [f, t, t, t, t, f, f, f, f, f, f, t]. The value f (**false**) in the first position means that 1 cannot be placed in (5,6) (1 is actually already present in the middle region of the grid). This auxiliary data structure is initialized before the first call, and its properties are maintained by the instances of *Do* and *Undo*.

The procedure *Sudoku2* is written according to these considerations:

1. **procedure** *Sudoku2*(r, c) **pre**
2. $r \in 1..9$ **and** $c \in 1..9$
3. **begin**
4.   **for** j ranging 1..9 **do**

5.   **if** $H[r,j]$ **and** $V[j,c]$ **and** $R\left[\left\lfloor \dfrac{r-1}{3}\right\rfloor + 1, \left\lfloor \dfrac{c-1}{3}\right\rfloor + 1, j\right]$ **then**

6. $X[r,c] \leftarrow j$;

7. $H[r,j] \leftarrow$ **false**; $V[j,c] \leftarrow$ **false**; $R\left[\left\lfloor \dfrac{r-1}{3}\right\rfloor + 1, \left\lfloor \dfrac{c-1}{3}\right\rfloor + 1, j\right] \leftarrow$ **false** ;

8.   **if** $r = 9$ **and** $c = 9$ **then**
9.   write(X)
10.   **else**
11.   **if** $c = 9$ **then**
12.   *Sudoku2*$(r + 1, 1)$
13.   **else**
14.   *Sudoku2*$(r, c + 1)$
15.   **end if**
16.   **end if**;

17. $H[r,j] \leftarrow$ **true**; $V[j,c] \leftarrow$ **true**; $R\left[\left\lfloor \dfrac{r-1}{3}\right\rfloor + 1, \left\lfloor \dfrac{c-1}{3}\right\rfloor + 1, j\right] \leftarrow$ **true**

18.   **end if**
19.   **end for**
20. **end**

The calling program is as follows:

1. **variables**
2. $H \in 1..9 \times 1..9 \rightarrow \mathbb{B}$ **and**
3. $V \in 1..9 \times 1..9 \rightarrow \mathbb{B}$ **and**
4. $R \in 1..3 \times 1..3 \times 1..9 \rightarrow \mathbb{B}$ **and**
5. $X \in 1..9 \times 1..9 \rightarrow 1..9$
6. **begin**

7. $H \leftarrow \begin{bmatrix} \text{true} & \cdots & \text{true} \\ \cdots & \cdots & \cdots \\ \cdots & \cdots & \cdots \\ \text{true} & \cdots & \text{true} \end{bmatrix} ; V \leftarrow \begin{bmatrix} \text{true} & \cdots & \text{true} \\ \cdots & \cdots & \cdots \\ \cdots & \cdots & \cdots \\ \text{true} & \cdots & \text{true} \end{bmatrix} ;$

8. $R[.,.,1] \leftarrow \begin{bmatrix} \text{true} & \text{true} & \text{true} \\ \text{true} & \text{true} & \text{true} \\ \text{true} & \text{true} & \text{true} \end{bmatrix} ; \ldots ; R[.,.,9] \leftarrow \begin{bmatrix} \text{true} & \text{true} & \text{true} \\ \text{true} & \text{true} & \text{true} \\ \text{true} & \text{true} & \text{true} \end{bmatrix} ;$

9. $Sudoku2(1,1)$
10. **end**

Answer 4.   Compared to the first stage (without any revealed square), there is a diffi-   63 - A 4
culty to overcome. It has to do with the existence of revealed squares on the grid. They are
"untouchable" and their value can never be changed. A solution consists in recording, in a
Boolean matrix D (for *Disclosed*), defined on the same domain as X, the status of the value
of $X[r, c]$, revealed (**true**) or not (**false**). The condition *Satisf* is enriched as follows. If the
position (r, c) is disclosed and if position j candidate for a placement is the same as $X[r, c]$,
construction can proceed. This is also the case if the position (r, c) is not disclosed and if j
is not present in the row, column or region. The arrays H, V and R must then be updated to
indicate that j is no longer available (this is optional if the position (r, c) is revealed) and,
in *Undo*, undo what was done in *Do*, on the sole condition that (r, c) is not a revealed position. The array R is created before the first call. The three arrays H, V and R are initialized
before the first call, from X, taking into account the revealed squares. The properties of H,
V and R are maintained in the instances of *Do* and *Undo*. The following procedure *Sudoku3*
can be deduced from that:

1. **procedure** *Sudoku3*(r, c) **pre**
2. $r \in 1..9$ **and** $c \in 1..9$
3. **begin**
4.   **for** j **ranging** $1..9$ **do**
5.   **if** $\left(\begin{array}{l} (D[r,c] \text{ and then } j = X[r,c]) \text{ or} \\ \left(H[r,j] \text{ and } V[j,c] \text{ and } R\left[\left\lfloor \dfrac{r-1}{3} \right\rfloor + 1, \left\lfloor \dfrac{c-1}{3} \right\rfloor + 1, j \right] \right) \end{array} \right)$ **then**
6. $X[r, c] \leftarrow j ;$
7. $H[r,j] \leftarrow \text{false}; V[j,c] \leftarrow \text{false}; R\left[\left\lfloor \dfrac{r-1}{3} \right\rfloor + 1, \left\lfloor \dfrac{c-1}{3} \right\rfloor + 1, j \right] \leftarrow \text{false};$
8.   **if** $r = 9$ **and** $c = 9$ **then**
9.   **write**(X)
10.   **else**
11.   **if** $c = 9$ **then**
12. $Sudoku3(r + 1, 1)$
13.   **else**
14. $Sudoku3(r, c + 1)$

15.   **end if**
16.   **end if;**
17.   **if not** D[r, c] **then**

18. $$H[r, j] \leftarrow \textbf{true}; V[j, c] \leftarrow \textbf{true}; R\left[\left\lfloor \frac{r-1}{3} \right\rfloor + 1, \left\lfloor \frac{c-1}{3} \right\rfloor + 1, j\right] \leftarrow \textbf{true}$$

19.   **end if**
20.   **end if**
21.   **end for**
22. **end**

The call can be made by the following program (the initialization of D, H, V and R is not made explicit):

1. **constants**
2. $D \in 1..9 \times 1..9 \rightarrow \mathbb{B}$ **and** $D = [\dots]$
3. **variables**
4. $X \in 1..9 \times 1..9 \rightarrow 1..9$ **and** $X = [\dots]$ **and**
5. $H \in 1..9 \times 1..9 \rightarrow \mathbb{B}$ **and**
6. $V \in 1..9 \times 1..9 \rightarrow \mathbb{B}$ **and**
7. $R \in 1..3 \times 1..3 \times 1..9 \rightarrow \mathbb{B}$
8. **begin**
9. $H \leftarrow [\dots] ; V \leftarrow [\dots] ; R \leftarrow [\dots] ;$
10.   *Sudoku3*(1, 1)
11. **end**

63 - A 5   **Answer** 5.   The procedure *Sudoku3* must be arranged so that it provides the number of solutions (and not the solutions themselves). Then we can:

- call this new procedure to ensure that the grid has one and only one solution.
- by using the same procedure, for each revealed square, check that its absence causes the character of uniqueness to be lost; if this is the case, the grid is actually minimal.

63 - A 6   **Answer** 6.   Evaluating the number of recursive calls is done simply by using a new global variable (named NbRecCall in the procedure code *Sudoku4* below) initialized to 0 in the calling program and incremented by 1 at each recursive call, then by displaying the value of this variable at the end of the execution. The new code is not presented. The only difference from the *Sudoku3* version is the use of the variable NbRecCall.

The grid *Blond platinum* requires 1 697 593 recursive calls while grid (b) in figure (a) on page 242 requires 88 217 461 calls.

63 - A 7   **Answer** 7.   The principle of the solution is simple. The grid is scanned from left to right and bottom up, and instead of starting with the square (1, 1), we start at the desired square, not forgetting to switch, if necessary, from the square (9, 9) to the square (1, 1). Concretely, it is necessary to declare two new variables (rd and cd) in the calling program and to initialize them with the coordinates (row and column) of the starting square. The condition for stopping the recursion of the procedure *Sudoku4* must provide for two special cases. The first one occurs when the starting square is (1, 1) and the last processed square is (9, 9). The second special case is when the starting square is in column 1 but not in row 1 and the last processed square is on the previous row, in column 9. The general case is when the starting column *is different* from column 1 and the last square processed is immediately to its left. This multiple condition appears in line 8 of the procedure *Sudoku4*. The recursive calls to be made and the corresponding conditions can easily be deduced

from this analysis. They appear from line 12 to line 18 of the procedure *Sudoku4*. The main call is identical to the one for the procedure *Sudoku3*.

1. **procedure** *Sudoku4*(r, c) **pre**
2. $r \in 1..9$ **and** $c \in 1..9$
3. **begin**
4.   **for** j **ranging** $1..9$ **do**
5.   **if** $\left(\begin{array}{l} (D[r, c] \text{ and then } j = X[r, c]) \text{ or} \\ \left(H[r, j] \text{ and } V[j, c] \text{ and } R\left[\left\lfloor \dfrac{r-1}{3} \right\rfloor + 1, \left\lfloor \dfrac{c-1}{3} \right\rfloor + 1, j \right] \right) \end{array} \right)$ **then**
6. $X[r, c] \leftarrow j; H[r, j] \leftarrow$ **false**; $V[j, c] \leftarrow$ **false**;
7. $R\left[\left\lfloor \dfrac{r-1}{3} \right\rfloor + 1, \left\lfloor \dfrac{c-1}{3} \right\rfloor + 1, j \right] \leftarrow$ **false** ;
8.   **if** $\left(\begin{array}{l} (rd = 1 \text{ and } cd = 1 \text{ and } r = 9 \text{ and } c = 9) \text{ or} \\ (rd \neq 1 \text{ and } cd = 1 \text{ and } r = ld - 1 \text{ and } c = 9) \text{ or} \\ (cd \neq 1 \text{ and } c = cd - 1 \text{ and } r = ld) \end{array} \right)$ **then**
9.   **write**(X)
10.   **else**
11. $NbRecCall \leftarrow NbRecCall + 1$;
12.   **if** $(r = 9 \text{ and } c = 9)$ **then**
13.   *Sudoku4*$(1, 1)$
14.   **elsif** $(r \neq 9 \text{ and } c = 9)$ **then**
15.   *Sudoku4*$(r + 1, 1)$
16.   **else**
17.   *Sudoku4*$(r, c + 1)$
18.   **end if**
19.   **end if**;
20.   **if not**$(D[r, c])$ **then**
21. $H[r, j] \leftarrow$ **true**; $V[j, c] \leftarrow$ **true**;
22. $R\left[\left\lfloor \dfrac{r-1}{3} \right\rfloor + 1, \left\lfloor \dfrac{c-1}{3} \right\rfloor + 1, j \right] \leftarrow$ **true**
23.   **end if**
24.   **end if**
25.   **end for**
26. **end**

Answer 8. To answer this question, it is sufficient to perform the sum of the number of recursive calls obtained by starting at each of the 81 squares and to calculate the average value.

63 - A 8

The grid *Blond platinum* requires an average of 16 436 954 recursive calls (significantly more than the value obtained by starting with square $(1, 1)$) while grid (b) of figure 5.17, page 242 demands 18 339 383 calls. According to this approach, the difficulties of the two grids are comparable.

63 - A 9   **Answer** 9.   Although of questionable mathematical rigor, this experiment makes it possible to estimate the gain obtained by the strengthening. Out of about 20 test sets, the ratio in favor of the version with strengthening is about 3.5.

Answers to problem 64. **Seven-Eleven**   *The problem is on page 242.*

64 - A 1   **Answer** 1.   The sum is equal to 711 cents (equivalent to 7.11$) and the product is 711 000 000 since as the product expressed in US dollar is 7.11 it is $7.11 \cdot 100^4$ in cents.

64 - A 2   **Answer** 2.   The minimal price of an item being two US cents, the maximal price is $(711 - (3 \cdot 2)) = 705$ cents.

64 - A 3   **Answer** 3.   The simplest answer is to take a total function from 1..4 to the interval 2..705 as the enumeration vector X. If it is a solution, such an X complies with two properties: $\sum_{k=1}^{4} X[k] = 711$ and $\prod_{k=1}^{4} X[k] = 711\,000\,000$. For $i \in 1..4$, we have $\sum_{k=1}^{i-1} X[k] < 711$ and $\prod_{k=1}^{i-1} X[k] < 711\,000\,000$. The appropriate pattern is *OneT*, page 213 (*One solution for Total functions*).

64 - A 4   **Answer** 4.   The pattern *OneT* is instantiated by applying a pruning that avoids considering sets of items whose price is excessive. The most elementary version is the following:

```
1.  procedure SevenEleven1(i) pre
2.     i ∈ 1..4 and
3.     j ∈ 2..706
4.  begin
5.     j ← 2 ;
6.     while not(j = 706 or Found) do
```

7.   if $\boxed{\sum_{k=1}^{i-1} X[k] + j \leqslant 711 \text{ and } \prod_{k=1}^{i-1} X[k] \cdot j \leqslant 711\,000\,000}$ then

8. $X[i] \leftarrow j$;

9.   if $i = 4$ and then $\boxed{\left(\sum_{k=1}^{4} X[k] = 711 \text{ and } \prod_{k=1}^{4} X[k] = 711\,000\,000 \right)}$

```
            then
10.               Found ← true ; write(X)
11.            elsif i ≠ 4 then
12.                SevenEleven1(i + 1)
13.            end if
14.         end if;
15.         j ← j + 1
16.     end while
17. end
```

with a call made through:

```
1.  variables
2.     X ∈ 1..4 → 2..705 and Found ∈ 𝔹
3.  begin
4.     Found ← false ;
5.     SevenEleven1(1)
6.  end
```

which delivers the solution $[1.20, 1.25, 1.50, 3.16]$ (prices in US dollars). It can be observed that, in this solution, calculations related to quantifiers are partly carried out several times. A significantly better solution is obtained by the strengthening of the recursion invariant. To do so, let us introduce two global variables Sum and Prod such that $(Sum = \sum_{k=1}^{i-1} X[k] \text{ and } Prod = \prod_{k=1}^{i-1} X[k])$ and let us modify the previous solution so that the previous formula remains invariant:

```
1.  procedure SevenEleven2(i) pre
2.      i ∈ 1..4 and
3.      j ∈ 1..2..706
4.  begin
5.      j ← 2;
6.      while not(j = 706 or Found) do
7.          if Sum + j ⩽ 711 and Prod · j ⩽ 711 000 000 then
8.              X[i] ← j; Sum ← Sum + j; Prod ← Prod · j;
9.              if i = 4 and Sum = 711 and Prod = 711 000 000 then
10.                 Found ← true; write(X)
11.             elsif i ≠ 4 then
12.                 SevenEleven2(i + 1)
13.             end if;
14.             Sum ← Sum − j; Prod ← Prod/j
15.         end if;
16.         j ← j + 1
17.     end while
18. end
```

Let us notice that, Prod being a multiple of j, the result of Prod/j is an integer. The following calling program (which establishes the invariant for $(i = 1)$)

```
1.  variables
2.      X ∈ 1..4 → 2..705 and
3.      Sum ∈ N and Prod ∈ N₁ and Found ∈ B
4.  begin
5.      Sum ← 0; Prod ← 1; Found ← false;
6.      SevenEleven2(1)
7.  end
```

returns the expected result. In terms of asymptotic complexity, these two versions are equivalent: the number of total functions from the interval 1 .. 4 to the interval 2 .. 705 is 704^4. However, this value widely overestimates the actual complexity, since, on the one hand, some prunings take place and, on the other hand, the program stops as soon as a solution is found. The actual number of calls is 24 984 613 and runtime is about 210 s. This latter solution improves the performances by a factor of about 10 with respect to the previous one.

Answer 5. The only way to make sure that the product of the prices is actually 64 - A 5
711 000 000 consists in taking a *total surjective* function from the interval 1 .. 15 to 1 .. 4 as the enumeration vector X. X then represents a "four element" partition from the bag $[2, 2, 2, 2, 2, 2, 3, 3, 5, 5, 5, 5, 5, 5, 79]$ (partition with no empty element due to surjectivity). The appropriate pattern is *OneTS*, whose code is obtained from that of *OneT* (see page 213) by adding the formula

$$\forall k \cdot (k \in 1 .. m \Rightarrow B[k])$$

to the condition in line 8. Let us recall that, in the procedure *TS* (see page 203), the array B is used to check surjectivity. It is the same in the pattern *OneTS*.

64 - A 6   **Answer** 6.   Let F be the constant array of 15 elements such that F = [2, 2, 2, 2, 2, 2, 3, 3, 5, 5, 5, 5, 5, 5, 79]. Developing the naïve solution is left to the reader and we directly focus on the "strengthened" solution where the vector V, defined on the interval 1 .. 4 and valued in the interval 1 .. 705, contains the prices already found from the vectors X[1 .. i − 1] and F[1 .. i − 1]. More precisely, for i ∈ 1 .. 15:

$$\forall k \cdot \left(k \in 1..4 \Rightarrow V[k] = \prod_{j \in 1..i-1 \text{ and } X[j]=k} F[X[j]] \right).$$

For the example $[[2, 2, 5, 5], [2, 2, 5, 5], [2, 3, 79], [2, 3, 5, 5]]$ of the statement, the articulation of the three relations F, X and V can be represented by the sagittal diagram in figure 5.29.

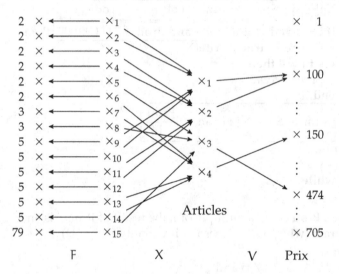

Fig. 5.29 – Articulation of the three relations F, X and V for the example $[[2, 2, 5, 5], [2, 2, 5, 5], [2, 3, 79], [2, 3, 5, 5]]$.

The corresponding procedure, *SevenEleven3* is as follows:

```
1. procedure SevenEleven3(i) pre
2.    i ∈ 1 .. 15 and
3.    j ∈ 1 .. 5 and Sav ∈ 𝔹
4. begin
5.    j ← 1;
6.    while not(j = 5 or Found) do
```

7.   **if** $\left| i < 4 \text{ or else } \sum_{k=1}^{4} V[k] \leqslant 711 \right|$ **then**

8.   X[i] ← j;

9. $\left| V[j] \leftarrow V[j] \cdot F[i] \; ; \; Sav \leftarrow B[j] \; ; \; B[j] \leftarrow \textbf{true} \; ; \right|$

10.   **if** i = 4 **and** $\left| \sum_{k=1}^{4} V[k] = 711 \text{ and } \forall k \cdot (k \in 1..4 \Rightarrow B[k]) \right|$ **then**

11.   Found ← **true** ; **write**(X)

12.   **elsif** $i \neq 4$ **then**
13. $SevenEleven3(i+1)$
14.   **end if**;

15. $\boxed{B[j] \leftarrow Sav \; ; V[j] \leftarrow \dfrac{V[j]}{F[i]}}$

16.   **end if**;
17. $j \leftarrow j + 1$
18.   **end while**
19. **end**

In the calling program, it is mandatory to initialize the vector V to 1, neutral element of the multiplication:

1. **constants**
2. $F \in 1..15 \rightarrow 2..79$ **and** $F = [2,2,2,2,2,2,2,3,3,5,5,5,5,5,5,79]$
3. **variables**
4. $X \in 1..15 \rightarrow 1..4$ **and**
5. $B \in 1..4 \rightarrow \mathbb{B}$ **and**
6. $V \in 1..4 \rightarrow 1..705$ **and**
7.   Found $\in \mathbb{B}$
8. **begin**
9. $V \leftarrow [1,1,1,1]$; $B \leftarrow 1..4 \times \{\mathbf{false}\}$; Found $\leftarrow$ **false** ;
10. $SevenEleven3(1)$
11. **end**

The number of calls necessary for the enumeration of all surjective functions from the interval 1 .. 15 to 1 .. 4 is 357 913 941 (see section 5.1.2.1, page 203) while the number of effective calls is 1 934 281 (about 13 times less than in question 3). The calculation is carried out in approximately 0.18 s. This latter solution improves the result in a factor of about 1 000 with respect to the second solution.

Answers to problem 65. **Decomposition of an integer** *The problem is on page 243.*

Answer 1.   The set involves the following ten elements (sets):   65 - A 1

$$\{\{1,2,3,4\},\{1,2,7\},\{1,3,6\},\{1,4,5\},\{2,3,5\},\{1,9\},\{2,8\},\{3,7\},\{4,6\},\{10\}\}.$$

Answer 2.   It is a matter of listing all the parts of a set (here of the interval 1 .. n).   65 - A 2
Therefore, a complete enumeration vector X represents a total function from 1 .. n to 0 .. 1, that can be interpreted as the characteristic vector of the considered subset (1 in position k if k is part of the subset, 0 otherwise) and such that the sum of the values of the interval 1..n filtered through X is equal to n. For the introductory example (decomposition of 6), the following configurations of X are found: $X = [1,1,1,0,0,0]$, for $\{1,2,3\}$, $X = [1,0,0,0,1,0]$, for $\{1,5\}$, $X = [0,1,0,1,0,0]$, for $\{2,4\}$ and $X = [0,0,0,0,0,1]$, for $\{6\}$. The pattern to be instantiated is thus *AllT* (see figure 5.7, page 211).

Answer 3.   The condition *SolFound*, instantiated in line 6 hereafter by the Boolean ex-   65 - A 3
pression $\sum_{k=1}^{i} k \cdot X[k] = n$, expresses the fact that, when the vector X is complete, the sum of the integers it represents is equal to n.

```
1. procedure DecompInteger1(i) pre
2.    i ∈ 1 .. n
3. begin
4.    for j ranging 0 .. 1 do
5.       X[i] ← j ;
```

6.   if $i = n$ and $\boxed{\sum_{k=1}^{i} k \cdot X[k] = n}$ then

```
7.          write(X)
8.       elsif i ≠ n then
9.          DecompInteger1(i + 1)
10.      end if
11.   end for
12. end
```

The calling program is:

```
1. constants
2.    n ∈ ℕ₁ and n = ...
3. variables
4.    X ∈ 1 .. n → 0 .. 1
5. begin
6.    DecompInteger1(1)
7. end
```

65 - A 4   **Answer 4.**   Since it is a pruning, it is necessary to introduce a conditional statement for the function *Satisf* of the pattern *AllT* specifying that the sum of the retained integers does not exceed n. So, we have:

```
1. procedure DecompInteger2(i) pre
2.    i ∈ 1 .. n
3. begin
4.    for j ranging 0 .. 1 do
```

5.   if $\boxed{\sum_{k=1}^{i-1} k \cdot X[k] + i \cdot j \leqslant n}$ then

```
6.          /%  ⋮ Idem lines 5 to 10 of DecompInteger1 %/
7.       end if
8.    end for
9. end
```

65 - A 5   **Answer 5.**   It is enough to introduce a global variable sum which, for each call to the procedure, with i as effective parameter, satisfies the property sum $= \sum_{k=1}^{i-1} k \cdot X[k]$. The following version takes this improvement into account:

```
1. procedure DecompInteger3(i) pre
2.    i ∈ 1 .. n
3. begin
4.    for j ranging 0 .. 1 do
```

5.   if $\boxed{som + i \cdot j \leqslant n}$ then

6.   X[i] ← j ; $\boxed{sum \leftarrow sum + i \cdot j}$;

7.   if $i = n$ and $\boxed{sum = n}$ then

```
  8.            write(X)
  9.          elsif i ≠ n then
 10.              DecompInteger3(i + 1)
 11.          end if;
 12.          | sum ← sum − i · j |
 13.        end if
 14.      end for
 15.  end
```

Let us notice that this version demands to "undo" (line 12) the update of sum carried out in line 6 so as to make it recover the value it had before the recursive call (see procedures *Do* and *Undo* of the pattern *AllT*, figure 5.7, page 211). The calling sequence is then:

```
1. constants
2.     n ∈ ℕ₁ and n = ...
3. variables
4.     X ∈ 1 .. n → 0 .. 1 and
5.     sum ∈ ℕ
6. begin
7.     sum ← 0 ;
8.     DecompInteger3(1)
9. end
```

Answer 6. It is enough to remove the conjunct $(i = n)$ from the condition in line 7 of   65 - A 6 the procedure *DecompInteger3* and complete X with 0's. Let us remark that, exceptionally, this pruning is not carried out inside the condition *Satisf*.

Experimental results and trends

Empirical tests lead to the following remarks:

- The solution based on "brute force" in the second question becomes rapidly inoperable (typically beyond $n = 25$) in terms of response time.
- The optimization in the third question (removal of branches whose sum exceeds n) is very fruitful, since the proportion of explored nodes reaches quickly $4/1\,000$ of those explored using "brute force".
- The optimization in the fourth question (strengthening through the variable sum) concerns only calculation time (not the number of explored nodes). It is a little insensitive for $n \leqslant 10$. On the other hand, one quickly reaches a calculation time that is of the order of $4/100$ of the time measured in the second question.
- The last solution (stopping exploration as soon as the solution is found) prunes about 10% of the nodes compared to the second and third solutions.

Answers to problem 66. **Madame Dumas and the Three Musketeers**

The problem is on page 244.

Answer 1. The vector X is an array defined over the interval 1 .. 5 valued in 1 .. 5. As   66 - A 1 preference 1 is handled directly, the initialization step puts 5 (*Porthos*) into X[1], and the problem reduces to the search for a bijection from 2 .. 5 to 1 .. 4. This bijection must also fit the four "separation" preferences. The appropriate pattern is *AllTI*, applied to bijections (see figure 5.7, page 211).

66 - A 2   **Answer** 2.   Figure 5.30, page 295, shows the complete recursion tree obtained by applying the above hypothesis dealing with the initialization of X[1] before the main call. Therefore, the single result is:

1	2	3	4	5
Porthos	*d'Artagnan*	*Aramis*	*Dumas*	*Athos*

66 - A 3   **Answer** 3.   There are several ways to handle preferences of type "$\mathcal{Y}$ prefers to be separated from $\mathcal{Z}$". One of the simplest is to store these preferences in the array (5×5) NotAside, such that NotAside[i, j] is **true** iff i wishes to be separated from j, or conversely. Therefore, this array is symmetric (see line 3 in the calling program hereafter).

66 - A 4   **Answer** 4.   The procedure *MmeDumas* is an instance of the pattern *AllTI*. Pruning (through the condition *Satisf*) is carried out using the array NotAside.

```
 1. procedure MmeDumas(i) pre
 2.    i ∈ 2..5
 3. begin
 4.    for j ∈ 1..4 − (codom(X[1..i−1])) do
 5.       if  not NotAside[X[I − 1, j]]  then
 6.          X[i] ← j ;
 7.          if i = 5 then
 8.             write(X)
 9.          else
10.             MmeDumas(i + 1)
11.          end if
12.       end if
13.    end for
14. end
```

The calling program is:

```
 1. constants
 2.    NotAside ∈ 1..5 × 1..5 → 𝔹 and
 3.    NotAside =
```

$$
\begin{bmatrix}
\text{false} & \text{true} & \text{false} & \text{false} & \text{false} \\
\text{true} & \text{false} & \text{true} & \text{false} & \text{true} \\
\text{false} & \text{true} & \text{false} & \text{true} & \text{false} \\
\text{false} & \text{false} & \text{true} & \text{false} & \text{false} \\
\text{false} & \text{true} & \text{false} & \text{false} & \text{false}
\end{bmatrix}
$$

```
 4. variables
 5.    X ∈ 1..5 → 1..5
 6. begin
 7.    X[1] ← 5 ;
 8.    MmeDumas(2)
 9. end
```

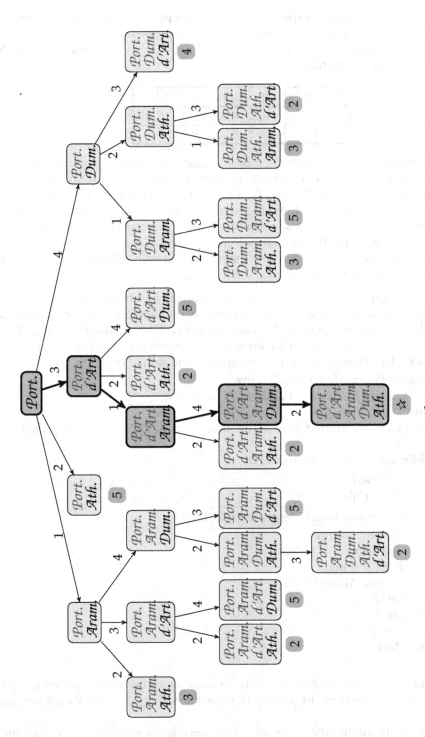

Fig. 5.30 – Recursion tree for Madame Dumas's problem with *Porthos* as the root. Nodes annotated ν mention the preference for which the branch is pruned. The single solution is in bold and dark grey.

Answers to problem 67. **Mini Master Mind**   *The problem is on page 245.*

67 - A 1   **Answer** 1.   To be the solution expected by the coder, a proposal must generate the same response as the one provided by the coder for each of the proposals in the history. Suppose for example that the code chosen by the coder is [R, O, N, V, B] and the game has reached the following configuration:

N° Prop.	Propositions	Rating
1	[N,O,B,V,R]	2
2	[N,R,B,O,V]	0

Any solution proposed by the decoder, compared to his two previous proposals, must provide as an answer 2 for the first one and 0 for the second one (see "Rating" column). This is the case with the proposal [B, O, R, V, N], which is therefore a candidate consistent with the history. On the other hand, the proposal [N, V, O, R, B] leads to the evaluation "1" for the two proposals already evaluated. This proposal is (doubly) inconsistent with the history; it cannot be the solution expected by the coder.

The reader will be able to verify that it is indeed this strategy which is applied by the decoder in the example of figure 5.18, page 246.

67 - A 2   **Answer** 2.   The appropriate pattern is *OneTI*, applied to bijections, since it is about discovering a permutation of colors. However, in order to avoid a refinement with which we are now familiar, we apply directly *UTI2*, refinement of *UTI*. (see figure 5.9, page 213). The condition *SolFound* is instantiated in the form of an expression that, when the vector X is complete, checks that it complies with the necessary condition of question 1.

```
1.  procedure PermutMasterMind1(i) pre
2.     i ∈ 1 .. n and j ∈ 1 .. n + 1 and L ∈ 1 .. n → 𝔹
3.  begin
4.     L ← (1 .. n − codom(X[1 .. i − 1]) × {true}) ∪ codom(X[1 .. i − 1]) × {false} ;
5.     j ← 1 ;
6.     while not(j = n + 1 or Found) do
7.        if  L[j]  then
8.           X[i] ← C[j] ;
9.           if i = n and then  CompatHisto(X)  then
10.              Found ← true ;
11.              write(X)
12.           elsif i ≠ n then
13.              PermutMasterMind1(i + 1)
14.           end if
15.        end if;
16.        j ← j + 1
17.     end while
18.  end
```

The refinement of the condition corresponding to *Satisf* (see line 7 above) is done using the technique presented to go from the pattern *TI*, page 205, to *TI2*, page 205. We are not going back on that.

Programming an algorithm where the role of the decoder is ensured by the machine is then easy to carry out. Assuming that the coder does not make any error, simply iterate on the procedure call *PermutMasterMind1* and ask the coder for his rating. The variable rep is intended to collect the coder's response, i.e. his rating of the last proposal. When he answers n, the code is discovered.

```
1.  constants
2.      C = [B, N, O, R, V] and n = |C|
3.  variables
4.      X ∈ 1 .. n → C and
5.      rep ∈ ℕ and Found ∈ 𝔹
6.  begin
7.      InitHisto ; rep ← 0;
8.      while rep ≠ n do
9.          Found ← false ;
10.         PermutMasterMind1(1) ;
11.         read(rep) ;
12.         InsertHisto(X, rep)
13.     end while
14. end
```

Answer 3.   The pruned recursion tree is presented in figure 5.31, page 298. Let us take   67 - A 3
as an example of pruning the one corresponding to the leftmost node in this latter figure (the branch ending in B). This pruning results from the fact that, when one confronts the first color of the third element of the history (the B of [B, V, O, R]), one discovers a correspondence with the B of the tree whereas, according to the history, there is none: this branch is sterile, it can be abandoned.

Answer 4.   Simply replace the condition in line 7 of the procedure *PermutMasterMind1*   67 - A 4
by:

$$C[j] \notin X[1 .. i-1] \text{ and then } PossibleHisto(C[j], i).$$

Answer 5.   Let *Last(C)* be the function that provides the last code on C (the one that has   67 - A 5
no successor). So, for C = {B, N, O, R, V}, *Last(C)* = [V, R, O, N, B]. The function *S* can be coded as follows:

```
1.  function S(p) pre
2.      p ∈ 1 .. n → C and
3.      i ∈ 1 .. n and j ∈ 1 .. n and k ∈ 1 .. n and l ∈ 1 .. n and aux ∈ 1 .. n and
4.      p ≠ Last(C)
5.  begin
6.      k ← n − 1 ;
7.      while not(p[k] < p[k + 1]) do
8.          k ← k − 1
9.      end while;
10.     l ← n ;
11.     while not(p[k] < p[l]) do
12.         l ← l − 1
13.     end while;
14.     aux ← p[k]; p[k] ← p[l]; p[i] ← aux; i ← k + 1;
15.     j ← n;
16.     while not(j ≤ i) do
17.         aux ← p[i]; p[i] ← p[j]; p[j] ← aux;
18.         i ← i + 1 ; j ← j − 1
19.     end while;
```

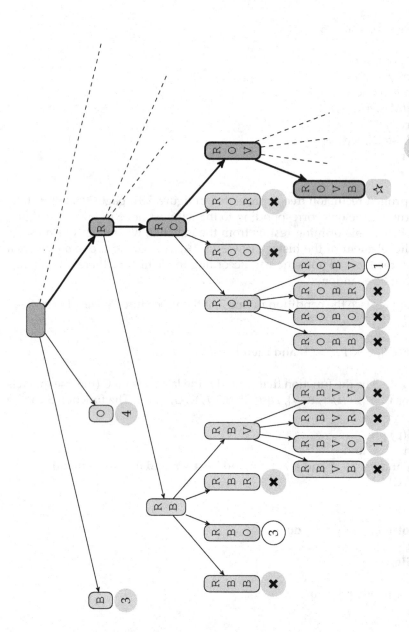

Fig. 5.31 – Recursion tree. In bold: the first solution found in a descending left-right course. The symbol Ⓘ placed under a node denotes a pruning caused by the ith step present in the history. The symbol Ⓘ denotes a node incompatible with the ith element of the history. The symbol ☆ represents the first permutation compatible with the history. The symbol ✖ represents a succession of colors containing a duplicate. The symbol Ⓘ denotes a node incompatible with the ith element of the history. Dotted branches are those that are not examined.

20.   **result** p
21. **end**

The first iteration searches the code p for the position k that precedes the beginning of the longest descending sequence s ($s = p[k+1..n]$) ending in position n. The second iteration searches for the position of the element immediately greater than p[k] in the sequence s. This is followed by the exchange described in the statement of the problem. Finally, the last iteration reverses the sequence $p[k+1..n]$. The complexity of this algorithm is in $\mathcal{O}(n)$.

Answer 6.   The resulting solution is: 67 - A 6

1. **constants**
2. $C = [B, N, O, R, V]$ **and** $n = |C|$
3. **variables**
4. $X \in 1..n \rightarrow C$ **and** $rep \in \mathbb{N}$
5. **begin**
6.   **for** $j \in 1..n$ **do**
7. $X[j] \leftarrow j$
8.   **end for;**
9.   *InitHisto;*
10.   **write**(X); **read**(rep);
11.   *InsertHisto*(X, rep);
12.   **while** $rep \neq n$ **do**
13. $X \leftarrow S(X);$
14.   **while not**(*CompatHisto*(X)) **do**
15. $X \leftarrow S(X)$
16.   **end while;**
17.   **write**(X); **read**(rep)
18.   **end while**
19. **end**

It should be noted that this solution does not fall within the usual framework of "Generate and test".

Answer 7.   Note that, in the three solutions studied, the history obtained is the same   67 - A 7
since the production is done in the lexicographical order of the colors. Let us discard the first solution which has no chance against the second one. The third option seems *a priori* better. However, an empirical test shows that this is not always the case. For fairly large values of n, the third solution is 1.5 times less efficient than the second. An initial explanation can be found in the fact that, if for example the coder's answer is 0, the second solution will eliminate (by pruning) all the permutations beginning with the first color at once, while, by construction, the third solution will sequentially go through all the permutations beginning with this color.

Remark

In [22], D. Knuth shows that, for the original game, there is a strategy allowing to find out the code with no more than five propositions.

Answers to problem 68. Crossword puzzle   *The problem is on page 247.*

Answer 1.   The enumeration structure X is a vector defined on the interval $1..H$ valued   68 - A 1
in the bag Dico. This vector represents a total *injective* function. Once the grid is completed,

the elements (bag of words) of Dico that have not been placed is identical to the bag of the vertical words in the grid. Leaving aside the fact that the codomain is a *bag*, the pattern to be retained is *OneTI* (see figure 5.9, page 213).

68 - A 2   **Answer** 2.   Figure 5.32, page 301, shows the tree browsed by a search of the type *OneSolution*.

68 - A 3   **Answer** 3.   The generic procedure *Satisf* is instantiated by the condition of line 6. It checks on the one hand that the word under test has not yet been placed, and on the other hand that its length is equal to that of the location under consideration. The generic procedure *SolFound* appears in the condition of line 9. This condition expresses that the bag of words still available (Free) is identical to the bag of words placed vertically. The generic procedure *Undo* is materialized by the adjunction, into the bag Free, of the value that has been deleted in line 8 (see page 249 for the definition of the functions *HorLocLength* and *VertWordsBag*).

```
1.  procedure CrosswordPuzzle1(i) pre
2.     i ∈ 1 .. H and j ∈ 1 .. N
3.  begin
4.     j ← 1 ;
5.     while not(j = N + 1 or Found) do
6.        if  Dico[j] ∈ Free and then |Dico[j]| = HorLocLength(i)  then
7.           X[i] ← Dico[j] ;
8.           Free ← Free ∸ [[Dico[j]]] ;
9.           if i = H and then  VertWordsBag = Free  then
10.              Found ← true ;
11.              write(X)
12.           elsif i ≠ H then
13.              CrosswordPuzzle1(i + 1)
14.           end if;
15.           Free ← Free ⊔ [[Dico[j]]]
16.        end if;
17.        j ← j + 1
18.     end while
19.  end
```

The call is made in the following way (the coding of the functions *HorLocLength* and *VertWordsBag* is left to the reader):

```
1.  constants
2.     l ∈ ℕ₁ and l = ... and c ∈ ℕ₁ and c = ... and
3.     Grid ∈ 1 .. l × 1 .. c → char and Grid = [...] and
4.     N ∈ ℕ₁ and N = ... and H ∈ ℕ₁ and H = ... and
5.     Dico ∈ 1 ... N → string and Dico = [[...]]
6.  variables
7.     Free ∈ bag(string) and
8.     X ∈ 1 .. H → string and
9.     Found ∈ 𝔹
10. begin
11.    Free ← BagConv(Dico) ;
12.    Found ← false ;
13.    CrosswordPuzzle1(1)
14. end
```

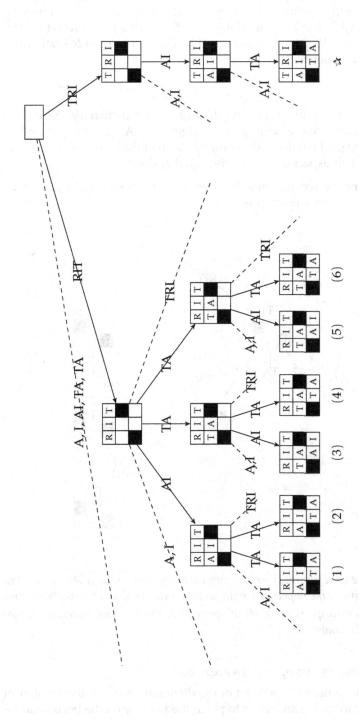

Fig. 5.32 – *Recursion tree for the example of figure 5.20, page 249. Dashed branches correspond to prunings for incompatible lengths between the word and the considered location. Leaves marked (1) to (6) fail because the bag of free words is different from the bag of vertically placed words. More precisely, for cases 1 and 2:* [**A, I, TA, TRI**] ≠ [**RA,IIT,I,TA**]*, for cases (3) and (5):* [**A, I, TA, TRI**] ≠ [**RT, IAA, T, I**]*, last for cases (4) and (6):* [**A, I, AI, TRI**] ≠ [**RT, IAT, T, A**]*.*

Complexity

The number of conditions evaluated is maximal when all the words of the lexicon Dico have the same length and the unique solution appears on the rightmost leaf of the recursion tree. The solution is then obtained by carrying out N tests on X[1], N − 1 tests on X[2], ..., N − H + 1 tests on X[H], that is a total of A_N^H tests. So, complexity at worst is in $\Theta(A_N^H)$. For the example of figure 5.19, page 248, the result is obtained in 1 820 243 calls, after over 7 000 s, which is about two hours.

Remark

In the above version, it is assumed that the data (grid and dictionary) have been pre-processed in order to facilitate the writing of the algorithm. A more elegant and flexible way to achieve the same goal would be to "compile" both of these components to produce the same information. This aspect of the exercise is not addressed here.

68 - A 4   **Answer** 4.   The principle recommended above leads to three prunings, as shown in figure 5.33. The approach seems promising.

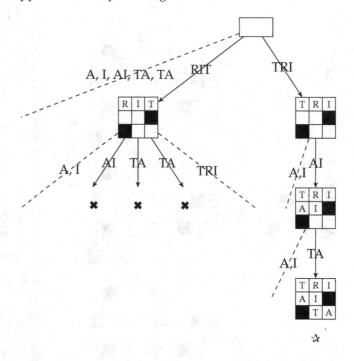

Fig. 5.33 – Recursion tree with prunings for the example of figure 5.20, page 249. Dotted branches correspond to prunings due to incompatible lengths between the word and the location considered. The branches marked ✖ *correspond to "vertical" prunings. The leaf that materializes the (first) success is marked with the symbol* ☆.

68 - A 5   **Answer** 5.   The following two operations are needed:

- *PrefixCheck*(w, k), where w is a word of the dictionary and k is the number of a horizontal location. We are about to place the word w on the horizontal location k. This function delivers **true** iff the prefixes of the vertical words leading to the kth horizontal location, completed by the corresponding character of the word w, all begin one of the words in the bag Free (see example on page 249).

- *WordStore*(w, k), where w is a word of the dictionary and k the number of a horizontal location. This procedure stores the word w in the kth horizontal location.

The generic procedure *Satisf* is simply expressed by the condition of line 9. As in the first solution, in order to be efficient, the implementation of the above two operations requires information allowing a quick access to the grid and the dictionary. The specification of these data structures is not addressed here. The function *PrefixCheck* may or may not locally update a copy of the bag Free. This heuristics has no impact on the result and has very little influence on the processing time. The procedure is then as follows (here, Grid is a variable):

1. **procedure** *CrosswordPuzzle2*(i) **pre**
2. $i \in 1 .. H$ **and** $j \in 1 .. N$
3. **begin**
4. $j \leftarrow 1$;
5.   **while not**$(j = N + 1$ **or** Found$)$ **do**
6.   **if** $\left(\begin{array}{l} \text{Dico}[j] \in \text{Free} \text{ and then} \\ |\text{Dico}[j]| = HorLocLength(i) \text{ and then} \\ PrefixCheck(\text{Dico}[j], i) \end{array} \right)$ **then**
7. $WordStore(\text{Dico}[j], i)$;
8.   Free $\leftarrow$ Free $\dot{-}$ $[\![\text{Dico}[j]]\!]$;
9.   **if** $i = H$ **then**
10.   Found $\leftarrow$ **true** ;
11.   **write**(Grid)
12.   **else**
13.   *CrosswordPuzzle2*$(i + 1)$
14.   **end if**;
15.   Free $\leftarrow$ Free $\sqcup$ $[\![\text{Dico}[j]]\!]$
16.   **end if**;
17. $j \leftarrow j + 1$
18.   **end while**
19. **end**

This version of the algorithm provides the solution to the problem of figure 5.19, page 248, after only 57 calls, which require about 0.0132 second, and are to be compared respectively to the 1 820 253 calls and 7 000 seconds required by the first pruning.

Answers to problem 69. **Self-referent arrays**   *The problem is on page 250.*

Answer 1. The following array: 69 - A 1

i	0	1	2	3
X[i]	2	0	2	0

is also a four element self-referent array.

69 - A 2   **Answer** 2.   The sum of the elements of a self-referent array of n elements is n. This is because each cell $X[i]$ references $X[i]$ different cells and all cells are referenced, so the total of the elements of X is n:

$$\sum_{i=0}^{n-1} X[i] = n. \tag{5.4}$$

69 - A 3   **Answer** 3.   We are looking for a total function from $0..n-1$ to $0..n-1$. So it is a matter of instantiation of the pattern *AllT* (see figure 5.7, page 211). A possible pruning, according to formula 5.4, consists in stopping the scan of a branch of the recursion tree when the sum of the elements of X is greater than n. On the other hand, rather than systematically recalculating the sum, a more efficient technique (applied many times in this chapter) is to strengthen the recursion invariant by introducing the variable s to designate the sum $\sum_{k=0}^{i-1} X[k]$. This requires, on the one hand, initializing s before the main call, and, on the other hand, instantiating the procedures *Do* and *Undo* in order to maintain this invariant. As to the generic function *SolFound*, it identifies with the formula 5.3, page 250. The following procedure can be deduced from this:

```
1. procedure SelfRefArr1(i) pre
2.    i ∈ 0..n − 1
3. begin
4.    for j ranging 0..n − 1 do
5.       if  s + j ⩽ n  then
6.          X[i] ← j;  s ← s + j ;
7.          if i = n−1 and then  ∀i · ( i ∈ 0..n − 1 ⇒
                                        X[i] = #j · (j ∈ 0..n − 1 and then X[j] = i) )
          then
8.             write(X)
9.          elsif  i ≠ n − 1  then
10.             SelfRefArr1(i + 1)
11.          end if;
12.          s ← s − j
13.       end if
14.    end for
15. end
```

The framed part of line 7 will have to be refined by a function that algorithmically verifies this condition. This part could be preceded by the conjunct $(s = n)$. The initial call is as follows:

```
1. constants
2.    n ∈ N₁ and n = ...
3. variables
4.    X ∈ 0..n − 1 → 0..n − 1 and s ∈ N
5. begin
6.    s ← 0;
7.    SelfRefArr1(0)
8. end
```

Answer 4. This pruning can be implemented by a strengthening of the recursion in-   69 - A 4
variant by introducing the array C (defined on the interval $0..n-1$ and valued on $0..n-1$)
aimed at counting the different values placed in the slice $X[0..i-1]$. The corresponding
program *SelfRefArr2* is:

```
 1. procedure SelfRefArr2(i) pre
 2.    i ∈ 0..n − 1
 3. begin
 4.    for j ranging 0..n − 1 do
 5.       if s + j ⩽ n and then  i > j ⇒ X[j] ≠ C[j]  then
 6.          X[i] ← j; s ← s + j;  C[j] ← C[j] + 1 ;
 7.          /%  ⋮ Idem lines 7 to 11 of SelfRefArr1 %/
 8.          s ← s − j ;  C[j] ← C[j] − 1
 9.       end if
10.    end for
11. end
```

The initial call is in the form:

```
1. constants
2.    n ∈ ℕ₁ and n = ...
3. variables
4.    X ∈ 0..n − 1 → 0..n − 1 and C ∈ 0..n − 1 → 0..n − 1 and s ∈ ℕ
5. begin
6.    s ← 0; C ← (0..n − 1) × {0};
7.    SelfRefArr2(0)
8. end
```

Remark

In a maximum of one minute of CPU time, the no-pruning version solves the problem for
$n \leqslant 9$. In the same conditions, the version *SelfRefArr1* (respectively *SelfRefArr2*) allows to
solve the problem for $n \leqslant 15$ (respectively $n \leqslant 18$).

Answer 5. There are $(n - 7 + 3)$ occurrences of the value 0, hence the value $(n - 4)$ in   69 - A 5
$X[0]$; the value 1 (respectively 2, $n - 4$) appears twice (respectively once, once).

Remark

If we are only interested in finding a single solution, we have here a basis for an extremely efficient algorithm in $\Theta(n)$. As the problem is stated, the search for all solutions
involves either executing the procedure *SelfRefArr2*, or demonstrating the conjecture of the
statement.

6

Branch and bound

L'esprit d'ordre est un capital de temps
(Being order-minded is a time capital).

H.-F. Amiel

6.1 Introduction

It is recommended to read this entire introduction, as well as that of Chapter 5 before starting to deal with problems.

6.1.1 Branch and bound: the principle

We consider a set C^1 whose elements are called *candidates*. Each element of C is associated with a constant cost $v: v \in C \to \mathbb{R}_+$, sometimes called "real cost" in the following. We are looking for any of the candidates c minimizing $v(c)^2$. Such candidates are called *solutions*. Of course, when C is empty, there is no solution[3].

A classic way to solve this type of problem is to list and evaluate all candidates in order to select one that minimizes the cost. When the cardinality of C is high, the disadvantage of this approach lies in the number of candidates to be considered and the resulting prohibitive temporal complexity.

Schematically, the "Branch and bound" method can be described as follows. Let $C_1, \ldots, C_n$ be a partition of C. All subsets C_i are collected in a data structure named OPEN. Each C_i is associated with an evaluation $f(C_i)$ which is an *underestimate* of the actual cost of all C_i candidates. One chooses (this is the *selection* phase) the most promising subset C_j (i.e. the one that minimizes the value of the evaluation function f), before partitioning it into different non-empty subsets $C_{j_1}, \cdots, C_{j_m}$ (this is the *separation* phase[4]). For each subset C_{j_k}, the value of $f(C_{j_k})$ is calculated (this is the evaluation). The subset C_i is then removed from OPEN while all C_{j_k} are inserted into it. The process is then reapplied to the new configuration of OPEN. Initially, OPEN contains only C. The algorithm ends either when the selected set C_i contains only one candidate, or when OPEN is empty. For "Branch and

---

[1]In general C is defined in intention, but cases where C is defined extensively (see problem 73, page 326) can be treated in the same way. The most frequent case is that of a finite set C, but the problem 72 page 323 deals with the case of a countable infinite set.

[2]Problems where we are looking to maximize cost are treated the same way.

[3]In the case of a definition of C in intention, it is generally difficult to know *a priori* if C is empty or not.

[4]Also called *burst*, *expansion* or *partitioning*.

DOI: 10.1201/b23251-6

bound" to provide a correct solution, several conditions, listed below, must be met (see the theorem on page 309). "Branch and bound" is then said to be *admissible*.

The remainder of this introduction explains the nature of the three phases mentioned above, before synthesizing them into a generic algorithm. A sufficient condition of admissibility is provided and demonstrated. An example is then detailed.

6.1.1.1 The separation phase

The successive separations can be represented in the form of a tree (called a search tree) where each node is identified with a subset C_j. A leaf is nothing but a subset reduced to a single element. This partition/tree duality is echoed down to the vocabulary, and we exploit it to ensure a better understanding. A "Branch and bound" algorithm traverses, without constructing it, all or part of the search tree, the objective being to use the estimation of nodes (subsets) and the selection strategy in order to limit the quantity of nodes developed.

Example

Let $C = \{a, b, c, d, e, f, g, h, i, j, k\}$ be a set of candidates. Figure 6.1 shows a possible complete search tree. The values attached to the nodes can be ignored for now.

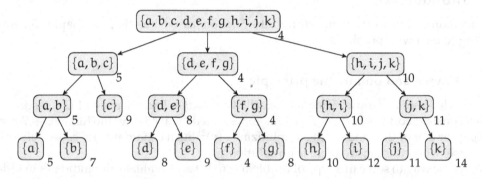

Fig. 6.1 – *Example of a search tree for the set* $\{a, \ldots, k\}$. *The set of children of a given node is a partition of this node.*

Two issues need to be addressed at this stage: (i) how to perform the separation?, and (ii) how to economically represent each of the nodes (of the subsets)? These choices depend on the considered problem, but it is not rare to find here the solutions adopted in the chapter devoted to "Generate and test" (see section 5.1, page 197): representation by an enumeration vector X and separation by instantiation of a position of this vector.

6.1.1.2 The selection phase

The order of development of the nodes here is not fixed in advance: priority is given to developing the nodes that are considered to be the most promising. To do this, each leaf of the current tree is present in a priority queue (see [17] for efficient implementations of priority queues). This is the OPEN structure mentioned earlier. Figure 6.2 shows a possible configuration at a given point of search (priorities are placed to the right of each node). The next selected node (expanded/split/partitioned) is then the node $\{f, g\}$, since it is assigned the highest priority. It can be noticed that during the search, three kinds of nodes are encountered: (i) those present in OPEN (in dark grey in the figure), which include in

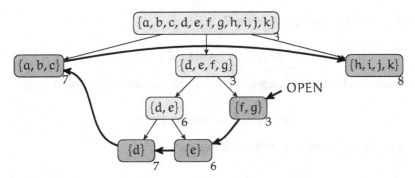

Fig. 6.2 – Example of configuration. Estimated costs are placed under the south-east corner of the nodes. The priority queue is pointed out. Although it has the same priority as node {a, b, c}, node {d}, more "developed", is located before in the queue.

particular the nodes likely to be developed, (ii) nodes already developed (in light grey above), which are no longer active, and (iii) nodes not yet created, which do not appear on the schema.

This step highlights the basically iterative nature of algorithms of type "Branch and bound", since it is a matter of developing the priority node at each step. The resulting disadvantage, compared to the "Generate and test" method, is that the priority queue can occupy a large memory space (however limited by the maximum weight of the search tree). This can be prohibitive for some large problems. On the other hand, one can hope to develop fewer nodes and thus achieve greater efficiency.

6.1.1.3 The evaluation phase

Before inserting a node into the queue OPEN, it must be assigned a *priority*. Let us define a function f^* whose profile is $f^* \in (\mathbb{P}(C) - \varnothing) \to \mathbb{R}_+$ and such that:

$$
\begin{aligned}
f^*(\{c\}) &= v(c) &\text{for any candidate } c\\
f^*(\{c_1, \ldots, c_n\}) &= \min_{c \in \{c_1, \ldots, c_n\}} (f^*(\{c\})) &\text{for } n > 1.
\end{aligned}
$$

$f^*(\{c_1, \ldots, c_n\})$ is therefore the optimal cost for all candidates in the set $\{c_1, \ldots, c_n\}$. For $E \subseteq C, f^*(E)$ is, by extension, called the *actual* cost of a node E and $f^*(C)$ the (actual) cost of the solutions (for the root set C).

The definition of the function f^* implies that it is increasing, in the sense that, if $E' \subseteq E$, $f^*(E) \leqslant f^*(E')$ (the function f^* increases when one goes through a branch from the root). In figure 6.1, page 308, an arbitrary but possible value for a function f^* is placed to the right of each node. The (only) solution is f, with a cost of 4. This figure illustrates the increase of f^*.

However, this actual cost cannot be used as a priority for the insertion of nodes in the queue OPEN, since it is (usually) unknown. Instead, a function f, with the same profile as f^*, called *evaluation function*, is used, which provides an estimated cost. This function f must satisfy the following theorem:

Theorem (Sufficient condition of admissibility of the "Branch and bound" algorithm):
If the function f meets the following two conditions:

1. *f is nonnegative and is never greater than f*:*

$$\forall E \cdot (E \subseteq C \Rightarrow f(E) \leqslant f^*(E)), \tag{6.1}$$

2. *for any candidate c, the value of f applied to {c} equals the value of f* applied to {c}:*

$$\forall c \cdot (c \in C \Rightarrow f(\{c\}) = f^*(\{c\})), \tag{6.2}$$

then the "Branch and bound" algorithm is admissible.

This theorem is demonstrated in the next section, dealing with the construction of the "Branch and bound" algorithm.

In the following section, we focus on building an abstract version of the generic program at the base of any solution of type "Branch and bound", assuming that an evaluation function f with the two above properties is available. It should be kept in mind that evaluating the function f has a cost (as well as the consultation and the maintenance of data structures), which should be limited as much as possible, so as not to lose the benefits of the "Branch and bound" method.

6.1.2   The generic "Branch and bound" algorithm

6.1.2.1   The priority queue

The generic algorithm we will develop is based on a data structure introduced in section 1.7 page 30: the priority queue OPEN. A clarification must be made concerning the operation *AddPQ*: in case of conflict (equality on priorities), preference is given to the most developed node (i.e. the lowest node in the search tree). If this criterion still does not make it possible to separate two subsets, preference is given to the one that is already present in the queue.

6.1.2.2   Construction of the generic "Branch and bound" algorithm

This algorithm is built according to the five classic points of the loop construction.

Invariant The priority queue OPEN contains a partition of the set C. Each element of this partition is accompanied by its priority. Some of them contain a single candidate, others are likely to be "separated". The queue is sorted on increasing priorities.

In figure 6.2, page 309, every node E of the schema is labeled with the value of the evaluation function $f(E)$ (which is both the estimated cost and the priority); the queue OPEN is drawn in bold and its constituents are grey. In this figure, the tree is only there for ease of understanding. It is not built by the algorithm.

Stopping condition The loop stops either when the queue OPEN is empty or when the head of the queue represents a *candidate* c (its priority is $f(\{c\})$). In the latter case, two observations can then be made.

  1. Since $\{c\}$ is the head of the queue OPEN and $f(\{c\}) = f^*(\{c\})$ (see formula 6.2, page 310), there is no better candidate in OPEN (although there may be equivalent candidates).
  2. Let E (card(E) > 1) be a subset of C present in OPEN, with priority the $f(E)$ ($f(\{c\}) \leqslant f(E)$). The invariant implies that $E \cap \{c\} = \emptyset$. We now show that $f(\{c\}) \leqslant f(E)$ implies that c is actually a solution.

$$f(\{c\}) \leqslant f(E)$$
$$\Rightarrow \qquad\qquad\qquad\qquad\qquad \text{property 6.1 } (f(E) \leqslant f^*(E)) \text{ and transitivity}$$
$$f(\{c\}) \leqslant f^*(E)$$
$$\Leftrightarrow \qquad\qquad\qquad\qquad\qquad \text{definition of } f^*, \text{ general case, see page 309}$$
$$f(\{c\}) \leqslant \min_{d \in E}(f^*(\{d\}))$$
$$\Leftrightarrow \qquad\qquad\qquad\qquad\qquad\qquad\qquad \text{definition of min}$$
$$\forall d \cdot (d \in E \Rightarrow f(\{c\}) \leqslant f^*(\{d\}))$$
$$\Leftrightarrow \qquad\qquad \text{property 6.2 } (f(\{c\}) = f^*(\{c\})) \text{ and substitution of equal elements}$$
$$\forall d \cdot (d \in E \Rightarrow f^*(\{c\}) \leqslant f^*(\{d\}))$$

This demonstration can be summarized by: for any element d of E, $f(\{c\}) = f^*(\{c\}) \leqslant f^*(E)) \leqslant f^*(\{d\})$. The last formula of this demonstration can be expressed as: a subset E (E $\subset$ C), present in OPEN and located after the head of file $\{c\}$, cannot give birth to a candidate better than c.

If the queue is empty, the invariant tells us that it contains a partition of the set C, so C is also empty. There is no candidate and no solution. If the queue is not empty, the conjunction of the invariant and the stopping condition results in the candidate c being a solution, demonstrating the admissibility of the algorithm (see page 309). Assuming the Boolean function *IsLeaf*(E), which determines whether or not the subset E is a leaf of the tree, is available, the stopping condition is expressed by *IsEmptyPQ*(OPEN) **or else** *IsLeaf*(*HeadPQ*(OPEN).ss)[5].

Progression The precondition of the progression specifies that the invariant is satisfied as well as the negation of the stopping condition. It can be deduced that the head of the queue OPEN exists and that it is a set of several candidates: therefore, it can be "separated". The progression consists in partitioning the head of the queue, removing it from the queue, calculating the priority of each of the elements in the partition, before introducing them into the queue, according to their priority. This step requires (usually) building a loop to restore the invariant. This construction is not made explicit here.

Initialization The invariant is established by placing C in the queue along with its priority.

Termination If C is finite, the algorithm ends since $\mathbb{P}(C)$ is also finite. A possible termination function consists in choosing the maximal weight of the search tree minus the number of nodes already built. If C is infinite countable and does not contain a solution, the algorithm does not terminate.

6.1.2.3 The generic "Branch and bound" algorithm itself

In the following algorithm, ElmtPQ is the type of elements to be placed in the queue: it is a pair whose first constituent ss (for subset) is a subset of C and the second, p, the priority. PQ is a type (see chapter 1, section 1.7) used to declare priority queues. For our example, this queue contains elements of type ElmtPQ. The function *Partition*(E) is assumed to be available. It delivers a partition of E excluding the empty set, according to a strategy to be defined on a case-by-case basis. The function that evaluates the estimated cost f is also assumed to be available.

1. **constants**
2. $C \subseteq \ldots$ **and** $C = \{\ldots\}$ **and** ElmtPQ $= \{(ss, p) \mid ss \in \mathbb{P}(C) - \varnothing$ **and** $p \in \mathbb{N}\}$
3. **variables**

---

[5]The field ss is used to extract the subset present in a node by discarding the priority.

4.   OPEN $\in$ PQ(ElmtPQ) **and** E $\subset$ C **and** E $\neq \emptyset$ **and** t $\in$ ElmtPQ

5. **begin**

6.   *InitPQ*(OPEN); *AddPQ*(OPEN, (C,*f*(C)));

7.   **while not** $\begin{pmatrix} IsEmptPQ\text{(OPEN)} \textbf{ or else} \\ IsLeaf\text{(}HeadPQ\text{(OPEN).ss)} \end{pmatrix}$ **do**

8.   t $\leftarrow$ *HeadPQ*(OPEN);

9.   *RemovePQ*(OPEN);

10.   **for** E $\in$ *Partition*(t.ss) **do**

11.   *AddPQ*(OPEN, (E,*f*(E))) ;

12.   **end for**

13.   **end while**;

14.   **if** *IsEmptyPQ*(OPEN) **then**

15.   **write**($\mathcal{N}o$ *solution*)

16.   **else**

17.   **write**(*HeadPQ*(OPEN))

18.   **end if**

19. **end**

Remarks

1. This version puts all items into the partition, including those for which the estimated cost is $+\infty$. It may be worthwhile to avoid cluttering up the queue with such uninteresting items. The above invariant must then be modified to take into account the fact that sets with infinite cost are not in the queue.

2. A second heuristics (called cleaning heuristics), which goes in the same direction as the previous one, can be systematically taken into account in order to limit the size of the priority queue. It is based on the following observation: as soon as a candidate c of cost $v(c)$ (with priority $p = v(c)$) is introduced in the priority queue (according to formula 6.2 page 310, p is then its real cost), it is useless to *introduce* or *retain* in the queue any candidate with an equal or higher priority.

6.1.3   An interesting special case for the functions f* and f

Frequently, each arc in the search tree is valued and the actual cost of a candidate c is the sum of the costs of the arcs that lead from the root C to the leaf {c}. The function f^* is then such that, for any node E, $f^*(E)$ is the cost of the optimal path from the root C and *passing through the node* E. This version of f^* is compatible with the generic version studied above. For any node E, $f^*(E)$ can be broken down into the sum of two functions:

$$f^*(E) = g^*(E) + h^*(E) \tag{6.3}$$

where $g^*(E)$ is the cost of the path between the root C and the node E, while $h^*(E)$ is the cost of the best path of the subtree rooted in E. The advantage that results from this scenario is that, when the node E is reached, $g^*(E)$ is known: it is the cost of the path already traveled. We can then define the evaluation function f by:

$$f(E) = g^*(E) + h(E) \tag{6.4}$$

h is called a "heuristic function". The evaluation of $h(E)$ concerns only the portion of the path remaining to reach a candidate. Then we have the following theorem:

Theorem (Sufficient condition of admissibility of the "Branch and bound" algorithm):
Let f be an evaluation function defined for any set E by:

$$f(E) = g^\star(E) + h(E),$$

where $g^\star$ is the cost of the path already traveled. If the heuristic function h satisfies:

$$0 \leqslant h(E) \leqslant h^\star(E)$$

then the "Branch and bound" algorithm is admissible.

This theorem is a direct consequence of the theorem given on page 309.

Example

Let us take again the example of figure 6.1, page 308, by assigning a value of $\mathbb{R}_+$ to each arc. In the tree below, the value noted in small print and italics represents the cost of each arc. For each candidate c, the value of $f^\star(\{c\})$ is placed under the leaves; it is the sum of the values of the corresponding branch.

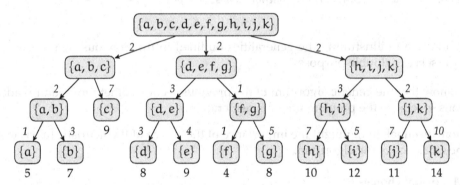

If we denote by $k(a, b)$ the cost of the arc (a, b), the new generic program is obtained by modifying the program in page 312 as follows. The new line 2 integrates the field $g^\star$ into a node:

$$\text{ElmtPQ} = \{(se, g^\star, p) \mid ss \in (\mathbb{P}(C) - \varnothing) \text{ and } g^\star \in \mathbb{N} \text{ and } p \in \mathbb{N}\}.$$

The new line 6 inserts an element whose field $g^\star$ is equal to zero into the queue and the field p is reduced to $h(C)$:

$$\textit{InitPQ}(\text{OPEN}); \textit{AddPQ}(\text{OPEN}, (C, 0, 0 + h(C)))$$

Finally, the new line 11 takes into account the value of $g^\star$ calculated from the value of the father of the node and the cost of the arc that joins them:

$$\textit{AddPQ}(\text{OPEN}, (E, t.g^\star + k(t.ss, E), t.g^\star + k(t.ss, E) + h(E)));$$

The closer to $h^\star$ is h (by lower value), the higher the efficiency[6]. More precisely, let h_1 and h_2 be two heuristic functions such that for any argument E, $h_1(E) \leqslant h_2(E)$, and let A_1 (respectively A_2) be a version of "Branch and bound" using the function h_1 (respectively h_2). At runtime, if the node w is expanded by A_2, it is also expanded by A_1. A trivial but inefficient solution is to choose h as the null function.

---

[6]Leaving aside the cost involved in calculating h.

6.1.4 An example: the traveling salesman

We find here the problem treated according to the "Generate and test" method in problem 57, page 233. Starting from an undirected graph[7] $G = (N, V, D)$ having n ($n \geqslant 2$) vertices, valued on $\mathbb{R}_+$, the point is to discover a solution starting at node 1, if any. The graph shown in figure 6.3 serves as the support for this example. The diagram (b) represents the matrix of distances D between the nodes $1, 2, 3$ and 4.

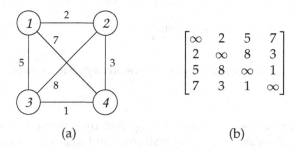

(a)   (b)

Fig. 6.3 – Example of an undirected valued graph. Schema (b) is the matrix representation D *of schema (a). The cycle* $[1, 3, 4, 2, 1]$ *is a solution, whose cost is 11.*

In addition to illustrating the generalities outlined in the previous two sections, this example serves a double purpose:

1. to show that the generic algorithm of the previous section sometimes requires adaptations specific to the problem under consideration,

2. more essential, to highlight the importance of the choice of the heuristic function h for the efficiency of the algorithm.

6.1.4.1 Initial choices

As suggested above, one must first decide on the representation of the subsets of candidates, as well as the partitioning strategy. For our problem, the set of candidates comes in the form of $\{[1, 2, 3, 4, 1], [1, 3, 2, 4, 1], [1, 4, 3, 2, 1]\}$. More generally, a candidate is thus a vector X of $n + 1$ elements beginning and ending with the value 1, and such that the first n elements constitute a permutation of the interval $1 .. n$.

6.1.4.2 The algorithm

The objective here is to instantiate the generic algorithm in order to take into account the peculiarities of the problem. It then appears that the progression of the main loop must distinguish between the general case (looking for a suitable permutation to place in the slice $X[1 .. n]$) and the particular case where one seeks to place 1 in $X[n + 1]$. Furthermore, in accordance with remark 1 on page 312, branches with infinite cost are discarded. In this part, an instance – still to be defined – of the function h is supposed to be available. Let us specify the nature of the nodes of the queue OPEN. As shown in the schema below, such a node consists of the three fields ss, g^* and p:

---

[7]The versions proposed below can easily be transposed to the case of *directed* graphs.

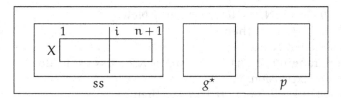

1. The field ss: it is the vector X along with its filling index i. This latter designates the next cell to complete. X has $n + 1$ cells (which allow to place a permutation of the interval $1 .. n$ plus the final node 1). The slice $X[1 .. i - 1]$ contains the instantiated positions and represents the subset of all candidates starting with these $(i - 1)$ values. Partitioning consists in instantiating position i with each of the values still available to get a partition. When X is complete, $i = n + 2$.

2. The field $g^\star$ is the value of the eponymous function in formula 6.3, page 312.

3. The field p is the priority of the element (i.e. the value of the evaluation function f in formula 6.4).

Let us now describe the main components of the algorithm that will be presented below. The set PC (reported on line 3) materializes all possible subsets of candidates (based on the representation choice adopted above). The set ElmtPQ (line 4) represents the structures placed in the priority queue (see above). ssNew, $g^\star$New and pNew are auxiliary variables used to construct the elements of the set ElmtPQ to be placed in the queue. Line 10 constructs the field ss of the initial node (which represents the set C), by placing the value 1 in $X[1]$ and 0 in the slice $X[2 .. n + 1]$ and initializing i to 2. Line 11 has the effect of placing in the queue OPEN the structure consisting of the three values ssNew (which has just been constructed) for the ss field, 0 for the field $g^\star$ and $0 + h(ssNew)$ for the field p. The difference between the general case and the special case related to the position $(n + 1)$ of the vector X is taken into account by the conditional statement starting at line 14. The elimination of nodes with infinite cost is achieved through the two conditional statements of lines 14 and 23. The sequence from line 16 to line 18 constructs and places a set of *one* candidate in the queue OPEN, while the sequence from line 24 to line 27 does the same when there is a set of at least two candidates (i.e. facing a structure whose vector X is not complete), which has the effect of restoring the invariant. The algorithm is as follows:

1. **constants**
2. $n \in \mathbb{N}_1 - \{1\}$ **and** $n = \ldots$ **and**
3. $PC = \{(X, i) \mid X \in 1 .. n + 1 \rightarrow 1 .. n \text{ and } i \in 1 .. n + 2\}$ **and**
4. $ElmtPQ = \{(se, g^\star, p) \mid se \in PC \text{ and } g^\star \in \mathbb{N} \text{ and } p \in \mathbb{N}\}$
5. **variables**
6. $OPEN \in PQ(ElmtPQ)$ **and** $t \in ElmtPQ$ **and**
7. $ssNew \in PC$ **and** $g^\star New \in \mathbb{N}$ **and** $pNew \in \mathbb{N}$
8. **begin**
9.   *InitPQ*(OPEN);
10. $ssNew \leftarrow (\{1 \mapsto 1\} \cup (2 .. n + 1 \times \{0\}), 2)$;
11.   *AddPQ*(OPEN, (ssNew, 0, 0 + h(ssNew)));
12.   **while not**(*IsEmptyPQ*(OPEN) **or else** *IsLeaf*(*HeadPQ*(OPEN).ss)) **do**
13. $t \leftarrow$ *HeadPQ*(OPEN) ; *RemovePQ*(OPEN) ;
14.   **if** $t.ss.i = n + 1$ **and then** $D[t.ss.X[t.ss.i - 1], 1] \neq +\infty$ **then**
15.   /% *Special case, back to the starting node:* %/
16. $ssNew \leftarrow (t.ss.X[1 .. n] \cup \{n + 1 \mapsto 1\}, n + 2)$;
17. $g^\star New \leftarrow t.g^\star + D[t.ss.X[t.ss.i - 1], 1]$;

18. $AddPQ(\text{OPEN}, (\text{ssNew}, g^*\text{New}, g^*\text{New}))$
19.   **elsif** $t.ss.i \neq n + 1$ **then**
20.   /% *General case:* %/
21.   **for** j **ranging** $(2 .. n) - \text{codom}(t.ss.X[2 .. t.ss.i - 1])$ **do**
22.   /% *Expansion:* %/
23.   **if** $D[t.ss.X[t.ss.i - 1], j] \neq +\infty$ **then**

24. $\text{ssNew} \leftarrow \left(\begin{pmatrix} t.ss.X[1 .. t.ss.i - 1] \cup \{i \mapsto j\} \cup \\ (t.ss.i + 1 .. n + 1 \times \{0\}) \\ t.ss.i + 1 \end{pmatrix}' \right);$

25. $g^*\text{New} \leftarrow t.g^* + D[t.ss.X[t.ss.i - 1], j];$
26. $\text{pNew} \leftarrow g^*\text{New} + h(\text{ssNew});$
27. $AddPQ(\text{OPEN}, (\text{ssNew}, g^*\text{New}, \text{pNew}))$
28.   **end if**
29.   **end for**
30.   **end if**
31.   **end while**;
32.   **if** $IsEmptyPQ(\text{OPEN})$ **then**
33.   **write**(*No solution*)
34.   **else**
35.   **write**($HeadPQ(\text{OPEN})$)
36.   **end if**
37. **end**

In the remainder of this section, for illustration, we consider two cases for h (a third one is studied in problem 71, page 322).

6.1.4.3   First case study: the zero heuristic function

The simplest case we can imagine is to take the zero function for the heuristic function h, which is equivalent to using the cost of the path already traveled as the priority, without using any estimation. The theorem on page 312 applies, and this technique can be used regardless of the problem treated by "Branch and bound". It guarantees the discovery of a solution, if any. Table 6.1 and the search tree of figure 6.4, page 317, offer two different (but equivalent) views of the result of applying the algorithm to the graph of figure 6.3, page 314.

Table 6.1 focuses on the content and structure of the priority queue. Each row corresponds to a configuration of the priority queue, with the nodes appearing in ascending order of priority (field f). For any row k beyond the first one, the greyed cells are the sons developed by the head of row $k - 1$. Some nodes are shown in a greyed and italicized font: these are the nodes that are out of the queue, or that are not introduced in it when the cleaning heuristic described in note 2, page 312, is applied. Thus, in row 6 of the table, the introduction of the candidate 12431 results in the deletion of the node *132***. In the following rows, all the nodes following 12431 are greyed and in italics: they cannot give rise to a solution better than 12431.

The tree of figure 6.4 shows similar information. The edges are labelled by their cost. Branches are associated with two numerical data. The one that appears on a grey background provides the order in which the node is taken into account for a (possible) development of its sons. The second one is the priority associated with the node (i.e. for this case, the cost of the path already traveled). Some nodes are shown in grey and italic font. These are the nodes that are out of the queue or not introduced when the heuristic described in note 2, page 312, is applied. Thus, when introducing candidate 12431, node

	node	f	node	f	node	f	node	f	node	f	node	f
1	1****	0										
2	12***	2	13***	5	14***	7						
3	124**	5	13***	5	14***	7	123**	10				
4	13***	5	1243*	6	14***	7	123**	10				
5	1243*	5	134**	6	14***	7	123**	10	132**	13		
6	134**	6	14***	7	123**	10	12431	11	132**	13		
7	14***	7	1342*	9	123**	10	12431	11	132**	13		
8	143**	8	1342*	9	123**	10	142**	10	12431	11	132**	13
9	1342*	9	123**	10	142**	10	12431	11	132**	13	1432*	16
10	123**	10	142**	10	12431	11	13421	11	132**	13	1432*	16
11	142**	10	12431	11	13421	11	1234*	11	132**	13	1432*	16
12	12431	11	13421	11	1243*	11	132**	13	1432*	16	1423*	18

Tab. 6.1 – Successive steps of the priority queue OPEN for the processing of the graph of figure 6.3, page 314, for the case h = 0. For each row k, the cells in grey represent the son at the head of row (k − 1). The cells in grey and italics are the nodes that can either be deleted or ignored due to the introduction of the candidate 12431.

132** is deleted, since it cannot generate a better solution than 12431. As for nodes 1234*, 13421, 1423* and 1432*, they are then simply not introduced into the queue.

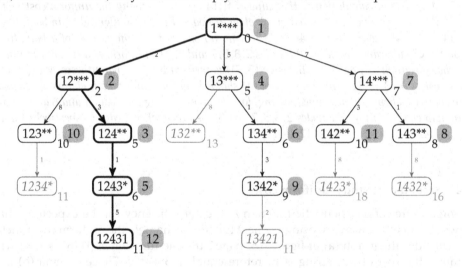

*Fig. 6.4 – Search tree for the processing of the graph of figure 6.3 page 314, for the case h = 0. The symbols * correspond to non instantiated positions of the vector X. The order of appearance of a node at the head of the priority queue is the number placed on a grey background. The cost of the path to the node is placed under the southeast corner of each node. The nodes in grey and italics are those that can either be deleted or ignored by the introduction of candidate 12431.*

For this example, the version that applies the cleaning heuristic of the remark 2, page 312, expands thirteen nodes (and deletes one already present) with a maximum queue size of 5. The base version (without cleaning) expands seventeen nodes for a maximum size of 6.

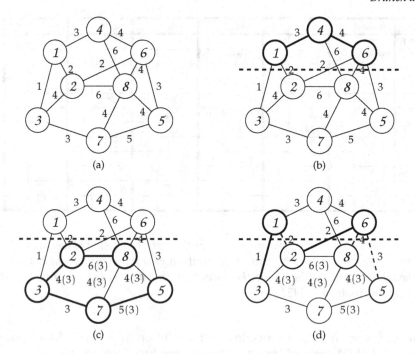

Fig. 6.5 – Example of calculation of the value of f([146 ∗ ∗ ∗ ∗]) *using the uniform cost method. Schema (a) shows a valued undirected graph of eight nodes. Figure (b) highlights, in bold, the cost of* g∗([146 ∗ ∗ ∗ ∗]), *which is* 3 + 4 = 7. *Schema (c) shows the uniform cost of a Hamiltonian chain on the G' subgraph including the nodes* 2, 3, 5, 7 *and* 8. *The uniform cost (the minimum edge cost of the sub-graph G', i.e.* 3, *for the edge* (3, 7)) *is written between parentheses. We get a total uniform cost of* 4 · 3 = 12. *Finally, schema (d) shows how the Hamiltonian chains of schema (c) and the chain of schema (b) are joined, taking, for the edges leaving the nodes* 1 *and* 6 *and joining a Hamiltonian chain built on the nodes* 2, 3, 5, 7 *and* 8, *the minimal cost edge (respectively* 1 *and* 2). *Finally,* f([146 ∗ ∗ ∗ ∗ ∗ ∗]) = 7 + 12 + (1 + 2) = 22.

6.1.4.4   Second case study: uniform cost

By using a more refined heuristic function h, greater efficiency can be expected. That is what we intend to show by choosing the next function h, namely the uniform cost function. Let us consider the graph (a) of figure 6.5, page 318. The function $g^*([146 ∗ ∗ ∗ ∗])$ which determines the cost of this string is therefore equal to 3 + 4 = 7 (see schema (b) in the figure). Let G' be the subgraph obtained from G by discarding the vertices of the chain already traversed. For our example, this subgraph consists of the vertices 2, 3, 5, 7 and 8, which appear below the dotted line in schema (b) of the figure. The uniform cost function h is defined as follows:

1. The minimum cost edge is chosen from G' (3 here for the edge (3, 7)) and this cost is applied uniformly to the Hamiltonian paths that we could build on G'. In our example, a Hamiltonian path on G' has four edges. In total, if all the edges were equal to 3, the cost would be 4 · 3 = 12.

2. We take the minimal cost to join the chain already traversed with a Hamiltonian chain on G' to get a Hamiltonian cycle. To do this, we choose the minimum cost edge between

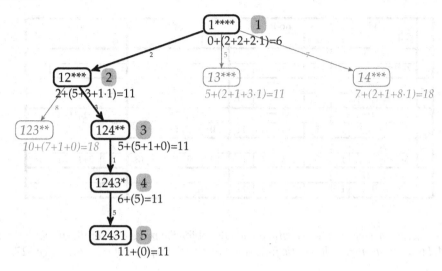

Fig. 6.6 – Search tree for the processing of the graph in figure 6.3 page 314, by the uniform cost heuristic function. See also the caption in figure 6.4, page 317. The branch in bold is the one that leads to the solution.

the vertex 1 and the graph G' (i.e. the edge $(1, 3)$ of cost 1) and the minimum cost edge between the vertex 6 and the graph G' (i.e. the edge $(6, 2)$ of cost 2). In total, the cost of this operation is $1 + 2 = 3$.

$h([146 * * * * * *])$ is thus equal to $12 + 3 = 15$.

The function h thus defined is, for any node, less than $h^\star$. It satisfies the condition of the theorem on page 312 which guarantees the admissibility of the algorithm.

Let us apply this function to the graph in figure 6.3, page 314. The principle is similar to the case of the null heuristic function. The results are presented, in two complementary forms, on the one hand in the table 6.2, page 320, and on the other hand in the tree of figure 6.6, page 319.

Table 6.2, page 320, focuses on the number of iterations necessary to get the result, namely 5. While adopting the same conventions as those of table 6.1, page 317, it also details the calculation of the evaluation function f.

In the light of the tree (see figure 6.6, page 319), the expression appearing under each node as $a + (b + c + d)$ denotes the cost of the evaluation function f. Specifically, a is the value of $g^\star$, and $(b + c + d)$ is the value of h. b (respectively c) is the minimum cost for the edge that leaves the node 1 (respectively the last node of the chain already traversed), d is a lower bound of the cost of a Hamiltonian chain on G'. In this example, the three nodes in shaded font and italics are nodes that are removed from the queue when the candidate 12431 is entered (according to the cleaning heuristic described in the note 2, page 312). This version thus develops eight nodes (compared to the thirteen nodes needed in the case of the null heuristic function). However, it must be insisted on the fact that evaluating complexity only in terms of the number of nodes developed can hide the additional cost generated by the evaluation of a sophisticated heuristic function.

	node			node			node			node		
	g^*	h	f	g^*	h	f	g^*	h	f	g^*	h	f
1		1****										
	0	2+2+2·1	6									
2		12***			13***			14***				
	2	5+3+1·1	11	5	2+1+3·1	11	7	2+1+8·1	18			
3		124**			13***			123**			14***	
	5	5+1+0	11	5	2+1+3·1	11	10	7+1+0	18	7	2+1+8·1	18
4		1243*			13***			123**			14***	
	6	5	11	5	2+1+3·1	11	10	7+1+0	18	7	2+1+8·1	18
5		12431			*13***			*123**			*14***	
	11	0	11	*5*	*2+1+3·1*	*11*	*10*	*7+1+0*	*18*	*7*	*2+1+8·1*	*18*

Tab. 6.2 – Successive steps of the priority queue OPEN *for the processing of the graph in figure 6.3 page 314, by the uniform cost heuristic function. See also the caption of table 6.1, page 317.*

6.2 What should be remembered about the "Branch and bound" approach

The problem of finding a solution that minimizes a certain cost can be approached by the "Branch and bound" method under the following conditions:

1. There is a finite set of candidates C, each candidate c having a nonnegative cost $v(c)$.

2. A set of at least two candidates can be partitioned into several nonempty subsets.

3. A subset of the candidates has an (actual) cost $f^*(\{c\})$ such that: (i) $f^*(\{c\}) = v(c)$, (ii) f^* is an increasing function in the broad sense.

4. Any subset of candidates can be assigned an estimated cost f such that: (i) for any candidate $c, f^*(\{c\}) = f(\{c\}) = v(c)$, (ii) $f \leqslant f^*$.

Therefore, the first two actions to take, before instantiating the generic program in section 6.1.2.2 page 310, are to choose:

1. a representation for the subsets of candidates,

2. a partitioning strategy for any set of candidates.

On the other hand, the choice of an evaluation function providing the estimated cost of a set of candidates can generally be deferred. It is not uncommon, however, that there is an interdependence between these three aspects (representation of candidates, partitioning strategy and choice of an evaluation function).

Like "Generate and test", the "Branch and bound" method inherently has an exponential complexity due to the number of candidates generated. We will therefore focus on the identification of efficient evaluation functions (especially the component h of the function f).

6.3 Problems

Problem 70. Task assignment ⦂

> In this problem, four evaluation functions f are studied. The lesson here is that it is important to be very careful to make sure that the theorem of page 312 (about a sufficient condition of admissibility) actually applies.

We consider n agents who must perform n tasks, each agent being assigned exactly one task. The point is that agents are not equally effective on all tasks. If the agent i performs the task j, the cost (e.g. in time) of this assignment is $D[i, j]$. Given a matrix of costs $D[1 .. n, 1 .. n]$, we try to minimize the cost of the assignment, obtained by adding up the costs on each agent. In the following, agents are noted in italics and the tasks in straight font. The term "assignment" is synonymous for this problem with the generic term "candidate" used in the introduction.

For example, for the four agents $1, 2, 3$ and 4 and the tasks 1, 2, 3 and 4, the matrix of costs D is the following:

	1	2	3	4
1	8	13	4	5
2	11	7	1	6
3	7	8	6	8
4	11	6	4	9

Thus, the assignment $\{1 \to 4, 2 \to 3, 3 \to 2, 4 \to 1\}$ assigns task 4 to agent 1, task 3 to agent 2, task 2 to agent 3 and task 1 to agent 4. Its (actual) cost is:

$$f^*(\{1 \to 4, 2 \to 3, 3 \to 2, 4 \to 1\}) = D[1,4] + D[2,3] + D[3,2] + D[4,1] = 25.$$

The objective of the problem is therefore to construct, according to the "Branch and bound" approach, an algorithm that produces any of the assignments of minimal cost.

Question 1. What is the set C of all candidates? What is its cardinality? Suggest a representation and a means of separation for a set of candidates.   70 - Q 1

Question 2. Now we are looking for an evaluation function f. The problem is well 70 - Q 2 suited to decomposing f into the sum of the two functions g^* (for the actual cost of the portion of the assignment already completed) and h for an optimistic estimate of the cost of the remainder of the assignment. A uniform cost strategy is to consider the lowest cost still available for h. Thus, for the above example, if the current set of candidates is represented by the vector $[3, *, *]$, the estimate for h is the smallest of the values of D present when the first row and the third column are removed, multiplied by the number of tasks remaining to be assigned, i.e. 6 (for $D[2,4]$ or $D[4,2]$, see table 6.3) multiplied by 3 (there are three tasks remaining to be assigned). Prove that h meets the admissibility theorem of page 312. Provide the "Branch and bound" search tree for this evaluation function and for the matrix D above.

Question 3. A better solution (*a priori*) would be, for each agent i remaining to be as- 70 - Q 3 signed, for h to take the smallest cost still available in the corresponding row of D. So, for

	1	2	3	4
1	8	13	4	5
2	11	7	1	6
3	7	8	6	8
4	11	6	4	9

Tab. 6.3 – Table of costs D. *The light grey areas are the values of* D *that become unavailable when task 3 is assigned to agent 1.*

the same example as previously, for agent 2 (respectively 3, 4), we would take 6 (respectively 7, 6). Redo the second question by applying this heuristic function.

70 - Q 4   **Question 4.**   In order to improve again the heuristic function h, we repeat the approach of the previous question by successively searching for the minimum for each row remaining to be processed, but this time we delete from future searches the column which produced this minimum. What can be said about the function f defined from this heuristic function?

70 - Q 5   **Question 5.**   A fourth strategy is sought, defined as follows. For the agents still to be assigned to a task, we search for the minimum on all the cells of D still available (and not, as in the previous question, the minimum on the row). The row and column that produced this minimum is removed from future searches. We reiterate as long as we can. Show, using a counterexample, that the theorem of page 312 does not apply.

The solution is on page 327.

Problem 71. The traveling salesman (iterative version)

> *This problem takes the example of the traveling salesman dealt with in the introduction, with the same assumptions. A third evaluation function is studied and its results are compared to those of the previous solutions.*

The traveling salesman problem was already dealt with in problem 57, page 233, in the chapter "Generate and test". It has also been taken as an example and developed in two different ways (by successively applying two evaluation functions) in the introduction to this chapter. In this problem, we define a new evaluation function based on a heuristic function f, which is finer than the other two.

Let us remind (see section 6.1.4, page 314) that we start with an undirected graph $G = (N, V, D)$ of n ($n \geqslant 2$) vertices, valued on $\mathbb{R}_+$, and that the objective is to find out a Hamiltonian cycle (if it exists) of minimal cost beginning and ending at vertex 1.

With the uniform cost method (see section 6.1.4.4, page 318), the value of the evaluation function f is made up of: (i) the cost g^* of the chain already traversed, (ii) the value of h, itself comprised of, on the one hand a lower bound of the cost of the potential Hamiltonian chains for the subgraph G' formed by the vertices not appearing in the chain already traversed, on the other hand the cost of the junction. The lower bound is obtained by the uniform application of the cost of the less costly edge to any edge of G' minus one (to ensure that cycles are ignored).

In the version studied here, we take inspiration from it, but, instead of systematically choosing the less costly edge of the subgraph G', the approach based on a local minimum, defined as follows, is chosen. We calculate the sum of the values of the less costly edges for the n' vertices of G', before subtracting the maximum value of these n' edges, in order to avoid cycles. In this way, the value obtained is indeed a lower bound of the cost of the potential Hamiltonian chains of G'.

The following schema illustrates how the value of $f([146******])$ is calculated. Part (a) shows an undirected valued graph, of eight vertices. Part (b) points out, in bold, the chain already traversed. Its cost $g^*([146*******])$ is $3 + 4 = 7$. Part (c) allows to know a lower bound of the cost of any Hamiltonian chain of the subgraph G' defined by the vertices $2, 3, 5, 7$ and 8. The minimal cost of each vertex is that of the edge carrying the arrow. In total, the cost $4 + 3 + 4 + 3 + 4 - \max(\{4, 3, 4, 3, 4\}) = 14$ is obtained. Last, part (d) shows how the chain already traversed (schema (b)) and the graph G' are joined, by taking the minimal cost edge from the vertex 1 (respectively 6) whose cost is 1 (respectively 2). All this leads to $f([146****]) = 7 + 14 + (1 + 2) = 24$.

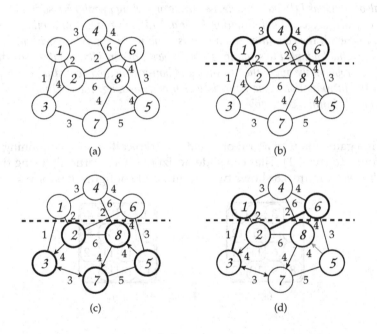

Question 1.   Let us consider the graph (a) of figure 6.7 where the part in bold is the 71-Q1 chain already traversed. Provide the value of f for this configuration. Do the same for the graph (b).

Question 2.   Let us now consider the graph (c) of figure 6.7. Build the search tree, first 71-Q2 with the uniform cost method (see page 318), then with the local minimum method described above.

The solution is on page 329.

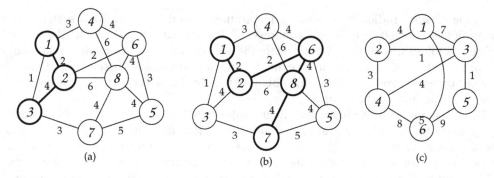

Fig. 6.7 – The three cases studied.

Problem 72. The 8-puzzle

> *8-puzzle (also known as L(l)oyd's puzzle, N-puzzle or sliding puzzle) is a solitary game where the aim is to reach a given final situation from an initial situation in a minimum number of moves. In general, the computer resolution is done using the A* algorithm, a variant of "Branch and bound" adapted to situations where the set of considered states is organized in a graph. In this problem, we apply the "Branch and bound" method according to the principles outlined in the introduction. One point is worth emphasizing: the cardinality of the set of candidates here is infinite countable.*

8-puzzle is a game made of a grid of size $n \times n$ (typically $n = 4$) containing $n^2 - 1$ tiles, numbered from 1 to $(n^2 - 1)$. Tiles can slide horizontally or vertically using the space left free (called *the hole*). Figure 6.8 shows two examples of configuration for $n = 4$:

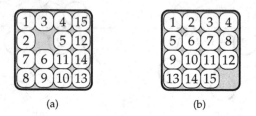

Fig. 6.8 – 8-puzzle: two examples of configuration.

From configuration (a), all at once, one can reach the four configurations appearing at the base of the schema below (the arrows represent the direction of movement of the hole):

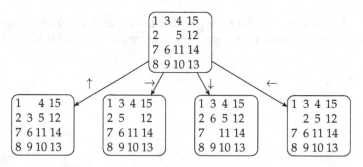

The goal of the game is, starting from a given configuration (for example configuration (a) in figure 6.8), to determine the shortest possible sequence of moves to reach the canonical configuration (b). The question of whether there is a finite sequence of moves between the start and end configuration is not insignificant since only a part of the possible configurations allows to reach the final configuration (b). To decide whether a configuration leads or not to the canonical configuration, one first considers the Manhattan distance d (see question 1 below) between the initial position and the final position ((n, n)) of the hole (for 8-puzzle of figure 6.8, $d = 4$). We then consider the permutation of the integers $1 .. n^2$ obtained by placing end to end the rows of the initial configuration and replacing the hole by the value n^2 (16 in schema (a) of figure 6.8). Let s be the number (even or odd) of inversions in this permutation (see problem 103, page 440). It can be shown[8] that the configuration leads to the final configuration if and only if d has the same parity as s. In case (a) of figure 6.8, s is odd (there are 37 inversions) and d is even, so the configuration cannot lead to the desired configuration. Let us notice that the calculation of this precondition, which will be considered satisfied in the following, is carried out by evaluating $\Theta(n^4)$ conditions.

Faced with such a problem, the temptation is great to consider that the state space to be taken into account is that of the configurations of the puzzle. However, this type of approach is not well suited to the application of the "Branch and bound" approach, since the same configuration may end up on two different branches of the search tree. It is preferable to consider that the set of candidates C is the set of *sequences* from the initial situation of the puzzle to the canonical situation. For a hypothetical example, C could be represented by the set $\{\langle \leftarrow, \leftarrow, \uparrow \rangle, \langle \downarrow, \leftarrow, \downarrow, \uparrow, \rightarrow \rangle, \langle \downarrow, \rightarrow, \downarrow, \uparrow, \uparrow \rangle, \ldots\}$. Here, given the loops that can be traveled, this set is infinite countable, but, as we will see, this characteristic does not have harmful consequences provided that the precondition mentioned above is satisfied. A *solution* is a *candidate* that minimizes the number of moves. As recommended in the introduction to this chapter, the first two steps in the realization of a "Branch and bound" algorithm consist in deciding on the representation of a subset of candidates and, for a given subset, in proposing a partitioning strategy.

Question 1. How to determine whether a move sequence is or is not a candidate?[9] 72 - Q 1
How can a set of candidates be partitioned into several non-empty subsets?

Now, let us turn our attention to the evaluation function f. For a non-empty set of candidates E, this function can be decomposed as follows: $f(E) = g^\star(E) + h(E)$. $g^\star(E)$ is the actual cost (i.e. the number of moves or the length of the sequence E). The heuristic function $h(E)$ is a lower estimate of the number of moves to be added to E in order to get a candidate. A naïve choice is to take $h = 0$. The tree traversal is then made width first. A smarter choice for h is the Manhattan distance. For any tile w of a configuration I of the puzzle, the Manhattan distance is the sum of horizontal and vertical moves necessary for w to attain its position in the final configuration F, or ($|w_{h_I} - w_{h_F}| + |w_{v_I} - w_{v_F}|$) where w_{h_x} (respectively w_{v_x}) is the horizontal (respectively vertical) coordinate of tile w in position X (initial or final). The Manhattan distance of a configuration is the sum of the Manhattan distance of its $(n^2 - 1)$ tiles, or: $\sum_{w=1}^{n^2-1} |w_{h_I} - w_{h_F}| + |w_{v_I} - w_{v_F}|$.

Question 2. Prove that this heuristic function obeys the condition of the theorem of 72 - Q 2
page 312. What is the Manhattan distance of the following configuration?

$$\begin{pmatrix} 4 & 1 & 3 \\ 7 & 2 & 5 \\ & 8 & 6 \end{pmatrix}$$

---

[8]See edouardlucas.free.fr/fr/liste_des_oeuvres.htm.
[9]Or, more exactly: a *set* containing a single candidate.

The availability of the heuristic function h now makes it easy to determine whether or not a sequence is a candidate. In what way? Provide the corresponding search tree and the solution found.

The solution is on page 331.

Problem 73. The nearest neighbor   ○ **:**

> *The characteristics of this problem force to issue a warning. Due to the very restrictive nature of its conditions of use and the existence of a naïve solution with acceptable performance, the sole objective of this problem is to put the "Branch and bound" method into practice, without any applicative ambition. Moreover, this problem illustrates two characteristics that are uncommon in implementations of the "Branch and bound" approach: on the one hand, the set of candidates is here defined in extension (whereas in general it is defined in comprehension) and, on the other hand, the evaluation function f does not break down into the sum of the two functions g^* and h.*

Let C be a non-empty set of points of the plane ($\mathbb{R}^2$) and let a be a point of this plane ($a \notin C$) "away" from the points of C in the Euclidian distance (d) sense. The objective is to identify any point of C closest to a. In other words, we are looking for a point c_0 such that:

$$d(c_0, a) = \min_{c \in C}(d(c, a)).$$

A simple efficient solution is to code the above formula as a sequential search. For purely didactic reasons, our choice is different.

Let R be a rectangle with sides parallel to the axes, which involves all the points of C, and let D be the disk circumscribed to R. In addition, the precondition of "deportation", $a \notin D$, is imposed. Let m be the center of the disc and let r be its radius. Figure 6.9 shows an example of such a situation (here R is indeed a square).

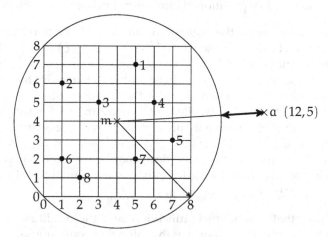

Fig. 6.9 – Example with a set of eight candidate points. The distance between a and the disc is the length of the double arrow in bold. Points are numbered from 1 to 8. The exact coordinates appear in table 6.4. The unique solution is point number 5.

#	coord.	#	coord.
1	(5,7)	5	(7,3)
2	(1,6)	6	(1,2)
3	(3,5)	7	(5,2)
4	(6,5)	8	(2,1)

Tab. 6.4 – Table of coordinates of the eight points in the example in figure 6.9.

As mentioned in page 320 of the introduction, two aspects must be addressed first and foremost: the representation of the set of candidates (the set of points in this problem) and the separation strategy. Above, we suggested that a set of candidates be represented by a rectangle. This one is up and right open (thus, points located on these limits do not belong to the rectangle) and down and left closed. This choice makes it possible to satisfy the partitioning constraint imposed by the "Branch and bound" method. As of separation, a solution is to break up a rectangle into four rectangles of the same size, by cutting it in half lengthwise and widthwise.

Let S be such a rectangle. A rough draft of the evaluation function f is to equate $f(S)$ with the distance between the reference point a and the disk circumscribed at S: $f(S) = (d(m, a) - r)$.

Question 1. The function f as outlined above does not guarantee the admissibility of the "Branch and bound" algorithm. Why? Refine this function, as well as the separation strategy, then demonstrate that the resulting version of f is correct.   73 - Q 1

Question 2. Apply the "Branch and bound" algorithm using the evaluation function of the previous question and provide the search tree for the example in figure 6.9, page 326, and table 6.4.   73 - Q 2

Question 3. Propose a second evaluation function and discuss it in relation to the first one.   73 - Q 3

The solution is on page 331.

6.4   Solutions

Answers to problem 70. Task assignment   *The problem is on page 321.*

Answer 1. The set C of all candidates is the set of permutations of the interval $1 .. n$ 70 - A 1
to the interval $1 .. n$. Its cardinality is $n!$. The following representation is chosen where the array $[t_1, \ldots, t_{i-1}, *, \cdots, *]$ represents all the candidates which assign the task t_1 to the agent $1, \ldots$, the task t_{i-1} to the agent $i - 1$ (the star symbols ($*$) playing the role of "jokers"). Separation consists in the instantiation of the position i of the array with the values of the interval $1 .. n$ still available to get a permutation.

Answer 2. By construction, $0 \leqslant h \leqslant h^\star$: admissibility is guaranteed. The search tree is   70 - A 2
given in figure 6.10.

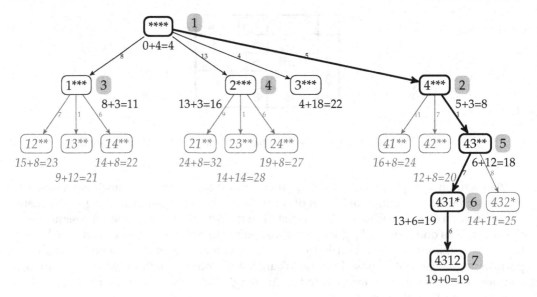

Fig. 6.10 – Search tree for the example.

In this tree, a star symbol (∗) corresponds to an uninstantiated position. The number that appears on a grey background corresponds to the order in which the nodes are taken into account. The estimated cost f is placed under each node. It comes in the form of $g^* + h = f$. The nodes in grey and italics font are the nodes that can be either deleted or ignored after the candidate 4312 has been entered. As an example, the value $f = 18$, obtained for the node 43∗∗, is calculated as follows. g^* is the sum of $D[1,4]$ and $D[2,3]$, i.e. $(5+6) = 11$. The value of h is the minimum of the matrix D when the first line and the fourth column, as well as the second line and the third column are suppressed, multiplied by the number of tasks remaining to be assigned (here 2), thus $6 \times 2 = 12$. Finally, $f = 6 + 12 = 18$.

It can be noticed that the beginning of the processing is going in the right direction until the second pass through the loop, before "getting lost" on the two left-hand branches. The solution expands seventeen nodes and the length of the OPEN queue is less than or equal to 11 (provided that the cleanup strategy presented on page 312 of the introduction is applied).

70 - A 3   **Answer** 3.   Admissibility is ensured for the same reasons as in the previous question. The graphical conventions of the previous answer remain valid for the search tree of figure 6.11, page 329.

The value $f = 19$, obtained for the node 43∗∗, is calculated as follows. $g^* = 6$ as in the answer to the second question, and $h = D[3,1] + D[4,2] = 7 + 6 = 13$. The final result (the assignment $[4,3,1,2]$) has a cost of 19 (it was predictable, it must not change). However, it is obtained by expanding only 11 nodes.

70 - A 4   **Answer** 4.   The function f defined from the heuristic function h does not agree with the admissibility sufficient condition of theorem in page 312. This can be seen by noticing that $h(****) = 23$ $(4+6+7+6)$, which is more than the actual cost $h^*(****) = 19$. The problem is that optimizing locally closes off more globally favorable opportunities. Since the theorem on page 312 deals with a sufficient condition, nothing can be said about the admissibility of the resulting algorithm.

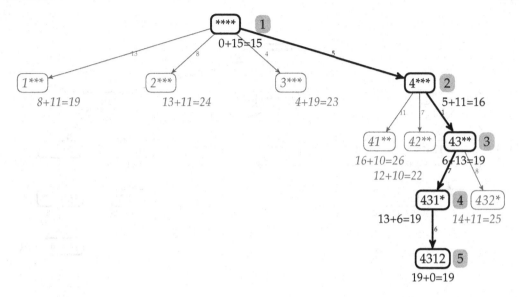

Fig. 6.11 – Search tree for task assignment, second version.

Answer 5.   Let us consider the following matrix D:

	1	2
1	2	1
2	8	2

. Notice that $h(**) = 9$ 70 - A 5

$(1 + 8)$, which is more than the actual cost $h^*(**) = 4$. As in the previous question, nothing can be be said about the admissibility of the resulting algorithm.

Answers to problem 71. The traveling salesman (iterative version)   *The problem is on page 322.*

Answer 1.   Let us consider the graph (a) of figure 6.7, page 324. g^* is equal to $(2+4) = 6$.   71 - A 1
The subgraph G′ is made of the vertices $4, 5, 6, 7$ and 8. The cost of putting side to side is the minimum cost for the edges coming from the vertex 1 (respectively 3) and ending in G′, i.e. 3 (respectively 3). Therefore, splicing costs $3 + 3 = 6$. Now let us try to underestimate the cost of a Hamiltonian chain of G′. The minimum cost for G′ edges from the vertex 4 (respectively $5, 6, 7, 8$) is 4 (respectively $3, 3, 4, 4$). The cost of any Hamiltonian chain on G′ is therefore lower bounded by $(4 + 3 + 3 + 4 - \max(\{4, 3, 3, 4, 4\}))$, which is 14. The value of h is then $6 + 14 = 20$. To get that of f, g^* must be added, which yields $(20 + 6) = 26$.
For the graph (b) of figure 6.7, page 324, g^* is equal to $(2 + 2 + 4 + 4) = 12$. The subgraph G′ consists of the vertices $3, 4$ and 5. The cost of splicing for vertex 1 (respectively 7) is 1 (respectively 3), i.e. a total of $(1 + 3) = 4$. On the other hand, G′ has isolated vertices (the three vertices 3, 4 and 5). Therefore there cannot exist a Hamiltonian chain in G′. Such a configuration does not need to be further developed.

Answer 2.   Applying the uniform cost method to the graph (c) of figure 6.7, page 324,   71 - A 2
leads to the search tree of figure 6.12, page 330. In this graph, the order in which the nodes are considered is the integer appearing on a grey background. The expressions placed under each node are of the form $g^* + h = f$; they do not require further explanation. The symbol ✂ marks a node that does not develop any sons. The solution found is the string $[1, 6, 5, 3, 4, 2, 1]$, for which 18 nodes are created after 11 iterations. Applying the lo-cal minium method produces the tree in figure 6.13, page 330.

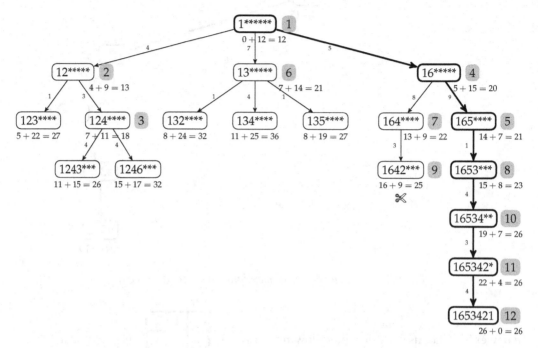

Fig. 6.12 – Search tree for the traveling salesman.

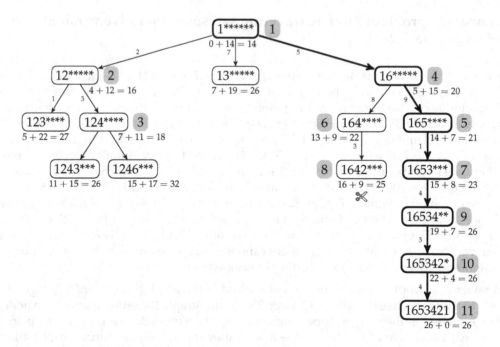

Fig. 6.13 – Search tree for the traveling salesman, second version.

Contrary to the previous case, the node $[1, 3, *, *, *, *]$ never reaches the head of the queue. The solution (the same string $[1, 6, 5, 3, 4, 2, 1]$ as in the uniform cost version) is obtained after 10 iterations (instead of 11 for the previous method) and the creation of 15 nodes. It can also be noticed that, for common nodes, as expected, the estimate obtained here is greater than or equal to the previous one.

Answers to problem 72. The 8-puzzle
The problem is on page 323.

Answer 1.   A sequence of moves s is a candidate iff the final targeted situation is reached by applying s to the initial situation. A sequence that is not a candidate represents the set of all the candidates beginning with this sequence. This answers the first objective (the representation of a subset of candidates). **72 - A 1**

Let us remark that, in a given situation, at most (respectively at least) four (respectively two if the hole is located in a corner) moves are possible. To partition a set of candidates, it is sufficient to add one of the (at most) four possible elementary moves to the current sequence in order to obtain (at most) four subsets.

Answer 2.   For a given tile w and given the move mode, the actual number of elementary moves is lower bounded by $|w_{h_I} - w_{h_F}| + |w_{v_I} - w_{v_F}|$, value that cannot be negative. Summing up over all the tiles, we get: **72 - A 2**

$$0 \leqslant \sum_{w=1}^{n^2-1} |w_{h_I} - w_{h_F}| + |w_{v_I} - w_{v_F}| \leqslant h^\star,$$

which ensures the admissibility of the "Branch and bound" algorithm using this distance. The following table provides the Manhattan distance for each of the eight tiles for a canonical configuration 3×3. The final value of the Manhattan distance is 6.

$$\begin{array}{ccc} 4_1 & 1_1 & 3_0 \\ 7_1 & 2_1 & 5_1 \\ & 8_0 & 6_1 \end{array}$$

A sequence is a candidate if the value of h is zero. The search tree is given in figure 6.14. In this schema, expressions of the form $g^\star + h = f$ placed under each node are self-explanatory. The number on a grey background specifies the order in which the nodes are considered for a separation.

Therefore, a possible solution is the following sequence of moves: $\langle \uparrow, \uparrow, \rightarrow, \downarrow, \rightarrow, \downarrow \rangle$.

Remark

The management of the priority queue OPEN could be optimized by avoiding the introduction of sets of candidates including loops (i.e. which involve elementary sequences of moves involving as many $\uparrow$ as $\downarrow$ and as many $\rightarrow$ as $\leftarrow$).

Answers to problem 73. The nearest neighbor
The problem is on page 326.

Answer 1.   Formulas 6.1 and 6.2 of the theorem in page 309 are sufficient admissibility conditions for the evaluation function. If we stuck to the draft function of the statement of the problem, the condition 6.2 would not be satisfied since a single candidate (a point of **73 - A 1**

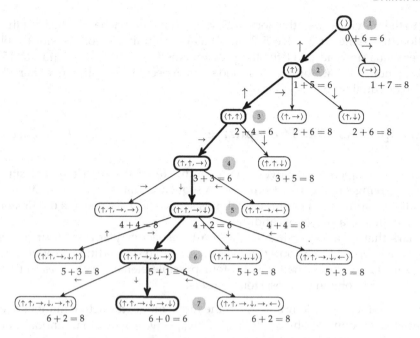

Fig. 6.14 – Search tree for the configuration of question 2.

C) would belong to a rectangle whose circumscribed disk would generally be at a distance of a less than (*not equal to*) the actual distance:

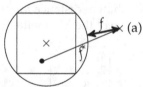

Therefore, the separation strategy must single out the case where there is only one point inside the rectangle, and, if this is the case, identify the rectangle at the coordinates of the point, before it is entered in the queue OPEN. Let us also remind that an empty set (here an empty rectangle of points) must not be placed in the queue.

As for formula 6.1 that imposes that the value of the evaluation function f be less than or equal to the real cost (the distance between the reference point and the disk), the precondition of the statement of the problem demanding that a be outside the initial disk, actually implies that f is a function underestimating the actual distance, as suggested by the previous diagram. Since both conditions of the theorem are met, the algorithm is admissible.

73 - A 2   **Answer** 2.   The diagram below answers the question. The iterated application of the "Branch and bound" approach will, as a consequence of a father's separation, produce rectangles of decreasing sizes. These rectangles are noted in bold in the following figure. For the four candidate leaves, these rectangles are identified by the single point considered. The set appearing under each node is the set of candidate numbers for that node. The value noted in italics is the estimated cost f for the considered node. The numbers on a grey background to the right of some nodes correspond to the successive heads of the priority queue OPEN. The greyed-out nodes are the nodes that can be either deleted or ignored after a candidate has been entered.

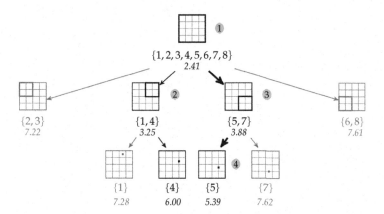

It can be noted that the algorithm starts in the wrong direction since at the end of the first iteration the head of the queue OPEN is the northeast rectangle, while the solution is on the southeast rectangle. This diagram confirms that point 5, with coordinates $(7, 3)$, is indeed the unique solution. It is situated at a distance of 5.39 from point a.

Answer 3. Another possible evaluation function is to systematically consider the smallest rectangle (with sides parallel to the axes) including the points under consideration. In this way, the case of a rectangle containing a single point fits naturally into the general case. On the other hand, it must always be determined whether the rectangle is empty or not. **73 - A 3**

Remark

The two solutions envisaged are very sensitive to the choice of the representation of the sets of points, an aspect overlooked above. A naïve representation – a list of points for example – will require a sequential scan through the set of points to determine whether or not the rectangle is empty (and in the case of the first evaluation function studied, to determine whether or not it contains a single point), thus losing all the interest of the "Branch and bound" approach in terms of temporal complexity. A solution to this problem requires a sophisticated representation of the points of a plane such as the kd-trees (see [17, 7] which are illustrated by the following two diagrams for the eight points in figure 6.9, page 326:

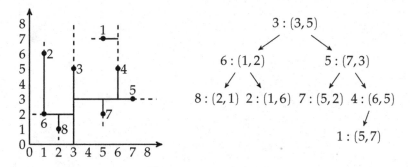

Such a data structure makes it possible to know the number of points inside a given rectangle with performances that make this algorithm a competitor to the naïve sequential search algorithm.

7

Greedy algorithms

> Un gourmet est un glouton qui se
> domine (A gourmet is a glutton who
> refrains himself).
>
> Francis Blanche

7.1 Introduction

7.1.1 Presentation

Like "Generate and test" algorithms (see Chapter 5) or "Branch and bound" algorithms (see Chapter 6), greedy algorithms are deterministic in the sense that they never question the choices they make.

A greedy algorithm can be seen as a direct descent from the root to a leaf in the tree traversed by the "Generate and test" technique. More precisely, at each node of this tree, a greedy algorithm applies a choice rule allowing to select a value of the domain of the considered variable, before moving on to the next node, until meeting a leaf.

One could think that a greedy algorithm is unlikely to find the solution it is looking for, since it actually builds a single one. There are, however, non-trivial problems for which a greedy algorithm always finds a solution. In this case, it is called an *exact* greedy algorithm, or an *optimal* greedy algorithm in the context of an optimization problem. Note that for some optimization problems for which no solution in terms of an optimal greedy algorithm is known, an *approximate* greedy algorithm can be used. Inasmuch as the result delivered is judged to be sufficiently close to the optimal sought, this low-cost approach is preferred to a non-greedy algorithm reaching the optimal at a high or even prohibitive price. Thereafter, we will mainly focus on exact greedy algorithms (problems 83 to 86) or optimal greedy algorithms (the example in section 7.1.3 and problems 74 to 82).

The advantage of greedy algorithms is obviously their low temporal complexity (polynomial), since they are based on the scan of an array or a queue. Therefore, attention will be paid more to the exact or optimal character of the considered algorithms than to their complexity.

A notable characteristic is that here more than anywhere else the discovery of a solution (i.e. the greedy choice rule) is primarily a matter of intuition. It is therefore essential to complete it with a proof of the exact or optimal character of the algorithm that is constructed (see next section), which can sometimes prove difficult, whereas showing a counter-example is enough to prove that the greedy choice strategy considered does not lead to an exact or optimal algorithm.

7.1.2 Proving that a greedy algorithm is exact or optimal

As mentioned before, a greedy algorithm is built like a loop and therefore obeys the methodology highlighted in Chapter 3. In most cases, the proof of the exact or optimal character will be integrated into the construction of the iteration (as part of the specification) and thus into the postcondition and the invariant. For various reasons (notably pedagogical, but see also problem 86, page 371), it happens that the proof is made *a posteriori*, i.e. after the construction of the solution. Since problems without optimality criteria do not pose any specific difficulties, thereafter we focus on the case of optimization problems. The integration of the proof into the construction aims at establishing that the algorithm makes a "lead run" from start to finish in the sense of the optimality criterion. In the technique of a proof *a posteriori*, the most commonly used version is the "exchange argument". Its starting point is an algorithm built from a specification that does not incorporate the optimality property. Then, from any version A of the solution, it must be shown that A is never better than a greedy version G. Other variants exist, such as the "transformation" technique which consists in considering, not any version A, but a fictitious optimal version O, and showing that O can be transformed into the greedy solution G, while remaining optimal, which proves the optimality of G.

We are going to use a common example to illustrate the application of the two techniques: "lead run" and proof *a posteriori*.

7.1.3 An example: task scheduling on a photocopier

Let us consider n photocopy tasks ($n \geqslant 0$), each of which can be performed only in the (closed, nonempty) time interval $I_i = (b_i, e_i)$, for $i \in 1 .. n$. Tasks cannot be split, which means that the necessary time spent on task i amounts to $(e_i - b_i)$. The goal is to plan the passages on the photocopier in order to accomplish as many tasks as possible, knowing that the photocopier accepts only one task at a given time t. Consider, for example, the case below, where the three tasks are represented by the following three intervals: $I_1 = (1, 4.5)$, $I_2 = (5.5, 10)$ and $I_3 = (4, 6)$. Here, the maximum number of tasks that can be performed is 2. Indeed, the only way to obtain this result is to perform the task I_1, then the task I_2. It is impossible to perform all three, nor to perform tasks I_1 and I_3 (which are said to be incompatible since their intervals overlap), nor tasks I_3 and I_2 which are also incompatible.

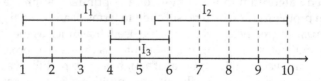

In the following, if I_k is an interval, we denote by $o(I_k)$ (respectively $e(I_k)$) the origin (respectively the end) of I_k. A candidate schedule CS consists of a list of (compatible) intervals $\langle g_1, \ldots, g_k \rangle$ such that, for any i, $o(g_i) < e(g_i)$ and $e(g_i) \leqslant o(g_{i+1})$.

7.1.4 The "lead run" method

As mentioned before, from the outset this technique integrates the optimality criterion in the specification of the algorithm. How to design a greedy strategy for the above problem? The first task must be chosen according to a certain criterion, then, among those still to be completed, the second according to the same criterion, etc. The greedy strategy forbids questioning the choices made. Before trying simple strategies, remember that the goal is to maximize the number of tasks performed on the photocopier.

- The first idea is to choose tasks by increasing duration. In the case of the diagram above, this leads to choose the task I_3 first. Then, no other task can be scheduled and the algorithm stops without having found the best solution. We have therefore proven, by a counter-example, that this greedy algorithm is not optimal.

- The tasks could be chosen in ascending order of their starting time. In our example, task I_1 would be scheduled first, then task I_2 (we discard task I_3, because it partially overlaps task I_1), and the optimum would be reached. But this does not prove the optimality of this greedy algorithm in general. A counter-example is easy to find, as shown in the diagram below with three tasks defined by the intervals $I_1 = (1,6)$, $I_2 = (2,3)$ and $I_3 = (4,5)$.

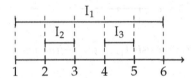

- It can also be seen that choosing the task that will be completed first leaves maximum time to place other tasks after it, with the hope that this will result in planning as many tasks as possible. On the two examples above, this algorithm works and we come up against a counter-example. Our goal is now to build the corresponding program, while demonstrating the optimality of this strategy.

The two principal data structures used in greedy algorithms are an input queue containing data to be processed (often it is a priority queue, see section 1.7, page 30) on the one hand and an output queue gathering the results on the other hand. In this case, both of these entities can be implemented by a FIFO queue (First In, First Out, see section 1.8, page 32). A procedure specific to the problem addressed here is added to the FIFO queues operation set:

procedure *InitFifo*(T, P : **modif**): if T is an array of intervals, this operation, which overwrites the original version of *InitFifo*, puts into the queue P the intervals of T sorted in ascending order on the ends of the intervals.

Designing the algorithm

Below, F is the input queue and R is the output queue. We apply the heuristic of the work partly done (see Chapter 3) and the solution is obtained after two attempts.

First attempt

Invariant Let us imagine that the first i intervals have been processed.

- R_i is the configuration of the output queue R when the greedy strategy has been applied to the list of interval $\langle I_1, \ldots, I_i \rangle$. $R_i = \langle g_1, \ldots, g_k \rangle$ is an optimal schedule for the list $\langle I_1, \ldots, I_i \rangle$.

- F_i is the configuration of the input queue F when the greedy strategy has been applied to the list of intervals $\langle I_1 \ldots, I_i \rangle$, i.e. $F_i = \langle I_{i+1}, \ldots, I_n \rangle$.

Example

Figure 7.1 illustrates such a situation when $i = 5$. Then we have $R_5 = \langle g_1, g_2 \rangle = \langle I_1, I_3 \rangle$. Dotted intervals are inconsistent with R_5. Notice that the list $\langle I_1, I_4 \rangle$ is also a solution. It is however not obtained by the greedy strategy defined above.

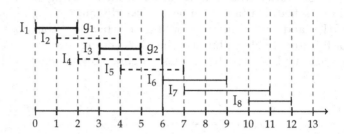

Fig. 7.1 – "Greedy" processing of the list $\langle I_1, \ldots, I_8 \rangle$. Situation reached when $i = 5$. $F_5 = \langle I_6, I_7, I_8 \rangle$ and $R_5 = \langle g_1, g_2 \rangle = \langle I_1, I_3 \rangle$.

Stopping condition The queue F is empty. The conjunction of this proposition and the invariant implies that R is an optimal solution.

Progression The head h of the list F is moved to the bottom of the list R and all intervals incompatible with the interval h are removed from F. This last action requires a loop. Its construction is not developed here. Applying it to the example of figure 7.1, we obtain $R_6 = \langle I_1, I_3, I_6 \rangle$ and $F_6 = \langle I_8 \rangle$. The interval I_7, incompatible with I_6, is removed from the queue F.

All properties of the invariant are trivially restored, with the *notable exception* of optimality. Is there any guarantee that the progression will not cause the greedy solution to lose its optimal character? In other words, can we rule out the following situation, where we have a greedy solution $R = \langle g_1, \ldots, g_k, \rangle$ and an optimal solution $R' = \langle o_1, \ldots, o_k \rangle$, as shown in the diagram below:

to reach, in the next step (see diagrams below), either the situation (a) where the greedy solution has lengthened by one interval, or the situation (b) where the solution R' has, for its part, lengthened by *two* intervals. That would show that the greedy solution is not optimal.

(a)   (b)

The transition to the situation (b) is only possible because $e(o_k) < e(g_k)$. Intuitively, this cannot happen since the greedy solution always chooses the interval that ends first. In order to show this property rigorously, we are going to strengthen the invariant by introducing this property. This leads us to our second attempt.

Second attempt

Invariant The previous version of the invariant is strengthened by modifying the first point as follows. R_i is the configuration of the output queue R when the greedy strategy has been applied to the list of intervals $\langle I_1, \ldots, I_i \rangle$. $R_i = \langle g_1, \ldots, g_k \rangle$ is thus an optimal solution for the list $\langle I_1, \ldots, I_i \rangle$, and there is no other optimal solution ending before $e(g_k)$.

Stopping condition The stopping condition remains unchanged. Its conjunction with the invariant implies the intended purpose.

Progression We focus on maintaining the optimality of the greedy solution. The conjunction of the invariant and the negation of the stopping condition means that there is at least one interval (I_{i+1}) to be processed. Let $R' = \langle o_1, \ldots, o_k \rangle$ be any optimal solution for the list $\langle I_1, \ldots, I_i \rangle$. Choosing a new compatible interval o_{k+1} results in $e(o_k) \leqslant o(o_{k+1})$. Also, according to the invariant, $e(g_k) \leqslant e(o_k)$. In total, by transitivity, we obtain $e(g_k) \leqslant o(o_{k+1})$. The interval o_{k+1} is thus compatible with g_k. But, the greedy strategy imposes to choose g_{k+1} so that $e(g_{k+1})$ is as small as possible – and in particular less than or equal to $e(o_{k+1})$ –, which restores the invariant.

Initialization To establish the invariant when $i = 0$, it is sufficient that R is empty and F consists of the list of the intervals to be considered sorted on their increasing extremities.

Termination At least one element of F is discarded at each step; therefore $|F|$ (the number of elements in the queue F) is a suitable termination function.

The following algorithm is thus deduced:

```
1. constants
2.    n ∈ ℕ₁ and n = ... and T ∈ 1..n → (ℝ₊ × ℝ₊) and T = [...]
3. variables
4.    F ∈ FIFO(ℝ₊ × ℝ₊) and R ∈ FIFO(ℝ₊ × ℝ₊) and t ∈ (ℝ₊ × ℝ₊)
5. begin
6.    InitFifo(T, F); /% Creation of F from the array T of intervals %/
7.    InitFifo(R);
8.    while not IsEmptyFifo(F) do
9.       t ← HeadFifo(F); RemoveFifo(F);
10.      AddFifo(R, t); /% Movement of t at the back of the queue R %/
11.      while not(IsEmptyFifo(F) or else d(HeadFifo(F)) ⩾ f(t)) do
12.         DeleteFifo(F)
13.      end while
14.   end while
15. end
```

In this algorithm, the most expensive operation is the sorting performed by the procedure *InitFifo*, which is assumed to be $\mathcal{O}(n \cdot \log_2(n))$. It is also the complexity of the algorithm.

The demonstration by the "lead run" method is used more generally in the *matroid theory*. Briefly, a matroid is a collection of subsets of a finite set in which each element is positively weighted; by definition, this collection must verify certain axioms. Under these axioms, the best subset of a matroid can be defined: the one whose sum of the weights of its elements is maximal, among those, called *independent*, which comply with a certain property. Matroids have particular properties, due to their axioms, such that it can be demonstrated that there is a greedy algorithm to discover this best subset. The correctness of this algorithm is proven by the "lead run" method.

When it is possible to identify the optimization problem to solve with the problem of finding the best independent subset of a matroid, an exact greedy algorithm is at hand. But this approach comes up against two pitfalls:

1. This identification can be impossible. There are optimization problems with a greedy solution that cannot be solved using the matroid method.

2. This identification may be so difficult to do that it is simpler (if one thinks there is a greedy solution) to attempt to directly demonstrate the optimality of the greedy algorithm by the "lead run" method.

To learn more about matroids and the theory of greedy algorithms, we recommend the book [9].

7.1.5   Proof *a posteriori*: the transformation technique

Let us take again the example of the photocopier. In accordance with the principles underlying this technique, we assume here that the algorithm is designed without taking optimality into account, and we realize the proof of it *after the fact*. For a given set of tasks, let $G = \langle g_1, \ldots, g_p \rangle$ be the p queries selected by the greedy algorithm above, and $O = \langle o_1, \ldots, o_q \rangle$ the q queries of any optimal solution ($p \leqslant q$, since O is optimal):

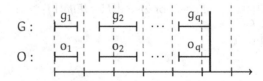

We will prove, by induction on q, that it is possible to transform the list O into the list G without making it lose its optimal status (which will show at the same time that G can be identified with O, and thus that G is also optimal).

Base   For $q = 0$, we also have $p = 0$ since $q \geqslant p$. In this case, we deduce that $G = O$ and that G is optimal.

Induction hypothesis   For $q \geqslant 0$, G and O are identical, and $p = q$:

We will prove, by induction on q, that it is possible to transform the list O into the list G without making it lose its optimal status (which will show at the same time that G can be identified with O, and thus that G is also optimal).

Induction   Two scenarios are to be considered. The first one is characterized by the absence of the element g_{q+1} in G (which thus ends in g_q), the second one by the existence of g_{q+1}. Let us remark that the situation where g_{q+1} exists but not o_{q+1} is to be discarded at once since it violates the condition $q \geqslant p$.

1. The first case is illustrated by the schema below:

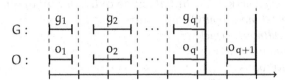

However, this case must be discarded because, according to its strategy, the greedy algorithm would have necessarily included o_{q+1} in its list G.

2. The second case, illustrated below,

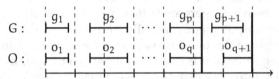

is where the first q elements of G and O are identical (this is the induction hypothesis) and where the end date of g_{q+1} is less than or equal to that of o_{q+1} (due to the greedy strategy used). To recover the induction hypothesis, let us simply replace o_{q+1} by g_{q+1}. This is possible without affecting the optimality of O:

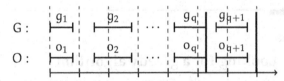

We have shown that it is possible to transform O into G while preserving its optimal character. We conclude that G, the greedy solution, was indeed optimal.

7.2   What to remember about greedy methods

To summarize, a greedy algorithm is based on the following three ingredients:

1. two data structures: usually an input queue (often a priority queue) and an output queue (mainly a FIFO queue) inside which the components of the solution are placed,

2. a strategy for handling elements that are extracted from the input queue, before joining (or not!) the output queue,

3. either a proof that the algorithm does indeed provide an exact or optimal solution, or a counter-example.

The following generic code can be proposed, where F is the input queue, R is the output queue, and t and t' are two auxiliary variables (the operation identifiers do not convey any assumptions about the type of queue used).

1. *InitInputQueue*(F) ; /% *Creation of the input queue %/*
2. *InitOutputQueue*(R) ; /% *Initialization of the output queue %/*
3. **while not** *IsEmptyInputQueue*(F) **do**
4.   t ← *HeadInputQueue*(F) ;
5.   *DeleteInputQueue*(F) ;
6.   *ElementProcessing*(t, t') ;
7.   *InsertOutputQueue*(R, t')
8. **end while**

This is only a general framework. As we have already said, the entry queue is most often a priority queue, but later on we come across variants where priorities are fixed from the outset, or successive integers are sufficient, or several elements are removed from the queue at once. The output queue is usually a FIFO queue. However, in some cases, it may be necessary to change the order or nature of the elements already entered. As for the element processing strategy, it is rarely as simple as a transfer from the input queue to the output queue: an iterative calculation, a breakdown or a selection of elements is most often necessary. The reader will have understood that a greedy solution to a particular problem turns out to be a more or less substantial variation around this algorithm.

7.3   Problems

Problem 74. Looking for a greedy algorithm   ⚇ •

> *This problem has already been studied in the introduction of the chapter titled "Generate and test" (see Chapter 5). Here, the point is to test several greedy strategies.*

We consider an array $T[1 .. n]$ of positive integers, where n is even and the elements of T are sorted in ascending order. We want to copy T in two bags B_1 and B_2, of the same size $n/2$ and of respective sums $Sum1$ and $Sum2$, so that $(Sum1 \leqslant Sum2)$ and $(Sum2 - Sum1)$ is minimum. Specifically, assuming that T represents the input queue, the postcondition of the algorithm consists of the following five conjuncts:

1. The bags have the same cardinality: $|S_1| = |S_2|$.

2. The sums $Sum1$ and $Sum2$ are such that $(Sum1 \leqslant Sum2)$.

3. The difference $(Sum2 - Sum1)$ is minimum.

4. The input queue is empty.

5. $S_1 \sqcup S_2$ is the bag of the initial values of T.

74 - Q 1   **Question** 1.   On the basis of this postcondition, imagine three greedy strategies to deal with this problem and show that they do not produce optimal solutions.

74 - Q 2   **Question** 2.   Does this prove that there is no greedy algorithm for this problem?

The solution is on page 375.

Problem 75. Binary search trees

> *The problem dealt with below is considered from a dynamic programming point of view in problem 135 page 669. Here, we stick to a greedy approach.*

A set of n integer values $\{x_1, \ldots, x_n\}$ is given, each of them associated with a probability $p(x_i)$. In order to facilitate a positive search (searching for an item that is known to be present in the set), these n values are stored in a binary search tree (bst for short). The *cost* of such a bst A is defined as:

$$\text{cost}(A) = \sum_{k=1}^{n} p(x_k) \cdot (d_k + 1), \qquad (7.1)$$

where d_k is the depth of node x_k in the tree A. The value $\text{cost}(A)$ is indeed the (mathematical) expectation of the number of comparisons to be made to find an element present in the tree A. The objective is to build the bst of minimal cost by a greedy approach.

Example

The figure below shows on the one hand a list of five values x_i each weighted by a probability $p(x_i)$, and on the other hand a bst constructed from these five values.

x_i	1	2	3	4	5	6
$p(x_i)$	0.15	0.19	0.17	0.18	0.14	0.17

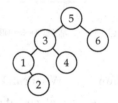

According to definition 7.1, the cost of this tree is

$$1 \cdot p(5) + 2 \cdot p(3) + 2 \cdot p(6) + 3 \cdot p(1) + 3 \cdot p(4) + 4 \cdot p(2),$$

i.e.

$$1 \cdot 0.14 + 2 \cdot 0.17 + 2 \cdot 0.17 + 3 \cdot 0.15 + 3 \cdot 0.18 + 4 \cdot 0.19,$$

expression whose value is 2.57.

Question 1. The idea of placing the most likely values as high as possible in the tree seems favorable to an optimal search. It can be obtained in a greedy way, either by constructing the tree by inserting at the leaves from a list of values sorted on increasing probabilities, or on the contrary by making an insertion at the root from a list of values sorted on decreasing probabilities. A leaf insertion of a value v in a bst is done by inserting v in the left or right subtree depending on the relative position of v with respect to the root, until an empty tree is reached. A root insertion is done by splitting the values of the initial tree into two sub-trees, depending on the value to be inserted, and then rooting these two sub-trees to v. Give the tree obtained from the test set above, by applying the first of these strategies ("leaf insertion"). How much does it cost? 75 - Q 1

Question 2. Still starting from the same test set, show, by a counter-example, that this strategy is not optimal. 75 - Q 2

The solution is on page 377.

Problem 76.   Relays for mobile phones   ⧉ •

This problem is close to the one presented in the introduction (task scheduling on a photo-copier). Consequently, it should be easily solved by the reader.

We consider a long straight country road, along which dwellings are scattered. Each house must be connected to the mobile phone network by an operator. A relay antenna on the network allows the use of the phone in a fixed remote area of $d/2$ around the relay (all antennas have the same power). The operator wants to install as few antennas as possible to "cover" all the houses.

The problem can be formalized in the following way. The array T ($T \in 1 .. n \rightarrow \mathbb{R}_+$) represents the position of each house along the road. We are looking for a list S of real values, having a minimal number of elements p, $S = \langle s_1, \ldots, s_p \rangle$, such that for any value T[i], there is a value s_j checking the constraint $(|T[i] - s_j| \leqslant d)$. S is an optimal list of relay antenna positions. In the diagram below, line T represents the position of the houses, line O shows an optimal coverage, with three relays, while line Q covers all the houses, but with four relays (and an overlap of the two relays on the right).

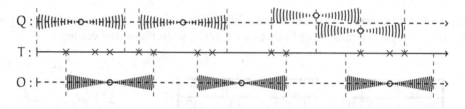

76 - Q 1   **Question 1.**   What can be said about the following two greedy strategies?

1. A relay is placed at each house.
2. Proceeding from left to right, a relay is placed at the level of each house which is not yet covered by the relays already installed.

76 - Q 2   **Question 2.**   Propose a third greedy strategy which can be expected to be optimal.

76 - Q 3   **Question 3.**   By developing a "lead run" strategy (see section 7.1.4, page 336), build an exact greedy algorithm solving the problem on the basis of the greedy strategy of the previous question. What is its complexity (that of a sort can serve as a reference)?

76 - Q 4   **Question 4.**   It is now assumed that the optimality of the solution has not been proven during the construction of the algorithm. Prove by a method *a posteriori* (see section 7.1.5, page 340), that the previous greedy strategy is optimal.

The solution is on page 378.

Problem 77.   Ordering purchases of varying prices   ⧉ ⦂

This problem is a simple illustration of the exchange argument method. No code is required.

The owner of a football club wants to buy some players at a training center. The *mercato* rules prohibits him from buying more than one player per month. The price of the players is the same at the beginning – it is noted s – but this price varies over time, differently for each player. Thus, since the price of player j is s at the start, it will be equal to $(s \cdot r_j^t)$ t months later. The r_j rate depends on how fast the player is progressing, but it is always strictly above 1. We rely on an estimated rate of progression, known at time $t = 0$, which is assumed to be different for each player. The objective is to define a greedy strategy that allows to buy one player per month and ensures to acquire the coveted players while spending as little money as possible. Last, it is assumed that the buyer has no competitors.

Question 1.   Give two simple strategies that can be used as a basis for a greedy algo-   77 - Q 1
rithm. Which strategy seems to be the best?

Question 2.   Show, by applying the exchange argument (see section 7.1.2, page 336),   77 - Q 2
that it is optimal.

The solution is on page 381.

Problem 78. Optimal broadcast

Prim and Dijkstra algorithms have many similarities: same date of publication (1959 although the first one was in fact "rediscovered" since it was originally published by V. Jarnik in 1930), algorithms aiming at "minimal costs" in graphs (connected undirected for the first one, directed for the second one), and last but not least, exact greedy algorithms. Both algorithms are textbook cases found in the literature under the rubric "graph" as well as "greedy". The present statement focuses on the correction of the loop they are relying on. A feature of Prim's proposed algorithm is that its result does not use a FIFO queue.

Two related issues

We are provided with a communication network consisting of n sites. We consider a first problem (for which Prim's algorithm is a solution) where sites are connected to each other by bidirectional links so that any site can reach any other (in the sense of information routing) through a series of links. One of the sites called source is distinguished from which information is broadcasted to all others. However, each link has its own usage cost (positive integer) and routing is sought such that the sum of the costs associated with the links used to reach all sites is minimal. In the second problem (solved by Dijkstra's algorithm), sites are connected by oriented links and there may be no path between one or more pairs of sites. The objective is the same as above, but the optimal routing is based on the sum of the costs associated with the links used to reach each site. Apart from the nature of the network, these two problems therefore differ essentially in the function to be minimized.

Many other problems lead to these same paradigms for finding an optimal solution, for example, determining the optimal cabling route for a group of buildings or choosing an optimal irrigation system for tiered plots from a water point above them.

Before continuing, let us illustrate these two problems. In figure 7.2, the optimal information broadcasting path for a network with five sites, described in part (a), is given in part (b). In part (a) of figure 7.3, we consider a directed network modeled on the previous one and we provide for each of the sites 2 to 5, on the one hand, the value of the shortest path from the source (site 1) in part (b), on the other hand, the tree associated with the optimal path in part (c).

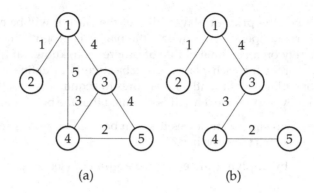

Fig. 7.2 – A network and the optimal associated route.

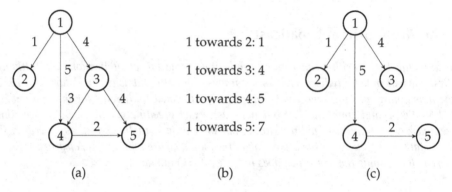

1 towards 2: 1

1 towards 3: 4

1 towards 4: 5

1 towards 5: 7

Fig. 7.3 – A network, minimal broadcasting costs from site 1 and the associated tree.

Remark

It can be observed that the results obtained do not "coincide". Indeed, according to part (b) of the first diagram, the routing of information from site 1 to site 4 (respectively 5) costs 7 (respectively 9) and is therefore not minimal, whereas the overall routing cost (in the sense of the first problem) for the second diagram has a value of 12 (arcs $(1,2), (1,3), (1,4)$ and $(4,5)$) and is not minimal either. This justifies (if need be) the existence of two quite distinct problems and therefore the need for different algorithms to solve them.

Prim's algorithm

Definitions and properties

Diverse notions and notations related to graphs and trees are used throughout this problem and the reader can refer to sections 1.5, page 22, and 1.6, page 27. Thereafter, $G = (N, A, P)$ denotes an undirected graph whose set of vertices (respectively edges) is N (respectively A), valued on positive integers ($P \in A \rightarrow \mathbb{N}_1$), that is connected, i.e. there is a string connecting any pair of distinct vertices. Similarly, $T = (N, A, P)$ denotes an undirected tree made of the set of vertices (respectively edges) N (respectively A), valued on positive integers. The weight of a tree is the sum of values of its edges (or branches). It can be remarked that a tree with k vertices has $(k - 1)$ edges on the one hand, that a unique elementary string connects any pair of vertices of a tree on the other hand. A covering tree of the graph $G = (N, A, P)$ is a tree (*a priori* non-rooted) involving all the vertices of G. A minimal cost covering tree of G is called minimal weight covering tree (mwct). It is easy to show that any graph G (connected) has at least one mwct and that any tree is its own mwct. With reference to a graph $G = (N, A, P)$, a tree T is said to be *promising* if it is a sub-tree (in the broad sense) of a mwct.

Property 5:
Adding to a tree an edge joining two of its vertices gives birth to an elementary cycle.

Question 1. Prove the validity of property 5. 78 - Q1

The idea behind Prim's algorithm is to set a vertex as the source, this latter constituting a promising tree (vertex number 1 afterward), and to "enrich" a promising tree by adding to it a new edge (and thus a new vertex) of the graph G that is to be covered. By virtue of property 5, such an addition can only be made with a *mixed* edge consisting of a pre-existing vertex of the initial tree (*inner* vertex) and a vertex not yet part of it (*outer* vertex). The question is therefore to determine which edge of $G = (N, A, P)$ can/should be inserted in a promising tree so that the new tree is also promising.

Property 6:
Let $G = (N, A, P)$ be a graph and $T = (N', A', P')$ with $N' \subset N$ be a sub-graph of G that is a promising tree. Adding to T one of the minimal value mixed *edges of G leads to a new promising tree.*

Question 2. Prove property 6. 78 - Q2

Construction of the algorithm

Prim's algorithm will be constructed as an exact greedy algorithm by adopting the "lead run" principle (see section 7.1.4, page 336). The postcondition of the program to be carried out can be stated as follows: "$T = (N', A', P')$ is a promising tree of $G = (N, A, P)$ and $card(A') = card(N') - 1 = card(N) - 1 = n - 1$". So it is natural to pose:

Invariant $T = (N', A', P')$ is a promising tree of G with $N' \subseteq N$.

Stopping condition $card(A') = n - 1$.

Progression By virtue of property 6, we integrate in the promising tree $T = (N', A', P')$ with $N' \subset N$, one of the minimum value *mixed* edges of G, that is to say an edge $(s1, s2)$ with s1 an outer vertex and s2 an inner vertex ($s2 \in N'$).

Termination $n - 1 - card(A')$.

Initialization The tree reduced to the single vertex 1 (the source) is taken as the initial promising tree.

It can be observed that the set of mixed edges can be represented by a total *function* mE associating to each outer vertex the nearest inner vertex in the sense of the value of the edges connecting the vertices (mE $\in 2..n \to 1..n$). This function should therefore be updated after inserting a mixed edge in the progression. Despite the orientation related to mE, the term edges is used afterward.

Among the many ways to represent the resulting tree, consistently with mE we choose an inverse tree rooted on the source (vertex 1). Consequently, the *total* function iE will represent the edges that are part of the tree (in progress) by associating to any vertex, source excluded, its father in this tree (iE $\in 2..n \rightarrow 1..n$).

The set of outer vertices and the set of inner vertices constitute a partition of the set N of vertices of G. This is the meaning to be given to line 6 of the code below. This remark will be fully exploited later, in the implementation of the algorithm.

P^T denotes the transposed matrix of the matrix P and since the considered graph is undirected, it is represented by a matrix P such that $P = P^T$. In these two matrices, the absence of an edge in the graph results in the conventional value $+\infty$.

Given these choices, the abstract version of the algorithm is presented below:

```
1.  constants
2.     n ∈ ℕ₁ and n = ... and P ∈ 1..n × 1..n → ℕ₁ and P = Pᵀ and P = [...] and
3.     IsConnected(G)
4.  variables
5.     iE ∈ 2..n → 1..n and mE ∈ 2..n → 1..n and
6.     dom(iE) ∪ dom(mE) = 2..n and dom(iE) ∩ dom(mE) = ∅
7.  begin
8.     iE ← ∅ ; mE ← 2..n × {1} ;
9.     for k ∈ 2..n do
10.        let e, i such that
11.           (e, i) ∈ mE and P(e, i) = min ({P(l, j) | (l, j) ∈ mE})
12.        begin
13.           iE ← iE ∪ {{e, i}}; mE ← mE − {(e, i)};
14.           /% mE update for the complete restoration of the invariant, i.e. for any
              outer vertex e, mE(e) means the inner vertex closest to e %/
15.           for e' ∈ dom(mE) do
16.              if P(e', e) < P(e', mE(e')) then
17.                 mE(e') ← e
18.              end if
19.           end for
20.        end
21.     end for;
22.     write(iE)
23. end
```

Implementations

Concerning the actual implementation, the two sets iE and mE are aggregated into the single array denoted Arc. This array is defined on the interval $2..n$ (vertex 1 is excluded because it is not the origin of any arc, but it is always part of the inner vertices) and has a value in $1..n$. The partition that distinguishes the outer vertices from the inner vertices is represented by the Boolean array External, also defined on the interval $2..n$.

78 - Q 3   **Question 3.**   Write the function *MinCostOutVertex* which refines lines 10 and 11 of the generic algorithm and searches for the outer vertex closest to an inner vertex. How complex is this function in terms of the number of conditions evaluated?

78 - Q 4   **Question 4.**   Give the code of Prim's algorithm for the proposed implementation and its complexity (number of conditions evaluated).

78 - Q 5   **Question 5.**   Apply the previous algorithm to the following graph:

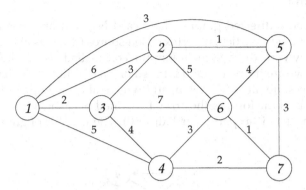

Question 6. It can be observed that the proposed implementation uses neither input, nor output queues. Specify their substitutes.

78 - Q 6

With an implementation based on a priority queue F as the input queue, the frame of the algorithm becomes:

1. **constants**
2.   /% *declaration of* n *and* P %/
3. **variables**
4.   /% *declaration of variables among which* iE *and* F %/
5. **begin**
6.   /% *initialization of* iE *and* F %/;
7.   **for** $k \in 2 .. n$ **do**
8.   /% *the (edge) head of queue* F *is put into* iE %/;
9.   /% *update of queue* F *for the complete restoration of the invariant; a loop traversing* F *is carried out in which the mixed edge relative to each outer vertex e is, where appropriate, replaced (deletion and insertion) by one of lesser value.* %/
10.   **end for;**
11.   **write**(aI)
12. **end**

Question 7. Deduce a minimum class of complexity (in terms of conditions evaluated) from such a solution and conclude as to its interest.

78 - Q 7

Remarks about Prim's algorithm

1. Prim's algorithm can be easily adapted to the search for a *maximum* weight coverage tree, as well as to graphs with valuations of any sign.

2. The reader will be able to check that, applied to the example of figure 7.2, page 346, Prim's algorithm delivers (apart from the inversion of orientation) the tree of part c.

3. Kruskal's algorithm solves the same problem as Prim's algorithm. Its complexity in $\Theta(m \cdot \log_2(m))$ with $m = \text{card}(A)$, is due to the preliminary sorting of the edges of the graph $G = (N, A, P)$ according to their increasing value. It has the advantage of being able to process non-connected graphs (by delivering one tree per connected component).

Dijkstra's algorithm

Let $G = (N, V, P)$ be a directed graph, where $\text{card}(N) = n$ and P is an arc (or arrow) valuation on $\mathbb{N}_1$. Let d be a particular vertex called source ($d = 1$ as above). The problem is to determine, for any vertex f of N, the minimum cost (called *distance* below) to go from d to f. The algorithm we are trying to build is based on an iteration such that, for a sub-graph G' of G, the distances are already known, and which, at each step, adds a new vertex to G'. The final result is in the form of the array L, defined over the interval $1 .. n$, where $L[i]$ is the distance from d to i (in particular $L[d] = 0$). The graph in figure 7.4 is used as an illustration thereafter.

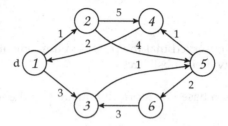

Fig. 7.4 – An example of a valued directed graph.

Notations

- Let c be a path in G; $\text{cost}(c)$ is the sum of the valuations of the arcs part of this path (in case of circuits, duplicate arcs are counted as many times as they occur).

- Let f be a vertex of G ($f \in N$); $\text{path}(f)$ is the set (possibly infinite) of all the paths from d to f; $\text{dist}(f)$ is the distance from d to f, i.e.:

$$\text{dist}(f) \;\widehat{=}\; \min_{c \in \text{path}(f)} (\text{cost}(c)).$$

For figure 7.4, with $d = 1$, we have:

- $\text{cost}(\langle 1, 2, 4 \rangle) = 6$,

- $\text{path}(4) = \{\langle 1, 2, 4 \rangle, \langle 1, 3, 5, 4 \rangle, \langle 1, 2, 4, 1, 2, 4 \rangle, \langle 1, 3, 5, 6, 3, 5, 4 \rangle, \ldots\}$,

- $\text{dist}(5) = 4$, $\text{dist}(6) = 6$.

Construction of the algorithm—first version

As with Prim's algorithm, we are looking for a "lead run" type solution (see section 7.1.4, page 336) and so it is a matter of building an iteration.

Invariant We use "the work partly done" strategy (see section 3.4, page 99). Let us formulate the assumption that array L contains the distances from d to all the vertices of N' ($N' \subseteq N$). More specifically:

$$I_1 \;\widehat{=}\; \forall f \cdot (f \in N' \Rightarrow L[f] = \text{dist}(f)).$$

Moreover, if N' is not empty, $d \in N'$:

$$I_2 \;\widehat{=}\; (N' \neq \varnothing \Rightarrow d \in N').$$

Let us introduce the variable N″ such that $(N'' \triangleq N - N')$ and let:

$$I_3 \triangleq (N = N' \cup N'') \text{ and } (N' \cap N'' = \varnothing).$$

In the example of figure 7.5, $d = 1$, $N' = \{1, 2, 3\}$ and the three distances between the vertex 1 and these three vertices are known. They appear in the lower part of each of these vertices.

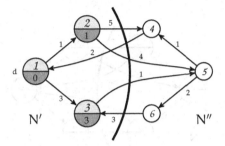

Fig. 7.5 – Situation after the insertion of three vertices into N′ (the value of L for these three vertices appear in the lower zone of these vertices).

Stopping condition

$$N'' = \varnothing.$$

It can be checked that the conjunction of the invariant and the stopping condition actually implies the goal: the distances from d to all vertices are known.

Progression A vertex of N″ to be moved to N′ must be selected while ensuring that the invariant is preserved. However, in the absence of additional information, it is difficult to choose such a vertex. This leads to propose a second version obtained by strengthening the invariant (I_1 **and** I_2 **and** I_3) with a fourth conjunct I_4 aimed at facilitating the construction of the progression.

Construction of the algorithm—second version

Invariant A greedy strategy consists in assigning to each vertex f of N″ an overestimation of the distance between d and f and, at each step of progression, to move the best vertex of N″ into N′. In order to have an exact greedy algorithm, the estimation for this vertex should be *exactly* the desired distance. Of course, the introduction of this overestimation property requires the addition of a fragment of code to maintain it. Before providing further details, it is necessary to complete the above notations.

- We call $ePath(f)$ (for e-path) the set of all the paths from the source d ($d \in N'$) to a vertex f of N″ such that all vertices belong to N′, except f.

- We denote by $eDist(f)$ (for e-distance) the lowest cost among those of the e-paths ($ePath$) from d to f:

$$eDist(f) \triangleq \min_{c \in ePath(f)} (cost(c)).$$

If $ePath(f) = \varnothing$ then $eDist(f) = +\infty$.

The predicate I_4 added to the previous invariant (I_1 **and** I_2 **and** I_3) specifies that for any element f of N″, L[f] is the e-distance from d to f:

$$I_4 \;\hat{=}\; \forall f \cdot (f \in N'' \Rightarrow L[f] = eDist(f)).$$

The example of figure 7.5 is then completed as shown in figure 7.6, where L[4] = $eDist(4) = 6$, L[5] = $eDist(5) = 4$. On the other hand, there is (yet) no e-path from d to vertex 6, therefore L[6] = $eDist(6) = +\infty$.

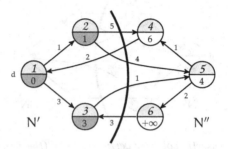

Fig. 7.6 – Situation after three progression steps. The values of dist(f), *for* f ∈ N′, *and* eDist(f), *for* f ∈ N″, *appear in the lower part of each vertex. They correspond to* L[f].

Once $d \in N'$, if $f \in N''$, any path from d to f has an e-path as a prefix (possibly itself). Let $\langle d, a_1, \ldots, a_p, f \rangle$ be a path. Its e-path is $\langle d, a_1, \ldots, a_i \rangle$ such that, for any j in the interval 1 .. i, $a_j \in N'$ and $a_{i+1} \in N''$. So, the schema below shows a path from d to f and, in bold, the corresponding e-path:

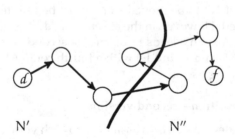

Therefore, such a path is never less expensive than the corresponding e-path, hence the following property (which is not formally demonstrated):

Property 7:
Let $f \in N''$, $d \in N'$, c *be a path from* d *to* f *and* c′ *be the corresponding e-path. We have* $cost(c') \leqslant cost(c)$.

In figure 7.5, page 351, $c = \langle 1, 2, 5, 6 \rangle$ is a path from $d = 1$ to $f = 6$, which has a cost of 7. The corresponding e-path is $c' = \langle 1, 2, 5 \rangle$, which has a cost of 5.

Stopping condition The stopping condition remains unchanged with respect to the first version.

Progression As mentioned above, among all of the elements of N″, we choose the one that is the closest to d, in terms of e-distance. At least one does exist since, according to the precondition of the progression, N″ is not empty. The code of the progression is thus obtained by introducing a local "constant" g, and the part of the code denoted by (C) is to be instantiated:

1. **let** g **such that**
2.   g ∈ N″ **and** $L[g] = \min_{f \in N''} (L[f])$
3. **begin**
4. $N'' \leftarrow N'' - \{g\}$; $N' \leftarrow N' \cup \{g\}$;
5.   ⋮ (C)
6. **end**

Question 8.   Prove that, if its construction can be achieved, this algorithm is an exact greedy algorithm (in other words, the selected vertex g is such that $L[g] = \text{dist}(g)$). In the example of figure 7.6, which situation is reached after executing line 4 of the progression?   78 - Q 8

Question 9.   Complete the construction of the progression (i.e. write the fragment of code (C) that restores the conjunct I_4 of the invariant). Based on the example in figure 7.6, what is the situation reached after the progression is executed?   78 - Q 9

Question 10.   Complete the construction of the algorithm and write its code.   78 - Q 10

Question 11.   What would happen to property 7 if the precondition that requires that the valuation of P never be negative was abandoned?   78 - Q 11

Question 12.   We envisage a refinement of the algorithm provided in response to question 10 based on the following elements: (i) the sets N′/N″ are represented by a characteristic vector W (W ∈ 1 .. n → 𝔹) and (ii) in order to avoid a complex evaluation of its stopping condition, the *while* loop is replaced by a *for* loop, whose body is executed n times. Give an informal description of the resulting algorithm. What is its complexity in terms of conditions evaluated?   78 - Q 12

Question 13.   In the perspective of a second refinement, heap type priority queues (see section 1.7, page 30) are under consideration. On this basis, describe informally the different data structures, as well as the steps of the algorithm, and provide its code. Analyze its temporal complexity (in terms of conditions evaluated) and compare it to that obtained in response to the previous question.   78 - Q 13

Question 14.   In the above, it has been suggested that the main *for* loop of the algorithm be executed n times. Explain how the number of steps could be limited to (n − 2) in the priority queue-based algorithm.   78 - Q 14

Question 15.   So far, we have only been concerned with distances. In general, an optimal *path* is also expected. The set of optimal paths from d to each vertex can be represented by a reverse tree (a son vertex designates its father) whose root is d, as shown in the following diagram for the example in figure 7.4, page 350:   78 - Q 15

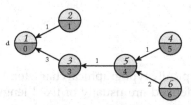

Indicate what changes need to be made to the algorithm to build this tree.

Question 16.   Dijkstra's original paper was about finding the distance between any two given vertices d and s of G. How can the algorithm given in answer to the question 10 be adapted to solve this variant of the problem discussed here?

Conclusion

The reader can check that, applied to the graph of part (a) in figure 7.3, page 346, Dijkstra's algorithm delivers the array L hereafter:

$$
\begin{array}{ccccc}
1 & 2 & 3 & 4 & 5 \\
\hline
\end{array}
$$

0	1	4	7	9

corresponding to the values given in the tree of part (b) in figure 7.3, page 346.

Dijkstra's algorithm can easily be adapted to the search for maximal value paths from a source with a directed graph whose arcs bear non-positive values.

Other minimal value paths algorithms are presented in problems 131 on page 660, 132 on page 661 and 133 on page 664 in Chapter 9.

With regard to the comparison of Prim and Dijkstra algorithms, it should be noted that:

- The values carried by the edges or arcs were integers, but could just as well be real.

- If Prim's algorithm can work with valuations of any sign, we saw in question 11 that Dijkstra's algorithm cannot (which may limit its use for some problems).

- The two algorithms are similar, having as a general structure a loop, which is not surprising since they are two greedy algorithms. But the similarity goes beyond that, because in both cases, one is led to: (i) partition all the vertices of the considered graph, (ii) choose a vertex constituting an optimal choice, and finally (iii) perform an update relative to the vertices which have not yet been chosen.

The solution is on page 382

Problem 79. Optimal data compression

> *The objective of this problem is to build an algorithm that provides a code for compacting data (i.e. compressing without loss of information). In many respects, the solution studied here holds a special place in the problems of this book. First of all, by its importance: despite its age (it was published in 1952), Huffman's algorithm often occupies one of the stages in data compression applications. By its apparent simplicity on the other hand, which takes the form of a very concise algorithm, which contrasts with the effort it takes to prove its optimality. Its efficiency could be added to its credit, as well as its coverage in terms of data structures, etc., in short an excellent problem.*

Introduction

Binary coding of symbols (typically typographical characters) is the subject of international standards. The codes thus defined are usually of fixed length (8 bits for the Ascii code,

16 bits for the UTF-16 code, etc.). However, due to their universal vocation, their use generally proves to be costly (in terms of space for file coding, in terms of time for transmission). Substantial improvement can be achieved by using an *ad hoc* code instead (depending only on the text considered) of *variable* length, which accounts for the frequency of each character in the text. Consider for example the following text t of 17 characters:

$$t = mammy \sqcup made \sqcup a \sqcup mead$$

expressed using the vocabulary $V = \{a, d, e, m, y, \sqcup\}$ (the character $\sqcup$ represents space). Using a fixed length eight bit code, this text occupies $17 \cdot 8 = 136$ bits. A fixed length three bit code (the best we can do here, using a fixed length code, for a vocabulary V of six symbols) requires $17 \cdot 3 = 51$ bits.

A variable length code is likely to improve the situation. That is what is shown by the one used in table 7.1 which allows to code the text t above by the following string of 49 (instead of 51) bits (the dot symbol denotes concatenation):

$$10 \cdot 1111 \cdot 10 \cdot 10 \cdot 00 \cdot 110 \cdot 10 \cdot 1111 \cdot 1110 \cdot 01 \cdot 110 \cdot 1111 \cdot 110 \cdot 10 \cdot 01 \cdot 1111 \cdot 1110$$

Intuitively, this will be even truer when shorter code words are assigned to the most frequent characters.

symbols	y	d	e	$\sqcup$	a	m
frequencies	1	2	2	3	4	5
code words	00	1110	01	110	1111	10

Tab. 7.1 – An example of code and frequencies for the vocabulary $V = \{a, d, e, m, y, \sqcup\}$ related to the previous text.

The objective of the problem is to build an algorithm (developed by D.A. Huffman in 1952) that, for a given text t (and therefore a given vocabulary and frequency table), provides an optimal code, i.e. which codes t with as few bits as possible.

Thereafter, the concepts of code and tree prefixes are introduced before defining the concepts of Huffman's code and tree.

Code/tree prefixes

A prefix code is a code inside which no two characters are such that the code word of one character is a prefix of the code word of the other. For instance, this forbids to code ℓ by 1 et e by 1011. The advantage of a prefix code lies in the decoding phase (passage from the bit string to the corresponding character string), insofar as this step can be carried out in a deterministic way[1]: as soon as a code word c is identified at the beginning of the string b to be decoded, it is sufficient to translate it to the corresponding character, remove it from b and reapply the process on what remains of b. Fixed length codes are, by construction, prefix codes as well as the one in table 7.1.

A prefix code can be represented as a complete binary tree (i.e. without any simple point, see section 1.6, page 27), whose left branches are labelled by 0's and right branches by 1's, and whose leaves are labelled by a character. The code of table 7.1 is represented by the tree (a) of figure 7.7.

---

[1]The focus here is only on deterministic codes, i.e. codes for which the coding process requires no backtracking.

Nevertheless, prefix is not a synonym of optimal: for the above text t (and therefore for the vocabulary V and frequencies of table 7.1), the code represented by the prefix tree (b) of figure 7.7 is better than that represented by tree (a) since it codes the text t with 42 bits instead of 49. On the other hand, it is known (claim assumed afterwards) that an optimal code can always be represented as a prefix code.

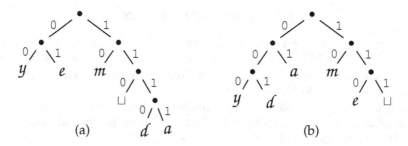

Fig. 7.7 – Two prefix trees for the vocabulary $V = \{a, d, e, m, y, \sqcup\}$. The tree (a) corresponds to the code in table 7.1 and the tree (b) is a second prefix tree.

The cost $L(A)$ of the prefix tree A is defined from both the length of the bit string resulting from coding the text t by A and the frequency of each of the words of the code used. More specifically, let $V = \{v_1, \ldots, v_n\}$ $(n \geqslant 2)$ be a vocabulary, f $(f \in V \to \mathbb{N}_1)$ be the frequency of the v_i's in the text t (their number of occurrences), and A be a prefix tree,

$$L(A) = \sum_{v \in V} f(v) \cdot l_A(v), \tag{7.2}$$

where $l_A(v)$ is the length of the code word of v (or the depth of the leaf v in A)[2].

Huffman code/tree

The prefix tree A represents a Huffman code if there is no (prefix) tree A' such that $L(A') < L(A)$. Generally, a Huffman tree A is not unique: there are trees A' such that $L(A') = L(A)$. For the pair (V, f) of table 7.1, page 355, a Huffman tree A is such that $L(A) = 42$.

79 - Q 1   **Question 1.**   Check that using the pair (V, f) previously quoted, the tree (b) in figure 7.7 is such that $L(b) = 42$. For the same pair (V, f), propose a second Huffman tree that is not obtained by subtree exchanges.

Huffman's algorithm

Trees produced by Huffman's algorithm are not perfectly identical to optimal prefix trees as described above. They are enriched (strengthened) by a redundant information which ease their construction: each node is completed by the sum of the frequencies of all its leaves. In addition, as far as we are concerned, we waive two pieces of information that are superfluous during the construction of the tree: the characters on the leaves and the labels on the branches. The diagram below shows how a Huffman tree (a) becomes an "optimal tree" (c) through an "external" tree (b) (i.e. a tree where non-structural information is carried only by the leaves).

---

[2]$L(A)$ is also called "length of the weighted path" of the tree A.

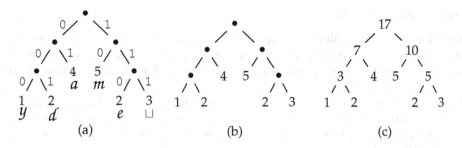

(a)   (b)   (c)

Frequency trees

Definition 5 (Frequency tree):
A (complete) frequency tree is an element of the set P *of complete binary trees, such that each node is labeled with the sum of the frequencies of its leaves.* P *is defined as:*

$$P = \{(/, h, /) \mid h \in F\} \cup \{(l, h, r) \mid l \in P \text{ and } r \in P \text{ and } h = l.h + r.h\}.$$

The left operand of the operator $\cup$ allows to obtain complete trees only. F is the bag of values taken by the leaves (the frequency bag). The tree (c) above is a frequency bag defined over the bag $[\![1, 2, 4, 5, 2, 3]\!]$.
The cost $L(A)$ of the frequency tree A over the frequency bag F is defined as:

$$L(A) = \sum_{k \in F} k \cdot l_A(k), \qquad (7.3)$$

where $l_A(k)$ is the depth of the leaf k in A. This definition is compatible with that of formula 7.2 page 356.

Property 8:
Let G (respectively D) be a frequency tree defined on the bag of frequencies F_G *(respectively* F_D*), let* $A = (G, G.h + D.h, D)$ *be the frequency tree defined on the bag of frequency* $F_G \sqcup F_D$*. A complies with the following property:*

$$L(A) = L(G) + G.h + D.h + L(D). \qquad (7.4)$$

Question 2. The above tree (c) is a frequency tree. Check that both formulas 7.3 and 7.4 yield the same cost for this tree. Prove property 8.   79 - Q 2

Optimal trees

Definition 6 (Optimal tree):
A frequency tree A (defined on the frequencies F) is an optimal tree iff there is no tree A' (for the same frequencies) such that $L(A') < L(A)$.

Question 3. Assuming that P represents the set of all frequency trees, formally define   79 - Q 3
H ($H \subseteq P$) the subset of optimal frequency trees of P.

Construction of an optimal tree

In a first step, the construction of an optimal tree is presented in an intuitive manner, before attention is turned to the construction of the algorithm. The main difficulty of this construction lies in the proof of optimality. We are looking for a solution of type "lead run" (see section 7.1.4, page 336).

There are two possibilities for the construction of the tree: descending or ascending and we opt for the latter. Initially, the different frequencies are placed in a list B, then at each iteration step, two frequencies are rooted in a tree whose root carries the sum of the two frequencies. Which frequencies to choose from the list? We are in a greedy approach, so we choose the two weakest frequencies. The process is reiterated. Each step decreases the length of the list by one unit: the algorithm ends when the list contains only one element. This is illustrated in the six diagrams below.

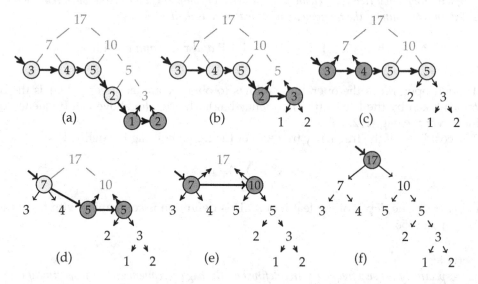

These six diagrams show the evolution of the list B (in bold) and the upward construction of the optimal tree. At each step, the list contains a forest [see for example diagram (d)] of optimal trees that is included in the tree finally constructed by the algorithm [diagram (f)]. A peculiarity of this example is that in the list B, two minimum frequencies are always next to each other. It may happen that the construction process provides a different tree, but still an optimal one. Concretely, as specified below, the algorithm represents B by a priority queue.

Tree list

The previous section leads us to define the notions of frequency tree list and optimal list (of frequency trees).

Definition 7 (Frequency list):
Let $A_1, \ldots, A_m$ m be frequency trees on respectively $F_1, \ldots, F_m$. $B = \langle A_1, \ldots, A_m \rangle$ is a frequency list on $F = F_1 \sqcup \ldots \sqcup F_m$.

Definition 8 (Cost of a list):
Let $B = \langle A_1, \ldots, A_m \rangle$ be a frequency list. Its cost is defined as $L(B) = \sum_{i=1}^{m} L(A_i)$.

Definition 9 (Optimal list):
B *is an optimal list (of frequencies) on* F *if, for any list* B' *on* F, $L(B) \leqslant L(B')$.

Question 4.   Prove that if $B = \langle A_1, \ldots, A_m \rangle$ is an optimal list, then each A_i is an optimal   79 - Q 4
tree.

Construction of Huffman's algorithm

The objective is to obtain an optimal tree on the bag of frequencies $F = F_1 \sqcup \cdots \sqcup F_n$. It is
an iterative algorithm based on an optimal sorted list (a priority queue) of frequency trees.
We propose an invariant from which the other components of the loop are designed.

Invariant $B = \langle A_1, \ldots, A_m \rangle$ $(m \in 1 \mathrel{..} n)$ is an optimal list on the respective frequencies
$F_1, \ldots, F_m$ with $F_1 \sqcup \cdots \sqcup F_m = F$.

Question 5.   Complete the construction of the loop. Write the text of Huffman's algo-   79 - Q 5
rithm and give its complexity.

The solution is on page 390.

Problem 80.   File merging   ○ ⋮

> *This problem is dealing with sequential files sorted on a given key. Contrary to what intuition*
> *suggests, the cost of merging* n *files, in terms of number of key comparisons, depends on*
> *the order according to which the files are pairwise merged. There is a greedy algorithm that*
> *determines this order.*

It is recommended to solve problem 79, page 354, on Huffman coding algorithm, as
well as problem 88, on page 424, on sort-merge, before tackling this one.
    Merging is an operation that allows the production of a sorted file F_3 from two sequen-
tial sorted files F_1 and F_2:

	F_1					F_2					F_3							
	3	5	10	12	⊢	⋀	1	5	7	⊢	=	1	3	5	5	7	10	12	⊢

Thereafter, it is considered that merging two files F_1 and F_2 of e_1 and e_2 records amounts
to $e_1 + e_2$ units of cost (for instance, number of conditions evaluated). Merging n $(n > 2)$
files can be achieved by successively merging pairs of files until a single file is obtained.
However, the total cost of the operation depends on the order according to which the pairs
to be processed are chosen. For example, consider the six files of $3, 4, 6, 8, 12$ and 14 records
processed in the figure below. In schema (a), the files are processed in ascending order of
the size of the six original files (framed in the schema). The resulting cost is 121. Indeed,
merging the two files of 3 and 4 elements gives a file of 7 elements (at a cost of 7); these
7 elements merge with the file of 6 elements to give 13 elements (at a cost of 20), etc. The
total cost is the sum of the circled values, i.e. $7 + 13 + 21 + 33 + 47 = 121$.

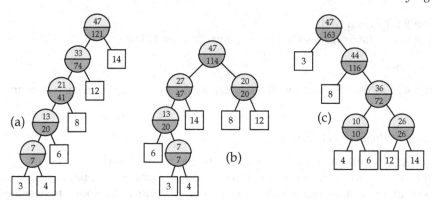

(a) (b) (c)

For schema (b), the cost is equal to 114, and the processing is characterized by the fact that the two smallest files are systematically merged, irrespective of their origin. As for schema (c), the cost is 163 with a random order for treating files.

The objective of the problem is to design a greedy algorithm that determines an optimal merging tree for any given set of n files.

80 - Q 1 **Question 1.** Knowing that for a set of files having respectively $5, 6, 7, 8, 9$ and 10 records the optimal cost amounts to 116 units, provide the optimal tree.

80 - Q 2 **Question 2.** Write the code of the greedy algorithm that determines an optimal tree for any set of files and prove its optimality.

The solution is on page 393.

Problem 81. The photocopier

> *This problem is a variant of the problem dealt with in the introduction of this chapter. It can be declined in many ways and be the source of a variety of more or less difficult related problems. This can be verified by looking for a permutation that maximizes the benefit of a task, or by considering only the ends of tasks that are penalizing, etc. This is its main interest.*

As in the introductory example of this chapter, a number of copy tasks must be performed, but customer demands are different. There are n tasks to carry out, all of them must be accomplished and they cannot be split. A task t_i requires a certain amount of time $d(t_i)$ and it can be placed anywhere in the copier schedule as long as it does not compete with another task. The end time of the task t_i is noted as $f(t_i)$. Each task has an expiry time $e(t_i)$ which is such that if t_i ends before the end time $e(t_i)$, the benefit is positive and is $(e(t_i) - f(t_i))$, if it ends after the end time, the benefit is negative and is (still) $(e(t_i) - f(t_i))$; and finally, if t_i ends exactly at the hour $e(t_i)$, the profit of the operation is zero.

The objective of the problem is the design of an exact greedy algorithm that determines an execution schedule of the n tasks optimizing (maximizing) the global benefit. More specifically, the "heart" of the problem consists in proving that the proposed greedy strategy is optimal.

Thereafter, it is assumed that there is an optimal strategy where the photocopier is used without downtime (the proof is easy). A solution of this type is expected.

Example

Consider the following three tasks a, b and c and their expiry times:

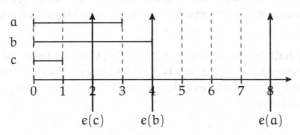

The six possible permutations are represented in the schema hereafter.

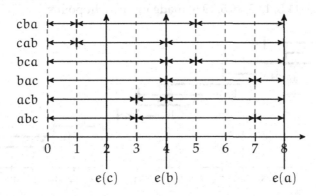

For example, the benefit obtained with the permutation abc is calculated as follows:

$$(e(a) - f(a)) + (e(b) - f(b)) + (e(c) - f(c))$$

$=$ arithmetics

$$(e(a) + e(b) + e(c)) - (f(a) + f(b) + f(c))$$

$=$ definition of $f(t_i)$

$$(e(a) + e(b) + e(c)) - (d(t(a)) + (d(t(a)) + d(t(b))) + (d(t(a)) + d(t(b)) + d(t(c))))$$

$=$ arithmetics

$$(e(a) + e(b) + e(c)) - (3 \cdot d(t(a)) + 2 \cdot d(t(b)) + 1 \cdot d(t(c)))$$

$=$ numeric application

$$(8 + 4 + 2) - (3 \cdot 3 + 2 \cdot 4 + 1 \cdot 1)$$

$=$ arithmetics

$$-4.$$

Question 1. Complete the calculation for the five other permutations. What can be concluded (as for optimality) about the greedy strategy where tasks are ordered according to their increasing expiry times?   81 - Q 1

Question 2. Using a pattern of type "exchange argument", prove that the greedy strategy based on the ordering of tasks according to their increasing durations is optimal. What is the complexity of the resulting algorithm?   81 - Q 2

The solution is on page 393.

Problem 82. The intervals stabbing problem

> *The main difficulty of this problem lies in the search for a greedy strategy and the proof of its optimality. The statement helps the reader in the identification of a solution.*

We consider the half-line of the real positives $\mathbb{R}^*_+$. Given a finite set I of n ($n \geqslant 0$) left-open closed-right intervals, a set of points T is said to *pin* I if each interval of I contains at least one point of T. The objective of the problem is to construct a greedy program that determines a minimal size set T.

Example

In the example illustrated hereafter, the twelve intervals $(I_1, \ldots, I_{12})$ are pinned by the set $T = \{1.5, 3.5, 6.5, 9.5, 11.5, 13.5, 16.5, 19.5\}$ made up of eight points.

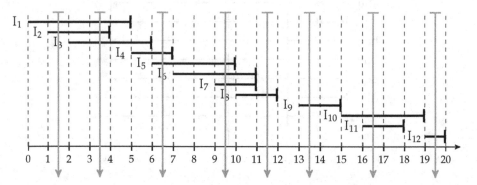

It can be easily seen that T is not minimal. For example, the point of abscissa 1.5 pins the intervals I_1 and I_2, which are also pinned by the point of abscissa 3.5. Since it does not pin any other intervals, the first point of T is therefore useless.

82 - Q 1   **Question 1.**   Is it possible to remove other points of T while preserving its status?

In the perspective of a greedy approach, two strategies for placing the points of T are being envisaged. These two strategies share the fact that they scan the input queue "from left to right" and that they pin intervals on their closed end (the right part of the interval). In the first case, the input queue F is sorted on increasing *origins*, in the second, it is sorted on increasing *ends*.

82 - Q 2   **Question 2.**   What happens when applying these two strategies to the above example? What can be concluded?

82 - Q 3   **Question 3.**   Write a greedy program based on one of the two strategies discussed in the second question. Prove that it is optimal. The "lead run" approach is recommended. How complex is this solution?

82 - Q 4   **Question 4.**   A pin can be placed at any point in an interval ending at the position determined in the previous questions without altering the optimality of the solution. How is this interval defined?

The solution is on page 394.

Problem 83. Two-color graph coloring

In this problem, as in those which follow, the problem to solve is not a matter of optimality. Here, we study an algorithm for coloring a graph with only two colors. A more general version (painting with any number of colors) is studied in problem 59, page 236. However, the present version is much more efficient. In addition, it is closely related to a category of graphs possessing numerous applications: bipartite graphs.

Given an undirected connected graph $G = (N, V)$ $(\text{card}(N) > 0)$, we intend to paint it (if it is feasible) in black and white so that no two adjacent vertices have the same color. Such a graph is then said to be *bicolored*. The greedy algorithm we plan to construct for this purpose is related to "breadth-first" exploration of a graph that we first study.

Breadth-first graph exploration: reminders

Introduction

First of all, let us define the notions of "distance between two vertices" and "breadth-first exploration" for an undirected connected graph.

Definition 10 (Distance between two vertices):
Let $G = (N, V)$ be an undirected connected graph, s and s' be two vertices of G. The length of the shortest path between s and s' is called the distance between s and s'.

Definition 11 (Breadth-first search):
Let G be an undirected connected graph and s be a vertex of G. Any process that encounters the vertices of G with increasing distances from s is referred to as a breadth-first exploration of G from s.

From the diagram (b) in figure 7.8 page 363, we can conclude that the list $\langle a, b, c, d, e, f, g, h \rangle$ corresponds to a "breadth-first" exploration from vertex a. The same is true for the list $\langle a, c, b, d, e, h, f, g \rangle$.

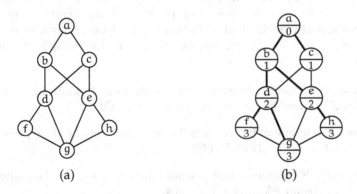

(a)   (b)

Fig. 7.8 – An example of a graph. Schema (a) presents the graph that illustrates the examples of the statement of the problem. Schema (b) shows, in bold lines, for the graph (a), and for each vertex, a shorter path from the vertex a to all other vertices. In schema (b), the integer that appears in each vertex is the distance with respect to the vertex a.

The loop invariant

We would like to construct an iterative algorithm, a greedy one and here we limit ourselves to search for a loop invariant, the rest of the construction being left up to the reader. Let us imagine that a part of the work has already been done (see section 3, page 93). Thus, for a partial graph $G' = (N', V')$ (sub-graph of G induced by N', containing the starting vertex s), we have a list associated with the "breadth-first" traversal of G', from s. Traditionally, this list is called CLOSE. Progressing consists in extending this list by adding a vertex, absent from CLOSE, as close as possible to s.

In the absence of other assumptions, progressing is possible but difficult to develop as well as costly, since any vertex absent from CLOSE is a possible candidate for transfer into CLOSE. We propose to enrich this first version of the invariant by adding a data structure (let us call it OPEN), containing all the vertices absent from CLOSE on the condition that they are neighbors of at least one of the vertices of CLOSE. *A priori*, OPEN appears as a priority queue managed on the distances of its elements from s, since the element to be moved into CLOSE is the one closest to s. We will see later that a simplified version of a priority queue is possible. To maintain this new version of the invariant, it is sufficient to move the head of OPEN to the end of CLOSE, and—as a counterpart to strengthening the invariant – to introduce the "new" neighbors of the moved element into OPEN, those that are neither in OPEN, nor in CLOSE (this is a greedy choice).

However, given an element e in OPEN, inquiring directly about the presence or absence of one of its neighbors in OPEN or CLOSE can be costly. A better solution consists in a (new) strengthening by the following proposition: in the perspective of the coloring to come, a "color" is allotted to each vertex of the graph, white if the summit is either in OPEN, or in CLOSE, and grey otherwise (in fact, here, the two colors play the role of Boolean values). Provided that direct access to the vertices is possible, updating OPEN is made easier. In the progression, the preservation of this complement of the invariant is obtained by painting in white any vertex that is moved to OPEN.

Let us come back to the OPEN queue management strategy. Is it possible to use a simple FIFO queue (see section 1.8, page 32) instead of a priority queue? If this is the case, the management of OPEN will be greatly simplified. To do this, when the vertex e leaves OPEN to join CLOSE, the neighbors of e candidates for entry into OPEN would have to be at a distance greater than or equal to all the elements present in OPEN, which would make it possible to have a sorted queue. This means that if e is at distance k from s, all the other elements of OPEN are at distance k or $(k + 1)$ from s, since the "grey" neighbors of e are at distance $(k + 1)$ from s. We add this assumption to our invariant. The reader is invited to check that it is actually established by initializing the loop. It remains to prove that it is preserved by the progression. Eventually, we propose the following invariant made up of four conjuncts.

1. CLOSE is the FIFO queue whose content represents a "breadth-first traversal" of the sub-graph of G induced by the vertices present in CLOSE.

2. OPEN is the FIFO queue of the vertices that are neighbors of those present in CLOSE. The set intersection of OPEN and CLOSE is empty.

3. If the head of OPEN contains a vertex whose distance to s is k, then other elements of OPEN are at the distance k or $(k + 1)$ from s.

4. In the graph G, the vertices present either in CLOSE or in OPEN are colored in white, others are in grey.

Figure 7.9, page 366, shows the diverse steps of the "breadth-first exploration" of the graph of figure 7.8, page 363. In each graph of the figure, vertices present in CLOSE appear in grey lines, those in OPEN are in double lines. Distances are only mentioned as a reminder, the algorithm does not exploit them. Let us for example comment on the step that leads from schema (e) to schema (f). In diagram (e), CLOSE contains the list of "breadth-first exploration" of the sub-graph induced by the vertices a, b, c and d. The vertex e, head of the queue OPEN, will move to the end of CLOSE. Which neighbors of e are intended to join OPEN? c and b are already in CLOSE, they are not concerned. g is already in OPEN, it is not affected. The only remaining vertex is h, which will join OPEN and be colored in white.

Data structures

Two types of data structure are used in this algorithm. The first one, FIFO queues, is described on page 32. The second one is about a "colored" variant of graphs.

The data structure called undirected colored graph

There is a need for coloring the vertices of a graph, accessing their color and exploring the list of neighbors, thus the following definitions (the set Colors is assumed to be defined):

- **procedure** *ColorGr*(G, s, col): operation which colors the vertex s of G using the color col.

- **function** *WhichColorGr*(G, s) **result** Colors: function that returns the color of the vertex s of G.

- **procedure** *OpenNeighborsGr*(G, s): operation which initialized the exploration of the list of the neighbors of the vertex s of G.

- **function** *EndListNeighborsGr*(G, s) **result** $\mathbb{B}$: function that delivers **true** iff the exploration of the list of the neighbors of the vertex s of G is over.

- **procedure** *ReadNeighborsGr*(G, s, s'): operation which stores in s' the identity of the vertex which is "under the readhead" of the list of the neighbors of s, then moves the readhead one position forward.

For this application, in terms of both algorithm expression and efficiency, the best refinement is the representation by an adjacency list (see schema (d) in figure 1.3 page 23 for a similar representation for directed graphs). The graph is thus defined as a "triple" $(G = (N, V, R))$ where R corresponds to colors (at the present time "white" and "grey").

The algorithm

In addition to the graph G, this algorithm uses the variables cv (the current vertex) and neighb to browse the list of neighbors.

1. **constants**
2. $n \in \mathbb{N}_1$ **and** $n = \ldots$ **and** $N = 1 .. n$ **and** Colors $= \{grey, white\}$ **and**
3. $V \in N \times N$ **and** $V = \{\ldots\}$
4. **variables**
5. $R \in N \rightarrow$ Colors **and** $G = (N, V, R)$ **and**
6. $s \in N$ **and** $cv \in N$ **and** neighb $\in N$ **and** CLOSE $\in$ FIFO(N) **and** OPEN $\in$ FIFO(N)
7. **begin**

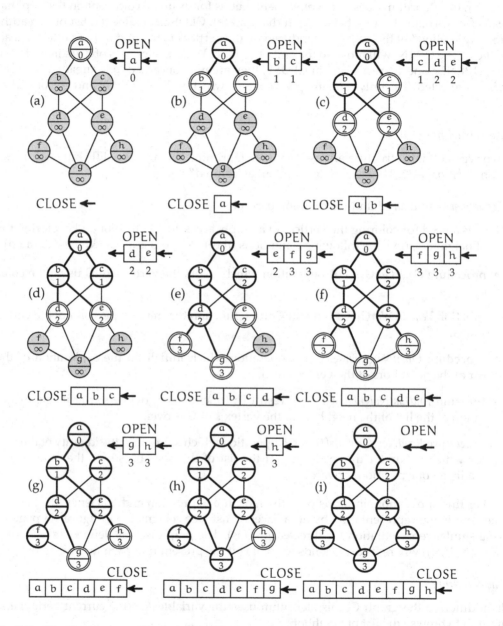

Fig. 7.9 – The diverse steps of the breadth-first exploration *of the graph of schema (a) in figure 7.8 page 363. Vertices circled in bold are the vertices of* CLOSE, *those double circled are the vertices of* OPEN. *The integer value that accompanies each vertex is the known distance from the vertex* a. *The two queues* OPEN *and* CLOSE *are represented at northeast and south of the graphs respectively.*

```
 8.    /% coloring all the vertices in grey: %/
 9.    for w ∈ N do
10.      ColorGr(G, w, grey)
11.    end for;
12.    InitFifo(CLOSE); InitFifo(OPEN);
13.    s ← ... ; /% choice of the initial vertex: %/
14.    ColorGr(G, s, white);
15.    AddFifo(OPEN, s);
16.    while not IsEmptyFifo(OPEN) do
17.      cv ← HeadFifo(OPEN); RemoveFifo(OPEN);
18.      AddFifo(CLOSE, cv);
19.      OpenNeighborsGr(G, cv) ;
20.      while not EndListNeighborsGr(G, cv) do
21.        ReadNeighborsGr(G, cv, neighb) ;
22.        if WhichColorGr(G, neighb) = grey then
23.          ColorGr(G, neighb, white) ;
24.          AddFifo(OPEN, neighb)
25.        end if
26.      end while
27.    end while;
28.    write(CLOSE)
29. end
```

Question 1. What is the asymptotic complexity of this algorithm in terms of conditions evaluated? 83 - Q 1

Question 2. Explain the principle of a greedy coloring algorithm based on this algorithm. 83 - Q 2

Two-color graph coloring algorithm

We are now equipped to address the problem at the heart of the problem: coloring a graph with both black and white. We will adapt the above algorithm in such a way as to color alternately in black and white, according to the depth in relation to the starting vertex, either until the summits are exhausted, or until an impossibility is discovered.

Question 3. Design the coloring algorithm. 83 - Q 3

Question 4. Show the different steps of the coloring from the vertex a of the graph in figure 7.8 page 363. 83 - Q 4

Question 5. Write the code of the algorithm and give its complexity. 83 - Q 5

Question 6. The problem 59, page 236, addresses the more general problem of coloring with m (m ⩾ 2) colors. Discuss the possibility of generalizing the algorithm provided in answer to the question 5, for m > 2. 83 - Q 6

Remark

An interesting characteristic property of bicolorable graphs is the following: a graph is bicolorable iff it does not contain any odd-length cycle. Nevertheless, this property is not constructive: observing it on a graph does not provide a coloring!

The solution is on page 397.

Problem 84. From a partial order to a total order   ⠿

> *Two versions of the topological sort are studied. The first one, naïve but not very efficient, is easy to design. The second one requires strengthening an invariant; implemented using pointers, it constitutes an excellent problem of both refinement and dynamic structures manipulation. The algorithm built here is close to that of Marimont intended for leveling a circuit-free graph.*

To tackle this problem, problem 2, page 33, must be first studied.

Let $(E, \prec)$ be a pair such that E is a finite set of n elements and $\prec$ be a partial order relation on E. We want to build on E a total order relation $\leqslant$ compatible with $\prec$, i.e. such that for any pair (a, b) of E: $(a \prec b) \Rightarrow (a \leqslant b)$. An element of $(E, \prec)$ without any predecessor is called a *minimal* element.

Example

In the context of a computer science cursus, $c_1 \prec c_2$ denotes the fact that the course c_1 must precede the course c_2 in order to comply with the prerequisites necessary to understand the latter. Let us consider the following courses:

a	First-order logic	b	Specification and imperative programming
c	Set theory	d	Information systems design
e	Databases	f	Data structures

An example of the relation $\prec$ is defined as:

$$a \prec b, a \prec c, b \prec d, c \prec b, c \prec d, c \prec e, c \prec f, e \prec d, f \prec e.$$

It can be represented by the following graph:

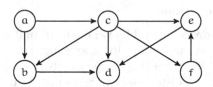

This type of graph is characterized by the fact that it is a directed one and that it does not contain any circuit; it is called a "directed acyclic graph" or DAG. In such a graph, an element without any predecessor (a minimal element of the partial order) is called an *entry point*.

The objective of the problem is to build a greedy algorithm which provides a total order compatible with the initial partial order. For the above example, one solution consists in proposing the total order $a \leqslant c \leqslant b \leqslant f \leqslant e \leqslant d$.

84 - Q 1   **Question 1.**   Prove that a non-empty DAG, deprived from any of its entry points, remains a DAG.

84 - Q 2   **Question 2.**   Let us denote by $G = (N, V)$ any graph and $n = \text{card}(N)$. Prove that some DAG's can be such that $\text{card}(V) \in \Theta(n^2)$.

We now sketch the construction of the "greedy" loop of the algorithm, before applying it to the above example. The construction method used is based on the technique of the "lead run". The next questions deal with the algorithm, its refinement and its complexity.

First construction attempt

Let $G = (E, V)$ be the n-vertice input DAG.

Invariant Let S be the output queue that contains the set E_S ($E_S \subseteq E$) of the vertices sorted in a total order compatible with $\prec$ and such that any vertex v of E not in E ($v \in (E - E_S)$) is greater than any vertex of E according to the partial order.

Stopping condition All of the vertices are in the queue S, i.e. $|S| = n$. The conjunction of the invariant and the previous condition actually entails that S is a list sorted in an order compatible with the partial order.

Progression The progression consists in inserting one of the vertices of $(E - E_S)$ into S. This results in this vertex being in the sub-graph *Induced*$(G, E - E_S)$ and the invariant will be strengthened in this direction.

In order to determine the vertex to be moved in the best conditions, it is necessary to introduce a data structure capable of exploiting the subgraph *Induced*$(G, E - E_S)$.

Second construction attempt

The graph G becomes a variable.

Invariant The predicate "G is a DAG" is added to the previous version of the invariant.

Stopping condition It remains unchanged.

Progression We are looking for one of the entry points of G in order to move this vertex of $(E - E_S)$ to the queue S. It can be easily checked that S satisfies the first version of the invariant and that G, the new induced sub-graph, is indeed a DAG (by virtue of the property established in answer to question 1).

Let us remark that G plays the role of the input queue of greedy algorithms and that the conjunction of the invariant and the stopping condition actually implies the desired objective.

Initialization The invariant is established starting from the empty queue S and the graph G that is the initial graph.

Termination $n - |S|$ is an appropriate termination function since an element is moved from G to S at each step of the progression.

Let us notice that this algorithm returns a correct result by construction. Obviously, it makes the "lead run".

Question 3. Apply the above algorithm to the introductory example. 84 - Q 3

Question 4. Assuming that both functions $d_G^-(s)$ returning the in-degree of the vertex s of G and *Induced* (see section 1.5, page 22, for notions related to graphs) are available, write the code of this algorithm. Assuming a representation of graphs by a list of successors (see figure 1.3, page 23), prove that the complexity of this algorithm is in $O(n^2)$ in terms of numbers of vertices visited. 84 - Q 4

Question 5. In the version obtained in answer to the question 4, from the point of view of complexity the penalizing factor is the search for a minimum among all the vertices still to be considered. On the basis of a strengthening of the above invariant, propose a more 84 - Q 5 efficient solution for non-dense graphs (a few arcs with respect to the square of the number of vertices). What can be concluded about the efficiency of this solution?

The solution is on page 400.

Problem 85. Tournaments and Hamiltonian paths

Here is a very strange greedy problem: an input queue without queue and an output queue constantly changing. In addition, an amazing similarity with sorting by simple insertion appears. All the ingredients are there to tickle the reader's curiosity.

Let $G = (N, V)$ be a directed loop-free graph ($card(N) = n$ and $n \geqslant 1$). G is called a tournament graph (or simply a tournament) if, for any pair of vertices u and v ($u \neq v$), one (and only one) of the two arcs (u, v) or (v, u) exists (either $(u, v) \in V$, or $(v, u) \in V$). The objective of the problem is to build an algorithm that searches for a Hamiltonian path in such a (tournament) graph.

Let us recall (see Chapter 1) that an elementary path in a directed graph is a path which does not involve more than one occurrence of any vertex, and that a Hamiltonian path is an elementary path including all the vertices of the graph. The graph of schema (a) in figure 7.10 is a tournament, while schema (b) illustrates a Hamiltonian path.

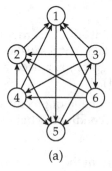 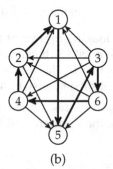

(a)   (b)

Fig. 7.10 – Schema (a) shows a six vertex tournament. Schema (b) highlights the Hamiltonian path $\langle 3, 6, 4, 2, 1, 5 \rangle$ in graph (a).

We will first constructively prove that every tournament has at least one Hamiltonian path, and then exploit this proof in a greedy algorithm delivering such a path. The following property is admitted: "let $N' \subset N$; the sub-graph G' induced from the tournament G by N' is a tournament as well" (the proof is easy to carry out by contradiction).

85 - Q 1   **Question 1.**   This first question is about a lemma used to prove the existence of a Hamiltonian path in a tournament. Let us consider a binary string of length $m \geqslant 2$, that begins with one *0* and finishes with one *1*. Prove that such a string involves at least once the sub-string *01*.

85 - Q 2   **Question 2.**   Prove by induction that any tournament has at least one Hamiltonian path.

Question 3.   Design an algorithm which produces an arbitrary Hamiltonian path in a 85 - Q 3 tournament and give its complexity.

The solution is on page 404.

Problem 86.   Odd-order magic squares

> *This problem has many peculiarities. First of all, it departs from the constructive approach advocated throughout this book: we limit ourselves to proving a posteriori that Bachet's algorithm (17th century and nothing is known about its genesis!), delivers a correct result. Moreover, here, there is no priority queue or FIFO queue in or out, and therefore no moves: does the solution to this problem about magic squares belong to the category of greedy algorithms? The reader will judge. What remains is a non-trivial demonstration and programming problem.*

We consider the construction of odd-order magic squares. A magic square of order n is a matrix $n \times n$ in which each of the integers of the interval $1 .. n^2$ appears once and only once and such that the sum of the values of the rows, columns and main diagonals is the same. This sum, noted M_n, is called "magic number of order n".

More specifically, the so-called Bachet's method is being studied (from Claude-Gaspard Bachet called de Méziriac, 1612). The starting point of this method is a crenellated checkerboard of $(n^2 + (n-1)^2)$ cells (41 cells for $n = 5$), as shown in the diagram below on the left for $n = 5$. In such a crenellated square, there are south-west/north-east diagonals alternately of n and $(n-1)$ cells, later called "large" diagonals and "small" diagonals respectively. The next step is to successively fill each of the n "large diagonals" with the n^2 values, going from their lower left corner to their upper right corner. Once this phase completed, the "small" diagonals are empty, but some values are already placed in the central square. They will not be moved.

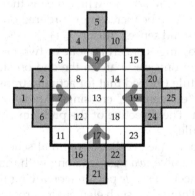

With regard to the other values (in grey on the diagram on the left), let C.-G. Bachet take the floor: "you will put them in the empty places that remain, using only transpositions, that is to say that those above you will be put below, and those below will be carried above; those on the left side will go to the right side, and those on the right side will go to the left side". The result of this last phase appears on the right-hand diagram (in grey the moved values): it is a magic square.

86 - Q 1   **Question** 1.   Give the formula that calculates M_n, the magic number of order n. What are the values of M_5 and M_7?

86 - Q 2   **Question** 2.   Using Bachet's method, fill the magic square of order 7.

86 - Q 3   **Question** 3.   Prove that, for any odd value n, this method actually produces magic squares. It will be sufficient to prove that the sum of the values located on the two main diagonals of the square, as well as that of any row, is equal to M_n.

86 - Q 4   **Question** 4.   Design the algorithm that produces a magic square of order n according to Bachet's method.

The solution is on page 406.

Problem 87.   The bridge and torch problem

> *This problem addresses the problem known as "the Bridge Puzzle", "the Four Men Puzzle", "the Flashlight Puzzle" among others as quoted in [29]. The objective is to help a group of people cross a bridge under some constraints over the admissible moves. The aim is the design of a greedy algorithm solving the problem and the focus is put on the (progressive) construction of an algorithm.*

The problem

It is night and a group of N (N $\geqslant$ 2) people are on the same side (D) of a bridge. The objective is to help them go to the other side (A) as quickly as possible (optimality criterion), knowing that: (i) a torch is necessary to cross the bridge (in both directions) in order to see and avoid possible obstacles, (ii) a maximum of two people can cross at the same time, (iii) each person p_i ($i \in 1..N$) walks at a given speed which induces his crossing time t_i expressed in a given unit of time, e.g. minutes, and (iv) when persons p_i and p_j cross the bridge together, they walk at the rate of the slowest one, which means that the time to cross is $\max(\{t_i, t_j\})$. The N people are supposed to be increasingly ordered on their crossing time (t is a function from 1..N to $\mathbb{N}$ in the broad sense), thus: $t_1 \leqslant t_2 \leqslant \cdots \leqslant t_{N-1} \leqslant t_N$. A schedule is a sequence of "elementary" crossings concerning one or two people (carrying the torch) such that the N people initially on side D are in the end on side A of the bridge. The duration associated with a schedule (indeed that for actually transferring the N people from D to A) is the sum of all its "elementary" crossings. An *optimal* schedule is one of those having the minimal duration. The objective of the problem is to build an algorithm whose output is an optimal schedule.

The following intuitive result can be proven (see [29]). An optimal schedule is such that: (i) "forward" moves from D to A *must* involve *two* people (along with the torch) and (ii) "backward" moves from A to D *must* concern a *single* person (conveying the torch) in order to allow a new pair of people to cross. Thereafter, such elementary crossings are represented as follows: $+\{i, j\}$ for a "forward" move related to p_i and p_j, $-\{i\}$ for a "backward" move where p_i goes back to side D with the torch.

Introductory examples

87 - Q 1   **Question** 1.   Give an optimal schedule for N = 2 and N = 3.

Two greedy strategies

We now consider situations where $N \geqslant 4$. A first strategy (Str_1) is based on the idea that "backward" crossings are made with the fastest person (p_1) who accompanies each other in "forward" moves. With $N = 6$ and $t_1 = 1, t_2 = 5, t_3 = 6$, $t_4 = 7, t_5 = 8$ and $t_6 = 10$, a schedule following this line is

$$S = \langle +\{1,2\}, -\{1\}, +\{1,3\}, -\{1\}, +\{1,4\}, -\{1\}, +\{1,5\}, -\{1\}, +\{1,6\} \rangle$$

for a total crossing time $T = 4t_1 + t_2 + t_3 + t_4 + t_5 + t_6 = 40$ (which is proven to be optimal in answer 11). Let us notice that the order over the "forward" moves does not matter. Unfortunately, with $t_1 = 1, t_2 = 2, t_3 = 5, t_4 = 10, t_5 = 12$ and $t_6 = 20$, the same schedule yields a total time $T = 53$, whereas the schedule

$$S' = \langle +\{1,2\}, -\{1\}, +\{5,6\}, -\{2\}, +\{1,2\}, -\{1\}, +\{3,4\}, -\{2\}, +\{1,2\} \rangle$$

performs better with a crossing time of 42. Here, $+\{5,6\}$ and $+\{3,4\}$ could commute. The schedule S' obeys a second strategy (Str_2) according to which "forward" moves concern two "neighbor slow" people p_i and p_{i-1} (crossing together), so that t_{i-1} does not contribute to the total time. Of course, the greater t_{i-1}, the higher the gain.

Question 2. Check that, when applied to $t_1 = 1, t_2 = 5, t_3 = 6, t_4 = 7, t_5 = 8$ and $t_6 = 10$, the schedule S' is not optimal.   87 - Q 2

A mixed approach as an optimal strategy?

The previous examples show that neither Str_1, nor Str_2 defines an optimal strategy. However, the key ideas behind these two strategies (minimizing the duration for returning the torch or skipping one out of two "slow" people in the total duration) seem to be promising and one may wonder about a strategy Str_3 "mixing" them in an *appropriate* way depending on the $t_i's$.

Question 3. Check that the schedule   87 - Q 3

$$S'' = \langle +\{1,2\}, -\{1\}, +\{5,6\}, -\{2\}, +\{1,4\}, -\{1\}, +\{1,3\}, -\{1\}, +\{1,2\} \rangle$$

is better than both schedules S and S' for $t_1 = 1, t_2 = 5, t_3 = 6, t_4 = 8, t_5 = 10$ and $t_6 = 15$.

At this point, it appears that S, S' and S'' can be considered three instances of an *overall* strategy (for $N = 6$ of course) where either p_6 and p_5 on the one hand and p_4 and p_3 on the other hand cross "together", or only the two slowest people (p_6 and p_5) cross together, or no such "slow" pair crosses. This would mean that the actual number of candidate schedules is indeed 3.

Question 4. Give the number of all candidate schedules *a priori* (i.e. the combinatorial   87 - Q 4
of the problem), for $N = 2, 3, 4$ and 5.

Some interesting properties

We will first assume that all the people walk at *different* rates.

Question 5. Prove that, in any optimal schedule, persons other than p_1 and p_2 cannot   87 - Q 5
move back to side D once arrived on side A.

From the previous question, it turns out that, in an optimal schedule, the possible "forward" moves are *a priori* of one of the following three types:

(a) $+\{1, x\}$ where $x \geqslant 2$,

(b) $+\{2, x\}$ where $x \geqslant 3$ (the case $+\{2, 1\}$ or equivalently $+\{1, 2\}$ is covered by the previous case),

(c) $+\{x, y\}$ where $x > 2, y > 2$ and $x \neq y$ (provided that a move $+\{1, 2\}$ took place before, otherwise the torch could not be returned to side D).

87 - Q 6   **Question 6.**   Prove that: (i) "forward" moves of type b cannot be part of an optimal schedule and (ii) if they occur, moves of type c must be such that $x = N - 2i$ and $y = N - 2i - 1$ (or conversely since x and y play the same role) for $i \in 0 .. \lfloor N/2 \rfloor - 1$.

87 - Q 7   **Question 7.**   Check that, when people may walk at the *same* speed (for some i, $t_i = t_{i+1}$), it is possible to restrict the components of optimal schedules to: (i) "backward" moves with only either p_1 or p_2 and (ii) "forward" moves of type a and c only.

87 - Q 8   **Question 8.**   According to the previous results, what is the number of candidate schedules regardless of the order over their components. Give its value for $N = 2, 3, 4$ and 5. Compare with the answer to question 4.

The algorithm

The point is now the design of a greedy algorithm generating an optimal schedule based on the previous observations. To do so, we first consider the transfer of p_{N-2i} and p_{N-2i-1} ($i \in 0 .. \lfloor N/2 \rfloor - 1$) from side D to side A assuming that p_1 and p_2 are on side D (which is the case in the initial situation).

87 - Q 9   **Question 9.**   Identify the possible sub-sequences for the transfer of p_{N-2i} and p_{N-2i-1} from side D to side A and the rationale for choosing one of these sub-sequences to build an optimal schedule.

87 - Q 10   **Question 10.**   Characterize the strategy Str_3 with respect to Str_1 and Str_2.

The algorithm answering the problem under consideration can be specified as follows:

Precondition N people (represented by the interval $1 .. N$) on side D of the bridge *with the torch* **and** none on side A **and** SCH is an empty list intended to contain an optimal schedule.

Postcondition N people on side A of the bridge *with the torch* **and** none on side D **and** the list SCH contains an optimal schedule.

A first line of development consists in strengthening the postcondition (by the introduction of a *new* variable) so that it can be split into an invariant and a stopping condition. Such a postcondition would be:

$(N - 2m - NumParN)$ people on side D **and** $2m + NumParN$ people on side A *with the torch* (where *NumParN* returns 0 if N is even and 1 if N is odd) **and** $m \in 1 .. \lfloor N/2 \rfloor$ **and** $m = \lfloor N/2 \rfloor$ **and** SCH contains an optimal schedule relating to the $2m + NumParN$ people on side A.

The interested reader is invited to work along this line to see that it leads to a long and tiresome specification mainly because of the progression and the initialization which depend on both the parity of N and the sign of the expression $2t_2 - t_1 - t_{N-2m-1}$. This is the reason why another approach is suggested. In Chapter 3, it has been seen that sequential composition (page 96) makes it possible to introduce an intermediate situation between the precondition and the postcondition, which may simplify the development of a solution. Of course, this implies the writing of two complementary pieces of code.

Question 11. Specify the construction of a solution based on the previous suggestion: a "greedy fragment" followed by a more classic one. Write the code. What are the schedules produced with the following data: 87 - Q 11

- $N = 4$ and $t_1 = 1, t_2 = 5, t_3 = 6, t_4 = 8$,
- $N = 6$ and $t_1 = 1, t_2 = 5, t_3 = 6, t_4 = 7, t_5 = 8, t_6 = 10$,
- $N = 6$ and $t_1 = 1, t_2 = 5, t_3 = 6, t_4 = 8, t_5 = 10, t_6 = 15$,
- $N = 6$ and $t_1 = 1, t_2 = 2, t_3 = 5, t_4 = 10, t_5 = 12, t_6 = 20$,
- $N = 7$ and $t_1 = 1, t_2 = 4, t_3 = 4, t_4 = 7, t_5 = 10, t_6 = 12, t_7 = 15$?

The solution is on page 409.

7.4 Solutions

Answers to problem 74. Looking for a greedy algorithm *The problem is on page 342.*

Answer 1. We saw in the introduction to this chapter (see section 7.2) that greedy methods are characterized by three ingredients: (i) queues (input and output), (ii) the strategy for handling items removed from the input queue, and (iii) the proof that the algorithm is exact/optimal (or not). In this problem, the input queue is represented by the array T, and the bags B_1 and B_2 represent the two FIFO output queues needed to handle this problem in a greedy fashion. The choice of the next element(s) to be processed is (implicitly) imposed by the statement of the problem: the smallest remaining element(s) is (are) selected since T is sorted in ascending order. As a result, our latitude is limited to determining how to handle items leaving the input queue. 74 - A 1
To build the greedy loop, we discard point 4 of the postcondition statement, which will be the stopping condition, and transform point 5 into 5': "$B_1 \sqcup B_2 \sqcup$ "the bag of values remaining in T" is the bag of initial values of T", in order to make the invariant. However, the careful observation of these four points convinces us that it will be difficult to preserve them together at every step of the progression. Consequently, we decided to found the three requested strategies on weakening this invariant in three different ways:

1. The elements in the input queue are extracted one by one. Conjuncts 2 and 3 are discarded and, since it is impossible to preserve conjunct 1 as it is, it is transformed into:
$$\left| |B_1| - |B_2| \right| \leqslant 1.$$
In addition, we avoid the violation of conjunct 2 when possible.

2. The elements in the priority queue are still extracted one by one. Conjuncts 1 and 3 are discarded and only conjuncts 5' and 2 ($Sum1 \leqslant Sum2$) are retained. The violation of conjunct 1 is avoided when possible.

3. This time, the elements of the priority queue are extracted two by two. Conjunct 3 is discarded and only conjuncts 1, 2 and 5' are retained. Whenever possible, we choose the solution that minimizes the difference $(Sum2 - Sum1)$.

Let us apply these three strategies to the following example in order to point out a counter-example for each of them: $T = [1, 3, 5, 6, 9, 11]$. Beforehand, let us remark that a solution to the considered problem is to choose $B_1 = [3, 5, 9]$ and $B_2 = [1, 6, 11]$, bags for which: $Sum2 - Sum1 = 18 - 17 = 1$.

First strategy The course of the algorithm is presented below. In the second step, the choice is between placing 1 in B_1 or in B_2; according to the heuristic stated above, this value is placed in B_2 so as to satisfy the property $Sum1 \leqslant Sum2$.

		Sum_1 / Sum_2	T
S_1	[ ]	0	$[1, 3, 5, 6, 9, 11]$
S_2	[ ]	0	
S_1	[ ]	0	$[3, 5, 6, 9, 11]$
S_2	[1]	1	
S_1	[3]	3	$[5, 6, 9, 11]$
S_2	[1]	1	
S_1	[3]	3	$[6, 9, 11]$
S_2	[1, 5]	6	
S_1	[3, 6]	9	$[9, 11]$
S_2	[1, 5]	6	
S_1	[3, 6]	9	$[11]$
S_2	[1, 5, 9]	15	
S_1	[3, 6, 11]	20	[ ]
S_2	[1, 5, 9]	15	

The result is not as expected, since $Sum1$ is greater than Sum_2 and the difference is not minimized. This example shows that this greedy strategy is not optimal.

Second strategy The trace of execution is presented below. It shows that the difference is actually minimized and that $(Sum1 \leqslant Sum2)$. On the other hand, the constraint on cardinalities is not satisfied. It is also a counter-example which shows that this strategy is not optimal.

		Sum_1 / Sum_2	T
S_1	[ ]	0	$[1, 3, 5, 6, 9, 11]$
S_2	[ ]	0	
S_1	[ ]	0	$[3, 5, 6, 9, 11]$
S_2	[1]	1	
S_1	[ ]	0	$[5, 6, 9, 11]$
S_2	[1, 3]	4	
S_1	[ ]	0	$[6, 9, 11]$
S_2	[1, 3, 5]	9	
S_1	[6]	6	$[9, 11]$
S_2	[1, 3, 5]	9	
S_1	[6]	6	$[11]$
S_2	[1, 3, 5, 9]	18	
S_1	[6, 11]	17	[ ]
S_2	[1, 3, 5, 9]	18	

Third strategy The conjunct $5'$ is actually an invariant and properties 1 and 2 of the post-condition are met, as shown in the table below (which is not surprising since they are part of the invariant of the loop). Unfortunately, the difference is not minimal: it is equal to 3 whereas 1 was expected. It is also a counter-example.

		Som_1/Som_2	T
S_1	$[\,]$	0	$[1,3,5,6,9,11]$
S_2	$[\,]$	0	
S_1	$[1]$	1	$[5,6,9,11]$
S_2	$[3]$	3	
S_1	$[1,6]$	7	$[9,11]$
S_2	$[3,5]$	8	
S_1	$[1,6,9]$	16	$[\,]$
S_2	$[3,5,11]$	19	

Remark

These three strategies can be seen as the heart of approximate greedy algorithms, as long as the properties not satisfied by their respective solutions are considered non-critical.

Answer 2. The answer is negative and nothing forbids to think that an optimal greedy strategy exists. To the best of our knowledge, given a specification, determining whether or not there is an optimal greedy strategy is an open problem.

74 - A 2

Answers to problem 75. Binary search trees   *The problem is on page 343.*

Answer 1. The strategy based on "leaf insertion" of the values sorted according to decreasing probabilities gives the following result:

75 - A 1

x_i	2	4	3	6	1	5
$p(x_i)$	0.19	0.18	0.17	0.17	0.15	0.14

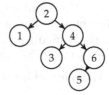

The cost of this tree is

$$1 \cdot 0.19 + 2 \cdot 0.15 + 2 \cdot 0.18 + 3 \cdot 0.17 + 3 \cdot 0.17 + 4 \cdot 0.14,$$

expression whose value is 2.42 and this tree is therefore better than the one proposed in the statement, whose cost is 2.57.

Answer 2. According to "leaf insertion", the list below leads to the tree on the right.

75 - A 2

x_i	4	2	6	1	3	5
$p(x_i)$	0.18	0.19	0.17	0.15	0.17	0.14

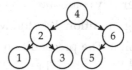

The cost of this tree is expressed by

$$1 \cdot 0.18 + 2 \cdot 0.19 + 2 \cdot 0.17 + 3 \cdot 0.15 + 3 \cdot 0.17 + 3 \cdot 0.14,$$

expression whose value is 2.28. This solution is therefore better than the one obtained in response to question 1. We ignore if it is optimal, but it invalidates the solution of question 1 as an optimal greedy solution.

Remarks

1. No optimal greedy solution is known for this problem.

2. On the other hand, an optimal solution is produced in the problem based on dynamic programming quoted in the statement.

3. In section 6.2.2, the book [22] provides a complete study of this problem, generalized to the case of failing search.

Answers to problem 76. Relays for mobile phones *The problem is on page 344.*

76 - A 1   **Answer 1.**   Clearly, the first strategy is not optimal. On the other hand, it shows that there is always at least one possible coverage. For the example of the the statement of the problem, the second strategy provides, as a counter-example, the following coverage:

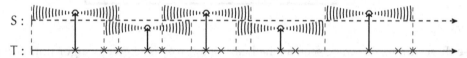

This coverage involves five relays, while two better solutions are proposed in the statement (see solutions O and Q on page 344). It is therefore not optimal.

76 - A 2   **Answer 2.**   We proceed from left to right. A relay is placed so that the left boundary of its coverage coincides with the first house not yet covered. For the example of the statement, the result is as follows:

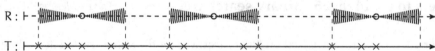

76 - A 3   **Answer 3.**   The input and output queues F and R can both be implemented as FIFO queues. The notations defined in the introductory example are used here (see section 7.1.4, page 336). The difficult part of the construction concerns the proof of optimality of the solution. Let us tackle the construction of the main loop.

Invariant The selected invariant is the conjunction of the following three properties:

1. The pair (R_i, F_i) is such that $R_i = \langle g_1, \ldots, g_k \rangle$ is the configuration of the output queue R when the greedy strategy is applied to the list $\langle T_1, \ldots, T_i \rangle$; $F_i = \langle T_{i+1}, \ldots, T_n \rangle$ is then the configuration of F.

2. R is an optimal solution.

3. Any other optimal solution (R'_i, F_i), with $R'_i = \langle o_1, \ldots, o_k \rangle$, is such that $(o_k \leqslant g_k)$ (R_i makes the "lead run"). This last property is related to the optimality of the greedy solution.

Stopping condition We stop when the queue F is empty, i.e. when *IsEmptyFifo*(F).

Progression The precondition of the progression guarantees that the invariant is satisfied while the stopping condition is not met (so there is a dwelling T_{i+1} that is not yet processed). The progression is done by placing the abscissa $(T_{i+1} + d/2)$ (i.e. (*HeadFifo*(F)+d/2)) in the output queue R so that the house T_{i+1} is covered by the next relay. This dwelling is removed from the queue F and all the dwellings covered by the relay that has just been placed are eliminated from F. This last operation is carried out by a loop that is not made explicit here. In summary, starting from the configuration

(R_i, F_i), the configuration (R_j, F_j) is obtained, with $j > i$, $R_j = \langle g_1, \ldots, g_k, g_{k+1} \rangle$ and $F_j = \langle T_{j+1}, \ldots, T_n \rangle$.

Let us demonstrate the optimality of the greedy solution. The greedy solution R_j obtained after a step of progression from the situation (R_i, F_i) covers the house of abscissa T_{i+1}. Any other optimal solution R'_j must also cover T_{i+1}. This requires, as shown in the two diagrams below, that $o_{k+1} \leqslant g_{k+1}$.

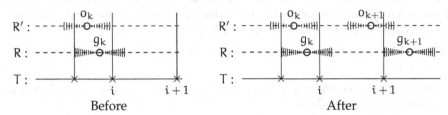

<table>
<tr><td>Before</td><td>After</td></tr>
</table>

It follows that there is no solution R'_j better than R_j: the greedy solution is optimal. Provided that the initialization and termination of the algorithm are correct, the solution R_n is therefore optimal.

Initialization F is the FIFO queue containing the intervals sorted on their increasing ends, and R is empty. At the end of these operations, the invariant is established.

Termination F decreases in length by at least 1 with each step of the progression. $|F|$, the size of F, is therefore a valid termination function.

The following algorithm can be deduced:

1. **constants**
2. $n \in \mathbb{N}_1$ **and** $n = \ldots$ **and** $d \in \mathbb{R}_+$ **and** $d = \ldots$ **and**
3. $T \in 1..n \rightarrow \mathbb{R}_+$ **and** $T = [\ldots]$ /% *Position of the dwellings* %/
4. **variables**
5. $F \in FIFO(\mathbb{R}_+)$ **and** $R \in FIFO(\mathbb{R}_+)$ **and** $t \in \mathbb{R}_+$
6. **begin**
7. $Sort(T)$; /% *sort of* T %/
8. $InitFifo(F, T)$; /% *Creation of the priority queue* F *from* T %/
9. $InitFifo(R)$;
10. **while not** $IsEmptyFifo(F)$ **do**
11. $t \leftarrow HeadFifo(F)$; $RemoveFifo(F)$;
12. $AddFifo\left(R, t + \dfrac{d}{2}\right)$;
13. **while not**$(IsEmptyFifo(F)$ **or else** $(HeadFifo(F) - t > d))$ **do**
14. $DeleteFifo(F)$
15. **end while**
16. **end while**
17. **end**

In this algorithm, the most time-consuming operation is the sort performed by the procedure *Sort* on line 7, which is $\mathcal{O}(n \cdot \log_2(n))$. It is also the complexity of this algorithm.

Answer 4.   In accordance with the principles underlying this technique, it is assumed   76 - A 4
here that the algorithm is designed without taking optimality into account and that the proof is done *a posteriori*. Consider a given succession T of dwellings. Let $T = \langle t_1, \ldots, t_i \rangle$ and let $G = \langle g_1, \ldots, g_p \rangle$ be the position of the p relays selected by the greedy strategy above, and let $O = \langle o_1, \ldots, o_q \rangle$ be the position of the q relays that would be discovered by any optimal solution ($q \leqslant p$ since O is optimal):

G : ⊢ - - - ⊩⊪⊪⊶O⊶⊪⊪⊩ - - -⊩⊪⊪⊶O⊶⊪⊪⊩ - - - ··· - ⊩⊪⊶⊶O⊶⊶⊪⊩ - ⌐

g_1 g_2 g_p

O : ⊢ - ⊣⊪⊶O⊶⊶⊪⊢ - - - ⊩⊶O⊶⊶⊪⊩ - - - - ··· ⊩⊶O⊶⊶⊪⊩ - - -

o_1 o_2 o_q

T : ⊢——✕——✕———✕——✕✕——————— ··· ——✕——✕—⌐

We will show by induction on q that it is possible to transform the list O into the list G without making it lose its optimal status (which will show at the same time that G can be identified with O, and therefore that the list G is also optimal).

Base For $q = 0$, we also have $p = 0$. In this case, we deduce that $G = O$ and that G is optimal.

Induction hypothesis For $q \geqslant 0$, the positions O and G are identical (all o_h's have been replaced by g_h's) and $p = q$:

G : ⊩⊪⊶O⊶⊪⊩ - - -⊩⊪⊶O⊶⊶⊪⊩ - - ··· - ⊩⊪⊶O⊶⊶⊪⊩ - ⌐

g_1 g_2 g_q

O : ⊩⊶O⊶⊶⊪⊩ - - -⊣⊩⊶O⊶⊶⊣⊢ - - ··· - ⊩⊶O⊶⊶⊪⊩ - -

o_1 o_2 o_q

T : ✶——✕———✕——✕✕——————— ··· ——✕——✕—

Induction Three scenarios are to be considered.

1. The coverage of the relay o_{q+1} starts before that of g_{q+1}:

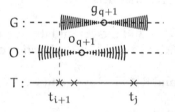

g_{q+1}

o_{q+1}

t_{i+1} t_j

   Two sub-cases must be singled out. Either o_{q+1} covers as many houses as g_{q+1}, or it covers fewer. In the first case, o_{q+1} can be replaced by g_{q+1}. On the other hand, the second case does not make it possible to restore the hypothesis of induction, since the two lists of covered dwellings are different. This case must be discarded.

2. The coverage of the relay o_{q+1} starts after that of g_{q+1}:

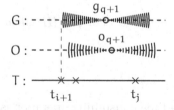

g_{q+1}

o_{q+1}

t_{i+1} t_j

   The dwelling t_{i+1} is not covered by o_{q+1}, which does not restore the induction hypothesis. This case must be ruled out as well.

3. The coverage of the relay o_{q+1} starts at the same position as that of g_{q+1}. These two relays cover the same area. o_{q+1} can then be replaced by g_{q+1} without affecting the optimality of O.

We have shown that, in any case, O can be transformed into G while preserving its optimal character. We conclude that the greedy solution G was already optimal.

Answers to problem 77. **Ordering purchases of varying prices** *The problem is on page 344.*

Answer 1.   There are two simple ways to order the players: by increasing or decreasing   77 - A 1
rate of progression. A greedy algorithm will choose the players one by one, according to
one of these two orders. A simple example shows that one of these methods seems better
than the other. If there are three players, with the rates $r_1 = 2$, $r_2 = 3$ and $r_3 = 4$, the
amount spent to acquire them is $s \cdot (2 + 3^2 + 4^3) = 75s$ in one case, $s \cdot (4 + 3^2 + 2^3) = 21s$ in
the other.

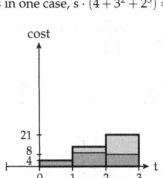

In this example, buying players on a decreasing rate basis is the best of both strategies, but
is it optimal?

Answer 2.   It must be shown that the amount paid by ordering the players to buy in   77 - A 2
descending order of their rate r_j is less than any amount corresponding to any other order.
In other words, it is to prove that choosing any other permutation of players is equivalent
to buying them at a higher price.
The demonstration is done in two steps. The first step is to show that in any permutation
R' of all players, if we swap two adjacent items appearing in ascending order in R' to get
the permutation R'', the cost decreases ($C(R'') < C(R')$). The second step is to show that
sorting an array of integers R in descending order can always be done by a succession of
transpositions (exchanges) of two adjacent elements in ascending order. This property is
easy to prove (it is particularly used in bubble sort, see [9]).

Example

Let us look at the set $2, 3, 4, 6$ and the permutation $R' = [4, 2, 6, 3]$. The table below shows
both a succession of exchanges leading to the table sorted in descending order, and the cost
obtained at the end of each stage. Initially, the cost is $C([4, 2, 6, 3]) = 4^1 + 2^2 + 6^3 + 3^4 = 305$.

	permutation at start	after exchange	cost
1	$[4, \underline{2}, \underline{6}, 3]$	$[4, 6, 2, 3]$	$4^1 + 6^2 + 2^3 + 3^4 = 129$
2	$[\underline{4}, \underline{6}, 2, 3]$	$[6, 4, 2, 3]$	$6^1 + 4^2 + 2^3 + 3^4 = 111$
3	$[6, 4, \underline{2}, \underline{3}]$	$[6, 4, 3, 2]$	$6^1 + 4^2 + 3^3 + 2^4 = 65$

The first step will therefore be sufficient to prove that the permutation in descending
order is optimal. Let $R' = [r_1, \ldots, r_i, r_{i+1}, \ldots, r_n]$ such that $r_i < r_{i+1}$, and let $R'' = [r_1, \ldots, r_{i+1}, r_i, \ldots, r_n]$ the permutation obtained after the exchange between r_i and r_{i+1}.

We have:

$$C(R') = s \cdot \sum_{j=1}^{n} r_j^j$$

and

$$C(R'') = s \cdot \left(\sum_{j=1}^{i-1} r_j^j + r_{i+1}^i + r_i^{i+1} + \sum_{j=i+2}^{n} r_j^j \right).$$

Let us prove that the cost decreases at each exchange, in other words that $C(R'')-C(R') < 0$.

$C(R'') - C(R')$

$=$ definitions of $C(R'')$ and $C(R')$

$$s \cdot \left(\sum_{j=1}^{i-1} r_j^j + r_{i+1}^i + r_i^{i+1} + \sum_{j=i+2}^{n} r_j^j \right) - s \cdot \sum_{j=1}^{n} r_j^j$$

$=$ arithmetics

$$s \cdot \left(r_{i+1}^i + r_i^{i+1} - r_i^i - r_{i+1}^{i+1} \right)$$

$=$ arithmetics

$$s \cdot \left(r_i^i \cdot (r_i - 1) - r_{i+1}^i \cdot (r_{i+1} - 1) \right)$$

$<$ overestimation: $r_i < r_{i+1}$

$$s \cdot \left(r_i^i \cdot (r_i - 1) - r_{i+1}^i \cdot (r_i - 1) \right)$$

$<$ overestimation: $r_i^i < r_{i+1}^i$

$$s \cdot \left(r_i^i \cdot (r_i - 1) - r_i^i \cdot (r_i - 1) \right)$$

$=$ arithmetics

$0.$

Therefore, $C(R'') - C(R') < 0$. So, the closer we get to the greedy solution, the lower the cost. The proposed greedy algorithm is indeed exact.

Answers to problem 78. Optimal broadcast   *The problem is on page 345.*

Prim's algorithm

78 - A 1   **Answer 1.**   We have seen that a unique elementary chain connects any pair of distinct vertices (s_i, s_j) of a T tree. If the edge (s_i, s_j) is added to T, the elementary chain linking s_i to s_j can be extended to form an elementary cycle including the vertices s_i and s_j.

78 - A 2   **Answer 2.**   A proof by contradiction is undertaken. Let $T = (N', A', P')$ be a promising tree with $N' \subset N$ (and therefore $A' \subset A$) and $U = (M, B, Q)$ a mwct of G containing T, but including none of the minimum value edges joining a vertex of N' (inner vertex) and a vertex of $(N - N')$ (outer vertex) making up the set of edges MVE. Let a_1 of value v_1 be one of the edges of MVE. According to property 5, its addition to U causes a cycle to appear since U is no longer a tree (U has card(N) vertices and card(N) edges). In this cycle, there are exactly two edges having one end in N' and the other in $(N - N')$: a_1 and another a_2 of value v_2 greater than v_1 since U does not contain any edge in MVE, thus with a value v_1 that is minimal (see the diagram below). Consider U' the tree issued from U by removing the edge a_2 and adding the edge a_1. U' is also a covering tree of G and its weight is strictly less than that of U, hence U cannot be a mwct.

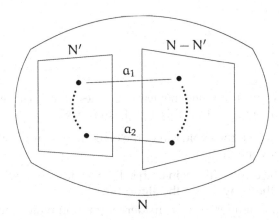

Answer 3.   The function *MinCostOutVertex* searches among all mixed edges of G, (one of) the minimum value edge(s) and returns the associated outer vertex. It then proceeds to examine the array Arc filtered by External, which yields the following code:

78 - A 3

1. **function** *MinCostOutVertex* **result** 2 .. n **pre**
2. $vm \in \mathbb{N}_1$ **and** vertex $\in 2 .. n$
3. **begin**
4. $vm \leftarrow +\infty$;
5.   **for** $i \in 2 .. n$ **do**
6.   **if** External[i] **and then** P[i, Arc[i]] $< vm$ **then**
7. $vm \leftarrow mE[i]$; vertex $\leftarrow i$
8.   **end if**
9.   **end for**;
10.   **result** vertex
11. **end**

This function is called in the context of the existence of at least one arc of finite length, which ensures that a value is assigned to the variable *vertex*. The number of conditions evaluated is in constant time in the *for* loop and therefore the complexity of this function is in $\Theta(n)$.

Answer 4.   In the context of the chosen implementation, the final result is given by the array Arc, in the form of a reverse tree rooted on the source. Therefore, Arc[i] = j is interpreted by the presence of the branch (j, i) in the mwct under construction. Prim's algorithm is written as:

78 - A 4

1. **constants**
2. $n \in \mathbb{N}_1$ **and** $n = \ldots$ **and** $P \in 1 .. n \times 1 .. n \rightarrow \mathbb{N}_1$ **and** $P = P^T$ **and** $P =$ [...] **and**
3.   IsConnected(G)
4. **variables**
5.   Arc $\in 2 .. n \rightarrow 1 .. n$ **and** External $\in 2 .. n \rightarrow \mathbb{B}$ **and** $g \in 2 .. n$
6. **begin**
7.   Arc $\leftarrow 2 .. n \times \{1\}$; External $\leftarrow 2 .. n \times \{$**true**$\}$;
8.   **for** $k \in 2 .. n$ **do**
9. $g \leftarrow$ MinCostOutVertex;
10.   External[g] $\leftarrow$ **false**;
11.   **for** $a \in 2 .. n$ **do**
12.   **if** External[a] **and then** P[a, g] $<$ P[a, Arc[a]] **then**
13.   Arc[a] $\leftarrow g$

```
14.        end if
15.        end for
16.    end for;
17.    write(Arc)
18. end
```

The computation of g (line 9) and the inner *for* loop (lines 11 to 15) have a linear complexity in terms of conditions evaluated, thus this algorithm is in $\Theta(n^2)$.

78 - A 5   **Answer 5.**   In figure 7.11, the evolution of the construction of a mwct for the proposed graph is presented, knowing that:

- The union of the arrows (those in both solid and dashed lines), from diagram (b), represents the array Arc of the algorithm.
- Schema (a) is a reminder of the considered graph in which the edges appear as dotted lines.
- On each diagram, the bold black curve delineates the boundary between the inner vertices (the part containing the vertex 1) and the outer vertices (the other part). This boundary has no algorithmic existence.
- The dotted greasy arrows represent mixed arcs, while the solid greasy arrows represent the reverse tree rooted on node 1.

The weight of the resulting covering tree, consisting of edges $(1, 3)$, $(3, 2)$, $(2, 5)$, $(5, 7)$, $(7, 6)$ and $(7, 4)$ is 12. Notice that at the second step of the iteration (from (b) to (c) in figure 7.11), there is a choice between the edges $(2, 3)$ and $(5, 1)$, both of value 3. However, the algorithm as written, leads to take the edge $(2, 3)$. The reader can check that the other possibility leads to the result of figure 7.12, corresponding to a mwct also of weight 12.

78 - A 6   **Answer 6.**   In the solution proposed in question 4, the role of the input (respectively output) queue is held by the array Arc in its part associated with the outer (respectively inner) vertices. Note that the order conveyed by a FIFO queue is conveyed here by the representation of the result as an reverse tree. Moreover, the absence of an explicit input queue forces a sequential search for the element of minimum value (function *MinCostOutVertex*).

78 - A 7   **Answer 7.**   According to the framework given in the statement of the problem, the condition associated with the control of the update loop of the queue F must be evaluated. This latter involves successively $(n - 1)$, then $(n - 2), \ldots, 1$ elements, hence a total number of conditions evaluated in the algorithm in $\Omega(n^2)$. Therefore, it appears that, asymptotically speaking, such an approach cannot be better than the one developed in question 4.

Dijkstra's algorithm

78 - A 8   **Answer 8.**   There are two cases to consider, depending on whether or not $d \in N'$. If $d \notin N'$ (this case occurs only initially), then d is the selected vertex; it must be moved to N', since the distance from d to d is zero and $L[d] = dist(d) = 0$. For the opposite case, we start with the definition of L for the vertices f of N' to which we add the assumption that $d \in N'$:

$$\forall f \cdot (f \in N'' \Rightarrow L[f] = eDist(f))$$

$$\Leftrightarrow \qquad\qquad\qquad\qquad\qquad\qquad\qquad\qquad\qquad\qquad \text{definition of } eDist$$

$$\forall f \cdot (f \in N'' \Rightarrow L[f] = \min_{h \in ePath(f)} (cost(h)))$$

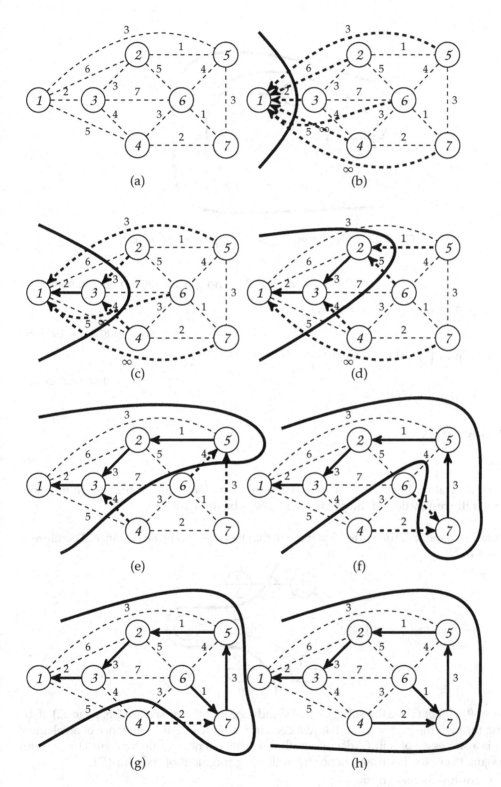

Fig. 7.11 – Trace of the execution of Prim's algorithm.

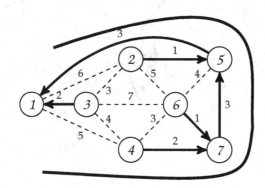

Fig. 7.12 – Another mwct *for the graph of question 5.*

$\Rightarrow$ $\qquad\qquad\qquad\qquad\qquad$ $N'' \neq \varnothing \Rightarrow \exists g \cdot (g \in N''$ **and** g achieves the double minimum)

$$L[g] = \min_{f \in N''} \left(\min_{h \in ePath(f)} (cost(h)) \right)$$

$\Rightarrow$ $\qquad\qquad\qquad\qquad\qquad\qquad\qquad$ property 7, page 352 $(d \in N')$

$$L[g] \leqslant \min_{f \in N''} \left(\min_{h \in path(f)} (cost(h)) \right)$$

$\Leftrightarrow$ $\qquad\qquad\qquad\qquad\qquad\qquad\qquad\qquad$ definition of dist

$$L[g] \leqslant \min_{f \in N''} (dist(f))$$

$\Rightarrow$ $\qquad\qquad\qquad\qquad\qquad\qquad\qquad\qquad\qquad$ for $f = g$

$$L[g] = dist(g).$$

Remark

This demonstration is an integral part of the proof of correction of the algorithm, since without it the restoration of the predicate I_1 would be impossible.

In figure 7.6, page 352, the vertex 5 is the one that has the smallest e-distance. Therefore, it is moved to N':

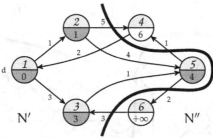

78 - A 9 $\quad$ **Answer** 9. $\quad$ Let G'' be the sub-graph of G induced by N'' (see section 1.5, page 22). If, by passing through the vertex g that has just been moved into N', the e-distance of an element h that is a successor of g in G' decreases, then we have a new value for $L[h]$. This restores the conjunct I_4 of the invariant, hence the following fragment of code for (C):

1. **for** $h \in Succ_{G''}(g)$ **do**
2. $\quad$ $L[h] \leftarrow \min(\{L[h], L[g] + P[g, h]\})$
3. **end for**

Looking at our example, passing through node 5 allows the e-paths to be shortened from 1 to 4 and from 1 to 6. The e-distance from 1 to 4 decreases from 6 to 5, and the e-distance from 1 to 6 decreases from $+\infty$ to 6, as shown in the diagram below:

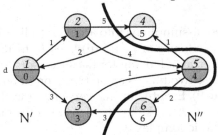

Answer 10.   The two items **Initialization** and **Termination** remain to be specified. 78 - A 10

Initialization To establish the invariant, L must be initialized by row d of P and N′ (respectively N″) must receive the value $\varnothing$ (respectively N):

    1. **for** $k \in 1 \ldots n$ **do**
    2. $L[k] \leftarrow P[d, k]$;
    3. **end for**;
    4. $N' \leftarrow \varnothing$; $N'' \leftarrow N$

It can be specifically noticed that the conjunct I_4 of the invariant is actually established by this program.

Termination Every step of progression makes the cardinality of N″ decrease by 1. The integer function $card(N'')$ is strictly decreasing and nonnegative and it ensures termination.

The code of the algorithm is as follows (G″ is the sub-graph of G induced by N″):

```
1.  constants
2.    n ∈ ℕ₁ and n = … and N = 1 .. n and P ∈ 1 .. n × 1 .. n → ℕ₁ and P =
      […] and
3.    d ∈ 1 .. n and d = 1
4.  variables
5.    L ∈ 1 .. n → ℕ₁ and N′ ⊆ N and N″ ⊆ N
6.  begin
7.    for k ∈ 1 .. n do
8.       L[k] ← P[d, k]
9.    end for;
10.   N′ ← ∅ ; N″ ← N ;
11.   while N″ ≠ ∅ do
12.      let g such that
13.         g ∈ N″ and L[g] = min (L[f])
                            f∈N″
14.      begin
15.         N″ ← N″ − {g} ; N′ ← N′ ∪ {g} ;
16.         for h ∈ Succ_G″(g) do
17.            L[h] ← min({L[h], L[g] + P[g, h]})
18.         end for
19.      end
20.   end while;
21.   write(L)
22. end
```

78 - A 11   **Answer 11.**   If the valuation of an arc could be negative, by lengthening, a path could see its cost decrease and the property 7, page 352, could not be proven. So it could not be used to answer question 8, which shows that the constructed algorithm is an exact greedy algorithm.

78 - A 12   **Answer 12.**   Taking these assumptions into account, (i) line 13 consists in a sequential search for a minimum in position g of L and (ii) lines 16 to 18 are refined by a *for* loop that runs through row g of array P looking for the successors h (filtered by W) of g and a possible update of L[h]. These two phases are in $\Theta(n)$ conditions evaluated, as well as the loop initializing L (lines 7 to 9). Eventually, this version of the algorithm is $\Theta(n^2)$ in terms of conditions evaluated. Let us remark that the density of the graph (the cardinality of V) does not impact the asymptotic complexity.

78 - A 13   **Answer 13.**   Let us now address the issue of a refinement based on a heap priority queue and let us make the following two strengthenings:

1. The priority queue F comes redundantly with the part of F previously filtered by W. An additional operation must enrich this data structure, namely *IncrPrio*(F, (id, prio)) that increases the priority of the element id of the queue F. Its new priority is prio. This new operation is assumed to be in $\mathcal{O}(\log_2(n))$. Some adjustments are necessary to introduce this operation in a heap implementation which requires some development, an aspect that is left to the reader.

2. The vector S representing the successors (for a vertex g, the list contains the successors of g in G) is added to the matrix representation P. This limits the scan of the internal loop (lines 16 to 18) to successors only.

Figure 7.13 shows a possible configuration as a result of this strengthening.

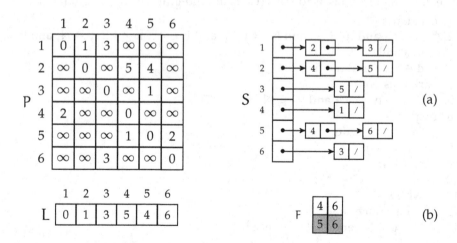

Fig. 7.13 – The situation reached after the progression described in answer 9. The graph is represented in part (a) of the figure, with the matrix P of distances on the left and the representation by a list of successors S on the right. Part (b) represents data structures that are built by the algorithm. L is the array of known distances dist *(respectively* eDist*) for the vertices 1, 2, 3 and 5 (respectively 4 and 6), and F is the priority queue.*

In the code below, PQ(ElmtPrio) represents the set of heap type priority queues (see section 1.7, page 30) whose elements are "records" of type ElmtPrio. Lines 9 to 11 initialize the array L and the priority queue F by copying the row designated by d in array P. As before, the main *while* loop is replaced by a *for* loop (lines 12 to 20). Line 13 extracts the priority element g along with its priority prio. Line 14 removes the head of queue F and stores the distance (now known) from d to g in L. The inner loop starting at line 15 corresponds to that of lines 16 to 18 of the generic algorithm, completed to take into account the possible change in priority of the elements of F. Its refinement would be to browse the list of successors of vertex g in G' (the sub-graph G induced by N'), starting at the entry S[g]. The alternative starting at line 16 updates the parallel structures L and F in case a better e-path from d to h is found.

1. **constants**
2. $n \in \mathbb{N}_1$ and $n = \ldots$ and $P \in 1..n \times 1..n \rightarrow \mathbb{N}_1$ and $P = [\ldots]$ and
3. $d \in 1..n$ and $d = 1$ and
4. $ElmtPrio = \{Node, Prior \mid Node \in \mathbb{N}_1 \text{ and } Prior \in \mathbb{R}_+\}$
5. **variables**
6. $L \in 1..n \rightarrow \mathbb{N}_1$ and $F \in PQ(ElmtPrio)$ and $g \in \mathbb{N}_1$ and $prio \in \mathbb{N}_1$
7. **begin**
8. $InitPQ(F)$;
9. **for** $k \in 1..n$ **do**
10. $AddPQ(F, (k, P[d, k]))$; $L[k] \leftarrow P[d, k]$
11. **end for;**
12. **for** $k \in 1..n$ **do**
13. $g \leftarrow HeadPQ(F).Node$; $prio \leftarrow HeadPQ(F).Prior$;
14. $RemovePQ(F)$; $L[g] \leftarrow prio$;
15. **for** $h \in Succ_{G''}(g)$ **do**
16. **if** $L[g] + P[g, h] < L[h]$ **then**
17. $L[h] \leftarrow L[g] + P[g, h]$; $IncrPrio(F, (h, L[g] + P[g, h]))$
18. **end if**
19. **end for**
20. **end for;**
21. **write**(L)
22. **end**

Now, let us turn our attention to the temporal complexity of this solution in terms of conditions evaluated. The loop for the initialization of the priority queue has a complexity in $\mathcal{O}(n \cdot \log_2(n))$. The body of the loop starting at line 12 is executed n times on a heap whose weight decreases by 1 at each step. The n executions of $RemovePQ(F)$, at line 14, therefore are in: $\mathcal{O}(\log_2(n) + \log_2(n-1) + \cdots + \log_2(1)) = \mathcal{O}(\log_2(n!))$. Yet, according to Stirling's formula, $\log_2(n!)$ behaves asymptotically as $n \cdot \log_2(n)$.

As for the complexity of the fragment between lines 15 and 19, we must first notice that, if we let $m = card(V)$, the *total* number of executions of the body of this loop is equal to m. The call of $IncrPrio(F, (h, L[g] + P[g, h]))$, on line 17, is therefore made at most m times. According to the hypothesis formulated in the statement, this call is in $\mathcal{O}(\log_2(n))$, that is to say in total for the loop a number of conditions evaluated in $\mathcal{O}(m \cdot \log_2(n))$. This solution is therefore in:

$$\mathcal{O}(\max(\{m, n\}) \cdot \log_2(n)).$$

In the case of a full or dense graph (intuitively: for which, the out-degree of any node is on average close to n), this solution can prove to be less good than the previous one since it is then in $\mathcal{O}(n^2 \cdot \log_2(n))$. On the other hand, in the case of hollow graphs (intuitively: m is of the order of $c \cdot n$ with c a small integer constant), this solution is asymptotically better since it is then in $\mathcal{O}(n \cdot \log_2(n))$.

78 - A 14   **Answer** 14.   First of all, let us notice that the initialization carried out in the algorithm proposed in the previous answer is based on the fact that initially, only e-distances are known. However, the case of the vertex d (the source) is such that its distance from the source (0) is also known. Therefore lines 9 to 10 can be replaced by

1. $L[1] \leftarrow 0$;
2. **for** $k \in 2 .. n$ **do**
3. $AddPQ(F, (k, P[d, k])); L[k] \leftarrow P[d, k]$
4. **end for**;

and in the main loop, "$k \in 1 .. n$" can be replaced by "$k \in 2 .. n$".

Note also that at the end of the penultimate step of the progression ($k = n - 1$), only one element remains in the queue F. This one is chosen at the next step with the certainty that its e-distance is in fact its distance. It can be deduced that the last step has no effect on L. Eventually, the main loop can therefore be performed only $(n - 2)$ times by modifying the initialization step appropriately.

78 - A 15   **Answer** 15.   The reverse tree can be represented by the array A such that, at the end of the process, $A[j]$ designates the predecessor of j in the optimal path connecting d and j. To obtain such a tree, its elements must be initialized with the value d (or 1), then each time a vertex s (which has just been moved to N′) updates the e-distance of a vertex g, the value of $A[g]$ is replaced by s. Note that a vertex whose predecessor has kept the value d (or 1) is in fact unattainable if the value associated with it in L is equal to $+\infty$.

78 - A 16   **Answer** 16.   When a vertex is moved from N″ to N′, its distance to the source is known. Therefore, if we are looking for the distance between the source d and another given vertex s, we just have to change the stopping condition that becomes: $s \in N'$.

Answers to problem 79. Optimal data compression *The problem is on page 354.*

79 - A 1   **Answer** 1.   For the tree (b) in figure 7.7, page 356, we have:

$L(b)$

$=$ definition 7.2 page 356

$f(y) \cdot l_b(y) + f(d) \cdot l_b(d) + f(e) \cdot l_b(e) + f(\sqcup) \cdot l_b(\sqcup) + f(a) \cdot l_b(a) + f(m) \cdot l_b(m)$

$=$ table 7.1 page 355

$1 \cdot 3 + 2 \cdot 3 + 2 \cdot 3 + 3 \cdot 3 + 4 \cdot 2 + 5 \cdot 2$

$=$ arithmetics

$42.$

A second optimal tree is presented hereafter:

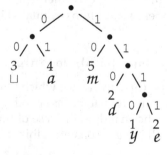

Answer 2. Formula 7.3, page 357, yields $L(c) = (1 \cdot 3 + 2 \cdot 3 + 4 \cdot 2) + (5 \cdot 2 + 2 \cdot 3 + 3 \cdot 3) = 42$. 79 - A 2
Formula 7.4 page 357 leads to $L(c) = (1 \cdot 2 + 2 \cdot 2 + 4 \cdot 1) + 7 + 10 + (5 \cdot 1 + 2 \cdot 2 + 3 \cdot 2) = 42$.

The starting point is the definition of $L(A)$:

$$L(A)$$
$$=$$ definition of L, formula 7.3 page 357
$$\sum_{k \in (F_G \sqcup F_D)} k \cdot l_A(k)$$
$$=$$ splitting of the quantifier
$$\sum_{k \in F_G} k \cdot l_A(k) + \sum_{k \in F_D} k \cdot l_A(k)$$
$$=$$ for $k \in F_G$, $l_A(k) = l_G(k) + 1$, ditto for F_D
$$\sum_{k \in F_G} k \cdot (l_G(k) + 1) + \sum_{k \in F_D} k \cdot (l_D(k) + 1)$$
$$=$$ arithmetics
$$\sum_{k \in F_G} k \cdot l_G(k) + \sum_{k \in F_G} k + \sum_{k \in F_D} k \cdot l_D(k) + \sum_{k \in F_G} k$$
$$=$$ property of frequency trees
$$\sum_{k \in F_G} k \cdot l_G(k) + G.h + \sum_{k \in F_D} k \cdot l_D(k) + D.h$$
$$=$$ arithmetics and definition of L, formula 7.3 page 357
$$L(G) + G.h + D.h + L(D).$$

Answer 3. The set H of optimal trees can be straightforwardly derived from the defi- 79 - A 3
nition of P:

$$H = \{A \mid A \in P \text{ and } \forall A' \cdot (A' \in P \Rightarrow L(A) \leqslant L(A'))\}.$$

Answer 4. Let us proceed by contradiction. If B is not optimal, in $B = \langle A_1, \ldots, A_m \rangle$, 79 - A 4
there is (at least) one A_i (on frequencies F_i's) that is not optimal. Let A'_i be an optimal tree
(on frequencies F_i's), let $B' = \langle A_1, \ldots, A'_i, \ldots, A_m \rangle$.

$$L(B)$$
$$=$$ definition 8 page 358
$$L(A_1) + \cdots + L(A_i) + \cdots + L(A_m)$$
$$>$$ A_i is not optimal
$$L(A_1) + \cdots + L(A'_i) + \cdots + L(A_m)$$
$$=$$ definition of B'
$$L(B').$$

The list B is therefore not optimal.

Answer 5. The four items of the construction of the loop remaining to be specified are 79 - A 5
presented hereafter.

Stopping condition It is simply defined as:

$$|B| = 1.$$

The conjunction of the answer to question 4, page 359, (all trees in the list B are optimal), of the invariant (B is an optimal list on F), and the stopping condition (the list contains a single element) entails that the (unique) tree of B is an optimal tree on F: that is the goal.

Progression On page 356 (Huffman's algorithm), it was seen that, assuming the invariant and the negation of the stopping condition are satisfied, the progression consists in rooting A_1 and A_2 on the root of value $A_1.h + A_2.h$, before inserting this new tree in the priority queue. We are going to apply a proof by contradiction in order to show that, in doing so, the invariant is actually preserved. Let us prove that, if we do not take the two smallest roots for rooting, the resulting list is not optimal. Let $B = \langle A_1, \ldots, A_m \rangle$ be the sorted list at the beginning of the progression. The list obtained at the end of the progression is $B' = \langle A_3, \ldots, (A_1, A_1.h + A_2.h, A_2), \ldots, A_m \rangle$. According to property 8, page 357, the cost of B' is $L(B') = L(B) + A_1.h + A_2.h$. On the other hand, if two trees A_i and A_j such that $A_i.h + A_j.h > A_1.h + A_2.h$ are rooted, the sorted list obtained is $B'' = \langle A_1, \ldots, A_{i-1}, A_{i+1}, \ldots, A_{j-1}, A_{j+1}, \ldots, (A_i, A_i.h + A_j.h, A_j), \ldots, A_n \rangle$. So we have:

$$L(B'')$$
$$=$$
$$\quad\quad L(B) + A_i.h + A_j.h \quad\quad\quad\quad\quad\quad\quad\quad\quad\quad\text{property 8, page 357}$$
$$>$$
$$\quad\quad L(B) + A_1.h + A_2.h \quad\quad\quad\quad\quad\quad\quad\quad\quad\quad\text{hypothesis above}$$
$$=$$
$$\quad\quad L(B') \quad\quad\quad\quad\quad\quad\quad\quad\quad\quad\quad\quad\quad\quad\text{definition of } B'$$

which establishes that the tree B'' is not optimal.

Initialization The invariant is established by placing the n components of the bag F of frequencies in the sorted list B. It is easy to check that it is an optimal list and that $F = F_1 \sqcup \ldots \sqcup F_n$.

Termination The length of the list B decreases by 1 at each step of progression, while being positive: $|B|$ is a convenient termination function.

Assuming that the cost function L is available and that the sorted list B is refined by a priority queue of optimal trees[3], the code of Huffman's algorithm is written:

```
 1. constants
 2.    P = {(/, h, /) | h ∈ ℕ₁} ∪ {(l, h, r) | l ∈ P and r ∈ P and h = l.h + r.h} and
 3.    H = {A | A ∈ P and ∀A' · (A' ∈ P ⇒ L(A) ⩽ L(A'))} and
 4.    n ∈ ℕ₁ and n = ... and F ∈ 1 .. n → ℕ₁ and F = [F₁, ..., Fₙ]
 5. variables
 6.    B ∈ PQ(H) and A1 ∈ H and A2 ∈ H
 7. begin
 8.    InitPQ(B) ;
 9.    for i ∈ 1 .. n do
10.       AddPQ(B, F[i])
11.    end for;
12.    while not(|B| = 1) do
13.       A1 ← HeadPQ(B) ; RemovePQ(B) ;
14.       A2 ← HeadPQ(B) ; RemovePQ(B) ;
15.       AddPQ(B, (A1, A1.h + A2.h, A2))
```

---

[3]It is considered here that the data structure *FdP* is set up to record optimal trees and that the priorities are the roots of these trees.

16.   **end while**;
17.   **write**(*HeadPQ*(B))
18. **end**

Complexity

The simplest choice for refining the priority queue is a heap (see section 1.7, page 30), for which the operations *AddPQ* and *RemovePQ* are in $\mathcal{O}(\log_2(n))$ conditions evaluated, for a queue of length n. For the first loop, the ith step costs at worst $\log_2(i)$. The n passes in this loop amount to $\log_2(1) + \cdots + \log_2(n) = \log_2(n!)$. But $\log_2(n!)$ behaves like $n \cdot \ln(n)$ (see Stirling formula, section 2.1.4 page 74). With the exception of a multiplicative factor, the same reasoning applies to the second loop. The complexity of the algorithm is thus in $\mathcal{O}(n \cdot \log_2(n))$ conditions evaluated.

Answers to problem 80. File merging
The problem is on page 359.

Answer 1.   The strategy used in schema (b) of the statement of the problem (which merges the two smallest files among those available) is optimal. For a set of files with $5, 6, 7, 8, 9$ and 10 records, it yields: 80 - A 1

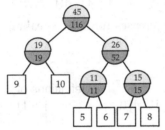

The cost of this tree is actually 116 units.

Answer 2.   It is a matter of construction of a binary tree in an ascending manner. In fact, it is a problem similar to Huffman's coding, whose algorithm construction and proof of optimality can be found on page 390. 80 - A 2

Answers to problem 81. The photocopier
The problem is on page 360.

Answer 1.   The calculation for the other five permutations yields: 81 - A 1

acb	=	$14 - (3 \cdot 3 + 2 \cdot 1 + 1 \cdot 4)$	=	-1
bac	=	$14 - (3 \cdot 4 + 2 \cdot 3 + 1 \cdot 1)$	=	-5
bca	=	$14 - (3 \cdot 4 + 2 \cdot 1 + 1 \cdot 3)$	=	-3
cab	=	$14 - (3 \cdot 1 + 2 \cdot 3 + 1 \cdot 4)$	=	1
cba	=	$14 - (3 \cdot 1 + 2 \cdot 4 + 1 \cdot 3)$	=	0

The permutation corresponding to a schedule of tasks based on increasing expiry times is cba, for which the profit is zero. This is not the best benefit, which is attained by the permutation cab. As a consequence, this strategy must be discarded.

81 - A 2   **Answer** 2.   First of all, let us observe that for the example of the statement, this strategy is actually optimal: the best possible benefit (1) is obtained with the permutation *cab*. Now, it is necessary to generalize and to prove that the benefit obtained by ordering tasks according to their increasing duration is at least equal to the profit given by any other permutation. The proof is done in two steps. In the first one, it is proven that if two adjacent elements appearing in decreasing order (of their duration) in any permutation P' are exchanged (which gives the new permutation P''), the benefit provided by P'' is enhanced (broadly speaking), i.e. $B(P'') \geqslant B(P')$. The second step consists in proving that sorting an array of integers can be achieved by a sequence of exchanges of two adjacent elements. This very obvious property is assumed (it is used in particular for *bubble sort*).

Let us prove the first point. Let $P' = [d(t_{i_1}), \ldots, d(t_{i_j}), d(t_{i_{j+1}}), \ldots, d(t_{i_n})]$ such that $d(t_{i_j}) \geqslant d(t_{i_{j+1}})$ and let $P'' = [d(t_{i_1}), \ldots, d(t_{i_j+1}), d(t_{i_j}), \ldots, d(t_{i_n})]$ be the permutation obtained after exchanging $d(t_{i_j})$ and $d(t_{i_{j+1}})$. We have:

$$B(P') = \sum_{i=1}^{n} e(t_i) - \left(\begin{array}{l} n \cdot d(t_{i_1}) + \cdots + (n-j+2) \cdot d(t_{i_{j-1}}) + \\ (n-j+1) \cdot d(t_{i_j}) + (n-j) \cdot d(t_{i_{j+1}}) + \\ (n-j-1) \cdot d(t_{(i_{j+2})}) + \cdots + 1 \cdot d(t_{i_n}) \end{array} \right)$$

and

$$B(P'') = \sum_{i=1}^{n} e(t_i) - \left(\begin{array}{l} n \cdot d(t_{i_1}) + \cdots + (n-j+2) \cdot d(t_{i_{j-1}}) + \\ (n-j+1) \cdot d(t_{i_{j+1}}) + (n-j) \cdot d(t_{i_j}) + \\ (n-j-1) \cdot d(t_{(i_{j+2})}) + \cdots + 1 \cdot d(t_{i_n}) \end{array} \right).$$

Let us prove that the benefit increases (broadly speaking) with this exchange, in other words that $B(P'') - B(P') \geqslant 0$:

$$B(P'') - B(P')$$

$=$ definitions of $B(P'')$ and $B(P')$ and arithmetics

$-(n-j+1) \cdot d(t_{i_j}) + (n-j) \cdot d(t_{i_{j+1}}) + ((n-j+1) \cdot d(t_{i_{j+1}}) + (n-j) \cdot d(t_{i_j}))$

$=$ arithmetics

$d(t_{i_j}) - d(t_{i_{j+1}})$

$\geqslant$ hypotheses about P' and P''

$0.$

Therefore, since $B(P'') - B(P') \geqslant 0$, the closer we get to the greedy solution, the more increased (broadly speaking) the profit. The greedy strategy proposed is thus optimal. The complexity of the algorithm is that of the sort of the tasks in ascending order of their durations, therefore it is in $\mathcal{O}(n \cdot \log_2(n))$.

Answers to problem 82. The intervals stabbing problem   *The problem is on page 362.*

82 - A 1   **Answer** 1.   No other point of T can be suppressed: if the point 3.5 (respectively 6.5) is removed, I_1, I_2 and I_3 (respectively I_4) are not pinned, etc. On the other hand, the points 9.5 and 11.5 can be replaced by the point 10.5 in order to obtain a six point set T.

82 - A 2   **Answer** 2.   The first strategy leads to the following solution:

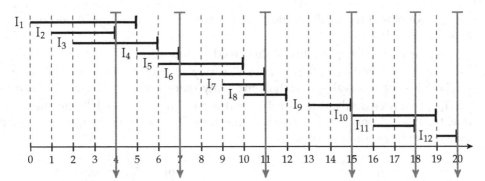

The second one yields:

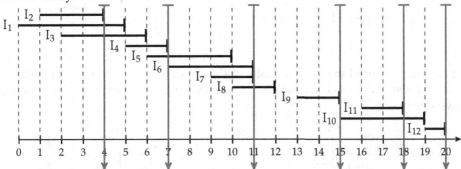

It can be noted that the two output queues T are the same in both cases: T = $\langle 4, 7, 11, 15, 18, 20 \rangle$. On the other hand, it appears that the second strategy (obtained with a sort on increasing ends) is easier to implement since we pin the first interval that is not yet pinned. This is not the case for the first strategy where some intervals must be put on hold to make sure that none is forgotten. For example, in the first diagram above, one should not pin I_1 at its end since in this case I_2 would be forgotten. The second strategy overcomes this difficulty.

Answer 3.   The development is carried out by applying the second strategy of the statement. Both input queue F and output queue T are implemented as FIFO queues. The notations defined in the introductory example are used here (see section 7.1.4, page 336). The difficult part of the construction is proving the optimality of the solution.   82 - A 3

Invariant The invariant taken here is the conjunction of the three following properties:

1. The pair (T_i, F_i) is such that $T_i = \langle g_1, \ldots, g_k \rangle$ is the configuration of the output queue T when the greedy strategy is applied to the list $\langle I_1, \ldots, I_i \rangle$, and $F_i = \langle I_{i+1}, \ldots, I_n \rangle$ is then the configuration of F.

2. T is an optimal solution.

3. Any other optimal solution (T'_i, F_i), with $T'_i = \langle o_1, \ldots, o_k \rangle$ is such that $o_k \leqslant g_k$ (T_i makes the "lead run"). This last property is related to the optimality of the greedy solution.

Stopping condition The process stops when the queue F is empty, i.e. when *IsEmptyFifo*(F).

Progression The precondition of the progression ensures that the invariant is met while the stopping condition is not (so there is an interval I_{i+1} which has not yet been processed). The progression is carried out by placing the abscissa of the extremity of the interval I_{i+1} (i.e. *HeadFifo*(F).end, cf. the second line of the program) in the output queue, while removing this interval from the queue F and eliminating from F all intervals that have a common intersection with I_{i+1}. This latter operation is carried out by a loop that is not built here. In summary, starting from the configuration

(T_i, F_i), we obtain the configuration (T_j, F_j), with $j > i$, $T_j = \langle g_1, \ldots, g_k, g_{k+1} \rangle$ and $F_j = \langle I_{j+1}, \ldots, I_n \rangle$.

Let us now prove the optimality of this greedy solution.

The greedy solution T_j obtained after one step of progression from the situation (T_i, F_i) pins the interval I_{i+1} at $I_{i+1}.\text{end}$. Any other optimal solution T_j' must also pin I_{i+1} (not necessarily at $I_{i+1}.\text{end}$). But this pin can be the $k + 1^{\text{th}}$ one, the $k + 2^{\text{th}}$ one, the $k + 3^{\text{th}}$ one, etc. The two schemas hereafter illustrate the transition for the case where I_{i+1} is pinned by o_{k+1}:

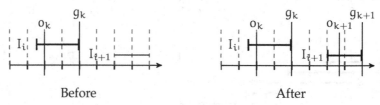

Before   After

It can be concluded that T_j' is actually optimal and that the point c of the invariant is actually restored. The case where I_{i+1} is pinned by o_{k+2} is illustrated by the following two schemas:

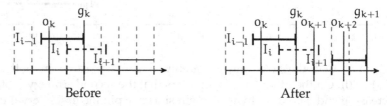

Before   After

It follows that T_j' is no longer an optimal solution; it has one point more than the greedy solution. The cases where I_{i+1} is pinned by o_{k+3}, o_{k+4}, etc. can be treated in the same way. Provided that the initialization and the termination of the algorithm are correct, T_n is therefore an optimal solution. The case where several intervals end at the same point does not raise any particular problem.

Initialization F is the FIFO queue containing the intervals sorted on their increasing ends, and T is empty. At the end of these operations, the invariant is established.

Termination F decreases in length by at least one unit with each step of progression. $|F|$, the size of F, is therefore a suitable termination function.

The program

The elements of the above construction are gathered to constitute the following program:

```
1.  constants
2.     Interval = {(beg, end) | beg ∈ ℝ*₊ and end ∈ ℝ*₊ and beg ⩽ end} and
3.     n ∈ ℕ₁ and n = ... and I ∈ 1..n → Interval and I = [...]
4.  variables
5.     t ∈ Interval and T ∈ FIFO(ℝ*₊) and F ∈ FIFO(Interval)
6.  begin
7.     InitFifo(F, I) ; /% Initialization of F and sort on increasing ends %/
8.     InitFifo(T);
9.     while not(IsEmptyFifo(F)) do
10.        t ← HeadFifo(F); RemoveFifo(F);
11.        AddFifo(T, t.end);
12.        while not(IsEmptyFifo(F) or else t.end ⩽ HeadFifo(F).beg) do
```

13.   *RemoveFifo*(F)
14.   **end while**
15.   **end while**;
16.   **write**(T)
17. **end**

Complexity

Each interval is taken into account once. The cost of the algorithm is that of the sort on line 7. So, it is in $\mathcal{O}(n \cdot \log_2(n))$.

Answer 4.   A pin can be placed at any point of the open/closed interval ending in t.end   82 - A 4
and starting at the origin with the largest abscissa among all the intervals deleted during a passage in the main loop. This is shown, in grey, in the diagram below, for the example of the statement:

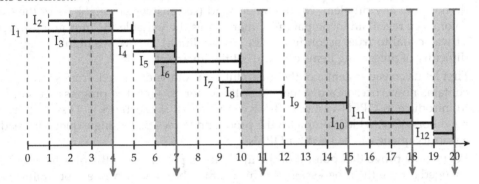

Answers to problem 83. Two-color graph coloring   *The problem is on page 363.*

Answer 1.   Assuming a representation of the graph by an adjacency matrix as sug-   83 - A 1
gested in the statement of the problem, the main loop (starting at line 16 of the algorithm of page 367) is traversed card(N) times, while the card(N) cumulative executions of the internal loop add up to card(V) traversals. The algorithm is therefore in $\Theta(\text{card}(N) + \text{card}(V))$ conditions evaluated.

Answer 2.   First of all, notice that the coloring algorithm should stop if it is impossible   83 - A 2
to use only two colors, contrary to the breadth-first exploration algorithm, which always produces a list associated with a breadth-first traversal of the graph. However, coloring (where possible) can be based on the following remarks: (i) vertices located at the same distance from the initial vertex of the exploration (s) must have the same color, (ii) coloring can be done when a vertex transits from the queue OPEN to the queue CLOSE, and (iii) coloring a vertex is only possible if none of its neighbors has already its color.

Answer 3.   The main loop is designed on the basis of the five classic items and some of   83 - A 3
the conjuncts of the invariant of the breadth-first exploration algorithm (see page 364). Let $G' = (N', V')$ be the sub-graph of G induced by the vertices present in CLOSE.

Invariant It consists of the following conjuncts:

1. CLOSE is a FIFO queue whose content represents a "breadth-first exploration" of G'.

2. OPEN is a FIFO queue involving the vertices that are neighbors of those present in CLOSE. The set intersection of OPEN and CLOSE is empty.

3. If the head of the queue OPEN contains a vertex whose distance to s is k, then all other vertices of OPEN are at a distance k or $(k + 1)$ to s.

4. The variable BiColor is equal to **true** iff the graph G′ is bicolored.

5. Vertices of G presents in either OPEN or CLOSE are white or black, others are grey.

Stopping condition The loop stops either when the OPEN queue is empty, or when the variable BiColor is equal to **false**. The conjunction of the invariant and the stopping condition actually entails that BiColor is equivalent to the proposal "G is bicolored".

Progression The precondition of the progression states that the queue OPEN is not empty. The head of the queue OPEN (cv) is moved to the end of the queue CLOSE (which can create a graph G′ that cannot be bicolored). It remains then to browse the list of neighbors of cv in G. Neighbors in grey are entered into OPEN with the color (white or black) opposite to that of cv. As for the neighbors of cv already present in the queue CLOSE (which are therefore already colored), those of the color opposite to that of cv do not pose any problem. On the other hand (see answer 2), neighbors of the same color as cv reveal an incompatibility that causes the variable BiColor going to **false** (it was equal to **true**, according to the precondition). Below, we highlight the dual difficulty of preserving items c) and d) of the invariant.

First let us consider item c of the invariant. cv is at the distance k from s, and OPEN contains no vertices at a distance other than k or $(k + 1)$. The progression will lead to introduce in OPEN vertices whose distance to s is exactly $(k + 1)$ since they are neighbors of cv, which completes the proof and shows that a single queue instead of a priority queue can be used for OPEN .

Let us now prove that point d of the invariant is preserved. If BiColor has not been changed during the progression, this means that the color of cv does not conflict with any other color in its neighborhood, in particular with any other color of G′. G′, the new sub-graph induced by the vertices present in CLOSE can therefore be bicolored:

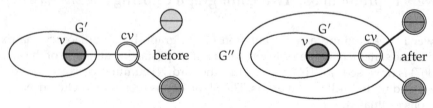

On the contrary, if BiColor takes the value **false**, it means that one (at least) of the neighbors of cv has the same color as cv. Two cases are *a priori* possible (they are illustrated by the diagrams below):

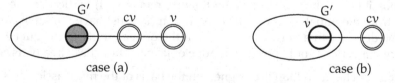

(a) This neighbor, v, is in OPEN. As soon as we consider moving v into CLOSE, its color will conflict with cv: the induced subgraph will not be bicolorable.

(b) v is in CLOSE (therefore in N′): the new sub-graph induced by moving cv into CLOSE is not bicolorable. However, this case cannot occur since it will have been anticipated by case (a).

Initialization The initial vertex s is placed into OPEN with an arbitrary color (for example black), all other vertices are grey: the induced sub-graph is empty, therefore it can be bicolored. The queue CLOSE is empty. The variable BiColor is equal to **true**. The invariant is established.

Termination At each step, a new vertex is transferred to CLOSE. The expression $(\text{card}(N) - \text{card}(\text{CLOSE}))$ is therefore a valid termination function.

Answer 4.   In the schema below, the conventions are the same as those in figure 7.9,   **83 - A 4** page 366, coloring excepted. Vertices not yet encountered are still in light grey. However, the vertices in either CLOSE or OPEN are colored either black (indeed dark grey), or white, depending on their depth. During the transition between steps (d) and (e), vertices f and g are colored white. In the step after step (f) all the already colored neighbors of the vertex f are considered in order to determine if their color is compatible with that of f. This is not the case for g which is white, hence coloring failure.

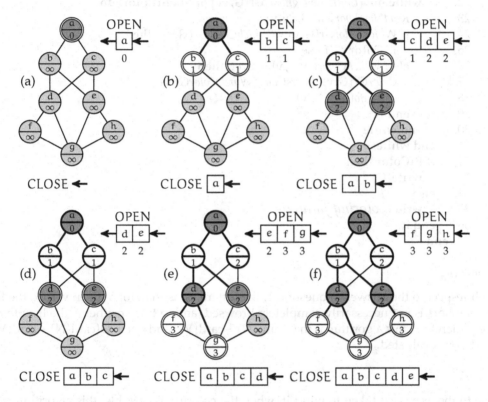

Answer 5.   The program given hereafter makes use of the same declarations as those of   **83 - A 5** the program of the statement. In addition, it is assumed that the color "black" is available. The operation *ReverseColor* switches between black and white.

```
1. constants
2.    n ∈ ℕ₁ and n = ... and N = 1 .. n and
3.    Colors = {grey, white, black} and V ∈ N × N and V = {...}
4. variables
5.    R ∈ N → Colors and G = (N, V, R) and
6.    s ∈ N and cv ∈ N and v ∈ N and BiColor ∈ 𝔹 and
7.    CLOSE ∈ FIFO(N) and OPEN ∈ FIFO(N)
8. begin
9.    /% coloring all the vertices in grey: %/
```

```
10.    for w ∈ N do
11.        ColorGr(G, w, grey)
12.    end for;
13.    InitFifo(CLOSE); InitFifo(OPEN);
14.    s ← ...; /% choice of the initial vertex %/
15.    ColorGr(G, s, black);
16.    AddFifo(OPEN, s);
17.    BiColor ← true;
18.    while not (IsEmptyFifo(OPEN) or not BiColor) do
19.        cv ← HeadFifo(OPEN); RemoveFifo(OPEN);
20.        AddFifo(CLOSE, cv);
21.        OpenNeighborsGr(G, cv) ;
22.        while not (EndListNeighborsGr(G, cv) or not BiColor) do
23.            ReadNeighborsGr(G, cv, v) ;
24.            if WhichColorGr(G, v) = WhichColorGr(G, cv) then
25.                BiColor ← false
26.            elsif WhichColorGr(G, v) = grey then
27.                ColorGr(G, v, ReversColor(WhichColorGr(G, cv))) ;
28.                AddFifo(OPEN, v)
29.            end if
30.        end while
31.    end while;
32.    if BiColor then
33.        write(G)
34.    else
35.        write(coloring failure)
36.    end if
37. end
```

Complexity

With respect to the answer to question 1, the difference is that, for a given vertex, the list of neighbors is not necessarily completely browsed, and in turn, neither is the list of vertices. Therefore, this algorithm is in $\mathcal{O}(\mathrm{card}(N) + \mathrm{card}(V))$ and not in $\Theta(\mathrm{card}(N) + \mathrm{card}(V))$ conditions evaluated.

Remark

Due to the approach taken to build it, when the coloring is possible, this algorithm provides not only a colored version of the graph G, but also (in CLOSE) a breadth-first path of G.

83 - A 6   **Answer 6.**   This method is not suitable for m (m > 2) colors, since the color of a vertex gives only a partial non-determining indication of the color to be assigned to each of its neighbors, unlike the case for two colors.

Answers to problem 84. From a partial order to a total order   *The problem is on page 368.*

84 - A 1   **Answer 1.**   A proof by contradiction is carried out. If the new graph is not a DAG, it contains (at least) one circuit. This latter was already present in the initial graph that therefore was not a DAG either.

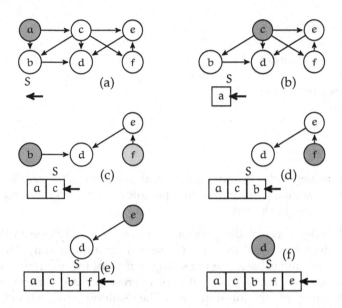

Fig. 7.14 – The six steps of the algorithm in answer to question 3 of problem 84.

Answer 2. Let $N = \{s_1, \ldots, s_n\}$. A graph G, such that for any i and any j > i there exists   84 - A 2
an arc of origin s_i and extremity s_j, is a DAG:

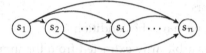

Its representation by an adjacency matrix (see section 1.5, page 22) is an upper triangular
matrix which contains $(1 + 2 + \cdots + (n-2) + (n-1)) = (n \cdot (n-1)/2)$ times the value 1.
This type of DAG fits the formula of the statement.

Answer 3. The six steps of the algorithm are shown in figure 7.14. Candidate nodes   84 - A 3
are in grey (light or dark); selected nodes are in dark grey. In the graph G, vertices in grey
are candidate to a transfer to the queue S. In part (c) of the diagram, vertices b and f are
candidates. The vertex b (in dark grey) is arbitrarily chosen.

The result reached after step (f) is a queue S containing the vertices a, c, b, f, e, d.

Answer 4. In the algorithm thereafter, vertices are integers. The predicate *IsDAG* en-   84 - A 4
sures that the graph in argument is a DAG.

```
 1. constants
 2.     EInit ⊂ N₁ and EInit = {...} and n = card(EInit)
 3. variables
 4.     E ⊂ N₁ and V ∈ E × E and G = (E, V) and IsDAG(G) and
 5.     S ∈ FIFO(EInit)
 6. begin
 7.     E ← EInit; V ← {...};
 8.     InitFifo(S);
 9.     while |S| ≠ n do
10.         let s such that
11.             s ∈ E and d⁻_G(s) = 0
12.         begin
```

```
13.        AddFifo(S, s);
14.        E ← E − {s};
15.        G ← Induced(G, E)
16.     end
17.  end while;
18.  write(S)
19. end
```

Complexity

During the first (respectively second, etc.) pass, at worst the n (respectively $(n − 1)$, etc.) vertices are scanned to find a minimum. In total, this algorithm is therefore in $\mathcal{O}(n^2)$ visits of vertices or conditions evaluated.

84 - A 5   Answer 5.   The high cost of the previous solution is mainly due to the search for a vertex whose in-degree is equal to 0 (i.e. the search for a minimum). The principle of a potentially better solution is based on the strengthening of the invariant by associating to each vertex its in-degree. Furthermore, it is of interest to place vertexes with a zero in-degree, and only those, into the input queue F. The resulting construction is the following:

Invariant Let S be the FIFO queue containing the set E_S of vertices ordered according to a total order compatible with $\prec$, and such that any vertex v of E not in E_S ($v \in (E−E_S)$) is greater than any vertex of E_S according to the partial order. Let F be the input queue containing the vertices of E not in E_S whose in-degree is equal to 0. Last let L be a structure containing the set of all other vertices associated with their in-degree and the set of their successors.

Stopping condition Again, we have the condition $n = |S|$.

Progression An element t is arbitrarily extracted from the input queue F, its identifier is placed into the output queue S, and its in-degree is decremented by 1 for each of its successors w. If value zero is reached, w is moved to the input queue.

Initialization The output queue S is empty; the set L is created from any representation of the graph and the entry points are put into the input queue F. All other vertices stay in L.

Termination A vertex is moved to the queue S at each step of progression: $n − |S|$ is an acceptable termination expression.

The algorithm

Hereafter, each element of L is made up of three components: id is the vertex identifier, di is its in-degree and suc is the list of its successors. The procedure *Construct* allows to get an adapted representation of the initial graph G in the data structure L. The input queue F can be implemented as a FIFO queue since its elements have the same priority.

```
1. constants
2.    LL = {(id, di, suc) | id ∈ E and di ∈ ℕ₁ and suc ⊆ E} and
3.    E ⊂ ℕ₁ and E = {...} and V ∈ E × E and V = {...} and
4.    G = (E, V) and IsDAG(G) and n = card(E)
5. variables
6.    S ∈ FIFO(E) and F ∈ FIFO(LL) and L ⊆ LL and t ∈ L
7. begin
8.    Construct(L, G); InitFifo(F);
9.    for v ∈ L do
10.      if v.di = 0 then
```

11. $L \leftarrow L - \{v\};$
12. $AddFifo(F, v)$
13.   **end if**
14.   **end for;**
15. $InitFifo(S);$
16.   **while** $|S| \neq n$ **do**
17. $t \leftarrow HeadFifo(F);$
18. $RemoveFifo(F);$
19. $AddFifo(S, t.id);$
20.   **for** $w \in t.suc$ **do**
21. $w.di \leftarrow w.di - 1;$
22.   **if** $w.di = 0$ **then**
23. $t.suc \leftarrow t.suc - \{w\};$
24. $AddFifo(F, w)$
25.   **end if**
26.   **end for**
27.   **end while;**
28.   **write**(F)
29. **end**

A last refinement based on pointers and dynamic structures provides the following representation for schema (b) of the answer to question 3:

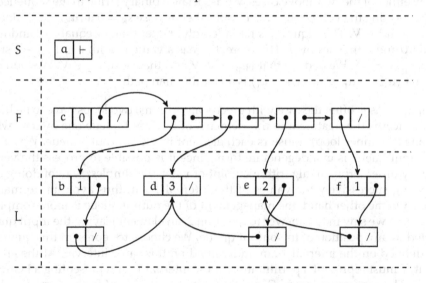

Complexity

It is reasonable to assume that the procedure *Construct* is in $\Theta(n + card(V))$. It is the case if the initial representation is based on lists of successors (see figure 1.3, page 23). Under these conditions, it appears that, for the rest of the algorithm, each vertex and each arc are taken into account once and the operations on the queues are in $\Theta(1)$. Consequently, the complexity of this solution is in $\Theta(n + card(V))$. In the worst case, this solution is not asymptotically better than the previous one since as mentioned in question 2, a DAG can have in the order of n^2 arcs. On the other hand, in the case of non-dense graphs ($card(V) \ll n^2$), this solution is better since it is in $\mathcal{O}(n + card(V))$.

Answers to problem 85. Tournaments and Hamiltonian paths *The problem is on page 370.*

85 - A 1   **Answer** 1.   Let $s = s_1 \ldots s_m$ ($m \geqslant 2$) be such a binary string. It has a longest prefix entirely composed of 0, whose length p is such that $p \in 1 .. m-1$. The sub-string $s_p s_{p+1}$ is the string 01 (we could also reason on the longest suffix).

85 - A 2   **Answer** 2.   As required in the statement, a proof by induction is carried out.

Base A tournament with a single vertex u is such that $\langle u \rangle$ is a Hamiltonian path for this graph.

Induction hypothesis Any tournament of i vertices ($i \geqslant 1$) has (at least) one Hamiltonian path. Let $\langle u_1, \ldots, u_i \rangle$ be one of them.

Induction Let v be a $(i+1)^{\text{th}}$ vertex. Three cases are to be taken into account depending on the direction of the arcs between v and u_1 and/or v and u_i.

* $(v, u_1) \in V$. In this case, $\langle v, u_1, \ldots, u_i \rangle$ is a Hamiltonian path.
* $(u_i, v) \in V$. In this case, $\langle u_1, \ldots, u_i, v \rangle$ is a Hamiltonian path.
* $(v, u_1) \notin V$ and $(u_i, v) \notin V$. Here, it is impossible to place v at one of the extremities of the (initial) Hamiltonian path of length i. The lemma of the first question is used to prove that it is always possible to place v somewhere inside $\langle u_1, \ldots, u_i \rangle$. Let us prior notice that this situation cannot occur for $i = 1$; this latter is taken into account by either of the two above cases. We associate a binary string to the sequence of arcs connecting the vertices $u_1, \ldots, u_i$ and v. Let us pose $s_k = 0$ if $(u_k, v) \in V$ and $s_k = 1$ if $(v, u_k) \in V$. The sequence s has a length greater than or equal to 2 and it begins by 0 and it finishes by 1. Therefore, there is a value p, with $p \in 1 .. i-1$ such that $s_p s_{p+1} = 01$. We deduce that $(u_p, v) \in V$ and that $(v, u_{p+1}) \in V$. We then observe that $\langle u_1, \ldots, u_p, v, u_{p+1}, \ldots, u_i \rangle$ is a Hamiltonian path.

85 - A 3   **Answer** 3.   As is often the case with greedy algorithms, two loops have to be built. The first one concerns the treatment of the elements of the input queue one by one, while the second one (the inner loop) transfers each element in the "output" queue. We can notice that the input queue is in a degenerate form since it is possible to process the vertices in an arbitrary order. From an algorithmic point of view, the simplest way of doing consists in processing successively the values of the interval $1 .. n$, thus avoiding to materialize the queue. On the other hand, the management of the output queue is more complex than usual since, as we saw in the answer to question 2, an element leaving the input queue can be inserted in any position of the output queue. We choose to represent this queue by the array T defined on the interval $1 .. n$ and valued on this same interval. At the end of the treatment, T must represent a permutation of the interval $1 .. n$ representing a Hamiltonian path in G. The representation of G can be limited to that of V in the form of a Boolean adjacency matrix (see Chapter 1).

Construction of the outer loop

The five points of the construction are successively presented.

Invariant The sub-array $T[1 .. i]$ represents a Hamiltonian path for the sub-graph of G induced by $N' = 1 .. i$.

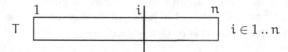

Stopping condition The condition $i = n$ is such that its conjunction with the invariant is the desired goal.

Progression The progression is inspired from the answer to question 2. By means of a loop, it intends to insert the value $(i + 1)$ into T, so that the sub-array $T[1 .. i + 1]$ represents a Hamiltonian path for the first $(i + 1)$ vertices. The invariant is then restored by the assignment $i \leftarrow i+1$. The development of this second loop is performed thereafter.

Initialization The program

     1. $i \leftarrow 1; T[1] \leftarrow 1$

establishes the invariant.

Termination The expression $(n - i)$ is nonnegative and strictly decreases at each step of progression. It is a convenient termination expression.

Construction of the inner loop

The role of this loop is to determine the position j where the value $(i + 1)$ will be inserted.

Invariant The shaded area below represents a "hole". Apart from this position, the sub-array $T[1 .. i + 1]$ represents a Hamiltonian path for the first i vertices of the graph.

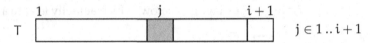

Stopping condition The stopping condition is made up of three sub-conditions expressing the result of question 2. It is presented in the program below. A refinement of this condition is possible, which ends up in a more concise version.

Progression We choose a "right to left" progression of the variable j and we get the following program:

     1. $T[j] \leftarrow T[j - 1]; j \leftarrow j - 1$

Initialization The following assignment establishes the invariant:

     1. $j \leftarrow i + 1$

Termination The expression j is always positive and it strictly decreases at each step of progression. This is an appropriate termination expression.

The algorithm

It is presented as follows:

     1. **constants**
     2. $n \in \mathbb{N}_1$ and $n = \ldots$ and $V \in 1 .. n \times 1 .. n \rightarrow \mathbb{B}$ and $V = [\ldots]$
     3. **variables**
     4. $T \in 1 .. n \rightarrow 1 .. n$ and $i \in 1 .. n$ and $j \in 1 .. i + 1$
     5. **begin**
     6. $i \leftarrow 1; T[1] \leftarrow 1;$
     7.   **while** $i \neq n$ **do**
     8. $j \leftarrow i + 1;$
     9.   **while not** $\left(\begin{array}{l} (j = i \textbf{ and then } V[i + 1, T[j + 1]]) \\ \textbf{or else} \\ (j = i + 1 \textbf{ and then } V[T[j - 1], i + 1]) \\ \textbf{or else} \\ (V[T[j - 1], i + 1] \textbf{ and then } V[i + 1, T[j + 1]]) \end{array} \right)$ **do**

10. $T[j] \leftarrow T[j-1]; j \leftarrow j-1$
11.   **end while**;
12. $T[j] \leftarrow i+1; i \leftarrow i+1$
13.   **end while**;
14.   **write**(T)
15. **end**

Complexity

This algorithm presents a very strong analogy with the sort by simple insertion. In particular, its complexity is also in $\mathcal{O}(n^2)$ in terms of conditions evaluated. This suggests that there could be a (non-greedy) algorithm similar to merge sort (see problem 88, page 424), more efficient than the version developed above. It turns out that it is actually the case, which relegates the solution discussed here to the rank of a "pure" problem.

Answers to problem 86. Odd-order magic squares   *The problem is on page 371.*

86 - A 1   **Answer 1.**   The sum of the n^2 values of any magic square is $(n^2 \cdot (n^2+1)/2)$. The sum of each row or column is then equal to $M_n = n \cdot (n^2+1)/2$, hence $M_5 = 65$ and $M_7 = 175$.

86 - A 2   **Answer 2.**   For $n = 7$, we get the diagrams below, which actually lead to a magic square of order 7:

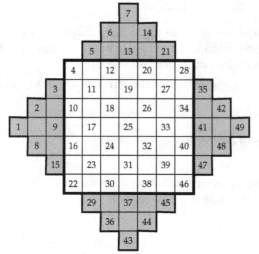

86 - A 3   **Answer 3.**   The proof is first made for $n = 5$ before generalizing for any odd value n.

Case of the "large" south-west/north-east diagonal of the central square This is the simplest case to take into account. For $n = 5$, the five central values of the interval $1 .. 25$ must be cumulated, i.e. $11 + 12 + 13 + 14 + 15 = 13 \cdot 5 = 65$. More generally, for any n:

$$\left(\left(\frac{n^2+1}{2} - \frac{n-1}{2} \right) + \left(\frac{n^2+1}{2} - \left(\frac{n-1}{2} - 1 \right) \right) + \cdots + \right.$$
$$\left. \left(\frac{n^2+1}{2} \right) + \cdots + \left(\frac{n^2+1}{2} + \left(\frac{n-1}{2} - 1 \right) \right) + \left(\frac{n^2+1}{2} + \frac{n-1}{2} \right) \right)$$
$$= \qquad\qquad\qquad\qquad\qquad\qquad\qquad\qquad\qquad\qquad\qquad\qquad\qquad \text{arithmetics}$$
$$n \cdot \left(\frac{n^2+1}{2} \right).$$

It is indeed M_n.

Case of the main north-west/south-east diagonal of the main square Here, the median values of the south-west/north-east diagonals of the crenellated checkerboard must be cumulated. For $n = 5$, we get $(5+1)/2 + (6+10)/2 + (11+15)/2 + (16+20)/2 + (21+25)/2 = 65$. In the general case:

$$\left(\frac{(0n+1)+n}{2} + \frac{(1n+1)+2n}{2} + \cdots + \frac{((i-1)\cdot n+1)+i\cdot n}{2} \right.$$
$$\left. + \cdots + \frac{((n-1)\cdot n+1)+n\cdot n}{2} \right)$$

use of the notation $\sum$

$$= \sum_{i=1}^{n} \frac{((i-1)\cdot n+1)+i\cdot n}{2}$$

arithmetics

$$= \frac{1}{2} \cdot \sum_{i=1}^{n} (2\cdot i\cdot n - n + 1)$$

quantifier breakup

$$= \frac{1}{2} \cdot \left(2n \cdot \sum_{i=1}^{n} i - n \cdot \sum_{i=1}^{n} 1 + \sum_{i=1}^{n} 1 \right)$$

arithmetics

$$= \frac{1}{2} \cdot (n^3 + n^2 - n^2 + n)$$

arithmetics

$$= n \cdot \left(\frac{n^2 + 1}{2} \right).$$

It is still M_n.

Case of any other row For example, let us consider the third row of the magic square of order 5 of the statement of the problem. Regarding the values that are in place after the first phase, the value 7 corresponds to the second value of the second diagonal, that is $1 \cdot 5 + 2$, the value 13 corresponds to the third value of the third diagonal, i.e. $2 \cdot 5 + 3$ and the value 19 to the fourth value of the fourth diagonal, i.e. $3 \cdot 5 + 4$. The values placed during the last phase, 25 and 1, correspond respectively to the fifth value of the fifth diagonal $(4 \cdot 5 + 5)$ and to the first value of the first diagonal $(0 \cdot 5 + 1)$. In total, by grouping the terms differently, we get $((0 \cdot 5 + 1 \cdot 5 + 2 \cdot 5 + 3 \cdot 5 + 4 \cdot 5) + (1 + 2 + 3 + 4 + 5))$. By proceeding in the same way on another line, we see that we obtain the same terms, initially in another order. The sum is actually equal to 65. For any (odd) n, the formula generalizes as follows:

$$\sum_{i=0}^{n-1} i \cdot n + \sum_{i=1}^{n} i$$

arithmetics

$$= \frac{n \cdot (n-1) \cdot n}{2} + \frac{n \cdot (n+1)}{2}$$

arithmetics

$$= n \cdot \left(\frac{n^2 + 1}{2} \right).$$

We find again M_n. The case of columns is treated in a similar way, which completes the demonstration.

Answer 4.   Let us first observe that, since we have proven that the result of Bachet's method does indeed produce a magic square of order n, it is useless to repeat this proof during the construction of the algorithm. A weakened form of invariant is sufficient. There are (at least) two ways to proceed: either Bachet's method is literally translated into computer terms, by carrying out two successive phases, or these two phases are merged into a single one. We choose the second method, which is the closest to the generic greedy algorithm (see section 7.2, page 341). Note that the coordinates of the north-west corner of the square to be constructed are $(1, 1)$ while those of the initial padding cell (where the value 1 is initially placed, to the left of the crenellated square) are $((n + 1)/2, -(n - 3)/2)$.

Invariant For $i \in 1 .. n^2 + 1$, the values of the interval $1 .. i - 1$ are placed on the central square according to Bachet's method.

Stopping condition $i = (n^2 + 1)$. In conjunction with the invariant, this proposition ensures that the square is filled in, and, given the demonstration above, it is a magic square.

Progression The values are virtually placed on the crenellated checkerboard at the position (r, c) and, for those outside the square, dragged inside the square according to the second phase of Bachet's method. The pair (r, c) is updated to traverse the n large diagonals of the checkerboard.

Initialization The following program:

$$1. \ i \leftarrow 1; r \leftarrow \frac{n + 1}{2}; c \leftarrow -\frac{n - 3}{2}$$

establishes the invariant.

Termination The expression $(n^2 + 1 - i)$ decreases at each step of progression while remaining nonnegative. This is the guarantee for the termination of the loop.

The program

We deduce the following code:

```
 1. constants
 2.    n ∈ ℕ₁ and n = ...
 3. variables
 4.    ms ∈ 1 .. n × 1 .. n → 1 .. n² and  /% ms: magic square %/
 5.    i ∈ 1 .. n² + 1 and r ∈ ℤ and c ∈ ℤ
 6. begin
 7.    i ← 1;
 8.    r ← (n+1)/2; c ← -(n-3)/2;
 9.    while i ≠ n² + 1 do
10.       if r < 1 then
11.          ms[r + n, c] ← i
12.       elsif r > n then
13.          ms[r - n, c] ← i
14.       elsif c < 1 then
15.          ms[r, c + n] ← i
16.       elsif c > n then
17.          ms[r, c - n] ← i
18.       else
19.          ms[r, c] ← i
20.       end if;
```

```
21.        r ← r − 1 ; c ← c + 1 ;
22.        i ← i + 1 ;
23.        if i mod n = 1 then
24.            r ← r + (n + 1) ; c ← c − (n − 1)
25.        end if
26.    end while;
27.    write(ms)
28. end
```

Let us try to identify this program with the greedy generic code of section 7.2, page 341. The priority queue is the sorted set of values in the range $1 .. n^2$. Given its characteristics, this queue does not need to be materialized. The FIFO queue does not exist here. It is replaced by the square ms. Line 7 represents the initialization of the priority queue. Line 8 is in a way the initialization of the FIFO queue. The body of the loop plays the role of removing the head element from the priority queue and then adding it to the FIFO queue. As we pointed out in the statement, there is no optimization function, although with a little imagination we can consider that looking for a set of rows, columns and diagonals of the same sum constitutes a minimization compared to other configurations.

Answers to problem 87. The bridge and torch problem   *The problem is on page 372.*

Answer 1.   When $N = 2$, the only possible schedule is: $\langle +\{1,2\}\rangle$, which is therefore optimal.   87 - A 1

When $N = 3$, six schedules are possible:

- $S_1 = \langle +\{1,2\}, -\{1\}, +\{1,3\}\rangle$ for a total crossing time $T_1 = t_2 + t_1 + t_3$,
- $S_2 = \langle +\{1,2\}, -\{2\}, +\{2,3\}\rangle$ for a total crossing time $T_2 = t_2 + t_2 + t_3 = 2t_2 + t_3$,
- $S_3 = \langle +\{1,3\}, -\{1\}, +\{1,2\}\rangle$ for a total crossing time $T_3 = t_3 + t_1 + t_2$,
- $S_4 = \langle +\{1,3\}, -\{3\}, +\{2,3\}\rangle$ for a total crossing time $T_4 = t_3 + t_3 + t_3 = 3t_3$,
- $S_5 = \langle +\{2,3\}, -\{2\}, +\{1,2\}\rangle$ for a total crossing time $T_5 = t_3 + t_2 + t_2 = 2t_2 + t_3$,
- $S_6 = \langle +\{2,3\}, -\{3\}, +\{1,3\}\rangle$ for a total crossing time $T_6 = t_3 + t_3 + t_3 = 3t_3$.

Due to the order over the t_i's, the two equivalent (from a temporal point of view) optimal schedules are S_1 and S_3.

Answer 2.   With $t_1 = 1, t_2 = 5, t_3 = 6, t_4 = 7, t_5 = 8$ and $t_6 = 10$, the schedule S' leads   87 - A 2
to a total time of 44, while 40 has been obtained with S, which shows that S' is not optimal.

Answer 3.   For $N = 6$ and $t_1 = 1, t_2 = 5, t_3 = 6, t_4 = 8, t_5 = 10, t_6 = 15$, the total   87 - A 3
crossing time is $T = 48$ if the schedule S is used and T' (respectively T'') = 50 (respectively 47) with S' (respectively S''). This shows that, in this case, S'' performs better than both S and S', but not yet that S'' is optimal (this is shown in answer 11).

Answer 4.   If N people are on side D of the bridge, there are two out of N choices for   87 - A 4
the first "forward" move and two possibilities for the first "backward" move, then two among $(N − 1)$ choices for the second "forward" crossing and three possibilities for the second "backward" crossing, and so on. For $N = 2$, this yields a single possible schedule. For $N = 3$, the number of possible schedules is $C_3^2 \cdot 2 = 6$. When $N = 4$, this number is $C_4^2 \cdot 2 \cdot C_3^2 \cdot 3 = 108$ and finally for $N = 5$, the number of possible schedules is $C_5^2 \cdot 2 \cdot C_4^2 \cdot 3 \cdot C_3^2 \cdot 4 = 4320$. It is clear that this problem is highly combinatorial and it would be hardly manageable using a "Generate and test" approach.

87 - A 5   **Answer 5.**   Let us consider a schedule S of type $\langle\ldots,-\{x\},\ldots\rangle$ where $-\{x\}$ is the *first* backward move with a person x ranked strictly over 2. Before $-\{x\}$, there has been a "forward" move either $+\{1,x\}$, or $+\{2,x\}$, or $+\{x,y\}$ where y is ranked strictly over 2.

In the first case, if p_2 is located on side D, the sub-sequence (of S) $\langle+\{1,x\},\ldots,-\{x\}\rangle$ can be replaced by $\langle+\{1,2\},\ldots,-\{2\}\rangle$ whose cost is strictly less and thus S is not an optimal schedule. If p_2 is on side A, he has crossed the bridge with another person y. But, the torch has to be returned to side D; since p_2 stays on side A and $-\{x\}$ is the first "backward" move, the torch is necessarily conveyed by p_1. Therefore, we have a sub-sequence (of S) of type $\langle+\{1,2\},-\{1\},\ldots,+\{1,x\},\ldots,-\{x\}\rangle$ which is indeed equivalent to $\langle+\{1,2\},\ldots,\ldots,\rangle$, but strictly more costly and the "backward" move $-\{x\}$ cannot appear in an optimal schedule in this situation.

The same reasoning applies for the second case by exchanging the roles of p_1 and p_2.

As for the last case, if any, "forward" moves preceding $+\{x,y\}$ must involve p_1 or p_2 (possibly both) for the torch to be returned on side D by a person ranked strictly under 3 (since $-\{x\}$ is the first "backward" move where $x > 2$). So, we are sure that p_1 or p_2 is located on side D when the move $+\{x,y\}$ takes place. Neglecting the cost of the elements represented by "$\ldots$", the partial cost of the sub-sequence $\langle+\{x,y\},\ldots,-\{x\}\rangle$ is $c = 2t_x$ if $t_x > t_y$ or $c' = t_x + t_y$ if $t_x < t_y$. The partial cost of the sub-sequence $\langle+\{1,y\},\ldots,-\{1\}\rangle$ is $c1 = t_1 + t_y$ and that of the sub-sequence $\langle+\{2,y\},\ldots,-\{2\}\rangle$ is $c2 = t_2 + t_y$. Since $c1 < c, c2 < c, c1 < c', c2 < c'$, it turns out that the sub-sequence $\langle+\{x,y\},\ldots,-\{x\}\rangle$ is more costly than both $\langle+\{1,y\},\ldots,-\{1\}\rangle$ and $\langle+\{2,y\},\ldots,-\{2\}\rangle$. This proves that, in this third case also, the "backward" move $-\{x\}$ (where x is ranked strictly over 2) cannot be part of an optimal schedule.

87 - A 6   **Answer 6.**   Let us deal with the *first* "forward" move of type b, i.e. $+\{2,x\}$ where $x \geqslant 3$. Either p_1 has never crossed the bridge and he is still on side D, or he has been involved at least once and he has been obliged to return the torch to side D. It appears that p_1 can only be on side D of the bridge and the move $+\{2,x\}$ must be followed by the move $-\{2\}$ to return the torch. But, the sub-sequence $\langle+\{1,x\},-\{1\}\rangle$ (of cost $c_1 = t_1 + t_x$) performs strictly better than the sub-sequence $\langle+\{2,x\},-\{2\}\rangle$ (of cost $c_2 = t_2 + t_x$), hence the move $+\{2,x\}$ is forbidden in an optimal schedule.

Let us now deal with moves of type c ($+\{x,y\}$ where $x > 2, y > 2$ and $x \neq y$). The schedule $S_1 = \langle\ldots,+\{N-1,N\},\ldots,+\{u,v\},\ldots\rangle$ where $u \geqslant 3, v > u$ and both differ from N and $N - 1$, induces the partial cost $pc_1 = \max(\{t_{N-1}, t_N\}) + \max(\{t_u, t_v\}) = t_N + t_v$, while the partial cost of the schedule $S_2 = \langle\ldots,+\{N-1,u\},\ldots,+\{N,v\},\ldots\rangle$ (u and v as before) is $pc_2 = \max(\{t_{N-1}, t_u\}) + \max(\{t_N, t_v\}) = t_{N-1} + t_N$. Since u and v are less than $N - 1$, we have $t_v < t_{N-1}$. Therefore S_2 cannot be an optimal schedule. We can now consider the remaining persons $p_1,\ldots,p_{N-2}$ onto which the same reasoning can be applied leading to prove that p_{N-2} and p_{N-3} must cross together, an so on for the next pairs of people. Therefore, it turns out that in any optimal schedule, the only pairs of people likely to cross together are on the one hand p_1 and p_2 and on the other hand p_{N-2i} and p_{N-2i-1} where $i \in 0 .. \lfloor N/2 \rfloor - 1$.

87 - A 7   **Answer 7.**   Let us look back to the components of optimal schedules outlined before in case of people likely to walk at the same rate. Concerning "backward" moves, if $t_2 = t_3 = \cdots = t_i$ ($i \in 3 .. N$), it is clear that any person p_j ($j \in 3 .. N$) can return the torch to side D, but the crossing time is not strictly decreased with respect to using only p_2 (such moves perform as well as $-\{2\}$, not strictly better). Similarly, if $t_1 = t_2 = \cdots = t_i$ ($i \in 2 .. N$), "forward" moves $+\{i,x\}$ ($i \in 2 .. N$) may appear in an optimal schedule but they do not contribute to improving crossing time. Last, regarding moves of type c ($+\{x,y\}$

where $x > 2, y > 2$ and $x \neq y$), p_N can cross the bridge with p_v if $t_v = t_{N-1}$, but here again the crossing time is not strictly decreased with respect to that of p_N crossing with p_{N-1}. In conclusion, it appears that optimal schedules can be restricted to containing "backward" moves with only persons p_1 and p_2, and "forward" moves either $+\{1, x\}$ where $x \geqslant 2$, or $+\{x, y\}$ where $x > 2, y > 2, x \neq y, x = N - 2i, y = N - 2i - 1$ for $i \in 0 .. \lfloor N/2 \rfloor - 1$, provided that a move $+\{1, 2\}$ took place before.

Answer 8.   Since two types of "forward" moves are allowed, there are only two possi-   87 - A 8
bilities for the transfer of persons p_{N-2i} and p_{N-2i-1} from side D to side A of the bridge. Therefore, the number of candidate schedules is $2^{\lfloor N/2 \rfloor - 1}$ which yields 1 (respectively 1, 2, 2) for $N = 2$ (respectively 3, 4, 5). It can be observed that the search space has been drastically decreased with respect to that given in the answer to question 4.

Answer 9.   As mentioned just before, there are only *two* possibilities for the transfer of   87 - A 9
persons p_{N-2i} and p_{N-2i-1} from side D to side A of the bridge:

1. Each of them is accompanied by the fastest person (p_1), which leads to the sub-sequence $+\{1, N - 2i\}, -\{1\}, +\{1, N - 2i - 1\}, -\{1\}$ whose partial crossing time is $2t_1 + t_{N-2i} + t_{N-2i-1}$ (strategy Str_1 mentioned earlier in the statement), or

2. They cross together (strategy Str_2), but first it is necessary that the two fastest persons (p_1 and p_2) cross the bridge so that it becomes possible later to move the torch back to side D (with either p_1, or p_2). The corresponding sub-sequence is $+\{1, 2\}, -\{1\}, +\{N - 2i, N - 2i - 1\}, -\{2\}$ or alternatively $+\{1, 2\}, -\{2\}, +\{N - 2i, N - 2i - 1\}, -\{1\}$, whose duration is $2t_2 + t_1 + t_{N-2i}$ in both cases.

If $2t_2 + t_1 + t_{N-2i}$ is less than (respectively greater than or equal to) $2t_1 + t_{N-2i} + t_{N-2i-1}$, i.e. $2t_2 - t_1 - t_{N-2i-1} < $ (respectively $\geqslant$) 0, the choice is the second (respectively first) sub-sequence for an optimal schedule. In case of equality, the duration is the same whatever the choice made.

Remark

Indeed, the order between sub-sequences does not really matter. For example, the schedules $\langle +\{1, 2\}, -\{1\}, +\{5, 6\}, -\{2\}, +\{1, 4\}, -\{1\}, +\{1, 3\}, -\{1\}, +\{1, 2\}\rangle$ and $\langle +\{1, 4\}, -\{1\}, +\{1, 3\}, -\{1\}, +\{1, 2\}, -\{1\}, +\{5, 6\}, -\{2\}, +\{1, 2\}\rangle$ (among many others) are equivalent regarding the total crossing time.

Answer 10.   It can be noticed that $2t_2 - t_1 - t_{N-2i-1}$ is an increasing function in i and   87 - A 10
thus, as soon as it is positive for a given i, Str_1 is the only strategy applicable further on. Consequently, the strategy Str_3 consists in applying Str_2 as long as $2t_2 - t_1 - t_{N-2i-1}$ remains negative (or zero), then Str_1.

Answer 11.   As mentioned in the statement, the solution under design first supposes   87 - A 11
the identification of an "appropriate" intermediate situation. In the answer to question 1, the sub-sequences of moves for the optimal transfer of "only" two or three people are exhibited and it is tempting to consider these two cases as constituting the intermediate situation. Consequently, the postcondition of the "greedy" component is:

m people on side D of the bridge *with the torch* **and** $(N - m)$ people on side A **and** $m \in 2 .. N$ **and** $m \leqslant 3$ (persons p_1, p_2 and possibly p_3 are still on side D) **and** SCH contains an optimal schedule relating to the $(N - m)$ people on side A.

On this basis, it is now possible to specify the five components of the loop associated with this first part of the algorithm.

Invariant From the previous postcondition, the following invariant can be derived:

m people on side D of the bridge *with the torch* **and** $(N - m)$ people on side A **and** $m \in 2 .. N$ **and** SCH contains an optimal sequence of moves relating to the $(N - m)$ people on side A.

Stopping condition $m \leqslant 3$. Clearly, the conjunction of the invariant and the stopping condition entails the postcondition.

Progression The objective is to generate the crossing of persons numbered m and $m - 1$ from side D to side A while restoring the invariant. The choice justified in answer 9 plays a key role to produce the following convenient sub-sequence of moves:

$$\langle +\{1, 2\}, -\{1\}, +\{m, m - 1\}, -\{2\} \rangle \text{ if } 2t_2 - t_1 - t_{m-1} < 0$$
$$\langle +\{1, m\}, -\{1\}, +\{1, m - 1\}, -\{1\} \rangle \text{ if } 2t_2 - t_1 - t_{m-1} \geqslant 0.$$

In both cases, two people "disappear" from side D and the value of m must be diminished by 2. In the end of the progression, as required by the final phase, m is equal to 2 or 3 and the torch is located on side D of the bridge.

Initialization Since $N \geqslant 2$, the invariant is established by the assignment of N to m.

Termination The number of people on side D of the bridge (m) decreases at each step of progression while remaining positive; m is an acceptable termination expression.

As mentioned before, the role of the second fragment of code is to generate the subsequence of moves for the transfer of the remaining 2 or 3 people from D to A (with the torch). In the "greedy" part of the algorithm, there is obviously no need for an explicit input queue since the persons are processed in decreasing order of their numbers. The algorithm is written hereafter.

```
1.  constants
2.    N ∈ ℕ₁ and N ⩾ 2 and N = ... and t ∈ 1 .. N → ℕ₁ and t = ... and
3.    /% SCHt : type of the list of crossings SCH %/
                ⎛ {/}∪                                                              ⎞
4.    SCHt =    ⎜ {{a, b}, succ | (a, b) ∈ 1 .. N − 1 × 2 .. N and succ ∈ SCHt}∪   ⎟
                ⎝ {{c}, succ | c ∈ 1 .. N and succ ∈ SCHt}                         ⎠
5.  variables
6.    SCH ∈ SCHt and m ∈ 0 .. N
7.  begin
8.    /% first part - greedy component %/
9.    SCH ← /; m ← N;
10.   while not(m ⩽ 3) do
11.     if 2 · t[2] − t[1] − t[m − 1] ⩽ 0 then
12.       SCH ← SCH · ⟨{1, 2}⟩ · ⟨{1}⟩ · ⟨{m − 1, m}⟩ · ⟨{2}⟩
13.     else
14.       SCH ← SCH · ⟨{1, m − 1}⟩ · ⟨{1}⟩ · ⟨{1, m}⟩ · ⟨{1}⟩
15.     end if;
16.     m ← m − 2
17.   end while;
18.   /% final processing %/
19.   if m = 3 then
20.     SCH ← SCH · ⟨{1, 3}⟩ · ⟨{1}⟩ · ⟨{1, 2}⟩
21.   else
22.     SCH ← SCH · ⟨{1, 2}⟩
```

23. **end if**;
24. **write**(SCH)
25. **end**

When run, this algorithm returns the following results:

- Case $N = 4$ and $t_1 = 1, t_2 = 5, t_3 = 6, t_4 = 8$.

  1. Greedy phase - Initialization: $m \leftarrow 4$.

  2. Greedy phase - step 1: $2t_2 - t_1 - t_3 = 3$ and the sub-list inserted into SCH is: $\langle\{1,3\}.\{1\}.\{1,4\}.\{1\}\rangle$; $m \leftarrow 2$.

  3. Final phase: the sub-list inserted into SCH is: $\langle\{1,2\}\rangle$.

  In its external form, the schedule produced is

  $$\langle +\{1,4\}, -\{1\}, +\{1,3\}, -\{1\}, +\{1,2\}\rangle$$

  for a total crossing time of 21.

- Case $N = 6$ and $t_1 = 1, t_2 = 5, t_3 = 6, t_4 = 7, t_5 = 8, t_6 = 10$.

  1. Greedy phase - Initialization: $m \leftarrow 6$.

  2. Greedy phase - step 1: $2t_2 - t_1 - t_5 = 1$ and the sub-list inserted into SCH is: $\langle\{1,6\}.\{1\}.\{1,5\}.\{1\}\rangle$; $m \leftarrow 4$.

  3. Greedy phase - step 2: $2t_2 - t_1 - t_3 = 3$ and the sub-list inserted into SCH is: $\langle\{1,4\}.\{1\}.\{1,3\}.\{1\}\rangle$; $m \leftarrow 2$.

  4. Final phase: the sub-list inserted into SCH is: $\langle\{1,2\}\rangle$.

  The schedule produced is

  $$\langle +\{1,6\}, -\{1\}, +\{1,5\}, -\{1\}, +\{1,4\}, -\{1\}, +\{1,3\}, -\{1\} + \{1,2\}\rangle$$

  for a total crossing time of 40.

- Case $N = 6$ and $t_1 = 1, t_2 = 5, t_3 = 6, t_4 = 8, t_5 = 10, t_6 = 15$.

  1. Greedy phase - Initialization: $m \leftarrow 6$.

  2. Greedy phase - step 1: $2t_2 - t_1 - t_5 = -1$ and the sub-list inserted into SCH is: $\langle\{1,2\}.\{1\}.\{6,5\}.\{2\}\rangle$; $m \leftarrow 4$.

  3. Greedy phase - step 2: $2t_2 - t_1 - t_3 = 3$ and the sub-list inserted into SCH is: $\langle\{1,4\}.\{1\}.\{1,3\}.\{1\}\rangle$; $m \leftarrow 2$.

  4. Final phase: the sub-list inserted into SCH is: $\langle\{1,2\}\rangle$.

  The final schedule is

  $$\langle +\{1,2\}, -\{1\}, +\{6,5\}, -\{2\}, +\{1,4\}, -\{1\}, +\{1,3\}, -\{1\}, +\{1,2\}\rangle$$

  hence the total crossing duration is 47.

- Case $N = 6$ and $t_1 = 1, t_2 = 2, t_3 = 5, t_4 = 10, t_5 = 12, t_6 = 20$.

  1. Greedy phase - Initialization: $m \leftarrow 6$.

  2. Greedy phase - step 1: $2t_2 - t_1 - t_5 = -9$ and the sub-list inserted into SCH is: $\langle\{1,2\}.\{1\}.\{6,5\}.\{2\}\rangle$; $m \leftarrow 4$.

  3. Greedy phase - step 2: $2t_2 - t_1 - t_3 = -2$ and the sub-list inserted into SCH is: $\langle\{1,2\}.\{1\}.\{4,3\}.\{2\}\rangle$; $m \leftarrow 2$.

4. Final phase: the sub-list inserted into SCH is: $\langle\{1,2\}\rangle$.

The final schedule is

$$\langle +\{1,2\}, -\{1\}, +\{6,5\}, -\{2\}, +\{1,2\}, -\{1\}, +\{4,3\}, -\{2\}, +\{1,2\}\rangle$$

hence the crossing duration is 42.

For these three cases, the total crossing time obtained is the one announced in the statement, which is proven to be optimal.

- Case $N = 7$ and $t_1 = 1, t_2 = 4, t_3 = 4, t_4 = 7, t_5 = 10, t_6 = 12, t_7 = 15$.

  1. Greedy phase - Initialization: $m \leftarrow 7$.

  2. Greedy phase - step 1: $2t_2 - t_1 - t_6 = -5$ and the sub-list inserted into SCH is: $\langle\{1,2\}.\{1\}.\{7,6\}.\{2\}\rangle$; $m \leftarrow 5$.

  3. Greedy phase - step 2: $2t_2 - t_1 - t_4 = 0$ and the sub-list inserted into SCH is: $\langle\{1,5\}.\{1\}.\{1,4\}.\{1\}\rangle$; $m \leftarrow 3$.

  4. Final phase: the sub-list inserted into SCH is: $\langle\{1,3\}.\{1\}.\{1,2\}\rangle$.

  The final schedule is thus

$$\langle +\{1,2\}, -\{1\}, +\{7,6\}, -\{2\}, +\{1,5\}, -\{1\}, +\{1,4\}, -\{1\}, +\{1,3\}, -\{1\}, +\{1,2\}\rangle$$

  for a total duration of 52.

8

Divide and conquer

À force de ruminer des choses...
voilà ce que nous découvrîmes:
fallait diviser pour résoudre !...
C'était l'essentiel !...
Tous les emmerdeurs en deux classes
!...
(By dint of brooding things...
that's what we discovered:
we had to divide up to solve! ... That
was the point! ... All troublemakers in
two classes!).

L. F. Céline

8.1 Introduction

8.1.1 Presentation and principle

The principle of the method called "Divide and conquer", DaC for short, is to break up a problem of size n into several sub-problems identical to (of the same nature as) the initial problem, whose sizes are strictly less than that of the initial one, to solve each sub-problem, then to gather the results to transform the solutions of sub-problems into a global one. In addition, it is necessary to identify one or several sizes for which the problem has not to be divided, since it can be "directly" solved. These sizes correspond to problems said to be *elementary*.

This approach is similar to that used in Chapter 4 ("Reduce and conquer, recursion"), which is generalized as for the sizes of sub-problems generated. In order to ensure the correctness of the proposed solution, most often an inductive construction (strong recurrence on $\mathbb{N}$, partition induction or inductive reasoning strictly speaking) is used involving four elements: (1) the *base* where elementary cases and their related solutions are made explicit, (2) the *induction hypothesis* where it is assumed that it is known how to resolve any problem of size $k < n$, (3) the *induction* itself where the resolution the problem $Pb(n)$ is proven using the induction hypothesis, and (4) the *termination* where it is checked that from any starting size, the cases dealt with in the base are reached.

By means of such a construction, the resolution model (or schema) by division of the considered problem can be specified, an equation whose solution gives the temporal complexity of the solution can be derived, and a code can be produced. This methodological approach thus allows to proceed step by step and to design an algorithm that is "safe by construction".

In the rest of this introduction, we will consider a generic one-dimensional problem Pb, which corresponds to many concrete situations and allows a simple and readable presentation. However, some problems will illustrate two-dimensional situations for which the proposed approach remains applicable by adapting the reasoning, calculations, division schema and coding described in the one-dimensional case.

How can this technique be applied in practice? Let us first illustrate it with an example.

8.1.2   An example: merge-sort

To present the DaC method, let us take the classical (and fundamental) problem of sorting. One of its versions inspired by the DaC approach is called "sorting by merging", or in short merge-sort. Here, we describe its principle; a few complements will be the subject of the problem 88, page 424.

An array of integers of size n ($n \geqslant 1$) is to be sorted in ascending order. Let us first notice that it is easy to design a sorting method whose complexity is in $\Theta(n^2)$ or in $O(n^2)$ (the elementary operation is the comparison). For example, we scroll through the entire array to find its smallest element and exchange it with the element of rank 1. Then we start again on the $(n-1)$ unsorted elements (from rank 2 to n), and so on until we the array is exhausted. This algorithm requires exactly $(n-1) + (n-2) + \cdots + 2 = (n \cdot (n-1)/2) - 1$ comparisons. Let us call *NaiveSort*$(1, n)$ this algorithm which sorts the elements from 1 to n of an array. Let us try the "Divide and conquer" method to sort this array. To simplify, we assume that $n = 2^p$, even if this assumption is not necessary as we will see in problem 88, page 424.

Let us first split the array into two halves and solve the two sub-problems. So we apply *NaiveSort*$(1, n/2)$ and *NaiveSort*$(n/2+1, n)$, which requires exactly $2 \cdot (n/2 \cdot (n/2-1)/2-1) = n^2/4 - n/2 - 2$ comparisons. We now have two sorted half arrays that need to be put together.

Interestingly, this problem of bringing together (here called *merge*) two sorted half arrays into a single sorted array is quite simple. Without going into details, it is easy to see that it is enough to proceed step by step in one half array or the other (comparing the element arrived at in each half array) in order to come up to a sorted array of size n. In problem 88, page 424, an example is used to see how this merging algorithm works and how it can be precisely written.

This merge phase certainly takes at most $2 \cdot n/2 = n$ comparisons. To simplify, we can say that it takes exactly n, a slightly pessimistic upper bound.

Let us go back to our initial problem: we know that the two sorting phases take $n^2/4 - n/2 - 2$ comparisons and that the gathering takes n. In total, the original array was sorted with $(n^2/4 + n/2 - 2)$ comparisons, which is better than the $(n^2/2 - n/2 - 1)$ initial comparisons (using *NaiveSort* only once). For example, if $n = 128$, we have made 4 158 comparisons instead of 8 127. This is a good starting point.

Why stopping on such a good way? Let us calculate how many comparisons the following technique would take:

- divide the array into four sub-arrays of size $n/4$,
- sort each sub-array,
- merge twice two sorted sub-arrays of size $n/4$,
- merge two sorted arrays of size $n/2$.

The calculation yields: $(n^2/8 + n/2 - 4 + (2n/2 + n))$, i.e. $(n^2/8 + 3n/2 - 4)$, thus $2\,236$ for $n = 128$. Better yet!

All that remains is to pursue the reasoning to the end and to divide until no sorting is necessary (in the sense of the use of *NaiveSort*) and only the gathering phases remain, since an array of size 1 is by definition sorted.

Base An array of size 1 is sorted.

Induction hypothesis It is assumed that sorting any array whose size m is a power of 2 with $m < n$, is known.

Induction In order to sort an array whose size n is a power of 2 ($n > 1$), it is divided into two halves of size $n/2$ that are first sorted (which is feasible according to the induction hypothesis), then merged thanks to the procedure called *Merge*.

Termination The size of the array strictly diminishes at each step and finally reaches 1 (the value of the base).

This reasoning can be described through the following *division model*:

$$
\begin{array}{ll}
\text{MrgSort}(1) \text{ elementary} & \\
\text{MrgSort}(n) \rightarrow 2 \cdot \text{MrgSort}\left(\dfrac{n}{2}\right) + \text{Merge}\left(\dfrac{n}{2}\right) & n > 1
\end{array}
$$

It is important to notice that building a DaC algorithm implies not trying to understand what happens beyond the division, but to reason by recurrence, assuming smaller problems solved. In pratice, one must therefore not proceed as in the example above, but seek from the outset a model of division of the type we have just given.

As far as coding is concerned, the algorithm that emerges is canonically derived from the division model. More precisely, it is a recursive procedure whose main part consists of two recursive calls and a call to the procedure *Merge* (of profile "**procedure** *Merge*(p, q, r)" which merges the two arrays $T[p\,..\,q]$ and $T[q+1\,..\,r]$) which will be studied in more details in problem 88, page 424. Here, the terminal case is empty since the basic problem consists in doing nothing. Note that choosing $n = 2^p$ ensures that the indices calculated during divisions by 2 are always integer values. If the array T to be sorted is a global variable, we have the following procedure and its calling program:

1. **procedure** *MergeSort*(i, j) **pre**
2. $i \in 1\,..\,n$ **and** $j \in i\,..\,n$
3. **begin**
4.   **if** $i \neq j$ **then**
5. $MergeSort\left(i, \dfrac{i+j}{2}\right)$;
6. $MergeSort\left(\dfrac{i+j}{2} + 1, j\right)$;
7. $Merge\left(i, \dfrac{i+j}{2}, j\right)$
8.   **end if**
9. **end**

1. **constants**
2. $n \in \mathbb{N}_1$ **and** $\exists p \cdot (p \in \mathbb{N}$ **and** $n = 2^p)$
   and $n = \ldots$
3. **variables**
4. $T \in 1\,..\,n \rightarrow \mathbb{N}$
5. **begin**
6. $T \leftarrow [\ldots]$;
7. $MergeSort(1, n)$
8. **end**

Complexity calculation of this algorithm (the elementary operation being the comparison) with an array of size $n = 2^p$ relies on the following recurrence equation:

$$C(1) = 0$$
$$C(n) = 2 \cdot C\left(\frac{n}{2}\right) + n \qquad\qquad n > 1.$$

As a matter of fact, the procedure *Merge* is used twice for data of size $n/2$ and the procedure *Merge* is called once for two arrays of size $n/2$.

In order to explicitly compute $C(n)$, the method of *summation factors* (also called *plug and chug*) can be used. It consists in writing the recurrence formula for the values n, $n/2$, $n/4$, ..., 1, which is made possible thanks to the assumption according to which $n = 2^p$:

$$C(n) = 2 \cdot C\left(\frac{n}{2}\right) + n$$
$$C(\frac{n}{2}) = 2 \cdot C\left(\frac{n}{4}\right) + \frac{n}{2}$$
$$\cdots$$
$$C(1) = 0$$

There are $p = \log_2(n)$ lines. By multiplying the first one by 1, the second one by 2, ..., the last one by 2^p and by adding all these formulas term to term, we get:

$$C(n) = n + 2 \cdot \frac{n}{2} + 4 \cdot \frac{n}{4} + \cdots + 2^{p-1} \cdot \frac{n}{2^{p-1}} + 0 = n + n + \cdots + n + 0 = (p-1) \cdot n \leqslant n \cdot \log_2(n).$$

By the DaC method, we thus end up with an algorithm of complexity $\mathcal{O}(n \cdot \log_2(n))$ whereas the naïve sorting algorithm is not in $\mathcal{O}(n \cdot \log_2(n))$, but in $\Theta(n^2)$.

8.1.3   General pattern for "Divide and conquer"

We now consider a generic DaC algorithm capable of solving a problem Pb of size n, denoted by $Pb(n)$. As mentioned before, the resolution mechanism is most often based on an inductive construction step leading to a division model with two constituents:

Terminal case It lists the sizes for which a direct solution to the problem under consideration is known (elementary problems).

General case The solution to $Pb(n)$ is expressed as the composition of the solutions to a (sub-)problems of the same nature as Pb, of sizes strictly smaller than n.

So, we have the generic division model:

$$\boxed{\begin{array}{ll} Pb(m_1) \text{ elementary}, \ldots, Pb(m_k) \text{ elementary} \\ Pb(n) \rightarrow a \cdot Pb(n_i) + Gather(n) \qquad\qquad \texttt{n with a non elementary size} \end{array}}$$

where $n_i < n$ and $a \geqslant 1$, and $Gather(n)$ is the function that gathers the results of a sub-problems of size $n_1, \ldots, n_a$ to construct that of problem Pb.

It is then possible to deduce (most often very easily) an algorithm itself, the generic version of which is written:

1. **procedure** *DaC*(m; GlobRes: **modif**)**pre**
2. $m \in \mathbb{N}$ **and** GlobRes ... **and** PartRes$_1$ ... **and** ... **and** PartRes$_a$ ... **and**
3. $n_1 \in \mathbb{N}$ **and** ... **and** $n_a \in \mathbb{N}$

```
 4. begin
 5.    if m ∈ {m₁, ..., mₖ} then
 6.       if m = m₁ then
 7.          GlobRes ← solution to the elementary problem
 8.          ...
 9.       elsif m = mₖ then
10.          GlobRes ← solution to the elementary problem
11.       end if
12.    else
13.       DaC(n₁, PartRes₁);
14.       ...;
15.       DaC(nₐ, PartResₐ);
16.       GlobRes ← Gather(PartRes₁, ..., PartResₐ)
17.    end if
18. end
```

whose calling program is in the form:

```
1. constants
2.    n ∈ ℕ₁ and n = ...
3. variables
4.    R...
5. begin
6.    DaC(n, R)
7. end
```

Thus, to solve a problem of size m, it is divided into a problems that provide partial results $PartRes_1$, ..., $PartRes_a$. These are then used by the procedure *Gather* for the construction of the global result $GlobRes$. A non-trivial step of identification and construction of the sub-problems may be necessary in some cases, as illustrated in problems 95, page 432, and 96, page 433. It was omitted in the previous generic procedure in order not to weigh it down.

Finally, let us note that a recurrence formula (in the usual sense) constitutes in itself a division model for particular problems where a numerical quantity is calculated (see problem 89, page 425). In this kind of situation, $Gather$ is simply made up of the set of calculations aggregating the terms of the recurrence.

8.1.4   A typology of "Divide and conquer" algorithms

In many algorithms of type "Divide and conquer", the division of the data is done "in half", i.e. for example in the case of an array $T[1 .. n]$, the division is done in *two contiguous* sub-arrays $T[1 .. \lfloor n/2 \rfloor]$ and $T[\lfloor n/2 \rfloor + 1 .. n]$. The division process then repeats itself regularly until reaching the size 1 for which a direct solution is known (Pb(1) is then the only elementary problem). Assuming that $n/2$ designates indifferently $\lfloor n/2 \rfloor$ or $\lceil n/2 \rceil$, we then end up with one of the two following patterns:

$$
\begin{cases}
\text{Pb}(1) \text{ elementary} \\
\begin{cases}
\text{Pb}(n) \to 2 \cdot \text{Pb}\left(\dfrac{n}{2}\right) + \text{Gather}(n) \\
\quad \text{or} \\
\text{Pb}(n) \to \text{Pb}\left(\dfrac{n}{2}\right)
\end{cases} & n > 1
\end{cases}
$$

depending on whether the resolution requires the solution of both sub-problems or only one of them.

Some algorithms related to arrays do not divide into 2, but into a *larger* number of parts. In some problems, it may happen that the division is not into contiguous sub-arrays, but *intertwined*. In this case, the data in an array can be divided into even index data and odd index data for example (see problem 110, page 464). Sometimes, the division is made in two contiguous arrays, but not by half: the division index is then chosen in a *non deterministic* way, or calculated by a more refined method. Another possibility is that the division is done at a location (for contiguous division) or according to a process (for intertwined division) that *depends on the data* being worked on, i.e. the algorithm will not choose the same division depending on whether it applies to one array or another (see problem 116, page 480). Finally, there is a[1] DaC algorithm whose number of divisions into sub-arrays depends partly on the *size* of the array. It is presented as the "egg problem" (problem 114, page 474).

To illustrate this great variety, we have chosen to present the types of DaC algorithms in figure 8.1, page 421 in the form of a decision tree (see chapter 1) in which the previous criteria are highlighted. The result is that the leaves of the tree, i.e. the distinct families according to our typology, are very variable in size. There is an abundant variety of algorithms of type 4, that is for which a division is made into two contiguous parts of equal (or different from 1) size. On the other hand, few algorithms have been encountered where the division is also in two contiguous but data-dependent parts; similarly, algorithms where the division is intertwined are exceptional[2].

Other algorithms are the only (or almost) representatives of their category. This can be due to either the extreme singularity of the problem (types 5 and 6), or the art of the inventors (types 2 and 7).

8.1.5   Complexity of "Divide and conquer"

8.1.5.1   Introduction to the master theorem

The temporal complexity of a DaC algorithm is expressed as a function of (at least) one elementary operation appearing in the instance of the division model. Most often, it is characteristic of the problem to be treated (evaluated condition for a search in a tabular structure, elementary drawing of segments in the realization of a drawing or weighing for the search of a fake coin). This complexity is highly dependent on the division model used to solve the problem under consideration. However, due to its high frequency, the following division model for a data of size n:

---

[1]The authors are not aware of any examples other than this one.

[2]Yet, the *Fast Fourier Transform*, or FFT, which is of this type, is one of the few most used algorithms in practice and is even found as a built-in function in Excel.

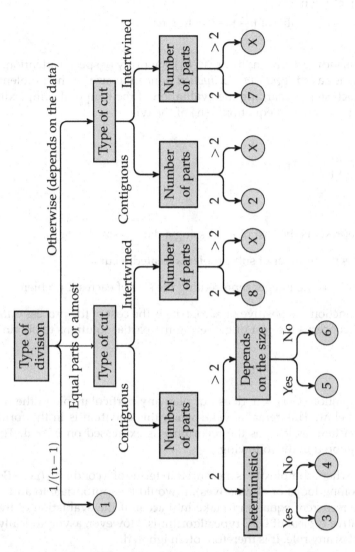

1. *Reduce and conquer* algorithms (regular recursion: see chapter 4)

2. Distance between sequences (problem 107, page 452)

3. Basic *Quicksort*. The selection problem (problem 95, page 432)

4. Merge-sort (problem 88, page 424). And many others . . .

5. The egg problem (problem 114, page 474)

6. The fake coin (problem 97, page 434)

7. The stuttering sub-sequence (problem 109, page 462)

8. The FFT (problem 110, page 464)

Fig. 8.1 – A typology of "Divide and conquer" algorithms. Leaves marked X have no representatives in the problems.

Problem(1) elementary

Problem(n) $\to$ a $\cdot$ Problem $\left(\dfrac{n}{b}\right)$ + Gather(n) $n > 1$

(n/b represents indifferently $\lfloor n/b \rfloor$ or $\lceil n/b \rceil$) is worthy of special attention.

This model is called *logarithmic reduction* since the size of the problem decreases by a factor b at each step. Regarding the evaluation of the temporal complexity, this generic model results in a recurrent equation $C(n)$ of the type:

$$
\begin{aligned}
C(1) &= c \\
C(n) &= a \cdot C\left(\frac{n}{b}\right) + f(n) \qquad\qquad\qquad n > 1
\end{aligned}
$$

where:

- c ($c \in \mathbb{N}$) represents the cost of processing a data of size 1,

- a ($a \in \mathbb{N}_1$) is the number of sub-problems treated recursively,

- n/b ($n/b \in \mathbb{N}$) is the integer representing the size of each subproblem ($b > 1$),

- Since the function f is positive or zero, $f(n)$ is the cost of the process *Gather* mentioned above and concerns the cost of gathering the partial solutions to obtain the global solution.

Remarks

1. The first equation, $C(1) = c$ does not play any particular role in the master theorem presented below. This remains valid when this equation is in the form $C(d) = c$, d being a constant, as long as the recurrence is expressed on $n > d$. This equation is therefore ignored in the following.

2. In the case where complexity is measured in terms of a condition (i.e. a Boolean expression controlling loops or alternatives), it would be appropriate to add 1 to each right part of the recurrent equation to take into account the evaluation of the condition of the alternative typical of DaC type algorithms. However, asymptotically this constant does not play any role. It is therefore often ignored.

3. In the case of passing parameters by value and depending on the elementary operation chosen, the cost of the copy may have to be taken into account in the equation.

Theorem (Master theorem):
Let $C(n) = a \cdot C(n/b) + f(n)$, *with* $a \geqslant 1$, $b > 1$, $f(n)$ *a positive or zero function and* n/b *representing indifferently* $\lfloor n/b \rfloor$ *or* $\lceil n/b \rceil$.

1. *If* $f(n) \in \mathcal{O}(n^{\log_b(a) - \varepsilon})$ *for a constant* $\varepsilon > 0$, *then* $C(n) \in \Theta(n^{\log_b(a)})$.

2. *If* $f(n) \in \Theta(n^{\log_b(a)})$, *then* $C(n) \in \Theta(n^{\log_b(a)} \cdot \log_b(n))$.

3. *If* $f(n) \in \Omega(n^{\log_b(a) + \varepsilon})$ *for a constant* $\varepsilon > 0$ *and if* $a \cdot f(n/b) \leqslant k \cdot f(n)$ *for a constant* $k < 1$ *and for* n *sufficiently large, then* $C(n) \in \Theta(f(n))$.

A proof of this theorem can be found in [9]. Its corollary is the following theorem.

Corollary of the master theorem Let $C(n)$ be the recurrence $C(n) = a \cdot C(n/b) + p(n)$, where a and b are two constants such that $a \in \mathbb{N}_1$, $b \in \mathbb{N}_1$ **and** $b > 1$ and $p(n)$ is a positive or zero polynomial of degree k.

1. If $a > b^k$, then $C(n) \in \Theta(n^{\log_b(a)})$.

2. If $a = b^k$, then $C(n) \in \Theta(n^k \cdot \log_b(n))$.

3. If $a < b^k$, then $C(n) \in \Theta(n^k)$.

These theorems make it possible to prove the following special cases that are frequently encountered in the remainder of this chapter:

$$C(n) = C\left(\frac{n}{2}\right) + p(n) \quad \begin{cases} k = 0, \text{ case 2 of the corollary: } C(n) \in \Theta(\log_2(n)) & (8.1) \\ k \geqslant 1, \text{ case 3 of the corollary: } C(n) \in \Theta(n^k) & (8.2) \end{cases}$$

$$C(n) = 2 \cdot C\left(\frac{n}{2}\right) + p(n) \quad \begin{cases} k = 0, \text{ case 1 of the corollary: } C(n) \in \Theta(n) & (8.3) \\ k = 1, \text{ case 2 of the corollary: } C(n) \in \Theta(n \cdot \log_2(n)) & (8.4) \\ k \geqslant 2, \text{ case 3 of the corollary: } C(n) \in \Theta(n^k) & (8.5) \end{cases}$$

$$C(n) = 4 \cdot C\left(\frac{n}{2}\right) + p(n) \quad \begin{cases} k \leqslant 1, \text{ case 1 of the corollary: } C(n) \in \Theta(n^2) & (8.6) \\ k = 2, \text{ case 2 of the corollary: } C(n) \in \Theta(n^2 \cdot \log_2(n)) & (8.7) \\ k \geqslant 3, \text{ case 3 of the corollary: } C(n) \in \Theta(n^k) & (8.8) \end{cases}$$

$$C(n) = 3 \cdot C\left(\frac{n}{2}\right) + p(n) \quad k \leqslant 1, \text{ case 1 of the corollary: } C(n) \in \Theta(n^{\log_2(3)}) \quad (8.9)$$

$$C(n) = 3 \cdot C\left(\frac{n}{4}\right) + p(n) \quad k = 1, \text{ case 3 of the corollary: } C(n) \in \Theta(n) \quad (8.10)$$

8.1.5.2 Other types of recurrence equations

On the other hand, the preceding theorems do not allow a conclusion regarding for example the following recurrence (where $c \in \mathbb{N}_1$):

$$C(n) = 2 \cdot C\left(\frac{n}{2}\right) + c \cdot n \cdot \log_2(n).$$

An example of this type appears in problem 106, page 448, where it is the subject of question 3. In this problem, it is proven that (i) the master theorem does not allow for a conclusion, (ii) $C(n) \in \Theta(n \cdot (\log_2(n))^2)$ (for n a power of 2).

It is not uncommon to come across equations of the form:

$$C(n) = a \cdot C\left(\frac{n}{b} + k\right) + c \cdot n + g$$

with $a \in \mathbb{N}_1$, $b \in \mathbb{N}_1$, $k \in \mathbb{N}_1$, $c \in \mathbb{N}_1$ and $g \in \mathbb{N}$. Strictly speaking, the master theorem does not apply (therefore nor its corollary). A case-by-case proof is possible. Thus, an instance of the theorem below (for $k = 1$, $e = 2$ and $g = 2$), is used and proven in the solution of problem 115, page 477.

Theorem:
Let $C(n)$ be the recurrence defined as $C(n) = C(\lfloor n/2 \rfloor + k) + c \cdot n + g$ with $k > 0$, $c \in \mathbb{N}_1$ and $g \in \mathbb{N}$. Then:

$$C(n) \in \mathcal{O}(n).$$

There is a wide variety of complexity classes associated with DaC algorithms. This leads us to systematically study their complexity in the following problems.

8.1.6 About the size of the problem

In general, the objective aimed at in the problems of this chapter consists in developing at least one "efficient" solution (in the sense of temporal complexity) and valid for any size n of problem. It may happen that we are first interested in a solution valid only for particular sizes. This is the case, for example, for merge-sort in the version studied previously. This can make it possible to simplify both the presentation of the solution and the associated complexity calculation, even if it means generalizing then (see problem 88, page 424, for merge-sort). Time complexity also depends on the size of the problem and it will always be the subject of questions. It will therefore concern either particular sizes, or the general case depending on the specification of the desired solution. Exceptionally, within the framework of a valid solution for any size n, we will restrict ourselves to calculate the (class of) complexity for particular sizes, either because this will be enough to characterize the complexity of the considered solution, or to avoid excessively long developments.

8.2 What to remember about the DaC approach

The DaC approach is an essential brick in the arsenal of methods available to computer scientists. It often appears as "miraculous" to the beginner's eyes. This is because its perfect mastering passes through the understanding of the intimate links it maintains with mathematical induction. This relationship being acquired, its application to a particular problem can then be seen as a workaround of this problem insofar as solving it amounts to (i) composing two or more solutions and (ii) finding a solution for a small problem. However, since the optimality of the solution in terms of complexity is not systematic, it is generally necessary to evaluate its effectiveness. Here also mathematics (the master theorem of page 422) can come to the developer's rescue. In synergy with other methods, such as dynamic programming (see for example problem 107, page 452) or domain transformation (see for example problem 110, page 464), the DaC approach can be the basis of algorithmic gems as aesthetic as they are efficient.

8.3 Problems

Problem 88. Merge-sort   8 •

The purely DaC aspect of this algorithm and the interest of this approach have been addressed in section 8.1.2, page 416. This problem is simply intended to expand on a few points left open in this introductory section. This is in particular the case of the merging algorithm. It is treated here in a purely iterative way.

The reader is invited to resume the elements of the presentation on page 416.

88 - Q 1   **Question 1.**   It is assumed that both slices $T[p..q]$ and $T[q+1..r]$ are sorted. The array T being supposed to be global, write the algorithm $Merge(p, q, r)$ which accepts the indices p, q and r as input and merges the slices $T[p..q]$ and $T[q+1..r]$ into a sorted array $T[p..r]$.

Question 2. How many comparisons between elements of T does it take to merge the   88 - Q 2
arrays [3, 6, 7, 9] and [4, 5, 10, 12]? the arrays [3, 4, 5, 6] and [7, 9, 10, 12]? the arrays [3,
5, 7, 10] and [4, 6, 9, 12]? In the worst case, how many conditions must be evaluated for
merging the arrays $T[p .. q]$ and $T[q + 1 .. r]$?

Question 3. What adaptations must be made in the *MergeSort* procedure if the size of   88 - Q 3
T is not a power of 2?

The solution is on page 491.

Problem 89. Fibonacci sequence: four constructions   8 ⦂

*This problem illustrates in a spectacular way how the application of the DaC principle makes
it possible to reduce the complexity of the solutions to a given problem. Four versions are
successively studied, from a first naïve one, whose complexity is exponential, to two DaC
versions, with logarithmic complexities.*

Consider the Fibonacci sequence:

$$\begin{cases} \mathcal{F}_0 = \mathcal{F}_1 = 1 \\ \mathcal{F}_n = \mathcal{F}_{n-1} + \mathcal{F}_{n-2} \qquad n \geqslant 2. \end{cases}$$

The problem studied in this problem is the calculation of $\mathcal{F}_n$ for any n. The trivial recursive solution whose structure mirrors the above definition, is very inefficient. Thus, for
example, the calculation of $\mathcal{F}_6$ leads to compute $\mathcal{F}_5$ and $\mathcal{F}_4$, that of $\mathcal{F}_5$ demands the computation of $\mathcal{F}_3$ and again that of $\mathcal{F}_4$. Each of the calculations of $\mathcal{F}_4$ leads to the computation
of $\mathcal{F}_3$, and so on. It can be noticed that, in terms of additions, this calculation exceeds very
quickly n, n^2, n^3, etc. It can be easily proven that the complexity of this algorithm (in terms
of additions or evaluated conditions) is in fact exponential.

A more efficient solution is to store the results already known in an array in order to
avoid recalculating them. This principle, called "memoization", is part of the techniques
applied in dynamic programming (see Chapter 9). If M is this array, this principle can be
applied as follows to the calculation of an element of the Fibonacci sequence:

```
1.  function Fibo1(n) result N₁ pre
2.     n ∈ 0 .. Maxi
3.  begin
4.     if n = 0 or n = 1 then
5.        result 1
6.     else
7.        if M[n] = 0 then
8.           M[n] ← Fibo1(n − 1) + Fibo1(n − 2)
9.        end if;
10.       result M[n]
11.    end if
12. end
```

As shown in the following calling context, the array M must be initialized to 0 before the
first call to *Fibo1*:

1. **constants**
2. $Maxi \in \mathbb{N}_1$ **and** $Maxi = \dots$ **and** $n \in 0 \,..\, Maxi$ **and** $n = \dots$
3. **variables**
4. $M \in (2 \,..\, Maxi) \to \mathbb{N}$
5. **begin**
6. $M \leftarrow (2 \,..\, Maxi) \times \{0\}$;
7.   **écrire**$(Fibo1(n))$
8. **end**

This solution is at worst (respectively at best) in $\Theta(n)$ (respectively $\Theta(1)$) additions or conditions evaluated. Furthermore, it is constrained by the precondition on the value of n. Is it possible to improve the complexity at worst? This is what is targeted through two DaC solutions.

In the presence of an order 2 linear recurrent sequence such as $\mathcal{F}_n$, it is often interesting to move to an order 1 linear recurrent sequence since the development becomes simpler. On the other hand, if the initial sequence is a scalar one, the transformation leads to a vector sequence. This principle is going to be applied by first developing an algorithm for the vector version before using it to get the scalar version of $\mathcal{F}_n$.

A first DaC solution

89 - Q 1   **Question 1.**   It will be shown that the Fibonacci sequence can be transformed into an order 1 vector sequence. To do this, let $\mathcal{V}_n = \begin{bmatrix} \mathcal{F}_{n-1} \\ \mathcal{F}_n \end{bmatrix}$ be a two-element colum vector and F be a 2×2 square matrix. Calculate the matrix F such that:

$$
\begin{vmatrix}
\mathcal{V}_1 = \begin{bmatrix} \mathcal{F}_0 \\ \mathcal{F}_1 \end{bmatrix} = \begin{bmatrix} 1 \\ 1 \end{bmatrix} \\
\mathcal{V}_n = F \times \mathcal{V}_{n-1}
\end{vmatrix}
\qquad n > 1.
$$

89 - Q 2   **Question 2.**   Prove that the solution to the corresponding recurrence equation can be written $\mathcal{V}_n = F^{n-1} \times \mathcal{V}_1$.

89 - Q 3   **Question 3.**   Assuming available the function of profile $MatProd(A, B)$ (A and B are two 2×2 matrices) that returns the matrix $A \times B$, according to the DaC approach design a function of profile $MatPower(M, n)$, that delivers the matrix M^n for any $n \in \mathbb{N}_1$. Deduce the procedure $FiboV(n; u, v : \textbf{modif})$ that, for a given $n \in \mathbb{N}_1$, calculates the values u and v such that $\mathcal{V}_n = \begin{bmatrix} u \\ v \end{bmatrix}$.

89 - Q 4   **Question 4.**   Show how the procedure $FiboV$ can be used in order to define the function $Fibo2(n)$ that returns $\mathcal{F}_n$, for $n \in \mathbb{N}$. Taking the product of 2×2 matrices as the elementary operation, provide the recurrence equation of the complexity of this function when n is in the form 2^k. What about the complexity in number of additions? Conclude.

89 - Q 5   **Question 5.**   Provide a lower and upper bound of the exact complexity of the function $MatPower$ in terms of products of 2×2 matrices. Specify the cases where the bounds are reached. How do these values translate into additions and multiplications of numbers?

89 - Q 6   **Question 6.**   Using the calculation of $Fibo2(15)$ as a counter-example, show that the algorithm $MatPower$ is not necessarily optimal to get the matrix M^n.

A second DaC solution

This solution is also based on a transformation of the sequence $\mathcal{F}_n$ into a vector sequence. However, this time, the new sequence is not linear.

Question 7. Prove by induction on p that: 89 - Q 7

$$\forall p \cdot (p \in \mathbb{N}_1 \Rightarrow \forall n \cdot (n \in \mathbb{N}_1 \Rightarrow \mathcal{F}_{n+p} = \mathcal{F}_n \cdot \mathcal{F}_p + \mathcal{F}_{n-1} \cdot \mathcal{F}_{p-1})).$$

Question 8. Apply the previous formula for $p = n$, $p = n - 1$ and $p = n + 1$, in order to deduce $\mathcal{F}_{2n}$, $\mathcal{F}_{2n-1}$ and $\mathcal{F}_{2n+1}$ in terms of $\mathcal{F}_n$ and $\mathcal{F}_{n-1}$. 89 - Q 8

Question 9. Denoting by W_n the vector $\begin{bmatrix} \mathcal{F}_{n-1} \\ \mathcal{F}_n \end{bmatrix}$, deduce that W_{2n} and W_{2n+1} can be calculated in terms of $\mathcal{F}_n$ and $\mathcal{F}_{n-1}$. 89 - Q 9

Question 10. We are looking for a DaC procedure *FiboW*($n; u, v$: **modif**) that, for a given value of n, delivers $W_n = \begin{bmatrix} u \\ v \end{bmatrix}$. 89 - Q 10

Design this procedure using the DaC principle. Deduce the division model that applies. Provide the code of the procedure *FiboW*. Show how the procedure *FiboW* can be used to define the function *Fibo3*(n) that delivers $\mathcal{F}_n$, for any $n \in \mathbb{N}$.

Question 11. Establish and solve the recurrence equation of complexity of the procedure *FiboW* in terms of the additions carried out. Compare the two DaC solutions. 89 - Q 11

The solution is on page 492.

Problem 90. Binary, ternary and interpolation searches

> *This problem on binary search is a classic of the application of the DaC principle. However, an extension to ternary search (i.e. recursive division by 3) is proposed. This raises the question of comparing the complexities of these two solutions. A complementary solution to the problem of searching for the existence of a value in an array is the subject of the last question: the search by interpolation. Although simple in principle, this algorithm requires thoroughness to obtain a correct solution.*

We consider an array $T[1 .. n]$ ($n \in \mathbb{N}_1$), of all different integers, sorted in ascending order and we want to know if the integer v is in it. The first two questions relate to the algorithms and their construction, questions 3, 4 and 5 are devoted to the comparison of the exact complexities, the last question concerns the search by interpolation.

Question 1. We are looking for a DaC solution based on a division into two sub-arrays of approximately equal sizes. Among the many possible versions, we focus on the so-called Bottenbruch version which tests *equality* between v and an element of the array only if the array in question has *a single* item. Design this solution and deduce the division model, then the code. 90 - Q 1

Question 2. We are now interested in a solution based on a ternary search. There are several ways to divide an array into three sub-arrays of approximately equal size: 90 - Q 2

- For example, the array (of length n) can be divided into three sub-arrays of respective sizes $\lfloor n/3 \rfloor$, $\lfloor n/3 \rfloor$ and $(\lfloor n/3 \rfloor + (n \bmod 3))$. Show that the curve which counts the comparisons for the search for $v \geqslant T[n]$ is not monotonic. Conclusion?

- There is also the so-called "by necessity" solution, which begins by considering the first sub-array of length $\lfloor n/3 \rfloor$ then, if necessary, divides the residual by 2 to provide a second sub-array of size $\lfloor (n - \lfloor n/3 \rfloor)/2 \rfloor$ and a third of size $\lceil (n - \lfloor n/3 \rfloor)/2 \rceil$. We again impose the Bottenbruch constraint: the test on *equality* between v and an element of the array only occurs if the array does not have more than two elements. Prove that the three sub-arrays have respective sizes of $\lceil (n-2)/3 \rceil$, $\lceil (n-1)/3 \rceil$ and $\lceil n/3 \rceil$. Build this solution and provide the division model, then the code.

In the next three questions, we are interested in the exact worst-case complexity of the two algorithms developed above, complexity expressed in number of comparisons between v and an element of the array. The stated objective is to prove that, in the worst case, the ternary solution is *never* better than the binary solution. To do this, we proceed as follows. We try to determine $C_2(n)$, complexity at the worst of the binary search. We do the same for $C_3(n)$ and the ternary search, before comparing the functions $C_2(n)$ and $C_3(n)$.

90 - Q 3 **Question 3.** The worst solution for dichotomous research[3] is reached when $v \geqslant T[n]$. Consequently, prove that the recurrent equation which defines $C_2(n)$ is as follows:

$$C_2(n) = \lceil \log_2(n) \rceil + 1. \tag{8.11}$$

90 - Q 4 **Question 4.** For the ternary search, we will highlight the recurrent equation $C_3(n)$, before looking for a solution.

a. For a given size n of the array, the set of possible executions of the ternary search algorithm can be represented by a decision tree (see Chapter 1 and problem 96, page 433, for another example using decision trees). In our case, the decision tree is a binary tree in which each node materializes a comparison (of type $\leqslant$, $>$, $\neq$ or $=$) between v and an element $T[i]$. Provide the decision trees A_n of the ternary search for $n \in 1..7$. By what relation is the height $h(A_n)$ of the tree linked to the worst-case complexity $C_3(n)$ of the algorithm?

b. By adopting the notation $\langle A_g, T[i], A_d \rangle$ to represent the decision tree $\begin{array}{c} T[i] \\ / \ \backslash \\ A_g \quad A_d \end{array}$, provide an inductive definition of A_n. Deduce an inductive definition for its height h. Prove that the function h is monotonic (in the broad sense). What can we conclude from this?

c. Provide the recurrence equation defining $C_3(n)$. Let E ($E \subset \mathbb{N}_1$) the set defined as:

$$E = \{3^0\} \cup \bigcup_{p \geqslant 0} (2 \cdot 3^p + 1 .. 3^{p+1})$$

and let 1_E be its characteristic function. Prove that:

$$C_3(n) = 2 \cdot \lceil \log_3(n) \rceil + 1_E(n). \tag{8.12}$$

---

[3]The reader dissatisfied with this statement can use question 4 to prove it.

Question 5. Using the representations of your choice for C_2 and C_3, prove that for all 90 - Q 5
$n \in \mathbb{N}_1, C_2(n) \leqslant C_3(n)$.

Question 6. This last question is devoted to search by interpolation. In general, the 90 - Q 6
search for an entry in a dictionary is not carried out by a binary search, but exploits the
estimation of the position of the value sought to open the dictionary on a page likely to
contain the entry in question. This is the principle of search by interpolation. Build the corresponding operation, provide the division model as well as the operation code. Compare
with binary research.

The solution is on page 497.

Problem 91. Searching for a fixpoint 8 :

> *At first glance, this problem is just one more example on binary search (see for example prob-
> lem 90, page 427). We therefore anticipate to obtain an algorithm whose complexity is in
> $\Theta(\log_2(n))$. However, and this is the originality of this problem, the fine exploitation of its
> specification leads to single out different scenarios. The second question is characterized by an
> extremely simple evaluation of the average complexity.*

Let $T[1..n]$ ($n \in \mathbb{N}_1$) be an array, sorted in ascending order, of *relative* integers all distinct.
We aim at the design of the operation "**function** *FixPoint* **result** $\mathbb{B}$" which makes it possible
to know if there is at least one fixpoint in T, i.e. if there is an index p such that $T[p] = p$ (the
value of p is not sought).

Question 1. Construct a solution to this problem. Write the code of the operation *Fix-* 91 - Q 1
Point (T is assumed to be a global array). What can be said about the complexity of this
operation?

Question 2. We now consider that T is an array, sorted in ascending order, of *positive* 91 - Q 2
integers all distinct. Give the new version of the operation "**function** *FixPoint* **result** $\mathbb{B}$", its
code and its average complexity.

The solution is on page 507.

Problem 92. Searching in a cyclic sorted array ○ :

> *The main advantage of the problem is to show that we can perform a search in an "almost
> sorted" array (in the sense of "cyclic array" defined below) with (asymptotically speaking) an
> efficiency comparable to that of the binary search in a sorted array.*

A cyclic sorted array $T[1 .. n]$ ($n \in \mathbb{N}_1$) is an array of natural integers (without duplicates), inside which there is a boundary f ($f \in 1 .. n$) such that the two sub-arrays $T[1 .. f]$
and $T[f + 1 .. n]$ are sorted in ascending order and such that all the elements of $T[1 .. f]$ are
greater than those of $T[f + 1 .. n]$.

For example, the following array T:

i	1	2	3	4	5	6	7
T[i]	9	11	12	13	2	5	8

is cyclic sorted, its boundary f is at position 4. Let us remark that, since duplicates are forbidden, in a cyclic sorted array the boundary is unique and that a non-empty sorted array is a cyclic sorted array.

More formally, by generalizing to arrays without duplicates on the interval i .. s, the predicate *IsSortedCyclic*(T[i .. s]) is defined as:

$$IsCyclicSorted(T[i..s]) \triangleq i \leqslant s \text{ and } \exists f \cdot \left(f \in i..s \text{ and } \left(\begin{array}{l} IsSorted(T[i..f]) \text{ and} \\ IsSorted(T[f+1..s]) \text{ and} \\ \forall(j,k) \cdot (j \in i..f \text{ and} \\ k \in f+1..s \Rightarrow T[j] > T[k]) \end{array} \right) \right).$$

92 - Q 1   **Question 1.**   Prove the following properties:

Property 9:
If IsCyclicSorted(T[i .. s]), *then the element (circularly) just after the boundary f in* T[i .. s] *is the smallest element of* T[i..s]. *More formally, if f is the boundary,* T[((f−i+1) *mod*(s−i+1))+i] = min(*codom*(T[i .. s])).

Property 10:
Let T[i..s] (i < s) *be a cyclic sorted array and* m ∈ i..s−1. *The sub-arrays* T[i..m] *and* T[m+1..s] *are cyclic sorted arrays and at least one of them is sorted.*

Property 11:
Let T[i .. s] (i < s) *be a cyclic sorted array and* m ∈ i .. s − 1. *If* T[m .. s] *is sorted, then the smallest element in* T[i .. s] *belongs to the sub-array* T[i .. m], *otherwise it belongs to the sub-array* T[m + 1 .. s].

Property 12:
Let T[i .. s] (i ⩽ s) *be a cyclic sorted array;* T[i .. s] *is sorted iff* T[i] ⩽ T[s].

92 - Q 2   **Question 2.**   According to the DaC approach, construct the operation "**function** *SmallestElement*(i, s)**result** ℕ" which returns the smallest element of the cyclic sorted array T[i .. s] (T is assumed to be a global array). In the inductive part of the reasoning, it is requested to prove how from the preceding properties can be deduced the criterion guiding the choice of the half-array in which to search for the smallest element of a cyclic sorted array T. Which division model applies? Provide the code for this operation. What is the complexity of this function in terms of conditions evaluated?

92 - Q 3   **Question 3.**   Once again according to the DaC approach, we now want to design the operation "**function** *Belong*(i, s, v) **result** 𝔹" which decides whether the value v is present or not in T[i .. s]. Build this operation. For the inductive case, describe with precision the conditions which guide the research in one or the other half-array. We aim for an order of growth of complexity in $\Theta(\log_2(n))$. Has this objective been achieved?

The solution is on page 510.

Problem 93. Local minimum in a binary tree ○ •

> *This is one of the only problems in the book that deals with an inductive data structure (in this case binary trees). As is often the case in this situation, the form of the reasoning developed here is inspired by the data structure. This is the main lesson here.*

We consider a *full* binary tree (see chapter 1) of weight n ($n > 0$): all nodes have zero or two sons, never a single one, and all leaves are at the same depth. n is of the form $2^p - 1$ and $p - 1$ is the height of the tree. Each node is assigned a different integer value and a node is a *local minimum* if it is (in terms of values) smaller than its father and its two sons (if any). In the examples below, the local minima are circled.

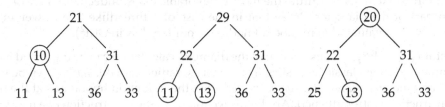

Question 1.   Show that in such a tree there is always (at least) one local minimum.   93 - Q 1

Question 2.   Construct the operation "**function** LocMin(a) **result** $\mathbb{Z}$" which delivers   93 - Q 2
one of the local minima (a complexity in $\mathcal{O}(\log_2(n))$ evaluated conditions is targeted). Specify the division model. Write the code of the operation along with its calling program. Does the operation have the expected complexity?

Question 3.   Is the proposed method applicable to any binary tree?   93 - Q 3

The solution is on page 513.

Problem 94. Diameter of a binary tree ○ ⦂

> *Three lessons can be drawn from this problem dealing with binary trees. The first concerns the improvement in complexity resulting from a strengthening of an induction hypothesis. A new example is given here. The second concerns the form of the reasoning developed there. It can profitably draw inspiration from that of the data structure. The third lesson relates to the use of tree structure to assess complexity. When the treatment to be performed on each node is in $\Theta(1)$ (this is the case here), it is sufficient—when it is possible—to count the nodes encountered during the computation.*

The main definitions as well as the most frequent vocabulary items related to binary trees are grouped in section 1.6 page 27. In the following, we consider that the type bt for unlabeled finite binary trees is defined by:

$$bt = \{/\} \cup \{(l, r) \mid l \in bt \text{ and } r \in bt\}$$

Therefore, an element of bt is either / (which *represents* the empty tree), or a pair (l, r) of which each constituent is a binary tree (bt).

94 - Q 1   **Question** 1.   Show by an example that, in a non-empty tree, a path whose length is the diameter of the tree does not necessarily pass through the root of the tree.

94 - Q 2   **Question** 2.   The height h of a binary tree is not defined for an empty tree. However, for the sake of brevity, we accept the following inductive definition:

$$\begin{cases} h(/) & = & -1 \\ h((l,r)) & = & \max(\{h(l), h(r)\}) + 1 \end{cases}$$

Taking as a basis the number of nodes encountered during the calculation, what is the complexity C_h of the associated function for a tree of weight n (i.e. of n nodes)? In a similar way, define the diameter d of a binary tree. Write the code of the operation "**function** $d(a)$ **result** $\mathbb{N} \cup \{-1\}$" which computes the diameter of the binary tree a. Regarding complexity, threadlike trees constitute the most unfavorable cases. Indeed, each arc of the tree is then part of the diameter. Prove that in the case of a threadlike tree of weight n the complexity C_d, evaluated in number of nodes encountered, is in $\Theta(n^2)$.

94 - Q 3   **Question** 3.   The previous version of the diameter calculation can be improved in terms of complexity using classic heuristics. This consists, rather than *calculating* a value needed at a given time, in *assuming this value available*. So, the induction hypothesis at the base of the construction is strengthened. Apply this technique to the construction of a new version of the diameter calculation and show (assuming the height is available) that by counting the nodes encountered we obtain a solution in $\Theta(n)$.

The solution is on page 515.

Problem 95.   The selection problem and the median element   8 ⁝

> *The originality of this problem lies in the use of a non-standard reasoning of type "partition induction" (see section 1.1.4, page 7). In addition, this problem illustrates (once again) that to solve a given problem (here that of the median element) it may pay off solving a more general one (here that of the selection), thus a priori more difficult. This problem is expressed (and solved) in a set-theoretic formalism. So, technical aspects related to implementation are postponed.*

We consider E a finite non-empty subset of $\mathbb{N}$ of n elements. We want to solve the problem of the *selection of the kth smallest element* $(1 \leqslant k \leqslant n)$: v is the kth smallest element of E if there are $(k-1)$ elements less than v in E. When k is equal to 1 or n, this problem is easily solved in $\Theta(n)$, with the comparison as the elementary operation. To what extent can the same performance be achieved for any k?

95 - Q 1   **Question** 1.   This first question concerns an auxiliary iterative algorithm used to solve the problem of the selection of the kth smallest element by a DaC approach. The corresponding procedure is called $BreakUp(E, E^-, E^+, a)$. One element of the set E is randomly selected (all elements are assumed to be equiprobable). This element, denoted a, is called the *pivot*. $BreakUp(E, E^-, E^+, a)$ separates the elements of the set $E - \{a\}$ into two other sets E^- and E^+, the first containing all the elements of E strictly less than the pivot, the second containing all the elements of E strictly greater than the pivot.

1. Give the constituents of an iterative construction of the procedure $BreakUp$.

2. In the perspective of refining this procedure, show how sets can be implemented as arrays. Infer that the complexity of $BreakUp$ is in $\Theta(n)$.

Question 2. Let "**function** *Selection*(E, k) **result** ℕ" be the operation which returns the kth smallest element of the set E. This operation is preconditioned by k ∈ 1 .. card(E).

95 - Q 2

1. Let a be an arbitrary element of E. What relationship between E, k and a allows us to claim that a is the sought element?

2. Assuming that the procedure *BreakUp* is available, construct a DaC solution to the selection problem. Which division model applies?

3. Deduce the code of the function *Selection*.

4. What are the specificities of this solution compared to the standard DaC model?

5. Give the elements of an algorithmic refinement.

6. What is the complexity at best of the function *Selection*? What order of growth of complexity is obtained if the procedure *BreakUp* cuts at each step the set E into two subsets E^- and E^+ of sizes equal or different from 1? What is the worst-case complexity of the function *Selection*? What do you think is the average complexity?

Question 3. How can the solution to the selection problem be adapted to obtain a solution to the problem of the median element, i.e. that of finding the $\lfloor card(E)/2 \rfloor^{th}$ element of E?

95 - Q 3

The solution is on page 517.

Problem 96. Nuts and bolts ○ ⦂

> *This problem is similar to a sort insofar as we are looking for a bijection endowed with certain properties (a sort is a permutation, therefore a bijection). It is therefore not surprising that we find here algorithmic methods and complexity calculation techniques close to those used in sorting problems.*

In a toolbox, there is in bulk a set E of n (n > 0) nuts of all different diameters and the set B of the corresponding n bolts. The difference in diameter is so small that it is impossible to visually compare the size of two nuts or bolts with each other. To find out if a bolt matches a nut, the only way is to try to put them together. The attempt at a bolt-nut pairing is the elementary operation chosen for the evaluation of the complexity of this problem. It provides one of three answers: either the nut is wider than the bolt, or it is narrower, or they have exactly the same diameter. The problem is to establish the bijection that associates each nut with its bolt.

Question 1. Give the principle of a naïve algorithm. What is its complexity at best? At worst?

96 - Q 1

Question 2. Construct a DaC algorithm that assembles each bolt with its nut. Which division model applies?

96 - Q 2

Question 3. Write a set-theoretic version of the operation "**procedure** *Matching*(E, B)" which assembles the n nuts of the set E to the n bolts of the set B. Show that the worst-case complexity is in $\Theta(n^2)$.

96 - Q 3

Question 4. Using the decision tree method (see chapter 1, page 27), we now try to determine a lower bound to the complexity of the worst-case nut and bolt problem. A decision tree for an algorithm solving the considered problem is a complete ternary tree that represents the comparisons made between nuts and bolts (see problem 90, page 427,

96 - Q 4

for another example using decision trees). In such a tree, a left (respectively central, right) sub-tree takes into account the response $>$ (respectively $=$, $<$) to the comparison. To each leaf of the tree is associated one of the possible bijections between E and B. Provide the decision tree for the naïve method in the case where $E = \{1, 2, 3\}$ and $B = \{a, b, c\}$. Knowing that $\log_3(n!) \in \Omega(n \cdot \log_3(n))$ (according to Stirling's formula), prove that any algorithm that solves the nut and bolt problem has a complexity at worst in $\Omega(n \cdot \log_3(n))$.

The solution is on page 520.

Problem 97. Discovering the fake coin

The problem addressed here is a classic weighing one, for which many variants exist. Strictly speaking, this is not a computer science problem (by the way no algorithm is required). In spite of this, it is actually a DaC problem. One of its characteristics is the contrast between the simplicity of the statement and the difficulty to find a thorough exhaustive solution.

Let us consider a set of $n \geqslant 1$ coins looking alike, among of which $(n - 1)$ are in gold and one in gold-plated light metal. We are provided with a two-pan weigh-scale which indicates, at each weighing, whether the weight placed on the left pan is less than, greater than or equal to the weight placed on the right pan. Note that it is only possible to use the result of a weighing if the number of pieces is identical on each pan.

The goal of the problem is to find the fake coin with the fewest possible weighings in the most unfavourable case (at worst). Two strategies are studied.

Three-pile division strategy

Let us consider the following strategy (called "three-pile strategy"), for which the n coins are separated into two piles of the same cardinality k and a third (possibly empty) pile containing the remaining coins (so k can vary from 0 to $\lfloor n/2 \rfloor$). The function $C_3(n)$ provides the number of weighings needed in the worst case.

Base If $n = 1$ (k is then 0), we are faced with a single coin which is the fake coin. No weighing is necessary: $C_3(1) = 0$.

Induction hypothesis For any m such that $1 \leqslant m < n$, it is known how to determine $C_3(m)$.

Induction Let $k \in 1 .. \lfloor n/2 \rfloor$. The principle of this strategy is to separate the n coins into three piles, two piles of k coins and one pile of $n - 2k$ coins. A weighing is performed by placing a pile of k coins in each pan of the weigh-scale. Two cases can then arise.

   First case The weigh-scale is out of balance. The fake coin is in the lightest pile. The number of weighings remaining to be carried out is therefore $C_3(k)$.

   Second case The weigh-scale is balanced. The fake coin is therefore in the third pile. The number of weighings remaining to be carried out is therefore $C_3(n - 2k)$[4].

In both cases, thanks to the induction hypothesis, the sought value can be found.

---

[4]Notice that when n is even and $k = \lfloor n/2 \rfloor$, $C_3(n - 2k) = C_3(0)$, but the fake coin is then in one of the two piles of k coins. We are back to the first case. From a calculation point of view, to get around this pitfall, in the following we admit that $C_3(0) = 0$.

Termination The number of coins weighed at each stage decreases, which ensures the termination of the process.

Question 1.   Give the recurrence equation for $C_3(n)$ with $n > 0$. 97 - Q 1

Question 2.   We will now try to simplify this equation. First prove (by induction on n) 97 - Q 2
that $C_3(n)$ is increasing. Deduce that the equation obtained in the first question is equivalent to the following recurrence equation:

$$
\begin{vmatrix}
C_3(1) = 0 \\
C_3(n) = 1 + C_3\left(\left\lceil \dfrac{n}{3} \right\rceil\right) & n > 1.
\end{vmatrix}
$$

Question 3.   Solve this equation. Deduce that the detection of the fake coin is done at 97 - Q 3
worst in $\lceil \log_3(n) \rceil$ weighings.

Four-pile division strategy

The three-pile strategy can be extended to four piles in many ways. We investigate one of them for which, if $n \geqslant 3$; the initial pile is separated into three piles *of the same cardinality* k, plus a pile of $(n - 3k)$ coins.

Question 4.   Redo the previous development for this strategy. 97 - Q 4

The solution is on page 524.

Problem 98. The missing value   8 •

> *This problem certainly concerns the application of the DaC principle, but the reader is invited to deal with the problem beforehand using iterative methods. This is an opportunity to remember that the best sort algorithms are not always at worst in $n \cdot \log_2(n)$: they can for example be linear! It depends on the precondition.*

A constant array $T[1..n]$ ($n \in \mathbb{N}_1$) contains all the integers in the interval $1..n+1$, except one. We would like to determine which is the missing integer in T. Complexity calculations will be based on the evaluation of conditions.

Question 1.   Design an algorithm which solves the problem in linear time without call- 98 - Q 1
ing on an auxiliary array.

Question 2.   The array is now assumed to be variable. We try *simultaneously* to deter- 98 - Q 2
mine the missing value and to sort the array. An additional square of T can be supposed available at position $n+1$. Build an iterative solution that solves the problem in linear time.

Question 3.   The array $T[1 .. n]$ is now assumed to be sorted. Build a DaC solution 98 - Q 3
based on binary search. Provide the division model as well as the algorithm. What is its complexity at worst?

98 - Q 4 **Question** 4.   Answer the previous three questions when the array contains *all but two* integers in the interval $1 .. n + 2$.

The solution is on page 531.

Problem 99.   The best interval (1)   o ⦂

> *This statement proposes the study of a DaC version of a problem also dealt with through "dynamic programming" in problem 118, page 642. This version constitutes a simple example of improvement of the efficiency of solutions found out for a given problem, improvements obtained first by the application of the DaC principle, then by an adequate strengthening of the postcondition. In terms of temporal complexity, the result is comparable to the dynamic programming solution.*

Let $T[1 .. n]$ ($n \geqslant 1$) be an array of real non-negative values ($T \in 1 .. n \rightarrow \mathbb{R}_+$). There are at least two indices, i and j, defining the interval $i .. j$, with $1 \leqslant i \leqslant j \leqslant n$, such that the value of the expression $T[j] - T[i]$ is maximum. We are looking for this maximum value (the value of the *best* interval). The special case where $i = j$ characterizes a monotonic array strictly decreasing: the value searched for is then zero.

An example for the application of this algorithm: the array T contains last month daily share values of a given company. One wonders today what the optimal gain would have been by buying a share and then selling it during the last month.

99 - Q 1 **Question** 1.   Let "**procedure** *BestInterval1*(beg, end; bi: **modif**)" be the operation that delivers the value of the best interval biv for the array $T[\text{beg} .. \text{end}]$.

1. Construct the procedure *BestInterval1* by applying the partition induction principle (see section 1.1.4, page 7).

2. What division model is this solution based on? Deduce its complexity in terms of number of conditions evaluated.

99 - Q 2 **Question** 2.   The above DaC version leads to superfluous calculations.

1. Which ones? Carrying out an improvement requires the strengthening of the postcondition, which implies the addition of parameters in the procedure. Specify this new procedure *BestInterval2* informally.

2. Specify this procedure. Provide the corresponding division model as well as the code of the procedure. What is the complexity of this solution. Compare it with that of *BestInterval1*.

The solution is on page 537.

Problem 100.   The sub-array of maximum sum   ⦂

> *The main interest of this problem lies in the succession of strengthenings of the induction hypothesis demanded by the search for an efficient solution and in their constructive nature. It illustrates once more that the development can most often be carried out in a rational manner and that the work already done turns out to be a guide for the work to be done. There are however exceptions to this rule, such as the problem 105, page 445, on finding a majority element.*

Let $T[1..n]$ $(n \geqslant 1)$ be an array of real numbers. We call *sum* of a sub-array of T the sum of the elements of this sub-array. We are looking for the maximum value taken the sum when all sub-arrays of T are considered (including the empty sub-array and T itself).

For example, in the following array:

i	1	2	3	4	5	6	7	8
$T[i]$	3.	1.	−4.	3.	−1.	3.	−0.5	−1.

5, the maximum value taken by the sum, is reached with the sub-array $T[4..6]$. On the other hand, in the following array:

i	1	2	3	4	5	6	7	8
$T[i]$	−5.	−4.	−4.	−3.	−1.	−8.	−0.5	−15.

any sub-array of length 0 (for instance $T[4..3]$) provides the solution which is 0.0.

Question 1. A naïve solution, where all the sub-arrays are explicitly examined, is of course possible. Nevertheless, it is costly in terms of temporal complexity (the addition being taken as the elementary operation). So, we are looking for a solution of type DaC of the form $SubArrMax1(beg, end; ms : \mathbf{modif})$ (where beg and end – input parameters – are the boundaries of the considered array and ms – output parameter – is the maximum sum obtained when all sub-arrays of $T[beg .. end]$ are taken into account). *100 - Q 1*

1. Characterize the elementary case.

2. Express the induction hypothesis that is the base of the general case. Describe the processing to be carried out to gather the two partial solutions obtained. Deduce the division model, then the code of the procedure $SubArrMax1$.

3. What is the complexity of this solution?

Question 2. In the previous solution, the existence of repetitive calculations in the gathering suggests a more efficient DaC type solution than this one. *100 - Q 2*

1. What strengthening of the induction hypothesis is it reasonable to formulate? Specify the header of the new version $SubArrMax2$ of this procedure.

2. Describe the processing to be carried out for the gathering of the results obtained in the inductive case. What is the associated division model?

3. Deduce the order of growth of the resulting complexity. Conclusion?
[1.]

Question 3. The answers to question 2 suggest a new possible strengthening. *100 - Q 3*

(a) What new strengthening of the induction hypothesis is reasonable? Specify the header of the new version $SubArrMax3$ of this procedure.

(b) How can the gathering described in question 2.b be arranged to take into account the new induction hypothesis? What is the associated division model? Deduce the code of the procedure $SubArrMax3$.

(c) What is the resulting order of growth of complexity?

The solution is on page 540.

Problem 101. Paving a chessboard with triminoes   ○ •

> *This is one of the few problems in which the initial problem breaks down into four sub-problems. In addition, the basic step is empty, as is the gathering step. The equation providing the complexity is part of the panel that accompanies the master theorem (see page 422). However, the statement here requires to solve this equation exactly.*

Let us consider a chessboard $n \times n$ such that $n = 2^m$ and $m \geqslant 0$, as well as the four types of triminos hereafter each of which is made up of a square 2×2 deprived of a square:

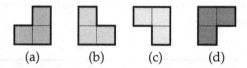

(a)   (b)   (c)   (d)

We would like to cover the whole chessboard, except for a particular given square (the "hole") of coordinates (hr, hc) (row of the hole and column of the hole), using the patterns above, so that each square is covered by a single pattern.

Example

We are provided with a eight-row, eight-column chessboard and the hole is in position $(2, 6)$: second row, sixth column.

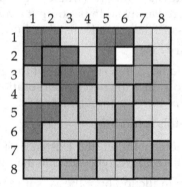

The objective of the problem is to design a DaC solution to this problem.

101 - Q 1   **Question 1.**   Prove by induction that for any positive integer m the expression $(2^{2m} - 1)$ is a multiple of 3. Conclusion?

101 - Q 2   **Question 2.**   Construct by induction the operation "**procedure** *Paving*(r, c, n, hr, hc)" which paves a chessboard of $n \times n$ squares (n is a power of 2), whose northwest corner is located at row r and at column c and for which the hole is located at row hr and at column hc.

101 - Q 3   **Question 3.**   Give the division model that applies.

101 - Q 4   **Question 4.**   Write the code of the procedure code *Paving*. The operation "**procedure** *Place*(r, c, td)" (which places a trimino of type td (td $\in$(a) .. (d)) so that its missing square is located in (r, c)) is assumed to be available. Establish that the exact complexity of this operation is equal to $((n^2 - 1)/3)$ if the placement of a trimino is taken as the elementary operation.

The solution is on page 544.

Problem 102. The saddle

> *In addition to its intrinsic interest linked to the exploitation of the order on the rows and columns of a matrix, this problem highlights the impact of the strictness or not of this order on the problem to be solved.*

Let us consider a two-dimensional array of positive integers such that the values of the same row and those of the same column are ordered, *not necessarily strictly*. Such an array is called a *saddle*.

Example

The array hereafter is a four-row, five-column saddle.

2	14	25	30	69
3	15	28	30	81
7	15	32	43	100
20	28	36	58	101

It should be noted that any sub-array of a saddle is itself a saddle, and this property is used implicitly in the following.

We study the search for a given value v in a saddle S. More precisely, if v is present, we want to know the coordinates of one of its occurrences, otherwise $(0,0)$ is delivered.

Reduce and conquer

A first solution is to scan S sequentially by row (or by column) until v is found.

Question 1. Describe the principle of this first strategy in terms of DaC.   102 - Q 1

Question 2. What is its class of complexity at worst (in terms of comparisons), when m is the number of rows and n the number of columns of S? Can it be improved knowing that both lines and columns are sorted?   102 - Q 2

"Divide and conquer" $(n/2, n/2)$

In the previous approach, the fact that S is a saddle has not been exploited (double sequential scan) or only partly (sequential scan on rows and binary search in a row). To take advantage of this property, we now consider a solution in the particular case where the saddle is a square of side $n = 2^k$ ($k \geqslant 1$), and we single out the two values: $x = S[n/2, n/2]$, $y = S[n/2 + 1, n/2 + 1]$.

Question 3. Prove that if the searched value v is such that $v > x$, a part (to be specified) of the saddle can be eliminated to continue the search. Specify what can be done when $v < y$.   102 - Q 3

Question 4. Deduce a resolution model of type DaC in logarithmic reduction and give the associated procedure.   102 - Q 4

Question 5. Establish the order of complexity at worst of this method (in terms of number of comparisons).   102 - Q 5

Question 6. How can this strategy be adapted to the case of any saddle?   102 - Q 6

More and more efficient

We now consider the search for a v value in a saddle S of any dimension (m rows, n columns) by distinguishing the value $z = S[1, n]$.

102 - Q 7   **Question 7.**   What should be done depending on whether z is equal to, greater than, or less than v?

102 - Q 8   **Question 8.**   Deduce a resolution model of type DaC in the form:

> $Pb(m, n) \rightarrow$ test related to the value z + $Pb(m', n')$

and specify the values m' and n'.

102 - Q 9   **Question 9.**   Write the corresponding recursive procedure, whose header is **procedure** *Saddle3*(rBeg, cEnd; row, col : **modif**), called in the main program by *Saddle3*(1, n, r, c), where the output parameters r and c are assigned the indexes of row and column of a square of the saddle $S[1 .. m, 1 .. n]$ containing the desired value, or $(0, 0)$ if this value is absent from S.

102 - Q 10   **Question 10.**   Establish the class of complexity at worst of this latter method (n terms of comparisons) and conclude about the approach to be taken to solve the addressed problem.

A related problem: counting zero values

102 - Q 11   **Question 11.**   We now assume that the saddle $S[1 .. m, 1 .. n]$ contains relative integers and that the objective is to count the number of 0's in S. Can the approach developed previously for finding the presence of a value based on eliminating rows or columns serve as a basis for solving this problem? What if the order was strict in the rows and columns?

The solution is on page 547.

Problem 103. Counting inversions in a list of numbers   ∘ ⦂

> *This problem is a new example of problem showing that applying the DaC principle is not a guarantee of algorithm complexity improvement. It also confirms that strengthening the postcondition of the specification (i.e. making "more" than initially requested) can sometimes be the key to the improvement sought.*

The goal of this problem is to build a fast algorithm to count the number of *inversions* present in a list without duplicates. A list of values without duplicates is stored in the array $T[1 .. n]$, and numbers i and j such that $1 \leqslant i < j \leqslant n$, are said to form an inversion if $T[i] > T[j]$.

For example, for $n = 8$, the number of inversions of the following list is 13.

i	1	2	3	4	5	6	7	8
$T[i]$	7	10	2	1	4	12	3	9

Written as a list of the pairs of indexes (i, j) such that $i < j$ and $T[i] > T[j]$, the inversions are the following:

$$\langle (1,3), (1,4), (1,5), (1,7), (2,3), (2,4), (2,5), (2,7), (2,8), (3,4), (4,7), (6,7), (6,8) \rangle.$$

Remark

Notice that the different versions of the algorithm under design in this problem make it possible to obtain the *signature* of a permutation[5] of the n first positive integers ($n \geqslant 1$). It suffices to take an array T valued in $1..n$ and to find the parity of the number of inversions in T.

Question 1. Build a naïve iterative algorithm that calculates the number of inversions 103 - Q 1 in a list without duplicates. Give the order of growth of complexity of this algorithm by taking the evaluation of conditions as the elementary operation.

It is now assumed that $n = 2^k$, for k integer greater than or equal to 1. For $k > 1$, inversions can be partitioned into three categories:

- those for which the two terms are located in the first part of T, for example: $(2, 3)$ in the above example,
- those for which the two terms are located in the second part of T, for example: $(6, 7)$,
- those for which the first term is in the first part of T and the second one in the second half of T, for example: $(2, 7)$.

Question 2. Design the operation "**function**$NbInv1(i, s)$ **result** $0..(n \cdot (n+1))/2$", such 103 - Q 2 that the call $NbInv1(1, n)$ computes the number of inversions present in the array $T[1..n]$ (T is a global variable) according to the DaC approach. Which division model applies? Provide the code of this function. Give the order of growth of complexity of this solution. What can be concluded with respect to the first question?

Question 3. To improve the efficiency of the solution, the idea is to avoid the com- 103 - Q 3 parison of all possible pairs. It is proposed to strengthen the post-condition, not only by looking for the number of inversions, but also by sorting the array T. Let us study the heart of this solution considering an array where each half is sorted as in the following example:

i	1	2	3	4	5	6	7	8
T[i]	2	3	7	12	1	4	9	10

1. Prove that, in a configuration such as:

where $T[1..mid]$ and $T[mid+1..n]$ are increasingly sorted, if $T[j] > T[k]$ then, for any $l \in j..mid$, $T[l] > T[k]$. What can be concluded?

2. Deduce an iterative algorithm that, in this case, counts the inversions in linear time.

Question 4. Construct (based on the previous question as well as the prob- 103 - Q 4 lem 88, page 424, which deals with sort-merge) the operation of type DaC "**procedure**$NbInv2(i, s; nb : $ **modif**$)$" such that the call $NbInv2(1, n, nbi)$ both sorts the array $T[1..n]$ (T is a global variable) and counts (in nbi) the number of inversions present in the initial configuration of $T[1..n]$. Improving the order of growth of complexity with respect to the solution of question 2 is expected. Provide the division model as well as the code.

---

[5]Which, by definition, is 1 if the number of inversions is even, -1 otherwise.

103 - Q 5   **Question** 5.   Is it possible to adapt the algorithms of the previous question to cope with the case where n is not a power of 2?

The solution is on page 550.

Problem 104. The skyline

> *One of the classic strategies for improving the efficiency of algorithms is to change the underlying data structure. In this problem, we start the development on the basis of a "naïve" data structure before optimizing it by eliminating a form of redundancy. This problem shows that the improvement expected by the use of a DaC approach is not always achieved.*

We consider the drawing of the downtown skyline with rectangular buildings by the seaside. The skyline (dashed in the diagrams below) is the line that separates the sky from the buildings, when standing far enough out to sea and looking towards the city. Part (a) of figure 8.2 shows the two-dimensional projection of a downtown area consisting of three buildings, and part (b) gives the corresponding skyline.

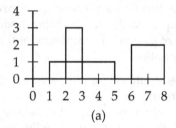
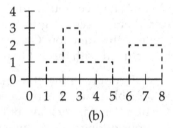

Fig. 8.2 – *Three buildings: (a) by projection and (b) the corresponding* skyline.

It is assumed that all dimensions are integer and that the buildings are constructed between the abscissa 0 and n ($n \geqslant 1$). The addition of a fourth building materializes as shown in parts (a) and (b) of figure 8.3, page 442.

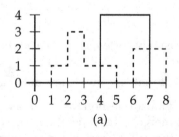
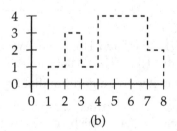

Fig. 8.3 – *Insertion of a building: (a) the new building and (b) the new* skyline.

A first approach

In this first part, a skyline is represented by the array $S[1 .. n]$, whose i^{th} constituent contains the height of the *skyline* between abscissas $i - 1$ and i. For the example of part (a) in figure 8.2, page 442, the skyline is thus represented by:

i	1	2	3	4	5	6	7	8
S[i]	0	1	3	1	1	0	2	2

We choose to represent a building by the *skyline* it would have if it were alone. The representation of the third building in figure 8.2, page 442, (the rightmost building) is therefore:

i	1	2	3	4	5	6	7	8
$I_3[i]$	0	0	0	0	0	0	2	2

An iterative construction algorithm

We intend to get the skyline of a set[6] I of m ($m \geqslant 0$) buildings ($I = \{I_1, \ldots, I_m\}$).

Question 1. Design the algorithm assuming that the set of buildings I is defined by $I \in 1 .. m \rightarrow (1 .. n \rightarrow \mathbb{N})$ (I is an array of m buildings; each building is an array of n heights). 104 - Q 1

Question 2. What is the exact complexity (in terms of conditions) of the calculation of the skyline of I, as a function of n and m? 104 - Q 2

A DaC algorithm

In the perspective of improving the efficiency of the algorithm, we wish to apply a DaC approach to calculate the skyline of the set $I[1 .. m]$ of buildings. The profile of the corresponding procedure is *SkyLine1*$(beg, end; S :$ **modif**$)$, where the set of buildings considered is the one represented by $I[deb .. fin]$ and where S is the corresponding skyline.

Question 3. Design the procedure *SkyLine1*. Deduce the division model that applies. Write the code of this procedure. 104 - Q 3

Question 4. Give the recurrence equation that characterizes the complexity of this procedure, based on the number of conditions evaluated. Deduce the class of complexity. Conclusion? 104 - Q 4

A second approach

An alternative way to try to improve the efficiency of an algorithm is to choose a better representation for the manipulated entities (here buildings and *skylines*). It can be seen that the previous representation is redundant, in that the sampling concerns *all* of the n points. Based on the skyline of figure 8.3, page 442, redrawn as follows:

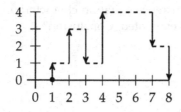

---

[6]Or a multi-set, if there are identical buildings.

it is possible to redefine a representation in which only the end coordinates of the vertical vectors are kept. We obtain a list of couples to which the pair $(n+1, 0)$ is added as a sentinel and completed by pairs $(0, 0)$ up to the $n+1$ position if necessary. The whole is stored in an array defined on the interval $0..n+1$. Thus, for the example above, the new representation is:

$$T[0..n+1] = [(0,0), (1,1), (2,3), (3,1), (4,4), (7,2), (8,0), (9,0), (0,0), (0,0)].$$

The list of pairs is sorted on the first coordinate, which constitutes an identifier. This new representation preserves all the information while avoiding redundancy. In the following, this representation is characterized by the predicate IsSkyLine.

104 - Q 5   **Question 5.**   Specify the representation of the skyline of figure 8.2, page 442.

An iterative algorithm

104 - Q 6   **Question 6.**   An iterative solution taking into account this new representation can be inspired by the answer to question 1. The outer loops are identical in both cases. On the other hand, the treatment that achieves the fusion of two *skylines* is a novelty. Two solutions can be considered. The first is a coarse merge with redundancies that must be eliminated in a later phase. This solution is fairly easy to build, but it is quite expensive and not very elegant. The second solution consists in obtaining the result in a single pass on the two *skylines*. It is the subject of this question. Specify its construction in the form of a procedure with the following profile: "*FusionSkyLines*(S1, S2; F : **modif**)" (S1 and S2 are the two *skylines* whose fusion is to be made, and F the resulting skyline).

Suggestion The main difficulty of the algorithm lies in the identification of the cascade of cases and sub-cases which appear in the progression of the loop. The reader is encouraged to clearly separate two phases, the highlighting of the various cases on the one hand and the optimization (factorization of the identical cases) on the other hand.

104 - Q 7   **Question 7.**   Based on the number of conditions evaluated, as a function of m, what is the worst-case complexity of the procedure *FusionSkyLines*?

104 - Q 8   **Question 8.**   Derive an iterative solution using the procedure *FusionSkyLines*. What is the order of growth of worst-case complexity (in number of evaluated conditions) of this iterative computation (as a function of m)?

A DaC algorithm

With the same representation, we are now looking for a DaC solution. The profile of the procedure is *SkyLine2*(beg, end; S : **modif**).

104 - Q 9   **Question 9.**   Construct the procedure *SkyLine2*. Deduce the division model that applies. Write the code of this procedure.

104 - Q 10   **Question 10.**   Give the recurrence equation characterizing the complexity of this procedure, in terms of conditions evaluated. Conclusion?

The solution is on page 556.

Problem 105. The majority element (recursive issue) 8 ⁝

> *Already covered in problem 40, page 119, this problem reviews three DaC solutions to the problem of finding a majority element in a bag. If the first solution is classic, the other two call for a more original technique. Indeed, in this book and in this chapter in particular, we have frequently exploited the proven heuristic which consists in strengthening the postcondition in order to obtain a good temporal efficiency. Here on the contrary, the postcondition is weakened. On the one hand, this last heuristic makes it possible to obtain a simple algorithm (but which only partially meets the specification), on the other hand it requires the addition of a complementary algorithm whose goal is to ensure that the result obtained in the first step meets (or not) the initial specification. This technique can profitably enrich the background of any developer. The last solution is similar to the one developed in problem 40, page 119.*

Let B be a bag of n ($n \geqslant 1$) strictly positive integers. B is said to be *majority* if there is an integer x such that:

$$\text{mult}(x, B) \geqslant \left\lfloor \frac{n}{2} \right\rfloor + 1$$

$\text{mult}(x, B)$ designating the function delivering the number of occurrences of x in B; x is then called *majority element* of B and is unique. The problem posed is that of finding a majority element in B. Determining a candidate who has got the absolute majority during a ballot or the design of fault-tolerant algorithms are possible applications of this problem.

Thereafter, complexity will be expressed in terms of the number of conditions evaluated.

In the three solutions below, the bag B is refined by an array of positive integers $T[1..n]$ ($n \geqslant 1$). It is difficult to imagine the identification of the majority element (if it exists), without knowing its number of occurrences (multiplicity). This is why we decide to immediately strengthen the postcondition, by transforming the search for the majority element into the search for the pair (x, nbx) (x being the majority element and nbx its number of occurrences or multiplicity).

A DaC algorithm in $\Theta(n \cdot \log_2(n))$

For $T[1 .. n]$, we calculate the pair (x, nbx) such that:

- if $T[1 .. n]$ is not majority, the pair $(0, 0)$ is returned,

- if $T[1 .. n]$ is majority, (x, nbx) is returned, where x is the majotity element and nbx its multiplicity.

The DaC technique envisaged works on two "halves" of $T[1 .. n]$ of equal sizes or different from 1. The pair (x, nbx) is then calculated from $(xl, nbxl)$ (associated with the left half of T) and $(xr, nbxr)$ (associated with the right half of T), by counting if necessary the majority value of a certain half in the opposite half.

Example

In the table below, the pair $(1, 8)$ calculated for the interval $1 .. 13$ appears at the bottom of the figure, between the indices 6 and 7. This means that 1 is the majority element and its multiplicity is 8. This result is obtained by "gathering" (in a way to be made explicit) the pair $(0, 0)$ obtained for the interval $1 .. 6$ and the pair $(1, 5)$ obtained for the interval $7 .. 13$.

1	2	3	4	5	6	7	8	9	10	11	12	13
2	1	1	3	1	2	3	1	1	1	1	2	1

$$2,1 \quad 1,1 \quad 1,1 \quad 3,1 \quad 1,1 \quad 2,1 \quad 3,1 \quad 1,1 \quad 1,1 \quad 1,1 \quad 1,1 \quad 2,1 \quad 1,1$$

$$(1,2) \qquad\qquad (0,0) \qquad\qquad (1,2) \qquad\qquad (1,2) \qquad\qquad (0,0)$$

$$(1,2) \qquad\qquad\qquad\qquad (0,0) \qquad\qquad\qquad (1,2) \qquad\qquad\qquad\qquad (1,3)$$

$$(0,0) \qquad\qquad\qquad\qquad\qquad\qquad\qquad\qquad (1,5)$$

$$(1,8)$$

In the general case of an array $T[beg .. end]$ of length lgt ($lgt = end - beg + 1$), we consider two contiguous half-arrays, $T[beg .. beg + \lfloor lgt/2 \rfloor - 1]$ for which we calculate $(xl, nbxl)$, and $T[beg + \lfloor lgt/2 \rfloor .. beg + lgt - 1]$ for which we calculate $(xr, nbxr)$.

105 - Q 1   **Question 1.**   Using a reasoning of type "partition induction" (see section 1.1.4, page 7), design the operation "**procedure** *Majority1*($beg, lgt; x, nbx$: **modif**)" where beg and lgt identify the sub-array $T[beg .. beg + lgt - 1]$ and (x, nbx) is the desired pair. The call *Majority1*$(1, n, me, nbme)$ calculates the pair $(me, nbme)$ for the array $T[1 .. n]$. Give the division model used, then the code of the procedure.

105 - Q 2   **Question 2.**   What is the worst-case complexity class of this solution? Compare with the iterative solution of problem 40, page 119.

A more efficient (linear) DaC algorithm

Theory (see section 3.3.1, page 96) tells that if X and Y are correct programs for the respective specifications (P, R) and (R, Q) then $X; Y$ is a correct program for the specification (P, Q). A particularly interesting use of this property of sequentiality occurs when R is a *weaker* predicate than Q ($Q \Rightarrow R$). Applied to our situation, rather than directly searching for the possible majority element, this property makes it possible to simply search for a *candidate* (to be majority element). That is the role of X. If the result turns out to be satisfactory with regard to complexity, the fragment Y that checks whether this candidate is (or not) the majority element of the array T, remains to be built.

Definition

The pair (x, mx) is said to be the majority candidate (MC) in the array T (made up of lgt positive elements) if and only if:

1. mx is an upper bound of the number of occurrences of x in T: $mult(x, T) \leqslant mx$,

2. mx is strictly greater than the default half-length of T: $mx > \lfloor lgt/2 \rfloor$,

3. for any y different from x, the number of occurrences of y in T is less than or equal to $lgt - mx$: $\forall y \cdot (y \in \mathbb{N}_1 \text{ and } y \neq x \Rightarrow mult(y, T) \leqslant lgt - mx)$.

By abuse of language, we will also say that x is MC in T if there is (at least) one mx such that the pair (x, mx) is MC in T.

Examples

1. In $T = [1, 1, 1, 6, 6]$, the pair $(1, 3)$ is MC. Indeed:

   - 3 is an upper bound of the number of occurrences of 1 in T,

   - $\lfloor \frac{5}{2} \rfloor < 3 \leqslant 5$,

   - 6 is present only twice and $2 \leqslant 5 - 3$.

2. In the array $T = [1, 1, 5, 5]$, the pair $(1, 3)$ is not MC. Indeed:

   - 3 is an upper bound of the number of occurrences of 1 in T,
   - $\lfloor \frac{4}{2} \rfloor < 3 \leqslant 4$,
   - but 5 is present twice and $2 \nleqslant 4 - 3$.

3. On the other hand, the pair $(1, 3)$ is MC in $T = [1, 1, 4, 5]$ but T *is not* majority.

4. The pairs $(1, 3)$ and $(1, 4)$ are both MC in the array $T = [1, 1, 1, 6, 5]$.

Question 3. We would like to construct the procedure $CandMaj1(beg, lgt; x, mx :$ 105 - Q 3
modif) that calculates a pair (x, mx) for the slice $T[beg .. beg + lgt - 1]$. This pair (x, mx) has the following meaning:
- if, in view of the current situation, it is *certain* that the considered sub-array *is not* majority, then the procedure returns $(0, 0)$,
- otherwise (there is one MC for sure) the procedure delivers the pair (x, mx) as the MC.

Design this procedure using a partition induction reasoning (see section 1.1.4, page 7). Give the division model used as well as the code of the procedure *CandMaj1*. What is its complexity?

Question 4. What additional processing must be done to obtain the expected result 105 - Q 4
(the value of the majority element if it exists)? What then is the complexity of the global processing?

Question 5. Apply the proposed solution to the following arrays: 105 - Q 5

   1. $T1 = [1, 2, 1, 3, 2, 1, 1, 3, 3, 2, 3, 1, 1, 1]$,
   2. $T2 = [2, 1, 1, 3, 1, 2, 3, 1, 1, 1, 1, 2, 1]$,
   3. $T3 = [1, 1, 2, 1, 3, 1, 3, 2, 2]$.

A second linear DaC solution, simple and original

We now point out an algorithm of linear complexity applicable to an array T of any size, based on another type of division of T. This algorithm also aims to determine a MC for the array T; it is built only from property 13.

Property 13:
If x is the majority element of $T[1 .. n]$ *and* $T[1 .. i]$ *is not majority, then x is the majority element of* $T[i + 1 .. n]$.

Question 6. Prove property 13. 105 - Q 6

Question 7. Give the principle of solution of type DaC based on the above property. 105 - Q 7
Give the division model used, as well as the elementary problems and the global complexity.

Question 8. Write the corresponding function *CandMaj2* of profile $CandMaj2(beg, lgt)$ 105 - Q 8
result $\mathbb{N}$ returning 0 if $T[beg .. beg + lgt - 1]$ has no majority element "for sure" and x $(x > 0)$ if x is the MC of $T[beg .. beg + lgt - 1]$.

Process the examples:

$$T1 = [1,2,1,3,2,1,1,3,3,2,3,1,1,1],$$
$$T2 = [2,1,1,3,1,2,3,1,1,1,1,2,1],$$

$$T3 = [1,1,2,1,3,1,3,2,2],$$
$$T4 = [1,2,1,1,2,3].$$

The solution is on page 561.

Problem 106. The two closest points in a plane

> *This problem illustrates two essential aspects of the development of algorithms: the refinement and the strengthening. Starting from a set-oriented specification, a first choice is made for the representation of sets. A naïve solution for this refinement first developed is not satisfactory from the point of view of complexity, which leads to strengthening the postcondition in order to obtain a solution in $\Theta(n \cdot \log_2(n))$.*

We are looking for an algorithm of type DaC to solve the following problem: we have a finite set E of n ($n \geqslant 2$) points in a plane. What is the distance between the two closest points[7]?

More formally: let $\mathbb{R}^2$ be the space endowed with the Euclidian metrics noted Δ. Let E be a finite set of n points in $\mathbb{R}^2$. Let $p = (p_x, p_y)$ and $q = (q_x, q_y)$ be two points of $\mathbb{R}^2$. $\Delta(p, q)$ denotes the Euclidian distance between p and q, i.e. $\Delta(p, q) = \sqrt{(p_x - q_x)^2 + (p_y - q_y)^2}$. We are looking for the positive real number d defined as

$$d = \min\left(\{a \in E \text{ and } b \in E \text{ and } a \neq b \mid \Delta(a, b)\}\right)$$

Example

For the set of points below:

d is the searched value.

Thereafter, complexity is expressed in number of conditions evaluated.

106 - Q 1   **Question 1.**   What is the order of complexity of the naïve calculation algorithm of d?

---

[7]There is never uniqueness of this pair of points since if (a, b) is such a pair, this is also the case for (b, a). The question of the identification of *the set* of such pairs leads to a trivial arrangement of the programs developed below. This question is not addressed later.

In the following, n is a power of 2. The operation "**function** $Closest1(S)$ **result** $\mathbb{R}_+$" delivers the distance between the closest neighbors in the set of points S. In the following calling context:

1. **constants**
2. $Coord = \{x, y \mid x \in \mathbb{R}$ **and** $y \in \mathbb{R}\}$ **and** $E \subset Coord$ **and** $E = \{\ldots\}$
3. **begin**
4.   **write**$(Closest1(E))$
5. **end**

the function *Closest1* below provides a first sketch:

1. **function** $Closest1(S)$ **result** $\mathbb{R}_+$ **pre**
2. $S \subset Coord$ **and** $\exists k \cdot (k \in \mathbb{N}_1$ **and** $card(S) = 2^k)$ **and** $S_1 \subset S$ **and** $S_2 \subset S$ **and**
3. $(S_1 \cap S_2) = \varnothing$ **and** $(S_1 \cup S_2) = S$ **and** $card(S_1) = card(S_2)$ **and**
4. $d \in \mathbb{R}_+^*$ **and** $d_1 \in \mathbb{R}_+^*$ **and** $d_2 \in \mathbb{R}_+^*$
5. **begin**
6.   **if** $card(S) = 2$ **then**
7.   **let** a, b **such that**
8. $a \in S$ **and** $b \in S$ **and** $a \neq b$
9.   **begin**
10.   **result** $\Delta(a, b)$
11.   **end**
12.   **else**
13. $d_1 \leftarrow Closest1(S_1)$;
14. $d_2 \leftarrow Closest1(S_2)$;
15. $d \leftarrow \min(\{d_1, d_2\})$;
16. $Gather1(\ldots)$;
17.   **result** $\ldots$
18.   **end if**
19. **end**

The existential quantifier specifies that the number of elements of S is a power of 2. The value d_1 (respectively d_2) is the smallest distance found in the subset S_1 (respectively S_2).

Question 2. Specify the four key points of the inductive construction of the function *Closest1* (here, we are doing a kind of "reverse engineering").   106 - Q 2

Question 3. What is the order of complexity of the function *Closest1* if the procedure *Gather1* is in $\Theta(n^2)$? in $\Theta(n \cdot \log_2(n))$? in $\Theta(n)$?   106 - Q 3

We are now trying to refine the representation of the sets S, S_1 and S_2. There are generally many ways to partition an even-sized set S into two subsets of the same size. For the sake of distance calculations, it is interesting to realize this partition by a *line* separator. The choice of a vertical or horizontal line is reasonable insofar as the distance between a point and this line is then limited to a calculation on *only one* of the coordinates of the point. Thereafter, it is arbitrarily considered that this line is presented vertically. The refinement of the set S can then be done by an array of pairs $T[i .. s]$ ($T[1 .. n]$ for the initial set E, so that, if $Coord$ is the set of pairs of real values (x, y), then $T[1 .. n] \in 1 .. n \rightarrow Coord$), sorted on increasing abscissas (this ensures that the proximity of the points to the separating line results in a proximity in the array). If $mid = \lfloor (i + s)/2 \rfloor$, the sets S_1 and S_2 are refined by the sub-arrays $T[i .. mid]$ and $T[mid + 1 .. s]$. d_1 and d_2 are refined by dl and dr (left and right distances). The point $T[mid]$ belongs to the dividing line. This is also the case for all points that have the same abscissa as $T[mid]$, whether they belong to S_1 or S_2. The function

Closest1 is then refined in the following way (T is here a global structure, only the bounds i and s are passed as parameters):

1. **function** *Closest2*(i, s) **result** $\mathbb{R}_+$ **pre**
2. $i \in 1 .. n$ **and** $s \in i + 1 .. n$ **and** $\exists k \cdot (k \in \mathbb{N}_1$ **and** $s - i + 1 = 2^k)$ **and**
3.   *IsSortedX*(T[i .. s]) **and** $mid \in i .. s - 1$ **and** $d \in \mathbb{R}_+^*$ **and** $dl \in \mathbb{R}_+^*$ **and** $dr \in \mathbb{R}_+^*$
4. **begin**
5.   **if** $s - i + 1 = 2$ **then**
6.   **result** $\Delta(T[i], T[s])$
7.   **else**
8. $mid \leftarrow \left\lfloor \dfrac{i + s}{2} \right\rfloor;$
9. $dl \leftarrow$ *Closest2*(i, mid);
10. $dr \leftarrow$ *Closest2*(mid + 1, s);
11. $d \leftarrow \min(\{dl, dr\});$
12.   *Gather2*(...);
13.   **result** ...
14.   **end if**
15. **end**

The conjunct *IsSortedX*(T[i .. s]) expresses that the sub-array T[i .. s] is sorted on increasing abscissas.

Example

The diagram below shows the previous example. Note that the point T[mid] is located on the dividing line and that seven points are to its left and eight to its right.

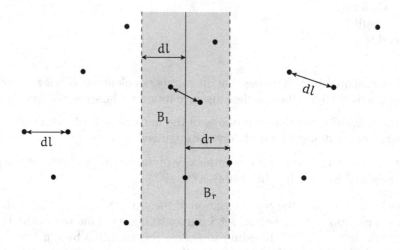

The value dl (respectively dr) is the best distance found in the left (respectively right) half. The value d is the smaller of the two values dl and dr (this is the d in line 11 of the code of *Closest2*).

Let $T[mid] = (m_x, m_y)$. B_l (respectively B_r) denotes the set of located in the vertical strip delimited by the lines of equation $x = m_x - d$ and $x = m_x$ (respectively $x = m_x$ and $x = m_x + d$). Therefore, if two points p_1 and p_2 are such that $p_1 \in T[i .. mid]$ **and** $p_2 \in T[mid + 1 .. s]$ **and** $\Delta(p_1, p_2) \leqslant d$ then $p_1 \in B_l$ and $p_2 \in B_r$.

Question 4.   Prove that any square window open on one of the two strips B_l or B_r 106 - Q 4
contains at most four points:

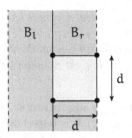

It is easy to conclude (since S is a *set* of points) that there are at most six points in a
rectangle of length 2d and height d spreading over the entire width of the strip:

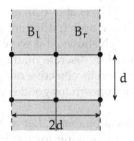

Question 5.   Assuming that the points belonging to the strips B_l and B_r are recorded   106 - Q 5
in an array Y, what must be imposed on this array so that the search for a better neighbor
for Y[j] is done in a sub-array of Y, *of bounded size*, beginning in Y[j + 1]? Give an upper
bound of this size.

Question 6.   Design   an   iterative   version   of   the   operation   "**procedure**   106 - Q 6
Gather2(beg, end; md : **modif**)", where beg and end are such that T[beg .. end] represents the set of points S, and where md is, as input, the best value found in S_1 or S_2 and,
as output, the best value found in S. This procedure begins by constructing the array Y
from the previous question before exploiting it to search for a possible better pair. What is
the order of complexity of this procedure? give the division model of the solution based
on *Closest2*. What is its complexity?

Question 7.   The previous solution is not entirely satisfactory in terms of complexity: 106 - Q 7
one would have expected complexity in $\Theta(n \cdot \log_2(n))$ and this goal is not achieved. Is it
possible to identify the origin of the observed extra cost? For better efficiency, it is suggested to strengthen the induction hypothesis in the following way: the operation *Closest3*
delivers (not only) the distance between the closest neighbors in T[i .. s] and (but also) a
version R[1 .. s − i + 1] of T[i .. s] sorted on the ascending ordinates. Build the operation
"**procedure** *Closest3*(i, s; d, R : **modif**)". Give its complexity.

Question 8.   How to deal with any arbitrary value of n (n ⩾ 2)?   106 - Q 8

The solution is on page 571.

Problem 107. Distance between sequences (1)

> *Understanding the statement of this problem demands having assimilated the introduction to the chapter on dynamic programming (see Chapter 9). This concerns a search algorithm for one of the longest common sub-sequences (in general there is no uniqueness), called* WFlg *and a search algorithm of the length of the longest common sub-sequences (*WFLgForward*).*

In its simplest version, Hirschberg's algorithm searches for one of the longest sub-sequences common to two strings (lgtssc). It is based on a DaC technique, but the division step uses the principle of dynamic programming. The claimed advantage of this method is to save space compared to methods based solely on the principle of dynamic programming. D.S. Hirschberg having imagined the algorithm in the 70s, this argument then had more force than nowadays (although if one deals with biological sequences of thousands of letters, if one exploits it to make the correction of dictations or for similarity searches on the web, it is still of some use). But it is above all an extraordinary example, unique to our knowledge, of the association of two such different techniques. Last, this algorithm is based on an optimality theorem which shows, if it were necessary, that it is often mandatory to have a minimum background in discrete mathematics to be able to methodically construct computer applications. Given its objective of optimizing memory resources, this problem is one of the few where the concern for good spatial complexity conditions development.

Let x and y be two strings on the alphabet Σ. Let m and n be the respective lengths of x and y ($m = |x|$ and $n = |y|$). We are looking for a sub-sequence common to x and y of maximum length. The set of the longest sub-sequences common to x and y is denoted by $LGTSSC(x, y)$. This set is never empty, since the empty string ε is a sub-sequence of any string. In the remainder of this problem, Σ is implicitly the Latin alphabet of 26 letters: $\Sigma = \{a, b, \ldots, z\}$.

Example

Let us consider the alphabet Σ and the two strings $u = attentat$ and $v = tante$. The string *teta* is a sub-sequence of u. The string *tnte* is a sub-sequence of v but *is not* a sub-sequence of u (the symbols do not appear in the same order). The strings ε, *tt*, *at* and *tnt* are sub-sequences common to u and v; thus they belong to $SSC(u, v)$. Here, $LGTSSC(u, v) = \{ant, ate, tat, tnt, tte\}$.

Notations

- If c (respectively $c[i \ldots s]$) is a string, we note $\overline{c}$ (respectively $\overline{c[i \ldots s]}$) the mirror string. If C is a set of strings, we note $\overline{C}$ the set of mirror strings of C. It can be noted that $\overline{\overline{c}} = c$ and $\overline{LGTSSC(\overline{x}, \overline{y})} = LGTSSC(x, y)$.

- By definition, all the elements of a given set $LGTSSC(x, y)$ have the same length denoted by $lg(LGTSSC(x, y))$.

The general principle behind Hirschberg's algorithm for searching for an element of $LGTSSC(x, y)$ consists in dividing x into two sub-strings, and for each part x_1 and x_2, to search for a prefix y_1 and a suffix y_2 of y (with $y_1 \cdot y_2 = y$), such that if $c_1 \in LGTSSC(x_1, y_1)$ and $c_2 \in LGTSSC(x_2, y_2)$ then

$$c_1 \cdot c_2 \in LGTSSC(x, y).$$

The same principle can then be applied to the pairs of strings (x_1, y_1) and (x_2, y_2). The main difficulty of the algorithm lies in finding appropriate sub-strings y_1 and y_2.

Example

For $u = attentat$, $u_1 = atte$, $u_2 = ntat$ and $v = tante$, table 8.1 lists the sets $LGTSSC(u_1, v_1)$ and $LGTSSC(u_2, v_2)$ for all the possible pairs (v_1, v_2) where $v_1 \cdot v_2 = v$. The penultimate column provides all possible concatenations between the elements of $LGTSSC(u_1, v_1)$ and those of $LGTSSC(u_2, v_2)$. The longest sub-sequences are obtained for the pairs $(v_1, v_2) = (tante, \varepsilon)$, $(v_1, v_2) = (ta, nte)$, $(v_1, v_2) = (t, ante)$ and $(v_1, v_2) = (\varepsilon, tante)$. Note that the set of longest sub-sequences appearing in the column "Concat." of table 8.1 (those of length 3) is equal to the set $LGTSSC(u, v)$. Let us temporarily assume that this is always the case: the result does not depend on the position at which x is cut. The confirmation is a consequence of the theorem of page 455.

$u_1 = atte$			$u_2 = ntat$				
v_1	(1)	$lg_1()$	v_2	(2)	$lg_2()$	Concat.	(3)
tante	$\{ate, tte\}$	3	ε	$\{\varepsilon\}$	0	$\{ate, tte\}$	3
tant	$\{at, tt\}$	2	e	$\{\varepsilon\}$	0	$\{at, tt\}$	2
tan	$\{a, t\}$	1	*te*	$\{t\}$	1	$\{at, tt\}$	2
ta	$\{a, t\}$	1	*nte*	$\{nt\}$	2	$\{ant, tnt\}$	3
t	$\{t\}$	1	*ante*	$\{at, nt\}$	2	$\{tat, tnt\}$	3
ε	$\{\varepsilon\}$	0	*tante*	$\{tat\}$	3	$\{tat\}$	3

Tab. 8.1 – Common sub-sequences and longest common sub-sequences. Column (1) (respectively (2) and (3)) represents LGTSSC(u_1, v_1) *(respectively* LGTSSC(u_2, v_2) *and* $lg_1() + lg_2()$).

Let us now detail this part of Hirschberg's algorithm. First of all, let us recall that the dynamic programming algorithm *WFlg* mentioned in the introduction, provides the length of the longest sub-sequence common to x' and y' (see diagram (a) of figure 8.4, page 454) in aa array of m columns and n rows and for each prefix x' of x and y' of y. In particular, the last column provides the length of the longest sub-sequence common to x and *all* the prefixes y' of y; the northeast corner (shaded in the diagram) is the length of the longest sub-sequence common to x and y. It can be deduced that each row and each column of the table are sorted (in a broad sense) in ascending order (the table is a saddle, see problem 102, page 439). In the following, the column of the position j is noted P_j and is defined by:

$$P_j[i] = lg(LGTSSC(x[1 .. j], y[1 .. i])) \text{ for } i \in 0 .. n.$$

Symmetrically, the dual algorithm that treats mirror strings provides, for each prefix x' of $\bar{x}$ and y' of $\bar{y}$, the length of the longest sub-sequence common to x' and y' (see diagram (b) of figure 8.4, page 454). In this case, the left column, read from top to bottom, provides the length of the longest sub-sequence common to $\bar{x}$ and all prefixes of $\bar{y}$. The southwest corner of the table (shaded in the diagram) is the length of the longest sub-sequence common to $\bar{x}$ and $\bar{y}$ (this length is of course the same as the one found for x and y). The column of the position j is noted P_j^* and it is defined by:

$$P_j^*[i] = lg(LGTSSC(\overline{x[j .. m]}, \overline{y[n-i+1 .. n]})) \text{ for } i \in 0 .. n.$$

It is now supposed that x is arbitrarily split into two parts x_1 ($x_1 = x[1 .. j]$) and x_2 ($x_2 = x[j+1 .. m]$) ($x = x_1 \cdot x_2$) and y into y_1 ($y_1 = y[1 .. i]$) and y_2 ($y_2 = y[i+1 .. n]$) ($y = y_1 \cdot y_2$),

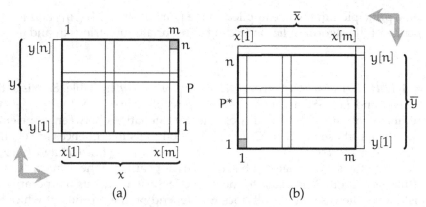

(a)   (b)

Fig. 8.4 – Search for the length of the longest common sub-sequence using dynamic programming. Diagram (a): table P for the strings x and y. Diagram (b): table P* for the strings $\overline{x}$ and $\overline{y}$.

before calculating the "forward" table for the pair (x_1, y_1) and the "backward" table for the pair $(\overline{x_2}, \overline{y_2})$. That is what is shown in the diagram (a) of figure 8.5. Let $c_1 \in \text{LGTSSC}(x_1, y_1)$ and $c_2 \in \overline{\text{LGTSSC}}(\overline{x_2}, \overline{y_2})$. Therefore, we have $|c_1| = P_j[i]$ and $|c_2| = P_{j+1}^*[n - i]$. If we let $c = c_1 \cdot c_2$ we have $|c| = P_j[i] + P_{j+1}^*[n - i]$. Looking for the longest sub-sequence common to x and y is equivalent to searching for the largest value taken by the expression $P_j[i] + P_{j+1}^*[n - i]$ when i ranges from 0 to n. That is what is suggested by part (b) of figure 8.5.

A DaC algorithm founded only on these considerations would have a spatial complexity in $\Omega(m \cdot n)$, which is not compatible with our expectations. The introduction of the chapter devoted to dynamic programming, page 631, provides a solution since it shows that it is possible to "linearize" the algorithm *WFlg* so as to obtain a new version (called *WFLgForward*) whose spatial complexity is in $\Theta(n)$. Part (c) of figure 8.5 illustrates how linearization makes it possible to reduce space used.

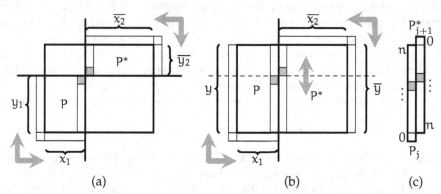

(a)   (b)   (c)

Fig. 8.5 – Principle of Hirschberg's algorithm.

Example

In the example of figure 8.6, page 455, greyed columns provide the vectors P_4 and P_5^* for the calls *WFLgForward*(***atte,atte***, P_4) and *WFLgBackward*(***atte,atte***, P_5^*). The other columns are present only for clarity.

		0	1	2	3	4	4	3	2	1	0			
		P_0	P_1	P_2	P_3	P_4	P_5^*	P_6^*	P_7^*	P_8^*	P_9^*		v	
			a	t	t	e	n	t	a	t				u
							0	0	0	0	0		0	
5	e	0	1	2	2	3	0	0	0	0	0	e	1	
4	t	0	1	2	2	2	1	1	1	1	0	t	2	
3	n	0	1	1	1	1	2	1	1	1	0	n	3	
2	a	0	1	1	1	1	2	2	2	1	0	a	4	
1	t	0	0	1	1	1	3	3	2	1	0	t	5	
0		0	0	0	0	0	0							
			a	t	t	e	n	t	a	t				
		P_0	P_1	P_2	P_3	P_4	P_5^*	P_6^*	P_7^*	P_8^*	P_9^*			
		0	1	2	3	4	5	6	7	8				

Fig. 8.6 – Calls to WFLgForward and WFLgBackward. The two vectors P_4 and P_5^* are to be read in opposite directions, bottom up for P_4, top to down for P_5^*.

In the context of figure 8.6, page 455, let us call M_4 (in reference to the next theorem) the largest value found among the six sums $P_4[0] + P_5^*[5]$, $P_4[1] + P_5^*[4]$, $P_4[2] + P_5^*[3]$, $P_4[3] + P_5^*[2]$, $P_4[4] + P_5^*[1]$, $P_4[5] + P_5^*[0]$. M_4 is equal to 3 and it is also the value of $lg(LGTSSC(x,y))$. This value is attained with four of the six sums: the first, second, third and sixth ones.

107 - Q 1

Question 1. We saw above that there is a need for the operation "**procedure** *WFLgBackward* $(x, y; Q : \textbf{modif})$", which provides in the vector Q, the length of the longest sub-sequences common to $\overline{x[1 .. m]}$ and $\overline{y[i+1 .. n]}$, for $i \in 0 .. n$. Arrange the code of the procedure *WFLgForward* (see section 9.2 page 635) so as to obtain that of the procedure *WFLgBackward*. What can be said about the temporal (in number of conditions evaluated related to the *WFLgForward* and *WFLgBackward*) and spatial complexities of this algorithm?

The development carried out above is formalized by the following theorem:

Theorem (of optimality from Hirschberg):

If

$$M_j = \max_{i \in 0..n} \left(P_j[i] + P_{j+1}^*[n - i] \right)$$

then

$$M_j = P_m[n]$$

for $j \in 0 .. m$.

In other words, referring to the example of figure 8.6, page 455, if for some given column j, M_j is the largest value obtained by the addition of the values $P_j[i]$ and $P_{j+1}^*[n - i]$ $(i \in 0 .. n)$, then j is a possible candidate for finding an appropriate splitting of y. This theorem is the keystone of Hirschberg's algorithm.

107 - Q 2

Question 2. Calculate the value M_5 for $u = esclandre$ and $v = scandale$. For which single k index of P_5 is this value reached? Search "by hand" the sets $LGTSSC(u[1..5], v[1..k])$ and $\overline{LGTSSC}(\overline{u[6 .. 9]}, \overline{v[k+1 .. 8]})$. Deduce the set $LGTSSC(u, v)$.

Question 3. What about the following suggestion: calculate the vector P^*_{j+1} using the algorithm *WFLgForward* applied to the suffixes x_2 and y_2?

Question 4. Prove Hirschberg's optimality theorem. Suggestion: prove on the one hand that $M_j \leqslant P_m[n]$ and on the other hand that $M_j \geqslant P_m[n]$.

Question 5. Describe the DaC reasoning underlying the construction of the operation "**procedure** *HirschLGTSSC*(x, y; c : **modif**)" that, provided that the actual input-output parameter corresponding to c is beforehand initialized with the empty string, delivers into this parameter any of the strings of the set $LGTSSC(x, y)$. Which division model applies? Knowing that a spatial complexity in $\mathcal{O}(\min(\{m, n\}))$ is targeted, provide the code of this operation. What can be said about the temporal complexity of this algorithm? To simplify, it is suggested to limit the calculations to the case where m is a power of 2.

We are now interested in the development of Hirschberg's algorithm in order to obtain no longer a chain but a trace. This notion is defined in problem 139, page 674. We limit ourselves here to the presentation of an example. Once again, consider the strings $u = attentat$ and $v = tante$. A possible trace between u and v is given by:

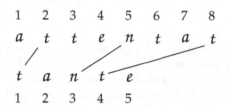

This structure can be materialized by the sorted list of the pairs of the trace relation: $\langle (2, 1), (5, 3), (8, 4) \rangle$. The search for a trace requires to have the "absolute" indices of the symbols in the strings. To do this, the strings x and y and their sub-strings are identified by the index of their ends (respectively ix, sx, iy and sy below).

Having a trace between two strings makes it easy to obtain the longest common subsequence, as well as the corresponding alignment, the edit trace (i.e. the optimal list of editing operations allowing the transformation of the first string into the second one), the cost of the transformation or even the distance between the two strings (see problem 139, page 674).

The objective of this question is to adapt Hirschberg's algorithm in order to calculate a trace between two strings. The focus is first put on the inductive part of the algorithm and more particularly on the gathering step. This time, it is no longer a matter of simply concatenating the optimal sequences of the left and right parts, but—if the situation requires it—to take into consideration the coordinates of a symbol common to x and y. Unlike the version developed in question 5, we must be able to compare the symbol which is in the middle of x with the symbol of y located on the line which separates y in two parts. The index q separator of y being supposed to be available, three situations are to be singled out (see figure 8.7).

The first case (see part (a) of figure 8.7) is the one where the separating index q is equal to iy − 1. In this case, the trace is to be found only on the rectangle going from the corner (mid +1, iy) to the corner (sx, sy) (the dark grey rectangle in the figure). This case is found in figure 8.6 if we choose q = 0 as the separator index. The second case (see part (b) of figure 8.7) is where x[mid] = y[q]. The pair (mid, q) must be inserted into the trace, and the search must continue on the two grey rectangles. This case is found in figure 8.6, page 455, if we choose q = 5. Last, the third case (see part (c) of figure 8.7) is where x[mid] ≠ y[q]. The symbol x[mid] is not aligned with any element of the string y[ix Uptoq]: we can eliminate

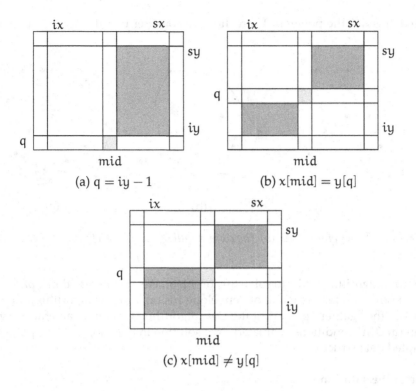

(a) q = iy − 1   (b) x[mid] = y[q]

(c) x[mid] ≠ y[q]

Fig. 8.7 – Calculation of the trace—the three cases to be considered.

the column mid to continue the search on the two grey rectangles. In figure 8.6, this case corresponds either to q = 1, or to q = 2.

Question 6.   Construct the procedure *HirschTrace* (to simplify, we can get rid of the con-   107 - Q 6
straints related to spatial complexity). Give the division model that applies, as well as the code of the procedure. To do this, we assume available the type Trace, a list of pairs of natural numbers, with the concatenation operator · and the constructor "ct(a, b)" (respectively *tv*) which creates a trace consisting of the pair (a, b) (respectively an empty trace).

The solution is on page 576.

Problem 108. The convex hull

> *The interest of this problem lies mainly in the following three points: (i) the choice of the data structure to represent a convex hull, which strongly conditions the efficiency of the result, (ii) the gathering phase which is implemented by a non-trivial iteration, and (iii) the strengthening of the induction hypothesis (subject of the fourth question), which simplifies the first solution and makes it more efficient.*

The objective of this problem is to search for the convex hull (or convex envelope or convex closure) of a finite non-empty set E of n points in a plane. The convex hull of E is a convex polygon P such that all the vertices of P belong to E and all other points of E are located "inside" the polygon. Thereafter, we consider that three points of E are never aligned[8].

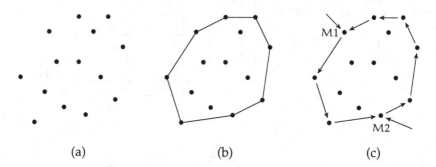

Fig. 8.8 – (a) The set of points E, *(b) The convex hull of* E, *and (c) The directed envelope of* E.

Numerous algorithms exist to solve this problem. We are interested in a particular DaC algorithm known under the name of "envelope fusion". In this algorithm, the main difficulty lies in the "gathering" part of the DaC algorithm. Obtaining an efficient gathering algorithm (in $O(n)$ conditions evaluated for a solution in $O(n \cdot \log_2(n))$) requires having a well-adapted data structure.

Principle of the solution

It is supposed (base case) that it is known to directly find the convex hull of a set containing one or two points. In the inductive case, the set of points is divided into two subsets (left and right) having approximately the same cardinality. All the points of the left (respectively right) subset have abscissas strictly lower (respectively strictly higher) than all the points of the right (respectively left) subset. To reach an efficient solution, this constraint requires that the set E be refined by an array T sorted on the increasing x-coordinates. It also has an impact on the separation algorithm, since two points of the same abscissa must belong to the same subset[9].

If, according to the induction hypothesis, it is known how to calculate the convex envelope of the left and right subsets, it remains—gathering phase—to find the two segments tangent to each of the two envelopes in order to merge the whole in a single envelope (see figure 8.9, page 459).

Definitions, notations, data structure and properties

Several notions necessary for understanding and implementing the solution are now presented. Instead of considering a convex hull P as a set of segments, P is represented as a *succession* of *vectors*, which endows P with an orientation. In the remainder, direct (i.e. according to the trigonometric direction) orientation is chosen, as in part (c) of figure 8.8, page 458.

As such, a convex hull is of little interest without (at least) one vertex through which to access it.

---

[8]Otherwise, it would be sufficient (so to speak) to keep only the two most distant points to obtain the desired envelope.

[9]It is the reason why the base case must consider the case of a set of *two* points. Indeed, otherwise, one could not exclude that cutting a set of two points gives on the one hand the empty set and on the other hand the initial set itself.

Definition and notation 1 (Keyed convex hull):
Let P be a directed convex hull. If M is a vertex of this envelope, $\widehat{M}$ denotes the pair (P, M) and M is the (input) key of P.

This definition presupposes that a vertex belongs to only one envelope, which happens to always be the case thereafter. Part (c) of figure 8.8, page 458, shows $\widehat{M1}$ and $\widehat{M2}$, two keyed envelopes of the same convex hull. In the following, the context makes it possible to determine whether it is a question of a simple envelope or of a key envelope.

The data structure

The refinement of the data structure "envelope" can be made using a double-linked list, for example. The identifier ConvEnv denotes all possible keyed convex hulls. The following operations are assumed to be defined on this data structure:

- **function** *CreateConvEnv1*(M) **result** ConvEnv: this function creates the envelope $\widehat{M}$ from a set made up of a single point M.

- **function** *CreateConvEnv2*(M1, M2) **result** ConvEnv: this function creates the envelope $\widehat{M1}$ from a set made up of the only two points M1 and M2.

- **function** *Succ*($\widehat{M}$) **result** point: this function returns the point that follows M in the envelope $\widehat{M}$.

- **function** *Pred*($\widehat{M}$) **result** point: this function returns the point that precedes M in the envelope $\widehat{M}$.

- **function** *Merge*(LR$_N$, LR$_S$) **result** ConvEnv: if LR$_N$ = $(\widehat{L_N}, \widehat{R_N})$ and LR$_S$ = $(\widehat{L_S}, \widehat{R_S})$, this function merges the two envelopes in order to form a third one, according to the principle illustrated by figure 8.9, page 459.

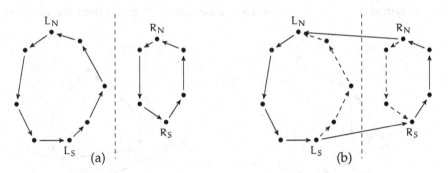

Fig. 8.9 – (a) Before merging and (b) After merging.

This operation requires as preconditions that (i) the two envelopes are located on either side of a vertical line, (ii) the line support of the vector $\overrightarrow{R_N L_N}$ (respectively $\overrightarrow{L_S R_S}$) is a lower (respectively upper) tangent[10] common to the two envelopes.

---

[10]The tangent of a convex polygone is a line which has one and only one point in common with the area delimited by the polygon.

Moreover, the set point of points of the plane plan is assumed to be defined by the identifier point which is such that point = {x, y | x ∈ ℝ **and** y ∈ ℝ}.

Definition 12 (Determinant of two vectors):

Let $\vec{v} = \begin{pmatrix} x \\ y \end{pmatrix}$ and $\vec{v'} = \begin{pmatrix} x' \\ y' \end{pmatrix}$ be two vectors of the directed plane. The determinant of $\vec{v}$ and $\vec{v'}$, denoted by $\det(\vec{v}, \vec{v'})$ is defined by the scalar $x \cdot y' - x' \cdot y$. If this determinant is positive, the angle made by the two vectors has the same orientation as the plane, if it is zero, the two vectors are co-linear, if it is negative, the orientation of the angle is the opposite of that of the plane.

Figure 8.10 illustrates this definition.

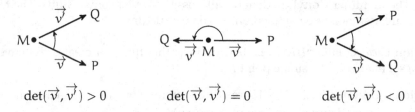

$$\det(\vec{v}, \vec{v'}) > 0 \qquad \det(\vec{v}, \vec{v'}) = 0 \qquad \det(\vec{v}, \vec{v'}) < 0$$

Fig. 8.10 – Sign of the determinant of two vectors.

The notion of determinant makes it possible to know whether a point is or not located outside a convex polygon. More interestingly in the scope of this problem, while avoiding explicit calculations of angles (expensive and subject to rounding errors), it also allows to decide whether from an external point a given side of a convex envelope is "seen" or not. The side PQ of an envelope is visible from the point M if $\det(\overrightarrow{MP}, \overrightarrow{MQ}) < 0$, and not visible if $\det(\overrightarrow{MP}, \overrightarrow{MQ}) > 0$. This is illustrated in figure 8.11. The case $\det(\overrightarrow{MP}, \overrightarrow{MQ}) = 0$ can only occur if the three points are aligned, which by hypothesis is excluded here, or if at least two of them are confused. The latter case is to be taken into account in the function *TangentSup* of question 2.

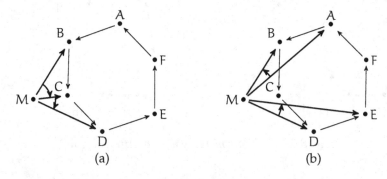

(a)   (b)

Fig. 8.11 – Visibility. Diagram (a): $\overrightarrow{BC}$ and $\overrightarrow{CD}$ are visible from M. $\det(\overrightarrow{MB}, \overrightarrow{MC}) < 0$ and $\det(\overrightarrow{MC}, \overrightarrow{MD}) < 0$; Diagram (b): $\overrightarrow{AB}$ and $\overrightarrow{DE}$ are not visible from M. $\det(\overrightarrow{MA}, \overrightarrow{MB}) > 0$ and $\det(\overrightarrow{MD}, \overrightarrow{ME}) > 0$.

Definition 13 (Bridge between two envelopes):
Let L and R be two envelopes located on either side of a vertical line. A bridge between L and R is a segment joining a vertex of L and a vertex of R, all points of which (except the ends) are outside L and R.

Part (a) of figure 8.12 lists the ten bridges existing between the two envelopes. A segment such as BI is not a bridge: it is partly located inside the left envelope. In general, three bridges (in bold) can be singled out: DI, which joins the rightmost point of the left envelope and the leftmost point of the right envelope. It is the only one that can be identified directly from the knowledge of the envelopes. AG (respectively CJ) is a particular bridge— the upper tangent (respectively the lower tangent) common to the two envelopes—which is characterized by the fact that no point of E is *above* (respectively *below*) the support line of the segment. These tangents are of great importance: they are the ones that must be taken into account in order to obtain a true envelope (see figure 8.9, page 459) during the merging phase.

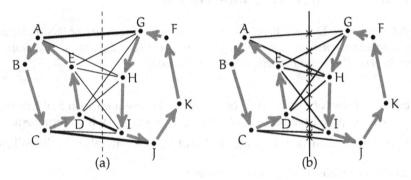

Fig. 8.12 – (a) The set of bridges between $\widehat{D}$ and $\widehat{I}$ and (b) Intersection between a vertical line and the bridges.

Part (b) of figure 8.12 emphasizes the points of intersection between a separating vertical line and the different bridges. These points—in finite number—are useful later on to prove the termination of the merging algorithm.

Question 1. Searching for the upper and lower tangents is done from the only directly $\quad$ 108 - Q 1
identifiable bridge, the one that links the rightmost vertex of the left envelope and the leftmost vertex of the right envelope, progressing from bridge to bridge. The coordinates of these two vertices are known following the cut. But to progress, it is also necessary to have access to the successor and predecessor nodes. It is therefore necessary to know their situations *within the envelopes*. The operation "**function** *Search*$(\widehat{e}, v)$ **result** ConvEnv" takes into account the envelope $\widehat{e}$ (envelope designated by the point e), the point of abscissa v, and delivers the same envelope but this time designated by v. Build this function on the basis of a sequential search. What can be said about its complexity in number of conditions evaluated?

Question 2. Now, we intend to build an iterative version of the operation "**function** $\quad$ 108 - Q 2
UpperTangent$(\widehat{l}, \widehat{r}, i)$ **result** ConvEnv × ConvEnv" which, from two envelopes $\widehat{l}$ and $\widehat{r}$ (separated vertically) and from the index i designating the leftmost point of $\widehat{r}$ in T, delivers the pair $(\widehat{L}, \widehat{R})$ such that the segment LR is the upper tangent of $\widehat{l}$ and $\widehat{r}$. What can be said about the complexity of this function in terms of the number of conditions evaluated?

Question 3.   The operation "**function** $Cut(lb, ub)$**result** $\mathbb{N}_1$" is assumed to be available such that if m is the delivered result, $T[lb \mathinner{.\,.} m - 1]$ and $T[m \mathinner{.\,.} ub]$ are the two sets of points from which the left and right envelope searches are made. Which division model applies? Provide the code of the operation "**function** $ConvexEnvelope(lb, ub)$ **result** $ConvEnv$", which delivers the convex envelope of the points of $T[lb \mathinner{.\,.} ub]$ using the DaC method described above. What can be said about the complexity of this solution, in terms of the conditions evaluated (depending on n)?

Question 4.   Although not affecting the complexity, calls to the function *Search* can prove to be penalizing. Describe the principle of a solution in which this function becomes unnecessary.

The solution is on page 583.

Problem 109.   The stuttering sub-sequence

> *Two solutions of type DaC are developed here. The main originality of this problem lies in the second solution, where the splitting step is more ingenious than the simple division by 2 practiced in general. The return benefit is better efficiency.*

Let Σ be an alphabet of cardinality s ($s \geqslant 1$). Let x be a sequence on Σ of length n ($n \geqslant s$) and let $y = a_1 \dots a_m$ be a sequence on Σ of length m ($m \geqslant s$). If a^i represents the string $\underbrace{a \dots a}_{i \text{ times}}$, $\overset{i}{y}$ denotes the sequence $a_1^i \dots a_m^i$. Without loss of generality, in the following, it is assumed that x as well as y use *all* the symbols of Σ.

We are looking for the largest value of i, denoted by $Maxi(x, y)$ for which $\overset{i}{y}$ is a sub-sequence of x. i is also called *stuttering degree* of y in x. Let us recall that the symbols of a sub-sequence are not necessarily contiguous in the sequence.

For example, with $\Sigma = \{a, b, c\}$, $y = abc$ and $x = cbbabaacbbabbcbbacccbac$, the stuttering degree $Maxi(x, y)$ is equal to 4 ($\overset{4}{y} = aaaabbbbcccc$), since $x = cbbabaacbbabbcbbacccbac$ and $\overset{5}{y}$ is not a sub-sequence of x.

Question 1.   Design an iterative version of the operation "**function**$Scan(x, y, i)$ **result** $\mathbb{B}$" which returns **true** if and only if $\overset{i}{y}$ is a sub-sequence of x. Prove that by choosing the evaluation of conditions as the elementary operation, its asymptotic complexity is in $\mathcal{O}(n + m)$.

Question 2.   Prove that $Maxi(x, y) \in 0 \mathinner{.\,.} \lfloor \frac{n}{m} \rfloor$.

Question 3.   We now have a finite interval over which $Maxi(x, y)$ takes its value and different techniques can be applied to determine this value among which sequential search. Binary search is also appealing to solving this problem and this is the solution considered later on in this question. Describe the DaC reasoning for constructing the function $Maxi0(x, y, lb, ub)$ that delivers the value of $Maxi(x, y)$ over the interval $lb \mathinner{.\,.} ub$ ($lb \mathinner{.\,.} ub \subseteq 0 \mathinner{.\,.} \lfloor \frac{n}{m} \rfloor$). Which division model applies? What is, in number of conditions evaluated, the order of growth of the complexity of this solution? The calculations can be limited to the case where $\lfloor \frac{n}{m} \rfloor$ is a power of 2.

Applied differently, would the DaC paradigm improve the previous result? Above, DaC has been applied over an interval of integers. Is there an alternative to this choice? One can think of applying DaC on the sequence x itself, but—the reader will be able to verify this—cutting x down the middle is a futile attempt in the search for better complexity.

There is another problem, dealt with in the next problem (the computation of the fast discrete Fourier transform, see problem 110, page 464), in which splitting is done not by cutting through the middle but by breaking down the elements according to the parity of their indices. The principle applied here is somehow similar to this latter, elements of x being broken down according to the parity of the indices *of each element of the alphabet* Σ. The following example illustrates this principle (symbols are indexed in order to ease readibility):

$$x = c_1 b_1 b_2 a_1 b_3 a_2 a_3 c_2 b_4 b_5 a_4 b_6 b_7 c_3 b_8 b_9 a_5 c_4 c_5 c_6 b_{10} a_6 c_7$$
$$Odd(x) = c_1 b_1 a_1 b_3 a_3 b_5 b_7 c_3 b_9 a_5 c_5 c_7$$
$$Even(x) = b_2 a_2 c_2 b_4 a_4 b_6 b_8 c_4 c_6 b_{10} a_6$$

By first proving that:

$$Maxi(x,y) \in \left(\begin{array}{c} Maxi(Odd(x),y) + Maxi(Even(x),y) - 1 \\ .. \\ Maxi(Odd(x),y) + Maxi(Even(x),y) + 1 \end{array} \right)$$

it would be possible to develop a DaC solution. However, this would have the disadvantage of requiring a double recursive call (on $Odd(x)$ and on $Even(x)$) which, according to the corollary of the master theorem and its particular case 8.4, page 423, would lead to a solution in $n \cdot \log_2(n)$, comparable to the previous binary solution from a complexity point of view. In the following, avoiding this double recursive call is the main goal.

Question 4. Explain the principle of the algorithm of the function $Odd(x)$ and prove that its complexity is in $\Theta(n)$ conditions evaluated. 109 - Q 4

Question 5. We want to prove that $Maxi(x,y)$ varies over a certain interval and that all the values of this interval can be reached. 109 - Q 5
Through an example, we first present the notion of segmentation $S(x,y)$ of x compared to y and that of segmentation of $Odd(x)$ induced by $S(x,y)$ compared to y. Let $X = Maxi(x,y)$ and $I = Maxi(Odd(x),y)$. For $x = a_1 b_1 a_2 a_3 a_4 a_5 a_6 b_2 c_1 c_2 a_7 c_3 c_4 c_5 c_6 c_7$ and $y = bac$, $S(x,y)$ is made up of segments since y involves three symbols. We have for example:

$$S(x,y) = \sigma_1, \sigma_2, \sigma_3$$

$$x = \| \overbrace{a_1 b_1 a_2 a_3 a_4 a_5 a_6 b_2}^{\sigma_1} \| \overbrace{c_1 c_2 a_7}^{\sigma_2} \| \overbrace{c_3 c_4 c_5 c_6 c_7}^{\sigma_3} \|$$
$$\underbrace{}_{2b} \quad \underbrace{}_{1a} \quad \underbrace{}_{5c}$$

$$y' = bbaccccc, \quad X = \min(\{2,1,5\})$$

y' is the sub-sequence of x appearing in bold. The segmentation is not unique and taking the example above, we also have:

$$S(x,y) = \sigma_1, \sigma_2, \sigma_3$$

$$x = \| \overbrace{a_1 \boldsymbol{b_1}}^{\sigma_1} \| \overbrace{a_2 a_3 a_4 a_5 a_6 \boldsymbol{b_2} c_1 c_2 \boldsymbol{a_7}}^{\sigma_2} \| \overbrace{\boldsymbol{c_3} \boldsymbol{c_4} \boldsymbol{c_5} \boldsymbol{c_6} \boldsymbol{c_7}}^{\sigma_3} \|$$

$$\underset{1b}{} \qquad \underset{6a}{} \qquad \underset{5c}{}$$

$$y' = \boldsymbol{baaaaaaccccc}, \quad X = \min(\{1, 6, 5\})$$

However, in both cases $X = 1$. Regarding the induced segmentation (by $S(x,y)$) of $Odd(x)$ with respect to y, the first example gives:

$$x = \| \overbrace{a_1 \boldsymbol{b_1} a_2 a_3 a_4 a_5 a_6 \boldsymbol{b_2}}^{\sigma_1} \| \overbrace{c_1 c_2 \boldsymbol{a_7}}^{\sigma_2} \| \overbrace{\boldsymbol{c_3} \boldsymbol{c_4} \boldsymbol{c_5} \boldsymbol{c_6} \boldsymbol{c_7}}^{\sigma_3} \|$$

$$S(Odd(x), y) = \sigma_1', \sigma_2', \sigma_3'$$

$$Odd(x) = \| \overbrace{a_1 \boldsymbol{b_1} a_3 a_5}^{\sigma_1'} \| \overbrace{c_1 \boldsymbol{a_7}}^{\sigma_2'} \| \overbrace{\boldsymbol{c_3} \boldsymbol{c_5} \boldsymbol{c_7}}^{\sigma_3'} \|$$

Of course, the relationship which binds X and I does not depend on the chosen segmentations. Prove that, in the case where X is even, $2I = X$, and that in the case where X is odd, we have either $2I + 1 = X$, or $2I - 1 = X$. Deduce that

$$Maxi(x, y) \in (2 \cdot Maxi(Odd(x), y) - 1) \,..\, (2 \cdot Maxi(Odd(x), y) + 1)$$

and that the three values of the interval can be taken by $Maxi(x, y)$.

109 - Q 6   **Question 6.**   According to the DaC principle, construct the operation "**function** *Maxi1*(x, y) **result** $\mathbb{N}$" based on the two previous questions. Which division model applies? Write the code of the operation *Maxi1*. Prove that the algorithm terminates. What can be said about its complexity? Compare the two DaC solutions from a complexity perspective.

The solution is on page 588.

Problem 110.   The Fast Fourier Transform

Many superlatives are associated to this fast Fourier transform algorithm. Useful, it is undoubtedly at the highest point. To be convinced, it suffices to list a few of its applications: speech recognition, filtering, spectrum analysis, product of polynomials, data compression, etc. The algorithm is certainly efficient, so much so that historically it is necessary to look for one of the keys to the preeminence of computers over analog computers and, indirectly, of the digital revolution that we know. In short, a remarkable algorithm, an excellent problem. Let us end with a quote from C. Villani (Medal Fields 2010, in [35], p. 35): "the influence of Joseph Fourier is now much more important than that of Hugo himself; his "great mathematical poem" (as Lord Kelvin said), taught in all countries of the world, is used every day by billions of humans who do not even realize it."

Definition of the discrete Fourier transform (DFT)

A DFT is a linear transform from $\mathbb{C}^n$ into $\mathbb{C}^n$ defined as follows. Let x be a vector of complex numbers defined on the interval $0 .. n - 1$. For any integer k, $k \in 0 .. n - 1$, the value $X[k]$ of the DFT from the vector x is defined as:

$$X[k] \;=\; \sum_{j=0}^{n-1} x[j] \cdot e^{-\frac{2\pi \cdot i}{n} \cdot j \cdot k} \tag{8.13}$$

where e is the base of the natural logarithm and i the complex number such that $i^2 = -1$.

Question 1.   From this definition, construct a "naïve" algorithm that calculates the discrete Fourier transform X of a vector x of n complex numbers. What is its complexity in number of exponentiations and in number of multiplications? | 110 - Q 1

Properties of the nth roots of unity, the basics

The focus is now on improving the efficiency of the previous solution through a DaC approach. To do so, we will exploit the properties of the complex n^{th} roots of unity. In the following, by hypothesis, n is always a power of 2. A complex root n^{th} root of unity is a complex number w_n such that $w_n^n = 1$. There are n n^{th} roots of unity which are, for $k \in 0 .. n - 1$: $e^{-\frac{2\pi \cdot i}{n} \cdot k}$. The particular root obtained for $k = 1$, $e^{-\frac{2\pi \cdot i}{n}}$ is called the principal root (or n-principal root if it is necessary to specify). It is denoted by W_n. The n roots of the unit are powers of W_n: $W_n^0, W_n^1, W_n^2, \ldots, W_n^{n-1}$.

Figure 8.13 represents n^{th} roots of unity for $n = 8$ in the complex plane.

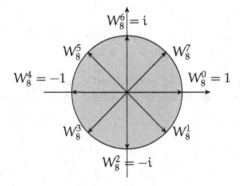

Fig. 8.13 – The nth roots of unity in the complex plane, for $n = 8$.

These roots are located at equidistant positions on the complex unity cercle.

Properties

(not proven here)

1. For any even value $n > 0$, the power $(n/2)^{\text{th}}$ of any n^{th} root of unity is equal to -1:

$$w_n^{\frac{n}{2}} = -1 \quad (n > 0 \text{ even}). \tag{8.14}$$

2. For any even value $n > 0$ and any $k \geqslant 0$, the square of the power W_n^k of the n-principal root is equal to the power $W_{\frac{n}{2}}^k$ of the $(n/2)$-principal root:

$$(W_n^k)^2 = W_{\frac{n}{2}}^k \quad \text{(for } n > 0 \text{ even)}. \tag{8.15}$$

Fast Fourier transform (FFT)

The fast Fourier transform (FFT) accelerates the naïve computing of the DFT by using the properties of the squares of the roots of the unit. The most direct application of the DaC principle would consist in cutting the vector x in its middle:

$$X[k]$$
$$=$$
$$\sum_{j=0}^{n-1} x[j] \cdot W_n^{j \cdot k}$$
formula 8.13 and definition of W_n

$$=$$
$$\sum_{j=0}^{\frac{n}{2}-1} x[j] \cdot W_n^{j \cdot k} + \sum_{j=\frac{n}{2}}^{n-1} x[j] \cdot W_n^{j \cdot k}.$$
cutting x in its middle

However, this approach leads to a dead end in terms of improving complexity (the reader is invited to verify this). We must look for another cut-off strategy. One solution consists in placing on one side the elements of even indices of x and on the other those of odd indices (used as a subscript, i means *odd* and should not be confused with the imaginary unit also noted i). To do this, we let:

$$x_e = \begin{bmatrix} x[0], & x[2], & \cdots, & x[2p], & \cdots, & x[n-2] \end{bmatrix}, \tag{8.16}$$
$$x_o = \begin{bmatrix} x[1], & x[3], & \cdots, & x[2p+1], & \cdots, & x[n-1] \end{bmatrix}. \tag{8.17}$$

For $k \in 0 .. n/2 - 1$, we then have $x_e[k] = x[2k]$ and $x_o[k] = x[2k+1]$. The Fourier transform X_e of x_e (for $k \in 0 .. n/2 - 1$) gives rise to the following calculation:

$$X_e[k]$$
$$=$$
$$\sum_{j=0}^{\frac{n}{2}-1} x_e[j] \cdot e^{-\frac{2\pi i}{\frac{n}{2}} \cdot j \cdot k}$$
formula 8.13

$$=$$
$$\sum_{j=0}^{\frac{n}{2}-1} x_e[j] \cdot W_{\frac{n}{2}}^{j \cdot k}.$$
definition of W_n $(W_n = e^{-\frac{2\pi i}{n}})$ and substitution
$$\tag{8.18}$$

For odd indexes and still for $k \in 0 .. n/2 - 1$, there is a similar formula:

$$X_o[k] = \sum_{j=0}^{\frac{n}{2}-1} x_o[j] \cdot W_{\frac{n}{2}}^{j \cdot k}. \tag{8.19}$$

The definition of Fourier transform for $k \in 0 .. n - 1$ gives rise to the following development:

$$X[k]$$

$$=$$ formula 8.13

$$\sum_{j=0}^{n-1} x[j] \cdot e^{-\frac{2\pi i}{n} \cdot j \cdot k}$$

$$=$$ definition of W_n $(W_n = e^{-\frac{2\pi i}{n}})$

$$\sum_{j=0}^{n-1} x[j] \cdot W_n^{j \cdot k}$$

$$=$$ separation between even and odd indexes

$$\sum_{j=0}^{\frac{n}{2}-1} x[2j] \cdot W_n^{2j \cdot k} + \sum_{j=0}^{\frac{n}{2}-1} x[2j+1] \cdot W_n^{(2j+1) \cdot k}$$

$$=$$ formulas 8.16 and 8.17

$$\sum_{j=0}^{\frac{n}{2}-1} x_e[j] \cdot W_n^{2j \cdot k} + \sum_{j=0}^{\frac{n}{2}-1} x_o[j] \cdot W_n^{(2j+1) \cdot k}$$

$$=$$ calculations on the indexes of W_n and factorization

$$\sum_{j=0}^{\frac{n}{2}-1} x_e[j] \cdot (W_n^{j \cdot k})^2 + W_n^k \cdot \sum_{j=0}^{\frac{n}{2}-1} x_o[j] \cdot (W_n^{j \cdot k})^2$$

$$=$$ property 8.15

$$\sum_{j=0}^{\frac{n}{2}-1} x_e[j] \cdot W_{\frac{n}{2}}^{j \cdot k} + W_n^k \cdot \sum_{j=0}^{\frac{n}{2}-1} x_o[j] \cdot W_{\frac{n}{2}}^{j \cdot k}. \tag{8.20}$$

Formula 8.20 is defined for $k \in 0 .. n-1$. It holds *a fortiori* for $k \in 0 .. n/2 - 1$. We can then continue the development by limiting ourselves to this last interval and using formulas 8.18 and 8.19, page 466:

$$\sum_{j=0}^{\frac{n}{2}-1} x_e[j] \cdot W_{\frac{n}{2}}^{j \cdot k} + W_n^k \cdot \sum_{j=0}^{\frac{n}{2}-1} x_o[j] \cdot W_{\frac{n}{2}}^{j \cdot k}$$

$$=$$ formulas 8.18 and 8.19, page 466, for $k \in 0 .. \frac{n}{2} - 1$

$$X_e[k] + W_n^k \cdot X_o[k],$$

which defines the first $n/2$ elements of the vector X in a DaC fashion. We must now complete the calculation on the interval $n/2 .. n-1$ in order to obtain the last $n/2$ elements of X in an analogous form. Starting again from formula 8.20 for $k \in 0 .. n/2 - 1$ we have:

$$X\left[k + \frac{n}{2}\right]$$

$$=$$ formula 8.20 for the substitution $k \leftarrow k + \frac{n}{2}$

$$\sum_{j=0}^{\frac{n}{2}-1} x_e[j] \cdot W_n^{2(k+\frac{n}{2}) \cdot j} + W_n^{k+\frac{n}{2}} \cdot \sum_{j=0}^{\frac{n}{2}-1} x_o[j] \cdot W_n^{2(k+\frac{n}{2}) \cdot j}$$

$$=$$ formula 8.14: $W_n^{k+\frac{n}{2}} = W_n^k \cdot W_n^{\frac{n}{2}} = -W_n^k$

$$\sum_{j=0}^{\frac{n}{2}-1} x_e[j] \cdot W_n^{2(k+\frac{n}{2}) \cdot j} - W_n^k \cdot \sum_{j=0}^{\frac{n}{2}-1} x_o[j] \cdot W_n^{2(k+\frac{n}{2}) \cdot j}$$

$$=$$ definition of W_n^n : $W_n^{2(k+\frac{n}{2}) \cdot j} = (W_n^n)^j \cdot W_n^{2k \cdot j} = 1 \cdot W_n^{2k \cdot j} = (W_n^{k \cdot j})^2$

$$\sum_{j=0}^{\frac{n}{2}-1} x_e[j] \cdot (W_n^{k \cdot j})^2 - W_n^k \cdot \sum_{j=0}^{\frac{n}{2}-1} x_o[j] \cdot (W_n^{k \cdot j})^2$$

$$=$$ formula 8.15

$$\sum_{j=0}^{\frac{n}{2}-1} x_e[j] \cdot W_{\frac{n}{2}}^{k \cdot j} - W_n^k \cdot \sum_{j=0}^{\frac{n}{2}-1} x_o[j] \cdot W_{\frac{n}{2}}^{k \cdot j}$$

$$=$$ formulas 8.18 and 8.19, page 466, for $k \in 0 .. \dfrac{n}{2} - 1$

$$X_p[k] - W_n^k \cdot X_i[k].$$

To summarize, it has been shown that, in the (induction) hypothesis where it is known how to compute $X_p[k]$ and $X_i[k]$ from the two half-vectors x_p and x_i, one knows how to compose the two partial results to obtain the Fourier transform X of x, by applying the two formulas:

$$
\begin{aligned}
X[k] &= X_e[k] + W_n^k \cdot X_o[k] \\
X\left[k + \frac{n}{2}\right] &= X_e[k] - W_n^k \cdot X_o[k]
\end{aligned}
$$

and this for $k \in 0 .. n/2 - 1$.

110 - Q 2   **Question 2.**   The function $Even(m, A)$ (respectively $Odd(m, A)$) which, for a vector A of even length m, delivers the sub-vector A containing the even (respectively odd) index elements, is assumed to be available. Deduce the function $DFT(n, x)$ allowing the calculation of the DFT X of a vector x, $x \in (0 .. n - 1) \rightarrow \mathbb{C}$, for n power of 2. Assuming that the elementary operations are multiplication (of numbers) and exponentiation, what is the complexity of this operation? Conclusion?

The solution is on page 595.

Problem 111. Multiplying polynomials

> *This problem shows that the application of the DaC principle does not systematically lead to a more efficient solution than an iterative one. But its main interest lies in a remarkable application of the Fast Fourier transform (see problem 110, page 464).*

We want to multiply two polynomials on $\mathbb{Z}$: $A(x) = a_{n-1} \cdot x^{n-1} + a_{n-2} \cdot x^{n-1} + \cdots + a_1 \cdot x + a_0$ and $B(x) = b_{m-1} \cdot x^{m-1} + b_{m-2} \cdot x^{m-2} + \cdots + b_1 \cdot x + b_0$. For example, using the traditional presentation for the multiplication of integers, we have:

		$2x^4$	$-$	$3x^3$	$+$	$4x$	$+$	5
$\times$						$2x^2$	$+$	3
		$6x^4$	$-$	$9x^3$	$+$ $0x^2$ $+$	$12x$	$+$	15
$+$	$4x^6$ $-$ $6x^5$ $+$ $0x^4$ $+$ $8x^3$			$+$ $10x^2$				
	$4x^6$ $-$ $6x^5$ $+$ $6x^4$ $-$ x^3			$+$ $10x^2$	$+$	$12x$	$+$	15

More generally, if $A(x)$ is defined as $\sum_{k=0}^{n-1} a_k \cdot x^k$ and $B(x)$ as $\sum_{k=0}^{m-1} b_k \cdot x^k$, the polynomial $C(x)$, product of $A(x)$ and $B(x)$, is defined as:

$$C(x) = \sum_{k=0}^{m+n-2} c_k \cdot x^k \quad \text{with} \quad c_k = \sum_{\substack{i+j=k \\ i\in 0..n-1 \\ j\in 0..m-1}} a_i \cdot b_j. \tag{8.21}$$

A naïve solution to calculate the coefficients c_k of $C(x)$ is to use the above quantified formulas. If the elementary operation chosen to evaluate complexity is the multiplication of coefficients a_i's and b_j's, the cost of this method is in $\Theta(n \cdot m)$. Our goal is to improve this situation using the DaC technique. In the following, the *size* of a polynomial is the number of its monomials.

Question 1.   In this question, it is assumed on the one hand that all the coefficients are different from 0 and on the other hand that $n = m = 2^k$ ($k \geqslant 0$). How is the DaC principle applied to achieve the calculation of $C(x)$? What are the criteria to retain to obtain a "good" representation of a polynomial? Deduce the division model that applies. Provide the code in the form of the operation "**function** *MultPolyn*(A, B) **result** polynom". What is the complexity of this solution in terms of multiplications (of numbers)? Conclusion?   111 - Q 1

Question 2.   111 - Q 2
From the previous solution, keeping the same hypotheses and using the identity:

$$a \cdot d + b \cdot c = (a+b)(c+d) - (a \cdot c) - (b \cdot d),$$

design a variant which diminishes complexity.

Question 3.   What to do when some coefficients are zero and/or when n and m are any natural numbers? Is the efficiency of the previous variant maintained?   111 - Q 3

Question 4.   (To tackle this question, it is necessary to have first answered problem 110, page 464, on the Fourier transform.) A more efficient solution exists which is a direct application of the Fourier transform. It is based on a classic scientific paradigm consisting in performing a change of representation space in order to simplify the processing[11]. Its principle relies on the existence of two types of representation for polynomials—the traditional representation by coefficients (used above) and the representation by samples—and to perform the product in the most efficient representation (here the representation by samples), preceded and followed by the necessary conversions. The representation by coefficients considers the vector of coefficients. The representation by samples consists, for a polynomial $P(x)$ of degree less than or equal to $(n-1)$, in evaluating $P(x)$ on (at least) n different abscissas x_i.   111 - Q 4

Example

Let us consider the two polynomials $D(x) = 2x + 1$ and $E(x) = x + 2$ along with their representations by coefficients that are $[2, 1]$ for $D(x)$ and $[1, 2]$ for $E(x)$. The representation by samples first needs the choice of the n (here 2) different abscissas. Let us take $x_0 = 0$ and $x_1 = 1$. $D(x)$ is then represented by $[(0, D(0)), (1, D(1))]$, or $[(0, 1), (1, 3)]$, whereas $E(x)$ is represented by $[(0, 2), (1, 3)]$.

The advantage of this representation lies in the fact that some operations are easier, notably the product, since it is then sufficient to multiply the values taken by the polynomials over all the samples. The calculation of the product however requires that, in the case of

---

[11] A classic example is the multiplication of numbers by adding their logarithms.

representation by samples, the sampling abscissas are identical for the two polynomials to be multiplied. The product of two polynomials of degree $(n-1)$ is a polynomial of degree $(2n-2)$ and we must be aware of the fact that it is therefore necessary to have $(2n-1)$ samples for each of the two polynomials to be multiplied.

In the above example, the sampling of $D(x)$ and $E(x)$ is completed on the abscissa 2. We then have:

$$D(x) = [(0,1),(1,3),(2,5)] \text{ and } E(x) = [(0,2),(1,3),(2,4)]$$

The result $R(x) = D(x) \cdot E(x)$ is obtained by multiplying the respective ordinates:

$$R(x) = [(0,1\cdot 2),(1,3\cdot 3),(2,5\cdot 4)].$$

We are therefore faced with the following problem. Given two polynomials represented by their coefficients, the best solution known to obtain their product is in $\Theta(n^{\log_2(3)})$ (see for example [22]). On the other hand, with a representation by samples, the solution is in $\Theta(n)$. Is it possible to do better than $\Theta(n^{\log_2(3)})$, by performing a change of representation? If this is the case, the treatment scheme is presented in figure 8.14.

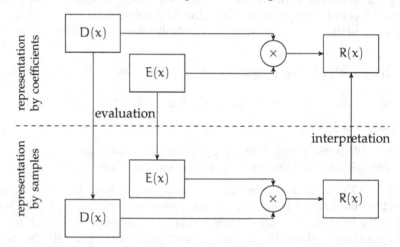

Fig. 8.14 – *Product of polynomials by a representation change. The upper part of the diagram illustrates the classic product, fully carried out by the representation by coefficients. The lower part is its counterpart for the representation by samples. The left part shows the change of representation of the two arguments (the evaluation), and the right part schematizes the change of representation of the result (the interpretation).*

From an algorithmic point of view, the conversion between the representation by coefficients and the representation by samples is easy (using Horner's scheme for example). On the other hand, it is costly (in the order of $\Theta(n^2)$). The reverse conversion between sample-based representation and coefficient-based representation, amounts to solve a linear equation system.

Thus, for the above example, to find the three coefficients a, b and c of $R(x) = a\cdot x^2 + b\cdot x + c$, the following linear system must be solved:

$$\begin{bmatrix} 0^2 & 0 & 1 \\ 1^2 & 1 & 1 \\ 2^2 & 2 & 1 \end{bmatrix} \begin{bmatrix} a \\ b \\ c \end{bmatrix} = \begin{bmatrix} 2 \\ 9 \\ 20 \end{bmatrix}$$

whose solution is $a = 2$, $b = 5$ and $c = 2$. However, here too, complexity is high (in the order of $\Theta(n^2)$). In appearance, we are facing a dead end. Yet . . .

A way out: Fourier transform

We have seen that the choice of the sampling abscissas is arbitrary. In particular, it is possible to evaluate each of the two polynomials to be multiplied on the $2n^{th}$ complex roots of unity. This is exactly what the Fourier transform does, efficiently if the DFT algorithm treated in problem 110, page 464, is used (complexity in the order of $\Theta(n \cdot \log_2(n))$). As for the reciprocal transformation, the interpolation, the inverse DFT must be used, which computes x from X. For n points, this is defined by:

$$x[k] \;=\; \frac{1}{n} \cdot \sum_{j=0}^{n-1} X[j] \cdot e^{\frac{2\pi \cdot i}{n} \cdot j \cdot k}$$

where e is the base of the natural logarithm and i is the complex number such that $i^2 = -1$. The corresponding algorithme is also in $\Theta(n \cdot \log_2(n))$.
In summary, a solution to the product of polynomials problem has been described, which is in $\Theta(n \cdot \log_2(n))$ multiplications (of numbers). It involves three main points:

1. evaluation phase: conversion of the two polynomials from the coefficient-based representation to the sample-based representation (complexity in $\Theta(n \cdot \log_2(n))$),

2. multiplication phase (complexity in $\Theta(n)$),

3. interpolation phase: conversion of the result in its representation by coefficients (complexity in $\Theta(n \cdot \log_2(n))$).

This is shown in the schema of figure 8.14, page 470. The work required in this question is to implement this solution in the form of the function *ProdPolynDFT*(n, P, Q), knowing that the two polynomials P and Q are represented by their coefficients and that they have the same size n, n being a power of 2.

The solution is on page 598.

Problem 112. Coulomb's law ○ ⁝

> *Strictly speaking, this problem involves no question of type DaC. However, solving it completely requires exploiting the answers provided to the questions of problem 111, page 468, (on the product of polynomials) and indirectly those of the problem on Fourier transform (problem 110, page 464). These two problems must therefore be tackled before beginning this one.*

In electrostatics, Coulomb's law expresses the electrical force $F_{1 \to 2}$ exerted by an electrical charge q_1 placed at a point M_1 on a charge q_2 placed at a point M_2. This law is expressed in a vectorial form by the following formula:

$$\overrightarrow{F}_{1 \to 2} = \frac{q_1 \cdot q_2}{4\pi\epsilon_0 \|\overrightarrow{r}_{12}\|^2} \cdot \overrightarrow{u},$$

where $\overrightarrow{u}$ is the unity vector of the line D, support of the two charges, and $\overrightarrow{r}_{12} = \overrightarrow{M_1 M_2}$ is the vector that connects the first material to the second one. ϵ_0 is a constant.
Let us now consider a set of n charges $\{q_1, q_2, \dots, q_n\}$ located at regular intervals (of length d) on the line D:

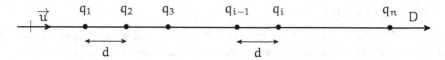

Let $\overrightarrow{F}_{\bullet i}$ the sum of the forces exerted by the $(n-1)$ other charges on the charge q_i.

112 - Q 1   **Question 1.**   Prove that the following relationship holds:

$$\|\overrightarrow{F}_{\bullet i}\| = |C \cdot q_i| \cdot \left| \sum_{j=1}^{i-1} \frac{q_j}{(i-j)^2} - \sum_{j=i+1}^{n} \frac{q_j}{(i-j)^2} \right|$$

where C is a constant.

112 - Q 2   **Question 2.**   Prove that it is possible to calculate $\|\overrightarrow{F}_{\bullet i}\|$ (for $i \in 1 .. n$) in $\Theta(n \cdot \log_2(n))$ multiplications. *Suggestion:* it may be fruitful to have a look at question 4 of problem 111, page 468, about the product of polynomials.

The solution is on page 604.

Problem 113. An efficient algorithm for multiplying integers   8 •

> *This problem addresses a concrete problem, namely the product of integers. The usual method, learned at school for positive numbers, is well known and it will be seen that its complexity, i.e. the number of elementary (single-digit) products, can be improved with a convenient DaC approach. In addition, it will be shown that the solution proposed also applies to negative integers.*

The usual way of doing a product—A "naïve" method

Thereafter, numbers in decimal representation (base 10) are considered, but all that is said applies to any base, in particular 2. For the moment, the objective is to multiply *two natural numbers* X and Y of length $n = 2^k$ digits ($k \geqslant 0$), assuming available the following elementary operations: addition of two integers, single-digit product, shift of a number with a cost proportional to the magnitude of the shift. In the remainder of this problem, numbers are assumed to have *exactly* $n = 2^k$ digits, the initial number being padded with as many leading 0's as necessary.

Example

Let us consider the multiplication of $X = 4\,279$ by $Y = 3\,621$, numbers of $n = 4$ digits ($k = 2$):

X   4279
Y   3621

```
          4279        n² = 16 single-digit products,
          8558x       (n − 1) = 3 additions of integers,
         25674xx      one 1 bit shift, one 2 bit shift, one 3 bit shift,
        12837xxx      thus a global magnitude equal to n(n − 1)/2 = 6 digits

        15294259
```

It turns out that, using this "naïve" method, the product is in $\Theta(n^2)$ regarding both single-digit products and shift magnitude, and it is in $\Theta(n)$ additions.

A first DaC approach

In the spirit of the DaC approach, the idea is to split the natural number N of length $n = 2^k$ ($k > 0$) into two halves N_l and N_r of length $n/2$. So, N is expressed as

$$N_l \cdot 10^{n/2} + N_r.$$

In this context, the product of $X = A \cdot 10^{n/2} + B$ by $Y = C \cdot 10^{n/2} + D$ is written:

$$A \cdot C \cdot 10^n + (A \cdot D + B \cdot C) \cdot 10^{n/2} + B \cdot D. \qquad (8.22)$$

Question 1. Specify the inductive schema and the division model related to formula 8.22. What is the resulting class of complexity? Conclude with respect to the naïve approach.

113 - Q 1

Interestingly enough, it can be noticed that formula 8.22 works *not only for natural numbers* but for relative numbers as well, provided that A and B (respectively C and D) the two halves of X (respectively Y) inherit the sign of X (resp Y). Consequently, from now on, the product of relative numbers is considered.

A second DaC approach—Karatsuba algorithm

The complexity of the previous DaC approach is strongly linked to the presence of four products in formula 8.22. Fortunately, it is possible to rewrite the product of X and Y (whatever their sign) as follows:

$$X \cdot Y = A \cdot C \cdot 10^n + (A \cdot C + B \cdot D - (A - B) \cdot (C - D)) \cdot 10^{n/2} + B \cdot D. \qquad (8.23)$$

The fact that subtractions appear in the expression above, does not matter since (i) relative numbers are taken into account and (ii) the length of the numbers $(A - B)$ and $(C - D)$ does not exceed $n/2$.

Question 2. Develop the tree (including the calculations carried out at each node) associated with the multiplication of $X = 4\,279$ by $Y = 3\,621$.

113 - Q 2

Question 3. Give the inductive schema and the division model related to the approach based on formula 8.23. What is the resulting class of complexity of the multiplication of $X = A \cdot 10^{n/2} + B$ by $Y = C \cdot 10^{n/2} + D$?

113 - Q 3

Question 4. Write the DaC algorithm performing the multiplication of two integers X and Y (having $n = 2^k$ digits, $k > 0$) on the basis of formula 8.23.

113 - Q 4

The solution is on page 605.

Problem 114. The egg problem (1)   8 ⋮

> *In most DaC algorithms, the division is done into s sub-problems (approximately) of the same size, where s is a number fixed in advance (typically 2). This is where the interest of this problem lies since in the second part (the rootchotomy), s depends on the size n of the problem. In the third part (the triangular method), s still depends on n and moreover the subproblems are of variable sizes. The first part of the problem is a simple application of sequential search. One possible application of the algorithms developed here is the optimization of destructive tests of samples. problem 130, page 657, considers a variant of this problem from the "dynamic programming" perspective.*

When an egg is dropped from a building window, it may or may not break: it depends on the height of the fall. We want to assess the resistance of the eggs, that is to say the height, expressed in number of floors (f), from which an egg breaks if it is dropped through the window. It is understood that all eggs are identical and that an egg always breaks if it falls from a level of rank greater than or equal to f and never if it falls from a level of rank less than f.

When an egg falls without breaking it can be picked up and reused. On the other hand, if it is broken, it can no longer be used. Floors are numbered starting at 1. Given a building of n ($n \geqslant 1$) floors and a certain number k ($k \geqslant 1$) of eggs, we want to find f. If the top floor is not high enough to break this sort of egg, the expected result is $(n+1)$. The goal is to minimize the number of releases for n and k given.

The function $Break(h)$ that drops an egg from floor h is assumed to be available. It delivers the value **true** if the egg breaks and **false** otherwise. If the egg breaks, the quota of available eggs decreases by 1, otherwise it remains unchanged. The precondition of this function is that there is still at least one egg available and that $h \in 1 .. n$.

A first technique: sequential search

114 - Q 1   **Question 1.**   We are given only one egg ($k = 1$). Specify the principle of the operation "$\text{function} Egg1(\text{lb}, \text{ub})$ **result** $\mathbb{N}_1$" which delivers the result for the portion of building between floors lb and ub and such that the call $Egg1(1, n)$ provides the expected result for the whole building. Deduce that the worst-case complexity $S_1(n)$ (for sequential with a single egg), expressed in number of drops, is equal to n.

A second technique: radixchotomy

114 - Q 2   **Question 2.**   We now take $k = 2$. This choice aims at improving complexity. If we want to make sure to conclude, we must keep one egg to end with a sequential search (in general). With the first egg, a possible strategy consists in dividing the number of floors into s segments of length e so that the number of drops associated with this division added to that of the sequential search is minimum in the worst case. Usually there is a residual segment of r floors and the three integer values s, e and r are linked by the relationship:

$$s \cdot e + r = n \text{ and } r \in 0 .. e - 1$$

which is nothing but the definition of the Euclidian division of n by e. For a given value of e, we thus have $s = \lfloor n/e \rfloor$ and $r = n - e \cdot \lfloor n/e \rfloor$. From an algorithmic point of view, the initial phase of search is a sequential search performed with a step e, while the second

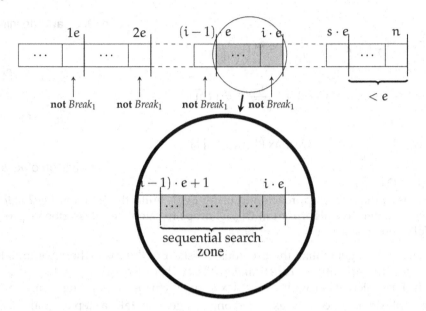

Fig. 8.15 – *The radixchotomy: the two steps of the search when two eggs are available.*

phase is a sequential search (with a step of 1) similar to that carried out in the first, as shown in figure 8.15.

The worst situation (in number of drops) is reached for $f = s \cdot e$ or $f = s \cdot e - 1$: the first phase stops at position $s \cdot e$, while the second phase explores the entire last segment up to the position $s \cdot e - 1$. The case of the search in the residual segment is never worse than the search for $f = s \cdot e - 1$ or $f = s \cdot e$; in the following calculation, we can therefore consider that n is a multiple of e. In this case, we perform at worst $R_2(n)$ (for radixchotomy with two eggs) drops. $R_2(n)$ is such that:

$$R_2(n)$$
$$= \binom{\text{s drops for the first phase (n/e drops)}}{\text{and $e - 1$ drops for the second one}}$$
$$\frac{n}{e} + (e - 1).$$

We now have to determine an appropriate value for e. Let us temporarily transform the problem the following way: let $g(e) = (e - 1) + n/e$ be a real function of a real variable. We are looking for a solution that minimizes $g(e)$. We also impose the constraint that e is of the form n^x. Therefore, the segments have the same length. So we have $g(e) = f(x) = (n^x - 1) + n/n^x$. The derivative $f'(x) = n^x \cdot \ln(n) - n^{1-x} \cdot \ln(n)$ is zero for $x = 0.5$, which is the desired result. Since an *integer* value is expected for e, $e = \lfloor \sqrt{n} \rfloor$ can be chosen. So we have[12]

$$R_2(n) = \lfloor \sqrt{n} \rfloor - 1 + \frac{n}{\lfloor \sqrt{n} \rfloor}.$$

Let us prove that $R_2(n) \in \Theta(\sqrt{(n)})$.

$$\sqrt{n} \in \Theta(\sqrt{n}) \text{ and for } n \geqslant 10 \quad \frac{1}{2} \cdot \frac{n}{\sqrt{n}} \leqslant \left\lfloor \frac{n}{\lfloor \sqrt{n} \rfloor} \right\rfloor \leqslant 2 \cdot \frac{n}{\sqrt{n}}$$

---

[12]Hence the term (a neologism?) of *radixchotomy*: the division of a data of size n is done in $\sqrt{n}$ parts, of size $\sqrt{n}$ or almost.

$\Rightarrow$ $\qquad\qquad\qquad\qquad\qquad$ $\lfloor x \rfloor \in \Theta(x)$ **and** definition of Θ

$$\lfloor \sqrt{n} \rfloor \in \Theta(\sqrt{n}) \text{ and } \lfloor \frac{n}{\lfloor \sqrt{n} \rfloor} \rfloor \in \Theta\left(\frac{n}{\sqrt{n}}\right)$$

$\Rightarrow$ $\qquad\qquad\qquad\qquad\qquad\qquad\qquad$ calculation

$$\left(\lfloor \sqrt{n} \rfloor - 1 \in \Theta(\sqrt{n})\right) \text{ and } \left(\frac{n}{\lfloor \sqrt{n} \rfloor} \in \Theta\left(\sqrt{n}\right)\right)$$

$\Rightarrow$ $\qquad\qquad\qquad\qquad\qquad\qquad\qquad$ rule of the addition

$$\lfloor \sqrt{n} \rfloor - 1 + \left\lfloor \frac{n}{\lfloor \sqrt{n} \rfloor} \right\rfloor \in \Theta\left(\max\left(\{\sqrt{n}, \sqrt{n}\}\right)\right)$$

$\Rightarrow$ $\qquad\qquad\qquad\qquad\qquad\qquad$ definition of R_2 and max

$$R_2(n) \in \Theta\left(\sqrt{n}\right).$$

On the basis of the above approach and using *Egg1*, build the function *Egg2Radix* which implements an iterative algorithm in $\mathcal{O}(\sqrt{n})$ drops to calculate f. Describe its progression for the following test set: $n = 34, f = 29$.

114 - Q 3 **Question 3.** We generalize the previous question to the case where we initially have k eggs. Build the operation "**function** *EggkRadix*(lb, ub) **result** $\mathbb{N}_1$" which is such that *EggkRadix*(1, n) calculates f with a complexity in $\mathcal{O}(\sqrt[k]{n})$ for a building of n floors. Prove that its complexity is indeed the expected one. Suggestion: take a step e equal to $\lfloor \sqrt[k]{n^{k-1}} \rfloor$.

A third technique: the triangular method

For the moment, we assume that we have two eggs ($k = 2$). In the previous method, we relied on the hypothesis of dividing the building into segments of uniform length. It is sometimes possible to obtain a better solution in the worst cases by cutting into segments of decreasing lengths. Let's take the example of a 36-floor building. If we use radixchotomy and the floor f sought is the 36th, we realize 11 drops. With a division into consecutive segments of $8, 7, 6, 5, 4, 3, 2$ and 1 floors, we will make a drop at floors $8, 15, 21, 26, 30, 33, 35$ and finally 36, for a total of eight drops. It should also be noted that, whatever the selected segment, if the desired stage is the last of the segment, it takes exactly eight releases each time. This property is due to the fact that 36 is the 8th triangular number. A triangular number t_i is a number of the form $\sum_{k=1}^{i} k$, where i is called the *seed* of the number t_i.

114 - Q 4 **Question 4.** How to proceed if the number of floors is not a triangular number? Develop the example with $n = 29$ and $f = 29$.

114 - Q 5 **Question 5.** Let $T_2(n)$ (for triangular with two eggs) be the complexity at worst in terms of drops in the context of this method. Prove by induction on n and i that $t_{i-1} < n \leqslant t_i \Rightarrow T_2(n) = i$. In other words, if t_i is the triangular number superior closest to n, then the strategy described above demands at worst exactly i drops (in the following, by abuse of language, i is called the *seed* of n). Deduce that this method is in $\mathcal{O}(\sqrt{n})$ drops.

114 - Q 6 **Question 6.** In the following, the method is generalized to any value k ($k \geqslant 2$). Implementing the corresponding DaC algorithm requires the availibility of the operation "**function** *Seed*(v) **result** $\mathbb{N}_1$" that, for a positive natural number v, delivers the seed of v. Specify the principle of a solution for this operation in $\Theta(1)$ drops.

114 - Q 7 **Question 7.** As with radixchotomy, as soon as a segment is identified, a new research phase can be started on the same principle, or, if there is only one egg, by a sequential search. The operation "**function** *TriangEggk*(lb, ub) **result** $\mathbb{N}_1$" is such that the expression *TriangEggk*(1, n) delivers the desired result. Specify the inductive development on which this operation is based. Deduce the division model that applies as well as the code of the function *TriangEgg*. Give its worst-case complexity equation, in number of drops.

Question 8. Using the programming language of your choice, experimentally compare the execution times of the two methods for $n \in 1..500$, for $f \in 1..n+1$ and for $k < \lceil \log_2(n) \rceil$ (if $k \geqslant \lceil \log_2(n) \rceil$, a binary search is possible and prevails over the methods studied above).

114 - Q 8

Remark

When $k < \lceil \log_2(n) \rceil$, an alternative solution is to start with a binary search and finish, when only one egg is left, with a sequential search. It is possible to prove that this solution is in $\mathcal{O}(k + n/2^{k-1})$ drops.

The solution is on page 607.

Problem 115. Searching for a duplicate in a bag   ⚇ ⁚

> *The main difficulty, but also the major interest of the problem, lies in the understanding and the implementation of the stage of separation into sub-problems. This is based on a heuristics which contributes to the good behavior of the algorithm in terms of complexity. The corresponding loop must be built very thoroughly. The inductive reasoning which allows the application of the DaC principle is very simple.*

Let B be a bag of n elements, $n \geqslant 2$, (this is the precondition) whose values are taken in the interval $lb..ub$ ($lb \leqslant ub$) such that $n > card(lb..ub)$. In addition, extreme values lb and ub belong to the bag. According to the principle called "pigeonholes" (see problem 2, page 33), such a bag contains at least one duplicate. The objective of the problem is the design of an algorithm that returns any of the duplicates present in B.

So, for the interval $lb..ub = 12..19$ and the bag $[\![14, 17, 12, 19, 14, 16, 12, 14, 15]\!]$ made up of nine elements, there are two duplicates (12 and 14). The result delivered can be either one or the other. A trivial solution exists. It consists in checking, for each value v of the bag B if it already exists in $B \stackrel{.}{-} [\![v]\!]$. The corresponding algorithm is in $\mathcal{O}(n^2)$.

The focus is put on a une solution of type DaC aiming at a better efficiency. Let us insist on the fact that the above precondition does not correspond to a general characterization of the presence of a duplicate in a bag. For example, the bag $[\![14, 16, 12, 12, 14]\!]$ contains duplicates without its size (5) exceeding that of the range of values appearing there (5 also).

Further on, B is refined by the array $T[1 .. n]$ valued in the interval $lb .. ub$. The array T is a global variable whose sub-arrays are identified by their bounds (ll left bound and rl right bound).

Here, the DaC principle applies to the interval $lb..ub$. The separation phase mentioned above consists in breaking down the values of T into two arrays T_l and T_r in relation to the value mid, middle of the interval $lb .. ub$, while maintaining the interval $llb .. lub$ of the values of T_l and the interval $rlb .. rub$ of the values of T_r until it is sure that one of these two arrays contains a duplicate, in which case, if its length exceeds 2, the same procedure can be reapplied to it.

Example

Let us go back to the above example. mid is equal to $\lfloor (12 + 19)/2 \rfloor = 15$. Therefore, T_l receives the values of T belonging to the interval 12 .. 15, while T_r receives those of the interval 16 .. 19 (see figure hereafter).

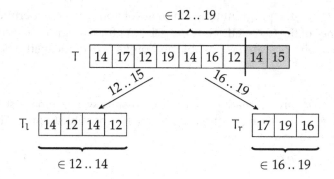

After having broken down the first seven elements of T in T_l and T_r, it can be observed that T_l contains four elements, which belong to the interval 12 .. 14 of length 3. It can be concluded that T_l contains (at least) one duplicate, and it becomes useless to continue the splitting; then the search is pursued in T_l.

Rather than using two auxiliary arrays T_l and T_r, the splitting will be made "on the spot" (i.e. moving the values intended for T_l and T_r to the ends of T) using the operation "**procedure** *Swap*(j, k)" which exchanges the values of T located at positions j and k.

The profile of the operation *Ventilate* is:

$$\textbf{procedure } \textit{Ventilate}(lb, ub, ll, rl; nbi, nbs, nbl, nbr : \textbf{modif}).$$

Schematically, this procedure starts from a sub-array $T[ll .. rl]$ containing a duplicate and provides a strictly smaller sub-array $T[nbl .. nbs]$ also containing a duplicate. In order to be operational, this specification must be strengthened in accordance with the following precondition and postcondition (see Chapter 3, page 98 and following):

Precondition P:

$$\in lb .. ub$$

$$\begin{array}{ccc} ll & & rl \\ T & \boxed{} \end{array}$$

1. The array $T[ll .. rl]$ is valued in the interval $lb .. ub$.

2. $card(ll..rl) > 2$ (this array has at least three elements, the case where the array has two elements and a duplicate being trivial).

3. $lb \in T[ll .. rl]$ and $ub \in T[ll .. rl]$ (possible extreme values actually belong to the array).

4. $card(ll .. rl) > card(lb .. ub)$ (there are more places in $T[ll .. rl]$ (i.e. $card(ll .. rl)$) than possible values in the set $lb .. ub$ (i.e. $card(lb .. ub)$): there is therefore at least one duplicate).

Postcondition Q:

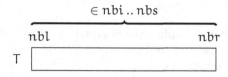

1. $nbl..nbr \subset ll..rl$ (the array $T[nbl..nbr]$ is strictly smaller than the array $T[ll..rl]$).

2. The array $T[nbl..nbr]$ is valued in the interval $nbi..nbs$.

3. $card(nbl..nbr) \geqslant 2$ (The array has at least two elements).

4. $card(nbl..nbr) = card(lb..ub) + 1$ (there is exactly one place more than possible values: there is therefore at least one duplicate).

5. $nbi \in T[nbl..nbr]$ and $nbs \in T[nbl..nbr]$ (possible extreme values actually belong to the array).

6. $T[nbl..nbr] \sqsubseteq T[ll..rl]$ (the bag of values of the array $T[nbl..nbr]$ is included in the bag of values of the array $T[ll..rl]$).

However, the postcondition Q is not well suited for the construction of a loop. An intermediate situation R must be inserted between the situations P and Q, which will constitute the postcondition of the loop. The program A specified by the Hoare triple "{R} A {Q}" will be made up of a conditional statement.

Intermediate situation R:

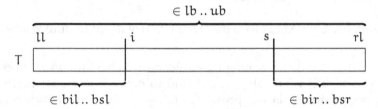

Four kinds of conjuncts are now singled out: general conjuncts (related to the entire array $T[ll..rl]$), conjuncts specific to the sub-array $T[ll..i-1]$, those specific to the sub-array $T[s+1..rl]$, last the conjunct common to both sub-arrays.

General conjuncts.

1. $mid = \lfloor (lb + ub)/2 \rfloor$.

2. $T[ll..rl]$ is a multiset permutation of the initial values. There is therefore always at least one duplicate in the array. This array is modified only by calls to the procedure *Swap* and the present conjunct can therefore be forgotten.

Conjuncts specific to the array $T[ll..i-1]$.

1. $i \in ll..rl-1$ (the sub-array is never the entire array).

2. $bil..bsl \subseteq bi..mid$.

3. The sub-array is valued in the interval $bil..bsl$.

4. $bil..bsl \neq \emptyset \Rightarrow (bil \in T[ll..i-1]$ **and** $bsl \in T[ll..i-1])$ (if the interval of the values of the sub-array is not empty, the extreme values of this interval are present in the array).

5. $card(ll..i-1) \in 0..card(bil..bsl)+1$ (the number of places in the sub-array lies between 0 and the number of possible values plus 1. This latter case implies the existence of at least one duplicate).

Conjuncts specific to the sub-array $T[s + 1 .. rl]$. They are similar to those of the sub-array $T[ll .. i - 1]$.

Conjunct common to both sub-arrays.
   $card(ll .. i - 1) = card(bil .. bsl) + 1$ **or** $card(s + 1 .. rl) = card(bir .. bsr) + 1$ (in one of the two sub-arrays, there are more places than possible values: two places contain the same value. This sub-array contains at least one duplicate).

115 - Q 1   **Question 1.**

a. Design the loop B of the specification $\{P\} B \{R\}$ for the procedure *Ventilate*.

b. Write the entire code of the procedure *Ventilate*.

c. Provide an execution trace of the main variables for the introductory example.

d. Give an upper bound for the number of conditions evaluated. Deduce the worst-case complexity of the procedure *Ventilate*.

e. Prove that the size of the output sub-array $T[nbl .. nbr]$ does not exceed half the size of the input array $T[ll .. rl]$ plus 1, that is:

$$card(nbl .. nbr) \leqslant \left\lfloor \frac{card(ll .. rl)}{2} \right\rfloor + 1. \tag{8.24}$$

This formula is to be used to prove the termination of the procedure *Ventilate* in the next question.

115 - Q 2   **Question 2.**   Deduce the reasoning by induction which allows to build the operation "**function** *DuplSearch*(ll, rl) **result** $lb .. ub$" and to prove it termination. This operation delivers any one of the duplicates present in the array $T[ll .. rl]$. Which division model applies? Provide the code for this operation. Prove that it is at worst in $\mathcal{O}(n)$ conditions evaluated.

The solution is on page 613.

Problem 116. The largest rectangle under a histogram

It turns out that this problem is an outstanding example from many points of view.

- *The two considered problems (square and rectangle) have close specifications. However, the techniques used are different and hardly transposable from one to another.*

- *The second problem (that of the rectangle) is tackled according to three different approaches (DaC, purely iterative method and method mixing recursion and iteration).*

- *The DaC solution (in its most elaborated version) leads to the study of an original and efficient data structure based on trees.*

- *The iterative solution makes an explicit use of a stack (see 1.8) which requires an ingenious refinement in order to reach an elegant and efficient solution.*

- *The icing on the cake, the last solution studied is an antidote to empiricism and to the "hack". The result, of rare conciseness and purity, can only be achieved by scrupulously applying the precepts advocated in this book.*

> Moreover, this is not a purely "academic" problem. Simple extensions find applications in image processing. Due to the wide variety of solutions discussed, the placement of this problem in this chapter is somewhat arbitrary.

The problem

Definition 14 (Histogram of an array of natural numbers):

Let t be an array defined on the interval a .. b valued in the interval i .. s. The array h defined on the interval i .. s valued in the interval $0 .. b - a + 1$ is the histogram of t if for each value v of the interval i .. s, h[v] counts the number of occurrences of v in t.

This definition can be formalized as follows. Let

$$t \in a .. b \to i .. s \quad \text{and} \quad h \in i .. s \to 0 .. b - a + 1.$$

The array h is the histogram of t if:

$$\forall k \cdot (k \in i .. s \implies h[k] = \#j \cdot (j \in a .. b \mid t[j] = k)).$$

Example Let t be the following array, defined on the interval $1 .. 25$ valued in the interval $1 .. 7$:

1	2	3	4	5	6	7	8	9	10	11	12	13	14	15	16	17	18	19	20	21	22	23	24	25
1	3	2	1	4	5	4	3	2	1	6	1	5	3	7	6	3	4	5	6	1	4	6	1	3

Its histogram h, defined on the interval $1 .. 7$ valued in the interval $0 .. 25$, is:

	1	2	3	4	5	6	7
h	6	2	5	4	3	4	1

Such an array is often represented as shown in figure 8.16 below.

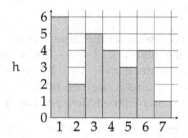

Fig. 8.16 – An example of histogram.

It can be noted (remark exploited hereafter) that it is possible to define the histogram of a histogram. Thus, the histogram h′ of h is defined on the interval $0 .. 25$ and valued in the interval $0 .. 7$. It looks like this:

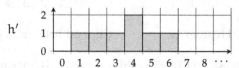

The objective of the problem is twofold. The first step is to find the side of the largest *square* under a histogram, then, in a second step, to find the area of the largest *rectangle* under a histogram. In each case, several solutions are studied. The problem ends with an application to black and white images. The complexity of the different solutions is measured in the number of conditions evaluated.

Searching for the side of the largest square under a histogram

For the example of figure 8.16, the expected value is 3. It is reached by two distinct squares:

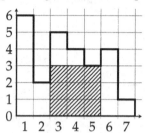 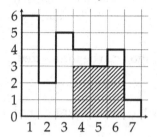

Two solutions are studied. The first one is iterative, in $\mathcal{O}(n^2)$; the second solution, in $\Theta(n)$, is an optimization of the previous one.

116 - Q 1   **Question** 1.   We have seen that there is generally no uniqueness of the solution. A situation where multiple solutions are vertically aligned may exist, as shown in the diagram below:

Prove that it is always possible to consider, in solving this problem, only the squares which touch the x-axis. This property is applied systematically further on.

Remark

Regarding more particularly the search for the largest square under a histogram h defined on the interval $i..s$ valued in the interval $0..b - a + 1$, it is easy to note that it is impossible to place a square whose side is greater than $s - i + 1$. In the following, we assume—without loss of generality—that the histograms concerned by the search for the largest square are clipped beyond $(s - i + 1)$, as shown in the following diagram:

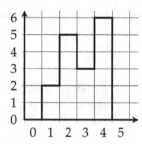
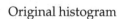 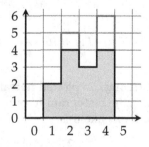

Original histogram   Clipped histogram (in grey)

The preprocessing necessary to satisfy this constraint is not carried out here.

Largest square under a histogram, naïve iterative version

Question 2.   Construct an iterative solution based on the following invariant: r is the 116 - Q 2 side of the largest square contained in the histogram $h[1 .. i - 1]$; the largest square adjacent to the position i – the only one that can still expand – has as side $(i - a)$, with $1 \leqslant a \leqslant i \leqslant n + 1$.

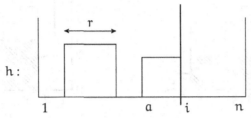

Check that complexity is in $O(n^2)$.

Largest square under a histogram, optimal iterative version

From the complexity point of view, the problem posed by the above naïve solution lies in the computation of a quantified expression, a computation for which the simplest solution is based on a loop. We already know that in the interval $a .. i - 1$, no value of h is less than $a - i$ (otherwise the considered square would not exist). If we had f, the histogram of $h[a .. i - 1]$, the refinement of the conditional expression $\min(h[a .. i - 1]) \geqslant i - a + 1$ would be reduced to $f[i - a] = 0$ (in fact $f[i - a] = 0$ means that no value of $h[a .. i - 1]$ is equal to $i - a$; we already knew that none of them is less than $i - a$).

Example Let us consider the following histogram $h[a .. i - 1]$:

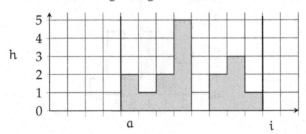

The histogram f of $h[a .. i - 1]$ is thus:

	0	1	2	3	4	5
f	1	2	3	1	0	1

or:

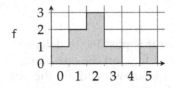

Thus, in $h[a .. i - 1]$, there are three positions equal to 2 (hence $f[2] = 3$).

Question 3.   Construct a new solution based on the above observation. Write the code. 116 - Q 3 Check that this solution is actually in $\Theta(n)$.

Searching for the area of the largest rectangle under a histogram

The objective of this part of the problem is to build a program that determines the area of the largest rectangle under a histogram. For the example of figure 8.16, page 481, this value is equal to 12. It is reached by two distinct rectangles:

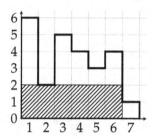 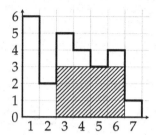

Three solutions are studied. The first one is of type DaC (two variants are proposed), the second one is an iterative solution and the last one, very original, effectively combines iteration and recursion.

Definition 15 (ma: maximum area):
For $1 \leqslant i \leqslant j \leqslant n + 1$, $ma(i, j)$ is the area of the largest rectangle under the portion of the histogram whose abscissas belong to the interval $i .. j - 1$.

For the example of figure 8.16, page 481, $ma(2, 5)$ is equal to 8:

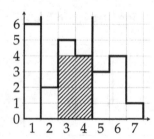

Largest rectangle under a histogram, naïve DaC version

Property 14 (of ma. Not proven):

1. $ma(i, i) = 0$ *for* $1 \leqslant i \leqslant n + 1$,

2. *if* $i \leqslant k < j$ *and* $h[k] = \min(h[i .. j - 1])$ *then* $ma(i, j) = \max(\{ma(i, k), (j - i) \cdot h[k], ma(k + 1, j)\})$.

This property expresses that it is possible to determine the area of the largest rectangle under a histogram, provided that, on the one hand, the position of an occurrence of the minimum of the histogram is known and, on the other hand, the area of the largest rectangles located on either side of this minimum.

Example For the following histogram:

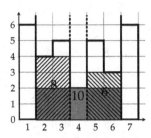

k = 4 and the value of $ma(2,7)$ is max$(\{8,6,10\})$, that is 10.

Question 4.   The function $PosMin(i,s)$ that delivers any of the locations of the mini-   116 - Q 4
mum of $h[i..s-1]$ is supposed to be available. By directly applying the property 14 above,
provide the DaC version of the operation "**function** $AmHDaC(i,s)$ **result** $\mathbb{N}$" which delivers the area of the largest rectangle present under the histogram $h[i .. s - 1]$. What is the
complexity of this operation if the function $PosMin$ is implemented by a sequential search?

Largest rectangle under a histogram, DaC version and minimum segment trees

The previous solution is based on a standard linear search (in $\Theta(n)$) of the minimum of
a histogram. However, a more efficient solution to this problem exists: the one that uses
minimum segment trees. The main definitions, as well as the most frequent vocabulary
elements relating to binary trees, are gathered in Chapter 1.

Minimum segment trees (segment trees for finding out the minimum)

Let $h \in i .. s \rightarrow \mathbb{N}$ be an array. A minimum segment tree for h is a binary tree such that
each vertex is composed of:

- the position p of (one of) the minimum of $h[i .. s]$,

- the interval $i .. s$ itself,

- the left minimum segment sub-tree corresponding to the first half of the interval $i .. s$,

- the right minimum segment sub-tree corresponding to the second half of the interval
  $i .. s$.

In the following, for readability purposes, the arrays are assumed to have a size n that
is a power of 2 ($n = 2^k$). The results obtained can be extended to any value of n.

Example Let h be defined as:

1	2	3	4	5	6	7	8
2	6	1	5	9	3	8	4

The corresponding minimum segment tree of A is:

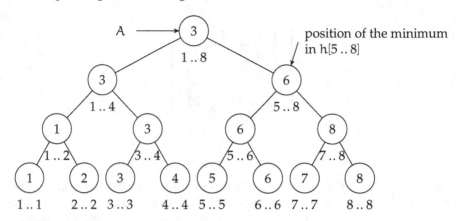

Such a tree is represented by the structure

$$mst = \{/\} \cup \{(l, (m, i, s), r) \mid m \in mst \text{ and } r \in mst \text{ and } m \in \mathbb{N}_1 \text{ and } i \in \mathbb{N}_1 \text{ and } s \in \mathbb{N}_1\}$$

where $i .. s$ is the integer interval of the considered vertex and m is the position of the minimum for the array. Let "**function** *PosMinAux*(a, p, q) **result** $\mathbb{N}$" be the operation that returns (one of) the position(s) of the minimum of $h[p .. q]$ in the minimum segment tree a.

116 - Q 5   **Question 5.**   Build this operation, provide its code and calculate its complexity in number of nodes visited first, conditions evaluated then. Deduce the complexity of the new version of the operation *AmHDaC*.

Largest rectangle under a histogram, iterative version

The principle of this version is similar to the one applied in the iterative versions of the search for the largest square. However, it deviates from it by the fact that generally there exist *several* rectangles which are candidates for enlargement to the right. This set of candidates is called "set of open rectangles", it is denoted by O and $k = \text{card}(O)$. In the following, it is assumed that h is extended into 0 and into $n + 1$ by 0. An open rectangle is represented by the pair (l, ht), where l is the leftmost abscissa of the rectangle and ht its height. Formally, for a given i, the open rectangle (l, ht) is defined as:

$$l \in 0 .. i - 1 \text{ and } ht = \min(h[l .. i - 1]) \text{ and } h[l - 1] < ht.$$

In figure 8.17, for $i = 10$, we have $O = \{(0, 0), (1, 1), (4, 3), (6, 4)\}$. The extension of h in 0 makes it possible to have permanently the "neutral" rectangle with coordinates $(0, 0)$ and area 0 (zero) in the stack O.

116 - Q 6   **Question 6.**   Prove the following property:

Lemma 1:
Let $P = \langle (l_1, ht_1), \ldots, (l_k, ht_k) \rangle$ be the list of open rectangles sorted on increasing l_j's. The list $\langle ht_1, \ldots, ht_k \rangle$ is also strictly increasing.

Without going into the details of what constitutes the next question, during the progression, either the rectangle with the greatest height (that is to say the last element of the list)

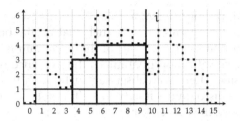

Fig. 8.17 – A histogram and the four open rectangles for $i = 10$.

is removed from the list P, or the width of the open rectangles is lengthened, by possibly creating at the tail of the list P, a new rectangle whose height is greater than those of all the rectangles present in P. Therefore, the list P behaves like a *stack*. The extension of h to $(n+1)$ allows, when i reaches this value, to unstack all open rectangles except the one with coordinates $(0,0)$, and then advance i to $n+2$.

The information in P is redundant. Indeed, the heights ht_j's can be found from the abscissas g_j's. In order to remove this redundancy, it is decided to refine the P stack by the stack P', which looks like this: $P' = < l_1 - 1, \ldots, l_k - 1, s >$, where the top s of the stack P' is the rightmost abscissa such that $s \in l_k + 1 \ldots i - 1$ and $(l_k, h[s])$ is the top of the stack P (P' contains one element more than P). Thus, if $P = < (0,0), (1,1), (4,3), (6,4) >$ (see figure 8.17), $P' = < -1, 0, 3, 5, 9 >$.

Question 7. Prove that this representation P' allows to find all the information present in P. 116 - Q 7

Question 8. 116 - Q 8
The data structure stack is defined section 1.8, page 32. Use the stack P' to construct the loop onto which this algorithm is based. What is its complexity?

Largest rectangle under a histogram, Morgan's version

Faced with the previous solution explicitly using a stack, it is legitimate to ask the question whether it is not possible to use the execution stack implicitly (instead). The solution studied here answers this question, even if it is not an adaptation of the previous solution, but an original approach due to the Australian computer scientist C. Morgan which uses it as an example of building a program from a formal specification (see [26], pages 209–216).

The histogram is extended in 0 and $n + 1$ so that $h[0] = h[n + 1] = -1$. These values serve as sentinels in the following.

Let $P(k) = k \in 0 \ldots n$ be a predicate. Let $AmHMorg(i, b, j)$ (where i is an input parameter and b as well as j are output parameters) be the procedure specified by:

Precondition : $P(i)$.

Postcondition : Q defined as $Q \cong Q_1$ **and** Q_2 **and** Q_3 **and** Q_4 where

$Q_1 \cong i < j \leqslant n + 1$
$Q_2 \cong h[i] \leqslant \min(h[i + 1 \ldots j - 1])$
$Q_3 \cong h[i] \geqslant h[j]$
$Q_4 \cong b = am(i + 1, j)$.

For a given abscissa i, calling *AmHMorg*(i, b, j) returns two results, j and b. The first one is the smallest abscissa (j) greater than i such that on the one hand $h[j] \leqslant h[i]$ and on the other hand the portion $h[i + 1 \mathrel{..} j - 1]$ of the histogram is greater than or equal to $h[i]$. Let us note that the specification guarantees the existence of j. Indeed, it is always possible to find such a j since there is an abscissa j such that $h[j]$ is less than or equal to all the previous values of the histogram – it is $(n + 1)$ $(h[n + 1] = -1)$ – and that, in case the interval $i + 1 \mathrel{..} j - 1$ is empty, the expression $\min(h[i + 1 \mathrel{..} j - 1])$ becomes $\min(\varnothing)$, which is $+\infty$ $(h[i] \leqslant +\infty)$. The second result, b, is the area of the largest rectangle under the portion of the histogram bounded by the interval $i + 1 \mathrel{..} j - 1$.

Example Let us come back to the example of figure 8.16, page 481, to evaluate *AmHMorg*$(2, b, j)$:

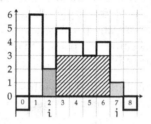

This call returns $j = 7$ and $b = 12$.
Let us take again the example of figure 8.16, page 481, to evaluate *AmHMorg*$(3, b, j)$:

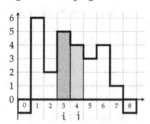

This time, the interval $i + 1 \mathrel{..} j - 1$ is empty. The area b of the largest rectangle under the portion $h[4 \mathrel{..} 3]$ is zero. This call thus delivers $j = 4$ and $b = 0$.

116 - Q 9   **Question 9.**   Let $Q_5 \mathrel{\hat{=}} h[j] \leqslant \min(h[i + 1 \mathrel{..} j - 1)$. Prove that $Q \Rightarrow Q_5$. In the following, the predicate (Q **and** Q_5) is denoted by Q'.

116 - Q 10   **Question 10.**   Prove that after the call *AmHMorg*$(0, b, j)$, j is equal to $(n + 1)$ and b is the area of the largest rectangle under the histogram $h[1 \mathrel{..} n]$.

A recursive solution of the form

```
 1. procedure AmHMorg(i; b, j : modif) pre
 2.    i ∈ N and b ∈ N and j ∈ N₁ and
 3.    c ∈ N and k ∈ N
 4. begin
 5.    Initialization;
 6.    while not SC do
 7.       AmHMorg(j, c, k);
 8.       EndProgression
 9.    end while
10. end
```

is sought.

If $I(i, b, j)$ and $SC(i, b, j)$ represent respectively the invariant of the loop and the stopping condition, The annotated version of the procedure *AmHMorg* is as follows:

1. **procedure** *AmHMorg*$(i; b, j :$ **modif**$)$ **pre**
2. $\quad i \in \mathbb{N}$ **and** $b \in \mathbb{N}$ **and** $j \in \mathbb{N}_1$ **and**
3. $\quad c \in \mathbb{N}$ **and** $k \in \mathbb{N}$
4. **begin**
5. $\quad \boxed{P(i)}$
6. $\quad$ *Initialization*;
7. $\quad \boxed{I(i, b, j)}$
8. $\quad$ **while** $\boxed{\text{not } SC(i, b, j)}$ **do**
9. $\qquad \boxed{I(i, b, j) \text{ and not } SCA(i, b, j)}$
10. $\qquad$ *AmHMorg*(j, c, k);
11. $\qquad \boxed{Q'(j, c, k) \text{ and } I(i, b, j) \text{ and not } SC(i, b, j)}$
12. $\qquad$ *EndProgression*
13. $\qquad \boxed{I(i, b, j)}$
14. $\quad$ **end while**
15. $\quad \boxed{I(i, b, j) \text{ and } SC(i, b, j)}$
16. $\quad \boxed{Q'(i, b, j)}$
17. **end**

Remarks

1. Since i is an input parameter, $P(i)$ is a predicate that always holds.

2. These annotations result from the fundamental theoretical elements of sequential programming (see Chapter 3).

3. In the annotation of line 11, the conjunct $Q'(j, c, k)$ is the postcondition resulting from the recursive call in line 10. The rest of formula ($I(i, b, j)$ **and not** $SC(i, b, j)$) is inherited directly from the precondition of the progression. Indeed, the call at line 10, *AmHMorg*(j, c, k), does not modify the value of the loop state variables (i, b and j).

4. Line 15 is the "natural" postcondition of the loop, whereas line 16 is the postcondition of the procedure. It can be logically concluded that

$$I(i, b, j) \text{ and } SC(i, b, j) \Rightarrow Q'(i, b, j). \tag{8.25}$$

5. P and Q' are known (given) predicates; on the other hand, I and SC are unknown. *Initialization* and *EndProgression* are unknown code fragments, to be built from their specifications. That of *EndProgression* is the pair of predicates of lines 11 (for the precondition) and 13 (for the postcondition). A trivial solution would be to choose the "empty" action, since the postcondition is already a conjunct of the precondition. However, this choice is to be excluded because it does not allow to prove that the program ends. A code fragment that restores the invariant $I(i, b, j)$ must be sought.

In the following questions, this loop is progressively developed by applying the classical principles of iteration construction (see Chapter 3).

116 - Q 11   **Question** 11.   These principles advocate first determining the invariant I and the stopping condition SC. Starting from formula 8.25, make a proposition for both I and SC.

116 - Q 12   **Question** 12.   Prove that it is legal to call the procedure *AmHMorg*(j, c, k) in line 10 (i.e. that the precondition $P(j)$ is implied by the predicate of line 9).

116 - Q 13   **Question** 13.   Let us now determine the code corresponding to *FinProgression*.

    a. If the following configuration

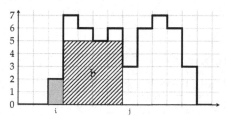

      is an instance of the predicate in line 9, what is the situation reached at line 11?

    b. Design a solution for the code fragment *EndProgression*. What is, on the considered example, the situation reached at line 13?

    c. What would have happened if Q was used instead of using the postcondition Q'?

116 - Q 14   **Question** 14.   Provide a solution for the code fragment *Initialization*.

116 - Q 15   **Question** 15.   Prove that the procedure terminates.

116 - Q 16   **Question** 16.   Write the code of the procedure.

116 - Q 17   **Question** 17.   This question aims at proving that the complexity of this solution is in $\Theta(n)$. To do so, let us count the calls to the procedure *AmHMorg*. This choice is (asymptotically) compatible with the initial one (count of conditions) since, if there are a recursive calls to the procedure, there are $(a + 1)$ evaluations of the condition of the loop. Prove by induction the following property: executing *AmHMorg*(i, c, j) causes $(j - i)$ recursive calls to *AmHMorg*.

Application: calculation of the area of the largest black rectangle in a black and white image

Consider a rectangular image made up of black (1) and white (0) pixels. We are looking for the largest totally black rectangular sub-image. More formally, given a Boolean matrix $T[1 .. m, 1 .. n]$ representing an image, we want to calculate the value a, the area of (one of) the largest black rectangle contained in T.

Example

In the image of figure 8.18, the area a the largest black rectangle is 6.

Fig. 8.18 – A black and white image.

Question 18.   Show how it is possible to apply the algorithms studied beforehand to 116 - Q 18 solve the problem. The temporal complexity of the proposed solution is required.

The solution is on page 618.

8.4   Solutions

Answers to problem 88. Merge-sort   *The problem is on page 424.*

Answer 1.   The algorithm consists of two parts. The first is to interclass the two sub- 88 - A 1 arrays $T[p..q]$ and $T[q+1..r]$ in the auxiliary array $S[p..r]$. An iterative solution is fine. At the end of this processing, one of the two sub-arrays has been completely transferred to S, the other has only been partially. The second part of the algorithm consists in completing S with the values remaining to be moved. The five constituents of the loop construction are shown hereafter:

Invariant The two sub-arrays $T[p..i-1]$ and $T[q+1..j-1]$ are interclassed in $S[p..k-1]$. Moreover, $i \in (p..q+1), j \in (q+1..r+1)$ **and** $(k=i+j-q-1)$.

Stopping condition One of the two sub-arrays $T[p..i-1]$ or $T[q+1..j-1]$ is processed, namely:

$$(i = q+1) \text{ or } (j = r+1).$$

It can be noted that the conjunction of the invariant and the stopping condition entails that the portion that is not yet processed can simply be transferred at the end of S.

Progression The smallest value between $T[i]$ and $T[j]$ is copied into S, and the invariant is restored by updating the indices i or j and k.

Initialization The program:

$$i \leftarrow p; j \leftarrow q+1; k \leftarrow p$$

establishes the invariant.

Termination k, scan index of S, increases by one at each step of progression. The expression $(r+1-k)$ is a suitable termination function.

Consequently, the code of the procedure is the following:

```
 1. procedure Merge(p, q, r) pre
 2.     p ∈ ℕ and q ∈ ℕ and r ∈ ℕ and p − 1 ⩽ q ⩽ r + 1 and
 3.     IsSorted(T[p .. q]) and IsSorted(T[q + 1 .. r]) and
 4.     S ∈ p .. r → ℕ and i ∈ p .. q + 1 and j ∈ q + 1 .. r + 1 and k ∈ p .. r + 1
 5. begin
 6.     /% First part: interclassification %/
 7.     i ← p; j ← q + 1; k ← p;
 8.     while not(i = q + 1 or j = r + 1) do
 9.         if T[i] < T[j] then
10.             S[k] ← T[i]; i ← i + 1
```

```
11.      else
12.          S[k] ← T[j]; j ← j + 1
13.      end if;
14.      k ← k + 1
15.   end while;
16.   /% Second part: transfer of remaining elements %/
17.   S[k .. k + (q − i)] ← T[i .. q];
18.   S[k .. k + (r − j)] ← T[j .. r];
19.   T ← S
20.· end
```

Regarding the second part, it can be noticed that, contrary to what is sometimes encountered, it is useless to choose, by a conditional statement, the sub-array of T which is to be transferred into S. This is because the other sub-array is empty, so it can easily be copied to S as well.

88 - A 2   **Answer 2.**   Merging arrays [3, 6, 7, 9] and [4, 5, 10, 12] requires six comparisons (3 <> 4,6 <> 4,6 <> 5,6 <> 10,7 <> 10,9 <> 10), that of arrays [3, 4, 5, 6] and [7, 9, 10, 12] only four (3 <> 7,4 <> 7,5 <> 7,6 <> 7) and that of arrays [3, 5, 7, 10] and [4, 6, 9, 12] is performed with seven comparisons (3 <> 4,5 <> 4,5 <> 6,7 <> 6,7 <> 9,10 <> 9,10 <> 12). Merging arrays $T[p .. q]$ and $T[q + 1 .. r]$ demands at most $(q − p + 4)$ comparisons. This value is reached when one of the two slices is exhausted and the last element of the other is reached (see for example the case of the arrays [3, 5, 7, 10] and [4, 6, 9, 12]). An exhaustive assessment of complexity cannot be confined to this formula; it would be necessary to add the implicit conditions of lines 17 to 19 of the procedure *Merge*.

88 - A 3   **Answer 3.**   For an arbitrary size of T, the only adaptation to be made in the procedure *Merge-sort* concerns the denotation of the "middle" index, which must be written $\lfloor (i+j)/2 \rfloor$ and no longer $(i + j)/2$ in the two recursive calls, as well as in the call to the procedure *Merge*.

Answers to problem 89. Fibonacci sequence: four constructions   *The problem is on page 425.*

89 - A 1   **Answer 1.**   Let us consider the following matrix $F = \begin{bmatrix} a & b \\ c & d \end{bmatrix}$ where a, b, c and d are to be determined. We have:

$$\mathcal{V}_n = F \times \mathcal{V}_{n-1}$$

$\Leftrightarrow$ définitions

$$\begin{bmatrix} \mathcal{F}_{n-1} \\ \mathcal{F}_n \end{bmatrix} = \begin{bmatrix} a & b \\ c & d \end{bmatrix} \times \begin{bmatrix} \mathcal{F}_{n-2} \\ \mathcal{F}_{n-1} \end{bmatrix}$$

$\Leftrightarrow$ matrix product

$$\begin{bmatrix} \mathcal{F}_{n-1} \\ \mathcal{F}_n \end{bmatrix} = \begin{bmatrix} a \cdot \mathcal{F}_{n-2} + b \cdot \mathcal{F}_{n-1} \\ c \cdot \mathcal{F}_{n-2} + d \cdot \mathcal{F}_{n-1} \end{bmatrix}$$

hence, from the definition of $\mathcal{F}_n$ and by identification:

$$F = \begin{bmatrix} 0 & 1 \\ 1 & 1 \end{bmatrix}.$$

89 - A 2   **Answer 2.**   Therefore, we have $\mathcal{V}_n = F \times \mathcal{V}_{n-1} = F \times (F \times \mathcal{V}_{n-2}) = \ldots = F^{n-1} \times \mathcal{V}_1.$

Answer 3.   We design the operation "**function** *MatPower*(M, n) **result** (1 .. 2) × (1 ..
2) → ℕ", that returns the matrix M^n for any $n \in \mathbb{N}_1$.

Base For $n = 1$, the result is M.

Induction hypothesis It is known how to calculate M^m for $1 \leqslant m < n$.

Induction It is known that:

$$
n = \begin{cases} \left\lfloor \dfrac{n}{2} \right\rfloor + \left\lfloor \dfrac{n}{2} \right\rfloor & \text{if n is even} \\[2mm] \left\lfloor \dfrac{n}{2} \right\rfloor + \left\lfloor \dfrac{n}{2} \right\rfloor + 1 & \text{if n is odd} \end{cases}
$$

It can be deduced that:

$$
M^n = \begin{cases} M^{\left\lfloor \frac{n}{2} \right\rfloor} \times M^{\left\lfloor \frac{n}{2} \right\rfloor} & \text{if n is even} \cdot \\[2mm] M^{\left\lfloor \frac{n}{2} \right\rfloor} \times M^{\left\lfloor \frac{n}{2} \right\rfloor} \cdot M & \text{if n is odd} \end{cases}
$$

From the induction hypothesis, it is known how to calculate $M^{\left\lfloor \frac{n}{2} \right\rfloor}$, thus also M^n.

Termination The power n is a positive integer that decreases at each step. This ensures the termination of the algorithm.

The code of the function *MatPower* comes straightforwardly:

```
 1. function MatPower(M, n) result (1 .. 2) × (1 .. 2) → ℕ pre
 2.    M ∈ (1 .. 2) × (1 .. 2) → ℕ and n ∈ ℕ₁ and
 3.    T ∈ (1 .. 2) × (1 .. 2) → ℕ
 4. begin
 5.    if n = 1 then
 6.       result M
 7.    else
 8.       T ← MatPower( M, ⌊n/2⌋ );
 9.       if Even(n) then
10.          result MatProd(T, T)
11.       else
12.          result MatProd(MatProd(T, T), M)
13.       end if
14.    end if
15. end
```

We deduce the procedure *FiboV*(n; u, v : **modif**):

```
 1. procedure FiboV(n; u, v : modif) pre
 2.    n ∈ ℕ₁ and (u, v) ∈ ℕ₁ × ℕ₁ and
 3.    T ∈ (1 .. 2) × (1 .. 2) → ℕ
 4. begin
 5.    if n = 1 then
 6.       u ← 1; v ← 1
 7.    else
 8.       T ← MatPower(F, n − 1);
 9.       u ← T[1, 1] + T[1, 2]; v ← T[2, 1] + T[2, 2]
10.    end if
11. end
```

89 - A 4   **Answer** 4.   The function *Fibo2* is then written:

```
1. function Fibo2(n) result ℕ₁ pre
2.     n ∈ ℕ and
3.     (y, z) ∈ ℕ₁ × ℕ₁
4. begin
5.     FiboV(n + 1, y, z);
6.     result y
7. end
```

Notice that calling *FiboV* must be performed with the value $(n + 1)$ as the first actual parameter in order to meet the precondition of *FiboV* ($n \in \mathbb{N}_1$) and to deliver a result y equal to $\mathcal{F}_n$ (indeed $y = \mathcal{F}_{(n+1)-1} = \mathcal{F}_n$). Calling this function is carried out in the context where the matrix F is appropriately initialized:

```
1. constants
2.     F ∈ (1..2) × (1..2) → ℕ and F = [0 1; 1 1] and n ∈ ℕ and n = ...
3. begin
4.     write(Fibo2(n))
5. end
```

Complexity

If $n = 2^k$, the function *FiboV* is called with $2^k + 1$ as the first argument, whereas the function *MatPower* is called with $2^k + 1 - 1$ as its second parameter. In this case, the recurrence equation of complexity for *MatPower* is written:

$$\left|\begin{array}{l} C(1) = 0 \\ C(n) = C\left(\dfrac{n}{2}\right) + 1 \end{array}\right. \qquad\qquad n > 1.$$

This equation matches the special case 8.1 of the corollary of the master theorem, page 423. The complexity is thus in $\Theta(\log_2(n))$. It is also that of *Fibo2* that does not involve matrix products other than those due to *MatPower*. This solution makes it possible to move from linear to logarithmic complexity.

89 - A 5   **Answer** 5.   The exact complexity of *MatPower* is now studied. The best case occurs for $n = 2^k$: a single matrix product is performed at each step, hence exactly k matrix products in total. For $n > 1$, the worst case is when $n = 2^k - 1$: two matrix products are performed at each step, hence $2(k-1)$ in total. The first values of the number of products of two matrices are displayed in the table hereafter (the row N represents the number of matrix products):

n	0	1	2	3	4	5	6	7	8	...	15	16	...
N	0	0	1	2	2	3	3	4	3	...	6	4	...

It can be proven that $N = \lfloor \log_2(n) \rfloor + \nu(n) - 1$ where $\nu(m)$ is the number of 1's appearing when m is written in base 2.

The product of 2×2 matrices requires four additions and eight multiplications. The table below provides the minimal and maximal number of additive and multiplicative operations for *MatPower*:

Operation:	Additions	Multiplications
Minimum, for $n = 2^k$	4k	8k
Maximum, for $n = 2^k - 1$	8k − 8	16k − 16

Answer 6. *Fibo2*(15) requires the calculation of F^{15}. As shown in the table, the method used above requires six matrix products. But, for 15, we can calculate M^3 with two calls: $M^3 = (M \times M) \times M$, then successively calculate: $M^6 = M^3 \times M^3$, $M^{12} = M^6 \times M^6$, $M^{15} = M^{12} \times M^3$. Eventually, only five matrix products are necessary. This technique (known as the *Knuth power tree* method, see [22]) relies on the decomposition of the exponent of M into prime factors. Depending on the value of n, it is sometimes better, sometimes worse than the DaC method. 89 - A 6

Answer 7. Let $Q(p) = \forall n \cdot (n \in \mathbb{N} \Rightarrow \mathcal{F}_{n+p} = \mathcal{F}_n \cdot \mathcal{F}_p + \mathcal{F}_{n-1} \cdot \mathcal{F}_{p-1})$. We must prove the proposition $\forall p \cdot (p \in \mathbb{N}_1 \Rightarrow Q(p))$. 89 - A 7

Base Since $\mathcal{F}_0 = 1$ and $\mathcal{F}_1 = 1$, the body of $Q(1)$ comes down to $\mathcal{F}_{n+1} = \mathcal{F}_n \cdot 1 + \mathcal{F}_{n-1} \cdot 1$, that can be simplified into $\mathcal{F}_{n+1} = \mathcal{F}_n + \mathcal{F}_{n-1}$ and the proposition $Q(1)$ holds.

Induction hypothesis It is the proposition $Q(p)$.

Induction $Q(p+1)$ must be proven assuming that the induction hypothesis holds. Let us start with the second member of the equality to recover the first one:

$$\mathcal{F}_n \cdot \mathcal{F}_{p+1} + \mathcal{F}_{n-1} \cdot \mathcal{F}_p$$

$=$ 　　　　　　　　　　　　　　　　　　　　　definition of $\mathcal{F}_{p+1}$

$$\mathcal{F}_n \cdot (\mathcal{F}_p + \mathcal{F}_{p-1}) + \mathcal{F}_{n-1} \cdot \mathcal{F}_p$$

$=$ 　　　　　　　　　　　　　　　　　　　　　arithmetics

$$(\mathcal{F}_n + \mathcal{F}_{n-1}) \cdot \mathcal{F}_p + \mathcal{F}_n \cdot \mathcal{F}_{p-1}$$

$=$ 　　　　　　　　　　　　　　　　　　　　　definition of $\mathcal{F}_{n+1}$

$$\mathcal{F}_{n+1} \cdot \mathcal{F}_p + \mathcal{F}_n \cdot \mathcal{F}_{p-1}$$

$=$ 　　　　induction hypothesis, substitution $n \leftarrow n+1$ and arithmetics

$$\mathcal{F}_{n+p+1}.$$

Answer 8. 89 - A 8

1. For $p = n$: $\mathcal{F}_{2n} = (\mathcal{F}_n)^2 + (\mathcal{F}_{n-1})^2$.

2. For $p = n - 1$:

$$\mathcal{F}_{2n-1}$$

$=$ 　　　　　　　　　　　　　　　　　　　　　above property

$$\mathcal{F}_n \cdot \mathcal{F}_{n-1} + \mathcal{F}_{n-1} \cdot \mathcal{F}_{n-2}$$

$=$ 　　　　　　　　　　　　　　　　　　　　　$\mathcal{F}_{n-2} = \mathcal{F}_n - \mathcal{F}_{n-1}$

$$\mathcal{F}_{n-1} \cdot (2\mathcal{F}_n - \mathcal{F}_{n-1}).$$

3. For $p = n + 1$: $\mathcal{F}_{2n+1} = \mathcal{F}_n \cdot (\mathcal{F}_n + 2\mathcal{F}_{n-1})$.

Answer 9. 89 - A 9

1.
$$W_{2n} = \begin{bmatrix} \mathcal{F}_{2n-1} \\ \mathcal{F}_{2n} \end{bmatrix} = \begin{bmatrix} \mathcal{F}_{n-1} \cdot (2\mathcal{F}_n - \mathcal{F}_{n-1}) \\ (\mathcal{F}_n)^2 + (\mathcal{F}_{n-1})^2 \end{bmatrix}.$$

2.
$$W_{2n+1} = \begin{bmatrix} \mathcal{F}_{2n} \\ \mathcal{F}_{2n+1} \end{bmatrix} = \begin{bmatrix} (\mathcal{F}_n)^2 + (\mathcal{F}_{n-1})^2 \\ \mathcal{F}_n \cdot (\mathcal{F}_n + 2\mathcal{F}_{n-1}) \end{bmatrix}.$$

Answer 10. We design the operation "**procedure** *FiboW*$(n; u, v : $ **modif**)" according to the following inductive pattern. 89 - A 10

Base The base case occurs when $n = 1$, and $W_1 = \begin{bmatrix} 1 \\ 1 \end{bmatrix}$.

Induction hypothesis It is assumed that $W_{\lfloor n/2 \rfloor} = \begin{bmatrix} w \\ z \end{bmatrix} = \begin{bmatrix} \mathcal{F}_{\lfloor n/2 \rfloor - 1} \\ \mathcal{F}_{\lfloor n/2 \rfloor} \end{bmatrix}$.

Induction The result W_n depends on the parity of n and it is obtained by applying the induction hypothesis from the formulas of the previous question. If n is even, $W_n = \begin{bmatrix} w \cdot (2z - w) \\ w \cdot w + z \cdot z \end{bmatrix}$ and otherwise $W_n = \begin{bmatrix} w \cdot w + z \cdot z \\ z \cdot (z + 2w) \end{bmatrix}$.

Termination The parameter n is a positive integer that diminishes at each step. This ensures the termination of the algorithm.

The underlying division model is:

$\text{FiboW}(1 \text{ elementary}$

$\text{FiboW}(m) \rightarrow \text{FiboW}\left(\dfrac{m}{2}\right) + \text{calculation of } u \text{ and } v \text{ from } w \text{ and } z \qquad\qquad m > 1$

The code of the procedure *FiboW* is then:

```
1.  procedure FiboW(n; u, v : modif) pre
2.     n ∈ ℕ₁ and (u, v) ∈ ℕ₁ × ℕ₁ and
3.     (w, z) ∈ ℕ₁ × ℕ₁
4.  begin
5.     if n = 1 then
6.        u ← 1; v ← 1
7.     else
8.        FiboW(⌊n/2⌋, w, z);
9.        if Even(n) then
10.          u ← w · (2z − w); v ← w · w + z · z
11.       else
12.          u ← w · w + z · z; v ← z · (z + 2w)
13.       end if
14.    end if
15. end
```

The function $Fibo3(n)$ makes use of the auxiliary procedure *FiboW*:

```
1.  function Fibo3(n) result ℕ₁ pre
2.     n ∈ ℕ and
3.     (s, t) ∈ ℕ₁ × ℕ₁
4.  begin
5.     FiboW(n + 1, s, t);
6.     result s
7.  end
```

Notice that calling *FiboW* is performed with $(n+1)$ as the first actual parameter in order to meet the precondition and to deliver the result s equal to $\mathcal{F}_n$ (indeed $s = \mathcal{F}_{(n+1)-1} = \mathcal{F}_n$).

89 - A 11   **Answer 11.**   In terms of additions, the recurrence equation of complexity for *FiboW* is given by:

$$\begin{vmatrix} C(1) = 0 \\ C(n) = C\left(\dfrac{n}{2}\right) + 2 \end{vmatrix} \qquad\qquad n > 1.$$

The special case 8.1 of the corollary of the master theorem, page 423, allows to deduce that the complexity of this operation is in $\Theta(\log_2(n))$ additions. It is also that of *Fibo3*. To go further in the comparison between the two DaC methods on the basis of arithmetic operations, it can be seen that in the best case the first method requires four additions and eight multiplications at each step of the key function *MatPower* while the second method systematically requires two additive operations and four multiplications[13] at each step of the key procedure *FiboW*. The second method is therefore better in all cases.

Answers to problem 90. Binary, ternary and interpolation searches *The problem is on page 427.*

Answer 1. We construct the operation "**function** *BinarySearch*(i, s, v)**result** $\mathbb{B}$" which delivers **true** iff v belongs to the sorted sub-array $T[i .. s]$. 90 - A 1

Base If $i = s$, the result is the one given by the evaluation of the expression $v = T[i]$.

Induction hypothesis Let $T[i'..s']$ be the sub-array such that $s' - i' + 1 \geqslant 1$ and $i'..s' \subset i..s$. It is known how to determine (using a binary search) whether v is or not present in $T[i' .. s']$.

Induction Let $s - i + 1 > 1$ and $mid = \lfloor (i + s)/2 \rfloor$. In the case where $v \leqslant T[mid]$, the value v is present in $T[i .. s]$ iff it is present in $T[i .. mid]$. The induction hypothesis allows to determine if v is present in $T[i .. mid]$. Symmetrically, if $v > T[mid]$, the value v is present in $T[i.. s]$ iff it is present in $T[mid + 1.. s]$ and the induction hypothesis allows to determine if v is present in $T[mid + 1 .. s]$.

Termination The search interval diminishes at each step while remaining positive and this ensures the termination of the algorithm.

The division model can therefore be formulated by:

$$\text{BinSearch}(1) \text{ elementary}$$
$$\text{BinSearch}(n) \rightarrow \begin{cases} \text{Compare the value } v \text{ to the one in the middle of the array} \\ + \\ \text{BinSearch}\left(\dfrac{n}{2}\right) \end{cases} \quad n > 1$$

The following code can be deduced:

```
1.  function BinarySearch(i, s, v) result 𝔹 pre
2.      i ∈ 1 .. n and s ∈ i .. n and v ∈ ℕ and
3.      mid ∈ i .. s and IsSorted(T[i .. s])
4.  begin
5.      if i = s then
6.          result v = T[i]
7.      else
8.          mid ← ⌊(i+s)/2⌋;
9.          if v ⩽ T[mid] then
10.             result BinarySearch (i, mid, v)
11.         else
12.             result BinarySearch (mid + 1, s, v)
```

---

[13]Assuming that multiplications by 2 are not performed by offsets and that a subtraction is equivalent to an addition.

13.   **end if**
14.   **end if**
15. **end**

A slightly different version of Bottenbruch's version above would be obtained by testing the equality between v and $T[mid]$ as soon as the value mid becomes available. In the worst case (looking for $T[n]$), this version is always worse than the above solution. However, the search for a value v such that $v > T[n]$ is done in constant time, which is not the case with the above solution. For reasons explained below, this type of solution is applied in the answer to question 6. The following program presents an example of a call to the function *BinarySearch*:

1. **constants**
2. $n \in \mathbb{N}_1$ and $n = \ldots$ and
3. $T \in 1 .. n \to \mathbb{N}$ and $T = [\ldots]$ and *IsSorted*$(T[1 .. n])$ and $w \in \mathbb{N}$ and $w = \ldots$
4. **begin**
5.   **write**$(BinarySearch(1, n, w))$
6. **end**

90 - A 2   **Answer 2.**

a. For $n = 4, 5, 6, 7$, the number of comparisons for $v \geqslant T[n]$ is $4, 5, 4, 5$ respectively. The corresponding curve is therefore not monotonous. Consequently, this solution does not guarantee that the search for $v \geqslant T[n]$ is the worst in terms of complexity. Indeed, an array of length $\lfloor n/3 \rfloor$ might require more comparisons than an array of length $\lfloor n/3 \rfloor + n \bmod 3$.

b. We have to prove that: (i) $\lfloor n/3 \rfloor = \lceil (n-2)/3 \rceil$, (ii) $\lfloor (n - \lfloor n/3 \rfloor)/2 \rfloor = \lceil (n-1)/3 \rceil$, and last (iii) $\lceil (n - \lfloor n/3 \rfloor)/2 \rceil = \lceil n/3 \rceil$. By construction:

$$n = \left\lfloor \frac{n}{3} \right\rfloor + \left\lfloor \frac{n - \lfloor \frac{n}{3} \rfloor}{2} \right\rfloor + \left\lceil \frac{n - \lfloor \frac{n}{3} \rfloor}{2} \right\rceil .$$

The property (see [15]):

$$n = \left\lceil \frac{n - m + 1}{m} \right\rceil + \cdots + \left\lceil \frac{n - 1}{m} \right\rceil + \left\lceil \frac{n}{m} \right\rceil \qquad \text{for } m > 0$$

allows to assert that

$$n = \left\lceil \frac{n - 2}{3} \right\rceil + \left\lceil \frac{n - 1}{3} \right\rceil + \left\lceil \frac{n}{3} \right\rceil .$$

It is therefore sufficient to prove, for example, that:

$$\left\lfloor \frac{n}{3} \right\rfloor = \left\lceil \frac{n - 2}{3} \right\rceil \quad \text{and} \quad \left\lceil \frac{n - \lfloor \frac{n}{3} \rfloor}{2} \right\rceil = \left\lceil \frac{n}{3} \right\rceil ,$$

the third equality will be deduced immediately. Let us prove these two properties.

$$\left\lfloor \frac{n}{3} \right\rfloor$$

$$= \qquad \text{property of } \lfloor \ \rfloor \text{ and } \lceil \ \rceil : \text{for } m > 0, \left\lfloor \frac{n}{m} \right\rfloor = \left\lceil \frac{n - m + 1}{m} \right\rceil$$

$$\left\lceil \frac{n - 2}{3} \right\rceil.$$

For the second property, a case analysis is performed according to the value of $(n \bmod 3)$, in order to remove the operator $\lfloor \ \rfloor$. The proof is performed only for $n \bmod 3 = 1$. Let us first observe that under this condition $\lfloor n/3 \rfloor = (n - 1)/3$.

$$\left\lceil \frac{n - \lfloor \frac{n}{3} \rfloor}{2} \right\rceil$$

$$= \qquad \text{hypothesis } n \bmod 3 = 1$$

$$\left\lceil \frac{n - \frac{n-1}{3}}{2} \right\rceil$$

$$= \qquad \text{arithmetics}$$

$$\left\lceil \frac{2n + 1}{2 \cdot 3} \right\rceil$$

$$= \qquad \text{arithmetics}$$

$$\left\lceil \frac{n}{3} + \frac{1}{6} \right\rceil$$

$$= \qquad \text{hypothesis } n \bmod 3 = 1$$

$$\left\lceil \frac{n}{3} \right\rceil.$$

We now build the operation "**function** *TernarySearch*(i, s, v) **result** $\mathbb{B}$", which delivers **true** iff v belongs to the sorted sub-array $T[i .. s]$.

Base If the length $(s - i + 1)$ of the sub-array is less than or equal to 2, v is directly compared to $T[i]$, then if necessary to $T[s]$.

Induction hyothesis Let $T[i' .. s']$ be a sub-array such that $s' - i' + 1 \geqslant 1$ and $i' .. s' \subset i .. s$. It is known how to determine by ternary search whether v is or not present in $T[i' .. s']$.

Induction Let $T[i .. s]$ be a sub-array of length greater than 2 $(s - i + 1 > 2)$, lg be its length $(lg = s - i + 1)$ and $OneThird$ be the end of the first third $(OneThird = i + \lceil (lg - 2)/3 \rceil - 1)$. In the case where $v \leqslant T[OneThird]$, the value v is present in $T[i .. s]$ iff it is present in $T[i .. OneThird]$ and the induction hypothesis is used to determine whether v is present or not in $T[i .. OneThird]$. Otherwise, let $TwoThirds = (s - \lceil lg/3 \rceil)$. If $v \leqslant T[TwoThirds]$, v is present in $T[i .. s]$ iff it is present in $T[OneThird + 1 .. TwoThirds]$ and the induction hypothesis is used to determine whether v is present or not in $T[OneThird + 1 .. TwoThirds]$. Finally, where needed, v is present in $T[i .. s]$ iff it is present in $T[TwoThirds + 1 .. s]$ and the induction hypothesis allows us to determine whether the value v is present in $T[TwoThirds + 1 .. s]$.

Termination The search interval decreases at each step (it is approximately divided by 3) while remaining positive, which guarantees the termination of the algorithm.

The division model can thus be formulated by:

$$
\begin{array}{l}
\text{TernSearch}(1)\ \text{elementary}\ \left(\begin{array}{l}\text{The element of the array of size}\\ \text{1 is or not the searched value } v\end{array}\right) \\[1em]
\text{TernSearch}(2)\ \text{elementary (the value } v \text{ is searched in } T[i \mathinner{\ldotp\ldotp} i+1]) \\[1em]
\text{TernSearch}(n) \rightarrow \left(\begin{array}{l}\text{Compare the value } v \text{ to that located at}\\ \text{the third of the array}\\ + \text{ if necessary:}\\ \text{Compare the value } v \text{ to that located}\\ \text{two thirds of the array}\\ +\\ \text{TernSearch}\left(\dfrac{n}{3}\right)\end{array}\right) \quad n > 2
\end{array}
$$

The following code can therefore be deduced:

```
 1.  function TernarySearch(i, s, v) result 𝔹 pre
 2.     i ∈ 1 .. n and s ∈ i .. n and v ∈ ℕ and
 3.     lg ∈ 1 .. i and OneThird ∈ i .. s and TwoThirds ∈ OneThird ..
          s and IsSorted(T[i .. s])
 4.  begin
 5.     if s − i + 1 ⩽ 2 then
 6.        if v = T[i] then
 7.           result true
 8.        else
 9.           result s > i and then v = T[s]
10.        end if
11.     else
```
$$12.\qquad lg \leftarrow s - i + 1;\ OneThird \leftarrow i + \left\lceil \frac{lg - 2}{3} \right\rceil - 1;$$
```
13.        if v ⩽ T[OneThird] then
14.           result TernarySearch(i, OneThird, v)
15.        else
```
$$16.\qquad\qquad TwoThirds \leftarrow s - \left\lceil \frac{lg}{3} \right\rceil;$$
```
17.           if v ⩽ T[TwoThirds] then
18.              result TernarySearch(OneThird + 1, TwoThirds, v)
19.           else
20.              result TernarySearch(TwoThirds + 1, s, v)
21.           end if
22.        end if
23.     end if
24.  end
```

90 - A 3　　**Answer 3.**　　Let us notice first of all that, in the best case, the ternary search is never worse than the binary search (in the first case we carry out the search in only a third of the array, and in the other in half).

The complexity at worst of the binary search is reached when the longest of the two sub-arrays (the one of size $\lceil n/2 \rceil$) is systematically treated. The corresponding equation $C_2(n)$ is as follows:

$$C_2(1) = 1$$
$$C_2(n) = C_2\left(\left\lceil\frac{n}{2}\right\rceil\right) + 1 \qquad\qquad n > 1.$$

Let us prove by induction on n that formula 8.11, page 428, is an exact solution to this equation.

Base For $n = 1$, we have on the one hand $C_2(1) = 1$, and on the other hand $\lceil\log_2(1)\rceil + 1 = 1$.

Induction hypothesis It is assumed that for any m such that $1 \leqslant m < n$, $C_2(m) = \lceil\log_2(m)\rceil + 1$.

Induction

$$C_2(n)$$
$$=$$
definition of C_2
$$C_2\left(\left\lceil\frac{n}{2}\right\rceil\right) + 1$$
$$=$$
induction hypothesis
$$\left(\left\lceil\log_2\left(\left\lceil\frac{n}{2}\right\rceil\right)\right\rceil + 1\right) + 1$$
$$=$$
case analysis: $\begin{cases} n \bmod 2 = 0 \Rightarrow \left\lceil\frac{n}{2}\right\rceil = \frac{n}{2} \\ n \bmod 2 = 1 \Rightarrow \left\lceil\frac{n}{2}\right\rceil = \frac{n+1}{2} \end{cases}$

$$\begin{cases} \left\lceil\log_2\left(\frac{n}{2}\right)\right\rceil + 2 & \text{for } n \text{ even} \\[2mm] \left\lceil\log_2\left(\frac{n+1}{2}\right)\right\rceil + 2 & \text{for } n \text{ odd} \end{cases}$$

$$=$$
property of $\log_2$ and $\lceil x + q\rceil = \lceil x\rceil + q$

$$\begin{cases} (\lceil\log_2(n)\rceil - 1) + 2 & \text{for } n \text{ even} \\ (\lceil\log_2(n+1)\rceil - 1) + 2 & \text{for } n \text{ odd} \end{cases}$$

$$=$$
arithmetics and $(q \bmod 2 = 1) \Rightarrow (\lceil\log_2(q)\rceil = \lceil\log_2(q+1)\rceil)$

$$\begin{cases} \lceil\log_2(n)\rceil + 1 & \text{for } n \text{ even} \\ \lceil\log_2(n)\rceil + 1 & \text{for } n \text{ odd.} \end{cases}$$

Figure 8.19, page 502, provides the graph of the function $C_2(n)$.

Answer 4.   90 - A 4

a. Figure 8.20, page 503, shows the seven decision trees for $n \in 1..7$.

   Since each node materializes a comparison between v and an element of the array, the complexity at worst $C_3(n)$ is given by the height h of the tree A_n: $C_3(n) = h(A_n)$.

b. The interpretation of the function *TernarySearch* yields the following inductive definition of A_n:

$$\begin{cases} A_1 = \langle /, T[1], /\rangle \\ A_2 = \langle /, T[1], \langle /, T[2], /\rangle\rangle \\ A_n = \left\langle A_{\lceil\frac{n-2}{3}\rceil}, T[Tiers], \left\langle A_{\lceil\frac{n-1}{3}\rceil}, T[DeuxTiers], A_{\lceil\frac{n}{3}\rceil}\right\rangle\right\rangle \qquad n > 2. \end{cases}$$

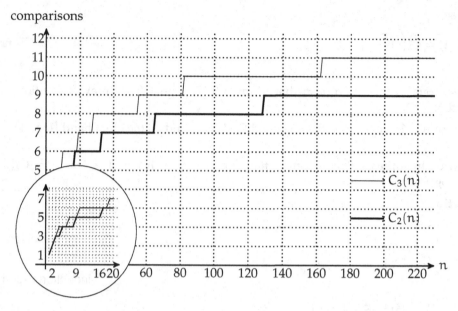

Fig. 8.19 – Complexity of binary and ternary searches for $v > T[n]$, with magnifying glass effect on the beginning of the curves.

The inductive definition of $h(A_n)$ is immediate:

$$
\begin{cases}
h(A_1) = 1 \\
h(A_2) = 2 \\
h(A_n) = \max \left(\left\{ \begin{array}{l} h\left(A_{\lceil \frac{n-2}{3} \rceil}\right), \\ h\left(\langle A_{\lceil \frac{n-1}{3} \rceil}, T[\text{DeuxTiers}], A_{\lceil \frac{n}{3} \rceil}\rangle\right) \end{array} \right\} \right) + 1 \qquad n > 2.
\end{cases}
$$

The third formula can be simplified into

$$
h(A_n) = \max \left(\left\{ h\left(A_{\lceil \frac{n-2}{3} \rceil}\right), h\left(A_{\lceil \frac{n-1}{3} \rceil}\right) + 1, h\left(A_{\lceil \frac{n}{3} \rceil}\right) + 1 \right\} \right) + 1.
$$

Now, let us prove that function h is monotonous. It is sufficient to prove that for any $n \in \mathbb{N}_1$, $h(A_n) \leqslant h(A_{n+1})$. This property is equivalent to "for any $n \in \mathbb{N}_1$ and for any $p \geqslant n$, $h(A_n) \leqslant h(A_p)$". The proof is carried out by induction on n. It is assumed (without any proof) that $\lceil (n-2)/3 \rceil \leqslant \lceil (n-1)/3 \rceil \leqslant \lceil n/3 \rceil$.

Base We have $h(1) \leqslant h(2)$ $(1 \leqslant 2)$ and $h(2) \leqslant h(3)$ $(2 \leqslant 3)$.

Induction hypothesis It is assumed that for any m such that $1 \leqslant m < n$, $h(A_m) \leqslant h(A_{m+1})$. It is also assumed that for any m such that $1 \leqslant m < n$ and for any $p \geqslant m, h(A_m) \leqslant h(A_p)$.

Induction

$$h(A_n) \leqslant h(A_p)$$

$\Leftrightarrow$ \hfill definition and property of h

$$
\begin{cases}
\max \left(\left\{ h\left(A_{\lceil \frac{n-2}{3} \rceil}\right), h\left(A_{\lceil \frac{n-1}{3} \rceil}\right) + 1, h\left(A_{\lceil \frac{n}{3} \rceil}\right) + 1 \right\} \right) + 1 \\
\leqslant \\
\max \left(\left\{ h\left(A_{\lceil \frac{p-2}{3} \rceil}\right), h\left(A_{\lceil \frac{p-1}{3} \rceil}\right) + 1, h\left(A_{\lceil \frac{p}{3} \rceil}\right) + 1 \right\} \right) + 1
\end{cases}
$$

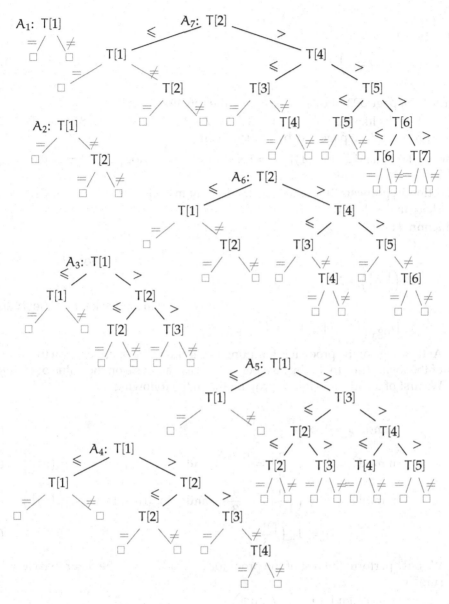

Fig. 8.20 – Decision trees A_1 to A_7 for ternary search.

$\Leftrightarrow$ induction hypothesis applied to each max

$$h\left(A_{\lceil \frac{n}{3} \rceil}\right) + 2 \leqslant h\left(A_{\lceil \frac{p}{3} \rceil}\right) + 2$$

$\Leftrightarrow$ induction hypothesis

true

It can be deduced that, in a decision tree, the right branch is the longest, or, if preferred, that the worst complexity is reached when looking for a v such that $v \geqslant T[n]$.

c. Given the equivalence between the height of the decision tree and the maximum number of comparisons, the equation $C_3(n)$ that provides the worst-case complexity of ternary search (for $v \geqslant T[n]$) is as follows:

$$C_3(1) = 1$$
$$C_3(2) = 2$$
$$C_3(n) = C_3\left(\left\lceil\frac{n}{3}\right\rceil\right) + 2 \qquad\qquad\qquad\qquad\qquad\qquad n > 2.$$

Figure 8.19, page 502, shows the graph of the function $C_3(n)$.

The set E looks like this: $E = 1 .. 1 \cup 3 .. 3 \cup 7 .. 9 \cup 19 .. 27 \cup 55 .. 81 \cup \cdots$ Let us now prove property 8.12, page 428, by induction on n.

Base $C_3(1) = 1$ and $2 \cdot \lceil\log_3(1)\rceil + 1 = 1$, $C_3(2) = 2$ and $2 \cdot \lceil\log_3(2)\rceil + 0 = 2 \cdot \lceil 0.63\ldots\rceil + 0 = 2$.

Induction hypothesis It is assumed that for any m such that $1 \leqslant m < n$, $C_3(m) = (2 \cdot \lceil\log_3(m)\rceil + 1_E(m))$.

Induction For $n > 2$:

$$C_3(n)$$
$$=\qquad\qquad\qquad\qquad\qquad\qquad\qquad\qquad\qquad \text{definition of } C_3(n) \text{ for } n > 2$$
$$C_3\left(\left\lceil\frac{n}{3}\right\rceil\right) + 2$$
$$=\qquad\qquad\qquad\qquad\qquad\qquad \left\lceil\frac{n}{3}\right\rceil < n\text{: the induction hypothesis applies}$$
$$2 \cdot \left\lceil\log_3\left(\left\lceil\frac{n}{3}\right\rceil\right)\right\rceil + 1_E\left(\left\lceil\frac{n}{3}\right\rceil\right) + 2.$$

At this stage of the proof, it is tempting to eliminate the operator $\lceil\ \rceil$ in the argument of the logarithm. To do this, we perform a case analysis on the value of $(n \bmod 3)$. We first of all admit, without proving them, the following results:

$$n \bmod 3 = 0 \Rightarrow \left\lceil\frac{n}{3}\right\rceil = \frac{n}{3} \qquad\qquad\qquad\qquad\qquad (8.26)$$

$$n \bmod 3 = 1 \Rightarrow \left(\left\lceil\frac{n}{3}\right\rceil = \frac{n+2}{3} \ \text{ and } \ \lceil\log_3(n+2)\rceil = \lceil\log_3(n)\rceil\right) \quad (8.27)$$

$$n \bmod 3 = 2 \Rightarrow \left(\left\lceil\frac{n}{3}\right\rceil = \frac{n+1}{3} \ \text{ and } \ \lceil\log_3(n+1)\rceil = \lceil\log_3(n)\rceil\right) \quad (8.28)$$

$$1_E(n) = 1_E\left(\left\lceil\frac{n}{3}\right\rceil\right). \qquad\qquad\qquad\qquad\qquad (8.29)$$

We only perform the rest of the proof for $(n \bmod 3) = 2$, the other two cases being similar:

$$2 \cdot \left\lceil\log_3\left(\left\lceil\frac{n}{3}\right\rceil\right)\right\rceil + 1_E\left(\left\lceil\frac{n}{3}\right\rceil\right) + 2$$
$$=\qquad\qquad\qquad\qquad\qquad\qquad\qquad\qquad\qquad \text{properties 8.28 and 8.29}$$
$$2 \cdot \left\lceil\log_3\left(\frac{n+1}{3}\right)\right\rceil + 1_E(n) + 2$$
$$=\qquad\qquad\qquad\qquad\qquad\qquad\qquad\qquad \text{property of } \log_3 \text{ and arithmetics}$$
$$2 \cdot \lceil\log_3(n+1) - 1\rceil + 1_E(n) + 2$$
$$=\qquad\qquad\qquad\qquad\qquad\qquad \text{property of } \lceil\ \rceil\text{: } \lceil x + q\rceil = \lceil x\rceil + q$$
$$2 \cdot \lceil\log_3(n+1)\rceil - 2 + 1_E(n) + 2$$
$$=\qquad\qquad\qquad\qquad\qquad\qquad\qquad \text{arithmetics and property 8.28}$$
$$2 \cdot \lceil\log_3(n)\rceil + 1_E(n).$$

90 - A 5 **Answer 5.** It remains to prove that $C_3(n) \geqslant C_2(n)$ for any $n \in \mathbb{N}_1$. We choose to use on the one hand the recurrent equation of C_3, on the other hand formula 8.11, page 428.

Base For $n = 1$: $\lceil \log_2(1) \rceil + 1 = 1$ and $C_3(1) = 1$. For $n = 2$: $\lceil \log_2(2) \rceil + 1 = 2$ and $C_3(2) = 2$.

Induction hypothesis For any m such that $1 \leqslant m < n$, $\lceil \log_2(m) \rceil + 1 \leqslant C_3(m)$.

Induction

$$C_3(n)$$

$= \qquad\qquad\qquad\qquad\qquad\qquad\qquad\qquad\qquad$ definition of C_3

$$C_3\left(\left\lceil \frac{n}{3} \right\rceil \right) + 2$$

$\geqslant \qquad\qquad\qquad\qquad\qquad$ $\left\lceil \frac{n}{3} \right\rceil < n$, the induction hypothesis applies

$$\left(\left\lceil \log_2\left(\left\lceil \frac{n}{3} \right\rceil \right) \right\rceil + 1 \right) + 2$$

$= \qquad\qquad\qquad\qquad\qquad\qquad\qquad\qquad\qquad$ commutativity of operator $+$

$$\left(\left\lceil \log_2\left(\left\lceil \frac{n}{3} \right\rceil \right) \right\rceil + 2 \right) + 1$$

$= \qquad\qquad\qquad\qquad\qquad\qquad$ property of $\lceil \ \rceil$: $\lceil x \rceil + q = \lceil x + q \rceil$

$$\left(\left\lceil \log_2\left(\left\lceil \frac{n}{3} \right\rceil \right) + 2 \right\rceil \right) + 1$$

$= \qquad\qquad\qquad\qquad\qquad\qquad\qquad\qquad\qquad$ property of $\log_2$

$$\left\lceil \log_2\left(4 \cdot \left\lceil \frac{n}{3} \right\rceil \right) \right\rceil + 1$$

$\geqslant \qquad\qquad\qquad\qquad\qquad\qquad$ $4 \cdot \left\lceil \frac{n}{3} \right\rceil > n$, monotonicity of log

$$\lceil \log_2 n \rceil + 1$$

$= \qquad\qquad\qquad\qquad\qquad\qquad\qquad\qquad\qquad$ definition

$$C_2(n).$$

It can be deduced that in the worst case ternary search is never better than binary search.

Answer 6. We begin by specifying the principle of the search by interpolation before constructing the operation. Let us first consider the case of an array $T[i..s]$ in which the values progress linearly from the position i to the position s (this is the case (a) in figure 8.21). To determine the presence of the element v in T, simply consider the position p defined by: $\qquad$ 90 - A 6

$$\frac{p - i}{s - i} = \frac{v - T[i]}{T[s] - T[i]},$$

or $p = i + \lfloor ((s - i) \cdot (v - T[i])) / (T[s] - T[i]) \rfloor$, before comparing v and $T[p]$. Generally, T does not exactly satisfy the condition of linearity assumed above: without prejudging the presence or absence of v in $T[i .. s]$, one can have $v \neq T[p]$. This is shown by the cases (b) and (c) in figure 8.21. Case (b) is quasi-linear, while case (c) is widely far from linear. Let us construct the operation "**function** *InterpSearch*(i, s, v) **result** $\mathbb{B}$" which determines the presence of v in the array $T[i .. s]$.

First attempt (inspired from the binary search):

Base If $i = s$, the result is that of the evaluation of the expression $v = T[i]$.

Induction hypothesis Let $T[i'..s']$ be the sub-array such that $s' - i' + 1 \geqslant 1$ and $i'..s' \subset i..s$. It can be determined by interpolation whether v is or not present in $T[i' .. s']$.

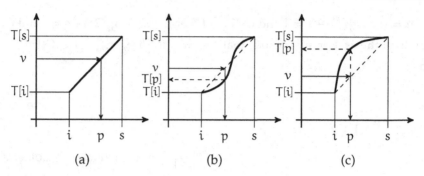

Fig. 8.21 – Principle of the search by interpolation.

Induction Let $s - i + 1 > 1$ and $p = i + \lfloor((s-i) \cdot (v - T[i]))/(T[s] - T[i])\rfloor$. In the case where $v \leqslant T[p]$, the value v is present in $T[i \mathinner{\ldotp\ldotp} s]$ iff it is present in $T[i \mathinner{\ldotp\ldotp} p]$. But the induction hypothesis requires that $i \mathinner{\ldotp\ldotp} p \subset i \mathinner{\ldotp\ldotp} s$, condition that is not guaranteed since s and p can designate the same position.

Therefore, it is necessary to make sure that the new search interval decreases with respect to $i \mathinner{\ldotp\ldotp} s$. One solution is to examine the case $v = T[p]$ separately; if this fails, the intervals on either side of p are shorter than those of $i \mathinner{\ldotp\ldotp} s$ and the induction hypothesis can be applied. A new base is required and the following induction construction is considered.

Base If $v \notin T[i] \mathinner{\ldotp\ldotp} T[s]$, v is absent from the array.

Induction hypothesis Unchanged.

Induction Let $(s - i + 1) > 1$ and $p = (i + \lfloor((s-i) \cdot (v - T[i]))/(T[s] - T[i])\rfloor)$. If $v = T[p]$, v is present in the array. Otherwise, for the case where $v < T[p]$, the value v is present in $T[i \mathinner{\ldotp\ldotp} s]$ iff it is present in $T[i \mathinner{\ldotp\ldotp} p - 1]$. The induction hypothesis allows to determine by interpolation if v is present in $T[i \mathinner{\ldotp\ldotp} p - 1]$. The case where $v > T[p]$ is symmetric.

Termination For an array of length n, the length of the new search interval is between $(n - 1)$ and $\lfloor n/2 \rfloor$[14]. The search interval therefore strictly decreases at each step while remaining positive. This ensures termination.

The division model can be formulated by:

$$
\text{IntSearch}(n) \rightarrow
\begin{cases}
\text{elementary} & \text{if } v \notin T[i] \mathinner{\ldotp\ldotp} T[s] \\
\text{Compute } p + \\
\text{Compare } v \text{ and } T[p]
\begin{cases}
\text{elementary} & \text{if } v = T[p] \\
\text{IntSearch}(m) \text{ with } \lfloor n/2 \rfloor \leqslant m \leqslant n - 1 & \text{if } v \neq T[p]
\end{cases}
\end{cases}
$$

The following program can be thus deduced:

1. **function** *InterpSearch*(i, s, v) **result** $\mathbb{B}$ **pre**
2. $i \in 1 \mathinner{\ldotp\ldotp} n$ **and** $s \in i \mathinner{\ldotp\ldotp} n$ **and** $v \in \mathbb{N}$ **and**
3. $p \in i \mathinner{\ldotp\ldotp} s$ **and** *IsSorted*$(T[i \mathinner{\ldotp\ldotp} s])$
4. **begin**
5.   **if** $v \notin T[i] \mathinner{\ldotp\ldotp} T[s]$ **then**
6.   **result false**

---

[14]The case where v is outside the bounds $T[i] \mathinner{\ldotp\ldotp} T[s]$ does not lead to a new search, this is the case handled by the base.

7. **else**
8. $p \leftarrow i + \left\lfloor \dfrac{(s-i) \cdot (v - T[i])}{T[s] - T[i]} \right\rfloor$;
9.   **if** $v = T[p]$ **then**
10.   **result true**
11.   **elsif** $v < T[p]$ **then**
12.   **result** *InterpSearch* $(i, p-1, v)$
13.   **else**
14.   **result** *InterpSearch* $(p+1, s, v)$
15.   **end if**
16.   **end if**
17. **end**

Although similar to binary search, interpolation search differs from it by at least two points: it requires a calculation on the values of the array (which limits its scope), and it is all the more efficient in terms of complexity as the array is "linear" (at worst, complexity can be reached in $\Theta(n)$ in situations similar to case (c) of figure 8.21, page 506). In the case of a uniform distribution of the values in the array T, it can be proven that the complexity is in $\mathcal{O}(\log_2(n))$, which is remarkable. However, empirical tests show that in terms of complexity the interpolation surpasses binary search only for very large values of n. A mixture of the two methods can then be envisaged.

Answers to problem 91. Searching for a fixpoint   *The problem is on page 429.*

Answer 1.   Figure 8.22, page 508, shows the principal cases to envisage (or to discard).   91 - A 1
We note [diagram (b)] that as soon as $T[1] > 1$ there can be no fixpoint since the function represented by T is strictly increasing and therefore cannot intersect the identity function. Consequently, there is an infinity of cases for which it can be concluded directly (i.e. in constant time) in the negative. Similarly, schema (c) is another case where one can also conclude in the negative. It is characterized simply by the fact that $T[n] < n$. On the other hand, schema (d) requires a search: T not being a continuous function, it may or may not have one (or more) fixpoint(s). In other words, only those functions T are considered that may cross "up" (or overlap) the identity function, the others may not contain a fixpoint.
It is proposed to structure the solution as follows. The operation "**function** *FixPoint* **result** $\mathbb{B}$" searched takes into account first of all the cases for which the conclusion is immediate; it calls the search operation only if necessary. This latter operation, whose header is "**function** *FixPointAux*(i, s)**result** $\mathbb{B}$" applies the DaC principle to perform a fixpoint search in $T[i .. s]$. We provide the code of the operation *FixPoint* before building the operation *FixPointAux*.

1. **function** *FixPoint* **result** $\mathbb{B}$
2. **begin**
3.   /% *We call* FixPointAux *only if necessary:* %/
4.   /% *case (d) of figure 8.22, page 508* %/
5.   **result** $(T[1] \leqslant 1 \text{ and } T[n] \geqslant n)$ **and then** *FixPointAux*$(1, n)$
6. **end**

The construction of the operation "**function** *FixPointAux*(i, s)**result** $\mathbb{B}$" is carried out as follows:

Base If $i = s$, the array has a fixpoint iff $T[i] = i$.

Induction hypothesis Let $T[i' .. s']$ such that $i' .. s' \subset i .. s$ and $i' \neq s' \Rightarrow T[i'] \leqslant i'$ and $T[s'] \geqslant s'$. We know how to determine if $T[i' .. s']$ has or not (at least) one fixpoint.

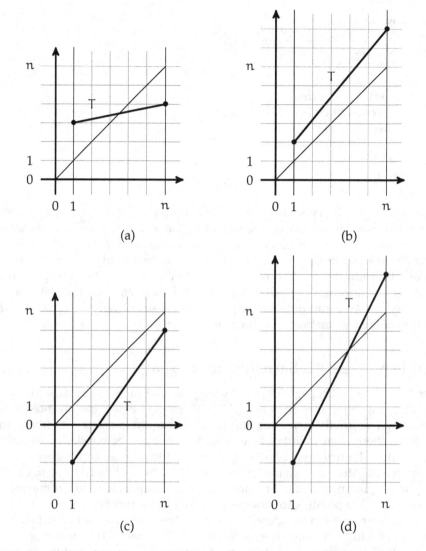

Fig. 8.22 – Location of T *with respect to the identity function: the main cases to consider. This figure (abusively) assimilates* T *to a continuous function. Schema (a) is impossible:* T *must have a slope greater than or equal to that of the identity. In schema (b),* $T[1] > 1$: T *cannot cross the identity function, there cannot be a fixpoint. In schema (c) since* $T[n] < n$, T *remains under the identity function: there can be no fixed point either. Last, in schema (d), the origin of* T *is below or on the identity function, and its end is on or above the identity function: there can be a fixpoint.*

Induction If $T\big[\lfloor(i+s)/2\rfloor\big] \geqslant \lfloor(i+s)/2\rfloor$, if there is a fixpoint in T, there is one in $T\big[i..\lfloor(i+s)/2\rfloor\big]$. Moreover, this latter sub-array meets the conditions of the induction hypothesis (and especially $i \neq \lfloor(i+s)/2\rfloor \Rightarrow T[i] \leqslant i$ **and** $T\big[\lfloor(i+s)/2\rfloor\big] \geqslant \lfloor(i+s)/2\rfloor$). We can therefore determine whether or not it has a fixpoint. The case $T\big[\lfloor(i+s)/2\rfloor\big] < \lfloor(i+s)/2\rfloor$ is analogous.

Termination The length of the considered sub-array decreases at each step while remaining positive. This ensures the termination of the algorithm.

The division model for this operation is the one we find in any binary search:

FixPtAux(1) elementary

$$\text{FixPtAux}(n) \rightarrow \begin{pmatrix} \text{Compare the value in the middle of the array} \\ \text{and the value of the index of this element } + \\ \text{FixPtAux}\left(\left\lfloor \dfrac{n}{2} \right\rfloor\right) \end{pmatrix} \qquad n > 1$$

and the code of the operation can be deduced:

1. **function** *FixPointAux*(i, s) **result** $\mathbb{B}$ **pre**
2. $i \in 1 .. n$ **and** $s \in i .. n$ **and**
3. $i \neq s \Rightarrow T[i] \leqslant i$ **and** $T[s] \geqslant s$
4. **begin**
5.   **if** $i = s$ **then**
6.   **result** $i = T[i]$
7.   **else**
8.   **if** $T\left[\left\lfloor \dfrac{i+s}{2} \right\rfloor\right] \geqslant \left\lfloor \dfrac{i+s}{2} \right\rfloor$ **then**
9.   **result** *FixPointAux*$\left(i, \left\lfloor \dfrac{i+s}{2} \right\rfloor\right)$
10.   **else**
11.   **result** *FixPointAux*$\left(\left\lfloor \dfrac{i+s}{2} \right\rfloor + 1, s\right)$
12.   **end if**
13.   **end if**
14. **end**

Complexity

The only cases leading to a binary search (known to be in $\Theta(\log_2(n))$) are those for which $T[1] \leqslant 1$ and $T[n] \geqslant n$. In all other cases, the complexity (in number of conditions evaluated) is in constant time. The complexity $C(n)$ for an array of n elements is therefore expressed as:

$$C(n) \in \begin{cases} \Theta(\log_2(n)) & \text{if } T[1] \leqslant 1 \text{ and } T[n] \geqslant n \\ \Theta(1) & \text{otherwise.} \end{cases}$$

Answer 2.   Since $T[1] \geqslant 1$, T is always on or above the identity function. If the set of fixpoints of T is not empty, 1 is one of them. So it is sufficient to compare $T[1]$ to 1: | 91 - A 2

1. **function** *FixPoint* **result** $\mathbb{B}$
2. **begin**
3.   **result** $T[1] = 1$
4. **end**

Complexity

The average complexity of this solution is trivially in constant time.

Answers to problem 92. Searching in a cyclic sorted array   *The problem is on page 429.*

The problem is on page 429.

92 - A 1   **Answer** 1.   *Proof of property 9*

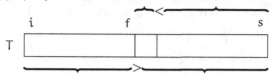

The case $f = s$ is trivial: $T[i .. s]$ is sorted and $T[i]$ is therefore the smallest element. As for the general case where $f \in i .. s - 1$, let:

$$m = \min(\mathrm{codom}(T[i .. f]))$$
$$m' = \min(\mathrm{codom}(T[f + 1 .. s]))$$
$$M' = \max(\mathrm{codom}(T[f + 1 .. s]))$$

which represent three of the *extrema* of each slice. On the one hand:

   $IsCyclicSorted(T[i .. s])$ **and** f is the boundary

$\Rightarrow$

   $m' \leqslant M'$ **and** $M' < m$

and on the other hand:

   $IsCyclicSorted(T[i .. s])$ **and** f is the boundary

$\Rightarrow$

   $IsSorted(T[f + 1 .. s])$

$\Rightarrow$

   $T[f + 1] = m'$.

Therefore:

$$T[f + 1] = m' \leqslant M' < m$$

$T[f + 1]$ is less than or equal to the two minima: $T[f + 1]$ is thus the smallest element of $T[i .. s]$.

Proof of property 10.
If $f \leqslant m$:

   $IsCyclicSorted(T[i .. s])$

$\Rightarrow$ f is the boundary

   $IsSorted(T[f + 1 .. s])$

$\Rightarrow$ hypothesis $f \leqslant m$

   $IsSorted(T[m + 1 .. s])$.

Therefore $T[m + 1 .. s]$ is a cyclic sorted array. As for $T[i .. m]$, $T[i .. f]$ is sorted, as well as $T[f + 1 .. m]$ and all elements of $T[i .. f]$ are greater than those of $T[f + 1 .. m]$. $T[i .. m]$ is therefore a cyclic sorted sub-array. If $m \leqslant f$, by a similar approach it can be proven that $T[i .. m]$ is sorted and that $T[m + 1 .. s]$ is cyclic sorted, which completes the proof of the property.

Proof of property 11. Let us proceed to a case-based analysis, starting with the case where $T[m .. s]$ is sorted:

   $IsSorted(T[m .. s])$

$\Rightarrow$ f is the boundary

   $f \in i .. m - 1$

$\Rightarrow$ property 9

$T[f+1] = \min(\text{codom}(T[i..s]))$

$\Rightarrow$ $\qquad\qquad\qquad\qquad\qquad\qquad\qquad\qquad\qquad\qquad f < m$

$\min(\text{codom}(T[i..s])) \in \text{codom}(T[i..m])$.

Therefore, the smallest element of $T[i..s]$ belongs to $T[i..m]$. Let us now deal with the case where $T[m..s]$ is not sorted.

not *IsSorted*$(T[m..s])$

$\Rightarrow$ $\qquad\qquad\qquad\quad$ f is the boundary and $f = s \Rightarrow$ *IsSorted*$(T[m..s])$

$f \in m..s-1$

$\Rightarrow$ $\qquad\qquad\qquad\qquad\qquad\qquad\qquad\qquad\qquad\qquad$ property 9

$T[f+1] = \min(\text{codom}(T[i..s]))$

$\Rightarrow$ $\qquad\qquad\qquad\qquad\qquad\qquad f \in m..s-1 \Rightarrow f+1 \in m+1..s$

$\min(\text{codom}(T[i..s])) \in \text{codom}(T[m+1..s]))$.

Therefore, the smallest element of $T[i..s]$ belongs to $T[m+1..s]$.

Proof of property 12. The direct part of the proof is simple and results immediately from the properties of a sorted array. For the reciprocal, let us carry out a case-based analysis, distinguishing between cases $f = s$ and $f < s$. If $f = s$, from the definition of a cyclic sorted array, $T[i..s]$ is sorted. The case $f < s$ is proven as follows:

IsCyclicSorted$(T[i..s])$

$\Rightarrow$

$\min(\text{codom}(T[i..f])) > \max(\text{codom}(T[f+1..s]))$

$\Rightarrow$ $\qquad\quad$ *IsCyclicSorted*$(T[i..s])$, *IsSorted*$(T[i..f])$ and *IsSorted*$(T[f+1..s])$

$T[i] > T[s]$

which contradicts the hypothesis $T[i] \leqslant T[s]$ and the case $f < s$ is indeed impossible.

Answer 2. We carry out a reasoning of type "partition induction" (see section 1.1.4, page 7). 92 - A 2

Base The base case $(i = s)$ is trivial.

Induction hypothesis Let p be such that $1 \leqslant p < n$. It is known how to find the smallest element of any cyclic sorted array of p elements.

Induction Let $T[i..s]$ be an array of n elements. We take the value $m = \lfloor(i+s)/2\rfloor$ to divide the array in two parts. According to property 10, page 430, the two sub-arrays $T[i..m]$ and $T[m+1..s]$ are cyclic sorted arrays, and according to property 11, page 430, if the sub-array $T[m..s]$ is not sorted (i.e. if $T[m] > T[s]$), $T[m+1..s]$ contains the smallest element. Otherwise $T[i..m]$ contains the smallest element and in any case, the induction hypothesis ensures that it is known how to find the smallest element of $T[i..s]$.

Termination The size of the processed array decreases at each step while remaining positive and this ensures the termination of the algorithm.

The division model that applies for an array of size n is then:

$\text{SmallestElt}(1)$ elementary

$\text{SmallestElt}(n) \rightarrow$ evaluate *IsSorted*$(T[m..s]) + \text{SmallestElem}\left(\dfrac{n}{2}\right)$ $\qquad n > 1$

The code of this function is:

1. **function** *SmallestElement*(i, s) **result** $\mathbb{N}$ **pre**
2. $\quad i \in 1..n$ **and** $s \in i..n$ **and** *IsCyclicSorted*$(T[i..s])$ **and** $m \in i..s-1$

3. **begin**
4.   **if** i = s **then**
5.   **result** T[i]
6.   **else**
7. $m \leftarrow \left\lfloor \dfrac{i+s}{2} \right\rfloor ;$
8.   **if** T[m] > T[s] **then**
9.   **result** *SmallestElement*(m + 1, s)
10.   **else**
11.   **result** *SmallestElement*(i, m)
12.   **end if**
13.   **end if**
14. **end**

Complexity

For an array of size n, the complexity equation (expressed in terms of conditions evaluated) is:

$$\left| \begin{array}{l} C(1) = 1 \\ C(n) = C\left(\dfrac{n}{2}\right) + 2 \end{array} \right. \qquad\qquad n > 1.$$

Hence, according to formula 8.1, page 423, $C(n) \in \Theta(\log_2(n))$.

92 - A 3   **Answer** 3.   Here again, a reasoning of the type "partition induction" is carried out (see section 1.1.4, page 7).

Base The base case (i = s) is trivial.

Induction hypothesis Let p be such that $1 \leqslant p < n$. For any cyclic sorted array of p elements, it is known how to determine whether or not v is present in T.

Induction The best information available for such a search is the character, sorted or unsorted, of the arrays under consideration. If an array is sorted and the value v is within the array boundaries, the search must be done in that array. If the array is sorted and the value v is not within the bounds of the sub-array, it is useless to search in the sub-array. Let T[i .. s] be an array of n elements. Let us apply this principle to the two sub-arrays T[i .. m] and T[m + 1 .. s], with $m = \lfloor (i+s)/2 \rfloor$. The search is performed in T[i .. m] if one of the following two conditions is met:

$$IsSorted(T[i .. m]) \textbf{ and } v \in T[i] .. T[m]$$

or else if

$$IsSorted(T[m + 1 .. s]) \textbf{ and } v \notin T[m + 1] .. T[s].$$

In all cases, the induction hypothesis ensures that it is possible to decide on the presence of v in one of the sub-arrays, and thus in T[i .. s].

Termination The size of the array under consideration decreases at each step while remaining positive and this ensures the termination of the algorithm.

Hence the following draft of the function *Belong*:

1. **function** *Belong*(i, s, v) **result** $\mathbb{B}$ **pre**
2. $i \in 1..n$ **and** $s \in i..n$ **and** $v \in \mathbb{N}$ **and** *IsCyclicSorted*$(T[i..s])$ **and** $m \in i..s-1$
3. **begin**
4.   **if** $i = s$ **then**
5.   **result** $T[i] = v$
6.   **else**
7. $m \leftarrow \left\lfloor \dfrac{i+s}{2} \right\rfloor;$
8.   **if** $\left(\begin{array}{l} (\textit{IsSorted}(T[i..m]) \textbf{ and } v \in T[i]..T[m]) \\ \textbf{or} \\ (\textit{IsSorted}(T[m+1..s]) \textbf{ and } v \notin T[m+1]..T[s]) \end{array} \right)$ **then**
9.   **result** *Belong*(i, m, v)
10.   **else**
11.   **result** *Belong*$(m+1, s, v)$
12.   **end if**
13.   **end if**
14. **end**

The condition of the inner alternative can easily be refined (especially using property 12, page 430) in the following form:

$$(T[i] \leqslant v \textbf{ and } v \leqslant T[m]) \textbf{ or } (T[m+1] \leqslant T[s] \textbf{ and not } (T[m+1] \leqslant v \textbf{ and } v \leqslant T[s])).$$

The division model as well as the complexity equation are similar to those of the second question. So we have a solution in $\Theta(\log_2(n))$ and the objective is achieved.

Answers to problem 93. Local minimum in a binary tree   *The problem is on page 431.*

Answer 1.   Since the tree is not empty, it certainly contains a node which has the smallest value. This node is therefore a global minimum and *a fortiori* a local minimum.   93 - A 1

Answer 2.   Let us carry out an inductive construction of the operation *LocMin*:   93 - A 2

Base Two cases are to be considered:

1. In a full tree reduced to its root, this latter is a local minimum.
2. In a full tree not reduced to its root, whose root is less than its two sons, the root is a local minimum.

Induction hypothesis It is known how to find a local minimum is a full tree of $((n-1)/2)$ nodes.

Induction We consider a full tree a with two nonempty subtrees l and r each having a root. One (at least) of the two roots is less than the root of a (otherwise we would be in the second base case). Let s be the corresponding subtree ($s = l$ or $s = r$). s has a local minimum (see question 1) that can be determined from the induction hypothesis, since each subtree of a has $((n-1)/2)$ nodes. If it is the root of s, it is also a local minimum of a (since this value is less than the root of a), otherwise it is still a local minimum of a. In all cases, the sought value is a local minimum of s.

Termination In the inductive part, the search is carried out in a tree of lower weight, which ensures the termination.

Like the construction above, the division model presents two cases for the base:

LMin(1) elementary	the tree reduced to its root.
LMin(n) elementary	$\left(\begin{array}{l} n > 1 \text{ and the root value is} \\ \text{less than that of its two sons.} \end{array}\right)$
$LMin(n) \rightarrow LMin\left(\dfrac{n-1}{2}\right)$	$\left(\begin{array}{l} n > 1 \text{ and the root value is greater} \\ \text{than that of one of its two sons.} \end{array}\right)$

The code of the function *LocMin* is written as follows:

```
1.  function LocMin(a) result Z pre
2.      a ∈ ft and a ≠ /
3.  begin
4.      if (a.l = /) or else (a.l.v > a.v and a.r.v > a.v) then
5.          result a.v
6.      else
7.          if a.l.v < a.v then
8.              result LocMin(a.l)
9.          else
10.             result LocMin(a.r)
11.         end if
12.     end if
13. end
```

Here is an example of calling program of the function *LocMin* for the first tree of the statement of the problem:

```
1. constants
2.     /% h(a): height of a binary tree a – see Chapter 1 %/
3.     ft = {/} ∪ {(l,v,r) | l ∈ ft and v ∈ Z and r ∈ ft and h(l) = h(r)}
4. variables
5.     t ∈ ft
6. begin
7.     t ← (((/,11,/),10,(/,13,/)),21,((/,36,/),31,(/,33,/)));
8.     write(LocMin(t))
9. end
```

Complexity

The complexity at worst of the function *LocMin* in terms of conditions evaluated is given by the following recurrence equation:

$$\begin{array}{l} C(1) = 1 \\ C(n) = C\left(\dfrac{n}{2}\right) + 2 \end{array} \qquad n > 1.$$

The worst case occurs when a leaf is found as a local minimum. From the particular case 8.3 of the corollary of the master theorem (see page 422), we have $C(n) \in \mathcal{O}(\log_2(n))$ (it is a logarithmic reduction).

Answer 3.   The proposed method can easily be adapted to any arbitrary binary tree.   93 - A 3
This is done by transforming the induction into a strong one and extending the reasoning
to nodes with 0, 1 or 2 descendant(s). Let us proceed to an induction reasoning.

Base Two cases are to be considered:

1. In a binary tree reduced to its root, this latter is a local minimum.
2. In a binary tree not reduced to its root, whose root value is less than that of its two
   sons, the root is a local minimum.

Induction hypothesis For $n \geqslant 2$, it is known how to find a local minimum in a binary
having less than n nodes.

Induction Two cases are to be considered, that of a binary tree a endowed with two non-
empty sub-trees and that of a binary tree a having a single non-empty sub-tree. The
first case is the same as the one of the induction developed in question 2, except that
the above extended induction hypothesis is used. As for it, the second case is a special
case of the first.

Termination In the inductive part, the search is carried out in a tree of lower weight, which
ensures the termination.

Answers to problem 94. Diameter of a binary tree   *The problem is on page 431.*

Answer 1.   Below are two examples of diameters that do not pass through the root.   94 - A 1

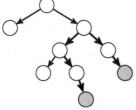   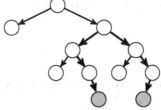

(a) diameter of five arcs   (b) diameter of six arcs

In diagram (a), there is also a diameter which goes through the root, whereas in diagram
(b) this is not the case.

Answer 2.   Each node is encountered once and only once. So we have $C_h(n) = n$, hence   94 - A 2
$C(n) \in \Theta(n)$.
In the first question, we have seen that a diameter does not necessarily go through the root.
We will therefore consider two cases to define the function d:

1. If the diameter can pass through the root, it is the height of the left subtree
   plus the height of the right subtree, plus 2 (to count each of the two arcs that
   connect a subtree to the root).
2. If no diameter passes through the root, the diameter is the larger of the two
   diameters of the root subtrees.

So we have:

$$\begin{cases} d(/) & = & -1 \\ d((l, r)) & = & \max(\{h(l) + h(r) + 2, d(l), d(r)\}). \end{cases}$$

The code of this function can be obtained directly from the definition above:

1. **function** $d(a)$ **result** $\mathbb{N} \cup \{-1\}$ **pre**
2. $\quad a \in bt$
3. **begin**
4. $\quad$ **if** $a = /$ **then**
5. $\quad\quad$ **result** -1
6. $\quad$ **else**
7. $\quad\quad$ **result** $\max(\{h(a.l) + h(a.r) + 2, d(a.l), d(a.r)\})$
8. $\quad$ **end if**
9. **end**

It can be noted that, in general, during a calculation, a given node is encountered several times.

Complexity

In the case of a threadlike tree, the recurrence equation is as follows:

$$
\begin{aligned}
C_d(0) &= 0 \\
C_d(n) &= C_d(n-1) + C_h(n-1) + 1 \qquad\qquad\qquad n > 0.
\end{aligned}
$$

For a non-empty tree, the root is visited (once) and its (single) sub-tree is visited twice (once for the height and once for the diameter). Let us start by simplifying the second formula:

$$C_d(n) = C_d(n-1) + C_h(n-1) + 1$$
$$\Leftrightarrow \qquad\qquad\qquad\qquad\qquad\qquad\qquad\qquad\qquad\qquad\qquad T_h(n) = n$$
$$C_d(n) = C_d(n-1) + n - 1 + 1$$
$$\Leftrightarrow \qquad\qquad\qquad\qquad\qquad\qquad\qquad\qquad\qquad\qquad \text{arithmetics}$$
$$C_d(n) = C_d(n-1) + n$$

By summation, it is easy to show that $C_d(n) = (n \cdot (n+1))/2$, and therefore that $C_d(n) \in \Theta(n^2)$.

94 - A 3 **Answer** 3. It suffices to transform the function d into the function dh which computes *simultaneously* the diameter and the height of a binary tree. We assume available the set DiamHeight such that DiamHeight $= \{$Diam, Height $\mid$ Diam $\in \mathbb{N} \cup \{-1\}$ **and** Height $\in \mathbb{N} \cup \{-1\}\}$. The construction of the operation "**function** $dh(a)$ **result** DiamHeight" which delivers the pair (diameter, height) is carried out as follows:

Base In the case of an empty tree, the result is the pair $(-1, -1)$.

Induction hypothesis It is known how to compute the diameter and height of any binary tree whose weight is less than n.

Induction Let $a = (l, r)$ be a binary tree of weight n ($n > 0$). Let dhl and dhr be respectively the pairs (diameter, height) for the trees l and r. From the induction hypothesis, it is known how to compute these two pairs. The diameter of a is equal to max({dhl.Height + dhr.Height + 2, dhl.Diam, dhr.Diam}) and its height is max({dhl.Height + dhr.Height}) + 1.

Termination The trees considered being finite, the weight of the subtrees a.l and a.r is strictly less than that of a. This ensures the termination of the algorithm.

The resulting division model is the following:

> dh(/) elementary (empty tree)
> dh((l, r)) → dh(l) + dh(r) + composition of the results

The code of this function looks like this:

```
1.  function dh(a) result DiamHeight pre
2.      a ∈ ab and
3.      dhr ∈ DiamHeight and dhl ∈ DiamHeight
4.  begin
5.      if a = / then
6.          result (−1, −1) /% empty tree %/
7.      else
8.          dhl ← dh(a.l); dhr ← dh(a.r);
9.          result ( max({dhl.Height + dhr.Height + 2, dhl.Diam, dhr.Diam}),
                     max({dhl.Height, dhr.Height}) + 1                        )
10.     end if
11. end
```

As in the case of function h, each node is encountered once and only once. The complexity is therefore in $\Theta(n)$ in terms of nodes visited. This solution is therefore better than the previous one.

Answers to problem 95. The selection problem and the median element
The problem is on page 432.

Answer 1. 95 - A 1

a. The problem can be solved in an iterative way. The loop is based on the following elements:

Invariant E' and E'' are two subsets that make up a partition of $E - \{a\}$ ($E - \{a\} = E' \cup E''$ and $E' \cap E'' = \emptyset$) such that all the elements of E' less (respectively greater) than a are put in E^- (respectively E^+). $E' - \{a\} = E^- \cup E^+$ (none of the elements of E'' has been viewed yet).

Stopping condition $E'' = \emptyset$ (all the elements of E'' have been viewed).

Progression If a is the pivot mentioned in the statement of the problem:

```
1.  let v such that
2.      v ∈ E''
3.  begin
4.      /% if v = a, v must not be moved according to the specification %/
5.      if v < a then
6.          E⁻ ← E⁻ ∪ {v}
7.      elsif v > a then
8.          E⁺ ← E⁺ ∪ {v}
9.      end if;
10.     E' ← E' ∪ {v}; E'' ← E'' − {v}
11. end
```

Initialization $E' ← \emptyset$; $E'' ← E$; $E^- ← \emptyset$; $E^+ ← \emptyset$.

Termination card(E''). This integer expression strictly decreases at each step of progression while remaining non-negative.

b. A set is represented by an array along with its actual (useful) size. A naïve implementation of this algorithm consists in a sequential scan of the the array which refines the set E, hence a complexity in $\Theta(n)$.

95 - A 2   **Answer 2.**

a. It suffices that the number of elements less than a in E is equal to $(k-1)$ to assert that a is the desired solution. This relationship is formalized by $\#w \cdot (w \in E \text{ and } w < a) = k-1$.

b. A reasoning by strong induction is carried out.

Base $\#w \cdot (w \in E \text{ and } w < a) = k - 1$. If this condition is met, a is the sought element.

Induction hypothesis It is known how to select the kth smallest element of any set of cardinality m for $1 \leqslant m < n$.

Induction If, after the call of the procedure $BreakUp(E, E^-, E^+, a)$, the number of elements of E^- is greater than or equal to k, the kth element of E is the kth element of E^-. Otherwise, the sought element is located in E^+, and it is its $(k - 1 - card(E^-))^{th}$ element. In both cases, the induction hypothesis allows to obtain the sought result.

Termination The cardinality of the set considered decreases with each step while remaining positive. This guarantees the termination of the algorithm.

The following division model is derived from this (a is any value in the set E):

$$
\text{Select}(n) \rightarrow \begin{cases} \text{elementary if there are } (k-1) \text{ elements less than } a \text{ in E} \\ \text{BreakUp} + \text{Select}(n'), \text{ with } k \leqslant n' < n \text{ otherwise.} \end{cases}
$$

c. The "set-theoretic" version of the algorithm looks like this:

```
1.  function Selection(E, k) result ℕ pre
2.     E ⊂ ℕ and E ≠ ∅ and k ∈ 1 .. card(E) and
3.     E⁻ ⊂ ℕ and E⁺ ⊂ ℕ
4.  begin
5.     let a such that
6.        a ∈ E
7.     begin
8.        if #w · (w ∈ E and w < a) = k − 1 then
9.           result a
10.       else
11.          BreakUp(E, E⁻, E⁺, a);
12.          if card(E⁻) ⩾ k then
13.             result Selection(E⁻, k)
14.          else
15.             result Selection(E⁺, k − 1 − card(E⁻))
16.          end if
17.       end if
18.    end
19. end
```

Remark

The control structure **let** and the expression $a \in E$ represent the *non-deterministic* choice of an element of E[15]. However, a refinement by random drawing (as specified in the statement) is immediate if the appropriate function is available. A deterministic refinement is also possible.

d. This solution differs from the classic DaC construction by the following points:

   i. Cutting is not done at a pre-determined position (most often half), which requires that the location be determined beforehand. This is precisely the role of the preparatory procedure *BreakUp*.

   ii. The process does not stop necessarily on a set of cardinality 1, but as soon as the cardinality of E^- is $(k-1)$.

   Remark For each call of the procedure *Selection*, only one of the recursive calls is performed. The resulting terminal recursion suggests an easy translation in an iterative form (see section 1.3, page 15).

e. Three points should be emphasized for the refinement of this function: (i) The non-deterministic choice must be translated into a random choice (see remark above). (ii) It suffices to take again the refinement of sets adopted in part b) of the first question (refinement by an array accompanied by its useful length). (iii) The condition of the outer alternative, which represents the count of the number of elements E smaller than the pivot a, also needs to be refined. Rather than coding this condition separately, it is possible—and more efficient—to move the call to the procedure *BreakUp* to the beginning of the imperative part of the function in order to take advantage of the availability of the set E^-, since the cardinality of E^- is precisely the number of elements of E smaller than the pivot.

f. The best-case complexity of the function *Selection* is obtained when the first call to the procedure *Selection* shows that the chosen pivot is the sought value, i.e. $(n-1)$ comparisons.

If, at each step, the procedure *BreakUp* cuts the set E in two subsets E^- and E^+ of sizes equal or different from 1, the division model is as follows:

$$
\begin{array}{ll}
\text{Select}(1) \text{ elementary} \\
\text{Select}(n) \rightarrow \text{BreakUp} + \text{Select}\left(\dfrac{n}{2}\right) & n > 1
\end{array}
$$

hence a division model in logarithmic reduction with a function $f(n)$ of linear complexity and a class of complexity in $\Theta(n)$ for the function *Selection* (see corollary of the master theorem, page 423, case 3 with $a < b$).

The worst-case complexity of the function *Selection* is reached when the procedure *BreakUp* produces a pair of sets E^- and E^+ one of which is empty and that the process does not stop (there is a need to continue with a recursive call). The division model is then:

$$
\begin{array}{ll}
\text{Select}(1) \text{ elementaire} \\
\text{Select}(n) \rightarrow \text{BreakUp} + \text{Select}(n-1) & n > 1
\end{array}
$$

---

[15]That is to say a choice for which *no assumption* (in particular of a probabilistic nature) is made on the selected element. So this is not a random choice.

The complexity in number of comparisons is given by:

$$\left|\begin{array}{l} C(1) = 0 \\ C(n) = C(n-1) + n - 1 \end{array}\right. \qquad n > 1.$$

and therefore $C(n) \in \Theta(n^2)$. In this situation, a sort-based solution is preferable.

It can be proven that the average complexity is in $\Theta(n)$ (see [9], p. 185). There are also variants of this algorithm, always with a random choice, the worst-case complexity of which is also in $\Theta(n)$ (see for example also [9]).

95 - A 3 **Answer** 3.   Who can do more can do less. The problem of finding the median (i.e. the $\lfloor \text{card}(E)/2 \rfloor^{\text{th}}$ element of E) is a direct application of the problem solved here. On the other hand, if we had approached the problem of the median directly, we would have found that a good solution consists in solving the problem of finding the kth element. This constitutes a new example (see also the problem 40, page 119) of the interest of generalizing a problem. The generalization is carried out by *weakening* the precondition, since to go from the problem of the median element to the problem of the kth element, we remove the conjunct which specifies that k is the middle position.

Answers to problem 96. Nuts and bolts   *The problem is on page 433.*

96 - A 1 **Answer** 1.   It is not possible to sort first nuts, then bolts – and thus solve the problem – since it is forbidden to compare two bolts with each other or two nuts with each other. The solutions to this problem can, however, be inspired by sorting methods, since in the problem of nuts and bolts, it is a question of finding the right bijection, while in the case of sorts the objective is to find a good permutation. A naïve method (inspired by straight insertion sorting) is to take a nut, attempt to screw it successively through all the bolts until the correct bolt is found, and then repeat the process on the two sets deprived from matched parts. If for a nut there is only one bolt left to consider, the comparison is useless.

Complexities

Best-case complexity is achieved when each nut is threaded onto the first bolt tested. We have the following recurrence equation:

$$\left|\begin{array}{l} C(1) = 0 \\ C(n) = C(n-1) + 1 \end{array}\right. \qquad n > 1$$

hence, by summation, $C(n) = n - 1$ and $C(n) \in \Theta(n)$.
Worst-case complexity is reached when each nut matches with the last remaining bolt. The corresponding equation is:

$$\left|\begin{array}{l} C(1) = 0 \\ C(n) = C(n-1) + n - 1 \end{array}\right. \qquad n > 1.$$

The term "$(n-1)$" comes from comparing a nut with the first $(n-1)$ bolts. By the summation factor method, it is easily shown that $C(n) \in \Theta(n^2)$.

Answer 2.   The DaC method hereafter is inspired from *quicksort*, sorting algorithm as-   96 - A 2
sumed to be known from the reader.

Base If both sets E and B are empty, they are matched.

Induction hypothesis It is known how to match two sets E and B of cardinal less than or
equal to n.

Induction Let E and B be of cardinality $n + 1$. A pivot nut ePiv is selected (non-
deterministically) and one successively tries to assemble all the bolts with it. This
makes it possible to find the pivot bolt bPiv that corresponds to ePiv, but also to divide the set of bolts B − {bPiv} into two subsets: the set of bolts (Binf) that have a
smaller diameter than bPiv and the set of bolts (Bsup) that have a larger diameter.
Then all the nuts except ePiv are tried on the bPiv bolt, which divides the set of nuts
E − {ePiv} into two subsets: the set of nuts (Einf) with a smaller diameter than ePiv,
and the set of nuts (Esup) with a diameter larger than ePiv. The result is twofold: on
the one hand a pair (ePiv, bPiv) of corresponding items has been found, on the other
hand the problem has been divided into two sub-problems of sizes smaller than $n+1$.
We know how to solve them according to the induction hypothesis.

Termination The size of the sub-problems is positive or zero and strictly decreases at each
step. This ensures termination.

The division model looks like this:

$$
\boxed{
\begin{array}{l}
\text{Match}(\varnothing, \varnothing) \text{ elementary since there is nothing to do, sets being empty} \\[2mm]
\text{Match}(E, B) \rightarrow \begin{array}{c} \text{determine the four} \\ \text{subsets} \end{array} \begin{pmatrix} \text{Binf,} \\ \text{Bsup,} \\ \text{Einf,} \\ \text{Esup} \end{pmatrix} + \begin{pmatrix} \text{Match(Einf, Binf)} \\ + \\ \text{Match(Esup, Bsup)} \end{pmatrix}
\end{array}
}
$$

Answer 3.   Below, the operation "**procedure** *Screw*(e, b)" screws the nut e onto the bolt   96 - A 3
b.

```
 1. procedure Matching(E, B) pre
 2.    E ⊆ N₁ and B ⊆ N₁ and E = B and
 3.    Einf ⊆ E and Esup ⊆ E and Einf ∩ Esup = ∅ and
 4.    card(Einf ∪ Esup) = card(E) − 1 and Binf = Einf and Bsup = Esup and
 5.    bPiv ∈ B
 6. begin
 7.    if E ≠ ∅ then
 8.       let ePiv such that
 9.          /% Non-deterministic selection of an element ePiv of E %/
10.          /% as the pivot for E: %/
11.          ePiv ∈ E
12.       begin
13.          Binf ← ∅; Bsup ← ∅;
14.          for b ∈ B do
15.             if ePiv = b then
16.                bPiv ← b; Screw(ePiv, bPiv)
17.             elsif ePiv < b then
18.                Bsup ← Bsup ∪ {b}
19.             else
20.                Binf ← Binf ∪ {b}
```

```
21.              end if
22.          end for;
23.          Einf ← ∅; Esup ← ∅;
24.          for e ∈ E − {ePiv} do
25.              if bPiv < e then
26.                  Esup ← Esup ∪ {e}
27.              else
28.                  Einf ← Einf ∪ {e}
29.              end if
30.          end for
31.      end;
32.      Matching(Einf, Binf) ;
33.      Matching(Esup, Bsup)
34.   end if
35. end
```

Complexity

For worst-case complexity, a solution consists in showing that it is in $\mathcal{O}(n^2)$, then to point out a solution in $\Theta(n^2)$. It is then possible to conclude that the complexity at worst is in $\Theta(n^2)$. As far as the number of assembly attempts is considered, the complexity at worst $C(n)$ is the solution of the following recurrence equation:

$$
\begin{vmatrix}
C(0) = 0 \\
C(n) = \max_{q \in 0..n-1} \left(C(q) + C(n - q - 1) \right) + f(n) & n > 0
\end{vmatrix}
$$

where $f(n) \in \Theta(n)$. Function f enumerates the assembly attempts appearing in both loops. There is therefore a positive constant d such that $f(n) \leqslant d \cdot n$. Moreover, $\text{card}(\text{Einf}) + \text{card}(\text{Esup}) = n - 1$. To prove that $C(n) \in \mathcal{O}(n^2)$, it suffices to show that there is a positive constant c such that $C(n) \leqslant c \cdot n^2$.

Base Obviously, $C(0) \in \mathcal{O}(n^2)$.

Induction hypothesis For any $q \in 0..n-1$, $C(q) \leqslant c \cdot q^2$ and $C(n-q-1) \leqslant c \cdot (n-q-1)^2$.

Induction

$\quad C(n)$

$=$ definition

$\quad \max_{q \in 0..n-1} (C(q) + C(n - q - 1)) + f(n)$

$\leqslant$ induction hypothesis and property of f

$\quad \max_{q \in 0..n-1} \left(c \cdot q^2 + c \cdot (n - q - 1)^2 \right) + d \cdot n$

$=$ calculation

$\quad c \cdot \max_{q \in 0..n-1} \left(2q^2 - 2(n - 1) \cdot q + (n - 1)^2 \right) + d \cdot n$

$=$ $\left\{ \begin{array}{l} \text{The real function } g(q) = 2q^2 - 2(n-1) \cdot q + (n-1)^2 \text{ is a parabola} \\ \text{whose minimum is reached for } q = (n-1)/2.0. \text{ The arc of the} \\ \text{parabola delimited by } q = 0 \text{ and } q = n-1 \text{ decreases from} \\ q = 0 \text{ to } q = (n-1)/2.0 \text{ and increases from } q = (n-1)/2.0 \\ \text{to } q = n-1. \text{ On the abscissa } q = 0 \text{ and } q = n-1, \text{ it reaches} \\ \text{the same maximum, namely } (n-1)^2. \end{array} \right.$

$\quad c \cdot (n - 1)^2 + d \cdot n$

$$= \atop \leqslant$$
$$c \cdot n^2 - c \cdot (2n-1) + d \cdot n$$
$$c \cdot n^2$$

arithmetics

for c sufficiently large $c \cdot (2n-1) \geqslant d \cdot n$

We therefore have $C(n) \in O(n^2)$. Let us now show a solution in $\Theta(n^2)$. Intuitively, the situation where one of the subsets (Einf for instance) is empty and the other one (Esup) contains $(n-1)$ elements may fall under this case. It is indeed a situation of extreme imbalance that deserves to be considered. The recurrence equation is then:

$$C(0) = 0$$
$$C(n) = C(0) + C(n-1) + f(n) \qquad\qquad n > 0.$$

(still with $f(n) \in \Theta(n)$.) This equation is to be compared with the one encountered in the worst case of the question 1. So we also have $C(n) \in \Theta(n^2)$. Hence the result sought for the worst case:

$$C(n) \in \Theta(n^2).$$

Answer 4. The decision tree for the method used in the first question in the case where $E = \{1,2,3\}$ and $B = \{a,b,c\}$ is shown in figure 8.23, page 524. The shaded squares represent the progress of the pairing, while the white squares represent the assembly attempts. Let a be a decision tree for the nut and bolt problem. Its height h corresponds to the maximum number of bolt-nut pairing attempts made by the underlying algorithm. Since in the statement of the problem it is asked to prove that any algorithm that solves the nut and bolt problem has a complexity at worst in $\Omega(n \cdot \log_3(n))$, it is sufficient to show that h, the maximum number of matching attempts, is also in $\Omega(n \cdot \log_3(n))$. The number of leaves f of a ternary tree complies with the relation $f \leqslant 3^h$. Moreover, there are $n!$ ways to match the nuts and bolts of sets E and B of the same cardinal n. To each leaf of a corresponds one of these $n!$ possibilities, and the $n!$ possibilities are covered (the leaf-bijection relation is a surjective function: there may be more leaves than possible matches, as shown in fig-

ure 8.23, page 524, where for example the pairing $\boxed{\begin{smallmatrix}1\,2\,3\\a\,c\,b\end{smallmatrix}}$ appears twice in the central part of

the tree), therefore $f \geqslant n!$. Hence, the following development:
$$3^h \geqslant f \geqslant n!$$
$$\Rightarrow$$ arithmetics
$$3^h \geqslant n!$$
$$\Leftrightarrow$$ switch to base 3 logarithm
$$h \geqslant \log_3(n!)$$
$$\Rightarrow$$ Stirling formula
$$h \in \Omega(n \cdot \log_3(n)).$$

It can be concluded that the worst-case solution to the nut and bolt problem has a complexity that cannot be better than $n \cdot \log_3(n)$.

96 - A 4

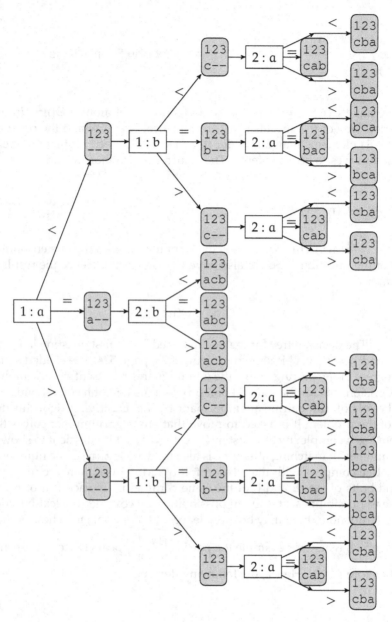

Fig. 8.23 – Nuts and bolts: the decision tree for a naïve solution.

Answers to problem 97. Discovering the fake coin *The problem is on page 434.*

97 - A 1   **Answer** 1.   In the worst case, the number of forthcoming weighings is:

$$\max(\{C_3(n-2k), C_3(k)\}).$$

We must take into account the fact that we are looking for a value k that *minimizes* the number of weighings in the worst case:

$$\min_{k \in 1..\lfloor \frac{n}{2} \rfloor} (\max(\{C_3(n-2k), C_3(k)\})), \qquad (8.30)$$

i.e. by accounting for the weighing already carried out:

$$C_3(n) = 1 + \min_{k \in 1..\lfloor \frac{n}{2} \rfloor} (\max(\{C_3(n-2k), C_3(k)\})). \tag{8.31}$$

We then get the following recurrence equation:

$$\left|\begin{array}{l} C_3(1) = 0 \\ C_3(n) = 1 + \min_{k \in 1..\lfloor \frac{n}{2} \rfloor} (\max(\{C_3(n-2k), C_3(k)\})) \end{array}\right. \qquad n > 1.$$

Answer 2. First of all, we admit the following result. 97 - A 2

Property 15:
The solution of the recurrence equation

$$\left|\begin{array}{l} f(1) = 0 \\ f(n) = 1 + f\left(\left\lfloor \frac{n}{2} \right\rfloor\right) \end{array}\right. \qquad n > 1$$

is $f(n) = \lfloor \log_2(n) \rfloor.$

The proof of the increase of C_3 is done using the following lemma:

Lemma 2:
For any n, $n \in \mathbb{N}_1$, $C_3(n) \leqslant \lfloor \log_2(n) \rfloor.$

Let us demonstrate this lemma by induction on n.
Base For $n = 1$, $C_3(1) = 0 = \lfloor \log_2(1) \rfloor.$
Induction hypothesis For any m such that $1 \leqslant m < n$, $C_3(m) \leqslant \lfloor \log_2(m) \rfloor.$
Induction Let now prove the property for n:

$$\begin{aligned}
&C_3(n) \\
=\ & \qquad\qquad\qquad\qquad\qquad\qquad\qquad\qquad\qquad \text{definition of } C_3 \\
& 1 + \min_{k \in 1..\lfloor \frac{n}{2} \rfloor} (\max(\{C_3(n-2k), C_3(k)\})) \\
\leqslant\ & \qquad\qquad\qquad\qquad\qquad\qquad\qquad\qquad\qquad \text{property of min} \\
& 1 + \min \left(\left\{ \begin{array}{l} \min_{k \in 1..\lfloor \frac{n}{2} \rfloor - 1} (\max(\{C_3(n-2k), C_3(k)\})), \\ \min_{k=\lfloor \frac{n}{2} \rfloor} (\max(\{C_3(n-2k), C_3(k)\})) \end{array} \right\} \right) \\
\leqslant\ & \qquad\qquad\qquad\qquad\qquad\qquad\qquad\qquad\qquad \min(a,b) \leqslant a \\
& 1 + \min_{k=\lfloor \frac{n}{2} \rfloor} (\max(\{C_3(n-2k), C_3(k)\})) \\
=\ & \qquad\qquad\qquad\qquad\qquad\qquad\qquad \text{property of min and substitution} \\
& 1 + \max \left(\left\{ C_3\left(n - 2\left\lfloor \frac{n}{2} \right\rfloor\right), C_3\left(\left\lfloor \frac{n}{2} \right\rfloor\right) \right\} \right).
\end{aligned}$$

At this stage of the proof, it is necessary to carry out a case-based analysis, depending on the parity of n.

Case n even

$$1 + \max\left(\left\{C_3\left(n - 2\left\lfloor\frac{n}{2}\right\rfloor\right), C_3\left(\left\lfloor\frac{n}{2}\right\rfloor\right)\right\}\right)$$

$$= \qquad\qquad\qquad\qquad\qquad\qquad\qquad \text{for } n \text{ even, } 2\cdot\left\lfloor\frac{n}{2}\right\rfloor = n$$

$$1 + \max\left(\left\{C_3(0), C_3\left(\left\lfloor\frac{n}{2}\right\rfloor\right)\right\}\right)$$

$$= \qquad\qquad \text{it is assumed that } C_3(0) = 0 \text{ and } C_3 \text{ is a positive or zero function}$$

$$1 + C_3\left(\left\lfloor\frac{n}{2}\right\rfloor\right)$$

$$= \qquad\qquad\qquad\qquad\qquad\qquad\qquad\qquad\qquad \text{property 15, page 525}$$

$$\lfloor\log_2(n)\rfloor.$$

Case n odd

$$1 + \max\left(\left\{C_3\left(n - 2\left\lfloor\frac{n}{2}\right\rfloor\right), C_3\left(\left\lfloor\frac{n}{2}\right\rfloor\right)\right\}\right)$$

$$= \qquad\qquad\qquad\qquad\qquad\qquad\qquad \text{for } n \text{ odd, } 2\cdot\left\lfloor\frac{n}{2}\right\rfloor = n - 1$$

$$1 + \max\left(\left\{C_3(1), C_3\left(\left\lfloor\frac{n}{2}\right\rfloor\right)\right\}\right)$$

$$= \qquad\qquad\qquad\qquad C_3(1) = 0 \text{ and } C_3 \text{ is a non-negative function}$$

$$1 + C_3\left(\left\lfloor\frac{n}{2}\right\rfloor\right)$$

$$= \qquad\qquad\qquad\qquad\qquad\qquad\qquad\qquad\qquad \text{property 15, page 525}$$

$$\lfloor\log_2(n)\rfloor.$$

Let us go back to the proof by induction of the growth of the function C_3. It is a matter of showing that, for any $n \in \mathbb{N}_1$, $C_3(n + 1) \geqslant C_3(n)$.

Base Let us prove that $C_3(2) \geqslant C_3(1)$.

$$C_3(2)$$

$$= \qquad\qquad\qquad\qquad\qquad\qquad\qquad\qquad\qquad \text{definition of } C_3$$

$$1 + \min_{k \in 1..\lfloor\frac{2}{2}\rfloor}(\max(\{C_3(2 - 2k), C_3(k)\}))$$

$$= \qquad\qquad\qquad\qquad\qquad\qquad\qquad\qquad\qquad\qquad\qquad k = 1$$

$$1 + \max(\{C_3(0), C_3(1)\})$$

$$= \qquad\qquad\qquad\qquad\qquad\qquad\qquad\qquad \text{assuming that } C_3(0) = 0$$

$$1 + C_3(1)$$

$$\geqslant \qquad\qquad\qquad\qquad\qquad\qquad\qquad\qquad\qquad\qquad \text{arithmetics}$$

$$C_3(1).$$

Induction hypothesis For any m such that $1 \leqslant m < n$, $C_3(m) \leqslant C_3(n)$.

Induction Let us prove that $C_3(n+1) \geqslant C_3(n)$. Once again, a case-based analysis is carried out depending on the parity of n. It is known that n even $\Rightarrow 1..\lfloor(n+1)/2\rfloor = 1..\lfloor n/2\rfloor$ and n odd $\Rightarrow 1..\lfloor(n+1)/2\rfloor = (1..\lfloor n/2\rfloor) \cup \{(n+1)/2\}$.

Case n even

$$C_3(n+1)$$

$=$ definition of $C_3(n+1)$ and substitution

$$1 + \min_{k \in 1..\lfloor \frac{n+1}{2} \rfloor} (\max(\{C_3(n+1-2k), C_3(k)\}))$$

$=$ above property for n even

$$1 + \min_{k \in 1..\lfloor \frac{n}{2} \rfloor} (\max(\{C_3(n+1-2k), C_3(k)\}))$$

$\geqslant$ induction hypothesis: $C_3(n+1-2k) \geqslant C_3(n-2k)$

$$1 + \min_{k \in 1..\lfloor \frac{n}{2} \rfloor} (\max(\{C_3(n-2k), C_3(k)\}))$$

$=$ definition of $C_3(n)$

$$C_3(n).$$

Case n odd

$$C_3(n+1)$$

$=$ definition of $C_3(n+1)$ and substitution

$$1 + \min_{k \in 1..\lfloor \frac{n+1}{2} \rfloor} (\max(\{C_3(n+1-2k), C_3(k)\}))$$

$=$ above property for n odd

$$1 + \min_{k \in (1..\lfloor \frac{n}{2} \rfloor) \cup \{\frac{n+1}{2}\}} (\max(\{C_3(n+1-2k), C_3(k)\}))$$

$=$ property of min

$$1 + \min \left(\left\{ \begin{array}{l} \min\limits_{k \in 1..\lfloor \frac{n}{2} \rfloor} (\max(\{C_3(n+1-2k), C_3(k)\})), \\ \min\limits_{k = \frac{n+1}{2}} (\max(\{C_3(n+1-2k), C_3(k)\})) \end{array} \right\} \right)$$

$=$ substitution of k by $\left\lfloor \dfrac{n+1}{2} \right\rfloor \left(= \dfrac{n+1}{2}\right)$ in the second min expression

$$1 + \min \left(\left\{ \begin{array}{l} \min\limits_{k \in 1..\lfloor \frac{n}{2} \rfloor} (\max(\{C_3(n+1-2k), C_3(k)\})), \\ \max\left(\left\{ C_3(0), C_3\left(\left\lfloor \dfrac{n+1}{2} \right\rfloor\right) \right\} \right) \end{array} \right\} \right)$$

$=$ properties of min

$$\min \left(\left\{ \begin{array}{l} 1 + \min\limits_{k \in 1..\lfloor \frac{n}{2} \rfloor} (\max(\{C_3(n+1-2k), C_3(k)\})), \\ 1 + \max\left(\left\{ C_3(0), C_3\left(\left\lfloor \dfrac{n+1}{2} \right\rfloor\right) \right\} \right) \end{array} \right\} \right)$$

$\geqslant$ induction hypothesis: $C_3(n+1-2k) \geqslant C_3(n-2k)$

$$\min \left(\left\{ \begin{array}{l} 1 + \min\limits_{k \in 1..\lfloor \frac{n}{2} \rfloor} (\max(\{C_3(n-2k), C_3(k)\})), \\ 11 + \max\left(\left\{ C_3(0), C_3\left(\left\lfloor \dfrac{n+1}{2} \right\rfloor\right) \right\} \right) \end{array} \right\} \right)$$

$=$ (with $C_3(0) = 0$) the function C_3 is positive and definition of $C_3(n)$

$$\min\left(\left\{C_3(n), 1 + C_3\left(\left\lfloor \frac{n+1}{2} \right\rfloor\right)\right\}\right)$$

$$= \min\left(\left\{C_3(n), \lfloor \log_2(n+1) \rfloor\right\}\right) \qquad \text{property 15, page 525}$$

$$\geqslant \min\left(\left\{C_3(n), \lfloor \log_2(n) \rfloor\right\}\right) \qquad \text{log is an increasing function}$$

$$= C_3(n). \qquad \text{lemma 2, page 525}$$

Therefore, the function $C_3(n)$ is increasing on n.

We now focus on expression 8.30, page 524. In a first step, we concentrate on the sub-expression max before searching for a value k minimizing this sub-expression. Given the nature of the two arguments of the expression max, if the argument curves of max "intersect", the graph of the function max is first decreasing then increasing over the interval $1 .. \lfloor n/2 \text{ rfloor}$. It then has (at least) one minimum and its abscissa is one of the integers closest to the solution of the equation $C_3(n - 2k) = C_3(k)$, i.e. $k = n/3$. If $n/3$ is an integer value (in this case $n/3 = \lceil n/3 \rceil$) this is the solution, otherwise the two candidate integers are $k = \lceil n/3 \rceil - 1$ and $k = \lceil n/3 \rceil$. Let us prove that $k = \lceil n/3 \rceil$ is always the solution we are looking for.

In $k = \lceil n/3 \rceil - 1$, the value of the function $C_3(n - 2k)$ is $C_3(n - 2 \cdot (\lceil n/3 \rceil - 1))$ and in $k = \lceil n/3 \rceil$, the value of the function $C_3(k)$ is $C_3(\lceil n/3 \rceil)$. We leave it to the reader to prove[16] that for any n $(n - 2 \cdot (\lceil n/3 \rceil - 1)) \geqslant \lceil n/3 \rceil$, before exploiting this property:

$$n - 2 \cdot \left(\left\lceil \frac{n}{3} \right\rceil - 1\right) \geqslant \left\lceil \frac{n}{3} \right\rceil$$

$$\Rightarrow \qquad \qquad \qquad \qquad \qquad \qquad \qquad \qquad C_3 \text{ is increasing}$$

$$C_3\left(n - 2 \cdot \left(\left\lceil \frac{n}{3} \right\rceil - 1\right)\right) \geqslant C_3\left(\left\lceil \frac{n}{3} \right\rceil\right).$$

For the second case, $\lceil n/3 \rceil$ is also the abscissa of the minimum. At the same time, we have proven that the curves actually "intersect". Figure 8.24, page 528, shows the different curves obtained for $n = 30$.

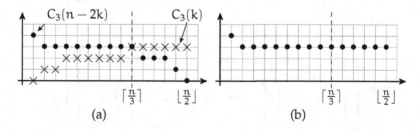

(a)   (b)

Fig. 8.24 – This figure concerns the case $n = 30$. Schema (a) shows the graph of the two curves $C_3(n - 2k)$ and $C_3(k)$, while schema (b) gives their maximum.

---

[16]For example, by carrying out a case-based analysis over the three possible values of $(n \bmod 3)$.

Remark

The function C_3 is not *strictly* increasing and several (consecutive) instances of the minimum. The value $\lceil n/3 \rceil$ is always one of them.

The expression max being minimum when $k = \lceil n/3 \rceil$, in formula 8.31, page 525, it is therefore possible to replace the expression min by $C_3(\lceil n/3 \rceil)$ and the simplified equation of the statement of the problem is obtained.

Answer 3. It is now time to solve this equation. We opt for the method of summation factors[17].

$$
\begin{aligned}
C_3\left(\left\lceil \frac{n}{3^0} \right\rceil\right) &= 1 + C_3\left(\left\lceil \frac{n}{3^1} \right\rceil\right) \\
+ \quad C_3\left(\left\lceil \frac{n}{3^1} \right\rceil\right) &= 1 + C_3\left(\left\lceil \frac{n}{3^2} \right\rceil\right) \\
+ \quad C_3\left(\left\lceil \frac{n}{3^2} \right\rceil\right) &= 1 + C_3\left(\left\lceil \frac{n}{3^3} \right\rceil\right) \\
+ \quad &\vdots \\
+ \quad C_3\left(\left\lceil \frac{n}{3^{\lceil \log_3(n) \rceil}} \right\rceil\right) &= C_3(1) \quad (= 0)
\end{aligned}
$$

and finally:

$$ C_3(n) = \lceil \log_3(n) \rceil \qquad n \neq 0. $$

For the considered strategy, the minimum number of weighings in the worst case is reached by separating the coins into three piles of respectively $\lceil n/3 \rceil$, $\lceil n/3 \rceil$ and $(n - 2 \cdot \lceil n/3 \rceil)$ coins.

Remark

The "binary" strategy, which would consist in separating into two piles of maximum size plus possible residue of a single coin, is a special case of the three-pile strategy, with $k = \lfloor n/2 \rfloor$. We have shown that this strategy is not optimal in general. Thus, for $n = 17$, the binary strategy requires at worst four weighings, while the strategy developed above requires only three.

Answer 4. The development is simply sketched out. The demonstrations are similar to those of the three-pile strategy, but there is an additional difficulty that we now emphasize.

The induction reasoning

Base If $n = 1$, we are facing the fake coin. No weighing is necessary: $C_4(1) = 0$. If $n = 2$, only one weighing is necessary: $C_4(2) = 1$.

Induction hypothesis For any m such that $1 \leqslant m < n$, it is known how to determine $C_4(m)$.

Induction Let $k \in 1 .. \lfloor n/3 \rfloor$. The n coins are separated into four piles (T1, T2, T3 and T4), three of them with k coins, the last one having $n - 3k$ coins. A first weighing is made between T1 and T2. Two cases may then occur:

---

[17]Let us recall that $\lceil \lceil n/a \rceil / b \rceil = \lceil n/(a \cdot b) \rceil$.

First case The weigh-scale is out of balance. The false coin is therefore in the lightest pile. The number of weighings remaining to be carried out is $C_4(k)$ and, from the induction hypothesis, it is known how to determine $C_4(k)$.

Second case The weigh-scale is balanced. The fake coin is therefore in T3 or in T4. A second weighing is performed by comparing T1 (or T2) to T3. Two sub-cases are to be considered.

> **First sub-case** The weigh-scale is out of balance. The false coin is thus in T3. There remains $C_4(k)$ weighings to perform and, from the induction hypothesis, it is known how to determine $C_4(k)$.

> **Second sub-case** The weigh-scale is balanced. The fake coin is in T4. $C_4(n-3k)$ weighings remain to be made and we know how to determine $C_4(n-3k)$ according to the induction hypothesis. (This case can only occur if $n \neq 3k$.)

Termination The number of coins decreases at each step, which ensures the termination of the process.

A development similar to that carried out for the three-pile strategy leads to the following recurrence equation, which provides, for this strategy, the minimum number of weighings to be carried out in the worst case:

$$
\begin{aligned}
&C_4(1) = 0 \\
&C_4(2) = 1 \\
&C_4(n) = 2 + \min_{k \in 1..\lfloor \frac{n}{3} \rfloor} (\max(\{C_4(n-3k), C_4(k)\})) \qquad\qquad n > 2.
\end{aligned}
$$

If $n = 3k$, it is assumed that $C_4(0) = 0$.

Increase of C_4

Proving that C_4 is increasing is made similarly to what has been done to demonstrate the increase of C_3.

Value of the minimum and simplification

Adapting blindly the reasoning applied for the three-pile strategy would lead to asserting that the minimum is reached here for $\lceil n/4 \rceil$, and therefore that the recurrence equation C_4 is simplified to:

$$
\begin{aligned}
&C_4(1) = 0 \\
&C_4(2) = 1 \\
&C_4(n) = 2 + C_4\left(\left\lceil \frac{n}{4} \right\rceil \right) \qquad\qquad n > 2.
\end{aligned}
$$

Strictly speaking, this reasoning is erroneous. Indeed, for $n = 5$:

$$
\left\lceil \frac{n}{4} \right\rceil \notin 1 .. \left\lfloor \frac{n}{3} \right\rfloor \quad (2 \notin 1..1).
$$

The natural number 5 is the only integer greater than 2 having this property (proof not developed and feasible by induction, with $n \in 6..11$ for the base, and an induction on the intervals of type $n \in 12k..12k+11$, for $k \geq 1$). The interval onto which the expression of the minimum applies ($k \in 1..\lfloor n/3 \rfloor$) comes down to $1..1$. The minimum cannot be reached for $k = \lceil n/4 \rceil (= 2)$. Let us evaluate the expression min in taking this remark into account:

$$\min_{k \in 1..\lfloor \frac{5}{3} \rfloor} (\max(\{C_4(5-3k), C_4(k)\}))$$

$$= \qquad\qquad\qquad\qquad\qquad\qquad\qquad\qquad\qquad \text{for } k=1$$

$$\min_{k=1}(\max(\{C_4(5-3k), C_4(k)\}))$$

$$= \qquad\qquad\qquad\qquad\qquad\qquad \text{property of min and substitution}$$

$$\max(\{C_4(5-3\cdot 1), C_4(1)\})$$

$$= \qquad\qquad\qquad\qquad\qquad\qquad\qquad\qquad\qquad\qquad \text{arithmetics}$$

$$\max(\{C_4(2), C_4(1)\})$$

$$= \qquad\qquad\qquad\qquad\qquad\qquad\qquad\qquad\qquad \text{definition of } C_4$$

$$\max(\{1, 0\})$$

$$= \qquad\qquad\qquad\qquad\qquad\qquad\qquad\qquad\qquad \text{definition of max}$$

$$1.$$

It can be deduced that $C_4(5) = 2 + 1 = 3$. Therefore, it is necessary to modify the definition of C_4 to obtain the following equation C_4':

$$\begin{vmatrix} C_4'(1) = 0 \\ C_4'(2) = 1 \\ C_4'(5) = 3 \\ \\ C_4'(n) = 2 + C_4'\left(\left\lceil \frac{n}{4} \right\rceil\right) \qquad\qquad\qquad n > 2 \text{ and } n \neq 5. \end{vmatrix}$$

However, it can be observed that $C_4'(5) = C_4(5)$. Eventually, the above version C_4 is appropriate.

Closed form for C_4

The solution of the quation $C_4(n)$ is given by:

$$C_4(n) = 2 \cdot \lceil \log_4(n) \rceil + \begin{cases} -1 & \text{if } n \in 2^{2i} + 1 .. 2^{2i+1} \\ 0 & \text{otherwise} \end{cases}.$$

It is easy to prove that this value is always greater than or equal to $\lceil \log_3(n) \rceil$. The (optimal) four-pile strategy proposed here is therefore never better than the optimal three-pile strategy.

Answers to problem 98. The missing value   *The problem is on page 435.*

Answer 1. Since $\sum_{i=1}^{m} i = (m \cdot (m+1))/2$, the missing integer x is such that: 98 - A 1

$$x = \frac{(n+1) \cdot (n+2)}{2} - \sum_{i=1}^{n} T[i].$$

The iterative computation of the sum is carried out by evaluating $(n+1)$ times the condition of the loop. The algorithm is therefore exactly in $\Theta(n)$.

Answer 2. There is a theorem[18] that establishes that all algorithms *based on the comparison between the items to be sorted* are in $\Omega(n \cdot \log_2(n))$. Many computer scientists conclude   98 - A 2

---

[18]See problems 96 page 433 (question 4), and 97 page 434 (question 2), to have an idea of the proof of this optimality theorem.

that "it is impossible to do better than $n \cdot \log_2(n)$". That is forgetting a bit quickly the restriction noted in italics. Certain situations may be encountered where the existence of a particular precondition leads to more efficient algorithms. Without going as far as the trivial case of sorting an array that is already sorted (in $\Theta(1)$), we can for example consider the case where $T[1 .. n]$ contains any permutation of the set $1 .. n$. The following sequence then performs the sorting in linear time:

1. **for** $i \in 1 .. n$ **do**
2. $T[i] \leftarrow i$
3. **end for**

The situation occuring in this problem is not very far from the previous one. It is legitimate to look for an efficient *ad hoc* algorithm. We can proceed as follows. In a first step, we build a loop which has as precondition that $T[1 .. n+1]$ is a permutation of the values of the interval $0 .. n$ and as postcondition that $T[1 .. n+1]$ is a permutation of the initial values such that for any j either $T[j] = 0$, or $T[j] = j$. It is then easy to deduce that the missing value i is the one such that $T[i] = 0$. The second step consists in identifying the missing value by an iteration (not constructed here), then to shift to the left all the values located to the right of position i. The postcondition of the first step is formalized as follows:

$$Permut(T, T_i) \textbf{ and } \forall j \cdot (j \in 1 .. n+1 \Rightarrow T[j] = 0 \textbf{ or } T[j] = j).$$

The predicate $Permut(T, T_i)$ expresses that T is a permutation of its initial values T_i. However, T is modified only through exchanges and this conjunct can be ignored further on.

Invariant A possible invariant is obtained by replacing the constant expression $(n+1)$ by $k-1$ in the postcondition (k is a fresh variable):

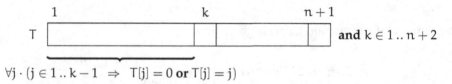

$$\forall j \cdot (j \in 1 .. k-1 \Rightarrow T[j] = 0 \textbf{ or } T[j] = j)$$

Stopping condition The expression $k = n+1$ is appropriate (in principle one should write $k = n+2$, but $\forall j \cdot (j \in 1..n \Rightarrow T[j] = 0 \textbf{ or } T[j] = j) \Rightarrow \forall j \cdot (j \in 1..n+1 \Rightarrow T[j] = 0 \textbf{ or } T[j] = j)$).

Progression Two cases are to be considered. If $(T[k] = 0 \textbf{ or } T[k] = k)$ the element located at position k is correctly placed, the invariant is recovered with the instruction $k \leftarrow k+1$ which decreases (only) the first term of the termination expression (see below). Otherwise ($T[k]$ is not correctly placed), we simply exchange the values located at positions k and $T[k]$ in order to increase the number of correctly placed elements. The invariant is not affected, on the other hand, the second term of the termination expression decreases.

Initialization The invariant is established by the assignment $k \leftarrow 1$.

Termination The progression carries out one of the following actions: either the index k is increased if $T[k]$ is correctly placed, or two elements of the array are exchanged in order to increase the number of correctly placed elements. These two cases are reflected in the termination function, which can be broken down into two terms: either the length of the sub-array remaining to be processed $(n+1-k+1)$ decreases by 1 at each step (first case of the progression), or the number of elements such as $T[j] = j$ increases by 1 (second case of the progression). The expression:

$$(n+1-k) \; + \; (n - \#j \cdot (j \in 1 .. n+1 \textbf{ and } T[j] = j))$$

ensures the termination of the loop.

The code of this algorithm is the following:

```
1.  constants
2.     n ∈ ℕ₁ and n = ...
3.  variables
4.     T ∈ 1 .. n + 1 → 0 .. n and
5.     i ∈ ℕ₁ and k ∈ ℕ₁ and aux ∈ 0 .. n
6.  begin
7.     read(T[1 .. n]); T[n + 1] ← 0; /% codom(T[1 .. n + 1]) = 0 .. n %/
8.     /% First step: %/
9.     k ← 1;
10.    while not(k = n + 1) do
11.       if T[k] = 0 or T[k] = k then
12.          k ← k + 1
13.       else
14.          aux ← T[k]; T[k] ← T[aux]; T[aux] ← aux
15.       end if
16.    end while;
17.    /% Second step: %/
18.    i ← 1;
19.    while T[i] = i do
20.       i ← i + 1
21.    end while;
22.    for j ∈ i .. n do
23.       T[j] ← j + 1
24.    end for;
25.    write(i)
26. end
```

Complexity

The point is to prove that the above solution is actually linear. Obviously, the second step is in $\Theta(n)$. As for the first step, the most favorable situation (in terms of complexity) is obtained when the **then** part of the conditional satement is systematically selected. The least favorable situation is the one that first makes n exchanges to correctly place the n elements, before ending with n passes in the **then** branch. In any case, the problem is solved in a time in the order of $\Theta(n)$.

Answer 3.   Let us design the operation "**function** *MissingValue*(i, s) **result** $(i .. s + 1)$"   98 - A 3 which considers the sorted sub-array $T[i .. s]$ containing all the values in the interval $i .. s + 1$ except one of them and which returns this missing value.

Base If $i = s$, two cases are to be considered. Either $T[i] = i$ and the missing value is $i + 1$, or $T[i] = i + 1$ and the missing value is i.

Induction hypothesis Let $T[i' .. s']$ be a sorted array of length greater than or equal to 1 such that $i' .. s' \subset i .. s$ containing all the values of the interval $i' .. s' + 1$ except one of them. It is known how to find out the missing value of this array.

Induction It is assumed that $(s - i + 1) > 1$. Let $mid = \lfloor (i + s)/2 \rfloor$. If $T[mid] = mid$, on the one hand $T[i .. mid]$ is a sorted array containing all the values of the interval $i .. mid$, and on the other hand $T[mid + 1 .. s]$ is a sorted array containing all the values of the interval $mid + 1 .. s + 1$ except one. The missing value can be found according to the induction hypothesis. Moreover, $T[mid] \neq mid$ implies that $T[mid] = mid + 1$ and this second case is treated symmetrically.

Termination The size of the processed sub-array decreases at each step while remaining positive which ensures the termination of the algorithm.

The underlying division model is the following:

$$
MissVal(1) \text{ elementary}
$$

$$
MissVal(n) \rightarrow \begin{pmatrix} \text{comparison between the} \\ \text{middle value and its in-} \\ \text{dex} \\ + \\ MissVal\left(\dfrac{n}{2}\right) \end{pmatrix} \qquad\qquad n > 1.
$$

The code of the corresponding procedure is:

```
 1. function MissingValue(i, s) result (i .. s + 1) pre
 2.    i ∈ 1 .. n and s ∈ i .. n and
 3.    mid ∈ i .. s and ∃x · (x ∈ i .. s + 1 and T[i .. s] = i .. s + 1 − {x})
 4. begin
 5.    if i = s then
 6.       if T[i] = i + 1 then
 7.          result i
 8.       else
 9.          result i + 1
10.       end if
11.    else
```
$$
12.\qquad mid \leftarrow \left\lfloor \frac{i+s}{2} \right\rfloor;
$$
```
13.       if T[mid] = mid then
14.          result MissingValue(mid + 1, s)
15.       else
16.          result MissingValue(i, mid)
17.       end if
18.    end if
19. end
```

Complexity

The equation $C_1(n)$ which provides the complexity at worst in terms of conditions evaluated is the following:

$$
\left|\begin{array}{l} C_1(1) = 2 \\ C_1(n) = C_1\left(\left\lceil \dfrac{n}{2} \right\rceil\right) + 2 \end{array}\right. \qquad\qquad n > 1.
$$

Formula 8.1, page 423 allows to say that the complexity at worst is in $\Theta(\log_2(n))$.

98 - A 4   **Answer 4.**   The algorithm of the first question can be adapted in the following way. Let x and y be the two missing values that are natural integers complying with the inequality $1 \leqslant x < y \leqslant n + 2$. Let $v = x + y$. Applying the remarkable identity

$\sum_{i=1}^{m} i = (m \cdot (m+1))/2$ leads to the equation:

$$v = \frac{(n+2) \cdot (n+3)}{2} - \sum_{i=1}^{n} T[i].$$

This equation is not sufficient to determine x and y. A second equation *independent* from the first one can be obtained from the sum of the squares of the two unknown:

$$x^2 + y^2 = w.$$

The remarkable identity $\sum_{i=1}^{m} i^2 = (m \cdot (m+1) \cdot (2m+1))/6$ allows to write:

$$w = \frac{(n+2) \cdot (n+3) \cdot (2 \cdot (n+2)+1)}{6} - \sum_{i=1}^{n} (T[i])^2.$$

We are now endowed with the system:

$$\begin{cases} v &= x+y \\ w &= x^2+y^2 \end{cases}$$

which, by applying the substitution $y = v-x$, is transformed into a second degree equation in x (equation constrained by the formula $x \in 1 .. n+1$)[19]:

$$2x^2 - 2v \cdot x + (v^2 - w) = 0$$

whose solution matching the previous constraint is given by (case of the coefficient of the even term in x):

$$x = \frac{v - \sqrt{2w - v^2}}{2}$$

hence, for the second unknown:

$$y = \frac{v + \sqrt{2w - v^2}}{2}.$$

By considering an evaluation in terms of conditions, the calculation of both sums is in $\Theta(n)$. The computation of the square root of the discriminant $2w - v^2$ can (in this particular case) be carried out by a binary search. The value of the discriminant is bounded by $4n^2 + 12n + 1$ (not detailed here) and therefore the search for its square root is in $\Theta(\log_2(n))$. The other operations do not involve any condition and the complexity of this solution is thus in $\Theta(n)$.

As for the second question, that of the simultaneous search of the two missing values and the sort of the array, the previous method can be be easily adapted (provided that two additional squares are made available), and the result remains in $\Theta(n)$.

Let us now come to the third question with two missing values. Let us build the operation "**function** *TwoMissingValues*(i, s) **result** $(i .. s + 1) \times (i + 1 .. s + 2)$", which considers the sorted sub-array $T[i..s]$ containing all the values of the interval $i..s+2$ except two of them, and which determines the two missing values.

Base If $i = s$, the array $T[i .. s]$ contains all the values of the interval $i .. (i + 2)$ except two of them. Consequently, if $T[i] = i$, the missing values are $(i + 1)$ and $(i + 2)$. If $T[i] = (i+2)$, the missing values are i and $(i+1)$. Last, if $T[i] = (i+1)$, the two missing values are i and $(i + 2)$, although we will see that this situation cannot occur.

---

[19]The nature of the problem guarantees the existence of two different integer solutions in the interval $1 .. n + 2$, and therefore the existence of one solution in the interval $1 .. n + 1$.

Induction hypothesis Let $T[i' .. s']$ be a sorted array of length greater than or equal to 1 such that $i' .. s' \subset i .. s$ containing all the values of the interval $i' .. s' + 2$ except two of them. It is known how to identify the two missing values in this array.

Induction Let $T[i .. s]$ be an array of length greater than 1 containing all the values of the interval $i .. s + 2$ except two of them. Let $mid = \lfloor (i + s)/2 \rfloor$. Three cases are to be considered:

1. $T[mid] = mid$. The two missing values are located in the sub-array $T[mid + 1 .. s]$. It is known how to find them out from the induction hypothesis.

2. $T[mid] = (mid + 2)$. The two missing values are located in the sub-array $T[i .. mid]$. It is known how to find them out from the induction hypothesis.

3. $T[mid] = (mid + 1)$. One of the missing values is to be searched in the sub-array $T[i .. mid]$. The case dealt with in question 3 is recovered and it is known how to solve it. The second missing value is to be searched in the sub-array $T[mid + 1 .. s]$. This sub-array contains all the values of the interval $mid + 2 .. s + 2$ except one of them. The problem to be solved differs from that of question 3 (although very close). This can be done, for example, by adapting the function *MissingValue* to determine the missing value over the interval $i + 1 .. s + 2$. Let "**function** *RightMissingValue*(i, s) **result** $i + 1 .. s + 2$" be this operation (not developed here). Its complexity is in $\mathcal{O}(\log_2(n))$. Note that the case considered here ($T[mid] = (mid + 1)$) is treated without using the induction hypothesis. This explains why this case does not have to be taken into account in the base.

Termination The length of the sub-array decreases at each step while remaining positive, which ensures the termination of the algorithm.

From the point of view of process modeling, the division model is as follows:

$$
\begin{array}{l}
\text{TwoMissVal}(1) \text{ elementary} \\[4pt]
\text{TwoMissVal}(n) \rightarrow \text{test on the ``middle'' value } + \\[4pt]
\left(
\begin{array}{l}
\text{TwoMissVal}\left(\dfrac{n}{2}\right) \text{ or} \\[8pt]
\text{MissVal}\left(\dfrac{n}{2}\right) + \text{RightMissingValue}\left(\dfrac{n}{2}\right)
\end{array}
\right) \qquad n > 1.
\end{array}
$$

The code of the function *TwoMissingValues* is written:

```
1.  function TwoMissingValues(i, s) result (i .. s + 1) × (i + 1 .. s + 2) pre
2.     i ∈ 1 .. n and s ∈ i .. n and mid ∈ i .. s and
3.     ∃(x, y) · (x ∈ i .. s + 1 and y ∈ i + 1 .. s + 2 and T[i .. s] = i .. s + 2 − {x, y})
4.  begin
5.     if i = s then
6.        if T[i] = i then
7.           result (i + 1, i + 2)
8.        else
9.           result (i, i + 1)
10.       end if
11.    else
12.       mid ← ⌊ (i + s)/2 ⌋ ;
13.       if T[mid] = mid then
14.          result TwoMissingValues(mid + 1, s)
15.       elsif T[mid] = mid + 2 then
```

16.   **result** *TwoMissingValues*(i, mid)
17.   **else**
18.   **result** $(MissingValues(i, mid), RightMissingValues(mid + 1, s))$
19.   **end if**
20. **end if**
21. **end**

Complexity

We limit ourselves to the case where n is a power of 2. The complexity at worst $C_2(n)$ is given by the recurrence:

$$\left|\begin{array}{l} C_2(1) = 2 \\ C_2(n) = \max\left(\left\{C_2\left(\left\lceil\frac{n}{2}\right\rceil\right), 2 \cdot C_1\left(\left\lceil\frac{n}{2}\right\rceil\right)\right\}\right) + 3 \end{array}\right. \qquad n > 1.$$

It is now shown that, whatever the case under consideration $C_2(n) \in \Theta(\log_2(n))$. Either:

$$\left|\begin{array}{l} C_2(1) = 2 \\ C_2(n) = C_2\left(\left\lceil\frac{n}{2}\right\rceil\right) + 3 \end{array}\right. \qquad n > 1,$$

or:

$$\left|\begin{array}{l} C_2(1) = 2 \\ C_2(n) = 2C_1\left(\left\lceil\frac{n}{2}\right\rceil\right) + 3 \end{array}\right. \qquad n > 1.$$

In the first case, according to formula 8.1, page 423, we can write $C_2(n) \in \Theta(\log_2(n))$. As for the second case, since $C_1(n) \in \Theta(\log_2(n))$, we have $c_1 \cdot \log_2(n) \leqslant C_1(n) \leqslant c_2 \cdot \log_2(n)$ for a given pair c_1, c_2 and for any n greater than or equal to a given n_1. It can thus be concluded that here also $C_2(n) \in \Theta(\log_2(n))$.

Answers to problem 99. The best interval (1)   *The problem is on page 436.*

Answer 1.   99 - A 1

a. **Base** The elementary case occurs when $beg = end$ and the result is then $bi = 0$.

   Induction hypothesis It is known how to determine the value of the best interval for any array of m elements such that $1 \leqslant m < n$.

   Induction Let $T[beg .. end]$ be an array of n ($n > 1$) elements and let $mid = \lfloor(beg + end)/2\rfloor$. According to the induction hypothesis, it is known how to determine the value of the best interval bli (respectively bri) for the left (respectively right) sub-array $T[beg .. mid]$ (respectively $T[mid + 1 .. end]$).

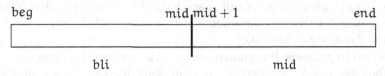

The best interval bi for T[beg .. end] is the largest valeur between bli, bri and (SupR − InfL) if SupR (respectively InfL) is the maximum (respectively minimum) of the right (respectively left) sub-array.

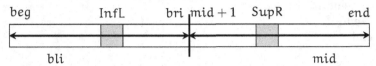

As suggested by the diagram above, the values InfL and SupR are calculated by a sequential scan of each of the two sub-arrays.

Termination Each step decreases the size of the arrays considered, which remains positive. This guarantees the termination of the algorithm.

b. The division model is then:

$$
\begin{array}{ll}
\text{BestInterval1}(1) \text{ elementary} & \\
\text{BestInterval1}(n) \rightarrow \left(\begin{array}{l} 2 \cdot \text{BestInterval1}\left(\dfrac{n}{2}\right) \\[4pt] + \text{loop for the computation of } \left\{\begin{array}{l}\text{InfL,}\\\text{SupR}\end{array}\right\} \\[6pt] + \text{computation (using max) of bi} \end{array}\right) & n > 1
\end{array}
$$

The complexity in number of conditions evaluated is given by the following recurrence equation (in which $\lfloor n/2 \rfloor$ and $\lceil n/2 \rceil$ are assimilated to $n/2$, as done in the master theorem page 422):

$$
\left|\begin{array}{l}
C(1) = 1 \\[4pt]
C(n) = 2 \cdot C\left(\dfrac{n}{2}\right) + n + 1
\end{array}\right. \qquad n > 1.
$$

The term n corresponds to the cost of the two sequential searches. According to the special case 8.4 of the corollary of the master theorem page 423, $C(n) \in \Theta(n \cdot \log_2(n))$.

99 - A 2   **Answer** 2.

a. The actual calculation of the InfL and SupR values should be avoidable. Let us strengthen the induction hypothesis of the previous question, assuming that we know not only the value of the best interval, but also—in both sub-arrays—their extrema:

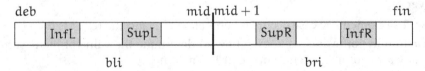

The new version has two additional output parameters, inf and sup, which represent the extrema of the array T[beg .. end]. Now, we have the operation: *BestInterval2*(beg, end; bi, inf, sup : **modif**)

b. **Base** The elementary case is still characterized by beg = end, but it is now necessary to assign the two new parameters with a value (indifferently T[beg] or T[end] since there is a single element).

Induction hypothesis It is known how to determine the best interval, the smallest and the largest element for any array of m elements such that $1 \leqslant m < n$.

Induction Let T[beg .. end] an array of n $(n > 1)$ elements and let $mid = \lfloor(beg + end)/2\rfloor$. According to the induction hypothesis it is known how to determine the value of the best interval as well as the extrema for the left (respectively right) sub-array T[beg..mid] (respectively T[mid+1..end]). bi is assigned the best of the three values bli, bri and $(SupR - InfL)$. But, this time, there is no need for scanning the the two sub-arrays to get the values inf and sup: it is sufficient to choose between InfL and InfR (respectively SupL and SupR) to obtain inf (respectively sup).

Termination See question 1.

The corresponding division model iss then:

$$
\begin{array}{|l r|}
\hline
\text{BestInterval2}(1)\ \text{elementary} & \\[2mm]
\text{BestInterval2}(n) \rightarrow \left(\begin{array}{l} 2\cdot\text{BestInterval2}\left(\dfrac{n}{2}\right) \\[3mm] + \text{computation (by max) of } \left\{\begin{array}{l} bi, \\ InfL, \\ SupR \end{array}\right\} \end{array}\right) & \quad n > 1 \\
\hline
\end{array}
$$

Assuming that T and n are global identifiers, the program is written:

1. **procedure** *BestInterval2*(beg, end; bi, inf, sup : **modif**) **pre**
2.   beg $\in 1 .. n$ **and** end $\in$ beg $.. n$ **and** bi $\in \mathbb{R}_+$ **and** inf $\in \mathbb{R}_+$ **and** sup $\in$ $\mathbb{R}_+$ **and**
3.   bli $\in \mathbb{R}_+$ **and** bri $\in \mathbb{R}_+$ **and**
4.   InfL $\in \mathbb{R}_+$ **and** SupL $\in \mathbb{R}_+$ **and** InfR $\in \mathbb{R}_+$ **and** SupR $\in \mathbb{R}_+$ **and** Middle $\in$ $1 .. n$
5. **begin**
6.   **if** beg $=$ end **then**
7.   bi $\leftarrow 0.0$; inf $\leftarrow$ T[beg]; sup $\leftarrow$ T[end]
8.   **else**
9.   Middle $\leftarrow \left\lfloor \dfrac{beg + end}{2} \right\rfloor$;
10.   *BestInterval2*(beg, Middle, bli, InfL, SupL);
11.   *BestInterval2*(Middle $+ 1$, end, bli, InfR, SupR);
12.   bi $\leftarrow$ max($\{$bli, bri, SupR $-$ InfL$\}$);
13.   inf $\leftarrow$ min($\{$InfL, InfR$\}$);
14.   sup $\leftarrow$ max($\{$SupL, SupR$\}$)
15.   **end if**
16. **end**

The gathering phase is the program made up of the calls to operators max and min (lines 12, 13 and 14). Here is an example of call to the procedure *BestInterval2*:

1. **constants**
2. $n \in \mathbb{N}_1$ **and** $n = \ldots$ **and** $T \in 1 .. n \rightarrow \mathbb{R}_+$ **and** $T = [\ldots]$
3. **variables**
4. $m \in \mathbb{R}_+$ **and** $i \in \mathbb{R}_+$ **and** $j \in \mathbb{R}_+$
5. **begin**
6.   *BestInterval2*(1, n, m, i, j) ;
7.   **write**(*The value of the best interval is* , m, *and its bounds are* , i, .., j)
8. **end**

The complexity in number of conditions evaluated is given by the recurrence equation (with the same hypotheses as for the previous question):

$$C(1) = 1$$
$$C(n) = 2 \cdot C\left(\frac{n}{2}\right) + 4 \qquad\qquad n > 1.$$

According to the special case 8.3 of the corollary of the master theorem, page 423, we have $C(n) \in \Theta(n)$. It can be observed that the new procedure causes a change in the class of complexity: we move from $\Theta(n \cdot \log_2(n))$ to $\Theta(n)$.

Answers to problem 100. The sub-array of maximum sum *The problem is on page 436.*

100 - A 1 **Answer** 1.

a. The elementary case occurs when beg = end. In this case, The desired result is the greatest of the two values 0.0 and T[beg].

b. For an array T[beg .. end] (end > beg) and for mid = $\lfloor$(beg + end)/2$\rfloor$, sml the maximum sum for T[beg .. mid] and smr the maximum sum for T[mid + 1 .. end] are known (induction hypothesis). The desired result for T[beg .. end] is either sml, or smr, or the sum for a sub-array of T[beg..end] whose left part is located at the right of T[beg..mid] and whose right part is located at the left of T[mid + 1 .. end]. The calculation of these values is carried out by scanning T[beg .. mid] from right to left in order to find the maximum sum smlr and similarly, by scanning T[mid + 1 .. end] from left to right in order to find msrl. Finally, the best of the three values msl, msr and mslr + msrl is taken.

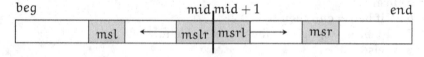

The division model is then:

SubArrMax1(1) elementary

SubArrMax1(n) $\to$ 2 · SubArrMax1 $\left(\frac{n}{2}\right)$ + $\left(\begin{array}{l}\text{computation of smlr} \\ \text{and msrl then ms}\end{array}\right)$ $\qquad$ n > 1

The algorithm is the following:

```
1.  procedure SubArrMax1(beg, end; ms : modif) pre
2.     beg ∈ 1 .. n and end ∈ beg .. n and ms ∈ ℝ₊ and
3.     msl ∈ ℝ₊ and msr ∈ ℝ₊ and mslr ∈ ℝ₊ and msrl ∈ ℝ₊ and
4.     srl ∈ ℝ₊ and slr ∈ ℝ₊ and mid ∈ 1 .. n
5.  begin
6.     if beg = end then
7.        ms ← max({T[beg], 0.0})
8.     else
9.        mid ← ⌊(beg + end)/2⌋;
10.       SubArrMax1(beg, mid, msl);
11.       SubArrMax1(mid + 1, end, msr);
12.       mslr ← 0.0; slr ← 0.0;
```

```
13.     for k ranging reverse beg .. mid do
14.         slr ← slr + T[k]; mslr ← max({mslr, slr})
15.     end for;
16.     msrl ← 0.0; srl ← 0.0;
17.     for k ranging mid + 1 .. end do
18.         srl ← srl + T[k]; msrl ← max({msrl, srl})
19.     end for;
20.     ms ← max({msl, mslr + msrl, msr})
21.     end if
22. end
```

An example of a calling program of this procedure is:

```
1.  constants
2.      n ∈ ℕ₁ and n = ... and T ∈ 1 .. n → ℝ and T = [...]
3.  variables
4.      mv ∈ ℝ₊
5.  begin
6.      SubArrMax1(1, n, mv);
7.      write(mv)
8.  end
```

c. The complexity of this algorithm is given by the following recurrence equation:

$$\begin{vmatrix} C(1) = 0 \\ C(n) = 2 \cdot C\left(\dfrac{n}{2}\right) + n \end{vmatrix} \qquad\qquad n > 1.$$

therefore $C(n) \in \Theta(n \cdot \log_2(n))$.

Answer 2.   100 - A 2

a. The computations carried out in the two loops so as to get the values $smlr$ and $smrl$ can be avoided. To do so, these two values are assumed to be available for the two sub-arrays $T[beg .. mid]$ and $T[mid + 1 .. end]$ (as well as their counterparts $smll$ and $smrr$ located at the other two ends):

beg		mid	mid + 1			end
msll	msl	mslr	msrl		msmr	msrr

The procedure acquires two new output parameters, msl and msr:

beg				end
msl		ms		msd

hence the header $SubArrMax2(beg, end; msl, msr, msm : \mathbf{modif})$.

b. How to obtain the value of msl (the case of msr is symmetrical) from the results coming from the processing of $T[beg .. mid]$ and $T[mid + 1 .. end]$? It is tempting to say that msl simply inherits the value of $msll$. This is not the case. Let us take the example of the array $[50, -10, 50]$ for which $smll = 50$. Yet $msl = 80$ $(50 - 10 - 10 + 50)$. The sum of the maximum left sub-array of $T[beg .. end]$ can thus capture elements located in the right sub-array $T[mid + 1 .. end]$! As a general rule, the right limit of the left maximum sub-array of $T[beg .. end]$ can only be one of the following two positions:

- the right limit of the maximum left sub-array of T[beg .. mid], or
- the right limit of the maximum left sub-array of T[mid + 1 .. end].

Indeed, the right limit of the left maximum sub-array of T[beg .. end] cannot be located:

- to the right of the old limit in the left sub-array, as this would contradict the fact that msll is indeed the maximum left sum of the sub-array T[beg .. mid],
- inside the maximum left sub-array of the right sub-array T[mid + 1 .. end], as it would be sufficient to drag this limit to the right to get a better value,
- in the right sub-array T[mid + 1 .. end], to the right of the maximum left sub-array of the latter, as this would contradict the fact that msll is indeed the maximum left sum of the right sub-array.

The new value can therefore only be the sum of the sub-array T[beg .. mid] plus the value msll or the old msll value. This is of course the greater of the two. As it stands, this solution requires two iterations to compute the sums of T[deb .. mid] and T[mid + 1 .. end].

The division model is then:

$$
\begin{array}{l}
\text{SubArrMax2}(1) \text{ elementary} \\[2mm]
\text{SubArrMax2}(n) \rightarrow 2 \cdot \text{SubArrMax2}\left(\dfrac{n}{2}\right) + \begin{pmatrix} \text{computation of the sums} \\ \text{of T[beg .. mid] and} \\ \text{T[mid + 1 .. end], then} \\ \text{msl, msl and ms} \end{pmatrix} \quad n > 1
\end{array}
$$

c. *Complexity*

The complexity of this algorithm is identical to that of *SubArrMax1*:

$$
\left|\begin{array}{l}
C(1) = 0 \\
C(n) = 2 \cdot C\left(\dfrac{n}{2}\right) + n
\end{array}\right. \qquad\qquad n > 1
$$

and thus $C(n) \in \Theta(n \cdot \log_2(n))$. There is no gain with respect to the first version. On the other hand, there is a way to improve this second solution: consider that the sums of the two sub-arrays are available.

100 - A 3   **Answer** 3.

a. The sums lsg and rs of the two sub-arrays T[beg..mid] and T[mid+1..end] are assumed to be known:

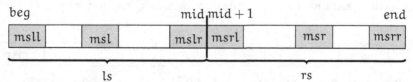

The parameter s which represents the sum of the array T[beg..end] must then be added to the existing output parameters (msl, ms and msr):

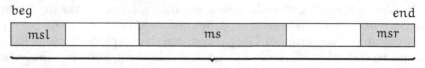

hence the header *SubArrMax3*(beg, end; msl, msr, s, ms : **modif**).

b. This time, the gathering is done without the need for iterative calculations, by using directly the values ls and rs values and assigning to s the sum of ls and rs. The division model is then:

$$
\boxed{
\begin{array}{ll}
\text{SubArrMax3}(1) \text{ elementary} & \\
\text{SubArrMax3}(n) \rightarrow 2 \cdot \text{SubArrMax3}\left(\dfrac{n}{2}\right) + \begin{pmatrix} \text{computation of} \\ \text{msl and msr,} \\ \text{then ms and s} \end{pmatrix} & n > 1
\end{array}
}
$$

The code of the procedure *SubArrMax3* is as follows:

```
 1. procedure SubArrMax3(beg, end; msl, msr, s, ms : modif) pre
 2.     beg ∈ 1 .. n and end ∈ beg .. n and
 3.     msl ∈ ℝ₊ and msr ∈ ℝ₊ and s ∈ ℝ and ms ∈ ℝ₊ and
 4.     msll ∈ ℝ₊ and mslr ∈ ℝ₊ and ls ∈ ℝ₊ and
 5.     msrl ∈ ℝ₊ and msrr ∈ ℝ₊ and rs ∈ ℝ₊ and mid ∈ beg .. end
 6. begin
 7.     if beg = end then
 8.         msl ← max({T[beg], 0.0}) ; msr ← max({T[end], 0.0}) ;
 9.         s ← T[beg]; ms ← max({T[beg], 0.0})
10.     else
11.         mid ← ⌊(beg + end)/2⌋;
12.         SubArrMax3(beg, mid, msll, mslr, ls, msl);
13.         SubArrMax3(mid + 1, end, msrl, msrr, rs, msr);
14.         msl ← max({msll, ls + msrl}); msr ← max({msrr, rs + mslr});
15.         s ← ls + rs; ms ← max({msl, mslr + msrl, msrd})
16.     end if
17. end
```

Here is an example of call of this procedure:

```
 1. constants
 2.     n ∈ ℕ₁ and n = ... and T ∈ 1 .. n → ℝ and T = [...]
 3. variables
 4.     mxl ∈ ℝ₊ and mxr ∈ ℝ₊ and tot ∈ ℝ and mx ∈ ℝ₊
 5. begin
 6.     SubArrMax3(1, n, mxl, mxr, tot, mx);
 7.     write(mx)
 8. end
```

c. The complexity of this algorithm is given by the recurrence equation hereafter:

$$
\left|
\begin{array}{ll}
C(1) = 0 & \\
C(n) = 2 \cdot C\left(\dfrac{n}{2}\right) + 3 & n > 1,
\end{array}
\right.
$$

hence $C(n) \in \Theta(n)$.

Answers to problem 101. Paving a chessboard with triminos *The problem is on page 438.*

101 - A 1   **Answer** 1.   We must prove that for any m there is an integer p such that $(2^{2m} - 1) = 3p$.

Base For $m = 0$, the value of the expression is $2^0 - 1$, or $3 \cdot 0 = 0$.

Induction hypothesis There is an integer p such that, for $m \geqslant 0$, $2^{2m} - 1 = 3p$.

Induction We must prove that the equality holds when m is replaced by $m+1$. For $m+1$, the expression becomes:

$$2^{2(m+1)} - 1$$
$$=\qquad\qquad\qquad\qquad\qquad\qquad\qquad\qquad\qquad\text{arithmetics}$$
$$2^2 \cdot 2^{2m} - 1$$
$$=\qquad\qquad\qquad\qquad\qquad\qquad\qquad\text{induction hypothesis}$$
$$4 \cdot (3p + 1) - 1$$
$$=\qquad\qquad\qquad\qquad\qquad\qquad\qquad\qquad\qquad\text{arithmetics}$$
$$3 \cdot (4p + 1).$$

This expression represents actually a multiple of 3. This predicate is a precondition for the existence of a solution to the considered problem. Indeed, in order to cover all the squares of a chessboard $2^m \cdot 2^m$, except one square, with triminos of three squares, $(2^m \cdot 2^m - 1)$ must be a multiple of 3. Moreover, $((2^{2m} - 1)/3)$ (or if preferred $((n^2 - 1)/3)$) is the number of triminos necessary for the paving.

101 - A 2   **Answer** 2.

Base If $m = 0$, the chessboard reduces to a single square which is the hole. It is known how to cover the chessboard with zero trimino (nothing to do).

Induction hypothesis It is known how to cover with triminos a chessboard $2^m \times 2^m$ (for $m \geqslant 0$) except one arbitrary square.

Induction We have to prove that it is known how to cover with triminos a chessboard $2^{m+1} \times 2^{m+1}$ except one arbitrary square.

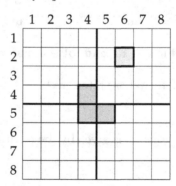

The chessboard is divided into for quarters $2^m \times 2^m$. The appropriate trimino is placed in the center of the chessboard, so that it does not encroach on the quarter where the hole is located. Each quarter now possesses a square that must not be covered, either because it is already covered by one of the squares of the "central" trimino just laid, or because it is the "initial" hole (see diagram above). From the induction hypothesis, it is known how to pave each quarter with triminos.

Termination The side of the square is divided by 2 at each step which ensures termination.

Answer 3. Te division model is given hereafter:

Pave(1) elementary

$Pave(2^m) \to 4 \cdot Pave(2^{m-1}) + \text{laying of a trimino}$ $\qquad m > 0$

Answer 4. The following diagram provides the diverse useful coordinates when a chessboard is divided into four quarters.

The procedure *Paving* is in the form:

1. **procedure** *Paving*(r, c, n, hr, hc) **pre**
2. $r \in \mathbb{N}$ and $c \in \mathbb{N}$ and $n \in \mathbb{N}_1$ and $\exists m \cdot (m \in \mathbb{N}$ and $n = 2^m)$ and
3. $hr \in 1..r + n - 1$ and $hc \in c..c + n - 1$ and
4. /% coordinates of the hole in each quarter: %/
5. $hr1 \in r..r + \dfrac{n}{2} - 1$ and $hc1 \in c..c + \dfrac{n}{2} - 1$ and
6. $hr2 \in r..r + \dfrac{n}{2} - 1$ and $hc2 \in c + \dfrac{n}{2}..c + n - 1$ and
7. $hr3 \in r + \dfrac{n}{2}..r + n - 1$ and $hc3 \in c..c + \dfrac{n}{2} - 1$ and
8. $hr4 \in r + \dfrac{n}{2}..r + n - 1$ and $hc4 \in c + \dfrac{n}{2}..c + n - 1$
9. **begin**
10. $\quad$ **if** $n \neq 1$ **then**
11. $\quad$ /% Default values of the holes (central squares): %/
12. $\quad$ $hr1 \leftarrow r + \dfrac{n}{2} - 1; hc1 \leftarrow c + \dfrac{n}{2} - 1;$
13. $\quad$ $hr2 \leftarrow r + \dfrac{n}{2} - 1; hc2 \leftarrow c + \dfrac{n}{2};$
14. $\quad$ $hr3 \leftarrow r + \dfrac{n}{2}; hc3 \leftarrow c + \dfrac{n}{2} - 1;$
15. $\quad$ $hr4 \leftarrow r + \dfrac{n}{2}; hc4 \leftarrow c + \dfrac{n}{2};$
16. $\quad$ **if** $hr \in r..r + \dfrac{n}{2} - 1$ and $hc \in c..c + \dfrac{n}{2} - 1$ **then**
17. $\quad$ /% The hole is in the first quarter %/
18. $\quad$ $Lay \left(r + \dfrac{n}{2} - 1, c + \dfrac{n}{2} - 1, 1\right);$
19. $\quad$ $hr1 \leftarrow hr; hc1 \leftarrow hc$

20.   **elsif** hr $\in$ r .. r $+ \dfrac{n}{2} - 1$ **and** hc $\in$ c $+ \dfrac{n}{2}$ .. c $+ n - 1$ **then**

21.   /% *The hole is in the second quarter* %/

22.   *Lay* $\left(r + \dfrac{n}{2} - 1, c + \dfrac{n}{2}, 2 \right)$;

23.   hr2 $\leftarrow$ hr; hc2 $\leftarrow$ hc

24.   **elsif** hr $\in$ r $+ \dfrac{n}{2}$ .. r $+ n - 1$ **and** hc $\in$ c .. c $+ \dfrac{n}{2} - 1$ **then**

25.   /% *The hole is in the third quarter* %/

26.   *Lay* $\left(r + \dfrac{n}{2}, c + \dfrac{n}{2} - 1, 3 \right)$;

27.   hr3 $\leftarrow$ hr; hc3 $\leftarrow$ hc

28.   **else**

29.   /% *The hole is in the fourth quarter* %/

30.   *Lay* $\left(r + \dfrac{n}{2}, c + \dfrac{n}{2}, 4 \right)$;

31.   hr4 $\leftarrow$ hr; hc4 $\leftarrow$ hc

32.   **end if;**

33.   *Paving* $\left(r, c, \dfrac{n}{2}, \text{hr1}, \text{hc1} \right)$;

34.   *Paving* $\left(r, c + \dfrac{n}{2}, \dfrac{n}{2}, \text{hr2}, \text{hc2} \right)$;

35.   *Paving* $\left(r + \dfrac{n}{2}, c, \dfrac{n}{2}, \text{hr3}, \text{hc3} \right)$;

36.   *Paving* $\left(r + \dfrac{n}{2}, c + \dfrac{n}{2}, \dfrac{n}{2}, \text{hr4}, \text{hc4} \right)$

37. **end if**

38. **end**

Complexity

If $C(n)$ stands for the complexity of this procedure for a chessboard $n \times n$, the number of triminos laid is given by the following recurrence equation:

$$
\begin{aligned}
C(1) &= 0 \\
C(n) &= 4 \cdot C\left(\dfrac{n}{2} \right) + 1
\end{aligned}
\qquad n > 1.
$$

The case 8.6 of the corollary of the master theorem (page 423) allows to conclude as for the order of growth of complexity: $\Theta(n^2)$. However, the question is about "exact" complexity. Since $n = 2^m$, let us make a variable change, letting $C(2^m) = C'(m)$. The following recurrence equation is obtained:

$$
\begin{aligned}
C'(0) &= 0 \\
C'(m) &= 4 \cdot C'(m - 1) + 1
\end{aligned}
\qquad m > 0.
$$

Using the summing factor method , we get

$$
C'(m) = \sum_{i=0}^{m-1} 4^i.
$$

The following development:

$$
\sum_{i=0}^{m-1} 4^i
$$

$$= \frac{4^m - 1}{3}$$
$$= \frac{n^2 - 1}{3}$$

remarkable identity: $\sum_{i=p}^{q} m^i = \dfrac{m^{q+1} - m^p}{m - 1}$

$n = 2^m$

yields the expected result:

$$C(n) = \frac{n^2 - 1}{3}.$$

It can be remarked that this value (which, it should be remembered, represents the number of triminos laid) is equal to the number of squares to be covered with triminos. This confirms *a posteriori* that the proposed solution is correct (every square of the chessboard except one is covered by one and only one trimino). Furthermore, the expected result is recovered: $C(n) \in \Theta(n^2)$.

Answers to problem 102. The saddle
The problem is on page 439.

Answer 1. The aim of this question is to highlight the fact that a sequential search can be seen as a mechanism of type DpR $(1, n - 1)$, i.e. of type "Reduce and conquer" (see Chapter 4). The first line is taken and a sequential search (which is itself of type "Reduce and conquer") is performed. If the desired value has not been found, we iterate over the array stripped of the first row (as long as there is at least one row remaining). Therefore, the division model is:

$SearchSad1(0, n)$ elementary	$n \geqslant 1$
$SearchSad1(m, n) \rightarrow \left(\begin{array}{l} SearchSadCol(n) \quad + \\ \text{if needed} \\ SearchSad1(m - 1, n) \end{array} \right)$	$m \geqslant 1$ and $n \geqslant 1$
$SearchSadCol(0)$ elementary	
$SearchSadCol(n) \rightarrow$ test + if needed $SearchSadCol(n - 1)$	$n \geqslant 1$

Obviously, the role of rows and columns can be exchanged.

Answer 2. This process requires at worst $m \cdot n$ comparisons. However, it can be improved by doing a binary search (see problem 90, page 427) in a line rather than a sequential search, in which case complexity at worst is equal to $m \cdot \log_2(n)$.

Answer 3. If $v > x$, the upper left quarter of the saddle S can be eliminated, as by definition any value of this portion is less than or equal to x. If $v < y$, the lower right quarter of the saddle S can be suppressed.

Answer 4. A test is performed on x and y if necessary; then, if needed (in the case where neither x, nor y is equal to v), the process continues with the three suitable saddles of dimension $n/2$, hence the division model:

102 - A 1
102 - A 2
102 - A 3
102 - A 4

SearchSad2(1) elementary

$$\text{SearchSad2}(n) \rightarrow \text{test}(x, y, v) + 3 \cdot \text{SearchSad2}\left(\frac{n}{2}\right) \qquad n > 1$$

Remark

If $x < v < y$, we have both $v > x$ and $v < y$; therefore v can only be located in one the two saddles top right or bottom left.

The proposed solution implements a kind of "call by necessity": a recursive call occurs only when the previous one does not yield a conclusion.

```
 1.  procedure Saddle2(v, i₁, j₁, i₂, j₂; row, col : modif) pre
 2.     v ∈ ℕ₁ and i₁ ∈ 1 .. n and i₂ ∈ 1 .. n and j₁ ∈ 1 .. n and j₂ ∈ 1 .. n and
 3.     i₂ − i₁ = j₂ − j₁ and  /% A square saddle is under consideration %/
 4.     ∃p · (p ∈ ℕ₁ and i₂ − i₁ + 1 = 2ᵖ) and  /% the side is a power of 2 %/
 5.     row ∈ 0 .. n and col ∈ 0 .. n and k ∈ i₁ .. i₂ and l ∈ j₁ .. j₂
 6.     /%
```

$$
\begin{array}{cc}
 & \begin{array}{cc} j_1 & \quad j_2 \end{array} \\
\begin{array}{c} i_1 \\[14pt] i_2 \end{array} &
\begin{array}{|c|c|}
\hline
1 & 2 \\
\hline
3 & 4 \\
\hline
\end{array}
\end{array}
$$

```
        %/
 7.     /% row and col stand for the coordinates of a square of the saddle %/
 8.     /% containing the desired value v ((0, 0) if this value is missing) %/
 9.  begin
10.     if i₁ = i₂ then
11.        if v = S[i₁, j₁] then
12.           row ← i₁; col ← j₁
13.        else
14.           row ← 0; col ← 0
15.        end if
16.     else
17.        k ←  (i₁ + i₂ − 1)/2 ; l ←  (j₁ + j₂ − 1)/2 ;
18.        Saddle2(v, k + 1, j₁, i₂, r, row, col);  /% sub-saddle 3 %/
19.        if row = 0 then
20.           Saddle2(v, i₁, l + 1, k, j₂, row, col);  /% sub-saddle 2 %/
21.           if row = 0 then
22.              if v ⩽ S[k, l] then
23.                 Saddle2(v, i₁, j₁, k, l, row, col)  /% sub-saddle 1 %/
24.              else
25.                 Saddle2(v, k + 1, l + 1, i₂, j₂, row, col)  /% sub-saddle 4 %/
26.              end if
27.           end if
28.        end if
29.     end if
30.  end
```

An example of call of this procedure is:

```
 1.  constants
 2.     n ∈ ℕ₁ and n = ... and
```

3. $S \in 1..n \times 1..n \to \mathbb{N}_1$ and *IsSaddle(S)* and $S = [...]$ and
4. $w \in \mathbb{N}_1$ and $w = ...$
5. **variables**
6. $l \in 0..n$ and $c \in 0..n$
7. **begin**
8. $Saddle2(w, 1, 1, n, n, l, c)$
9. **end**

Answer 5.   From the model of resolution established previously and the particular case   102 - A 5
8.1 of the corollary of the master theorem, page 423, the complexity of this solution is in
$\mathcal{O}(n^{\log_2(3)})$.

Answer 6.   A non-square saddle can be completed with a very large conventional value   102 - A 6
to come up to a square saddle of side $n = 2^k$.

Answer 7.   If $z = v$, an occurrence of v has been found and the search ends. If $z > v$ 102 - A 7
(respectively $z < v$), column m (respectively row 1) can be eliminated before continuing
the search by the same process.

Answer 8.   The resolution model of type "Reduce and conquer" is: 102 - A 8

$$
\begin{array}{ll}
SearchSad3(0, n) \text{ elementary (failure)} & n > 0 \\
SearchSad3(m, 0) \text{ elementary (failure)} & m > 0 \\
SearchSad1(m, n) \to \left(\begin{array}{l} \text{test } (v = z) : stop - success \\ \text{test } (v < z) : SearchSad3(m, n - 1) \\ \text{test } (v > z) : SearchSad3(m - 1, n) \end{array} \right) & m \geqslant 1 \text{ and } n \geqslant 1
\end{array}
$$

Answer 9.   The associated procedure is given hereafter: 102 - A 9
1. **procedure** *SearchSaddle3*$(v, rBeg, cEnd; row, col :$ **modif**$)$ **pre**
2. $v \in \mathbb{N}$ and $rBeg \in 1..m$ and $cEnd \in 1..n$ and $row \in 0..m$ and $col \in 0..n$
3.   /% *rBeg: upper row of the saddle, cEnd: its last column* %/
4.   /% *row and col stand for the coordinates of one of the squares* %/
5.   /% *of the saddle containing the desired value* v $((0, 0)$ *if none)* %/
6. **begin**
7.   **if** $rBeg = m + 1$ **or** $cEnd = 0$ **then**
8. $row \leftarrow 0; col \leftarrow 0$
9.   **else**
10.   **if** $v = S[rBeg, cEnd]$ **then**
11. $row \leftarrow rBeg; col \leftarrow cEnd$
12.   **else**
13.   **if** $v < S[rBeg, cEnd]$ **then**
14. $Saddle3(v, rBeg, cEnd - 1, row, col)$
15.   **else**
16. $Saddle3(v, rBeg + 1, cEnd, row, col)$
17.   **end if**
18.   **end if**
19.   **end if**
20. **end**

An example of call of the procedure *Saddle3* is:

1. **constants**
2. $m \in \mathbb{N}_1$ **and** $m = \ldots$ **and** $n \in \mathbb{N}_1$ **and** $n = \ldots$ **and**
3. $S \in 1 .. n \times 1 .. n \rightarrow \mathbb{N}_1$ **and** *IsSaddle*(S) **and** $S = [\ldots]$ **and**
4. $w \in \mathbb{N}$ **and** $w = \ldots$
5. **variables**
6. $r \in 0 .. m$ **and** $c \in 0 .. n$
7. **begin**
8. $Saddle3(w, 1, n, r, c)$
9. **end**

102 - A 10   **Answer 10.**   At worst, all columns and all rows except one must be eliminated, hence a complexity in $\mathcal{O}(m+n)$. We thus passed successively from a complexity in $\mathcal{O}(m \cdot n)$ with a double sequential search (or in $\min\left(\mathcal{O}(n \cdot \log_2(m)), m \cdot \log_2(n)\right)$) by combining sequential and binary search), to a complexity in $\mathcal{O}(n^{\log_2(3)})$ (i.e. about $\mathcal{O}(n^{1.58})$), then in $\mathcal{O}(m + n)$, thus linear. This latter approach can be advocated since it applies to any saddle and has the lowest complexity.

102 - A 11   **Answer 11.**   The method based on the elimination of rows and columns cannot be used as a basis for the solution of the problem of counting zeros in a saddle S. Indeed, the rows and the columns are not strictly increasing, and one can only delete a row or a column if the upper right corner contains a value other than zero. When a zero is found, there may be others in the associated row and column; they must therefore be examined sequentially in order to carry out the count.

On the other hand, if the order is strict in the rows and the columns, nothing prevents to be inspired by the method of deleting row or column, since then the presence of a zero in the upper right corner guarantees that it is the only one in the associated row and column. We can then delete the line *and* the column as well!

Answers to problem 103. Counting inversions in a list of numbers   *The problem is on page 440.*

103 - A 1   **Answer 1.**   A first solution is based on the nesting of two **for** loops. Here, we choose a different approach where a single loop is used[20]. For this example, the only advantage of this solution is that it focuses on a technique that, on other occasions, may prove to be almost indispensable (this would be the case, for example, in the problem of searching for the existence of a certain value in a rectangular array, in an interative way, as in problem 32, page 111). Let us build this solution.

Invariant The variable nbi counts the inversions. In the following configuration:

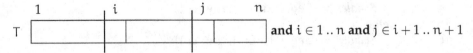

   and $i \in 1 .. n$ **and** $j \in i + 1 .. n + 1$

nbi is the sum of the number of inversions between each element $T[k]$ of $T[1 .. i - 1]$ and the sub-array $T[k+1 .. n]$ on the one hand and $T[i]$ and the sub-array $T[i+1 .. j-1]$ on the other hand.

---

[20] Any algorithm can be coded with a single loop. To be convinced of this, it is simply enough to note that the virtual machine that interprets a "bytecode" is itself made up of a single loop.

Stopping condition When $(i = n$ **and** $j = n+1)$, nbi is actually the number of inversions. Note that $i = n \Rightarrow j = n+1$. The stopping condition is therefore simplified into $i = n$.

Progression The precondition of the progression is the conjunction of the invariant and the negation of the stopping condition. i and j are therefore in the interval $1 .. n$. So, $T[j]$ does exist and it is possible to compare $T[i]$ and $T[j]$ and update nbi if necessary. It then remains to restore the invariant (see the code below).

Initialization The following program:

    1. $nbi \leftarrow 0; i \leftarrow 1; j \leftarrow 2$

establishes the invariant.

Termination Let us count the passages remaining to be made in the body of the loop. The value $(n - j + 1)$ represents the number of passages in the loop necessary to confront $T[i]$ with the elements of $T[j .. n]$. The value $(((n-i) \cdot (n-i-1))/2)$ counts the passages in the loop which allow the comparison of each of the elements beyond $T[i]$ with their successors. Finally, the expression $((n-j+1) + ((n-i) \cdot (n-i-1))/2)$ constitutes a valid termination expression: it decreases at each step while remaining non-negative.

The following code is obtained:

    1. **constants**
    2. $n \in \mathbb{N}_1$ **and** $n = ...$ **and** $T \in 1 .. n \rightarrow 1 .. n$ **and** $T = [...]$
    3.   /% T *represents a bijection* %/
    4. **variables**
    5. $nbi \in \mathbb{N}$ **and** $i \in 1 .. n$ **and** $j \in i .. n+1$
    6. **begin**
    7. $nbi \leftarrow 0; i \leftarrow 1; j \leftarrow 2;$
    8.   **while** $i \neq n$ **do**
    9.   **if** $T[i] > T[j]$ **then**
    10. $nbi \leftarrow nbi + 1$
    11.   **end if**;
    12. $j \leftarrow j + 1;$
    13.   **if** $j = n + 1$ **then**
    14. $i \leftarrow i + 1; j \leftarrow i + 1$
    15.   **end if**
    16.   **end while**
    17. **end**

Remark

The maximum number of possible inversions is reached when the array is decreasingly sorted. For an array of n elements, this number is $((n \cdot (n-1))/2)$. In the program below, nbi could be declared by: $nbi \in 0 .. ((n \cdot (n-1))/2)$.

Complexity

To assess complexity, it is enough to count the passages in the loop. The conditions of the alternatives do not affect the order of growth of complexity. There are $((n-1) \cdot n)/2$ passages in the loop, the complexity is therefore in $\Theta(n^2)$.

    Answer 2.   The construction is made using "partition induction" (see section 1.1.4, page 7) on the size $s - i + 1$ of the array.   103 - A 2

Base If $i = s$, the array $T[i .. s]$ has a single element and thus there is no inversion.

Induction hypothesis Let $m = 2^{k-1}$ ($k \geqslant 1$) be the number of elements of $T[i .. s]$. It is known how to compute the number of inversions present in $T[i .. s]$.

Induction Let $n = 2^k$ be the number of elements of the array $T[i .. s]$ and let $\text{mid} = \lfloor (i+s)/2 \rfloor$. The sub-arrays $T[i .. \text{mid}]$ and $T[\text{mid}+1 .. s]$ have 2^{k-1} elements. From the induction hypothesis, it is known how to compute the number of inversions present in each of them. The number of "crossed" inversions between these two sub-arrays is calculated by considering all pairs (v, w) such that $v \in T[i .. \text{mid}]$ and $w \in T[\text{mid}+1 .. s]$. Those that are such that $T[v] > T[w]$ are related to the inversions.

Termination The length of the array considered is divided by 2 at each step, while remaining positive. This ensures the termination of the algorithm.

The division model that applies is as follows:

$$
\begin{array}{|l}
\text{nbInv1}(1) \text{ elementary} \\[4pt]
\text{nbInv1}(n) \to 2 \cdot \text{nbInv1}\left(\dfrac{n}{2}\right) + \begin{pmatrix} \text{crossed comparison in} \\ \text{the two half-arrays} \end{pmatrix} \qquad\qquad n > 1
\end{array}
$$

The code of the operation *NbInv1* is as follows:

```
 1. function NbInv1(i, s) result ℕ pre
 2.    i ∈ 1 .. n and s ∈ i .. n and ∃k · (k ∈ ℕ₁ and s − i + 1 = 2^k) and
 3.    mid ∈ i .. s and NbiLr ∈ ℕ
 4. begin
 5.    if i = s then
 6.        result 0
 7.    else
 8.        mid ← ⌊(i + s)/2⌋;
 9.        NbiLr ← 0;
10.        for j ranging i .. mid do
11.          for k ranging mid + 1 .. s do
12.            if T[i] > T[j] then
13.                NbiLr ← NbiLr + 1
14.            end if
15.          end for
16.        end for;
17.        result NbInv1(i, mid) + NbInv1(mid + 1, s) + NbiLr
18.    end if
19. end
```

Complexity

The recurrence equation C_1 that provides the number of conditions evaluated by this algorithm depending on the size n of the array is of the form:

$$
\left|
\begin{array}{l}
C_1(1) = 1 \\[4pt]
C_1(n) = C_1\left(\dfrac{n}{2}\right) + g(n) \quad \text{where } g(n) \in \Theta(n^2) \qquad\qquad n > 1.
\end{array}
\right.
$$

The special case 8.2 of the corollary of the master theorem, page 423, allows to deduce that this solution is in $\Theta(n^2)$. From an asymptotic point of view, this solution does not improve the (iterative) one of the first question. Once again, we see that the application of the DaC paradigm does not systematically lead to better efficiency.

Answer 3.   103 - A 3

a. The sub-array T[j .. mid] is sorted. Since T[j] > T[k], it can be concluded by transitivity that each element of T[j .. mid] is greater than T[k]. As soon as an inversion between T[j] and T[k] is found out it can be deduced that there are $(mid - j + 1)$ inversions between the elements of T[j .. mid] and those of T[k]; this result is obtained "for free" (without making any further comparisons) and this is the crux of a possible improvement.

b. Let us build the corresponding loop.

Invariant We consider, as stated, the case where T[1 .. mid] and T[mid + 1 .. n] are sorted. nbi is the number of inversions between T[p] and T[q] for $p \in 1 .. j - 1$ and $q \in mid + 1 .. k - 1$, plus, for each $p \in 1 .. j - 1$ such that T[p] > T[q], the number of inversions between T[p'] and T[q] for $p' \in p + 1 .. mid$ (this latter value is equal to $(mid - p)$ according to the previous question). Let us come back to the example of the statement:

$$
T \quad \begin{array}{|c|c|c|c|c|c|c|c|}
\hline
2 & 3 & 7 & 12 & 1 & 4 & 9 & 10 \\
\hline
\end{array}
$$

with positions 1 2 3 4 5 6 7 8, j pointing at position 4 (value 12) and k at position 6 (value 4).

The following (partial) result is obtained:

Comparison	Induced result	nb of inv.
T[1] > T[5]	T[2] > T[5], T[3] > T[5] and T[4] > T[5]	4
T[3] > T[6]	T[4] > T[6]	2

$$nbi = 6$$

The heart of the invariant is formalized by (reminder: # is the quantifier "count"):

$$
nbi = \left(
\begin{array}{l}
\#(p, q) \cdot \left(
\begin{array}{l}
p \in 1 .. j - 1 \text{ and} \\
q \in mid + 1 .. k - 1 \text{ and} \\
T[p] > T[q]
\end{array}
\right) \\
\quad + \\
\#(p, q, r) \cdot \left(
\begin{array}{l}
p \in 1 .. j - 1 \text{ and} \\
q \in mid + 1 .. k - 1 \text{ and} \\
r \in p + 1 .. mid \text{ and } T[r] > T[q]
\end{array}
\right)
\end{array}
\right).
$$

Stopping condition The process stops when either j or k exceeds the right limit of its respective sub-array, i.e.: $(j = mid + 1 \text{ or } k = n + 1)$.

Progression A conditional statement compares T[j] with T[k], and depending on the result, updates j, k and nbi to restore the invariant (see the code hereafter).

Termination The expression $(mid - j + 1)$ (respectively $(k + 1 - s + 1)$) represents the number of squares remaining to be compared in the first (respectively second) sub-array. The expression $((mid - j + 1) + (k + 1 - s + 1))$ ensures the termination of the itération.

The related code is:

1. **constants**
2. $n \in \mathbb{N}_1$ **and** $n = \ldots$ **and** $\exists k \cdot (k \in \mathbb{N}_1 \text{ and } n = 2^k)$ **and**
3. $mid \in 1 .. n$ **and** $mid = \left\lfloor \dfrac{n+1}{2} \right\rfloor$ **and**

4. $T \in 1 .. n \to \mathbb{N}$ **and** *IsInjective*(T) **and** $T = [\dots]$ **and**

5.   *IsSorted*(T[1 .. mid]) **and** *IsSorted*(T[mid + 1 .. n])

6. **variables**

7. $nbi \in 0 .. \dfrac{n \cdot (n-1)}{2}$ **and**

8. $j \in 1 ..$ mid **and** $k \in$ mid $+ 1 .. n$

9. **begin**

10.   nbi $\leftarrow$ 0; j $\leftarrow$ 1; k $\leftarrow$ mid $+ 1$;

11.   **while not** (j = mid + 1 **or** k = n + 1) **do**

12.   **if** T[j] < T[k] **then**

13.   j $\leftarrow$ j + 1

14.   **else**

15.   k $\leftarrow$ k + 1; nbi $\leftarrow$ nbi + (mid - j + 1)

16.   **end if**

17.   **end while**

18. **end**

Complexity

In the body of the loop, either j or k is incremented. This algorithm is actually in $\Theta(n)$ conditions evaluated.

103 - A 4   **Answer 4.**   Let us build this solution starting with the procedure *NbInv2*. It calls the operation "**procedure** *NbInvMerge*(i, s; nb : **modif**)", which—from two sorted half-arrays of T[i .. s]—computes the number of inversions on either side of the middle while merging the two sub-arrays.

Base If i = s, the array T[i .. s] has a single element, there is no inversion and it is sorted.

Induction hypothesis Let $m = 2^{k-1}$ ($k \geqslant 1$) be the number of elements of the sorted array T[i .. s]. It is known how to compute the number of inversions present in T[i .. s].

Induction Let $n = 2^k$ be the number of elements of the array T[i .. s] and let mid $= \lfloor (i + s)/2 \rfloor$. The sub-arrays T[i .. mid] and T[mid + 1 .. s] are sorted and they have 2^{k-1} elements. From the induction hypothesis, it is known how to compute the number of inversions present in each of them. It then remains to calculate the number of inversions present on either side of the middle while merging the two halves into a single sorted array. This is carried out by the procedure *NbInvMerge* quoted above, which incorporates the computing technique presented in question 4 (see problem 88, page 424) in the merging procedure.

Termination The length of the considered array is divided by 2 at each step while remaining positive. This ensures the termination of the algorithm.

The division model that applies is:

$$
\begin{array}{ll}
\text{nbInv2}(1) \text{ elementary} & \\
\text{nbInv2}(n) \to 2 \cdot \text{nbInv2}\left(\dfrac{n}{2}\right) + \text{nbInvMerge}(n) & n > 1
\end{array}
$$

The code of this procedure is:

1. **procedure** *NbInv2*(i, s; nb : **modif**) **pre**

2. $i \in 1 .. n$ **and** $s \in i .. n$ **and** $\exists k \cdot \left(k \in \mathbb{N}_1 \text{ and } s - i + 1 = 2^k \right)$ **and**

3.   mid $\in i .. s$ **and** NbiL $\in \mathbb{N}$ **and** NbiR $\in \mathbb{N}$ **and** NbiLr $\in \mathbb{N}$

4. **begin**
5.   **if** $i = s$ **then**
6. $nb \leftarrow 0$
7.   **else**
8. $mid \leftarrow \left\lfloor \dfrac{i+s}{2} \right\rfloor$;
9. $NbInv2(i, mid, NbiL)$;
10. $NbInv2(mid + 1, s, NbiR)$;
11. $NbInvMerge(i, s, NbiLr)$;
12. $nb \leftarrow NbiL + NbiR + NbiLr$
13.   **end if**
14. **end**

The procedure *NbInvMerge* is founded on an iteration built from the five following components (A is an auxiliary array intended to receive the result of the merge of the two halves of T):

Invariant The following conjunct:

$$A[i .. l] = IsMerge(T[i .. j - 1], T[mid + 1 .. k - 1]),$$

is added to the invariant proposed in response to question 3. It specifies that the sub-array $A[i .. l]$ is actually the merge of the sub-arrays $T[i .. j - 1]$ and $T[mid + 1 .. k - 1]$.

Stopping condition It is unchanged with respect to that in response to question 3.

Progression The update of the array A is added to the progression in response to question 3.

Initialization The assignment $l \leftarrow i$ is added to the initialization program produced in response to question 3 to establish the invariant.

Termination The termination expression is the same as that given in response to question 3.

The associated code is written:

1. **procedure** $NbInvMerge(i, s; nb : $ **modif**$)$ **pre**
2. $i \in 1 .. n$ **and** $s \in i .. n$ **and** $\exists k \cdot \left(k \in \mathbb{N}_1 \text{ and } s - i + 1 = 2^k\right)$ **and** $nbi \in$ $\mathbb{N}$ **and**
3. $mid \in i .. s$ **and** $j \in i .. mid + 1$ **and** $k \in mid + 1 .. s + 1$ **and** $l \in i .. s$ **and**
4. $IsSorted(T[i .. mid])$ **and** $IsSorted(T[mid + 1 .. s])$ **and** $A \in i .. s \rightarrow 1 .. n$
5. **begin**
6. $mid \leftarrow \left\lfloor \dfrac{i+s}{2} \right\rfloor$;
7. $j \leftarrow i; k \leftarrow mid + 1; nbi \leftarrow 0; l \leftarrow i$;
8.   **while not**$(j = mid + 1$ **or** $k = s + 1)$ **do**
9.   **if** $T[j] < T[k]$ **then**
10. $A[l] \leftarrow T[j]; j \leftarrow j + 1$
11.   **else**
12. $A[l] \leftarrow T[k]; k \leftarrow k + 1; nbi \leftarrow nbi + (mid - j + 1)$
13.   **end if**;
14. $l \leftarrow l + 1$
15.   **end while**;
16. $A[l .. l + s - k] \leftarrow T[k .. s]$;
17. $A[l .. l + mid - j] \leftarrow T[j .. mid]$;
18. $T[i .. s] \leftarrow A$
19. **end**

Complexity

The assessment of the complexity of the procedure *NbInvMerge* is carried out similarly to question 3. This procedure is therefore in $\Theta(n)$ conditions evaluated. The recurrence equation C_2 for the procedure *NbInv2* is:

$$\left|\begin{array}{l} C_2(1) = 1 \\ C_2(n) = 2 \cdot C_2\left(\dfrac{n}{2}\right) + g(n) \quad \text{where } g(n) \in \Theta(n) \end{array}\right. \qquad n > 1.$$

From the special case 8.4 of the corollary of the master theorem, page 423, this solution is in $\Theta(n \cdot \log_2(n))$ conditions evaluated.

103 - A 5   **Answer 5.**   The answer to this question is positive. The algorithms are correct for any value of n, since the equality property of the sizes of the arrays is never exploited. The only consequence is the difficulty this could cause in complexity calculations. But we know, according to the master theorem (see page 422), that in general there are no consequences on the solution of the recurrence equations.

Answers to problem 104. The skyline   *The problem is on page 442.*

104 - A 1   **Answer 1.**   This construction does not raise any specific problem. The reader is invited to specify the stopping condition, the initialization and the termination expression. The iteration is based on the following invariant: S is the skyline of the buildings $I[1]$ to $I[j-1]$, for $j \in 1 .. m + 1$. The progression is itself an iteration whose invariant is: S is the result of the fusion between the fragment of the jth building going from position 1 to position $k - 1$ and the homologous fragment of the skyline S. The progression of this nested iteration is to store the largest element between $S[k]$ and $I[j][k]$ in $S[k]$ (then to restore the invariant by updating k). These iterations are easily expressed by **for** loops:

```
1.  constants
2.    m ∈ N and m = ... and n ∈ N and n = ... and I ∈ 1 .. m → (1 ..
        n → N) and I = [...]
3.  variables
4.    S ∈ 1 .. n ↣ N
5.  begin
6.    S ← (1 .. n) × {0}; /% initialization of the skyline S with 0's %/
7.    for j ranging 1 .. m do
8.      for k ranging 1 .. n do
9.        S[k] ← max({S[k], I[j][k]})
10.     end for
11.   end for;
12.   write(S)
13. end
```

104 - A 2   **Answer 2.**   The number of conditions evaluated is equal to $((m+1) \cdot (2n+1))$. Indeed, if we consider that the evaluation of a max requires one condition, the outer (respectively inner) loop requires the evaluation of $m + 1$ (reps. $(n + 1)$) conditions, i.e., in total $((m + 1) \cdot (2n + 1))$. Since n is constant, the complexity is therefore in $\Theta(m)$.

104 - A 3   **Answer 3.**   The procedure *SkyLine1*(beg, end; S : **modif**) built by strong induction on the number of buildings. Let $p = (end - beg + 1)$ be this number.

Base The elementary case occurs when $p = 1$, i.e. when the set of buildings is reduces to a single one. The skyline is then I[beg].

Induction hypothesis It is known how to calculate the *skyline* of a set of q buildings, for any q such that $1 \leqslant q < p$.

Induction Let $p > 1$ and $mid = \lfloor (beg + end)/2 \rfloor$. From the induction hypothesis, it is known how to calculate the *skylines* S1 of I[beg .. mid] and S2 of I[mid + 1 .. end]. The desired result is then the merging of S1 and S2 (i.e., the greater of the two heights between S1[j] and S2[j] when j crosses the interval 1 .. n).

Termination The number of buildings is divided by 2 at each step while remaining positive. This ensures the termination of the algorithm.

Thus, the division model is:

$$
\boxed{
\begin{array}{ll}
\text{SkyLine1}(1) \text{ elementary} & \\
\text{SkyLine1}(m) \rightarrow 2 \cdot \text{SkyLine1}\left(\dfrac{m}{2}\right) + \text{merging of S1 and S2} & m > 1
\end{array}
}
$$

The code of the procedure *SkyLine1* is as follows:

```
1.  procedure SkyLine1(beg, end; S : modif) pre
2.      beg ∈ 1 .. m and end ∈ beg .. m and S ∈ 1 .. n → ℕ and
3.      mid ∈ beg .. end and S1 ∈ 1 .. n → ℕ and S2 ∈ 1 .. n → ℕ
4.  begin
5.      if beg = end then
6.          S ← I[beg]
7.      else
8.          mid ← ⌊(beg + end)/2⌋;
9.          SkyLine1(beg, mid, S1);
10.         SkyLine1(mid + 1, end, S2);
11.         for j ∈ 1 .. n do
12.             S[j] ← max({S1[j], S2[j]})
13.         end for
14.     end if
15. end
```

This procedure can be called by the program:

```
1.  constants
2.      m ∈ ℕ and m = ... and n ∈ ℕ and n = ... and
3.      I ∈ 1 .. m → (1 .. n → ℕ) and I = [...]
4.  variables
5.      T ∈ 1 .. n → ℕ
6.  begin
7.      SkyLine1(1, m, T);
8.      write(T)
9.  end
```

Answer 4. If n is considered constant, the recurrence relation accounting for the complexity as a function of m is:

104 - A 4

$$C(1) = 1$$
$$C(m) = 2 \cdot C\left(\frac{m}{2}\right) + g(n) \text{ where } g(n) \in \Theta(n) \qquad\qquad m > 1.$$

The special case 8.3 of the master theorem, page 423, states that $C(m) \in \Theta(m)$ ($g(n)$ is constant with respect to m). From an asymptotic point of view, complexity is not enhanced!

104 - A 5   **Answer 5.**   The representation of the skyline of figure 8.2, page 442, is the following:
$T[0 .. n+1] = [(0,0), (1,1), (2,3), (3,1), (5,0), (6,2), (8,0), (9,0), (0,0), (0,0)]$.

104 - A 6   **Answer 6.**   The loop is founded on the five following components.

Invariant The "natural" invariant constitutes a starting base for the construction of the iteration. It is represented by the diagram below:

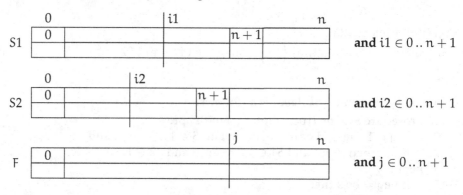

$F[0..j-1]$ is the skyline resulting from the merge of $S1[0..i1-1]$ and $S2[0..i2-1]$ (except the sentinels $(n+1, 0)$). The following propositions (connected with six fresh variables $hts1, hts2, p1, p2, h1$ and $h2$) come into play for strengthening this invariant:

- $hts1$ is the height (second component) of the pair $S1[i1-1]$ if $i1 \in 1..n+1$, -1 if $i1 = 0$,
- $hts2$ is the height of the couple $S2[i2-1]$ if $i2 \in 1..n+1$, -1 if $i2 = 0$,
- $p1$ (respectively $p2$) is the first component of the couple $S1[i1]$ (respectively $S2[i2]$),
- $h1$ (respectively $h2$) is the second component of the couple $S1[i1]$ (respectively $S2[i2]$).

Stopping condition The stopping condition expresses that the two sentinels are reached by the indexes $i1$ and $i2$ ($p1 = n+1$ **and** $p2 = n+1$). It is therefore necessary to generate a sentinel in F at the end of the loop.

Progression The progression is the most difficult part of the construction. It can be designed in considering three cases according the relative position of $p1$ and $p2$:

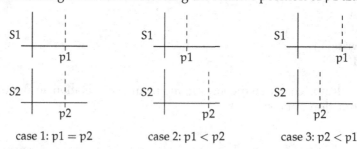

case 1: $p1 = p2$ case 2: $p1 < p2$ case 3: $p2 < p1$

Below, only the first case ($p1 = p2$) is detailed. Let m be the greater value between $h1$ and $h2$. Two sub-cases can be singled out: $hts1 > hts2$ and $hts2 \geqslant hts1$. Let us consider the first one. Five (sub-)sub-cases are then to be taken into account according to the relative position of $m, hts1$ and $hts2$. Below, the diagrams on the left show the relative position of the three variables ($hts1$ represents the current end of the *skyline* F), while the diagrams on the right show how the skyline extends on F:

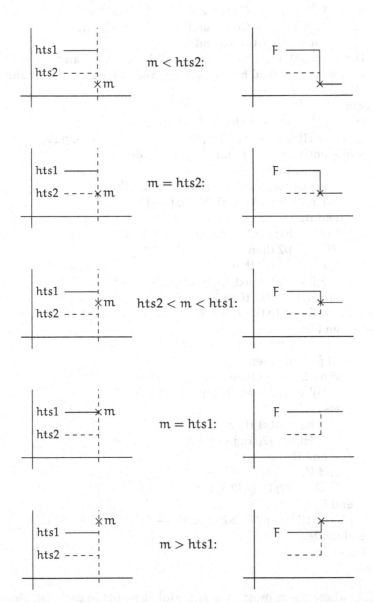

Note that, in the case where $m = hts1$, there is no creation of a new pair for F, since the current height does not change. The study of these five cases shows that, taking into account the similarity of certain situations after the treatment, factorizations are possible. The procedure presented later takes this into account.

Initialization The initialization of the loop is trivial (as long as the variables $hts1$ and $hts2$ are correctly assigned).

Termination The expression $((n + 2 - i1) + (n + 2 - i2))$ constitutes a suitable termination expression.

The following procedure can be derived:

```
1.  procedure MergingSkyLines(S1, S2; F : modif) pre
2.      Coord = {x, y | x ∈ ℕ and y ∈ ℕ} and
3.      S1 ∈ (0 .. n + 1) → Coord and IsSkyLine(S1) and
4.      S2 ∈ (0 .. n + 1) → Coord and IsSkyLine(S2) and
5.      F ∈ (0 .. n + 1) → Coord and
6.      i1 ∈ 0 .. n + 1 and i2 ∈ 0 .. n + 1 and j ∈ 0 .. n + 1 and
7.      hts1 ∈ ℕ∪{−1} and hts2 ∈ ℕ∪{−1} and (p1, p2) ∈ (ℕ × ℕ) and (h1, h2) ∈
        (ℕ × ℕ)
8.  begin
9.      i1 ← 0; i2 ← 0; j ← 0; hts1 ← −1; hts2 ← −1;
10.     p1 ← S1[i1].x; p2 ← S2[i2].x; h1 ← S1[i1].y; h2 ← S2[i2].y;
11.     while not(p1 = n + 1 and p2 = n + 1) do
12.        if p1 = p2 then
13.           if max({hts1, hts2}) ≠ max({h1, h2}) then
14.               F[j] ← (p1, max({h1, h2})); j ← j + 1
15.           end if;
16.           hts1 ← h1; hts2 ← h2; i1 ← i1 + 1; i2 ← i2 + 1
17.        elsif p1 < p2 then
18.           if hts1 > hts2 then
19.               F[j] ← (p1, max({h1, hts2})); j ← j + 1
20.           elsif h1 > hts2 then
21.               F[j] ← S1[i1]; j ← j + 1
22.           end if;
23.           hts1 ← h1; i1 ← i1 + 1
24.        elsif p2 < p1 then
25.           if hts2 > hts1 then
26.               F[j] ← (p2, max({h2, hts1})); j ← j + 1
27.           else
28.              if h2 > hts1 then
29.                  F[j] ← S2[i1]; j ← j + 1
30.              end if
31.           end if;
32.           hts2 ← h2; i1 ← i2 + 1
33.        end if;
34.        p1 ← S1[i1].x; p2 ← S2[i2].x; h1 ← S1[i1].y; h2 ← S2[i2].y
35.     end while;
36.     F[j] ← (n + 1, 0)
37.  end
```

104 - A 7   **Answer 7.**   There are at most $(n + 1)$ useful elements in each list. Since n is constant, complexity at worst is in $\Theta(1)$.

104 - A 8   **Answer 8.**   The inner loop is performed in the procedure *MergingSkyLines*. The initialization must place a sentinel in S. Note also that S cannot be both the first input parameter of the procedure and the output parameter at the same time, hence the use of an auxiliary array V.

1. **constants**
2. $m \in \mathbb{N}$ **and** $m = \ldots$ **and** $n \in \mathbb{N}$ **and** $n = \ldots$ **and**
3. $I \in 1 .. m \rightarrow (1 .. n \rightarrow \mathbb{N})$ **and** $I = [\ldots]$
4. **variables**
5. $S \in 1 .. n \rightarrow \mathbb{N}$ **and** $V \in 1 .. n \rightarrow \mathbb{N}$
6. **begin**
7. /% *creation of a sentinel on* S: %/
8. $S \leftarrow (0 \mapsto (n+1, 0)) \cup (1 .. n) \times (0, 0)$;
9. **for** j **ranging** $1 .. m$ **do**
10. *FusionSkyLines*$(S, I[j], V)$;
11. $S \leftarrow V$
12. **end for**;
13. **write**(S)
14. **end**

Like the previous iterative version, this version is in $\Theta(m)$.

Answer 9. Except for the gathering phase, which uses the procedure *SkyLine2*, the construction of this solution as well as its division model are similar to those of the question 3. The code of the procedure is the following: 104 - A 9

1. **procedure** *SkyLine2*$(beg, end; S:$ **modif**$)$ **pre**
2. $beg \in 1 .. m$ **and** $end \in beg .. m$ **and** $S \in (0 .. n+1) \rightarrow (\mathbb{N} \times \mathbb{N})$ **and**
3. $mid \in beg..end$ **and** $S1 \in (0..n+1) \rightarrow (\mathbb{N} \times \mathbb{N})$ **and** $S2 \in (0..n+1) \rightarrow (\mathbb{N} \times \mathbb{N})$
4. **begin**
5. **if** $beg = end$ **then**
6. $S \leftarrow I[beg]$
7. **else**
8. $mid \leftarrow \left\lfloor \dfrac{beg + end}{2} \right\rfloor$;
9. *SkyLine2*$(beg, mid, S1)$;
10. *SkyLine2*$(mid + 1, end, S2)$;
11. *MergingSkyLines*$(S1, S2, S)$
12. **end if**
13. **end**

Answer 10. The recurrence equation of complexity is identical to that of function *Sky-Line1*. Therefore, the algorithm is still in $\Theta(m)$. From an asymptotic point of view, the use of a more sophisticated data structure does not yield a better solution. This result is easily understandable since the gain brought by the new data structure is at worst zero. In addition, the algorithm proves to be more difficult to build. The improvement should be sought on average complexity. 104 - A 10

Answers to problem 105. The majority element (recursive issue) *The problem is on page 445.*

The proofs used later on make use of the following proposition (whose demonstration is left to the reader) relating to the operator "floor" $\lfloor \ \rfloor$, for two positive real numbers x and y:

$$\lfloor x \rfloor + \lfloor y \rfloor \leqslant \lfloor x + y \rfloor \leqslant \lfloor x \rfloor + \lfloor y \rfloor + 1. \tag{8.32}$$

Answer 1.   The solution presented is based on the following inductive reasoning.

Base The base case occurs when the array has a single element T[beg .. beg] (which is majority), and the result is then (T[beg], 1).

Induction hypothesis It is known how to calculate the pair (x, mbx) for any array of size m such that $1 \leqslant m < lgt$.

Induction In this part of the reasoning, the array T[beg .. beg + lgt − 1] of size lgt greater than 1 is under consideration. In order to simplify the notations, we denote by T the array T[beg .. beg + lgt − 1]. The left half-array T[beg .. beg + ⌊lgt/2⌋ − 1] (respectively the right half-array T[beg + ⌊lgt/2⌋ .. beg + lgt − 1]) is denoted by Tl (respectively Tr) and its size ⌊lgt/2⌋ (respectively ⌈lgt/2⌉) is denoted by lgtl (respectively lgtr). One has lgtl + lgtr = lgt. From the induction hypothesis, it is known how to calculate the pairs $(xl, nbxl)$ and $(xr, nbxr)$ for each of these two arrays. Five cases are to be singled out:

1. $xl > 0, xr > 0$ and $xl = xr$: the value xl (or equivalently xr) has nbxl (nbxl $\geqslant$ (⌊lgtl/2⌋ + 1)) occurrences in Tl and nbxr (nbxr $\geqslant$ (⌊lgtr/2⌋ + 1)) occurrences in Tr. Now:

$$
\left\lfloor \frac{lgtl}{2} \right\rfloor + 1 + \left\lfloor \frac{lgtr}{2} \right\rfloor + 1
$$

$$
\geqslant \qquad\qquad\qquad\qquad\qquad \text{formula 8.32, page 561}
$$

$$
\left\lfloor \frac{lgtl}{2} + \frac{lgtr}{2} \right\rfloor + 1
$$

$$
= \qquad\qquad\qquad\qquad\qquad\qquad\qquad \text{arithmetics}
$$

$$
\left\lfloor \frac{lgt}{2} \right\rfloor + 1.
$$

   xl (or equivalently xr) is thus majority in T, and the result is $(xl, nbxl + nbxr)$.

2. $xl = 0, xr = 0$: any value y has a number of occurrences at most equal to ⌊lgtl/2⌋ (respectively ⌊lgtr/2⌋) in Tl (respectively Tr). Now:

$$
\left\lfloor \frac{lgtl}{2} \right\rfloor + \left\lfloor \frac{lgtr}{2} \right\rfloor
$$

$$
\leqslant \qquad\qquad\qquad\qquad\qquad \text{formula 8.32, page 561}
$$

$$
\left\lfloor \frac{lgtl}{2} + \frac{lgtr}{2} \right\rfloor
$$

$$
= \qquad\qquad\qquad\qquad\qquad\qquad\qquad \text{arithmetics}
$$

$$
\left\lfloor \frac{lgt}{2} \right\rfloor.
$$

   T is thus not majority and the result returned is $(0, 0)$, or $(xl, nbxl + nbxr)$. This result is indeed identical to the previous one.

3. $xl > 0, xr > 0, xl \neq xr$: we compute the number of occurrences ndxl of xl in Tr. If nbxl + nrxl > ⌊lgt/2⌋ $(xl, nbxl + ndxl)$ is returned, otherwise we compute the number of occurrences nlxr of xr in Tl, and $(xr, nbxr + nlxr)$ is returned if (nbxl + nlxr) > ⌊lgt/2⌋, otherwise the result is $(0, 0)$.

4. $xl > 0$ and $xr = 0$: we compute the number of occurrences nrxl of xl in Tr and $(xl, nbxl + nrxl)$ is returned if (nbxl + nrxl) > ⌊lgt/2⌋, $(0, 0)$ otherwise.

5. $xr > 0$ and $xl = 0$: this case is the symmetrical of the preceding one.

Termination The size of the arrays dealt with decreases at each step while remaining positive. This ensures the termination of the algorithm.

The division model used is:

$$
\begin{array}{|l|}
\hline
\text{Majority1}(1) \text{ elementaire} \\[2mm]
\text{Majorite1}(t) \rightarrow \left(
\begin{array}{l}
\text{Majorite1}\left(\left\lfloor \dfrac{\text{lgt}}{2} \right\rfloor\right) + \text{Majority1}\left(\left\lceil \dfrac{\text{lgt}}{2} \right\rceil\right) + \\[2mm]
\text{computation of the result from } (xl, nbxl) \text{ and } (xr, nbxr)
\end{array}
\right) \quad \text{lgt} > 1. \\
\hline
\end{array}
$$

The associated code is given hereafter:

1. **procedure** *Majority1*(beg, lgt; x, nbx : **modif**) **pre**
2.   beg $\in \mathbb{N}_1$ **and** lgt $\in \mathbb{N}_1$ **and** x $\in \mathbb{N}$ **and** nbx $\in \mathbb{N}$ **and**
3.   xl $\in \mathbb{N}$ **and** xr $\in \mathbb{N}$ **and** nbxl $\in \mathbb{N}$ **and** nbxr $\in \mathbb{N}$ **and** nrxl $\in \mathbb{N}$ **and** nlxr $\in \mathbb{N}$
4. **begin**
5.   **if** lgt $= 1$ **then**
6.   x $\leftarrow$ T[beg] ; nbx $\leftarrow 1$
7.   **else**
8.   *Majority1*$\left(\text{beg}, \left\lfloor \dfrac{\text{lgt}}{2} \right\rfloor, xl, nbxl\right)$;
9.   *Majority1*$\left(\text{beg} + \left\lfloor \dfrac{\text{lgt}}{2} \right\rfloor, \left\lceil \dfrac{\text{lgt}}{2} \right\rceil, xr, nbxr\right)$;
10.   **if** xl $=$ xr **then**
11.   x $\leftarrow$ xl; nbx $\leftarrow$ nbxl $+$ nbxr
12.   **elsif** xl > 0 **and** xr > 0 **and** xl $\neq$ xr **then**
13.   nrxl $\leftarrow$ mult$\left(xl, T\left[\text{beg} + \left\lfloor \dfrac{\text{lgt}}{2} \right\rfloor .. \text{beg} + \text{lgt} - 1\right]\right)$;
14.   **if** nrxl $+$ nbxl $> \left\lfloor \dfrac{\text{lgt}}{2} \right\rfloor$ **then**
15.   x $\leftarrow$ xl; nbx $\leftarrow$ nbxl $+$ nrxl
16.   **else**
17.   nlxr $\leftarrow$ mult$\left(xr, T\left[\text{beg} .. \text{beg} + \left\lfloor \dfrac{\text{lgt}}{2} \right\rfloor - 1\right]\right)$;
18.   **if** nlxr $+$ nbxr $> \left\lfloor \dfrac{\text{lgt}}{2} \right\rfloor$ **then**
19.   x $\leftarrow$ xr; nbx $\leftarrow$ nbxr $+$ nlxr
20.   **else**
21.   x $\leftarrow 0$; nbx $\leftarrow 0$
22.   **end if**
23.   **end if**
24.   **elsif** xl $\neq 0$ **and** xr $= 0$ **then**
25.   nrxl $\leftarrow$ mult$\left(xl, T\left[\text{beg} + \left\lfloor \dfrac{\text{lgt}}{2} \right\rfloor .. \text{beg} + \text{lgt} - 1\right]\right)$;
26.   **if** nrxl $+$ nbxl $> \left\lfloor \dfrac{\text{lgt}}{2} \right\rfloor$ **then**
27.   x $\leftarrow$ xl; nbx $\leftarrow$ nbxl $+$ nrxl

```
28.        else
29.            x ← 0; nbx ← 0
30.        end if
31.    else
```

32. $\quad\quad$ $nlxr \leftarrow mult\left(xr, T\left[beg \mathbin{..} beg + \left\lfloor \dfrac{lgt}{2} \right\rfloor - 1\right]\right);$

33. $\quad\quad$ **if** $nlxr + nbxr > \left\lfloor \dfrac{lgt}{2} \right\rfloor$ **then**

```
34.            x ← xr; nbx ← nbxr + nlxr
35.        else
36.            x ← 0 ; nbx ← 0
37.        end if
38.    end if
39.  end if
40. end
```

105 - A 2   **Answer 2.**   The procedure *Majority1* calls the function mult of linear complexity. By counting all the tests, the worst-case complexity of *Majority1* is therefore the solution of the recurrence equation:

$$\left|\begin{array}{l} C(1) = 1 \\[2mm] C(lgt) = 2 \cdot C\left(\dfrac{lgt}{2}\right) + lgt + 4 \end{array}\right. \qquad\qquad\qquad lgt > 1.$$

According to formula 8.4, page 423, it can be deduced that $C(lgt) \in \Theta(lgt \cdot \log_2(lgt))$. The complexity of the solution obtained is less good than that of the iterative version.

105 - A 3   **Answer 3.**   The solution proposed is based on the following inductive reasoning.

Base   As before, the base case occurs when the array to be processed has only one element $T[beg]$; the result is the pair $(T[beg], 1)$.

Induction hypothesis   It is known how to compute the pair (x, mbx) for any array of size m such that $1 \leqslant m < lgt$.

Induction   In the inductive case (array $T[beg \mathbin{..} beg + lgt - 1]$ of size lgt, $lgt > 1$), several sub-cases are to be studied. The same notations as before are used ($T, Tl, Tr, lgtl$ and $lgtr$), and we have (proposition not proven):

$$\left\lfloor \frac{tl}{2} \right\rfloor + \left\lceil \frac{tr}{2} \right\rceil \geqslant \left\lfloor \frac{lgt}{2} \right\rfloor. \tag{8.33}$$

Seven cases (or sub-cases) are to be considered. The seven following properties (16 to 22) account for them. They are the basis of the treatment to be carried out following recursive calls, in order to restore the induction hypothesis. The associated proofs are based on the following properties (not proven) of the operators $\lfloor \rfloor$ and $\lceil \rceil$ for positive real numbers x and y:

$$\lfloor x \rfloor \leqslant \lceil x \rceil \tag{8.34}$$

$$\lfloor x \rfloor + \lceil y \rceil \leqslant \lfloor x + y \rfloor \tag{8.35}$$

$$\lfloor y \rfloor \geqslant 2 \cdot \left\lfloor \frac{y}{2} \right\rfloor \tag{8.36}$$

and on the following property, where m and n are two natural numbers:

$$2m \leqslant n \Rightarrow m \leqslant \left\lfloor \frac{n}{2} \right\rfloor. \tag{8.37}$$

Property 16:
If Tl and Tr are not majority, then T is not majority.

This property has been proven in the answer to question 1.

Property 17:
If (xl, mxl) is MC in Tl, if (xr, mxr) is MC in Tr and if $xl = xr$, then $(xl, mxl + mxr)$ is MC in T.

Proof of property 17. It must be proven that under the three hypotheses "(xl, mxl) is MC in Tl", "(xr, mxr) is MC in Tr" and "$xl = xr$", $(xl, mxl + mxr)$ is MC in T. The three clauses of the definition of a MC are to be considered.
Clause 1. It must be proven that $\mathrm{mult}(xl, T) \leqslant mxl + mxr$. We start from formula $(\mathrm{mult}(xl, Tl) \leqslant mxl$ **and** $\mathrm{mult}(xr, Tr) \leqslant mxr)$ that is the conjunction of the induction hypothesis on the left and on the right.

$\mathrm{mult}(xl, Tl) \leqslant mxl$ **and** $\mathrm{mult}(xr, Tr) \leqslant mxr$
$\Rightarrow$ 　　　　　　　　　　　　　　arithmetics and propositional calculus
$\mathrm{mult}(xl, Tl) + \mathrm{mult}(xr, Tr) \leqslant mxl + mxr$
$\Leftrightarrow$ 　　　　　　　　　　　　　　　　　　hypothesis $xl = xr$
$\mathrm{mult}(xl, Tl) + \mathrm{mult}(xl, Tr) \leqslant mxl + mxr$
$\Leftrightarrow$ 　　　　　　　　　　　　　　　definition of T, Tl and Tr
$\mathrm{mult}(xl, T) \leqslant mxl + mxr.$

Clause 2. It must be proven that $\lfloor lgt/2 \rfloor < mxl + mxr$. First

$$mxr > \left\lfloor \frac{lgtr}{2} \right\rfloor \qquad \text{induction hypothesis on the right}$$
$$\Rightarrow \qquad\qquad\qquad\qquad\qquad\qquad \text{arithmetics on integers}$$
$$mxr \geqslant \left\lfloor \frac{lgtr}{2} \right\rfloor + 1.$$

From this result:

$$mxl + mxr$$
$$> \qquad\qquad \text{induction hypothesis on the left and previous result}$$
$$\left\lfloor \frac{lgtl}{2} \right\rfloor + \left(\left\lfloor \frac{lgtr}{2} \right\rfloor + 1 \right)$$
$$\geqslant \qquad\qquad\qquad \text{property of } \lfloor\ \rfloor, \text{ formula 8.32, page 561}$$
$$\left\lfloor \frac{lgtl + lgtr}{2} \right\rfloor$$
$$= \qquad\qquad\qquad\qquad\qquad\qquad\qquad lgt = lgtl + lgtr$$
$$\left\lfloor \frac{lgt}{2} \right\rfloor.$$

Clause 3. It must be proven that for any y different from xl, $mult(y, T) \leqslant lgt - (mxl + mxr)$. We start from the induction hypothesis on the left and on the right:

$$mult(y, Tl) \leqslant lgtl - mxl \quad \textbf{and} \quad mult(z, Tr) \leqslant lgtr - mxr$$

$\Rightarrow$ in particular for $y = z$

$$mult(y, Tl) + mult(y, Tr) \leqslant lgtl + lgtr - (mxl + mxr)$$

$\Leftrightarrow$ definitions of T, Tl, Tr and $lgt, lgtl, lgtr$

$$mult(y, T) \leqslant lgt - (mxl + mxr)$$

Property 18:
If (xl, mxl) is MC in Tl, if (xr, mxr) is MC in Tr, if $(xl \neq xr)$ and if $(mxl + (lgtr - mxr)) = (mxr + (lgtl - mxl))$, then T is not majority.

In other words, if the majority candidates in Tl and Tr are different and if the number of majority elements on the left plus the number of non majority elements on the right is equal to the number of majority elements on the right plus the number of non majority elements on the left, then T is not majority.

Property 19:
If (xl, mxl) is MC in Tl, if (xr, mxr) is MC in Tr, if $xl \neq xr$ and if $(mxl + (lgtr - mxr)) > (mxr + lgtl - mxl))$, then $(xl, mxl + (lgtr - mxr))$ is MC in T.

Property 20:
If (xl, mxl) is MC in Tl, if (xr, mxr) is MC in Tr, if $xl \neq xr$ and if $(mxl + (lgtr - mxr)) < (mxr + (lgtl - mxl))$, then $(xr, mxr + (lgtl - mxl))$ is MC in T.

Property 21:
If (xr, mxr) is MC in Tr and if Tl is not majority, then $(xr, mxr + \lceil lgtl/2 \rceil)$ is MC in T.

Property 22:
If (xl, mxl) is MC in Tl and if Tr is not majority, then $(xl, mxl + \lceil lgtr/2 \rceil)$ is MC in T.

The proofs of proprerties 18 to 22 are similar to that of property 17 and thus left to the reader.

Termination The size of the arrays processed decreases at each step wile remaining positive. This ensures the termination of the algorithm.

The division model used is:

$$
\boxed{
\begin{array}{ll}
\text{CandMaj1}(1) \text{ elementary} & \\[1em]
\text{CandMaj1}(lgt) \rightarrow \left(\begin{array}{l} \text{CandMaj1}\left(\left\lfloor \dfrac{lgt}{2} \right\rfloor \right) + \text{CandMaj1}\left(\left\lceil \dfrac{lgt}{2} \right\rceil \right) + \\ \text{calculation of } (x, mx) \text{ from } (xl, mxl) \text{ and } (xr, mxr) \end{array} \right) & lgt > 1
\end{array}
}
$$

The code of the procedure *CandMaj1* stems directly from the above properties:

```
1.  procedure CandMaj1(beg, lgt; x, mx : modif) pre
2.     beg ∈ 1 .. n and lgt ∈ 1 .. n − beg + 1 and x ∈ N and mx ∈ 0 .. lgt and
3.     xl ∈ N and xr ∈ N and mxl ∈ 0 .. ⌊lgt/2⌋ and mxr ∈ 0 .. ⌈lgt/2⌉ and
4.     lgtl ∈ N and lgtr ∈ N
5.  begin
6.     if lgt = 1 then
7.        x ← T[beg]; mx ← 1
8.     else
9.        lgtl ← ⌊lgt/2⌋ ; mgtr ← ⌈lgt/2⌉ ;
10.       CandMaj1(beg, lgtl, xl, mxl);
11.       CandMaj1(beg + lgtr, tr, xr, mxr);
12.       if xl = 0 and xr = 0 then
13.          x ← 0; mx ← 0 /% property 16 %/
14.       elsif xl ≠ 0 and xr ≠ 0 then
15.          if xl = xr then
16.             x ← xl ; mx ← mxl + mxr /% property 17 %/
17.          else
18.             if mxl + (lgtr − mxr) = mxr + (lgtl − mxl) then
19.                x ← 0; mx ← 0 /% property 18 %/
20.             elsif mxl + (lgtr − mxr) > mxr + (lgtl − mxl) then
21.                x ← xl; mx ← mxl + (lgtr − mxr) /% property 19 %/
22.             elsif mxl + (lgtr − mxr) < mxr + (lgtl − mxl) then
23.                x ← xr; mx ← mxr + (lgtl − mxl) /% property 20 %/
24.             end if
25.          end if
26.       elsif xl = 0 and xr ≠ 0 then
27.          x ← xr; mx ← mxr + ⌈lgtl/2⌉ /% property 21 %/
28.       elsif xl ≠ 0 and xr = 0 then
29.          x ← xl; mx ← mxl + ⌈lgtr/2⌉ /% property 22 %/
30.       end if
31.    end if
32. end
```

Complexity

The restoration of the induction hypothesis (i.e. the computation of the pair (x, mx)) is done in constant time. Indeed, at most six conditions are evaluated after the recursive calls. The recurrence equation expressing complexity is written:

$$
\begin{cases}
C(1) = 1 \\
C(lgt) = 2 \cdot C\left(\dfrac{lgt}{2}\right) + e & lgt > 1 \text{ and } 1 \leqslant e \leqslant 6.
\end{cases}
$$

Formula 8.3, page 423, makes it possible to deduce that $C(lgt) \in \Theta(lgt)$.

Answer 4.   Any call to the procedure *CandMaj1* must be completed by a fragment of program checking if the possible candidate found is actually a majority element:

1. **constants**
2. $n \in \mathbb{N}_1$ **and** $n = \ldots$ **and** $T \in 1..n \rightarrow \mathbb{N}_1$ **and** $T = [\ldots]$
3. **variables**
4. $v \in \mathbb{N}$ **and** $MajV \in 0..n$
5. **begin**
6.   *CandMaj1*$(1, n, v, MajV)$;
7.   **if** $v = 0$ **or else** $\text{mult}(v, T) \leqslant \left\lfloor \dfrac{n}{2} \right\rfloor$ **then**
8.   write(*No majority element in this array*)
9.   **else**
10.   write(v, *is the majority element in this array*)
11.   **end if**
12. **end**

Complexity

The complexity of the program following the call to the procedure *CandMaj1*, in charge of checking whether the candidate v is or not the majority element, is in $\Theta(n)$ (complexity of the refinement of the expression $\text{mult}(v, T) \leqslant \lfloor n/2 \rfloor$). The complexity of the whole processing is thus in $\Theta(n)$.

Answer 5.   Application to the tables proposed in the statement of the problem.

1. For table T1:

1	2	3	4	5	6	7	8	9	10	11	12	13	14
1	2	1	3	2	1	1	3	3	2	3	1	1	1

$$1,1 \quad 2,1 \quad 1,1 \quad 3,1 \quad 2,1 \quad 1,1 \quad 1,1 \quad 3,1 \quad 3,1 \quad 2,1 \quad 3,1 \quad 1,1 \quad 1,1 \quad 1,1$$
$$(0,0) \qquad 0,0 \qquad (1,2) \qquad (0,0) \qquad 0,0 \qquad (1,2)$$
$$(1,2) \qquad\qquad (1,3) \qquad\qquad (3,2) \qquad\qquad (1,3)$$
$$(1,5) \qquad\qquad\qquad\qquad (1,4)$$
$$(1,9)$$

The value 1 has only seven occurrences in T1, which is not majority.

2. For table T2:

1	2	3	4	5	6	7	8	9	10	11	12	13
2	1	1	3	1	2	3	1	1	1	1	2	1

$$2,1 \quad 1,1 \quad 1,1 \quad 3,1 \quad 1,1 \quad 2,1 \quad 3,1 \quad 1,1 \quad 1,1 \quad 1,1 \quad 1,1 \quad 2,1 \quad 1,1$$
$$(1,2) \qquad (0,0) \qquad (1,2) \qquad 1,2 \qquad (0,0)$$
$$(1,2) \qquad\qquad (3,2) \qquad\qquad (1,2) \qquad\qquad (1,3)$$
$$(0,0) \qquad\qquad\qquad\qquad (1,5)$$
$$(1,8)$$

The value 1 has eight occurrences in T2, which is thus majority.

3. For table T3:

1	2	3	4	5	6	7	8	9
1	1	2	1	3	1	3	2	2

$$1,1 \quad 1,1 \quad 2,1 \quad 1,1 \quad 3,1 \quad 1,1 \quad 3,1 \quad 2,1 \quad 2,1$$
$$(1,2) \qquad (0,0) \qquad (0,0) \qquad (2,2)$$
$$(1,3) \qquad\qquad (2,3)$$
$$(0,0)$$

Table T3 is claimed non majority without calling on the function $\text{mult}(v, T)$.

Answer 6. Property 13, page 447, is demonstrated as follows. If $T[1 .. i]$ is not majority, 105 - A 6
x is not the majority element of $T[1 .. i]$:

$$\text{mult}(x, T) \geqslant \left\lfloor \frac{n}{2} \right\rfloor + 1 \quad \textbf{and} \quad i \in 1 .. n - 1 \quad \textbf{and} \quad \text{mult}(x, T[1 .. i]) < \left\lfloor \frac{i}{2} \right\rfloor + 1$$

$\Leftrightarrow$ property of mult

$$\left(\begin{array}{l} \text{mult}(x, T[1 .. i]) + \text{mult}(x, T[i + 1 .. n]) \geqslant \left\lfloor \dfrac{n}{2} \right\rfloor + 1 \\[2mm] \textbf{and } i \in 1 .. n - 1 \textbf{ and} \\[2mm] \text{mult}(x, T[1 .. i]) < \left\lfloor \dfrac{i}{2} \right\rfloor + 1 \end{array} \right)$$

$\Rightarrow$ arithmetics

$$\left\lfloor \frac{i}{2} \right\rfloor + 1 + \text{mult}(x, T[i + 1 .. n]) > \left\lfloor \frac{n}{2} \right\rfloor + 1 \quad \textbf{and} \quad i \in 1 .. n - 1$$

$\Rightarrow$ arithmetics

$$\left\lfloor \frac{i}{2} \right\rfloor + 1 + \text{mult}(x, T[i + 1 .. n]) > \left\lfloor \frac{n - i + i}{2} \right\rfloor + 1 \quad \textbf{and} \quad i \in 1 .. n - 1$$

$\Rightarrow$ property of $\lfloor \ \rfloor$: $\left\lfloor \dfrac{m + n}{2} \right\rfloor \geqslant \left\lfloor \dfrac{m}{2} \right\rfloor + \left\lfloor \dfrac{n}{2} \right\rfloor$

$$\left\lfloor \frac{i}{2} \right\rfloor + \text{mult}(x, T[i + 1 .. n]) > \left\lfloor \frac{n - i}{2} \right\rfloor + \left\lfloor \frac{i}{2} \right\rfloor \quad \textbf{and} \quad i \in 1 .. n - 1$$

$\Leftrightarrow$ arithmetics

$$\text{mult}(x, T[i + 1 .. n]) \geqslant \left\lfloor \frac{n - i}{2} \right\rfloor + 1 \quad \textbf{and} \quad i \in 1 .. n - 1.$$

This result expresses that x is the majority element of $T[i + 1 .. n]$.

Answer 7. From property 13, page 447, it can be deduced that the DaC algorithm 105 - A 7
sketched below is correct. We are looking for a starting sub-array T that does not have
a majority element, knowing that we start from the first element which is the majority element in the sub-array of size 1. If the second element differs from the first, the (sub-)array
containing the first two elements does not have a majority element: we start again with
the array deprived from these two elements. Otherwise, we continue by accumulating the
number of occurrences of the first element until either detecting that it is not a majority
element (we start again with the array cut off from the slice without a majority element),
or have processed the whole of the initial array. The MC of T is that of the last slice examined. As in the previous solution (after the execution of *CandMaj1*), we are then led to
check whether it is actually the majority element or not.

The underlying division model is:

$CandMaj2(0)$ elementary (T has no majority element "for sure")

$CandMaj2(1)$ elementary (the value $T[beg .. beg]$ is the MC in T)

$$CandMaj2(lgt) \rightarrow CandMaj2(lgt - k) + \left(\begin{array}{l} \text{removal of a slice of size k beginning} \\ \text{the(sub-)array of T dealt with that has} \\ \text{no majority element or detection of a} \\ \text{majority candidate} \end{array} \right)$$

$$lgt > 1.$$

It should be noted that this model illustrates the case of an original division with "dynamic
cut" to find a sub-problem of the same nature as the initial one. Moreover, this approach

is much simpler to specify than the previous solution, the validity of which requires the (fairly technical) proof of seven properties.

Complexity

The global complexity of this solution is linear, since $(n-1)$ comparisons are performed before concluding. At worst one call, which consumes the entire initial array T, is performed and then $(n-1)$ comparisons, or at best $\lceil n/2 \rceil$ calls, during which only one comparison is performed (no succession of the same value is encountered).

105 - A 8   **Answer** 8.   The function associated with this majority element search is as follows:

```
1.  function CandMaj2(beg, lgt) result ℕ pre
2.     beg ∈ ℕ₁ and lgt ∈ ℕ and i ∈ ℕ₁ and eMajC ∈ ℕ₁ and nbo ∈ ℕ
3.  begin
4.     if lgt = 0 then
5.        result 0
6.     elsif lgt = 1 then
7.        result T[beg]
8.     else
9.        i ← beg + 1; eMajC ← T[beg]; nbo ← 1 ;
10.       while i ⩽ beg + lgt − 1 and nbo > 0 do
11.          if T[i] = eMajC then
12.             nbo ← nbo + 1
13.          else
14.             nbo ← nbo − 1
15.          end if;
16.          i ← i + 1
17.       end while;
18.       if nbo = 0 then
19.          result CandMaj2(i, lgt − (i − beg))
20.       else
21.          result eMajC
22.       end if
23.    end if
24. end
```

The calling program for *CandMaj2* is:

```
1.  constants
2.     n ∈ ℕ₁ and n = ... and T ∈ 1..n → ℕ₁ and T = [...]
3.  variables
4.     v ∈ ℕ
5.  begin
6.     v ← CandMaj2(1, n) ;
7.     if mult(v, T) ⩽ ⌊n/2⌋ then
8.        write(No majority element in this array)
9.     else
10.       write(v, is the majority element in this array)
11.    end if
12. end
```

The treatment of the array T1 = $[1, 2, 1, 3, 2, 1, 1, 3, 3, 2, 3, 1, 1, 1]$ leads to the elimination of the slice $[1, 2]$, then $[1, 3]$, then $[2, 1]$, then $[1, 3]$, then $[3, 2]$, then $[3, 1]$ and $[1, 1]$ exhausts T1 with 1 as the majority candidate, which in the end is not a majority element of T1.

With the array T2 = $[2, 1, 1, 3, 1, 2, 3, 1, 1, 1, 2, 1]$, there is successive elimination of $[2, 1]$, $[1, 3]$, $[1, 2]$, $[3, 1]$. The slice $[1, 1, 1, 2, 1]$ in which 1 is a current majority element leads to returning 1 as a majority candidate, which turns out to be actually a majority element of T2.

With T3 = $[1, 1, 2, 1, 3, 1, 3, 2, 2]$, the slice $[1, 1, 2, 1, 3, 1, 3, 2]$ is eliminated and 2 (alone in its slice and therefore stop with $\mathsf{lgt} = 1$) is returned as the majority candidate who is not a majority element of T3.

Last, with T4 = $[1, 2, 1, 1, 2, 3]$, the slices $[1, 2]$ and $[1, 1, 2, 3]$ are successively eliminated, without any majority element having been found (stop with $\mathsf{lgt} = 0$) and the value 0 is returned, indicating with certainty that there is no majority element in T4.

Answers to problem 106. The two closest points in a plane *The problem is on page 448.*

Answer 1. The naïve algorithm requires the evaluation of in the order of $\Theta(n^2)$ conditions. Indeed, the first point must be compared to the following $(n-1)$, the i^e point must be compared to the following $(n-i)$, and so on. [106 - A 1]

Answer 2. The four components of the construction are: [106 - A 2]

Base If S has only two elements, the result is the distance between these two points.

Induction hypothesis Let p be the cardinality of S ($2 \leqslant p < n$ and p is a power of 2). It is known how to calculate the distance that separates the closest two points of S.

Induction S is partitioned into two subsets S1 and S2 of the same cardinality 2^{n-1}. According to the induction hypothesis, it is known how to calculate the distance d_1 (respectively d_2) which separates the two nearest points of S1 (respectively S2). The calculation of the distance between the two points closest in S (gathering step) is done by taking the smallest of the three values d_1, d_2 on the one hand and the smallest distance between pairs where one point is in S1 and the second in S2 on the other hand.

Termination Each step divides the cardinality of the considered sets by 2. These cardinalities remain positive and this ensures the termination of the algorithm.

Answer 3. If the procedure *Gather1* is in the order of $\Theta(n^2)$, formula 8.5, page 423, makes it possible to conclude that the DaC algorithm is in $\Theta(n^2)$. Therefore, it has the same complexity as the naïve one. To improve it, *Gather1* must be in an order of complexity less than $\Theta(n^2)$. If the version of *Gather1* is in $\Theta(n \cdot \log_2(n))$, the master theorem (see page 422) does not make it possible to conclude. Indeed, we then have (case 3 of the master theorem) $a = 2, b = 2, f(n) = n \cdot \log_2(n)$ and $n^{\log_b(a)} = n$. Since $f(n) \in \Omega(n^{\log_b(a)})$, $f(n)$ is asymptotically greater than n but, for any $\epsilon > 0$, $f(n) \notin \Omega(n^{\log_b(a)+\epsilon})$. The first condition of case 3 is violated and the master theorem does not apply. However, it is possible to directly solve the recurrence equation that counts the conditions being evaluated. Since n is a power of 2, this equation is as follows (ignoring the term 1 corresponding to the condition that is evaluated in the recursive case): [106 - A 3]

$$C(2) = 1$$
$$C(n) = 2 \cdot C\left(\frac{n}{2}\right) + n \cdot \log_2(n) \qquad \text{for } n > 2.$$

A resolution strategy is to proceed to a variable change before applying the summation factors technique. Let $n = 2^m$ (hence $m = \log_2 n$). The second equation becomes:

$$C(2^m) = 2 \cdot C(2^{m-1}) + m \cdot 2^m.$$

Now let $S(m) = C(2^m)$. We get the new recurrence equation:

$$S(1) = 1$$
$$S(m) = 2 \cdot S(m-1) + m \cdot 2^m \qquad m > 1,$$

equation onto which is applied the summation factors technique by multiplying each row by the factor 2^{m-i}:

$$\sum_{i=1}^{m} 2^{m-i} \cdot S(i) = 2^{m-1} + \sum_{i=2}^{m} \left(2^{m-i+1} \cdot S(i-1) + i \cdot 2^m\right)$$

$$\Leftrightarrow \qquad \qquad \text{arithmetics}$$

$$S(m) = 2^{m-1} + 2^m \cdot \sum_{i=2}^{m} i$$

$$\Leftrightarrow \qquad \qquad \text{arithmetics} \left(\sum_{i=2}^{m} i = \frac{m^2}{2} + \frac{m}{2} - 1\right)$$

$$S(m) = 2^{m-1} \cdot m^2 + 2^{m-1} \cdot m - 2^{m-1}.$$

Hence, by performing the reverse change of variable to recover $C(n)$:

$$C(n) = \frac{n}{2}(\log_2(n))^2 + \frac{n}{2}\log_2(n) - \frac{n}{2}$$

and thus $C(n) \in \Theta(n \cdot (\log_2(n))^2)$.
If *Gather1* is in $\Theta(n)$, according to formula 8.4, page 423, the algorithm is in $\Theta(n \cdot \log_2(n))$.

106 - A 4   **Answer 4.**   It is obvious that four points can be placed at the four corners of the square. Let us reason by contradiction. We will prove that if there exists a fifth point (different from the four others) located at a distance d' greater than d from a corner B, then this point is at a distance d" less than d of the corner D opposite to B in the square.
In the diagram of figure 8.25, the triangle BCD is such that BC $=$ d. The function giving the distance b between the points C and D when $0 \leqslant \alpha < \pi/4$ is expressed as:

$$b = d\sqrt{3 - 2\sqrt{2} \cdot \cos \alpha}$$

(this equation is an elementary consequence of the generalized Pythagore's theorem expressing the relationships between an angle α and the three sides of any triangle: $b^2 = c^2 + d^2 - 2 \cdot c \cdot d \cdot \cos \alpha$). The function $b(\alpha)$ is continuous and strictly increasing on $0 \leqslant \alpha < \pi/4$: $(1 - \sqrt{2})d \leqslant b < d$. It follows that any point of the square located beyond the point C with respect to B is located at a distance of D less than d, and therefore that d is not the minimum distance between two points of the strip considered, hence the contradiction.

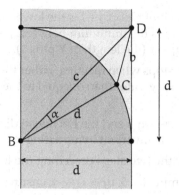

Fig. 8.25 – Figure for answer 4.

Answer 5.   The array Y must be sorted on the ordinates. Indeed, if this array is browsed   106 - A 5
according to the increasing ordinates, the point represented by Y[j] must be confronted
with the five points (at most) which follow it in the array (six points at most per rectangle
minus the point considered, i.e. five). Beyond this limit, it is impossible to find a point at
a distance less than d from Y[j]). If any of them improve the score by d, the distance is
updated. However, browsing the table does not require consulting the five (at most) next
elements. It suffices to stop the search as soon as the vertical distance between the two
points considered reaches or exceeds d.

Answer 6.   The processing of the procedure *Gather2* is done in three steps: building the   106 - A 6
strip Y, sorting Y and exploiting Y for a distance better than d. The first step is to consider
each point of S and to keep in Y only the points which are at a distance less than d from
the dividing line. In the diagram below only the points B and C are kept.

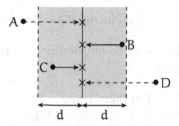

The second step, the sorting of Y according to ascending ordinates, is not developed here
and it is assumed that a sort in $\mathcal{O}(n \cdot \log_2(n))$ at worst is used. The third step is to browse
the array Y for a solution that improves on the best known solution. To do this, two nested
loops are needed. The first one, a **for** loop (which is not built here), takes into account
each of the elements of Y (Y[j]) in the order of increasing indices. The second one, a **while**
loop, evaluates the distance between each Y[j] and the points following Y[j] and keeps the
smallest value md. This loop is constructed as follows:

Invariant It is in the form:

$$j+1 \leqslant k \leqslant \min(\{j+5, ly+1\}) \textbf{ and } md = \min\left(\left\{\begin{array}{l} \textit{best value in } T[i..m], \\ \textit{in } T[m+1..s] \textit{ and in} \\ Y[1..k-1] \end{array}\right\}\right).$$

The variable ly is the useful length of the array Y built in the first step of the procedure
Gather2 (construction of the strip). The variable j controls the outer **for** loop, while k

plays the same role for the inner loop. $j+1$ is the lower bound of the variation domain of k while its upper bound is the minimum between $j+5$ (the maximum number of points to consider) and $ly+1$ (the length of Y plus 1).

Stopping condition The loop stops when meeting, either the end of the array Y, or a point that, for sure, is at a distance greater than or equal to the best value already found (see question 5).

Progression The best value between b and the Euclidean distance between Y[j] and Y[k] is selected, before restoring the invariant by updating k.

Initialization It is realized by the two steps preceding the loop itself.

Termination The expression $\min(\{j+5, ly+1\}) - k$ ensures termination.

The procedure *Gather2*(beg, end; md : **modif**) is written (Coord is the set of points of the plane defined in the statement):

```
 1. procedure Gather2(beg, end; md : modif) pre
 2.    beg ∈ 1 .. n and end ∈ deb + 1 .. n and md ∈ ℝ and
 3.    Y ∈ 1 .. end − beg + 1 → Coord and ly ∈ 0 .. end − beg + 1 and
 4.    m ∈ beg .. end and k ∈ 1 .. end − beg + 2
 5. begin
 6.    /% first step: construction of the strip Y: %/
 7.    m ← ⌊ (beg + end) / 2 ⌋;
 8.    ly ← 0;
 9.    for j ∈ beg .. end do
10.       if |T[j].x − T[m].x| < md then
11.          ly ← ly + 1 ; Y[ly] ← T[j]
12.       end if
13.    end for;
14.    /% second step: sorting Y on increasing ordinates: %/
15.    SortY(Y[1 .. ly]) ;
16.    /% third step: looking for a better solution for md: %/
17.    for j ranging 1 .. ly do
18.       k ← j + 1;
19.       while not (k = ly + 1 or then Y[k].y − Y[j].y ⩾ md) do
20.          md ← min({md, Δ(Y[j], Y[k])}); k ← k + 1
21.       end while
22.    end for
23. end
```

In line 10 of the procedure *Gather2*, the absolute value is the distance between the point T[j] and the dividing line.

The code of the function *Closest2* of the statement is to be completed by replacing lines 12 and 13 by:

```
12. Gather2(i, s, d);
13. result d
```

If n denotes the cardinality of S, the first step of this procedure is in $\Theta(n)$, the second one, sorting, is in $\Theta(n \cdot \log_2(n))$ and the third one (since the inner loop is bounded) is in $\Theta(n)$. Therefore, *Gather2* is in $\Theta(n \cdot \log_2(n))$. The division model is:

Closest2(2) elementary

$$\text{Closest2}(n) \rightarrow 2 \cdot \text{Closest2}\left(\frac{n}{2}\right) + \text{Gather2}(n) \qquad\qquad n > 2.$$

From the answer to question 3, it can be concluded that this solution is in $\Theta(n \cdot (\log_2(n))^2)$.

Answer 7. The problem stems from the sorting performed inside the procedure *Gather2*, the cost of which is in $\Theta(n \cdot \log_2(n))$. Strengthening the postcondition makes it possible to recover a version of the set S (or if one prefers of the array $T[i \mathinner{..} s]$) *ordered on the ordinates* on return from a call. The new version of *Gather* is the operation "**procedure** *Gather3*(beg, end, Zl, Zr; md, Z : **modif**)". The parameters beg, end and md are unchanged, Zl (respectively Zr) is a version of $T[i \mathinner{..} mid]$ (respectively $T[mid + 1 \mathinner{..} s]$) sorted on ordinates, and Z, output parameter, is a version of $T[i \mathinner{..} s]$ also sorted on Y-axis. The operation "**procedure** *Gather3*(beg, end, Zl, Zr; md, Z : **modif**)" is divided into two parts. The first one consists in merging the two arrays Zl and Zr on the ordinates while constructing the strip Y. Merging is done in the array Z, which then contains the same set of values as $T[i \mathinner{..} s]$. The merging operation has been studied in detail (see section 8.1.2 and problem 88, page 424), that of the construction of the strip as well. We do not go back to that here. Let us simply recall that this first part is in $\Theta(n)$. Last, the second part, the search for a better solution for md, is identical to the one built in the version *Gather2* above. The division model is the same as in the previous question, but here *Gather3* is in $\Theta(n)$. The procedure *Gather3* is given hereafter:

1. **procedure** *Closest3*(i, s; d, R : **modif**) **pre**
2. $\exists k \cdot \left(k \in \mathbb{N}_1 \text{ and } s - i + 1 = 2^k\right)$ **and**
3. $i \in 1 \mathinner{..} n$ **and** $s \in i + 1 \mathinner{..} n$ **and** $d \in \mathbb{R}_+^*$ **and** $R \in 1 \mathinner{..} s - i + 1 \rightarrow$ **Coord and**
4. *IsSortedX*($T[i \mathinner{..} s]$) **and** $dl \in \mathbb{R}_+^*$ **and** $dr \in \mathbb{R}_+^*$ **and**
5. $Rl \in 1 \mathinner{..} \dfrac{s - i + 1}{2} \rightarrow$ **Coord and** $Rr \in 1 \mathinner{..} \dfrac{s - i + 1}{2} \rightarrow$ **Coord and** $mid \in i \mathinner{..} s$
6. **begin**
7.   **if** $s - i + 1 = 2$ **then**
8. $d \leftarrow \Delta(T[i], T[s])$;
9.   **if** $T[i].y < T[s].y$ **then**
10. $R \leftarrow T$
11.   **else**
12. $R[1] \leftarrow T[s]; R[2] \leftarrow T[i]$
13.   **end if**
14.   **else**
15. $mid \leftarrow \left\lfloor \dfrac{i + s}{2} \right\rfloor$;
16.   *Closest3*(i, mid, dl, Rl);
17.   *Closest3*(mid + 1, s, dr, Rr);
18. $d \leftarrow \min(\{dl, dr\})$;
19.   *Gather3*(i, s, Rl, Rr, d, R)
20.   **end if**
21. **end**

Taking into account these modifications, the procedure *Closest3* is in $\Theta(n \cdot \log_2(n))$. Below is an example of a call to the procedure *Closest3*:

1. **constants**
2. $Coord = \{x, y \mid x \in \mathbb{R} \text{ and } y \in \mathbb{R}\}$ **and**
3. $n \in \mathbb{N}_1$ **and** $n \geqslant 2$ **and** $n = \ldots$ **and** $\exists k \cdot (k \in \mathbb{N}_1 \text{ and } n = 2^k)$
4. **variables**

106 - A 7

```
5.    T ∈ 1..n  →  Coord and V ∈ 1..n  →  Coord and dist ∈ ℝ*₊
6. begin
7.    T ← [...];
8.    SortX(T); /% to establish the precondition of Closest3 %/
9.    Closest3(1, n, dist, V);
10.    write(dist)
11. end
```

106 - A 8   **Answer** 8.   The extension to any value of n does not raise any difficulty. However, it must be ensured that the set of points considered contains at least two elements. This is reflected in the algorithm by the fact that the base case must treat an array of three as well as of two elements (indeed, the successive division by 2 of any integer greater than 3 results in the values 2 and 3).

Answers to problem 107. Distance between sequences (1)   *The problem is on page 452.*

107 - A 1   **Answer** 1.   According to the statement of the problem, the procedure *WFLgBackward* is designed to browse the strings x and y from the endpoint to the origin. Calls to this procedure therefore do not require the strings to be reversed beforehand.

```
1. procedure WFLgBackward(x, y; Q : modif) pre
2.    x ∈ string(Σ) and y ∈ string(Σ) and Q ∈ 0..|y| → ℕ and h ∈ 0..|y| × 0..
      1 → ℕ
3. begin
4.    let m, n such that
5.        m ∈ ℕ and m = |x| and n ∈ ℕ and n = |y|
6.    begin
7.        for j ∈ 0..n do
8.            h[j, 1] ← 0
9.        end for;
10.       for i ranging reverse 1..m do
11.           /% Column offset of h: %/
12.           for j ∈ 0..n do
13.               h[j, 0] ← h[j, 1]
14.           end for;
15.           for j ranging reverse 1..n do
16.               if x[i] = y[j] then
17.                   h[j − 1, 1] ← h[j, 0] + 1
18.               else
19.                   h[j − 1, 1] ← max({h[j, 1], h[j − 1, 0]})
20.               end if
21.           end for
22.       end for;
23.       for k ∈ 0..n do
24.           Q[n − k] ← h[k, 1]
25.       end for
26.   end
27. end
```

As for the operation *WFLgForward*, the temporal complexity of *WFLgBackward* is in $\Theta(m \cdot n)$ while spatial complexity is in $\Theta(n)$.

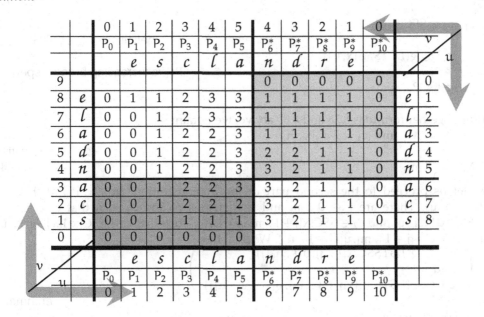

Fig. 8.26 – Calcuation of the vectors related to answer 2.

Answer 2. Figure 8.26 page 577, provides the vectors P_5 and P_6^*, from which the best sum between $0+3, 1+3, \ldots, 3+0$ is calculated. This is $3+3$, value that is reached only for $i=3$. So we have $lg(LGTLSSC(\textit{esclandre, scandale})) = 6$.

107 - A 2

We now have the information to divide y into two parts $y_1 = \textit{sca}$ and $y_2 = \textit{ndale}$. We can search for $LGTSSC(\textit{escla}, y_1)$ and $\overline{LGTSSC}(\textit{erdn}, \overline{y_2})$. We get respectively $\{\textit{sca}\}$ and $\{\textit{nde}\}$ which allow to conclude that $LGTSSC(\textit{scandal, esclandre}) = \{\textit{scande}\}$.

Answer 3. In terms of temporal complexity, this is a clumsy solution since it requires invoking $(n+1)$ times *WFLgForward* to calculate the $(n+1)$ values of P_{j+1}^*. On the other hand, it would be possible to use *WFLgForward* on mirror chains. We opt for another choice.

107 - A 3

Answer 4. Let us do the first part of the proof: $M_j \leqslant P_m[n]$. Let $i_0 \in 0 \mathinner{.\,.} n$ be one of the indices such that $M_j = P_j[i_0] + P_{j+1}^*[n - i_0]$. Let $c_1 \in LGTSSC(x[1 \mathinner{.\,.} j], y[1 \mathinner{.\,.} i_0])$ and $c_2 \in \overline{LGTSSC}(x[j+1 \mathinner{.\,.} m], y[i_0 + 1 \mathinner{.\,.} n])$. We first have:

107 - A 4

$$c_1 \in LGTSSC(x[1 \mathinner{.\,.} j], y[1 \mathinner{.\,.} i_0]) \ \textbf{and} \ c_2 \in \overline{LGTSSC}(x[j+1 \mathinner{.\,.} m], \overline{y[i_0 + 1 \mathinner{.\,.} n]})$$

$\Rightarrow$ $\left\{ \begin{array}{l} \text{For } c_1\text{: } P_j \text{ is increasing (broadly speaking), thus } P_j[i_0] \text{ is the} \\ \text{length of the longest sub-sequence common to } x[1 \mathinner{.\,.} j] \text{ and} \\ y[1 \mathinner{.\,.} i_0]. \text{ Idem for } c_2. \end{array} \right.$

$$|c_1| = P_j[i_0] \ \textbf{and} \ |c_2| = P_{j+1}^*[n - i_0]$$

$\Rightarrow$ arithmetics

$$|c_1| + |c_2| = P_j[i_0] + P_{j+1}^*[n - i_0]$$

$\Rightarrow$ property of concatenation and definition of i_0 and M_j

$$|c_1 \cdot c_2| = M_j. \tag{8.38}$$

We also have:

$$c_1 \in LGTSSC(x[1 \mathinner{.\,.} j], y[1 \mathinner{.\,.} i_0]) \ \textbf{and} \ c_2 \in \overline{LGTSSC}(x[j+1 \mathinner{.\,.} m], \overline{y[i_0 + 1 \mathinner{.\,.} n]})$$

$\Rightarrow$ $\qquad\qquad c_1 \in SSC(x[1 \mathinner{.\,.} j], y[1 \mathinner{.\,.} i_0]) \ \textbf{and} \ c_2 \in SSC(x[j+1 \mathinner{.\,.} m], y[i_0 + 1 \mathinner{.\,.} n])$

$c_1 \cdot c_2 \in SSC(x,y)$

$\Rightarrow$ definition of $lg(LGTSSC(x,y))$

$|c_1 \cdot c_2| \leqslant lg(LGTSSC(x,y))$

$\Leftrightarrow$ P_m is increasing broadly speaking

$|c_1 \cdot c_2| \leqslant P_m[n].$ (8.39)

Putting together formulas 8.38 and 8.39 above, we obtain:

$|c_1 \cdot c_2| = M_j$ **and** $|c_1 \cdot c_2| \leqslant P_m[n]$

$\Rightarrow$ transitivity

$M_j \leqslant P_m[n].$ (8.40)

Now let us proceed to the second part of the demonstration: $M_j \geqslant P_m[n]$. Let $c \in LGTSSC(x,y)$. There are $j \in 0 .. m$ and two strings c_1 and c_2 such that $c = c_1 \cdot c_2$, $c_1 \in SSC(x[1..j],y)$ and $c_2 \in SSC(x[j+1..m],y)$. Let i_0 such that $c_1 \in SSC(x[1..j],y[1..i_0])$ and $c_2 \in SSC(x[j+1..m],y[i_0+1..n])$. We then have:

$$\left(\begin{array}{l} |c_1| \leqslant lg(LGTSSC(x[1..j],y[1..i_0])) \\ \textbf{and} \\ |c_2| \leqslant lg(LGTSSC(x[j+1..m],y[i_0+1..n])) \end{array} \right)$$

$\Rightarrow$ arithmetics

$$\left(\begin{array}{l} |c_1| + |c_2| \\ \leqslant \\ lg(LGTSSC(x[1..j],y[1..i_0])) + lg(LGTSSC(x[j+1..m],y[i_0+1..n])) \end{array} \right)$$

$\Rightarrow$ property of concatenation

$$\left(\begin{array}{l} |c_1 \cdot c_2| \\ \leqslant \\ lg(LGTSSC(x[1..j],y[1..i_0])) + lg(\overline{LGTSSC}(\overline{x[j+1..m]},\overline{y[i_0+1..n]})) \end{array} \right)$$

$\Rightarrow$ property of the operation "mirror", definition of c_1, c_2 and $lg(C)$

$|c| \leqslant P_j[i_0] + P^*_{j+1}[n - i_0]$

$\Leftrightarrow$ P_m is increasing broadly speaking

$P_m[n] \leqslant P_j[i_0] + P^*_{j+1}[n - i_0]$

$\Leftrightarrow$ definition of M_j and i_0: $P_j[i_0] + P^*_{j+1}[n - i_0] \leqslant M_j$

$P_m[n] \leqslant M_j.$ (8.41)

Formulas 8.40 and 8.41 above establish the proof of the theorem on page 455.

107 - A 5   **Answer 5.**   The DaC reasoning underlying the construction of the operation "**procedure** *HirschLGTSSC*$(x,y;c:$ **modif**$)$" is the following:

Base The base case is characterized by a situation where the string x is made up of a single symbol which is present in the other string; this symbol lengthens the string c.

Induction hypothesis It is known how to calculate one of the elements of $LGTSSC(x[1 .. \lfloor m/2 \rfloor], y[1 .. q])$ using Hirschberg's algorithm, as well as $\overline{LGTSSC}(x[\lfloor m/2 \rfloor + 1 .. m], y[q+1 .. n])$, for $m > 1$ and $q \in 0 .. n$.

Induction The main objective of the separation step is to discover an index q allowing the chain y to be split into two sub-strings. To do this, we rely on the work done in the previous questions and on Hirschberg's optimality theorem, page 455. The procedures *WFLgForward* and *WFLgBackward* calculate the vectors $P_{\lfloor m/2 \rfloor}$ and $P^*_{\lfloor m/2 \rfloor + 1}$ (named Pfo and Pbk in the algorithm below). It then remains to choose an index q among all the indices that maximize the sum Pfo[i] + Pbk[i + 1]. The gathering step is reduced to its simplest form, since each of the two recursive calls will suitably lengthen the string c.

Termination The size of the first parameter (x) diminishes at each step, that of the second parameter does not increase: this ensures the termination of the algorithm.

The division model is described as follows:

$$
\begin{aligned}
&\text{HirschLGTSSC}(m, n) \rightarrow \text{possible lengthening of the lgtssc by } x[1] \qquad \text{if } m \leqslant 1 \\[4pt]
&\text{HirschLGTSSC}(m, n) \rightarrow
\left(
\begin{aligned}
&\text{search for an index q to split } y\ + \\
&\text{HirschLGTSSC}\left(\left\lceil \frac{m}{2} \right\rceil, q\right) + \\
&\text{HirschLGTSSC}\left(\left\lfloor \frac{m}{2} \right\rfloor, n - q\right)
\end{aligned}
\right)
\qquad \text{if } m > 1
\end{aligned}
$$

The code of the operation *HirschLGTSSC* is given below.

```
 1.  procedure HirschLGTSSC(x, y; c : modif) pre
 2.     x ∈ string(Σ) and y ∈ string(Σ) and c ∈ string(Σ)
 3.  begin
 4.     let m, n, q, mid, Pfo, Pbk, sum such that
 5.        m ∈ ℕ and m = |x| and n ∈ ℕ and n = |y| and
 6.        q ∈ 0 .. n and mid ∈ 1 .. m and
 7.        Pfo ∈ 0 .. n → ℕ and Pbk ∈ 0 .. n → ℕ and sum ∈ ℕ
 8.     begin
 9.        if m ≤ 1 then
10.           WFLgForward(x, y, Pfo);
11.           if Pfo[n] ≠ 0 then
12.              c ← c · x[1]
13.           end if
14.        else
15.           mid ← ⌊m/2⌋;
16.           WFLgForward(x[1 .. mid], y, Pfo);
17.           WFLgBackward(x[mid + 1 .. m], y, Pbk);
18.           /% choice of an index that maximizes Pfo[i] + Pbk[i + 1]: %/
19.           q ← 0; sum ← 0;
20.           for i ∈ 0 .. n do
21.              if sum < Pfo[i] + Pbk[n − i] then
22.                 sum ← Pfo[i] + Pbk[n − i]; q ← i
23.              end if
24.           end for;
25.           HirschLGTSSC(x[1 .. mid], y[1 .. q], c);
26.           HirschLGTSSC(x[mid + 1 .. m], y[q + 1 .. n], c)
27.        end if
28.     end
29.  end
```

Below is a possible calling program.

```
1.  constants
2.     u ∈ string(Σ) and u = ... and v ∈ string(Σ) and v = ...
3.  variables
4.     lgtssc ∈ string(Σ)
```

```
5. begin
6.    lgtssc ← ε;
7.    HirschLGTSSC(u, v, lgtssc);
8.    write(lgtssc)
9. end
```

Several important remarks regarding the above code related to spatial and temporal complexities are now discussed.

Complexities

First of all, we are concerned with spatial complexity. The analysis assumes that the input strings (x and y and the corresponding effective parameters) are managed by the position of their ends and not by passing these strings as parameters. It is also assumed that x is the longest string (otherwise, just reverse the arguments in the operation call). Recall that, to simplify the calculations, we admit that m is a power of 2. $S(m, n)$, the spatial complexity equation, is defined by:

$$
\begin{aligned}
S(m, n) &= S'(m, n) + f(n) & \text{where } f(n) \in \mathcal{O}(n) \\
S'(m, n) &= S'\left(\left\lceil \frac{m}{2} \right\rceil, i \right) + S'\left(\left\lfloor \frac{m}{2} \right\rfloor, n - i \right) & m > 1 \\
S'(m, n) &= 0 & m \leqslant 1.
\end{aligned}
$$

$S'(m, n)$ is the spatial complexity of the operation obtained by disregarding the blocks **let** present in the code. The function $f(n)$ specifically accounts for space occupied by the two vectors Pfo and Pbk located in a block **let**. These two vectors are allocated when entering the block and deallocated when leaving it, so they must be counted separately. The second line of the equation accounts for space occupied by the two recursive calls, which are made on a rectangle of respective heights i and $n - i$ (i disappears during calculations). Scalar variables or constants presents in the algorithm are not counted. The third line of the equation is about the base case. Let us prove, by induction on m, that $S'(m, n)$ is in $\mathcal{O}(n)$. It will then be easy to conclude that $S(m, n)$ is also in $\mathcal{O}(n)$. We must prove that there is a positive constant d such that

$$
S'(m, n) \leqslant d \cdot n.
$$

Base The base equation holds for any $d \geqslant 1$.

Induction hypothesis For any m' such that $m' < m$, $S'(m', n) \leqslant d \cdot n$.

Induction It must be proven that $S'(m, n) \leqslant d \cdot n$:

$$
\begin{aligned}
& S'(m, n) \\
={}& & \text{m is a power of 2} \\
& S'\left(\frac{m}{2}, i \right) + S'\left(\frac{m}{2}, n - i \right) \\
\leqslant{}& & \text{induction hypothesis} \\
& d \cdot i + d \cdot (n - i) \\
={}& & \text{arithmetics} \\
& d \cdot n.
\end{aligned}
$$

Thus we have $S'(m, n) \in \mathcal{O}(n)$ (as well as $S(m, n) \in \mathcal{O}(n)$ since S and S' only differ by one term in $\mathcal{O}(n)$). x being assumed to be the longest string, more generally we have:

$$
S(m, n) \in \mathcal{O}(\min(\{m, n\})).
$$

Let us now turn to the computation of the worst-case time complexity in terms of conditions evaluated. Neglecting the cost of the iteration (in $\mathcal{O}(n)$), the recurrence equation is written:

$$
\left|
\begin{array}{ll}
C(m, n) = m \cdot n & m \leqslant 1 \\
C(m, n) = C\left(\left\lceil \dfrac{m}{2} \right\rceil, i\right) + C\left(\left\lfloor \dfrac{m}{2} \right\rfloor, n - i\right) + n \cdot \left\lfloor \dfrac{m}{2} \right\rfloor + n \cdot \left\lceil \dfrac{m}{2} \right\rceil & m > 1.
\end{array}
\right.
$$

The two terms $n \cdot \lfloor m/2 \rfloor$ and $n \cdot \lceil m/2 \rceil$ come from the calls to *WFLgForward* and *WFLgBackward*. Let us prove by induction that $C(m, n) \in \mathcal{O}(m \cdot n)$. It must be proven that there exists a positive constant d such that

$$
C(m, n) \leqslant d \cdot n \cdot m.
$$

Base The base equation holds for $d = 2$.

Induction hypothesis For any m' such that $m' < m$, $C(m', n) \leqslant d \cdot n \cdot m'$.

Induction $C(m, n)$

$$
=
$$
m is a power of 2

$$
C\left(\frac{m}{2}, i\right) + C\left(\frac{m}{2}, n - i\right) + n \cdot \frac{m}{2} + n \cdot \frac{m}{2}
$$

$$
\leqslant
$$
calculation

$$
d \cdot \frac{m}{2} \cdot n + m \cdot n
$$

$$
=
$$
for $d = 2$

$$
d \cdot \frac{m}{2} \cdot n + d \cdot \frac{m}{2} \cdot n
$$

$$
=
$$
substitution, $d = 2$

$$
2 \cdot m \cdot n.
$$

It is proven that:

$$
C(m, n) \in \mathcal{O}(n \cdot m).
$$

Moreover, since $d = 2$, at least for m power of 2, the cost in computation time is "only (at most) doubled" compared to the Wagner-Fischer algorithm for finding the longest common sub-sequence. In a way, we traded a little bit of time for a lot of space.

Remarks

1. As it has been observed in the example of figure 8.6, page 455, several indices can be candidates for the cutoff of y. The above algorithm, due to the non-deterministic nature of the loop **for** used, does not allow any prediction on the index obtained. A refinement of this part of the algorithm would select the index closest to the middle of the interval $0 .. n$, so that y is split into two strings minimizing the size difference.

2. What would happen if the variables Pfo and Pbk are declared locally to the procedure *HirschLGTLSSC* rather than in a block **let**? It would be necessary to count the size n of these vectors in the recurrence equation $S'(m, n)$, which would become $S'(m, n) = S'(\lceil m/2 \rceil, i) + S'(\lfloor m/2 \rfloor, n - i) + 2n$. This solution of this equation is in $\mathcal{O}(n \cdot \log_2(m))$, not in $\mathcal{O}(n)$. An alternative would be to declare these vectors as global variables.

3. Passing the result (the longest common sub-sequence) by an *input-output* parameter is an essential choice. Indeed, it makes it possible not to count the size of this result in the recurrence equation (since this result is located in the space of the calling program). A less elegant alternative would be to use a global string to do this. On the other hand, a solution in which the input-output parameter is replaced by an output parameter would lead to the recurrence equation $S'(m, n) = S'(\lceil m/2 \rceil, i) + S'(\lfloor m/2 \rfloor, n - i) + n$,

equation whose drawbacks are known. The choice of a function instead of a procedure would present the same flaw. Few authors pay attention to this detail and most of the solutions presented in the literature are announced as linear in space, whereas they are in fact in $\mathcal{O}(n \cdot \log_2(m))$.

In summary, in order to obtain a linear solution in space, it is recommended (i) to pass only *the bounds* of the strings x and y as parameters (unlike what is done for readability in the above version of the *HirschLGTSSC* procedure, but which is carried out in the procedure *HirschTrace* below), (ii) to declare the vectors Pfo and Pbk as locally as possible, but in no way locally to the procedure *HirschLGTSSC*, and (iii) to pass the result *via* an input-output parameter.

107 - A 6   **Answer** 6.   The construction of the procedure *HirschTrace* is based on the following inductive reasoning:

Base This step is similar to that of the procedure *HirschLGTSSC*, but instead of recording the symbol (if necessary), its position in each of the two strings is retained.

Induction hypothesis This step is also similar to that of the procedure *HirschLGTSSC*.

Induction It is the development presented in the statement.

Termination The width of the rectangles remaining to be considered strictly decreases at each step (their height does not increase), which ensures termination.

The division model is described as follows:

$$
\begin{array}{ll}
\text{HirschTrace}(m, n) \rightarrow \begin{pmatrix} \text{possible lengthening of the} \\ \text{trace by a pair } (mid, py) \end{pmatrix} & m \leqslant 1 \\[2em]
\text{HirschTrace}(m, n) \rightarrow \begin{pmatrix} \text{search for an index } q \text{ to split } y + \\ \text{HirschTrace}\left(\left\lceil \dfrac{m}{2} \right\rceil, q\right) + \text{if needed:} \\ \text{lengthening of the trace by the pair} \\ (mid, q) + \text{HirschTrace}\left(\left\lfloor \dfrac{m}{2} \right\rfloor, n - q\right) \end{pmatrix} & m > 1.
\end{array}
$$

The code of the operation *HirschTrace* is presented hereafter (u and v are global strings on the vocabulary Σ).

```
 1. procedure HirschTrace(ix, sx, iy, sy; t : modif) pre
 2.    ix ∈ 1 .. |u| and sx ∈ 1 .. |u| and iy ∈ 1 .. |v| and sy ∈ 1 .. |v| and
 3.    t ∈ Trace and sum ∈ ℕ
 4. begin
 5.    let m, n, Pfo, Pbk, mid, q such that
 6.       m ∈ ℕ and m = sx − ix + 1 and n ∈ ℕ and n = sy − iy + 1 and
 7.       Pfo ∈ 0 .. n → ℕ and Pbk ∈ 0 .. n → ℕ and mid ∈ ix .. sx and q ∈ 0 .. n
 8.    begin
 9.       if m ⩽ 1 then
10.          WFLgForward(ix, sx, iy, sy, Pfo);
11.          if Pfo[n] ≠ 0 then
12.             let py such that v[py] = u[sx] begin t ← t · ct(sx, py) end
13.          end if
14.       else
15.          mid ← ⌊ (ix + sx) / 2 ⌋;
```

```
16.        WFLgForward(ix, mid, iy, sy, Pfo);
17.        WFLgBackward(mid + 1, sx, iy, sy, Pbk);
18.        /% choice of an index that maximizes Pfo[i] + Pbk[i + 1]: %/
19.        q ← 0; sum ← 0;
20.        for i ∈ 0 .. n do
21.           if sum < Pfo[i] + Pbk[n − i] then
22.              sum ← Pfo[i] + Pbk[n − i]; q ← i
23.           end if
24.        end for;
25.        q ← iy + q − 1;
26.        if q = iy − 1 then
27.           HirschTrace(mid + 1, sx, q + 1, sy, t)
28.        elsif u[mid] = v[q] then
29.           HirschTrace(ix, mid − 1, iy, q − 1, t);
30.           t ← t · ct(mid, q);
31.           HirschTrace(mid + 1, sx, q + 1, sy, t)
32.        else
33.           HirschTrace(ix, mid − 1, iy, q, t);
34.           HirschTrace(mid + 1, sx, q + 1, sy, t)
35.        end if
36.     end if
37.   end
38. end
```

The block **let** of the branch **then** determines a position py in $v[iy .. sy]$ such that $v[py]$ is equal to (the only) character of the string $u[ix .. sx]$ ($ix = sx$ in this case), then lengthens the trace t with the pair (sx, py). To obtain a solution linear in time, it remains to localize the declaration of the vectors Pfo and Pbk. Below is a possible calling program.

```
1. constants
2.    u = ... and v = ...
3. variables
4.    tr ∈ Trace
5. begin
6.    tr ← tv ; /% Intialization to the empty trace %/
7.    HirschTrace(1, |u|, 1, |v|, tr);
8.    write(tr)
9. end
```

Answers to problem 108. The convex hull
The problem is on page 457.

Answer 1.   We proceed to a classic unbounded sequential search and the components   108 - A 1
of the loop are the following:

Invariant v is the abscissa of none of the vertices between e and $Pred(i)$.

Stopping condition The loop stops when $i.x = v$.

Progression The vertex next to i becomes the current vertex i.

Initialization If $\widehat{e}$ is the envelope under consideration, The assignment $i \leftarrow e$ establishes the invariant.

Termination The number of vertices between i and e is a suitable termination expression.

1. **function** *Search* $(\hat{e}, v)$ **result** ConvEnv **pre**
2. $\hat{e} \in$ ConvEnv **and** $v \in \mathbb{R}$ **and**
3.   *there is at least one vertex of abscissa v in* $\hat{e}$ **and**
4. $\hat{i} \in$ ConvEnv
5. **begin**
6. $i \leftarrow e$;
7.   **while not**$(i.x = v)$ **do**
8. $i \leftarrow Succ\left(\hat{i}\right)$
9.   **end while**;
10.   **result** $\hat{i}$
11. **end**

An alternate version might as well use *Pred* instead of *Succ*. If n is the number of points of the set E, the complexity of this algorithm is in $\mathcal{O}(n)$ evaluated conditions.

108 - A 2   **Answer** 2.   The segment LR is the upper tangent between the left envelope $\hat{l}$ and the right envelope $\hat{r}$, if and only if, on the one hand LR is a bridge, on the other hand the point L *does not see* the predecessor of R and, conversely, the point R *does not see* the successor of L (see segment AG of figure 8.12, page 461). A classic loop construction strategy is applied by breaking down this definition into two parts, which will constitute the invariant and the stopping condition.

Invariant The segment LR is a bridge between $\hat{l}$ and $\hat{r}$.

Stopping condition The point L does not see the predecessor of R in $\hat{r}$; the point R does not see the successor of L in $\hat{l}$.

Progression How to get a new bridge that is "closer" to the upper tangent? Since at least one of the elementary conditions of the stopping condition is not satisfied, we can go back to one of the ends which is visible, as shown in the following diagram:

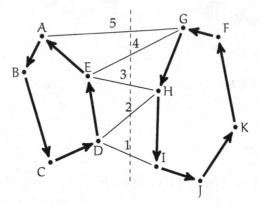

It is worth noticing that in general only part of the bridges located between the initial bridge (DI above) and the tangent (AG above) is taken into account in this progression: the bridges EI and AH are ignored. But whatever the way to proceed, we end up with the upper tangent AG.

Initialization The only directly calculable bridge is obtained by applying the function *Search* twice.

Termination The list F of the intersections between the bridges and a separating vertical is finite (see diagram (b) of figure 8.12, page 461). For the search for the upper tangent, the points of intersection obtained during the progression are encountered according to strictly increasing ordinates. They constitute a sublist of F. The number of points between the current intersection and that of the tangent constitutes a suitable termination function.

It can be easily checked that (i) the conjunction of the invariant and the stopping condition is identical to the goal (and thus entails it as required by the theory), (ii) the progression is a solution to the specification pre-post defined by the pair (invariant **and** negation of the stopping condition, invariant), (iii) the initialization establishes the invariant and (iv) the progression decreases the termination function.The algorithmic translation of the stopping condition is done using the notion of determinant (see figures 8.10, page 460, and 8.11, page 460). In this condition, the case of equality makes it possible to take into account the envelopes made up of a single vertex, for which this vertex is itself its own successor and its own predecessor. We obtain the following algorithm:

1. **function** *UpperTangent* $\left(\hat{l}, \hat{r}, i\right)$ **result** ConvEnv × ConvEnv **pre**
2. $\hat{l} \in$ ConvEnv **and** $\hat{r} \in$ ConvEnv **and** $i \in$ dom(T) **and**
3.   T[i − 1] *is the point of* $\hat{l}$ *of maximum abscissa* **and**
4.   T[i] *is the point of* $\hat{r}$ *of minimum abscissa* **and**
5. $\hat{L} \in$ ConvEnv **and** $\hat{R} \in$ ConvEnv
6. **begin**
7. $\hat{L} \leftarrow$ *Search* $\left(\hat{l}, T[i − 1].x\right)$; $\hat{R} \leftarrow$ *Search* $(\hat{r}, T[i].x)$;
8.   **while not** $\left(\det\left(\overrightarrow{RL}, \overrightarrow{R\,Succ(L)}\right) \geqslant 0 \text{ and } \det\left(\overrightarrow{LR}, \overrightarrow{L\,Pred(R)}\right) \leqslant 0\right)$ **do**
9.   **if** $\det\left(\overrightarrow{RL}, \overrightarrow{R\,Succ(L)}\right) < 0$ **then**
10. $L \leftarrow$ *Succ* $\left(\hat{L}\right)$
11.   **else**
12. $R \leftarrow$ *Pred* $\left(\hat{R}\right)$
13.   **end if**
14.   **end while**;
15.   **result** $\left(\hat{L}, \hat{R}\right)$
16. **end**

It is of course possible to avoid the repeated calculation of the determinants by factoring the calculation of the expression $\det(\overrightarrow{RL}, \overrightarrow{R\,Succ(L)})$, which is carried out at the same time in the condition of the loop and in that of the alternative (this refinement is not carried out here). Regarding complexity (in terms of conditions evaluated), the initialization, where the function *Search* is called on two occasions, is in $\mathcal{O}(n)$; the loop is executed at most $\text{card}(\hat{l}) + \text{card}(\hat{r})$ times. Now, $\text{card}(\hat{l}) + \text{card}(\hat{r}) \leqslant n$. The algorithm is therefore in $\mathcal{O}(n)$ conditions evaluated.

Answer 3.   The case of the operation "**function** *LowerTangent*$(\hat{l}, \hat{g}, i)$ **result** ConvEnv × ConvEnv" is similar to that of *UpperTangent*. The division model of *ConvexEnvelope* is: 108 - A 3

$$\begin{array}{|ll|}\hline \text{ConvexEnvelope(1) and ConvexEnvelope(2) elementary} & \\ \text{ConvexEnvelope(n)} \rightarrow \left(\begin{array}{l} 2 \cdot \text{ConvexEnvelope}\left(\frac{n}{2}\right) + \\ \text{calculation of the tangents then merging} \end{array}\right) & n > 2 \\ \hline \end{array}$$

Based on the principle of the algorithm widely detailed above, the code is:

```
1.  function ConvexEnvelope(lb, ub) result ConvEnv pre
2.     lb ∈ 1 .. n and ub ∈ 1 .. n and lb ⩽ ub and
3.     EnvL ∈ ConvEnv and EnvR ∈ ConvEnv and mid ∈ lb .. ub and
4.     TgtNth ∈ ConvEnv × ConvEnv and TgtSth ∈ ConvEnv × ConvEnv
5.  begin
6.     if ub − lb ⩽ 1 then
7.        if lb = ub then
8.           result CrateConvEnv1(T[lb])
9.        else
10.          result CrateConvEnv2(T[lb], T[ub])
11.       end if
12.    else
13.       mid ← Cut(lb, ub);
14.       EnvL ← ConvexEnvelope(lb, mid − 1);
15.       EnvR ← ConvexEnvelope(mid, ub);
16.       TgtNth ← UpperTangent(EnvL, EnvR, mid);
17.       TgtSth ← LowerTangent(EnvL, EnvR, mid);
18.       result Fusion(TgtNth, TgtSth)
19.    end if
20. end
```

Below, a calling program is presented:

```
1.  constants
2.     ConvEnv = {...} and n ∈ ℕ₁ and n = ... and
3.     T ∈ 1 .. n → ℝ × ℝ and T = [...] and
4.     Not3PointsAligned(T) and IsSortedOnAbscissa(T)
5.  begin
6.     write(ConvexEnvelope(1, n))
7.  end
```

Complexity

The complexity inequation (in terms of conditions evaluated) is:

$$
\left|
\begin{array}{ll}
C(n) = 1 & n \leqslant 2 \\
C(n) \leqslant 2 \cdot C\left(\dfrac{n}{2}\right) + f(n) & \text{where } f(n) \in \mathcal{O}(n) \text{ and } n > 2
\end{array}
\right.
$$

hence $C(n) \in \mathcal{O}(n \cdot \log_2(n))$.

108 - A 4   **Answer 4.**   A strengthening of the induction hypothesis is made for the function *ConvexEnvelope* (which becomes *ConvexEnvelopeBis*). As usual, the principle is to assume that initially missing information is now available. The new induction hypothesis states that operation delivers the convex envelope, with the leftmost and rightmost points as access (input) points. In this way, by passing the appropriate arguments to the tangent calculation operations, it becomes unnecessary to explicitly search for these points. Some parameters become redundant and they can be removed. The operation *ConvexEnvelopeBis* is a procedure that delivers the desired convex envelope in $\hat{l}$ and $\hat{r}$, with l and r as leftmost and rightmost access points. The calls for the calculation of the tangents are made with the two envelopes (resulting from the induction) named by the rightmost (respectively leftmost) access points for the left (respectively right) envelope, i.e. $\widehat{lr}$ (respectively $\widehat{rl}$).

Les operations *CreateConvEnv1*, *CreateConvEnv2* and *Fusion* are transformed in procedures (and renamed respectively *CrateConvEnv1Bis*, *CreateConvEnv2Bis* and *FusionBis*).

1. **procedure** *ConvexEnvelopeBis* $\left(lb, ub; \widehat{l}, \widehat{r} : \textbf{modif} \right)$ **pre**

2. $lb \in 1 .. n$ **and** $ub \in 1 .. n$ **and** $lb \leqslant ub$ **and** $\widehat{l} \in$ ConvEnv **and** $\widehat{r} \in$ ConvEnv **and**

3. $\widehat{lr} \in$ ConvEnv **and** $\widehat{rl} \in$ ConvEnv **and** $mid \in lb .. ub$ **and**

4. $TgtNth \in$ ConvEnv $\times$ ConvEnv **and** $TgtSth \in$ ConvEnv $\times$ ConvEnv

5. **begin**

6.   **if** $ub - lb \leqslant 1$ **then**

7.   **if** $lb = ub$ **then**

8.   *CreateConvEnv1Bis* $\left(T[lb], \widehat{l}, \widehat{r} \right)$

9.   **else**

10.   *CreateConvEnv2Bis* $\left(T[lb], T[ub], \widehat{l}, \widehat{r} \right)$

11.   **end if**

12.   **else**

13. $mid \leftarrow Cut(lb, ub)$;

14.   *ConvexEnvelopeBis* $\left(lb, mid - 1, \widehat{l}, \widehat{lr} \right)$;

15.   *ConvexEnvelopeBis* $\left(mid, ub, \widehat{rl}, \widehat{r} \right)$;

16. $TgtNth \leftarrow$ *UpperTangentBis* $\left(\widehat{lr}, \widehat{rl} \right)$;

17. $TgtSth \leftarrow$ *LowerTangentBis* $\left(\widehat{lr}, \widehat{rl} \right)$;

18.   *FusionBis*(TgtNth, TgtSth)

19.   **end if**

20. **end**

The function *UpperTangent* (as well as *LowerTangent*) is modified accordingly: the initialization of the loop no longer requires a sequential search to discover the bridge from which the progression is made, since these two points are passed as parameters. This is the only modification compared to the initial version. The operation *Search* becomes unnecessary but the operations *UpperTangentBis* and *LowerTangentBis*, although more efficient, remain in $\mathcal{O}(n)$ evaluated conditions.

1. **function** *UpperTangentBis*$(\widehat{l}, \widehat{r})$ **result** ConvEnv $\times$ ConvEnv **pre**

2. $\widehat{l} \in$ ConvEnv **and** $\widehat{r} \in$ ConvEnv **and**

3. $\widehat{L} \in$ ConvEnv **and** $\widehat{R} \in$ ConvEnv

4. **begin**

5. $\widehat{L} \leftarrow \widehat{l}; \widehat{R} \leftarrow \widehat{r}$;

6.   : *Idem lines 8 to 15 of UpperTangent*

7. **end**

The calling context should also be slightly modified to take into account the change in the status of the operation and the role of the parameters:

1. **constants**

2.   ConvEnv $= \dots$ **and** $n \in \mathbb{N}_1$ **and** $n = \dots$ **and**

3. $T \in 1 .. n \rightarrow \mathbb{R} \times \mathbb{R}$ **and** $T = [\dots]$ **and**

4.   Not3PointsAligned(T) **and** IsSortedOnAbscissa(T)

5. **variables**

6. $\widehat{l} \in$ ConvEnv **and** $\widehat{r} \in$ ConvEnv

7. **begin**

8. $ConvexEnvelopeBis\left(1, n, \widehat{l}, \widehat{r}\right)$;

9.   **write** $\left(\widehat{l}\right)$

10. **end**

Answers to problem 109. The stuttering sub-sequence   *The problem is on page 462.*

The problem is on page 462.

109 - A 1   **Answer 1.**   If $y = a_1 \ldots a_m$, the function $Scan(x, y, i)$ is intended to ensure that, in the sequence x, there is indeed (at least) i occurrences of a_1, then (at least) i occurrences of a_2, etc. Below, the sequence x (respectively y) is represented by the character string x (respectively y) defined on the domain $1 \ldots n$ (respectively $1 \ldots m$). The five points of the loop construction are shown below. The variable j (respectively k) iterates over x (respectively y).

Invariant It is formulated via the following expression:

$$k \in 1 \ldots m + 1 \text{ and } j \in 1 \ldots n + 1 \text{ and } cpt \in 0 \ldots i \text{ and } (k \leqslant m \Rightarrow \overset{i}{\overbrace{y_1 \ldots y_{k-1}}} \overset{cpt}{\overbrace{y_k}} \text{ is a}$$

sub-sequence of $x_1 \ldots x_{j-1}$) **and** $(k = m + 1 \Rightarrow \overset{i}{y}$ is a sub-sequence of $x_1 \ldots x_{j-1})$.

Stopping condition It is expressed as:

$(k = m + 1 \text{ or } j = n + 1 \text{ or } (k = m \text{ and } cpt = i))$.

Progression See the code below.

Initialization The sequence $k \leftarrow 1; j \leftarrow 1; cpt \leftarrow 0$ establishes the invariant.

Termination The expression $((n + 1) - j + 1 + (m + 1) - k + 1)$ ensures termination.

The output result of this loop is worthy of some comments. In the case where the loop ends with the condition $(k = m + 1)$, the invariant makes it possible to assert that $\overset{i}{y}$ is a sub-sequence of $x_1 \ldots x_{j-1}$, and therefore of x. Otherwise, $\overset{i}{y}$ is a sub-sequence of x only if on the one hand k has reached the end of y and on the other hand the occurrence counter cpt is equal to i.

```
1.  function Scan(x, y, i) result 𝔹 pre
2.     x ∈ string and y ∈ string and i ∈ ℕ₁
3.  begin
4.     let n, m, j, k, cpt such that
5.        n = |x| and m = |y| and j ∈ 1 .. n + 1 and k ∈ 1 .. m + 1 and cpt ∈ 0 .. i
6.     begin
7.        k ← 1; j ← 1; cpt ← 0;
8.        while not(k = m + 1 or j = n + 1 or (k = m and cpt = i)) do
9.           if cpt < i then
10.             if y[k] = x[j] then
11.                cpt ← cpt + 1
12.             end if;
13.             j ← j + 1
14.          else
15.             k ← k + 1; cpt ← 0
16.          end if
17.       end while;
18.       result k = m + 1 or (k = m and cpt = i)
```

19. **end**

20. **end**

The body of the loop is executed at most $(n + m)$ times and the stopping condition is therefore evaluated at most $(n + m + 1)$ times. The asymptotic complexity is in $O(n + m)$ (hence in $\max(\{m, n\})$) evaluated conditions.

Answer 2. $Maxi(x, y)$ reaches its lower bound when y is not a sub-sequence of x and then $Maxi(x, y) = 0$. In general, therefore $0 \leqslant Maxi(x, y)$ and the upper bound is reached when $x = \overset{i}{y}$.   109 - A 2

$$x = \overset{i}{y}$$
$$\Rightarrow \qquad\qquad\qquad\qquad \text{consequence on the length of the sequences}$$
$$n = m \cdot i$$
$$\Leftrightarrow \qquad\qquad\qquad\qquad \text{arithmetics } (m > 0)$$
$$i = \left\lfloor \frac{n}{m} \right\rfloor.$$

In general, we therefore have $i \leqslant \lfloor \frac{n}{m} \rfloor$, hence $Maxi(x, y) \in 0 .. \lfloor \frac{n}{m} \rfloor$. In addition, it can be noticed that all the values of the interval $0 .. \lfloor \frac{n}{m} \rfloor$ can be reached.

Answer 3. The DaC reasoning for the construction of the function $Maxi0(x, y, lb, ub)$ is based on the following elements: 109 - A 3

Base If $lb = ub$, the interval is of length 1. It is then sufficient to make sure [by invoking $Scan(x, y, bi)$] that $\overset{bi}{y}$ is a sub-sequence of x, in which case the value lb is delivered. Otherwise, the value 0 is returned.

Induction hypothesis Let $mid = \lfloor \frac{(bi + bs)}{2} \rfloor$. It is assumed that it is known how to evaluate $Maxi0(x, y, mb, mid)$, as well as $Maxi0(x, y, mid + 1, ub)$.

Induction $Scan(x, y, mid + 1)$ is first evaluated and, depending on the result, we evaluate either $Maxi0(x, y, mid + 1, ub)$ or $Maxi0(x, y, lb, mid)$.

The division model is described below:

$Maxi0(1) \to$ Scan with the current value (lb or ub)		
$Maxi0\,(q) \to Maxi0\left(\frac{q}{2}\right) +$	$\begin{pmatrix} \text{Scan to determine} \\ \text{which half of the} \\ \text{interval must be} \\ \text{treated} \end{pmatrix}$	$q > 1$ and $q = lb .. ub$

Complexity

Regarding the complexity equation, we have:

$$\begin{vmatrix} C(1) = (n + m + 1)_{Scan} + 1 \\ C(q) = C\left(\frac{q}{2}\right) + (n + m + 1)_{Scan} + 1 \end{vmatrix} \qquad\qquad q > 1.$$

The first part of the equation counts conditions evaluated when calling the function *Scan* (i.e. $n + m + 1$) and the condition that determines that the length of the considered interval is 1. The second part counts the number of conditions evaluated by the recursive call, the evaluation of the function *Scan* and the condition of the alternative. The desired result is $C(\lfloor \frac{n}{m} \rfloor)$ (or $C(\lfloor \frac{n}{m} + 1 \rfloor)$ to be more precise). The master theorem (see page 422) seems to be relevant to solve this equation, but this is not the case, because the "constants" $m + n$ are not independent of the variable q. However, it can be solved directly when $\frac{n}{m}$ is a power of 2 (and therefore $n \geqslant m$). Let $\frac{n}{m} = 2^p$; by additions, we get:

$$C\left(\frac{n}{m}\right) = (n + m + 2) \cdot p + (n + m + 2).$$

The following development stems:

$$C\left(\frac{n}{m}\right) = (n + m + 2) \cdot p + (n + m + 2)$$

$$\Leftrightarrow \qquad\qquad\qquad\qquad\qquad\qquad\qquad\qquad\qquad p = \log_2\left(\frac{n}{m}\right)$$

$$C\left(\frac{n}{m}\right) = (n + m + 2) \cdot \log_2\left(\frac{n}{m}\right) + (n + m + 2)$$

$$\Rightarrow \qquad\qquad\qquad\qquad\qquad\qquad\qquad\qquad\qquad \text{definition of } \mathcal{O}$$

$$C\left(\frac{n}{m}\right) \in \mathcal{O}\left((n + m) \cdot \log_2\left(\frac{n}{m}\right)\right)$$

$$\Rightarrow \qquad\qquad\qquad\qquad\qquad\qquad\qquad\qquad\qquad n \geqslant m, \text{ overestimation}$$

$$C\left(\frac{n}{m}\right) \in \mathcal{O}\left(n \cdot \log_2\left(\frac{n}{m}\right)\right)$$

$$\Rightarrow \qquad\qquad\qquad\qquad\qquad\qquad\qquad\qquad\qquad \text{overestimation}$$

$$C\left(\frac{n}{m}\right) \in \mathcal{O}\left(n \cdot \log_2(n)\right). \tag{8.42}$$

109 - A 4 **Answer 4.** For each symbol of Σ, a Boolean variable initialized to **false** is maintained. A single pass over x is sufficient. For each letter encountered in x, the value of its Boolean variable is switched and the occurrence of this letter is kept (respectively rejected) if its Booleab variable is equal to 1 (respectively 0). The sequence of letters kept constitutes the string $Odd(x)$. The array of Boolans is accessed directly ($\Theta(1)$ for each access), the string x is traversed only once and the complexity of this function is thus in $\Theta(n)$ conditions evaluated. Note the following property of $Odd(x)$: all symbols present in x (i.e. all symbols in Σ) are also present in the string $Odd(x)$. This property is not shared by $Even(x)$.

109 - A 5 **Answer 5.** Let $S(x, y)$ be a segmentation of x and let σ_j be one of the sequences of $S(x, y)$ such that a_j appears exactly X times (a_j^X is an optimal sub-sequence of σ_j). Lets $\alpha = a_j$. A case-based analysis performed according to the parity of X.

Case where X is even

Let us start with the case where X is even and let $X = 2k$. Since one α out of two is withdrawn, the sequence σ_j' contains $I = k$ symbols α. It can be deduced that $2I = X$.
Let us illustrate this case by considering that, in the sequence σ_j, the first α is located at a position p of even index ($p = 2q + 1$). Therefore, for x and $Odd(x)$ the configuration is:

Case where X is odd

Let us now consider the case where X is odd. Two sub-cases are to be singled out depending on depending on whether, in x, the first symbol α of the segment σ_j has an even or odd index. Let us start with the even case. Let $X = 2k + 1$:

$$x = \| \ldots \ldots \| \overbrace{\underbrace{\ldots \ldots}_{\neq \alpha} \alpha_{2q} \overbrace{\cdots \cdots \cdots \cdots}^{X=2k+1 \text{ occ. of } \alpha} \alpha_{2q+2k} \underbrace{\ldots \ldots}_{\neq \alpha}}^{\sigma_j} \| \ldots \ldots \|$$

$$Odd(x) = \| \ldots \| \overbrace{\underbrace{\ldots \ldots}_{\neq \alpha} \alpha_{2q+1} \underbrace{\cdots \cdots \cdot}_{I = \lfloor (2k+1)/2 \rfloor \text{ occ. of } \alpha} \alpha_{2q+2k-1} \underbrace{\ldots \ldots}_{\neq \alpha}}^{\sigma'_j} \| \ldots \|.$$

We then have $2I + 1 = X$. Still on the assumption that X is odd, if in x the first symbol α of the segment $sigma_j$ has an odd index, the situation can be schematized by:

$$x = \| \ldots \ldots \| \overbrace{\underbrace{\ldots \ldots}_{\neq \alpha} \alpha_{2q+1} \overbrace{\cdots \cdots \cdots \cdots}^{X=2k+1 \text{ occ. of } \alpha} \alpha_{2q+2k+1} \underbrace{\ldots \ldots}_{\neq \alpha}}^{\sigma_j} \| \ldots \ldots \|$$

$$Odd(x) = \| \ldots \ldots \| \overbrace{\underbrace{\ldots \ldots}_{\neq \alpha} \alpha_{2q+1} \underbrace{\cdots \cdots \cdot}_{I = \lfloor (2k+1)/2 \rfloor + 1 \text{ occ. of } \alpha} \alpha_{2q+2k+1} \underbrace{\ldots \ldots}_{\neq \alpha}}^{\sigma'_j} \| \ldots \ldots \|.$$

We then have $2I - 1 = X$.

In the above, it was considered somewhat quickly that if the value X comes from the segment σ_j of $S(x, y)$, then the value I comes from the segment σ'_j of $S(Odd(x), y)$. Would not it be possible to find a "better" I on another segment of $S(Odd(x), y)$? The following example, still with $y = bac$, suggests that this is not the case.

$$x = \| \overbrace{c_1 b_1 b_2 b_3}^{\sigma_1} \underset{X_1=3}{\|} \overbrace{a_1 a_2 a_3 a_4}^{\sigma_2} \underset{X_2=4}{\|} \overbrace{c_2 c_3 c_4 c_5 c_6}^{\sigma_3} \underset{X_3=5}{\|}$$

$$Odd(x) = \| \overbrace{c_1 b_1 b_3}^{\sigma'_1} \underset{I_1=2}{\|} \overbrace{a_1 a_3}^{\sigma'_2} \underset{I_2=2}{\|} \overbrace{c_3 c_5}^{\sigma'_3} \underset{I_3=2}{\|}.$$

Indeed, X_2 (X evaluated on the segment σ_2) and X_3 are both greater than X_1. Taking into account what has just been demonstrated, I_2 and I_3 cannot be less than I_1. The complete demonstration is left to the reader.

It has been proven that

$$Maxi(x, y) \in (2 \cdot Maxi(Odd(x), y) - 1) \, .. \, (2 \cdot Maxi(Odd(x), y) + 1)$$

and that the three values of the interval can be reached by $Maxi(x, y)$.

Answer 6. The base case is characterized by the fact that the length of the sequence x is less than or equal to that of the sequence y. In this situation, if the two lengths are equal, it is sufficient to compare x to y to know if the degree of stuttering of y in x is 1 or 0. Otherwise (we then have $|x| < |y|$), the degree of stuttering is 0.

The induction hypothesis assumes that it is known how to determine the degree of stuttering i of y in any string of length strictly less than n. It suffices then to apply the result of the previous question to deliver either $2i + 1$, or $2i$, or $2i - 1$ (since $Scan(x, y, 2i + 1) \Rightarrow Scan(x, y, 2i)$, the order according to which the calls to this function are made is not significant).

Therefore, the division model is:

$$
\boxed{
\begin{array}{ll}
Maxi1_m(n) \rightarrow \left(\begin{array}{l}\text{determination of the degree of}\\ \text{stuttering (0 or 1) of } y \text{ in } x\end{array}\right) & n \leqslant m \\[2em]
Maxi1_m(n) \rightarrow Maxi1_m\left(\left\lfloor \dfrac{n+s-1}{2}\right\rfloor\right) + \left(\begin{array}{l}\text{determination of the degree of}\\ \text{stuttering of } y \text{ in } x \text{ through (at}\\ \text{most) two calls to } Scan\end{array}\right) & n > m
\end{array}}
$$

The justification for the argument ($\lfloor(n+s-1)/2\rfloor$) in the first formula (and not ($\lfloor n/2 \rfloor$)) is given below. The algorithm then looks as follows:

```
1.  function Maxi1(x, y) result ℕ pre
2.      x ∈ string and y ∈ string and
3.      i ∈ ℕ
4.  begin
5.      if |x| ≤ |y| then
6.          if x = y then
7.              result 1
8.          else
9.              result 0
10.         end if
11.     else
12.         i ← Maxi1(Odd(x), y);
13.         if Scan(x, y, 2i + 1) then
14.             result 2i + 1
15.         elsif Scan(x, y, 2i) then
16.             result 2i
17.         else
18.             result 2i − 1
19.         end if
20.     end if
21. end
```

In order to guarantee the termination of the algorithm, we must now ensure that, in the branch **else**, the recursive call applies to a string (the string $Odd(x), y)$) of length *strictly less* than n. Since s is the cardinality of Σ, we have:

$$ s \leqslant m < n \tag{8.43} $$

The first inequality accounts for the fact that y uses all the characters of Σ at least once and the second inequality stems from the fact that we are in the branch **else** of the alternative. In x, some symbols may be present an odd number of times (this is for example the case of a, b and c in $a_1 b_1 b_2 b_3 c_1 d_1 d_2$). Let x' be the string obtained from x by adding as many symbols as necessary to have systematically an even number of each symbol and such that $Odd(x) = Odd(x')$ (for the example, $x' = a_1 b_1 b_2 b_3 c_1 d_1 d_2 a_2 b_4 c_2$). The length of x' is upper bounded by $n+s-1$, because in x there is at least one symbol with an even index (otherwise one would have $m \geqslant n$); the completion is thus done with at most $(s-1)$ symbols). We then have:

$|x'| \leqslant n + s - 1$

$\Rightarrow$ division by 2, $card(x')$ is even by construction

$$|Odd(x')| \leqslant \left\lfloor \frac{n+s-1}{2} \right\rfloor$$

$\Leftrightarrow$ $\qquad\qquad\qquad\qquad\qquad Odd(x) = Odd(x')$

$$|Odd(x)| \leqslant \left\lfloor \frac{n+s-1}{2} \right\rfloor \qquad\qquad\qquad\qquad (8.44)$$

$\Rightarrow$ $\qquad\qquad\qquad\qquad$ inequality 8.43 and $\lfloor a \rfloor \leqslant a$

$$|Odd(x)| < \frac{n+n}{2}$$

$\Leftrightarrow$ $\qquad\qquad\qquad\qquad\qquad\qquad\qquad$ arithmetics

$$|Odd(x)| < n.$$

Hence, in the function *Maxi1*, the recursive call is done with a string strictly shorter, which ensures the termination of the algorithm.

Complexity

Assuming that the refinement of the function $|\dots|$ applied to any string is in $\Theta(1)$, the worst-case complexity is represented by the following recurrence equation (the cost of the condition $|x| \leqslant |y|$ is ignored):

$$\left|\begin{array}{ll} C_m(n) = n & m \geqslant n \\[2mm] C_m(n) = C_m\left(\left\lfloor \frac{n+s}{2} \right\rfloor\right) + 3n + 2m & n > m. \end{array}\right.$$

The first part of the equation expresses the cost of the condition $x = y$. This condition requires at worst n elementary comparaisons[21]. The second part accounts for the evaluation of the function $Odd(x)$ (for a cost of n), of the two evaluations of the function *Scan* (for a cost of $2 \cdot (n+m)$), as well as of the cost of the recursive call. This latter operates on a string of at most $\lfloor (n+s-1)/2 \rfloor$ characters (as shown by formula 8.44 earlier), which is overestimated by $\lfloor (n+s)/2 \rfloor$ to simplify the calculations.

$$C_m(n) \in \mathcal{O}(n + m \cdot \log_2(n)).$$

For the term n, this conjecture is justified by the kinship of the complexity equation with that of the special case 8.2 of the corollary of the master theorem (page 423), whose solution is in $\Theta(n)$. For the second term, $m \cdot \log_2(n)$, unfolding $C_m(n)$, shows the term $2m$ at each step (except the last one). It must therefore be modulated by a factor dependent on n. The presence of the division by 2 incites to introduce the factor $\log_2(n)$ to propose $m \cdot \log_2(n)$. The proof is made by induction. It must be demonstrated that there exists a positive constant c such that

$$C_m(n) \leqslant c \cdot (n + m \cdot \log_2(n)).$$

To do this, we prove (inductive part of the proof) that if (induction hypothesis)

$$C_m\left(\left\lfloor \frac{n+s}{2} \right\rfloor\right) \leqslant c \cdot \left(\left\lfloor \frac{n+s}{2} \right\rfloor + m \cdot \log_2\left(\left\lfloor \frac{n+s}{2} \right\rfloor\right)\right), \qquad (8.45)$$

then $C_m(n) \leqslant c \cdot (n + m \cdot \log_2(n))$. We succeed in simply demonstrating this implication for $c \geqslant 11$ and for all $n \geqslant n_0$ (with $n_0 = c \cdot s$). In the following, we retain $c = 11$. Under

---

[21]Due to the cost of comparing two strings, it is necessary to consider the elementary underlying conditions.

these conditions, it remains to demonstrate (this is the base) that the induction hypothesis is satisfied for n_0, that is:

$$C_m\left(\left\lfloor\frac{n_0+s}{2}\right\rfloor\right) \leqslant c \cdot \left(\left\lfloor\frac{n_0+s}{2}\right\rfloor + m \cdot \log_2\left(\left\lfloor\frac{n_0+s}{2}\right\rfloor\right)\right).$$

Now let us perform the full proof.

Induction hypothesis There is a value $c > 0$ such that formula 8.45 holds.

Induction

$C_m(n)$

$\leqslant$ definition, arithmetics, induction hypothesis and $\lfloor a \rfloor \leqslant a$

$$c \cdot \frac{n}{2} + c \cdot \frac{s}{2} + c \cdot m \cdot \log_2\left(\frac{n+s}{2}\right) + 3n + 2m$$

$\leqslant$ $s \leqslant m < n$

$$c \cdot \frac{n}{2} + c \cdot \frac{s}{2} + c \cdot m \cdot \log_2\left(\frac{2n}{2}\right) + 5n$$

$=$ arithmetics

$$c \cdot \frac{n}{2} + c \cdot \frac{s}{2} + c \cdot m \cdot \log_2(n) + 5n. \tag{8.46}$$

Overestimating the expression $(c \cdot s/2 + 5n)$ by $(c \cdot n/2)$ would be of interest. Under what condition is this possible?

$$c \cdot \frac{s}{2} + 5n \leqslant c \cdot \frac{n}{2}$$

$\Leftrightarrow$ arithmetics

$$c \cdot s \leqslant (c - 10) \cdot n.$$

A solution is to choose $c = 11$. This choice entails that $n \geqslant 11s$. Let $n_0 = 11s$. Under this condition, starting from formula 8.46:

$$c \cdot \frac{n}{2} + c \cdot \frac{s}{2} + c \cdot m \cdot \log_2(n) + 5n$$

$\leqslant$ $c = 11$ and $n \geqslant 11s$

$$c \cdot \frac{n}{2} + c \cdot \frac{n}{2} + c \cdot m \cdot \log_2(n)$$

$=$ arithmetics

$$c \cdot (n + m \cdot \log_2(n)),$$

which completes the inductive part of the demonstration.

Base Formula 8.45, page 593, must be proven for $c = 11$ and $n = n_0$:

$$C_m\left(\left\lfloor\frac{11s+s}{2}\right\rfloor\right) \leqslant 11 \cdot \left(\left\lfloor\frac{11s+s}{2}\right\rfloor + m \cdot \log_2\left(\left\lfloor\frac{11s+s}{2}\right\rfloor\right)\right)$$

$\Leftrightarrow$ arithmetics

$$C_m(6s) \leqslant 11 \cdot (6s + m \cdot \log_2(6s)) \tag{8.47}$$

Let us find the value of $C_m(6s)$ by summation (we assume that $2s > m$ in order to apply the base $(C_m(n) = n)$ on s:

$$C_m(6s) \;=\; C_m\left(\left\lfloor \frac{6s+s}{2} \right\rfloor\right) + 18s + 2m$$

$$+$$

$$C_m(3s) \;=\; C_m\left(\left\lfloor \frac{3s+s}{2} \right\rfloor\right) + 9s + 2m$$

$$+$$

$$C_m(2s) \;=\; C_m\left(\left\lfloor \frac{2s+s}{2} \right\rfloor\right) + 6s + 2m$$

$$+$$

$$\underline{\quad C_m(s) \;=\; s \qquad\qquad\qquad\qquad\qquad\qquad}$$

$$C_m(6s) \;=\; 34s + 6m$$

Let us try to establish proposal 8.47 by upper bounding its first member:

$$
\begin{array}{ll}
C_m(6s) & \\
= & \text{above calculation} \\
34s + 6m & \\
\leqslant & \text{arithmetics} \\
66s + 11m & \\
\leqslant & s \geqslant 1 \\
11 \cdot (6s + m \cdot \log_2(6s)) & \\
= & \text{for } c = 11 \text{ and } n = 6s \\
c \cdot (n + m \cdot \log_2(n)). &
\end{array}
$$

Hence it can be concluded that:

$$C_m(n) \in \mathcal{O}(n + m \cdot \log_2(n)). \tag{8.48}$$

Formulas 8.42, page 590, and 8.48, that evaluate the complexity of the two solutions, are *a priori* incomparable. The first one depends only on the argument n/m (although the corresponding function is independent of m),and the second one on both m and n. In order to attempt a comparison anyway, let us assume that m is constant (and $n \gg m$). For formula 8.42, let $C'(n) = n \cdot \log_2(n)$. We then have:

$$
\begin{array}{ll}
C'(n) & \in \quad \mathcal{O}(n \cdot \log_2(n)) \\
C\left(\dfrac{n}{m}\right) & \in \quad \mathcal{O}(C'(n)).
\end{array}
$$

Regarding formula 8.48, let $C''(n) = n + m \cdot \log_2(n)$. We have:

$$
\begin{array}{ll}
C''(n) & \in \quad \mathcal{O}\,(n + m \cdot \log_2(n)) \\
C_m(n) & \in \quad \mathcal{O}(C''(n)).
\end{array}
$$

The calculation rules on the operator $\mathcal{O}$ allow to write that:

$$C''(n) \in \mathcal{O}\,(n).$$

Under the considered hypothesis, the first solution is in $\mathcal{O}(n \cdot \log_2(n))$, whereas the second one is in $\mathcal{O}(n)$.

Answers to problem 110. The Fast Fourier Transform

The problem is on page 464.

Answer 1. The naïve version of the calculation of the discrete Fourier transform is: 110 - A 1

1. **constants**

2. $n \in \mathbb{N}_1$ **and** $n = \ldots$ **and**
3. $x \in (0 .. n - 1) \rightarrow \mathbb{C}$ **and** $x = [\ldots]$ **and**
4. $W \in \mathbb{C}$ **and** $W = e^{-\frac{2\pi \cdot i}{n}}$
5. **variables**
6. $X \in (0 .. n - 1) \rightarrow \mathbb{C}$
7. **begin**
8. **for** l **ranging** $0 .. n - 1$ **do**
9. $X[l] \leftarrow 0;$
10. **for** c **ranging** $0 .. n - 1$ **do**
11. $X[l] \leftarrow X[l] + W^{l \cdot c} \cdot x[c]$
12. **end for**
13. **end for**
14. **end**

This algorithm requires $2n^2$ multiplications of complex numbers and n^2 complexe exponentiations. Therefore, it is in $\Theta(n^2)$. However, it is easy to decrease the underlying multiplicative factor (the asymptotic complexity remaining unchanged) by suitably strengthening the invariants of the two loops (the outer loop by $wl = W^l$ and the inner loop by $wlc = wl^c$). We then obtain:

1. **constants**
2. $\cdots$
3. **variables**
4. $\cdots$
5. **begin**
6. $wl \leftarrow 1;$
7. **for** l **ranging** $0 .. n - 1$ **do**
8. $X[l] \leftarrow 0;$
9. $wlc \leftarrow 1;$
10. **for** c **ranging** $0 .. n - 1$ **do**
11. $X[l] \leftarrow X[l] + wlc \cdot x[c];$
12. $wlc \leftarrow wlc \cdot wl$
13. **end for;**
14. $wl \leftarrow wl \cdot W$
15. **end for**
16. **end**

This version requires $(2n^2 + n)$ multiplications of complex numbers and no exponentiation. It is therefore also in $\Theta(n^2)$. What should be remembered here is that, as is often the case, local "arrangements" generally do not decrease the asymptotic complexity. We must try another paradigm and it will be the "DaC" one.

110 - A 2   **Answer** 2.   The division model is the following:

DFT(1) elementary	
$\text{DFT}(m) \rightarrow 2 \cdot \text{DFT}\left(\frac{m}{2}\right) + \begin{pmatrix} \text{composition of the re-} \\ \text{sults according to the} \\ \text{schema of the statement} \end{pmatrix}$	$m > 1$

However, it must be emphasized that this is not a simple division by 2 of the initial vector, but the use of two interlaced sub-vectors in the initial vector.

1. **function** $DFT(n, x)$ **result** $(0 .. (n - 1) \rightarrow \mathbb{C})$ **pre**
2. $n \in \mathbb{N}_1$ **and** $\exists k \cdot (k \in \mathbb{N}_1$ **and** $n = 2^k)$ **and** $x \in (0 .. n - 1) \rightarrow \mathbb{C}$ **and**

3. $Xe \in \left(0..\dfrac{n}{2} - 1\right) \to \mathbb{C}$ and $Xo \in \left(0..\dfrac{n}{2} - 1\right) \to \mathbb{C}$ and

4. $X \in (0..n-1) \to \mathbb{C}$

5. **begin**

6. **let** W **such that**

7. $W \in \mathbb{C}$ **and** $W = e^{-\frac{2\pi \cdot i}{n}}$

8. **begin**

9. **if** $n = 1$ **then**

10. **result** x

11. **else**

12. $Xe \leftarrow DFT\left(\dfrac{n}{2}, Even(n, x)\right);$

13. $Xo \leftarrow DFT\left(\dfrac{n}{2}, Odd(n, x)\right);$

14. **for** $j \in 0..\dfrac{n}{2} - 1$ **do**

15. $X[j] \leftarrow Xe[j] + W^j \cdot Xo[j];$

16. $X\left[j + \dfrac{n}{2}\right] \leftarrow Xe[j] - W^j \cdot Xo[j]$

17. **end for;**

18. **result** X

19. **end if**

20. **end**

21. **end**

Below is an example of a call to the function *DFT*.

1. **write** $\left(DFT\left(8, [1.0 + 8i, \pi i, e + 9.4i, 6 + 0.8i, 0.07, 12 + 9.6i, i, 0.6 + 0.7i]\right)\right)$

Complexity

Denoting an exponentiation by e and a product by p, the recurrence equation providing the complexity of this algorithm is:

$$\begin{vmatrix} C(1) = 1 \\ C(n) = 2 \cdot C\left(\dfrac{n}{2}\right) + n \cdot e + n \cdot p \end{vmatrix} \qquad n > 1 \text{ power of 2}$$

hence, according to formula 8.4, page 423, a complexity in $\Theta(n \cdot \log_2(n))$ for both operations. This is a significant improvement over the solution of question 1. Historically, many other improvements have been brought to this algorithm, but so far none have blown up the "wall" of $\Theta(n \cdot \log_2(n))$. A simple improvement consists on the one hand in factorizing the double calculation of $W^j \cdot Xo[j]$, and on the other hand in removing the exponentiations present in the loop by strengthening its invariant (by the conjunct $Wj = W^j$). The branch **else** of the alternative then becomes:

1. $Xe \leftarrow DFT\left(\dfrac{n}{2}, Even(n, x)\right);$

2. $Xo \leftarrow DFT\left(\dfrac{n}{2}, Odd(n, x)\right);$

3. $Wj \leftarrow 1;$

4. **for** j **ranging** $0..\dfrac{n}{2} - 1$ **do**

5. $aux \leftarrow Wj \cdot Xo[j];$

6. $X[j] \leftarrow Xe[j] + aux;$

7. $X\left[j + \dfrac{n}{2}\right] \leftarrow Xe[j] - aux;$

8. $Wj \leftarrow Wj \cdot W$

9. **end for;**
10. **result** X

The recurrence equation becomes:

$$\left|\begin{array}{l} C(1) = 1 \\ C(n) = 2 \cdot C\left(\dfrac{n}{2}\right) + n \cdot p \end{array}\right. \qquad\qquad n > 1 \text{ power of } 2.$$

The complexity in terms of exponentiations drops to $\Theta(1)$, while in number of multiplications it remains in $\Theta(n \cdot \log_2(n))$.

Overcoming the constraint of a size n which is a power of 2 can be done by using variants of the above algorithm. Such variants exist in particular in the case where the vector x consists of real numbers (and not of complex numbers), or even when n is prime or the product of two integers which are prime between them. The solution based on "stuffing with 0's" the vector x alters the result and should, if possible, be avoided. Many other solutions exist. Their study goes beyond the objectives of this problem.

Answers to problem 111. Multiplying polynomials *The problem is on page 468.*

111 - A 1   **Answer 1.**   An induction is performed on the size n ($n > 0$) of the polynomials A and B.

Base When A and B are polynomials of degree 0 (of size 1), the result is $(a_0 \cdot b_0) \cdot x^0$.

Induction hypothesis It is known how to multiply two polynomials of size $n/2$ ($1 \leqslant n/2$).

Induction Let $n > 1$. The polynomial $A(x) = a_{n-1} \cdot x^{n-1} + a_{n-2} \cdot x^{n-2} + \cdots + a_1 \cdot x + a_0$ can be put in the form:

$$A(x) = \left(a_{n-1} \cdot x^{\frac{n}{2}-1} + \cdots + a_{\frac{n}{2}}\right) \cdot x^{\frac{n}{2}} + \left(a_{\frac{n}{2}-1} \cdot x^{\frac{n}{2}-1} + \cdots + a_0\right).$$

It is the same with $B(x) = b_{n-1} \cdot x^{n-1} + b_{n-2} \cdot x^{n-2} \cdots + b_1 \cdot x + b_0$. Letting:

$$A1 = \quad a_{n-1} \cdot x^{\frac{n}{2}-1} + \cdots + a_{\frac{n}{2}}$$
$$A0 = \quad a_{\frac{n}{2}-1} \cdot x^{\frac{n}{2}-1} + \cdots + a_0$$

we have $A(x) = A1 \cdot x^{\frac{n}{2}} + A0$; similarly $B(x) = B1 \cdot x^{\frac{n}{2}} + B0$. The product of the two polynomials $A(x)$ and $B(x)$ can then be rewritten:

$$A(x) \cdot B(x) = (A1 \cdot B1) \cdot x^n + (A0 \cdot B1 + A1 \cdot B0) \cdot x^{\frac{n}{2}} + (A0 \cdot B0). \qquad (8.49)$$

From the induction hypothesis, it is known how to multiply polynomials of size $n/2$. The initial problem of the multiplication of two polynomials of degree $(n-1)$ has been transformed to the problem of four multiplications (plus three additions and two multiplications of a polynomial by a monomial of the form $1 \cdot x^i$) of polynomials of degree $(n/2 - 1)$.

Getting an efficient representation of a polynomial must take into account the following criteria:

(a) cutting a given polynomial into two polynomials of the same size must be immediate,

(b) multiplying a polynomial by a monomial of type x^i must not require costly operations.

The first point excludes a linked list representation and solution based on arrays can be adopted. The second point requires not to tie the bounds to the degree of the polynomial. We opt for the following solution: a polynomial is a quadruple made up of (i) an array of sufficient size, where the coefficients are recorded, (ii) the two bounds of the array delimiting the sub-array containing the coefficients and (iii) a variable representing the degree of the polynomial. Thus, the following diagram (P is the array, ia and sa the two bounds delimiting the sub-array and da the degree of the polynomial):

$$
\begin{array}{c}
\quad la \qquad\qquad ua \qquad\qquad\qquad da \\
P \quad \boxed{\begin{array}{|c|c|c|c|c|c|c|} \hline & & 1 & 5 & -3 & 2 & \\ \hline \end{array}} \qquad \boxed{3} \\
\qquad\quad 7 \ \ 8 \ \ 9 \ \ 10
\end{array}
$$

is a possible representation for the polynomial $2x^3 - 3x^2 + 5x + 1$.

Being provided with an explicit representation of the degree does not appear useful *a priori* since it seems that $da = ua - la$. However, formula 8.49 above shows that it is necessary to increase the degree of a polynomial without modifying its size, which the representation proposed with an explicit degree makes possible in a simple way.

Termination The size of the polynomials is positive and it is divided by 2 at each step. This ensures the termination of the algorithm.

The division model is the following:

MultPol(1) elementary
$\text{MultPol}(n) \rightarrow 4 \cdot \text{MultPol}\left(\dfrac{n}{2}\right) + \left(\begin{array}{l}\text{composition of the} \\ \text{four solutions ac-} \\ \text{cording to formula} \\ 8.49\end{array}\right) \qquad n > 1.$

Assuming that $P + Q$ represents the sum of the two polynomials P and Q and $P \uparrow i$ stands for the multiplication of the polynomial P by the monomial x^i, a possible implementation of this algorithm is given by:

1. **function** *MultPolyn*(A, B) **result** polynomial **pre**
2. $A \in$ polynomial **and** $B \in$ polynomial **and** /% *see below for the type* polynomial %/
3. $A.da = B.da$ **and** /% *polynomials of the same degree* %/
4. $A.ua - A.la = B.ua - B.la$ **and** /% *polynomials of the same size* %/
5.   P11, P10, P01, P00 $\in$ polynomial $\times$ polynomial $\times$ polynomial $\times$ polynomial **and**
6.   MidA $\in \mathbb{N}$ **and** MidB $\in \mathbb{N}$ **and** hd $\in \mathbb{N}$ /% *middles and half-degree* %/
7. **begin**
8.   **if** $A.la = A.ua$ **then**
9.   **result** $([A.Ta[A.ua] \cdot B.Tb[B.ua], 0,0,0,0,0,0,0], 0,0,0)$
10.   **else**
11. $\text{MidA} \leftarrow \left\lfloor \dfrac{A.la + A.ua}{2} \right\rfloor; \text{MidB} \leftarrow \left\lfloor \dfrac{B.la + B.ua}{2} \right\rfloor;$
12. $\text{hd} \leftarrow \left\lfloor \dfrac{A.da}{2} \right\rfloor;$
13. $\text{P11} \leftarrow \textit{MultPolyn}((A.Ta, \text{MidA} + 1, A.ua, \text{hd}), (B.Ta, \text{MidB} + 1, B.ua, \text{hd}));$

14. $P10 \leftarrow MultPolyn\,((A.Ta, MidA + 1, A.ua, hd)\,, (B.Ta, B.la, MidB, hd));$
15. $P01 \leftarrow MultPolyn\,((A.Ta, A.la, MidA, hd)\,, (B.Ta, MidB + 1, B.ua, hd));$
16. $P00 \leftarrow MultPolyn\,((A.Ta, A.la, MidA, hd)\,, (B.Ta, B.la, MidB, hd))\,;$
17.   **result** $(P11 \uparrow (A.da + 1)) + ((P10 + P01) \uparrow (hd + 1)) + P00$
18.   **end if**
19. **end**

The precondition of the function *MultPolyn* specifies that the two arguments A and B are polynomials of the same degree and size. The set $\texttt{polynomial}$, defined hereafter, is made up of de quadruples representing respectively the array of coefficients, the lower bound, the upper bound and the degree. The size of a polynomial is a power of 2, and its degree is in the form $(2^k - 1)$. An example of calling program is presented hereafter (here the polynomials have a maximum degree of 7):

1. **constants**
2.   /% *array of coefficients, lower bound, upper bound, degree:* %/
3. $\texttt{aux} = (0..7 \rightarrow \mathbb{Z}) \times 0..7 \times 0..7 \times 0..7$
4. $\texttt{polynomial} =$
5. $$\left\{ (Ta, la, ua, da) \,\middle|\, (Ta, la, ua, da) \in \texttt{aux} \textbf{ and } \begin{pmatrix} \exists k \cdot \begin{pmatrix} k \in \mathbb{N} \textbf{ and} \\ da = 2^k - 1 \end{pmatrix} \\ \textbf{and} \\ \exists k \cdot \begin{pmatrix} k \in \mathbb{N} \textbf{ and} \\ ua - la = 2^k - 1 \end{pmatrix} \end{pmatrix} \right\}$$
6. **begin**
7.   /% *product of* $5x^3 + 3x^2 - 2x + 4$ *and* $2x^3 - 4x^2 - 3x + 1$: %/
8. $\texttt{write}(MultPolyn(([4, -2, 3, 5, 0, 0, 0, 0], 0, 3, 3), ([1, -3, -4, 2, 0, 0, 0, 0], 0, 3, 3)))$
9. **end**

Complexity

Regarding complexity in terms of coefficient multiplications, it can be seen that this type of operation only occurs in the base case (branch **then**) and, indirectly, in the four recursive calls to the function *MultPolyn*. Hence, if n is the size of each of the polynomials in argument, the following equation:

$$\left| \begin{aligned} C(1) &= 1 \\ C(n) &= 4 \cdot C\left(\frac{n}{2}\right) \end{aligned} \right. \qquad\qquad n > 1.$$

The term $n/2$ comes from the fact that each of the arrays has been divided by 2 while the factor 4 relates to the number of sub-problems generated and therefore of recursive calls. Formula 8.6, page 423, allows to say that $C(n) \in \Theta(n^2)$. It can be observed that this DaC solution is not better than the naïve solution mentioned at the beginning of the statement of the problem! The reader can check that taking into account the number of additive operations (including the multiplications by a monomial of type x^i) does not change this result. A possible improvement involves reducing the number of sub-problems generated which is the subject of the next question.

111 - A 2   **Answer** 2.   The solution below relies on the fact that the three values $A0 \cdot B0$, $(A0 \cdot B1 + A1 \cdot B0)$ and $A1 \cdot B1$ can be calculated with only three multiplications of polynomials. From the suggestion made in the statement, it can be observed that:

$$A0 \cdot B1 + A1 \cdot B0 = (A0 + A1) \cdot (B0 + B1) - A0 \cdot B0 - A1 \cdot B1$$

and it can be thus concluded that the following program (where the operator $-$ represents the subtraction of polynomials):

1. $P00 \leftarrow A0 \cdot B0$;
2. $P11 \leftarrow A1 \cdot B1$;
3. $R \leftarrow (A0 + A1) \cdot (B0 + B1) - P00 - P11$

provides the three desired values respectively in P00, R and P11. Applied to the previous algorithm, this technique makes it possible to replace lines 13 to 17 of the conditional statement of the previous operation (renamed *MultPolynBis*) by:

15. $P11 \leftarrow MultPolynBis((A.Ta, MidA + 1, A.ua, hd), (B.Ta, MidB + 1, B.ua, hd))$;
16. $P00 \leftarrow MultPolynBis ((A.Ta, A.la, MidA, hd) , (B.Ta, B.la, MidB, hd))$;
17. $Y \leftarrow MultPolynBis \left(\begin{array}{l} (A.Ta, A.la, MidA, hd) + (A.Ta, MidA + 1, B.ua, hd), \\ (B.Ta, B.la, MidB, hd) + (B.Ta, MidB + 1, B.ua, hd) \end{array} \right)$;
18. **result** $(P11 \uparrow (da + 1)) + ((Y - P00 - P11) \uparrow (hd + 1)) + P00$

Complexity

If n is the size of each of the argument polynomials, the equation of complexity (in terms of products of polynomials, is:

$$\left| \begin{array}{l} C(1) = 1 \\ C(n) = 3 \cdot C \left(\dfrac{n}{2} \right) \end{array} \right. \qquad n > 1.$$

From formula 8.9, page 423, the solution of this equation is such that $C(n) \in \Theta(n^{\log_2(3)})$. This is actually an improvement since $\log_2(3) \approx 1.585 \; (< 2)$.

Answer 3. In algebra, the degree of the polynomial $P(x) = a_{n-1} \cdot x^{n-1} + \cdots a_0 \cdot x^0$ 111 - A 3
is traditionally the largest index i for which $a_i \neq 0$ (it may be the polynomial zero). In the following, we call *explicit degree* of the polynomial $Q(x) = a_{n-1} \cdot x^{n-1} + a_{n-2} \cdot x^{n-1} + \cdot + a_1 \cdot x + a_0$ the value $n - 1$, and this whatever the value of the coefficient a_{n-1}. Thus, if $R(x) = 3x^2 + 5$ and $R'(x) = 0x^4 + 3x^2 + 5$, the polynomials R and R' have the same degree; however the explicit degree of R is 2, while that of R' is 4.
A first solution to the problem of the multiplication of any polynomials approached in this question is that of "padding": in order to satisfy the conditions of the first two questions, it suffices to add as many zero coefficient monomials as necessary so that:

- the explicit degrees $(n - 1)$ and $(m - 1)$ are identical,
- n is a power of 2.

For example, let us consider the polynomials $A(x) = 3x^8 - 2x$ and $B(x) = x^4 + 3x$. The solution presented above consists in working with the two following representations:

$$A(x) = 0x^{15} + \cdots + 0x^9 + 3x^8 + 0x^7 + 0x^6 + 0x^5 + 0x^4 + 0x^3 + 0x^2 - 2x + 0$$
$$B(x) = 0x^{15} + \cdots + 0x^9 + 0x^8 + 0x^7 + 0x^6 + 0x^5 + 1x^4 + 0x^3 + 0x^2 + 3x + 0.$$

However, it is clear that this solution can lead to unnecessary calculations due to the presence of padding monomials.
A second solution is based on the fulfillment of the following conditions:

- the two polynomials have the same size,
- the two polynomials have the same explicit degree,
- the two conditions above apply recursively to any pair of polynomials obtained by separating the original polynomials in 2.

A consequence of these conditions is that the size of the two polynomials must be a power of 2. Let us consider again the two polynomials $A(x) = 3x^8 - 2x$ and $B(x) = x^4 + 3x$. How can they be transformed so that they match the conditions above? We start by adding monomials with zero coefficients in order to have the same powers explicited in each polynomial. We obtain:

$$A(x) = 3x^8 + 0x^4 - 2x$$
$$B(x) = 0x^8 + 1x^4 + 3x.$$

Finally, we complete the polynomials in order to reach a size (4 is here a minimum) that is a power of 2:

$$A(x) = 0x^9 + 3x^8 + 0x^4 - 2x$$
$$B(x) = 0x^9 + 0x^8 + 1x^4 + 3x.$$

The principle of the two algorithms developed in the previous questions remains valid, but the data structure chosen to represent the polynomials must be revised. In fact, the degrees of the monomials represented are generally not contiguous; each coefficient must therefore be accompanied by its degree. However, for polynomials satisfying the conditions of the first two questions, the asymptotic complexities remain unchanged.

Conditions a) to c) above constitute—beyond the precondition—minimum conditions to be fulfilled in order to guarantee the correctness of the two algorithms. In particular, any pair of polynomials matching the conditions of the first two questions fulfill the latter three conditions. The reciprocal is false.

111 - A 4   **Answer 4.**   The function $ProdPolynDFT(n, P, Q)$ calls on functions $DFT(n, x)$ and $DFTRev(n, X)$ that calculate respectively the DFT of the complex vector x and the reverse DFT of the complex vector X. The first one is studied in problem 110, page 464. The second one calls on the auxiliary function $DFTRevAux$ that is in charge of the calculation properly DaC. The function $DFTRevAux$, in its optimized version, is as follows:

```
 1. function DFTRevAux(n, X) result (0 .. (n − 1) → ℂ) pre
 2.    n ∈ ℕ₁ and ∃k · (k ∈ ℕ₁ and n = 2ᵏ) and X ∈ (0 .. (n − 1)) → ℂ and
 3.    Xe ∈ (0 .. n/2 − 1) → ℂ and Xo ∈ (0 .. n/2 − 1) → ℂ and
 4.    x ∈ (0 .. n − 1) → ℂ and
 5.    Wj ∈ ℂ and aux ∈ ℂ
 6. begin
 7.    let W such that
 8.       W ∈ ℂ and W = e^(2π·i/n)
 9.    begin
10.       if n = 1 then
11.          result X
12.       else
13.          Xe ← DFTRevAux (n/2, Even(n, X));
14.          Xo ← DFTRevAux (n/2, Odd(n, X));
15.          Wj ← 1;
16.          for j ranging 0 .. n/2 − 1 do
17.             aux ← Wj · Xo[j]; x [j] ← Xe[j] + aux;
18.             x [j + n/2] ← Xe[j] − aux;
19.             Wj ← Wj · W
```

20.   **end for**;
21.   **result** x
22.   **end if**
23.   **end**
24. **end**

According to the definition of the reverse DFT, the function *DFTRev* simply divides (each element of) the vector returned by a call to *DFTRevAux* par n:

1. **function** $DFTRev(n, X)$ **result** $(0 .. n - 1) \rightarrow \mathbb{C}$ **pre**
2. $n \in \mathbb{N}_1$ **and** $\exists k \cdot (k \in \mathbb{N}_1$ **and** $n = 2^k)$ **and** $X \in (0 .. n - 1) \rightarrow \mathbb{C}$
3. **begin**
4.   **result** $\dfrac{1}{n} \cdot DFTRevAux(n, X)$
5. **end**

The function *ProdPolynDFT*(n, P, Q) considers two polynomials P and Q of degree $(n - 1)$, in the coefficient-based representation, and it perform their product by the DFT method. Although represented by real coefficients, the polynomials P and Q are below the arguments of the function *DFT*, which deals with a vector of complex numbers. This conversion is assumed to have been carried out.

1. **function** $ProdPolynDFT(n, P, Q)$ **result** $(0 .. n - 1) \rightarrow \mathbb{C}$ **pre**
2. $n \in \mathbb{N}_1$ **and** $\exists k \cdot (k \in \mathbb{N}_1$ **and** $n = 2^k)$ **and**
3. $P \in 0 .. (n - 1) \rightarrow \mathbb{C}$ **and** $Q \in (0 .. n - 1) \rightarrow \mathbb{C}$
4. **begin**
5.   **result** $DFTRev(n, DFT(n, P) \cdot DFT(n, Q))$
6. **end**

The call to the function *ProdPolynDFT*(n, P, Q) can be made as shown in the forthcoming example where the role of the function *Double*(n, P) is to obtain a representation by means of $(2n - 1)$ samples as indicated in the example of the statement. This function takes into account the polynomial P of degree $(n - 1)$ in its representation by coefficients (according to increasing powers), and doubles its degree by complementing it with zero coefficients. This function is not detailed here. The example is illustrated using the polynomials $D(x)$ and $E(x)$ defined in the statement.

1. **constants**
2. $n \in \mathbb{N}_1$ **and** $n = 2$ **and**
3. $D \in (0 .. n - 1) \rightarrow \mathbb{C}$ **and** $D = [1 + 0i, 2 + 0i]$ **and**
4. $E \in (0 .. n - 1) \rightarrow \mathbb{C}$ **and** $E = [2 + 0i, 1 + 0i]$
5. **variables**
6. $D1 \in (0 .. 2n - 1) \rightarrow \mathbb{C}$ **and** $E1 \in (0 .. 2n - 1) \rightarrow \mathbb{C}$
7. **begin**
8. $D1 \leftarrow Double(n, D);$ /% $D1 = [1 + 0i, 2 + 0i, 0 + 0i, 0 + 0i]$ %/
9. $E1 \leftarrow Double(n, E);$ /% $E1 = [2 + 0i, 1 + 0i, 0 + 0i, 0 + 0i]$ %/
10.   **write**$(ProdPolynDFT(2n, D1, E1))$
11. **end**

The result is in the form of a vector of complex numbers. However, given the problem at hand, the imaginary part is null[22].

---

[22] If we disregard the rounding errors inherent in floating arithmetic.

Answers to problem 112. Coulomb's law

The problem is on page 471.

112 - A 1   **Answer 1.**   We have $d = \|\vec{r}_{12}\|$. Let $C = \dfrac{1}{4\pi\epsilon_0 d^2}$. Then we have:

$$\vec{F}_{1 \to 2} = C \cdot q_1 \cdot q_2 \cdot \vec{u}.$$

Now, we would like to express $\vec{F}_{j \to i}$ for $j \in 1 .. i - 1$. From the definition, we have:

$$\vec{F}_{j \to i} = \frac{q_j \cdot q_i}{4\pi\epsilon_0 \|\vec{r}_{ji}\|^2} \cdot \vec{u}.$$

Yet $\vec{r}_{ji} = \overrightarrow{M_j M_i}$ and thus $\|\overrightarrow{M_j M_i}\| = d \cdot (i - j)$. Then:

$$\vec{F}_{j \to i} = C \cdot \frac{q_j \cdot q_i}{(i - j)^2} \cdot \vec{u}.$$

The case $j \in i + 1 .. n$ is dealt with in the same way (see figure 8.27):

$$\vec{F}_{j \to i} = C \cdot \frac{q_j \cdot q_i}{(i - j)^2} \cdot -\vec{u}.$$

By summing the $(n - 1)$ vectors, we have the following development:

$$\vec{F}_{\bullet i} = \sum_{j \in (1..n) - \{i\}} \vec{F}_{j \to i}$$

$\Leftrightarrow$ development under the quantifier

$$\vec{F}_{\bullet i} = \sum_{j=1}^{i-1} \frac{C \cdot q_i \cdot q_j}{(i - j)^2} \cdot \vec{u} + \sum_{j=i+1}^{n} \frac{C \cdot q_i \cdot q_j}{(i - j)^2} \cdot -\vec{u}$$

$\Rightarrow$ passage to the module ($\|\vec{u}\| = 1$)

$$\|\vec{F}_{\bullet i}\| = \left| \sum_{j=1}^{i-1} \frac{C \cdot q_i \cdot q_j}{(i - j)^2} - \sum_{j=i+1}^{n} \frac{C \cdot q_i \cdot q_j}{(i - j)^2} \right|$$

$\Leftrightarrow$ property of the operator $|\ |$

$$\|\vec{F}_{\bullet i}\| = |C \cdot q_i| \cdot \left| \sum_{j=1}^{i-1} \frac{q_j}{(i - j)^2} - \sum_{j=i+1}^{n} \frac{q_j}{(i - j)^2} \right|.$$

112 - A 2   **Answer 2.**   Let $G[i] = (\sum_{j=1}^{i-1} \frac{q_j}{(i-j)^2} - \sum_{j=i+1}^{n} \frac{q_j}{(i-j)^2})$ for $i \in 1 .. n$. We then have $\|\vec{F}_{\bullet i}\| = |C \cdot q_i| \cdot |G[i]|$. We now focus on the calculation of the vector G. Letting $q = [q[1], \ldots, q[n]]$ and f, defined on the interval $-(n-1) .. (n-1)$, as $f = [-1/(n-1)^2, -1/(n-2)^2, \ldots, -1/2^2, -1/1^2, 0, 1^2, 1/2^2, \ldots, 1/(n-1)^2]$, we get:

$$G[i] = \sum_{\substack{k+j=i \\ k \in 1..n \\ j \in -(n-1)..(n-1)}} q[k] \cdot f[j]. \qquad (8.50)$$

It is possible to check that the development of formula 8.50 actually yields the definition of G. Formula 8.50 looks similar to formula 8.21 in the statement of problem 111, page 468, about the product of polynomials, formula which provides the coefficient of each monomial of the product. In the fourth question of the problem about the product of polynomials, it has been shown that this product can be performed in $\Theta(n \cdot \log_2(n))$ multiplications using the FFT. It can be deduced that G can be calculated in $\Theta(n \cdot \log_2(n))$ multiplications as well. It is the same for $\|\vec{F}_{\bullet i}\|$, for $i \in 1 .. n$.

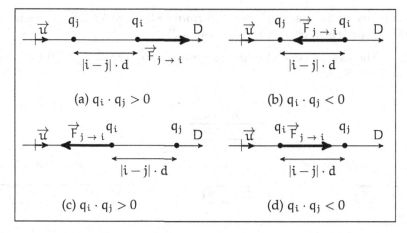

Fig. 8.27 – Coulomb's law—The four action cases of q_j on q_i.

Remark

It can also be proven that

$$G[i] = \sum_{k=1}^{n} q[k] \cdot f[i-k] \quad \text{for } i \in 1 \,..\, n.$$

This formula is similar to the convolution product of q and f (here restricted to its computation over the interval $1 \,..\, n$). As suggested by this formula, each value $G[i]$ can simply be calculated by an iteration.

Answers to problem 113. **An efficient algorithm for multiplying integers**
The problem is on page 472.

Answer 1.   According to formula 8.22, the multiplication of two natural numbers of length 2^k ($k \geqslant 0$) obeys the following inductive schema. 113 - A 1

Base If $k = 0$, the multiplication of two natural numbers of length 1 comes down to a single-digit product.

Induction hypothesis It is assumed thay it is known how to multiply two natural numbers of length 2^m where $0 \leqslant m < k$.

Induction Formula 8.22 makes explicit how to perform the multiplication of two natural numbers of length $n = 2^k$ by means of four multiplications of numbers of length $n/2 = 2^{k-1}$.

Termination The length of the numbers decreases by a factor 2 at each step while remaining positive and this ensures the termination of the algorithm.

The division model can therefore be formulated by:

Multiply1(1) elementary (one single-digit product)
Multiply1(n) $\rightarrow 4 \cdot$ Multiply1 $\left(\dfrac{n}{2}\right) + \left(\begin{array}{l}\text{shift of magnitude } 3n/2 \\ \text{and 3 additions}\end{array}\right)$ $n > 1$.

From the corollary of the master theorem (formula 8.3, page 423), the complexity of this type of multiplication is in $\Theta(n^2)$ (since $\log_2(4) = 2$).

113 - A 2   **Answer** 2.   The tree associated with the multiplication of $X = 4\,279$ by $Y = 3\,621$ is displayed in figure 8.28.

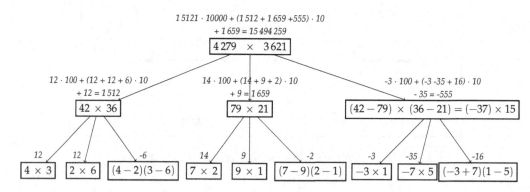

Fig. 8.28 – *The recursion tree for the multiplication of $4\,279$ by $3\,621$. The results related to the calculations carried out at each node appear in italics over the node.*

Let us notice that, instead of 16, using the approach based on formula 8.22, only nine single-digit products are performed with this strategy.

113 - A 3   **Answer** 3.   In this DaC approach, the inductive schema is close to that given for the previous method, except that formula 8.23 is used instead of formula 8.22. Thus, the resulting division model is:

$$\boxed{\begin{array}{l}
\text{Multiply2}(1)\ \text{elementary (one single-digit product)} \\[4pt]
\text{Multiply2}(n) \rightarrow 3 \cdot \text{Multiply2}\left(\dfrac{n}{2}\right) + \left(\begin{array}{l}\text{shift of magnitude } 3n/2 \text{ and} \\ 6 \text{ additions/subtractions}\end{array}\right) \qquad n > 1.
\end{array}}$$

The corollary of the master theorem (formula 8.3, page 423) tells that the complexity of the model above is in $\Theta(n^{\log_2(3)})$ ($\approx \Theta(n^{1.585})$).

113 - A 4   **Answer** 4.   The function $LeftHalf(\text{NB}, n)$ (respectively $RightHalf(\text{NB}, n)$) that delivers the left (respectively right) half (made up of $n/2$ digits) of the integer NB (made up of $n = 2^k$ ($k > 0$) digits) is assumed available. Let us recall that these halves bear *the same sign* as the integer they come from. Moreover, the division by 2 and the powers of 10 are supposed to be performed by shifts to cope with the complexity pointed out before[23]. In this context, the algorithm carrying out the product of the two integers X and Y is written as follows:

1. **function** $MultNb(X, Y, n)$ **pre**
2. $n \in \mathbb{N}_1$ **and** $\exists k \cdot (k \in \mathbb{N}$ **and** $n = 2^k)$ **and** $n \geqslant \max(\{\text{nbdg}(X), \text{nbdg}(Y)\})$ **and**
3. $n/2 < \max(\{\text{nbdg}(X), \text{nbdg}(Y)\})$ **and** $X \in \mathbb{Z}$ **and** $Y \in \mathbb{Z}$ **and** $A \in \mathbb{Z}$ **and**
4. $B \in \mathbb{Z}$ **and** $C \in \mathbb{Z}$ **and** $D \in \mathbb{Z}$ **and** $ac \in \mathbb{Z}$ **and** $bd \in \mathbb{Z}$ **and** $midt \in \mathbb{Z}$

---

[23]If, instead of a decimal representation, we consider a binary representation for which the negative numbers are coded by two's complement, the splitting of a negative number N into two halves (of the same sign) N_l and N_r cannot be done as simply as for a natural number. It is necessary first of all to take the two's complement of N, before proceeding to the separation and then to take the two's complement of each half. The complexity in terms of multiplications is not affected since only three two's complements are added (compared to the case of natural numbers)

5. /% nbdg(I) *returns the number of digits (power of 2) required to write*
    the integer I %/
6. **begin**
7. **if** $n = 1$ **then**
8.   **result** $X * Y$
9. **else**
10. $A \leftarrow LeftHalf(X, n); B \leftarrow RightHalf(X, n);$
11. $C \leftarrow LeftHalf(Y, n); D \leftarrow RightHalf(Y, n);$
12. $ac \leftarrow MultNb(A, C, n/2); bd \leftarrow MultNb(B, D, n/2);$
13. $midt \leftarrow ac + bd - MultNb(A - B, C - D, n/2);$
14.   **result** $ac * 10^n + midt * 10^{n/2} + bd$
15. **end if**
16. **end**

The following code illustrates the use of the above function:

1. **write**(*The product of* , 142, *and* , 67935, *is equal to* , $MultNb(142, 67935, 8)$)

Remark

Let us mention the existence of more efficient algorithms for multiplying integers also based on the DaC approach (see https://en.wikipedia.org/wiki/Multiplication_algorithm). Most of them are all the more of interest as the size of the numbers increases. The reader interested in recent advances on this topic may consult https://www.quantamagazine.org/mathematicians-discover-the-perfect-way-to-multiply-20190411/.

Answers to problem 114. The egg problem (1) *The problem is on page 474.*

Answer 1. This is a direct application of the bounded linear search (see section 3.5, page 107). From an operational point of view, the execution of **function** $Egg1(1, n)$ can be described as follows: the egg is dropped from the second floor. If it breaks, 1 is delivered, otherwise, it is picked up and dropped from the second floor ans so on. At worst, the egg is dropped n times, hence $S_1(n) = n$.

114 - A 1

Answer 2. If e represents the size of the different fragments, the first step is, as in the previous question, a bounded linear search which results in a loop having as step of progression $e = \lfloor \sqrt{n} \rfloor$ (except for the residual), as invariant $i \in 1 .. s + 1$ **and** $\forall h \cdot (h \in 1 .. \min(\{(i-1) \cdot e, n\}) \Rightarrow$ **not** $Break(h))$ and termination the expression $(s + 1 - i)$. The second step is similar to the one described in the answer to the first question, hence the call to the function $Egg1$ with the appropriate arguments.

114 - A 2

1. **function** $Egg2Radix$ **result** $\mathbb{N}_1$
2. **begin**
3.   **let** e, s, i **such that**
4.   /% *e: number of floors per segment; s: number of segments:* %/
5. $e = \lfloor \sqrt{n} \rfloor$ **and** $s = \lfloor \frac{n}{e} \rfloor$ **and** $i \in \mathbb{N}_1$
6.   **begin**
7. $i \leftarrow 1;$
8.   **while not** $(i \cdot e > n$ **or else** $Break(i \cdot e))$ **do**
9. $i \leftarrow i + 1$
10.   **end while**;
11.   **result** $Egg1(1 + (i - 1) \cdot e, \min(\{i \cdot e - 1, n\}))$

12.   **end**
13. **end**

It can be noticed that the answer to the first question is a special case of the second for a step of $\left\lfloor \sqrt[1]{n^0} \right\rfloor$ (instead of $\left\lfloor \sqrt[2]{n^1} \right\rfloor$). This remark is generalised and exploited in the following question. For $n = 34$ (and $f = 29$), the length of the segments is $\lfloor \sqrt{34} \rfloor$ floors (i.e. five floors), there are six segments to which is added a residual segment of four floors. The dropping floor is subscripted by the number of the egg used: $5_1, 10_1, 15_1, 20_1, 25_1$ and 30_1 (the first egg breaks), then $26_2, 27_2, 28_2$ and 29_2 (the second egg breaks). The answer is 29 for a total of ten drops.

114 - A 3   **Answer** 3.   The construction of the function $EggkRadix(lb, ub)$ is based on a DaC reasoning which originality lies in the fact that the reduction is not logarithmic but bears on a radical having the size of the problem[24]. Let $l = (ub - lb + 1)$ be the size of the problem and k be the number of eggs.

Base If $(ub + 1) = lb$, the interval is of length zero (this case can especially occur when $f = (ub + 1)$) and the result is lb.

Induction hypothesis It is known how to solve the problem for any segment of size less than l, $l \geqslant 0$.

Induction The division consists in searching (by an iteration of steps $\left\lfloor \sqrt[k]{l^{k-1}} \right\rfloor$) the segment of length $e = \left(\left\lfloor \sqrt[k]{l^{k-1}} \right\rfloor - 1 \right)$ allowing to conclude before calling the function $EggkRadix$ on this segment.

The division model can be described as:

$EggkRadix_k(0)$ elementary since the interval is of length zero.	for any k
$EggkRadix_k(l) \rightarrow EggkRadix_{k-1}\left(\left\lfloor \sqrt[k]{l^{k-1}} \right\rfloor - 1 \right) + \left(\begin{array}{l} \text{Iteration to deter-} \\ \text{mine the segment} \\ \text{to be dealt with.} \end{array} \right)$	and $k > 1$

The iteration is based on the following invariant:

$$\left(i \in 1 .. \left\lfloor \frac{n}{e} \right\rfloor + 1 \text{ and } \forall h \cdot \left(\begin{array}{l} h \in lb .. \min(\{lb + (i - 1) \cdot e - 1, ub\}) \\ \Rightarrow \text{not } Break(h) \end{array} \right) \right).$$

The expression $(\lfloor n/e \rfloor + 1 - i)$ ensures its termination. The code of the function $EggkRadix$ in in the form:

1. **function** $EggkRadix(lb, ub)$ **result** N_1 **pre**
2. $lb \in 1 .. n + 1$ **and** $ub \in 1 .. n + 1$ **and** $ub - lb + 1 \geqslant 0$ **and**
3. $e \in \mathbb{N}$ **and** $i \in \mathbb{N}$
4. **begin**
5.   **let** l **such that**
6. $l = ub - lb + 1$
7.   **begin**
8.   **if** $ub + 1 = lb$ **then**
9.   **result** lb

---

[24]In the equation of complexity, the quotient will therefore not be constant and it can be predicted that the master theorem will not apply.

```
10.        else
11.            i ← 1; e ← ⌊ᵏ√(l^(k-1))⌋;
12.            while not(lb + i · e − 1 > ub or else Break(lb + i · e − 1)) do
13.                i ← i + 1
14.            end while;
15.            result EggkRadix(lb + (i − 1) · e, min({lb + i · e − 2, ub}))
16.        end if
17.    end
18. end
```

The code given hereafter represents a calling context (k, global variable modified by the function *Break* is the number of initially available eggs):

```
1. variables
2.     k ∈ ℕ₁
3. begin
4.     k ← 4;
5.     write(EggkRadix(1, 56))
6. end
```

Complexity

Regarding the (in)equation of complexity, it must be considered that, in the worst case, an egg is broken at each step. $T_k(l)$ is an upper bound of the number of drops for k eggs available and for a section of l floors:

$$
\begin{vmatrix}
T_1(0) = 0 \\
\\
T_k(l) \leqslant T_{k-1}\left(\left\lfloor \sqrt[k]{l^{k-1}} \right\rfloor - 1\right) + \left\lfloor \dfrac{l}{\left\lfloor \sqrt[k]{l^{k-1}} \right\rfloor} \right\rfloor \qquad \qquad l > 0 \text{ and } k > 1.
\end{vmatrix}
$$

The origin of the inequality lies in the fact that if a certain step takes place in the worst situation, that will not necessarily be the case with the next one. Indeed, if an egg breaks on the penultimate position (worst case), we only take the $(e-1)$ first floors of this last segment and the egg will therefore break on the last floor, and no longer on the penultimate. To solve this inequality, we take as induction hypothesis the suggestion of the statement of the problem, that is $T_q(h) \in \mathcal{O}(\sqrt[q]{h})$. After having verified this hypothesis on the base $(T_1(0) \in \mathcal{O}(\sqrt{0}))$, the development which follows effectively makes it possible to conclude. We admit for the second term that $\left\lfloor l/\lfloor \sqrt[k]{l^{k-1}} \rfloor \right\rfloor \in \mathcal{O}\left(\sqrt[k]{l}\right)$. In the following, c' and c'' are positive constants and l is "fairly large". We start from the induction hypothesis:

$$T_{k-1}(l) \in \mathcal{O}(\sqrt[k-1]{l})$$

$\Leftrightarrow$ definition of $\mathcal{O}$

$$T_{k-1}(l) \leqslant c' \cdot \sqrt[k-1]{l}$$

$\Rightarrow$ substitution of l by $\left\lfloor \sqrt[k]{l^{k-1}} \right\rfloor - 1$

$$T_{k-1}\left(\left\lfloor \sqrt[k]{l^{k-1}} \right\rfloor - 1\right) \leqslant c' \cdot \sqrt[k-1]{\left\lfloor \sqrt[k]{l^{k-1}} \right\rfloor - 1}$$

$\Rightarrow$ $\sqrt[k-1]{\left\lfloor \sqrt[k]{l^{k-1}} \right\rfloor - 1} \in \mathcal{O}\left(\sqrt[k]{l}\right)$ and transitivity

$$T_{k-1}\left(\left\lfloor \sqrt[k]{l^{k-1}} \right\rfloor - 1\right) \leqslant c'' \cdot \sqrt[k]{l}$$

$\Leftrightarrow$ definition of $\mathcal{O}$

$$T_{k-1}\left(\left\lfloor \sqrt[k]{l^{k-1}} \right\rfloor - 1\right) \in \mathcal{O}\left(\sqrt[k]{l}\right).$$

The two terms of the inequation are in $\mathcal{O}\left(\sqrt[k]{l}\right)$ and it can be concluded that $T_k(l) \in \mathcal{O}\left(\sqrt[k]{l}\right)$.

114 - A 4   **Answer 4.**   We look for the triangular number superior closest (here it is still 36), and the cutting is done as for 36, to the top (29) of the building:

The drops are then done as follows (the number of the egg used as a subscript): 8_1, 15_1, 21_1, 26_1, 29_1, the first egg breaks. The sequential phase is carried out on the interval $27_2, 28_2$: $27_2, 28_2$, the second egg does not break to provide the result $f = 29$ with seven drops. The interested reader can check that taking the closest triangular number *inferior* (26 here) requires more drops (eight here).

114 - A 5   **Answer 5.**   Let us prove by induction on both i and n that $t_{i-1} < n \leqslant t_i \Rightarrow T_2(n) = i$.

Base For $n = 1$ and $i = 1$, we have $t_0(= 0) < n \leqslant t_1(= 1)$. A single drop makes it possible to conclude.

Induction hypothesis

$$\forall (m, j) \cdot (m < n \text{ and } j \leqslant i \Rightarrow (t_{j-1} < m \leqslant t_j \Rightarrow T_2(m) = j))$$

Induction It must be proven that if $t_i < n \leqslant t_{i+1}$, then $T_2(n) = i + 1$. In accordance with the adopted strategy, the first drop takes place on floor $i + 1$. Two cases are then to be considered.

(a) The egg breaks and (at most) $1_1 + i_2$ drops are necessary to conclude, in total $i + 1$ drops.

(b) The egg does not break and the n-floor problem becomes a $n - (i+1)$-floor problem.

$t_i < n \leqslant t_{i+1}$

$\Leftrightarrow$ definition of t_i and $n - (i+1) > 0$

$$\sum_{j=1}^{i} j - (i+1) < n - (i+1) \leqslant \sum_{j=1}^{i+1} j - (i+1)$$

$\Leftrightarrow$ arithmetics

$$\left(\sum_{j=1}^{i-1} j\right) - 1 < n - (i+1) \leqslant \sum_{j=1}^{i} j$$

$\Leftrightarrow$ definition of t_i and arithmetics

$t_{i-1} \leqslant n - (i+1) \leqslant t_i$

Two sub-cases are to be considered. If $t_{i-1} = (n - (i+1))$, $(i-1)$ drops are sufficient for $(n - (i+1))$ floors and thus i drops for n floors. Otherwise, the induction hypothesis applies and i drops are necessary for $(n-(i+1))$ floors and thus $(i+1)$ drops for n floors.

Complexity

We have actually $T_2(n) = i$. In the case where $n = t_i$ ($t_i = i \cdot (i+1)/2$), it can be easily deduced (it is the positive solution of the equation $i^2 + i - 2n = 0$) that $i = (-1 + \sqrt{8n+1})/2$, hence $i \in \Theta\left(\sqrt{2n}\right)$, i.e. $T_2(n) \in \Theta\left(\sqrt{2n}\right)$. For $k = 2$, the triangular method is therefore always in $\mathcal{O}\left(\sqrt{n}\right)$ drops.

Answer 6. For a given integer v, the question is to find the seed g satisfying the double inequality $t_{g-1} < v \leqslant t_g$. If v is exactly a triangular number, g is the integer $((-1 + \sqrt{8v+1})/2)$ (see previous question); otherwise, the solution h of the equation $h^2 + h - 2v = 0$ is such that $((-1 + \sqrt{8v+1})/2 - 1) < h < ((-1 + \sqrt{8v+1})/2)$. g is then the "ceiling" of h, i.e. $\lceil (-1 + \sqrt{8v+1})/2 \rceil$. This formula is suitable in all cases and the calculation of the germ $g = \lceil (-1 + \sqrt{8v+1})/2 \rceil$ is done in constant time. `114 - A 6`

Answer 7. The induction is first presented, then the construction of the iteration contained in the inductive part is detailed. `114 - A 7`

Base Two cases are to be considered. Either a single egg remains, or the height l of the segment being analyzed is zero ($l = ub - lb + 1$). In the first case, a sequential search is performed using the function *Egg1* of the first question. The second case arises when l is not a triangular number and the search has been completed to the end. The result is then lb (i.e. the last floor plus one).

Induction hypothesis It is known how to solve the problem for a size less than 1.

Induction The division phase consists in finding, by a loop of decreasing step of 1 at each iteration, a segment allowing to conclude, before in general applying the function *TriangEggk* on this segment.

The construction of the loop is based on the following elements:

Invariant

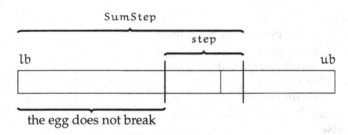

$$\left(\begin{array}{c} lb \in \mathbb{N}_1 \text{ and } ub \in \mathbb{N}_1 \text{ and } l = (ub - lb + 1) \text{ and } l \geqslant 0 \text{ and} \\ \\ step \in 0 \mathbin{..} Seed(l) \text{ and } SumStep \in Seed(l) \mathbin{..} l \text{ and } SumStep = \sum_{j=step}^{Seed(l)} j \end{array} \right)$$

Stopping condition (and loop exit processing) Three cases are to be considered for the stopping condition:

1. $step = 0$. This happens when l is a triangular number and the endpoint ub has been reached. In the code at the exit of the loop, we can then either directly deliver the value $ub + 1$ or make a recursive call with the bounds $lb + SumStep$ and ub. This second solution is implemented below.

2. $lb + SumStep - 1 > ub$. This case occurs when l is not a triangular number and the segment to be treated is the last one. A recursive call is made with the bounds $lb + SumStep$ and ub.

3. *Break*$(lb + SumStep - 1)$. This case should be evaluated by short-circuiting in order to avoid unnecessary drops. The egg breaks on the last floor of the segment to be processed. A recursive call is made with the bounds $(lb + SumStep - step)$ and $(lb + SumStep - 2)$ (the floor $(lb + SumStep - 1)$ has just been tested, no need to take it into account again).

Progression The variables $step$ and $SumStep$ are updated.

Initialization The variables $step$ and $SumStep$ take the value of the seed of l.

Termination The step strictly decreases with each iteration while remaining positive or zero. The expression $step$ is therefore suitable as a termination function.

The division model is described as follows:

$$TriangEggk_1(l) \rightarrow \begin{pmatrix} \text{elementary case, se-} \\ \text{quential phase on a} \\ \text{segment of length } l \end{pmatrix}$$

$$TriangEggk_k(l) \rightarrow TriangEggk_{k-1}(g') + \begin{pmatrix} \text{Loop of } g'' \text{ itera-} \\ \text{tions to determine} \\ \text{the segment to be} \\ \text{dealt with} \end{pmatrix} \quad \begin{array}{l} l > 0, k > 1 \text{ and} \\ g' + g'' = Seed(l) \end{array}$$

The code of the function *TriangEggk* is written as follows:

```
 1. function TriangEggk(lb, ub) result ℕ₁ pre
 2.    lb ∈ 1 .. n + 1 and ub ∈ 1 .. n + 1 and ub − lb + 1 ⩾ 0 and
 3.    step ∈ ℕ and SumStep ∈ 1 .. n
 4. begin
 5.    let l such that
 6.       l = ub − lb + 1
 7.    begin
 8.       if k = 1 or else lb = ub + 1 then
 9.          if k = 1 then
10.             result Egg1(lb, ub)
11.          else
12.             result lb
13.          end if
14.       else
15.          step ← Seed(l); SumStep ← step;
16.          while not ⎛ step = 0 or else         ⎞ do
                      ⎜ lb + SumStep − 1 > ub or else ⎟
                      ⎝ Break(lb + SumStep − 1)      ⎠
17.             step ← step − 1;
18.             SumStep ← SumStep + step
19.          end while;
20.          if step = 0 or lb + SumStep − 1 > ub then
21.             result TriangEggk(lb + SumStep − step, ub)
22.          else
23.             result TriangEggk(lb + SumStep − step, lb + SumStep − 2)
24.          end if
25.       end if
26.    end
27. end
```

Complexity

The complexity of this function is now addressed. To simplify, it is assumed that l is a triangular number. This case is easily generalized to any natural integer. The two basic equations are $T_1(l) = l$ ($l \geqslant 0$) and $T_k(0) = 0$ ($k \geqslant 1$). The first equation is justified by the fact that if only one egg remains, a sequential search is necessary. The second one is trivial: if there is no floor, there is no drop. The inductive case $T_k(l)$ is more complex. It is necessary *a priori* to take the largest value between $T_{k-1}(Seed(l) - 1) + 1$, $T_{k-1}(Seed(l) - 2) + 2$, ..., $T_{k-1}(0) + Seed(l)$. The expression $T_{k-1}(Seed(l) - i) + i$ expresses that the approach is applied with one egg less on the ith triangular segment minus its last element (for which a drop has already been done). A closer look reveals that, for every i, every $T_{k-1}(Seed(l) - i) + i$ is at worst equal to $Seed(l)$[25]. So we have the following simplified equation:

$$\left| \begin{array}{lr} T_1(l) = l & l \geqslant 0 \\ T_k(0) = 0 & k \geqslant 1 \\ T_k(l) = Seed(l) & l > 0 \text{ and } k > 1. \end{array} \right.$$

This equation is not a reccurence equation. When $k > 1$, $Seed(l)$ behaves like $2 \cdot \sqrt{l}$. We get:

$$T_k(l) \in \mathcal{O}(\sqrt{l}) \qquad k > 1.$$

Answer 8. For $k = 2$, the two methods reveal comparable execution times in 9% of cases, the triangular method performs better in 50% of cases and radixchotomy in 41% of cases. Four $k \in 3 \ .. \ 10$, radixchotomy significantly outperforms the triangular method. Beyond 10, no test has been carried out and we are reduced to extrapolating this result.

114 - A 8

Answers to problem 115. Searching for a duplicate in a bag *The problem is on page 477.*

Answer 1.

115 - A 1

a. The specification of the loop being provided in the statement of the problem, its various constituents remain to be developed.

Invariant Let us apply the classic invariant discovery heuristic (see Chapter 3), by separating the postcondition into two parts. The most difficult conjunct to establish, the one that is common to the two sub-arrays, is discarded to keep the other conjuncts, namely:

- $mid = \lfloor (lb + ub)/2 \rfloor$.
- $T[ll \ .. \ rl]$ is a multiset permutation of the initial values.
- $i \in ll \ .. \ rl - 1$.
- $bil \ .. \ bsl \subseteq ll \ .. \ mid$.
- The sub-array is valued in the interval $bil \ .. \ bsl$.
- $(bil \ .. \ bsl \neq \varnothing) \Rightarrow (bil \in T[ll \ .. \ i - 1] \textbf{ and } bsl \in T[ll \ .. \ i - 1])$.

---

[25]Let us take for example the equation $T_{k-1}(Seed(l) - 1) + 1$. If $k = 1$, $Seed(l)$ drops are required. On the other hand, if there are enough eggs, we will achieve less than $Seed(l)$ drops. This can be checked for example for $l = 36$ and $k = 10$, values for which $T_{10}(36)$, $T_9(7)$, $T_8(3)$, $T_7(1)$ and $T_6(0)$ drops are done, i.e. four releases in total.

- $\text{card}(\text{ll}\mathbin{..}i-1) \in 0\mathbin{..}\text{card}(\text{bil}\mathbin{..}\text{bsl}) + 1$.
- The conjuncts similar to those of the sub-array $T[\text{ll}\mathbin{..}i{-}1]$ for the sub-array $T[s+1\mathbin{..}\text{rl}]$.

Stopping condition As mentioned above, the discarded conjunct is retained:

$$\text{card}(\text{ll}\mathbin{..}i-1) = \text{card}(\text{bil}\mathbin{..}\text{bsl}) + 1 \textbf{ or } \text{card}(s+1\mathbin{..}\text{rl}) = \text{card}(\text{bir}\mathbin{..}\text{bsr}) + 1.$$

By construction, the conjunction of the invariant and the stopping condition actually entails the postcondition of the loop.

Progression As stated by the theory, the progression consists in preserving the invariant under the assumption of the negation of the stopping condition. This is done by comparing the element $T[i]$ to mid and updating either $T[\text{ll}\mathbin{..}i{-}1]$ or $T[s+1\mathbin{..}\text{rl}]$ and its attributes (see code below).

Initialization The sub-arrays $T[\text{ll}\mathbin{..}i-1]$ and $T[s+1\mathbin{..}\text{rl}]$ must be empty. To do this, the variables i and s take the values ll and rl respectively. The ranges $\text{bil}\mathbin{..}\text{bsl}$ and $\text{bir}\mathbin{..}\text{bsr}$ must be initialized to $\varnothing$, which is expressed in lines 6 and 7 in the code hereafter.

Termination $s + 1 - i$ is a non-negative expression which decreases at each step of progression, which ensures the termination of the loop.

b. At the end of the loop, (at least) one of the two sub-arrays $T[\text{ll}\mathbin{..}i{-}1]$ or $T[s+1\mathbin{..}\text{ub}]$ is the array $T[\text{nbl}\mathbin{..}\text{nbr}]$ wanted. This remark makes it possible to complete the construction of the procedure *Ventilate* by writing the code of the final alternative:

```
1.  procedure Ventilate(lb, ub, ll, rl; nbi, nbs, nbl, nbr : modif) pre
2.     lb, ub ∈ ℤ × ℤ and ll, rl ∈ 1 .. n × 1 .. n and
3.     nbi, nbs ∈ ℤ × ℤ and nbl, nbr ∈ 1 .. n × 1 .. n and
4.     /% see the predicate P of the statement %/
5.  begin
6.     i ← ll; bil ← mid + 1; bsl ← lb − 1;
7.     s ← rl; bir ← ub + 1; bsr ← mid;
8.     while not ( card(ll .. i − 1) = card(bil .. bsl) + 1 or
                  card(s + 1 .. rl) = card(bir .. bsr) + 1 ) do
9.        if T[i] ⩽ mid then
10.          bil ← min({bil, T[i]}); bsl ← max({bsl, T[i]});
11.          i ← i + 1
12.       else
13.          bir ← min({bir, T[i]}); bsr ← max({bsr, T[i]});
14.          Swap(i, s);
15.          s ← s − 1
16.       end if
17.    end while;
18.    if card(ll .. i − 1) = card(bil .. bsl) + 1 then
19.       nbi ← bil; nbs ← bsl; nbl ← ll; nbr ← i − 1
20.    else
21.       nbi ← bir; nbs ← bsr; nbl ← s + 1; nbr ← rl
22.    end if
23. end
```

c. Figure 8.29 shows a trace of this algorithm on the example of the statement. Initially, we have: $\text{lb} = 12, \text{ub} = 19, \text{ll} = 1, \text{rl} = 9$ and $\text{mid} = 15$.

step	0	1	2	3	4	5	6	7
T[1]	14	14	14	14	14	14	14	14
T[2]	17	17	**15**	15	15	15	15	15
T[3]	12	12	12	12	12	12	12	12
T[4]	19	19	19	19	19	**14**	14	14
T[5]	14	14	14	14	14	14	14	14
T[6]	16	16	16	16	16	16	16	16
T[7]	12	12	12	12	12	12	12	12
T[8]	14	14	14	14	14	**19**	19	19
T[9]	15	15	**17**	17	17	17	17	17
i	1	**2**	2	**3**	**4**	4	**5**	**6**
s	9	9	**8**	8	8	**7**	7	7
bil	16	**14**	14	14	**12**	12	12	12
bsl	11	**14**	14	**15**	15	15	15	15
bir	20	20	**17**	17	17	17	17	17
bsr	15	15	**17**	17	17	**19**	19	19
stop. cond.	false	false	false	false	false	false	false	true

Fig. 8.29 – Trace of the algorithm on the example of the statement.

At the end of step 7, there are only four values (12 to 15) in the sub-array $T[1..5]$ and the stopping condition is met ($card(ll\ Uptoi-1) = card(1..5) = 5$, while $card(bil..bsl) = card(12..15) = 4$). The associated assignments are carried out to obtain $nbi = 12, nbs = 15, nbl = 1, nbr = 5$.

d. The number of iteration steps is bounded by $n = card(ll..rl)$; the progression involves an alternative. At worst, $2n + 1$ conditions are evaluated. The complexity of this operation is thus in $\mathcal{O}(n)$.

e. Regarding formula 8.24, page 480, two cases are singled out depending on whether the procedure is exited by the branch **then** or by the branch **else**. For the branch **then**, we have the following development:

$$\left\lfloor \frac{card(ll..rl)}{2} \right\rfloor$$

$\geqslant$ precondition $card(ll..rl) > card(lb..ub)$

$$\left\lfloor \frac{card(lb..ub)}{2} \right\rfloor$$

$=$ definition of mid

$card(lb..mid)$

$\geqslant$ $bil..bsl \subseteq lb..mid$ (invariant of the loop)

$card(bil..bsl)$

$=$ exiting condition of the loop

$card(ll..i-1) - 1$

$=$ assignment of the branch **then**

$card(nbl..nbr) - 1.$

By transitivity, formula 8.24 is deduced for the branch **then**. The case of the branch **else** is dealt with in the same way.

Answer 2.   The principal elements of the construction have been presented above. Let $n = \text{card}(ll .. rl)$.

Base If $T[ll .. rl]$ contains a duplicate and has exactly two elements, the duplicate is one of them, $T[ll]$ for example.

Induction hypothesis It is known how to find out a duplicate in any array of size less than or equal to $(\lfloor n/2 \rfloor + 1)$ (for $n \geqslant 2$).

Induction The elements are broken down according to the method depicted in the first question. An array of size less than or equal to $(\lfloor n/2 \rfloor + 1)$ is obtained. It is known how to deal with it from the induction hypothesis.

Termination Formula 8.24 guarantees that the size of the new sub-array is less than or equal to $(\lfloor n/2 \rfloor + 1)$. In addition, for $n > 2$, $(\lfloor n/2 \rfloor + 1) < n$. The size of the new sub-array is therefore strictly less than that of the old one. This ensures the termination of the algorithm.

The division model is:

DuplicateSearch(2) trivial case		
DuplicateSearch(n) → DuplicateSearch(m) +	$\begin{pmatrix} \text{Iteration to} \\ \text{construct} \\ \text{and to de-} \\ \text{termine the} \\ \text{sub-array to} \\ \text{be dealt with} \end{pmatrix}$	$n > 2$ and $m \leqslant \lfloor n/2 \rfloor + 1$

The code of the function *DuplSearch* is as follows:

```
 1. function DuplSearch(lb, ub, ll, rl) result lb .. ub pre
 2.     lb, ub ∈ ℤ × ℤ and ll, rl ∈ 1 .. n × 1 .. n and
 3.     /% see predicate P of the statement deprived from the conjunct card(ll ..
        rl) > 2 %/
 4. begin
 5.     if card(ll .. rl) = 2 then
 6.         result T[ll]
 7.     else
 8.         Ventilate(lb, ub, ll, rl, nbi, nbs, nbl, nbr);
 9.         result DuplSearch(nbi, nbs, nbl, nbr)
10.     end if
11. end
```

It can be noted that the structure of this operation (based on a terminal recursion) is well suited for a transformation into an iterative form (transformation not developed here).

Complexity

The equation of complexity at worst in terms of conditions evaluated is the following:

$$\left| \begin{array}{l} C(2) = 1 \\ C(n) = C\left(\left\lfloor \dfrac{n}{2} \right\rfloor + 1\right) + 2n + 2 \end{array} \right. \qquad\qquad n > 2.$$

This equation is not part the panel of solutions provided by the master theorem (see page 422). However, it approaches sufficiently the corollary of the master theorem, page 423, to conjecture a solution in $\mathcal{O}(n)$. The proof is done by induction. It must be proven that there exists a positive constant c such that

$$C(n) \leqslant c \cdot n.$$

To do this, we prove (inductive part of the demonstration) that if (induction hypothesis)

$$C\left(\left\lfloor \frac{n}{2} \right\rfloor + 1\right) \leqslant c \cdot \left(\left\lfloor \frac{n}{2} \right\rfloor + 1\right) \tag{8.51}$$

then $C(n) \leqslant c \cdot n$. We succeed in proving this implication for $c \geqslant 5$ and for any $n \geqslant n_0$ (with $n_0 = 2c + 4$). In the following, $c = 5$ is retained. Under these conditions, it remains to demonstrate (this is the base) that the induction hypothesis is satisfied for n_0, that is:

$$C\left(\left\lfloor \frac{n_0}{2} \right\rfloor + 1\right) \leqslant c \cdot \left(\left\lfloor \frac{n_0}{2} \right\rfloor + 1\right).$$

Now let us perform the full proof.

Induction hypothesis There is a value $c > 0$ such that formula 8.51 holds.

Induction

$$\begin{aligned} &C(n) \\ \leqslant \quad &\text{definition, arithmetics, induction hypothesis and } \lfloor x \rfloor \leqslant x \\ &c \cdot \frac{n}{2} + c + 2n + 2 \tag{8.52} \end{aligned}$$

It would be interesting to overestimaye the expression $(c + 2n + 2)$ by $(c \cdot n/2)$. Under what condition is this possible?

$$\begin{aligned} &c + 2n + 2 \leqslant c \cdot \frac{n}{2} \\ \Leftrightarrow \quad &\text{arithmetics} \\ &2c + 4 \leqslant c \cdot n - 4n \end{aligned}$$

A solution consists in choosing $c = 5$. This choice implies imposes that $n \geqslant 14$. Let $n_0 = 14$. Under this condition, from formula 8.52 above, we have:

$$\begin{aligned} &c \cdot \frac{n}{2} + c + 2n + 2 \\ \leqslant \quad &\text{for } c = 5 \text{ and } n \geqslant 14 \\ &c \cdot \frac{n}{2} + c \cdot \frac{n}{2} \\ = \quad &\text{arithmetics} \\ &c \cdot n \end{aligned}$$

which completes the inductive part of the proof.

Base Formula 8.51 above must be proven with $c = 5$ and $n = n_0$:

$$\begin{aligned} &C\left(\left\lfloor \frac{14}{2} \right\rfloor + 1\right) \leqslant 5 \cdot \left(\left\lfloor \frac{14}{2} \right\rfloor + 1\right) \\ \Leftrightarrow \quad &\text{arithmetics} \\ &C(8) \leqslant 40 \tag{8.53} \end{aligned}$$

Let us calculate by summation the value of $C(8)$ in order to verify the previous proposition:

$$C(8) = C\left(\left\lfloor\frac{8}{2}\right\rfloor + 1\right) + 2 \cdot 8 + 2$$

$$+ \quad C(5) = C\left(\left\lfloor\frac{5}{2}\right\rfloor + 1\right) + 2 \cdot 5 + 2$$

$$+ \quad C(3) = C\left(\left\lfloor\frac{3}{2}\right\rfloor + 1\right) + 2 \cdot 3 + 2$$

$$+ \quad C(2) = \qquad\qquad 1$$

$$\overline{\qquad C(8) = \qquad\qquad 39}$$

Formula 8.53, page 617, thus holds and it is possible to conclude that $C(n) \in \mathcal{O}(n)$.

Answers to problem 116. The largest rectangle under a histogram   *The problem is on page 480.*

116 - A 1   **Answer 1.**   Given the nature of a histogram, the existence of a square which does not touch the x-axis implies the existence of another square of the same size "lower" in the histogram (the converse is false).

116 - A 2   **Answer 2.**   On the basis of the invariant proposed in the statement of the problem, the construction of the iteration continues as follows:

Stopping condition   The conjunction of the condition $(i = n + 1)$ and the invariant entails the postcondition. Therefore, this is a safe stopping condition.

Progression   Three cases are to be considered.

1. The square adjacent to i can expand by one unit to i and can also expand by one unit in height:

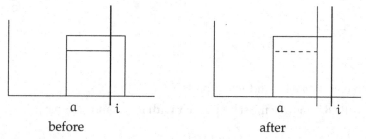

before   after

The condition determining this case is formulated by a conjunction. First of all, $h[i] \geqslant (i - a + 1)$ expresses that there is room in column i to *widen* the square to the right. Then, $\min(h[a .. i - 1]) \geqslant i - a + 1$ expresses the fact that there is room above the square to *enlarge it in height*. The variable r has to be be updated if needed. Let us note from now on that the expression $\min(h[a .. i - 1])$ cannot remain as it is, it must be refined and we will come back to this.

2. The height of column i does not allow the existing square to expand:

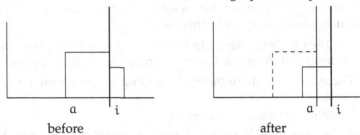

before   after

The corresponding condition is expressed as $h[i] < (i - a + 1)$. The variable a must be updated (see the following) but the best known solution does not change, since the area of the new square adjacent to the new value of i diminishes.

3. The height of column i would make it possible to expand the existing square, but there is no room above this square. The best we can do is to shift the square "to the right":

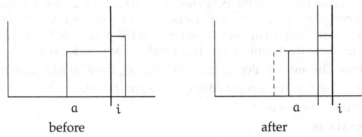

before   after

The condition determining this case can be expressed as $h[i] \geqslant (i - a + 1)$ **and** $\min(h[a .. i - 1]) < (i - a + 1)$. The variable a must be updated, but the value of r does not change.

The code corresponding to this progression is the following (the update of i is made after the conditional statement):

1. **if** $h[i] \geqslant i - a + 1$ **and** $\min(h[a .. i - 1]) \geqslant i - a + 1$ **then**
2. $r \leftarrow \max(r, i - a + 1)$
3. **elsif** $h[i] < i - a + 1$ **then**
4. $a \leftarrow i - h[i] + 1$
5. **else**
6. $a \leftarrow a + 1$
7. **end if**;
8. $i \leftarrow i + 1$

Initialization   1. $a \leftarrow 1; i \leftarrow 1; r \leftarrow 0$

Termination The value of i increases at each step, the expression $(n + 1 - i)$ ensures termination.

Complexity

The expression min present in the progression must be refined. The first idea that comes to mind consists in strengthening the invariant by the expression $m = \min(h[a .. i - 1])$. However, without doing the development, it is easy to see that m cannot be updated efficiently: the second case of the alternative would require a loop to do so. A naïve solution is to precede the alternative by calculating the value of the minimum. This solution is easy to implement (it is left to the reader). From a complexity point of view, in the worst case (the one where the value of a does not change), the various calculations of the minimum are done on lengths $0, 1, \ldots, n - 1$, hence a complexity in $\mathcal{O}(n^2)$ conditions evaluated. We will see that it is possible to improve this result.

116 - A 3   **Answer** 3.   The idea is to take again the naïve solution by appropriately strengthening the invariant starting from the considerations presented in the statement.

Invariant The invariant is strengthened by adding the proposition: f is the histogram of $h[a \,..\, i - 1]$.

Stopping condition It remains unchanged.

Progression We have already seen that the refinement of the expression related to the minimum can be easily done, provided that the histogram f is available. However, we must not lose sight of the fact that, in each of the three cases of progression, a code fragment must be written to restore the part of the invariant that has been added. In all three cases listed in the first version, the "window" $h[a \,..\, i - 1]$ moves globally to the right requiring an update of f. In the first case, only i progresses (by 1). It is sufficient to update $f[h[i]]$. In the third case, i and a progress (by 1) in the same way. This is a case similar to the previous one. The second case is more delicate since, if i is still progressing by 1, the new value of a is $i - h[i] + 1$. The update corresponding to f requires a loop to update the set of affected positions. The code presented below specifies these treatments. Some factorizations are carried out.

Initialization The initialization of f: $f \leftarrow 0 \,..\, n \times \{0\}$, must be added to the previous one.

Termination The function proposed before is appropriate.

The corresponding code is:

```
1.  constants
2.      n ∈ ℕ₁ and n = ... and h ∈ 1 .. n → 0 .. n and h = [...]
3.  variables
4.      f ∈ 0 .. n → 0 .. n and a ∈ 1 .. n + 1 and i ∈ a .. n + 1 and r ∈ 0 .. n
5.  begin
6.      a ← 1; i ← 1; r ← 0;
7.      f ← 0 .. n × {0};
8.      while i ≠ n + 1 do
9.          if h[i] ⩾ i − a + 1 and f[i − a] = 0 then
10.             r ← max({r, i − a + 1})
11.         elsif h[i] < i − a + 1 then
12.             for k ∈ a .. i − h[i] do
13.                 f[h[k]] ← f[h[k]] − 1
14.             end for;
15.             a ← i − h[i] + 1
16.         else
17.             f[h[a]] ← f[h[a]] − 1;
18.             a ← a + 1
19.         end if;
20.         f[h[i]] ← f[h[i]] + 1;
21.         i ← i + 1
22.     end while
23. end
```

Complexity

Very often nested loops as in the code above originates a quadratic complexity. However, this is not the case here because it can be observed that:

- the inner loop is such that, if we aligned by thought all its executions, the variable k would *at worst* browse the interval 1 .. n, without any overlap,
- the variable i visits the entire interval 1 .. n,
- each element of h is considered at most twice regarding its relation to the array f: once to increment one of the f[k]'s, and at most once to decrement it.

It can be deduced that the complexity of this solution is in $\Theta(n)$ conditions evaluated. This solution is actually asymptotically optimal: it is obviously impossible to solve the problem without considering all of the (n) values of h.

Answer 4. The code below results directly from the application of property 14, page 484. 116 - A 4

```
1. function AmHDaC(i, s) result ℕ pre
2.    i ∈ ℕ and s ∈ ℕ and s ⩾ i and
3.    k ∈ i .. s − 1 and lft ∈ ℕ and rgt ∈ ℕ
4. begin
5.    if i = s then
6.       result 0
7.    else
8.       k ← PosMin(i, s);
9.       lft ← AmHDaC(i, k);
10.      rgt ← AmHDaC(k + 1, s);
11.      result max({lft, (s − i) · h[k], rgt})
12.   end if
13. end
```

The result is obtained by the call $AmHDaC(1, n + 1)$.

Complexity

The number of conditions evaluated is considered. If the operation *PosMin* is implemented by a linear search, of complexity function $f(n)$, the worst complexity of this DaC version is the solution of the following recurrence equation:

$$\left| \begin{array}{l} T(0) = 1 \\ T(n) = T(n − 1) + f(n) \end{array} \right. \qquad n \geqslant 1, \text{ where } f(n) \in \mathcal{O}(n),$$

that is $T(n) \in \mathcal{O}(n^2)$.

Answer 5. The function *PosMinAux*(a, p, q) is based on the following inductive construction: 116 - A 5

Base If $p .. q = a.i .. a.s$, then the minimum of $h[p .. q]$ is $a.m$.

Induction hypothesis For any interval $a.i' .. a.s'$ such that $a.i' .. a.s' \subseteq a.i .. a.s$ and for any pair (p, q) such that $p .. q \subseteq a.i' .. a.s'$, it is known how to find the position of (one of) the minimum of the array $h[p .. q]$.

Induction Since we are not in the base case and $p..q \subseteq a.i..a.s$, we have $p..q \subseteq (a.i+1)..a.s$ (and) or $p .. q \subseteq a.i .. (a.s − 1)$. Let mid be the middle of the interval $a.i .. a.s$. Three cases are to be considered. (i) Either p and q are on either side of mid (more precisely mid $\in p .. q − 1$), and in this case the position of the minimum $h[p .. mid]$ must be sought in the left sub-tree (it is known how to do it according to the induction hypothesis) and the position of the minimum of $h[mid + 1 .. q]$ in the right sub-tree (it is know how to do it according to the induction hypothesis) and the position that designates the smallest value is retained. (ii) Or p and q are in the first half of the interval $a.i .. a.s$ (in other words $q \leqslant mid$), in which case the result to be returned is the position of the minimum of $h[p .. q]$ in the left sub-tree (it is known how to do it according to the induction hypothesis). (iii) Or p and q are in the second half of the interval $a.i .. a.s$ (i.e. $p > mid$). This case is the symmetrical of the previous one. In all cases, the new values of $p, q, a.i, a.s$ are such that $p .. q \subseteq a.i .. a.s$.

Termination The height of the considered trees (or tree, depending on the cases) decreases by 1 at each step while remaining positive. This ensures the termination of the algorithm.

The code of the function *PosMinAux* is as follows:

```
1.  function PosMinAux(a, p, q) result ℕ₁ pre
2.      a ∈ mst and p .. q ⊆ a.i .. a.s and
3.      mid ∈ a.i .. a.s and ml ∈ a.i .. a.s and mr ∈ a.i .. a.s
4.  begin
5.      if p .. q = a.i .. a.s then
6.          result a.m
7.      else
8.          mid ← ⌊ (a.i + a.s) / 2 ⌋ ;
9.          if mid ∈ p .. q − 1 then
10.             ml ← PosMinAux(a.l, p, mid);
11.             mr ← PosMinAux(a.r, mid + 1, q);
12.             if h[ml] < h[mr] then
13.                 result ml
14.             else
15.                 result mr
16.             end if
17.         elsif q ≤ mid then
18.             result PosMinAux(a.l, p, q)
19.         else
20.             result PosMinAux(a.r, p, q)
21.         end if
22.     end if
23. end
```

The tree A being supposed to be built from the histogram h, the operation "**function** *PosMin*(p, q) **result** $\mathbb{N}_1$" called in the function *AmHDaC* is:

```
1.  function PosMin(p, q) result ℕ₁ pre
2.      p .. q − 1 ⊆ A.i .. A.s
3.  begin
4.      result PosMinAux(a, p, q − 1)
5.  end
```

Complexity of the operation PosMinAux

It is chosen to count the nodes visited in the tree a built from an array of $n = 2^k$ elements when searching on the interval $p .. q$. A rough evaluation consists in considering complexity at worst and observing that if, at each step of the algorithm, the branch making two recursive calls is executed (lines 10 and 11 of the algorithm), *all* the nodes of the tree ($(2n − 1)$ nodes) would be visited. It can be deduced that $PosMinAux(a, p, q) \in \mathcal{O}(n)$.

A closer look reveals that this result is pessimistic since there is no configuration that systematically uses this sequence of two calls. Indeed, let us consider the examples in figure 8.30, page 623. The square nodes are those that complete the induction (the selected nodes), the greyed round nodes are those that are *consulted* during the search. Let $\mathcal{S}(p, q)$ be the set of selected nodes and $\mathcal{C}(p, q)$ be the set of consulted nodes. Let us take the example (c) in figure 8.30, page 623, where a node is identified by the interval it represents. This example is the search for the minimum of the interval 1 .. 6. At the root of the tree, the search is split to the two sons 1 .. 4 and 5 .. 7. The interval 1 .. 4 is the base case, it is a selected node. For this branch, the search stops there. For the interval 5 .. 7, the search is done on the left, in the node 5 .. 7 which is also a base case. In total, the nodes 1 .. 4 and 5 .. 6 are the *selected* nodes, while 1 .. 8, 1 .. 4, 5 .. 7 and 5 .. 6 are the *consulted* nodes. It can be observed that:

- whatever $m \in \mathcal{S}(p, q)$, none of the ascendants or descendants of m belong to $\mathcal{S}(p, q)$,
- two brother nodes cannot belong to $\mathcal{S}(p, q)$ (if it was the case, their father should belong to $\mathcal{S}(p, q)$),
- the union of the intervals represented in the set $\mathcal{S}(p, q)$ constitutes the interval p .. q (there are no "holes"),
- the set $\mathcal{C}(p, q)$ is the union of $\mathcal{S}(p, q)$ and the ascendants of the nodes of $\mathcal{S}(p, q)$.

Let us consider the diagram (b) in figure 8.31, page 624. It concerns the search for the minimum on the interval 2 .. 15. This is done by consulting 13 nodes. If the size of the interval is increased, for example by taking 1 .. 15, the consultation is carried out on only eight nodes. On the contrary, if we decrease the size of the interval, for example to 3 .. 15, the search requires to consult only 11 nodes. It seems that the studied configuration is a maximum in terms of the number of nodes to consult. We admit the following result: when p and q vary, the maximum of $\operatorname{card}(\mathcal{C}(p, q))$ is reached only for $\mathcal{C}(2, n-1)$, i.e. when looking for the position of the minimum of the array deprived from its two ends (see figure 8.31 for examples). Our objective is to prove that $\operatorname{card}(\mathcal{C}(p, q)) \in \mathcal{O}(\log_2(n))$.

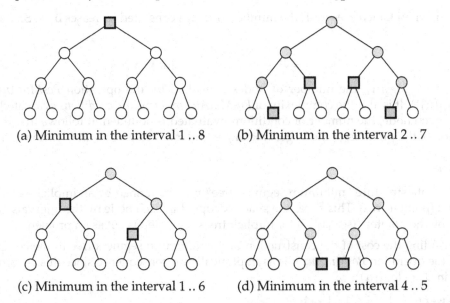

(a) Minimum in the interval 1 .. 8   (b) Minimum in the interval 2 .. 7

(c) Minimum in the interval 1 .. 6   (d) Minimum in the interval 4 .. 5

Fig. 8.30 – Examples of search for the minimum in an array defined on the interval 1 .. 8. Square-shaped nodes are the selected nodes and shaded nodes are consulted nodes.

Theorem:
Let $n = 2^k$, where $k \geqslant 2$. For a tree of $2^{k+1} - 1$ nodes from an array of n elements, $\text{card}(\mathcal{C}(2, n - 1)) = 4k - 3$.

As shown in figure 8.31, page 624, the change from $n = 2^k$ to $n = 2^{k+1}$ is done by hooking 2^{k+1} leaves to the existing 2^k leaves.

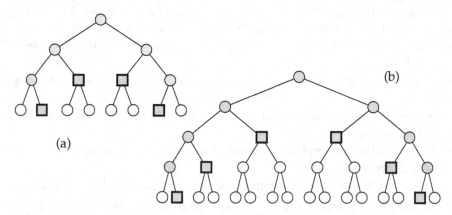

Fig. 8.31 – Search for the minimum of $h[2 .. n - 1]$ *for* $n = 2^3$ *and* $n = 2^4$.

Let c_k be the series providing the cardinality of the set $\mathcal{C}(2, n - 1)$ for $n = 2^k$ and $k \geqslant 2$. The series c_k is written:

$$\left| \begin{array}{ll} c_2 = 5 \\ c_k = c_{k-1} + 4 & k > 2. \end{array} \right.$$

Indeed, when k increases by 1, the number of nodes consulted increases by 4. So the solution is:

$$c_k = 4k - 3 \qquad \text{for } k \geqslant 2.$$

Since $k = \log_2(n)$, the number of nodes consulted by the operation *PosMinAux* is in $\mathcal{O}(\log_2(n))$. It is also the complexity of *PosMinAux* in terms of *conditions* evaluated since, for a given node, the number of conditions evaluated is bounded. It follows that the DaC version of the problem of the largest rectangle under a histogram is in $\mathcal{O}(n \cdot \log_2(n))$.

Remarks

1. The data structure "minimum segment tree" may be refined by an implicit representation (pointer free). This saves the space occupied in each node by the intervals, as well as by the pointers (see [17, 7] for implicit trees. This step is left as an problem.

2. Including the cost of the construction of the minimum segment tree in the complexity of the operation *PosMinAux* has asymptotically no consequence since this construction is in $\mathcal{O}(n \cdot \log_2(n))$.

116 - A 6   **Answer 6.**   Let $j \in 1 .. k - 1$:
$$ht_j = \min(h[g_j .. i - 1])$$
$\Rightarrow$
$$ht_j \leqslant h[g_{j+1}]$$

definition of open rectangles

$\min(h[g_j .. i - 1]) \leqslant h[g_{j+1}]$ and transitivity

$\Rightarrow$ $\qquad\qquad h[g_{j+1}] < ht_{j+1}$ (definition of open rectangles) and transitivity
$ht_j < ht_{j+1}$.

Answer 7. If P' is given, P is obtained by the formula hereafter: 116 - A 7

$$P = \langle (P'[1] + 1, h[P'[2]]), (P'[2] + 1, h[P'[3]]), \ldots, (P'[k] + 1, h[P'[k + 1]]) \rangle,$$

that is for the example: $P = \langle (0,0), (1,1), (4,3), (6,4) \rangle$. The expected configuration is actually returned.

Answer 8. The loop is built in the following way. 116 - A 8

Invariant m is the area of the largest rectangle in the portion of the histogram $h[0 .. i - 1]$, $i \in 0 .. n + 1, k \in 1 .. n + 1$ and $P' = \langle g_1 - 1, \ldots, g_k - 1, s \rangle$ is the stack representing the open rectangles. This stack is never empty: $g_1 - 1 = -1$.

Progression Three cases are to be considered depending on the relative situation relative of $h[i]$ and $h[topStack(P')]$.

First case

If $h[i] < h[topStack(P')]$, the invariant is restored by unfolding P', then updating m.

Example

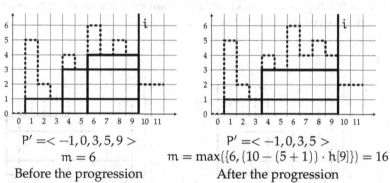

$P' = < -1, 0, 3, 5, 9 >$ $\qquad\qquad$ $P' = < -1, 0, 3, 5 >$
$m = 6$ $\qquad\qquad$ $m = \max(\{6, (10 - (5 + 1)) \cdot h[9]\}) = 16$
Before the progression $\qquad\qquad$ After the progression

In the left part of the diagram, the value 6 is issued from the (closed) rectangle constituted by column 6. The square starting at column 6 cannot expand, it closes and its area becomes the best: m takes the value 16. The new value of P' actually satisfies the invariant. In particular, the top of the stack P' (which is equal to 5) is indeed the rightmost abscissa s such that $(4, h[s])$ would be the top of the stack P. During the next iteration, the open rectangle $(4, 3)$ will close and m will take the value 18.

Second case

If $h[i] = h[topStack(P')]$, the invariant is recoverd by replacing the top of the stack by i before incrementing i.

Example

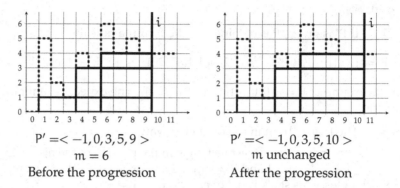

$$P' =< -1, 0, 3, 5, 9 >$$
$$m = 6$$
Before the progression

$$P' =< -1, 0, 3, 5, 10 >$$
m unchanged
After the progression

The value of m is not affected, since no open rectangle closes. The new value of P' actually satisfies the invariant. In particular, the top of the stack P' (which is equal to 10) is indeed the rightmost abscissa s such that $(6, h[s])$ would be the top of the stack P.

Third case

If $h[i] > h[\text{topStack}(P')]$, all open rectangles can expand and a new open rectangle is created (at the top of the stack). m is unchanged since no open rectangle closes. The boundary i moves one unit to the right.

Example

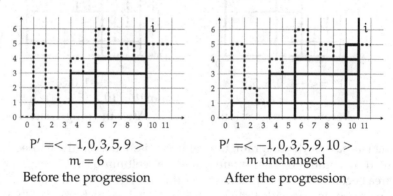

$$P' =< -1, 0, 3, 5, 9 >$$
$$m = 6$$
Before the progression

$$P' =< -1, 0, 3, 5, 9, 10 >$$
m unchanged
After the progression

The new value of P' actually meets the invariant. In particular, the top of the stack P' (which is equal to 10) is indeed the rightmost abscissa s such that $(10, h[s])$ would be the top of the stack P.

Stopping condition Let us recall that the value 0 has been placed in $h[n+1]$ as a sentinel. Moreover, the open rectangle of height 0 is always at the basis of the stack. When i takes the value $(n+1)$, $(k-1)$ iterations are carried out, whose effect is notably to close all the open rectangles of positive height (applying the first case of the progression). Only the rectangle of height 0 remains on the stack. Applying the second case of the progression then increases the width of this rectangle by 1—without affecting the value of m—and makes i take the value $n+2$. The algorithm is complete.

Initialization The extension of the histogram in 0 by 0 leads to initialize the stack P' to $\langle -1.0 \rangle$. Furthermore, i takes the value 1 and m the value 0. These assignments actually establish the invariant.

Termination This aspect is discussed below.

The stack P′ is supposed to be global. The code of the algorithm is:

```
 1. constants
 2.    n ∈ ℕ₁ and n = ...
 3. variables
 4.    h ∈ 0 .. n + 1 → ℕ and i ∈ 1 .. n + 2 and m ∈ ℕ and ht ∈ ℕ₁
 5. begin
 6.    read(h[1 .. n]);
 7.    h[0] ← 0; h[n + 1] ← 0;
 8.    initStack(P′); Stack(P′, −1); Stack(P′, 0); m ← 0; i ← 1;
 9.    while i ≠ n + 2 do
10.       if h[i] < h[topStack(P′)] then
11.          ht ← h[topStack(P′)];
12.          unStack(P′);
13.          m ← max({m, (i − (topStack(P′) + 1)) · ht})
14.       elsif h[i] = h[topStack(P′)] then
15.          unStack(P′);
16.          Stack(P′, i);
17.          i ← i + 1
18.       else
19.          Stack(P′, i) ;
20.          i ← i + 1
21.       end if
22.    end while;
23.    write(m)
24. end
```

Termination and complexity

When looking at the code, it can be observed that in the progression either i increases, or the height of the stack diminishes. If d is the number of calls to the operation *unStack* in the branch **then** of the alternative (in the branch **elsif** the operations *Stack* and *unStack* "cancel each other out"), then the value of the expression $(2n − (i + d))$ decreases at each step, while remaining positive or zero. This ensures the termination of the algorithm.

Concerning the complexity of this algorithm, in the body of the loop each value of the interval $1 .. n + 1$ is stacked once. As only previously stacked values can be unstacked, it can be deduced that the algorithm is in $\Theta(n)$ conditions evaluated. This is a significant improvement over the previous version. It is easy to notice that the problem cannot be solved without taking into consideration all the values of the histogram: it is an asymptotically optimal solution.

Q_3 and Q_2

= definition

$\quad h[j] \leqslant h[i] \text{ and } h[i] \leqslant \min(h[i + 1 .. j − 1])$

⇒ transitivity

$\quad h[j] \leqslant \min(h[i + 1 .. j − 1]).$

Answer 9.   The *only* abscissa j greater than $i(= 0)$ which satisfies both $h[0] \leqslant \min(h[1 .. j − 1]), h[j] \leqslant \min(h[1 .. j − 1])$ and $h[0] \geqslant h[j]$ is $(n + 1)$. By substitution, we get $b = am(1, n + 1)$, which is the expected result.   116 - A 9

Answer 10.   The classical heuristic consisting in the breakup of the goal (i.e. the predicate $Q'(i, b, j)$) is applied to discover an invariant and a stopping condition. Moreover,   116 - A 10 the invariant must be easy to implement and the stopping condition must not contain a quantifier. A possible solution is to take $I(i, b, j) \;\hat{=}\; Q_1$ **and** Q_2 **and** Q_4 **and** Q_5 **and** $CA(i, b, j) \;\hat{=}\; Q_3$, that is:

$$I(i, b, j) \quad \hat{=} \quad \begin{cases} i < j \leqslant n + 1 \textbf{ and} \\ h[i] \leqslant \min(h[i + 1 .. j - 1]) \textbf{ and} \\ b = am(i + 1, j) \textbf{ and} \\ h[j] \leqslant \min(h[i + 1 .. j - 1]) \end{cases}$$

$$SC(i, b, j) \quad \hat{=} \; h[i] \geqslant h[j].$$

116 - A 11   **Answer** 11.   It must be proven that $(I(i, b, j) \textbf{ and not } SC(i, b, j)) \Rightarrow P(j)$:

$I(i, b, j) \textbf{ and not } SC(i, b, j)$

$\Leftrightarrow$ $P(i)$ always holds

$I(i, b, j) \textbf{ and not } SC(i, b, j) \textbf{ and } P(i)$

$\Rightarrow$ definition of predicates I, SC and P

$i < j \leqslant n + 1 \textbf{ and } h[i] < h[j] \textbf{ and } i \in 0 .. n$

$\Rightarrow$ $h[i] < h[j] \Rightarrow j \neq n + 1$

$i < j < n + 1 \textbf{ and } i \in 0 .. n$

$\Rightarrow$ arithmetics and propositional calculus

$0 \leqslant i < j < n + 1$

$\Rightarrow$ arithmetics and propositional calculus

$j \in 1 .. n$

$\Rightarrow$ definition of P

$P(j)$.

116 - A 12   **Answer** 12.

a. For the considered example, the situation reached at line 12 is:

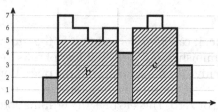

b. The invariant of the loop is restored as long as the following two operations are performed:

- the assignment $j \leftarrow k$,
- the calculation of the new value of b, that is $max(\{b, c, (k - i - 1) \cdot h[j]\})$. Indeed, property 14 page 484 is applicable, since $h[j]$ is a minimum of h over the interval $i + 1 .. k - 1$ and that we know the maximum areas (b and c) on either side of j.

The situation that is reached is:

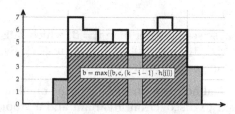

c. If we had used Q instead of Q', it would have been impossible to prove that the code proposed above for *EndProgression* restores the invariant, since we would have no information on the position of h[j] with respect to $\min(h[i+1\mathinner{..}j-1])$.

Answer 13. The program   116 - A 13

   1. $b \leftarrow 0; j \leftarrow i+1$

establishes the invariant. Therefore, it is a good candidate for the code fragment *Initialization*.

Answer 14. The value of the expression $n+1-j$ strictly decreases at each step of the   116 - A 14
progression while remaining positive or zero. This ensures the termination of the algorithm.

Answer 15. The following code from the construction carried out before: 116 - A 15

```
1.  procedure AmHMorg(i; b, j : modif) pre
2.     i ∈ N and b ∈ N and j ∈ N₁ and
3.     c ∈ N and k ∈ N
4.  begin
5.     b ← 0; j ← i + 1;
6.     while h[j] > h[i] do
7.        AmHMorg(j, c, k);
8.        b ← max({b, c, (k − i − 1) · h[j]});
9.        j ← k
10.    end while
11. end
```

Answer 16. The complexity of this solution is assessed in terms of calls to the procedure *AmHMorg*.   116 - A 16

Base The initialization of the loop consists of the "main" call $AmHMorg(i', b', j')$, followed by $b \leftarrow 0; j \leftarrow i+1$. This program actually establishes the property (i.e. $i+1-i = 1$ call to *AmHMorg*).

Induction hypothesis Before any step of the progression, the situation is:

The induction hypothesis states that reaching this situation required $(j-i)$ calls to the procedure *AmHMorg*.

Induction After executing the call $AmHMorg(j, c, k)$ appearing in the body of the loop, the situation is:

which, from the induction hypothesis, has required on the one hand $(j-i)$ calls to *AmHMorg*, on the other hand $(k-j)$ calls to this same procedure, that is a total of $(k-i)$ calls to *AmHMorg*. The assignment $j \leftarrow k$ makes it possible to recover the property to be proven.

Since the main call is of the form $AmHMorg(0, b', j')$ and the actual parameter j' takes the value $n+1$, it is easy to conclude that this algorithm is in $\Theta(n)$.

Answer 17.   It is sufficient to process the histogram corresponding to each line (for example) and to take the best rectangle found among all the histograms constructed. For the example of figure 8.18, page 490, the following histograms are considered (by processing the image from bottom to top):

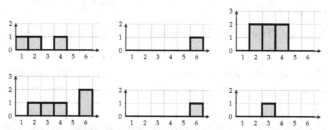

For a m-line n-column image, a preprocessing must be carried out making it possible to obtain, in an auxiliary array $TA[1 .. m, 1 .. n]$, the m histograms before processing each of them. Leaving aside the preprocessing, the best algorithms (with explicit stack or Morgan's approach) for this problem are therefore in $\Theta(n \cdot m)$ conditions evaluated.

To obtain this class of complexity, it is important that the construction of the array TA leads to the evaluation of $\mathcal{O}(n \cdot m)$ conditions. A method of filling TA from T, requiring to evaluate $\Theta(n \cdot m)$ conditions (related to loop control), consists in using an algorithm based on the following recurrence:

$$
\begin{array}{ll}
TA[m, j] = T[m, j] & 1 \leqslant j \leqslant n \\
TA[i, j] = T[i, j] \cdot (1 + TA[i + 1, j]) & 1 \leqslant j \leqslant n \text{ and } 1 \leqslant i \leqslant m - 1.
\end{array}
$$

9

Dynamic programming

Se rappeler quelque chose est encore le
meilleur moyen de ne pas l'oublier.
(Remembering things is certainly the
best way not to forget them.)

P. Dac

9.1 Overview

As "Divide and conquer", dynamic programming makes it possible to solve problems
by combining the solutions to sub-problems. A major difference between these two approaches lies in the fact that dynamic programming only concerns problems of calculating
the optimal value of a numerical quantity. Therefore, dividing into subproblems *must* result in an equation of recurrence. This method is of prime interest when the sub-problems
themselves have sub-problems in common (overlapping sub-problems) and a sub-problem
is evaluated only once, its solution being explicitly stored: this technique is called *memoization*. Another difference between "Divide and conquer" and "Dynamic Programming" is
due to the nature of the programs associated with them: recursive (in general) in the first
case, iterative in the other one.

As a simple illustration, let us consider the following integer number pyramid

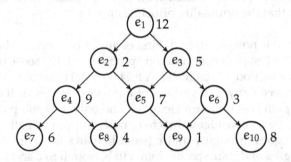

represented as a directed graph (see section 1.5, page 22), where each vertex labelled from
e_1 to e_{10} has the value appearing on its right side. We look for the path going from e_1 (top
of the pyramid) to any of the base elements (e_7, e_8, e_9 or e_{10}) crossing numbers whose sum
is maximum. The calculation of the maximum value path associated with the element e_8
denoted by $\mathrm{sopt}(e_8)$ is given by:

$$\mathrm{sopt}(e_8) = 4 + \max(\{\mathrm{sopt}(e_4), \mathrm{sopt}(e_5)\}).$$

Similarly, for e_9:

$$\text{sopt}(e_9) = 1 + \max(\{\text{sopt}(e_5), \text{sopt}(e_6)\})$$

and, in turn, the calculations of $\text{sopt}(e_4)$, $\text{sopt}(e_5)$ and $\text{sopt}(e_6)$ call on common values ($\text{sopt}(e_2)$ and $\text{sopt}(e_3)$). Thus, it can be observed that identical calculations are required to make others, which correspond to the presence of common sub-problems.

It is one of the strong points of dynamic programming to carry out these calculations only once thanks to the use of a table storing the solution of each sub-problem. In the previous example, the array $V[1..10]$ will record the values associated with the recurrence sopt. Note that, in this particular problem, if it is certain that the sought value is indeed in V, it is not localized *a priori*, but must be determined as the maximum of the sub-array $V[7..10]$.

In general, the chosen tabular structure will be filled thanks to a previously established recurrence. But it is *essential* to proceed in such a way that the value of any cell related to a recurring term can be calculated exclusively from *already filled* cells. It is therefore necessary to define a *progression* or *evolution* of the calculation offering this guarantee. In the previous example, one *must* make the calculation evolve by considering the elements by successive lines of the pyramid, since the calculation associated with an element of line l ($l > 1$) calls upon one or two elements of line $(l-1)$.

Another aspect of dynamic programming is that we have to solve an optimization problem, that is to say that it aims to find a solution that minimizes a cost or maximizes a gain, which is the case in the example of the pyramid.

The problems to be solved must however satisfy *Bellman's optimality principle* [1], according to which the[2] optimal solution to a problem can be obtained from optimal solutions to sub-problems. This principle is stated as follows:

Any *sub-policy* of an optimal *policy* is itself optimal.

The term "policy" is obviously specific to each problem. Two scenarios can thus be envisaged: (i) first making sure (generally using a proof by contradiction) that the *optimality principle* applies to the optimal solution, thus that relying on dynamic programming makes sense (however, nothing is guaranteed) or (ii) searching for a recurrence relation whose main term corresponds to the optimal quantity sought. In the problems proposed further on, this second approach is used with rare exceptions since establishing a recurrence proves *de facto* that the optimality principle applies.

Bellman's principle is now illustrated. First of all, let us wonder about its applicability to two quite close "shortest path computation" problems (in the sense of their length) in an undirected graph (see section 1.5, page 22). A first (classic) example consists in calculating the shortest path between any two vertices of a directed graph G. It is easy to prove by contradiction that a path is of minimum length if and only if its sub-paths are of minimum length. Indeed, let G be us consider a directed graph and p be a path from a to d of minimum length, which goes through b and c (solid line arcs in figure 9.1). The length of p is the sum of the lengths of the sub-paths from a to b, from b to c and from c to d. Suppose that there is a path from b to c in the graph G that costs less (dotted line in the figure) than the chosen path from b to c; then there is a shorter path from a to d, which is contrary to the fact that the path from a to d is of minimum length.

---

[1] Richard Bellman, researcher at the Rand Corporation, wrote he chose in 1950 the term "dynamic programming" to avoid the words "research" and "mathematics". See [31].

[2] A problem does not necessarily have a unique optimal solution.

Fig. 9.1 – Application of the optimality principle to the search for a shortest path in a directed graph.

Let us now take a second example, finding the longest *circuit free* path between any two vertices of a directed graph. Let us consider the graph of figure 9.2. The longest circuit free path from a to c is of length 2 $\langle a, b, c \rangle$, the longest circuit free path from a to b is of length 2 $\langle a, c, b \rangle$ and the longest circuit free path from b to c is of length 1. The longest circuit free path from a to c is therefore not obtained by composition of circuit free paths, which shows that the optimality principle is not met in this case.

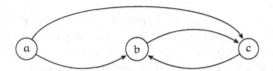

Fig. 9.2 – A (counter-)example where the optimality principle dos not apply.

However, the above considerations do not *prove* that dynamic programming cannot be applied. Indeed, there could be another way of defining a policy. Nevertheless, there are strong reasons to think that this problem can only be solved using the "Generate and test" approach (see Chapter 5), therefore at the cost of a high complexity.

Let us now take up the problem of finding the best path (in the sense defined above) in a pyramid of numbers. Here, instead of verifying *a priori* the applicability of Bellman's principle, a recurrence will be established. Let us consider the pyramid of height h having $n = \left(\sum_{k=1}^{h+1} k \right)$ elements (figure 9.3). Let $v(i)$ be the value of the element e_i, $prl(i)$ and $prr(i)$ be the numbers of (at most) two possible predecessors (left and right) of e_i on any path from e_1 to e_i. The value $sopt(i)$ generally depends on those of its two predecessors and the case of elements having only one or no predecessor must be treated separately, hence the recurrence:

$$
\begin{array}{ll}
sopt(1) = v(1) & \\
sopt(i) = v(i) + sopt(prr(i)) & i \in I_l \\
sopt(i) = v(i) + sopt(prl(i)) & i \in I_r \\
sopt(i) = v(i) + \max \left(\left\{ \begin{array}{l} sopt(prl(i)), \\ sopt(prr(i)) \end{array} \right\} \right) & 1 < i < n \text{ and } i \notin I_r \text{ and } i \notin I_l
\end{array}
$$

where I_r (respectively I_l) stands for the set of the indices of the rightmost (respectively leftmost) branch of the pyramid. $I_r = \{3, 6, 10, 15, 21, \ldots\}$ is the set of triangular integers (i.e. of the form $i = \sum_{k=1}^{j} k$, see also problem 114, page 474) of the interval $2 .. n$. $I_l = \{2, 4, 7, 16, 22, \ldots\}$ is the set of the integers successors of a triangular number of this same interval. Here, the fact of having been able to define sopt recursively means that Bellman's principle is applied.

In general, writing a dynamic programming algorithm therefore requires expressing the problem in terms of sub-problems of smaller size and establishing a recurrence relation

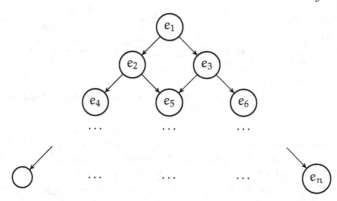

Fig. 9.3 – A pyramid of numbers.

between them (as in the example of the pyramid). Often, several recurrences are possible (stemming from different correct approaches and for a given point of view from the fact that forward or backward recurrence are generally possible), one of which being possibly chosen according to considerations of implementation efficiency.

Once the recurrence has been established, a tabular structure is determined in which the values associated with the sub-problems (thus the elements of the recurrence) will be stored. This table can be a vector or an array of any number of dimensions (in practice, 2-dimensional arrays are rarely exceeded). Filling this table will then be done iteratively by exploiting the recurrence relation. It can thus be seen that the construction of a dynamic programming algorithm is in fact that of a particular iterative algorithm, the constituent elements of which are based on the recurrence and its use to progress in filling the table. It is worth noticing that a dynamic programming algorithm fills a table containing the costs or gains of the optimal solutions of the sub-problems (and finally of the problem) and not the solution itself. Thus, in the example of the pyramid of numbers, an element of the array is used to store the optimal cost associated with a vertex e_i and not the optimal path going from the top of the pyramid to e_i. In order to build an optimal solution, it is necessary to enrich the table during its construction; we will then speak of "Tom Thumb's method", since "a trace" is left about the choice made to obtain the optimal of each of the sub-problems. The optimal solution is obtained by going through the table in an appropriate order, after its construction is complete.

What if there are *several* distinct optimal solutions of the same optimal cost? Usually, finding *one* of them is satisfying, and the choice of which is sort of random: it is made according to the ordering of the data and/or to tests in the code. For example, changing a "$\leqslant$" into a "$<$" may lead to the first optimal solution according to a certain order, instead of the last. Finding *all* optimal solutions is relevant of the "Generate and test" techniques (see Chapter 5).

Finally, it should be noted that the low (polynomial) complexity of the algorithms obtained is precisely due to the fact that we do not seek to calculate all the solutions in order to extract the best (as it is done using the "Generate and test" technique, see Chapter 5), dynamic programming reducing the search space by applying the optimality principle.

Dynamic programming algorithms using an explicit tabular structure, the study of the temporal complexity of the solutions proposed is completed by that of their spatial complexity. Regarding the first one, it is most often expressed in terms of evaluated conditions due to the fact that an algorithm relating to dynamic programming seeks an optimal value and, for this purpose, is based on a cost comparison. In problems where it is not specified, the elementary operation is therefore the evaluation of conditions.

9.2 An example: the longest sub-sequence common to two sequences

The interests of this example

Searching for the longest sub-sequence common to two sequences illustrates the approach described above through an example of medium difficulty as for establishing the recurrence. In addition, it serves as a basis for problem 107, page 452, in Chapter 8. Basics on strings (sequences) are given in chapter 1.

The problem

Given two sequences x and y, the problem is to find the length of their longest common sub-sequence(s). For example, for the strings *altitude* and *piteous*, this length is equal to 3 because *ite* and *itu* are their longest common sub-sequence(s).

As a sequence x has $2^{|x|}$ sub-sequences, including x itself and the empty word ε, a "simplistic" way to find the longest sub-sequence common to two sequences x and y consists in calculating and comparing all the pairs of sub-sequences, which is in complexity $\mathcal{O}(2^{|x|+|y|})$ (the elementary operation being the comparison of two symbols). It will be seen that dynamic programming provides a way to do much better.

For example, consider again *itu*, one of the two longest common sub-sequences of u $(= x) = $ *altitude* and $v (= y) = $ *piteous*. Its prefix *it* is certainly the longest sub-sequence common to at least one prefix of u and one prefix of v, for example to *altit* and *pite*. Can we use this remark in a systematic way?

Decomposition into sub-problems

The solution consists in defining a family of sub-problems on which a recurrence relation can be built. In our case, calling "sub-problem" the search for the longest sub-sequence common to a prefix of x and to a prefix of y would reduce to a number of comparisons in $\mathcal{O}(|x| \cdot |y|)$ (because $|x|$ (respectively $|y|$) is the number of prefixes of x (respectively y), assuming that the resolution of this set of sub-problems is sufficient to solve the initial problem). This is where the difficulty lies: it is necessary to prove by induction how this decomposition solves the initial problem.

Let $|x| = m$ be the length of x and $|y| = n$ be that of y. Let us start by defining $\text{lssc}(i, j)$, where $i \in 0 \ldots n$ and $j \in 0 \ldots m$, as the length of (one of) the longest sub-sequence common to the prefix of length i of y and the prefix of length j of x. If this construction can be completed correctly, by increasing the length of the prefixes, the solution will be calculated by $\text{lssc}(n, m)$. For example, if u $(= x) = $ *altitude* and $v (= y) = $ *piteous*, $\text{lssc}(1,6) = \text{lssc}(2,3) = 0$ and $\text{lssc}(2,5) = 1$.

The complete processing of the problem

The problem is now fully addressed in the form of questions and answers. The first question aims to highlight the fact that the problem calls on three sub-problems of the same nature as the initial problem. The second one is the step which makes it possible to prove by induction that this decomposition is sufficient. The next one concerns the implementation and the use of "Tom Thumb's" method to recover the optimal solution. The aspects related to the complexity of the *WFlg* algorithm obtained are also tackled. The last question aims to obtain a version called *WFLgForward* of the *WFlg* algorithm improving spatial complexity, but limited to the sole calculation of the length of the (a) longest sub-sequence common to two sequences. This latter algorithm is used in problem 107, page 452.

Question 1. Let $z = z[1 .. k]$ be a longest sub-sequence common to à x and y. Prove that:

- either $x[m] = y[n]$ and then: i) $z[k] = x[m] = y[n]$, and ii) $z[1 .. k - 1]$ is a longest sub-sequence common to à $x[1 .. m - 1]$ and $y[1 .. n - 1]$,

- or $x[m] \neq y[n]$ and then z is the longest between on the one hand the longest sub-sequence common to $x[1 .. m - 1]$ and y, on the other hand the longest sub-sequence common to x and $y[1 .. n - 1]$.

Answer 1. The two cases evoked in the question are successively examined. Let us first take the case $x[m] = y[n] = g$. Let w be a longest sub-sequence common to $x[1 .. m - 1]$ and $y[1 .. n - 1]$. The sequence $w \cdot g$ is a sub-sequence common to x and y, of length 1 greater than that of w and therefore maximum.

Now suppose that $x[m] \neq y[n]$. The longest sub-sequence common to x and y, denoted by w, can only be constructed in two ways, and the better will be taken. The first choice is to start from z, the longest sub-sequence common to $x[1 .. m - 1]$ and $y[1 .. n - 1]$, and to see what causes the adjunction of the last symbol of x, $x[m]$. The other choice is offered by the symmetric case, namely starting from z and seeing what causes the addition of $y[n]$ to the last symbol of y. Let us take the first case: the symbol $x[m]$ finds or not a symbol in y beyond the last one ($y[n]$), which was used to construct z. In other words, the candidate sequence w is the longest sub-sequence common to x and $y[1 .. n - 1]$. Symmetrically, the candidate sequence w is the longest sub-sequence common to $x[1 .. m - 1]$ and y.

Question 2. Deduce the formula which allows in the general case to calculate $lssc(i, j)$ as a function of $lssc(i-1, j-1)$, $lssc(i-1, j)$ and $lssc(i, j-1)$, then give the complete recurrence of computation of lssc.

Answer 2. For the general case, we can rely on what was established in the previous question by considering the prefixes $x[1 .. j]$ on the one hand and $y[1 .. i]$ on the other part, not empty. If $x[j] = y[i]$, a longest sub-sequence common to $x[1 .. j]$ and $y[1 .. i]$ is constructed as a longest sub-sequence common to $x[1 .. j - 1]$ and $y[1 .. i - 1]$ extended by $x[j] = y[i]$. Otherwise, two sub-problems have to be solved: find a longest sub-sequence common to $x[1 .. j]$ and $y[1 .. i - 1]$ and a longest sub-sequence common to $x[1 .. j - 1]$ and $y[1 .. i]$. Afterwards, there is just choose the longest of the two, or either of the two if they are the same length.

Noticing that the longest sub-sequence common to the sequence ε of length zero and any other sequence is itself ε, the following recurrence can be deduced:

$$\left|\begin{array}{ll} lssc(0, j) = 0 & \qquad\qquad 0 \leqslant j \leqslant m \\ lssc(i, 0) = 0 & \qquad\qquad 1 \leqslant i \leqslant n \end{array}\right.$$

$$\begin{vmatrix} lssc(i,j) = lssc(i-1,j-1)+1 & x[j] = y[i] \textbf{ and } 1 \leqslant i \leqslant n \textbf{ and } 1 \leqslant j \leqslant m \\ lssc(i,j) = \max \left(\left\{ \begin{array}{l} lssc(i,j-1), \\ lssc(i-1,j) \end{array} \right\} \right) & x[j] \neq y[i] \textbf{ and } 1 \leqslant i \leqslant n \textbf{ and } 1 \leqslant j \leqslant m. \end{vmatrix}$$

Question 3. Propose an evolution for the calculation of the previous recurrence, then write the dynamic programming algorithm called *WFlg* which, given two sequences x and y of respective lengths m and n, calculates the length of their longest common sub-sequence(s) and allows to recover one of the longest common sub-sequences. Specify where is the value of the length associated with the optimal solution. What are the spatial and temporal complexities of this algorithm by taking the evaluation of conditions as an elementary operation? Treat as an example the sequences $u = abcbdab$ and $v = bdcaba$.

Answer 3. The tabular structure LSSC[0 .. n, 0 .. m] in connection with the m symbols of x and the n symbols of y will be filled. The length of one of the longest sub-sequences common to the sequences x and y will be in the cell LSSC[n, m].

The first two terms of the recurrence result in the row and the column with index 0 of LSSC being initialized to 0. It can be observed that any other element LSSC[i, j] with i and j strictly positive depends either on its neighbor from the previous column and from the previous row according to the last term of the recurrence, or on its neighbor of the previous diagonal according to the third term of the recurrence. Therefore the calculation can proceed column by column and from bottom to top in each column. Note that one could just as easily proceed by line or diagonal and that these three types of fill are the most common for two-dimensional arrays.

To find one of the longest common sub-sequences by "Tom Thumb's method" (sowing pebbles to find his way), the array LSSC[0..n, 0..m] is doubled by the array PTH[0..n, 0..m] of "white pebbles" built in parallel. Each cell of this array contains information (1, 2 or 3) indicating which of the three possibilities of the recurrence created the value retained in the element of LSSC of the same indices. Browsing PTH from PTH[n, m] up to PTH[0, 0] (or any cell with index row or column equal to 0) allows to find deterministically a longer sub-sequence common to x and y. If there are several possibilities, the selected sub-sequence depends on the order of the tests carried out in the program. The algorithm *WFlg* below, which displays the value of lssc(n, m) is derived from what precedes:

```
 1.  constants
 2.    x ∈ string(Σ) and x  =  ... and y ∈  string(Σ) and y  =  ... and m  =
         |x| and n = |y|
 3.  variables
 4.    LSSC ∈ 0 .. n × 0 .. m → ℕ and PTH ∈ 0 .. n × 0 .. m → {1, 2, 3}
 5.  begin
 6.    for j ∈ 0 .. m do
 7.      LSSC[0, j] ← 0; PTH[0, j] ← 2
 8.    end for;
 9.    for i ∈ 1 .. n do
10.      LSSC[i, 0] ← 0; PTH[i, 0] ← 3
11.    end for;
12.    for j ranging 1 .. m do
13.      for i ranging 1 .. n do
14.        if x[j] = y[i] then
15.          LSSC[i, j] ← LSSC[i − 1, j − 1] + 1; PTH[i, j] ← 1
```

```
16.        else
17.            if LSSC[i − 1, j] > LSSC[i, j − 1] then
18.                LSSC[i, j] ← LSSC[i − 1, j]; PTH[i, j] ← 3
19.            else
20.                LSSC[i, j] ← LSSC[i, j − 1]; PTH[i, j] ← 2
21.            end if
22.        end if
23.      end for
24.    end for;
25.    write(LSSC[n, m])
26. end
```

The tabular structure used requires $(n + 1)$ rows and $(m + 1)$ columns; therefore spatial complexity is in $\Theta(m \cdot n)$. The number of comparisons is at least $m \cdot n$ and at most $2 \cdot m \cdot n$ (neglecting loop control). Temporal complexity is thus as well in $\Theta(m \cdot n)$.

6 a	0 ↓	1 ↙	2 ↓	2 ←	3 ↓	3 ←	4 ↙	4 ←
5 b	0 ↓	1 ↓	2 ↙	2 ←	3 ↙	3 ←	3 ←	4 ↙
4 a	0 ↓	1 ↙	1 ←	2 ↓	2 ←	2 ←	3 ↙	3 ←
3 c	0 ↓	0 ←	1 ↓	2 ↙	2 ←	2 ←	2 ←	2 ←
2 d	0 ↓	0 ←	1 ↓	1 ←	1 ←	2 ↙	2 ←	2 ←
1 b	0 ↓	0 ←	1 ↙	1 ←	1 ↙	1 ←	1 ←	1 ↙
0 ε	0 ←	0 ←	0 ←	0 ←	0 ←	0 ←	0 ←	0 ←
i v/u	ε	a	b	c	b	d	a	b
j	0	1	2	3	4	5	6	7

The longest sub-sequence common to $u = abcbdab$ and $v = bdcaba$ found by the previous algorithm is $bcba$. There are also two others: $bcab$ and $bdab$. The calculation table is given above. Following path indications ($\swarrow$ (respectively $\leftarrow, \downarrow$) corresponding to 1 (respectively 2, 3) in the algorithm) leads to the path whose cells are greyed out. By keeping the values of the symbols associated with cells with the indication $\swarrow$, $abcb$ is obtained, which is the mirror string of the one sought.

Question 4. Explain why a version of the previous algorithm of less spatial complexity can be envisaged, provided that one is only interested in the length of the longest common sub-sequence and not in the reconstruction of the associated sub-sequence. Write the code of the operation "**procedure** *WFLgForward*(x, y; P : **modif**)" that returns in vector P the length of the longest sub-sequence common to $x[0 .. m]$ and $y[0 .. i]$ for $i \in 0 .. n$. Give its spatial complexity.

Answer 4. As it was mentioned, the computation associated with the cell (i, j) of the array LSSC calls only on the contents of its three neighbors $LSSC[i − 1, j − 1]$, $LSSC[i − 1, j]$

and LSSC[i, j − 1]. Therefore, a calculation using a two-column table, h[0 .. n, 0 .. 1] can take place. The code of the associated procedure *WFLgForward* is:

```
1.  procedure WFLgForward(x, y; P : modif) pre
2.     x ∈ string(Σ) and y ∈ string(Σ) and const m = |x| and const n = |y| and
3.     P ∈ 0 .. n → ℕ and h ∈ 0 .. n × 0 .. 1 → ℕ
4.  begin
5.     for i ∈ 0 .. n do
6.        h[i, 1] ← 0
7.     end for
8.     for j ranging 1 .. m do
9.        for i ∈ 0 .. n do
10.          h[i, 0] ← h[i, 1]
11.       end for;
12.       for i ranging 1 .. n do
13.          if x[j] = y[i] then
14.             h[i, 1] ← h[i − 1, 0] + 1
15.          else
16.             h[i, 1] ← max({h[i − 1, 1], h[i, 0]})
17.          end if
18.       end for
19.    end for;
20.    for k ∈ 0 .. n do
21.       P[k] ← h[k, 1]
22.    end for
23. end
```

Thanks to the use of the arrays h and P, the spatial complexity of this procedure is in $\Theta(n)$.

9.3   What should be remembered to apply dynamic programming

As for the other approaches seen previously, the construction of a dynamic programming algorithm is part of a methodological process that guides its development. This can be synthesized by the following steps:

1. identify the numerical quantity g which will be calculated (this one can somewhat "deviate" from that appearing initially in the problem, see for example the problems 118, page 642 and 137, page 673),

2. establish a recurrence relation allowing the calculation of g which is complete, that is to say which covers all the admissible values of the indices it contains,

3. define the tabular structure T associated with the calculation (dimensions and size of each of them) and check that the solution to the problem posed will be found there (the location of the optimal value is generally known *a priori*, but it may happen that it is not not the case—see the problem of the pyramid—and it is then determined by means of a complementary treatment),

4. determine an evolution of the calculation of g that guarantees the compatibility with dynamic programming, i.e. that ensures that the calculation of an element relies only on values already calculated,

5. if needed, introduce the elements necessary for the calculation of the optimal solution itself ("Tom Thumb") by completing the tabular structure T, in order to record the choice making it possible to obtain the optimal value for each cell of T [the principle of the algorithm then exploiting this information in order to build the (one) optimal solution must be made explicit],

6. specify the spatial (in connection with the tabular structure) and temporal complexity of the proposed solution (when the latter is expressed in terms of comparisons, which is the most frequent, the conditions falling under the control of loops which introduce only one multiplicative factor will not be taken into account),

7. when possible, make improvements [limitation of the calculation to only the necessary elements, reduction of the size (or even elimination) of the tabular structure, etc.],

8. write the code of the algorithm.

9.4 Problems

The following problems offer a variety of topics for which dynamic programming is relevant. They are classified according to different themes: cutting or sharing, problems relating to sequences, trees or graphs, images and games and finally the illustration of a pseudo-polynomial problem. Due to the systematic nature of the production of the algorithm from the recurrence and the filling strategy of the tabular structure chosen, the code of the algorithm is only requested occasionally when revealing a particular interest. Finally, unless explicitly stated otherwise, temporal complexity is measured as the number of conditions evaluated in connection with the operations "minimum" and "maximum" of the recurrence.

9.4.1 Cutting and sharing: one-dimensional problems

Problem 117. Approximation of a sampled function by a broken line

This problem illustrates the notion of optimal approximation by means of dynamic programming. It shows the very significant reduction brought by this method in terms of complexity compared to a naïve approach such as "Generate and test".

Let P be a set of n points of the plan, where $n \geqslant 1$, whose abscissas are $1, 2, \ldots, n$ and whose ordinates are any natural numbers. The objective is to find the best approximation of this set by a broken line defined as a succession of straight line segments whose ends are points of P. It can be represented by the succession of abscissas onto which it relies. We impose that the first number is 1 and the last n, in other words that the first point of P is the start of the first line segment and its last point the end of the last line segment. In the four examples below, the broken lines are successively: $(1,4,8)$, $(1,5,8)$, $(1,4,7,8)$ and $(1,3,4,8)$.

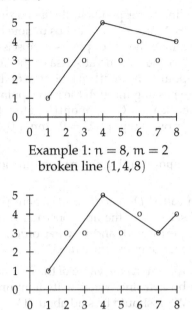

Example 1: $n = 8$, $m = 2$
broken line $(1,4,8)$

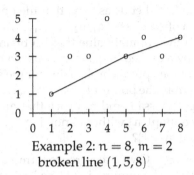

Example 2: $n = 8$, $m = 2$
broken line $(1,5,8)$

Example 3: $n = 8$, $m = 3$
broken line $(1,4,7,8)$

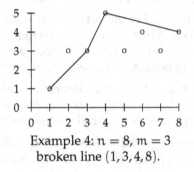

Example 4: $n = 8$, $m = 3$
broken line $(1,3,4,8)$.

The quality of the approximation of P by a broken line is *partly* measured by calculating the sum *sed* of the Euclidean distances from each point of P to the line segment whose extremities surround it. Consequently, any point of origin or end of a segment of the approximation induces a zero distance. For the example 1, this sum is made up of two parts:

- the distance of points $1, 2, 3$ and 4 to the segment built over points 1 and 4, i.e. $(0 + 0.4 + 0.4 + 0) = 0.8$,

- the distance of points $4, 5, 6, 7$ and 8 to the segment built over points 4 and 8, i.e. about $(0 + 1.75 + 0.5 + 1.25 + 0) = 3.5$.

A positive term $(m - 1) \cdot C$ is added to this sum, proportional to the number m of straight line segments of the broken line. In the example of the first figure, if $C = 2$, this term is equal to 2 since $m = 2$. The approximation is all the better as the cost $(sed + (m - 1) \cdot C)$ is small.

In the first example, this cost is about $0.8 + 3.5 + 2 = 6.3$. Similarly, for example 3, we calculate, $sed = (0 + 0.4 + 0.4 + 0) + (0 + 1.1 + 0.3 + 0) + (0 + 0) = 2.2$; the cost of the approximation is $2.2 + 2 \cdot 2 = 6.2$. This latter approximation is thus a bit better than the previous one. The second and fourth examples lead to approximations of respective costs, about 7.9 and 8.1, worse than the first one. The best of the four approximations considered is therefore the third one. However, the approximation consisting of the two segments $(1, 2)$ and $(2, 8)$ even better than this one, since its cost is about 5.4.

Given a set P of n points and C, the general problem is to find the optimal broken line, i.e. the one that minimizes the cost $(sed + m \cdot C)$.

117 - Q 1   **Question 1.**   What can be said about the approximations when $n \cdot C$ is very small (and therefore C too) or C is very large?

117 - Q 2   **Question 2.**   Let us assume that the optimal broken line corresponds to the increasing succession of abscissas $(a_1, a_2, \ldots, a_{m-1}, a_m)$, where $a_1 = 1$ and $a_m = n$. Let us denote by $appopt(i)$ the optimal value that is obtained to approximate the set of points of abscissa $(1, \ldots, i)$ by a broken line. Now let us denote by $k = a_{m-1}$ the starting abscissa of the last segment of the optimal broken line for the set P of the n points and $sed(k, n)$ the sum of the distances from the points of abscissa $(k, \ldots, n)$ to the line passing through the two P points having as abscissa k and n. Prove that $appopt(n) = sed(k, n) + C + appopt(k)$. How to calculate $appopt(n)$ without knowing k, but assuming known $appopt(1) = 0$, $appopt(2)$, $\ldots$, $appopt(n-1)$?

117 - Q 3   **Question 3.**   Give a recurrence formula to calculate $appopt(i)$ $(1 \leqslant i \leqslant n)$ as a function of $appopt(1), \ldots, appopt(i-1)$, $sed(j, i)$ and C.

117 - Q 4   **Question 4.**   Let us assume that there is a function called *Distance*(j, i, k), where $j \leqslant k \leqslant i$, that calculates the distance from the point of abscissa k to the line constructed on the points j and i What calculations are needed to be performed, and in what order, to calculate $appopt(n)$? Where is the expected result in the tabular structure used?

117 - Q 5   **Question 5.**   Deduce an algorithm which computes $appopt(n)$ the value of the optimal approximation of an arbitrary set P of n points by a broken line. What is its temporal complexity in number of calls to the function *Distance*? What should be said about it?

117 - Q 6   **Question 6.**   How should this algorithm be modified so that it also produces the abscissas of the points of the optimal broken line?

The solution is on page 690.

Problem 118.   The best interval (2)   ○ ●

> *This problem proposes an alternative solution to the one developed with the DaC approach in problem 99, page 436. It illustrates a borderline (rare) case where there is a solution requiring no tabular storage structure, and therefore of constant spatial complexity.*

Let us first recall the problem, already presented in problem 99, page 436. We have an array $T[1 .. n]$ $(n \geqslant 1)$ of real positive values. There are (at least) two indices i and j, defining the interval $i .. j$, with $1 \leqslant i \leqslant j \leqslant n$, such that the value $T[j] - T[i]$ is maximum. We look for this maximum value called the value of (a) best interval. For example, if $T = [9, 15, 10, 12, 8, 18, 20, 7]$, the best interval of value 12 is unique and obtained for $i = 5$ and $j = 7$.

Remark If the array is monotonically decreasing, this value is zero and corresponds to any interval of type $i .. i$ for $1 \leqslant i \leqslant n$.

A solution of linear complexity (in terms of conditions evaluated) has been proposed in problem 99, page 436 and the objective is to design another one using dynamic programming of the same order of complexity if possible (trying to do better is illusory).

118 - Q 1   **Question 1.**   Let us call $biv(k)$ the value of the (one best interval finishing *exactly* in position k. Specify how to get the value of the (one) best interval of the array T from $biv(1), \ldots, biv(n)$. Give a recurrence relation for the calculation of $biv(k)$.

Question 2. Deduce a filling strategy of an appropriate tabular structure. What are its temporal and spatial complexities? Check that the temporal complexity meets the desired objective. 118 - Q 2

Question 3. How to proceed to determine the best interval itself, in other words its bounds? 118 - Q 3

Question 4. Write the code of the corresponding program. 118 - Q 4

Question 5. Apply this algorithm to the array T[1 .. 14] =[14, 11, 16, 12, 20, 7, 3, 3, 19, 24, 24, 3, 5, 16]. 118 - Q 5

Question 6. Suggest a variant (principle and code) of the previous solution improving spatial complexity. 118 - Q 6

Question 7. Compare the two solutions for this problem: (a) DaC version of problem 99, page 436, and (b) that given in answer to the previous question. 118 - Q 7

The solution is on page 692.

Problem 119. Locating gas stations ○ •

> *This problem illustrates a fairly simple problem for which the value associated with the optimal solution sought is in a predetermined location in the tabular structure. Particular attention is paid to the step of reconstructing the optimal solution itself.*

A fuel company FC obtains the concession of gas stations along a highway under construction. The rule is the following: the company in charge of the highway HC indicates the n locations envisaged for installing the gas stations. Each location is numbered by an integer i, and its position is given by its mileage from the highway entrance. For each possible location, the HC company gives the estimated amount that a gas station placed at this location will bring in each year (in M$). It also indicates the "distance to preserve" in miles in the following sense: if it is decided to install a gas station at one location, it is not allowed to install another (towards the entrance to the highway) at a distance less than or equal to the distance to be preserved. It is assumed that the locations are numbered by increasing distance from the entrance to the highway. For example, with the following data:

Location #	Position	Annual gain	Distance to preserve
1	40	5	0
2	90	7	70
3	130	1	50
4	200	5	120

if it is chosen to install a station at site 4, the sites 3 and 2 can no longer be equipped since these gas stations would be at a distance of less than 120 miles. It is therefore only possible to make the following combinations of locations to install the service stations: $\langle 1 \rangle$, $\langle 2 \rangle$, $\langle 3 \rangle$, $\langle 4 \rangle$, $\langle 1, 3 \rangle$ and $\langle 1, 4 \rangle$.

119 - Q 1   **Question** 1.   Among the six possible configurations in this example, which one is the most profitable?

The problem is to place gas stations among the n locations considered, so that the gain is maximum. Let optgain(i) be the maximum gain that gas stations can bring if only locations 1 to i are taken into account (optgain(n) is therefore the final value sought). In addition, e(i) denotes the number of the nearest location (in the direction of the entrance) where it is possible to set up a gas station if there is one at the location i (taking into account the distance to be preserved). If no gas station can be put before the one in position i, e(i) is equal to 0. Finally, let g(i) be the annual gain of the gas station located at location i.

119 - Q 2   **Question** 2.   Explain why a "virtual location" with number 0 must be introduce and specify the value of g(0).

119 - Q 3   **Question** 3.   Give the recurrence for the calculation of optgain(i), the maximum gain associated with an optimal location relative to the locations 0 to i.

119 - Q 4   **Question** 4.   Specify the main elements of the program implementing this recurrence (tabular structure and progression of its filling, location of the optimal value sought, spatial and temporal complexities in terms of the number of conditions evaluated).

119 - Q 5   **Question** 5.   Give the principle of reconstitution of the optimal configuration.

119 - Q 6   **Question** 6.   Apply it to the example:

Location #	Position	Annual gain	Distance to preserve
1	20	6	0
2	80	7	70
3	170	2	100
4	200	3	50
5	260	1	80
6	280	5	100
7	340	2	90

The solution is on page 694.

Problem 120.   Traveling in the desert   ○ ●

This problem shows that, depending on the cost function considered, a simple greedy solution (see Chapter 7) works or that, on the other hand, it is necessary to call on a solution based on a recurrence, which requires a slightly more elaborate specification. Here again, the cost of the optimal solution is located in a predetermined cell of the tabular structure.

A traveler wants to go from one oasis to another without dying of thirst. He knows the position of the wells on the route (numbered from 1 to n, the well number 1 (respectively n) being the starting (respectively arrival) oasis). The traveler knows that his consumption is exactly one liter of water per mile. He is provided with a full gourd when he leaves. When he arrives at a well, he chooses between two possibilities: (i) continue his journey or (ii) fill his gourd. If he makes the second choice, he empties his gourd in the sand before filling it completely at the well in order to have fresh water. On arrival, he empties the gourd.

Question 1.   The traveler wants to make as few stops as possible. Highlight an optimal   120 - Q 1
greedy strategy (see Chapter 7) achieving this objective.

Question 2.   The traveler wants to pour as few liters of water as possible into the sand.   120 - Q 2
Show that the previous greedy strategy is still optimal.

Question 3.   At each well, including that of the arrival oasis, a guard makes him pay as   120 - Q 3
many units of the local currency as the square of the number of liters of water he has just
poured at the arrival of the section that he has traveled. The point is to choose the wells
where it must stop in order to pay as little as possible. Show with the data of the example
of question 5 that the previous greedy strategy is no longer optimal.

Question 4.   Specify a solution based on dynamic programming whose elements are: 120 - Q 4

- $apopt(i)$: minimum amount paid in total from well number 1 (the starting oasis) to well number i, given that the traveler empties his gourd at well number
  i,
- $d(i,j)$: number of miles between well number i and well number j,
- D: capacity of the gourd

whose recurrence, tabular structure used, evolution of its filling and temporal (in number
of conditions evaluated) and spatial complexities of the resulting program will be given
(the code is not requested).

Question 5.   Apply this solution with a ten-liter gourd and wells located at 8, 9, 16, 18,   120 - Q 5
24 and 27 miles from the starting oasis, arrival being located at 32 miles from the starting
oasis.

The solution is on page 695.

Problem 121.   Formatting a paragraph   ○ •

> *This problem illustrates an application of dynamic programming to a simple text formatting*
> *problem for which the minimization of a cost associated with spaces appearing in lines is*
> *expected. Strong analogies with the previous problem can be noted, especially the form of the*
> *recurrence.*

In the context of a word processing application, the aim is to arrange the sequence of
words which form a paragraph so as to best distribute the spaces in a sense which will
be specified later. To simplify, we consider a text without punctuation marks, therefore
consisting only of words (series of letters) and spaces. The rules are the following:

- each word—unbreakable—has a length equal to its number of characters and
  less than or equal to one line,
- the words of a line are separated by a space,
- any line begins with a left justified word,
- the length of a space is that of a letter,
- the length of a line cannot be exceeded.

For example, with lines of 25 characters, the two following formattings are possible, among
a large number (spaces are represented by the character "=");

```
A=short=text=is=formatted        A=short=text=is==========
according=to=different===        formatted=according=to===
strategies===============        different=strategies=====
```

The first formatting has 4 spaces on the first line, 5 on the second line, and 15 on the third one. The second has 13 spaces on the first line, 5 on the second one, and 6 on the last line. Both have 24 spaces and we would like to break this kind of equality. To this end, the quality of a formatting is measured by its *cost* fc given as the sum of the squares of the total number of spaces on each of the lines. The cost of the first formatting is $4^2 + 5^2 + 15^2 = 266$, that of the second $13^2 + 5^2 + 6^2 = 230$ and, therefore, the second is better than the first.

The goal of this problem is to find, for a given text and a given line length, a formatting of minimum cost.

121 - Q 1   Question 1.   What about two formattings of the same text using the same number of lines, if we take as cost fc' the number of spaces and not fc?

121 - Q 2   Question 2.   Consider the following two formattings (line length is equal to 28) of the text: "This short text is formatted in two extremely different ways".

```
This=short=text=is=formatted     This=short=text=is==========
in=two=extremely=different==     formatted=in=two=extremely==
ways========================     different=ways==============
```

What about a greedy algorithm (see Chapter 7) consisting in filling each line as much as possible?

121 - Q 3   Question 3.   With lines of length 10, give all the ways to format the sentence "Molina was an American".

121 - Q 4   Question 4.   We consider the N words $m_1, \ldots, m_N$ of the text to be formatted, their length $lg(m_1), \ldots, lg(m_N)$ and L the length of the line. Let us denote by $sl(i,j)$ the cost which results from writing the words $m_i, \ldots, m_j$ on the same line. Taking into account the principles mentioned above, there are two cases:

- $m_i, \ldots, m_j$ can be all written on a line ($\sum_{k=i}^{j} lg(m_k)+(j-i) \leqslant L$), then $sl(i,j) = (L-\sum_{k=i}^{j} lg(m_k))^2$, the square of the total number of spaces appearing on the line,
- the words $m_i, \ldots, m_j$ cannot be contained on a single line ($\sum_{k=i}^{j} lg(m_k)+(j-i) > L$), then $sl(i,j)$ takes an arbitrary large value, denoted by $+\infty$.

We call optcost(i) the optimal cost of writing the words $m_i, \ldots, m_N$ under the constraint that m_i is at the start of a line. Give the recurrence formula which computes optcost(i).

121 - Q 5   Question 5.   Deduce the principle of a program which, knowing the values of sl, calculates the formatting of minimum cost for a text and allows it to be written later. Specify the spatial and temporal complexities of this program.

121 - Q 6   Question 6.   Deal with the example of the question 3.

121 - Q 7   Question 7.   In the proposed approach, we started from optcost(i), the optimal cost of writing $m_i, \ldots, m_N$. Could we have proceeded otherwise?

Question 8. Other choices could be made regarding the counting of spaces, such as 121 - Q 8 taking the sum of the squares of the numbers of spaces appearing on a line. What impact would this have on the previously proposed solution?

The solution is on page 696.

Problem 122. Optimal coding

> *This problem illustrates an optimal text compression application, given sequences of symbols defining the code used. Establishing a recurrence is a bit more difficult than in previous problems. In addition, we are interested here in explaining the procedure for reconstituting the optimal coding.*

Let $\mathcal{C}$ be a set of m words on the alphabet Σ, all with lengths less than or equal to k ($\mathcal{C}$ is called the *code*). We also have another word D of length n on the alphabet Σ, which we try to encode using the fewest possible occurrences of words of $\mathcal{C}$. For example, if $\mathcal{C} = a$, b, ba, $abab$} and $D = babbaababa$, a possible encoding of D is ba ba b ba, using six occurrences of $\mathcal{C}$. There may be no solution, as for the encoding of $D = abbc$ with the code $\mathcal{C} = a$, bc}. A sufficient condition for any string to be encoded (and thus admit optimal encoding) is that Σ be included (in a broad sense) in $\mathcal{C}$.

Question 1. Give a recurrence to calculate the minimum number of occurrences of 122 - Q 1 words of the code $\mathcal{C}$ necessary for encoding D. By convention, this minimum number is equal to $+\infty$ if D cannot be encoded with $\mathcal{C}$.

Question 2. The elementary operation being the comparison of the letters of the al- 122 - Q 2 phabet Σ, write an algorithm in $\mathcal{O}(n \cdot m \cdot k)$ which finds the cost of the optimal coding and allows to produce it later (if it exists).

Question 3. Specigy the algorithm making possible to reconstitute the optimal coding 122 - Q 3 when it exists.

Question 4. Apply this algorithm to: (i) the code $\mathcal{C} = \{a, b, ba, abab\}$ and the word 122 - Q 4 $D = bababbaababa$ and (ii) the code $\mathcal{C} = \{a, bc\}$ and the word $D = abbc$.

The solution is on page 698.

Problem 123. Cutting a metal bar

> *The only point in this problem that deserves special attention concerns the establishment of recurrences.*

Given a metal bar of length n (centimeters) and a table of increasing unit selling prices USP of the metal segments for the lengths $i = 1, \ldots, n$, we try to cut the bar into segments so as to maximize its selling price. The following table is an example of a selling price table for lengths ranging from 1 to 7.

Length i of the segment	1	2	3	4	5	6	7
Selling price USP[i]	3	7	10	13	16	20	24

123 - Q 1   **Question 1.**   In this example, what is the optimal cut for a bar of length 4?

123 - Q 2   **Question 2.**   Give a recurrence formula for the optimal price $\text{optsell}(n)$ of the cut of a bar of length n.

123 - Q 3   **Question 3.**   Derive the principle of a dynamic programming algorithm that calculates this price. Specify its temporal (number of conditions evaluated) and spatial complexity.

123 - Q 4   **Question 4.**   How to proceed to know not only the optimal price, but also the length of the segments that make up the optimal cut?

123 - Q 5   **Question 5.**   Deal with the cas of a bar of length 7 with the selling price table given before.

123 - Q 6   **Question 6.**   How to proceed so that in case of an identical optimal selling price between a possibility with cutting and another one without cutting, the latter is chosen by the algorithm?

It is now assumed that segments can only be produced (and sold) for a certain number m of lengths $LG[1] = 1$ to $LG[m] = p$ with $p > m$, for which the unit selling price $USP[i]$ ($1 \leqslant i \leqslant m$) is known. For example, for $m = 4$, we could have $LG[1] = 1, LG[2] = 3, LG[3] = 4$, $LG[4] = 6$ and $SP[1] = 3, SP[2] = 8, SP[3] = 13, SP[4] = 20$. In general, any bar longer than p must be cut, which is always possible since $LG[1] = 1$.

123 - Q 7   **Question 7.**   Give the new recurrence for the calculation of $\text{optsell}(n)$, the optimal selling price of a bar of any length n (positive integer). What is the temporal complexity (in number of conditions evaluated) of the associated algorithm?

123 - Q 8   **Question 8.**   How to proceed now to obtain the length of each of the segments making up the (one) optimal cut?

123 - Q 9   **Question 9.**   Deal with the case of a bar of length 11 to be cut with the following data:

Number i of the segment	1	2	3	4	5	6
Length $LG[i]$ of the segment i	1	2	4	6	7	9
Selling price $USP[i]$ of the segment i	2	5	11	15	17	24

The solution is on page 700

9.4.2 Cutting and sharing: two-dimensional problems

Problem 124. Assigning staff to tasks   ○ ⁝

> *The main interest of this problem lies in the attention to pay to establishing a recurrence which reveals some peculiarities.*

Let us consider n tasks $T_1, \ldots, T_n$, to be performed in parallel, each of which can be performed with different numbers of employees (integers from 1 to k). Any employee is able to contribute to any task T_i, but once assigned to one of them, he devotes himself to it until its term and then ceases his activity. The duration of each task varies according to the staff assigned to it; $d(i, e)$ the duration of task i performed with e employees is expressed in units of time (integers from 10 to 200). For each task T_i, the duration $d(i, e)$ decreases as the staff e assigned to it increases, unless the task is not feasible for the staff assigned, in which case it is not for any higher either. As an example, with $n = 4$ and $k = 5$, we can have the table of durations below:

staff e	1	2	3	4	5
$i =$ 1	110	90	65	55	$+\infty$
2	120	90	70	50	40
3	90	70	65	60	$+\infty$
4	65	60	55	$+\infty$	$+\infty$

$+\infty$ indicating that the task cannot be performed with this workforce. Here, the tasks $1, 3$ and 4 cannot be done with five employees, and the task 4 cannot even be performed with four.

The problem to be solved consists in finding an optimal allocation of staff to each of the tasks considered in the following sense: for a fixed overall staff E available for all the tasks to be performed, e_i designating the staff assigned to the task T_i ($E = \sum_{i=1}^{n} e_i$), the sum of the durations $SD = \sum_{i=1}^{n} d(i, e_i)$ is minimum. It is assumed that the global workforce E does not make it possible to assign to each task the workforce ensuring it the minimum duration, otherwise the solution is trivial. Thus, in the previous example, we will assume $E < 16$. We call $\texttt{optsd}(i, e)$ the cost associated with the optimal assignment of e employees to the tasks T_1 to T_i.

Question 1. Give the complete recurrence for the calculation of $\texttt{optsd}(i, e)$.   124 - Q 1

Question 2. Specify the tabular structure used and the evolution of its filling.   124 - Q 2

Question 3. Show that the spatial complexity of the algorithm is in $\Theta(n \cdot E)$ and that its temporal complexity is in $\mathcal{O}(k^2 \cdot n^2)$ conditions evaluated.   124 - Q 3

Question 4. Give the result obtained for the example given above with $E = 10$.   124 - Q 4

The solution is on page 702.

Problem 125. Matrix chained product

This problem takes place in the domain of numerical calculation and it elegantly and efficiently solves the crucial question of choosing the order in which to perform a succession of matrix products. The solution relies on a two-element recurrence, with the optimal cost being in a predefined location of the tabular structure used. The ultimate goal is not so much to find the optimal cost and parentheses as to be able to use these elements to build an effective program that achieves the matrix product in question.

Let us consider the product of real matrixes $M_1 \times M_2 \times \cdots \times M_n$ which is expected to be performed with as few multiplications of real numbers as possible. The dimensions of these matrixes are described in the array $D[0 .. n]$, where $M_i[1 .. D[i-1], 1 .. D[i]]$. Let us denote by $\texttt{optprod}(i, j)$ the minimum number of multiplications to perform the product of the partial chain of matrices $(M_i \times \cdots \times M_{i+j})$. We are therefore looking for the value $\texttt{optprod}(1, n-1)$.

125 - Q 1   **Question 1.**   Let $M_1[10, 20]$, $M_2[20, 50]$, $M_3[50, 1]$ and $M_4[1, 100]$ be four matrices. Compare the number of multiplications when the operations are done in the order given by the parentheses $(M_1 \times (M_2 \times (M_3 \times M_4)))$ with the one resulting from the bracketing $((M_1 \times (M_2 \times M_3)) \times M_4)$.

125 - Q 2   **Question 2.**   Give the number of possible bracketed expressions for the product $M_1 \times \cdots \times M_n$.

125 - Q 3   **Question 3.**   Propose a recurrence for the calculation of $\mathrm{optprod}(i, j)$.

125 - Q 4   **Question 4.**   Design the program that calculates $\mathrm{optprod}(1, n)$ (and finds the corresponding optimal bracketed expression) after pointing out the tabular structure used and the progression of its filling. What is the order of growth of spatial and temporal (in number of conditions evaluated) complexity of this program? Compare the temporal complexity to the naïve method (examining all the writings with parentheses).

125 - Q 5   **Question 5.**   Apply this program to the example of the four matrices $M_1[10, 20]$, $M_2[20, 50]$, $M_3[50, 1]$ and $M_4[1, 100]$ to calculate the minimum number of multiplications necessary for the product $M_1 \times M_2 \times M_3 \times M_4$.

125 - Q 6   **Question 6.**   Specify the principle of the program returning the optimal way for performing the product (bracketed expression). Apply it to the previous example.

The solution is on page 703.

Problem 126. Cutting a wooden board   8 ⋮

> *Although apparently close to the bar cutting problem, the latter proves to be more complicated regarding the establishment of the recurrence. It is indeed necessary to specify here a two-variable recurrence.*

Let us consider a board of length N (integer value) that we want to cut into n segments of lengths $l_1, l_2, \ldots, l_n$ (integer values) with $\sum_{i=1}^{n} l_i = N$. The segments should cut the board from left to right according to their index. For example, if $N = 10$, $l_1 = 2$, $l_2 = 5$ and $l_3 = 3$, the cuts must be made at the abscissas 2 and 7 on the board.

The objective is to minimize the cost of cutting, based on the following principle: cutting a segment of size m in 2 costs m units (the segment of size m must be transported to the saw). We are looking in which order to make the cuts to minimize the total cost. In the previous example, there are only two ways to do this:

- Cut the board first at the abscissa 7, then at the abscissa 2, which costs $10 + 7 = 17$ units. This is represented by the following cutting diagram:

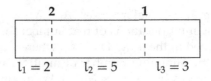

or by the bracketing $((l_1\ l_2)\ l_3)$.

- Proceed in reverse order, which costs $10 + 8 = 18$ units and is represented by the cutting diagram:

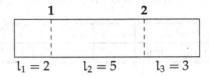

$$l_1 = 2 \qquad l_2 = 5 \qquad l_3 = 3$$

or by the bracketing $(l_1 \, (l_2 \, l_3))$.

Question 1. What is the number of possible distinct cuts? What other problem does this one bring to mind in terms of combinatorial? 126 - Q 1

Question 2. Give the recurrence which calculates the value of the optimal cut and specify the complexity of the associated procedure (which is not requested). Apply it to the example given in the statement of the problem. 126 - Q 2

Question 3. Deal with the problem (recurrence, complexity in particular) when the board is circular (a flat donut), as in the example below: 126 - Q 3

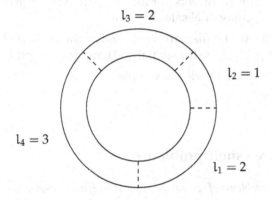

The solution is on page 705.

Problem 127. The safecrackers

> *Establishing the recurrence associated with this problem relies on a reasoning similar to that developed in problem 117 on page 640, according to which a finite nonempty list has necessarily a last element. However, taking into account a property of the problem dealt with here, it will be possible to simplify the calculations, which is the major interest of this problem.*

Thieves break into the bank vault, where safes are lined up along the wall. These thieves want to open all the safes as quickly as possible. The problem comes from the fact that the safes come from different manufacturers, so they need different times to be opened. Each safe is assigned to a thief, and the thieves are all equally skilled at the task. They decide to divide the wall into sectors made up of adjoining safes and assign a sector to each one.

Example

To illustrate, let us say that there are three thieves and nine safes, which are numbered from left to right along the wall and whose opening time, in minutes, is distributed as follows:

Safe #	1	2	3	4	5	6	7	8	9
Opening time	5	7	3	5	6	3	2	5	3

127 - Q 1　　**Question 1.**　　Consider the strategy of assigning the sector $(1, 2, 3)$ to the first thief, the sector $(4, 5, 6)$ to the second, and the sector $(7, 8, 9)$ to the third. Thieves leave after 15 minutes, the time taken by the slowest (first) thief. Point out a better solution than the one based on this strategy.

127 - Q 2　　**Question 2.**　　In general, there are N safes and p thieves. Let $etso(i)$ be the time necessary for the opening of the ith safe by any of the thieves, and let $optgtso(n, k)$ the optimal global time, that is say the minimum time necessary for the opening of n safes $(1 \leqslant k \leqslant N)$ by k thieves $(1 \leqslant k \leqslant p)$. What is the value of $optgtso(n, k)$ when: (i) $n = 1$ (there is only one safe to open), (ii) $k = 1$ (only one thief must open all safes), (iii) $k > n$ (the number of thieves is greater than the number of safes to be opened) and (iv) $k \leqslant n$?

127 - Q 3　　**Question 3.**　　Deduce the recurrence for the calculation of $optgtso(N, p)$, the minimum time necessary for the opening of N safes by p thieves.

127 - Q 4　　**Question 4.**　　Describe the tabular structure used by the associated algorithm, as well as the strategy for its filling. What are the spatial and temporal complexities of this algorithm?

127 - Q 5　　**Question 5.**　　Deal with the previous example.

The solution is on page 707.

Problem 128.　Three shelf problems

> *In this problem, three problems of storing books in a shelf are considered, with different storage constraints depending on whether the number of shelves or the height or width of the shelf is set.*

A shelf is used to store books of various thicknesses and heights. The depth of the books, as well as that of the shelf, does not play a role here, so they are ignored afterward. The shelf consists of one or more spokes of fixed or variable height having a certain width, on which the books are placed. To simplify, it is assumed that the boards which form the spokes have zero thickness. The top spoke is topped with a board that defines the total height of the shelf.

Different storage problems will be considered according to the parameters set at the start (number and height(s) of shelves, width of the shelf, order of books in particular). In the first part, there are N books $B_1, \ldots, B_N$ of different heights to be arranged in this order, a given width of shelf W, and we look for the number of shelves (and the minimum total height) of the shelf for storing all the books. In the next part, we try again to arrange all the books $B_1, \ldots, B_N$ in this order, in a fixed number K of shelves. These have the same height, as well as the books, and we are looking for the minimum width of the shelf (and its spokes). In the third and last part, there are N books $B_1, \ldots, B_N$ of the same height and a shelf with K spokes of given width W. The problem here is to determine the maximum number of books that can be stored while complying with their order.

Minimum height shelf

There are N books $B_1, \ldots, B_N$ to be stored on the shelf under the following constraints:

- the order in which the books are arranged is fixed: B_1 must be at the extreme left of the top spoke, B_2 is next to B_1 or, failing that, at the extreme left of the bottom spoke, and so on,

- the shelf (and thus each of its spokes) has a fixed width W, but the number of shelves is adjustable as well as the height of each shelf,

- each book B_i is characterized by its height h_i and its thickness t_i.

With books of thickness t_i and height h_i as follows:

i	1	2	3	4	5
t_i	3	3	2	3	2
h_i	5	7	9	3	10

the figure below gives two different ways to store $N = 5$ books on a shelf of width $W = 10$.

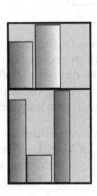 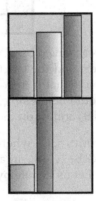

The overall height of the first shelf is $7 + 10 = 17$, that of the second $9 + 10 = 19$.

The problem is figuring out how to arrange the spokes of the shelf so that it has a minimum overall height (regardless of the number of spokes).

Question 1. Let us denote by hgmin(i) the minimum overall height of a shelf of width W on which the books $B_i, \ldots, B_N$ ($1 \leqslant i \leqslant N$) are stored, with the convention hgmin(N + 1) = 0 for the height of the shelf in which we do not put any books. Let us denote by sh(i, j) the height of the spoke where the series of books starting with B_i and ending with B_j (with $j \geqslant i$) are stored. We have:

$$
sh(i, j) = \begin{cases} \max_{k \in i..j} (h_k) & \text{if } \sum_{k=i}^{j} t_k \leqslant W \\ +\infty & \text{otherwise.} \end{cases}
$$

Find a descending (or backward) recurrence relation defining hgmin(i).

Question 2. Deduce the characteristics of a dynamic programming algorithm to calculate hgmin(1), the time complexity of which will be given.

128 - Q 1

128 - Q 2

128 - Q 3   **Question 3.**   Apply this algorithm to the following example:

i	1	2	3	4	5	6
t_i	1	2	1	1	2	1
h_i	1	2	5	4	3	1

with $W = 4$.

Minimum width shelf

The objective is now to store all the books $B_1, \ldots, B_N$ in a shelf with K (fixed) adjustable spokes of width W. The order in which the books are arranged is imposed as before (B_1 must be at the extreme left of the top spoke, B_2 is tight to the right of B_1 or at the extreme left of the shelf of the below, etc.). Each book B_i is characterized by its thickness t_i, and, without loss of generality, all the books are assumed to be of the same height.

We are looking for the smallest possible value W which allows us to store all the books $B_1, \ldots, B_N$. In other words, it is a matter of partitioning $B_1, \ldots, B_N$ into K sections so that the width of the largest of the sections is as small as possible. For example, with $K = 3$ spokes and $N = 6$ books whose widths are as follows:

i	1	2	3	4	5	6
t_i	5	3	4	1	3	2

the optimal storage is achieved by placing the first book on the top spoke, the second and third books on the next and the last three on the bottom spoke. The width of the widest spoke is equal to 7. Note that if the order of the books did not matter, a storage on three shelves of width 6 would be possible, for example by putting the books B_1 and B_4 on the first spoke, the books B_2 and B_5 on the second and, finally, the books B_3 and B_6 on the last.

Let us denote by $wdmin(n, k)$, where $1 \leqslant n \leqslant N$ the minimum width which allows to store the n first books $B_1, \ldots, B_n$ in a shelf made up of k spokes (which are therefore of width $wdmin(n, k)$). Let us denote by $st(i, j) = t_i + \cdots + t_j$ the sum of the thicknesses of the books $B_i, \ldots, B_j$.

128 - Q 4   **Question 4.**   Prove that, for any n, with $1 \leqslant n \leqslant N$, we have $wdmin(n, 1) = st(1, n)$.

128 - Q 5   **Question 5.**   Consider a situation where there are n books and k spokes, with $n \leqslant k$. Prove that it is possible to have a single book per spoke. Establish that therefore $wdmin(n, k) = max(\{t_1, \ldots, t_n\})$.

128 - Q 6   **Question 6.**   Let us now consider an optimal arrangement of n books on k spokes, with $n > k$, the last spoke containing the books $B_m, \ldots, B_n$. Prove that either $wdmin(n, k) = wdmin(m - 1, k - 1)$, or $wdmin(n, k) = st(m, n)$.

128 - Q 7   **Question 7.**   Deduce from the previous questions a recurrence relation to calculate $wdmin(N, K)$.

128 - Q 8   **Question 8.**   Specify the progression of the calculation carried out by the related dynamic programming algorithm and prove that its time complexity is in $\mathcal{O}(K \cdot N^2)$.

128 - Q 9   **Question 9.**   Deal with the previous example, where $N = 6$ (books) and $K = 3$ (spokes).

A maximum number of books on a shelf

We have a shelf of width W composed of K spokes of the same height (W and K fixed) and of N books $B_1, \ldots, B_N$ of thickness $t_1, \ldots, t_N$, all the same height (slightly less than the spokes of the shelf). The books are numbered from 1 to N, in alphabetical order of the authors.

Let us suppose that all the books cannot fit on the shelf (especially if $\sum_{i=1}^{N} t_i > K \cdot W$) and a maximum of M of books among the N must be stored in the shelf, preserving their alphabetical order. For example, if there are four books of widths given below:

i	1	2	3	4
t_i	3	3	2	2

and $W = 5$, $K = 2$, only three ($M = 3$) out of the four books can be stored in one of the following ways:

- B_1 on the first spoke, B_2 and B_3 on the second,
- B_1 on the first spoke, B_2 and B_4 on the second,
- B_1 on the first spoke, B_3 and B_4 on the second,
- B_2 on the first spoke, B_3 and B_4 on the second,
- B_1 and B_3 on the first spoke, B_4 on the second,
- B_2 and B_3 on the first spoke, B_4 on the second.

However, the total thickness of the books is 10, and if it was possible to change their order, we could put them all away by putting for example B_1 and B_3 on the first spoke, B_2 and B_4 on the second.

Let us denote by $wdnec(i, j)$ the minimum width necessary for the storage of an ordered subset of j books among i books. If these j books are distributed over several spokes, it is necessary to take into account in $wdnec(i, j)$ any space lost at the end of the first rows (but not the one lost on the last). Continuing with the previous example, the value 7 is obtained for $wdnec(4, 3)$ with the last two placements in the list above.

Question 10. It is first assumed that there is only one spoke in the shelf ($K = 1$). What is the combinatorial of the problem *a priori*?   128 - Q 10

Question 11. Give a recurrence formula to calculate $wdnec(i, j)$. Deduce the principle   128 - Q 11 of the associated dynamic programming algorithm, the way of determining the sought value M and the temporal complexity of this algorithm. Deal with the previous example with the four books of thicknesses 3, 3, 2 and 2 with $W = 5$.

Question 12. Let us now consider the case where $K = 2$. Give a recurrence to calculate   128 - Q 12 $wdnec(i, j)$. Deduce the principle of the associated dynamic programming algorithm, the way of determining the sought value M and the temporal complexity of this algorithm.

Question 13. Write an algorithm for any value of K ($K \geqslant 1$). Specify how to determine   128 - Q 13 the desired value M. Give the temporal and spatial complexities of this algorithm. Apply it with $W = 5$ and $K = 3$ to the eight books whose thickness is given below:

i	1	2	3	4	5	6	7	8
t_i	3	3	1	2	4	2	3	4

The solution is on page 710.

Problem 129. Choosing skis   8 :

> *This problem deals with an optimal resource allocation problem with two neighboring "opti-*
> *mality criteria". The key to optimality lies in a simple property of the function of assigning*
> *pairs of skis to skiers. In the particular case where there are as many skiers as there are pairs*
> *of skis, it turns out that the solution can be reached by a greedy process (see Chapter 7). In*
> *the general case of a resolution by dynamic programming, a simplification of the calculations*
> *is studied.*

A ski school has m pairs of skis to be assigned to n skiers, with $m \geqslant n \geqslant 1$. One pair of skis—and only one—must be assigned to each skier and the objective is to maximize the global satisfaction of the skiers, knowing that a skier is all the more satisfied as the length of length of the skis assigned to him is close to his height.

More formally, let $h_1, \ldots, h_n$ be the sizes (heights) of the skiers and $s_1, \ldots, s_m$ the lengths of the skis. The goal is to find an optimal injective function $asf \in 1 .. n \rightarrow 1 .. m$. It must maximize the value of the global satisfaction associated with the assignment defined by asf, thus minimize the sum of the deviations (in absolute value):

$$sde(n, m, asf) = \sum_{k=1}^{n} |h_k - s_{asf(k)}|.$$

Without loss of generality, it is assumed that both lengths of skis and heights of skiers are ordered: $s_1 \leqslant \cdots \leqslant s_m$ and $h_1 \leqslant \cdots \leqslant h_n$.

129 - Q 1   **Question 1.**   Give the combinatorial *a priori* of this problem.

129 - Q 2   **Question 2.**   Prove that a monotonic function asf makes it always possible to reach an optimal assignment.

129 - Q 3   **Question 3.**   Deduce that, in the presence of as many skiers as there are pairs of skis, a greedy process (to be explained) makes it possible to solve the problem.

129 - Q 4   **Question 4.**   Let $optasg(i, j)$ be the sum of the deviations (in absolute value) corresponding to the optimal assignment that makes use of skis numbered from 1 to j to equip skiers from ranks 1 to i, where $1 \leqslant i \leqslant j$. Either the pair of skis of rank j is assigned to a skier, or it is not used. Prove that, in the first case, the pair of ski numbered j must be assigned to skier i.

129 - Q 5   **Question 5.**   Deduce the complete recurrence defining $optasg(i, j)$.

129 - Q 6   **Question 6.**   Give the principle of a dynamic programming algorithm implementing this calculation. What are its spatial and temporal complexities (number of conditions evaluated)? Specify how the (one) optimal function asf can be determined.

129 - Q 7   **Question 7.**   Solve the problem with $m = 5, n = 3$, skis of lengths $s_1 = 158, s_2 = 179, s_3 = 200, s_4 = 203, s_5 = 213$ and skiers of heights $h_1 = 170, h_2 = 190, h_3 = 210$.

129 - Q 8   **Question 8.**   Propose a strategy filling the array associated with $optasg$ only partly.

129 - Q 9   **Question 9.**   A new optimality criterion is now considered. The objective is still to find an optimal injective function $asf \in 1 .. n \rightarrow 1 .. m$, but in the sense of minimizing the largest deviation between the height of the skier and the length of the pair of skis assigned to him,

that is:

$$\mathrm{lgdev}(n, m, asf) = \max_{k \in 1..n} (|h_k - s_{asf(k)}|).$$

Is it possible to adapt the previous solution?

The solution is on page 716.

Problem 130. The egg problem (2)

This problem returns to the problem dealt with in problem 114, page 474, in chapter "Divide and conquer". However, it is strengthened here by requiring that the guarantee of determining egg resistance be achieved with the least amount of drops in the worst case. After having examined two approaches based on recurrences, we compare them to each other and to the "Divide and conquer" solution called radixchotomy. *Finally, a link is established between the problem of dropping eggs and that of identifying any number of an interval of integers by a given number of questions and a limited number of negative answers.*

Let us first recall the problem *Egg1*, presented in problem 114, page 474, in chapter "Divide and conquer". We have a set of identical eggs and we want to know their resistance, that is to say the height (number f of floors) from which they break if we drop them by the window of a building. An egg that has not broken can be reused, whereas if it has broken it is permanently discarded. Given a building of n (n ⩾ 1) floors and an initial number k (k ⩾ 1) of eggs, the value of f is searched. If the eggs do not break even when dropped from the top floor, the value of f is set to n + 1, which is equivalent to considering that the eggs necessarily break with a building having a floor of more than really. One of the objectives of the problem 114, page 474, was also to limit the number of drops for n and k given, while guaranteeing the determination of f since the number of drops was the elementary operation considered.

The problem *Egg2* very similar to the previous one is now studied. We always want to guarantee the determination of f for a given pair (n, k), but with a minimum number of egg drops *in the worst case*. Thus, after having dropped one of the eggs available from the fourth of the ten floors of a building, we will consider the greatest number of drops necessary for the exploration of the first three floors on the one hand, of the last six of the other, depending on whether or not the egg is broken. In addition, for the sake of simplification, the process is extended to the case of buildings of zero size (n = 0).

A "direct" approach

Question 1. Let nbdmin(i, j) be the minimum number of drops necessary to determine f in the *worst case*, knowing that we are provided with i eggs and that the building has j floors. Prove that nbdmin can be defined by the recurrence:

130 - Q 1

nbdmin(i, 0) = 0	1 ⩽ i ⩽ k
nbdmin(i, 1) = 1	1 ⩽ i ⩽ k
nbdmin(1, j) = j	1 < j ⩽ n

$$\left| \; nbdmin(i,j) = 1 + \min_{p \in 1..j} \left(\max \left(\left\{ \begin{array}{l} nbdmin(i-1, p-1), \\ nbdmin(i, j-p) \end{array} \right\} \right) \right) \right. \qquad \left\{ \begin{array}{c} 1 < i \leqslant k \\ \textbf{and} \\ 1 < j \leqslant n \end{array} \right. .$$

130 - Q 2   **Question 2.**   Propose the principle of the algorithm *EggDyn1* stemming canonically from the previous recurrence, storing the values of $nbdmin$ in the array $NBDM[1..k, 0..n]$. What is the temporal complexity?

130 - Q 3   **Question 3.**   Use this algorithm to calculate $nbdmin(3, 8)$. Check that $nbdmin(i, j)$ is increasing on j in this example, and prove it in the genaral case. Deduce the principle of the algorithm *EggDyn2* calculating $nbdmin(k, n)$ in $\mathcal{O}(k \cdot n \cdot \log_2(n))$. What can be concluded about the interest for the algorithm *EggDyn1*?

130 - Q 4   **Question 4.**   In order to determine a sequence of drops associated with any value $NBDM[i, j]$ (or any pair (i, j)), such that $i \geqslant 1, j \geqslant 0$), NBDM is doubled with the array $PTH[1..k, 0..n]$ in which $PTH[i, j]$ is equal to:

- the (one) value of p associated with the optimal value $NBDM[i, j]$, for $2 \leqslant i \leqslant k$ and $2 \leqslant j \leqslant n$,
- 1 for $j = 1$ and $1 \leqslant i \leqslant k$ on the one hand, $1 < j \leqslant n$ and $i = 1$ on the other hand.

Remark

Cells $PTH[i, 0]$ have no interest since then there are no floors left to examine.

Explain how to use the array PTH for determining a sequence of drops corresponding to a given pair (i, j).

Subsequently, let us take the table $PTH[1..3, 0..8]$ below:

j	0	1	2	3	4	5	6	7	8
i = 1	/	1	1	1	1	1	1	1	1
2	/	1	1	2	1	2	3	1	2
3	/	1	1	2	1	2	3	4	1

Give the sequence of drops for: i) $k = 2, n = 8, f = 5$, ii) $k = 2, n = 6, f = 3$, iii) $k = 2, n = 4, f = 5$, iv) $k = 2, n = 5, f = 1$.

A solution relying on a "close" problem

130 - Q 5   **Question 5.**   Consider now the problem *Egg3* aiming at the calculation of the maximum height of a building (expressed as a number of floors) $bhmax(i, j)$, for which the value of f can be identified *for sure* with at most i eggs and j drops. Specify the recurrence calculating $bhmax(k, nbd)$. What is the difference between this one and the one proposed for the problem *Egg2*? Calculate the value $bhmax(4, 12)$.

130 - Q 6   **Question 6.**   Elaborate on the coherence of the values $nbdmin(i, j)$ (or $NBDM[i, j]$) and $bhmax(i, l)$ (or $BHM[i, l]$), where i is the number of eggs, j the number of floors of the building and nd is the number of drops.

130 - Q 7   **Question 7.**   Show how to use $bhmax$ to solve the problem *Egg2* (identification of f *for sure* with a minimum number of drops at worst with k eggs for a building of n floors).

Specify the principle of the algorithm *Egg3* carrying out the calculation and give its time complexity.

Question 8. Specify the principle of the algorithm that reconstitutes the sequence of drops associated with k eggs and a building of n floors from the array BH. 130 - Q 8

Question 9. Apply this algorithm with the following data: (i) $k = 2, n = 9, f = 5$ and (ii) $k = 2, n = 7, f = 3$, these two cases corresponding to those of question 4, page 658. What can be observed about the drop sequences produced? Apply it also to $k = 3, n = 42, f = 4$. 130 - Q 9

An alternative calculation of $bhmax(i, j)$

Question 10. Prove the following property: 130 - Q 10

$$bhmax(i, j) = \sum_{p=0}^{i} C_j^p \quad 1 \leqslant j \leqslant n, 1 \leqslant i \leqslant k.$$

Question 11. Deduce the principle of the algorithm *EggDyn4* calculating the minimum number of drops *at worst* with k eggs and a building of n floors (in the sense of the problem *Egg2*) whose time complexity is in $\Theta(k \cdot \log_2(n))$, knowing that on the one hand the property $C_n^{p+1} = (C_n^p \cdot (n - p))/(p + 1)$ holds for $0 \leqslant p \leqslant n$ and $n \geqslant 0$, on the other hand the inequality $bhmax(i, r) \geqslant hmax(i, r - 1)$ is valid for any $r \geqslant 1$ (which stems from $C_r^p \geqslant C_{r-1}^p$). 130 - Q 11

Question 12. Specify the phase intended for the reconstitution of the sequence of drops associated with $bhmax(i, j)$. Give its complexity and compare it to that of the procedure given for question 8. 130 - Q 12

Synthesis: choice of a method

Question 13. The different methods of solving the egg drop problem are now compared: DaC approach called *radixchotomy* in problem 114, page 474, and algorithms based on dynamic programming *EggDyn2*, *EggDyn3* or *EggDyn4*. Discuss the choice of one of these approaches (the aspect related to the calculation of the sequence of drops can be ignored). 130 - Q 13

Question 14. Consider the configurations $k = 2, n = 3, 1 \leqslant f \leqslant 4$. Give the sequence of drops obtained on the one hand by means of the array PTH shown in question 4, for the algorithm *EggDyn2*, on the other hand with *radixchotomy*. What can be concluded regarding the number of drops necessary for the determination of f? 130 - Q 14

Exhaustive identification of elements of an interval

Question 15. The objective is now to identify any number x of the interval 1 .. N with at most Q questions of type "is x greater than v?" and at most NA negative answers. How does this problem, called *IntervIdent*, relate to the problem *Egg3*? When does it admit (at least) one solution? When this is the case, how is the sequence of questions answering the problem identified? 130 - Q 15

Question 16. The solution to the problem *IntervIdent* will be represented by a binary tree where each node is label by the value v of the question asked and each leaf is the identified value. Complete (label) the partial tree below for $N = 299, Q = 12, NA = 3$, the root corresponding to the first question to be asked. 130 - Q 16

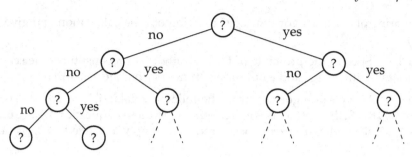

130 - Q 17 **Question** 17.   If the interval considered is no longer $1..299$, but $1..296$, what is the first question to ask?

130 - Q 18 **Question** 18.   Characterize the lengths of intervals for which the query tree is unique.

The solution is on page 719.

9.4.3 Graphs and trees

Several problems related to graphs and trees are now dealt with. Relevant definitions and notions are given in sections 1.5 on page 22, and 1.6 on page 27.

Problem 131. Best path in a conform graph   8 •

> *This problem addresses the problem of traversing a specific weighted directed graph: a circuit free graph with only one entry point and one exit point. We are looking for a path of minimum value between these two vertices. The interest of the problem lies in the absence of restrictions on the valuation of the graph, but also in the low complexity of the solution which is constructed.*

Let G be a directed nonweighted graph with the following characteristics:

- the graph has no loop,
- vertices (or nodes) of G are labelled by integers from 1 to n,
- if the arc (i, j) exists in G, then $i < j$.

Such a graph G is said to be "with conform numbering" or also "conform".

131 - Q 1 **Question** 1.   Prove that a conform graph G is circuit free and that it does have *at least* one entry point (vertex without predecessor) and one exit point (vertex without successor).

In the following, we consider a directed weighted graph $GV = (N, V, P)$ having in addition the following properties:

- the vertex numbered 1 is an entry point and the vertex numbered n is an exit point,
- any other vertex has at least one predecessor and one successor,
- each arc has a value *a real number*, GV being represented by a n-row, n-column matrix MGV, where the value of the element $MGV[i, j]$ corresponds to that of the arc (i, j) ($+\infty$ is the conventional value used if this arc does not exist).

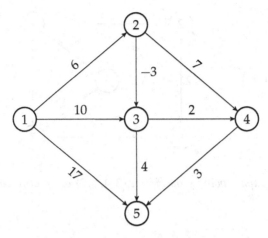

Fig. 9.4 – A conform graph.

Question 2. Give the recurrence for the calculation of the number of paths from 1 to n 131 - Q 2
in a weighted graph GV complying with the previous conditions, $nbpth(j)$ standing for
the number of paths from 1 to j. Specify the value of $nbpth(5)$ for the graph of figure 9.4.

Question 3. Give the characteristics (recurrence, tabular structure, filling strategy) of   131 - Q 3
a dynamic programming algorithm that calculates the value of the (one) minimum value
path between the vertices 1 and n. What are its time and space complexities?

Question 4. Deal with the example of the graph in figure 9.4.   131 - Q 4

The solution is on page 730.

Problem 132. Best paths from a source

> *Bellman-Ford's algorithm is one of the great classics of dynamic programming algorithms*
> *relating to directed weighted graphs, of which there are many variants. It deals with a more*
> *general problem than the previous one, since here the value of the optimal paths between a*
> *given origin vertex and any other vertex is searched. Its main advantage is that it is less re-*
> *strictive than Dijkstra's one (see problem 78, page 345) as to the values carried by the arcs. In*
> *this problem, we take sides for the construction of an algorithm based on dynamic program-*
> *ming. Other algorithms, more efficient or solving a "similar" problem, are also discussed.*

In the following, the graph $WG = (N, V, P)$ considered is valued (on $\mathbb{R}$), has no loop
and its vertices are labeled from 1 to n. The vertex 1 plays a special role and it is called
source and it is denoted by sc. The value of the (one) path of minimum value between sc
and any other vertex of the graph WG ($+\infty$ if there is no path) is searched. The possible
presence of a circuit of positive value does not interfere, since a path of minimum value
cannot include such a circuit (there is a path without this circuit of lesser value). It is the
same for a circuit of negative value whose vertices are not reachable starting from sc as in
the graph of figure 9.5.

Here, there is no path from vertex 1 to vertices $3, 4$ and 5 and the value of the optimal
path from 1 to $3, 4$ and 5 is $+\infty$. The only problematic case is that of a circuit of negative
value accessible from sc, since then the value of the optimal path from sc to any vertex of

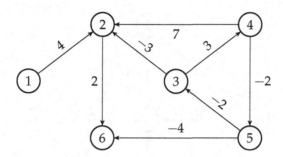

Fig. 9.5 – Example of a graph involving the circuit $\langle 3, 4, 5, 3 \rangle$ of negative value (-1) not accessible from 1.

the circuit is asymptotically $-\infty$ (case occurring by replacing the arc $(5,6)$ by $(6,5)$ in the graph of figure 9.5.

For the moment, the graph WG is supposed to be free of circuit(s) of negative value accessible from the source. If there is (at least) one elementary path from the source to another vertex v_{i_p}, there is (at least) a path of minimum value from sc to v_{i_p}. Let $\text{pth}_1 = \langle sc, v_{i_1}, \ldots, v_{i_p} \rangle$ $(p \geqslant 1)$ be an optimal path from sc to v_{i_p}, then $\text{pth}_2 = \langle sc, v_{i_1}, \ldots, v_{i_{p-1}} \rangle$ is an optimal path from sc to $v_{i_{p-1}}$ (Bellman's optimality principle) which has the property of having an arc less than pth_1. From this observation, comes the idea of defining a recurrence relating to the number of arcs of the optimal paths. We denote by $\text{valpthvmin}(v, i)$ the value of (an) optimal path from the source to the vertex v comprising at most i arcs.

132 - Q 1   **Question 1.**   Give the recurrence formula defining $\text{valpthvmin}(s, i)$.

First version of the algorithm

132 - Q 2   **Question 2.**   A weighted graph WG is considered, with n vertices and m arcs. It is represented by the table of its arcs $\text{AWG}[1..m, 1..2]$ and the vector of its values $\text{VWG}[1..m]$. $\text{AWG}[p, 1]$ is the origin of arc p and $\text{AWG}[p, 2]$ its end, whereas $\text{VWG}[p]$ is the value of arc p. Deduce the version Bellman-Ford's algorithm that uses the tabular structure $\text{VPTHVMIN}[1..n, 1..2]$ instead of $\text{VPTHVMIN}[1..n, 0..n-1]$. Specify its time complexity in number of conditions evaluated.

132 - Q 3   **Question 3.**   Apply this algorithm to the two graphs of figure 9.6.

132 - Q 4   **Question 4.**   Give the principle of a solution that makes it possible to reconstruct the (one) optimal path from the source sc to any other vertex. Use the graph WG_1 of figure 9.6 to illustrate this principle.

Variant with "on the spot" calculation

132 - Q 5   **Question 5.**   The following algorithm is envisaged:

    1. **constants**
    2. $n \in \mathbb{N}_1$ **and** $n = \ldots$ **and** $m \in \mathbb{N}_1$ **and** $m = \ldots$ **and**
    3. $\text{AWG} \in 1..m \times 1..2 \to \mathbb{N}_1$ **and** $\text{AWG} = [\ldots]$ **and** $\text{VWG} \in 1..m \to \mathbb{R}$ **and**
    4. $\text{VWG} = [\ldots]$ **and** $\text{NegativeCircuitFree(WG)}$
    5.   /% *AWG is the matrix associated with the arcs of the graph WG considered and VWG is the vector giving their values; the arc (t, s) of value v is*

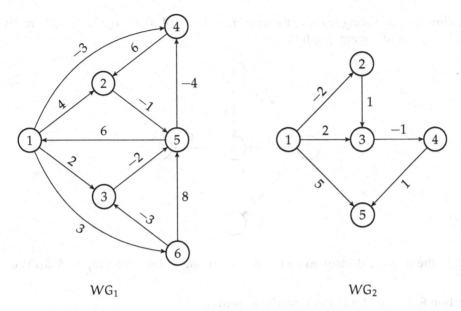

WG_1 WG_2

Fig. 9.6 – Two graphs for question 3.

represented by $AWG[k, 1] = t$, $AWG[k, 2] = s$, $VWG[k] = v$; VPTHVMIN
is the vector of the values of minimum value paths from the source (vertex 1) to any other vertex; NegativeCircuitFree(WG) indicates that WG
is free from any circuit of negative value %/

6. **variables**
7.   VPTHVMIN $\in 1..n \to \mathbb{R}$
8. **begin**
9.   VPTHVMIN[1] $\leftarrow 0$;
10.   **for** v **ranging** $2..n$ **do**
11.   VPTHVMIN[v] $\leftarrow +\infty$
12.   **end for;**
13.   **for** i **ranging** $1..n-1$ **do**
14.   /% calculation (update) of the value of the minimum value path for any
           vertex other than the source (1) %/
15.   **for** $a \in 1..m$ **do**
16.   VPTHVMIN[$AWG[a, 2]$] $\leftarrow$
17. $\min\left(\left\{ \begin{array}{l} \text{VPTHVMIN}[AWG[a, 2]], \\ \text{VPTHVMIN}[AWG[a, 1]] + VWG[a] \end{array} \right\}\right)$
18.   **end for**
19.   **end for;**
20.   write(VPTHVMIN)
21. **end**

What is the main advantage of this version?

Question 6.   Explain why this algorithm also solves the problem of minimum value   132 - Q 6
paths from the source (vertex 1) to any other vertex. Check that with the graphs WG_1 and
WG_2 by taking in order the arcs $(5, 1)$, $(1, 2)$, $(4, 2)$, $(1, 3)$, $(6, 3)$, $(1, 4)$, $(5, 4)$, $(2, 5)$, $(3, 5)$,
$(6, 5)$, $(1, 6)$ for WG_1 and $(1, 2)$, $(1, 3)$, $(2, 3)$, $(3, 4)$, $(1, 5)$, $(4, 5)$ for WG_2.

132 - Q 7   **Question 7.**   By taking in order the arcs $(1,2)$, $(3,2)$, $(4,3)$, $(1,4)$, $(5,4)$, $(1,5)$, apply this algorithm to the following graph WG_3:

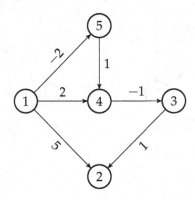

What are the comments inspired by the use of this algorithm with graphs WG_1, WG_2 and WG_3?

132 - Q 8   **Question 8.**   Could this algorithm be improved?

132 - Q 9   **Question 9.**   Compare the interpretation of the value VPTHVMIN[s] after its computation at step j to its counterpart in the algorithm given in response to question 2.

Additional aspects

132 - Q 10   **Question 10.**   How could these algorithms be completed so that they can also return a Boolean specifying whether or not there is (at least) one circuit of negative value accessible from the source?

132 - Q 11   **Question 11.**   How to solve the problem of finding the (one) minimum value path between any vertex and a given vertex called *well* (as opposed to source)?

132 - Q 12   **Question 12.**   What about the problem of finding the (one) maximum value path from a given source to any vertex?

The solution is in page 731.

Problem 133. Best paths algebras   ⠶

> *Floyd's algorithm is also one of the great classics of dynamic programming algorithms relating to directed weighted graphs. It concerns a more general tracking problem than that of the previous problem, since here optimal paths are searched for all pairs of vertices. The interest of this problem is twofold: (i) Floyd's algorithm is built as an adaptation of Roy-Warshall's algorithm, which calculates the transitive closure of a graph (but does not relate to dynamic programming strictly speaking since there is no search for an optimum) and (ii) it serves as the basis for a family of algorithms for calculating optimal paths in various senses: the shortest, the longest, that of minimum (or maximum) probability or capacity, etc.*

Preliminary: existence of paths, transitive closure and Roy-Warshall's algorithm

We consider a non weighted graph $G = (N, V)$ where:

- there is no loop,
- vertices are labeled from 1 to n.

We are first interested in the calculation of the transitive closure G^+ of G, i.e. the graph G^+ such that the existence of the path $\langle x * y \rangle$ in G yields the arc (x, y) in G^+. Roy-Warshall's algorithm performing this calculation relies on a recurrence bearing on the highest number of the *intermediary* vertices appearing in the paths constructed at a given step. At step i, the arc (x, y) is inserted in G^+ if the two arcs (x, i) and (i, y) are present in G^+. This expresses the fact that if there is in G a path from x to i and a path from i to y whose intermediary vertices have a number at most equal to $(i - 1)$, there is actually the path $\langle x * i * y \rangle$ with intermediary vertices of number not exceeding i. Denoting by $path(x, y, i)$ the predicate representing the existence of such a path in G, the recurrence is;

$$
\begin{array}{ll}
path(x, y, 0) = (x, y) \in V & 1 \leqslant x \leqslant n \text{ and } 1 \leqslant y \leqslant n \\[2mm]
path(x, y, i) = \left(\begin{array}{c} path(x, y, i-1) \text{ or} \\ \left(\begin{array}{c} path(x, i, i-1) \text{ and} \\ path(i, y, i-1) \end{array} \right) \end{array} \right) &
\left\{ \begin{array}{l} 1 \leqslant i \leqslant n \text{ and} \\ 1 \leqslant x \leqslant n \text{ and} \\ 1 \leqslant y \leqslant n \end{array} \right. .
\end{array}
$$

Question 1. Prove that this recurrence takes into account ("sees") all the *elementary* 133 - Q 1 paths and circuits, even if it is limited to their origins and ends.

Question 2. Concerning *non-elementary* paths, some are "seen" but their recognition 133 - Q 2 depends on the numbering of the vertices. The graphs G_1 and G_2:

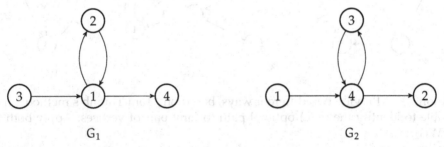

$$G_1 \qquad\qquad\qquad\qquad G_2$$

are identical, except for the numbering of the vertices. Explain why the path $\langle 3, 1, 2, 1, 4 \rangle$ "is seen" in G_1, but not its counterpart $\langle 1, 4, 3, 4, 2 \rangle$ in G_2.

Question 3. Write the code of the algorithm canonically derived from this recurrence, 133 - Q 3 by adopting the matrix representation MG (respectively MG^+) of the graph $G = (N, V)$ (respectively $G^+ = (N, V^+)$). What are the spatial and temporal complexities by taking the access to graphs G and G^+ as the elementary operation?

Question 4. Since the calculation of $path(x, y, i)$ uses only elements of last index $(i-1)$, 133 - Q 4 two two-dimensional arrays $1 .. n \times 1 .. n$, can be used, one relating to i and the other to $(i - 1)$. But, in fact, Roy-Warshall's algorithm only uses one $1 .. n \times 1 .. n$ array and it performs an "on the spot" computation. Explain why such a structure is sufficient for the calculation and establish the new recurrence resulting from this simplification.

133 - Q 5   **Question 5.**   Temporal complexity can also be improved by getting rid of the disjunction present in the recurrence and by noting that the absence of a path from x to i induces that of a path from x to y passing through i. Give the final Roy-Warshall's algorithm taking into account all the preceding remarks and specify its spatial and temporal complexities (in number of accesses to graphs).

Floyd's algorithm

The problem solved by Floyd's algorithm is the computation of the value of the (one) optimal path, i.e. of minimum value for any pair of vertices of a directed weighted graph $WG = (N, V, P)$. In other words, if in WG there are several paths originating in v_i and ending in v_j, the value of the one of least value for the pair (v_i, v_j) is kept.

133 - Q 6   **Question 6.**   The principle of Floyd's algorithm consists in taking advantage of Roy-Warshall's algorithm, through an adaptation, as long as the problem can be solved in the space of elementary paths. What about the presence of circuits of positive, zero or negative value in the graph WG?

133 - Q 7   **Question 7.**   Propose a recurrence for the calculation of the value of the (one) optimal path for any pair of vertices (x, y) of the weighted graph WG with no problematic circuits.

133 - Q 8   **Question 8.**   Deduce the code of Floyd's algorithm. specify its spatial and temporal complexities.

133 - Q 9   **Question 9.**   Apply this algorithm to the graphs WG_1 and WG_2 given further. Apply it also to the graph WG_3 below by releasing the precondition on negative value circuits. In this context, how to characterize the presence of negative value circuit(s)?

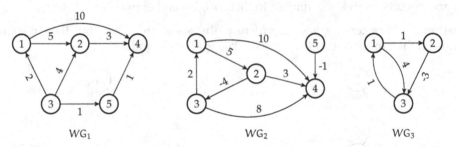

WG_1 $\qquad\qquad\qquad\qquad$ WG_2 $\qquad\qquad\qquad\qquad$ WG_3

133 - Q 10   **Question 10.**   Provide two different ways, based on "Tom Thumb's method", making it possible to identify the (one) optimal path for any pair of vertices. Apply both to the graph WG_2.

Path algebras

An adaptation of Roy-Warshall's algorithm has been dealt with and some others "of interest" can be imagined. By analogy with Floyd's algorithm, such an adaptation is possible under two conditions:

- The problem considered consists in searching for an optimal value relative to all the pairs of vertices of a weighted graph. This makes it possible to answer the problem posed for specific pairs of vertices, for example: (i) from a given vertex to any other vertex, (ii) from any vertex $x \neq v_k$ to a given vertex v_k or (iii) from a given vertex v_i to another given vertex v_j.
- The problem can be solved in the space of elementary paths, i.e. no circuit is likely to impair the result delivered by the program resulting from the adaptation.

In Roy-Warshall's algorithm, paths are "manipulated" by means of two operations, the disjunction (logical "or") and the conjunction (logical "and"), as illustrated by the recurrence given in the statement of the problem. These operators have been replaced in Floyd's algorithm by two others (minimum and addition) which allow the appropriate computation of minimum value paths. We speak of a *path algebra* associated with the problem treated.

Question 11.   For each of the following problems, discuss the possibility of adapting   133 - Q 11
Roy-Warshall's algorithm by specifying: (1) the pair of operators applying to paths, (2) the initialization of the graph used to calculate the desired result, and (3) the types of circuit causing problem (if any):

- the value of the maximum value path for any pair of vertices,
- the length of the shortest path for any pair of vertices (the length of a path is defined as the number of its arcs),
- the length of the longest path for any pair of vertices,
- knowing that the value associated with an arc represents a probability value and that the value of the path corresponding to the concatenation of several arcs is the product of probabilities attached to them,
  (a) the probability of the minimum probability path for any pair of vertices,
  (b) the probability of the maximum probability path for any pair of vertices,
- knowing that the value associated with an arc represents a capacity value (the capacity of a path is that of its minimum capacity arc),
  (a) the capacity of the minimum probability path for any pair of vertices,
  (b) the capacity of the maximum probability path for any pair of vertices.

Question 12.   Give the principle of the algorithm calculating the number of paths for   133 - Q 12
any pair of vertices, then its code.

Two variants of the minimum value path problem

Question 13.   For any pair of vertices, we want to calculate the value of the (one) path   133 - Q 13
of minimum value not involving the *intermediate vertex* of number k (k given). Specify under what condition this problem can be solved by an adaptation of Floyd's algorithm, then give the associated recurrence.

Question 14.   For any pair of vertices (x, y), we want to calculate the value of the (one)   133 - Q 14
minimum value path passing through the *intermediate vertex* of number k (k given). What about an adaptation of Floyd's algorithm?

The solution is on page 736.

Problem 134. Best path in an array   ○ ●

> *In this problem, the focus is put on a traversal problem in a square array. Indeed, the initial problem is reformulated as a tracking problem in a weighted graph, which justifies its place in the chapter on dynamic programming. The solution developed here will be compared to other tracking algorithms in the graphs studied previously in this chapter.*

Let us consider the array $TJ[1 .. n, 1 .. n]$ $(n > 1)$ for which we are interested in the calculation of the (one) "best" path from the cell $(n, 1)$ to the cell $(1, n)$, knowing that:

- each cell is provided with an integer value (positive, negative or zero), called a penalty later on; the cost of a path of the array is the sum of the cells it is made up with,
- the (one) best path is a minimum cost path,
- without loss of generality, numbering is assumed to be topdown from 1 to n for rows and from left to right for columns,
- the following moves are permitted:
  - a) $(i,j) \longrightarrow (i, j+1)$ $(\rightarrow)$ if the precondition $(j+1 \leqslant n)$ holds,
  - b) $(i,j) \longrightarrow (i-1, j-1)$ $(\nwarrow)$ if the precondition $((1 \leqslant i-1 \leqslant n) \text{ and } (1 \leqslant j-1 \leqslant n))$ is met,
  - c) $(i,j) \longrightarrow (i-1, j+1)$ $(\nearrow)$ if the precondition $((1 \leqslant i-1 \leqslant n) \text{ and } (1 \leqslant j+1 \leqslant n))$ is valid.

Let us remark that with such moves, no circuit(s) can appear in a path from the cell $(n,1)$ to the cell $(1,n)$.

Example of an array and a path.

	1	2	3	4	5	6
1	−1	−1	5	2→1→3		
2	1	1	−1	0	0	0
3	−1	−2	−3	7	0	6
4	0	−5	2	0→0		6
5	1	−2	3	1	5	−3
6	2→5→4→0				−2	7

The path taken above is: $\langle (6,1), (6,2), (6,3), (6,4), (5,5), (4,4), (3,6), (2,5), (1,4), (1,5), (1,6) \rangle$. Its cost is 28.

The objective is to calculate by dynamic programming the value $\text{pmc}(n,1)$ representing the cost of a minimum cost path from the cell $(n,1)$ to the cell $(1,n)$.

134 - Q 1   **Question 1.**   Reformulate the problem as the search for a minimum value path in a particular weighted directed graph. Specify the graph associated with the array TJ below:

	1	2	3	4
1	2	−4	1	0
2	−6	2	−1	3
3	5	−2	−3	3
4	0	10	2	7

134 - Q 2   **Question 2.**   Knowing the values associated with the cells in the array TJ, establish the recurrence formula to calculate $\text{pmc}(i,j)$, the cost associated with the (one) best path from cell (i,j) to cell $(1,n)$ where $1 \leqslant i \leqslant n, 1 \leqslant j \leqslant n$.

134 - Q 3   **Question 3.**   Specify the the evolution of the calculation performed by the algorithm implementing this recurrence. What are the spatial and temporal complexities (in number of evaluated conditions) of the algorithm for calculating $\text{pmc}(i,j)$.

Question 4.   Specify how the best path can be reconstructed.   134 - Q 4

Question 5.   Give the values of pmc as well as the optimal path for the array TJ in   134 - Q 5
question 1.

Question 6.   What would have happened if the values in cells $(4, 1)$ and $(1, 4)$ of TJ had   134 - Q 6
been 9 and 5?

Question 7.   Which other recurrence could have been the basis for the solution to this   134 - Q 7
problem?

The solution is on page 745.

Problem 135. Weighted binary search trees   8 :

> *Binary search trees (bst) constitute a data structure (see Chapter 1) making it possible to manage the order over the values carried by the nodes of the tree, for example values lower (respectively higher) than that of the root in the left (respectively right) subtree. Here, we study a peculiar value search problem in a bst, with a probabilistic hypothesis relative to the values it contains. A certain similarity between this problem and the chained product of matrices (problem 125, page 649) is pointed out.*

Here are considered *binary search trees* (bst) where values are the integers $x_1, x_2, \ldots, x_n$
such that $x_1 < x_2 < \cdots < x_n$. There are many ways to proceed to their construction. For
example, in the special case where for any i in 1 to 5, $x_i = i$, at least two bst's are possible
(see figure 9.7).

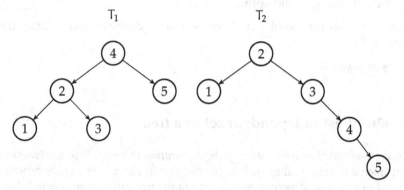

Fig. 9.7 – T_1 and T_2, two possible bst with 1, 2, 3, 4, and 5 as values.

To simplify, any node of such a bst is assimilated to the value x_i it contains. Any value
x_i has the probability $p(x_i)$ of being searched. The value $\text{cbst}(A) = \sum_{k=1}^{n} p(x_k) \cdot (d_k + 1)$,
denotes the *cost* of a bst T, where d_k is the depth of x_k in T (the root depth being 0. The
value $\text{cbst}(T)$ is actually the expectation of the number of comparisons to be made to
find an existing item in the bst T. The objective is to construct the bst of minimum cost,
knowing the pairs $(x_i, p(x_i))$. For the two trees in figure 9.7, the respective costs are:

$3 \cdot p(1) + 2 \cdot p(2) + 3 \cdot p(3) + p(4) + 2 \cdot p(5)$ for T_1,
$2 \cdot p(1) + p(2) + 2 \cdot p(3) + 3 \cdot p(4) + 4 \cdot p(5)$ for T_2.

135 - Q 1 **Question 1.**   What is the number of binary search trees containing the values $x_1, \ldots, x_n$?

135 - Q 2 **Question 2.**   Let $lst(T)$ (respectively $rst(T)$) be the left (respectively right) subtree of the bst T and $spr(T)$ the sum of the probabilities associated with the values of the nodes of T. If R is empty, let $spr(T) = 0$. Prove that:

$$cbst(T) = cbst(lst(T)) + cbst(rst(T)) + spr(T).$$

Check this formula on the trees T_1 and T_2 in figure 9.7, page 669. Deduce that the left and right subtrees of minimum cost bst are themselves of minimum cost, which validates Bellman's principle.

135 - Q 3 **Question 3.**   It can be remarked that, in the context of this problem, the left (respectively right) subtree of any bst contains consecutive index values. Let us call $T_{i,t}$ the bst whose values are $x_i, \ldots, x_{i+t-1}$, and let $sp(i, t) = spr(A_{i,t})$. Give the complete recurrence for the calculation of $copt(1, n)$, the optimal (minimum) cost of the bst $T_{1,n}$.

135 - Q 4 **Question 4.**   Specify the principle of the dynamic programming algorithm implementing the computation of $copt(1, n)$. Give the spatial and temporal complexities of this algorithm. Elaborate on the gain afforded by this solution compared to the combinatorial evoked in question 1.

135 - Q 5 **Question 5.**   Let us consider the pairs of values (x_i, p_i) of the following table:

i	1	2	3	4	5
x_i	1	2	3	4	5
p_i	0.05	0.1	0.2	0.15	0.5

Calculate $copt(1, 5)$ and give the optimal bst $T_{1,5}$.

135 - Q 6 **Question 6.**   Situate this problem with respect to the chained product of matrices (problem 125, page 649).

The solution is on page 746.

Problem 136.   Best independent set in a tree   ∘ ⦂

> *This problem is situated in the context of the exploration of a tree. It presents several peculiarities compared to almost all of those in the chapter: (i) the elements of the recurrence will not be stored in a tabular structure, but directly in the tree, (ii) the constructed algorithm is not iterative but recursive and (iii) the construction of the optimal solution itself is done at the same time as the computation of the value associated with it.*

Let t be a non-empty tree, unordered (i.e. whose children of a node are considered as a *set* of nodes). Every node u (leaves included) has a weight (positive integer) denoted by $wght(u)$. The weight $W(S)$ of a subset S of nodes of t is defined as the sum of the weights of its nodes:

$$W(S) = \sum_{u \in S} wght(u).$$

Two nodes u and v are said to be *adjacent* when u is the father of v or when v is the father of u. A set of two or more nodes is said to be *independent* if it involves no pair of adjacent nodes. The objective is to find a subset S^*, such that S^* is an independent set of nodes of t of maximum weight and its weight $W(S^*)$. Figure 9.8 shows an example of tree and of an independent subset.

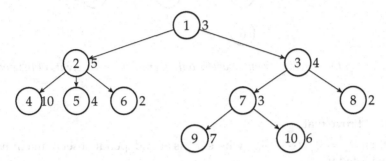

Fig. 9.8 – An example of tree. The weight of a node is placed next to its identifier which is circled. The weight of the independent set $\{1, 4, 5, 6, 7, 8\}$ is 24.

In the following, arbitrary unordered trees are considered where each node has the structure:

1. identifier id,

2. weight wght,

3. optimal value opvl of the subtree rooted in u,

4. set sidop of the identifiers of the nodes of the optimal weight independent subset of maximum weight rooted in u,

5. set schild of the identifiers of the children of u.

This type of tree is defined inductively, as binary trees (see section 1.6, page 27). The program hereafter illustrates the use of the tree of figure 9.9, page 672:

1. **constants**
2.   tqe $= \{/\} \cup \{($id, wght, opvl, sidop, schild$) \mid$ id $\in \mathbb{N}_1$ **and** wght $\in \mathbb{N}_1$ **and**
3.   opvl $\in \mathbb{N}_1$ **and** sidop $\subset \mathbb{N}_1$ **and** schild $\subset$ tqe$\}$
4. **variables**
5.   t $\in$ tqe
6. **begin**
7.   t $\leftarrow (1, 7, 15, \{1, 6\}$,
8. $\{(2, 1, 1, \{2\}, /), (3, 4, 8, \{6\}, \{(6, 8, 8, \{6\}, /)\}), (4, 2, 2, \{4\}, /), (5, 2, 2, \{5\}, /)\})$;
9.   **for** e $\in$ t.schild **do**
10.   **write**(*the node identified by* , e.id, *has the weight* , e.wght)
11.   **end for**
12. **end**

So, tqe is the set of all trees with the considered structure and this programme writes the identifier and the weight of each of the sons of the root of the tree t of figure 9.9, page 672.

Let u be a node of t whose sons are $v_1, \ldots, v_c$ and the grand-sons are $w_1, \ldots, w_g$. S_u^* denotes an independent subset of maximum weight for the tree rooted in u.

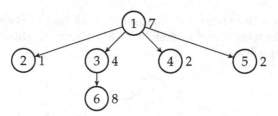

Fig. 9.9 – The tree of the program example where only identifiers and weights of the nodes appear.

136 - Q 1   **Question** 1.   Prove that:

- if $u \notin S^*$, then $S_u^* = S_{v_1}^* \cup \cdots \cup S_{v_c}^*$, where $S_{v_i}^*$ is an independent set of maximum weight for the tree rooted in v_i,

- if $u \in S^*$, then $S_u^* = \{u\} \cup S_{w_1}^* \cup \cdots \cup S_{w_g}^*$, where $S_{w_i}^*$ is an independent set of maximum weight for the tree rooted in w_i.

136 - Q 2   **Question** 2.   Deduce a recurrence relation for the calculation of the weight of $S^* = S_r^*$, the independent subset of maximum weight of the tree t rooted in r.

136 - Q 3   **Question** 3.   We assume available the operation "**procedure** *Collect*(t;vchild, vgchild, schild, sgchild : **modif**)" delivering for the tree t rooted in r:

- vchild the value $\sum_{u \in \text{children}(r)} P(S_u^*)$,
- vgchild the value $\sum_{u \in \text{grand-children}(r)} P(S_u^*)$,
- schild the identifiers of the nodes of the maximum weight independent set of each of the sons of r,
- sgchild the identifiers of the nodes of the maximum weight independent set of each of the grand-sons of r.

This procedure must be called for a tree whose five components id, wght, opvl, sidop and schild are informed for any node other than the root. So, this procedure is limited to the extraction of the values it must return without any proper calculation.

Example

With the tree

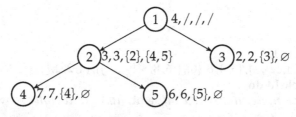

where any node is labelled by its identifier and completed by its other four components; the call *Collect* returns 5 for vchild, 13 for vgchild, $\{2,3\}$ for schild and $\{4,5\}$ for sgchild.

Specify a dynamic programming algorithm for the simultaneous calculation of S^* and its weight. What is its time complexity in terms of visits of nodes?

Question 4.   Apply thsi algorithm to the tree of figure 9.8, page 671, in order to deter- 136 - Q 4
mine the (one) maximum weight independent set.

The solution is on page 749.

9.4.4 Sequences

Problem 137. Longest ascending sub-sequence   8 •

> *Besides the fact that this is a classic problem on sequences, this problem illustrates a case where the optimal value sought is not found at a predetermined location in the tabular structure used.*

Sequences of length at least equal to 2 made up of positive integers are considered. For example, such a sequence is $u = \langle 11,5,2,8,7,3,1,6,4,2 \rangle$, of length 10. Generally, a sequence of length $n \geq 1$ is denoted by $x = \langle x[1],\ldots,x[i],\ldots,x[n] \rangle$. A sequence of length less than or equal to n is said to be an *ascending sub-sequence* (ASS) of x, of which:

- the elements are taken from left to right in x,
- the elements are strictly increasing from left to right.

For example, $\langle 2,3,4 \rangle$ and $\langle 1,6 \rangle$ are two ASS's of u. The second one is special, since its elements follow each other in u. It is called an ascending *contiguous* (ACSS) sub-sequence of u.

The goal of this problem is to find the length of the longest ACSS and ASS of any sequence x, denoted by $lacss(x)$ and $lass(x)$. For example, the longest ICSS's of u are $\langle 2,8 \rangle$ and $\langle 1,6 \rangle$, so $lacss(u) = 2$. The longest ASS's of u are $\langle 2,3,4 \rangle$ and $\langle 2,3,6 \rangle$, which leads to $lass(u) = 3$. The elementary operation for the evaluation of the complexity is the comparison between numbers of the sequence x considered.

Question 1.   Prove that for any sequence x: $lass(x) \geq lacss(x)$.   137 - Q 1

Question 2.   Give the principle of an algorithm in $\Theta(n)$ to compute $lacss(x)$.   137 - Q 2

Question 3.   Why is it not possible to calculate $lass(x)$ in $\Theta(n)$ with an algorithm simi- 137 - Q 3
lar to the previous one?

Question 4.   A dynamic programming algorithm will be built that computes $lasst(i)$ 137 - Q 4
the length of the longest sub-sequence of x whose *the last element* is $x[i]$. In the previous example:

i	1	2	3	4	5	6	7	8	9	10
u[i]	11	5	2	8	7	3	1	6	4	2
lssct(i)	1	1	1	2	2	2	1	3	3	2

Given $lasst(1),\ldots,lasst(n)$, the calculation of $lass(x)$ is immediate by means of a loop searching for the maximum of $lasst(i)$ for $i \in 1 .. n$. Give the recurrence defining $lasst(i)$. Deduce the program calculating $lass(x)$ for any sequence x of length n, allowing moreover to identify subsequently a sub-sequence of this length. Specify its spatial and temporal complexities.

137 - Q 5 **Question** 5.   Apply this algorithm to the sequence $u = \langle 11, 5, 2, 8, 7, 3, 1, 6, 4, 2 \rangle$.

The solution is on page 751.

Problem 138.   Shortest common super-sequence   8 •

> *This problem is quite similar to the one treated as an example in the introduction of this chapter and can be seen as its inverse. The main interest lies in establishing the recurrence and the property linking the length of a longest sub-sequence and a shortest super-sequence common to two sequences.*

At the beginning of the chapter, the problem of finding the longest sub-sequence common to two sequences was studied and the problem of determining the shortest super-sequence common to two sequences is now addressed. For example, if $u = actuality$ and $v = acquire$, the sequence $actuquialirety$ is a super-sequence common to both of length 14. However, one of their shortest common super-sequences is $actqulirety$ of length 11, and their single longest common sub-sequence is $acui$ of length 4.

Let x and y be two sequences and let us denote by $lcsbs(i, j)$ (respectively $scsps(i, j)$ the length of the (one) longest sub-sequence (respectively shortest super-sequence) common to the prefixes of length j of x and of length i of y.

138 - Q 1 **Question** 1.   On the basis of that established in the problem dealt with at the beginning of this chapter, give a complete recurrence for the calculation of scsps.

138 - Q 2 **Question** 2.   Deduce the principle of an algorithm calculating the length of the shortest super-sequence common to the sequences x and y (and the super-sequence itself). Specify its spatial and temporal complexities.

138 - Q 3 **Question** 3.   Apply this algorithm to the sequences $u = vague$ and $v = veal$.

138 - Q 4 **Question** 4.   Prove that for any pair of sequences x, y such that $|x| = m$ and $|y| = n$:

$$lcsbs(n, m) + scsps(n, m) = m + n.$$

Check that this formula holds for $u = vague$ ($n = |u| = 5$) and $v = veal$ ($m = |v| = 4$).

The solution is on page 753.

Problem 139.   Distance between sequences (2)   8 :

> *This problem may be seen as a variant of that addressed in the introduction of this chapter. It finds its application in the field of processing of character strings and the genome.*

9.4.4.1   Definitions

It is assumed that it is possible to insert as many symbols ε as desired in a sequence x without altering its meaning, namely that of the sequence without symbols ε; the sequence

x' with such insertions is called a "super-sequence" of x. For example, if $u = bcaa$, a super-sequence of u is $\varepsilon bc\varepsilon\varepsilon aa$. We will say that the length of this super-sequence is 7.

Let x and y be two sequences and consider two super-sequences of x and y of same length built on the alphabet Σ. An "alignment" between x and y is the letter-to-letter mapping of the two super-sequences. For example, between the sequences $u = bcaa$ and $v = acbca$, the following alignment can be created:

$$
\begin{array}{cccccc}
\varepsilon & \varepsilon & b & c & a & a \\
| & | & | & | & | & | \\
a & c & b & \varepsilon & c & a
\end{array}
$$

where $u' = \varepsilon\varepsilon bcaa$ and $v' = acb\varepsilon ca$.

An alternative formulation of the alignment between two sequences is that of "trace", in which the sequences without inserting the character ε is used. The trace corresponding to the previous example is:

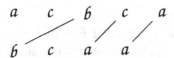

A trace must be such that two association lines between letters never intersect. Under this constraint, one can construct an[3] alignment equivalent to a trace and uniquely build an alignment from a trace. An alignment or a trace can be interpreted as a series of *elementary editing operations* between sequences: insertions, deletions and transformations of letters to form the second sequence from the first. In the previous example, the alignment is interpreted as the following sequence of transformations:

1. insertion of a
2. insertion of c
3. transformation of b into b

4. deletion of c
5. transformation of a into c
6. transformation of a into a

To give a value to the costs of insertions, deletions and transformations, a matrix δ of non-negative real numbers is used. It is defined on $(|\Sigma|+1) \times (|\Sigma|+1)$ which corresponds to a distance: it is symmetrical, of zero diagonal and complies with the triangular inequality. The value of an element of this matrix can be interpreted as the cost to transform one symbol into another or as the cost of deletion and insertion for each symbol. For example, on the alphabet Σ made up of the three letters a, b and c, such a matrix could be:

	ε	a	b	c
ε	0	1	1	1
a	1	0	1.5	1.2
b	1	1.5	0	1.7
c	1	1.2	1.7	0

---

[3]Sometimes several, but they have the same interpretation.

In this example, the deletion cost of a is 1 ($\delta[a, \varepsilon] = 1$), the insertion cost of b est 1 ($\delta[\varepsilon, b] = 1$) and the transformation cost of a into c is 1.2 ($\delta[a, c] = 1.2$).

Let us call *alignment cost* the sum of the elementary costs of its constitutive operations. The cost of the alignment:

$$
\begin{array}{cccccc}
\varepsilon & \varepsilon & b & c & a & a \\
| & | & | & | & | & | \\
a & c & b & \varepsilon & c & a
\end{array}
$$

is thererfore: 1 (insertion of a) + 1 (insertion of c) + 0 (transformation of b into b) + 1 (deletion of c) + 1.2 (transformation of a into c) + 0 (transformation of a into a) = 4.2. Another alignment between the words u = $bcaa$ and v = $acbca$ is for example:

$$
\begin{array}{ccccc}
b & c & a & \varepsilon & a \\
| & | & | & | & | \\
a & c & b & c & a
\end{array}
$$

for a (lesser) cost of 1.5 (transformation of b into a) + 0 (transformation of c into c) + 1.5 (transformation of a into b) + 1 (insertion of c) + 0 (transformation of a into a) = 4.

Note that an alignment associating pairs of symbols ε is of no interest. Indeed, such an alignment $algn$ is equivalent in the sense of cost to another alignment $algn'$ deprived of the pairs of symbols ε, since for any matrix δ, $\delta(\varepsilon, \varepsilon) = 0$. For example, the alignment $algn$:

$$
\begin{array}{cccccccc}
\varepsilon & \varepsilon & \varepsilon & b & c & a & \varepsilon & a \\
| & | & | & | & | & | \\
\varepsilon & a & c & b & \varepsilon & c & \varepsilon & a
\end{array}
$$

has the same cost as the alignment $algn'$:

$$
\begin{array}{cccccc}
\varepsilon & \varepsilon & b & c & a & a \\
| & | & | & | & | & | \\
a & c & b & \varepsilon & c & a
\end{array}
$$

In the following, only alignments not associating any pair of symbols ε are considered.

9.4.4.2 The problem

The problem is to find the cost of an optimal alignment, that is to say the least expensive, between two sequences x and y. Let us call $\Delta(x, y)$ the cost of the (one) optimal alignment between the sequences x and y, and $calopt(i, j)$ the cost of the optimal alignment between the prefix of length i of y and the prefix of length j of x. Thus the value $\Delta(x, y) = calopt(|y|, |x|) = calopt(n, m)$ is sought.

139 - Q 1   **Question 1.**   This question aims to establish a recurrence relation of the computation of $calopt\ (i, j)$. To do this, the problem is reformulated as a problem of finding a path of minimum value in a graph. However, taking into account the particular form of the graph to be processed, a specific solution (adapted to the "particular topology" of the graph) is

developed, as has already been done in problem 134, page 667. It can be noticed that an alignment can be interpreted as a path in a graph, as the following example illustrates. The path between the node labeled (0/0) and the node labeled (4/5) (arcs in bold) in the graph below represents the alignment:

$$
\begin{array}{ccccccc}
a & c & b & \varepsilon & c & a \\
| & | & | & | & \times & | & | \\
\varepsilon & \varepsilon & b & c & a & a
\end{array}
$$

between the sequences $u = acbca$ and $v = bcaa$.

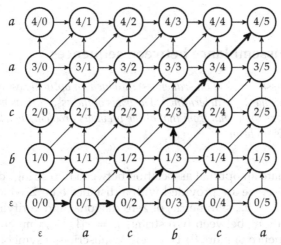

(a) Define such a graph in the general case of two arbitrary sequences x and y (in particular give the value assigned to arcs) and prove that an optimal alignment between two sequences corresponds to the calculation of a minimum value path in this graph.

(b) Calculate the number of different alignments between two sequences x and y.

(c) Due to the peculiar form of the graph, give a recurrence relation to calculate $calopt(i, j)$ as the value of the (one) minimum value path between node (0/0) and node (i/j) of this graph.

Question 2. Give the algorithm (so called Wagner-Fischer's—*WF* algorithm) that computes the cost $\Delta(x, y)$ of the (one of the) minimum cost alignment(s) between two arbitrary sequences, given the matrix δ. What are its spatial and temporal complexities as a function of $m = |x|$ and $n = |y|$? What "standard" shortest path computation algorithms could have been envisaged? Situate their temporal complexity in relation to that of the *WF* algorithm.　139 - Q 2

Question 3. We take the usual alphabet with:　139 - Q 3

- for any letter α: $\delta[\alpha, \varepsilon] = \delta[\varepsilon, \alpha] = 2$;
- for any letter α: $\delta[\alpha, \alpha] = 0$;
- if α and β are two different consonants or vowels: $\delta[\alpha, \beta] = \delta[\beta, \alpha] = 1$;
- if α is a consonant and β is a vowel: $\delta[\alpha, \beta] = \delta[\beta, \alpha] = 3$.

Calculate $\Delta(dakoury, lemur)$.

Question 4. How is it possible to reconstitute the (an) optimal alignment? Show an optimal alignment for the previous example, as well as for the strings $u = art$ and $v = deal$.　139 - Q 4

139 - Q 5 **Question 5.**   Explain why it is possible to find a solution whose space complexity is reduced to $\Theta(n)$. Write the corresponding algorithm, called "linear" Wagner-Fischer's algorithm (*LWF*).

139 - Q 6 **Question 6.**   If $\bar{x}$ and $\bar{y}$ designate the mirror sequences of x and y, how to calculate the (one) optimal alignment between $\bar{x}$ and $\bar{y}$ from an optimal alignment between x and y?

139 - Q 7 **Question 7.**   Show that, since δ defines a distance, then Δ also defines a distance (hence the title of this problem). How to take advantage of the symmetry property to improve the spatial complexity of the algorithm *LWF*?

The solution is on page 755.

Problem 140. Dissemblance between sequences   ⚇ ⦂

> *This problem is a classic problem on sequences, in which an optimal cost of transforming one sequence into another has to be determined. The basis of the associations between the symbols of the sequences differs somewhat from that of the previous problem, which partly constitutes the originality of this problem.*

We want to calculate an optimal association between two strings defined on an alphabet Σ. For this purpose, we are provided with a distance δ on Σ which is represented by a matrix defined on $|\Sigma| \times |\Sigma|$, symmetric, of zero diagonal and verifying the triangular inequality. An "association" between two strings $x = x[1], \ldots, x[m]$ and $y = y[1], \ldots, y[n]$ corresponds to a sequence of pairs (k, l), where k subscribes a symbol of x and l a symbol of y, which must respect the following constraints:

- no symbol can be deleted or inserted, each symbol in x must therefore correspond to at least one in y and vice versa,
- if several symbols of x (respectively y) correspond to a symbol of y (respectively x), they must be contiguous,
- the pair (k, l) is followed by the pair (k', l') such that $k' = k + 1$ or (non-exclusive) $l' = l + 1$.

For example, between the sequences $u = bcaa$ and $v = acbca$, among many others the association:

$$\langle (b, a), (b, c), (b, b), (c, b), (c, c), (a, a), (a, a) \rangle$$

can be established. It is described on the indices by:

$$\langle (1,1), (1,2), (1,3), (2,3), (2,4), (3,5), (4,5) \rangle$$

or by the figure:

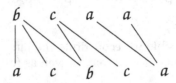

More formally, an association is a sequence of pairs of indices such that:

- the first term of the sequence is the pair $(1,1)$,
- the last term of the sequence is the pair (m,n),
- the term (k,l), except (m,n), can only be followed by one of the three terms $(k,l+1)$, $(k+1,l)$ or $(k+1,l+1)$.

Each pair (k,l) making up an association corresponds to a value in the matrix δ: the distance between the letters of rank k ($x[k]$) and l ($y[l]$) in Σ. The *cost of the association* is defined as the sum of the values of all its pairs. For example, for the following matrix δ defined on $\Sigma = \{a, b, c\}$:

	a	b	c
a	0	2	1.5
b	2	0	1
c	1.5	1	0

the association between the sequences $u = bcaa$ and $v = acbca$ proposed before:

$$\langle(1,1),(1,2),(1,3),(2,3),(2,4),(3,5),(4,5)\rangle$$

has a cost of:

$$\delta[b,a] + \delta[b,c] + \delta[b,b] + \delta[c,b] + \delta[c,c] + \delta[a,a] + \delta[a,a] =$$
$$2+1+0+1+0+0+0 = 4.$$

The *dissemblance between two sequences* is defined as the cost of the association which has the lowest cost among all the possible associations between these two sequences. We are looking for an *efficient* algorithm to calculate it.

Question 1. What is the dissemblance between the sequences $u = a$ and $v = aa$ for the matrix δ given above? Between the sequences $u = aab$ and $v = abb$? Between the sequences $u = ab$ and $v = bac$? Give a non-trivial example of a pair of sequences of zero dissemblance. 140 - Q 1

Question 2. Propose a recurrence relation calculating the dissemblance between two sequences x and y. *Indication*: use the fact that, for any pair of sequences, the last symbol of the first one is associated with the last symbol of the second one. 140 - Q 2

Question 3. Specify the data structure to be used and the evolution of its filling, then write the program performing the calculation of the dissemblance between two sequences. What are its spatial and temporal complexities? 140 - Q 3

Question 4. Apply this algorithm for $u = acbca$ and $v = bcaa$ for the matrix δ given before. 140 - Q 4

Question 5. Explain how to reconstitute the (one) optimal association. Give one for the previous example. 140 - Q 5

140 - Q 6 **Question 6.** How could such a program be used in a word processing spell checker (whose limitations are to be highlighted)?

The solution is on page 760.

Problem 141. The best elephant team   8 ⦂

> *This problem presents two main interests. The first resides in the fact that it can be solved by reformulating it as a sequence problem. The second relates to the progressiveness of the questions leading from the resolution of a restricted case to that of the general case.*

Let us consider a set E of n ($n \geqslant 2$) elephants. Besides its number i ($i \in 1 .. n$), each elephant is represented by a triple $(wght(i), int(i), val(i))$ where $wght(i)$ is the weight of the elephant i, $int(i)$ is a measure of its intelligence and $val(i)$ is its market value. We are looking for the (one) subset S of E which complies with the following conditions:

1. for any pair (i, j) of S, $(wght(i) < wght(j)) \Leftrightarrow (int(i) < int(j))$,

2. there is no pair (i, j) of S with $i \neq j$, such that $wght(i) = wght(j)$ **and** $int(i) = int(j)$,

3. the value $\sum\limits_{i \in S} val(i)$ is maximum (in other words, for any subset T meeting the two above conditions: $\sum\limits_{i \in S} val(i) \geqslant \sum\limits_{i \in T} val(i)$).

For example, if $E = \{(1, 2300, 7, 10), (2, 2000, 14, 80), (3, 2800, 13, 40), (4, 2100, 11, 50), (5, 2500, 6, 20), (6, 2600, 9, 15), (7, 2000, 17, 50)\}$, eight subsets of more than one elephant satisfy the first two conditions: $\{1, 3\}, \{1, 6\}, \{3, 4\}, \{3, 5\}, \{3, 6\}, \{5, 6\}, \{1, 3, 6\}, \{3, 5, 6\}$. Among them, the best one is $\{3, 4\}$ for a value of 90 (which exceeds the value of any single elephant, in particular $\{2\}$).

141 - Q 1 **Question 1.** Give the principle of a "Generate and test" solution. What is its complexity at worst in terms of conditions evaluated?

It is envisaged to reduce the resolution of this problem of sets (and subsets) to the search for an optimal sub-sequence common to two elephant sequences x and y. More precisely, x and y have the same length n and are constructed appropriately (see subsequent questions) from the set of elephants E. In the end, the resulting common sub-sequence is seen as a refinement of the initially desired subset S.

141 - Q 2 **Question 2.** State a necessary (respectively sufficient) condition on the order in which the elephants i and j must appear in the sequences x and y so that they can both (respectively so that one only at most can) belong to a sub-sequence common to x and y.

First of all we deal with the special case where all the elephants present in E have different intelligences and weights.

141 - Q 3 **Question 3.** Express the problem posed as the identification of an optimal (in a sense to be specified) sub-sequence common to the sequences of elephants x and y (that will be made explicit).

141 - Q 4 **Question 4.** Deduce the principle of a solution based on dynamic programming solving this problem by pointing out the recurrence used. It is asked to specify the tabular structure and the evolution of its filling.

Question 5.   Give the temporal (in number of conditions evaluated) and spatial com-   141 - Q 5
plexities of the resulting algorithm (which is not required), then compare its temporal complexity with that of the solution obtained with the "Generate and test" approach.

In the forthcoming questions, the algorithm works on two sequences of size n, i.e. relative
to the entire set E of elephants. These sequences result from a preliminary processing based
on appropriate sorts of which criteria (sort keys) will be specified.

Let us now consider the case of a set E that may involve a subset (of cardinality greater than
or equal to 2) of elephants having same weight but with distinct intelligences called of type
E_{swdi} (the symmetric case of a subset of type E_{sidw} of elephants having same intelligence
but different weights could be considered as well).

Question 6.   How must the two sequences of elephants issued from E be constructed   141 - Q 6
so that the method developed in questions 3 and 4 leads to a correct result?

We now take into account a situation where E may contain a subset of elephants of type
E_{swi} having same weight and same intelligence (but no subset of type E_{swdi} or E_{sidw}). By
virtue of the second condition of membership to the solution set S, at most one elephant of
type E_{swi} can be integrated into it.

Question 7.   How then to solve the problem posed?   141 - Q 7

Question 8.   Synthesize the processing of an arbitrary set E of elephants and specify its   141 - Q 8
temporal complexity in number of conditions evaluated.

Question 9.   Apply this procedure to the example made up of the set of elephants   141 - Q 9
E = {(1, 1500, 15, 32), (2, 1200, 25, 27), (3, 1400, 22, 17), (4, 1000, 20, 20), (5, 1500, 15, 10),
(6, 1800, 26, 15), (7, 1500, 15, 8), (8, 1400, 12, 23)}.

The constraints imposed on the solution set S are revised by waiving the second condition.
So, the solution set S may now involve several elephants of same weight and intelligence.
A "broader" acceptance is thus adopted by also allowing elephants "as heavy as intelli-
gent".

Question 10.   How can the problem be solved in the presence of an arbitrary set E of   141 - Q 10
elephants?

Question 11.   Deal with the example of question 9.   141 - Q 11

The solution is on page 763.

9.4.5   Images

Problem 142.   The best triangulation of a convex polygon

> *This problem addresses a question whose application lies in the field of 3D imaging. Estab-
> lishing the recurrence first requires finding a "good" triangulation strategy, which is one of
> the key points of the solution.*

A n-vertex ($n \geqslant 3$) polygon $\mathcal{P}$ of the plane is by definition *convex* if and only if, when drawing a line between any two consecutive vertices, the $(n-2)$ remaining vertices are on the same side of this line. A *chord* of a convex polygon is defined as the segment joining two non-adjacent vertices. A *triangulation* of a convex polygon $\mathcal{P}$ is a set of chords such that:

- two chords do not intersect,
- the chords completely divide the polygon into triangles.

From the coordinates of the n vertices of a convex polygon $\mathcal{P}$, the *length* of a triangulation of $\mathcal{P}$ is defined as the sum of the lengths of the chords which compose it. The problem is as follows: given a convex polygon $\mathcal{P}$, find a *minimal triangulation* of $\mathcal{P}$, i.e. a triangulation of $\mathcal{P}$ of minimum length. Subsequently it is assumed that the considered polygon has n vertices labeled clockwise (also called retrograde or counter-trigonometric) noted s_0, s_1, ..., s_{n-1}.

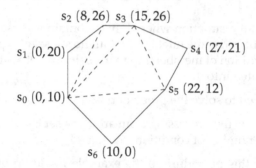

Fig. 9.10 – *An heptagon and a triangulation of approximate value 77.56.*

A first triangulation strategy (called *OneTrOnePol*) that comes quite naturally to mind is to separate a polygon with n sides ($n > 3$) into a triangle and a polygon with $(n-1)$ sides. Such an approach has the major disadvantage of having to consider the same triangulation several times. For example, with the heptagon of figure 9.10, the partial triangulation of figure 9.11 is obtained: (i) by separating the initial polygon into a triangle of vertices s_0, s_1 and s_2 and a polygon of vertices s_0, s_2, s_3, s_4, s_5, s_6, then by separating this last polygon into a triangle of vertices s_3, s_4 and s_5 and a polygon of vertices s_0, s_2, s_3, s_5, s_6, but also (ii) by doing the opposite by separating the initial polygon into a triangle of vertices s_3, s_4 and s_5 and a polygon of vertices s_0, s_1, s_2, s_3, s_5, s_6, then by separating this last polygon into a triangle of vertices s_0, s_1 and s_2 and a polygon of vertices s_0, s_2, s_3, s_5, s_6. With this approach, the number of triangulations $nbtr1(n)$ examined for a polygon of n sides is given by:

$$
\begin{aligned}
&nbtr1(3) = 1 \\
&nbtr1(4) = 2 \\
&nbtr1(n) = n \cdot nbtr1(n-1) \qquad\qquad\qquad\qquad\qquad\qquad n \geqslant 5
\end{aligned}
$$

that is $nbtr1(n) = n!/12$ for $n > 3$, which is "worse" than exponential.

It is therefore desirable to look for an alternative strategy to *OneTrOnePol* avoiding the previous pitfall, that is to say still taking into account *all* the possible triangulations (completeness), but without duplicates (minimality). First it can be noticed that any side of the

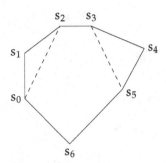

Fig. 9.11 – A partial triangulation of the heptagon of figure 9.10.

initial polygon belongs to one and only one of the triangles of a triangulation. A side denoted (s_i, s_{i+1}) is chosen and the strategy *OneTrTwoPol* consists in drawing from any vertex other than s_i and s_{i+1}, a triangle of which (s_i, s_{i+1}) is a side, which is summarized in figure 9.12. The reader is invited to check that the set of triangulations obtained does indeed have the two desired properties (completeness and minimality).

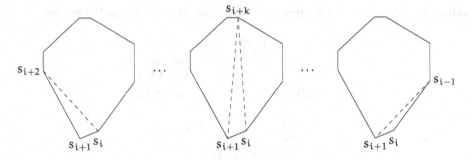

Fig. 9.12 – The adopted triangulation strategy.

Question 1. Calculate the number $nbtr2(n)$ of triangulations generated by the strategy *OneTrTwoPol* for a n-side polygon. Express it as a Catalan number (see page 11) and compare it to $nbtr1(n)$, the number of triangulations obtained with the strategy *OneTrOnePol*. What other problems of this chapter does $nbtr2(n)$ suggest? 142 - Q 1

Question 2. The strategy *OneTrTwoPol* proposed is valid in particular if the reference side (s_{n-1}, s_0) is chosen which breaks up the initial polygon into: 142 - Q 2

- a triangle of vertices s_0, s_j ($j \in 1 .. n-2$) and s_{n-1},
- a polygon of vertices s_0 to s_j (not existing for $j = 1$),
- a polygon of vertices s_j to s_{n-1} (not existing for $j = n-2$).

The two polygons thus generated having vertices of increasing numbers, we are freed from the management of questions related to the circularity of the problem. So, in a general way, we will consider the minimal triangulation of the polygon of vertices $s_i, \ldots, s_{i+t-1}$ having t sides such that $i + t - 1 < n$, by taking the reference side (s_i, s_{i+t-1}), as shown in the following figure:

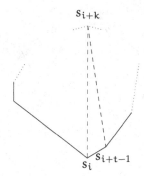

where k ranges from 2 to $(t-2)$. Explain why the polygon $\mathcal{P}$ *must* be convex for this strategy to be convenient.

142 - Q 3   **Question 3.**   Let us call $\texttt{lgmintr}(i, t)$ the length of the (one) optimal triangulation of the polygon whose vertices are $s_i, \ldots, s_{i+t-1}$ where $i + t - 1 < n$. Give the recurrence for the calculation of $\texttt{lgmintr}(i, t)$.

142 - Q 4   **Question 4.**   Specify the elements (tabular structure, filling strategy, location of the solution value) of an algorithm stemming from the previous recurrence. Give its spatial and temporal complexities.

142 - Q 5   **Question 5.**   Apply this algorithm to the example of the polygon hereafter:

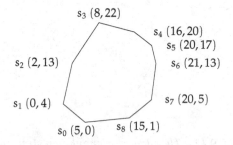

computing not only the value of the optimal triangulation, but also the identification of its chords.

The solution is on page 766.

Problem 143. Largest black square in an image   8 ⁞

> *The interest of this problem lies in the comparison between two approaches to solve the addressed problem, one iterative, the other based on dynamic programming.*

Consider a rectangular image of width n and of height m made up of black (1) and white (0) pixels represented by the matrix IMG$[1 .. m, 1 .. n]$. The objective is to identify the side c of the largest square sub-image in IMG that is fully black. For example, in the image of figure 9.13, where $m = 6$ and $n = 8$, the biggest black square is unique. Its side is 3 and it spreads over rows 2 to 4 and columns 2 to 4 (with the numbering convention of rows bottom up and columns from left to right used throughout the problem).

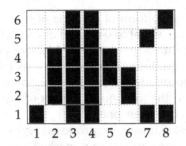

Fig. 9.13 – A black and white 6 × 8 image and its largest black square (framed).

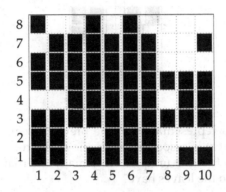

Fig. 9.14 – A black and white 8 × 10 image.

Question 1. First, an iterative solution is designed that uses the procedure defined in problem 116, page 480, calculating the side of the largest square under a histogram. Specify the principle of this solution and determine its temporal complexity in terms of conditions evaluated. Apply it to the image of figure 9.14, page 685. 143 - Q 1

Question 2. Now, the resolution of the problem is undertaken using the dynamic programming paradigm. Let $slbs(i, j)$ be the side of the largest black square whose northwest corner coordinates are (i, j). Give the recurrence calculating $slbs$. 143 - Q 2

Question 3. Specify the tabular structure to be used for the implementation and the strategy to fill it in. 143 - Q 3

Question 4. Write the corresponding dynamic programming algorithm and give its space and time complexities. Compare the temporal complexity to that of the iterative solution. 143 - Q 4

Question 5. Apply this algorithm to the image of figure 9.14. 143 - Q 5

The solution is on page 769.

Problem 144. Trimming an image

The originality of this problem lies in the fact that it is the only one in this book in which spatial and temporal complexities of a dynamic programming algorithm are of course polynomial, but with a degree greater than 3.

Consider a binary image in the form of a matrix of pixels IMG[1 .. m, 1 .. n] (m rows, n columns), whose elements are equal to 0 (white) or to 1 (black). The objective is to partition (or segment) the image into a set of entirely black or entirely white rectangles. The technique used is that of the "guillotine", whose rule is as follows: given a rectangle, it is permitted to divide it into two smaller rectangles either by a horizontal line or by a vertical line. The problem is to find the minimum number of guillotine strokes to completely separate the black pixels from the white ones.

In the example below of a 4×5 image, the proposed segmentation (which is not claimed optimal) requires seven guillotine strokes (lines marked with an arrow).

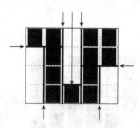

144 - Q 1   **Question 1.**   Propose a representation of the previous segmentation as a tree where each node (including leaves) is associated with one of the rectangles (for instance using Cartesian coordinates). Is the tree unique? How many internal (non-leaf) nodes does it contain? What property do the leaves have?

144 - Q 2   **Question 2.**   How to insert a numbering of guillotine strokes in this tree?

144 - Q 3   **Question 3.**   Give a recurrence relation to calculate the minimum number of guillotine moves required to segment any image of m rows and n columns (m, n ⩾ 1).

144 - Q 4   **Question 4.**   Propose a tabular structure and specify the strategy governing its filling.

144 - Q 5   **Question 5.**   Write the code of the optimal segmentation algorithm. What are its space and time complexities?

144 - Q 6   **Question 6.**   Apply this algorithm to the 3 × 4 image below:

The solution is on page 775.

9.4.6   Games

Problem 145.   Stacking bricks   8 ⦂

> *This problem, as some others, requires a preliminary analysis step resulting in a new formulation of the problem. Indeed, the initial problem considers an infinite number of bricks, which cannot be managed from an algorithmic point of view. Indeed, after having identified a finite useful number of bricks, it becomes quite easy to establish the recurrence serving as the basis for the resolution by dynamic programming.*

We are provided with bricks of n different types, and for each type an unlimited number of copies are available. A brick of type i is a rectangular parallelepiped whose sides are s_i^1, s_i^2 and s_i^3, with $s_i^1 \leqslant s_i^2 \leqslant s_i^3$.

The objective is to make a stack of maximum height. First, a brick is placed on one of its faces, then a second on the first, *sides in parallel*, then a third, etc. The constraint is that a brick can only be laid on the pile under construction if the face that is laid is strictly included in its two dimensions in the upper face of the previous brick. In other words, with each new brick, the stack shrinks *strictly*.

Question 1. Prove that there are at most three really different ways of laying a new brick on a brick already laid. 145 - Q 1

Question 2. Prove that in a stack there can be at most two bricks of a given type. 145 - Q 2

Question 3. Reformulate the problem as an optimal stacking, with a choice no longer among an unlimited number of bricks, but among $3n$ different objects. 145 - Q 3

Question 4. Give the recurrence formula for the construction of the highest stacking. 145 - Q 4 Specify the tabular structure used in the associated algorithm and the evolution of the calculation. Give the time complexity of this algorithm in terms of conditions evaluated.

Question 5. Apply the algorithm to the situation with three types of bricks B1, B2 and 145 - Q 5 B3 of respective dimensions $10 \times 12 \times 16$, $8 \times 9 \times 18$ and $4 \times 6 \times 25$.

The solution is on page 781.

Problem 146. Winning the Patagonian game ∘ •

> In this problem, we come back to the Patagon game already addressed in problem 18, page 42. The objective of this game is to maximize the gain of the player who chooses values from a table in succession (or draws "valued" cards arranged face-up), without being able to take two consecutive ones.

We saw in problem 18, page 42, the definition of the Patagon game. In a slightly different form, it can be said that, given an array $T[1..n]$ of strictly positive integers, it consists in finding the maximum value, $\mathrm{sopt}(n) = \sum_{i \in I} T[i]$, obtained from a set I of indices between 1 and n ($n > 1$) such that I does not contain two consecutive indices.

In problem 18, page 42, the number of "reasonable" ways of playing denoted by nbRWP, in other words the combinatorial of the game. It turns out to be exponential since with a n-size array T, nbRWP is the integer closest to $(1.324 \cdots)^{n-1}/1.045 \cdots$. It will be shown that the value $\mathrm{sopt}(n)$ can be found without exploring this exhaustive set of candidates.

Question 1. What about the greedy algorithm which proceeds by pair of values of T 146 - Q 1 and chooses, as long as the constraint is met, the greatest value?

Question 2. Establish a complete recurrence relation for calculating $\mathrm{sopt}(n)$. 146 - Q 2

146 - Q 3 **Question** 3. Deduce a dynamic programming algorithm which computes sopt and subsequently produces an associated set I. What is its time complexity? Compare it with respect to nbRWP.

146 - Q 4 **Question** 4. Specify the calculation of the optimal set of indices I.

146 - Q 5 **Question** 5. Deal with the example where $n = 9$ and $T = [2, 5, 7, 3, 1, 4, 1, 8, 4]$.

The solution is on page 782.

Problem 147. The game of extremes ⚬ ⦙

> *This problem concerns a two-player game for which two game strategies are successively studied. The first one aims at determining the maximum winning for the player starting first. This gain constitutes an upper bound of that which can be reached in the other (classic) strategy in which each player wants to amass a maximum gain. The algorithms obtained in each case turn out to be simple and fairly similar.*

Two players face a table with $2n$ cards ($n \geqslant 1$) lined up with a number written on each. The set of cards is visible to both players at all times. Each player, in turn, takes one of the two cards at the ends of the line. The card then disappears from the deck, and the player's winnings increase by the number written on the card.

Collaborative approach

First, the objective is to determine what the maximum payoff would be for the player who plays first, which is the same as assuming that his opponent collaborates with him as much as possible.

147 - Q 1 **Question** 1. Show on an example that the maximum payout is not always equal to the sum of the n highest card values.

147 - Q 2 **Question** 2. Give a recurrence for the calculation of the maximum final payoff of the player playing first.

147 - Q 3 **Question** 3. Deduce an algorithm of spatial and temporal complexities in $\Theta(n^2)$ that computes this optimum.

147 - Q 4 **Question** 4. Provide a trace of the execution of this algorithm with the line of cards:

12	7	6	10	8	5

147 - Q 5 **Question** 5. Prove that, according to this approach, the player playing first cannot do worse than a draw with the other player.

Competitive approach

It is now assumed that both players are looking to win.

147 - Q 6 **Question** 6. Give a recurrence for the calculation of the maximum final winning of the player playing first, taking into account that each player seeks to maximize his own gain.

Question 7.   Describe the principle of the algorithm computing this optimum. Specify   147 - Q 7
where are the maximum gain of the player starting the game and that of his opponent in
the tabular structure used. Situate the algorithm in relation to that of the question 3.

Question 8.   Apply this algorithm to the six-card line given previously.   147 - Q 8

Question 9.   Suggest a greedy strategy whereby the player playing first wins or draws.   147 - Q 9
Deduce that the same is true with the strategy based on dynamic programming. Does this
greedy strategy lead to maximum gain?

The solution is on page 784.

9.4.7   Pseudo-polynomial problems
Problem 148. Currency change (2)   ⁞

> In this problem, which is a standard, the composition of a fixed sum with a given monetary
> system is studied. The objective is mainly to build a dynamic programming solution such that
> the number of coins returned is minimal, for any monetary system. This solution turns out
> to be simple and efficient as long as the amounts considered remain "reasonable".

We are interested in giving change (with coins only) when a customer pays a shopkeeper with a sum greater than the amount of his purchase. The problem is to arrive at
exactly a given sum N by choosing from the cash register a multi-set (or bag) of coins
each having a given value. For example, in the Eurozone system, if the customer makes a
purchase of 8.10 Euros and gives 10 Euros, the problem is for the merchant to compose a
multi-set of coins that totals 1.90 Euros. There are a large number of solutions, including:

- one coin of 1 €, one coin of 50c, two coins of 20c,
- two coins of 50c, four coins of 20c, two coins of 5c,
- 19 coins of 10c, etc.

Let us call $C = \{c_1, \ldots, c_n\}$ the set of coins of the monetary system used comprising n
different (types of) coins. It is assumed that the retailer has an unlimited number of each of
them. The coin c_i has the value d_i. In the Eurozone, the set C is of size 8, with the values:
$d_1 = 2€, d_2 = 1€, d_3 = 50c, d_4 = 20c, d_5 = 10c, d_6 = 5c, d_7 = 2c, d_8 = 1c$, or, in cents:
$d_1 = 200, d_2 = 100, d_3 = 50, d_4 = 20, d_5 = 10, d_6 = 5, d_7 = 2, d_8 = 1$. Coming back to
the previous example, the first solution can be noted by the multiset $[\![c_2, c_3, c_4, c_4]\!]$ or by a
vector of size n indicating how many coins of each type were taken for the solution, here
$[0, 1, 1, 2, 0, 0, 0]$.

To complete the definition of the problem, the shopkeeper is assumed to seek to give
back as few coins as possible. It can therefore be called RCOW as "returning change in
an optimal way" and state it as follows. A set C is given and to each element c_i of C is
associated a value d_i, a strictly positive integer, just like N, the sum to be returned. Find a
multiset S composed of elements of C such that:

- the sum of the values of the elements of S amounts exactly to N,
- the number of elements in S is minimum.

If no multi-set meets the first of the two criteria above, the problem is declared insoluble.
This situation may arise in particular if the monetary system does not have a coin of unit
value.

A fast greedy algorithm, but not always exact

The method typically used by a retailer can be described as follows: use the coins in descending order of value, taking as many as possible of each. It is this greedy algorithm that, in the introductory example, produces the first solution $[\![c_2, c_3, c_4, c_4]\!]$.

148 - Q 1   **Question 1.**   Show that it does not solve the RCOW problem when $\mathcal{C} = \{c_1, c_2, c_3\}$, with $d_1 = 6, d_2 = 4, d_3 = 1$ and $N = 8$. Find another non-trivially deduced pair $(\mathcal{C}, N)$ from this one for which this algorithm is not suitable either.

Remark

It can be proven that this algorithm solves the RCOW problem only when $\mathcal{C}$ has certain properties that are possessed in particular by the European coin system or by systems of the type $\{1, 2, 4, 8, \ldots\}$. We are not interested in these properties here.

An exact algorithm

In the spirit of the method used in problem 20, page 44, relating to yellow coins in the European currency system, let us define $\mathrm{nbcmin}(i, j)$ as the minimum number of coins necessary to form the sum j by allowing only the subset of coins $\{c_1, \ldots, c_i\}$. If this is not possible, $\mathrm{nbcmin}(i, j)$ takes an arbitrarily large value. The objective is therefore to calculate $\mathrm{nbcmin}(n, N)$. The coins involved in $\mathcal{C}$ are not assumed to be arranged in descending (or ascending) order.

148 - Q 2   **Question 2.**   Give the complete recurrence defining nbcmin.

148 - Q 3   **Question 3.**   Deduce the principle of a pseudo-polynomial algorithm (see section 2.1.8, page 78) based on dynamic programming, determining the number of coins involved in the optimal solution. Specify its time complexity.

148 - Q 4   **Question 4.**   Apply this algorithm to $N = 12$ and the currency system $\mathcal{C} = \{c_1, c_2, c_3\}$, where $d_1 = 4, d_2 = 5, d_3 = 1$.

148 - Q 5   **Question 5.**   How to complete the algorithm to know which coins are returned and in what quantities?

The solution is on page 788.

9.5   Solutions

Answers to problem 117. Approximation of a sampled function by a broken line
The problem is on page 640.

117 - A 1   **Answer 1.**   When $n \cdot C$ is very small, $m \cdot C$ is also since $m < n$. The best broken line relies on n points. It has $(n - 1)$ segments and a very small cost. When C is very large, it would be tempting to minimize $m \cdot C$, so take $m = 1$, and construct a broken line with a single segment based on the points 1 and n. However, this technique does not necessarily produce the optimal segmentation. For example, for three points of abscissa 1, 2 and 3 and

ordinate 0, h and 0, the cost of the broken line with only one segment is $h + C$, that of the line with two segments $2C$. If $h > C$, the second is better. Therefore, nothing obvious can be stated in the case where C is very large.

Answer 2.   Any broken line approximating the n points of the set P is made up of two   117 - A 2
parts: a first broken line (possibly empty) ending in k, followed by a last segment. In the particular case of the optimal broken line, by definition, the associated cost is: $appopt(n) = appopt(k) + sed(k, n) + C$. If k is not known, but the values $appopt(1), \ldots, appopt(n-1)$ are, we can however write:

$$appopt(n) = \min_{j \in 1..n-1} \left(sed(j, n) + C + appopt(j) \right).$$

The value of j for which the minimum is realized is k, which corresponds to the beginning of the last segment (which ends in n).

Answer 3.   The calculation of $appopt(i)$ is based on the application of the reasoning of   117 - A 3
the previous question. The recurrence relation thus is:

$$
\begin{aligned}
& appopt(1) = 0 \\
& appopt(i) = \min_{j \in 1..i-1} \left(sed(j, i) + C + appopt(j) \right) \qquad\qquad 1 < i \leqslant n.
\end{aligned}
$$

Answer 4.   The recurrence is used to fill the array $OA[1 .. n]$, in which the values   117 - A 4
$appopt(1), appopt(2), \ldots, appopt(n)$ are put in order. The result is in $OA[n]$.

Answer 5.   The corresponding algorithm is: 117 - A 5

```
1.  constants
2.     n ∈ N₁ and n = ... and C ∈ R₊ and C = ...
3.  variables
4.     sed ∈ R₊ and OA ∈ 1 .. n → R₊
5.  begin
6.     OA[1] ← 0 ;
7.     for i ranging 2 .. n do
8.        OA[i] ← +∞ ;
9.        for j ranging 1 .. i − 1 do
10.          sed ← 0 ;
11.          for k ranging j .. i do
12.             sed ← sed+ Distance(j, i, k)
13.          end for;
14.          OA[i] ← min({OA[i], sed + C + OA[j]})
15.       end for
16.    end for;
17.    write(AO[n])
18. end
```

The complexity in number of calls to *Distance* is:

$$
\sum_{i=2}^{n} \sum_{j=1}^{i} \sum_{k=j}^{i} 1 = \sum_{i=2}^{n} \sum_{j=1}^{i} (i - j + 1) = \sum_{i=2}^{n} \frac{i \cdot (i+1)}{2} \in \Theta(n^3)
$$

since $\sum_{i=1}^{n} i^2 = (n \cdot (n+1) \cdot (2n+1))/6$.

The combinatorial of this problem is exponential, as the number of possible broken lines for a set P of n points is 2^{n-2} and as the function *Distance* must be called at least once for each of them (except that passing through the n points). Thus, it can be seen that resolving the problem using dynamic programming brings a very substantial gain (from an exponential to a polynomial complexity).

117 - A 6   **Answer 6.**   To identify the optimal broken line, "Tom Thumb's technique" is used. For each cell OA[i, the index j which made it possible to reach the optimal (the segment of origin j and end i ends the optimal approximation of the points 1 to i) is stored in IND[i]. The array IND will be browsed later from IND[n] in a chained way until finding the value 1 corresponding to the first point of the optimal broken line (i.e. the list $\langle \mathrm{IND}[n], \mathrm{IND}[\mathrm{IND}[n]], \dots, 1 \rangle$ is browsed).

Answers to problem 118. The best interval (2)   *The problem is on page 642.*

118 - A 1   **Answer 1.**   The value of the (one) best interval of the array T is obtained by taking the maximum of the values $biv(1), \dots, biv(n)$, which is in $\Theta(n)$.

Of course, $biv(1) = 0$. Let l $(1 \leqslant l \leqslant k-1)$ be the starting index of the best interval finishing exactly in $k - 1$. We have:

$$T[k] - T[l] = (T[k] - T[k-1]) + (T[k-1] - T[l]) = T[k] - T[k-1] + biv(k-1).$$

If $T[k] - T[k-1] + biv(k-1)$ is negative, the interval k .. k is the best interval ending in k and its value is 0. The following recurrence can be derived:

$$\left| \begin{array}{l} biv(1) = 0 \\ biv(k) = \max \left(\left\{ \begin{array}{l} 0, \\ T[k] - T[k-1] + biv(k-1) \end{array} \right\} \right) \end{array} \right. \qquad 1 < k \leqslant n.$$

118 - A 2   **Answer 2.**   The calculation of the previous recurrence is performed by filling the array BI of size n. In the general case (second term of the recurrence), the calculation of an element depends only on the value of its predecessor and thus BI can be filled by increasing index values, after initializing the first element thanks to the first term of the recurrence. The number of conditions evaluated (including loop control) is in $\Theta(n)$; therefore temporal and spatial complexities of this procedure are in $\Theta(n)$. It can be noticed that the complementary phase of searching for the value of the best interval of the array T considered, that is to say the search for the maximum of BI, does not modify the linear time complexity of the complete solution.

118 - A 3   **Answer 3.**   Finding the (one) best interval itself can rely on "Tom Thumb's technique". The starting index in T of the (of a) best interval ending in k is stored in the array PTH[1..n] for each value of k (1 for k = 1 and then k if BI[k] is 0, the index associated with k − 1 otherwise).

118 - A 4   **Answer 4.**   The code is:

```
1. constants
2.    n ∈ ℕ₁ and n = ... and T ∈ 1 .. n → ℝ₊ and T = [...]
3. variables
4.    biv ∈ ℝ and i ∈ 1..n and j ∈ 1..n and BI ∈ 1..n→ℝ₊ and PTH ∈ 1..n→ℕ₁
5. begin
```

```
 6.    BI[1] ← 0; PTH[1] ← 1;
 7.    for k ranging 2 .. n do
 8.       BI[k] ← max({0, BI[k − 1] + T[k] − T[k − 1]});
 9.       if BI[k] = 0 then
10.          PTH[k] ← k
11.       else
12.          PTH[k] ← PTH[k − 1]
13.       end if
14.    end for;
15.    /% additional phase for the search of the value of the best interval and its
       bounds %/
16.    biv ← BI[1]; i ← 1; j ← 1;
17.    for k ∈ 2 .. n do
18.       if BI[k] > biv then
19.          biv ← BI[k]; i ← PTH[k]; j ← k
20.       end if
21.    end for;
22.    write(the value of the best interval is , biv , and its bounds are ,
23.          i , .., j )
24. end
```

Answer 5.   For the proposed example, we get: 118 - A 5

k	1	2	3	4	5	6	7	8	9	10	11	12	13	14
T[k]	14	11	16	12	20	7	3	3	19	24	24	3	5	16
BI[k]	0	0	5	1	9	0	0	0	16	21	21	0	2	13
PTH[k]	1	2	2	2	2	6	7	8	8	8	8	12	12	12

Going through BI and PTH, the value of the best interval found is 21, corresponding to the interval 8 .. 10 (there are three more besides).

Answer 6.   Since on the one hand the computation of an element only calls on its prede-   118 - A 6
cessor, and on the other hand the complementary phase aims to find the maximum value
of the array BI[1 .. n] and the bounds of best interval, these values can be kept "on the fly"
(variables Best, i and j), which leads to the algorithm:

```
 1. constants
 2.    n ∈ ℕ₁ and n = ... and T ∈ 1 .. n → ℝ₊ and T = [...]
 3. variables
 4.    Curr ∈ ℝ₊ and Best ∈ ℝ₊ and CurrBi ∈ 1 .. n and i ∈ 1 .. n and j ∈ 1 .. n
 5. begin
 6.    Curr ← 0; CurrBi ← 1; Best ← 0; i ← 1; j ← 1 ;
 7.    for k ∈ 2 .. n do
 8.       Curr ← max({0, Curr + T[k] − T[k − 1]});
 9.       if Curr = 0 then
10.          CurrBi ← k
11.       elsif Curr > Best then
12.          Best ← Curr; i ← CurrBi; j ← k
13.       end if
14.    end for;
15.    écrire(the value of the best interval is , Best , and its bounds are ,
```

16.   i, .., j)
17. **end**

118 - A 7   **Answer 7.**   As we have seen, in the two design paradigms used, we end up with a solution of linear time complexity and of constant "actual" spatial complexity. Moreover, both approaches lead to concise code. If the approach by invariant seems "natural" for this problem, the solution using dynamic programming is quite easy to design thanks to its systematic nature.

Answers to problem 119. Locating gas stations   *The problem is on page 643.*

119 - A 1   **Answer 1.**   Among the six possible configurations, $\langle 1, 4 \rangle$, which brings in 10 M\$, is the best one.

119 - A 2   **Answer 2.**   As no gas station can be set up before that in position 1, $e(1)$ is equal to 0 and locations 0 to n must therefore be considered thereafter. The "virtual" gas station numbered 0 has an annual gain of zero ($g(0) = 0$).

119 - A 3   **Answer 3.**   In the general case, for a given location i different from 0 and 1, only two choices are open:

- to set up a gas station there; the overall gain is then that of the station i increased by the optimal gain associated with the closest authorized location,
- not to put a station there; the optimal gain is then identical to that of the previous location $(i - 1)$.

This yields the recurrence:

$$
\left|
\begin{array}{l}
optgain(1) = g(1) \\
optgain(i) = \max \left(\left\{ \begin{array}{l} optgain(e(i)) + g(i), \\ optgain(i-1) \end{array} \right\} \right)
\end{array}
\right.
\qquad 1 < i \leqslant n.
$$

119 - A 4   **Answer 4.**   The tabular structure of the associated dynamic programming algorithm is a vector $OPTGN[0..n]$, whose filling is carried out by increasing values of index thanks to the above recurrence. The gain brought in by the optimal configuration is found at the end of execution in $OPTGN[n]$. The spatial complexity of the associated algorithm is therefore in $\Theta(n)$, as is the number of conditions evaluated.

119 - A 5   **Answer 5.**   In order to obtain the optimal configuration, the array $PTH[0..n]$ initialized to 0 is used. The cell $PTH[i]$ is set to 1 if, during the calculation of $OPTGN[i]$, the maximum has been obtained by setting up a station at location i (first alternative of the calculation of the maximum). The subsequent scan of PTH is done starting from the end. If $PTH[j]$ is equal to 1, a station is set up at location j and $PTH[e(j)]$ is examined (unless $e(j)$ is equal to 0 in which case the process stops). If $PTH[j]$ is equal to 0, no station is set up at location j and we look for the predecessor of j such that $PTH[j] = 1$ (the process stops if the index 1 is reached without having found such a predecessor).

119 - A 6   **Answer 6.**   Applying this method to the example proposed leads to:

i	0	1	2	3	4	5	6	7
e(i)	0	0	0	1	2	3	3	4
g(i)	0	6	7	2	3	1	5	2
OPTGN[i]	0	6	7	8	10	10	13	13
PTH[i]		1	1	1	1	0	1	0

It can be deduced that the optimal solution brings in 13 M$; this corresponds to the locations $(1,3,6)$.

Answers to problem 120. Traveling in the desert   *The problem is on page 644.*

Answer 1.   A greedy strategy is to go each time fill the gourd at the most distant well   120 - A 1
without dying of thirst. Why is this strategy optimal? The "lead run" method is applied
(see section 7.1.4, page 336) and the numbers of the wells (or, which amounts to the same
thing, the distance traveled from the starting oasis) are compared for the same number
of stops i between the greedy strategy and a non-greedy strategy. Let $gr(i)$ and $ngr(i)$ be
these values. There is necessarily a value i for which $ngr(i) < gr(i)$, otherwise the non-
greedy strategy would be greedy. After this step, it is impossible to find a value j strictly
greater than i such that $ngr(j) > gr(j)$. The existence of a step such that $ngr(j-1) < gr(j-1)$
and $ngr(j) > gr(j)$ would mean that with the greedy strategy the chosen well was not the
one located as far as possible, which is contrary to the very definition of this strategy.
The greedy strategy can possibly be "caught up with" the non-greedy one, we can have
$gr(j) = ngr(j)$, but not be "passed". The greedy strategy is therefore optimal. However, it
may not be the only one, since it can be "caught up with". Thus, with wells located at 8,
9, 16, 18, 24, 27 and 32 miles from the starting oasis, the greedy strategy leads to stops at
oases 2, 4, 6 and 7, the non-greedy strategy with stops at oases 1, 4, 5 and 7, doing equally
well in terms of number of stops and "catching up with" twice the greedy strategy.

Answer 2.   The total number of liters emptied is equal to the total number of liters   120 - A 2
put into the bottle minus the number of liters consumed. The first is proportional to the
number of stops, the second is constant whatever the strategy. Minimizing the number of
liters emptied therefore amounts to minimizing the number of stops.

Answer 3.   With the example of the following question, the greedy strategy involves   120 - A 3
the traveler filling his gourd at the wells located at 9, 18 and 27 miles. He empties $1 + 1 +$
$1 + 5 = 8$ liters and pays $1 + 1 + 1 + 25 = 28$ units. Another strategy is to stop at wells
located at 8, 16 and 24 miles. He empties $2 + 2 + 2 + 2 = 8$ liters and pays $4 + 4 + 4 + 4 = 16$
units. We therefore see that the greedy strategy can be surpassed by another non-greedy
one.

Answer 4.   By definition, $apopt(i)$ is the minimum price to pay if the traveler empties   120 - A 4
the gourd at well number i, thus $apopt(n)$ is the sought value. Arrived at well number i
where he empties his gourd, the best thing the traveler may have done is to have stopped
at an earlier well j so that: (i) he was able to reach the well number i (he did not die of
thirst), and (ii) the minimum price associated with the well number j increased by what
it pays to well number i is as low as possible. We therefore choose the value of j minimizing $(apopt(j) + (D - d(j,i))^2)$, provided that $d(j,i)$ does not exceed D. This yields the
recurrence:

$apopt(1) = 0$

$$\text{apopt}(i) = \min_{\substack{j \in 1..i-1 \\ \text{and } d(j,i) \leqslant D}} \left(\text{apopt}(j) + (D - d(j,i))^2\right) \qquad\qquad 1 < i \leqslant n.$$

Implementing this recurrence can be carried out thanks to the array $\text{APO}[1..n]$ associated with apopt, which is filled by increasing values of index after initialization of its first element $\text{APO}[1]$ thanks to the first term of the recurrence. The temporal complexity of the corresponding program is in $\mathcal{O}(n^2)$ conditions evaluated and the spatial complexity in $\Theta(n)$.

120 - A 5   **Answer** 5.   For the example, the values obtained are:

$\text{APO}[1] = 0$; j optimal $= 1$

$\text{APO}[2] = 4$ since $\text{APO}[1] + d(1,2) = 0 + (2-0)^2$; j optimal $= 1$

$$\text{APO}[3] = \min \left\{ \begin{array}{lll} j = 1 & d(1,3) = 9 & \text{APO}[1] + (10-9)^2 = 1 \\ j = 2 & d(2,3) = 1 & \text{APO}[2] + (10-1)^2 = 4 + 81 \end{array} \right\} = 1;$$

j optimal $= 1$

$$\text{APO}[4] = \min \left\{ \begin{array}{lll} j = 2 & d(2,4) = 8 & \text{APO}[2] + (10-8)^2 = 4+4 \\ j = 3 & d(3,4) = 7 & \text{APO}[3] + (10-7)^2 = 1+9 \end{array} \right\} = 8;$$

j optimal $= 2$

$$\text{APO}[5] = \min \left\{ \begin{array}{lll} j = 2 & d(2,5) = 10 & \text{APO}[2] + (10-10)^2 = 4+0 \\ j = 3 & d(3,5) = 9 & \text{APO}[3] + (10-9)^2 = 1+1 \\ j = 4 & d(4,5) = 2 & \text{APO}[4] + (10-2)^2 = 8+64 \end{array} \right\} = 2;$$

j optimal $= 3$

$$\text{APO}[6] = \min \left\{ \begin{array}{lll} j = 4 & d(4,6) = 9 & \text{APO}[4] + (10-8)^2 = 8+4 \\ j = 5 & d(5,6) = 2 & \text{APO}[5] + (10-6)^2 = 2+16 \end{array} \right\} = 12;$$

j optimal $= 4$

$$\text{PO}[7] = \min \left\{ \begin{array}{lll} j = 5 & d(5,7) = 9 & \text{APO}[5] + (10-9)^2 = 2+1 \\ j = 6 & d(6,7) = 3 & \text{APO}[6] + (10-3)^2 = 12+49 \end{array} \right\} = 3;$$

j optimal $= 5$

$$\text{APO}[8] = \min \left\{ \begin{array}{lll} j = 6 & d(6,8) = 8 & \text{APO}[6] + (10-8)^2 = 12+4 \\ j = 7 & d(7,8) = 5 & \text{APO}[7] + (10-5)^2 = 3+25 \end{array} \right\} = 16;$$

j optimal $= 6$.

The optimal sequence of stops can be reconstructed from the value j associated with each step, leading to the sequence of stops at wells 2, 4, 6 and 8, for a total cost of 16 units (as expected).

Answers to problem 121. Formatting a paragraph   *The problem is on page 645.*

121 - A 1   **Answer** 1.   Two formattings of the same text using the same number of lines have the same cost with fc' as shown in the initial example of the statement of the problem, as well as in the case treated in the second question.

121 - A 2   **Answer** 2.   The cost of the first of these two formattings, resulting from the application of the greedy strategy suggested is:

$$(1+1+1+1)^2 + (1+1+1+2)^2 + 24^2 = 617,$$

while the cost of the second is:

$$(1 + 1 + 1 + 10)^2 + (1 + 1 + 1 + 2)^2 + (1 + 14)^2 = 419.$$

On this example, it can be observed that the greedy strategy filling the lines to the maximum does not necessarily provide the best solution.

Answer 3. There are three ways to arrange the four words, two over three lines and one (trivial) over four lines: 121 - A 3

```
Molina=was        Molina====        Molina====
                                     was=======
an========        was=an====        an========
American==        American==        American==
```

Answer 4. Provided that this is possible, the choices for formatting the succession of words $m_i, \ldots, m_N$ are: 121 - A 4

- write m_i alone on the first line and format the other words on the following lines in an optimal fashion,
- write m_i and m_{i+1} on the first line and format the other words on the following lines in an optimal fashion,
- ...
- write $m_i, m_{i+1}, \ldots, m_{N-1}$ on the first line and m_N alone on the last line,
- write $m_i, m_{i+1}, \ldots, m_N$ together on the same line.

The cost associated with the generic term is therefore $sl(i, j) + optcost(j + 1)$ (this last term must be zero when j is equal to N), and we end up with the recurrence:

$$\begin{vmatrix} optcost(N + 1) = 0 \\ optcost(i) = \min_{j \in i..N} \ (sl(i,j) + optcost(j + 1)) \end{vmatrix} \qquad 1 \leqslant i \leqslant N.$$

Answer 5. To produce a program, the array $SL[1..N, 1..N]$ allowing to store the values of sl is supposed to be available. The array $OC[1..N + 1]$ is associated with the previous recurrence and the array $PTH[1..N]$ is used. It is such that $PTH[i]$ stores the choice made (value of j) for the computation of the optimal value of $OC[i]$ (the reader can easily convince himself that $PTH[N + 1]$ is irrelevant to reconstitute the optimal formatting). The cell $OC[1]$ contains the optimal cost associated with writing the words m_1 to m_N. It can be seen that, in the general term of the recurrence defining $optcost(i)$, the element of index i references elements of higher index, and OC is filled by decreasing values of the index starting by $OC[N + 1]$ thanks to the first term of the recurrence. The spatial complexity of this program is in $\Theta(N^2)$ (arrays SL and OC). Its time complexity is in $\Theta(N^2)$ evaluated conditions, both to fill SL and OC. 121 - A 5

Answer 6. For the proposed example, $N = 4$ and the array SL is: 121 - A 6

j	1	2	3	4
i = 1	$4^2 = 16$	$1^2 = 1$	$+\infty$	$+\infty$
2		$7^2 = 49$	$5^2 = 25$	$+\infty$
3			$8^2 = 64$	$+\infty$
4				$2^2 = 4$

The values of OC and PTH are the following:

$OC[5] = 0$
$OC[4] = 4$; $PTH[4] = 4$
$OC[3] = \min(\{sl(3,3) + OC[4], sl(3,4) + OC[5]\}) = \min(\{64 + 4, +\infty + 4\}) = 68$; $PTH[3] = 3$
$OC[2] = \min(\{sl(2,2) + OC[3], sl(2,3) + OC[4], ml(2,4) + OC[5]\}) = \min(\{49 + 68, 25 + 4, +\infty + 5\}) = 29$; $PTH[2] = 3$
$OC[1] = \min(\{sl(1,1) + FO[2], sl(1,2) + OC[3], ml(1,3) + OC[4], sl(1,4) + OC[5]\}) = \min(\{16 + 29, 1 + 68, +\infty + 29, +\infty + 4\}) = 45$; $PTH[1] = 1$.

The optimal solution of cost 45 is:

line 1	m_1	...	$m_{PTH[1]=1}$	Molina====
line 2	m_2	...	$m_{PTH[2]=3}$	was=an====
line 3	m_4	...	$m_{PTH[4]=4}$	American==

121 - A 7 **Answer 7.** In the previous solution, the quantity to calculate is optcost(i) the optimal cost for writing $m_i, \ldots, m_N$, and its value is sought for $i = 1$ (backward recurrence). The optimal cost optcost' for writing $m_1, \ldots, m_i$ and finding its value for $i = N$ could also have chosen (forward recurrence).

121 - A 8 **Answer 8.** In the proposed approach, the cost of spaces is taken into account in sl. Changing the cost of spaces is equivalent to modifying the calculation of sl accordingly and does not impact the dynamic programming algorithm itself.

Answers to problem 122. Optimal coding   *The problem is on page 647.*

122 - A 1 **Answer 1.** The problem is dealt with considering the diverse suffixes of the words, but it would also be possible to proceed with the prefixes. Let $D[i .. n]$ be the suffix for which the optimal coding is sought. This suffix may be encoded by means of the code $\mathcal{C}$ under two conditions: (i) it starts with a word of $\mathcal{C}$ of length j and (ii) the new suffix $D[i + j .. n]$ can also be encoded using the code $\mathcal{C}$. When there are several ways to code $D[i .. n]$, the (one) encoding using a minimum number of words of the code is chosen. More formally, by calling optcod(i) the minimum number of word occurrences of $\mathcal{C}$ to encode $D[i .. n]$, $S[1 .. m]$ the array containing the words of the code $\mathcal{C}$ and $LG[1 .. m]$ the array of lengths of each of them, we look for the word of length j of $\mathcal{C}$ minimizing: $1 + optcod(i + j)$. To meet the first condition mentioned above, it is necessary to make sure on the one hand that the length of the word to be coded $((i + LG[j] - 1) \leqslant n)$ is not exceeded, then that the chosen word matches the beginning of the suffix $D[i .. n]$ $(D[i .. (i + LG[j] - 1)] = S[j])$. Finally, the recurrence is:

$$\left|\begin{array}{l} optcod(n + 1) = 0 \\ optcod(i) = \min_{\substack{(j \in 1..m) \text{ and} \\ ((i+LG[j]-1\leqslant n) \text{ and then} \\ (D[i..(i+LG[j]-1)]=S[j]))}} (1 + optcod(i + LG[j])) \qquad 1 \leqslant i \leqslant n. \end{array}\right.$$

If no encoding is possible for the suffix $D[i .. n]$ (in other words, no value of j fits in the second term of the recurrence), the operand set of the minimum is empty and thus

$optcod(i) = +\infty$. Therefore, if $D[1 .. n]$ cannot be encoded, the value of $optcod(1)$ is also $+\infty$.

Answer 2.   The program uses an array $OC[1 .. n+1]$ associated with the computation 122 - A 2 of $optcod$. The cell $OC[i]$ stores the element $optcod(i)$ and the choice corresponding to the optimal value is recorded each time in the array PTH. The minimum number of word occurrences of the code $\mathcal{C}$ used to encode the string $D[1 .. n]$ is contained in the cell $OC[1]$. The recurrence shows that the calculation can be based on a filling by decreasing values of the index of the array OC (as well as of PTH). The following algorithm calculates and writes $CO[1]$ the cost of the optimal coding:

```
1.  constants
2.     n ∈ N₁ and n  =  ... and m ∈ N₁ and m  =  ... and D ∈ 1 ..
       n → char and D = ... and
3.     S ∈ 1 .. m → string(Σ) and S = ... and LG ∈ 1 .. m → N and LG = [...]
4.  variables
5.     OC ∈ 1 .. n + 1 → N and PTH ∈ 1 .. n + 1 → N
6.  begin
7.     OC[n + 1] ← 0; PTH[n + 1] ← 0;
8.     for i ranging inverse 1 .. n do
9.        OC[i] ← +∞;
10.       for str ranging 1 .. m do
                 ⎛ (i + LG[str] − 1) ⩽ n and then            ⎞
11.          if ⎜ D[i .. (i + LG[str] − 1)] = S[str] and then ⎟ then
                 ⎝ (1 + OC[i + LG[str]]) < OC[i]              ⎠
12.             OC[i] ← 1 + OC[i + LG[str]];
13.             PTH[i] ← str
14.          end if
15.       end for
16.    end for;
17.    if OC[1] ≠ +∞ then
18.       write(the minimum number of occurrences of elements of the
          code necessary for coding the considered word is , OC[1])
19.    else
20.       write(the considered word cannot be encoded with the proposed
          code)
21.    end if
22. end
```

The temporal complexity of this program is in $\mathcal{O}(n \cdot m \cdot k)$, since the outer (respectively inner) loop involves n (respectively m) steps, while the conditional statement beginning the inner loop requires up to k comparisons of characters of the alphabet Σ.

Answer 3.   The program hereafter recomposes the optimal coding thanks to the array 122 - A 3 $PTH[1 .. n+1]$ that has been used to store "Tom Thumb's" pebbles. It is assumed that it is run only if the value returned by the previous program differs from $+\infty$.

```
1.  constants
2.     n ∈ N₁ and n = ... and S ∈ 1 .. m → string and S = ... and
3.     LG ∈ 1 .. m → N and LG = [...]
4.  variables
```

```
5.    PTH ∈ 1..n + 1 → ℕ and i ∈ ℕ
6. begin
7.    i ← 1;
8.    while PTH[i] ≠ 0 do
9.        write(S[PTH[i]]); i ← i + LG[PTH[i]]
10.   end while
11. end
```

122 - A 4   **Answer** 4.   For the first example, we have: $n = 12, m = 4, S[1] = a, S[2] = b, S[3] = ba$, $S[4] = abab$, $LG[1] = LG[2] = 1, LG[3] = 2, LG[4] = 4$. The results obtained at the end of the execution of the first program are:

i	1	2	3	4	5	6	7	8	9	10	11	12	13
D[i]	b	a	b	a	b	b	a	a	b	a	b	a	
OC[i]	5	4	5	5	4	3	3	2	2	2	1	1	0
PTH[i]	2	4	3	1	2	3	1	4	3	1	3	1	0

The optimal coding obtained after running the second program uses five occurrences of words of the code $\mathcal{C}$, that is: $b\ abab\ ba\ abab\ a$, thus doing better than the coding mentioned in the statement on page 647.

For the second example, we have: $n = 4, m = 2, S[1] = a, S[2] = bc, LG[1] = 1, LG[2] = 2$. The results of running the program calculating the minimum cost of encoding $abbc$ with the code $\mathcal{C} = \{a, bc\}$ are:

i	1	2	3	4	5
D[i]	a	b	b	c	
OC[i]	+∞	+∞	1	+∞	0

which expresses that $abbc$ cannot be coded with $\mathcal{C} = \{a, bc\}$.

Answers to problem 123. Cutting a metal bar   *The problem is on page 647.*

123 - A 1   **Answer** 1.   There is only one way to cut the bar of length 4 into four segments: $(1, 1, 1, 1)$ which yields $3 + 3 + 3 + 3 = 12$. There are three ways to cut this bar into three segments: $(1, 2, 1), (1, 1, 2)$ and $(2, 1, 1)$ each of which bringing in $3 + 3 + 7 = 13$. There are three ways to cut this bar into two segments: $(3, 1)$ and $(1, 3)$ which yields $3 + 10 = 13$ and $(2, 2)$ which yields $7 + 7 = 14$. Finally, there is only one way to cut this bar into a segment (actually no cut), which brings in 13. So the optimal way is to cut the bar into two segments of length 2.

123 - A 2   **Answer** 2.   In general, and as the example of the previous question illustrates, the bar of length i (positive integer) can be first cut into a segment of length 1 and a bar of length $(i - 1)$ to cut or cut the bar into a segment of length 2 and a bar of length $(i - 2)$ remains to be cut or ... or cut the bar into a segment of length i, that is, the bar is not actually cut. So, we can say that the optimal cut of a bar consists of a segment of length j and an optimal cut of the remaining bar of length $(i - j)$. We must therefore find the index j maximizing the selling price of the cut made, knowing that j can be equal at least to 1 and at most to i. The optimal selling price of a bar of length zero (associated with the choice $j = i$) must be introduced and this yields the recurrence:

$$optsell(0) = 0$$
$$optsell(i) = \max_{j \in 1..i} (USP[j] + optsell(i - j)) \qquad\qquad 1 \leqslant i \leqslant n.$$

Answer 3. The related algorithm uses the vector OPTSP[0..n] where OPTSP[i] contains   123 - A 3
the maximum selling price optsell(i) of the bar cut of length i and therefore the sought
result is located in OPTSP[n]. Taking into account the form of the recurrence, the filling of
the vector is done by increasing value of index. The spatial complexity of this algorithm is
in $\Theta(n)$ and the number of conditions evaluated in $\Theta(n^2)$.

Answer 4. To determine the cut itself, it is necessary to keep in the array PTH associ- 123 - A 4
ated with OPTSP the value of j for which the maximum was found. The subsequent traversal of this array exploring PTH[n], PTH[n − PTH[n]], PTH[n − PTH[n] − PTH[n − PTH[n]]],
..., stopping as soon as PTH[i] = i (expressing that the bar of length i does not have to be
cut), allows to find the optimal cut.

Answer 5. With the proposed data, assuming that the loop over j (calculating the max- 123 - A 5
imum) is performed by increasing values (from 1 to i) and that a choice is selected if it is
strictly better than the current optimal, we get:

i	0	1	2	3	4	5	6	7
UP[i]		3	7	10	13	16	20	24
OPTSP[i]	0	3	7	10	14	17	21	24
PTH[i]		1	2	1	2	1	2	1

i being the length of the bar to be cut. The optimal cut of the bar of length 7 brings in 24 and
it corresponds to one segment of length 1 (PTH[7] = 1), then the remaining bar of length
6 is cut in one segment of length 2 (PTH[6] = 2), then the remaining bar of length 4 is cut
in one segment of length 2 (PTH[4] = 2) and finally a last segment of length 2 uncut since
PTH[2] = 2.

Answer 6. For example, the loop over j can be carried out by decreasing values of j 123 - A 6
(thus from i to 1) and a new choice is kept only if it performs strictly better than the current
optimal. Thus, in the example proposed previously, the bar of length 7 would not be split
since we would then have CH[7] = 7 (which corresponds to another optimal strategy with
OPTSP[7] = USP[7] = 24). The same is true for bars of length 2 and 3.

Answer 7. The principle of the optimal cut is the same as before, except that: (i) the seg- 123 - A 7
ment produced must have one of the m lengths allowed (and the remaining bar must then
be cut out optimally) and (ii) a segment can be selected only if its length does not exceed
that of the bar to be cut. The recurrence calculating optsell(n) stems from the above:

$$optsell(0) = 0$$
$$optsell(i) = \max_{\substack{j \in 1..m \\ \text{and } LG[j] \leqslant i}} (USP[LG[j]] + optsell(i - LG[j])) \qquad\qquad 1 \leqslant i \leqslant n.$$

It can be deduced that the algorithm implementing this recurrence (that also fills the vector
OPTSP by increasing values of the index) evaluates a number of conditions in $\mathcal{O}(m \cdot n)$.

Answer 8. To obtain the cut itself, the array PTH associated with OPTSP contains the 123 - A 8
length of the segment which led to the optimal. We then proceed as described in answer 4.
The segment number could be stored in PTH, but then the construction mechanism of the
optimal cut should be adapted, LG[PTH[i]] replacing PTH[i].

Answer 9.   With the proposed data and the same calculation hypotheses as in answer 5, we get:

i	0	1	2	3	4	5	6	7	8	9	10	11
USP[i]		2	5		11		15	17		24		
OPTSP[i]	0	2	5	7	11	13	16	18	22	24	27	29
PTH[i]		1	2	1	4	1	2	1	4	1	2	1

The optimal cut of the bar of length 11 brings in 29 and it corresponds to a first segment of length 1 (PTH[11] = 1), a second one of length 2 (PTH[10] = 2), a third one of length 4 (PTH[8] = 4) and a last one of length 4 as well since PTH[4] = 4.

Answers to problem 124. Assigning staff to tasks   *The problem is on page 648.*

Answer 1.   If we have e employees and we assign j ($1 \leqslant j \leqslant k$) of them to the task i, there are $(e - j)$ left for the tasks 1 to $(i - 1)$. However, we can make two remarks:

- i tasks cannot run with less than i employees, nor with more than $\min(\{E, i \cdot k\})$ employees, so if $e < i$ or $e > \min(\{E, i \cdot k\})$, it is not possible to assign e employees to tasks T_1 to T_i,
- since any task requires at least one employee for its achievement, if $(e - j) < (i - 1)$, it is not possible to assign $(e - j)$ employees to tasks T_1 to T_{i-1}.

Under the assumption of satisfaction of the two constraints established above, the optimal value of $\mathrm{optsd}(i, e)$ is obtained by taking as the value of j ($1 \leqslant j \leqslant k$) that minimizes the expression $d(i, j) + \mathrm{optsd}(i - 1, e - j)$, expressing in particular that the tasks 1 to $(i - 1)$ must themselves also be the object of the optimal allocation of $(e - j)$ employees who are assigned to them. We therefore end up with the following recurrence defining $\mathrm{optsd}(i, e)$:

$$
\begin{cases}
\mathrm{optsd}(1, e) = d(1, e) & 1 \leqslant e \leqslant k \\
\mathrm{optsd}(1, e) = +\infty & k < e \leqslant E \\
\mathrm{optsd}(i, e) = \min\limits_{\substack{(j \in 1..k)\text{ and} \\ ((i-1) \leqslant (e-j))}} (d(i, j) + \mathrm{optsd}(i - 1, e - j)) & \begin{cases} 1 < i \leqslant n \text{ and} \\ i \leqslant e \leqslant \min(\{E, i \cdot k\}) \end{cases} \\
\mathrm{optsd}(i, e) = +\infty & \begin{cases} ((1 < i \leqslant n) \text{ and} \\ (1 \leqslant e < i \text{ or } (e \leqslant E \text{ and } e > i \cdot k))) \end{cases}
\end{cases}
$$

Answer 2.   The tabular structure involved in the calculation program of optsd is an array $\mathrm{OSD}[1 .. n, 1 .. E]$. Since the calculation of the cell $\mathrm{OSD}[i, e]$ depends only on the values of cells of index $(i - 1)$, the filling is done by increasing values of the index of row (the first row is calculated thanks to the first two terms of the recurrence and the following ones thanks to the last two). In a row, the filling order is irrelevant. The final result, namely the optimal time to complete n tasks with E employees, is found in the cell $\mathrm{OSD}[n, E]$. Taking into account the remarks made previously, we know that for any row i, only cells of column index i to $i \cdot k$ need to be filled, hence the general structure of OSD:

	1	...	k	k+1	...	p	...	p·k	p·k+1	...	E
1	...	...	...	+∞	+∞	+∞	+∞	+∞	+∞	+∞	+∞
...	+∞	...	...	...	...	...	...	...	...	...	...
p	+∞	+∞	+∞	+∞	+∞	...	...	...	+∞	+∞	+∞
...	+∞	+∞	+∞	+∞	+∞	+∞	...	...	...	...	...

Answer 3. The spatial complexity of the algorithm is in $\Theta(n \cdot E)$, corresponding to the array OSD. Regarding its temporal complexity, an upper bound of the number of conditions evaluated for a cell of OSD is $k + 2$ (3 for the control of loops and $(k - 1)$ for the comparisons related to the innermost loop relative to j). The number of cells to be filled is limited by that of OSD, that is to say at most $n \cdot E$. Noticing that $E \leqslant n \cdot k$, it can be asserted that the temporal complexity of the algorithm is in $\mathcal{O}(k^2 \cdot n^2)$.

124 - A 3

Answer 4. The table OSD hereafter is obtained for the proposed example ($E = 10$):

124 - A 4

	1	2	3	4	5	6	7	8	9	10
1	110	90	65	55	+∞	+∞	+∞	+∞	+∞	+∞
2	+∞	230	200	180	155	135	115	105	95	+∞
3	+∞	+∞	320	290	270	245	225	205	185	175
4	+∞	+∞	+∞	385	355	335	310	290	270	250

The optimal duration is therefore 250. It can be checked that a staff assignment yielding this value is: 1 for task 4, 2 for taske 3, 4 for task 2 and last 3 for task 1.

Answers to problem 125. Matrix chained product   *The problem is on page 649.*

Answer 1. The bracketing $(M_1 \times (M_2 \times (M_3 \times M_4)))$ leads to:

125 - A 1

- $(M_3 \times M_4)$ resulting in $M_{34}[50, 100]$ with $5,000$ multiplications,
- $(M_2 \times M_{34})$ resulting in $M_{234}[20, 100]$ with $100,000$ multiplications,
- $(M_1 \times M_{234})$ returning the final result M_{1234} with $20,000$ multiplications,

that is a total of $125,000$ multiplications. The expression $((M_1 \times (M_2 \times M_3)) \times M_4)$ calls on:

- $(M_2 \times M_3)$ resulting in $M_{23}[20, 1]$ with $1,000$ multiplications,
- $(M_1 \times M_{23})$ resulting in $M_{123}[10, 1]$ ith 200 multiplications,
- $(M_{123} \times M_4)$ delivering the final result M_{1234} with $1,000$ multiplications,

that is $2,200$ multiplications in total. We can see that the number of multiplications varies greatly depending on the way of operating.

Answer 2. A bracketing of $M_1 \times \cdots \times M_n$ is obtained by "cutting" the chain of matrices to form two sub-expressions, then by bracketing again each of them. Knowing that a chain made up of a single matrix M_1 admits the unique bracketing (M_1), it can be deduced that the number $nbbr(n)$ of possible bracketings of $M_1 \times \cdots \times M_n$ is given by the recurrence:

125 - A 2

$$
\begin{vmatrix}
nbbr(1) = 1 \\
nbbr(n) = \sum_{k=1}^{n-1} nbbr(k) \cdot nbbr(n - k) & \qquad n > 1.
\end{vmatrix}
$$

Therefore, we have $nbbr(2) = 1, nbbr(3) = 2, nbbr(4) = 5, \ldots$. This definition fits exactly that of Catalan numbers given page 11. Thus:

$$nbbr(n) = Cat(n) = \frac{1}{n} \; C_{2n-2}^{n-1} \approx \frac{4^{n-1}}{n\sqrt{\pi n}}.$$

125 - A 3   **Answer** 3.   Finding $optprod(i, j)$ comes down to identifying the least expensive bracketing among:

$$(M_i) \times (M_{i+1} \times \cdots \times M_{i+j})$$
$$\cdots$$
$$(M_i \times \cdots \times M_{i+k}) \times (M_{i+k+1} \times \cdots \times M_{i+j})$$
$$\cdots$$
$$(M_i \times \cdots \times M_{i+j-1}) \times (M_{i+j}).$$

The generic term leads to perform in an optimal way the product $(M_i \times \cdots \times M_{i+k})$ of cost $optprod(i, k)$ delivering the matrix MI_1 with $D[i-1]$ rows and $D[i+k]$ columns, as well as the product $(M_{i+k+1} \times \cdots \times M_{i+j})$ of cost $optprod(i+k+1, j-k-1)$ returning the matrix MI_2 with $D[i+k]$ rows and $D[i+j]$ columns, and last the product of MI_1 and MI_2 requiring $D[i-1] \cdot D[i+k] \cdot D[i+j]$ multiplications. Therefore, the recurrence is:

$$\left| \begin{array}{l} optprod(i, 0) = 0 \\[2mm] optprod(i, j) = \displaystyle\min_{k \in 0..j-1} \left(\begin{array}{l} optprod(i, k) + \\ optprod(i+k+1, j-k-1) + \\ D[i-1] \cdot D[i+k] \cdot D[i+j] \end{array} \right) \end{array} \right. \quad \begin{array}{c} 1 \leqslant i \leqslant n \\[2mm] \left\{ \begin{array}{c} 1 \leqslant j \leqslant n-1 \\ \textbf{and} \\ 1 \leqslant i \leqslant n-j \end{array} \right. \end{array}.$$

125 - A 4   **Answer** 4.   For the requested calculation, the array $OPROD[1..n, 0..n-1]$ is associate with $optprod$. It can be observed that the calculation of $OPROD[i, j]$ uses cells with a second index strictly lower than j and we choose to perform the calculation by column of increasing number after initialization of column 0 thanks to the first term of recurrence. A column can be filled in by increasing values of the row index. In order to reconstitute the (one) optimal bracketing, for each cell of OPROD the value of k associated with the optimal choice is stored in the array $PTH[1..n, 0..n-1]$. We obtain:

1. **constants**
2. $n \in \mathbb{N}_1$ **and** $n = \ldots$ **and** $D \in 0..n \rightarrow \mathbb{N}_1$ **and** $D = [\ldots]$
3. **variables**
4. $OPROD \in 1..n \times 0..n-1 \rightarrow \mathbb{N}$ **and** $PTH \in 1..n \times 0..n-1 \rightarrow \mathbb{N}$ **and** $currv \in \mathbb{N}$
5. **begin**
6.   **for** i **ranging** $1..n$ **do**
7. $OPROD[i, 0] \leftarrow 0$; $PTH[i, 0] \leftarrow 0$
8.   **end for**;
9.   **for** j **ranging** $1..n-1$ **do**
10.   **for** i **ranging** $1..n-j$ **do**
11. $OPROD[i, j] \leftarrow +\infty$; $PTH[i, j] \leftarrow 0$;
12.   **for** k **ranging** $0..j-1$ **do**
13. $currv \leftarrow OPROD[i, k] + OPROD[i+k+1, j-k-1] + D[i-1] \cdot D[i+k] \cdot D[i+j]$;
14.   **if** $currv < OPRODM[i, j]$ **then**
15. $OPROD[i, j] \leftarrow currv$; $PTH[i, j] \leftarrow k$
16.   **end if**

17.   **end for**
18.   **end for**
19.   **end for;**
20.   **write**(OPROD[1, n − 1])
21. **end**

The spatial complexity of this program is in $\Theta(n^2)$ and its time complexity in $\Theta(n^3)$ conditions evaluated. The naïve method based on the comparison of the costs of all bracketings requires an exponential number of comparaisons (due to the exponential number of bracketings—see answer 2). The gain brought by dynamic programming is again very substantial compared to a naïve solution.

Answer 5.   We have D[0..4] = [10, 20, 50, 1, 100]. Putting the values of OPROD and PTH   125 - A 5
in a single cell, the table hereafter is obtained:

j	0		1		2		3	
i = 1	0	0	10,000	0	1,200	0	2,200	2
2	0	0	1,000	0	3,000	1		
3	0	0	5,000	0				
4	0	0						

Answer 6.   In general, PTH[i, j] is the value of the index k that led to the optimal result   125 - A 6
of the product $M_i \times M_{i+j}$. In particular, if PTH[1, n − 1] = k, it is known that the optimal
bracketing of the initial matrix product $M_1 \times \cdots \times M_{i+k} \times M_{i+k+1} \times \cdots \times M_n$ is $(M_1 \times \cdots \times M_{i+k}) \times (M_{i+k+1} \times \cdots \times M_n)$. The reconstitution of the (one) optimal bracketing is thus
based on a recursive program composing the optimal bracketing of the product of matrices
$(M_i \times \cdots \times M_{i+j})$ by a double recursive call for the products $(M_i \times \cdots \times M_{i+CH[i,j]})$ and
$(M_{i+CH[i,j]+1} \times \cdots \times M_{i+j})$. The first (respectively second) recursive call is made only if
PTH[i, j] $\neq$ 0 (respectively PTH[i, j] $\neq$ (i + j − 1)), i.e. in the presence of a product of at least
two matrices.
In the proposed example, the cell PTH[1, 3] is equal to 2, which yields the bracketing
$(M_1 \times M_2 \times M_3) \times (M_4)$. The second product being made up of a single matrix, only the
bracketing of the first product is to be carried out (only one recursive call takes place). The
same process applies starting from the cell PTH[1, 2] = 0 which leads to the bracketing
$(M_1) \times (M_2 \times M_3)$. Here again, a single recursive call is triggered to bracket the product
$M_2 \times M_3$. In the end, the optimal bracketing: $((M_1) \times (M_2 \times M_3)) \times (M_4)$ has been produced and we can verify that its cost is $(20 \cdot 50 \cdot 1) + (10 \cdot 20 \cdot 1) + (10 \cdot 1 \cdot 100) = 2,200$ as
expected.

Answers to problem 126. Cutting a wooden board   *The problem is on page 650.*

Answer 1.   The possible cuts of a segment to be divided in total in $(k + 1)$ pieces are   126 - A 1
obtained by successive cuts in two pieces. The number of possible distinct cuts nbcut(k)
is given by:

$$\begin{vmatrix} nbcut(1) = 1 \\ nbcut(k) = \sum_{i=1}^{k-1} nbcut(i) \cdot nbcut(k-i) \end{vmatrix} \qquad\qquad k > 1.$$

We have $nbcut(k) = Cat(k)$ (k^{th} Catalan number); thus it can be seen that in terms of combinatorial this problem is analogous to the chained product of matrices (problem 125, page 649), studied just before.

126 - A 2   **Answer** 2.   The ends and cut points are numbered from 0 to n. In so doing, the segment of rank i and length l_i is located between the cutting points $(i-1)$ and i, of respective abscissas $x(i-1)$ and $x(i)$. Consider the optimal cut of the segment between the cut points i and j ($j > i$) and denote by $bestcut(i,j)$ its cost. Its transport cost $TC(i,j)$ corresponds to its length, that is $l_{i+1} + \cdots + l_j = x(j) - x(i+1)$. The cut can start at the point $(i+1)$ – and it remains to optimally cut the segment between the points $(i+1)$ and j – or at the point $(i+2)$ – and the segment between the points i and $(i+2)$ on the one hand and the segment between the points $(i+2)$ and j on the other – or ... or at point $(j-1)$ – and it remains to optimally cut the segment between the points i and $(j-1)$. Among these possibilities, the case inducing the minimum cost is chosen. By noticing that for $i \in 0..n-1$, $bestcut(i, i+1) = 0$, the recurrence is:

$$
\left|
\begin{array}{l}
bestcut(i, i+1) = 0 \\[2mm]
bestcut(i,j) = \displaystyle\min_{k \in i+1..j-1} \left(\begin{array}{l} bestcut(i,k) + \\ bestcut(k,j) + \\ TC(i,j) \end{array} \right)
\end{array}
\right.
\qquad
\begin{array}{c}
0 \leqslant i \leqslant n-1 \\[2mm]
\left\{ \begin{array}{c} 0 \leqslant i \leqslant (n-2) \\ \textbf{and} \\ (i+2) \leqslant j \leqslant n \end{array} \right.
\end{array}.
$$

The calculations made to deal with the proposed example are now detailed.

Initialization $bestcut(0,1) = 0$; $bestcut(1,2) = 0$; $bestcut(2,3) = 0$.

Recurrence $bestcut(0,2) = bestcut(0,1) + bestcut(1,2) + TC(0,2) = 0 + 0 + 7 = 7$,
$bestcut(1,3) = bestcut(1,2) + bestcut(2,3) + TC(1,3) = 0 + 0 + 8 = 8$,
$$
bestcut(0,3) = \min \left(\left\{ \begin{array}{l} bestcut(0,1) + bestcut(1,3) + TC(0,3), \\ bestcut(0,2) + bestcut(2,3) + TC(0,3) \end{array} \right\} \right)
$$
$$
\min(\{0 + 8 + 10, 7 + 0 + 10\}) = 17.
$$

The spatial complexity of the procedure associated with this recurrence is in $\Theta(n^2)$ (array $BESTCT[0..n-1, 1..n]$) and time complexity in $\Theta(n^3)$ since, in general, calculating $bestcut(i,j)$ requires a loop to evaluate the minimum.

126 - A 3   **Answer** 3.   If you have a flat donut to cut, the new point concerns the circularity of the problem. Indeed, we must express the cost of the best cut of any arc of length less than or equal to n. Thus, in the proposed example where the numbers of the cutting points (from 0 to 3) are added in italics:

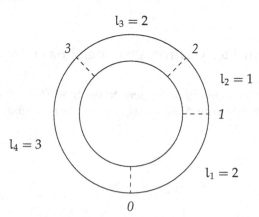

$l_3 = 2$

3   *2*

$l_2 = 1$

1

$l_4 = 3$

$l_1 = 2$

0

it is necessary to speak of the segment $(0,3)$, but also of $(2,0)$ or of $(3,2)$. A simple way to proceed is to associate the donut with a "double board", i.e. the juxtaposition of two identical segments corresponding to the donut "unfolded". In the example above, we will have:

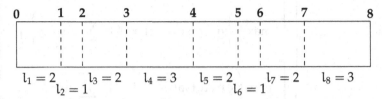

The best cut of the segment (i,j) is calculated as the choice of the best saw cut (cutting point with the optimal number k) cutting this segment into two pieces which will also be cut optimally. The final result is obtained by taking the cut of length n of minimum value among those starting at each of the cutting points $(0, 1, \ldots, n-1)$. The recurrence used is exactly the same as previously and time complexity remains in $\Theta(n^3)$, since the complementary phase that is added to the filling of the tabular structure $BESTCT'[0..n-1, 1..2n]$ to determine the minimum value among $BESTCT'[0, n-1]$, $BESTCT'[1, n], \ldots, BESTCT'[n-2, 1]$, $BESTCT'[n-1, 0]$, is linear in number of conditions evaluated.

Answers to problem 127. The safecrackers *The problem is on page 651.*

Answer 1. It has been seen in the statement of the problem that if each thief is in charge of three safes, the thieves leave after 15 minutes. By assigning the safes 1 and 2 to the first thief, the safes 3, 4 and 5 to the second and the other four to the third, the thief who finishes last is the second, in only 14 minutes. 127 - A 1

Answer 2. If there is a single safe to open ($n = 1$), $\text{optgtso}(1,k)$ is given by the opening time of this safe, i.e. $\text{optgtso}(1,k) = \text{etso}(1)$. When only one thief has to open n safes, he opens them one after the other so we have $\text{optgtso}(n,1) = \sum_{i=1}^{n} \text{etso}(i)$. When the number k of thieves is greater than the number n of safes to be opened, $(k-n)$ thieves are inactive. Each of the active thieves opens one of the safes, and the minimum time required to open all the safes is $\text{optgtso}(n,k) = \max(\{\text{etso}(1), \ldots, \text{etso}(n)\})$. Finally, if there are at least as many safes to open as there are thieves ($n \geqslant k$), $(k-1)$ thieves open j safes ($j < n$ so that there is at least one safe left to open), and the last thief takes care of the remaining $(n-j)$ safes. The best way to operate is obtained by opening the j safes optimally and choosing the value of j minimizing the expression: 127 - A 2

$$\max\left(\left\{\text{optgtso}(j, k-1), \sum_{i=j+1}^{n} \text{etso}(i)\right\}\right).$$

Therefore:

$$\text{optgtso}(n, k) = \min_{j \in 1..n-1}\left(\max\left(\left\{\text{optgtso}(j, k-1), \sum_{i=j+1}^{n} \text{etso}(i)\right\}\right)\right).$$

This expression can be refined, because by expanding it, we get:

$$optgtso(n, k) = \min \left(\begin{cases} \max \left(\left\{ optgtso(1, k-1), \sum_{i=2}^{n} etso(i) \right\} \right), \\ \dots \\ \max \left(\left\{ optgtso(k-1, k-1), \sum_{i=k}^{n} etso(i) \right\} \right), \\ \dots \\ \max \left(\left\{ optgtso(n-1, k-1), \sum_{i=n}^{n} etso(i) \right\} \right) \end{cases} \right).$$

For $m > 1$:

$$\max \left(\left\{ optgtso(k-m, k-1), \sum_{i=k-m+1}^{n} etso(i) \right\} \right)$$

$$\geqslant \max \left(\left\{ optgtso(k-1, k-1), \sum_{i=k}^{n} etso(i) \right\} \right)$$

since on the one hand $optgtso(k-m, k-1) = optgtso(k-1, k-1) = \max_{i=1}^{k-1} etso(i)$, on the other hand $\sum_{i=k-m+1}^{n} etso(i) \geqslant \sum_{i=k}^{n} etso(i)$.

Thus, any term $\max \left(\left\{ optgtso(k-m, k-1), \sum_{i=k-m+1}^{n} etso(i) \right\} \right)$ where $m > 1$ cannot produce a new value for the minimum sought, since $(k-1)$ thieves are assigned to strictly less than $(k-1)$ safes. Therefore the values of j less than $(k-1)$ can be omitted, which yields:

$$optgtso(n, k) = \min_{j \in k-1..n-1} \left(\max \left(\left\{ optgtso(j, k-1), \sum_{i=j+1}^{n} etso(i) \right\} \right) \right).$$

127 - A 3   **Answer 3.**   In order to be able to calculate $optgtso(N, p)$, the minimum opening time of N safes by p thieves, the four cases treated in the previous question (which cover all the situations that may occur) are inserted in the recurrence and therefore:

$$\begin{vmatrix} optgtso(1, k) = etso(1) & 1 \leqslant k \leqslant p \\ optgtso(n, 1) = \sum_{i=1}^{n} etso(i) & 1 < n \leqslant N \\ optgtso(n, k) = optgtso(n, n) & 1 < n \leqslant N \text{ and } 1 < k \leqslant p \text{ and } k > n \\ optgtso(n, k) = \min_{j \in k-1..n-1} \left(\max \left(\left\{ \begin{array}{c} optgtso(j, k-1), \\ \sum_{i=j+1}^{n} etso(i) \end{array} \right\} \right) \right) & \left\{ \begin{array}{c} 1 < n \leqslant N \text{ and} \\ 1 < k \leqslant p \end{array} \right. \end{vmatrix}$$

127 - A 4   **Answer 4.**   The algorithm performing this calculation uses the array $OTGSO[1..N, 1..p]$, hence a spatial complexity in $\Theta(p \cdot N)$; the value sought is in the cell $OTGSO[N, p]$. This array is filled with increasing column index values, since, according to the general term of recurrence, the calculation of a cell uses the cell values of the previous column. The first column is initialized thanks to the second term of the recurrence. In a given column, we proceed by row index of increasing value, knowing that the first element is filled thanks to the first term of the recurrence and the others thanks to one of the last two according to whether the row index (n) exceeds or not the column index (k). For optimization purposes, the partial sums $\sum_{i=j+1}^{n} \text{etso}(i)$ are precomputed (in $\Theta(N^2)$ additions and comparisons) and they are stored in an annex array.

In general, the filling of a cell leads to at most $(N-1)$ operations "maximum" and $(N-2)$ operations "minimum"; the total number of comparisons carried out to fill OTGSO is thus in $\mathcal{O}(p \cdot N^2)$. Indeed, the number of operations "maximum" and "minimum" is:

$$\left(\sum_{i=1}^{N-1} i^2\right) - \left(\sum_{i=1}^{N-p} i^2\right) = (p-1) \cdot \left(N^2 - p \cdot N + \frac{p \cdot (2p-1)}{6}\right).$$

This expression is equal to 0 when $p = 1$ (in accordance with the first term of the recurrence); it is in the order of $p \cdot N^2$ when p est small compared to N or when p is close to N.

Answer 5.   In the example of the statement, we have $N = 9$ and $p = 3$ and the array   127 - A 5
OTGSO[1 .. 9, 1 .. 3] is:

k	1	2	3
i = 1	5	5	5
2	12	7	7
3	15	10	7
4	20	12	8
5	26	14	11
6	29	15	12
7	31	16	12
8	36	20	14
9	39	20	14

As an illustration, let us detail the calculation of OTGSO[7,3]:

$$OTGSO[7,3] = \min \left(\left\{ \begin{array}{l} \max\left(\left\{OTGSO[2,2], \sum_{i=3}^{7} \text{etso}(i)\right\}\right), \\ \max\left(\left\{OTGSO[3,2], \sum_{i=4}^{7} \text{etso}(i)\right\}\right), \\ \max\left(\left\{OTGSO[4,2], \sum_{i=5}^{7} \text{etso}(i)\right\}\right), \\ \max\left(\left\{OTGSO[5,2], \sum_{i=6}^{7} \text{etso}(i)\right\}\right), \\ \max\left(\left\{OTGSO[6,2], \sum_{i=7}^{7} \text{etso}(i)\right\}\right) \end{array} \right\} \right)$$

$$= \min\left(\left\{ \begin{array}{l} \max(\{7,19\}), \max(\{10,16\}), \max(\{12,11\}), \\ \max(\{14,5\}), \max(\{15,2\}) \end{array} \right\}\right)$$
$$= \min(\{19, 16, 12, 14, 15\}) = 12.$$

It can be seen that the minimum time necessary for the opening of the nine safes (in cell $(9,3)$) is 14 minutes. The solution proposed in the answer to the first question (first two safes assigned to the first thief, safes 3, 4 and 5 assigned to the second and last four safes opened by the third thief) is actually optimal and it delivers this result.

Answers to problem 128. Three shelf problems *The problem is on page 652.*

128 - A 1 **Answer** 1. The idea is to found the recurrence on the fact that $sh(i,j)$ allows by definition to check if it is possible to place books B_i to B_j on the same spoke. Optimal ordering of books B_i to B_N consists in considering the best way (optimal value j) of constituting a spoke starting with B_i and ending in B_j, then in optimally ordering the books B_{j+1} to B_N. The recurrence relation is therefore the following:

$$\begin{vmatrix} \text{hgmin}(N+1) = 0 \\ \text{hgmin}(i) = \min_{j \in i..N} \left(sh(i,j) + \text{hgmin}(j+1) \right) \end{vmatrix} \qquad 1 \leqslant i \leqslant N.$$

This recurrence is actually descending (or backward) since it starts from $\text{hgmin}(N+1)$ and "descends" to $\text{hgmin}(1)$; the spokes are therefore built from the bottom (spoke with the highest number) to the top (spoke numbered 1).

128 - A 2 **Answer** 2. The algorithm associated with the calculation of $\text{hgmin}(1)$ consists of two steps. The first aims to calculate (in $SH[1..N, 1..N]$) the values of $sh(i,j)$ as defined previously from the thicknesses and heights of the books $B_1, \ldots, B_N$. In the second phase, the array $HGM[1..N+1]$ is filled. The progression of the calculation is done by decreasing values of the index (initialization of $HGM[N+1]$ thanks to the first term of the recurrence, then from $HGM[N]$ to $HGM[1]$ using the second term), the desired result being in $HGM[1]$. The first (respectively second) step of this algorithm requires $(N(N-1))/2$ (respectively $(N(N+1))/2$) comparisons (neglecting loop control). Therefore, complexity is in $\Theta(N^2)$ comparisons.

128 - A 3 **Answer** 3. In the example considered, the array $SH[1..6, 1..6]$ takes the following values:

j	1	2	3	4	5	6
i = 1	1	2	5	$+\infty$	$+\infty$	$+\infty$
2		2	5	5	$+\infty$	$+\infty$
3			5	5	5	$+\infty$
4				4	4	4
5					3	3
6						1

$HGM(7)$ is initialized with 0, and the calculations are:

$$HGM[6] = \min(\{SH[6,6] + HGM[7] = 1 + 0\}) = 1$$

$$HGM[5] = \min \left(\left\{ \begin{array}{l} SH[5,5] + HGM[6] = 3+1 \\ SH[5,6] + HGM[7] = 3+0 \end{array} \right\} \right) = 3$$

$$HGM[4] = \min \left(\left\{ \begin{array}{l} SH[4,4] + HGM[5] = 4+3 \\ SH[4,5] + HGM[6] = 4+1 \\ SH[4,6] + HGM[7] = 4+0 \end{array} \right\} \right) = 4$$

$$HGM[3] = \min \left(\left\{ \begin{array}{l} SH[3,3] + HGM[4] = 5+4 \\ SH[3,4] + HGM[5] = 5+3 \\ SH[3,5] + HGM[6] = 5+1 \\ SH[3,6] + HGM[7] = +\infty + 0 \end{array} \right\} \right) = 6$$

$$HGM[2] = \min \left(\left\{ \begin{array}{l} SH[2,2] + HGM[3] = 2+6 \\ SH[2,3] + HGM[4] = 5+4 \\ SH[2,4] + HGM[5] = 5+3 \\ SH[2,5] + HGM[6] = +\infty + 1 \\ SH[2,6] + HGM[7] = +\infty + 0 \end{array} \right\} \right) = 8$$

$$HGM[1] = \min \left(\left\{ \begin{array}{l} SH[1,1] + HGM[2] = 1+8 \\ SH[1,2] + HGM[3] = 2+6 \\ SH[1,3] + HGM[4] = 5+4 \\ SH[1,4] + HGM[5] = +\infty + 3 \\ SH[1,5] + HGM[6] = +\infty + 1 \\ SH[1,6] + HGM[7] = +\infty + 0 \end{array} \right\} \right) = 8.$$

Here, the height of the optimal shelf is 8. To know its composition in terms of spokes, at each step the value j for which the optimum has been reached must be kept. In this example, it can be observed that for HGM[1] $j = 2$, for HGM[3] the value of j realizing the optimal is 5, and that finally HGM[6] $= 1$ is reached with $j = 6$. It can be deduced that the upper spoke (of height 2) contains books B_1 and B_2, that the second shelf, of height 5, includes B_3 , B_4 and B_5, B_6 being alone on the lower spoke (of height 1) according to the following diagram:

Answer 4. In the presence of a single spoken ($K = 1$), all the books must be put there, and therefore for $1 \leqslant n \leqslant N$: $W = wdmin(n,1) = st(1,n)$.   128 - A 4

Answer 5. If there are as many spokes as books ($n \leqslant k$), it is possible to place at most one book on each spoke (some shelves are left vacant if $n < k$); the minimum width of the shelf is therefore that of the thickest book, that is $wdmin(n,k) = \max(\{t_1,\ldots,t_n\})$. Let us notice that the calculation of $W = wdmin(N,K)$ (the width of the shelf with K spokes allowing to store books B_1 to B_N) is non trivial only when $N > K$.   128 - A 5

Answer 6. When $n > k$ (general case), either the last spoke containing books $B_m,\ldots,B_n$ is the widest and $wdmin(n,k) = st(m,n)$, or the largest spoke has a rank strictly less than k and then: $wdmin(n,k) = wdmin(m-1,k-1)$.   128 - A 6

Answer 7. In the previous question, it was established that for a given m and $n > k$:   128 - A 7

$$wdmin(n,k) = \max(\{wdmin(m-1,k-1), st(m,n)\}).$$

The shelf of minimum width is obtained by taking the value of m minimizing $wdmin(n,k)$. If m varies from 1 to n *a priori*, it turns out that only values of the interval $k \mathinner{.\,.} n$ can lead to the optimal. Indeed, intuitively, a storage with more spokes than books ($k > m$) results in leaving at least one spoke vacant, with the books $B_m, \ldots, B_n$ on the last spoke occupied and $m - k$ empty lower spokes. The interested reader will easily prove that the storage obtained by putting the book B_m on the mth spoke and the books $B_{m+1}, \ldots, B_n$ on the $(m + 1)^{th}$ spoke is equal to or better (in terms of width) than the initial arrangement. In conclusion, it suffices to vary m from k to n, hence the recurrence of calculation of $wdmin(n, k)$ below:

$$\left| \begin{aligned} &wdmin(n, 1) = \sum_{i=1}^{n} t_i = st(1, n) \\ &wdmin(n, k) = \max_{i \in 1..n} (t_i) && 1 < n \leqslant k \leqslant K \\ &wdmin(n, k) = \min_{m \in k..n} \left(\max \left(\left\{ \begin{aligned} &wdmin(m - 1, k - 1), \\ &st(m, n) \end{aligned} \right\} \right) \right) && 2 \leqslant k \leqslant K \text{ and } k < n \leqslant \\ &N. \end{aligned} \right.$$

128 - A 8   **Answer** 8.   The dynamic programming algorithm performing the effective calculation uses the arrays $WDM[1..N, 1..K]$ and $T[1..N, 1..N]$ associated respectively with $wdmin$ and st. The filling of ST is trivial and that of WDM can be done by increasing values of column index value since, the computation of an element of column k calls only on values located in column $(k - 1)$. The first column is filled with the first term of the recurrence using ST. In any other index column k, the index elements row n greater than 1 and less than or equal to k are calculated using the second term of the recurrence, then the following ones (row index n greater than k) with the last term.

Considering the number of comparisons made (linked to operations min and max), it can be observed that the first column does not require any. The number of comparisons for cells in columns $k = 2$ to 4 is explained below:

i	1	2	3	4	5	...	N
$k = 2$	0	1	3	5	7	...	$2N - 3$
3	0	1	2	3	5	...	$2N - 5$
4	0	1	2	3	3	...	$2N - 7$

The number of comparisons is maximum for $k = 2$ and for the calculation of $WDM[N, K]$, the total number of comparisons is upper bounded by $((K - 1) \cdot \sum_{i=1}^{N-1}(2i - 1)) = (K - 1) \cdot (N - 1)^2$, hence a time complexity in $\mathcal{O}(K \cdot N^2)$.

128 - A 9   **Answer** 9.   In the example proposed, ST and WDM are given hereafter:

j	1	2	3	4	5	6
$i = 1$	5	8	12	13	16	18
2		3	7	8	11	13
3			4	5	8	10
4				1	4	6
5					3	5
6						2

k	1	2	3
$n = 1$	5	5	5
2	8	5	5
3	12	7	5
4	13	8	5
5	16	8	7
6	18	10	7

Here, $WDM[N, K] = WDM[6, 3] = 7$, which means that a shelf of width 7 is necessary for the storage of the six books on the three spokes, according to the assertion of the statement. Using "Tom Thumb's" technique (not detailed here), the following storage is found:

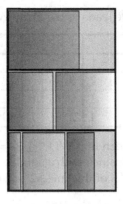

Remark

This algorithm can be used to determine whether it is possible to store N books of the same height and given thicknesses in a shelf with K spokes of width W (N, K and W assumed to be given).

Answer 10.   In the presence of a single spoke shelf (K = 1), a naïve solution (of type "Generate and test", see Chapter 5) consists in studying all the subsets of the N books in order to find out the optimal one (in the sense of a maximum number of books with an occupied space less than or equal to W), hence a complexity in $\mathcal{O}(2^N)$. **128 - A 10**

Answer 11.   With a single spoke shelf, the case j = i leads to a necessary space equal to the sum of the thicknesses of the i books; if only one book is taken (j = 1) among i, the one of minimum thickness is chosen. In the general case, to have j books among i $(1 < j < i)$, from a situation with $(i-1)$ books, the book number i is taken and the necessary space increases by its thickness t_i or it is left and j books among the first $(i-1)$ must be taken. The following recurrence can be deduced: **128 - A 11**

$$
\begin{vmatrix}
\mathrm{wdnec}(i,1) = \min_{j \in 1..i} (t_j) & 1 \leqslant i \leqslant N \\
\mathrm{wdnec}(i,i) = \sum_{j=1}^{i} t_i & 2 \leqslant i \leqslant N \\
\mathrm{wdnec}(i,j) = \min \left(\left\{ \begin{array}{l} \mathrm{wdnec}(i-1,j-1) + t_i, \\ \mathrm{wdnec}(i-1,j) \end{array} \right\} \right) & 2 \leqslant j < i \leqslant N.
\end{vmatrix}
$$

The associated algorithm fills the array WDN[1 .. N, 1 .. N] corresponding to wdnec by increasing values of the row index. Thanks to the first (respectively second) term of the recurrence, the first (respectively i^{th}) element of row i can be filled. The other cells (with column indices 2 to $i-1$) are filled using the last term of the recurrence. It should be noted that the cells of the upper right triangle of the table WDN are irrelevant since they correspond to the case j > i which does not make sense.
To determine the value M sought representing the maximum number of books that can be stored in the shelf, it suffices to search in the last row (index N) the index j (giving the maximum number M of books that can be stored on the single spoke) maximum such that WDN[N, j] is less than or equal to W.

One comparison is therefore performed for the first and second rows, two for the third row, ..., N − 1 for the calculations of the last row, hence an algorithm in $\Theta(N^2)$.

Applying the above to the example leads to the array WDN[1 .. 4, 1 .. 4] below:

j	1	2	3	4
i = 1	3			
2	3	6		
3	2	5	8	
4	2	4	7	10

Looking at the last line, it can be seen that $WDN[4,2] = 4$ (< 5) and $WDN[4,3] = 7$ (> 5), hence $M = 2$, which was expected, since with a single spoke shelf of width 5, the choice is between on the one hand two books of thickness 2 and on the other hand one of thickness 2 and one of thickness 3.

128 - A 12 **Answer 12.** With a two spoke shelf, the essential difference compared to the previous case is that it is necessary to manage any empty space on the first shelf. A spoke change must occur when, in the previous recurrence, the term $wdnec(i-1, j-1) + t_i$ exceeds the length W. In this case, one cannot consider putting the book on the same shelf as its predecessor, and the classic "addition" in the equations becomes inappropriate. One solution consists in defining a particular associative and non-commutative addition, denoted $\oplus$, as follows:

$$a \oplus b = \begin{cases} W + b & \text{if } a < W \text{ and } a + b > W \\ a + b & \text{otherwise.} \end{cases}$$

The first case corresponds to spoke change; in this case, the width of the first spoke is set to W. As for $K = 1$, it is supposed that the last spoke has a width as large as desired. The recurrence becomes:

$$
\begin{vmatrix}
wdnec(i, 1) = \min_{j \in 1..i} (t_j) & 1 \leqslant i \leqslant N \\
wdnec(i, i) = wdnec(i, i) = t_1 \oplus \cdots \oplus t_i & 2 \leqslant i \leqslant N \\
wdnec(i, j) = \min \left(\left\{ \begin{array}{l} wdnec(i-1, j-1) \oplus t_i, \\ wdnec(i-1, j) \end{array} \right\} \right) & 2 \leqslant j < i \leqslant N.
\end{vmatrix}
$$

The dynamic programming algorithm obeys the same principle as before and its complexity is of the same order regarding the number of comparisons. The determination of M is done by looking for the index j (giving the maximum number M of books that can be stored on the two spokes of the shelf) maximum such as $WDN[N, j] \leqslant 2 \cdot W$.

Dealing with the example leads to the following array WDN:

j	1	2	3	4
i = 1	3			
2	3	8		
3	2	5	10	
4	2	4	7	12

The value 8 in the cell $WDN[2, 2]$ results from the operation $3 \oplus 3$. Ultimately, the value of M, the maximum number of books that can be stored, is 3. This corresponds to putting a book of thickness 3 on the first spoke (B_1 or B_2) and B_3 of thickness 2, and the book B_4 alone on the second spoke. These two solutions appear in the (exhaustive) list given in the statement (see page 655).

Answer 13.   To take into account any number K of spokes, the operation ⊕ must be   128 - A 13
generalized by setting $p = \lceil a/W \rceil$, as follows:

$$a \oplus b = \begin{cases} p \cdot W + b & \text{if } (a \bmod W) + b > W \text{ and } p < K \\ a + b & \text{otherwise.} \end{cases}$$

It is easy to check that in the case where $K = 2$, the result of this expression coincides with
that given for the previous question. Indeed, if $K = 2$, p can only take the value 1 and therefore a/W is equal to 0, which means that a is less than W. If $K = 1$, the only possibility is
to do the classic addition as it appeared in the answer to the question assigned to this case.

The recurrence remains unchanged with respect to the case $K = 2$ and, letting T be the
array containing the thicknesses t_i of the books, we end up with the following algorithm
for any value of K:

```
1.  constants
2.     N ∈ ℕ₁ and N = ... and W ∈ ℕ₁ and W = ... and T ∈ 1..N → ℕ₁ and
                                                n
3.     E = [...] and K ∈ ℕ₁ and K = ... and   ∑  E[i] > K · L
                                               i=1
4.  variables
5.     WDN ∈ 1..N × 1..N → ℕ₁
6.  begin
7.     /% filling of the first column and the diagonal %/
8.     WDN[1, 1] ← T[1];
9.     for i ranging 2..N do
10.       WDN[i, 1] ← min({WDN[i − 1, 1], T[i]});
11.       WDN[i, i] ← WDN[i − 1, i − 1] ⊕ T[i]
12.    end for;
13.    /% filling of the other cells of each row %/
14.    for i ranging 2..N do
15.       for j ranging 2..i − 1 do
16.          WDN[i, j] ← min({WDN[i − 1, j − 1] ⊕ T[i], WDN[i − 1, j]})
17.       end for
18.    end for;
19.    j ← 1;
20.    while WDN[N, j] ⩽ K · W do
21.       j ← j + 1
22.    end while;
23.    if j > 1 then
24.       write(it is possible to store , WDN[N, j − 1], books on the shelf)
25.    else
26.       write(no book can be stored on the shelf)
27.    end if
28. end
```

The value of M is determined by looking for the index j (giving the maximum number
M of books that can be stored on the K spokes of the shelf) such as $WDN[N, j] \leqslant K \cdot W$,
which generalizes the particular cases dealt with in the two previous questions ($K = 1$ and
$K = 2$).

The spatial complexity of this algorithm is in $\Theta(N^2)$ (array WDN), as well as its time complexity in terms of conditions evaluated. The treatment of the example proposed with eight books, $K = 3$ and $W = 5$, leads to the array WDN below:

j	1	2	3	4	5	6	7	8
i = 1	3							
2	3	8						
3	1	4	9					
4	1	3	7	12				
5	1	3	7	12	16			
6	1	3	5	9	14	18		
7	1	3	5	8	13	17	21	
8	1	3	5	8	13	17	21	25

For example, the values WDN[5, 4] and WDN[8, 7] are computed as follows:

$$WDN[5,4] = \min(\{WDN[4,3] \oplus T[5], WDN[4,4]\}) = \min(\{7 \oplus 4, 12\}) = \min(\{14, 12\}) = 12,$$
$$WDN[8,7] = \min(\{WDN[7,6] \oplus T[8], WDN[7,7]\}) = \min(\{17 \oplus 4, 25\}) = \min(\{21, 25\}) = 21.$$

Finally, the value of M is 5, corresponding to the book B_1 of thickness 3 on the first spoke, books B_2 and B_3 on the second spoke and books B_4 and B_6 on the last spoke (use of "Tom Thumb's" method not developed here).

Answers to problem 129. Choosing skis

The problem is on page 656.

129 - A 1 **Answer 1.**   The number of assignments of one pair of skis among m to each of the n skiers corresponds to the choice of n elements out of m. It is thus the number of arrangements of n elements out of m, i.e. $m!/(m - n)!$ (see also page 204 in Chapter 5).

129 - A 2 **Answer 2.**   Let us consider two assignments that differ only on the pairs of skis of ranks i and j. In the first one, s_i (respectively s_j) is associated with h_p (respectively h_q), whereas in the second one s_i (respectively s_j) is associated with h_q (respectively h_p), where $p < q$ and therefore $h_p \leqslant h_q$. Let us first remark that when $s_i = s_j$ or $h_p = h_q$, these two assignments result in the same global satisfaction of the skiers. Examining the six cases that can occur with $s_i < s_j$ and $h_p < h_q$, it appears that the sum dv_1 of the deviations $|s_i - h_p|$ and $|s_j - h_q|$ is always less than or equal to the sum dv_2 of the deviations $|s_i - h_q|$ and $|s_j - h_p|$. In other words, the first ski assignment always does at least as well as the second. For example, if $s_i \leqslant h_p < h_q \leqslant s_j$, we have:

$$dv_1 = |s_i - h_p| + |s_j - h_q| = h_p - s_i + s_j - h_q$$
$$dv_2 = |s_i - h_q| + |s_j - h_p| = h_q - s_i + s_j - h_p$$

hence $dv_2 - dv_1 = 2 \cdot (h_q - h_p) > 0$.

It can be deduced that an assignment with an increasing function asf is preferable to an assignment where the order (in the sens of the lengths) over the pairs of skis involves at least one inversion with respect to the order (in the sense of heights) over the skiers.

129 - A 3 **Answer 3.**   When there are as many skiers as there are pairs of skis ($n = m$), any pair of skis is allocated to a skier. By virtue of the result established in the previous question, a monotonic assignment function asf can only assign the smallest pair of skis to the smallest skier, the second smallest pair of skis to the second smallest skier, and so on. after. This assignment strategy can be seen as a greedy process, where $asf(k) = k$ for any $k \in 1 .. n$.

Answer 4.   Consider the case where the skiers of rank 1 to i (h_1 to h_i) are equipped   129 - A 4
with pairs of skis taken in $s_1, \ldots, s_j$. If the last pair of skis (of rank j) is assigned to another
skier than the last (h_i), the assignment function asf is non-monotonic. According to the
result established above, such an assignment is in general not optimal and should not be
made to maximize the overall satisfaction of the skiers.

Answer 5.   The previous question is the key to the strategy to adopt, since in the pres-   129 - A 5
ence of i skiers and j pairs of skis ($j \geqslant i$), we only have the choice between assigning the
pair of skis of rank j to the skier of rank i and make an optimal allocation of the $(j-1)$
remaining pairs of skis to the $(i-1)$ first skiers or not allocate it to anyone by making an
optimal allocation of the $(j-1)$ remaining pairs of skis to the i skiers. The most favorable
of these two possibilities is chosen, that is to say the one associated with the smallest of
the two values obtained. This corresponds to the general case, when $j > i$ and $i > 1$. Two
particular cases occur when $i = 1$ (the single skier is assigned the pair of skis of length
closest to his height) and $i = j$ (case dealt with in question 3). The recurrence is:

$$
\left|
\begin{aligned}
&optasg(1, j) = \min_{k \in 1..j} (|h_1 - s_k|) && 1 \leqslant j \leqslant m \\[2mm]
&optasg(i, i) = \sum_{k=1}^{i} |h_k - s_k| && 1 < i \leqslant n \\[2mm]
&optasg(i, j) = \min \left(\left\{ \begin{aligned} &optasg(i, j{-}1), \\ &optasg(i{-}1, j{-}1) + |h_i - s_j| \end{aligned} \right\} \right) && \left\{ \begin{aligned} &i < j \text{ and} \\ &1 < i \leqslant n \text{ and} \\ &1 < j \leqslant m \end{aligned} \right. \;.
\end{aligned}
\right.
$$

Answer 6.   The principle of the dynamic programming algorithm associated with the   129 - A 6
computation of $optasg(n, m)$ consists in filling the array $OASG[1..n, 1..m]$. In the end,
the optimal overall satisfaction value for the distribution of m pairs of skis to n skiers
($m \geqslant n$) is found in the cell $OASG[n, m]$. The progression of the calculation can take place
by increasing values of the row index (for example), knowing that the first is filled thanks
to the first term of the recurrence. In any row of index i between 2 and n, the cell $OASG[i, i]$
is filled using the second term of the recurrence, and the cells $OASG[i, j]$ with $1 < j \leqslant m$
and $i < j$ are filled using the last term.
The spatial complexity of this algorithm is in $\Theta(m \cdot n)$ (due to the array $OASG$), just like its
temporal complexity in number of conditions evaluated (provided that the calculation of
the cells of the first row is performed in an optimized way, and therefore in $\Theta(m)$ instead
of $\Theta(m^2)$ with a "naïve computation").
"Tom Thumb's" method is applied to determine the values of the optimal function asf.
The array $ASF[1..n, 1..m]$ is filled "in parallel" of $OASG$ in the following way, depending
on the term of the recurrence used:

- when using the first term of the recurrence, the value $ASF[1, j]$ is assigned the
  value of k having achieved the minimum of $OASG[1, j]$,
- filling the cell $OASG[i, i]$ ($1 < i \leqslant n$) leads to $ASF[i, i] = i$,
- when the last term of the recurrence is used, the value of $ASF[i, j]$ is $ASF[i, j-1]$
  or j depending on whether the minimum is achieved by the first or the second
  expression.

The reconstitution of the optimal allocation is carried out starting from the value $ASF[n, m]$
and going up diagonally until being in row 1.

Answer 7.   With the three skiers of heights $h_1 = 170, h_2 = 190, h_3 = 210$ and the five   129 - A 7
pairs of skis of lengths $s_1 = 158, s_2 = 179, s_3 = 200, s_4 = 203, s_5 = 213$, the following

results are obtained (the values of optasg and asf are gathered in the same cell of the array $A[1..3, 1..5]$):

	$j = 1$ $s_1 = 158$	$j = 2$ $s_2 = 179$	$j = 3$ $s_3 = 200$	$j = 4$ $s_4 = 203$	$j = 5$ $s_5 = 213$
$i = 1$ $h_1 = 170$	12 1	9 2	9 2	9 2	9 2
$i = 2$ $h_2 = 190$		23 2	19 3	19 3	19 3
$i = 3$ $h_3 = 210$			33 3	26 4	22 5

Here, the reconstitution of the optimal assignment yields $asf(3) = 5$, $asf(2) = 3$ and $asf(1) = 2$, which corresponds to the optimal solution: $h_1 - s_2, h_2 - s_3, h_3 - s_5$, whose global satisfaction value is 22.

129 - A 8   **Answer** 8.   It can be observed that the cells of the "left lower triangle" (cells $OASG[i, j]$ such that $j < i$) are not filled since they correspond to situations where the problem has no solution (more skiers than pairs of skis). Moreover, the calculation of the value of cell $OASG[n, m]$ requires the knowledge of $OASG[n - 1, m - 1]$ and $OASG[n, m - 1]$, but not that of $OASG[n - 1, m]$ whose computation is therefore useless. For the same reason, the calculations of $OASG[n - 1, m]$ and $OASG[n - 2, m - 1]$ can also be omitted, and more generally those of the values of the cells of the "right upper triangle", that is $OASG[i, j]$ where $j > m - n + i$. Four $m = 9$ and $n = 6$, the array $OASG$ obtained is of the form:

j	1	2	3	4	5	6	7	8	9
i = 1	×	×	×	×					
2		×	×	×	×				
3			×	×	×	×			
4				×	×	×	×		
5					×	×	×	×	
6						×	×	×	×

where only the cells crossmarked, forming a diagonal of thickness $(m - n + 1)$, are to be filled.

It can be checked that, although meaningful, this simplification does not change the order of magnitude of time complexity.

129 - A 9   **Answer** 9.   By analogy with what was done previously, we will first show that for this new optimization criterion, the function asf must also be monotonic. Consider again (see answer 2, page 716) two assignments which differ only on pairs of skis of ranks i and j. In the first, s_i (respectively s_j) is associated with h_p (respectively h_q), while in the second, s_i (respectively s_j) is associated with h_q (respectively h_p) with $p < q$ and therefore $h_p \leqslant h_q$. If $s_i = s_j$ or $h_p = h_q$, these two assignments give the same overall satisfaction for skiers. In the six other cases that may arise, knowing that $s_i < s_j$ and $h_p < h_q$, it turns out that the maximum dv_1 of the deviations $|s_i - h_p|$ and $|s_j - h_q|$ is always less than or equal to the maximum dv_2 of the deviations $|s_i - h_q|$ and $|s_j - h_p|$. For example, for $s_i < s_j \leqslant h_p < h_q$, we have:

$$dv_1 = \max(\{|s_i - h_p|, |s_j - h_q|\}) = \max(\{h_p - s_i, h_q - s_j\})$$
$$dv_2 = \max(\{|s_i - h_q|, |s_j - h_p|\}) = h_q - s_i.$$

But, $h_q - s_i > h_p - s_j$ and $h_q - s_i > h_q - s_j$, thus $dv_1 < dv_2$. Therefore, the recurrence is:

$$
\begin{aligned}
&\text{optasg}'(1,j) = \min_{k \in 1..j} (|h_1 - s_k|) && 1 \leqslant j \leqslant m \\[4pt]
&\text{optasg}'(i,i) = \sum_{k=1}^{i} |h_k - s_k| && 1 < i \leqslant n \\[4pt]
&\text{optasg}'(i,j) = \min \left(\left\{ \begin{array}{l} \text{optasg}'(i,j-1), \\ \max \left(\left\{ \begin{array}{l} \text{optasg}'(i-1,j-1), \\ |h_i - s_j| \end{array} \right\} \right) \end{array} \right\} \right) && \begin{array}{l} i < j \text{ and} \\ 1 < i \leqslant n \text{ and} \\ 1 < j \leqslant m \end{array}
\end{aligned}
$$

whose first two terms are unchanged with respect to the initial recurrence. As a result, the algorithm obtained is very similar to the previous one, in particular regarding cells to be filled and time complexity.

Answers to problem 130. The egg problem (2) *The problem is on page 657.*

Answer 1. Consider the general case of a drop with at least two eggs and a building 130 - A 1 having more than one floor. When one of the i eggs is dropped from floor p, either it breaks and the process continues with $(i-1)$ eggs to explore the $(p-1)$ "lower" floors (possibly none when $p = 1$), or it does not break and the $(j-p)$ "upper" floors are explored (possibly none when $p = j$) with the same i eggs. Since the worst case is envisaged, we take the maximum number of drops necessary in each of these two situations and we search for the value of p that minimizes this maximum. In the presence of a building with a unique (respectively no) floor, a single drop is sufficient inasmuch as at least one egg is available (respectively no drop takes place – $f = 1$). Last, when a single egg is available, floors must be examined upwards one after the other so that the determination of f is ensured *for sure*. Thus, the recurrence is:

$$
\begin{aligned}
&\text{nbdmin}(i,0) = 0 && 1 \leqslant i \leqslant k \\
&\text{nbdmin}(i,1) = 1 && 1 \leqslant i \leqslant k \\
&\text{nbdmin}(1,j) = j && 1 < j \leqslant n \\[4pt]
&\text{nbdmin}(i,j) = 1 + \min_{p \in 1..j} \left(\max \left(\left\{ \begin{array}{l} \text{nbdmin}(i-1,p-1), \\ \text{nbdmin}(i,j-p) \end{array} \right\} \right) \right) && \begin{array}{l} 1 < i \leqslant k \\ \text{and} \\ 1 < j \leqslant n \end{array}
\end{aligned}
$$

Answer 2. The algorithm implementing the above recurrence in a canonical way uses 130 - A 2 the array $\text{NBDM}[1..k, 0..n]$ filled as follows:

(a) the first row ($i = 1$) is initialized thanks to the first and third terms of the recurrence,

(b) in any row i from 2 to k, the first element $\text{NBDM}[i, 0]$ is set to 0, the second $\text{NBDM}[i, 1]$ to 1, and others ($\text{NBDM}[i, j]$, j varying from 2 to n) are calculated by means of the general term of the recurrence.

The computation of the value $\text{NBDM}[i, j]$ in the general case requires $2j$ comparisons (related to minimum and maximum operations), the entire row i thus $\sum_{j=2}^{n} 2j$. It follows that the temporal complexity of the algorithm is in $\Theta(k \cdot n^2)$ comparisons.

Answer 3. The elements for the calculation of $\text{nbdmin}(3, 8)$ are gathered in the array 130 - A 3 $\text{NBDM}[1..3, 0..8]$ hereafter:

j	0	1	2	3	4	5	6	7	8
i = 1	0	1	2	3	4	5	6	7	8
2	0	1	2	2	3	3	3	4	4
3	0	1	2	2	3	3	3	3	4

It can be observed that $\mathrm{nbdmin}(i,j)$ increases (non strictly) on the number of floors j, whereas it decreases (non strictly) on the number of eggs i, which is in accordance with intuition.

Monotonicity of $\mathrm{nbdmin}(i,j)$ on j is now proven. The recurrence established in the previous question leads to single out the cases $i = 1$ and $i > 1$.

When $i = 1$, $\mathrm{nbdmin}(1,j) = j$ strictly increases on j.

The case $i > 1$, which relies on the last term of the recurrence, is less simple and two lemmas are established before proving the main expected result.

Notations.

Let $t1(p) = \max(\{\mathrm{nbdmin}(i - 1, p - 1), \mathrm{nbdmin}(i, m + 1 - p)\})$ and $t2(p) = \max(\{\mathrm{nbdmin}(i - 1, p - 1), \mathrm{nbdmin}(i, m - p)\})$.

The two lemmas are proven under the hypothesis H according to which $\mathrm{nbdmin}(i,j)$ is increasing on j for any j between 1 and m.

Lemma 3:
$t1(p) \geqslant t2(p)$ *for any* $p \in 1 .. m$.

Proof. We have:

$$t2(p)$$
$$= \qquad\qquad\qquad\qquad\qquad\qquad\qquad\qquad\qquad\qquad\text{definition}$$
$$\max(\{\mathrm{nbdmin}(i - 1, p - 1), \mathrm{nbdmin}(i, m - p)\})$$
$$\leqslant \qquad\qquad\qquad\qquad\qquad\qquad\qquad\qquad\qquad\text{hypothesis H}$$
$$\max(\{\mathrm{nbdmin}(i - 1, p - 1), \mathrm{nbdmin}(i, m + 1 - p)\})$$
$$= \qquad\qquad\qquad\qquad\qquad\qquad\qquad\qquad\qquad\qquad\text{definition}$$
$$t1(p).$$

Lemma 4:
$t1(m + 1) \geqslant t1(m)$.

Proof. We have on the one hand:

$$t1(m + 1)$$
$$= \qquad\qquad\qquad\qquad\qquad\qquad\qquad\qquad\qquad\qquad\text{definition}$$

$$\max(\{nbdmin(i-1,m), nbdmin(i,0)\})$$
$$=\qquad\qquad nbdmin(i,0)=0$$
$$nbdmin(i-1,m)$$

and on the other hand:

$$t1(m)$$
$$=\qquad\qquad \text{definition}$$
$$\max(\{nbdmin(i-1,m-1), nbdmin(i,1)\})$$
$$=\qquad\qquad nbdmin(i,1)=1$$
$$\max(\{nbdmin(i-1,m-1),1\}).$$

Moreover:

$$nbdmin(i-1,m)$$
$$\geqslant\qquad\qquad \text{hypothesis H}$$
$$nbdmin(i-1,m-1)$$

and

$$nbdmin(i-1,m)$$
$$\geqslant\qquad\qquad m\geqslant 1$$
$$1$$

therefore, $t1(m+1)\geqslant t1(m)$.

Let us now prove that $nbdmin(i,j)$ increases on j for $i>1$, by induction on $\mathbb{N}_1$ (strong induction).

Base For any $i>1$, $nbdmin(i,0)=0$ and $nbdmin(i,1)=1$ from the recurrence established in the first question; the increase (here strict) of $nbdmin(i,j)$ is therefore met.

Induction hypothesis For any $j\in 1..m$, the property holds, thus: $nbdmin(i,j)\geqslant nbdmin(i,j-1)$ for any $i>1$. That is precisely the hypothesis that makes it possible to use the two lemmas proven beforehand.

Induction We want to establish the property for $j=m+1$. We have:

$$nbdmin(i,m+1)$$
$$=\qquad\qquad \text{definition}$$
$$1+\min_{p\in1..m+1}(t1(p))$$
$$=\qquad\qquad \text{quantifier burst } (m\neq 0)$$
$$1+\min(\{\min_{p\in1..m}(t1(p)), t1(m+1)\})$$
$$\geqslant\qquad\qquad \text{lemma 1}$$
$$1+\min(\{\min_{p\in1..m}(t2(p)), t1(m+1)\})$$
$$\geqslant\qquad\qquad \text{lemma 2}$$
$$1+\min(\{\min_{p\in1..m}(t2(p)), t1(m)\})$$
$$\geqslant\qquad\qquad \text{lemma 1}$$
$$1+\min(\{\min_{p\in1..m}(t2(p)), t2(m)\})$$
$$=\qquad\qquad t2(m) \text{ appears twice}$$
$$1+\min_{p\in1..m}(t2(p))$$
$$=\qquad\qquad \text{definition}$$
$$nbdmin(j,m).$$

Let $f1(p) = \text{nbdmin}(i-1, p-1)$ and $f2(p) = \text{nbdmin}(i, i-p)$. From the previous monotonicity property, $f1(p)$ (respectively $f2(p)$) increases (respectively decreases) on p. These two curves "cross each other" and the calculation of $\text{nbdmin}(i, j)$ amounts to searching the local minimum of their maximum. A possible filling of the array NBDM can be deduced, in $\mathcal{O}(k \cdot n \cdot \log_2(n))$ comparisons instead of $\mathcal{O}(k \cdot n^2)$ initially.

Subsequently, the algorithm *EggDyn2* is preferable to *EggDyn1*, as its (asymptotic) complexity is better.

130 - A 4   **Answer** 4.   In the general case, PTH$[i, j]$ contains the (one) value p having led to the minimum of expression $\max(\{\text{nbdmin}(i-1, p-1), \text{nbdmin}(i, j-p)\})$, in other words the floor from which the first egg must be dropped when i eggs are available and floors 1 to j of the building are considered. In the special case where only one egg is available ($i = 1$), the first must be performed from the first floor to ensure that the value of f is determined *for sure*; PTH$[1, j]$ therefore has the value 1 for any j of the interval $1 .. n$. Finally, if there is only one stage ($j = 1$), the drop is made from this floor, hence PTH$[i, 1]$ also takes the value 1.

Remark

It is worth noticing that as a building with floors $1, 2, \ldots, n$ is considered, examining a portion of a building whose floors are $bg, \ldots, nd$ requires "shifting" the value of PTH$[i, j]$ to obtain the correct value of the floor where the drop must be performed. This remark is used in the following.

The principle of the algorithm determining a sequence of drops is now described. In general, we must determine a sequence of drops corresponding to the examination of a slice of floors $bg .. nd$, i.e. $j = nd - bg + 1$ floors with i eggs ensuring the identification of f with at most NBDM$[i, j]$ drops (at the beginning, $bg = 1, nd = n, i = k$). The drop is performed from the floor (PTH$[i, j] + db - 1$). If the egg breaks, we iterate with the interval $bg .. \text{PTH}[i, j] + bg - 2$ with $(i-1)$ eggs. If the egg does not break, we iterate with the interval PTH$[i, j] + bg .. nd$ with i eggs. The process stops when either the number of eggs available is zero, or the interval to be dealt with is empty.
The previous algorithm is applied to the four proposed cases and the results are shown in the following tables.

$k = 2, n = 8, f = 5$ NBDM$[2, 8] = 4$ thus four drops at worst

drop #	interval to consider	drop from floor #	break
1	1 .. 8	PTH$[2, 8] + 1 - 1 = 2$	no
2	3 .. 8	PTH$[2, 6] + 3 - 1 = 5$	yes
3	3 .. 4	PTH$[1, 2] + 3 - 1 = 3$	no
4	4 .. 4	PTH$[1, 1] + 4 - 1 = 4$	no

Conclusion: $f = 5$, the determination of f is achieved with exactly four drops and there is one egg remaining.

$k = 2, n = 6, f = 3$ NBDM$[2, 6] = 3$ thus three drops at worst

drop #	interval to consider	drop from floor #	break
1	1 .. 6	PTH$[2, 6] + 1 - 1 = 3$	yes
2	1 .. 2	PTH$[1, 2] + 1 - 1 = 1$	no
3	2 .. 2	PTH$[1, 1] + 2 - 1 = 2$	no

Conclusion: $f = 3$, the determination of f is achieved with exactly three drops and there is one egg remaining.

$k = 2, n = 4, f = 5$ NBDM$[2, 4] = 3$ thus three drops at worst

drop #	interval to consider	drop from floor #	break
1	1 .. 4	PTH$[2, 4] + 1 - 1 = 1$	no
2	2 .. 4	PTH$[2, 3] + 2 - 1 = 3$	no
3	4 .. 4	PTH$[2, 1] + 4 - 1 = 4$	no

Conclusion: $f = 5$, the determination of f is achieved with exactly three drops and no egg has broken.

$k = 2, n = 5, f = 1$ NBDM$[2, 5] = 3$ thus three drops at worst

drop #	interval to consider	drop from floor #	break
1	1 .. 5	PTH$[2, 5] + 1 - 1 = 2$	yes
2	1 .. 1	PTH$[1, 1] + 1 - 1 = 1$	yes

Conclusion: $f = 1$, the determination of f is achieved with only two drops and the two eggs initially available have broken.

Answer 5.   Suppose that we are provided with i eggs ($i > 1$) and that j drops ($j > 1$) are allowed. When an egg is dropped (whatever the floor), either it breaks and $(i - 1)$ are remaining for the $(j-1)$ further drops, or it does not break and we can proceed to the $(j-1)$ future drops with the same number i of eggs. The identification capability of the breaking floor is therefore the sum of what can be identified in each of these two cases. If only one egg is available, the determination of a breaking floor can only be ensured by proceeding sequentially, exhausting the number j of drops allowed. Last, with only one drop and at least one egg, the determination *for sure* can only be guaranteed if two floors are present. Consequently, the recurrence for calculating bhmax(k, nbd) is:

$$
\left|
\begin{array}{ll}
\text{bhmax}(1, j) = j + 1 & 1 \leqslant j \leqslant nbd \\
\text{bhmax}(i, 1) = 2 & 1 \leqslant i \leqslant k \\
\text{bhmax}(i, j) = \text{bhmax}(i - 1, j - 1) + \text{bhmax}(i, j - 1) & \left\{ \begin{array}{c} 1 < i \leqslant k \\ \textbf{and} \\ 1 < j \leqslant nbd \end{array} \right.
\end{array}
\right.
$$

A difference between this recurrence and the one seen in the first question lies in the fact that the calculation of bhmax does not look for an optimal value (neither min, nor max in the general term of the recurrence).

The table below gathers the calculations related to bhmax(4, 12):

j	1	2	3	4	5	6	7	8	9	10	11	12
i = 1	2	3	4	5	6	7	8	9	10	11	12	13
2	2	4	7	11	16	22	29	37	46	56	67	79
3	2	4	8	15	26	42	64	93	130	176	232	299
4	2	4	8	16	31	57	99	163	256	386	562	794

130 - A 6   **Answer** 6.   At first glance, it is expected that, if $nbdmin(i, j)$ is equal to l, then the value of $bhmax(i, l)$ is equal to j. But, it can be seen that, for example, $nbdmin(2, 6) = 3$, while $bhmax(2, 3) = 7$. This "shift" is explained by the fact that the number of floors taken into account in the problem *Egg2* does not include the additional virtual floor for which the egg necessarily breaks if it has not broken before. The property linking $nbdmin$ and $bhmax$ is:

$$bhmax(i, l) = j \Rightarrow nbdmin(i, j - 1) = l,$$

and these two values are thus coherent.

130 - A 7   **Answer** 7.   Solving the problem *Egg3* assumes that the number of eggs and releases is known, while *Eggs2* starts with the number of eggs and floors in the building. For i given, j is the minimum number of drops allowing to identify f *for sure* for buildings having between $bhmax(i, j - 1) + 1$ and $bhmax(i, j)$ floors. Solving the problem *Egg2* can be seen as using the recurrence $bhmax$ solving the problem *Egg3* to compute nbd, the smallest x such that $bhmax(k, x) > n$. Strict superiority comes from what was said in the previous answer about the difference of 1 between the number of floors taken into account in the problems *Egg2* and *Egg3*.

More precisely, the principle of the algorithm *EggDyn3* calculating the value nbd consists in filling the array $BHM[1 .. k, 1 .. n]$ until finding a value greater than n in row of index k. The filling of BHM is operated as follows:

(a) the value $(j + 1)$ is assigned to each cell of column index j in the first row according to the first term of the recurrence,

(b) each of the following rows is then successively filled, the first cell with the value 2 according to the second term of the recurrence, the following ones (2 to n) thanks to the general term.

The resulting algorithm is therefore in $O(k \cdot n)$ additions and comparisons (loop control).

130 - A 8   **Answer** 8.   From what has been said previously, in the general case, we know that f is identifiable *for sure* with k eggs for a building having n floors with at worst nbd drops, nbd being the smallest x such that $BHM[k, x] > n$. Let us drop an egg from the floor numbered $BHM[k - 1, nbd - 1]$. If the egg breaks, it is known that f can be identified *for sure* with $(k - 1)$ eggs for a building with $BHM[k - 1, nbd - 1]$ floors with at worst $(nbd - 1)$ drops. It is thus sure that with this first the value of f can be identified *for sure* with k eggs for a building with up to $BHM[k, nbd - 1] + BHM[k - 1, nbd - 1] = BHM[k, nbd]$ floors.

It can be deduced that the algorithm determining the sequence of drops on this basis proceeds as follows. We consider i eggs ($i > 1$) to be available to examine the interval $bg .. nd$, with at worst j drops ($j > 1$). At the beginning, we have $i = k, j = nbd, bg = 1, nd = n$. A drop is performed from floor $BHM[i - 1, j - 1] + bg - 1$. If the egg breaks, we consider the interval $bg .. BHM[i - 1, j - 1] + bg - 2$, which will be examined with $(i - 1)$ eggs and at worst $(j - 1)$ drops. The two families of special cases ($i = 1, j = 1$) and ($i > 1, j = 1$) are now dealt with. For the first one, only one egg is available. It is released from floor bg. If it breaks, it is concluded that $f = bg$, otherwise we iterate with the interval $bg+1..nd$. In the second type of particular case, a single drop is allowed with an interval of type $bg..bg+1$. This drop is performed from floor bg and the conclusion is $f = bg$ (respectively $bg + 1$) if there is break (respectively non-break).

Answer 9.   This algorithm is applied to each of the proposed situations and the results are shown in the forthcoming tables. 130 - A 9

$k = 2, n = 9, f = 5$ $BHM[2,4] = 11 > 9$ thus four drops at worst

drop #	interval to consider	drop from floor #	break
1	1..9	$BHM[1,3] + 1 - 1 = 4$	no
2	5..9	$BHM[1,2] + 5 - 1 = 7$	yes
3	5..6	$bg = 5$	yes

Conclusion: $f = 5$, the determination of f is achieved with only three drops and two eggs broken.

$k = 2, n = 7, f = 3$ $BHM[2,3] = 7$ thus three drops at worst

drop #	interval to consider	drop from floor #	break
1	1..7	$BHM[1,2] + 1 - 1 = 3$	yes
2	1..2	$bg = 1$	no
3	2..2	$bg = 2$	no

Conclusion: $f = 3$, the determination of f is achieved with three drops and one egg is remaining.

It can be observed that in the first example, the sequence of drops $4 - 7 - 5$ is obtained while in question 4, page 658, a sequence of four drops $2 - 5 - 3 - 4$ was given. This is not surprising since: (i) the value $PTH[2,8] = 2$ used in question 4, page 658, is only one of those possible, and (ii) the value 4 is also suitable since $1 + \max(\{nbdmin(1,3), nbdmin(2,4)\})$ $= 1 + \max(\{3,3\}) = 1 + \max(\{nbdmin(1,1), nbdmin(2,6)\}) = 1 + \max(\{1,3\}) = 4$. By taking the appropriate values in the array PTH, the same sequence of three drops would be obtained.
Regarding the second example, the drop sequences obtained coincide $(3 - 1 - 2)$.

The third example is now dealt with.

$k = 3, n = 42, f = 4$ $BHM[3,6] = 42$ thus six drops at worst

drop #	interval to consider	drop from floor #	break
1	1..42	$BHM[2,5] + 1 - 1 = 16$	yes
2	1..15	$BHM[1,4] + 1 - 1 = 5$	yes
3	1..4	$bg = 1$	no
4	2..4	$bg = 2$	no
5	3..4	$bg = 3$	no
4	4..4	$bg = 4$	yes

Conclusion: $f = 4$, the determination of f is achieved with exactly six drops and all the eggs have broken.

Answer 10. It is proven that the expression using combination numbers is identical to each of the terms of the recurrence defining $bhmax$.

For any $i \geqslant 1$, we have:

$$\sum_{p=0}^{i} C_1^p$$

$=$ expansion

$$C_1^0 + C_1^1 + \cdots + C_1^i$$

$=$ definition of C_n^p

$$1 + 1 + 0 + \cdots + 0 = 2$$

$=$ definition of $bhmax$

$$bhmax(i, 1).$$

Similarly, for any $j \geqslant 1$, we have:

$$\sum_{p=0}^{1} C_j^p$$

$=$ expansion

$$C_j^0 + C_j^1$$

$=$ definition of C_n^p

$$1 + j$$

$=$ definition of $bhmax$

$$bhmax(1, j).$$

Now, the expression $\sum_{p=0}^{i} C_j^p$ is treated for any i and j strictly greater than 1:

$$\sum_{p=0}^{i} C_j^p$$

$=$ partial expansion

$$C_j^0 + \sum_{p=1}^{i} C_j^p$$

$=$ definition of C_j^0

$$1 + \sum_{p=1}^{i} C_j^p$$

$=$ identity $C_j^p = C_{j-1}^p + C_{j-1}^{p-1}$

$$1 + \sum_{p=1}^{i} (C_{j-1}^p + C_{j-1}^{p-1})$$

$=$ property of addition

$$1 + \sum_{p=1}^{i} C_{j-1}^p + \sum_{p=1}^{i} C_{j-1}^{p-1}$$

$=$ $C_{j-1}^0 = 1$

$$\sum_{p=0}^{i} C_{j-1}^{p} + \sum_{p=1}^{i} C_{j-1}^{p-1}$$

$$=$$

variable change: $p - 1$ becomes p

$$\sum_{p=0}^{i} C_{j-1}^{p} + \sum_{p=0}^{i-1} C_{j-1}^{p}.$$

Let $g(i, j) = \sum_{p=0}^{i} C_{j}^{p}$. From the previous equality, it comes:

$$g(i, j) = g(i, j - 1) + g(i - 1, j - 1)$$

and by identification $bhmax(i, j) = g(i, j) = \sum_{p=0}^{i} C_{j}^{p}$.

Answer 11.   We have:

130 - A 11

$$bhmax(k, r) = \sum_{p=0}^{k} C_{r}^{p} = C_{r}^{0} + \cdots + C_{r}^{k}$$

and:

$$C_{r}^{p+1} = \frac{(C_{r}^{p} \cdot (n - p))}{(p + 1)}.$$

It can be deduced that for k and r given, $bhmax(k, r) = \sum_{p=0}^{k} C_{r}^{p}$ can be computed through a loop whose body carries out a multiplication and a division. In total, the calculation of $bhmax(k, r)$ requires k multiplications, divisions and comparisons (loop control).

As mentioned in the statement of the problem, $C_{r}^{p} \geqslant C_{r-1}^{p}$ and therefore $bhmax(k, r) \geqslant bhmax(k, r - 1)$; in other words, $bhmax(k, r)$ is increasing on its second argument. We also have $bhmax(k, n) > n$ (proof left to the reader). The algorithm *EggDyn4* can thus be envisaged to compute nbd, the smallest x such that $bhmax(k, x) > n$, using binary search and the following inductive schema on the search interval $bg \mathinner{..} nd$ (at the beginning $bg = 1, nd = n$).

Base When the length of the interval is 1, if $bhmax(k, bg) > n$ (respectively $\leqslant n$), the search value nbd is bg (respectively $bg + 1$).

Induction hypothesis It is assumed that it is known how to compute the value nbd by binary search for any interval $bg' \mathinner{..} nd'$ such that $nd' - bg' + 1 \geqslant 1$ and $bg' \mathinner{..} nd' \subset bg \mathinner{..} nd$.

Induction Let $nd - bg + 1 > 1$ and $mid = \lfloor (bg + nd)/2 \rfloor$. In the case where $bhmax(k, mid) > n$, the value nbd is in $bg \mathinner{..} mid$, and according to the induction hypothesis, it is known how to find it. Symmetrically, if $bhmax(k, mid) \leqslant n$, nbd is found in $mid + 1 \mathinner{..} nd$ and the induction hypothesis ensures that it is known how to calculate it.

Termination The length of the interval decreases strictly at each step to reach 1 the value of the base in the end.

There are $\lceil \log_2(n) \rceil$ steps to find nbd, each of them with a complexity in k (comparisons), thus in total a complexity of the calculation of $bhmax(k, nbd)$ in $\Theta(k \cdot \log_2(n))$ comparisons.

130 - A 12   **Answer** 12.   The reconstitution of the drop sequence associated with the pair (i, j) obeys the principle described in answer 8, page 724. However, and this is the new point, it is necessary to perform at each step the calculation of $bhmax(i-1, j-1)$ (corresponding to the cell $BHM[i-1, j-1]$ when the array BHM was available) giving the floor from which the drop must be performed. We therefore have a complexity in $\mathcal{O}(i \cdot nbd)$ comparisons, while in the answer to question 8 on page 659, the complexity was in $\Theta(nbd)$ comparisons, nbd being the value of the number of drops found for i eggs and j floors.

130 - A 13   **Answer** 13.   Before being able to validly proceed to the comparison on the complexity, it is important to note that if that of the solutions by dynamic programming is expressed in number of comparisons, the solution by *radixchotomy* is constructed by taking the number of drops as the operation elementary. However, it is easy to see that, in this approach, the number of drops is of the same order as the number of comparisons induced by the control of the loops, which makes the complexities of all these approaches comparable.

The characteristics of the four algorithms are gathered in the table below (k number of eggs, n number of floors of the building and nbd number of drops made):

method / algorithm	minimality of the number of drops at worst	class of asymptotic complexity
radixchotomy	no	$\mathcal{O}(\sqrt[k]{n})$
EggDyn2	yes	$\mathcal{O}(k \cdot n \cdot \log_2(n))$
EggDyn3	yes	$\mathcal{O}(k \cdot n)$
EggDyn4	yes	$\Theta(k \cdot \log_2(n))$

These elments show that:

1) the algorithm *EggDyn4* is the best if the guarantee of minimum number of releases at worst is demanded,

2) *radixchotomy* is the most appropriate if an efficient algorithm is desired without worrying about minimizing the number of drops at worst,

3) the more eggs available, the more efficient *radixchotomy*; this is fairly intuitive. Algorithms based on dynamic programming suffer from the increase in the number of eggs. The situation here is unusual as dynamic programming is doing very noticeably less well in terms of complexity, due to the very use of a tabular structure of which the number of eggs is one of the dimensions. This is the price to pay for the guarantee of the optimality of the solution provided!!!

130 - A 14   **Answer** 14.   In each of the following tables, we successively study what happens for the two approaches for f ranging from 1 to 4.

$f = 1$

		EggDyn2	*radixchotomy*
drop # 1	floor	2	1
	break	yes	yes
drop # 2	floor	1	/
	break	yes	/

f = 2

		EggDyn2	radixchotomy
drop # 1	floor	2	1
	break	yes	no
drop # 2	floor	1	2
	break	no	yes

f = 3

		EggDyn2	radixchotomy
drop # 1	floor	2	1
	break	no	no
drop # 2	floor	3	2
	break	yes	no
drop # 2	floor	/	3
	break	/	yes

f = 4

		EggDyn2	radixchotomy
drop # 1	floor	2	1
	break	no	no
drop # 2	floor	3	2
	break	no	no
drop # 2	floor	/	3
	break	/	no

Here, it can be observed that dynamic programming systematically requires two drops, while *radixchotomy* leads to one, two or even three drops. So, *in the worst case*, as expected, dynamic programming is optimal in the number of drops. After carrying out experiments, the authors conjecture that, in the worst case, *radixchotomy*, although not optimal, is on par with the optimal solution or requires only one drop more than it.

130 - A 15

Answer 15. Consider the following problem *IntervIdent2*: determine the maximum interval length of which any number x can be identified (for sure) with at most Q questions of the type "x is greater than v ?" and at most NA negative answers.
The problem *IntervIdent* admits (at least) one answer if the answer to the problem *IntervIdent2* is a value at least equal to N. However, it appears that *IntervIdent2* is isomorphic to *Egg3* by establishing the following correspondences:

- interval length (N) $\longleftrightarrow$ number of floors of the building (n),
- asking a question $\longleftrightarrow$ dropping an egg,
- negative answer to a question $\longleftrightarrow$ break of the egg.

Remark

Note that the problems *IntervIdent* and *IntervIdent2* are meaningless when the number of negative responses (NA) is greater than the number of questions (Q), while the problem of egg dropping is meaningful even if the number of eggs (k) is greater than the number of floors (n).

To know if the problem *IntervIdent* admits (at least) one solution, it is therefore sufficient to solve the problem *Egg3* with the algorithm *EggDyn3* or *EggDyn4*. The conclusion is positive (respectively negative) if the value of bhmax(NA, Q) is greater than (respectively less than or equal) to N.

When the problem *IntervIdent* admits (at least) one solution, building a sequence of questions to ask consists in finding the value v associated with each of them. By isomorphism, this amounts to identifying the stage from which a release is performed in the problem *Eggs3*. A sequence of questions to be asked can therefore be reconstituted by applying the algorithm *EggDyn3* (respectively *EggDyn4*), then the strategy described in the answer to question 8 (respectively 12).

130 - A 16   **Answer 16.**   With $N = 299, Q = 12, RN = 3$, the partial tree is:

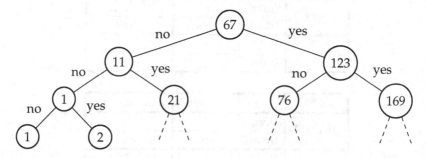

130 - A 17   **Answer 17.**   For the interval 1..296, it is of course possible to ask the same first question as for the interval 1 .. 299. Indeed, any element of each of the resulting intervals (1 .. 67 and 68 .. 296) can certainly be identified, with at worst 11 questions and two (respectively three) negative answers for the first (respectively second). However, the question can also be "is x greater than 66?", since any element of the intervals 1 .. 66 and 67 .. 296 (of width 230) can also be identified for sure with at worst 11 questions and two (respectively three) negative answers for the first (respectively second), as shown in the table of the answer to the question 5, page 658. For the same reason, the first question can be: "is x greater than 65?" or even "is x greater than 64?".

Taking into account what was said in the previous question, the intervals for which the question tree is unique are those whose length corresponds to a value of bhmax(NA, Q), knowing that Q questions are asked with at most NA negative answers. This is the case in particular for any interval 1 .. N with only one egg. But this is also the case for example for the intervals: (i) 1 .. 299, with three negative answers and twelve questions, (ii) 1 .. 46, with two negative answers and nine questions or (iii) 1 .. 16, with two negative answers and five questions or four negative answers and four questions.

Answers to problem 131. Best path in a conform graph   *The problem is on page 660.*

131 - A 1   **Answer 1.**   Let us make a proof by contradiction. Consider a conform graph G with n vertices ($n \geqslant 2$), and suppose that it involves the $\langle k, j_1, \ldots, j_p, k \rangle$ ($p \geqslant 1$ since there is no loop). We have:

$$k < j_1 < \ldots < j_p < k$$

which is impossible. Thus, a conform graph cannot involve a circuit.

Suppose now that the conform graph G has no entry (respectively exit) point. Let k be any vertex. The vertex k has at least one predecessor (respectively successor) j_1. The reasoning about the existence of a predecessor (respectively successor) j_2 for j_1 can be repeated, and as much as desired as any vertex has at least one predecessor (respectively successor).

However, the vertices $j_1, j_2, \ldots$ thus displayed are all different, since G has no circuit and has a finite number n of vertices. Therefore, it is not possible to construct a succession of predecessors (respectively successors) as long as desired. A contradiction arises which allows to assert that the conform graph G has at least one entry point and one exit point.

Answer 2.   Let $Pred(i)$ be set of the predecessors of i. All the vertices of $Pred(i)$ have a   131 - A 2
number strictly less than i, since G is a conform graph. Let k be one of the predecessors of i
$(k \in Pred(i))$ for which there are p $(p \geqslant 1)$ paths from the vertex number 1 $(nbpth(k) = p)$.
These paths can be "extended" by adjoining the terminal vertex i; in so doing, p paths are
built from 1 to i. This process can take place for any vertex k of $Pred(i)$, hence it comes that
the number of paths that originate in 1 and ends in i is given by:

$$
\left|
\begin{aligned}
&nbpth(1) = 1 \\
&nbpth(i) = \sum_{k=1}^{i-1} nbpth(k) \qquad\qquad 2 \leqslant i \leqslant n.
\end{aligned}
\right.
$$

With the proposed graph, we have:

$\quad nbpth(1) = 1; nbpth(2) = nbpth(1) = 1;$
$\quad nbpth(3) = nbpth(1) + nbpth(2) = 2;$
$\quad nbpth(4) = nbpth(2) + nbpth(3) = 3;$
$\quad nbpth(5) = nbpth(1) + nbpth(3) + nbpth(4) = 6.$

It can be checked that the number of paths from 1 to 5 are: $\langle 1, 5 \rangle$, $\langle 1, 2, 3, 5 \rangle$, $\langle 1, 2, 4, 5 \rangle$,
$\langle 1, 2, 3, 4, 5 \rangle$, $\langle 1, 3, 5 \rangle$ and $\langle 1, 3, 4, 5 \rangle$.

Answer 3.   Let $pvmin(i)$ be the value of the minimum value path that originates in 1   131 - A 3
and ends in i. The reasoning used in the previous question still applies and it yields:

$$
\left|
\begin{aligned}
&pvmin(1) = 0 \\
&pvmin(i) = \min_{k \in 1..i-1} (pvmin(k) + MGV[k, i]) \qquad\qquad 1 < i \leqslant n.
\end{aligned}
\right.
$$

The vector PVM$[1 .. n]$ is associated with pvmin and the searched value (that of the (one) path of minimum value from 1 to n) is located in PVM$[n]$. Due to the form of the recurrence defining pvmin, the progression of the filling of PVM progresses from left to right (increasing values of index i) starting with PVM$[1]$ thanks to the first term of the recurrence and using the second term to compute of the following elements (PVM$[2 .. n]$). The spatial complexity of this algorithm is in $\Theta(n^2)$ corresponding to the matrix MGV representing the considered graph, as well its temporal complexity in terms of conditions evaluated.

Remark

Let us recall that the values associated with the arcs of the graph GV are arbitrary.

Answer 4.   Applied to the graph given as an example, this algorithm produces the vec-   131 - A 4
tor PVM $= [0, 6, 3, 5, 7]$; the value of the path $\langle 1, 2, 3, 5 \rangle$ of minimum value from 1 to 5 is
thus 7.

Answers to problem 132. Best paths from a source   *The problem is on page 661.*

Answer 1.   In the general case, either the optimal path from the source and the vertex   132 - A 1
v uses less than i arcs and its value is $valpthvmin(v, i-1)$, or it involves exactly i arcs and
then its value is $valpthvmin(t, i-1)$, that of the best path from the source to t the vertex

predecessor of v on the optimal path from the source to s, increased by the value $P(t, v)$ of the arc (t, v). Hence, the recurrence:

$$\left| \begin{array}{l} valpthvmin(1,0) = 0 \\ valpthvmin(s,0) = +\infty \\ valpthvmin(s,i) = \min \left(\left\{ \begin{array}{l} valpthvmin(s, i-1), \\ \min_{t \in Pred(s)} \left(\begin{array}{l} valpthvmin(t, i-1)+ \\ P(t,s) \end{array} \right) \end{array} \right\} \right) \end{array} \right. \quad \begin{array}{l} 1 < s \leqslant n \\ \\ 1 < s \leqslant n \\ \textbf{and} \\ 1 \leqslant i \leqslant n-1 \end{array}$$

$Pred(s)$ denoting the set of predecessors of the vertex v.

132 - A 2   **Answer** 2.   It would be possible to design an algorithm stemming directly from the above recurrence. However, it can be noticed that traversing the set of predecessors of each vertex amounts to processing the set of arcs of WG. We can therefore use the representation of the graph WG by the table of its arcs. Moreover, instead of filling in the structure VPTHVMIN$[1 .. n, 0 .. n-1]$, the array VPTHVMIN$[1 .. n, 1 .. 2]$ is preferred, since in the recurrence the calculation of the second index element i uses only second index elements $(i - 1)$. This leads to the algorithm:

1. **constants**
2. $n \in \mathbb{N}_1$ and $n = \ldots$ and $m \in \mathbb{N}_1$ and $m = \ldots$ and AWG $\in 1 .. m \times 1 .. 2 \rightarrow \mathbb{N}_1$ and
3.   AWG $= [\ldots]$ **and** VWG $\in 1 .. m \rightarrow \mathbb{R}$ **and** VWG $= [\ldots]$ **and**
4.   NegativeCircuitFree(GV)
5.   /% *AWG is the matrix associated with the arcs of the graph WG considered and VWG is the vector giving their value;* NegativeCircuitFree(WG) *is a predicate that qui indicates that WG is free from any circuit of negative value* %/
6. **variables**
7.   VPTHVMIN $\in 1 .. n \times 1 .. 2 \rightarrow \mathbb{R}$
8.   /% *VPTHVMIN is the matrix giving the value of the minimum value path from the source (vertex 1) to any other vertex* %/
9. **begin**
10.   VPTHVMIN$[1, 1] \leftarrow 0$; VPTHVMIN$[1, 2] \leftarrow 0$;
11.   **for** $v \in 2 .. n$ **do**
12.   VPTHVMIN$[v, 1] \leftarrow +\infty$
13.   **end for**;
14.   **for** i **ranging** $1 .. n-1$ **do**
15.   /% *calculation (update of the value of the minimum value path for any vertex other than the source)* %/
16.   **for** $v \in 2 .. n$ **do**
17.   VPTHVMIN$[AWG[a, 2], 2] \leftarrow +\infty$
18.   **end for**;
19.   **for** $a \in 1 .. m$ **do**
20.   VPTHVMIN$[AWG[a, 2], 2] \leftarrow$
$$\min \left(\left\{ \begin{array}{l} \text{VPTHVMIN}[AWG[a, 2], 2], \\ \text{VPTHVMIN}[AWG[a, 2], 1], \\ \text{VPTHVMIN}[AWG[a, 1], 1] + \text{VWG}[a] \end{array} \right\} \right)$$
21.   **end for**;
22.   /% *remplacement of column 1 by column 2* %/

```
23.      for v ∈ 1 .. n do
24.          VPTHVMIN[s, 1] ← VPTHVMIN[s, 2]
25.      end for
26.   end for;
27.   for s ranging 1 .. n do
28.       write(VPTHVMIN[s, 2])
29.   end for
30. end
```

Time complexity of this algorithm is in $\Theta(m \cdot n)$ conditions evaluated.

Remark

A direct implementation of the recurrence with a matrix representation MWG of WG would lead to the same complexity in terms of the number of conditions evaluated, but would require $\Theta(n^3)$ access to MWG, since finding the predecessors of a vertex then requires n access to MWG.

Answer 3.   Applying this algorithm to the graph WG_1 leads to the following succession of matrices VPTHVMIN:

132 - A 3

	1	2
1	0	0
2	$+\infty$	4
3	$+\infty$	2
4	$+\infty$	-3
5	$+\infty$	$+\infty$
6	$+\infty$	3

	1	2
1	0	0
2	4	3
3	2	0
4	-3	-3
5	$+\infty$	0
6	3	3

	1	2
1	0	0
2	3	3
3	0	0
4	-3	-4
5	0	-2
6	3	3

	1	2
1	0	0
2	3	2
3	0	0
4	-4	-6
5	-2	-2
6	3	3

	1	2
1	0	0
2	2	0
3	0	0
4	-6	-6
5	-2	-2
6	3	3

With the graph WG_2, we get:

	1	2
1	0	0
2	$+\infty$	-2
3	$+\infty$	2
4	$+\infty$	$+\infty$
5	$+\infty$	5

	1	2
1	0	0
2	-2	-2
3	2	-1
4	$+\infty$	1
5	5	5

	1	2
1	0	0
2	-2	-2
3	-1	-1
4	1	-2
5	5	2

	1	2
1	0	0
2	-2	-2
3	-1	-1
4	-2	-2
5	2	-1

Answer 4.   In order to be able to reconstruct the optimal paths themselves, the idea is to memorize the number of the predecessor for which the optimal is reached ("Tom Thumb's technique"). This is done at each effective update of VPTHVMIN (line 20 of the algorithm). For the graph WG_1, we will have the tracking information: $2 \rightarrow 4, 3 \rightarrow 6, 4 \rightarrow 5, 5 \rightarrow 3$ and last $6 \rightarrow 1$. To reconstruct the optimal path from 1 to 2, we "go up" the path from the end to the origin using this tracking information, i.e. the optimal path: $\langle 1, 6, 3, 5, 4, 2 \rangle$.

132 - A 4

Answer 5.   The difference between this variant and the version given in answer to question 2 lies in the use of a vector VPTHVMIN[1..n] instead of a matrix VPTHVMIN[1.. n, 1 .. 2], because the calculation of the values of the optimal paths is done "on the spot". There is thus a gain in memory space with a spatial complexity divided by 2.

132 - A 5

132 - A 6   **Answer 6.**   In this version, the value of VPTHVMIN[s] resulting from the calculation at iteration step i can be used for other vertices during this same step i. It can be said that updates are potentially "accelerated" by dissociating the iteration step and the maximum number of arcs appearing in the optimal path (at this stage). This is perfectly legal, since the use of the value $VPTHVMIN[s_i]$ for the calculation of $VPTHVMIN[s_j]$ relies on the existence of an optimal path (for the moment) between vertices 1 and s_i. Since a minimum value is calculated, the result would be the same if one waited for a subsequent iteration step. What has just been said is illustrated on the graphs WG_1 and WG_2, for which the vector resulting from the successive iteration steps is given below by considering the arcs in the prescribed order:

$$WG_1$$

vertex	init.	i = 1	i = 2	i = 3	i = 4	i = 5
1	0	0	0	0	0	0
2	$+\infty$	4	3	2	0	0
3	$+\infty$	2	0	0	0	0
4	$+\infty$	-3	-4	-6	-6	-6
5	$+\infty$	0	-2	-2	-2	-2
6	$+\infty$	3	3	3	3	3

$$WG_2$$

vertex	init.	i = 1	i = 2	i = 3	i = 4
1	0	0	0	0	0
2	$+\infty$	-2	-2	-2	-2
3	$+\infty$	-1	-1	-1	-1
4	$+\infty$	-2	-2	-2	-2
5	$+\infty$	-1	-1	-1	-1

132 - A 7   **Answer 7.**   Applied to the graph WG_3 according to the order of the given arcs, this algorithm computes the succession of vectors:

vertex	init.	i = 1	i = 2	i = 3	i = 4
1	0	0	0	0	0
2	$+\infty$	5	5	2	-1
3	$+\infty$	$+\infty$	1	-2	-2
4	$+\infty$	2	-1	-1	-1
5	$+\infty$	-2	-2	-2	-2

Three points can be highlighted: (i) as expected, the same final results are obtained for WG_1 and WG_2, whatever the algorithm used, (ii) the same optimal path values is obtained for GV_2 and GV_3 by correlating the numbers and (iii) the second algorithm applied to the graph WG_1 highlights the uselessness of the last step (i = 5); on the other hand, with WG_2 all the values of the optimal paths are calculated at the end of the first iteration step (1), whereas with WG_3 only the last iteration step (4) allows to obtain them.

132 - A 8   **Answer 8.**   It can be seen that with this algorithm it may be useless to go to the end of the iteration on i. It would therefore be possible to stop as soon as no change takes place at a given iteration step compared to the preceding one.

Answer 9.   With the algorithm given in response to question 2, at the end of step j, the   132 - A 9
value VPTHVMIN[s, 2] is interpreted as the value of the optimal path between the source
and the vertex v having at most j arcs. With the proposed variant, the value VPTHVMIN[s]
at the end of step j is an upper bound of the value of the optimal path between the source
and s (there is no longer correlation between the iteration step and the number of arcs).

Answer 10.   If there exists a circuit of negative value accessible from the source in the   132 - A 10
weighted graph WG, an additional iteration step (i = n) will cause changes in the value
of the optimal path from the source to each of the peaks of this circuit. To detect such a
circuit, it is therefore sufficient to add an iteration step after line 18 of the algorithm given
in the statement of question 5, then to check whether or not there has been a change of the
minimum value associated with (at least) one vertex.

Example. Let us consider the graph:

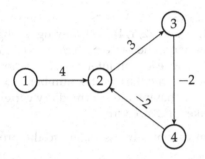

By adding the iteration step 4 and by releasing the precondition on the circuits, the succession of the values of the vector VPTHVMIN is:

vertex	init.	i = 1	i = 2	i = 3	i = 4 additional step
1	0	0	0	0	0
2	$+\infty$	3	2	1	0
3	$+\infty$	7	6	5	4
4	$+\infty$	5	4	3	2

It can be observed (as expected) that the value associated with the vertices 1, 2 and 3 has
changed between the iteration steps 3 and 4, and that therefore the considered graph has
(at least) one circuit of negative value.

Answer 11.   Finding the value of the path of minimum value from any vertex to the   132 - A 11
vertex 1 (well) of a graph WG is easy (provided that the well is not reachable by any circuit
of negative value). Indeed, it suffices to construct the graph TRWG transposed from WG
(the arc (v_i, v_j) of WG becomes the arc (v_j, v_i) in TRWG while keeping its value). We then
apply Bellman-Ford's algorithm to the graph TRWG, and the value of the optimal path
between the vertices v and 1 in WG is the optimal value found in TRWG between 1 and s.

Answer 12.   The computation of the maximum value from a source sc to any other   132 - A 12
vertex v of a valued graph WG can be considered according to the reasoning followed for
the computation of the minimum value. The two main differences relate to: (i) the need for
the absence of circuit(s) of *positive* value accessible from sc and (ii) the replacement in the
recurrence of the two instances of the minimum operator by the maximum operator (and
consequently, this same substitution in the derived algorithms).

Answers to problem 133. Best paths algebras   *The problem is on page 664.*

133 - A 1   **Answer 1.**   A proof by induction is used (strong recurrence on $\mathbb{N}_1$).

Base The recurrence "sees" any path without any intermediary vertex, since at the beginning all arcs of the graph G are taken into account.

Induction hypothesis the recurrence "sees" any path whose intermediary vertices are numbered $i < k$.

Induction Let $\langle x, v_{i_1}, \ldots, v_{i_p}, y \rangle$ be an elementary path from x to y in G such that k is the greatest number among $\{i_1, \ldots, i_p\}$. This path is taken into account in the recurrence for $i = k$, since elementary paths $\langle x, v_{i_1}, \ldots, v_k \rangle$ on the one hand and $\langle v_k, \ldots, v_{i_p}, y \rangle$ on the other hand have been taken into account previously from the induction hypothesis. It can be noticed that no special hypothesis being made about vertices x and y, the case of elementary circuits is implicitly dealt with in this proof.

133 - A 2   **Answer 2.**   In G_1, the path $\langle 3, 1, 2, 1, 4 \rangle$ is "seen" at step $i = 2$, as it results from the concatenation of paths $\langle 3, 1, 2 \rangle$ and $\langle 2, 1, 4 \rangle$ both having a single intermediary vertex of number 1 (< 2). On the other hand, the same path in G_2, $\langle 1, 4, 3, 4, 2 \rangle$, can be decomposed in neither $\langle 1, 4 \rangle$ and $\langle 4, 3, 4, 2 \rangle$ (since 4 is an intermediary vertex of this latter path), nor in $\langle 1, 4, 3 \rangle$ and $\langle 3, 4, 2 \rangle$ (since the intermediary vertex number 4 (> 3) belongs to both), nor in $\langle 1, 4, 3, 4 \rangle$ and $\langle 4, 2 \rangle$ (the first path having the intermediary vertex number 4). Consequently, the path $\langle 1, 4, 3, 4, 2 \rangle$ is not taken into account.

133 - A 3   **Answer 3.**   The algorithm canonically associated to the proposed recurrence is given below:

```
1. constants
2.    n ∈ ℕ₁ and n = ... and MG ∈ 1..n × 1..n → 𝔹 and MG = [...]
3.    /% MG is the adjacence square matrix associated with the considered
      graph G %/
4. variables
5.    MG⁺ ∈ 1..n × 1..n × 0..n → 𝔹
6.    /% MG⁺ is the three-dimension matrix such that at the end of execution
      MG⁺[i, j, n] is equal to true if there is a path from i to j in G, false other-
      wise %/
7. begin
8.    for i ∈ 1..n do
9.       for j ∈ 1..n do
10.         MG⁺[i, j, 0] ← MG[i, j]
11.      end for
12.   end for;
13.   for i ranging 1..n do
14.      for x ∈ 1..n do
15.         for y ∈ 1..n do
16.            MG⁺[x, y, i] ← MG⁺[x, y, i − 1] or else ( MG⁺[x, i, i − 1] and
                                                         MG⁺[i, y, i − 1]  )
17.         end for
18.      end for
19.   end for;
20.   write(MG⁺)
21. end
```

Given the three-dimensional nature of the matrix MG^+, the spatial complexity of this algorithm is in $\Theta(n^3)$. The initialization phase (lines 8 to 12) requires n^2 accesses to the matrices MWG and MWG^+, and the main calculation step (lines 13 to 19) requires between $2n^3$ and $4n^3$ accesses. The temporal complexity of this algorithm is therefore in $\Theta(n^3)$ accesses to graphs.

Answer 4. Looking at the recurrence, it can be observed that at step i, only $\text{path}(x, i, i-1)$ and $\text{path}(i, y, i-1)$ are "re-used". The fact that these elements are replaced respectively by $\text{path}(x, i, i)$ and $\text{path}(i, y, i)$ may seem hazardous, but it turns out that: $\qquad$ 133 - A 4

- $\text{path}(x, i, i) = \text{path}(x, i, i-1)$ **or** $(\text{path}(x, i, i-1)$ **and** $\text{path}(i, i, i-1))$
$$= \text{path}(x, i, i-1)$$
- $\text{path}(i, y, i) = \text{path}(i, y, i-1)$ **or** $(\text{path}(i, i, i-1)$ **and** $\text{path}(i, y, i-1))$
$$= \text{path}(i, y, i-1).$$

Consequently, the recurrence can be simplified into:

$$
\left|
\begin{aligned}
\text{path}(x, y) &= (x, y) \in V & \left\{ \begin{aligned} & 1 \leqslant x \leqslant n \text{ and} \\ & 1 \leqslant y \leqslant n \end{aligned} \right. \\[1em]
\text{path}(x, y) &= \left(\begin{aligned} & \text{path}(x, y) \text{ or} \\ & \left(\begin{aligned} & \text{path}(x, i) \text{ and} \\ & \text{path}(i, y)) \end{aligned} \right) \end{aligned} \right) & \left\{ \begin{aligned} & 1 \leqslant i \leqslant n \text{ and} \\ & 1 \leqslant x \leqslant n \text{ and} \\ & 1 \leqslant y \leqslant n \end{aligned} \right.
\end{aligned}
\right.
$$

Answer 5. In the program, the disjunction appearing in the general term of recurrence can be removed, by setting the value of $MG^+[x, y]$ to **true** when a path from x to y is found $\qquad$ 133 - A 5 at step i. Moreover, rather than trying to find a path from x to any y passing through i in the innermost loop, this can be done only if a path $\langle x * i \rangle$ exists by introducing a conditional statement, hence the following final algorithm (called Roy-Warshall's algorithm):

```
1.  constants
2.     n ∈ ℕ₁ and n = ... and MG ∈ 1..n × 1..n → 𝔹 and MG = [...]
3.     /% MG is the square matrix associated with the considered graph G %/
4.  variables
5.     MG⁺ ∈ 1..n × 1..n → 𝔹
6.     /% MG⁺ is the matrix representing the resulting graph, i.e. the transitive
       closure G⁺ of G %/
7.  begin
8.     MG⁺ ← MG;
9.     for i ranging 1..n do
10.      for x ∈ 1..n do
11.        if MG⁺[x, i] then
12.          for y ∈ 1..n do
13.            if MG⁺[i, y] then
14.              MG⁺[x, y] ← true
15.            end if
16.          end for
17.        end if
18.      end for
19.    end for
20. end
```

The spatial complexity of this algorithm is in $\Theta(n^2)$ (matrices MG and MG^+) and its time complexity in $\mathcal{O}(n^3)$ accesses to graphs.

133 - A 6   **Answer 6.**   We consider on the one hand the elementary path $pth_1 = \langle x * z * y \rangle$ of value $vpth_1$ and on the other hand the non-elementary path $pth_2 = \langle x * z, v_{i_1}, \ldots, v_{i_p}, z * y \rangle$ identical to pth_1 except the circuit $c = \langle z, v_{i_1}, \ldots, v_{i_p}, z \rangle$ "around z", of value $vpth_2$. The three cases of value $valc$ of the circuit c are studied:

- If $valc > 0$, it is clear that $vpth_2 > vpth_1$. Therefore it can be asserted that a path of minimum value between two vertices x and y cannot include a circuit of positive value. The fact that such a circuit may not be "seen" by the algorithm is thus not a problem.

- If $valc = 0$, the values $vpth_1$ and $vpth_2$ are identical, and here also the fact that the circuit may be ignored has no consequence.

- If $valc < 0$, the value of the path of minimum value between x and y is asymptotically $-\infty$. If the circuit c is not taken into account, the result returned by the algorithm is $vpth_1$ and if it is, the algorithm will return $vpth_2 = vpth_1 + valc < vpth_1$. In both cases, this answer is erroneous, from which it is concluded that Floyd's algorithm adapted from that of Roy-Warshall's one delivers an incorrect result in the presence of circuit(s) of negative value.

133 - A 7   **Answer 7.**   For any pair of vertices (x, y), the idea is to compare the value of the "new" path $\langle x * y \rangle$ obtained by concatenation of $\langle x * i \rangle$ and $\langle i * y \rangle$, *when it exists*, with that of the optimal path from x to y known until then. It is admitted that the graph $WG = (N, V, P)$ is such that if the arc (x, y) does not exist, $P(x, y)$ takes the conventional value $+\infty$ (neutral element for the minimum). So, the recurrence is:

$$\left| \begin{array}{l} Pthvalmin(x, y, 0) = P(x, y) \\[2ex] Pthvalmin(x, y, i) = \min \left(\left\{ \begin{array}{l} Pthvalmin(x, y, i-1), \\ Pthvalmin(x, i, i-1) + \\ Pthvalmin(i, y, i-1) \end{array} \right) \right\} \right) \end{array} \right. \quad \left\{ \begin{array}{l} 1 \leqslant x \leqslant n \text{ and} \\ 1 \leqslant y \leqslant n \\ 1 \leqslant i \leqslant n \text{ and} \\ 1 \leqslant x \leqslant n \text{ and} \\ 1 \leqslant y \leqslant n \end{array} \right. .$$

133 - A 8   **Answer 8.**   Floyd's algorithm can be easily deduced from this recurrence, since it obeys the structure of Roy-Warshal's one with, here again, a calculation "on the spot" whose justification is the same as that developed in the answer to question 3:

```
 1.  constants
 2.     n ∈ ℕ₁ and n = ... and MWG ∈ 1..n × 1..n → ℝ and MWG = [...] and
 3.     NegativeCircuitFree(WG)
 4.     /% MWG is the square matrix associated with the weighted graph WG
        considered and
        NegativeCircuitFree(WG) is the predicate indicating the absence of neg-
        ative value circuit in WG %/
 5.  variables
 6.     MWGVMIN ∈ 1..n × 1..n → ℝ
 7.     /% MWGVMIN is the matrix resulting from the calculation of the values
        of minimum value paths %/
 8.  begin
 9.     MWGVMIN ← MGV;
10.     for i ranging 1..n do
11.        for x ∈ 1..n do
12.           if MWGVMIN[x, i] ≠ ∞ then
13.              for y ∈ 1..n do
```

14.   **if** MWGVMIN[i, y] $\neq \infty$ **then**

15.   MWGVMIN[x, y] $\leftarrow$

16. $\min \left(\left\{ \begin{array}{l} \text{MWGVMIN}[x, y], \\ \text{MWGVMIN}[x, i] + \text{MWGVMIN}[i, y] \end{array} \right\} \right)$

17.   **end if**
18.   **end for**
19.   **end if**
20.   **end for**
21.   **end for;**
22.   **write**(MWGVMIN)
23. **end**

The spatial complexity of this algorithm is in $\Theta(n^2)$ (matrices MWG and MWGVMIN). Its temporal complexity – like that of Roy-Warshall's algorithm – is in $\mathcal{O}(n^3)$ in terms of evaluated conditions.

Answer 9.   We begin by applying Floyd's algorithm to the graph WG_1 (without circuit) for which the successive iterations are detailed (limiting ourselves to those that produce a change, the new values appearing in italics), then the sagittal representation of the starting and resulting graphs. The new arcs appear in bold and those of value $+\infty$ are omitted (these conventions also apply to the other two examples).   133 - A 9

	1	2	3	4	5
1	$+\infty$	5	$+\infty$	10	$+\infty$
2	$+\infty$	$+\infty$	$+\infty$	3	$+\infty$
3	2	4	$+\infty$	$+\infty$	1
4	$+\infty$	$+\infty$	$+\infty$	$+\infty$	$+\infty$
5	$+\infty$	$+\infty$	$+\infty$	1	$+\infty$

WG_1: matrix representation (MWG_1)

	1	2	3	4	5
1	$+\infty$	5	$+\infty$	10	$+\infty$
2	$+\infty$	$+\infty$	$+\infty$	3	$+\infty$
3	2	4	$+\infty$	*12*	1
4	$+\infty$	$+\infty$	$+\infty$	$+\infty$	$+\infty$
5	$+\infty$	$+\infty$	$+\infty$	1	$+\infty$

$MWGVMIN_1$ after iteration step 1

	1	2	3	4	5
1	$+\infty$	5	$+\infty$	*8*	$+\infty$
2	$+\infty$	$+\infty$	$+\infty$	3	$+\infty$
3	2	4	$+\infty$	*7*	1
4	$+\infty$	$+\infty$	$+\infty$	$+\infty$	$+\infty$
5	$+\infty$	$+\infty$	$+\infty$	1	$+\infty$

$MWGVMIN_1$ after iteration step 2

	1	2	3	4	5
1	$+\infty$	5	$+\infty$	8	$+\infty$
2	$+\infty$	$+\infty$	$+\infty$	3	$+\infty$
3	2	4	$+\infty$	*2*	1
4	$+\infty$	$+\infty$	$+\infty$	$+\infty$	$+\infty$
5	$+\infty$	$+\infty$	$+\infty$	1	$+\infty$

$MWGVMIN_1$ after iteration step 5

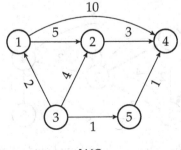

WG_1

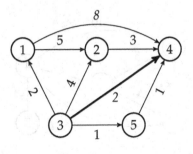

final graph

The iteration steps for i =3 and i =4 produce no change, since the vertex 3 has no prede-cessor (entry point) and the vertex 4 has no successor (exit point).

We now move to the graph WG_2 (involving the circuit of positive value $\langle 1,2,3,1 \rangle$). We give in figure 9.15 (respectively 9.16) the matrix (respectively sagittal) representation of the initial graph and of the graph resulting from the application of Floyd's algorithm.

	1	2	3	4	5
1	$+\infty$	5	$+\infty$	10	$+\infty$
2	$+\infty$	$+\infty$	-4	3	$+\infty$
3	2	$+\infty$	$+\infty$	8	$+\infty$
4	$+\infty$	$+\infty$	$+\infty$	$+\infty$	$+\infty$
5	$+\infty$	$+\infty$	$+\infty$	-1	$+\infty$

	1	2	3	4	5
1	3	5	1	8	$+\infty$
2	-2	3	-4	3	$+\infty$
3	2	7	3	8	$+\infty$
4	$+\infty$	$+\infty$	$+\infty$	$+\infty$	$+\infty$
5	$+\infty$	$+\infty$	$+\infty$	-1	$+\infty$

Fig. 9.15 – *Matrices representing the graph WG_2 (initial MWGVMIN$_2$) and the graph resulting from Floyd's algorithm (final MWGVMIN$_2$).*

Note that the iteration steps for i = 4 and i = 5 produce no change, since the vertex 4 has no successor (exit point) and the vertex 5 has no predecessor (entry point).

We end with the graph WG_3, assuming that the precondition relating to the circuits has been released. We give the matrices and the initial and final sagittal representations:

	1	2	3
1	$+\infty$	1	4
2	$+\infty$	$+\infty$	-3
3	1	$+\infty$	$+\infty$

	1	2	3
1	-1	0	-3
2	-2	-1	-4
3	0	1	-2

WG_3: matrix representation (MWG$_3$)   MWGVMIN$_3$ after iteration step 3

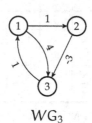

WG$_3$

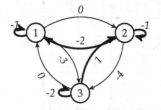

final graph

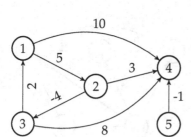

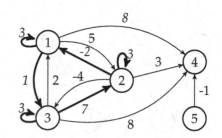

Fig. 9.16 – *The graph WG_2 (initial MWGVMIN$_2$) and the graph resultant from Floyd's algorithm (MWGVVMIN$_2$ final).*

It can be observed that the values on the diagonal of the final matrix $MWGVMIN_1$ are all equal to $+\infty$, which guarantees the absence of a circuit in this graph. It may also be noticed that the first three values of the diagonal of the final matrix $MWGVMIN_2$ are positive and different from $+\infty$, which testifies to the fact that the vertices $1, 2$ and 3 belong to a circuit (the same in fact). However, this circuit being of positive value, it does not contribute to "construct" a path of minimum value and does not interfere, as established in the answer to question 4. As for WG_3, it includes the circuit of negative value $\langle 1, 2, 3, 1 \rangle$, and it is known that the result of the algorithm is inaccurate (one of the objectives being to highlight it with this "simple" graph). The values appearing on the diagonal of $MWGVMIN_3$ are all negative, because the vertices $1, 2$ and 3 belong to the same circuit of negative value (-1). As expected, the values returned by the algorithm are wrong, since here the "exact" value of any path is (asymptotically) $-\infty$. In the presence of large graphs where the presence of negative value circuit(s) is not easily detectable, Floyd's algorithm can be applied to examine the diagonal of the resulting matrix. Indeed, the presence of negative values reveals the existence of at least one circuit of negative value and therefore makes it possible to know that the result obtained is inaccurate.

Answer 10.   To get not only the value of the (one) optimal path, but also this path itself, 133 - A 10
"Tom Thumb's" technique is applied. The matrix PTHVMIN[1 .. n, 1 .. n] is adjoined to MWGVMIN.
A first approach consists in filling PTHVMIN[x, y] with the vertex i (in the sense of the algorithm) for which the optimal value is found. The elements associated with the arcs of WG_2 are initialized to 0. So, we have:

	1	2	3	4	5
1	$+\infty$	0	$+\infty$	0	$+\infty$
2	$+\infty$	$+\infty$	0	0	$+\infty$
3	0	$+\infty$	$+\infty$	0	$+\infty$
4	$+\infty$	$+\infty$	$+\infty$	$+\infty$	$+\infty$
5	$+\infty$	$+\infty$	$+\infty$	0	$+\infty$

initial $PTHVMIN_2$

	1	2	3	4	5
1	3	0	2	2	$+\infty$
2	3	3	0	0	$+\infty$
3	0	1	2	0	$+\infty$
4	$+\infty$	$+\infty$	$+\infty$	$+\infty$	$+\infty$
5	$+\infty$	$+\infty$	$+\infty$	0	$+\infty$

final $PTHVMIN_2$

8 is found as the value of the optimal path between vertices 1 and 4 (see figure 9.15, page 740) for $i = 2$. The optimal path between these two vertices thus consists in going from 1 to 2 and from 2 to 4 in an optimal way. The mechanism is recursively repeated on these two paths (in a way similar to what is described page 705 in the answer to question 6 in problem 125), for which the process stops immediately as $PTHVMIN_2[1, 2] = PTHVMIN_2[2, 4] = 0$. The optimal path to go from 1 to 4 is $\langle 1, 2, 4 \rangle$. The value of the optimal path between the vertices 2 and 2 (see figure 9.15) is 3 and it is found for $i = 3$. The optimal path between 2 and 3 is the arc $(2, 3)$, and the one between 3 and 2 is decomposed in $(3, 1)$ and $(1, 2)$ (since $PTHVMIN_2[3, 2] = 1$). The optimal path from 2 to 2 is thus $\langle 2, 3, 1, 2 \rangle$.

Another way consists in putting in PTHVMIN[x, y] the (one) successor of x on the (one) optimal path connecting x to y. For any arc (x, y), PTHVMIN[x, y] is initialized to y and when the path $\langle x * i * y \rangle$ is optimal, PTHVMIN[x, y] is updated by the value PTHVMIN[x, i]. Applied to the graph WG_2, this strategy leads to the following initial and final arrays PTHVMIN[x, i]:

	1	2	3	4	5
1	$+\infty$	2	$+\infty$	4	$+\infty$
2	$+\infty$	$+\infty$	3	4	$+\infty$
3	1	$+\infty$	$+\infty$	4	$+\infty$
4	$+\infty$	$+\infty$	$+\infty$	$+\infty$	$+\infty$
5	$+\infty$	$+\infty$	$+\infty$	4	$+\infty$

	1	2	3	4	5
1	2	2	2	2	$+\infty$
2	3	3	3	4	$+\infty$
3	1	1	1	4	$+\infty$
4	$+\infty$	$+\infty$	$+\infty$	$+\infty$	$+\infty$
5	$+\infty$	$+\infty$	$+\infty$	4	$+\infty$

For the optimal path between the vertices 1 and 4, $PTHVMIN_2[1,4] = 2$. The optimal path is therefore $\langle 1, 2, \ldots \rangle$. the process continues with $PTHVMIN_2[2,4]$, which is equal to 4 (the end to be reached); the process stops and the the path $\langle 1, 2, 4 \rangle$ is found as with the other method. The same process applied to the optimal path between the vertices 2 and 2 leads first to 3, then to 1 and finally to 2. Here again, the optimal path $\langle 2, 3, 1, 2 \rangle$ is identified. Note that a "symmetric" method would consist in putting in $PTHVMIN[x, y]$ the (one) predecessor of y on the (one) optimal path from x to y .

133 - A 11   **Answer 11.**   The calculation of the value of the maximum value path between any pair of vertices is close to that solved by Floyd's algorithm. The "logical or" in the initial recurrence becomes the maximum instead of the minimum in Floyd's algorithm, and the "logical and" is replaced by then sum as in Floyd's algorithm. The matrix MWG associated with the graph WG considered (and thus the matrix that will be calculated) is initialized so that if the arc (x, y) does not exist in WG, its value is $-\infty$ (neutral element for the maximum). In this framework, any positive value circuit raises a problem and the algorithm must not be used.

Searching for the shortest (respectively longest) path for any pair of vertices constitutes a special case of the calculation of the value of the minimum (respectively maximum) value path. The algebras used remain unchanged (minimum, $+$) for the shortest ones and (maximum, $+$) for the longest. In the matrix MWG associated with the graph WG, the value of an arc is 1 if it exists and $+\infty$ or $-\infty$ otherwise. For the shortest paths, no circuit is problematic since they all have a positive value. *A contrario*, any circuit raises a problem for the longest paths, since if a path involving a circuit can be built between x and y, an infinity may be built and the length of the longest path between x and y is therefore (asymptotically) $+\infty$.

When the arcs carry probability values, the algebra is (minimum, $\cdot$) for the paths of minimum probability and (maximum, $\cdot$) for those of maximum probability. In the matrix MWG associated with the graph WG, the value associated with an arc that does not exist is $+\infty$ for paths of minimum probability and $-\infty$ for those of maximum probability. Any circuit with a probability other than 1 poses a problem for paths of minimum probability (since passing through such a circuit decreases the probability of the path "passing through" this circuit), while no circuit is problematic for maximum probability paths.

When arcs represent capacities, the algebra is (minimum, minimum) for minimum capacity paths and (maximum, minimum) for those of maximum capacity ones. In the matrix MWG associated with the graph WG, the value associated with an arc that does not exist is $+\infty$ for minimum capacity paths and $-\infty$ fot those of maximum capacity. Circuits do not disturb for maximum capacity paths. Indeed, if the capacity of the elementary path $\langle x * k * y \rangle$ is c_1, c_2 that of the non-elementary path $\langle x * k * y \rangle$ is such that $c_1 \geqslant c_2$. The case of paths of minimum capacity is more delicate. Let us consider the two graphs G_1 and G_2 below.

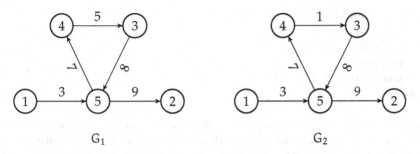

G_1 G_2

In G_1, paths $\langle 1, 5, 2 \rangle$ and $\langle 1, 5, 4, 3, 5, 2 \rangle$ have the same capacity (3), the latter being due to that of the arc $(1, 5)$. On the other hand, in G_2, the capacity of the path $\langle 1, 5, 2 \rangle$ is 3, while that of the path $\langle 1, 5, 4, 3, 5, 2 \rangle$ is 1. It would suffice that the circuit $\langle 5, 4, 3, 5 \rangle$ be "seen" once for the result to be correct, since any path of type $\langle 1, 5, \{4, 3, 5\}^+, 2 \rangle$ has a capacity equal to 1. But, the path $\langle 1, 5, 4, 3, 5, 2 \rangle$ is not "seen". Indeed, $\langle 1, 5, 4, 3, 5, 2 \rangle$ does not break down into $\langle 1, 5 \rangle$ and $\langle 5, 4, 3, 5, 2 \rangle$, nor into $\langle 1, 5, 4 \rangle$ and $\langle 4, 3, 5, 2 \rangle$, nor in $\langle 1, 5, 4, 3 \rangle$ and $\langle 3, 5, 2 \rangle$, nor in $\langle 1, 5, 4, 3, 5 \rangle$ nor in $\langle 5, 2 \rangle$ (see question 2).

Answer 12.   Although it is not a matter of optimal value calculation, counting the paths   133 - A 12
between any pair of vertices can be done thanks to an adaptation of Roy-Warshall's algorithm as long as the graph G concerned does not have any circuit(s). The initial graph G is unweighted, and for the initialization of the adapted algorithm, it is associated with a valued graph $WG' = (N, V, W')$ where $W' \in V \to 0\,..\,1$. The algebra $(+, \cdot)$ replaces the algebra (or, and), and this algorithm only provides a correct result if G is free of circuits. We therefore have the recurrence:

$$\left|
\begin{array}{ll}
\text{nbpath}(x, y, 0) = W'(x, y) & 1 \leqslant x \leqslant n \text{ and } 1 \leqslant y \leqslant n \\[2mm]
\text{nbpath}(x, y, i) = \left(\begin{array}{l} \text{nbpath}(x, y, i-1) + \\ \text{nbpath}(x, i, i-1) \cdot \text{nbpath}(i, y, i-1) \end{array} \right) & \left\{ \begin{array}{l} 1 \leqslant i \leqslant n \text{ and} \\ 1 \leqslant x \leqslant n \text{ and} \\ 1 \leqslant y \leqslant n \end{array} \right.
\end{array}
\right.$$

from which stems the following algorithm:

```
1.  constants
2.    n ∈ ℕ and n = ... and MWG ∈ 1..n × 1..n → 0..1 and MWG = [...] and
3.    IsCircuitFree(WG)
4.    /% MWG is the square matrix associated with the weighted graph WG'
      considered, IsCircuitFree(WG) specifies that the graph WG id free from
      circuit(s) %/
5.  variables
6.    MWGNBC ∈ 1..n × 1..n → ℕ
7.    /% MWGNBC is the matrix resulting from the count of paths between all
      pairs of vertices %/
8.  begin
9.    MWGNBC ← MWG;
10.   for i ∈ 1..n do
11.     for x ∈ 1..n do
12.       if MWGNBC[x, i] ≠ 0 then
13.         for y ∈ 1..n do
14.           MWGNBC[x, y]   ←   MWGNBC[x, y]  +  MWGNBC[x, i] ·
              MWGNBC[i, y]
```

15.   **end for**
16.   **end if**
17.   **end for**
18.   **end for**;
19.   **write**(MWGNBC)
20. **end**

133 - A 13   **Answer** 13.   The problem posed can be seen as a constrained version of that solved by Floyd's algorithm (the value of the (one) path of minimum value for all pairs of vertices). It is therefore clear that any circuit of negative value not passing through the vertex k raises a problem. The other circuits (of non-negative value or of negative value passing through k) do not prevent from using the algorithm. Under the hypothesis of the absence of a circuit of negative value passing through the vertex k, Floyd algorithm's is adapted by noting that:

- any initial arc is a path not passing through the intermediary vertex k,
- a path from x to y obtained by concatenation of $\langle x * i \rangle$ and $\langle i * y \rangle$ does not pass through the intermediary vertex k ($k \neq i$), iff none of the two paths $\langle x * i \rangle$ and $\langle i * y \rangle$ does not include the intermediary vertex k.

The recurrence at the basis of the adapted algorithm is therefore:

$$\left|\begin{array}{ll} \mathrm{pthvmpk}(x,y,0) = P'(x,y) & 1 \leqslant x \leqslant n \text{ and } 1 \leqslant y \leqslant n \\[4pt] \mathrm{pthvmpk}(x,y,i) = \min\left(\left\{\begin{array}{c} \mathrm{pthvmpk}(x,y,i-1), \\ \mathrm{pthvmpk}(x,i,i-1) + \\ \mathrm{pthvmpk}(i,y,i-1) \end{array}\right\}\right) & \begin{array}{l} 1 \leqslant i \leqslant n \text{ and} \\ i \neq k \text{ and} \\ 1 \leqslant x,y \leqslant n \end{array} \end{array}\right. .$$

133 - A 14   **Answer** 14.   The computation of the value of the (one) path of minimum value passing through the intermediate vertex k given by an algorithm adapted from that of Floyd is only possible if it is based only on elementary paths. This is not the case with the following WG graph:

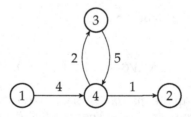

in which there is no elementary path going from 1 to 2 passing through 3. On the other hand, there is a path between 1 and 2 passing through the intermediary vertex 3 of minimum value, namely $\langle 1,4,3,4,2 \rangle$, but it is a *non-elementary* one that is not "seen" by Floyd's algorithm. Indeed, the path $\langle 1,4,3,4,2 \rangle$ does not break down into $\langle 1,4 \rangle$ and $\langle 4,3,4,2 \rangle$, nor in $\langle 1,4,3 \rangle$ and $\langle 3,4,2 \rangle$, nor in $\langle 1,4,3,4 \rangle$ and $\langle 4,2 \rangle$. In conclusion, an adaptation of Floyd's algorithm is only possible for graphs free from circuits. Note that it is then necessary to maintain both the paths between all the pairs of vertices and the paths passing through the intermediate vertex k. Indeed, when taking into account the path $\langle x * i * y \rangle$ (by concatenation), the paths $\langle x * i \rangle$ and $\langle i * y \rangle$ must *both* exist, and it suffices that at least *one of them* passes through the intermediary vertex k or that i be equal to k.

Answers to problem 134. Best path in an array   *The problem is on page 667.*

Answer 1.   The problem can be reformulated in the context of graphs in the following   134 - A 1
way (for instance). Any cell c of the array TJ is the vertex v of the graph WG. If the cell c_2
can be reached from the cell c_1 by means of one authorized move, an arc is placed between
the corresponding vertices v_1 and v_2 in WG. The value of the arc (v_1, v_2) is that of the cell c_1
associated with v_1, except if v_1 is the cell $(n, 1)$ of TJ, in which case the value of the arc is the
sum of the values of the cells associated with both v_1 and v_2. The problem then becomes a
matter of moving between the two vertices corresponding to the cells $(n, 1)$ and $(1, n)$ in
the weighted directed graph WG.

The graph WG associated with the array TJ mentioned at the beginning of statement of
the problem is:

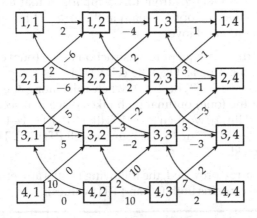

Answer 2.   The principle of calculating the cost associated with the (one) best path   134 - A 2
going from cell (i, j) to cell $(1, n)$ is now described. When in the cell (i, j), the associated
penalty (TJ[i, j]) must be paid and it is necessary to choose, among the three "accessible"
cells (in the case general), the one from which the value of the minimum cost path is the
lowest. The special cases concern the cells (i, j) such that $i = 1$ (only the first movement is
authorized), $j = 1$ (only the first and third movements are authorized) and $j = n$ (only the
second displacement is possible). Therefore, the following recurrence can be deduced:

$$
\begin{vmatrix}
\begin{aligned}
&\mathrm{pmc}(1, n) = TJ[1, n] \\
&\mathrm{pmc}(1, j) = TJ[1, j] + \mathrm{pmc}(1, j + 1) & & 1 \leqslant j < n \\
&\mathrm{pmc}(i, n) = TJ[i, n] + \mathrm{pmc}(i - 1, n - 1) & & 1 < i \leqslant n \\
&\mathrm{pmc}(i, 1) = TJ[i, 1] + \min \left(\left\{ \begin{array}{l} \mathrm{pmc}(i, 2), \\ \mathrm{pmc}(i - 1, 2) \end{array} \right\} \right) & & 1 < i \leqslant n \\
&\mathrm{pmc}(i, j) = TJ[i, j] + \min \left(\left\{ \begin{array}{l} \mathrm{pmc}(i, j + 1), \\ \mathrm{pmc}(i - 1, j - 1), \\ \mathrm{pmc}(i - 1, j + 1) \end{array} \right\} \right) & & \left\{ \begin{array}{c} 1 < i \leqslant n \\ \text{and} \\ 1 < j < n \end{array} \right.
\end{aligned}
\end{vmatrix}
$$

Answer 3.   The computation is done using the array OC[1 .. n, 1 .. n] whose upper row   134 - A 3
is initialized using the first two terms of the recurrence. Then, for any row, the element of
column n can be calculated from the element of column $(n - 1)$ of the previous row (3rd
term); any other element except the first can be calculated from its upper left neighbor, its
upper right neighbor and its right neighbor (5th term); the first element of the row can be
calculated from its upper right neighbor and from its right neighbor (4th term). In summary, the calculation can be performed topdown per row and in a row from right to left.

The spatial complexity of the algorithm is in $\Theta(n^2)$ and the temporal complexity in number of conditions evaluated also, since one carries out at most two comparisons to fill any cell of OC.

The minimum value path calculation algorithms studied in problems 132 page 661, and 133 page 664, can be applied to the graph WG associated with the array TJ since it has no circuit. Bellman-Ford's algorithm has a time complexity in $\Theta(M \cdot N)$, where N (respectively M) is the number of vertices (respectively arcs) of the treated graph. However, the graph WG associated with TJ has n^2 vertices and $(3n^2 - 5n + 2)$ arcs, n being the side of the (square) array TJ. Consequently, the use of Bellman-Ford's algorithm would have a complexity in $\Theta(n^4)$. For its part, Floyd's algorithm has a complexity in $\mathcal{O}(N^3)$, where N is the number of vertices of the considered graph. Its application would therefore lead to a complexity in $\mathcal{O}(n^6)$. It emerges from this comparison that the specific computation developed previously to find the optimal path in the array TJ far surpasses the "general" algorithms of Bellman-Ford and Floyd.

134 - A 4   **Answer 4.**   To allow the subsequent reconstruction of the (one) optimal path, the array PTH is filled in at the same time as OC. The cell PTH[i, j] is assigned the choice that was made for the next move "$\nwarrow$", "$\nearrow$" or "$\rightarrow$"), when calculating the value of OC[i, j]. The actual reconstruction of the (one) optimal path takes place in a second step; it is done as follows: starting with PTH[n, 1], we then go to PTH[i, j+1], PTH[i−1, j+1] or PTH[i−1, j−1] depending on whether "$\rightarrow$", "$\nearrow$" or "$\nwarrow$" is found in cell PTH[i, j]. The process stops when the cell PTH[1, n] is reached.

134 - A 5   **Answer 5.**   With the array provided, the following results are returned by the algorithm (a cell of the table below contains both OC and PTH values):

j	1	2	3	4
i = 1	−1 →	−3 →	1 →	0 /
2	−9 ↗	−2 →	−4 ↖	4 ↖
3	−6 →	−11 ↖	−5 ↖	−1 ↖
4	−11 ↗	1 →	−9 ↖	2 ↖

The strategy described in the previous answer yields the optimal path: $\langle (4, 1), (3, 2), (2, 1), (1, 2), (1, 3), (1, 4) \rangle$ of value −11.

134 - A 6   **Answer 6.**   As the two cells $(1, n)$ and $(n, 1)$ belong to any path, their values do not influence the determination of the optimal path. With the proposed alternative values, the optimal path would be the same, but would have the value −7 instead of −11.

134 - A 7   **Answer 7.**   In question 2, it is asked to establish the recurrence calculating the value $pmc(i, j)$ of the optimal path from the cell (i, j) to the cell $(1, n)$ of the array TJ. Therefore, the value of the optimal path going from $(n, 1)$ to $(1, n)$ corresponds to $pmc(n, 1)$. Another way to proceed would be to calculate the value of $pmc'(i, j)$, value of the optimal path from cell $(n, 1)$ to cell (i, j), $pmc'(1, n)$ then corresponding to the sought value.

Answers to problem 135. Weighted binary search trees   *The problem is on page 669.*

135 - A 1   **Answer 1.**   To construct a bst A composed of the values $x_1, \ldots, x_n$, x_k is chosen as the root, and on the one hand $x_1, \ldots, x_{k-1}$ are put in the left subtree and on the other hand $x_{k+1}, \ldots, x_n$ are placed in the right subtree. The number $nbbst(n)$ of binary search trees (bst's) having n values is thus given by:

$$nbbst(0) = 1$$

$$nbbst(n) = \sum_{k=1}^{n} nbbst(k-1) \cdot nbbst(n-k) \qquad n > 0$$

the solution of which is a Catalan number (see page 11):

$$nbbst(n) = Cat(n+1) = \frac{1}{n+1} \cdot C_{2n}^{n} \approx \frac{4^n}{(n+1)\sqrt{\pi(n+1)}}.$$

Answer 2. If the bst T is empty, its left (respectively right) subtree ($lst(T)$) (respectively $rst(T)$) are empty too, and: 135 - A 2

$$cbst(lst(T)) = 0; cbst(rst(T)) = 0; spr(T) = 0; cbst(T) = 0$$

and the equality holds.

Now let us consider a non-empty bst T. The values contained in T are partitioned into r, that of the probability root $p(r)$ and those in the left $lst(T)$ and right $rst(T)$ subtrees (possibly empty). Let $stNd(lsd(T))$ (respectively $stNd(rsd(T))$) be the sum of the nodes of $lst(T)$ (respectively $rst(T)$). We have:

$$cbst(T) = \sum_{k=1}^{n} p(x_k) \cdot (d_k + 1)$$

$$= p(r) + \sum_{k|x_k \in stNd(lst(T))} p(x_k) \cdot (d_k + 1) + \sum_{k|x_k \in stNd(rst(T))} p(x_k) \cdot (d_k + 1)$$

$$= p(r) + \sum_{k|x_k \in stNd(lst(T))} p(x_k) + \sum_{k|x_k \in stNd(rst(T))} p(x_k) +$$

$$\sum_{k|x_k \in stNd(lst(T))} p(x_k) \cdot d_k + \sum_{k|x_k \in stNd(rst(T))} p(x_k) \cdot d_k.$$

But, on the one hand:

$$p(r) + \sum_{k|x_k \in stNd(lst(T))} p(x_k) + \sum_{k|x_k \in stNd(rst(T))} p(x_k) = spr(T),$$

on the other hand, if the node of value x_k is at depth d_k in T, its depth d_k' is $d_k - 1$ in $lst(T)$ or $rst(T)$. Hence:

$$\sum_{k|x_k \in stNd(lst(T))} p(x_k) \cdot d_k = \sum_{k|x_k \in stNd(lst(A))} p_k \cdot (d_k' + 1) = cbst(lst(T))$$

$$\sum_{k|x_k \in stNd(lst(T))} p_k \cdot d_k = \sum_{k|x_k \in stNd(lst(T))} p_k \cdot (d_k' + 1) = cbst(lst(T))$$

and finally: $cbst(T) = spr(T) + cbst(lst(T)) + cbst(rst(T))$.

For the bst T_1 of figure 9.7, page 669, the initial definition of the cost of a bst yields:

$$cbst(T_1) = 3 \cdot p(1) + 2 \cdot p(2) + 3 \cdot p(3) + p(4) + 2 \cdot p(5)$$
$$= 1 + 2 \cdot p(1) + p(2) + 2 \cdot p(3) + p(5).$$

Applying the previously established formula, it comes:

$$spr(T_1) = 1; cbst(lst(T_1)) = p(2) + 2 \cdot p(1) + 2 \cdot p(3); cbst(rst(T_1)) = p(5)$$

hence $cbst(T_1) = spr(T_1) + cbst(lst(T_1)) + cbstr(rst(T_1))$.

Similarly, with T_2, the other bst in figure 9.7, we have:

$$cbst(T_2) = 2 \cdot p(1) + p(2) + 2 \cdot p(3) + 3 \cdot p(4) + 4 \cdot p(5)$$
$$= 1 + p(1) + p()3 + 2 \cdot p(4) + 3 \cdot p(5)$$
$$spr(T_2) = 1; cbst(lst(T_2)) = p(1); cbst(rst(T_2)) = p(3) + 2 \cdot p(4) + 3 \cdot p(5)$$

and the equality here also holds.

Given the additive nature of the formula linking the cost of a bst T and its left $lst(T)$ and right $rst(A)$ subtrees, it is trivial to prove by contradiction that $cbst(T)$ cannot be minimum if $cbst(lst(T))$ or $cbst(rst(T))$ is not.

135 - A 3   **Answer** 3.   Let us study the various possible organizations of the t values $x_i, \ldots, x_{i+t-1}$ making a bst $T_{i,t}$. In the presence of a single value ($t = 1$), the organization is unique; otherwise, the organization of the values $x_i, \ldots, x_{i+t-1}$ is as follows. A root of value x_{i+k} ($k \in 0 .. t-1$) is chosen, and the left (respectively right) subtree of $T_{i,t}$ contains the values $x_i, \ldots, x_{i+k-1}$ (respectively $x_{i+k+1}, \ldots, x_{i+t-1}$). According to the cost formula established in question 2, the cost $cbst(T_{i,t})$ is expressed as:

- $cbst(T_{i,t}) = cbst(lst(T_{i,t})) + sp(i, t)$ if $k = 0$ (empty left subtree),
- $cbst(T_{i,t}) = cbst(rst(T_{i,t})) + sp(i, t)$ if $k = t - 1$ (empty right subtree),
- $cbst(T_{i,t}) = cbst(lst(T_{i,t})) + cbst(rst(T_{i,t})) + sp(i, t)$ if $k \in 1 .. t - 2$.

The optimal value k – i.e. the one producing the minimum value of $cbst(T_{i,t})$ – must therefore be searched assuming the left and right subtrees themselves optimal. By noticing that there is no bst $T_{n,2}$ (which implies that the upper bound of variation of i is $(n-1)$), the recurrence is:

$$
\left|
\begin{aligned}
& cbst(i, 1) = p_i && 1 \leqslant i \leqslant n \\
& cbst(i, t) = \min \left(\left\{ \begin{aligned} & cbst(i+1, t-1), \\ & cbst(i, t-1), \\ & \min_{k \in 1..t-2} \left(\begin{aligned} cbst(i, k) + \\ cbst(i+k+1, t-k-1) \end{aligned} \right) \end{aligned} \right\} \right) \\
& \qquad + sp(i, t) && \left\{ \begin{aligned} & 1 \leqslant i \leqslant n-1 \textbf{ and} \\ & 2 \leqslant t \leqslant n-i+1 \end{aligned} \right.
\end{aligned}
\right.
$$

135 - A 4   **Answer** 4.   The implementation of the previous recurrence first requires computing the sp values stored in the array $SP[1 .. n, 1 .. n]$. The array $OC[1 .. n, 1 .. n]$ can then be filled in to store the values cbst. It can be observed that filling the cell $OC[i, t]$ uses cell values with column index less than t and row index greater than $(i-1)$. The calculation is chosen to progress by decreasing values of the row index (but this is not the only possibility), and in a row by increasing values of the column index. In the line of index i, $OC[i, 1]$ is filled in with the first term of the recurrence and each of the following values (from 2 to $n - i + 1$) with its second term. Note that the last line contains only one value, $OC[n, 1]$; the penultimate line has two values, $OC[n-1, 1]$ and $OC[n-1, 2]$, and so on until the first line is completely filled in. The value sought is $OC[1, n]$, the last cell calculated.

The spatial complexity of this algorithm is in $\Theta(n^2)$ (arrays SP and OC), and its time complexity in $\Theta(n^3)$ in terms of conditions evaluated.

The gain brought by this solution is significant since it has been seen in the question 1 that a naïve solution exploring any n-value bst is exponential, whereas dynamic programming offers a solution of polynomial complexity.

Answer 5. The arrat SP is:

t	1	2	3	4	5
i = 1	0.05	0.15	0.35	0.5	1
2	0.1	0.3	0.45	0.95	
3	0.2	0.35	0.85		
4	0.15	0.65			
5	0.5				

The computation of $\text{copt}(1,5)$ corresponds to that of $OC[1,5]$, which requires the complete filling of the upper left triangle of OC. We get:

t	1	2	3	4	5
i = 1	0.05	0.2	0.55	0.85	1.85
2	0.1	0.4	0.7	1.65	
3	0.2	0.5	1.35		
4	0.15	0.8			
5	0.5				

By keeping during the previous calculation the value of k that led to the optimal value, we can easily reconstruct the optimal bst given below.

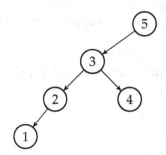

The cost of this bst can be calculated using the formula given at the beginning of the statement, namely $\text{cbst}(T) = \sum_{k=1}^{n} p(x_k) \cdot (d_k + 1)$, which leads to $p(5) + 2 \cdot p(3) + 3 \cdot p(2) + 3 \cdot p(4) + 4 \cdot p(1) = 0.5 + 0.4 + 0.3 + 0.45 + 0.2 = 1.85$. This value corresponds to the optimal value $OC[1,5]$ in the array shown in the previous answer.

Answer 6. This problem is very similar to that of the chained product of matrices (problem 125, page 649), as the form of the general of the recurrence is the same; hence, this is also the case for the associated program and its temporal and spatial complexities.

Answers to problem 136. Best independent set in a tree   *The problem is on page 670.*

Answer 1. The two cases $u \notin S^*$ and $u \in S^*$ are successively studied.

If $u \notin S^*$, all its sons are considered. A proof by contradiction is performed and it is supposed that there exists a value i such that $S^*_{v_i}$ is not optimal (is not of maximum weight) for the tree rooted in v_i. Therefore, there is another set which is optimal for this tree. Let $S^{**}_{v_i}$ be this set. In this case, $(S^* - S^*_{v_i}) \cup S^{**}_{v_i}$ has a weight greater than S^*, which contradicts the fact that S^* is optimal.

If $u \in \mathcal{S}^*$, a similar reasoning is used to prove the desired result by taking a value of i for which $\mathcal{S}^*_{w_i}$ is not optimal.

136 - A 2 **Answer** 2.   The calculation of a maximum weight independent subset of a tree t rooted in r depends on its height. For a tree t of height 0 (a single leaf), the optimal independent set associated with t has this leaf as a unique element. For a tree t of height 1, the optimal independent set associated with t is made up of either its root, or the union of all its leaves. For a subtree t rooted in u of height greater than or equal to 2, the choice is between the two sets specified in the answer to the previous question. The recurrence for the calculation of the weight of the maximum weight independent subset of the tree rooted in u is written:

$$\left|\begin{array}{ll} W(\mathcal{S}^*_u) = wght(u) & u \text{ is a leaf} \\[2mm] W(\mathcal{S}^*_u) = \max\left(\left\{\begin{array}{l} wght(u), \\ wght(v_1) + \cdots + wght(v_c) \end{array}\right\}\right) & \left\{\begin{array}{l} u \text{ is the root of a sub-} \\ \text{tree of height equal to 1} \end{array}\right. \\[4mm] W(\mathcal{S}^*_u) = \max\left(\left\{\begin{array}{l} W(\mathcal{S}^*_{v_1} \cup \cdots \cup \mathcal{S}^*_{v_c}), \\ W(\mathcal{S}^*_{w_1} \cup \cdots \cup \mathcal{S}^*_{w_g}) \end{array}\right\}\right) & \left\{\begin{array}{l} u \text{ is the root of a subtree} \\ \text{of height at least equal to 2} \end{array}\right. \end{array}\right.$$

and the weight $W(\mathcal{S}^*)$ of the maximum weight independent subset of the tree t rooted in r is given by $W(\mathcal{S}^*_r)$.

136 - A 3 **Answer** 3.   The principle of the algorithm consists in, on the one hand using the recurrence, on the other hand "hang up" the result of the calculations to the tree itself without calling on an array as it is usually done. The tree is explored top down from left to right and the calculations related to a node are carried out once its sons are treated (postfixed order). This leads to the following (recursive) procedure *OptIndepSubSet*:

```
 1.  procedure OptIndepSubSet(t) pre
 2.    t ∈ tqe and a = ... and Vopts ∈ ℕ and Voptgs ∈ ℕ and Sopts ⊂ ℕ₁ and
 3.    Soptgs ⊂ ℕ₁
 4.    /% the tree t must be non-empty %/
 5.  begin
 6.    if t.schild = ∅ then
 7.       /% case of a leaf %/
 8.       t.opvl ← t.wght; t.sidop ← {t.id}
 9.    else
10.       for e ∈ t.schild do
11.          OptIndepSubSet(e)
12.       end for;
13.       Collect(t, Vopts, Voptgs, Sopts, Soptgs);
14.       if Voptgs = 0 then
15.          /% case of a tree of height 1 %/
16.          if t.wght > Vopts then
17.             t.opvl ← t.wght; t.sidop ← {t.id}
18.          else
19.             t.opvl ← Vopts; t.sidop ← Sopts
20.          end if
21.       else
22.          /% case of a subtree of height at least equal to 2 %/
23.          if t.wght + Voptgs > Vopts then
24.             t.opvl ← t.wght + Voptgs; t.sidop ← {t.id} ∪ Soptgs
25.          else
26.             t.opvl ← Vopts ; t.sidop ← Sopts
```

27.　　　**end if**
28.　　　**end if**
29.　　**end if**
30. **end**

that is called through the program:

1. **variables**
2.　　at ∈ tqe
3. **begin**
4.　　at ← ...; *OptIndepSubSet*(at);
5.　　write(*an optimal independent subset of the tree*, at, *is*, at.sidop,
6.　　　　　*of weight*, at.opvl)
7. **end**

The complexity associated with this (generic) call is linear in terms of the number of vertices visited. Indeed, any vertex (except the root and its children) is visited three times (including two by *Collect*), the root is visited only once and each of its children twice.

Answer 4. For the proposed example, the results are gathered in the table hereafter (which is another representation of the considered tree) respecting the filling order of the vertices: 136 - A 4

vertex	weight	$P(S_u^*)$	optimal set of vertices
4	10	10	$\{4\}$
5	4	4	$\{5\}$
6	2	2	$\{6\}$
2	5	16	$\{4,5,6\}$
9	7	7	$\{9\}$
10	6	6	$\{10\}$
7	3	13	$\{9,10\}$
8	2	2	$\{8\}$
3	4	17	$\{3,9,10\}$
1	3	34	$\{1,4,5,6,9,10,8\}$

Answers to problem 137. Longest ascending sub-sequence *The problem is on page 673.*

Answer 1. Any contiguous increasing sub-sequence is an increasing sub-sequence, but not the opposite; for any sequence x, therefore we have: $lass(x) \geqslant lacss(x)$. 137 - A 1

Answer 2. The algorithm relies on a loop whose components are the following. 137 - A 2

Invariant The variable ls (respectively lacss) is the length of the longest ICSS ending in $x[i-1]$ (respectively found so far from $x[1]$ to $x[i-1]$).

Stopping condition $i = n + 1$.

Progression At each step, the element $x[i]$ of the sequence x is taken into account. If $x[i] > x[i-1]$, ls increases by 1 and lacss is updated if the new value of ls exceeds it. If $x[i] \leqslant x[i-1]$, $x[i]$ becomes the first element of a new ACSS and the invariant is restored by setting ls to 1.

Initialization The assignment of 1 to i, 0 to ls and $lacss$ establishes the invariant.

Termination The expression $(n + 1 - i)$ decreases while remaining positive or zero, which guarantees the termination.

The resulting algorithm can be easily deduced from the above and it has a linear temporal complexity, since $(n - 1)$ comparisons are made between numbers in the sequence x.

137 - A 3   **Answer** 3.   An algorithm similar to the previous one cannot be applied for the computation of the longest ascending sub-sequence, because, when a decrease $(x[i] \leqslant x[i - 1])$ is encountered, the symbol $x[i]$ can be part of several ascending sub-sequences starting before it (contrary to the previous case, where it could only start a new contiguous ascending sub-sequence).

137 - A 4   **Answer** 4.   In the general case, the longest ascending sub-sequence – which ends in $x[i]$ – is composed of $x[i]$ and, if it exists, of the longest ascending sub-sequence which ends before $x[i]$ (therefore of index $j < i$) on a value less than $x[i]$. The longest ascending sequence in a sequence s of length 1 is s itself; therefore, it has a length of 1 and $lasst(1) = 1$. The following recurrence of calculation of $lasst$ can be deduced:

$$
\begin{vmatrix}
lasst(1) = 1 \\
lasst(i) = 1 & i > 1 \text{ and } (\not\exists j \cdot (1 \leqslant j < i \text{ and } x[j] < x[i])) \\
lasst(i) = 1 + \max_{\substack{1 \leqslant j < i \text{ and} \\ x[j] < x[i]}} (lasst(j)) & i > 1 \text{ and } (\exists j \cdot (1 \leqslant j < i \text{ and } x[j] < x[i])).
\end{vmatrix}
$$

The program that calculates $lass(x)$ for any sequence x of length n is based on the use of the array $L[1 .. n]$ associated with $lasst$. The variable $lmax$ maintains the greatest value of $lasst$ calculated so far. The array $ID[1 .. n]$ is also introduced. $ID[i]$ identifies the index j corresponding to the optimal value found ($x[j] < x[i]$ and $L[j]$ maximum for $j \in 1 .. i - 1$). The progression of the calculation accounts for the fact that the value $lasst(i)$ calls on all the preceding values in order to fill $L[i]$ ($i \geqslant 2$), all the elements of $L[1 .. i - 1]$ must be scanned in order to find the best index j. This yields the following algorithm:

```
 1. constants
 2.    n ∈ ℕ₁ and n = ... and x ∈ 1 .. n → ℕ₁ and x = [...]
 3. variables
 4.    L ∈ 1 .. n → ℕ₁ and ID ∈ 1 .. n → ℕ₁ and lmc ∈ ℕ₁ and lMax ∈ ℕ₁ and
 5.    iMax ∈ ℕ₁
 6.    /% lmc is used for the calculation of the length of the longest ascend-
       ing sub-sequence located to the left of x[i]; the variables lMax and iMax
       represent respectively the length of the longest ascending sub-sequence
       ascendante and the index of its last element %/
 7. begin
 8.    lMax ← 1; iMax ← 1; L[1] ← 1; ID[1] ← 1
 9.    for i ranging 2 .. n do
10.       lmc ← 0; L[i] ← 1; ID[i] ← i;
11.       for j ranging 1 .. i − 1 do
12.          if x[i] > x[j] and L[j] > lmc then
13.             L[i] ← L[j] + 1; lmc ← L[j]; ID[i] ← j
14.          end if
15.       end for;
16.       if L[i] > lMax then
17.          lMax ← L[i]; iMax ← i
```

18.   **end if**
19.   **end for;**
20.   write(*the longest ascending sub-sequence ends in* , iMax,
21.   *and its length is* , lMax)
22. **end**

The temporal complexity of this algorithm is in $\Theta(n^2)$, while its spatial complexity is in $\Theta(n)$.

The longest ascending sub-sequence of x is identified from ID and iMax. The vector ID is scanned starting from the index iMax (of the last element of the longest ascending sub-sequence of x), in order to extract its components. The value $j = ID[iMax]$ gives the index of the preceding element of the longest ascending sub-sequence (except if $lMax = 1$). The process is iterated until the number of elements of the longest ascending sub-sequence (lMax) is exhausted.

Answer 5.   Applied to the sequence $u = \langle 11, 5, 2, 8, 7, 3, 1, 6, 4, 2 \rangle$, this algorithm results in: 137 - A 5

i	1	2	3	4	5	6	7	8	9	10
u[i]	11	5	2	8	7	3	1	6	4	2
L[i]/ID[i]	1/1	1/2	1/3	2/2	2/2	2/3	1/7	3/6	3/6	2/7

and the value of lMax and iMax are respectively 3 and 8. The reconstitution of the longest ascending sub-sequence begins with $u[8] = 6$ and $ID[8] = 6$. The preceding element is thus $u[6] = 3$. As $ID[6] = 3$, the element $u[3] = 2$ is reached and the process stops since the sub-sequence of three elements $\langle 2, 3, 6 \rangle$ has been found.

Answers to problem 138. Shortest common super-sequence   *The problem is on page 674.*

Answer 1.   The reasoning followed to establish the computation recurrence of scsps is   138 - A 1
very similar to that developed for the computation of the length of the longest common sub-sequence (lcsbs). It is clear that, if one of the sequences is empty, the shortest common super-sequence is the other sequence. If the last symbol considered is the same in both sequences ($x[j] = y[i]$), this character must be added to the shortest common super-sequence $x[1 .. j-1]$ and $y[1 .. i-1]$. On the other hand, if they are different, the choice is between adding the symbol $x[j]$ at the end of the shortest super-sequence common to the sequences $x[1 .. j-1]$ and $y[1 .. i]$ and add the symbol $y[i]$ at the end of the shortest super-sequence common to the sequences $x[1 .. j]$ and $y[1 .. i-1]$. Hence, the following recurrence:

$$
\begin{vmatrix}
scsps(0, j) = j & 0 \leqslant j \leqslant m \\
scsps(i, 0) = i & 1 \leqslant i \leqslant n \\
scsps(i, j) = scsps(i-1, j-1) + 1 & x[j] = y[i] \text{ and } 1 \leqslant i \leqslant n \text{ and } 1 \leqslant j \leqslant m \\
scsps(i, j) = \min \left(\left\{ \begin{array}{l} scsps(i, j-1), \\ scsps(i-1, j) \end{array} \right\} \right) + 1 & x[j] \neq y[i] \text{ and } 1 \leqslant i \leqslant n \text{ and } 1 \leqslant j \leqslant m.
\end{vmatrix}
$$

Answer 2.   The implementation of the previous recurrence goes through the tabular   138 - A 2
structure SCSPS[0 .. n, 0 .. m] in connection with the m symbols of x and the n symbols of y. The length of the shortest super-sequence will be in SCSPS[n, m]. The row and the column of index 0 are initialized thanks to the first two terms of the recurrence. Let us

observe that any other element SCSPS[i, j] with strictly positive values of i and j depends either on its neighbor from the previous column and from the previous row, or from its neighbor from the previous diagonal. Therefore the calculation can be performed row by row and in each row by increasing values of the column index (filling by column or by diagonal would also be suitable).

To find the (one of the) shortest common super-sequence(s) using "Tom Thumb's method", the array SCSPS[0..n, 0..m] is doubled by the array PTH[0..n, 0..m] built in parallel. With reference to a Cartesian representation, each cell of this array contains an indication ($\leftarrow$, $\downarrow$ or $\nearrow$) about which of the three possibilities of the recurrence created the value retained in the element of SCSPS of the same indices. Browsing PTH starting from PTH[n, m] allows to find in a deterministic way a shorter super-sequence common to x and y by following the arrows until reaching PTH[0, 0]. If there are several solutions, only one can be reconstituted from PTH and it depends on the order of the tests performed in the program.

The spatial complexity of this algorithm is in $\Theta(m \cdot n)$ (arrays SCSPS and PTH). At most $m \cdot n$ comparisons are performed between symbols of sequences (case reached when x and y have no common symbol); the temporal complexity is therefore in $\mathcal{O}(m \cdot n)$.

138 - A 3   **Answer** 3.   The length of the shortest super-sequence common to $u = \textit{vague}$ and $v = \textit{veal}$ is 7 (cell $(4, 5)$ of the array below). The construction of the shortest common super-sequence can be performed on the basis of the tracking information found in PTH (path in "grey tint"). When $\leftarrow$ or $\nearrow$ (respectively $\downarrow$) is encountered, the symbole of u (respectively v) is retained. The shortest super-sequence common to $u = \textit{vague}$ and $v = \textit{veal}$ found by the algorithm is $\textit{vagueal}$ as illustrated by the table below:

4	*l*	4 $\downarrow$	4 $\downarrow$	4 $\leftarrow$	5 $\uparrow$	6 $\downarrow$	7 $\downarrow$
3	*a*	3 $\downarrow$	3 $\downarrow$	3 $\leftarrow$	4 $\leftarrow$	5 $\leftarrow$	6 $\downarrow$
2	*e*	2 $\downarrow$	2 $\downarrow$	3 $\leftarrow$	4 $\leftarrow$	5 $\leftarrow$	5 $\nearrow$
1	*v*	1 $\downarrow$	1 $\nearrow$	2 $\leftarrow$	3 $\leftarrow$	4 $\leftarrow$	5 $\leftarrow$
0	ε	0 $\downarrow$	1 $\leftarrow$	2 $\leftarrow$	3 $\leftarrow$	4 $\leftarrow$	5 $\leftarrow$
i	v/u	ε	*v*	*a*	*g*	*u*	*e*
j		0	1	2	3	4	5

138 - A 4   **Answer** 4.   The shortest super-sequence common to to x and y involves all the symbols of x, as well as those of y minus those that are forming one of their longest common subsequences, hence $scsps(n, m) = n + m - lcsbs(n, m)$ or:

$$scsps(n, m) + lcsbs(n, m) = n + m.$$

For the example of the sequences $u = \textit{vague}$ and $v = \textit{veal}$, one of their longest common sub-sequences is $\textit{va}$ and one of their shortest super-sequences is $\textit{vealgue}$. Therefore:

$$scsps(4, 5) + lcsbs(4, 5) = 7 + 2 = 5 + 4 = 9.$$

Answers to problem 139. Distance between sequences (2)   *The problem is on page 674.*

Answer 1.

(a) Let us consider the construction of an alignment between the sequences x and y. Suppose that we have paired the prefix of length i of y and the prefix of length j of x. In the next step, three options are available: pair $x[j+1]$ and $y[i+1]$, or pair $x[j+1]$ and ε (deletion of $x[j+1]$), or pair ε and $y[i+1]$ (insertion of $y[i+1]$). We will therefore construct the graph in which the vertex denoted (i/j) associated with the state described previously admits three successors $(i+1/j+1)$ (choice 1, transform of $x[j+1]$ into $y[i+1]$), $(i/j+1)$ (choice 2, deletion of $x[j+1]$) and $(i+1/j)$ (choice 3, insertion of $y[i+1]$). Each of these arcs has the corresponding value in δ, namely $\delta[x[j+1], y[i+1]]$ in the first case, $\delta[x[j+1], \varepsilon]$ in the second and $\delta[\varepsilon, y[i+1]]$ in the last. So, a graph with positive or zero valuations having $(n+1) \cdot (m+1)$ vertices is obtained, each of the vertices having three successors in general (except the vertices of the form (n/j) or (i/m)). An alignment is therefore represented by a path from the vertex $(0/0)$ to the vertex (n/m) and its value by that of the associated path, that is to say the sum of the values of the arcs composing it. An optimal alignment is therefore a path of minimum value between the vertex $(0/0)$ and the vertex (n/m).

(b) Taking into account what was said previously about the graph describing the set of alignments, the number of different alignments between two sequences x and y having respectively m and n letters, denoted by $nbal(n, m)$, is given by the following recurrence:

$$\left| \begin{array}{l} nbal(0,j) = 1 \\ nbal(i,0) = 1 \\ nbal(i,j) = \left(\begin{array}{l} nbal(i,j-1) + \\ nbal(i-1,j) + \\ nbal(i-1,j-1) \end{array} \right) \end{array} \right. \qquad \begin{array}{c} 0 \leqslant j \leqslant m \\ 1 \leqslant i \leqslant n \\ \left\{ \begin{array}{c} 1 \leqslant i \leqslant n \\ \text{and} \\ 1 \leqslant j \leqslant m \end{array} \right. \end{array}.$$

This recurrence corresponds to Delannoy numbers, a sample of which is given in the table below:

j	0	1	2	3	4	5	6
i = 0	1	1	1	1	1	1	1
1	1	3	5	7	9	11	13
2	1	5	13	25	41	61	85
3	1	7	25	63	129	231	377
4	1	9	41	129	321	681	1289

It can be seen (easy proof left to the reader) that $nbal(i,j) \geqslant 3^{\min(\{m,n\})}$ and thus increases very rapidly.

(c) It was said in the statement of the problem that, in the general case $(i > 0$ and $j > 0)$, the vertex (i, j) can be accessed in three different ways: i) from the vertex $(i-1, j-1)$ by transforming $x[j]$ into $y[i]$, ii) from the vertex $(i, j-1)$ by removing $x[j]$, or iii) from the vertex $(i-1, j)$ by inserting $y[i]$. Since a minimum cost alignment is searched for, the best of these three choices (the one leading to the minimum) will be chosen. The following recurrence for the calculation of $calopt$ can be deduced:

$$calopt(0,0) = \delta[\varepsilon, \varepsilon] = 0$$
$$calopt(0,j) = calopt(0,j-1) + \delta[x[j], \varepsilon] \qquad\qquad 1 \leqslant j \leqslant m$$
$$calopt(i,0) = calopt(i-1,0) + \delta[\varepsilon, y[i]] \qquad\qquad 1 \leqslant i \leqslant n$$
$$calopt(i,j) = \min \left(\left\{ \begin{array}{l} calopt(i-1,j-1) + \delta[x[j], y[i]], \\ calopt(i-1,j) + \delta[\varepsilon, y[i]], \\ calopt(i,j-1) + \delta[x[j], \varepsilon] \end{array} \right\} \right) \quad \left\{ \begin{array}{c} 1 \leqslant i \leqslant n \\ \textbf{and} \\ 1 \leqslant j \leqslant m \end{array} \right. .$$

139 - A 2   **Answer 2.**   The implementation of this recurrence is founded on an algorithm calculating the matrix CALO (associated with calopt), by first filling the index column 0 thanks to the first and third terms of the recurrence, then the index columns 1 to n. In a given column of index j, the cell $(0,j)$ is first filled (second term of the recurrence), then the cells $(1,j)$ to (m,j) using the last term of the recurrence. Filling in by line or diagonal could apply as well. We end up with the following program called *WF*:

```
1.  constants
2.      x ∈ string(Σ) and x = … and y ∈ string(Σ) and y = … and m = |x| and
3.      n = |y| and δ ∈ Σ × Σ → ℝ₊ and δ = [...]
4.  variables
5.      CALO ∈ 0 .. n × 0 .. m → ℝ₊
6.  begin
7.      CALO[0, 0] ← 0;
8.      for i ranging 1 .. n do
9.          CALO[i, 0] ← CALO[i − 1, 0] + δ[ε, y[i]]
10.     end for;
11.     for j ranging 1 .. m do
12.         CALO[0, j] ← CALO[0, j − 1] + δ[x[j], ε] ;
13.         for i ranging 1 .. n do
```

$$14. \qquad CALO[i,j] \leftarrow \min \left(\left\{ \begin{array}{l} CALO[i-1,j-1] + \delta[x[j], y[i]], \\ CALO[i-1,j] + \delta[\varepsilon, y[i]], \\ CALO[i,j-1] + \delta[x[j], \varepsilon] \end{array} \right\} \right)$$

```
15.         end for
16.     end for;
17.     write(CALO[n, m])
18. end
```

The spatial complexity of this algorithm corresponds to the array CALO; it is thus in $\Theta(n \cdot m)$. Its time complexity in terms of comparisons ranges from $n \cdot m$ at best to $2 \cdot n \cdot m$ at worst; it is therefore in $\Theta(n \cdot m)$ as well. It can be observed that we have passed from a complexity greater than $3^{\min(\{m,n\})}$ for a naïve canonical algorithm to $\Theta(n \cdot m)$, hence a tremendous gain.

Let us recall that no algorithm specifically calculating the minimum value of the paths for a fixed pair of vertices is known. We could have used:

- Dijkstra's algorithm (see problem 78, page 345), since the arcs valuations are all positive or zero here; its complexity is in $\mathcal{O}(N^2)$ where N is the number of vertices of the graph, i.e. here a complexity in $\mathcal{O}((m \cdot n)^2)$ with a "canonical" implementation; with a more sophisticated implementation [4], the complexity is reduced to $\mathcal{O}((N + M) \cdot \log_2(N))$ where M (respectively N) is the number of arcs (respectively of vertices) of the graph, i.e. here in $\mathcal{O}((m \cdot n) \cdot (\log_2(m) + \log_2(n)))$,

---

[4]See for example https://en.wikipedia.org/wiki/Dijkstra's_algorithm.

- Bellman-Ford's algorithm (see problem 132, page 661) of complexity $\Theta(M \cdot N)$ where N (respectively M) is the number of vertices (respectively arcs) of the graph; here, the complexity will therefore be in $\Theta((m \cdot n)^2)$, since the graph has about $3m \cdot n$ arcs,
- Bellman-Ford's algorithm (see problem 132, page 661) of complexity $\Theta(M \cdot N)$ where N (respectively M) is the number of vertices (respectively arcs) of the graph; here, the complexity would be in $\Theta((m \cdot n)^2)$, since the graph has in the order of $3m \cdot n$ arcs,
- Floyd's algorithm (see problem 133, page 664), in $\mathcal{O}((m \cdot n)^3)$, which would therefore be even less efficient.

The design of a solution specific to the graph associated with this problem is thus totally justified.

Answer 3. Applied to the proposed example, the algorithm leads to the matrix CALO below: 139 - A 3

5	r	10	9	8	7	6	7	5	7
4	u	8	7	6	5	4	5	7	9
3	m	6	5	4	3	5	7	9	11
2	e	4	3	2	4	6	8	10	12
1	l	2	1	3	5	7	9	11	13
0	ε	0	2	4	6	8	10	12	14
i	v / u	ε	d	a	k	o	u	r	y
	j	0	1	2	3	4	5	6	7

hence $\Delta(\textit{reveals, nodal}) = 7$.

Answer 4. To reconstitute the (an) optimal alignment, the usual "Tom Thumb's tech-   139 - A 4
nique" is used. Therefore, the filling of an array containing the indication of the optimal choice made for each cell filling of CALO ($\swarrow$ for the transformation of x[j] into y[i], $\downarrow$ for inserting y[i], $\leftarrow$ for deleting x[j]) is added into the algorithm. This array is then scanned from the cell (n, m) until it reaches the cell $(0, 0)$.
In the previous example, by showing only the set of optimal choices in each cell of the array, we obtain:

5	r	$\downarrow$	$\downarrow\swarrow$	$\downarrow$	$\downarrow\swarrow$	$\downarrow$	$\downarrow\swarrow$	$\swarrow$	$\leftarrow$
4	u	$\downarrow$	$\downarrow$	$\downarrow\swarrow$	$\downarrow$	$\swarrow$	$\swarrow$	$\leftarrow$	$\leftarrow$
3	m	$\downarrow$	$\downarrow\swarrow$	$\leftarrow$	$\swarrow$	$\leftarrow$	$\leftarrow$	$\leftarrow\swarrow$	$\leftarrow$
2	e	$\downarrow$	$\downarrow$	$\swarrow$	$\leftarrow$	$\leftarrow\swarrow$	$\leftarrow\swarrow$	$\leftarrow$	$\leftarrow\swarrow$
1	l	$\downarrow$	$\swarrow$	$\leftarrow$	$\leftarrow\swarrow$	$\leftarrow$	$\leftarrow$	$\leftarrow\swarrow$	$\leftarrow$
0	ε	$\downarrow$	$\leftarrow$	$\leftarrow$	$\leftarrow$	$\leftarrow$	$\leftarrow$	$\leftarrow$	$\leftarrow$
i	v/u	ε	d	a	k	o	u	r	y
	j	0	1	2	3	4	5	6	7

The scan of the array from the northeast corner (cell $(5,7)$) goes through the cells: $(5,6)$ for the deletion of y from *dakoury*, $(4,5)$ for the transformation of r into r, $(3,4)$ for the transformation of u into u, $(3,3)$ for removing o from *dakoury*, $(2,2)$ for transforming k into m, $(1,1)$ for the transformation of a into e, $(0,0)$ for the transformation of d into l.

This leads to the following unique optimal alignment (because in each of these cells there is only one choice):

$$
\begin{array}{ccccccc}
d & a & k & o & u & r & y \\
| & | & | & | & | & | & | \\
l & e & m & \varepsilon & u & r & \varepsilon
\end{array}
$$

for a cost of 7.

With the sequences $u = art$ and $v = deal$, the array CALO (completed to account for the optimal alignments themselves) is:

4	l	8 ↓	6 ↓	5 ↙	7 ←↙
3	a	6 ↓	4 ↙	6 ←↙	8 ↓←↙
2	e	4 ↓	3 ↙	5 ↓←	6 ↙
1	d	2 ↓	3 ↙	3 ↙	5 ←↙
0	ε	0 ↓	2 ←	4 ←	6 ←
i	v / u	ε	a	r	t
	j	0	1	2	3

It is easy to observe that there are three optimal alignments of same cost (7):

$$
\begin{array}{cccc}
\varepsilon & a & r & t \\
| & | & | & | \\
d & e & a & l \\
2 & 1 & 3 & 1
\end{array}
\qquad
\begin{array}{ccccc}
\varepsilon & \varepsilon & a & r & t \\
| & | & | & | & | \\
d & e & a & \varepsilon & l \\
2 & 2 & 0 & 2 & 1
\end{array}
\qquad
\begin{array}{ccccc}
\varepsilon & \varepsilon & a & r & t \\
| & | & | & | & | \\
d & e & a & l & \varepsilon \\
2 & 2 & 0 & 1 & 2
\end{array}
$$

139 - A 5   **Answer 5.**   The general recurrence term defining $calopt$ shows that the computation of the cell (i, j) only uses the cells $(i-1, j)$, $(i, j-1)$ and $(i-1, j-1)$. It is therefore unnecessary to keep the entire array CALO to calculate the value $calopt(n, m) = CALO[n, m] = \Delta(u, v)$ (this is valid provided that we do not then try to calculate the optimal alignment as in the previous question). Therefore two columns of the array CALO containing the current column (of index j) and the previous one (of index $j - 1$) will be used (note that this could be done with two rows as well). The resulting algorithm requires $2 \cdot (n + 1)$ cells; its spatial complexity is in $\Theta(n)$ (it would be in $\Theta(m)$ if the calculation was performed in row rather than in column). The associated algorithm *LWF* looks like this:

```
 1. constants
 2.    x ∈ string(Σ) and x = ... and y ∈ string(Σ) and y = ... and m = |x| and
 3.    n = |y| and δ ∈ Σ × Σ → ℝ₊ and δ = [...]
 4. variables
 5.    CALO ∈ 0..n × 0..1 → ℝ₊
 6. begin
 7.    /% calculation of column 1 %/
 8.    CALO[0, 1] ← 0;
 9.    for i ranging 1..n do
10.       CALO[i, 1] ← CALO1[i − 1, 1] + δ[ε, y[i]]
11.    end for;
12.    for j ranging 1..m do
13.       /% shift of columns j − 1 (0) and j (1) %/
14.       for i ∈ 0..n do
```

15.   CALO[i, 0] ← CALO[i, 1]
16.   **end for**;
17.   /% *calculation of column j* (1) %/
18.   CALO[0, 1] ← CALO[0, 0] + $\delta[x[j], \varepsilon]$;
19.   **for** i **ranging** 1 .. n **do**

20.   CALO[i, 1] ← min $\left(\left\{ \begin{array}{l} CALO[i-1, 0] + \delta[x[j], y[i]], \\ CALO[i-1, 1] + \delta[\varepsilon, y[i]], \\ CALO[i, 0] + \delta[x[j], \varepsilon] \end{array} \right\} \right)$

21.   **end for**
22.   **end for**;
23.   **write**(CALO[n, 1])
24. **end**

Answer 6.   Any alignment between two sequences x and y is also an alignment be-   139 - A 6
tween the mirror sequences $\bar{x}$ and $\bar{y}$, and conversely. It can be deduced that the set of
alignments between x and y is equal to that of the alignments between $\bar{x}$ and $\bar{y}$ and that
an optimal alignment between x and y is also an optimal alignement for $\bar{x}$ and $\bar{y}$. Consequently, the algorithms previously given (*WF* and *LWF*) calculate the cost of an optimal
alignment between x and y as well as between $\bar{x}$ and $\bar{y}$.

Answer 7.   For Δ to define a distance, the following three properties must hold: 139 - A 7

(a) zero diagonal: if x is an arbitrary sequence over Σ of length m ($m \geqslant 0$),
the value of the optimal alignment between x and itself is equal to 0, that is
$calopt(m, m) = \Delta(x, x) = 0$,

(b) symmetry: if x and y are two sequences over Σ of respective lengths m and n,
the value of an optimal alignment between x and y ($\Delta(x, y) = calopt(n, m)$)
is equal to that of an optimal alignment between y and x, i.e. $\Delta(x, y) = \Delta(y, x)$,

(c) triangular inequality: if $x1, y1, x2, y2$ are arbitrary sequences over Σ of respective lengths $m1, n1, m2, n2$, the value of an optimal alignment between
$x1 \cdot x2$ and $y1 \cdot y2$ ($\cdot$ denoting sequence concatenation) must be less than
or equal to the sum of the values of an optimal alignment between $x1$ and
$y1$ and an optimal alignment between $x2$ and $y2$, i.e. $\Delta(x1 \cdot x2, y1 \cdot y2) \leqslant \Delta(x1 \cdot y1) + \Delta(x2 \cdot y2)$.

The first property is trivially verified since $\delta(\alpha, \alpha) = 0$ for any symbol α of Σ. To form the
optimal alignment (of zero cost) between a sequence x and itself, it suffices to transform
any symbol of x into itself.
Any alignment between x and y is also an alignment between y and x. A transformation
between two symbols other than ε has the same cost seen as an alignment between x and
y or between y and y. The transformation of a symbol into ε (removal of this symbol) in
an alignment between x and y corresponds to the transformation of ε into this symbol
(insertion) in an alignment between y and x. The converse is obviously valid, and the
symmetry of δ means that these pairs of transformations have an identical cost. The second
property is therefore also verified.
Regarding the last property, consider the graph associated with the alignments between
$x1 \cdot x2$ and $y1 \cdot y2$ in the following diagram:

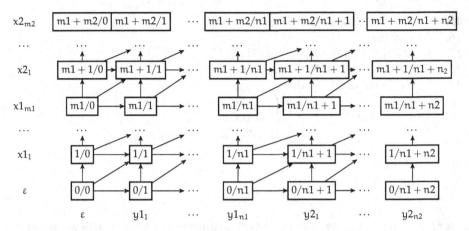

An optimal alignment between x1 and y1 corresponds to a path of minimum cost from the vertex $(0/0)$ to the vertex $(m1/n1)$, that is $\Delta(x1, y1) = \text{calopt}(n1, m1)$. Likewise, an optimal alignment between x2 and y2 corresponds to a path of minimum cost from the vertex $(m1/n1)$ to the vertex $(m1 + m2/n1 + n2)$, that is $\Delta(x2, y2)$. A possible alignment between $x1 \cdot x2$ and $y1 \cdot y2$ corresponds to the optimal path going from the vertex $(0/0)$ to the vertex $(m1/n1)$, then from this latter to the vertex $(m1 + m2/n1 + n2)$ but this is not necessarily the globally optimal path to go from $(0/0)$ to $(m1 + m2/n1 + n2)$. We therefore deduce that $\Delta(x1 \cdot x2, y1 \cdot y2) \leqslant \Delta(x1, y1) + \Delta(x2, y2)$.

A consequence of the symmetry property of Δ is that it is possible to calculate the value of an optimal alignment between the sequences x and y or y and x indifferently. It follows that in the algorithm *LWF*, it is possible to work with an array *CALO* of length $\min(\{m, n\})$ by inverting if necessary x and y; we have a spatial complexity in $\Theta(\min(\{m, n\}))$.

Remark

The symmetry property of δ entails that:

- the cost of insertion and symbol of Σ is equal to that of its deletion,
- the costs of the transformation of the symbol α into β ($\alpha \neq \beta$) is identical to that of the transformation of β into α.

Answers to problem 140. Dissemblance between sequences   *The problem is on page 678.*

140 - A 1   **Answer** 1.   The only possible association between a and aa is:

The dissemblance between $u = a$ and $v = aa$ is thus zero.

Between $u = aab$ and $v = abb$, there is a zero cost association:

These two sequences have therefore a zero dissemblance.

Between $u = ab$ and $v = bac$, therer are five possible associations:

whose respective costs are: $3, 5, 4.5, 5$ and 5. The dissemblance between these two sequences is equal to 3.

The pairs of sequences of type $\{a^+ b^+\}^k$, where a^+ stands for a sequence having at least one symbol a, associate "series" of a and b for a zero cost; their dissemblance is thus zero. For example, $u = aabbaabbbaababb$ and $v = ababbbabaaaaabbbb$ have a zero dissemblance, as it is possible to make the association:

Answer 2. Let $\mathrm{mincoasso}(i, j)$ be the value of the least costly association between the prefix of length i of y ($y[1], \ldots, y[i]$) and that of length j of x ($x[1], \ldots, x[j]$). The computation of $\mathrm{mincoasso}(i, j)$ relies on the fact that, for any pair of strings x and y, the last letter of x is associated with the last letter of y. Three families of association of the prefix of length i of y and that of length j of x can be singled out:

140 - A 2

$$
\begin{array}{ccc}
x[1] \cdots x[j-1]\ x[j] & \quad x[1] \cdots x[j-1]\ x[j] & \quad x[1] \cdots x[j-1]\ x[j] \\[2pt]
\big| \qquad \big| & \qquad \diagup \quad \big| & \qquad \diagdown \quad \big| \\[2pt]
y[1] \cdots y[i-1]\ y[i] & \quad y[1] \cdots y[i-1]\ y[i] & \quad y[1] \cdots y[i-1]\ y[i]
\end{array}
$$

In the first case, $x[j]$ and $y[i]$ are only associated with each other, and the resulting best association cost is $\mathrm{mincoasso}(i-1, j-1) + \delta(x[j], y[i])$. In the second case, $x[j]$ is associated with both $y[i]$ and a sequence of symbols $y[i - p], \ldots, y[i - 1]$ ($p \geqslant 1$); the best association cost is obtained for the configuration corresponding to the minimum cost association between the prefix of length j of x and the prefix of length $(i - 1)$ of y plus $\delta[x[j], y[i]]$, i.e. $\mathrm{mincoasso}(i - 1, j) + \delta[x[j], y[i]]$. The last case is the symmetrical of the previous one; the best cost of association is then $\mathrm{mincoasso}(i, j - 1) + \delta[x[j], y[i]]$. The calculation of the cost of the best association is therefore given by the recurrence:

$$
\left|
\begin{array}{ll}
\mathrm{mincoasso}(1, 1) = \delta[x[1], y[1]] & \\
\mathrm{mincoasso}(1, j) = \mathrm{mincoasso}(1, j - 1) + \delta[x[j], y[1]] & \quad 2 \leqslant j \leqslant m \\
\mathrm{mincoasso}(i, 1) = \mathrm{mincoasso}(i - 1, 1) + \delta[x[1], y[i]] & \quad 2 \leqslant i \leqslant n \\
\mathrm{mincoasso}(i, j) = \min \left(\left\{ \begin{array}{l} \mathrm{mincoasso}(i - 1, j - 1), \\ \mathrm{mincoasso}(i, j - 1), \\ \mathrm{mincoasso}(i - 1, j) \end{array} \right\} \right) + \delta[x[j], y[i]] & \begin{array}{c} 2 \leqslant i \leqslant n \\ \textbf{and} \\ 2 \leqslant j \leqslant m \end{array}
\end{array}
\right. .
$$

Remark

It would have been possible to reason from right to left on the sequences and so to end up with a "backward" recurrence.

Answer 3. The algorithm calculating the dissemblance between two sequences x and y uses the matrix MCA (associated with $\mathrm{mincoasso}$), by first filling the row of index 1 thanks to the first two terms of the recurrence, then lines 2 to n. In a given row of index i, the cell $(i, 1)$ is first filled in (third term of the recurrence), then the cells $(i, 2)$ to (i, m)

140 - A 3

using the last term of the recurrence. One could as well advance the calculation by column or by diagonal. The resulting program is:

```
 1.  constants
 2.    x ∈ string(Σ) and x = ... and y ∈ string(Σ) and y = ... and m = |x| and
 3.    n = |y| and δ ∈ Σ × Σ → ℝ₊ and δ = [...]
 4.  variables
 5.    MCA ∈ 1..n × 1..m → ℝ₊
 6.  begin
 7.    MCA[1,1] ← δ[x[1],y[1]];
 8.    for j ranging 2..m do
 9.      MCA[1,j] ← MCA[1,j−1] + δ[x[j],y[1]]
10.    end for;
11.    for i ranging 2..n do
12.      MCA[i,1] ← MCA[i−1,1] + δ[x[1],y[i]];
13.      for j ranging 2..m do
```

$$14. \quad MCA[i,j] \leftarrow \min\left(\left\{ \begin{array}{l} MCA[i-1,j-1], \\ MCA[i,j-1], \\ MCA[i-1,j] \end{array} \right\}\right) + \delta[x[j],y[i]]$$

```
15.      end for
16.    end for;
17.    write(MCA[n,m])
18. end
```

The spatial complexity of this algorithm corresponds to the array MCA; it is therefore in $\Theta(m \cdot n)$. Its temporal complexity in number of conditions evaluated is between $m \cdot n$ at best and $2 \cdot m \cdot n$ at worst; it is therefore in $\Theta(m \cdot n)$. Note that we could also "linearize" this algorithm (see problem 139, page 674) to obtain a lower spatial complexity ($\Theta(\min(\{m, n\}))$).

140 - A 4   **Answer 4.**   Applied to the strings $u = acbca$ and $v = bcaa$, the algorithm leads to the matrix MCA below:

4	*a*	3.5	5	5.5	5.5	3
3	*a*	3.5	3.5	4	4.5	2
2	*c*	3.5	2	3	3	4.5
1	*b*	2	3	3	4	6
i	v / u	*a*	*c*	*b*	*c*	*a*
	j	1	2	3	4	5

hence a dissemblance between $u = acbca$ and $v = bcaa$ of 3.

140 - A 5   **Answer 5.**   To reconstitute an optimal association, the usual "Tom Thumb's technique" is used. The filling of an additional array is therefore inserted in the algorithm. Each of its cells contains the indication of the optimal choice made for the corresponding cell of MCA ($\nearrow$ for the first choice, $\leftarrow$ for the second choice, $\downarrow$ for the third choice). This array is then scanned from cell (n, m) until $(1, 1)$ is reached.

Applied to the previous example, we start in $(4, 5)$ that contains $\downarrow$, then $(3, 5)$ that contains $\nearrow$, then $(2, 4)$ with two possibilities $\leftarrow$ and $\nearrow$. The first one leads to cell $(2, 3)$ where $\leftarrow$ is found, then in $(2, 2)$ that contains $\nearrow$, and the terminal cell $(1, 1)$ is reached. The second choice leads to $(1, 3)$ that contains $\leftarrow$, then in $(1, 2)$ that contains $\leftarrow$ and finally to the final cell $(1, 1)$. Therefore there are two optimal associations of cost 3:

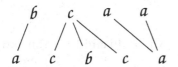 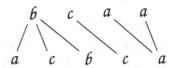

Answer 6.   This program makes it possible to fix words in which letters are wrongly 140 - A 6
doubled or on the contrary not wrongly doubled; for example, *girafe* and *giraffe* will
have zero dissemblance. On the other hand, inversions cannot be fixed for free as in *importance* and *improtance*. The matrix δ could be designed so as to favor certain faults,
for example the proximity of letters on a keyboard or the proximity of sounds ("p" and
"b" for example).

Answers to problem 141. The best elephant team   *The problem is on page 680.*

Answer 1.   The "Generate and test"-based solution examines all subsets of elephants 141 - A 1
meeting the first two constraints related to weight and intelligence, and it selects the best
(in the sense of the sum of the values of the elephants involved in it). The resolution pattern
OT is used (see section 5.1.3, page 210) with an enumeration vector representing a total
function of $1 .. n$ to $0 .. 1$ and the number of conditions evaluated is in $\mathcal{O}(2^n)$.

Answer 2.   The very definition of a sub-sequence common to two arbitrary sequences 141 - A 2
s_1 and s_2 requires that the selected elements appear in the same order in s_1 and s_2. In particular, i) so that the elephants i and j belong to a sub-sequence common to the sequences
of elephants x and y, it is necessary that they appear in the same order in both of them,
and ii) so that at most one of the elephants i or j belongs to a sub-sequence common to the
sequences of elephants x and y, it suffices that they appear in reverse order in both.

Answer 3.   According to the necessary condition stated previously, by ordering the ele- 141 - A 3
phants on the one hand by increasing intelligence to constitute the sequence s_i $(= x)$, on the
other hand by increasing weight to form the sequence s_w $(= y)$, it is guaranteed that any
sub-sequence common to s_i and s_w is such that any of its pairs of elephants (i, j) satisfies
the constraint:

$$(\text{wght}(i) < \text{wght}(j)) \Leftrightarrow (\text{int}(i) < \text{int}(j)).$$

The second constraint also holds since here the elephants have all different intelligences
and weights. The search for the (one) sub-sequence of maximum value ensures the desired optimality. It can be observed that this problem can be reformulated as the search
for a sub-sequence s_{co} *of maximum value* common to the two sequences s_i and s_w and the
identification of s_{co}.

Answer 4.   The problem solved in the presentation of this chapter (see page 635) is very 141 - A 4
similar to this one since it is a matter of length of the *longest* sub-sequence common to two
sequences. The adaptation to be carried out resides in establishing the recurrence making it
possible to manage the optimality criterion, by noting that here the sequences both concern
the same n elephants and therefore have the same length n. Let us call $\text{mvcss}(i, j)$ the value
of the sub-sequence common to the prefix of length i of the sequence y and to the prefix of
length j of the sequence x, of maximum value. By analogy with the recurrence established
for the problem of the longest sub-sequence common to two strings, we have:

$$
\begin{aligned}
&\text{mvcss}(0,j) = 0 && 0 \leqslant j \leqslant n \\
&\text{mvcss}(i,0) = 0 && 0 \leqslant i \leqslant n \\
&\text{mvcss}(i,j) = \text{mvcss}(i-1,j-1) + \text{val}(y[i]) && x[j] = y[i] \text{ and } 1 \leqslant i \leqslant n \text{ and } 1 \leqslant j \leqslant n \\
&\text{mvcss}(i,j) = \max\left(\left\{ \begin{array}{l} \text{mvcss}(i,j-1), \\ \text{mvcss}(i-1,j) \end{array} \right\}\right) && \left\{ \begin{array}{l} x[j] \neq y[i] \text{ and} \\ 1 \leqslant i \leqslant n \text{ and } 1 \leqslant j \leqslant n \end{array} \right. \quad \cdot
\end{aligned}
$$

As long as the algorithm manages the tracking information ("Tom Thumb's technique"), it is possible to produce in a second step a sub-sequence associated with the optimal value, sub-sequence implementing the subset S wanted. The dynamic programming algorithm corresponding to the calculation of mvcss implements an array $MVCSS[0..n,0..n]$. The filling of MVCSS is carried out by row, column or diagonal as for the problem treated in the presentation of this chapter (see its third question).

141 - A 5   **Answer 5.**   This algorithm has a spatial complexity in $\Theta(n^2)$ and it evaluates a number of conditions in $\Theta(n^2)$. In terms of time, the gain is substantial compared to the exponential complexity of the solution resorting to "Generate and test".

141 - A 6   **Answer 6.**   In the presence of a subset of type E_{swdi} in E, it must be ensured that the algorithm does not take into account more than one elephant of such a subset to produce the optimal value. By applying the sufficient condition stated previously, the preprocessing phase constructs a sequence s_w ordered by increasing weight and decreasing intelligence in the event of equality of weight and a sequence s_i ordered by increasing intelligence. In so doing, it is ensured that the elephants of the subset of type E_{swdi} are in reverse order in the sequences s_w and s_i, while maintaining the satisfaction of the first condition binding weight and intelligence. This strategy is suitable if E contains several subsets of type E_{swdi} and it is suitable for the case where E contains subsets of type E_{sidw} in which the elephants have same intelligence, but different weights.

141 - A 7   **Answer 7.**   Let E be a set of elephants that can contain a subset E_1 of type E_{swi} of elephants of same weight and intelligence, but none of type E_{swdi} or E_{sidw}. So that at most one of the elephants of E_1 appears in the result S, the preprocessing phase builds on the one hand a sequence s_w ordered by increasing weight, and by increasing market value in case of equal weight (in fact double equality of weight and intelligence given the absence of a subset of type E_{swdi} in E), on the other hand a sequence s_i ordered by increasing intelligence, and by decreasing market value in case of equal intelligence (in fact double equality of intelligence and weight due to the absence of a subset of type E_{sidw} in E). Thus it is guaranteed that at most one of the elephants of E_1 can be selected by the algorithm defined previously since the elephants appear there in reverse order in the sequences s_w and s_i. This procedure is also suitable in the case where several subsets of type E_{swi} are present in E.

141 - A 8   **Answer 8.**   In the presence of an arbitrary set of elephants E, the processing must integrate the possible presence of subsets of types E_{swdi}, E_{sidw} or even E_{swi}. The unification of the preprocessings (explained in the two previous questions) consists in building the following two sequences:

- a sequence s_w in which the elephants are ordered by increasing weight, by decreasing intelligence in case of equal weight, and finally by increasing value in case of double equality of weight and intelligence,
- a sequence s_i in which the elephants are ordered by increasing intelligence, by decreasing weight in the case of equal intelligence, and finally by decreasing value in the case of double equality of intelligence and weight.

The algorithm for finding a sub-sequence OSS of maximum value M common to s_w and s_i computes M and finally makes it possible to build a sub-sequence OSS refining a subset S of E of value M.

The proposed preprocessing is based on sorts constructing the sequences s_w and s_i. By taking a suitable sorting algorithm, this step will have a complexity in $O(n \cdot \log_2(n))$, dominated by that of the common sub-sequence search algorithm, which is in $\Theta(n^2)$ (cf. answer 5).

Answer 9. The preprocessing of the example leads to the sequences: 141 - A 9

- $s_w = \langle 4, 2, 3, 8, 7, 5, 1, 6 \rangle$
- $s_i = \langle 8, 1, 5, 7, 4, 3, 2, 6 \rangle$.

Note that: 1) the order of elephants 1, 5 and 7 (of same weight 1500 and same intelligence 15) is reversed in the sequences s_w and s_i and therefore only 1 is likely to appear in the final result, and 2) elephants 3 and 8 of same weight (1400) and different intelligences appear in reverse order in s_w and s_i so that at most one can appear in the result (we do not know which one *a priori*). The table gathering on the one hand the optimal value for each pair of prefixes of s_w and s_i, on the other hand the path indication, is given below:

8	6	0 ↓	20 ↓	47 ↓	47 ←	47 ←	47 ←	47 ←	55 ↓	70 ✓
7	2	0 ↓	20 ↓	47 ✓	47 ←	47 ←	47 ←	47 ←	55 ↓	55 ←
6	3	0 ↓	20 ↓	20 ←	37 ✓	37 ←	37 ←	37 ←	55 ↓	55 ←
5	4	0 ↓	20 ✓	20 ←	20 ←	23 ↓	31 ↓	33 ↓	55 ↓	55 ←
4	7	0 ↓	0 ←	0 ←	0 ←	23 ↓	31 ✓	33 ↓	55 ↓	55 ←
3	5	0 ↓	0 ←	0 ←	0 ←	23 ↓	23 ←	33 ✓	55 ↓	55 ←
2	1	0 ↓	0 ←	0 ←	0 ←	23 ↓	23 ←	23 ←	55 ✓	55 ←
1	8	0 ↓	0 ←	0 ←	0 ←	23 ✓	23 ←	23 ←	23 ←	23 ←
0	ε	0 ←	0 ←	0 ←	0 ←	0 ←	0 ←	0 ←	0 ←	0 ←
i	s_i/s_w	ε	4	2	3	8	7	5	1	6
	j	0	1	2	3	4	5	6	7	8

The optimal sub-sequence $\langle 6, 1, 8 \rangle$ of value 70 includes one of the elephants of the subset of type E_{swi} {1, 5, 7}, as well as one of those of type E_{swdi} {3, 8}. It is obtained by traversing the path "greyed out" from the cell (8, 8). The elephants associated with the cells where the path indication "✓" appears are retained, corresponding to the integration of a new elephant in the common sub-sequence of maximum value (use of the third term of the recurrence).

Answer 10. With the removal of the second rule, the dynamic programming algorithm must be able to take into account all the elephants of a subset of type E_{swi}. In accordance with the necessary condition stated in answer 2, this implies that the elements of such subsets of elephants are identically ordered in the sequences s_w and s_i. The preprocessing phase is similar to that described in answer 8 with the difference that in the sequence s_i, the elephants are ordered by increasing intelligence, by decreasing weight in case of equal weight, and finally by increasing market value in the event of double equality of intelligence and weight (as in the sequence s_w).   141 - A 10

Answer 11. In this example, the operand sequences of the algorithm are: 141 - A 11

- $s_w = \langle 4, 2, 3, 8, 7, 5, 1, 6 \rangle$
- $s_i = \langle 8, 7, 5, 1, 4, 3, 2, 6 \rangle$.

The table combining the optimal value and the path indication for each prefix pair of s_w and s_i, is as follows:

i	s_i									
8	6	0 ↓	20 ↓	47 ↓	47 ←	47 ←	47 ←	47 ←	73 ↓	88 ↙
7	2	0 ↓	20 ↓	47 ↙	47 ←	47 ←	47 ←	47 ←	73 ↓	73 ←
6	3	0 ↓	20 ↓	20 ←	37 ↙	37 ←	37 ←	41 ↓	73 ↓	73 ←
5	4	0 ↓	20 ↙	20 ←	20 ↓	23 ↓	31 ↓	41 ↓	73 ↓	73 ←
4	1	0 ↓	0 ←	0 ←	0 ←	23 ↓	31 ↙	41 ↓	73 ↙	73 ←
3	5	0 ↓	0 ←	0 ←	0 ←	23 ↓	31 ←	41 ↙	41 ←	41 ←
2	7	0 ↓	0 ←	0 ←	0 ←	23 ↓	31 ←	31 ←	31 ↙	31 ←
1	8	0 ↓	0 ←	0 ←	0 ←	23 ↙	23 ←	23 ←	23 ←	23 ←
0	ε	0 ←	0 ←	0 ←	0 ←	0 ←	0 ←	0 ←	0 ←	0 ←
i	s_i / s_w	ε	4	2	3	8	7	5	1	6
	j	0	1	2	3	4	5	6	7	8

The optimal sub-sequence $\langle 8, 7, 5, 1, 6 \rangle$ of value 8 is obtained as before using the routing information. Note that, as expected, it contains the three elephants $1, 5$ and 7 of same weight and intelligence.

Answers to problem 142. The best triangulation of a convex polygon *The problem is on page 681.*

142 - A 1   **Answer 1.**   For a n-side convex polygon, figure 9.12, page 683, shows that the strategy *OneTrTwoPol* proposed leads to proceed to the triangulation of a $(n-1)$-side polygon for $k = 2$ and $k = n - 1$ and, for any vertex s_{i+k} such that $k \in 3 .. n - 2$, a first k-side polygon and another one having $(n + 1 - k)$ sides. This process thus generates a number of triangulations $nbtr2(n)$ given by:

$$nbtr2(3) = 1$$
$$nbtr2(n) = 2 \cdot nbtr2(n-1) + \sum_{k=3}^{n-2} nbtr2(k) \cdot nbtr2(n+1-k) \qquad n > 3.$$

It is now proven that $nbtr2(n)$ is nothing but the $(n-1)^{\text{th}}$ Catalan number for $n > 1$. Let us recall that the nth Catalan number is defined as:

$$Cat(1) = 1$$
$$Cat(n) = \sum_{i=1}^{n-1} Cat(i) \cdot Cat(n-i) \qquad n > 1.$$

For $n > 2$, we have:

$$Cat(n) = 2 \cdot Cat(n-1) + \sum_{i=2}^{n-2} Cat(i) \cdot Cat(n-i)$$

and for $n > 3$:

$$Cat(n-1) = 2 \cdot Cat(n-2) + \sum_{i=2}^{n-3} Cat(i) \cdot Cat(n-i-1).$$

Letting $X(n) = Cat(n-1)$, we have $X(3) = Cat(2) = 1$, and for $n > 3$ it comes:

$$X(n) = 2 \cdot X(n-1) + \sum_{i=2}^{n-3} X(i+1) \cdot X(n-i)$$

$$= 2 \cdot X(n-1) + \sum_{i=3}^{n-2} X(i) \cdot X(n-i+1).$$

It turns out that the recurrences defining $X(n)$, the $(n-1)^{th}$ Catalan number on the one hand, $nbtr2(n)$ on the other hand, are identical.

Using the strategy *OneTrTwoPol*, the number of generated triangulations, $nbtr2(n)$, is less than $nbtr1(n)$, the one obtained with the strategy *OneTrOnePol* initially considered. Indeed, $nbtr1(n)$, in $\Theta(n!)$, increases much faster than $nbtr2(n)$, which is in $\mathcal{O}(4^{n-1})$. For example, on the one hand $nbtr1(5) = 10$ and $nbtr2(5) = 5$, on the other hand $nbtr1(10) = 302,400$ and $nbtr2(10) = 440$. This is because, unlike *OneTrOnePol*, *OneTrTwoPol* produces no duplicates.

With the strategy *OneTrTwoPol*, the number of triangulations is in the same order of magnitude as: (i) the number of bracketings in problem 125, page 649, (ii) the number of cuts in problem 126, page 650, and (iii) the number of binary trees in problem 135, page 669.

Answer 2.   In the chosen strategy, any chord drawn becomes the side of a polygon to be   142 - A 2
triangulated. If the polygon $\mathcal{P}$ is not convex, a chord can be partly outside the polygon; the polygon using it thus has a part which does not belong to the initial polygon, as illustrated below by the chord (s_4, s_8):

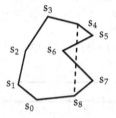

Answer 3.   No chord is drawn for the triangulation of any two- or three-sided polygon,   142 - A 3
so $lgmintr(i,t) = 0$ for $t \leqslant 3$. In the general case, the optimal triangulation of any polygon of t adjacent vertices of ascending numbers is calculated. So, from what has been said in the statement, the vertex s_{i+k} is identified such that the triangulation of the polygon $s_i, \ldots, s_{i+t-1}$ obtained $(i + t - 1 < n)$ is minimal. The recurrence for the calculation of $lgmintr(i,t)$ thus is:

$$
\begin{vmatrix}
lgmintr(i,t) = 0 & & 0 \leqslant i \leqslant n-1 \text{ and } 2 \leqslant t \leqslant 3 \\
lgmintr(i,t) = \min_{k \in 1..t-2} \left(\begin{array}{l} lgmintr(i, k+1) + \\ lgmintr(i+k, t-k) + \\ lgcrd(i, i+k) + \\ lgcrd(i+k, i+t-1) \end{array} \right) & & \begin{cases} 3 < t \leqslant n \\ \text{and} \\ 0 \leqslant i \leqslant n-t \end{cases}
\end{vmatrix}
$$

$lgcrd(i,j)$ denoting the length of the string joining the vertices s_i and s_j (if the vertices s_i and s_j are adjacent, $lgcrd(i,j) = 0$). Note that any chord is counted only once, since it then acts as the side of a polygon.

Answer 4. The associated algorithm uses the array $LMT[0 .. n-1, 2 .. n]$ whose first coordinate corresponds to s_i the starting vertex of the polygon and the second to its size t in number of vertices (or sides), the sought solution (i.e. the length of the optimal triangulation of the initial polygon) being located in the cell $LMT[0, n]$. The lengths of the various chords are assumed to be available in the symmetric zero diagonal array $LGC[0 .. n-1, 0 .. n-1]$ calculated beforehand. The evolution of the calculation consists in initializing the columns of indices 2 and 3 to 0 (first term of the recurrence), then to fill LMT by increasing values of the column index in accordance with the fact that, according to the second term of the recurrence, a cell of second index t only calls on cells of second index less than t. In a column, we can proceed in any order since no cell in this same column is required. Note that, in the array LMT, cells $LMT[i, t]$ such that $i \in n-t+1 .. n-1$ are not used.

The spatial complexity of the algorithm is in $\Theta(n^2)$ due to the presence of the arrays LMT and LGC. Its time complexity in terms of comparisons is in $\Theta(n^3)$. Once again, it can be seen that for an exponential initial combinatorial problem (Catalan number), a solution of polynomial complexity is found, hence a very significant gain compared to a naïve solution.

Answer 5. To identify the chords of the (one) best triangulation, "Tom Thumb's technique" is used. The array LMT is completed by the array PTH memorizing the (one) value of k for which the minimum is obtained. Secondly, to obtain the optimal triangulation itself (i.e. the chords that compose it) from the array PTH, a ternary tree is built whose root represents the initial polygon $\mathcal{P}$. The descendants of a node associated with a polygon represent the three elements which result from this polygon during its minimal triangulation. Thus, the left and right children correspond to the two polygons and the central child to the triangle which was produced (note that this type of node has no descendant). A left-right descending path makes it possible "to collect" the chords present in the central nodes to identify the optimal triangulation.

For the example of the nine-vertex polygon proposed, the arrays LMT and PTH are first grouped together below:

t	2	3	4	5	6	7	8	9
i = 0	0 /	0 /	13.3 2	29 2	44.8 2	56.6 2	72.8 2	87.7 2
1	0 /	0 /	15.7 2	31.4 2	43.3 2	59.5 2	74.4 2	/ /
2	0 /	0 /	13 3	24.3 4	39.8 4	56.7 6	/ /	/ /
3	0 /	0 /	86.0 4	24.1 4	37.8 6	/ /	/ /	/ /
4	0 /	0 /	86.0 6	22.0 6	/ /	/ /	/ /	/ /
5	0 /	0 /	12 7	/ /	/ /	/ /	/ /	/ /
6	0 /	0 /	/ /	/ /	/ /	/ /	/ /	/ /
7	0 /	0 /	/ /	/ /	/ /	/ /	/ /	/ /
8	0 /	0 /	/ /	/ /	/ /	/ /	/ /	/ /

It can be deduced that the value of the optimal triangulation obtained is 87.7 (cell $LMT[0, 9]$). From the array PTH, the ternary tree below is constructed in which: i) a polygon is given by the list of its vertices and the reference to PTH allowing to triangulate it in an optimal way (when it is not a triangle), and ii) for a triangle, its vertices and the strings having been drawn to build it are specified. For the example considered, the tree is as follows:

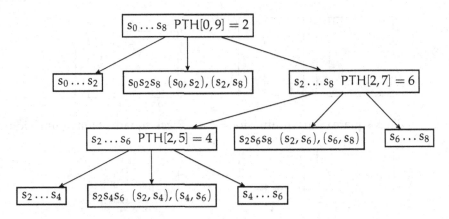

and it represents the triangulation:

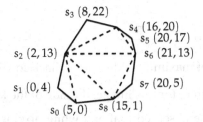

The (rounded) value of the triangulation (87.7) is that of the sum of the (rounded) lengths of the chords (s_2, s_4), (s_2, s_6), (s_2, s_8), (s_0, s_2), (s_4, s_6) and (s_6, s_8), that is $15.7 + 19 + 17.7 + 13.3 + 8.6 + 13.4 = 87.7$.

Answers to problem 143. Largest black square   *The problem is on page 684.*

Answer 1.   The principle consists in constructing successive histograms from the image   143 - A 1
of height m and width n to be processed (see last question of the problem 116, page 480) with a complexity in $\mathcal{O}(m \cdot n)$. For each of them, the optimal iterative procedure defined for the calculation of the side of the largest black square under a histogram of complexity in $\Theta(n)$ is applied. The maximum value found on all the histograms is retained and therefore the overall complexity is in $\Theta(m \cdot n)$.

Applying this to the proposed image (proceeding bottom up) leads to the following histograms and results:

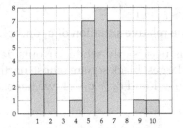

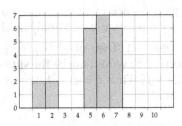

Black square of maximum side = 3   Black square of maximum side = 3

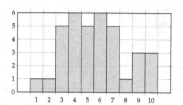

Black square of maximum side = 5

Black square of maximum side = 4

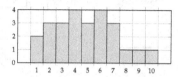

Black square of maximum side = 3

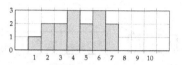

Black square of maximum side = 2

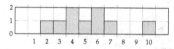

Black square of maximum side = 1

Black square of maximum side = 1

from which it is concluded that, for this image, the side of the largest black square is 5.

143 - A 2   **Answer** 2.   First, it can be observed that any white pixel is the northwest corner of a black square of side 0. Now consider a black pixel of coordinates (i, j). Let c (respectively c_1, c_2, c_3) be the side of the largest northwest square whose northwest corner is (i, j) (respectively $(i, j+1), (i-1, j), (i-1, j+1)$). It turns out that, if c_1 or c_2 or c_3 is zero, then $c = 1 = 1 + \min(\{c_1, c_2, c_3\})$. In the following, it is proven that this property also holds when c_1, c_2 and c_3 are all positive.

Let us remark that c_3 cannot be less than $\max(\{c_1, c_2\}) - 1$, as illustrated by the figure below:

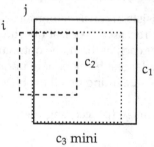

c_3 mini

and it can be deduced that $c_3 \geqslant c_1 - 1$ and $c_3 \geqslant c_2 - 1$.

Let us carry out a case-based analysis about the relative situation of c_1 and c_2.

Case 1 $c_1 < c_2 - 1$ Thee pixel $(i, j + c_1 + 1)$ is necessarily white (or outside the image), otherwise c_1 would not be the side of the largest black square whose northwest corner is $(i, j+1)$. Thus $c = c_1 + 1$, ans as $c_2 > c_1 + 1$ and $c_3 \geqslant c_2 - 1$, we have: $c = 1 + c_1 = 1 + \min(\{c_1, c_2, c_3\})$.

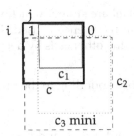

Case 2 $c_1 = c_2 - 1$ At least one of the pixels $(i - c_2, j + c_1 + 1), \ldots, (i, j + c_1 + 1)$ is white (or they all are outside the image), otherwise c_1 would not be the side of the largest black square whose northwest corner is $(i, j + 1)$. Therefore, here again $c = c_1 + 1$. As $c_2 = c_1 + 1$ and $c_3 \geqslant c_2 - 1$, it can be deduced that $c = 1 + c_1 = 1 + \min(\{c_1, c_2, c_3\})$.

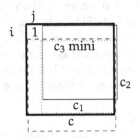

Case 3 $c_2 < c_1 - 1$ This situation is similar to case 1 by reversing the roles of c_1 and c_2.

Case 4 $c_2 = c_1 - 1$ This situation is similar to case 2 by reversing the roles of c_1 and c_2.

Case 5 $c_1 = c_2$ Two sub-cases must be distinguished depending on the color of the pixel $(i - c_1, j + c_1 + 1)$. If it is white, we have $c_3 = c_1 - 1$ and $c = 1 + c_3 = 1 + \min(\{c_1, c_2, c_3\})$. If it is black, at least one of the pixels $(i - c_1, j + c_1 + 1), \ldots, (i, j + c_1 + 1)$ is white (or they all are outside the image), otherwise c_1 would not be the side of the largest black square whose northwest corner is $(i, j + 1)$. So, $c_3 \geqslant c_1$ and $c = 1 + c_1 = 1 + \min(\{c_1, c_2, c_3\})$.

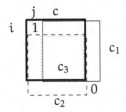 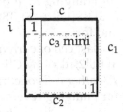

From the above comes the recurrence:

$$
\begin{vmatrix}
slbs(i, n) = IMG[i, n] & 1 \leqslant i \leqslant m \\
slbs(1, j) = IMG[1, j] & 1 \leqslant j < n \\
slbs(i, j) = 1 + \min\left(\left\{ \begin{array}{l} slbs(i, j+1), \\ slbs(i-1, j), \\ slbs(i-1, j+1) \end{array} \right\} \right) & \begin{array}{c} 1 < i \leqslant m \\ \text{and} \\ 1 \leqslant j < n \end{array}
\end{vmatrix}
$$

Answer 3.   The canonical tabular structure associated with this recurrence consists of the matrix $SLBS[1..m, 1..n]$. However, in view of the form of the general term (the cell (i, j) only requires the knowledge of the cells $(i, j+1)$, $(i-1, j)$ and $(i-1, j+1)$), the matrix can be limited to two rows (or two columns), provided that the current optimal value and the

143 - A 3

coordinates of the associated pixel are stored, which will constitute the desired result. At initialization, the second term of recurrence is used. Then, a row is filled in starting with the last column (first term), then the other cells by decreasing index using the general term of the recurrence.

143 - A 4   **Answer** 4.   The algorithm corresponding to the proposed strategy is:

```
 1. constants
 2.    m ∈ ℕ₁ and m = … and n ∈ ℕ₁ and n = … and
 3.    IMG ∈ 1 .. m × 1 .. n → 0 .. 1 and IMG = [...]
 4.    /% IMG is the matrix representing the initial image made up of white (0)
          oo black (1) pixels %/
 5. variables
 6.    SLBS ∈ 1 .. 2 × 1 .. n → 0 .. n and LgbsAbs ∈ 1 .. n and
 7.    LgbsOrd ∈ 1 .. m and LgbsSide ∈ 0 .. m
 8.    /% SLBS is the 2-row n-column matrix slidingly storing the values of the
          side of the largest black square associated with each of the pixels in a row
          of the image; LgbsAbs and LgbsOrd are the coordinates of the pixel asso-
          ciated with the current largest black square of side LgbsSide %/
 9. begin
10.    /% initializations %/
11.    LgbsSide ← 0 ; LgbsAbs ← n ; LgbsOrd ← 1 ;
12.    for j ∈ 1 .. n do
13.       SLBS[2, j] ← IMG[2, j] ;
14.       if SLBS[2, j] = 1 then
15.          LgbsAbs ← j ; LgbsSide ← 1
16.       end if
17.    end for;
18.    /% processing of rows 2 to m %/
19.    for i ranging 2 .. m do
20.       /% update of row 1 by assignment of row 2 %/
21.       for j ranging 1 .. n do
22.          SLBS[1, j] ← SLBS[2, j]
23.       end for;
24.       /% last cell of current row %/
25.       SLBS[2, n] ← IMG[i, n] ;
26.       /% other cells of current row %/
27.       for j ranging reverse 1 .. n − 1 do
28.          if IMG[i, j] = 0 then
29.             SLBS[2, j] ← 0
30.          else
```

31.
$$
SLBS[2,j] \leftarrow 1 + \min \left(\left\{ \begin{array}{l} SLBS[1,j], \\ SLBS[2,j+1], \\ SLBS[1,j+1] \end{array} \right\} \right) ;
$$

```
32.          if SLBS[2, j] > LgbsSide then
33.             LgbsSide ← SLBS[2, j] ; LgbsAbs ← j ; LgbsOrd ← i
34.          end if
35.          end if
36.       end for
37.    end for;
```

38.   **write**(*the northwest corner of the largest black square is in:* (,

39.   LgbsAbs, LgbsOrd,) *and its side is* , LgbsSide)

40. **end**

The spatial complexity of this algorithm is in $\Theta(m \cdot n)$ due to the presence of the matrix IMG (the matrix SLBS requiring only 2n cells). The temporal complexity is in $\Theta(m \cdot n)$ conditions evaluated. Indeed: i) the outer loop is performed for each row except the first, i.e. $(m - 1)$ times, and ii) the calculation associated with each cell of a row except the last one requires the evaluation of one or two conditions, that is to say between $(n - 1)$ and $2(n - 1)$. Therefore the complexity of this solution is the same as that of the one based on the iterative solution of the first question.

Answer 5.   Below are given the pairs of rows of the matrix SLBS and the values of the side (LgbsSide) of the largest square and its coordinates (LgbsAbs and LgbsOrd) at the end of the initialization and each of the successive seven iteration steps on i for the image of figure 9.14, page 685:

143 - A 5

initialization

	1	2	3	4	5	6	7	8	9	10
2	1	1	0	0	1	1	1	0	0	0
1										

LgbsSide = 1; LgbsAbs = 7; LgbsOrd = 1

iteration i = 2

	1	2	3	4	5	6	7	8	9	10
2	2	1	0	0	2	2	1	0	0	0
1	1	1	0	0	1	1	1	0	0	0

LgbsSide = 2; LgbsAbs = 6; LgbsOrd = 2

iteration i = 3

	1	2	3	4	5	6	7	8	9	10
2	2	1	1	1	3	2	1	1	1	1
1	2	1	0	0	2	2	1	0	0	0

LgbsSide = 3; LgbsAbs = 5; LgbsOrd = 3

iteration i = 4

	1	2	3	4	5	6	7	8	9	10
2	0	0	2	2	3	2	1	0	2	1
1	2	1	1	1	3	2	1	1	1	1

LgbsSide = 3; LgbsAbs = 5; LgbsOrd = 3 (unchanged values)

iteration $i = 5$

	1	2	3	4	5	6	7	8	9	10
2	1	1	3	3	3	2	1	1	2	1
1	0	0	2	2	3	2	1	0	2	1

$\text{LgbsSide} = 3; \text{LgbsAbs} = 5; \text{LgbsOrd} = 3$ (unchanged values)

iteration $i = 6$

	1	2	3	4	5	6	7	8	9	10
2	2	2	4	4	3	2	1	0	0	0
1	1	1	3	3	3	2	1	1	2	1

$\text{LgbsSide} = 4; \text{LgbsAbs} = 4; \text{LgbsOrd} = 6$

iteration $i = 7$

	1	1	3	4	5	6	7	8	9	10
2	0	3	5	4	3	2	1	0	0	1
1	2	2	4	4	3	2	1	0	0	0

$\text{LgbsSide} = 5; \text{PgcnAbs} = 3; \text{LgbsOrd} = 7$

iteration $i = 8$

	1	2	3	4	5	6	7	8	9	10
2	1	0	0	1	0	1	0	0	0	0
1	0	3	5	4	3	2	1	0	0	1

$\text{LgbsSide} = 5; \text{LgbsAbs} = 3; \text{LgbsOrd} = 7$ (unchanged values)

Therefore, the side of the largest black square is 5 and its northwest corner is in $(3, 7)$; it is the only one here (while there are four black squares with side 4). It is visualized below:

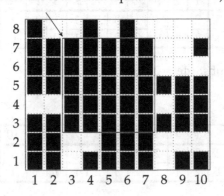

Answers to problem 144. Trimming an image   *The problem is on page 685.*

The problem is on page 685.

Answer 1.   A segmentation can be represented as a tree having the following structure: 144 - A 1

- the root corresponds to the entire image IMG$[1 .. m, 1 .. n]$,
- any other node (leaves excluded) is associated with a non homogeneous (from a color perspective) rectangle IMG$[i_1 .. i_2, j_1 .. j_2]$,
- any leaf corresponds to a homogeneous (either totally black, or fully white) rectangle IMG$[i_1 .. i_2, j_1 .. j_2]$.

The tree related to the segmentation of the proposed example is:

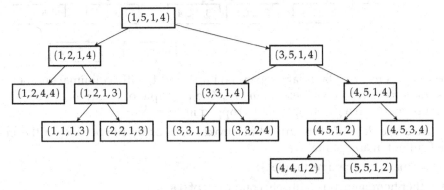

where each node is labeled with the values i_1, i_2, j_1, j_2 of the associated rectangle.

Several trees can be associated with a given segmentation, firstly by inverting the left and right subtrees, secondly by choosing another root (when possible, which is the case here where the cutting of the initial rectangle IMG$[1 .. 3, 1 .. 4]$ and IMG$[4 .. 5, 1 .. 4]$) could be also chosen.

Internal nodes (not leaves) of any tree associated with a segmentation are equal in number to the number of guillotine strokes (seven in the example).

Leaves correspond to homogeneous rectangles of the image and other nodes to non homogeneous rectangles.

Answer 2.   In fact, the order of the guillotine strokes is not critical in this problem.   144 - A 2
However, if one peculiar order is desired, it suffices to attach to each internal node the number corresponding to the order in which the guillotine strokes are made. The only constraint to respect is that the number associated with a node cannot be lower than that of its father. A "standard" way to do this is to assign the number on a downward left-right (or right-left) traversal. Thus, in the example treated, with a prefixed path, the tree is:

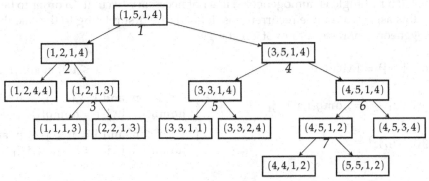

where the number assigned to a node appears below it in italics. However, the following numbering is also suitable, even if it does not correspond to a "standard" traversal:

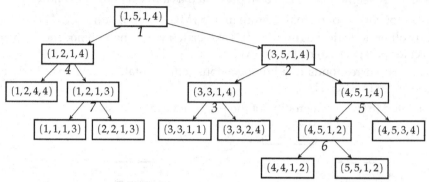

144 - A 3   **Answer** 3.   A rectangular image separated into 0 and 1, with a minimal number of guillotine strokes, is said to be *optimally cropped*. The principle of recurrence is based on the following property. In a given optimally cropped image:

(a) any rectangle delimited by guillotine strokes and/or by the borders of the image is itself cut out in an optimal way,

(b) any optimally cropped rectangle is:
  - either homogeneous (entirely composed of 0's or 1's),
  - or decomposable by a guillotine stroke into two smaller sub-rectangles optimally cropped.

For example, in the figure of the statement, let us number rows bottom up and lines from left to right and note $IMG[1 .. 8, 1 .. 8]$ this image. If the given cut is optimal, then the rectangle $IMG[4..8, 1..5]$ is optimally cut and the rectangles $IMG[4..6, 1..5]$ and $IMG[6..8, 1..5]$ are themselves optimally cropped.

Let us denote by:
  - $nbgs(i_1, i_2, j_1, j_2)$ the number of guillotine strokes required for the optimal cut of the rectangle $IMG[i_1 .. i_2, j_1 .. j_2]$,
  - $homg(i_1, i_2, j_1, j_2)$ the homogeneity (or not) of the rectangle $IMG[i_1 .. i_2, j_1 .. j_2]$ which is 0 (respectively 1) if it is completely made up of 0's (respectively 1's), 2 otherwise.

According to what has been said previously, in the general case, the optimal cutting of the *not homogeneous* rectangle $IMG[i_1 .. i_2, j_1 .. j_2]$ consists in looking for the horizontal or vertical guillotine stroke cutting it optimally. Special cases correspond to situations where a rectangle is reduced to a line (only vertical guillotine strokes are considered) or to a column (only horizontal guillotine strokes are considered), or even to a single pixel (no cutting is necessary). If a rectangle is homogeneous, it is not necessary to cut it. In order to be able to integrate this aspect, a double recurrence is defined, the first relating to the calculation of the homogeneous character or not of a rectangle:

$$homg(i, i, j, j) = IMG[i, j] \qquad 1 \leqslant i \leqslant m \text{ and } 1 \leqslant j \leqslant n$$

$$homg(i, i, j_1, j_2) = homg(i, i, j_1, j_1) \qquad \begin{cases} 1 \leqslant i \leqslant m \text{ and } 1 \leqslant j_1 < j_2 \leqslant n \text{ and} \\ homg(i, i, j_1, j_1) = homg(i, i, j_1 + 1, j_2) \end{cases}$$

$$homg(i, i, j_1, j_2) = 2 \qquad \begin{cases} 1 \leqslant i \leqslant m \text{ and } 1 \leqslant j_1 < j_2 \leqslant n \text{ and} \\ homg(i, i, j_1, j_2) \neq homg(i, i, j_1 + 1, j_2) \end{cases}$$

$$\text{homg}(i_1, i_2, j, j) = \text{homg}(i_1, i_1, j, j) \qquad \begin{cases} 1 \leqslant i_1 < i_2 \leqslant m \text{ and } 1 \leqslant j \leqslant n \text{ and} \\ \text{homg}(i_1, i_1, j, j) = \text{homg}(i_1 + 1, i_2, j, j) \end{cases}$$

$$\text{homg}(i_1, i_2, j, j) = 2 \qquad \begin{cases} 1 \leqslant i_1 < i_2 \leqslant m \text{ and } 1 \leqslant j \leqslant n \text{ and} \\ \text{homg}(i_1, i_1, j, j) \neq \text{homg}(i_1 + 1, i_2, j, j) \end{cases}$$

$$\text{homg}(i_1, i_2, j_1, j_2) = \text{homg}(i_1, i_1, j_1, j_2) \qquad \begin{cases} 1 \leqslant i_1 < i_2 \leqslant m \text{ and } 1 \leqslant j_1 < j_2 \leqslant n \text{ and} \\ \left(\begin{array}{l} \text{homg}(i_1, i_1, j_1, j_2) = \\ \text{homg}(i_1 + 1, i_2, j_1, j_2) \end{array} \right) \end{cases}$$

$$\text{homg}(i_1, i_2, j_1, j_2) = 2 \qquad \begin{cases} 1 \leqslant i_1 < i_2 \leqslant m \text{ and } 1 \leqslant j_1 < j_2 \leqslant n \text{ and} \\ \text{homg}(i_1, i_1, j_1, j_2) \neq \text{homg}(i_1 + 1, i_2, j_1, j_2) \end{cases}$$

the other one concerning the optimal number of guillotine strokes necessary to its cutting:

$$\text{nbgs}(i, i, j, j) = 0 \qquad 1 \leqslant i \leqslant m \text{ and } 1 \leqslant j \leqslant n$$

$$\text{nbgs}(i, i, j_1, j_2) = 0 \qquad \begin{cases} 1 \leqslant i \leqslant m \text{ and} \\ 1 \leqslant j_1 < j_2 \leqslant n \text{ and} \\ \text{homg}(i, i, j_1, j_2) \neq 2 \end{cases}$$

$$\text{nbgs}(i, i, j_1, j_2) = \min_{j \in j_1..j_2 - 1} \left(\begin{array}{l} 1 + \text{nbgs}(i, i, j_1, j) + \\ \text{nbgs}(i, i, j + 1, j_2)) \end{array} \right) \qquad \begin{cases} 1 \leqslant i \leqslant m \text{ and} \\ 1 \leqslant j_1 < j_2 \leqslant n \text{ and} \\ \text{homg}(i, i, j_1, j_2) = 2 \end{cases}$$

$$\text{nbgs}(i_1, i_2, j, j) = 0 \qquad \begin{cases} 1 \leqslant i_1 < i_2 \leqslant m \text{ and} \\ 1 \leqslant j \leqslant n \text{ and} \\ \text{homg}(i_1, i_2, j, j) \neq 2 \end{cases}$$

$$\text{nbgs}(i_1, i_2, j, j) = \min_{i \in i_1..i_2 - 1} \left(\begin{array}{l} \text{nbgs}(i_1, i, j, j) \\ + \text{nbgs}(i, i_2, j, j) \\ + 1 \end{array} \right) \qquad \begin{cases} 1 \leqslant i_1 < i_2 \leqslant m \\ \text{and } 1 \leqslant j \leqslant n \text{ and} \\ \text{homg}(i_1, i_2, j, j) = 2 \end{cases}$$

$$\text{nbgs}(i_1, i_2, j_1, j_2) = 0 \qquad \begin{cases} 1 \leqslant i_1 < i_2 \leqslant m \text{ and} \\ 1 \leqslant j_1 < j_2 \leqslant n \text{ and} \\ \text{homg}(i, i, j_1, j_2) \neq 2 \end{cases}$$

$$\text{nbgs}(i_1, i_2, j_1, j_2) = \min \left(\left\{ \begin{array}{l} \min_{i \in i_1..i_2 - 1} \left(\begin{array}{l} 1 + \text{nbgs}(i_1, i, j_1, j_2) \\ + \text{nbgs}(i + 1, i_2, j_1, j_2) \end{array} \right), \\ \min_{j \in j_1..j_2 - 1} \left(\begin{array}{l} 1 + \text{nbgs}(i_1, i_2, j_1, j) + \\ \text{nbgs}(i_1, i_2, j + 1, j_2) \end{array} \right) \end{array} \right\} \right)$$

$$\begin{cases} 1 \leqslant i_1 < i_2 \leqslant m \text{ and} \\ 1 \leqslant j_1 < j_2 \leqslant n \text{ and} \\ \text{homg}(i, i, j_1, j_2) = 2 \end{cases} .$$

Answer 4. Implementation calls on two matrices, ONGS[1 .. m, 1 .. m, 1 .. n, 1 .. n] associated with the computation of nbgs and HG[1 .. m, 1 .. m, 1 .. n, 1 .. n] connected with homg. The final result is located in the cell ONGS[1, m, 1, n]. $\qquad$ 144 - A 4

The calculation evolves in accordance with the recurrences. The two matrices are filled together starting with HG, since the value attached to a cell is required to calculate the value of the cell of ONGS of same coordinates. Taking into account the recurrences, the calculation goes from "simple" rectangles (each point of the image) towards larger and larger rectangles through the rows and columns of increasing sizes.

Answer 5. The algorithm is the following: $\qquad$ 144 - A 5

1. constants
2. $\quad m \in \mathbb{N}_1$ and $m = \ldots$ and $n \in \mathbb{N}_1$ and $n = \ldots$ and

3. $\text{IMG} \in 1..m \times 1..n \rightarrow \{0,1\}$ **and** $\text{IMG} = [\ldots]$

4.   /% IMG *is the matrix representing the initial image made up of pixels 0 or 1 %/*

5. **variables**

6. $\text{HG} \in 1..m \times 1..m \times 1..n \times 1..n \rightarrow 0..2$ **and**

7. $\text{ONGS} \in 1..m \times 1..m \times 1..n \times 1..n \rightarrow \mathbb{N}_1$

8.   /% HG *is the matrix storing the homogeneity (0 or 1) or not (2) of a rectangle and ONGS is the optimal number of guillotine strokes to cut this rectangle %/*

9. **begin**

10.   /% *processing of points %/*

11.   **for** $i \in 1..m$ **do**

12.   **for** $j \in 1..n$ **do**

13. $\text{HG}[i,i,j,j] \leftarrow \text{IMG}[i,j]; \text{ONGS}[i,i,j,j] \leftarrow 0$

14.   **end for**

15.   **end for;**

16.   /% *processing of rows from the shortest ones (wd = 2, i.e. two points) to the longest (wd = n, i.e. n points) %/*

17.   **for** i **ranging** $1..m$ **do**

18.   **for** wd **ranging** $2..n$ **do**

19.   **for** bg **ranging** $1..n-wd+1$ **do**

20.   **if** $\text{HG}[i,i,bg,bg] = \text{HG}[i,i,bg+1,bg+wd-1]$ **then**

21. $\text{HG}[i,i,bg,bg+wd-1] \leftarrow \text{HG}[i,i,bg,bg]$

22.   **else**

23. $\text{HG}[i,i,bg,bg+wd-1] \leftarrow 2$

24.   **end if;**

25.   **if** $\text{HG}[i,i,bg,bg+wd-1] < 2$ **then**

26. $\text{ONGS}[i,i,bg,bg+wd-1] \leftarrow 0$

27.   **else**

28. $\text{ONGS}[i,i,bg,bg+wd-1] \leftarrow +\infty \ ;$

29.   **for** j **ranging** $bg..bg+wd-2$ **do**

30. $\text{ONGS}[i,i,bg,bg+wd-1] \leftarrow$

31. $\min\left(\left\{\begin{array}{l} \text{ONGS}[i,i,bg,bg+wd-1], \\ \left(\begin{array}{l}1+\text{ONGS}[i,i,bg,j]+ \\ \text{ONGS}[i,i,j+1,bg+wd-1]\end{array}\right)\end{array}\right\}\right)$

32.   **end for**

33.   **end if**

34.   **end for**

35.   **end for**

36.   **end for;**

37.   /% *processing of columns from the shortest ones (ht = 2, i.e. two points) to the longest (ht = m, i.e. m points) %/*

38.   **for** j **ranging** $1..n$ **do**

39.   **for** ht **ranging** $2..m$ **do**

40.   **for** bg **ranging** $1..m-ht+1$ **do**

41.   **if** $\text{HG}[bg,bg,j,j] = \text{HG}[bg+1,bg+ht-1,j,j]$ **then**

42. $\text{HG}[bg,bg+ht-1,j,j] \leftarrow \text{HG}[bg,bg,j,j]$

43.   **else**

44. $\text{HG}[bg,bg+ht-1,j,j] \leftarrow 2$

45.   **end if;**

46.   **if** $\text{HG}[bg,bg+ht-1,j,j] < 2$ **then**

47. $\text{ONGS}[\text{bg}, \text{bg} + \text{ht} - 1, j, j] \leftarrow 0$

48.   **else**

49. $\text{ONGS}[\text{bg}, \text{bg} + \text{ht} - 1, j, j] \leftarrow +\infty$;

50.   **for** i **ranging** $\text{bg} .. \text{bg} + \text{ht} - 2$ **do**

51. $\text{ONGS}[\text{bg}, \text{bg} + \text{ht} - 1, j, j] \leftarrow$

52. $\min \left(\left\{ \begin{array}{l} \text{ONGSO}[\text{bg}, \text{bg} + \text{ht} - 1, j, j], \\ \left(\begin{array}{l} 1 + \text{ONGS}[\text{bg}, i, j, j] \\ \text{ONGS}[i + 1, \text{bg} + \text{ht} - 1, j, j] \end{array} \right) \end{array} \right\} \right)$

53.   **end for**

54.   **end if**

55.   **end for**

56. **end for**

57. **end for**;

58. /% *processing of rectangles from the smallest ones* ($\text{ht} = \text{wd} = 2$) *to the largest* ($\text{ht} = m, \text{wd} = n$) %/

59. **for** ht **ranging** $2 .. m$ **do**

60. **for** wd **ranging** $2 .. n$ **do**

61.   **for** i **ranging** $1 .. m - \text{ht} + 1$ **do**

62.   **for** j **ranging** $1 .. n - \text{lg} + 1$ **do**

63.   /% *scan of all the rectangles of width* wd, *height* ht *whose lower left corner has* (i, j) *as coordinates; the homogeneous character of the rectangle is first calculated; then if necessary, segmentation takes place, first by vertical guillotine strokes, then horizontal ones* %/

64.   **if** $\text{HG}[i, i, j, j + \text{wd} - 1] = \text{HG}[i + 1, i + \text{ht} - 1, j, j + \text{wd} - 1]$ **then**

65. $\text{HG}[i, i + \text{ht} - 1, j, j + \text{wd} - 1] \leftarrow \text{HG}[i, i, j, j + \text{wd} - 1]$

66.   **else**

67. $\text{HG}[i, i + \text{ht} - 1, j, j + \text{wd} - 1] \leftarrow 2$

68.   **end if**;

69.   **if** $\text{HG}[i, i + \text{ht} - 1, j, j + \text{wd} - 1] < 2$ **then**

70. $\text{ONGS}[i, i + \text{ht} - 1, j, j + \text{wd} - 1] \leftarrow 0$

71.   **else**

72. $\text{ONGS}[i, i + \text{ht} - 1, j, j + \text{wd} - 1] \leftarrow +\infty$;

73.   **for** k **ranging** $j .. j + \text{wd} - 2$ **do**

74. $\text{ONGS}[i, i + \text{ht} - 1, j, j + \text{wd} - 1] \leftarrow$

75. $\min \left(\left\{ \begin{array}{l} \text{ONGS}[i, i + \text{ht} - 1, j, j + \text{wd} - 1], \\ \left(\begin{array}{l} 1 + \text{ONGS}[i, i + \text{ht} - 1, j, k] + \\ \text{ONGS}[i, i + \text{ht} - 1, k + 1, j + \text{wd} - 1] \end{array} \right) \end{array} \right\} \right)$

76.   **end for**;

77.   **for** k **ranging** $i .. i + \text{ht} - 2$ **do**

78. $\text{ONGS}[i, i + \text{ht} - 1, j, j + \text{wd} - 1] \leftarrow$

79. $\min \left(\left\{ \begin{array}{l} \text{ONGS}[i, i + \text{ht} - 1, j, j + \text{wd} - 1], \\ \left(\begin{array}{l} 1 + \text{ONGS}[i, k, j, j + \text{wd} - 1] + \\ \text{ONGS}[k + 1, i + \text{ht} - 1, j, j + \text{wd} - 1] \end{array} \right) \end{array} \right\} \right)$

80.   **end for**

81.   **end if**

82.   **end for**

83.   **end for**

84. **end for**

85. **end for**;

86.   **write**(*the number of guillotine strokes for the segmentation is* ,
ONCS[1, m, 1, n])
87. **end**

The spatial complexity of this algorithm corresponds to the matrices HG and ONGS; it is therefore in $\Theta((m \cdot n)^2)$. As for the number of conditions evaluated, it is in $\Theta((m+n) \cdot (m \cdot n)^2)$.

144 - A 6   **Answer** 6.   Below are given the "useful" values of the matrices HG[1 .. 3, 1 .. 3, 1 .. 4, 1 .. 4] and ONGS[1 .. 3, 1 .. 3, 1 .. 4, 1 .. 4]:

- for pixels:

    HG/ONGS[1, 1, 1, 1] = 1/0 ; HG/ONGS[1, 1, 2, 2] = 1/0 ;
    HG/ONGS[1, 1, 3, 3] = 0/0 ; HG/ONGS[1, 1, 4, 4] = 1/0 ;
    HG/ONGS[2, 2, 1, 1] = 0/0 ; HG/ONGS[2, 2, 2, 2] = 0/0 ;
    HG/ONGS[2, 2, 3, 3] = 0/0 ; HG/ONGS[2, 2, 4, 4] = 1/0 ;
    HG/ONGS[3, 3, 1, 1] = 0/0 ; HG/ONGS[3, 3, 2, 2] = 0/0 ;
    HG/ONGS[3, 3, 3, 3] = 1/0 ; HG/ONGS[3, 3, 4, 4] = 1/0 ;

- for rows:

    HG/ONGS[1, 1, 1, 2] = 1/0 ; HG/ONGS[1, 1, 2, 3] = 2/1 ; HG/ONGS[1, 1, 3, 4] = 2/1 ;
    HG/ONGS[1, 1, 1, 3] = 2/1 ; HG/ONGS[1, 1, 2, 4] = 2/2 ; HG/ONGS[1, 1, 1, 4] = 2/2 ;
    HG/ONGS[2, 2, 1, 2] = 0/0 ; HG/ONGS[2, 2, 2, 3] = 0/0 ; HG/ONGS[2, 2, 3, 4] = 2/1 ;
    HG/ONGS[2, 2, 1, 3] = 0/0 ; HG/ONGS[2, 2, 2, 4] = 2/1 ; HG/ONGS[2, 2, 1, 4] = 2/1 ;
    HG/ONGS[3, 3, 1, 2] = 0/0 ; HG/ONGS[3, 3, 2, 3] = 2/1 ; HG/ONGS[4, 4, 3, 4] = 1/0 ;
    HG/ONGS[3, 3, 1, 3] = 2/1 ; HG/ONGS[3, 3, 2, 4] = 2/1 ; HG/ONGS[3, 3, 1, 4] = 2/1 ;

- for columns:

    HG/ONGS[1, 2, 1, 1] = 2/1 ; HG/ONGS[2, 3, 1, 1] = 0/0 ; HG/ONGS[1, 3, 1, 1] = 2/1;
    HG/ONGS[1, 2, 2, 2] = 2/1 ; HG/ONGS[2, 3, 2, 2] = 0/0 ; HG/ONGS[1, 3, 2, 2] = 2/1;
    HG/ONGS[1, 2, 3, 3] = 0/0 ; HG/ONGS[2, 3, 3, 3] = 2/1 ; HG/ONGS[1, 3, 3, 3] = 2/1;
    HG/ONGS[1, 2, 4, 4] = 1/0 ; HG/ONGS[2, 3, 4, 4] = 1/0 ; HG/ONGS[1, 3, 4, 4] = 1/0;

- for rectangles:

    HG/ONGS[1, 2, 1, 2] = 2/1 ; HG/ONGS[1, 2, 2, 3] = 2/2 ; HG/ONGS[1, 2, 3, 4] = 2/1;
    HG/ONGS[2, 3, 1, 2] = 0/0 ; HG/ONGS[2, 3, 2, 3] = 2/2 ; HG/ONGS[2, 3, 3, 4] = 2/2;
    HG/ONGS[1, 2, 1, 3] = 2/2 ; HG/ONGS[1, 2, 2, 4] = 2/3 ;
    HG/ONGS[2, 3, 1, 3] = 2/2 ; HG/ONGS[2, 3, 2, 4] = 2/3 ;
    HG/ONGS[1, 2, 1, 4] = 2/3 ; HG/ONGS[2, 3, 1, 4] = 2/3 ;
    HG/ONGS[1, 3, 1, 2] = 2/1 ; HG/ONGS[1, 3, 2, 3] = 2/3 ; HG/ONGS[1, 3, 3, 4] = 2/2;
    HG/ONGS[1, 3, 1, 3] = 2/3 ; HG/ONGS[1, 3, 2, 4] = 2/4 ; HG/ONGS[1, 3, 1, 4] = 2/4.

As ONGS[1, 3, 1, 4] = 4, it can be deduced that four guillotine strokes are necessary for the optimal segmentation of this image. One optimal segmentation (that could be obtained from tracking information associated with the computation of ONGS − ("Tom Thumb's technique") is given hereafter:

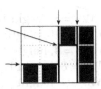

Answers to problem 145. Stacking bricks   *The problem is on page 686.*

Answer 1.   To lay a brick of type j on a brick of type i, the case which offers the most   145 - A 1
possibilities occurs when $s_j^1 \leqslant s_j^2 \leqslant s_j^3 < s_i^1 \leqslant s_i^2 \leqslant s_i^3$. Suppose that the upper face of
the brick of type i is composed of the sides of length s_i^1 and s_i^2 (this assumption does not
change anything afterwards). A brick of type j can be placed on the face composed of the
sides s_j^1 and s_j^2 in two different ways *a priori*, but in reality equivalent from the point of
view of the surface available for the following stacking. The brick j can also be put on the
face composed of the sides s_j^1 and s_j^3, or s_j^2 and s_j^3, hence three different ways to put the
brick j on the brick i.

Answer 2.   Consider two bricks of type i (of sides $s_i^1 \leqslant s_i^2 \leqslant s_i^3$). A second brick can be   145 - A 2
put only if the face of the first one is $s_i^2 \times s_i^3$. The face of the top brick can only be $s_i^1 \times s_i^2$.
Then no more brick of type i can be stacked. Note: to be able to make this stacking, it is
mandatory to have $s_i^1 < s_i^2 < s_i^3$.

Answer 3.   A brick of type i placed on the face corresponding to the sides s_i^1 and s_i^2 145 - A 3
becomes the object of width W_i (with $W_i = s_i^1$), length L_i (with $L_i = s_i^2$) and height H_i (with
$H_i = s_i^3$). A brick of type i can also become the other object defined by $W_i = s_i^1$, $L_i = s_i^3$
and $H_i = s_i^2$. A third possibility for this brick is to become the object defined by $W_i = s_i^2$,
$L_i = s_i^3$ and $H_i = s_i^1$. The constraint expressed in the statement of the problem imposes
that each of these objects can only be present once. Therefore the problem is reduced to the
choice of an optimal stacking of all the objects associated with each type of brick.

Answer 4.   Objects are sorted by decreasing surface area. Indeed, an object j can only   145 - A 4
be placed on an object k with a surface area greater than its own, and provided that the
length of the object j is less than that of the object k and that the width of the object j is
less than that of the object k. Let us define $\mathrm{htmax}(i)$ as the maximum height that can be
obtained with objects of rank less than or equal to i. So we have:

$$
\begin{aligned}
&\mathrm{htmax}(1) = h_1 \\
&\mathrm{htmax}(i) = h_i + \max_{\substack{k \in 1..i-1 \text{ and} \\ W_i < W_k \text{ and } L_i < L_k}} (\mathrm{htmax}(k)) && 2 \leqslant i \leqslant 3n.
\end{aligned}
$$

Implementation requires a vector $\mathrm{HTM}[1..3n]$ to store the values of the recurrence htmax,
resulting in linear spatial complexity. This vector is filled by increasing values of the index
i, since the cell $\mathrm{HTM}[i]$ potentially requires the knowledge of all values of lower index. The
calculation of $\mathrm{HTM}[i]$ associated with $\mathrm{htmax}(i)$ requires from 0 to $(i-1)$ comparisons, and
the maximum total number of comparisons is therefore in $\mathcal{O}(n^2)$.

Answer 5.   With the three bricks B1, B2 and B3 of respective dimensions $10 \times 12 \times 16$,   145 - A 5
$8 \times 9 \times 18$ and $4 \times 6 \times 25$, the nine objects (once sorted by decreasing surface area) are given
below:

    o_1 (B1) of length $L_1 = 16$, width $W_1 = 12$, height $H_1 = 10$ and surface $s1 = 192$,
    o_2 (B2) of length $L_2 = 18$, width $W_2 = 9$, height $H_2 = 8$ and surface $s2 = 162$,
    o_3 (B1) of length $L_3 = 16$, width $W_3 = 10$, height $H_3 = 12$ and surface $s3 = 160$,
    o_4 (B3) of length $L_4 = 25$, width $W_4 = 6$, height $H_4 = 4$ and surface $s4 = 150$,

o_5 (B2) of length $L_5 = 18$, width $W_5 = 8$, height $H_5 = 9$ and surface $s5 = 144$,
o_6 (B1) of length $L_6 = 12$, width $W_6 = 10$, height $H_6 = 16$ and surface $s6 = 120$,
o_7 (B3) of length $L_7 = 25$, width $W_7 = 4$, height $H_7 = 6$ and surface $s7 = 100$,
o_8 (B2) of length $L_8 = 9$, width $W_8 = 8$, height $H_8 = 18$ and surface $s8 = 72$,
o_9 (B3) of length $L_9 = 6$, width $W_9 = 4$, height $H_9 = 25$ and surface $s9 = 24$.

The following values of HTM are obtained:

$\text{HTM}[1] = \text{htmax}(1) = h_1 = 10$,
$\text{HTM}[2] = \text{htmax}(2) = h_2 = 8$,
$\text{HTM}[3] = \text{htmax}(3) = h_3 = 12$,
$\text{HTM}[4] = \text{htmax}(4) = h_4 = 4$,
$\text{HTM}[5] = \text{htmax}(5) = h_5 = 9$,
$\text{HTM}[6] = \text{htmax}(6) = h_6 + \text{htmax}(1) = 16 + 10 = 26$,
$\text{HRM}[7] = \text{htmax}(7) = h_7 = 6$,
$\text{HTM}[8] = \text{htmax}(8) = h_8 + \max(\{10, 8, 12, 26\}) = 18 + 26 = 44$,
$\text{HTM}[9] = \text{htmax}(9) = h_9 + \max(\{10, 8, 12, 4, 9, 26, 44\}) = 25 + 44 = 69$.

The optimal stacking thus reaches a height of 69 and corresponds to the successive stacking of objects: o_1 (B1), o_6 (B1), o_8 (B2) and o_9 (B3), i.e. two bricks B1, one brick B2 and one brick B3.

Remark

The sequence of values $\text{HTM}[1]$, $\text{HTM}[2]$, ..., $\text{HTM}[3n]$ is not monotonous, which makes it impossible to simplify the generic term of recurrence.

Answers to problem 146. Winning the Patagon game
The problem is on page 687.

146 - A 1   **Answer 1.**   The greedy solution proposed does not always deliver an optimal solution as shown by the example $T[1 .. 4] = [6, 7, 4, 1]$. In fact, the first pair of values considered is $(6, 7)$ and 7 is taken, then the pair $(4, 1)$ is examined and 1 must be taken given the previous choice. Thus, the sum collected is 8, whereas the optimal sum is 10.

146 - A 2   **Answer 2.**   sopt(j) $(1 \leqslant j \leqslant n)$ denotes the optimal sum for the slice $T[1 .. j]$, while obeying the constraint of non-contiguity of the values taken. From two things one:

- Either j lies in the optimal set of indices for the array $T[1 .. j]$, and then $(j - 1)$ cannot. The best that can be done then is to add the optimal sum for the array slice $T[1 .. j - 2]$ to the value $T[j]$.
- Or j is not part of the optimal set of indices for $T[1 .. j]$, and in this case: $\text{sopt}(j) = \text{sopt}(j - 1)$.

The following complete recurrence cab be built:

$$\left|\begin{array}{l} \text{sopt}(1) = T[1] \\ \text{sopt}(2) = \max(\{T[1], T[2]\}) \\ \text{sopt}(j) = \max\left(\left\{\begin{array}{l} \text{sopt}(j - 2) + T[j], \\ \text{sopt}(j - 1) \end{array}\right\}\right) \end{array}\right. \qquad 3 \leqslant j \leqslant n.$$

Answer 3.   Implementing this recurrence goes through the array SO[1..n] in which the   146 - A 3
values of sopt are stored. In the end of the calculation, SO[n] contains the optimal value
sought. The filling of SO is done by increasing values of the index according to the form
of the generic term of the recurrence, after having initialized the first two elements thanks
to the two corresponding terms of the recurrence. In order to subsequently be able to construct the set of indices I associated with the optimal value sopt(n), SO is doubled by the
array PTH[1 .. n] memorizing the choice made at each not (1 if the ith element is taken, 0
otherwise). So the algorithm is:

```
 1. constants
 2.     n ∈ ℕ₁ − {1} and n = ... and T ∈ 1 .. n → ℕ₁ and T = [...]
 3. variables
 4.     SO ∈ 1 .. n → ℕ₁ and PTH ∈ 1 .. n → 0 .. 1
 5. begin
 6.     SO[1] ← T[1]; PTH[1] ← 1;
 7.     if T[1] > T[2] then
 8.         SO[2] ← T[1]; PTH[2] ← 0
 9.     else
10.         SO[2] ← T[2]; PTH[2] ← 1
11.     end if;
12.     for j ranging 3 .. n do
13.         if SO[j − 2] + T[i] > SO[j − 1] then
14.             SO[j] ← SO[j − 2] + T[j]; PTH[j] ← 1
15.         else
16.             SO[j] ← SO[j − 1]; PTH[j] ← 0
17.         end if
18.     end for;
19.     write(SO[n])
20. end
```

The complexity of this algorithm is in $\Theta(n)$, both temporally and spatially. From an exponential combinatorial corresponding to the number of reasonable ways to play (nbRWP),
we end up to a linear complexity using dynamic programming.

Answer 4.   The construction of the optimal set of indices I relies on a right to left scan   146 - A 4
of the array of choices PTH. A value 1 means that the corresponding index value has been
taken in T, but not the previous one, which therefore has not to be examined. A value
0 corresponds to a value of T not taken in the optimal solution, and the previous one is
treated. The stop occurs for the indices 1 or 2. Therefore the algorithm for the construction
of I is:

```
 1. constants
 2.     n ∈ ℕ₁ and n = ... and PTH ∈ 1 .. n → 0 .. 1 and PTH = [...]
 3. variables
 4.     I ⊆ 1 .. n and j ∈ ℕ₁
 5. begin
 6.     j ← n ; I ← ∅;
 7.     while j ⩾ 3 do
 8.         if PTH[j] = 1 then
 9.             I ← I ∪ {j}; j ← j − 2
10.         else
11.             j ← j − 1
```

12.   **end if**
13.   **end while**;
14.   **if** $j = 2$ **then**
15.   **if** PTH[2] $= 1$ **then**
16. $I \leftarrow I \cup \{2\}$
17.   **else**
18. $I \leftarrow I \cup \{1\}$
19.   /% *indeed, an optimal solution must involve one of the first two ele-ments of the array* T %/
20.   **end if**
21.   **elsif** PTH[1] $= 1$ **then**
22. $I \leftarrow I \cup \{1\}$
23.   **end if**;
24.   **write**(I)
25. **end**

146 - A 5   **Answer 5.**   With the data of the example, the values obtained are:

i	1	2	3	4	5	6	7	8	9
T[i]	2	5	7	3	1	4	1	8	4
SO[i]	2	5	9	9	10	13	13	21	21
PTH[i]	1	1	1	0	1	1	0	1	0

and the complementary calculation using PTH delivers the set $I = \{1, 3, 6, 8\}$.

Answers to problem 147. The game of extremes   *The problem is on page 688.*

147 - A 1   **Answer 1.**   Consider the following row of cards:

$$\boxed{1} \; \boxed{3} \; \boxed{10} \; \boxed{8} \; \boxed{10} \; \boxed{2}$$

The sum of the three highest value cards is 28, while the player playing first can only take the card of value 2 (the other takes the card of value 1), then the card of value 10 (the other taking the one with a value of 3) and finally the second card with a value of 10, for a total of 22. This phenomenon generally occurs when the cards at the ends (initial or current) of the deck are part of the p out of $2p$ remaining cards of lower value.

147 - A 2   **Answer 2.**   Let $V[1 .. 2n]$ be the array of values in the row of $2n$ cards. Consider a row of cards $V[i .. s]$ with start index i, end index s and even size $(s - i + 1 \geqslant 4)$. The maximum gain for the first player, with a collaborative opponent $gmco(i, s)$, is obtained with the best of the following four game possibilities:

- the first player takes the card $V[i]$ and the second the card $V[i + 1]$, leading to the new line of cards $V[i + 2 .. s]$,
- the first player takes the card $V[i]$ and the second takes the card $V[s]$, leading to the new line of cards $V[i + 1 .. s - 1]$,
- the first player takes the card $V[s]$ and the second the card $V[i]$, leading to the new line of cards $V[i + 1 .. s - 1]$,
- the first player takes the card $V[s]$ and the second takes the card $V[s - 1]$, leading to the new line of cards $V[i .. s - 2]$.

Whatever choices both players make, they are faced with a $(s - i - 1)$-size line of cards. If $(s - i - 1) \geqslant 4$, the same reasoning can be reproduced, otherwise $(s - i + 1) = 2$, the line has two cards and there are only two playing possibilities, with the first player choosing the most favorable one. We thus end up with the recurrence:

$$
\begin{aligned}
&\text{gmco}(i, i+1) = \max(\{V[i], V[i+1]\}) &&1 \leqslant i \leqslant 2n - 1 \\
&\text{gmco}(i, s) = \max \left(\left\{ \begin{array}{l} \text{gmco}(i+2, s) + V[i], \\ \text{gmco}(i+1, s-1) + V[i], \\ \text{gmco}(i+1, s-1) + V[s], \\ \text{gmco}(i, s-2) + V[s] \end{array} \right\} \right) &&\left\{ \begin{array}{l} 1 \leqslant i \leqslant 2n - 3 \text{ and} \\ 4 \leqslant s \leqslant 2n \text{ and} \\ \exists k \cdot \left(\begin{array}{l} k \in \mathbb{N}_1 - \{1\} \text{ and} \\ s - i + 1 = 2k \end{array} \right) \end{array} \right.
\end{aligned}
$$

Answer 3. The construction of the associated program is based on the tabular structure GMCO $[1..2n - 1, 2..2n]$ which contains the values of gmco, hence a spatial complexity in $\Theta(n^2)$. Only cells GMCO$[i, s]$ such that $(s - i + 1)$ is a multiple of 2 are filled. We proceed by diagonals of equation $(s - i) = c$ where c is a constant. We start with $c = 1$ using the first term of the recurrence, then $c = 3, \ldots$, and finally $(2n - 1)$ using the second term. At the end of the calculation, the cell GMCO$[1, 2n]$ contains the maximum gain obtained by the player playing first with a cooperative opponent. The corresponding code is given below: 147 - A 3

```
1. constants
2.    n ∈ ℕ₁ and n = ... and V ∈ 1..2n → ℕ₁ and V = [...]
3. variables
4.    GMCO ∈ 1..2n × 1..2n → ℕ₁
5. begin
6.    for i ∈ 1..2n − 1 do
7.        GMCO[i, i + 1] ← max({V[i], V[i + 1]})
8.    end for;
9.    for k ranging 3..2n − 1 by 2 do
10.       for i ranging 1..2n − k do
11.           GMCO[i, i + k] ←
12.               max ({ GMCO[i + 2, i + k] + V[i],
                          GMCO[i + 1, i + k − 1] + V[i],
                          GMCO[i + 1, i + k − 1] + V[i + k],
                          GMCO[i, i + k − 2] + V[i + k] })
13.           /% i + k plays the role of s, the second index of the recurrence %/
14.       end for
15.   end for;
16.   write(GMCO[1, 2n])
17. end
```

Clearly this algorithm requires $(2n - 1)$ comparisons for the first loop. Then it evaluates $(2n - 3)$ conditions for $k = 3$, then $(2n - 5)$ for $k = 5, \ldots$, and finally a single condition for $k = 2n - 1$. The total number of comparisons evaluated is therefore in $\Theta(n^2)$.

Answer 4. With the line of cards proposed $(V = [12, 7, 6, 10, 8, 5])$, we obtain: 147 - A 4

s	2	3	4	5	6
i = 1	12		22		30
2		7		18	
3			10		16
4				10	
5					8

The maximum gain is therefore 30 and it is obtained as follows: the first player takes the card of value 12, then the second player takes the card of value 5, then the first player takes the card of value 8, then the second player takes the card of value 7, and finally the first player takes the card of value 10 value card by the first player, followed by the second player picking up the card of value 6 thus completing the game.

Remark

In general, the sequence of draws of the two players can be reconstructed by associating with GMCO an array containing in the cells (i, s) such that $(s - i + 1)$ is even, the choice of each of the two players corresponding to the optimal retained during the calculation of GMCO$[i, s]$ ("Tom Thumb's method").

147 - A 5   **Answer** 5.   Let us prove by induction (simple induction on $\mathbb{N}_1$) that the player playing first cannot do worse than draw with his opponent.

Base By definition of the recurrence defining $\operatorname{gmco}(i, s)$, in the presence of two cards, the player playing first chooses the one of higher value, so that he can only beat the other player or draw if both cards have the same value.

Induction hypothesis It is assumed that, for $k \geqslant 1$, the line $V[i .. s]$ with $s - i + 1 = 2k$ is such that the player playing first beats the other or at worst draws.

Induction Consider the situation where the player playing first is faced with a line having $2k + 2$ cards. We have seen that four situations could occur. If $V[i] \geqslant V[s]$ and if the first player takes the card of rank i and the other that of rank s (first case) or of rank $i + 1$ (second case), the player playing first at worst draws at this stage and in the following ones (induction hypothesis); we are therefore certain that he will not do worse than a draw in the end. If $V[i] \leqslant V[s]$, a similar reasoning is valid and deals with the third and fourth cases. There will necessarily be a draw at this stage if $V[i] = V[i + 1] = V[s] = V[s - 1]$, and therefore in the end if and only if all the cards are of value identical. In any case, the player starting the game cannot be beaten by his opponent with the chosen game strategy.

147 - A 6   **Answer** 6.   In a situation where each of the two players seeks to amass the maximum gain, *a priori* they follow the same process; the first (respectively second) player faces a line with an even (respectively odd) number of cards. The maximum gain (without collaboration) gmwc that a player can amass is the sum of the values of the cards of rank i to s facing him (denoted by $\operatorname{sum}(i, s)$), reduced by the maximum gain that the other player can amass on the next move. The terminal situation arises when a single card, necessarily picked up by the second player, remains on the table. The maximum gain of the player starting first is given by the following recurrence:

$$\operatorname{gmwc}(i, i) = V[i] \qquad\qquad\qquad 1 \leqslant i \leqslant 2n$$

$$\text{gmwc}(i, s) = \max \left(\left\{ \begin{array}{l} \text{sum}(i, s) - \text{gmwc}(i+1, s), \\ \text{sum}(i, s) - \text{gmwc}(i, s-1) \end{array} \right\} \right) \qquad 1 \leqslant i < s \leqslant 2n.$$

Remark

The last line may also be written:

$$\text{gmwc}(i, s) = \text{sum}(i, s) - \min \left(\left\{ \begin{array}{l} \text{gmwc}(i+1, s), \\ \text{gmwc}(i, s-1) \end{array} \right\} \right).$$

Answer 7.   In addition to the arrays $V[1 .. 2n]$ and $\text{SUM}[1 .. 2n, 1 .. 2n]$, the dynamic   147 - A 7
programming algorithm uses, the array $\text{GMWC}[1 .. 2n, 1 .. 2n]$ allowing to store the values
of the preceding recurrence. This one is filled by diagonal of equation $s - i = c$ where c is a
constant as in the previous case (but the calculation could proceed by row or by column as
well). The algorithm is quite similar to the one given in response to question 3 in terms of
general structure (the step of the outer loop being 1 instead of 2), and of spatial and temporal complexities both equally in $\Theta(n^2)$. It can be noticed that the cells $\text{GMWC}[j, k]$ such that
$(k - j + 1)$ is even (respectively odd) correspond to the optimal gains of the player playing
first (respectively second), whose maximum gain is found in $\text{GMWC}[1, 2n]$ (respectively
$\text{GMWC}[1, 2n - 1]$ or $\text{GMWC}[2, 2n]$ depending on the first card—$V[n]$ or $V[1]$—picked up
by the first player).

Answer 8.   With the same row of cards as before ($V = [12, 7, 6, 10, 8, 5]$), we get: 147 - A 8

s	1	2	3	4	5	6
i = 1	12	12	18	19	26	27
2		7	7	16	17	21
3			6	10	14	15
4				10	10	15
5					8	8
6						5

It can be observed that the maximum gain (27) of the player playing first is here strictly
lower than the value 30 reached when the other player cooperated (which is not surprising). By reconstituting the optimal solution ("Tom Thumb's technique" not detailed here),
it can be seen that the player playing first (respectively second) successively takes the cards
of value 12 (respectively 7) , 5 (respectively 8), 10 (respectively 6). The gain collected by the
other player is 21 (48 the total sum of the cards minus 27 the gain of the first player) and is
located in $\text{GMWC}[2, 6]$, since the first card drawn is $V[1]$.

Answer 9.   It can be noticed that the player starting the game has the choice between   147 - A 9
an even rank card (the last one) and an odd rank card (the first one). If he takes the first (respectively last), his opponent has the choice between two cards of even rank (respectively
odd). It can therefore be seen that the first player can, at his discretion, "force" his opponent to draw only cards of even or odd rank. A greedy strategy is to exploit this property
in the following way. The player playing first calculates the sum of the values of the cards
of even rank *sver* on the one hand, odd rank *svor* on the other hand. If *sver* > *svor*, he will
take all cards of even rank, the other being "forced" to take cards of odd rank. Thus, the
player going first is sure to beat his opponent. If *svor* > *sver*, the player playing first will
proceed in the opposite way, that is to say draw the cards of odd rank, so that his opponent
takes all the cards of even rank, and thus ensure his victory. If *sver* = *svor*, regardless of
whether the player playing first chooses odd or even ranked cards, there will be a draw. It

can therefore be seen that the greedy strategy proposed ensures that the first player never loses.

Since the dynamic programming method seen previously leads to the maximum payoff for the player playing first, this strategy is at least as good as the greedy strategy, with which the player playing first cannot lose. It can be concluded that the player going first wins or draws by following the strategy developed for the dynamic programming solution.

Let us apply the greedy strategy to the example of the line of cards $V = [12, 7, 6, 10, 8, 5]$. The sum of odd-ranked cards is equal to 26 and those of even-ranked cards is 22. Therefore the player playing first will amass a gain of 26 by adopting the greedy strategy, whereas with the dynamic programming he obtained 27. This proves that the greedy strategy does not lead to the maximum gain in general (it is not optimal with respect to the problem posed).

Answers to problem 148. Currency change (2)   *The problem is on page 689.*

148 - A 1   **Answer** 1.   With the proposed system, $\mathcal{C} = \{c_1, c_2, c_3\}$, where $d_1 = 6$, $d_2 = 4$, $d_3 = 1$, for $N = 8$ the multiset of coins obtained is $S = [6, 1, 1]$. There is another way to form $N = 8$, more "economical" in number of coins, namely $S' = [4, 4]$ (two coins instead of three). Another case where this greedy algorithm fails is: $\mathcal{C} = \{10, 6, 3, 1\}$ and $N = 18$, since it delivers $S = [10, 6, 1, 1]$ while there is a solution with only three coins: $S' = [6, 6, 6]$.

148 - A 2   **Answer** 2.   The establishment of the calculation recurrence of $\mathrm{nbcmin}(i, j)$, where i is the number of coins of the monetary system and j the sum to be formed, is detailed below. In the case where the sum to form j is greater than or equal to d_i and the monetary system has at least two coins, there are two options of which the best is chosen: i) either the optimal solution $\mathrm{nbcmin}(i, j)$ does not include the coin of rank i, in which case the optimal solution is $\mathrm{nbcmin}(i - 1, j)$, ii) or j is formed with a coin of rank i and it remains to form in an optimal way the amount $j - d_i$; the optimal number of coins is then $1 + \mathrm{nbcmin}(i, j - d_i)$. If the currency system has at least two coins and the value d_i exceeds the amount to be formed, the optimal solution is obtained by $\mathrm{nbcmin}(i - 1, j)$. If the monetary system has a single coin c_1 of value d_1 greater than (respectively less than or equal to) the sum to form j, there is no solution (respectively the optimal number of coins is $1 + \mathrm{nbcmin}(1, j - d_1)$). Finally, if the amount to be formed is zero ($j = 0$), no coin is necessary. The following recurrence can be deduced:

$$
\left|
\begin{array}{lr}
\mathrm{nbcmin}(i, 0) = 0 & 1 \leqslant i \leqslant n \\
\mathrm{nbcmin}(1, j) = \infty & 0 < j < d_1 \\
\mathrm{nbcmin}(1, j) = 1 + \mathrm{nbcmin}(1, j - d_1)) & d_1 \leqslant j \leqslant N \\
\mathrm{nbcmin}(i, j) = \mathrm{nbcmin}(i - 1, j) & 1 < i \leqslant n \text{ and } j < d_i \\
\mathrm{nbcmin}(i, j) = \min\left(\left\{ \begin{array}{l} \mathrm{nbcmin}(i - 1, j), \\ 1 + \mathrm{nbcmin}(i, j - d_i) \end{array} \right\} \right) & \left\{ \begin{array}{l} 1 < i \leqslant n \text{ and} \\ d_i \leqslant j \leqslant N \end{array} \right.
\end{array}
\right.
$$

Remark

If the value of the coin c_1 of $\mathcal{C}$ is $d_1 = 1$, the seconde line of the recurrence may be suppressed supprimée, as the associated situation cannot occur.

148 - A 3   **Answer** 3.   The associated program uses the array $D[1 .. n]$ corresponding to the elements of the monetary system $\mathcal{C}$, as well as the array $T[1 .. n, 0 .. N]$ allowing to store the elements of the recurrence. The desired result is located in the cell $T[n, N]$. The general case

of the recurrence highlights the fact that the computation of the cell $T[i,j]$ uses $T[i-1,j]$ and $T[i, j - D[i]]$. Therefore T can be filled by increasing values of the row index and in a row by increasing values of the column index. More precisely, the first line ($i = 1$) is initialized using the first three terms of the recurrence. For each following row of index i, $T[i, 0]$ is initialized to 0 (first term of the recurrence), then the following cells thanks to the last two terms of the recurrence (depending on whether j is or is not less than $D[i]$).

The temporal (and spatial) complexity is in $\Theta(n \cdot N)$, so the problem is pseudo-linear in n (see section 2.1.8, page 78).

Answer 4.   The example of the amount $N = 12$ to be formed is now dealt with using   148 - A 4
the currency system $\mathcal{C} = \{c_1, c_2, c_3\}$, where $d_1 = 4, d_2 = 5, d_3 = 1$. The procedure described
previously is therefore applied, which leads to the table:

j	0	1	2	3	4	5	6	7	8	9	10	11	12
$d_1 = 4$	0	∞	∞	∞	1	∞	∞	∞	2	∞	∞	∞	3
$d_2 = 5$	0	∞	∞	∞	1	1	∞	∞	2	2	2	∞	3
$d_3 = 1$	0	1	2	3	1	1	2	3	2	2	2	3	3

The minimum number of coins used to make up the sum $n = 1$ is 3 (three coins of value 4).

Answer 5.   To be able to identify the optimal combination of coins, the array PTH asso-   148 - A 5
ciated with T is used in which the choice made for each cell of T is stored, namely 1 if the
value of $T[i, j]$ is $T[i-1, j]$, or 2 if it is $1 + T[i, j - D[i]]$ ("Tom Thumb's method"). After filling
in PTH (at the same time as T), it is traversed as follows (as long as the value $T[n, N]$ is not
∞) to produce the multiset S of optimal coins. The starting point is $PTH[n, N]$. If 1 is found
in $PTH[i, j]$, the next element examined is $PTH[i - 1, j]$; if 2 is found there, a copy of coin i
(c_i of value $D[i]$) is added to the bag S and the next element examined is $PTH[i, j - D[i]]$.
This process continues until arriving in $PTH[i, 0]$. In the previous example, the multiset
$S = [\![4, 4, 4]\!]$ is thus built.

Notations

$exp_1 \mathrel{\hat{=}} exp_2$	definition
$\forall\, ident \cdot exp_1 \Rightarrow exp_2$	universal quantifier
$\exists\, ident \cdot exp_1 \text{ and } exp_2$	existential quantifier
$\displaystyle\sum_{exp_1} exp_2$	$\left\{\begin{array}{l}\text{Addition quantifier}\\\text{Sum of the values } exp_2 \text{ when } exp_1 \text{ is satisfied.}\end{array}\right.$
$\#ident \cdot exp$	counting operator: number of times when predicate exp is satisfied
$\lceil exp \rceil$	"ceiling" operator: the least integer greater than or equal to exp
$\lfloor exp \rfloor$	"floor" operator: the greatest integer less than or equal to exp
$\lvert exp \rvert$	absolute value or size of some entity (list, bag, etc.)
$\{exp_1, \ldots, exp_n\}$	set definition by extension
$\{\text{ListeIdent} \mid exp\}$	set definition by comprehension
$exp_1 .. exp_2$	interval of relatives
$exp_1 - exp_2$	subtraction of sets
$exp_1 \times exp_2$	cartesian product
(exp_1, exp_2)	couple (element of a cartesian product)
$(exp_1, \ldots, exp_n)$	tuple (extension of the notion of couple)
$exp_1 \circ exp_2$	relation composition
$exp_1 \to exp_2$	$\left\{\begin{array}{l}exp_1\text{: interval or cartesian product of intervals,}\\ exp_2\text{: any set,}\\ \text{set of the functions from } exp_1 \text{ to } exp_2\end{array}\right.$
$ident[exp_1, \ldots, exp_n]$	element of an array $ident$, with n dimensions
$ident[exp .. exp]$	slice of a one-dimensional array
$[exp_1, \ldots, exp_n]$	constant: one-dimensional array
$\begin{bmatrix} exp_{1,1} & \cdots & exp_{1,n} \\ \vdots & \cdots & \vdots \\ exp_{m,1} & \cdots & exp_{m,n} \end{bmatrix}$	constant: two-dimensional array
$\varnothing$	constant: empty bag
$exp_1 \mathrel{\in\!\!\!\!-} exp_2$	predicate: belonging to a bag
$[\![exp_1, \ldots, exp_n]\!]$	definition of a bag by extension
$exp_1 \dot{-} exp_2$	subtraction of bags
$exp_1 \sqcap exp_2$	intersection of bags
$exp_1 \sqcup exp_2$	union of bags
$exp_1 \sqsubset exp_2$	predicate: proper inclusion between bags
$exp_1 \not\sqsubset exp_2$	predicate: non proper inclusion between bags
$exp_1 \sqsubseteq exp_2$	predicate: inclusion between bags
$exp_1 \not\sqsubseteq exp_2$	predicate: non inclusion between bags
$\langle exp_1, \ldots, exp_n \rangle$	list of n values
$\mathbb{B}$	set of Booleans (\{**true, false**\})
$\mathbb{C}$	complex numbers
$card(exp) \quad \mid$	cardinal of a set
string	the set of strings
string(exp)	the set of strings on the vocabulary exp
$codom(exp)$	codomain of relation exp
$dom(exp)$	domain of relation exp
$im(exp)$	imaginary part of the complex number exp
$max(exp)$	greatest element of a set of numbers (when empty: $-\infty$)

$\max_{exp_1}(exp_2)$	$\begin{cases} \text{Quantifier max. Greatest element of expression } exp_2 \\ \text{when } exp_1 \text{ is satisfied.} \end{cases}$
$\min(exp)$	least element of a set of numbers (when empty: ∞)
$\min_{exp_1}(exp_2)$	$\begin{cases} \text{min quantifier. Least element of expression } exp_2 \\ \text{when } exp_1 \text{ is satisfied.} \end{cases}$
$mult(exp_1, exp_2)$	multiplicity of element exp_1 in the bag exp_2
$\mathbb{N}$	natural numbers (integers)
$\mathbb{N}_1$	$\mathbb{N} - \{0\}$
$pred(exp_1, exp_2)$	predecessor of element exp_1 in the binary relation exp_2
$\mathbb{P}(exp)$	set of the finite parts of set exp
$\mathbb{R}$	real numbers
$\mathbb{R}_+$	real numbers greater than or equal to 0
$\mathbb{R}_+^*$	real numbers greater than 0
$re(exp)$	imaginary part of the complex number exp exp
bag(exp)	set of the finite sub-bags of bag exp
$\begin{cases} \textbf{let } v_1, \dots, v_2 \textbf{ such as} \\ \quad exp \\ \textbf{begin} \\ \quad instr \\ \textbf{end} \end{cases}$	instruction specifying the variables $v_1, \dots, v_n$ and localizing their declaration
$bmax(exp)$	greatest of a bag of numbers (when empty: $-\infty$)
$bmin(exp)$	least of a bag of numbers (when empty: ∞)
$succ(exp_1, exp_2)$	suvcessor of element exp_1 in the binary relation exp_2
$\mathbb{Z}$	relative integer numbers
$\lceil x \rceil$	when x is real, $\lceil x \rceil \triangleq \min(\{m \in \mathbb{Z} \mid m \geqslant x\})$ (see [14])
$\lfloor x \rfloor$	when x is real, $\lfloor x \rfloor \triangleq \max(\{m \in \mathbb{Z} \mid m \leqslant x\})$ (see [14])
$\bigcup_{exp1} exp2$	quantifier that generalizes the operator $\cup$ (set union)
$\bigcap_{exp1} exp2$	quantifier that generalizes the operator $\cap$ (set intersection)

Remarks

1. The set definition by extension ($\{\texttt{ListeIdent} \mid exp\}$) is used to define "records". For example, $\{x, y \mid x \in \mathbb{R} \textbf{ and } y \in \mathbb{R}\}$ defines the set of points in the plane, $pt \in \{x, y \mid x \in \mathbb{R} \textbf{ and } y \in \mathbb{R}\}$ declares a variable (or a constant) with its first field being the "abcissa" x and the second being the "ordinate" y. By convention, the notation $pt.x$ (respectively $pt.y$) denotes this abcissa (respectively this ordinate).

2. The definition of inductive structures (lists, binary trees, etc.) is also done by using the notion of set defined by comprehension.

   For example, $liste = \{/\} \cup \{val, suiv \mid val \in \mathbb{N} \textbf{ and } suiv \in liste\}$ defines $liste$ as the union between the empty list (denoted $/$) and the set of couples composed of an integer and of a list of intgers. It is necessary to precise that all structures are here *finite* and that the structure $liste$ defined in this way is the *smallest* set satisfying the equation $liste$ $liste = \{/\} \cup \{val, suiv \mid val \in \mathbb{N} \textbf{ and } suiv \in liste\}$.

3. The counting operator # produces a natural integer. For example, when defined, the expression $\#i \cdot (i \in 1 .. 10 \textbf{ and } T[i] = 0)$ counts the number of 0 in the slice $T[1 .. 10]$ of the array T.

4. For the purposes of notation, the field **variables** (respectively **constants**) can contain in some programs — in addition to the declaration of the variables (respectively of the constants)—, a proposition that plays the role of a *precondition* (respectively of a *constraint*).

List of problems

Bibliography

[1] J.-R. ABRIAL, *The B-Book*, Cambridge University Press, 1996.

[2] J. ARSAC, *Préceptes pour programmer*, Dunod, 1991.

[3] S. BAASE AND A. V. GELDER, *Computer Algorithms*, Addison-Wesley Longman, 2000.

[4] J. BENTLEY, *Programming Pearls*, Addison-wesley, 1986.

[5] ———, *More Programming Pearls. Confessions of a Coder*, Addison-wesley, 1988.

[6] P. BERLIOUX AND P. BIZARD, *The Construction, Proof, and Analysis of Programs*, John Wiley and Sons, 1986.

[7] P. BRASS, *Advanced Data Structures*, Cambridge University Press, 2008.

[8] G. BRASSARD AND P. BRADLEY, *Fundamentals of Algorithmics*, Prentice-Hall, 1996.

[9] T. CORMEN, C. LEISERSON, C. STEIN, AND R. RIVEST, *Introduction to Algorithms*, The MIT Press, 3rd ed., 2009.

[10] M. CROCHEMORE, C. HANCART, AND T. LECROQ, *Algorithms on Strings*, Cambridge University Press, 2007.

[11] J.-P. DELAHAYE, *La suite du lézard et autres inventions*, Pour La Science, No 353, (2007).

[12] J. EDMONDS, *How to Think about Algorithms*, Cambridge, 2008.

[13] M. GOODRICH AND R. TAMASSIA, *Algorithm Design*, Wiley, 2001.

[14] R. GRAHAM, D. KNUTH, AND O. PATASHNIK, *Concrete Mathematics: A Foundation for Computer Science*, Addison-Wesley Professional, 2nd ed., 1994.

[15] D. GRIES, *The Science of Programming*, Springer, 1983.

[16] D. GRIES AND F. SCHNEIDER, *A Logical Approach to Discrete Mathematics*, Springer, 1993.

[17] M. GUYOMARD, *Structures de données et méthodes formelles*, Springer, 2011.

[18] C. HOARE, *Procedures and Parameters: An Axiomatic Approach*, in Proceedings of the Symposium on Semantics of Algorithmic Languages, 1971.

[19] E. HOROWITZ, S. SAHNI, AND S. RAJASEKARAN, *Computer Algorithms*, Silicon Press, 2nd ed., 1998.

[20] R. JOHNSONBAUGH AND M. SCHAEFFER, *Algorithms*, Pearson, Prentice-Hall, 2004.

[21] J. KLEINBERG AND E. TARDOS, *Algorithm Design*, Addison Wesley, 2006.

[22] D. KNUTH, *The Art of Computer Programming*, Addison-Wesley, 1968-2015.

[23] E. LEHMAN, F. LEIGHTON, AND A. MEYER, *Mathematics for Computer Science*, Media Services, 2017. Free on-line version available.

[24] A. LEVITIN, *The Design and Analysis of Algorithms*, Addison-Wesley, 2003.

[25] U. MANBER, *Introduction to Algorithms : a Creative Approach*, Addison Wesley, 1989.

[26] C. MORGAN, *Programming from Specifications*, Prentice-Hall, 1990.

[27] R. NEAPOLITAN AND K. NAIMIPOUR, *Foundations of Algorithms*, Jones and Barlett, 2004.

[28] I. PARBERRY, *Problems on Algorithms*, Prentice-Hall, 2nd ed., 2002.

[29] G. ROTE, *Crossing the bridge at night*, Bulletin of the European Association for Theoretical Computer Science., 78 (2002), pp. 241–246.

[30] T. ROUGHGARDEN, *Algorithms Illuminated (four volumes)*, Soundlikeyourself Publishing, 2017.

[31] S. RUSSELL AND P. NORVIG, *Artificial Intelligence: A Modern Approach*, Pearson, 4th ed., 2021.

[32] S. SKENIA, *The Algorithm Design Manual*, Springer, 2010.

[33] D. STINSON, *Techniques for Designing and Analyzing Algorithms*, CRC Press, 2022.

[34] G. VALIENTE, *Algorithms on Trees and Graphs*, Springer-Verlag, 2nd ed., 2021.

[35] C. VILLANI, *Birth of a Theorem: A Mathematical Adventure*, Farrar, Straus and Giroux, 2016.

Index

Printed in the United States
by Baker & Taylor Publisher Services